Organization Theory and Design

NINTH EDITION

Richard L. Daft
VANDERBILT UNIVERSITY

THOMSON
™
SOUTH-WESTERN

Australia · Brazil · Canada · Mexico · Singapore · Spain · United Kingdom · United States

THOMSON

SOUTH-WESTERN™

Organization Theory and Design, Ninth Edition

Richard L. Daft

With the Assistance of Patricia G. Lane

Vice President/Editorial Director:
Jack W. Calhoun

Vice President/Editor-in-Chief:
Dave Shaut

Senior Acquisitions Editor:
Joe Sabatino

Senior Developmental Editor:
Emma F. Guttler

Marketing Manager:
Kimberly Kanakas

Senior Production Project Manager:
Cliff Kallemeyn

Technology Project Editor:
Kristen Meere

Web Coordinator:
Karen Schaffer

Art Director:
Tippy McIntosh

Senior Manufacturing Coordinator:
Doug Wilke

Photo Editor:
Deanna Ettinger

Production House:
Graphic World Inc.

Printer:
CTPS

Library of Congress Control Number:
2005937447

For more information about our products, contact us at:

Thomson Learning Academic Resource Center

1-800-423-0563

Thomson Higher Education
5191 Natorp Boulevard
Mason, OH 45040
USA

About the Author

Richard L. Daft, Ph.D., is the Brownlee O. Currey, Jr., Professor of Management in the Owen Graduate School of Management at Vanderbilt University. Professor Daft specializes in the study of organization theory and leadership. Professor Daft is a Fellow of the Academy of Management and has served on the editorial boards of *Academy of Management Journal, Administrative Science Quarterly,* and *Journal of Management Education.* He was the Associate Editor-in-Chief of *Organization Science* and served for three years as associate editor of *Administrative Science Quarterly.*

Professor Daft has authored or co-authored 12 books, including *Management* (Thomson Learning/South-Western, 2005), *The Leadership Experience* (Thomson Learning/South-Western, 2005), and *What to Study: Generating and Developing Research Questions* (Sage, 1982). He recently published *Fusion Leadership: Unlocking the Subtle Forces That Change People and Organizations* (Berrett-Koehler, 2000, with Robert Lengel). He has also authored dozens of scholarly articles, papers, and chapters. His work has been published in *Administrative Science Quarterly, Academy of Management Journal, Academy of Management Review, Strategic Management Journal, Journal of Management, Accounting Organizations and Society, Management Science, MIS Quarterly, California Management Review,* and *Organizational Behavior Teaching Review.* Professor Daft has been awarded several government research grants to pursue studies of organization design, organizational innovation and change, strategy implementation, and organizational information processing.

Professor Daft is also an active teacher and consultant. He has taught management, leadership, organizational change, organizational theory, and organizational behavior. He has been involved in management development and consulting for many companies and government organizations, including the American Banking Association, Bell Canada, National Transportation Research Board, NL Baroid, Nortel, TVA, Pratt & Whitney, State Farm Insurance, Tenneco, the United States Air Force, the United States Army, J. C. Bradford & Co., Central Parking System, Entergy Sales and Service, Bristol-Myers Squibb, First American National Bank, and the Vanderbilt University Medical Center.

Brief Contents

Preface   xv

Part 1: Introduction to Organizations   1
1. Organizations and Organization Theory   2

Part 2: Organizational Purpose and Structural Design   53
2. Strategy, Organization Design, and Effectiveness   54
3. Fundamentals of Organization Structure   88

Part 3: Open System Design Elements   135
4. The External Environment   136
5. Interorganizational Relationships   170
6. Designing Organizations for the International Environment   204

Part 4: Internal Design Elements   243
7. Manufacturing and Service Technologies   244
8. Information Technology and Control   286
9. Organization Size, Life Cycle, and Decline   319

Part 5: Managing Dynamic Processes   357
10. Organizational Culture and Ethical Values   358
11. Innovation and Change   398
12. Decision-Making Processes   441
13. Conflict, Power, and Politics   481

Integrative Cases   517
1.0 It Isn't So Simple: Infrastructure Change at Royce Consulting   518
2.0 Custom Chip, Inc.   522
3.0 W. L. Gore & Associates, Inc. Entering 1998   528
4.0 XEL Communications, Inc. (C): Forming a Strategic Partnership   543
5.0 Empire Plastics   549
6.0 The Audubon Zoo, 1993   552
7.0 Moss Adams, LLP   566
8.1 Littleton Manufacturing (A)   577
8.2 Littleton Manufacturing (B)   589

Glossary   591
Name Index   601
Corporate Name Index   610
Subject Index   614

Contents

Preface   xv

Part 1: Introduction to Organizations   1

Chapter 1: Organizations and Organization Theory   2

A Look Inside: Xerox Corporation   3
Organization Theory in Action   6
   Topics, 6 • Current Challenges, 6
Leading by Design: The Rolling Stones   7
   Purpose of This Chapter, 10
What Is an Organization?   10
   Definition, 10 • Types of Organizations, 11 • Importance of Organizations, 12
Book Mark 1.0: The Company: A Short History of a Revolutionary Idea   12
Perspectives on Organizations   14
   Open Systems, 14 • Organizational Configuration, 16
Dimensions of Organization Design   17
   Structural Dimensions, 17 • Contextual Dimensions, 20

In Practice: W. L. Gore & Associates   21
   Performance and Effectiveness Outcomes, 22
In Practice: Federal Bureau of Investigation   24
The Evolution of Organization Theory and Design   25
   Historical Perspectives, 25 • Contemporary Organization Design, 27 • Efficient Performance versus the Learning Organization, 28
In Practice: Cementos Mexicanos   32
Framework for the Book   33
   Levels of Analysis, 33 • Plan of the Book, 34 • Plan of Each Chapter, 36
Summary and Interpretation   36

Chapter 1 Workbook: Measuring Dimensions of Organizations   38
Case for Analysis: Perdue Farms Inc.: Responding to 21st Century Challenges   39

Part 2: Organizational Purpose and Structural Design   53

Chapter 2: Strategy, Organization Design, and Effectiveness   54

A Look Inside: Starbucks Corporation   55
   Purpose of This Chapter, 56
The Role of Strategic Direction in Organization Design   56
Organizational Purpose   58
   Mission, 58 • Operative Goals, 59

Leading by Design: Wegmans   61
   The Importance of Goals, 62
A Framework for Selecting Strategy and Design   62
   Porter's Competitive Strategies, 63
In Practice: Ryanair   64
   Miles and Snow's Strategy Typology, 65

Book Mark 2.0: What Really Works:
The 4 + 2 Formula for Sustained Business Success   66

  *How Strategies Affect Organization
  Design, 67 • Other Factors Affecting
  Organization Design, 69*

Assessing Organizational Effectiveness   70

Contingency Effectiveness Approaches   70

  Goal Approach, 71

In Practice: Chevrolet   72

  *Resource-based Approach, 73 • Internal
  Process Approach, 74*

An Integrated Effectiveness Model   75

In Practice: The Thomson Corporation   78

Summary and Interpretation   79

Chapter 2 Workbook: Identifying Company Goals
and Strategies   80

Case for Analysis: The University Art Museum   81

Case for Analysis: Airstar, Inc.   84

Chapter 2 Workshop: Competing Values
and Organizational Effectiveness   85

**Chapter 3: Fundamentals
of Organization Structure   88**

A Look Inside: Ford Motor Company   89

  Purpose of This Chapter, 90

Organization Structure   90

Information-Processing Perspective on Structure   91

Book Mark 3.0: The Future of Work: How the New
Order of Business Will Shape Your Organization, Your
Management Style, and Your Life   92

  Vertical Information Linkages, 93

In Practice: Oracle Corporation   94

  Horizontal Information Linkages, 95

Organization Design Alternatives   99

  *Required Work Activities, 99 • Reporting
  Relationships, 100 • Departmental
  Grouping Options, 100*

Functional, Divisional, and Geographical Designs   102

  Functional Structure, 102

In Practice: Blue Bell Creameries, Inc.   103

  *Functional Structure with Horizontal
  Linkages, 104 • Divisional Structure, 104*

In Practice: Microsoft   106

  Geographical Structure, 107

Matrix Structure   108

  *Conditions for the Matrix, 109 • Strengths
  and Weaknesses, 110*

In Practice: Englander Steel   111

Horizontal Structure   113

  Characteristics, 114

In Practice: GE Salisbury   115

  Strengths and Weaknesses, 116

Virtual Network Structure   117

  How the Structure Works, 117

In Practice: TiVo Inc.   118

  Strengths and Weaknesses, 118

Hybrid Structure   120

Applications of Structural Design   122

  *Structural Alignment, 122 • Symptoms of
  Structural Deficiency, 123*

Summary and Interpretation   124

Chapter 3 Workbook: You and Organization
Structure   126

Case for Analysis: C & C Grocery Stores, Inc.   126

Case for Analysis: Aquarius Advertising Agency   129

Part 3: Open System Design Elements   135

Chapter 4: The External Environment   136

A Look Inside: Nokia   137

  Purpose of This Chapter, 138

The Environmental Domain   138

  *Task Environment, 138 • General
  Environment, 140 • International
  Context, 141*

In Practice: Ogilvy & Mather   142

Environmental Uncertainty   142

  *Simple–Complex Dimension, 143 •
  Stable–Unstable Dimension, 144*

Book Mark 4.0: Confronting Reality: Doing What Matters
to Get Things Right   144

  Framework, 145

Adapting to Environmental Uncertainty   147

  *Positions and Departments, 147 • Buffering
  and Boundary Spanning, 147*

In Practice: Genesco   149

   *Differentiation and Integration, 149 •
   Organic versus Mechanistic Management
   Processes, 151 • Planning, Forecasting, and
   Responsiveness, 152*

Leading by Design: Rowe Furniture Company   153

Framework for Organizational Responses
   to Uncertainty   154

Resource Dependence   154

Controlling Environmental Resources   156

   *Establishing Interorganizational Linkages,
   156*

In Practice: Verizon and SBC Communications Inc.   157

   *Controlling the Environmental Domain,
   159*

In Practice: Wal-Mart   160

   *Organization–Environment Integrative
   Framework, 161*

Summary and Interpretation   161

Chapter 4 Workbook: Organizations You Rely On   164

Case for Analysis: The Paradoxical Twins:
Acme and Omega Electronics   165

Chapter 5: Interorganizational Relationships   170

A Look Inside: International Truck
and Engine Corporation   171

   Purpose of This Chapter, 172

Organizational Ecosystems   172

   Is Competition Dead? 173

In Practice: Amazon.com Inc.   173

   *The Changing Role of Management, 174 •
   Interorganizational Framework, 176*

Resource Dependence   177

   *Resource Strategies, 177 • Power Strategies,
   178*

Collaborative Networks   178

   *Why Collaboration? 179 • From
   Adversaries to Partners, 180*

Book Mark 5.0: Managing Strategic Relationships:
The Key to Business Success   181

In Practice: Bombardier   182

Population Ecology   183

   *Organizational Form and Niche, 184 •
   Process of Ecological Change, 185*

Leading by Design: Shazam—It's Magic!   186

   Strategies for Survival, 187

In Practice: Genentech   188

Institutionalism   188

In Practice: Wal-Mart   189

   *The Institutional View and Organization
   Design, 190 • Institutional Similarity, 190*

Summary and Interpretation   193

Chapter 5 Workbook: Management Fads   195

Case for Analysis: Oxford Plastics Company   195

Case for Analysis: Hugh Russel, Inc.   196

Chapter 5 Workshop: Ugli Orange Case   199

Chapter 6: Designing Organizations for the International Environment   204

A Look Inside: Gruner + Jahr   205

   Purpose of This Chapter, 206

Entering the Global Arena   206

   *Motivations for Global Expansion, 206 •
   Stages of International Development, 209 •
   Global Expansion through International
   Strategic Alliances, 210*

Designing Structure to Fit Global Strategy   211

   *Model for Global versus Local
   Opportunities, 211 • International
   Division, 214 • Global Product Division
   Structure, 215 • Global Geographical
   Division Structure, 215*

In Practice: Colgate-Palmolive Company   217

   Global Matrix Structure, 218

In Practice: Asea Brown Boveri Ltd. (ABB)   219

Building Global Capabilities   220

   The Global Organizational Challenge, 220

In Practice: Sony   223

   Global Coordination Mechanisms, 224

Cultural Differences in Coordination and Control   227

   *National Value Systems, 227 • Three
   National Approaches to Coordination
   and Control, 227*

Book Mark 6.0: Cross-Cultural Business Behavior:
Marketing, Negotiating and Managing
Across Cultures   228

The Transnational Model of Organization   230

Summary and Interpretation   233

Chapter 6 Workbook: Made in the U.S.A.?   235

Case for Analysis: TopDog Software   235

Case for Analysis: Rhodes Industries   236

Chapter 6 Workshop: Comparing Cultures   239

Part 4: Internal Design Elements

243

Chapter 7: Manufacturing and Service Technologies

244

A Look Inside: American Axle & Manufacturing (AAM)   245

Purpose of This Chapter, 247

Core Organization Manufacturing Technology   248

Manufacturing Firms, 248 • Strategy, Technology, and Performance, 250

In Practice: Printronix   251

Book Mark 7.0: Inviting Disaster: Lessons from the Edge of Technology   252

Contemporary Applications   253

Flexible Manufacturing Systems, 253 • Lean Manufacturing, 254

In Practice: Autoliv   255

Leading by Design: Dell Computer   256

Performance and Structural Implications, 257

Core Organization Service Technology   259

Service Firms, 259 • Designing the Service Organization, 262

In Practice: Pret A Manger   263

Non-Core Departmental Technology   264

Variety, 264 • Analyzability, 264 • Framework, 264

Department Design   266

In Practice: Parkland Memorial Hospital   268

Workflow Interdependence among Departments   269

Types, 269 • Structural Priority, 271 • Structural Implications, 272

In Practice: Athletic Teams   273

Impact of Technology on Job Design   274

Job Design, 274 • Sociotechnical Systems, 275

Summary and Interpretation   276

Chapter 7 Workbook: Bistro Technology   278

Case for Analysis: Acetate Department   280

Chapter 8: Information Technology and Control

286

A Look Inside: The Progressive Group of Insurance Companies   287

Purpose of This Chapter, 289

Information Technology Evolution   289

In Practice: Anheuser-Busch   290

Information for Decision Making and Control   291

Organizational Decision-Making Systems, 291 • Feedback Control Model, 293 • Management Control Systems, 293

In Practice: eBay   295

The Balanced Scorecard, 296

Adding Strategic Value: Strengthening Internal Coordination   298

Intranets, 298 • Enterprise Resource Planning, 299 • Knowledge Management, 300

Book Mark 8.0: The Myth of the Paperless Office   302

In Practice: Montgomery-Watson Harza   303

Adding Strategic Value: Strengthening External Relationships   304

Leading by Design: Corrugated Supplies   304

The Integrated Enterprise, 305 • Customer Relationship Management, 307 • E-Business Organization Design, 307

In Practice: Tesco.com   308

IT Impact on Organization Design   309

Summary and Interpretation   311

Chapter 8 Workbook: Are You Fast Enough to Succeed in Internet Time?   313

Case for Analysis: Century Medical   315

Case for Analysis: Product X   316

Chapter 9: Organization Size, Life Cycle, and Decline

319

A Look Inside: Interpol   320

Purpose of This Chapter, 321

Organization Size: Is Bigger Better?   321

Pressures for Growth, 321 • Dilemmas of Large Size, 322

Book Mark 9.0: Execution: The Discipline of Getting Things Done   325

Organizational Life Cycle   326

Stages of Life Cycle Development, 326

In Practice: Nike   329

Organizational Characteristics during the Life Cycle, 330

Organizational Bureaucracy and Control   331

What Is Bureaucracy? 332

In Practice: United Parcel Service   333

Size and Structural Control, 334

Bureaucracy in a Changing World   335

*Organizing Temporary Systems for
Flexibility and Innovation, 336* • *Other
Approaches to Reducing Bureaucracy, 337*

Leading by Design: The Salvation Army   338

Organizational Control Strategies   339

Bureaucratic Control, 339 • *Market
Control, 340*

In Practice: Imperial Oil Limited   341

Clan Control, 341

In Practice: Southwest Airlines   342

Organizational Decline and Downsizing   343

Definition and Causes, 343 • *A Model of
Decline Stages, 344*

In Practice: Brobeck, Phleger & Harrison LLP   346

Downsizing Implementation, 346

In Practice: Charles Schwab & Company   348

Summary and Interpretation   348

Chapter 9 Workbook: Control Mechanisms   350

Case for Analysis: Sunflower Incorporated   351

Chapter 9 Workshop: Windsock, Inc.   352

Part 5: Managing Dynamic Processes   357

Chapter 10: Organizational Culture and Ethical Values   358

A Look Inside: Boots Company PLC   359

Purpose of This Chapter, 360

Organizational Culture   361

What Is Culture? 361 • *Emergence and
Purpose of Culture, 361* • *Interpreting
Culture, 363*

Book Mark 10.0: Good to Great: Why Some
Companies Make the Leap . . . And Others Don't   364

Organization Design and Culture   367

The Adaptability Culture, 368 • *The
Mission Culture, 368*

In Practice: J.C. Penney   369

The Clan Culture, 369 • *The Bureaucratic
Culture, 369* • *Culture Strength and
Organizational Subcultures, 370*

In Practice: Pitney Bowes Credit Corporation   371

Organizational Culture, Learning, and Performance   371

Leading by Design: JetBlue Airways   372

Ethical Values and Social Responsibility   374

*Sources of Individual Ethical Principles,
374* • *Managerial Ethics and Social
Responsibility, 375* • *Does It Pay to Be
Good? 377*

Sources of Ethical Values in Organizations   378

Personal Ethics, 378 • *Organizational
Culture, 379* • *Organizational Systems, 379*
• External Stakeholders, 380

How Leaders Shape Culture and Ethics   381

Values-based Leadership, 381

In Practice: Kingston Technology Co.   382

Formal Structure and Systems, 382

In Practice: General Electric   385

Corporate Culture and Ethics in a Global
Environment   386

Summary and Interpretation   387

Chapter 10 Workbook: Shop 'til You Drop:
Corporate Culture in the Retail World   389

Case for Analysis: Implementing Change at
National Industrial Products   390

Case for Analysis: Does This Milkshake Taste
Funny?   392

Chapter 10 Workshop: The Power of Ethics   394

Chapter 11: Innovation and Change   398

A Look Inside: Toyota Motor Corporation   399

Purpose of This Chapter, 400

Innovate or Perish: The Strategic Role
of Change   400

Incremental versus Radical Change, 400 •
Strategic Types of Change, 402

Leading by Design: Google   403

Elements for Successful Change   405

Technology Change   407

The Ambidextrous Approach, 407 •
*Techniques for Encouraging Technology
Change, 408*

In Practice: W. L. Gore   411

New Products and Services   412

New Product Success Rate, 412 • *Reasons
for New Product Success, 412* •
Horizontal Coordination Model, 413

In Practice: Procter & Gamble   415

Achieving Competitive Advantage: The Need for Speed, 416

Strategy and Structure Change   417

The Dual-Core Approach, 417 • Organization Design for Implementing Administrative Change, 418

In Practice: Tyco International   419

Culture Change   420

Forces for Culture Change, 420

In Practice: X-Rite Inc.   421

Organization Development Culture Change Interventions, 422

Strategies for Implementing Change   424

Book Mark 11.0: The Change Monster: The Human Forces That Fuel or Foil Corporate Transformation and Change   424

Leadership for Change, 425 • Barriers to Change, 426 • Techniques for Implementation, 426

Summary and Interpretation   429

Chapter 11 Workbook: Innovation Climate   430

Case for Analysis: Shoe Corporation of Illinois   432

Case for Analysis: Southern Discomfort   436

Chapter 12: Decision-Making Processes   441

A Look Inside: Maytag   442

Purpose of This Chapter, 443

Definitions   443

Individual Decision Making   445

Rational Approach, 445

In Practice: Alberta Consulting   448

Bounded Rationality Perspective, 448

Leading by Design: Motek   450

Book Mark 12.0: Blink: The Power of Thinking without Thinking   452

In Practice: Paramount Pictures   453

Organizational Decision Making   453

Management Science Approach, 453

In Practice: Continental Airlines   454

Carnegie Model, 456

In Practice: Encyclopaedia Britannica   457

Incremental Decision Process Model, 458

In Practice: Gillette Company   461

The Learning Organization   462

Combining the Incremental Process and Carnegie Models, 462 • Garbage Can Model, 463

In Practice: I ♥ Huckabees   466

Contingency Decision-Making Framework   467

Problem Consensus, 467 • Technical Knowledge about Solutions, 468 • Contingency Framework, 468

Special Decision Circumstances   471

High-Velocity Environments, 471 • Decision Mistakes and Learning, 472 • Escalating Commitment, 473

Summary and Interpretation   473

Chapter 12 Workbook: Decision Styles   475

Case for Analysis: Cracking the Whip   476

Case for Analysis: The Dilemma of Aliesha State College: Competence versus Need   477

Chapter 13: Conflict, Power, and Politics   481

A Look Inside: Morgan Stanley   482

Purpose of This Chapter, 483

Intergroup Conflict in Organizations   483

Sources of Conflict, 484

Leading by Design: Advanced Cardiovascular Systems   486

Rational versus Political Model, 487

Power and Organizations   488

Individual versus Organizational Power, 489 • Power versus Authority, 489 • Vertical Sources of Power, 490 • Horizontal Sources of Power, 494

In Practice: University of Illinois   496

In Practice: HCA and Aetna Inc.   498

Political Processes in Organizations   498

Definition, 499 • When Is Political Activity Used? 500

Using Power, Politics, and Collaboration   500

Tactics for Increasing Power, 501 • Political Tactics for Using Power, 502

Book Mark 13.0: Influence: Science and Practice   504

In Practice: Yahoo!   505

Tactics for Enhancing Collaboration, 505

In Practice: Aluminum Company of America/
International Association of Machinists   506
Summary and Interpretation   508
Chapter 13 Workbook: How Do You Handle
Conflict?   510
Case for Analysis: The Daily Tribune   511
Case for Analysis: Pierre Dux   512

Integrative Cases   **517**
1.0 It Isn't So Simple: Infrastructure Change
    at Royce Consulting   518
2.0 Custom Chip, Inc.   522
3.0 W. L. Gore & Associates, Inc. Entering 1998   528

4.0 XEL Communications, Inc. (C): Forming
    a Strategic Partnership   543
5.0 Empire Plastics   549
6.0 The Audubon Zoo, 1993   552
7.0 Moss Adams, LLP   566
8.1 Littleton Manufacturing (A)   577
8.2 Littleton Manufacturing (B)   589

Glossary   **591**

Name Index   **601**

Corporate Name Index   **610**

Subject Index   **614**

Preface

My vision for the Ninth Edition of *Organization Theory and Design* is to integrate contemporary problems about organization design with classic ideas and theories in a way that is interesting and enjoyable for students. Significant changes in this edition include updates to every chapter that incorporate the most recent ideas, new case examples, new book reviews, new end-of-chapter cases, and new end-of-book integrative cases. The research and theories in the field of organization studies are rich and insightful and will help students and managers understand their organizational world and solve real-life problems. My mission is to combine the concepts and models from organizational theory with changing events in the real world to provide the most up-to-date view of organization design available.

Distinguishing Features of the Ninth Edition

Many students in a typical organization theory course do not have extensive work experience, especially at the middle and upper levels, where organization theory is most applicable. To engage students in the world of organizations, the Ninth Edition adds and expands significant features: Leading by Design boxes with current examples of companies that are successfully using organization design concepts to compete in today's complex and uncertain business world, student experiential activities that engage students in applying chapter concepts, new Book Marks, new In Practice examples, and new end-of-chapter and integrative cases for student analysis. The total set of features substantially expands and improves the book's content and accessibility. These multiple pedagogical devices are used to enhance student involvement in text materials.

Leading by Design The Leading by Design features describe companies that have undergone a major shift in organization design, strategic direction, values, or culture as they strive to be more competitive in today's turbulent global environment. Many of these companies are applying new design ideas such as network organizing, e-business, or temporary systems for flexibility and innovation. The Leading by Design examples illustrate company transformations toward knowledge sharing, empowerment of employees, new structures, new cultures, the breaking down of barriers between departments and organizations, and the joining together of employees in a common mission. Examples of Leading by Design organizations include Wegmans Supermarkets, Google, The Salvation Army, JetBlue, Corrugated Supplies, Shazam, the Rolling Stones, and Dell Computer.

Book Marks Book Marks, a unique feature of this text, are book reviews that reflect current issues of concern for managers working in real-life organizations. These reviews describe the varied ways companies are dealing with the challenges of today's changing environment. New Book Marks in the Ninth Edition include *The Future of Work: How the New Order of Business Will Shape Your Organization, Your Management Style, and Your Life; Execution: The Discipline of Getting Things Done; What Really Works: The 4 + 2 Formula for Sustained Business Success; Blink: The Power of Thinking without Thinking; The Company: A Short History of a Revolutionary Idea;* and *Confronting Reality: Doing What Matters to Get Things Right.*

New Case Examples This edition contains many new examples to illustrate theoretical concepts. Many examples are international, and all are based on real organizations. New chapter opening cases for the Ninth Edition include Gruner + Jahr, International Truck and Engine Company, Morgan Stanley, Ford Motor Company, Boots Company PLC, Maytag, Toyota, and American Axle & Manufacturing. New In Practice cases used within chapters to illustrate specific concepts include TiVo Inc., General Electric, J.C. Penney, Genentech, Ryanair, Charles Schwab and Company, Nike, Verizon Communications, eBay, Tyco International, Sony, and the Federal Bureau of Investigation.

A Look Inside This feature introduces each chapter with a relevant and interesting organizational example. Many examples are international, and all are based on real organizations. New cases include Boots Company PLC, International Truck and Engine Company, Gruner + Jahr, Morgan Stanley, Toyota, and American Axle & Manufacturing.

In Practice These cases also illustrate theoretical concepts in organizational settings. New In Practice cases used within chapters to illustrate specific concepts include J.C. Penney, Charles Schwab and Company, eBay, the Federal Bureau of Investigation, Ryanair, Chevrolet, Genentech, Tyco International, and Sony.

Manager's Briefcase Located in the chapter margins, this feature tells students how to use concepts to analyze cases and manage organizations.

Text Exhibits Frequent exhibits are used to help students visualize organizational relationships, and the artwork has been redone to communicate concepts more clearly.

Summary and Interpretation The summary and interpretation section tells students how the chapter points are important in the broader context of organizational theory.

Case for Analysis These cases are tailored to chapter concepts and provide a vehicle for student analysis and discussion.

Integrative Cases The integrative cases at the end of the text are positioned to encourage student discussion and involvement. These cases include Royce Consulting; Custom Chip, Inc.; W. L. Gore & Associates, Inc.; XEL Communications, Inc.; Empire Plastics; The Audubon Zoo; Moss Adams, LLP; and Littleton Manufacturing.

New Concepts

Many concepts have been added or expanded in this edition. New material has been added on culture, learning, and performance; virtual network organization structures; applying ethics to create socially responsible organizations; outsourcing; lean manufacturing; customer relationship management; political tactics for increasing and using manager power; applying business intelligence; and the use of global coordination mechanisms for transferring knowledge and innovation. Many ideas are aimed at helping students learn to design organizations for an environment characterized by uncertainty; a renewed emphasis on ethics and social responsibility; and the need for a speedy response to change, crises, or shifting customer expectations. In addition, coping with the complexity of today's global environment is explored thoroughly in Chapter 6.

Chapter Organization

Each chapter is highly focused and is organized into a logical framework. Many organization theory textbooks treat material in sequential fashion, such as "Here's View A, Here's View B, Here's View C," and so on. *Organization Theory and Design* shows how they apply in organizations. Moreover, each chapter sticks to the essential point. Students are not introduced to extraneous material or confusing methodological squabbles that occur among organizational researchers. The body of research in most areas points to a major trend, which is reported here. Several chapters develop a framework that organizes major ideas into an overall scheme.

This book has been extensively tested on students. Feedback from students and faculty members has been used in the revision. The combination of organization theory concepts, book reviews, examples of leading organizations, case illustrations, experiential exercises, and other teaching devices is designed to meet student learning needs, and students have responded favorably.

Supplements

Instructor's Manual with Test Bank (ISBN: 0-324-40543-X) The Instructor's Manual contains chapter overviews, chapter outlines, lecture enhancements, discussion questions, discussion of workbook activities, discussion of chapter cases, Internet activities, case notes for integrative cases, and a guide to the videos available for use with the text. The Test Bank consists of multiple choice, true/false, and short answer questions.

PowerPoint Lecture Presentation Available on the Instructor's Resource CD-ROM and the Web site, the PowerPoint Lecture Presentation enables instructors to customize their own multimedia classroom presentations. Prepared in conjunction with the text and instructor's resource guide, the package contains approximately 150 slides. It includes figures and tables from the text, as well as outside materials to supplement chapter concepts. Material is organized by chapter and can be modified or expanded for individual classroom use. PowerPoints are also easily printed to create customized transparency masters.

ExamView A computerized version of the Test Bank is available upon request. ExamView contains all of the questions in the printed test bank. This program is easy-to-use test creation software compatible with Microsoft Windows. Instructors can add or edit questions, instructions, and answers and can select questions (randomly or numerically) by previewing them on the screen. Instructors can also create and administer quizzes online, whether over the Internet, a local area network (LAN), or a wide area network (WAN).

Instructor's Resource CD-ROM (ISBN: 0-324-40579-0) Key instructor ancillaries (Instructor's Manual, Test Bank, ExamView, and PowerPoint slides) are provided on CD-ROM, giving instructors the ultimate tool for customizing lectures and presentations.

WebTutor™ Toolbox (0-324-43106-6 on WebCT or 0-324-43109-0 on Black-Board) WebTutor is an interactive, Web-based student supplement on WebCT and/or BlackBoard that harnesses the power of the Internet to deliver innovative learning aids that actively engage students. The instructor can incorporate WebTutor as an integral part of the course, or the students can use it on their own as a study guide.

Web Site (http://daft.swlearning.com) The Daft Web site is a comprehensive, resource-rich location for both instructors and students to find pertinent information. The Instructor Resources section contains an Instructor's Manual download, Test Bank download, PowerPoint download, and case material.

Experiential Exercises in Organization Theory and Design, Second Edition By H. Eugene Baker III and Steven K. Paulson of the University of North Florida

Tailored to the Table of Contents in Daft's *Organization Theory and Design*, Ninth Edition, the core purpose of *Experiential Exercises in Organization Theory and Design* is to provide courses in organizational theory with a set of classroom exercises that will help students better understand and internalize the basic principles of the course. The chapters of the book cover the most basic and widely covered concepts in the field. Each chapter focuses on a central topic, such as organizational power, production technology, or organizational culture, and provides all necessary materials to fully participate in three different exercises. Some exercises are intended to be completed by individuals, others in groups, and still others can be used either way. The exercises range from instrumentation-based and assessment questionnaires to actual creative production activities.

Acknowledgments

Textbook writing is a team enterprise. The Ninth Edition has integrated ideas and hard work from many people to whom I am grateful. Reviewers and focus group participants made an especially important contribution. They praised many features, were critical of things that didn't work well, and offered valuable suggestions.

David Ackerman
University of Alaska, Southeast

Michael Bourke
Houston Baptist University

Suzanne Clinton
Cameron University

Jo Anne Duffy
Sam Houston State University

Cheryl Duvall
Mercer University

Patricia Feltes
Missouri State University

Robert Girling
Sonoma State University

John A. Gould
University of Maryland

Ralph Hanke
Pennsylvania State University

Bruce J. Hanson
Pepperdine University

Guiseppe Labianca
Tulane University

Jane Lemaster
University of Texas–Pan American

Steven Maranville
University of Saint Thomas

Rick Martinez
Baylor University

Janet Near
Indiana University

Julie Newcomer
Texas Woman's University

Asbjorn Osland
George Fox University

Laynie Pizzolatto
Nicholls State University

Samantha Rice
Abilene Christian University

Richard Saaverda
University of Michigan

W. Robert Sampson
University of Wisconsin, Eau Claire

Amy Sevier
University of Southern Mississippi

W. Scott Sherman
Pepperdine University

Thomas Terrell
Coppin State College

Jack Tucci
Southeastern Louisiana University

Judith White
Santa Clara University

Jan Zahrly
University of North Dakota

Among my professional colleagues, I am grateful to my friends and colleagues at Vanderbilt's Owen School—Bruce Barry, Ray Friedman, Neta Moye, Rich Oliver, David Owens, and Bart Victor—for their intellectual stimulation and feedback. I also owe a special debt to Dean Jim Bradford and Senior Associate Dean Joe Blackburn for providing the time and resources for me to stay current on the organization design literature and develop the revisions for the text.

I want to extend special thanks for my editorial associate, Pat Lane. She skillfully drafted materials on a variety of topics and special features, found resources, and did an outstanding job with the copyedited manuscript and page proofs. Pat's personal enthusiasm and care for the content of this text enabled the Ninth Edition to continue its high level of excellence.

The team at South-Western also deserves special mention. Joe Sabatino did a great job of designing the project and offering ideas for improvement. Emma Guttler was superb as Developmental Editor, keeping the people and project on schedule while solving problems creatively and quickly. Cliff Kallemeyn, Production Editor, provided superb project coordination and used his creativity and management skills to facilitate the book's on-time completion.

Finally, I want to acknowledge the love and contributions of my wife, Dorothy Marcic. Dorothy has been very supportive of my textbook projects and has created an environment in which we can grow together. She helped the book take a giant step forward with her creation of the Workbook and Workshop student exercises. Perhaps best of all, Dorothy lets me practice applying organization design ideas as co-producer of her theatrical productions. I also want to acknowledge the love and support of my daughters, Danielle, Amy, Roxanne, Solange, and Elizabeth, who make my life special during our precious time together.

PART 1

Introduction to Organizations

1. Organizations and
   Organization Theory

1 Organizations and Organization Theory

Organization Theory in Action
Topics • Current Challenges • Purpose of This Chapter

What Is an Organization?
Definition • Types of Organizations • Importance of Organizations

Perspectives on Organizations
Open Systems • Organizational Configuration

Dimensions of Organization Design
Structural Dimensions • Contextual Dimensions • Performance and Effectiveness Outcomes

The Evolution of Organization Theory and Design
Historical Perspectives • Contemporary Organization Design • Efficient Performance versus the Learning Organization

Framework for the Book
Levels of Analysis • Plan of the Book • Plan of Each Chapter

Summary and Interpretation

A Look Inside

Xerox Corporation

Xerox was once an icon of innovation and corporate success in the business of copying and digital imaging. On the eve of the twenty-first century, the company seemed on top of the world, with fast-rising earnings, a soaring stock price, and a new line of computerized copier-printers that were technologically superior to rival products. Less than 2 years later, many considered Xerox a has-been, destined to fade into history. Consider the following events:

- Sales and earnings plummeted as rivals caught up with Xerox's high-end digital machines, offering comparable products at lower prices.
- Xerox's losses for the opening year of the twenty-first century totaled $384 million, and the company continued to bleed red ink. Debt mounted to $17 billion.
- The stock fell from a high of $64 to less than $4, amid fears that the company would file for federal bankruptcy protection. Over an 18-month period, Xerox lost $38 billion in shareholder wealth.
- Twenty-two thousand Xerox workers lost their jobs, further weakening the morale and loyalty of remaining employees. Major customers were alienated, too, by a restructuring that threw salespeople into unfamiliar territories and tied billing up in knots, leading to mass confusion and billing errors.
- The company was fined a whopping $10 million by the Securities and Exchange Commission (SEC) for accounting irregularities and alleged accounting fraud.

What went wrong at Xerox? The company's deterioration is a classic story of organizational decline. Although Xerox appeared to fall almost overnight, the organization's recent problems are connected to a series of organizational blunders over a period of many years.

Background

Xerox was founded in 1906 as the Haloid Company, a photographic supply house that developed the world's first xerographic copier, introduced in 1959. Without a doubt, the "914" copier was a money-making machine. By the time it was retired in the early 1970s, the 914 was the best-selling industrial product of all time, and the new name of the company, Xerox, was listed in the dictionary as a synonym for photocopying.

Joseph C. Wilson, Haloid's longtime chairman and president, created a positive, people-oriented culture continued by his successor, David Kearns, who steered Xerox until 1990. The Xerox culture and its dedicated employees (sometimes called "Xeroids") were the envy of the corporate world. In addition to values of fairness and respect, Xerox's culture emphasized risk taking and employee involvement. Wilson wrote the following for early recruiting materials: "We seek people who are willing to accept risk, willing to try new ideas and have ideas of their own . . . who are not afraid to change what they are doing from one day to the next, and from one year to the next . . . who welcome new people and new positions." Xerox continues to use these words in its recruiting efforts today, but the culture the words epitomize began to erode years ago.

"Burox" Takes Hold

Like many profitable organizations, Xerox became a victim of its own success. Leaders no doubt knew that the company needed to move beyond copiers to sustain its growth, but they found it difficult to look beyond the 70 percent gross profit margins of the 914.

Xerox's Palo Alto Research Center (PARC), established in 1970, became known around the world for innovation—many of the most revolutionary technologies in the computer industry, including the personal computer, graphical user interface, Ethernet, and laser printer, were invented at PARC. But the copier bureaucracy, or *Burox* as it came to be known, blinded Xerox leaders to the enormous potential of these innovations. While Xerox was plodding along selling copy machines, younger, smaller, and hungrier companies were developing PARC technologies into tremendous money-making products and services. "At Xerox, unless there's a crisis in the organization, as long as the stock prices are acceptable, it doesn't move very fast," says a former Xerox manager.

The dangers of Burox became dramatically clear in the early 1970s, when the company's xerography patents began expiring. Suddenly, Japanese rivals such as Canon and Ricoh were selling copiers at the cost it took Xerox to make them. Market share declined from 95 percent to 13 percent by 1982. And with no new products to make up the difference, the company had to fight hard to cut costs and reclaim market share by committing to Japanese-style techniques and total quality management. Through the strength of his leadership, CEO Kearns was able to rally the troops and rejuvenate the company by 1990. However, he also set Xerox on a path to future disaster. Seeing a need to diversify, Kearns moved the company into insurance and financial services on a large scale. By the time he turned leadership over to Paul Allaire in 1990, Xerox's balance sheet was crippled by billions of dollars in insurance liabilities.

Entering the Digital Age

Allaire wisely began a methodical, step-by-step plan for extricating Xerox from the insurance and financial services business. At the same time, he initiated a mixed strategy of cost-cutting and new-product introductions to get the stodgy company moving again. Xerox had success with a line of digital presses and new high-speed digital copiers, but it fumbled again by underestimating the threat of the inkjet printer. By the time Xerox introduced its own line of desktop printers, the game was already over.

Desktop printers, combined with increasing use of the Internet and e-mail, cut heavily into Xerox's sales of copiers. People didn't need to make as many photocopies, but there was a huge increase in the number of documents being created and shared. Rebranding Xerox as "The Document Company," Allaire pushed into the digital era, hoping to remake Xerox in the image of the rejuvenated IBM, offering not just "boxes (machines)" but complete document management solutions.

As part of that strategy, Allaire picked Richard Thoman, who was then serving as Louis Gerstner's right-hand man at IBM, as his successor. Thoman came to Xerox as president, chief operating officer, and eventually CEO, amid high hopes that the company could regain the stature of its glory years. Only 13 months later, as revenues and the stock price continued to slide, he was fired by Allaire, who had remained as Xerox chairman.

Playing Politics

Allaire and Thoman blamed each other for the failure to successfully implement the digital strategy. Outsiders, however, believe the failure had much more to do with Xerox's dysfunctional culture. The culture was already slow to adapt, and some say that under Allaire it became almost totally paralyzed by politics. Thoman was brought in to shake things up, but when he tried, the old guard rebelled. A management struggle developed, with the outsider Thoman and a few allies on one side lined up against Allaire and his group of insiders who were accustomed to doing things the Xeroid way. Recognized for his knowledge, business experience, and intensity, Thoman was also considered to be somewhat haughty and unapproachable. He was never able to exert substantial influence with key managers and employees, nor to gain the support of board members, who continued to rally behind Allaire.

The failed CEO succession illustrates the massive challenge of reinventing a nearly 100-year-old company. By the time Thoman arrived, Xerox had been going through various rounds of restructuring, cost-cutting, rejuvenating, and reinventing for nearly two decades, but little had really changed. Many believe Thoman tried to do too much too soon. He saw the urgency for change but was unable to convey that urgency to others within the company and inspire them to take the difficult journey real transformation requires.

Others doubt that anyone can fix Xerox, because the culture has become too dysfunctional and politicized. "There was always an in-crowd and an out-crowd," says one former executive. "They change the branches, but when you look closely, the same old monkeys are sitting in the trees."

The Insider's Insider

Enter Anne Mulcahy, the consummate insider. In August 2001, Allaire turned over the CEO reins to the popular twenty-four-year veteran, who had started at Xerox as a copier saleswoman and worked her way up the hierarchy. Despite her insider status, Mulcahy says she's more than willing to challenge the status quo at Xerox.

Mulcahy is a strong decision maker. She launched a multi-billion dollar turnaround plan that included massive cost-cutting and closing of several money-losing operations, including the belatedly launched line of inkjet printers. She personally negotiated the settlement of a long investigation into fraudulent accounting practices, insisting that her personal involvement was necessary to signal a new commitment to ethical business practices. She has introduced numerous new products and services in high-growth areas such as digital technology, document services, color products, and consulting. The company launched forty new products in 2004 alone, and sales and profits are growing as debt continues to shrink. Moreover, a renewed focus on innovation signals that Mulcahy and her management team are concentrating on areas that provide a solid foundation for future growth. Although the stock price is nowhere near the highs of the late 1990s, it is on a strong upturn.

By getting Xerox off the critical list, Mulcahy has gained respect and admiration from employees, labor leaders, customers, creditors, and the press. She was recognized by *Business Week* magazine as one of the best managers of the year in 2004. However, Mulcahy can't afford to rest on her laurels. Xerox faces stiff competition from Hewlett-Packard, Canon, and other technology companies. Mulcahy has to keep her management team focused on growth while also maintaining the cost controls that stabilized the company. As Xerox struggles to regain the prestige it once held, the corporate world is watching with guarded optimism. In the rapidly changing world of organizations, nothing is ever certain.[1]

Welcome to the real world of organization theory. The shifting fortunes of Xerox illustrate organization theory in action. Xerox managers were deeply involved in organization theory each day of their working lives—but they never realized it. Company managers didn't fully understand how the organization related to the environment or how it should function internally. Familiarity with organization theory can help Anne Mulcahy and her management team analyze and diagnose what is happening and the changes needed to keep the company competitive. Organization theory gives us the tools to explain the decline of Xerox and understand Mulcahy's turnaround. It helps us explain what happened in the past, as well as what may happen in the future, so that we can manage organizations more effectively.

Organization Theory in Action

■ Topics

Each of the topics to be covered in this book is illustrated in the Xerox case. Consider, for example, Xerox's failure to respond to or control such elements as competitors, customers, and creditors in the fast-paced external environment; its inability to implement strategic and structural changes to help the organization attain effectiveness; ethical lapses within the organization; difficulties coping with the problems of large size and bureaucracy; lack of adequate cost controls; the negative use of power and politics among managers that created conflict and allowed the organization to drift further into chaos; and an outmoded corporate culture that stifled innovation and change. These are the subjects with which organization theory is concerned.

Briefcase

As an organization manager, keep these guidelines in mind:

Do not ignore the external environment or protect the organization from it. Because the environment is unpredictable, do not expect to achieve complete order and rationality within the organization. Strive for a balance between order and flexibility.

Of course, the concepts of organization theory are not limited to Xerox. Managers at AirTran Airways applied organization theory concepts to expand their business during a difficult time. Even as many carriers were slashing costs and seeking federal loans to combat huge losses, AirTran maintained a course of steady growth by developing strong interorganizational partnerships.[2] IBM, Hewlett-Packard, and Ford Motor Company have all undergone major structural transformations using concepts based in organization theory. Organization theory also applies to nonprofit organizations such as the Girl Scouts, the American Humane Association, local arts organizations, colleges and universities, and the Make-a-Wish Foundation, which grants wishes to terminally ill children. Even rock groups such as the Rolling Stones benefit from an appreciation of organization theory, as described in this chapter's Leading by Design box.

Organization theory draws lessons from organizations such as the Rolling Stones, IBM, and Xerox and makes those lessons available to students and managers. The story of Xerox's decline is important because it demonstrates that even large, successful organizations are vulnerable, that lessons are not learned automatically, and that organizations are only as strong as their decision makers. Organizations are not static; they continuously adapt to shifts in the external environment. Today, many companies are facing the need to transform themselves into dramatically different organizations because of new challenges in the environment.

■ Current Challenges

Research into hundreds of organizations provides the knowledge base to make Xerox and other organizations more effective. For example, challenges facing organizations today are quite different from those of the past, and thus the concept of organizations and organization theory is evolving. For one thing, the world is changing more rapidly than ever before. Surveys of top executives indicate that coping with rapid change is the most common problem facing managers and organizations.[3] Some specific challenges are dealing with globalization, maintaining high standards of ethics and social responsibility, responding rapidly to environmental changes and customer needs, managing the digital workplace, and supporting diversity.

Globalization. The cliché that the world is getting smaller is dramatically true for today's organizations. With rapid advances in technology and communications, the time it takes to exert influence around the world from even the most remote loca-

Leading by Design

The Rolling Stones

They may be old, but they keep on rocking and rolling after more than 40 years in the music business. The Rolling Stones have enjoyed phenomenal commercial success in recent decades, generating billions of dollars in revenue from record sales, song rights, concert tickets, sponsorships, and merchandising.

The Rolling Stones group was recently cited as one of the world's ten most enduring organizations, according to a study commissioned by Booz Allen Hamilton. One reason for the Stones' success is that the band operates like an effective global business organization. The Stones have set up a solid organizational structure, with different divisions to run different aspects of the business, such as touring or merchandising. At the top of the organization is a core top management team made up of the four band members: Mick Jagger, who acts as a sort of CEO, Keith Richards, Charlie Watts, and Ronnie Wood. This core team manages a group of somewhat autonomous yet interlocking companies that include Promotour, Promopub, Promotone, and Musidor, each dedicated to a particular part of the overall business. At times, depending on what's happening in the organization, each company might employ only a few dozen people. When the band is touring, on the other hand, head count goes way up and the organization resembles a flourishing start-up company. Jagger himself keeps a close eye on the market-price range for concert tickets so that the band can keep their prices competitive. That sometimes means cutting costs and increasing efficiency to make sure the organization turns a profit.

The Stones also recognize the importance of interorganizational partnerships, cutting sponsorship deals with big companies such as Sprint, Anheuser-Busch, and Microsoft, which reportedly paid $4 million for the rights to "Start Me Up" for the launch of Windows 95. And they hire lawyers, accountants, managers, and consultants to keep in touch with changes in the environment and manage relationships with customers (fans), partners, employees, record companies, promoters, and tour sites. Jagger learned from the early days that creativity and talent aren't enough to ensure success—in the mid-1960s, the band was selling millions of records but still living hand to mouth. Today, effective control systems and widespread information sharing make sure that doesn't happen.

"You don't start to play your guitar thinking you're going to be running an organization that will maybe generate millions," Jagger says. Yet by understanding and applying organization theory, the Rolling Stones have become one of the most successful organizations ever in the music industry—and the wealthiest rock 'n' roll band on the planet.

Source: Andy Serwer, "Inside the Rolling Stones Inc.," *Fortune* (September 30, 2002), 58–72; and William J. Holstein, "Innovation, Leadership, and Still No Satisfaction," *The New York Times* (December 19, 2004), Section 3, 11.

---

tions has been reduced from years to only seconds. Markets, technologies, and organizations are becoming increasingly interconnected.[4] Today's organizations have to feel "at home" anywhere in the world. Companies can locate different parts of the organization wherever it makes the most business sense: top leadership in one country, technical brainpower and production in other locales. A related trend is to contract out some functions to organizations in other countries or to partner with foreign organizations to gain global advantage. India's Wipro Ltd. used to sell cooking oils; today, its 15,000 employees develop sophisticated software applications, design semiconductors, and manage back-office solutions for giant companies from all over the world, including CNA Life, Home Depot, and Sony. Korea's Samsung Electronics, which has manufacturing plants in fourteen countries, has long supplied components for U.S. computer firms, and it recently designed a new laptop that it will manufacture for Texas-based Dell Computer Corp. Many of Intel's new chip circuits are designed by companies in India and China. These organizations can do the job for 50 to 60 percent less than organizations based in the United States, creating new advantages as well as greater competition for U.S.-based firms.[5]

This growing interdependence means that the environment for companies is becoming extremely complex and extremely competitive. Organizations have to learn to cross lines of time, culture, and geography in order to survive. Companies large and small are searching for the right structures and processes that can help them reap the advantages of global interdependence and minimize the disadvantages.

Ethics and Social Responsibility. Ethics and social responsibility have become some of the hottest topics in corporate America. The list of executives and major corporations involved in financial and ethical scandals continues to grow. The sordid story of high-flying Enron Corporation, where managers admitted they inflated earnings and hid debt through a series of complex partnerships, was just the beginning. Executives profited handsomely from the fraud at Enron, but when the company collapsed, employees and average investors lost billions. Arthur Andersen LLP, the company's auditor, was found guilty of obstruction of justice for improperly shredding documents related to the Enron investigation. Martha Stewart, who built a multimillion-dollar style empire, has served time in jail, convicted of lying about why she unloaded shares of ImClone Systems stock just before the price plunged. And Yale University's School of Management is forcing out the head of its corporate governance institute over alleged expense-account abuse.[6] Pick up any major newspaper on almost any day, and the front page will contain news about some organization embroiled in an ethical scandal. This is corporate corruption on a scale never before seen, and the effects within organizations and society will be felt for years to come.

Although some executives and officials continue to insist that it is a few bad apples involved in all the wrongdoing, the "man on the street" is quickly forming the opinion that all corporate executives are crooks.[7] The public is disgusted with the whole mess, and leaders will face tremendous pressure from the government and the public to hold their organizations and employees to high ethical and professional standards.

Speed of Responsiveness. A third significant challenge for organizations is to respond quickly and decisively to environmental changes, organizational crises, or shifting customer expectations. For much of the twentieth century, organizations operated in a relatively stable environment, so managers could focus on designing structures and systems that kept the organization running smoothly and efficiently. There was little need to search for new ways to cope with increased competition, volatile environmental shifts, or changing customer demands. Today, globalization and advancing technology has accelerated the pace at which organizations in all industries must roll out new products and services to stay competitive.

Today's customers also want products and services tailored to their exact needs. Companies that relied on mass production and distribution techniques must be prepared with new computer-aided systems that can produce one-of-a-kind variations and streamlined distribution systems that deliver products directly from the manufacturer to the consumer. Another shift brought about by technology is that the financial basis of today's economy is *information*, not machines and factories. For example, in the mid-1900s tangible assets represented 73 percent of the assets of nonfinancial corporations in the United States. By 2002, the percentage had shrunk to about 53 percent, and it continues to decline.[8] One result of concern to organizational leaders is that the primary factor of production becomes knowledge, to which managers must respond by increasing the power of employees. Employees, not production machinery, have the power and knowledge needed to keep the company competitive.

Considering the turmoil and flux inherent in today's world, the mindset needed by organizational leaders is to expect the unexpected and be prepared for rapid change and potential crises. Crisis management has moved to the forefront in light of terrorist attacks all over the world; a tough economy, rocky stock market, and weakening consumer confidence; widespread ethical scandals; and, in general, an environment that may shift dramatically at a moment's notice.

The Digital Workplace. Many traditional managers feel particularly awkward in today's technology-driven workplace. Organizations have been engulfed by information technology that affects how they are designed and managed. In today's workplace, many employees perform much of their work on computers and may work in virtual teams, connected electronically to colleagues around the world. In addition, organizations are becoming enmeshed in electronic networks. The world of e-business is booming as more and more business takes place by digital processes over a computer network rather than in physical space. Some companies have taken e-business to very high levels to achieve amazing performance. Dell Computer Corp. pioneered the use of end-to-end digital supply-chain networks to keep in touch with customers, take orders, buy components from suppliers, coordinate with manufacturing partners, and ship customized products directly to consumers. This trend toward *disintermediation*—eliminating the middleman—is affecting every industry, prompting a group of consultants at a Harvard University conference to conclude that businesses today must either "Dell or Be Delled."[9] These advances mean that organizational leaders not only need to be technologically savvy but are also responsible for managing a web of relationships that reaches far beyond the boundaries of the physical organization, building flexible e-links between a company and its employees, suppliers, contract partners, and customers.[10]

Diversity. Diversity is a fact of life that no organization can afford to ignore. As organizations increasingly operate on a global playing field, the workforce—as well as the customer base—is changing dramatically. Many of today's leading organizations have an international face. Look at the makeup of consulting firm McKinsey & Co. In the 1970s, most consultants were American, but by the turn of the century, McKinsey's chief partner was a foreign national (Rajat Gupta from India), only 40 percent of consultants were American, and the firm's foreign-born consultants came from forty different countries.[11]

The demographics of the U.S. population and workforce are also shifting. Today's average worker is older, and many more women, people of color, and immigrants are seeking job and advancement opportunities. During the 1990s, the foreign-born population of the United States nearly doubled, and immigrants now make up more than 12 percent of the U.S. workforce. By 2050, it is estimated that 85 percent of entrants into the workforce will be women and people of color. Already, white males, the majority of workers in the past, represent less than half of the workforce.[12] This growing diversity brings a variety of challenges, such as maintaining a strong corporate culture while supporting diversity, balancing work and family concerns, and coping with the conflict brought about by varying cultural styles.

People from diverse ethnic and cultural backgrounds offer varying styles, and managing diversity may be one of the most rewarding challenges for organizations competing on a global basis. For example, research has indicated that women's style of doing business may hold important lessons for success in the emerging global world of the twenty-first century. Yet the glass ceiling persists, keeping women from reaching positions of top leadership.[13]

■ Purpose of This Chapter

The purpose of this chapter is to explore the nature of organizations and organization theory today. Organization theory has developed from the systematic study of organizations by scholars. Concepts are obtained from living, ongoing organizations. Organization theory can be practical, as illustrated in the Xerox case. It helps people understand, diagnose, and respond to emerging organizational needs and problems.

The next section begins with a formal definition of organization and then explores introductory concepts for describing and analyzing organizations. Next, the scope and nature of organization theory are discussed more fully. Succeeding sections examine the history of organization theory and design, the development of new organizational forms in response to changes in the environment, and how organization theory can help people manage complex organizations in a rapidly changing world. The chapter closes with a brief overview of the themes to be covered in this book.

What Is an Organization?

Organizations are hard to see. We see outcroppings, such as a tall building, a computer workstation, or a friendly employee; but the whole organization is vague and abstract and may be scattered among several locations, even around the world. We know organizations are there because they touch us every day. Indeed, they are so common that we take them for granted. We hardly notice that we are born in a hospital, have our birth records registered in a government agency, are educated in schools and universities, are raised on food produced on corporate farms, are treated by doctors engaged in a joint practice, buy a house built by a construction company and sold by a real estate agency, borrow money from a bank, turn to police and fire departments when trouble erupts, use moving companies to change residences, receive an array of benefits from government agencies, spend 40 hours a week working in an organization, and are even laid to rest by a funeral home.[14]

■ Definition

Organizations as diverse as a church, a hospital, and Xerox have characteristics in common. The definition used in this book to describe organizations is as follows: **organizations** are (1) social entities that (2) are goal-directed, (3) are designed as deliberately structured and coordinated activity systems, and (4) are linked to the external environment.

The key element of an organization is not a building or a set of policies and procedures; organizations are made up of people and their relationships with one another. An organization exists when people interact with one another to perform essential functions that help attain goals. Recent trends in management recognize the importance of human resources, with most new approaches designed to empower employees with greater opportunities to learn and contribute as they work together toward common goals.

Managers deliberately structure and coordinate organizational resources to achieve the organization's purpose. However, even though work may be structured into separate departments or sets of activities, most organizations today are striving for greater horizontal coordination of work activities, often using teams of employees from different functional areas to work together on projects. Boundaries between departments, as well as those between organizations, are becoming more flexible and diffuse as companies face the need to respond to changes in the external environment more rapidly. An organization cannot exist without interacting with customers, suppliers, competitors, and other elements of the external environment. Today, some companies are even cooperating with their competitors, sharing information and technology to their mutual advantage.

Types of Organizations

Some organizations are large, multinational corporations. Others are small, family-owned shops. Some manufacture products such as automobiles or computers, whereas others provide services such as legal representation, banking, or medical services. Later in this text, Chapter 7 will look at the distinctions between manufacturing and service technologies. Chapter 9 discusses size and life cycle and describes some differences between small and large organizations.

Another important distinction is between for-profit businesses and *nonprofit organizations*. All of the topics in this text apply to nonprofit organizations such as the Salvation Army, the World Wildlife Fund, the Save the Children Foundation, and Chicago's La Rabida Hospital, which is dedicated to serving the poor, just as they do to such businesses as Starbucks Coffee, eBay, or Holiday Inns. However, there are some important dissimilarities to keep in mind. The primary difference is that managers in businesses direct their activities toward earning money for the company, whereas managers in nonprofits direct their efforts toward generating some kind of social impact. The unique characteristics and needs of nonprofit organizations created by this distinction present unique challenges for organizational leaders.[15]

Financial resources for nonprofits typically come from government appropriations, grants, and donations rather than from the sale of products or services to customers. In businesses, managers focus on improving the organization's products and services to increase sales revenues. In nonprofits, however, services are typically provided to nonpaying clients, and a major problem for many organizations is securing a steady stream of funds to continue operating. Nonprofit managers, committed to serving clients with limited funds, must focus on keeping organizational costs as low as possible and demonstrating a highly efficient use of resources.[16] Another problem is that, since nonprofit organizations do not have a conventional "bottom line," managers often struggle with the question of what constitutes organizational effectiveness. It is easy to measure dollars and cents, but nonprofits have to measure intangible goals such as "improve public health" or "make a difference in the lives of the disenfranchised."

Managers in nonprofit organizations also deal with many diverse stakeholders and must market their services to attract not only clients (customers) but also volunteers and donors. This can sometimes create conflict and power struggles among organizations, as illustrated by the Make-a-Wish Foundation, which is butting heads with small, local wish-granting groups as it expands to cities across the United States. The more kids a group can count as helping, the easier it is to raise money. As charitable donations in general have declined with the economy, the issue has become serious. Small groups are charging that Make-a-Wish is abusing the power of its national presence to overwhelm or absorb the smaller groups. "We should not have to compete for children and money," says the director of the Indiana Children's Wish Fund. "They [Make-a-Wish] use all their muscle and money to get what they want."[17]

Thus, the organization design concepts discussed throughout this book, such as setting goals and measuring effectiveness, coping with environmental uncertainty, implementing effective control mechanisms, satisfying multiple stakeholders, and dealing with issues of power and conflict, apply to nonprofit organizations such as the Make-a-Wish Foundation just as they do to Microsoft Corp., UPS, or Xerox, as described in the chapter opening. These concepts and theories are adapted and revised as needed to fit unique needs and problems.

◼ Importance of Organizations

It may seem hard to believe today, but organizations as we know them are relatively recent in the history of humankind. Even in the late nineteenth century there were few organizations of any size or importance—no labor unions, no trade associa-

Book Mark 1.0 (HAVE YOU READ THIS BOOK?)

The Company: A Short History of a Revolutionary Idea
By John Micklethwait and Adrian Wooldridge

"The limited liability corporation is the greatest single discovery of modern times," is one conclusion of the concise and readable book, *The Company: A Short History of a Revolutionary Idea* by John Micklethwait and Adrian Wooldridge. Companies are so ubiquitous today that we take them for granted, so it may come as a surprise that the company as we know it is a relatively recent innovation. Although people have joined together in groups for commercial purposes since ancient Greek and Roman times, the modern company has its roots in the late nineteenth century. The idea of a *limited liability company* that was legally an "artificial person" began with the Joint Stock Companies Act, enacted by the London Board of Trade in 1856. Today the company is seen as "the most important organization in the world." Here are a few reasons why:

- The corporation was the first autonomous legal and social institution that was within society yet independent of the central government.
- The concept of a limited liability company unleashed entrepreneurs to raise money because investors could lose only what they invested. Increasing the pool of entrepreneurial capital spurred innovation and generally enriched the societies in which companies operated.
- The company is the most efficient creator of goods and services that the world has ever known. Without a company to harness resources and organize activities, the cost

to consumers for almost any product we know today would be impossible to afford.
- Historically, the corporation has been a force for civilized behavior and provided people with worthwhile activities, identity, and community, as well as a paycheck.
- The Virginia Company, a forerunner of the limited liability corporation, helped introduce the revolutionary concept of democracy to the American colonies.
- The modern multinational corporation began in Britain in the third quarter of the 1800s with the railroads, which built rail networks throughout Europe by shipping into each country the managers, materials, equipment, and labor needed.

During the past few years, it seems that large corporations have been increasingly in conflict with societies' interests. Yet large companies have been reviled throughout modern history—consider the robber barons at the beginning of the twentieth century—and the authors suggest that recent abuses are relatively mild compared to some incidents from history. Everyone knows that corporations can be scoundrels, but overall, Micklethwait and Wooldridge argue, their force has been overwhelmingly for the cumulative social and economic good.

The Company: A Short History of a Revolutionary Idea, by John Micklethwait and Adrian Wooldridge, is published by The Modern Library.

tions, and few large businesses, nonprofit organizations, or governmental departments. What a change has occurred since then! The development of large organizations transformed all of society, and, indeed, the modern corporation may be the most significant innovation of the past 100 years.[18] This chapter's Book Mark examines the rise of the corporation and its significance in our society. Organizations are central to people's lives and exert a tremendous influence.

Organizations are all around us and shape our lives in many ways. But what contributions do organizations make? Why are they important? Exhibit 1.1 lists seven reasons organizations are important to you and to society. First, organizations bring together resources to accomplish specific goals. Consider Northrup Grumman Newport News (formerly Newport News Shipbuilding), which builds nuclear-powered, Nimitz-class aircraft carriers. Putting together an aircraft carrier is an incredibly complex job involving 47,000 tons of precision-welded steel, more than 1 million distinct parts, 900 miles of wire and cable, about 40 million skilled-worker hours, and more than 7 years of hard work by the organization's 17,800 employees.[19]

Organizations also produce goods and services that customers want at competitive prices. Bill Gates, who built Microsoft into a global powerhouse, asserts that the modern organization "is one of the most effective means to allocate resources we've ever seen. It transforms great ideas into customer benefits on an unimaginably large scale."[20]

Companies look for innovative ways to produce and distribute desirable goods and services more efficiently. Two ways are through e-business and through the use of computer-based manufacturing technologies. Redesigning organizational structures and management practices can also contribute to increased efficiency. Organizations create a drive for innovation rather than a reliance on standard products and outmoded ways of doing things.

Organizations adapt to and influence a rapidly changing environment. Consider Google, provider of the Internet's most popular search engine, which continues to

EXHIBIT 1.1
Importance of Organizations

Organizations exist to do the following:

1. *Bring together resources to achieve desired goals and outcomes*

2. *Produce goods and services efficiently*

3. *Facilitate innovation*

4. *Use modern manufacturing and information technologies*

5. *Adapt to and influence a changing environment*

6. *Create value for owners, customers, and employees*

7. *Accommodate ongoing challenges of diversity, ethics, and the motivation and coordination of employees*

adapt and evolve along with the evolving Internet. Rather than being a rigid service, Google is continually adding technological features that create a better service by accretion. At any time, Google's site features several technologies in development so that engineers can get ideas and feedback from users.[21] Some large businesses have entire departments charged with monitoring the external environment and finding ways to adapt to or influence that environment. One of the most significant changes in the external environment today is globalization. Organizations such as Coca-Cola, AES Corporation, Heineken Breweries, and IBM are involved in strategic alliances and partnerships with companies around the world in an effort to influence the environment and compete on a global scale.

Through all of these activities, organizations create value for their owners, customers, and employees. Managers analyze which parts of the operation create value and which parts do not; a company can be profitable only when the value it creates is greater than the cost of resources. JetBlue, a rapidly growing low-fare airline, for example, creates value by keeping labor costs low and offering extras such as leather seats and 24 channels of satellite TV.[22] Finally, organizations have to cope with and accommodate today's challenges of workforce diversity and growing concerns over ethics and social responsibility, as well as find effective ways to motivate employees to work together to accomplish organizational goals.

Organizations shape our lives, and well-informed managers can shape organizations. An understanding of organization theory enables managers to design organizations to function more effectively.

Perspectives on Organizations

There are various ways to look at and think about organizations and how they function. Two important perspectives are the open-systems approach and the organizational-configuration framework.

Open Systems

One significant development in the study of organizations was the distinction between closed and open systems.[23] A **closed system** would not depend on its environment; it would be autonomous, enclosed, and sealed off from the outside world. Although a true closed system cannot exist, early organization studies focused on internal systems. Early management concepts, including scientific management, leadership style, and industrial engineering, were closed-system approaches because they took the environment for granted and assumed the organization could be made more effective through internal design. The management of a closed system would be quite easy. The environment would be stable and predictable and would not intervene to cause problems. The primary management issue would be to run things efficiently.

An **open system** must interact with the environment to survive; it both consumes resources and exports resources to the environment. It cannot seal itself off. It must continuously adapt to the environment. Open systems can be enormously complex. Internal efficiency is just one issue—and sometimes a minor one. The organization has to find and obtain needed resources, interpret and act on environmental changes, dispose of outputs, and control and coordinate internal activities in the face of environmental disturbances and uncertainty. Every system that must interact with the environment to survive is an open system. The human being is an open system. So is the planet Earth, the city of New York, and Xerox Corp. Indeed, one problem at Xerox was that top managers seemed to forget they were part of an open system. They isolated themselves within the bureaucratic culture and failed to pay close attention to what was going on with their customers, suppliers, and competitors. The rapid changes over the past few decades, including globalization and increased competition, the explosion of the Internet and e-business, and the growing diversity of the population and workforce, have forced many managers to reorient toward an open-systems mindset and recognize their business as part of a complex, interconnected whole.

To understand the whole organization, we must view it as a system. A **system** is a set of interacting elements that acquires inputs from the environment, transforms them, and discharges outputs to the external environment. The need for inputs and outputs reflects dependency on the environment. Interacting elements mean that people and departments depend on one another and must work together.

Exhibit 1.2 illustrates an open system. Inputs to an organization system include employees, raw materials and other physical resources, information, and financial resources. The transformation process changes these inputs into something of value that can be exported back to the environment. Outputs include specific products and services for customers and clients. Outputs may also include employee satisfaction, pollution, and other by-products of the transformation process.

A system is made up of several **subsystems**, as illustrated at the bottom of Exhibit 1.2. These subsystems perform the specific functions required for organizational survival, such as production, boundary spanning, maintenance, adaptation, and management. The production subsystem produces the product and service outputs of the organization. Boundary subsystems are responsible for exchanges with the external environment. They include activities such as purchasing supplies or marketing products. The maintenance subsystem maintains the smooth operation and upkeep of the organization's physical and human elements. The adaptive subsystems are responsible for organizational change and adaptation. Management is a distinct subsystem, responsible for coordinating and directing the other subsystems of the organization.

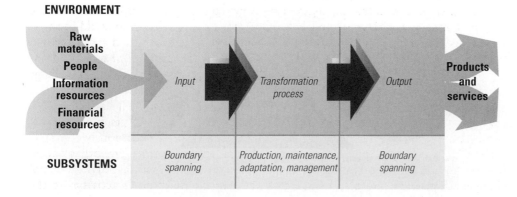

EXHIBIT 1.2
An Open System and its Subsystems

ENVIRONMENT

Raw materials
People
Information resources
Financial resources

Input   Transformation process   Output   Products and services

SUBSYSTEMS   Boundary spanning   Production, maintenance, adaptation, management   Boundary spanning

■ Organizational Configuration

Various parts of the organization are designed to perform the key subsystem functions illustrated in Exhibit 1.2. One framework proposed by Henry Mintzberg suggests that every organization has five parts.[24] These parts, illustrated in Exhibit 1.3, include the technical core, top management, middle management, technical support, and administrative support. The five parts of the organization may vary in size and importance depending on the organization's environment, technology, and other factors.

Technical Core. The technical core includes people who do the basic work of the organization. It performs the production subsystem function and actually produces the product and service outputs of the organization. This is where the primary transformation from inputs to outputs takes place. The technical core is the production department in a manufacturing firm, the teachers and classes in a university, and the medical activities in a hospital. At Xerox, the technical core produces copiers, digital presses, and document management services for customers.

Technical Support. The technical support function helps the organization adapt to the environment. Technical support employees such as engineers and researchers scan the environment for problems, opportunities, and technological developments. Technical support is responsible for creating innovations in the technical core, helping the organization change and adapt. Technical support at Xerox is provided by departments such as technology, research and development (R&D), and marketing research. Investment in R&D, for example, enabled Xerox to produce more than 500 patents in 2004, enabling Xerox to enrich existing products, develop next-generation products, and explore potentially disruptive technologies so the company can adapt as the environment changes.[25]

Administrative Support. The administrative support function is responsible for the smooth operation and upkeep of the organization, including its physical and human elements. This includes human resource activities such as recruiting and hiring, establishing compensation and benefits, and employee training and development, as well as maintenance activities such as cleaning of buildings and service and repair of machines. Administrative support functions in a corporation such as Xerox might

EXHIBIT 1.3
Five Basic Parts of an Organization
Source: Based on Henry Mintzberg, *The Structuring of Organizations* (Englewood Cliffs, N.J.: Prentice-Hall, 1979), 215–297; and Henry Mintzberg, "Organization Design: Fashion or Fit?" *Harvard Business Review* 59 (January-February 1981): 103–116.

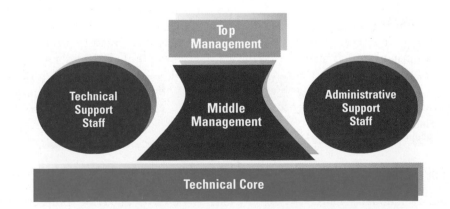

include the human resource department, organizational development, the employee cafeteria, and the maintenance staff.

Management. Management is a distinct subsystem, responsible for directing and coordinating other parts of the organization. Top management provides direction, strategy, goals, and policies for the entire organization or major divisions. Middle management is responsible for implementation and coordination at the departmental level. In traditional organizations, middle managers are responsible for mediating between top management and the technical core, such as implementing rules and passing information up and down the hierarchy.

In real-life organizations, the five parts are interrelated and often serve more than one subsystem function. For example, managers coordinate and direct other parts of the system, but they may also be involved in administrative and technical support. In addition, several of the parts serve the *boundary spanning* function mentioned in the previous section. For example, in the administrative support realm, human resource departments are responsible for working with the external environment to find quality employees. Purchasing departments acquire needed materials and supplies. In the technical support area, R&D departments work directly with the external environment to learn about new technological developments. Managers perform boundary-spanning as well, such as when Anne Mulcahy of Xerox negotiated directly with the SEC regarding accounting irregularities. The important boundary-spanning subsystem is embraced by several areas, rather than being confined to one part of the organization.

Dimensions of Organization Design

The systems view pertains to dynamic, ongoing activities within organizations. The next step for understanding organizations is to look at dimensions that describe specific organizational design traits. These dimensions describe organizations in much the same way that personality and physical traits describe people.

Organizational dimensions fall into two types: structural and contextual, illustrated in Exhibit 1.4. **Structural dimensions** provide labels to describe the internal characteristics of an organization. They create a basis for measuring and comparing organizations. **Contextual dimensions** characterize the whole organization, including its size, technology, environment, and goals. They describe the organizational setting that influences and shapes the structural dimensions. Contextual dimensions can be confusing because they represent both the organization and the environment. Contextual dimensions can be envisioned as a set of overlapping elements that underlie an organization's structure and work processes. To understand and evaluate organizations, one must examine both structural and contextual dimensions.[26] These dimensions of organization design interact with one another and can be adjusted to accomplish the purposes listed earlier in Exhibit 1.1.

Structural Dimensions

1. *Formalization* pertains to the amount of written documentation in the organization. Documentation includes procedures, job descriptions, regulations, and policy manuals. These written documents describe behavior and activities.

Formalization is often measured by simply counting the number of pages of documentation within the organization. Large state universities, for example, tend to be high on formalization because they have several volumes of written rules for such things as registration, dropping and adding classes, student associations, dormitory governance, and financial assistance. A small, family-owned business, in contrast, may have almost no written rules and would be considered informal.

2. *Specialization* is the degree to which organizational tasks are subdivided into separate jobs. If specialization is extensive, each employee performs only a narrow range of tasks. If specialization is low, employees perform a wide range of tasks in their jobs. Specialization is sometimes referred to as the division of labor.

3. *Hierarchy of authority* describes who reports to whom and the span of control for each manager. The hierarchy is depicted by the vertical lines on an organization chart, as illustrated in Exhibit 1.5. The hierarchy is related to span of control (the number of employees reporting to a supervisor). When *spans of control* are narrow, the hierarchy tends to be tall. When spans of control are wide, the hierarchy of authority will be shorter.

4. *Centralization* refers to the hierarchical level that has authority to make a decision. When decision making is kept at the top level, the organization is centralized. When decisions are delegated to lower organizational levels, it is decentralized. Organizational decisions that might be centralized or decentralized include purchasing equipment, establishing goals, choosing suppliers, setting prices, hiring employees, and deciding marketing territories.

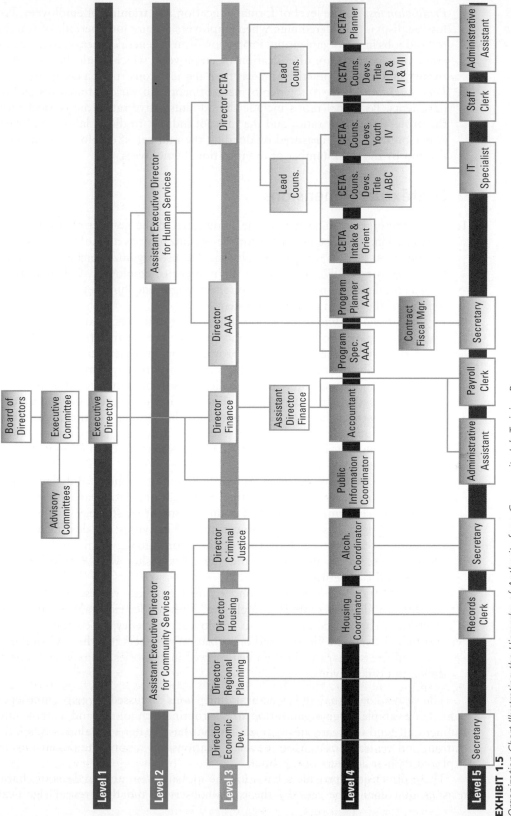

EXHIBIT 1.5
Organization Chart Illustrating the Hierarchy of Authority for a Community Job Training Program

5. *Professionalism* is the level of formal education and training of employees. Professionalism is considered high when employees require long periods of training to hold jobs in the organization. Professionalism is generally measured as the average number of years of education of employees, which could be as high as twenty in a medical practice and less than ten in a construction company.
6. *Personnel ratios* refer to the deployment of people to various functions and departments. Personnel ratios include the administrative ratio, the clerical ratio, the professional staff ratio, and the ratio of indirect to direct labor employees. A personnel ratio is measured by dividing the number of employees in a classification by the total number of organizational employees.

■ Contextual Dimensions

1. *Size* is the organization's magnitude as reflected in the number of people in the organization. It can be measured for the organization as a whole or for specific components, such as a plant or division. Because organizations are social systems, size is typically measured by the number of employees. Other measures such as total sales or total assets also reflect magnitude, but they do not indicate the size of the human part of the system.
2. *Organizational technology* refers to the tools, techniques, and actions used to transform inputs into outputs. It concerns how the organization actually produces the products and services it provides for customers and includes such things as flexible manufacturing, advanced information systems, and the Internet. An automobile assembly line, a college classroom, and an overnight package delivery system are technologies, although they differ from one another.
3. The *environment* includes all elements outside the boundary of the organization. Key elements include the industry, government, customers, suppliers, and the financial community. The environmental elements that affect an organization the most are often other organizations.
4. The organization's *goals and strategy* define the purpose and competitive techniques that set it apart from other organizations. Goals are often written down as an enduring statement of company intent. A strategy is the plan of action that describes resource allocation and activities for dealing with the environment and for reaching the organization's goals. Goals and strategies define the scope of operations and the relationship with employees, customers, and competitors.
5. An organization's *culture* is the underlying set of key values, beliefs, understandings, and norms shared by employees. These underlying values may pertain to ethical behavior, commitment to employees, efficiency, or customer service, and they provide the glue to hold organization members together. An organization's culture is unwritten but can be observed in its stories, slogans, ceremonies, dress, and office layout.

The eleven contextual and structural dimensions discussed here are interdependent. For example, large organization size, a routine technology, and a stable environment all tend to create an organization that has greater formalization, specialization, and centralization. More detailed relationships among the dimensions are explored in later chapters of this book.

These dimensions provide a basis for the measurement and analysis of characteristics that cannot be seen by the casual observer, and they reveal significant information about an organization. Consider, for example, the dimensions of W. L. Gore & Associates compared with those of Wal-Mart and a governmental agency.

When Jack Dougherty began work at W. L. Gore & Associates, Inc., he reported to Bill Gore, the company's founder, to receive his first assignment. Gore told him, "Why don't you find something you'd like to do." Dougherty was shocked at the informality but quickly recovered and began interrogating various managers about their activities. He was attracted to a new product called Gore-Tex, a membrane that was waterproof but breathable when bonded to fabric. The next morning, he came to work dressed in jeans and began helping feed fabric into the maw of a large laminator. Five years later, Dougherty was responsible for marketing and advertising in the fabrics group.

Bill Gore died in 1986, but the organization he designed still runs without official titles, orders, or bosses. One of the key tenets of the organization is that employees (called associates) figure out what they want to do and where they think they can make a contribution. The company has some 6,000 associates in forty-five locations around the world. The plants are kept small—up to 200 people—to maintain a family atmosphere. "It's much better to use friendship and love than slavery and whips," Bill Gore said. Several professional associates are assigned to act as "sponsors" for new product development, but the administrative structure is lean. Good human relations is a more important value than is internal efficiency, and it works. The company has seven times been named one of *Fortune* magazine's "100 Best Companies to Work For in America," and Gore continues to grow and prosper.

Contrast that approach to Wal-Mart, where efficiency is the goal. Wal-Mart achieves its competitive edge through employee commitment and internal cost efficiency. A standard formula is used to build each store, with uniform displays and merchandise. Wal-Mart operates about 1,600 discount stores, as well as 1,100 Supercenters, 500 Sam's Clubs, and more than 1,000 international stores. Its administrative expenses are the lowest of any chain. The distribution system is a marvel of efficiency. Goods can be delivered to any store in less than two days after an order is placed. Stores are controlled from the top, but store managers have also been given some freedom to adapt to local conditions. Performance is high, and employees are satisfied because the pay is fair and more than half of them share in corporate profits.

An even greater contrast is seen in many government agencies or nonprofit organizations that rely heavily on public funding. Most state humanities and arts agencies, for example, are staffed by only a small number of highly trained employees, but workers are overwhelmed with rules and regulations and swamped by paperwork. Employees who have to implement rule changes often don't have time to read the continuous stream of memos and still keep up with their daily work with community arts organizations. Employees must require extensive reporting from their clients in order to make regular reports to a variety of state and federal funding sources. Agency workers are frustrated and so are the community-based organizations they seek to serve. These smaller organizations sometimes refuse assistance because of the extensive paperwork involved.[27]

Exhibit 1.6 illustrates several structural and contextual dimensions of Gore & Associates, Wal-Mart, and the state arts agency. Gore & Associates is a medium-sized manufacturing organization that ranks very low with respect to formalization, specialization, and centralization. A number of professional staff are assigned to nonworkflow activities to do the R&D needed to stay abreast of changes in the fiber industry. Wal-Mart is much more formalized, specialized, and centralized. Efficiency is more important than new products, so most activities are guided by standard regulations. The percentage of nonworkflow personnel is kept to a minimum. The arts

EXHIBIT 1.6
Characteristics of Three
Organizations

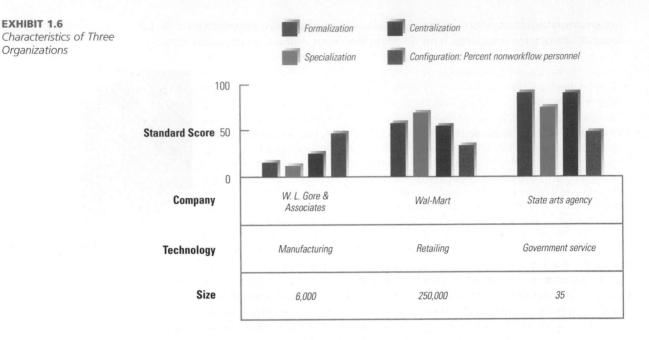

agency, in contrast to the other organizations, reflects its status as a small part of a large government bureaucracy. The agency is overwhelmed with rules and standard procedures. Rules are dictated from the top. Most employees are assigned to work-flow activities, although in normal times a substantial number of people are devoted to administration and clerical support.

Structural and contextual dimensions can thus tell a lot about an organization and about differences among organizations. Organization design dimensions are examined in more detail in later chapters to determine the appropriate level of each dimension needed to perform effectively in each organizational setting.

■ Performance and Effectiveness Outcomes

The whole point of understanding varying perspectives and the structural and contextual dimensions of organizations is to design the organization in such a way as to achieve high performance and effectiveness. Managers adjust structural and contextual dimensions and organizational subsystems to most efficiently and effectively transform inputs into outputs and provide value. **Efficiency** refers to the amount of resources used to achieve the organization's goals. It is based on the quantity of raw materials, money, and employees necessary to produce a given level of output. **Effectiveness** is a broader term, meaning the degree to which an organization achieves its goals.

To be effective, organizations need clear, focused goals and appropriate strategies for achieving them. Strategy, goals, and approaches to measuring effectiveness will be discussed in detail in Chapter 2. Many organizations are using new technology to improve efficiency and effectiveness. For example, the State of Illinois is applying technology to meet customer service and business development goals, such as providing trucking firms with one-stop access to state and federal permits over the Internet. Illinois was also one of the first states to go to a paperless system for school board meetings, allowing the public to view agendas and reports online. In the business world, UPS is using technologically sophisticated package-handling equipment

Briefcase

As an organization manager, keep this guideline in mind:

Consider the needs and interests of all stake-holders when setting goals and designing the organization to achieve effectiveness.

and computerized logistics systems to cut one day from the average delivery time for ground packages to major metropolitan areas.[28]

However, achieving effectiveness is not always a simple matter because different people want different things from the organization. For customers, the primary concern is high-quality products and services at a reasonable price, whereas employees are mostly concerned with adequate pay, good working conditions, and job satisfaction. Managers carefully balance the needs and interests of various stakeholders in setting goals and striving for effectiveness. This is referred to as the **stakeholder approach**, which integrates diverse organizational activities by looking at various organizational stakeholders and what they want from the organization. A **stakeholder** is any group within or outside of the organization that has a stake in the organization's performance. The satisfaction level of each group can be assessed as an indication of the organization's performance and effectiveness.[29]

Exhibit 1.7 illustrates various stakeholders and what each group wants from the organization. Organizations often find it difficult to simultaneously satisfy the demands of all groups. A business might have high customer satisfaction, but the organization might have difficulties with creditors or supplier relationships might be poor. Consider Wal-Mart. Customers love its efficiency and low prices, but the low-cost emphasis the company uses with suppliers has caused friction. Some activist groups argue that Wal-Mart's tactics are unethical because they force suppliers to lay off workers, close factories, and outsource to manufacturers from low-wage countries. One supplier said clothing is being sold at Wal-Mart so cheaply that many U.S. companies couldn't compete even if they paid their workers nothing. The challenges of managing such a huge organization have also led to strains in relationships with employees and other stakeholder groups, as evidenced by recent gender discrimination suits and complaints about low wages.[30]

EXHIBIT 1.7
Major Stakeholder Groups and What They Expect

Stakeholder interests sometimes conflict, such as when unions demand wage increases that might hurt shareholders' financial returns or require a switch to lower-cost suppliers. In nonprofit organizations, the needs and interests of clients sometimes conflict with restrictions on use of government funds or contributions from donors. In reality, it is unreasonable to assume that all stakeholders can be equally satisfied. However, if an organization fails to meet the needs of several stakeholder groups, it is probably not meeting its effectiveness goals. Recall from the opening case Xerox's problems with satisfying employees, customers, creditors, stockholders, and government regulators.

Research has shown that the assessment of multiple stakeholder groups is an accurate reflection of organizational effectiveness, especially with respect to organizational adaptability.[31] Moreover, both profit and nonprofit organizations care about their reputations and attempt to shape stakeholders' perceptions of their performance.[32]

Managers strive to at least minimally satisfy the interests of all stakeholders. When any one group becomes seriously dissatisfied, it may withdraw its support and hurt future organizational performance. Satisfying multiple stakeholders can be challenging, particularly as goals and priorities change, as illustrated by the following example.

In Practice

Federal Bureau of Investigation

Few will deny that homeland security and battling terrorism should be a top priority for the United States, and since the attacks of September 11, 2001, the Federal Bureau of Investigation (FBI) has channeled more and more resources into the domestic war on terrorism.

Sounds good so far, right? The only problem is, the new focus means pulling hundreds of agents off their regular beats, where they investigated everything from drug smuggling to kidnapping to white collar crime. "Just about everyone here is involved in terror cases, one way or another," says agent Ron Buckley. "Everything else is on the back burner."

That's putting a heavy burden on police departments and other law enforcement agencies around the country. These organizations don't have the personnel, investigative resources, or know-how to fight the kinds of crime FBI agents once handled. For example, even when local departments have adequate manpower, crimes often go unsolved because of lack of access to the FBI's high-tech forensic labs. State and local police aren't happy about the diversion of federal resources, even though they understand the need. Many of these departments are already woefully underfunded and understaffed, and some have resorted to using volunteers to take crime reports for nonviolent crimes. Local communities are also distressed because they fear more drugs in their neighborhoods and more violent crime on their streets. Although the U.S. public is worried about terrorism, they also want their own little piece of the world protected from criminal activity.

Some of the FBI agents aren't particularly happy about the change either. An agent who has spent most of his 25-year career poring over financial statements investigating fraud, for example, has to make a huge mental shift to feel comfortable traveling around town in an unmarked car with submachine guns, stun grenades, body armor—and a toothbrush—prepared for the next long stakeout.[33]

This example provides a glimpse of how difficult it can be for managers to satisfy multiple stakeholders. In all organizations, managers have to evaluate stakeholder concerns and establish goals that can achieve at least minimal satisfaction for major stakeholder groups.

The Evolution of Organization Theory and Design

Organization theory is not a collection of facts; it is a way of thinking about organizations. Organization theory is a way to see and analyze organizations more accurately and deeply than one otherwise could. The way to see and think about organizations is based on patterns and regularities in organizational design and behavior. Organization scholars search for these regularities, define them, measure them, and make them available to the rest of us. The facts from the research are not as important as the general patterns and insights into organizational functioning.

Historical Perspectives

Organization design and management practices have varied over time in response to changes in the larger society.

You may recall from an earlier management course that the modern era of management theory began with the classical management perspective in the late nineteenth and early twentieth century. The emergence of the factory system during the Industrial Revolution posed problems that earlier organizations had not encountered. As work was performed on a much larger scale by a larger number of workers, people began thinking about how to design and manage work in order to increase productivity and help organizations attain maximum efficiency. The classical perspective, which sought to make organizations run like efficient, well-oiled machines, is associated with the development of hierarchy and bureaucratic organizations and remains the basis of much of modern management theory and practice. In this section, we will examine the classical perspective, with its emphasis on efficiency and organization, as well as other perspectives that emerged to address new concerns, such as employee needs and the role of the environment. Elements of each perspective are still used in organization design, although they have been adapted and revised to meet changing needs.

Efficiency is Everything. Pioneered by Frederick Winslow Taylor, **scientific management** postulates that decisions about organizations and job design should be based on precise, scientific study of individual situations.[34] To use this approach, managers develop precise, standard procedures for doing each job, select workers with appropriate abilities, train workers in the standard procedures, carefully plan work, and provide wage incentives to increase output. Taylor's approach is illustrated by the unloading of iron from railcars and reloading finished steel for the Bethlehem Steel plant in 1898. Taylor calculated that with correct movements, tools, and sequencing, each man was capable of loading 47.5 tons per day instead of the typical 12.5 tons. He also worked out an incentive system that paid each man $1.85 per day for meeting the new standard, an increase from the previous rate of $1.15. Productivity at Bethlehem Steel shot up overnight. These insights helped to establish organizational assumptions that the role of management is to maintain stability and efficiency, with top managers doing the thinking and workers doing what they are told.

How to Get Organized. Another subfield of the classical perspective took a broader look at the organization. Whereas scientific management focused primarily on the technical core—on work performed on the shop floor—**administrative**

principles looked at the design and functioning of the organization as a whole. For example, Henri Fayol proposed fourteen principles of management, such as "each subordinate receives orders from only one superior" (unity of command) and "similar activities in an organization should be grouped together under one manager" (unity of direction). These principles formed the foundation for modern management practice and organization design.

The scientific management and administrative principles approaches were powerful and gave organizations fundamental new ideas for establishing high productivity and increasing prosperity. Administrative principles in particular contributed to the development of **bureaucratic organizations**, which emphasized designing and managing organizations on an impersonal, rational basis through such elements as clearly defined authority and responsibility, formal recordkeeping, and uniform application of standard rules. Although the term *bureaucracy* has taken on negative connotations in today's organizations, bureaucratic characteristics worked extremely well for the needs of the Industrial Age. One problem with the classical perspective, however, is that it failed to consider the social context and human needs.

What About People? Early work on industrial psychology and human relations received little attention because of the prominence of scientific management. However, a major breakthrough occurred with a series of experiments at a Chicago electric company, which came to be known as the **Hawthorne Studies**. Interpretations of these studies concluded that positive treatment of employees improved their motivation and productivity. The publication of these findings led to a revolution in worker treatment and laid the groundwork for subsequent work examining treatment of workers, leadership, motivation, and human resource management. These human relations and behavioral approaches added new and important contributions to the study of management and organizations.

However, the hierarchical system and bureaucratic approaches that developed during the Industrial Revolution remained the primary approach to organization design and functioning well into the 1970s and 1980s. In general, this approach worked well for most organizations until the past few decades. However, during the 1980s, it began to lead to problems. Increased competition, especially on a global scale, changed the playing field.[35] North American companies had to find a better way.

The 1980s produced new corporate cultures that valued lean staff, flexibility, rapid response to the customer, motivated employees, caring for customers, and quality products.

Over the past 2 decades, the world of organizations has undergone even more profound and far-reaching changes. The Internet and other advances in information technology, globalization, rapid social and economic changes, and other challenges from the environment call for new management perspectives and more flexible approaches to organization design.

Don't Forget the Environment. Many problems occur when all organizations are treated as similar, which was the case with scientific management and administrative principles approaches that attempted to design all organizations alike. The structures and systems that work in the retail division of a conglomerate will not be appropriate for the manufacturing division. The organization charts and financial procedures that are best for an entrepreneurial Internet firm like eBay or Google will not work for a large food processing plant.

Contingency means that one thing depends on other things, and for organizations to be effective, there must be a "goodness of fit" between their structure and the conditions in their external environment.[36] What works in one setting may not work in another setting. There is not one best way. Contingency theory means "it depends." For example, some organizations experience a certain environment, use a routine technology, and desire efficiency. In this situation, a management approach that uses bureaucratic control procedures, a hierarchical structure, and formal communication would be appropriate. Likewise, free-flowing management processes work best in an uncertain environment with a nonroutine technology. The correct management approach is contingent on the organization's situation.

Today, almost all organizations operate in highly uncertain environments. Thus, we are involved in a significant period of transition, in which concepts of organization theory and design are changing as dramatically as they did with the dawning of the Industrial Revolution.

■ Contemporary Organization Design

To a great extent, managers and organizations are still imprinted with the hierarchical, bureaucratic approach that arose more than a century ago. Yet the challenges presented by today's environment—globalization, diversity, ethical concerns, rapid advances in technology, the rise of e-business, a shift to knowledge and information as organizations' most important form of capital, and the growing expectations of workers for meaningful work and opportunities for personal and professional growth—call for dramatically different responses from people and organizations. The perspectives of the past do not provide a road map for steering today's organizations. Managers can design and orchestrate new responses for a dramatically new world.

Today's organizations and managers may be seen as shifting from a mindset based on mechanical systems to one based on natural and biological systems. These changing beliefs and perceptions affect how we think about organizations and the patterns of behavior within organizations.

For most of the twentieth century, eighteenth-century Newtonian science, which suggests that the world functions as a well-behaved machine, continued to guide managers' thinking about organizations.[37] The environment was perceived as orderly and predictable and the role of managers was to maintain stability. This mindset worked quite well for the Industrial Age.[38] Growth was a primary criterion for organizational success.

Organizations became large and complex, and boundaries between functional departments and between organizations were distinct. Internal structures grew more complex, vertical, and bureaucratic. Leadership was based on solid management principles and tended to be autocratic; communication was primarily through formal memos, letters, and reports. Managers did all the planning and "thought work," while employees did the manual labor in exchange for wages and other compensation.

The environment for today's companies, however, is anything but stable. With the turbulence of recent years, managers can no longer maintain an illusion of order and predictability. The science of **chaos theory** suggests that relationships in complex, adaptive systems—including organizations—are nonlinear and made up of numerous interconnections and divergent choices that create unintended effects and render the universe unpredictable.[39] The world is full of uncertainty, characterized by surprise, rapid change, and confusion. Managers can't measure, predict, or control in traditional ways the unfolding drama inside or outside the organization. However, chaos theory also recognizes that this randomness and disorder occurs within certain larger patterns of order. The ideas of chaos theory suggest that organizations should be viewed more as natural systems than as well-oiled, predictable machines.

Many organizations are shifting from strict vertical hierarchies to flexible, decentralized structures that emphasize horizontal collaboration, widespread information sharing, and adaptability. This shift can clearly be seen in the U.S. Army, once considered the ultimate example of a rigid, top-down organization. Today's army is fighting a new kind of war that demands a new approach to how it trains, equips, and uses soldiers. Fighting a fluid, fast-moving, and fast-changing terrorist network means that junior officers in the field who are experts on the local situation have to make quick decisions, learning through trial and error and sometimes departing from standard Army procedures. For example, when Captain Nicholas Ayers was leading a unit in Iraq, he says he often had to come up with new solutions to situations the Army had never before encountered. Ayers and other junior officers share what they learn via e-mail and on Web sites. A lesson learned in one unit is often applied successfully elsewhere. "This is entirely a bottom-up war," says Major John Nagl, third-in-command of a battalion near Fallujah, Iraq. "It is the platoon leaders and company commanders that are fighting it."[40]

Although the stakes might not be as high, business and nonprofit organizations today also need greater fluidity and adaptability. Many managers are redesigning their companies toward something called the **learning organization**. The learning organization promotes communication and collaboration so that everyone is engaged in identifying and solving problems, enabling the organization to continuously experiment, improve, and increase its capability. The learning organization is based on equality, open information, little hierarchy, and a culture that encourages adaptability and participation, enabling ideas to bubble up from anywhere that can help the organization seize opportunities and handle crises. In a learning organization, the essential value is problem solving, as opposed to the traditional organization designed for efficient performance.

■ Efficient Performance versus the Learning Organization

As managers struggle toward the learning organization, they are finding that specific dimensions of the organization have to change. Exhibit 1.8 compares organizations designed for efficient performance with those designed for continuous learning by looking at five elements of organization design: structure, tasks, systems, culture, and strategy. As shown in the exhibit, all of these elements are interconnected and influence one another.

From Vertical to Horizontal Structure. Traditionally, the most common organizational structure has been one in which activities are grouped together by common work from the bottom to the top of the organization. Generally little collaboration occurs across functional departments, and the whole organization is coordinated and controlled through the vertical hierarchy, with decision-making authority residing with upper-level managers. This structure can be quite effective. It promotes efficient production and in-depth skill development, and the hierarchy of authority provides a sensible mechanism for supervision and control in large organizations. However, in a rapidly changing environment, the hierarchy becomes overloaded. Top executives are not able to respond rapidly enough to problems or opportunities.

Briefcase

As an organization manager, keep these guidelines in mind:

When designing an organization for learning and adaptation in a turbulent environment, include elements such as horizontal structure, shared information, empowered roles, collaborative strategy, and adaptive culture. In stable environments, organizations can achieve efficient performance with a vertical structure, formal information and control systems, routine tasks, competitive strategy, and a stable culture.

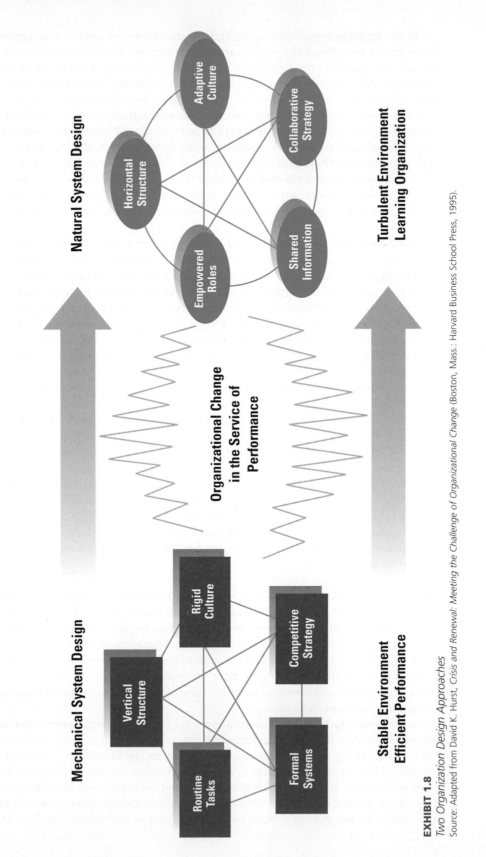

Natural System Design

Adaptive Culture

Collaborative Strategy

Horizontal Structure

Empowered Roles

Shared Information

Turbulent Environment Learning Organization

Organizational Change in the Service of Performance

Mechanical System Design

Rigid Culture

Competitive Strategy

Vertical Structure

Routine Tasks

Formal Systems

Stable Environment Efficient Performance

EXHIBIT 1.8
Two Organization Design Approaches
Source: Adapted from David K. Hurst, *Crisis and Renewal: Meeting the Challenge of Organizational Change* (Boston, Mass.: Harvard Business School Press, 1995).

In the learning organization, the vertical structure that creates distance between managers at the top of the organization and workers in the technical core is disbanded. Structure is created around horizontal workflows or processes rather than departmental functions. The vertical hierarchy is dramatically flattened, with perhaps only a few senior executives in traditional support functions such as finance or human resources. Self-directed teams are the fundamental work unit in the learning organization. Boundaries between functions are practically eliminated because teams include members from several functional areas. In some cases, organizations do away with departments altogether. For example, at Oticon Holding A/S, a Danish company that introduced the world's first digital hearing aid, there are no organization charts, no departments, no functions, and no titles. Employees are continuously forming and reforming into self-directed teams that work on specific projects.[41]

From Routine Tasks to Empowered Roles. Another shift in thinking relates to the degree of formal structure and control placed on employees in the performance of their work. Recall that scientific management advocated precisely defining each job and how it should be performed. A **task** is a narrowly defined piece of work assigned to a person. In traditional organizations, tasks are broken down into specialized, separate parts, as in a machine. Knowledge and control of tasks are centralized at the top of the organization, and employees are expected to do as they are told. A **role**, in contrast, is a part in a dynamic social system. A role has discretion and responsibility, allowing the person to use his or her discretion and ability to achieve an outcome or meet a goal. In learning organizations, employees play a role in the team or department and roles may be continually redefined or adjusted. There are few rules or procedures, and knowledge and control of tasks are located with workers rather than with supervisors or top executives. Employees are encouraged to take care of problems by working with one another and with customers. The U.S. Army again provides an excellent example. Four-star General John Abizaid, who took charge of U.S. Central Command (all of the forces in the Middle East) in July 2003, has long advocated an expanded role for soldiers in the field. He knows that today's soldiers have to do more than just shoot rifles and follow orders. During the peacekeeping operations in Iraq, low-ranking soldiers on a daily basis have to use intelligence, emotional understanding, and cultural sensitivity to defuse potentially dangerous situations.[42]

From Formal Control Systems to Shared Information. In young, small organizations, communication is generally informal and face-to-face. There are few formal control and information systems because the top leaders of the company usually work directly with employees in the day-to-day operation of the business. However, when organizations grow large and complex, the distance between top leaders and workers in the technical core increases. Formal systems are often implemented to manage the growing amount of complex information and to detect deviations from established standards and goals.[43]

In learning organizations, information serves a very different purpose. The widespread sharing of information keeps the organization functioning at an optimum level. The learning organization strives to return to the condition of a small, entrepreneurial firm in which all employees have complete information about the company so they can act quickly. Ideas and information are shared throughout the organization. Rather than using information to control employees, a significant part of a manager's job is to find ways to open channels of communication so that ideas flow in all directions. In addition, learning organizations maintain open lines of communication with customers, suppliers, and even competitors to enhance learning capability. At JetBlue Airways, CEO and founder David Neeleman promotes widespread information sharing by regularly going on flights to talk with employees and customers. Neeleman believes this is where he gets his best ideas for improving JetBlue.[44] Information technology also plays a key role in keeping people across the organization connected.

From Competitive to Collaborative Strategy. In traditional organizations designed for efficient performance, strategy is formulated by top managers and imposed on the organization. Top executives think about how the organization can best respond to competition, efficiently use resources, and cope with environmental changes. In the learning organization, in contrast, the accumulated actions of an informed and empowered workforce contribute to strategy development. Since all employees are in touch with customers, suppliers, and new technology, they help identify needs and solutions and participate in strategy making. In addition, strategy emerges from partnerships with suppliers, customers, and even competitors. Organizations become collaborators as well as competitors, experimenting to find the best way to learn and adapt. Boundaries between organizations are becoming diffuse, with companies often forming partnerships to compete globally, sometimes joining in modular or virtual network organizations that are connected electronically.

From Rigid to Adaptive Culture. For an organization to remain healthy, its culture should encourage adaptation to the external environment. A danger for many organizations is that the culture becomes fixed, as if set in concrete. Organizations that were highly successful in stable environments often become victims of their own success when the environment begins to change dramatically. This is what happened at Xerox Corp., as described in the opening case, when managers became stuck in the Burox culture and were unable to respond to rapid changes in the technological environment. The cultural values, ideas, and practices that helped attain success were detrimental to effective performance in a rapidly changing environment.

In a learning organization, the culture encourages openness, equality, continuous improvement, and change. People in the organization are aware of the whole system, how everything fits together, and how the various parts of the organization interact with one another and with the environment. This whole-system mindset minimizes boundaries within the organization and with other companies. In addition, activities and symbols that create status differences, such as executive dining rooms or reserved parking spaces, are discarded. Each person is a valued contributor and the organization becomes a place for creating a web of relationships that allows people to develop and apply their full potential. Consider QuikTrip, a chain of convenience stores, where most of the top managers started out at the store level, and everyone is considered a vital part of the chain's success. "The purpose of QuikTrip," says CEO Chester Cadieux II, "is to give our employees the opportunity to grow and succeed."[45] The emphasis on treating everyone with care and respect creates a climate in which people feel safe to experiment, take risks, and make mistakes, all of which encourages learning.

No company represents a perfect example of a learning organization, although many of today's most competitive organizations have shifted toward ideas and forms based on the concept of a living, dynamic system. Some of these organizations are spotlighted throughout this book in the Leading by Design boxes.

As illustrated in Exhibit 1.8, today's managers are involved in a struggle as they attempt to change their companies into learning organizations. The challenge for managers is to maintain some level of stability as they actively promote change toward the new way of thinking, to navigate between order and chaos.

One organization that is transforming into a learning organization is Mexico's Cementos Mexicanos (Cemex).

In Practice

Cementos Mexicanos

Cementos Mexicanos (Cemex), based in Monterrey, Mexico, has been making and delivering concrete for nearly a century. But the organization is on the cutting edge of organization design, a model of what it takes to succeed in the complex environment of the twenty-first century.

Cemex specializes in delivering concrete in developing areas of the world, places where anything can, and usually does, go wrong. Even in Monterrey, Cemex copes with unpredictable weather and traffic conditions, spontaneous labor disruptions, building permit snafus, and arbitrary government inspections of construction sites. In addition, more than half of all orders are changed or canceled by customers, usually at the last minute. Considering that a load of concrete is never more than ninety minutes from spoiling, those chaotic conditions mean high costs, complex scheduling, and frustration for employees, managers, and customers.

To help the organization compete in this environment, managers looked for both technological and organizational innovations. Leaders call their new approach "living with chaos." Rather than trying to change the customers, Cemex resolved to do business on the customers' own terms and design a system in which last-minute changes and unexpected problems are routine.

A core element of this approach is a complex information technology system, including a global positioning satellite system and onboard computers in all delivery trucks, which is fed with streams of day-to-day data on customer orders, production schedules, traffic problems, weather conditions, and so forth. Now Cemex trucks head out every morning to cruise the streets. When a customer order comes in, an employee checks the customer's credit status, locates a nearby truck, and relays directions for delivery. If the order is cancelled, computers automatically direct the plant to scale back production.

Cemex also made managerial and organizational changes to support the new approach. The company enrolled all its drivers, who had an average of 6 years of formal schooling, in weekly secondary-education classes and began training them in delivering not just cement but quality service. In addition, many strict and demanding work rules were abolished so that workers had more discretion and responsibility for identifying and rapidly responding to problems and customer needs. As a result, Cemex trucks now operate as self-organizing business units, run by well-trained employees who think like businesspeople. According to Francisco Perez, operations manager at Cemex in Guadalajara, "They used to think of themselves as drivers. But anyone can deliver concrete. Now our people know that they're delivering a service that the competition cannot deliver."

Cemex has transformed the industry by combining extensive networking technology with a new management approach that taps into the mindpower of everyone in the company. People at Cemex are constantly learning—on the job, in training classes, and through visits to other organizations. As a result, the company has a startling capacity to anticipate customer needs, solve problems, and innovate quickly. In addition, Cemex freely shares what it knows with other organizations, even competitors, believing the widespread sharing of knowledge and information is the best way to keep the organization thriving in a world of complexity. This philosophy has helped transform a once-sleepy cement company into a global powerhouse, with 2,200 operating units in 22 countries.[46]

Framework for the Book

What topic areas are relevant to organization theory and design? How does a course in management or organizational behavior differ from a course in organization theory? The answer is related to the concept called level of analysis.

Levels of Analysis

In systems theory, each system is composed of subsystems. Systems are nested within systems, and one **level of analysis** has to be chosen as the primary focus. Four levels of analysis normally characterize organizations, as illustrated in Exhibit 1.9. The individual human being is the basic building block of organizations. The human being is to the organization what a cell is to a biological system. The next higher system level is the group or department. These are collections of individuals who work together to perform group tasks. The next level of analysis is the organization itself. An organization is a collection of groups or departments that combine into the total organization.

Organizations themselves can be grouped together into the next higher level of analysis, which is the interorganizational set and community. The interorganizational set is the group of organizations with which a single organization interacts. Other organizations in the community also make up an important part of an organization's environment.

Organization theory focuses on the organizational level of analysis but with concern for groups and the environment. To explain the organization, one should look not only at its characteristics but also at the characteristics of the environment and of the departments and groups that make up the organization. The focus of this book is to help you understand organizations by examining their specific characteristics, the nature of and relationships among groups and departments that make up the organization, and the collection of organizations that make up the environment.

Are individuals included in organization theory? Organization theory does consider the behavior of individuals, but in the aggregate. People are important, but they are not the primary focus of analysis. Organization theory is distinct from organizational behavior.

Briefcase

As an organization manager, keep this guideline in mind:

Make yourself a competent, influential manager by using the frameworks that organization theory provides to interpret and understand the organization around you.

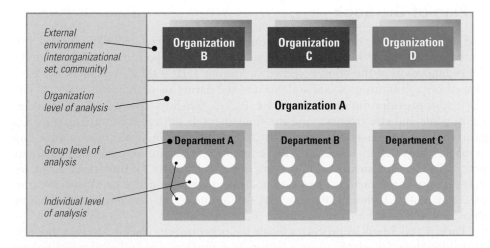

EXHIBIT 1.9
Levels of Analysis in Organizations
Source: Based on Andrew H. Van De Ven and Diane L. Ferry, *Measuring and Assessing Performance* (New York: Wiley, 1980), 8; and Richard L. Daft and Richard M. Steers, *Organizations: A Micro/Macro Approach* (Glenview, Ill.: Scott, Foresman, 1986), 8.

Organizational behavior is the micro approach to organizations because it focuses on the individuals within organizations as the relevant units of analysis. Organizational behavior examines concepts such as motivation, leadership style, and personality and is concerned with cognitive and emotional differences among people within organizations.

Organization theory is a macro examination of organizations because it analyzes the whole organization as a unit. Organization theory is concerned with people aggregated into departments and organizations and with the differences in structure and behavior at the organization level of analysis. Organization theory is the sociology of organizations, while organizational behavior is the psychology of organizations.

A new approach to organization studies is called *meso theory*. Most organizational research and many management courses specialize in either organizational behavior or organization theory. **Meso theory** (*meso* means "in between") concerns the integration of both micro and macro levels of analysis. Individuals and groups affect the organization and the organization in return influences individuals and groups. To thrive in organizations, managers and employees need to understand multiple levels simultaneously. For example, research may show that employee diversity enhances innovation. To facilitate innovation, managers need to understand how structure and context (organization theory) are related to interactions among diverse employees (organizational behavior) to foster innovation, because both macro and micro variables account for innovations.[47]

For its part, organization theory is directly relevant to top- and middle-management concerns and partly relevant to lower management. Top managers are responsible for the entire organization and must set goals, develop strategy, interpret the external environment, and decide organization structure and design. Middle management is concerned with major departments, such as marketing or research, and must decide how the department relates to the rest of the organization. Middle managers must design their departments to fit work-unit technology and deal with issues of power and politics, intergroup conflict, and information and control systems, each of which is part of organization theory. Organization theory is only partly concerned with lower management because this level of supervision is concerned with employees who operate machines, input data, teach classes, and sell goods. Organization theory is concerned with the big picture of the organization and its major departments.

■ Plan of the Book

The topics within the field of organization theory are interrelated. Chapters are presented so that major ideas unfold in logical sequence. The framework that guides the organization of the book is shown in Exhibit 1.10. Part 1 introduces the basic idea of organizations as social systems and the nature of organization theory. This discussion provides the groundwork for Part 2, which is about strategic management, goals and effectiveness, and the fundamentals of organization structure. Organizations are open systems that exist for a purpose. This section examines how managers help the organization achieve its purpose, including the design of an appropriate structure, such as a functional, divisional, matrix, or horizontal structure. Part 3 looks at the various open system elements that influence organization structure and design, including the external environment, interorganizational relationships, and the global environment.

Parts 4 and 5 look at processes inside the organization. Part 4 describes how organization design is related to such factors as manufacturing and service technology,

Part 1 Introduction to Organizations

CHAPTER 1
Organizations and Organization Theory

EXHIBIT 1.10
Framework for the Book

Part 2 Organizational Purpose and Structural Design

CHAPTER 2
Strategy, Organization Design, and Effectiveness

CHAPTER 3
Fundamentals of Organization Structure

Part 3 Open System Design Elements

CHAPTER 4
The External Environment

CHAPTER 5
Interorganizational Relationships

CHAPTER 6
Designing Organizations for the International
Environment

Part 4 Internal Design Elements

CHAPTER 7
Manufacturing and Service Technologies

CHAPTER 8
Information Technology and Control

CHAPTER 9
Organizational Size, Life Cycle, and Decline

Part 5 Managing Dynamic Processes

CHAPTER 10
Organizational Culture and Ethical Values

CHAPTER 11
Innovation and Change

CHAPTER 12
Decision-Making Processes

CHAPTER 13
Conflict, Power, and Politics

organizational size and life cycle, and information and control systems. Part 5 shifts to dynamic processes that exist within and between major organizational departments and includes topics such as innovation and change, culture and ethical values, decision-making processes, managing intergroup conflict, and power and politics.

■ Plan of Each Chapter

Each chapter begins with an organizational case to illustrate the topic to be covered. Theoretical concepts are introduced and explained in the body of the chapter. Several *In Practice* segments are included in each chapter to illustrate the concepts and show how they apply to real organizations. *Book Marks* are included in most chapters to present organizational issues that managers face right now. These book reviews discuss current concepts and applications to deepen and enrich your understanding of organizations. The *Leading by Design* examples illustrate the dramatic changes taking place in management thinking and practice. Key points for designing and managing organizations are highlighted in the *Briefcase* items throughout the chapter. Each chapter closes with a "Summary and Interpretation" section that reviews and explains important theoretical concepts.

Summary and Interpretation

One important idea in this chapter is that organizations are systems. In particular, they are open systems that must adapt to the environment to survive. Various parts of the organization are designed to perform the key subsystem functions of production, adaptation, maintenance, management, and boundary spanning. Five parts of the organization are the technical core, top management, middle management, technical support, and administrative support.

The focus of analysis for organization theory is not individual people but the organization itself. Relevant concepts include the dimensions of organization structure and context. The dimensions of formalization, specialization, hierarchy of authority, centralization, professionalism, personnel ratios, size, organizational technology, environment, goals and strategy, and culture provide labels for measuring and analyzing organizations. These dimensions vary widely from organization to organization. Subsequent chapters provide frameworks for analyzing organizations with these concepts.

Many types of organizations exist. One important distinction is between for-profit businesses, in which managers direct their activities toward earning money for the company, and nonprofit organizations, in which managers direct their efforts toward generating some kind of social impact. Managers strive to design organizations to achieve high performance and effectiveness. Effectiveness is complex because different stakeholders have different interests and needs that they want satisfied by the organization.

Turbulence and complexity have replaced stability and predictability as defining traits for today's organizations. Some of the specific challenges managers and organizations face include coping with globalization; maintaining high standards of ethics and social responsibility; achieving rapid response to environmental changes, organizational crises, or new customer expectations; shifting to a technology-based workplace; and supporting diversity.

These challenges are leading to changes in organization design and management practices. The trend is away from highly structured systems based on a mechanical model toward looser, more flexible systems based on a natural, biological model. Many managers are redesigning companies toward the learning organization, which is characterized by a horizontal structure, empowered employees, shared information, collaborative strategy, and an adaptive culture.

Finally, most concepts in organization theory pertain to the top- and middle-management levels of the organization. This book is concerned more with the topics of those levels than with the operational-level topics of supervision and motivation of employees, which are discussed in courses on organizational behavior.

Key Concepts

administrative principles	open system
bureaucratic organizations	organization theory
chaos theory	organizational behavior
closed system	organizations
contextual dimensions	role
contingency	scientific management
effectiveness	stakeholder
efficiency	stakeholder approach
Hawthorne Studies	structural dimensions
learning organization	subsystems
level of analysis	system
meso theory	task

Discussion Questions

1. What is the definition of *organization*? Briefly explain each part of the definition.
2. What is the difference between an open system and a closed system? Can you give an example of a closed system? How is the stakeholder approach related to this concept?
3. Explain how Mintzberg's five basic parts of the organization perform the subsystem functions shown at the bottom of Exhibit 1.2. If an organization had to give up one of these five parts, which one could it survive the longest without? Discuss.
4. A handful of companies on the *Fortune* 500 list are more than 100 years old, which is rare. What organizational characteristics do you think might explain 100-year longevity?
5. What is the difference between formalization and specialization? Do you think an organization high on one dimension would also be high on the other? Discuss.
6. What does *contingency* mean? What are the implications of contingency theories for managers?
7. What are the primary differences between an organization designed for efficient performance and one designed for learning and change? Which type of organization do you think would be easier to manage? Discuss.
8. Why is shared information so important in a learning organization as compared to an efficient-performance organization? Discuss how an organization's approach to information sharing might be related to other elements of organization design, such as structure, tasks, strategy, and culture.
9. What are some differences one might expect among stakeholder expectations for a nonprofit organization versus a for-profit business? Do you think nonprofit managers have to pay more attention to stakeholders than do business managers? Discuss.
10. Early management theorists believed that organizations should strive to be logical and rational, with a place for everything and everything in its place. Discuss the pros and cons of this approach for today's organizations.

Chapter 1 Workbook: Measuring Dimensions of Organizations*

Analyze two organizations along the dimensions shown below. Indicate where you think each organization would fall on each of the scales. Use an X to indicate the first organization and an * to show the second.

You may choose any two organizations you are familiar with, such as your place of work, the university, a student organization, your church or synagogue, or your family.

Formalization
Many written rules   1   2   3   4   5   6   7   8   9   10   Few rules

Specialization
Separate tasks and roles   1   2   3   4   5   6   7   8   9   10   Overlapping tasks

Hierarchy
Tall hierarchy of authority   1   2   3   4   5   6   7   8   9   10   Flat hierarchy of authority

Technology
Product   1   2   3   4   5   6   7   8   9   10   Service

External Environment
Stable   1   2   3   4   5   6   7   8   9   10   Unstable

Culture
Clear norms and values   1   2   3   4   5   6   7   8   9   10   Ambiguous norms and values

Professionalism
High professional training   1   2   3   4   5   6   7   8   9   10   Low professional training

Goals
Well-defined goals   1   2   3   4   5   6   7   8   9   10   Goals not defined

Size
Small   1   2   3   4   5   6   7   8   9   10   Large

Organizational Mindset
Mechanical system   1   2   3   4   5   6   7   8   9   10   Biological system

Questions
1. What are the main differences between the two organizations you evaluated?
2. Would you recommend that one or both of the organizations have different ratings on any of the scales? Why?

Case for Analysis: Perdue Farms Inc.: Responding to 21ST Century Challenges*

Background and Company History

"I have a theory that you can tell the difference between those who have inherited a fortune and those who have made a fortune. Those who have made their own fortune forget not where they came from and are less likely to lose touch with the common man." (Bill Sterling, 'Just Browsin' column in Eastern Shore News, *March 2, 1988)*

The history of Perdue Farms Inc. is dominated by seven themes: quality, growth, geographic expansion, vertical integration, innovation, branding, and service. Arthur W. Perdue, a Railway Express Agent and descendent of a French Huguenot family named Perdeaux, founded the company in 1920 when he left his job with Railway Express and entered the egg business full-time near the small town of Salisbury, Maryland. Salisbury is located in a region immortalized in James Michener's *Chesapeake* that is alternately known as "the Eastern Shore" or "the Delmarva Peninsula." It includes parts of *Delaware, Maryland* and *Virginia.* Arthur Perdue's only child, Franklin Parsons Perdue, was born in 1920.

A quick look at Perdue Farms' mission statement (Exhibit 1.11) reveals the emphasis the company has always put on quality. In the 1920s, "Mr. Arthur," as he was called, bought leghorn breeding stock from Texas to improve the quality of his flock. He soon expanded his egg market and began shipments to New York. Practicing small economies such as mixing his own chicken feed and using leather from his old shoes to make hinges for his chicken coops, he stayed out of debt and prospered. He tried to add a new chicken coop every year.

By 1940, Perdue Farms was already known for quality products and fair dealing in a tough, highly competitive market. The company began offering chickens for sale when Mr. Arthur realized that the future lay in selling chickens, not eggs. In 1944, Mr. Arthur made his son Frank a full partner in A.W. Perdue and Son, Inc.

In 1950, Frank took over leadership of the company, which employed 40 people. By 1952, revenues were $6,000,000 from the sale of 2,600,000 broilers. During this period, the company began to vertically integrate, operating its own hatchery, starting to mix its own feed formulations and operating its own feed mill. Also, in the 1950s, Perdue Farms began to contract with others to grow chickens for them. By furnishing the growers with peeps (baby chickens) and feed, the company was better able to control quality.

In the 1960s, Perdue Farms continued to vertically integrate by building its first grain receiving and storage facilities and Maryland's first soybean processing plant. By 1967, annual sales had increased to about $35,000,000. But, it became clear to Frank that profits lay in processing chickens. Frank recalled in an interview for *Business Week* (September 15, 1972) "processors were paying us 10c a live pound for what cost us 14c to produce. Suddenly, processors were making as much as 7c a pound."

A cautious, conservative planner, Arthur Perdue had not been eager for expansion, and Frank Perdue was reluctant to enter poultry processing. But, economics forced his hand and, in 1968, the company bought its first processing plant, a Swift and Company operation in Salisbury.

From the first batch of chickens that it processed, Perdue's standards were higher than those of the federal government. The state grader on the first batch has often told the story of how he was worried that he had rejected too many chickens as not Grade A. As he finished his inspections for that first day, he saw Frank Perdue headed his way and he could tell that Frank was not happy. Frank started inspecting the birds and never argued over one that was rejected. Next, he saw Frank start to go through the ones that the state grader had passed and began to toss some of them over with the rejected birds. Finally, realizing that few met his standards, Frank put all of the birds in the reject pile. Soon, however, the facility was able to process 14,000 Grade A broilers per hour.

From the beginning, Frank Perdue refused to permit his broilers to be frozen for shipping, arguing that it resulted in unappetizing black bones and loss of flavor and moistness when cooked. Instead, Perdue chickens were (and some still are) shipped to market packed in ice, justifying the company's advertisements at that time that it sold only "fresh, young broilers." However, this policy also limited the company's market to those locations that could be

*Adapted from George C. Rubenson and Frank M. Shipper, Department of Management and Marketing, Franklin P. Perdue School of Business, Salisbury University. Copyright 2001 by the authors.

Acknowledgements: The authors are indebted to Frank Perdue, Jim Perdue, and the numerous associates at Perdue Farms, Inc., who generously shared their time and information about the company. In addition, the authors would like to thank the anonymous librarians at Blackwell Library, Salisbury State University, who routinely review area newspapers and file articles about the poultry industry—the most important industry on the DelMarVa peninsula. Without their assistance, this case would not be possible.

EXHIBIT 1.11
Perdue Mission 2000

Stand on Tradition
Perdue was built upon a foundation of quality,
a tradition described in our Quality Policy. . .

Our Quality Policy
"We shall produce products and provide services at all times which meet or exceed the expectations of our customers."

"We shall not be content to be of equal quality to our competitors."

"Our commitment is to be increasingly superior."

"Contribution to quality is a responsibility shared by everyone in the Perdue organization."

Focus on Today
Our mission reminds us of the purpose we serve. . .

Our Mission
"Enhance the quality of life with great food and agricultural products."

While striving to fulfill our mission, we use our values to guide our decisions. . .

Our Values
- **Quality:** We value the needs of our customers. Our high standards require us to work safely, make safe food and uphold the Perdue name.
- **Integrity:** We do the right thing and live up to our commitments. We do not cut corners or make false promises.
- **Trust:** We trust each other and treat each other with mutual respect. Each individual's skill and talent are appreciated.
- **Teamwork:** We value a strong work ethic and ability to make each other successful. We care what others think and encourage their involvement, creating a sense of pride, loyalty, ownership and family.

Look to the Future
Our vision describes what we will become and the qualities
that will enable us to succeed. . .

Our Vision
"To be the leading quality food company with $20 billion in sales in 2020."

Perdue in the Year 2020
- **To our customers:** We will provide food solutions and indispensable services to meet anticipated customer needs.
- **To our consumers:** A portfolio of trusted food and agricultural products will be supported by multiple brands throughout the world.
- **To our associates:** Worldwide, our people and our workplace will reflect our quality reputation, placing Perdue among the best places to work.
- **To our communities:** We will be known in the community as a strong corporate citizen, trusted business partner and favorite employer.
- **To our shareholders:** Driven by innovation, our market leadership and our creative spirit will yield industry-leading profits.

serviced overnight from the Eastern Shore of Maryland. Thus, Perdue chose for its primary markets the densely populated towns and cities of the East Coast, particularly New York City, which consumes more Perdue chicken than all other brands combined.

Frank Perdue's drive for quality became legendary both inside and outside the poultry industry. In 1985, Frank and Perdue Farm, Inc. were featured in the book, *A Passion for Excellence*, by Tom Peters and Nancy Austin.

In 1970, Perdue established its primary breeding and genetic research programs. Through selective breeding, Perdue developed a chicken with more white breast meat than the typical chicken. Selective breeding has been so successful that Perdue Farms chickens are desired by other processors. Rumors have even suggested that Perdue chickens have been stolen on occasion in an attempt to improve competitor flocks.

In 1971, Perdue Farms began an extensive marketing campaign featuring Frank Perdue. In his early advertisements, he became famous for saying things like "If you want to eat as good as my chickens, you'll just have to eat my chickens." He is often credited with being the first to brand what had been a commodity product. During the 1970s, Perdue Farms also expanded geographically to areas north of New York City such as Massachusetts, Rhode Island, and Connecticut.

In 1977, "Mr. Arthur" died at the age of 91, leaving behind a company with annual sales of nearly $200,000,000, an average annual growth rate of 17% compared to an industry average of 1% a year, the potential for processing 78,000 broilers per hour, and annual production of nearly 350,000,000 pounds of poultry per year. Frank Perdue said of his father simply "I learned everything from him."

In 1981, Frank Perdue was in Boston for his induction into the Babson College Academy of Distinguished Entrepreneurs, an award established in 1978 to recognize the spirit of free enterprise and business leadership. Babson College President Ralph Z. Sorenson inducted Perdue into the academy, which, at that time, numbered 18 men and women from four continents. Perdue had the following to say to the college students:

"There are none, nor will there ever be, easy steps for the entrepreneur. Nothing, absolutely nothing, replaces the willingness to work earnestly, intelligently towards a goal. You have to be willing to pay the price. You have to have an insatiable appetite for detail, have to be willing to accept constructive criticism, to ask questions, to be fiscally responsible, to surround yourself with good people and, most of all, to listen." (Frank Perdue, speech at Babson College, April 28, 1981)

The early 1980s saw Perdue Farms expand southward into Virginia, North Carolina, and Georgia. It also began to buy out other producers such as Carroll's Foods, Purvis Farms, Shenandoah Valley Poultry Company, and Shenandoah Farms. The latter two acquisitions diversified the company's markets to include turkey. New products included value-added items such as "Perdue Done It!," a line of fully cooked fresh chicken products.

James A. (Jim) Perdue, Frank's only son, joined the company as a management trainee in 1983 and became a plant manager. The late 1980s tested the mettle of the firm. Following a period of considerable expansion and product diversification, a consulting firm recommended that the company form several strategic business units, responsible for their own operations. In other words, the firm should decentralize. Soon after, the chicken market leveled off and then declined for a period. In 1988, the firm experienced its first year in the red. Unfortunately, the decentralization had created duplication and enormous administrative costs. The firm's rapid plunge into turkeys and other food processing, where it had little experience, contributed to the losses. Characteristically, the company refocused, concentrating on efficiency of operations, improving communications throughout the company, and paying close attention to detail.

On June 2, 1989, Frank celebrated 50 years with Perdue Farms, Inc. At a morning reception in downtown Salisbury, the Governor of Maryland proclaimed it "Frank Perdue Day." The Governors of Delaware and Virginia did the same. In 1991, Frank was named Chairman of the Executive Committee and Jim Perdue became Chairman of the Board. Quieter, gentler and more formally educated, Jim Perdue focused on operations, infusing the company with an even stronger devotion to quality control and a bigger commitment to strategic planning. Frank Perdue continued to do advertising and public relations. As Jim Perdue matured as the company leader, he took over the role of company spokesperson and began to appear in advertisements.

Under Jim Perdue's leadership, the 1990s were dominated by market expansion south into Florida and west to Michigan and Missouri. In 1992, the international business segment was formalized, serving customers in Puerto Rico, South America, Europe, Japan and China. By fiscal year 1998, international sales were $180 million per year. International markets are beneficial for the firm because U.S. customers prefer white meat, whereas customers in most other countries prefer dark meat.

Food-service sales to commercial customers has also become a major market. New retail product lines focus on value-added items, individually quick-frozen items, home-meal replacement items, and products for the delicatessen. The "Fit 'n Easy" label continues as part of a nutrition campaign, using skinless, boneless chicken and turkey products.

The 1990s also saw the increased use of technology and the building of distribution centers to better serve the customer. For example, all over-the-road trucks were equipped with satellite two-way communications and geographic positioning, allowing real-time tracking, rerouting if needed, and accurately informing customers when to expect product arrival.

Currently, nearly 20,000 associates have increased revenues to more than $2.5 billion.

MANAGEMENT & ORGANIZATION

From 1950 until 1991, Frank Perdue was the primary force behind Perdue Farms' growth and success. During Frank's years as the company leader, the industry entered its high growth period. Industry executives had typically developed professionally during the industry's infancy. Many had little formal education and started their careers in the barnyard, building chicken coops and cleaning them out. They often spent their entire careers with one company, progressing from supervisor of grow-out facilities to management of processing plants to corporate executive positions. Perdue Farms was not unusual in that respect. An entrepreneur through and through, Frank lived up to his marketing image of "it takes a tough man to make a tender chicken." He mostly used a centralized management style that kept decision making authority in his own hands or those of a few trusted, senior executives whom he had known for a lifetime. Workers were expected to do their jobs.

In later years, Frank increasingly emphasized employee (or "associates" as they are currently called) involvement in quality issues and operational decisions. This emphasis on employee participation undoubtedly eased the transfer of power in 1991 to his son, Jim, which appears to have been unusually smooth. Although Jim grew up in the family business, he spent almost 15 years earning an undergraduate degree in biology from Wake Forest University, a master's degree in marine biology from the University of Massachusetts at Dartmouth and a doctorate in fisheries from the University of Washington in Seattle. Returning to Perdue Farms in 1983, he earned an EMBA from Salisbury State University and was assigned positions as plant manager, divisional quality control manager, and vice president of Quality Improvement Process (QIP) prior to becoming Chairman.

Jim has a people-first management style. Company goals center on the three Ps: People, Products, and Profitability. He believes that business success rests on satisfying customer needs with quality products. It is important to put associates first, he says, because "If [associates] come first, they will strive to assure superior product qual-ity—and satisfied customers." This view has had a profound impact on the company culture, which is based on Tom Peters's view that "Nobody knows a person's 20 square feet better than the person who works there." The idea is to gather ideas and information from everyone in the organization and maximize productivity by transmitting these ideas throughout the organization.

Key to accomplishing this "employees first" policy is workforce stability, a difficult task in an industry that employs a growing number of associates working in physically demanding and sometimes stressful conditions. A significant number of associates are Hispanic immigrants who may have a poor command of the English language, are sometimes undereducated, and often lack basic health care. In order to increase these associates' opportunity for advancement, Perdue Farms focuses on helping them overcome these disadvantages.

For example, the firm provides English-language classes to help non-English speaking associates assimilate. Ultimately associates can earn the equivalent of a high-school diploma. To deal with physical stress, the company has an ergonomics committee in each plant that studies job requirements and seeks ways to redesign those jobs that put workers at the greatest risk. The company also has an impressive wellness program that currently includes clinics at 10 plants. The clinics are staffed by professional medical people working for medical practice groups under contract to Perdue Farms. Associates have universal access to all Perdue-operated clinics and can visit a doctor for anything from a muscle strain to prenatal care to screening tests for a variety of diseases. Dependent care is available. While benefits to the employees are obvious, the company also benefits through a reduction in lost time for medical office visits, lower turnover, and a happier, healthier, more productive and stable work force.

MARKETING

In the early days, chicken was sold to butcher shops and neighborhood groceries as a commodity, that is, producers sold it in bulk and butchers cut and wrapped it. The customer had no idea which firm grew or processed the chicken. Frank Perdue was convinced that higher profits could be made if the firm's products could be sold at a premium price. But, the only reason a product can command a premium price is if customers ask for it by name—and that means the product must be differentiated and "branded." Hence, the emphasis over the years on superior quality, broader breasted chickens, and a healthy golden color (actually the result of adding marigold petals in the feed to enhance the natural yellow color that corn provided).

Today, branded chicken is ubiquitous. The new task for Perdue Farms is to create a unified theme to market a wide variety of products (e.g., both fresh meat and fully prepared and frozen products) to a wide variety of customers (e.g., retail, food service, and international). Industry experts believe that the market for fresh poultry has peaked while sales of value added and frozen products continue to grow at a healthy rate. Although domestic retail sales accounted for about 60% of Perdue Farms' revenues in the 2000 fiscal year, food service sales now account for 20%, international sales account for 5%, and grain and oilseed contribute the remaining 15%. The company expects food service, international, and grain and oilseed sales to continue to grow as a percentage of total revenues.

DOMESTIC RETAIL

Today's retail grocery customer is increasingly looking for ease and speed of preparation, that is, value-added products. The move toward value-added products has significantly changed the meat department in the modern grocery store. There are now five distinct meat outlets for poultry:

1. The fresh meat counter—traditional, fresh meat—includes whole chicken and parts
2. The delicatessen—processed turkey, rotisserie chicken
3. The frozen counter—individually quick-frozen items such as frozen whole chickens, turkeys, and Cornish hens
4. Home meal replacement—fully prepared entrees such as Perdue brand "Short Cuts" and Deluca brand entrees (the Deluca brand was acquired and is sold under its own name) that are sold along with salads and desserts so that you can assemble your own dinner
5. Shelf stable—canned products

Because Perdue Farms has always used the phrase "fresh young chicken" as the centerpiece of its marketing, value-added products and the retail frozen counter create a possible conflict with past marketing themes. Are these products compatible with the company's marketing image, and, if so, how does the company express the notion of quality in this broader product environment? To answer that question, Perdue Farms has been studying what the term "fresh young chicken" means to customers who consistently demand quicker and easier preparation and who admit that they freeze most of their fresh meat purchases once they get home. One view is that the importance of the term "fresh young chicken" comes from the customer's perception that "quality" and "freshness" are closely associated. Thus, the real issue may be trust, that is, the customer must believe that the product, whether fresh or frozen, is the freshest, highest quality possible, and future marketing themes must develop that concept.

OPERATIONS

Two words sum up the Perdue approach to operations—quality and efficiency—with emphasis on the first over the latter. Perdue, more than most companies, represents the Total Quality Management (TQM) slogan, "Quality, a journey without end." Some of the key events in Perdue's quality improvement process are listed in Exhibit 1.12.

Both quality and efficiency are improved through the management of details. Exhibit 1.13 depicts the structure and product flow of a generic, vertically integrated broiler company. A broiler company can choose which steps in the process it wants to accomplish in-house and which it wants suppliers to provide. For example, the broiler company could purchase all grain, oilseed, meal, and other feed products. Or it could contract with hatcheries to supply primary breeders and hatchery supply flocks.

Perdue Farms chose maximum vertical integration to control every detail. It breeds and hatches its own eggs (19 hatcheries), selects its contract growers, builds Perdue-engineered chicken houses, formulates and manufactures its own feed (12 poultry feedmills, 1 specialty feedmill, 2 ingredient-blending operations), oversees the care and feeding of the chicks, operates its own processing plants (21 processing and further processing plants), distributes via its own trucking fleet, and markets the products (see Exhibit 1.13). Total process control formed the basis for Frank Perdue's early claims that Perdue Farms poultry is, indeed, higher quality than other poultry. When he stated in his early ads that "A chicken is what it eats . . . I store my own grain and mix my own feed . . . and give my Perdue chickens nothing but well water to drink. . . ," he knew that his claim was honest and he could back it up.

Total process control also enables Perdue Farms to ensure that nothing goes to waste. Eight measurable items—hatchability, turnover, feed conversion, livability, yield, birds per man-hour, utilization, and grade—are tracked routinely.

Perdue Farms continues to ensure that nothing artificial is fed to or injected into the birds. No shortcuts are taken. A chemical-free and steroid-free diet is fed to the chickens. Young chickens are vaccinated against disease. Selective breeding is used to improve the quality of the chicken stock. Chickens are bred to yield more white breast meat because that is what the consumer wants.

To ensure that Perdue Farms poultry continues to lead the industry in quality, the company buys and analyzes competitors' products regularly. Inspection associates grade these products and share the information with the highest levels of management. In addition, the company's Quality Policy is displayed at all locations and taught to all associates in quality training (Exhibit 1.14).

EXHIBIT 1.12

Milestones in the Quality Improvement Process at Perdue Farms

1924 — Arthur Perdue bought leghorn roosters for $25
1950 — Adopted the company logo of a chick under a magnifying glass
1984 — Frank Perdue attends Philip Crosby's Quality College
1985 — Perdue recognized for its pursuit of quality in *A Passion for Excellence*
     — 200 Perdue managers attended Quality College
     — Adopted the Quality Improvement Process (QIP)
1986 — Established Corrective Action Teams (CAT's)
1987 — Established Quality Training for all associates
     — Implemented Error Cause Removal Process (ECR)
1988 — Steering Committee formed
1989 — First Annual Quality Conference held
     — Implemented Team Management
1990 — Second Annual Quality Conference held
     — Codified Values and Corporate Mission
1991 — Third Annual Quality Conference held
     — Customer Satisfaction defined
1992 — Fourth Annual Quality Conference held
     — How to implement Customer Satisfaction explained to team leaders and Quality Improvement Teams (QIT)
     — Created Quality Index
     — Created Customer Satisfaction Index (CSI)
     — Created "Farm to Fork" quality program
1999 — Launched Raw Material Quality Index
2000 — Initiated High Performance Team Process

RESEARCH AND DEVELOPMENT

Perdue is an acknowledged industry leader in the use of research and technology to provide quality products and service to its customers. The company spends more on research as a percent of revenues than any other poultry processor. This practice goes back to Frank Perdue's focus on finding ways to differentiate his products based on quality and value. It was research into selective breeding that resulted in the broader breast, an attribute of Perdue Farms chicken that was the basis of his early advertising. Although other processors have also improved their stock, Perdue Farms believes that it still leads the industry. A list of some of Perdue Farms technological accomplishments is given in Exhibit 1.15.

As with every other aspect of the business, Perdue Farms tries to leave nothing to chance in R&D. The company employs specialists in avian science, microbiology, genetics, nutrition, and veterinary science. Because of its R&D capabilities, Perdue Farms is often involved in United States Drug Administration (USDA) field tests with pharmaceutical suppliers. Knowledge and experience gained from these tests can lead to a competitive advantage. For example, Perdue has the most extensive and expensive vaccination program in the industry. Currently, the company is working with and studying the practices of several European producers who use completely different methods.

The company has used research to significantly increase productivity. For example, in the 1950s, it took 14 weeks to grow a 3 pound chicken. Today, it takes only seven weeks to grow a 5 pound chicken. This gain in efficiency is due principally to improvements in the conversion rate of feed to chicken. Feed represents about 65% of the cost of growing a chicken. Thus, if additional research can further improve the conversion rate of feed to chicken by just 1%, it would represent estimated additional income of $2.5-3 million per week or $130-156 million per year.

ENVIRONMENT

Environmental issues present a constant challenge to all poultry processors. Growing, slaughtering, and processing poultry is a difficult and tedious process that demands absolute efficiency to keep operating costs at an acceptable level. Inevitably, detractors argue that the process is dangerous to workers, inhumane to the poultry, hard on the environment, and results in food that may not be safe. Thus, media headlines such as "Human Cost of Poultry Business

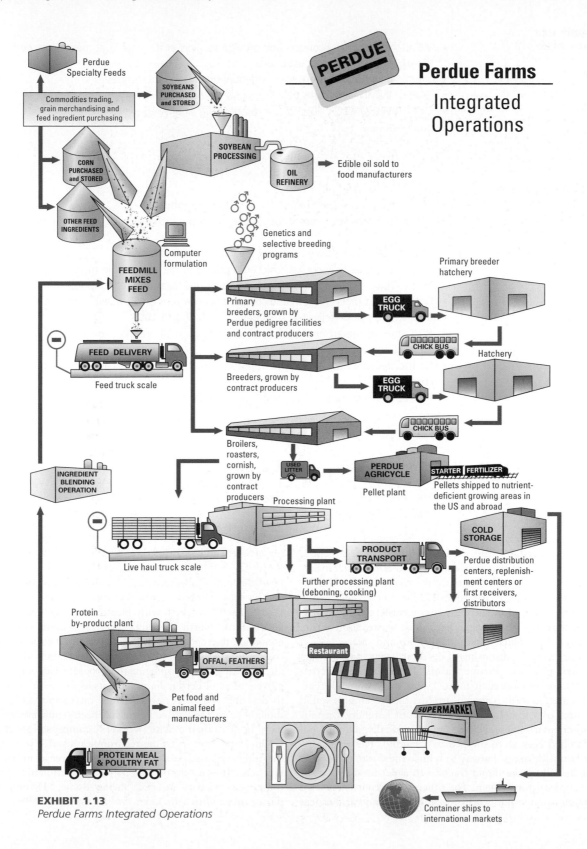

EXHIBIT 1.13
Perdue Farms Integrated Operations

EXHIBIT 1.14
Quality Policy

- WE SHALL produce products and provide services at all times that meet or exceed the expectations of our customers.
- WE SHALL not be content to be of equal quality to our competitors.
- OUR COMMITMENT is to be increasingly superior.
- CONTRIBUTION TO QUALITY is a responsibility shared by everyone in the Perdue organization.

EXHIBIT 1.15
Perdue Farms Inc. Technological Accomplishments

- Conducts more research than all competitors combined
- Breeds chickens with consistently more breast meat than any other bird in the industry
- First to use digital scales to guarantee weights to customers
- First to package fully-cooked chicken products in microwaveable trays
- First to have a box lab to define quality of boxes from different suppliers
- First to test both its chickens and competitors' chickens on 52 quality factors every week
- Improved on time deliveries 20% between 1987 and 1993
- Built state of the art analytical and microbiological laboratories for feed and end product analysis
- First to develop best management practices for food safety across all areas of the company
- First to develop commercially viable pelletized poultry litter

Bared," "Animal Rights Advocates Protest Chicken Coop Conditions," "Processing Plants Leave Toxic Trail," or "EPA Mandates Poultry Regulations" are routine.

Perdue Farms tries to be proactive in managing environmental issues. In April 1993, the company created an Environmental Steering Committee. Its mission is ". . . . to provide all Perdue Farms work sites with vision, direction, and leadership so that they can be good corporate citizens from an environmental perspective today and in the future." The committee is responsible for overseeing how the company is doing in such environmentally sensitive areas as waste water, storm water, hazardous waste, solid waste, recycling, bio-solids, and human health and safety.

For example, disposing of dead birds has long been an industry problem. Perdue Farms developed small composters for use on each farm. Using this approach, carcasses are reduced to an end-product that resembles soil in a matter of a few days. The disposal of hatchery waste is another environmental challenge. Historically, manure and unhatched eggs were shipped to a landfill. However, Perdue Farms developed a way to reduce the waste by 50 percent by selling the liquid fraction to a pet-food processor that cooks it for protein. The other 50 percent is recycled through a rendering process. In 1990, Perdue Farms spent

$4.2 million to upgrade its existing treatment facility with a state-of-the-art system at its Accomac, Virginia, and Showell, Maryland, plants. These facilities use forced hot air heated to 120 degrees to cause the microbes to digest all traces of ammonia, even during the cold winter months.

More than 10 years ago, North Carolina's Occupational Safety and Health Administration cited Perdue Farms for an unacceptable level of repetitive stress injuries at its Lewiston and Robersonville, North Carolina, processing plants. This sparked a major research program in which Perdue Farms worked with Health and Hygiene Inc. of Greensboro, North Carolina, to learn more about ergonomics, the repetitive movements required to accomplish specific jobs. Results have been dramatic. Launched in 1991 after 2 years of development, the program videotapes employees at all of Perdue Farms' plants as they work in order to describe and place stress values on various tasks. Although the cost to Perdue Farms has been significant, results have been dramatic with workers' compensation claims down 44 percent, lost-time recordables just 7.7 percent of the industry average, an 80 percent decrease in serious repetitive stress cases and a 50 percent reduction in lost time for surgery for back injuries (Shelley Reese, "Helping Employees get a Grip", *Business and Health*, Aug. 1998).

Despite these advances, serious problems continue to develop. Some experts have called for conservation measures that might limit the density of chicken houses in a given area or even require a percentage of existing chicken houses to be taken out of production periodically. Obviously this would be very hard on the farm families who own existing chicken houses and could result in fewer acres devoted to agriculture. Working with AgriRecycle Inc. of Springfield, Missouri, Perdue Farms has developed a possible solution. The plan envisions the poultry companies processing excess manure into pellets for use as fertilizer. This would permit sales outside the poultry growing region, better balancing the input of grain. Spokesmen estimate that as much as 120,000 tons, nearly one third of the surplus nutrients from manure produced each year on the Delmarva peninsula, could be sold to corn growers in other parts of the country. Prices would be market driven but could be $25 to $30 per ton, suggesting a potential, small profit. Still, almost any attempt to control the problem potentially raises the cost of growing chickens, forcing poultry processors to look elsewhere for locations where the chicken population is less dense.

In general, solving industry environmental problems presents at least five major challenges to the poultry processor:

- How to maintain the trust of the poultry consumer
- How to ensure that the poultry remain healthy
- How to protect the safety of the employees and the process
- How to satisfy legislators who need to show their constituents that they are taking firm action when environmental problems occur
- How to keep costs at an acceptable level

Jim Perdue sums up Perdue Farms' position as follows: ". . . . we must not only comply with environmental laws as they exist today, but look to the future to make sure we don't have any surprises. We must make sure our environmental policy statement [see Exhibit 1.16] is real, that there's something behind it and that we do what we say we're going to do."

LOGISTICS AND INFORMATION SYSTEMS
The explosion of poultry products and increasing number of customers during recent years placed a severe strain on the existing logistics system, which was developed at a time when there were far fewer products, fewer delivery points, and lower volume. Hence, the company had limited ability to improve service levels, could not support further growth, and could not introduce innovative services that might provide a competitive advantage.

In the poultry industry, companies are faced with two significant problems—time and forecasting. Fresh poultry has a limited shelf life—measured in days. Thus forecasts must be extremely accurate and deliveries must be timely. On one hand, estimating requirements too conservatively results in product shortages. Mega-customers such as Wal-Mart will not tolerate product shortages that lead to empty shelves and lost sales. On the other hand, if estimates are overstated, the result is outdated products that cannot be sold and losses for Perdue Farms. A common expression in the poultry industry is "you either sell it or smell it."

Forecasting has always been extremely difficult in the poultry industry because the processor needs to know approximately 18 months in advance how many broilers will be needed in order to size hatchery supply flocks and contract with growers to provide live broilers. Most customers (e.g., grocers and food-service buyers) have a much shorter planning window. Additionally, there is no way for Perdue Farms to know when rival poultry processors will put a particular product on special, reducing Perdue Farms sales, or when bad weather and other uncontrollable problems may reduce demand.

In the short run, information technology (IT) has helped by shortening the distance between the customer and Perdue Farms. As far back as 1987, personal computers (PCs) were placed directly on each customer-service associate's desk, allowing the associate to enter customer orders directly. Next, a system was developed to put dispatchers in direct contact with every truck in the system so that they would have accurate information about product inventory and truck location at all times. Now, IT is moving to further shorten the distance between the customer and the Perdue Farms service representative by putting a PC on the customer's desk. All of these steps improve communication and shorten the time from order to delivery.

To control the entire supply chain management process, Perdue Farms purchased a multi-million dollar information technology system that represents the biggest non-tangible asset expense in the company's history. This integrated, state-of-the-art information system required total process re-engineering, a project that took 18 months and required training 1200 associates. Major goals of the system were to (1) make it easier and more desirable for the customer to do business with Perdue Farms, (2) make it easier for Perdue Farms associates to get the job done and (3) take as much cost out of the process as possible.

INDUSTRY TRENDS
The poultry industry is affected by consumer, industry, and governmental regulatory trends. Currently, chicken is the number one meat consumed in the United States, with a 40 percent market share. The typical American consumes about 81 pounds of chicken, 69 pounds of beef, and 52

EXHIBIT 1.16
*Perdue Farms
Environmental Policy
Statement*

Perdue Farms is committed to environmental stewardship and shares that commitment with its farm family partners. We're proud of the leadership we're providing our industry in addressing the full range of environmental challenges related to animal agriculture and food processing. We've invested—and continue to invest—millions of dollars in research, new technology, equipment upgrades, and awareness and education as part of our ongoing commitment to protecting the environment.

• Perdue Farms was among the first poultry companies with a dedicated Environmental Services department. Our team of environmental managers is responsible for ensuring that every Perdue facility operates within *100 percent compliance of all applicable environmental regulations and permits*.

• Through our joint venture, Perdue AgriRecycle, Perdue Farms is investing $12 million to build in Delaware a first-of-its-kind pellet plant that will convert surplus poultry litter into a starter fertilizer that will be marketed internationally to nutrient deficient regions. The facility, which will serve the entire DelMarVa region, is scheduled to begin operation in April, 2001.

• We continue to explore new technologies that will reduce water usage in our processing plants without compromising food safety or quality.

• We invested thousands of man-hours in producer education to assist our family farm partners in managing their independent poultry operations in the most environmentally responsible manner possible. In addition, all our poultry producers are required to have nutrient management plans and dead-bird composters.

• Perdue Farms was one of four poultry companies operating in Delaware to sign an agreement with Delaware officials outlining our companies' voluntary commitment to help independent poultry producers dispose of surplus chicken litter.

• Our Technical Services department is conducting ongoing research into feed technology as a means of reducing the nutrients in poultry manure. We've already achieved phosphorous reductions that far exceed the industry average.

• We recognize that the environmental impact of animal agriculture is more pronounced in areas where development is decreasing the amount of farmland available to produce grain for feed and to accept nutrients. That is why we view independent grain *and* poultry producers as vital business partners and strive to preserve the economic viability of the family farm.

At Perdue Farms, we believe that it is possible to preserve the family farm; provide a safe, abundant and affordable food supply; and protect the environment. However, we believe that can best happen when there is cooperation and trust between the poultry industry, agriculture, environmental groups and state officials. We hope Delaware's effort will become a model for other states to follow.

pounds of pork annually (USDA data). Additionally, chicken is becoming the most popular meat in the world. In 1997, poultry set an export record of $2.5 billion. Although exports fell 6% in 1998, the decrease was attributed to Russia's and Asia's financial crisis and food-industry experts expect this to be only a temporary setback. Hence, the world market is clearly a growth opportunity for the future.

Government agencies whose regulations impact the industry include the Occupational Safety and Health Administration (OSHA) for employee safety and the Immigration and Naturalization Service (INS) for undocumented workers. OSHA enforces its regulations via periodic inspections, and levies fines when non-compliance is found. For example, a Hudson Foods poultry plant was fined more than a million dollars for alleged willful violations causing ergonomic injury to workers. The INS also uses periodic inspections to find undocumented workers. It estimates that undocumented aliens working in the industry vary from 3 to 78 percent of the workforce at individual plants. Plants that are found to use undocumented workers, especially those that are repeat offenders, can be heavily fined.

THE FUTURE

The marketplace for poultry in the twenty-first century will be very different from that of the past. Understanding the wants and needs of generation Xers and echo-boomers will be key to responding successfully to these differences.

Quality will continue to be essential. In the 1970s, quality was the cornerstone of Frank Perdue's successful marketing program to "brand" his poultry. However, in the twenty-first century, quality will not be enough. Today's customers expect—even demand—all products to be high quality. Thus, Perdue Farms plans to use customer service to further differentiate the company. The focus will be on learning how to become indispensable to the customer by taking cost out of the product and delivering it exactly the way the customer wants it, where and when the customer wants it. In short, as Jim Perdue says, "Perdue Farms wants to become so easy to do business with that the customer will have no reason to do business with anyone else."

Notes

1. This case is based on: Anthony Bianco and Pamela L. Moore, "Downfall: The Inside Story of the Management Fiasco at Xerox," *Business Week* (March 5, 2001), 82–92; Robert J. Grossman, "HR Woes at Xerox," *HR Magazine* (May 2001), 34–45; Jeremy Kahn, "The Paper Jam from Hell," *Fortune* (November 13, 2000), 141–146; Pamela L. Moore, "She's Here to Fix the Xerox," *Business Week* (August 6, 2001), 47–48; Claudia H. Deutsch, "At Xerox, the Chief Earns (Grudging) Respect," *The New York Times* (June 2, 2002), section 3, 1, 12; Olga Kharif, "Anne Mulcahy Has Xerox by the Horns," *Business Week Online* (May 29, 2003); "Focus on Innovation at Xerox Produces More Than 500 Patents in 2004, Provides Sound Foundation for Future Growth," *Business Wire* (January 13, 2005), 1; Amy Yee, "Xerox Comeback Continues to Thrive," *Financial Times* (January 26, 2005), 30; and "The Best and Worst Managers of the Year: Anne Mulcahy," *Business Week* (January 10, 2005), 55, 62. All quotes are from Grossman, "HR Woes at Xerox."

2. Martha Brannigan, "Air Pressure: Discount Carrier Lands Partners in Ill-Served Cities," *The Wall Street Journal* (July 16, 2002), A1, A10.

3. Harry G. Barkema, Joel A. C. Baum, and Elizabeth A. Mannix, "Management Challenges in a New Time," *Academy of Management Journal* 45, no. 5 (2002), 916–930. Eileen Davis, "What's on American Managers' Minds?" *Management Review* (April 1995), 14–20.

4. Barkema et al., "Management Challenges."

5. Keith H. Hammonds, "Smart, Determined, Ambitious, Cheap: The New Face of Global Competition," *Fast Company* (February 2003), 91–97; William J. Holstein, "Samsung's Golden Touch," *Fortune* (April 1, 2002), 89–94; Pete Engardio, Aaron Bernstein, and Manjeet Kripalani, "Is Your Job Next?" *Business Week* (February 3, 2003), 50–60.

6. Rebecca Smith and Jonathan Weil, "Ex-Enron Directors Reach Settlement," *The Wall Street Journal* (January 10, 2005), C3; Kara Scannell and Jonathan Weil, "Supreme Court to Hear Andersen's Appeal of Conviction," *The Wall Street Journal* (January 10, 2005), C1; "ImClone to Pay

$75 Million to Settle 2002 Suit," *The New York Times* (January 25, 2005), C3; Joann S. Lublin, "Travel Expenses Prompt Yale to Force Out Institute Chief," *The Wall Street Journal* (January 10, 2005), B1.

7. David Wessel, "Venal Sins: Why the Bad Guys of the Boardroom Emerged en Masse," *The Wall Street Journal* (June 20, 2002), A1, A6.

8. Greg Ip, "Mind Over Matter—Disappearing Acts: The Rapid Rise and Fall of the Intangible Asset," *The Wall Street Journal* (April 4, 2002), A1, A6.

9. Bernard Wysocki Jr., "Corporate Caveat: Dell or Be Delled," *The Wall Street Journal* (May 10, 1999), A1.

10. Andy Reinhardt, "From Gearhead to Grand High Poohbah," *Business Week* (August 28, 2000), 129–130.

11. G. Pascal Zachary, "Mighty is the Mongrel," *Fast Company* (July 2000), 270–284.

12. Steven Greenhouse, N.Y. Times News Service, "Influx of Immigrants Having Profound Impact on Economy," *Johnson City Press* (September 4, 2000), 9; Richard W. Judy and Carol D'Amico, *Workforce 2020: Work and Workers in the 21st Century* (Indianapolis, Ind.: Hudson Institute, 1997); statistics reported in Jason Forsythe, "Diversity Works," special advertising supplement to *The New York Times Magazine* (September 14, 2003), 75–100.

13. Debra E. Meyerson and Joyce K. Fletcher, "A Modest Manifesto for Shattering the Glass Ceiling," *Harvard Business Review* (January-February 2000), 127–136; Annie Finnigan, "Different Strokes," *Working Woman* (April 2001), 42–48; Joline Godfrey, "Been There, Doing That," *Inc.* (March 1996), 21–22; Paula Dwyer, Marsha Johnston, and Karen Lowry Miller, "Out of the Typing Pool, into Career Limbo," *Business Week* (April 15, 1996), 92–94.

14. Howard Aldrich, *Organizations and Environments* (Englewood Cliffs, N.J.: Prentice-Hall, 1979), 3.

15. This section is based largely on Peter F. Drucker, *Managing the Non-Profit Organization: Principles and Practices* (New York: HarperBusiness, 1992); and Thomas Wolf, *Managing a Nonprofit Organization* (New York: Fireside/Simon & Schuster, 1990).

16. Christine W. Letts, William P. Ryan, and Allen Grossman, *High Performance Nonprofit Organizations* (New York: John Wiley & Sons, Inc., 1999), 30–35.

17. Lisa Bannon, "Dream Works: As Make-a-Wish Expands Its Turf, Local Groups Fume," *The Wall Street Journal* (July 8, 2002), A1, A8.

18. Robert N. Stern and Stephen R. Barley, "Organizations and Social Systems: Organization Theory's Neglected Mandate," *Administrative Science Quarterly* 41 (1996): 146–162.

19. Philip Siekman, "Build to Order: One Aircraft Carrier," *Fortune* (July 22, 2002), 180[B]–180[J].

20. Brent Schlender, "The New Soul of a Wealth Machine," *Fortune* (April 5, 2004), 102–110.

21. Schlender, "The New Soul of a Wealth Machine," and Keith H. Hammonds, "Growth Search," *Fast Company* (April 2003), 75–80.

22. Arlyn Tobias Gajilan, "The Amazing JetBlue," *FSB* (May 2003), 51–60.

23. James D. Thompson, *Organizations in Action* (New York: McGraw-Hill, 1967), 4–13.

24. Henry Mintzberg, *The Structuring of Organizations* (Englewood Cliffs, N.J.: Prentice-Hall, 1979), 215–297; and Henry Mintzberg, "Organization Design: Fashion or Fit?" *Harvard Business Review* 59 (January-February 1981), 103–116.

25. "Focus on Innovation at Xerox Produces More Than 500 Patents in 2004."

26. The following discussion was heavily influenced by Richard H. Hall, *Organizations: Structures, Processes, and Outcomes* (Englewood Cliffs, N.J.: Prentice-Hall, 1991); D. S. Pugh, "The Measurement of Organization Structures: Does Context Determine Form?" *Organizational Dynamics* 1 (Spring 1973), 19–34; and D. S. Pugh, D. J. Hickson, C. R. Hinings, and C. Turner, "Dimensions of Organization Structure," *Administrative Science Quarterly* 13 (1968), 65–91.

27. Ann Harrington, "Who's Afraid of a New Product?" *Fortune* (November 10, 2003), 189–192; *http://www.gore.com*, accessed on August 28, 2002; "The 100 Best Companies to Work For," *Fortune* (January 20, 2003), 127–152; John Huey, "The New Post-Heroic Leadership," *Fortune* (February 21, 1994), 42–50; John Huey, "Wal-Mart: Will It Take Over the World?" *Fortune* (January 30, 1989), 52–61; *http://www.walmartstores.com*, accessed on August 28, 2002.

28. Paul Merrion, "Profile: Georgia Marsh—Using the Web to Untangle State Government Bureaucracy," *Crain's Chicago Business* (September 9, 2002), 11; Carolyn Bower, "School Boards Are Going Paperless," *St. Louis Post-Dispatch* (June 28, 2004), B1; Rick Brooks, "Leading the News: UPS Cuts Ground Delivery Time; One-Day Reduction Aims to Repel FedEx Assault on Company's Dominance," *The Wall Street Journal* (October 6, 2003), A3.

29. T. Donaldson and L. E. Preston, "The Stakeholder Theory of the Corporation: Concepts, Evidence, and Implications,"

Academy of Management Review 20 (1995), 65–91; Anne S. Tusi, "A Multiple-Constituency Model of Effectiveness: An Empirical Examination at the Human Resource Subunit Level," *Administrative Science Quarterly* 35 (1990), 458–483; Charles Fombrun and Mark Shanley, "What's in a Name? Reputation Building and Corporate Strategy," *Academy of Management Journal* 33 (1990), 233–258; Terry Connolly, Edward J. Conlon, and Stuart Jay Deutsch, "Organizational Effectiveness: A Multiple-Constituency Approach," *Academy of Management Review* 5 (1980), 211–217.

30. Charles Fishman, "The Wal-Mart You Don't Know—Why Low Prices Have a High Cost," *Fast Company* (December 2003), 68–80.

31. Tusi, "A Multiple-Constituency Model of Effectiveness."

32. Fombrun and Shanley, "What's in a Name?"

33. Gary Fields and John R. Wilke, "The Ex-Files: FBI's New Focus Places Big Burden on Local Police," *The Wall Street Journal* (June 30, 2003), A1, A12.

34. Ann Harrington, "The Big Ideas," *Fortune* (November 22, 1999), 152–154; Robert Kanigel, *The One Best Way: Frederick Winslow Taylor and the Enigma of Efficiency* (New York: Viking, 1997); and Alan Farnham, "The Man Who Changed Work Forever," *Fortune* (July 21, 1997), 114. For a discussion of the impact of scientific management on American industry, government, and nonprofit organizations, also see Mauro F. Guillén, "Scientific Management's Lost Aesthetic: Architecture, Organization, and the Taylorized Beauty of the Mechanical," *Administrative Science Quarterly* 42 (1997), 682–715.

35. Amanda Bennett, *The Death of the Organization Man* (New York: William Morrow, 1990).

36. Johannes M. Pennings, "Structural Contingency Theory: A Reappraisal," *Research in Organizational Behavior* 14 (1992), 267–309.

37. This discussion is based in part on Toby J. Tetenbaum, "Shifting Paradigms: From Newton to Chaos," *Organizational Dynamics* (Spring 1998), 21–32.

38. William Bergquist, *The Postmodern Organization* (San Francisco: Jossey-Bass, 1993).

39. Based on Tetenbaum, "Shifting Paradigms: From Newton to Chaos," and Richard T. Pascale, "Surfing the Edge of Chaos," *Sloan Management Review* (Spring 1999), 83–94.

40. Greg Jaffe, "Trial by Fire: On Ground in Iraq, Capt. Ayers Writes His Own Playbook," *The Wall Street Journal* (September 22, 2004), A1.

41. Polly LaBarre, "This Organization Is Disorganization," *Fast Company* (June-July 1996), 77–81.

42. Sydney J. Freedberg, Jr., "Abizaid of Arabia," *The Atlantic Monthly* (December 2003), 32–36.

43. David K. Hurst, *Crisis and Renewal: Meeting the Challenge of Organizational Change* (Boston, Mass.: Harvard Business School Press, 1995), 32–52.

44. Norm Brodsky, "Learning from JetBlue," *Inc.* (March 2004), 59–60.

45. Ann Harrington, note on QuikTrip, in Robert Levering and Milton Moskowitz, "100 Best Companies to Work For," *Fortune* (January 20, 2003), 127–152.

46. Thomas Petzinger, *The New Pioneers: The Men and Women Who Are Transforming the Workplace and Marketplace* (New York: Simon & Schuster, 1999), 91–93; and "In Search of the New World of Work," *Fast Company* (April 1999), 214–220; Peter Katel, "Bordering on Chaos," *Wired* (July 1997), 98–107; Oren Harari, "The Concrete Intangibles," *Management Review* (May 1999), 30–33; and "Mexican Cement Maker on Verge of a Deal," *The New York Times* (September 27, 2004), A8.

47. Robert House, Denise M. Rousseau, and Melissa Thomas-Hunt, "The Meso Paradigm: A Framework for the Integration of Micro and Macro Organizational Behavior," *Research in Organizational Behavior* 17 (1995): 71–114.

PART 2

Organizational Purpose and Structural Design

2. Strategy, Organization Design, and Effectiveness

3. Fundamentals of Organization Structure

2

Strategy, Organization Design, and Effectiveness

www.starbucks.com

The Role of Strategic Direction in Organization Design

Organizational Purpose
Mission • Operative Goals • The Importance of Goals

A Framework for Selecting Strategy and Design
Porter's Competitive Strategies • Miles and Snow's Strategy Typology • How Strategies Affect Organization Design • Other Factors Affecting Organization Design

Assessing Organizational Effectiveness

Contingency Effectiveness Approaches
Goal Approach • Resource-based Approach • Internal Process Approach

An Integrated Effectiveness Model

Summary and Interpretation

A Look Inside

Starbucks Corporation

Which U.S.-based company has had the greatest influence over the past decade on how we live our everyday lives? Many would argue that it is Starbucks, which has influenced everything from the routes we take to work, to our vocabulary, to the colors we prefer (yes, indeed, designers say, brown—or rather shades of latte, espresso, and cappuccino—is the new black).

The Starbucks phenomenon began in Seattle as a small specialty-coffee retailer with 11 stores and 100 employees in 1987. By early 2005, the company had 9,000 stores in 39 countries, with plans for continued expansion. Starbucks has always pursued a strategy of growth based on promoting its uniqueness. Today, more than ever before, the company isn't just selling coffee but "the Starbucks Experience," a phrase that is routinely used in the company's promotional materials. Chairman Howard Schultz and retiring CEO Orin Smith have steered Starbucks through a tremendous period of growth, but Schultz emphasizes that the company has goals to tap into all sorts of new markets, new customers, and new products and services. The overall goal stated by Schultz and incoming CEO Jim Donald is to spur greater growth by transforming Starbucks more broadly into a retail chain rather than just a coffee shop. Here are some of the company's goals and plans for achieving that overall goal:

- Expand the company's food service. In 2005, the company began selling lunch in five new markets, bringing to 2,500 the total number of stores offering lunch. Starbucks is also testing sales of hot breakfast at its Seattle stores, and indicates the company is close to a nationwide rollout.
- Become the first national retailer to offer CD-burning stations. The company's HearMusic media bars offer customers 200,000 songs to burn onto compact discs in the store. Current plans call for getting HearMusic stations into half of all U.S. outlets.
- Partner with music production companies to co-release, market, and distribute innovative, quality music selections exclusively for Starbucks customers, providing people with a unique way to discover new music. One project in the works features Herbie Hancock with John Mayer, Carlos Santana, Annie Lennox, and Sting.
- Open 1,500 more retail outlets in 2005, many in international markets, and add more stores with drive-through capabilities. Eventually, the company wants to have 25,000 stores all over the world.

The new goals and plans are a bold push beyond Starbucks' coffee roots. Some observers think the company's foray into music is particularly foolhardy, but Schultz and Donald believe it fits right in with Starbucks' strategy. "Providing our customers with innovative and unique ways to discover and acquire all genres of great music is another way we are enhancing the Starbucks Experience," Schultz says.[1]

Top managers such as Howard Schultz and Jim Donald are responsible for positioning their organizations for success by establishing goals and strategies that can help the company be competitive. An **organizational goal** is a desired state of affairs that the organization attempts to reach.[2] A goal represents a result or end point toward which organizational efforts are directed. The goals for Starbucks in 2005 include adding 1,500 new outlets, co-releasing a new exclusive music compilation, and expanding the company's food offerings. The goals fit with the company's overall strategy of differentiating Starbucks from the competition by creating an overall "experience." The choice of goals and strategy affects organization design, as we will discuss in this chapter.

■ Purpose of This Chapter

Top managers give direction to organizations. They set goals and develop the plans for their organization to attain those goals. The purpose of this chapter is to help you understand the types of goals that organizations pursue and some of the competitive strategies managers use to reach those goals. We will examine two significant frameworks for determining strategic action and look at how strategies affect organization design. The chapter also describes the most popular approaches to measuring the effectiveness of organizational efforts. To manage organizations well, managers need a clear sense of how to measure effectiveness.

The Role of Strategic Direction in Organization Design

An organization is created to achieve some purpose, which is decided by the chief executive officer (CEO) and the top management team. Top executives decide on the end purpose the organization will strive for and determine the direction it will take to accomplish it. It is this purpose and direction that shapes how the organization is designed and managed. Indeed, *the primary responsibility of top management is to determine an organization's goals, strategy, and design, therein adapting the organization to a changing environment.*[3] Middle managers do much the same thing for major departments within the guidelines provided by top management. The relationships through which top managers provide direction and then design are illustrated in Exhibit 2.1.

The direction-setting process typically begins with an assessment of the opportunities and threats in the external environment, including the amount of change, uncertainty, and resource availability, which we discuss in more detail in Chapter 4. Top managers also assess internal strengths and weaknesses to define the company's distinctive competence compared with other firms in the industry.[4] The assessment of internal environment often includes an evaluation of each department and is shaped by past performance and the leadership style of the CEO and top management team. The next step is to define overall mission and official goals based on the correct fit between external opportunities and internal strengths. Specific operational goals or strategies can then be formulated to define how the organization is to accomplish its overall mission.

In Exhibit 2.1, organization design reflects the way goals and strategies are implemented. Organization design is the administration and execution of the strategic plan. Organization direction is implemented through decisions about structural form, including whether the organization will be designed for a learning or an efficiency orientation, as discussed in Chapter 1, as well as choices about information and control systems, the type of production technology, human resource policies, culture, and linkages to other organizations. Changes in structure, technology, human resource policies, culture, and interorganization linkages will be discussed in subsequent chapters. Also note the arrow in Exhibit 2.1 running from organization design back to strategic direction. This means that strategies are often made within the current structure of the organization, so that current design constrains or puts limits on goals and strategy. More often than not, however, the new goals and strat-

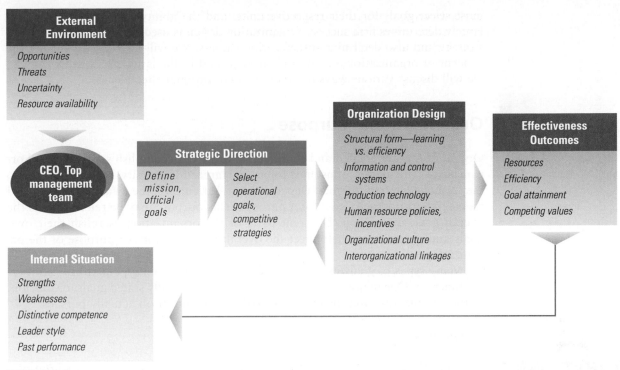

EXHIBIT 2.1

Top Management Role in Organization Direction, Design, and Effectiveness

Source: Adapted from Arie Y. Lewin and Carroll U. Stephens, "Individual Properties of the CEO as Determinants of Organization Design," unpublished manuscript, Duke University, 1990; and Arie Y. Lewin and Carroll U. Stephens, "CEO Attributes as Determinants of Organization Design: An Integrated Model," *Organization Studies* 15, no. 2 (1994), 183–212.

egy are selected based on environmental needs, and then top management attempts to redesign the organization to achieve those ends.

Finally, Exhibit 2.1 illustrates how managers evaluate the effectiveness of organizational efforts—that is, the extent to which the organization realizes its goals. This chart reflects the most popular ways of measuring performance, each of which is discussed later in this chapter. It is important to note here that performance measurements feed back into the internal environment, so that past performance of the organization is assessed by top management in setting new goals and strategic direction for the future.

The role of top management is important because managers can interpret the environment differently and develop different goals. For example, when William Weldon took over as head of Johnson & Johnson, he perceived a need for greater collaboration and information sharing among Johnson & Johnson's disparate divisions. Johnson & Johnson is an extremely complex organization, made up of more than 200 different companies organized into three divisions: drugs, medical devices, and diagnostics. The company has thrived by giving its various businesses almost complete autonomy. However, Weldon believes the system has to change to thrive in today's shifting environment. Weldon has set new goals that require managers to build alliances across the three major divisions.[5]

The choices top managers make about goals, strategies, and organization design have a tremendous impact on organizational effectiveness. Remember that goals and strategy are not fixed or taken for granted. Top managers and middle managers must select goals for their respective units, and the ability to make these choices largely determines firm success. Organization design is used to implement goals and strategy and also determines organization success. We will now discuss further the concept of organizational goals and strategy, and in the latter part of this chapter, we will discuss various ways to evaluate organizational effectiveness.

Organizational Purpose

Organizations are created and continued in order to accomplish something. All organizations, including Johnson & Johnson, Harvard University, New Line Cinema, the Catholic Church, the U.S. Department of Agriculture, the local dry cleaner, and the neighborhood deli, exist for a purpose. This purpose may be referred to as the overall goal, or mission. Different parts of the organization establish their own goals and objectives to help meet the overall goal, mission, or purpose of the organization.

Many types of goals exist in an organization, and each type performs a different function. One major distinction is between the officially stated goals, or mission, of the organization and the operative goals the organization actually pursues.

Mission

The overall goal for an organization is often called the **mission**—the organization's reason for existence. The mission describes the organization's vision, its shared values and beliefs, and its reason for being. It can have a powerful impact on an organization.[6] The mission is sometimes called the **official goals**, which refers to the formally stated definition of business scope and outcomes the organization is trying to achieve. Official goal statements typically define business operations and may focus on values, markets, and customers that distinguish the organization. Whether called a mission statement or official goals, the organization's general statement of its purpose and philosophy is often written down in a policy manual or the annual report. The mission statement for State Farm is shown in Exhibit 2.2. Note how the overall mission, values, and goals are all defined.

One of the primary purposes of a mission statement is to serve as a communication tool.[7] The *mission statement* communicates to current and prospective employees, customers, investors, suppliers, and competitors what the organization stands for and what it is trying to achieve. A mission statement communicates legitimacy to internal and external stakeholders, who may join and be committed to the organization because they identify with its stated purpose. Most top leaders want employees, customers, competitors, suppliers, investors, and the local community to look on them in a favorable light, and the concept of legitimacy plays a critical role.[8] The corporate concern for legitimacy is real and pertinent. Consider the accounting firm Arthur Andersen, which was accused of obstructing justice by shredding accounting documents related to the Enron investigation. Once the previously respected global firm lost legitimacy with clients, investors, and the public, it was all but dead. In the post-Enron environment of weakened trust and increasing regulation, many organizations face the need to redefine their purpose and mission to emphasize the firm's purpose in more than financial terms.[9] Companies where managers are sincerely guided by mission statements

Briefcase

As an organization manager, keep these guidelines in mind:

Establish and communicate organizational mission and goals. Communicate official goals to provide a statement of the organization's mission to external constituents. Communicate operational goals to provide internal direction, guidelines, and standards of performance for employees.

EXHIBIT 2.2
State Farm's Mission Statement
Source: "News and Notes from State Farm," Public Affairs Department, 2500 Memorial Boulevard, Murfreesboro, TN 37131.

STATE FARM INSURANCE
Our Mission, Our Vision, and Our Shared Values

State Farm's mission is to help people manage the risks of everyday life, recover from the unexpected, and realize their dreams.

We are people who make it our business to be like a good neighbor; who built a premier company by selling and keeping promises through our marketing partnerships; who bring diverse talents and experiences to our work of serving the State Farm customer.

Our success is built on a foundation of shared values—quality service and relationships, mutual trust, integrity, and financial strength.

Our vision for the future is to be the customer's first and best choice in the products and services we provide. We will continue to be the leader in the insurance industry and we will become a leader in the financial services arena. Our customers' needs will determine our path. Our values will guide us.

---

that focus on their social purpose, such as Medtronic's "To restore people to full life and health" or Liberty Mutual's "Helping people live safer, more secure lives," typically attract better employees, have better relationships with external parties, and perform better in the marketplace over the long term.[10]

Operative Goals

Operative goals designate the ends sought through the actual operating procedures of the organization and explain what the organization is actually trying to do.[11] Operative goals describe specific measurable outcomes and are often concerned with the short run. Operative versus official goals represent actual versus stated goals. Operative goals typically pertain to the primary tasks an organization must perform, similar to the subsystem activities identified in Chapter 1.[12] These goals concern overall performance, boundary spanning, maintenance, adaptation, and production activities. Specific goals for each primary task provide direction for the day-to-day decisions and activities within departments.

Overall Performance. Profitability reflects the overall performance of for-profit organizations. Profitability may be expressed in terms of net income, earnings per share, or return on investment. Other overall performance goals are growth and output volume. Growth pertains to increases in sales or profits over time. Volume pertains to total sales or the amount of products or services delivered. For example, General Motors Corp.'s Chevrolet division has a growth goal of increasing sales by 15 percent, to 3 million vehicles a year.[13]

Government and nonprofit organizations such as social service agencies or labor unions do not have goals of profitability, but they do have goals that attempt to specify the delivery of services to clients or members within specified expense levels.

The Internal Revenue Service has a goal of providing accurate responses to 85 percent of taxpayer questions about new tax laws. Growth and volume goals also may be indicators of overall performance in nonprofit organizations. Expanding their services to new clients is a primary goal for many social service agencies, such as Contact USA, which provides helpline services to people in crisis.

Resources. Resource goals pertain to the acquisition of needed material and financial resources from the environment. They may involve obtaining financing for the construction of new plants, finding less expensive sources for raw materials, or hiring top-quality technology graduates. Resource goals for Harvard University include attracting top-notch professors and students. Honda Motor Company has resource goals of obtaining high-quality auto parts at low cost. For Contact USA, resource goals include recruiting dedicated telephone volunteers and expanding the organization's funding base.

Market. Market goals relate to the market share or market standing desired by the organization. Market goals are the responsibility of marketing, sales, and advertising departments. An example of a market goal is Honda's desire to overtake Toyota Motor Company as the number-one seller of cars in Japan. Honda recently surpassed Nissan to become number two in Japan, and the recently introduced Fit subcompact has eclipsed the Toyota Corolla as the best-selling car in that market. In the toy industry, Canada's Mega Bloks Inc. achieved its goal of doubling its share of the toy building block market to 30 percent. The giant of the industry, Denmark's Lego, is reevaluating strategies to try to regain the market share it has lost.[14]

Employee Development. Employee development pertains to the training, promotion, safety, and growth of employees. It includes both managers and workers. Strong employee development goals are one of the characteristics common to organizations that regularly show up on *Fortune* magazine's list of "100 Best Companies to Work For." For example, family-owned Wegmans Food Markets, which has appeared on the list every year since its inception and rocketed to number 1 in 2005, has a motto of "Employees First, Customers Second," reflecting the company's emphasis on employee development goals.[15] Wegmans' unique approach to employee development is further described in this chapter's Leading by Design.

Innovation and Change. Innovation goals pertain to internal flexibility and readiness to adapt to unexpected changes in the environment. Innovation goals are often defined with respect to the development of specific new services, products, or production processes. 3M Co. has a goal that 30 percent of sales come from products that are less than four years old.[16]

Productivity. Productivity goals concern the amount of output achieved from available resources. They typically describe the amount of resource inputs required to reach desired outputs and are thus stated in terms of "cost for a unit of production," "units produced per employee," or "resource cost per employee." Managers at Akamai Technologies, which sells Web content delivery services, keep a close eye on sales per employee to see if the company is meeting productivity goals. Akamai's chief financial officer, Timothy Weller, sees this statistic as "the single easiest measure of employee productivity." Boeing Company installed a new moving

Leading by Design

Wegmans

Supermarkets aren't typically considered great places to work. The pay is low, the hours are grueling, and you don't get much appreciation from anyone. Most supermarkets have annual turnover rates of 19 to 20 percent and as much as 100 percent for part-timers. But the situation is different at Wegmans, a chain of sixty-seven stores in New York, Pennsylvania, New Jersey, and Virginia. Annual turnover is just 6 percent for full-time employees. About 6,000 Wegmans workers have at least 10 years of service, and more than 800 have worked at Wegmans stores for a quarter of a century.

Wegmans is one of the most successful supermarket chains in the industry. Its operating margins are about double that of the other four big chains (Albertson's, Kroger, Safeway, and Ahold USA). Sales per square foot are 50 percent higher than the industry average. An annual survey conducted by Cannondale Associates found that Wegmans beat all other retailers—even Wal-Mart—in merchandising savvy.

Employee commitment and satisfaction is an important factor in Wegmans success, and managers consider meeting goals for employee development just as important as meeting sales, profit, or productivity targets. "You cannot separate their strategy as a retailer from their strategy as an employer," says consultant Darrell Rigby, head of Bain & Company's global retail practice. Hourly wages and annual salaries at Wegmans are among the highest in the industry, but that's only a small part of the story. What really sets Wegmans apart is that it creates an environment and provides the resources to enable employees to develop to their fullest potential. The company has invested $54 million for college scholarships to more than 17,500 full- and part-time employees over the past 20 years. It thinks nothing of sending employees on trips to visit wineries in California or cheesemakers in Italy. "It's our knowledge that can help the customer," says president Danny Wegman. "So the first pump we have to prime is our own people." Employees are empowered to do just about anything to satisfy a customer, without checking with a higher-up. Operations chief Jack DePeters says only half-jokingly that Wegmans is "a $3 billion company run by 16-year-old cashiers."

Priming the pump is illustrated by the opening of a new Wegmans store in Dulles, Virginia, where the company spent $5 million on training alone. The company refuses to open a new store until everyone is fully prepared. Wegmans could have easily opened in November 2003, in time for the critical holiday sales season, but chose to wait until February. The emphasis on development over dollars pays off. Wegmans attracts high-quality employees, both for management and store positions. Eighty-six-year-old Robert Wegman, chairman of the company, explains why he's always emphasized employee development goals despite the high costs: "I have never given away more than I got back."

Source: Matthew Boyle, "The Wegmans Way," *Fortune* (January 24, 2005), 62–68.

assembly line for the 737 aircraft to increase productivity. Once the wings and landing gear are attached, each plane is dragged toward the door at two inches a minute, with workers moving along with it on a floatlike apparatus. Boeing's productivity goal is to push a 737 out the door in five days, down from the eleven it currently takes.[17]

Successful organizations use a carefully balanced set of operative goals. Although profitability goals are important, some of today's best companies recognize that a single-minded focus on bottom-line profits may not be the best way to achieve high performance. Innovation and change goals are increasingly important, even though they may initially cause a *decrease* in profits. Employee development goals are critical for helping to maintain a motivated, committed workforce.

EXHIBIT 2.3
Goal Type and Purpose

Type of Goals	Purpose of Goals
Official goals, mission:	Legitimacy
Operative goals:	Employee direction and motivation
	Decision guidelines
	Standard of performance

■ The Importance of Goals

Both official goals and operative goals are important for the organization, but they serve very different purposes. Official goals and mission statements describe a value system for the organization; operative goals represent the primary tasks of the organization. Official goals legitimize the organization; operative goals are more explicit and well defined.

Operative goals serve several specific purposes, as outlined in Exhibit 2.3. For one thing, goals can provide employees with a sense of direction, so that they know what they are working toward. This can help to motivate employees toward goal accomplishment, especially if employees are involved in setting the targets. The events at Iraq's notorious Abu Ghraib prison provide a negative illustration of the motivating power of goals. Analysts say U.S. soldiers guarding prisoners at Abu Ghraib were under so much pressure to meet quotas on the number of interrogations and intelligence reports they generated that they resorted to unethical approaches and even abuse.[18] Managers need to understand the power of goals and use care when setting and implementing them. Another important purpose of goals is to act as guidelines for employee behavior and decision making. Appropriate goals can act as a set of constraints on individual behavior and actions so that employees behave within boundaries that are acceptable to the organization and larger society.[19] They help to define the appropriate decisions concerning organization structure, innovation, employee welfare, or growth. Finally, goals provide a standard for assessment. The level of organizational performance, whether in terms of profits, units produced, degree of employee satisfaction, level of innovation, or number of customer complaints, needs a basis for evaluation. Operative goals provide this standard for measurement.

A Framework for Selecting Strategy and Design

To support and accomplish the direction determined by organizational mission and operative goals, managers have to select specific strategy and design options that will help the organization achieve its purpose and goals within its competitive environment. In this section, we examine a couple of practical approaches to selecting strategy and design.

A **strategy** is a plan for interacting with the competitive environment to achieve organizational goals. Some managers think of goals and strategies as interchangeable, but for our purposes, *goals* define where the organization wants to go and *strategies* define how it will get there. For example, a goal might be to achieve

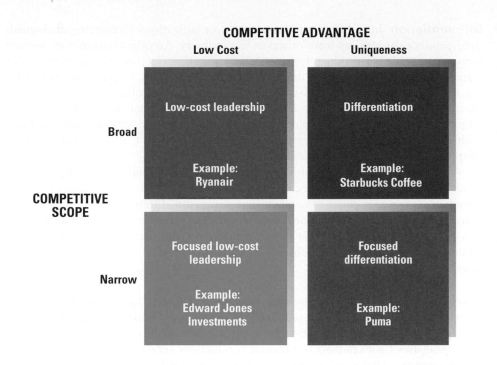

COMPETITIVE ADVANTAGE

EXHIBIT 2.4
Porter's Competitive Strategies
Source: Adapted with the permission of The Free Press, a Division of Simon & Schuster Adult Publishing Group, from *Competitive Advantage: Creating and Sustaining Superior Performance* by Michael E. Porter. Copyright © 1985, 1988 by Michael E. Porter.

15 percent annual sales growth; strategies to reach that goal might include aggressive advertising to attract new customers, motivating salespeople to increase the average size of customer purchases, and acquiring other businesses that produce similar products. Strategies can include any number of techniques to achieve the goal. The essence of formulating strategies is choosing whether the organization will perform different activities than its competitors or will execute similar activities more efficiently than its competitors do.[20]

Two models for formulating strategies are the Porter model of competitive strategies and Miles and Snow's strategy typology. Each provides a framework for competitive action. After describing the two models, we will discuss how the choice of strategies affects organization design.

Porter's Competitive Strategies

Michael E. Porter studied a number of businesses and introduced a framework describing three competitive strategies: low-cost leadership, differentiation, and focus.[21] The focus strategy, in which the organization concentrates on a specific market or buyer group, is further divided into *focused low cost* and *focused differentiation*. This yields four basic strategies, as illustrated in Exhibit 2.4. To use this model, managers evaluate two factors, competitive advantage and competitive scope. With respect to advantage, managers determine whether to compete through lower cost or through the ability to offer unique or distinctive products and services that can command a premium price. Managers then determine whether the organization will compete on a broad scope (competing in many customer segments) or a narrow scope (competing in a selected customer segment or group of segments). These choices determine the selection of strategies, as illustrated in Exhibit 2.4.

Briefcase

As an organization manager, keep these guidelines in mind:

After goals have been defined, select strategies for achieving those goals. Define specific strategies based on Porter's competitive strategies or Miles and Snow's strategy typology.

Differentiation. In a **differentiation** strategy, organizations attempt to distinguish their products or services from others in the industry. An organization may use advertising, distinctive product features, exceptional service, or new technology to achieve a product perceived as unique. This strategy usually targets customers who are not particularly concerned with price, so it can be quite profitable. Harley-Davidson motorcycles, Tommy Hilfiger clothing, and Jaguar automobiles are examples of products from companies using a differentiation strategy. Service firms such as Aflac Insurance, Four Seasons Hotels, and Starbucks Coffee, described in the chapter opening, can use a differentiation strategy as well.

A differentiation strategy can reduce rivalry with competitors and fight off the threat of substitute products because customers are loyal to the company's brand. However, companies must remember that successful differentiation strategies require a number of costly activities, such as product research and design and extensive advertising. Companies that pursue a differentiation strategy need strong marketing abilities and creative employees who are given the time and resources to seek innovations.

Low-Cost Leadership. The **low-cost leadership** strategy tries to increase market share by emphasizing low cost compared to competitors. With a low-cost leadership strategy, the organization aggressively seeks efficient facilities, pursues cost reductions, and uses tight controls to produce products or services more efficiently than its competitors. One good example of a low-cost leadership strategy is the Irish airline Ryanair.

In Practice

Ryanair

Fifteen or so years ago, Michael O'Leary took a trip that would change his life—and transform the Irish air carrier Ryanair into Europe's most successful, most profitable airline. O'Leary, who had been brought in as chief executive of Ryanair to save the ailing carrier, flew around America on Southwest Airlines and learned the tricks of running a low-cost airline.

O'Leary says of his corporate strategy: "It's the oldest, simplest formula: Pile 'em high and sell 'em cheap . . . We want to be the Wal-Mart of the airline business. Nobody will beat us on price. EVER." And sell 'em cheap he does. One industry expert says ticket prices on Ryanair are so inexpensive that it's "nearly a no-fare carrier." A Minneapolis office worker, for example, spent less than $150 to fly Ryanair from London to Bologna, Italy, then from Venice, Italy, to Dublin, Ireland, and from Dublin back to London.

Ryanair is able to offer such low fares because it keeps costs at rock bottom, lower than anyone else in Europe. The company's mantra is cheap tickets, not customer care. The carrier offers no business class, maximizes seating space, turns around an aircraft in 25 minutes rather than the 45 or so required by traditional carriers, and doesn't offer travel agent commissions. Most tickets are sold over the Internet, and Ryanair is the most requested Web site in Ireland. Instead of giving away snacks or food, Ryanair sells it. Staff costs are kept low too. In one recent year, the airline employed fewer than 2,000 people to fly 24 million passengers a year, while the German carrier Lufthansa employed about 30,000 people to fly 37 million.

Ryanair's passenger numbers continue to grow. They soared from 3.9 million in 1998 to more than 24 million in 2005. The airline industry is increasingly competitive, and other low-cost carriers are encroaching on Ryanair's territory. But O'Leary knows that Ryanair can beat anyone on price and cost control. As long as the airline keeps its disciplined approach, Ryanair will continue to soar.[22]

Although Ryanair is expanding, continuing to add new routes, the low-cost leadership strategy is concerned primarily with stability rather than taking risks or seeking new opportunities for innovation and growth. A low-cost position means a company can undercut competitors' prices and still offer comparable quality and earn a reasonable profit.

A low-cost strategy can help a company defend against current competitors because customers cannot find lower prices elsewhere. In addition, if substitute products or potential new competitors enter the picture, the low-cost producer is in a better position to prevent loss of market share.

Focus. With Porter's third strategy, the **focus strategy**, the organization concentrates on a specific regional market or buyer group. The company will try to achieve either a low-cost advantage or a differentiation advantage within a narrowly defined market. One good example of a focused low-cost strategy is Edward Jones, a St. Louis–based brokerage house. The firm has succeeded by building its business in rural and small-town America and providing investors with conservative, long-term investments.[23] An example of a focused differentiation strategy is Puma, the German athletic-wear manufacturer. Ten years ago, Puma was on the brink of bankruptcy. CEO Jochen Zeitz, then only 30 years old, revived the brand by targeting selected customer groups, especially armchair athletes, and creating stylish shoes and clothes that are setting design trends. Puma is "going out of its way to be different," says analyst Roland Könen, and sales and profits reflect the change. Puma has been profitable every year since 1994, and its sales are growing faster than those of competitors.[24]

When managers fail to adopt a competitive strategy, the organization is left with no strategic advantage and performance suffers. Porter found that companies that did not consciously adopt a low-cost, differentiation, or focus strategy, for example, achieved below-average profits compared to those that used one of the three strategies. Many Internet companies have failed because they did not develop competitive strategies that would distinguish them in the marketplace.[25] On the other hand, eBay and Google have been highly successful with coherent differentiation strategies. The ability of managers to devise and maintain a clear competitive strategy is one of the defining factors in an organization's success, as further discussed in this chapter's Book Mark.

Miles and Snow's Strategy Typology

Another business strategy typology was developed from the study of business strategies by Raymond Miles and Charles Snow.[26] The Miles and Snow typology is based on the idea that managers seek to formulate strategies that will be congruent with the external environment. Organizations strive for a fit among internal organization characteristics, strategy, and the external environment. The four strategies that can be developed are the prospector, the defender, the analyzer, and the reactor.

Prospector. The **prospector** strategy is to innovate, take risks, seek out new opportunities, and grow. This strategy is suited to a dynamic, growing environment, where creativity is more important than efficiency. FedEx Corporation, which innovates in both services and production technology in the rapidly changing shipping, document management, and information services industry, exemplifies the prospector strategy, as do today's leading high-tech companies, such as Microsoft.

Defender. The **defender** strategy is almost the opposite of the prospector. Rather than taking risks and seeking out new opportunities, the defender strategy is concerned with stability or even retrenchment. This strategy seeks to hold onto current customers, but it neither innovates nor seeks to grow. The defender is concerned primarily with internal efficiency and control to produce reliable, high-quality products for steady customers. This strategy can be successful when the organization exists in a declining industry or a stable environment. Paramount Pictures has

Book Mark 2.0 (HAVE YOU READ THIS BOOK?)

What Really Works: The 4 + 2 Formula for Sustained Business Success
By William F. Joyce, Nitin Nohria, and Bruce Roberson

In *What Really Works: The 4 + 2 Formula for Sustained Business Success*, William Joyce, Nitin Nohria, and Bruce Roberson contend that there are certain reliable indicators of enduring organizational success. The book is based on a large-scale, rigorous research project that involved 5 years of analyzing data collected over a decade from 160 companies representing 40 different industries. The findings indicate that there is a direct connection between high financial performance and sustained excellence in six key practices.

WHAT IS THE 4 + 2 FORMULA?
The authors say there are four key practices at which *all* outstanding companies excel, no matter what their size or industry:
- *Stay Clear on Strategy.* First and foremost is the ability to devise and maintain a clearly stated, focused strategy. Compare Target and Kmart. During the years of the study, Target rose to become the nation's second-largest discounter, behind Wal-Mart, by focusing on providing unique and higher-end merchandise at value prices. During the same time, Kmart floundered time and time again as managers shifted from one strategy to another—for example, shifting to pursue a more affluent fashion-conscious consumer, then shifting back to compete with Wal-Mart on price.
- *Maintain flawless operational execution.* Winning companies implement and maintain operational changes that increase their productivity by about twice the industry average. They don't try to outperform competitors on every facet of operations, but focus their energies on core

competencies, such as Wal-Mart's use of sophisticated information technology to scrupulously manage inventory.
- *Build a performance-driven culture.* Outstanding companies encourage both individual and team contributions and hold everyone accountable for results. One example is Home Depot, which gives everyone from the janitor to the top executive a sense of ownership over the stores.
- *Maintain a fast, flexible structure.* The most successful companies keep bureaucracy to a minimum, trimming unnecessary layers of management, cutting out excessive rules and regulations, and doing away with boundaries that inhibit communication and collaboration. Nucor, a steel company, confines its management structure to four layers—foreman, department head, plant manager, and CEO.

In addition to these four primary practices, the authors found that winning companies embrace two out of four secondary practices: *talent of employees, leadership and governance, innovation,* or *mergers and partnerships.*

DOES IT REALLY WORK?
Over the 10-year period, investors in the 4 + 2 companies saw their money multiply nearly tenfold, with a total return to shareholders of 945 percent. The losing companies produced only 62 percent in total returns over the same decade. Anecdotes from the companies are interesting and instructive for general readers and managers alike.

What Really Works: The 4 + 2 Formula for Sustained Business Success, by William Joyce, Nitin Nohria, and Bruce Roberson, is published by Harper Business.

been using a defender strategy for several years.[27] Paramount turns out a steady stream of reliable hits but few blockbusters. Managers shun risk and sometimes turn down potentially high-profile films to keep a lid on costs. This has enabled the company to remain highly profitable while other studios have low returns or actually lose money.

Analyzer. The **analyzer** tries to maintain a stable business while innovating on the periphery. It seems to lie midway between the prospector and the defender. Some products will be targeted toward stable environments in which an efficiency strategy designed to keep current customers is used. Others will be targeted toward new, more dynamic environments, where growth is possible. The analyzer attempts to balance efficient production for current product lines with the creative development of new product lines. Sony Corp. illustrates an analyzer strategy. Sony's strategy is to defend its position in traditional consumer electronics, but also build a business in the "integrated home entertainment" market, such as with its innovative Vaio computer.[28]

Reactor. The **reactor** strategy is not really a strategy at all. Rather, reactors respond to environmental threats and opportunities in an ad hoc fashion. In a reactor strategy, top management has not defined a long-range plan or given the organization an explicit mission or goal, so the organization takes whatever actions seem to meet immediate needs. Although the reactor strategy can sometimes be successful, it can also lead to failed companies. Some large, once highly successful companies, such as Xerox and Kodak, are struggling because managers failed to adopt a strategy consistent with consumer trends. In recent years, managers at McDonald's, long one of the most successful fast-food franchises in the world, have been floundering to find the appropriate strategy. McDonald's had a string of disappointing quarterly profits as competitors continued to steal market share. Franchisees grew aggravated and discouraged by the uncertainty and lack of clear strategic direction for the future. Recent innovations such as healthier food options have revived sales and profits, but managers still are struggling to implement a coherent strategy.[29]

The Miles and Snow typology has been widely used, and researchers have tested its validity in a variety of organizations, including hospitals, colleges, banking institutions, industrial products companies, and life insurance firms. In general, researchers have found strong support for the effectiveness of this typology for organization managers in real-world situations.[30]

■ How Strategies Affect Organization Design

Choice of strategy affects internal organization characteristics. Organization design characteristics need to support the firm's competitive approach. For example, a company wanting to grow and invent new products looks and "feels" different from a company that is focused on maintaining market share for long-established products in a stable industry. Exhibit 2.5 summarizes organization design characteristics associated with the Porter and Miles and Snow strategies.

With a low-cost leadership strategy, managers take an efficiency approach to organization design, whereas a differentiation strategy calls for a learning approach. Recall from Chapter 1 that organizations designed for efficiency have different characteristics from those designed for learning. A low-cost leadership strategy (efficiency) is associated with strong, centralized authority and tight control, standard

EXHIBIT 2.5
*Organization Design
Outcomes of Strategy*

Porter's Competitive Strategies	Miles and Snow's Strategy Typology
Strategy: Differentiation	**Strategy:** Prospector
Organization Design:	**Organization Design:**
• Learning orientation; acts in a flexible, loosely knit way, with strong horizontal coordination	• Learning orientation; flexible, fluid, decentralized structure
• Strong capability in research	• Strong capability in research
• Values and builds in mechanisms for customer intimacy	**Strategy:** Defender
• Rewards employee creativity, risk taking, and innovation	**Organization Design:**
Strategy: Low-Cost Leadership	• Efficiency orientation; centralized authority and tight cost control
Organization Design:	• Emphasis on production efficiency; low overhead
• Efficiency orientation; strong central authority; tight cost control, with frequent, detailed control reports	• Close supervision; little employee empowerment
• Standard operating procedures	**Strategy:** Analyzer
• Highly efficient procurement and distribution systems	**Organization Design:**
• Close supervision; routine tasks; limited employee empowerment	• Balances efficiency and learning; tight cost control with flexibility and adaptability
	• Efficient production for stable product lines; emphasis on creativity, research, risk-taking for innovation
	Strategy: Reactor
	Organization Design:
	• No clear organizational approach; design characteristics may shift abruptly, depending on current needs

Source: Based on Michael E. Porter, *Competitive Strategy: Techniques for Analyzing Industries and Competitors* (New York: The Free Press, 1980); Michael Treacy and Fred Wiersema, "How Market Leaders Keep Their Edge," *Fortune* (February 6, 1995), 88–98; Michael Hitt, R. Duane Ireland, and Robert E. Hoskisson, *Strategic Management* (St. Paul, Minn.: West, 1995), 100–113; and Raymond E. Miles, Charles C. Snow, Alan D. Meyer, and Henry J. Coleman, Jr., "Organizational Strategy, Structure, and Process," *Academy of Management Review* 3 (1978), 546–562.

operating procedures, and emphasis on efficient procurement and distribution systems. Employees generally perform routine tasks under close supervision and control and are not empowered to make decisions or take action on their own. A differentiation strategy, on the other hand, requires that employees be constantly experimenting and learning. Structure is fluid and flexible, with strong horizontal coordination. Empowered employees work directly with customers and are rewarded for creativity and risk taking. The organization values research, creativity, and innovativeness over efficiency and standard procedures.

The prospector strategy requires characteristics similar to a differentiation strategy, and the defender strategy takes an efficiency approach similar to low-cost leadership. Because the analyzer strategy attempts to balance efficiency for stable product lines with flexibility and learning for new products, it is associated with a mix of characteristics, as listed in Exhibit 2.5. With a reactor strategy, managers have left the organization with no direction and no clear approach to design.

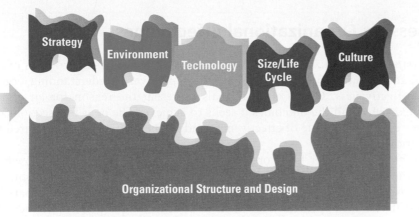

EXHIBIT 2.6
Contingency Factors Affecting Organization Design

The Right Mix of Design Characteristics Fits the Contingency Factors

■ Other Factors Affecting Organization Design

Strategy is one important factor that affects organization design. Ultimately, however, organization design is a result of numerous contingencies, which will be discussed throughout this book. The emphasis given to efficiency and control versus learning and flexibility is determined by the contingencies of strategy, environment, size and life cycle, technology, and organizational culture. The organization is designed to "fit" the contingency factors, as illustrated in Exhibit 2.6.

For example, in a stable environment, the organization can have a traditional structure that emphasizes vertical control, efficiency, specialization, standard procedures, and centralized decision making. However, a rapidly changing environment may call for a more flexible structure, with strong horizontal coordination and collaboration through teams or other mechanisms. Environment will be discussed in detail in Chapters 4 and 5. In terms of size and life cycle, young, small organizations are generally informal and have little division of labor, few rules and regulations, and ad hoc budgeting and performance systems. Large organizations such as Coca-Cola, Sony, or General Electric, on the other hand, have an extensive division of labor, numerous rules and regulations, and standard procedures and systems for budgeting, control, rewards, and innovation. Size and stages of the life cycle will be discussed in Chapter 9.

Design must also fit the workflow technology of the organization. For example, with mass production technology, such as a traditional automobile assembly line, the organization functions best by emphasizing efficiency, formalization, specialization, centralized decision making, and tight control. An e-business, on the other hand, might need to be informal and flexible. Technology's impact on design will be discussed in detail in Chapters 7 and 8. A final contingency that affects organization design is corporate culture. An organizational culture that values teamwork, collaboration, creativity, and open communication among all employees and managers, for example, would not function well with a tight, vertical structure and strict rules and regulations. The role of culture is discussed in Chapter 10.

One responsibility of managers is to design organizations that fit the contingency factors of strategy, environment, size and life cycle, technology, and culture. Finding the right fit leads to organizational effectiveness, whereas a poor fit can lead to decline or even the demise of the organization.

Assessing Organizational Effectiveness

Understanding organizational goals and strategies, as well as the concept of fitting design to various contingencies, is a first step toward understanding organizational effectiveness. Organizational goals represent the reason for an organization's existence and the outcomes it seeks to achieve. The next few sections of the chapter explore the topic of effectiveness and how effectiveness is measured in organizations.

Recall from Chapter 1 that organizational effectiveness is the degree to which an organization realizes its goals.[31] *Effectiveness* is a broad concept. It implicitly takes into consideration a range of variables at both the organizational and departmental levels. Effectiveness evaluates the extent to which multiple goals—whether official or operative—are attained.

Efficiency is a more limited concept that pertains to the internal workings of the organization. Organizational efficiency is the amount of resources used to produce a unit of output.[32] It can be measured as the ratio of inputs to outputs. If one organization can achieve a given production level with fewer resources than another organization, it would be described as more efficient.[33]

Sometimes efficiency leads to effectiveness. In other organizations, efficiency and effectiveness are not related. An organization may be highly efficient but fail to achieve its goals because it makes a product for which there is no demand. Likewise, an organization may achieve its profit goals but be inefficient.

Overall effectiveness is difficult to measure in organizations. Organizations are large, diverse, and fragmented. They perform many activities simultaneously, pursue multiple goals, and generate many outcomes, some intended and some unintended.[34] Managers determine what indicators to measure in order to gauge the effectiveness of their organizations. One study found that many managers have a difficult time with the concept of evaluating effectiveness based on characteristics that are not subject to hard, quantitative measurement.[35] However, top executives at some of today's leading companies are finding new ways to measure effectiveness, including the use of such "soft" indications as "customer delight" and employee satisfaction. A number of approaches to measuring effectiveness look at which measurements managers choose to track. These *contingency effectiveness approaches*, discussed in the next section, are based on looking at which part of the organization managers consider most important to measure. Later, we will examine an approach that integrates concern for various parts of the organization.

Contingency Effectiveness Approaches

Contingency approaches to measuring effectiveness focus on different parts of the organization. Organizations bring resources in from the environment, and those resources are transformed into outputs delivered back into the environment, as shown in Exhibit 2.7. The **goal approach** to organizational effectiveness is concerned with the output side and whether the organization achieves its goals in terms of desired levels of output.[36] The **resource-based approach** assesses effectiveness by observing the beginning of the process and evaluating whether the organization effectively obtains resources necessary for high performance. The **internal process approach** looks at internal activities and assesses effectiveness by indicators of internal health and efficiency.

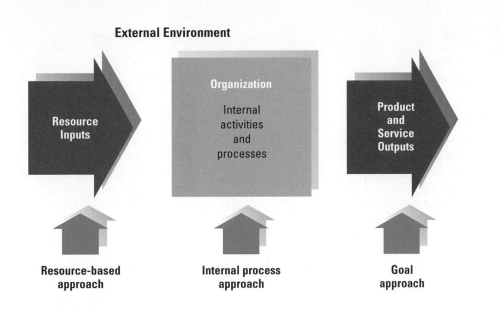

Goal Approach

The goal approach to effectiveness consists of identifying an organization's output goals and assessing how well the organization has attained those goals.[37] This is a logical approach because organizations do try to attain certain levels of output, profit, or client satisfaction. The goal approach measures progress toward attainment of those goals. For example, an important measure for the Women's National Basketball Association is number of tickets sold per game. During the league's first season, President Val Ackerman set a goal of 4,000 to 5,000 tickets per game. The organization actually averaged nearly 9,700 tickets per game, indicating that the WNBA was highly effective in meeting its goal for attendance.[38]

Indicators. The important goals to consider are operative goals. Efforts to measure effectiveness have been more productive using operative goals than using official goals.[39] Official goals tend to be abstract and difficult to measure. Operative goals reflect activities the organization is actually performing.

One example of multiple goals is from a survey of U.S. business corporations.[40] Their reported goals are shown in Exhibit 2.8. Twelve goals were listed as being important to these companies. Although the survey was conducted more than two decades ago, these twelve goals continue to be critical objectives for most businesses. These goals represent outcomes that cannot be achieved simultaneously. They illustrate the array of outcomes organizations attempt to achieve.

Usefulness. The goal approach is used in business organizations because output goals can be readily measured. Business firms typically evaluate performance in terms of profitability, growth, market share, and return on investment. However, identifying operative goals and measuring performance of an organization are not always easy. Two problems that must be resolved are the issues of multiple goals and subjective indicators of goal attainment.

Since organizations have multiple and conflicting goals, effectiveness often cannot be assessed by a single indicator. High achievement on one goal might mean low achievement on another. Moreover, there are department goals as well as overall

EXHIBIT 2.8
Reported Goals of U.S.
Corporations

Goal	% Corporations
Profitability	89
Growth	82
Market share	66
Social responsibility	65
Employee welfare	62
Product quality and service	60
Research and development	54
Diversification	51
Efficiency	50
Financial stability	49
Resource conservation	39
Management development	35

Source: Adapted from Y. K. Shetty, "New Look at Corporate Goals," *California Management Review* 22, no. 2 (1979), 71–79.

performance goals. The full assessment of effectiveness should take into consideration several goals simultaneously. Most organizations use a balanced approach to measuring goals.

The other issue to resolve with the goal approach is how to identify operative goals for an organization and how to measure goal attainment. For business organizations, there are often objective indicators for certain goals, such as profit or growth. However, subjective assessment is needed for other goals, such as employee welfare or social responsibility. Someone has to go into the organization and learn what the actual goals are by talking with the top management team. Once goals are identified, subjective perceptions of goal attainment have to be used when quantitative indicators are not available. Managers rely on information from customers, competitors, suppliers, and employees, as well as their own intuition, when considering these goals. Consider the case of General Motors Chevrolet division.

In Practice

Chevrolet

Chevy ruled the road in the 1960s and 1970s, but the brand has been steadily losing market share since the 1980s. Recently, General Motors outlined a new set of ambitious goals for the Chevrolet division.

Goals included introducing ten new car and truck models over a 20-month period, boosting the level of sales by 15 percent to 3 million vehicles a year, and unseating Ford to regain first-place position in car-truck sales. Managers are focused on measuring the effectiveness of the Chevrolet division by looking primarily at sales numbers and market share.

Things seemed to get off to a slow start, with many of the new vehicle models not making much of a splash in the marketplace. However, with the use of heavy incentives, Chevrolet was rapidly gaining on Ford by the fall of 2004. For the first 6 months of that year, Ford was still way ahead, leading by 107,157 vehicles at mid-year. Yet by the end of September, Chevy had reduced that lead to only 8,303 vehicles. Whereas Ford's car sales were down 14.6 percent in 2004, Chevrolet's were up 13.5 percent. While Chevrolet has not yet reached its goal of boosting sales by 15 percent, it is making steady progress toward achieving it.

Managers at GM and Chevrolet must also take into consideration that achieving sales goals might mean other goals are not met. Chevrolet's level of incentives in 2004 was the highest of any major U.S. automaker, which lowers the division's profits. In addition, the heavy push for sales could possibly weaken employee satisfaction or dealer morale. To fully measure effectiveness, managers have to look at a balanced set of goals for the Chevrolet division and use subjective as well as objective assessment of goal accomplishment.[41]

The goal approach works well for Chevrolet in terms of measuring sales and market share. Although the goal approach seems to be the most logical way to assess organizational effectiveness, managers should keep in mind that the actual measure of effectiveness is a complex process.

■ Resource-based Approach

The resource-based approach looks at the input side of the transformation process shown in Exhibit 2.7. It assumes organizations must be successful in obtaining and managing valued resources in order to be effective. From a resource-based perspective, organizational effectiveness is defined as the ability of the organization, in either absolute or relative terms, to obtain scarce and valued resources and successfully integrate and manage them.[42]

Indicators. Obtaining and successfully managing resources is the criterion by which organizational effectiveness is assessed. In a broad sense, indicators of effectiveness according to the resource-based approach encompass the following dimensions:
- Bargaining position—the ability of the organization to obtain from its environment scarce and valued resources, including financial resources, raw materials, human resources, knowledge, and technology
- The abilities of the organization's decision makers to perceive and correctly interpret the real properties of the external environment
- The abilities of managers to use tangible (e.g., supplies, people) and intangible (e.g., knowledge, corporate culture) resources in day-to-day organizational activities to achieve superior performance
- The ability of the organization to respond to changes in the environment

Usefulness. The resource-based approach is valuable when other indicators of performance are difficult to obtain. In many not-for-profit and social welfare organizations, for example, it is hard to measure output goals or internal efficiency. Some for-profit organizations also use a resource-based approach. For example, Mathsoft, Inc., which provides a broad range of technical-calculation and analytical software for business and academia, evaluates its effectiveness partly by looking at how many top-rate Ph.D.s it can recruit. CEO Charles Digate believes Mathsoft has a higher ratio of Ph.D.s to total employees than any other software company, which directly affects product quality and the company's image.[43]

Although the resource-based approach is valuable when other measures of effectiveness are not available, it does have shortcomings. For one thing, the approach only vaguely considers the organization's link to the needs of customers in the external environment. A superior ability to acquire and use resources is important only if resources and capabilities are used to achieve something that meets a need in the environment. Critics have challenged that the approach assumes stability in the marketplace and fails to adequately consider the changing value of various resources as the competitive environment and customer needs change.[44] The resource-based approach is most valuable when measures of goal attainment cannot be readily obtained.

■ Internal Process Approach

In the internal process approach, effectiveness is measured as internal organizational health and efficiency. An effective organization has a smooth, well-oiled internal process. Employees are happy and satisfied. Department activities mesh with one another to ensure high productivity. This approach does not consider the external environment. The important element in effectiveness is what the organization does with the resources it has, as reflected in internal health and efficiency.

Indicators. One indicator of internal process effectiveness is the organization's economic efficiency. However, the best-known proponents of a process model are from the human relations approach to organizations. Such writers as Chris Argyris, Warren G. Bennis, Rensis Likert, and Richard Beckhard have all worked extensively with human resources in organizations and emphasize the connection between human resources and effectiveness.[45] Writers on corporate culture and organizational excellence have stressed the importance of internal processes. Results from a study of nearly 200 secondary schools showed that both human resources and employee-oriented processes were important in explaining and promoting effectiveness in those organizations.[46]

There are seven indicators of an effective organization as seen from an internal process approach:
1. Strong corporate culture and positive work climate
2. Team spirit, group loyalty, and teamwork
3. Confidence, trust, and communication between workers and management
4. Decision making near sources of information, regardless of where those sources are on the organizational chart
5. Undistorted horizontal and vertical communication; sharing of relevant facts and feelings
6. Rewards to managers for performance, growth, and development of subordinates and for creating an effective work group
7. Interaction between the organization and its parts, with conflict that occurs over projects resolved in the interest of the organization[47]

Briefcase

As an organization manager, keep these guidelines in mind:

Use the goal approach, internal process approach, and resource-based approach to obtain specific pictures of organizational effectiveness. Assess competing values to obtain a broader, more balanced picture of effectiveness.

Usefulness. The internal process approach is important because the efficient use of resources and harmonious internal functioning are ways to assess organizational effectiveness. Today, most managers believe that happy, committed, actively involved employees and a positive corporate culture are important measures of effectiveness. For example, the giant aerospace company Boeing is struggling partly because internal processes are not functioning smoothly. Although technical processes for building planes have been improved, as described earlier, human relations and corporate culture are a mess. Hiring, promotion, and compensation practices are under fire. Twenty-eight thousand female employees have filed suit charging that the company systematically pays women less than men. Depositions describe a hostile work environment, including groping and offensive language on the part of male colleagues and bosses. CEO Harry Stonecipher was recently forced out because of improprieties related to an affair with a female executive. These internal human resources issues, combined with ethics scandals related to Boeing's external environment, have seriously damaged the company. In contrast, Four Seasons Hotels, a luxury chain of hotels with headquarters in Toronto, reflects smooth internal processes. Treating employees well is considered key to the organization's success. Workers at each hotel select a peer to receive the Employee of the Year award, which includes an expenses-paid vacation and a $1,000 shopping spree.[48]

The internal process approach also has shortcomings. Total output and the organization's relationship with the external environment are not evaluated. Another problem is that evaluations of internal health and functioning are often subjective, because many aspects of inputs and internal processes are not quantifiable. Managers should be aware that this approach alone represents a limited view of organizational effectiveness.

An Integrated Effectiveness Model

The three approaches—goal, resource-based, internal process—to organizational effectiveness described earlier all have something to offer, but each one tells only part of the story. The **competing values model** tries to balance a concern with various parts of the organization rather than focusing on one part. This approach to effectiveness acknowledges that organizations do many things and have many outcomes.[49] It combines several indicators of effectiveness into a single framework.

The model is based on the assumption that there are disagreements and competing viewpoints about what constitutes effectiveness. Managers sometimes disagree over which are the most important goals to pursue and measure. In addition, stakeholders have competing claims on what they want from the organization, as described in Chapter 1. One tragic example of conflicting viewpoints and competing interests comes from NASA. After seven astronauts died in the explosion of the space shuttle Columbia in February 2003, an investigative committee found deep organizational flaws at NASA, including ineffective mechanisms for incorporating dissenting opinions between scheduling managers and safety managers. External pressures to launch on time overrode safety concerns with the Columbia launch. As Wayne Hale, the NASA executive charged with giving the go-ahead for the next shuttle launch, puts it, "We dropped the torch through our own complacency, our arrogance, self-assurance, sheer stupidity, and through continuing attempt[s] to please everyone." NASA is an extremely complex organization that operates not only with different viewpoints internally but also from the U.S. Congress, the president, and the expectations of the American public.[50]

The competing values model takes into account these complexities. The model was originally developed by Robert Quinn and John Rohrbaugh to combine the diverse indicators of performance used by managers and researchers.[51] Using a comprehensive list of performance indicators, a panel of experts in organizational effectiveness rated the indicators for similarity. The analysis produced underlying dimensions of effectiveness criteria that represented competing management values in organizations.

EXHIBIT 2.9
*Four Approaches to
Effectiveness Values*
Source: Adapted from
Robert E. Quinn and John
Rohrbaugh, "A Spatial Model
of Effectiveness Criteria: Toward
a Competing Values Approach
to Organizational Analysis,"
Management Science 29
(1983), 363–377; and Robert E.
Quinn and Kim Cameron,
"Organizational Life Cycles
and Shifting Criteria of
Effectiveness: Some Preliminary
Evidence," *Management
Science* 29 (1983), 33–51.

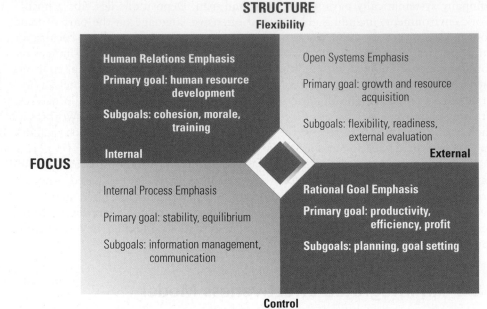

STRUCTURE
Flexibility

Human Relations Emphasis

Primary goal: human resource development

Subgoals: cohesion, morale, training

Internal

Open Systems Emphasis

Primary goal: growth and resource acquisition

Subgoals: flexibility, readiness, external evaluation

External

FOCUS

Internal Process Emphasis

Primary goal: stability, equilibrium

Subgoals: information management, communication

Rational Goal Emphasis

Primary goal: productivity, efficiency, profit

Subgoals: planning, goal setting

Control

Indicators. The first value dimension pertains to organizational **focus**, which is whether dominant values concern issues that are *internal* or *external* to the firm. Internal focus reflects a management concern for the well-being and efficiency of employees, and external focus represents an emphasis on the well-being of the organization itself with respect to the environment. The second value dimension pertains to organization **structure**, and whether *stability* versus *flexibility* is the dominant structural consideration. Stability reflects a management value for efficiency and top-down control, whereas flexibility represents a value for learning and change.

The value dimensions of structure and focus are illustrated in Exhibit 2.9. The combination of dimensions provides four approaches to organizational effectiveness, which, though seemingly different, are closely related. In real organizations, these competing values can and often do exist together. Each approach reflects a different management emphasis with respect to structure and focus.[52]

A combination of external focus and flexible structure leads to an **open systems emphasis**. Management's primary goals are growth and resource acquisition. The organization accomplishes these goals through the subgoals of flexibility, readiness, and a positive external evaluation. The dominant value is establishing a good relationship with the environment to acquire resources and grow. This emphasis is similar in some ways to the resource-based approach described earlier.

The **rational goal emphasis** represents management values of structural control and external focus. The primary goals are productivity, efficiency, and profit. The organization wants to achieve output goals in a controlled way. Subgoals that facilitate these outcomes are internal planning and goal setting, which are rational management tools. The rational goal emphasis is similar to the goal approach described earlier.

The **internal process emphasis** is in the lower-left section of Exhibit 2.9; it reflects the values of internal focus and structural control. The primary outcome is a

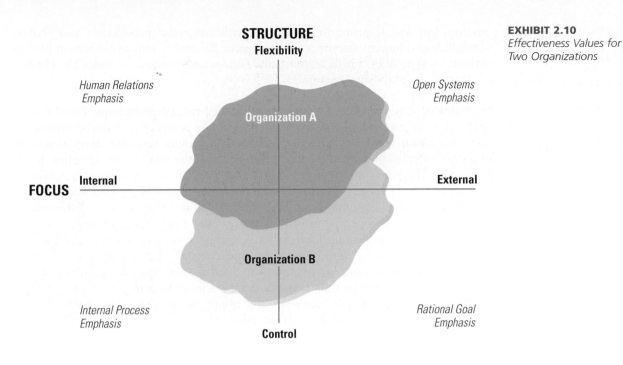

EXHIBIT 2.10
Effectiveness Values for Two Organizations

stable organizational setting that maintains itself in an orderly way. Organizations that are well established in the environment and simply want to maintain their current position would reflect this emphasis. Subgoals include mechanisms for efficient communication, information management, and decision making. Although this part of the competing values model is similar in some ways to the internal process approach described earlier, it is less concerned with human resources than with other internal processes that lead to efficiency.

The **human relations emphasis** incorporates the values of an internal focus and a flexible structure. Here, management concern is for the development of human resources. Employees are given opportunities for autonomy and development. Management works toward the subgoals of cohesion, morale, and training opportunities. Organizations adopting this emphasis are more concerned with employees than with the environment.

The four cells in Exhibit 2.9 represent opposing organizational values. Managers decide which goal values will take priority in the organization. The way two organizations are mapped onto the four approaches is shown in Exhibit 2.10.[53] Organization A is a young organization concerned with finding a niche and becoming established in the external environment. Primary emphasis is given to flexibility, innovation, the acquisition of resources from the environment, and the satisfaction of external constituencies. This organization gives moderate emphasis to human relations and even less emphasis to current productivity and profits. Satisfying and adapting to the environment are more important. The attention given to open systems values means that the internal process emphasis is practically nonexistent. Stability and equilibrium are of little concern.

Organization B, in contrast, is an established business in which the dominant value is productivity and profits. This organization is characterized by planning and goal setting. Organization B is a large company that is well established in the environment and is primarily concerned with successful production and profits. Flexibility and human resources are not major concerns. This organization prefers stability and equilibrium to learning and innovation because it wants to take advantage of its established customers.

Usefulness. The competing values model makes two contributions. First, it integrates diverse concepts of effectiveness into a single perspective. It incorporates the ideas of output goals, resource acquisition, and human resource development as goals the organization tries to accomplish. Second, the model calls attention to effectiveness criteria as management values and shows how opposing values exist at the same time. Managers must decide which values they wish to pursue and which values will receive less emphasis. The four competing values exist simultaneously, but not all will receive equal priority. For example, a new, small organization that concentrates on establishing itself within a competitive environment will give less emphasis to developing employees than to the external environment.

The dominant values in an organization often change over time as organizations experience new environmental demands or new top leadership.

The following example describes the dominant effectiveness values for the Thomson Corporation, which owns the company that published the textbook you are reading.

In Practice

The Thomson Corporation

When Richard Harrington took over as CEO of the Thomson Corporation in 1997, he began a process that has transformed the company from primarily a publisher of regional newspapers into a thriving information services enterprise. Today, Thomson is a leader in electronic publishing and providing integrated information solutions to corporate customers in a variety of industries. The line of newspapers was sold, and managers rebuilt Thomson into an organization providing a wide variety of information products and services to four strategic market groups: Legal and Regulatory, Learning, Financial, and Science and Healthcare.

The new goals and strategy took Thomson out of the business it knew best and thrust it into a new, highly competitive environment. Financial results were sure to suffer in the short term. The company had to acquire new businesses, new knowledge, new skills, and other resources to fit the new strategy and goals. Thomson spent several years acquiring more than 200 different businesses and melding them into a coherent whole. Growth became more important than productivity, efficiency, or even profit.

Making the revamped company successful required a strong focus on understanding customer needs and building good relationships with the external environment. Business unit managers were expected to thoroughly understand their potential customers, markets, and competitors. At the same time, however, they also had to make the internal people changes that were necessary. As a knowledge-based organization, Thomson considers employee development and a unified corporate culture fundamental to the company's success.[54]

The picture of Thomson mapped onto the competing values framework would look very much like Organization A in Exhibit 2.10. The company's transformation required a strong open systems emphasis with fairly strong emphasis on human relations as well. The rational goal emphasis and internal process emphasis are much weaker. Adapting to the environment and understanding and meeting customer needs are much more important now than internal control and cost efficiency, but goal emphasis could change in the future.

Summary and Interpretation

This chapter discussed organizational goals and the strategies that top managers use to help organizations achieve those goals. Goals specify the mission or purpose of an organization and its desired future state; strategies define how the organization will reach its goals. The chapter also discussed the impact of strategy on organization design and how designing the organization to fit strategy and other contingencies can lead to organizational effectiveness. The chapter closed with an examination of the most popular approaches to measuring effectiveness, that is, how well the organization realizes its purpose and attains its desired future state.

Organizations exist for a purpose; top managers define a specific mission or task to be accomplished. The mission statement, or official goals, makes explicit the purpose and direction of an organization. Official and operative goals are a key element in organizations because they meet these needs—establishing legitimacy with external groups and setting standards of performance for participants.

Managers must develop strategies that describe the actions required to achieve goals. Strategies may include any number of techniques to achieve the stated goals. Two models for formulating strategies are Porter's competitive strategies and the Miles and Snow strategy typology. Organization design needs to fit the firm's competitive approach to contribute to organizational effectiveness.

Assessing organizational effectiveness reflects the complexity of organizations as a topic of study. No easy, simple, guaranteed measure will provide an unequivocal assessment of performance. Organizations must perform diverse activities well—from obtaining resource inputs to delivering outputs—to be successful. Contingency approaches use output goals, resource acquisition, or internal health and efficiency as the criteria of effectiveness. The competing values model is a balanced approach that considers multiple criteria simultaneously. Organizations can be assessed by evaluating competing values for effectiveness. No approach is suitable for every organization, but each offers some advantages that the others may lack.

From the point of view of managers, the goal approach to effectiveness and measures of internal efficiency are useful when measures are available. The attainment of output and profit goals reflects the purpose of the organization, and efficiency reflects the cost of attaining those goals. Other factors such as top-management preferences, the extent to which goals are measurable, and the scarcity of environmental resources may influence the use of effectiveness criteria. In nonprofit organizations, where internal processes and output criteria are often not quantifiable, resource acquisition may be the best available indicator of effectiveness.

From the point of view of people outside the organization, such as academic investigators or government researchers, the competing values model of organizational effectiveness may be preferable. This model acknowledges different areas of focus (internal, external) and structure (flexibility, stability) and allows for managers to choose among approaches—human relations, open systems, rational goal, or internal process—in order to emphasize the values they wish to pursue.

Key Concepts

analyzer	mission
competing values model	official goals
defender	open systems emphasis
differentiation	operative goals
focus	organizational goal
focus strategy	prospector
goal approach	rational goal emphasis
human relations emphasis	reactor
internal process approach	resource-based approach
internal process emphasis	strategy
low-cost leadership	structure

Discussion Questions

1. Discuss the role of top management in setting organizational direction.
2. How might a company's goals for employee development be related to its goals for innovation and change? To goals for productivity? Can you discuss ways these types of goals might conflict in an organization?
3. What is a goal for the class for which you are reading this text? Who established this goal? Discuss how the goal affects your direction and motivation.
4. What is the difference between a goal and a strategy as defined in the text? Identify both a goal and a strategy for a campus or community organization with which you are involved.
5. Discuss the similarities and differences in the strategies described in Porter's competitive strategies and Miles and Snow's typology.
6. Do you believe mission statements and official goal statements provide an organization with genuine legitimacy in the external environment? Discuss.
7. Suppose you have been asked to evaluate the effectiveness of the police department in a medium-sized community. Where would you begin, and how would you proceed? What effectiveness approach would you prefer?
8. What are the advantages and disadvantages of the resource-based approach versus the goal approach for measuring organizational effectiveness?
9. What are the similarities and differences between assessing effectiveness on the basis of competing values versus the stakeholder approach described in Chapter 1? Explain.
10. A noted organization theorist once said, "Organizational effectiveness can be whatever top management defines it to be." Discuss.

Chapter 2 Workbook: Identifying Company Goals and Strategies*

Choose three companies, either in the same industry or in three different industries. Search the Internet for information on the companies, including annual reports. In each company look particularly at the goals expressed. Refer back to the goals in Exhibit 2.8 and also to Porter's competitive strategies in Exhibit 2.4.

*Copyright 1996 by Dorothy Marcic. All rights reserved.

	Goals from Exhibit 2.8 articulated	Strategies from Porter used
Company #1		
Company #2		
Company #3		

Questions

1. Which goals seem most important?
2. Look for differences in the goals and strategies of the three companies and develop an explanation for those differences.
3. Which of the goals or strategies should be changed? Why?
4. *Optional:* Compare your table with those of other students and look for common themes. Which companies seem to articulate and communicate their goals and strategies best?

Case for Analysis: The University Art Museum*

Visitors to the campus were always shown the University Art Museum, of which the large and distinguished university was very proud. A photograph of the handsome neoclassical building that housed the museum had long been used by the university for the cover of its brochures and catalogs.

The building, together with a substantial endowment, was given to the university around 1912 by an alumnus, the son of the university's first president, who had become very wealthy as an investment banker. He also gave the university his own small, but high-quality, collections—one of Etruscan figurines, and one, unique in America, of English pre-Raphaelite paintings. He then served as the museum's unpaid director until his death. During his tenure he brought a few additional collections to the museum, largely from other alumni of the university. Only rarely did the museum purchase anything. As a result, the museum housed several small collections of uneven quality. As long as the founder ran the museum, none of the collections were ever shown to anybody except a few members of the university's art history faculty, who were admitted as the founder's private guests.

After the founder's death, in the late 1920s, the university intended to bring in a professional museum director.

Indeed, this had been part of the agreement under which the founder had given the museum. A search committee was to be appointed; but in the meantime a graduate student in art history, who had shown interest in the museum and who had spent a good many hours in it, took over temporarily. At first, Miss Kirkoff did not even have a title, let alone a salary. But she stayed on acting as the museum's director and over the next 30 years was promoted in stages to that title. But from the first day, whatever her title, she was in charge. She immediately set about changing the museum altogether. She cataloged the collections. She pursued new gifts, again primarily small collections from alumni and other friends of the university. She organized fund raising for the museum. But, above all, she began to integrate the museum into the work of the university.

When a space problem arose in the years immediately following World War II, Miss Kirkoff offered the third floor of the museum to the art history faculty, which moved its offices there. She remodeled the building to include

*Case #3, "The University Art Museum: Defining Purpose and Mission" (pp. 28–35), from *Management Cases* by Peter F. Drucker. Copyright © 1977 by Peter F. Drucker. Reprinted by permission of the author.

classrooms and a modern and well-appointed auditorium. She raised funds to build one of the best research and reference libraries in art history in the country. She also began to organize a series of special exhibitions built around one of the museum's own collections, complemented by loans from outside collections. For each of these exhibitions, she had a distinguished member of the university's art faculty write a catalog. These catalogs speedily became the leading scholarly texts in the fields.

Miss Kirkoff ran the University Art Museum for almost half a century. But at the age of 68, after suffering a severe stroke, she had to retire. In her letter of resignation she proudly pointed to the museum's growth and accomplishment under her stewardship. "Our endowment," she wrote, "now compares favorably with museums several times our size. We never have had to ask the university for any money other than our share of the university's insurance policies. Our collections in the areas of our strength, while small, are of first-rate quality and importance. Above all, we are being used by more people than any museum of our size. Our lecture series, in which members of the university's art history faculty present a major subject to a university audience of students and faculty, attracts regularly three hundred to five hundred people; and if we had the seating capacity, we could easily have a larger audience. Our exhibitions are seen and studied by more visitors, most of them members of the university community, than all but the most highly publicized exhibitions in the very big museums ever draw. Above all, the courses and seminars offered in the museum have become one of the most popular and most rapidly growing educational features of the university. No other museum in this country or anywhere else," concluded Miss Kirkoff, "has so successfully integrated art into the life of a major university and a major university into the work of a museum."

Miss Kirkoff strongly recommended that the university bring in a professional museum director as her successor. "The museum is much too big and much too important to be entrusted to another amateur such as I was forty-five years ago," she wrote. "And it needs careful thinking regarding its direction, its basis of support, and its future relationship with the university."

The university took Miss Kirkoff's advice. A search committee was duly appointed and, after one year's work, it produced a candidate whom everybody approved. The candidate was himself a graduate of the university who had then obtained his Ph.D. in art history and in museum work from the university. Both his teaching and his administrative record were sound, leading to his current museum directorship in a medium-sized city. There he converted an old, well-known, but rather sleepy museum to a lively, community-oriented museum whose exhibitions were well publicized and attracted large crowds.

The new museum director took over with great fanfare in September 1981. Less than 3 years later he left—with less fanfare, but still with considerable noise. Whether he resigned or was fired was not quite clear. But that there was bitterness on both sides was only too obvious.

The new director, upon his arrival, had announced that he looked upon the museum as a "major community resource" and intended to "make the tremendous artistic and scholarly resources of the museum fully available to the academic community as well as to the public." When he said these things in an interview with the college newspaper, everybody nodded in approval. It soon became clear that what he meant by "community resource" and what the faculty and students understood by these words were not the same. The museum had always been "open to the public" but, in practice, it was members of the college community who used the museum and attended its lectures, its exhibitions, and its frequent seminars.

The first thing the new director did, however, was to promote visits from the public schools in the area. He soon began to change the exhibition policy. Instead of organizing small shows, focused on a major collection of the museum and built around a scholarly catalog, he began to organize "popular exhibitions" around "topics of general interest" such as "Women Artists through the Ages." He promoted these exhibitions vigorously in the newspapers, in radio and television interviews, and, above all, in the local schools. As a result, what had been a busy but quiet place was soon knee-deep with schoolchildren, taken to the museum in special buses that cluttered the access roads around the museum and throughout the campus. The faculty, which was not particularly happy with the resulting noise and confusion, became thoroughly upset when the scholarly old chairman of the art history department was mobbed by fourth-graders who sprayed him with their water pistols as he tried to push his way through the main hall to his office.

Increasingly, the new director did not design his own shows, but brought in traveling exhibitions from major museums, importing their catalog as well rather than have his own faculty produce one.

The students, too, were apparently unenthusiastic after the first 6 or 8 months, during which the new director had been somewhat of a campus hero. Attendance at the classes and seminars held at the art museum fell off sharply, as did attendance at the evening lectures. When the editor of the campus newspaper interviewed students for a story on the museum, he was told again and again that the museum had become too noisy and too "sensational" for students to enjoy the classes and to have a chance to learn.

What brought all this to a head was an Islamic art exhibit in late 1983. Since the museum had little Islamic art, nobody criticized the showing of a traveling exhibit, offered on very advantageous terms with generous financial assistance from some of the Arab governments. But then, instead of inviting one of the university's own faculty members to deliver the customary talk at the opening of the exhibit, the director brought in a cultural attaché of one of the Arab embassies in Washington. The speaker, it was reported, used the occasion to deliver a violent attack on Israel and on the American policy of supporting Israel against the Arabs. A week later, the university senate decided to appoint an advisory committee, drawn mostly from members of the art history faculty, which, in the future, would have to approve all plans for exhibits and lectures. The director thereupon, in an interview with the campus newspaper, sharply attacked the faculty as "elitist" and "snobbish" and as believing that "art belongs to the rich." Six months later, in June 1984, his resignation was announced.

Under the bylaws of the university, the academic senate appoints a search committee. Normally, this is pure formality. The chairperson of the appropriate department submits the department's nominees for the committee who are approved and appointed, usually without debate. But when the academic senate early the following semester was asked to appoint the search committee, things were far from "normal." The dean who presided, sensing the tempers in the room, tried to smooth over things by saying, "Clearly, we picked the wrong person the last time. We will have to try very hard to find the right one this time."

He was immediately interrupted by an economist, known for his populism, who broke in and said, "I admit that the late director was probably not the right personality. But I strongly believe that his personality was not at the root of the problem. He tried to do what needs doing, and this got him in trouble with the faculty. He tried to make our museum a community resource, to bring in the community and to make art accessible to broad masses of people, to the blacks and the Puerto Ricans, to the kids from the ghetto schools and to a lay public. And this is what we really resented. Maybe his methods were not the most tactful ones—I admit I could have done without those interviews he gave. But what he tried to do was right. We had better commit ourselves to the policy he wanted to put into effect, or else we will have deserved his attacks on us as 'elitist' and 'snobbish.' "

"This is nonsense," cut in the usually silent and polite senate member from the art history faculty. "It makes absolutely no sense for our museum to become the kind of community resource our late director and my distinguished colleague want it to be. First, there is no need. The city has

one of the world's finest and biggest museums, and it does exactly that and does it very well. Secondly, we have neither the artistic resources nor the financial resources to serve the community at large. We can do something different but equally important and indeed unique. Ours is the only museum in the country, and perhaps in the world, that is fully integrated with an academic community and truly a teaching institution. We are using it, or at least we used to until the last few unfortunate years, as a major educational resource for all our students. No other museum in the country, and as far as I know in the world, is bringing undergraduates into art the way we do. All of us, in addition to our scholarly and graduate work, teach undergraduate courses for people who are not going to be art majors or art historians. We work with the engineering students and show them what we do in our conservation and restoration work. We work with architecture students and show them the development of architecture through the ages. Above all, we work with liberal arts students, who often have had no exposure to art before they came here and who enjoy our courses all the more because they are scholarly and not just 'art appreciation.' This is unique and this is what our museum can do and should do."

"I doubt that this is really what we should be doing," commented the chairman of the mathematics department. "The museum, as far as I know, is part of the graduate faculty. It should concentrate on training art historians in its Ph.D. program, on its scholarly work, and on its research. I would strongly urge that the museum be considered an adjunct to graduate and especially to Ph.D. education, confine itself to this work, and stay out of all attempts to be 'popular,' both on campus and outside of it. The glory of the museum is the scholarly catalogs produced by our faculty, and our Ph.D. graduates who are sought after by art history faculties throughout the country. This is the museum's mission, which can only be impaired by the attempts to be 'popular,' whether with students or with the public."

"These are very interesting and important comments," said the dean, still trying to pacify. "But I think this can wait until we know who the new director is going to be. Then we should raise these questions with him."

"I beg to differ, Mr. Dean," said one of the elder statesmen of the faculty. "During the summer months, I discussed this question with an old friend and neighbor of mine in the country, the director of one of the nation's great museums. He said to me: 'You do not have a personality problem; you have a management problem. You have not, as a university, taken responsibility for the mission, the direction, and the objectives of your museum. Until you do this, no director can succeed. And this is your decision. In fact, you cannot hope to get a good director until you can tell that person what your basic objectives are. If your late director is to blame—I know him and I know that he is abrasive—it is for being willing to take on a job when you, the university, had not faced up to the basic management decisions. There is no point talking about who should manage until it is clear what it is that has to be managed and for what.'"

At this point the dean realized that he had to adjourn the discussion unless he wanted the meeting to degenerate into a brawl. But he also realized that he had to identify the issues and possible decisions before the next senate meeting a month later.

Case for Analysis: Airstar, Inc.*

Airstar, Inc. manufactures, repairs, and overhauls pistons and jet engines for smaller, often previously owned aircraft. The company had a solid niche, and most managers had been with the founder for more than 20 years. With the founder's death 5 years ago, Roy Morgan took over as president at Airstar. Mr. Morgan has called you in as a consultant.

Your research indicates that this industry is changing rapidly. Airstar is feeling encroachment of huge conglomerates like General Electric and Pratt & Whitney, and its backlog of orders is the lowest in several years. The company has always been known for its superior quality, safety, and customer service. However, it has never been under threat before, and senior managers are not sure which strategic direction to take. They have considered potential acquisitions, imports and exports, more research, and additional repair lines. The organization is becoming more chaotic, which is frustrating Morgan and his vice presidents.

Before a meeting with his team, he confides to you, "Organizing is supposed to be easy. For maximum efficiency, work should be divided into simple, logical, routine tasks. These business tasks can be grouped by similar kinds of work characteristics and arranged within an organization under a particularly suited executive. So why are we having so many problems with our executives?"

Morgan met with several of his trusted corporate officers in the executive dining room to discuss what was happening to corporate leadership at Airstar. Morgan went on to explain that he was really becoming concerned with the situation. There had been outright conflicts between the vice president of marketing and the controller over merger and acquisition opportunities. There had been many instances of duplication of work, with corporate officers trying to outmaneuver each other.

"Communications are atrocious," Morgan said to the others. "Why, I didn't even get a copy of the export finance report until my secretary made an effort to find one for me. My basis for evaluation and appraisal of corporate-executive performance and goal accomplishment is fast becoming obsolete. People have been working up their own job descriptions, and they all include overlapping responsibilities. Changes and decisions are being made on the basis of expediency and are perpetuating too many mistakes. We must take a good look at these organizational realities and correct the situation immediately."

Jim Robinson, vice president of manufacturing, pointed out to Morgan that Airstar was not really following the "principles of good organization." "For instance," explained Robinson, "let's review what we should be practicing as administrators." Some of the principles Robinson believed they should be following were:

1. Determine the goals, policies, programs, plans, and strategies that will best achieve the desired results for the company.
2. Determine the various business tasks to be done.
3. Divide the business tasks into a logical and understandable organizational structure.
4. Determine the suitable personnel to occupy positions within the organizational structure.
5. Define the responsibility and authority of each supervisor clearly in writing.
6. Keep the number and kinds of levels of authority at a minimum.

Robinson proposed that the group study the corporate organizational chart, as well as the various corporate business tasks. After reviewing the corporate organizational chart, Robinson, Morgan, and the others agreed that the number and kinds of formal corporate authority were logical and not much different from other corporations. The group then listed the various corporate business tasks that went on within Airstar.

Robinson continued. "How did we ever decide who should handle mergers or acquisitions?" Morgan answered, "I guess it just occurred over time that the vice president of marketing should have the responsibility." "But," Robinson queried, "where is it written down? How would the controller know it?" "Aha," Morgan exclaimed. "It looks like I'm part of the problem. There isn't anything in writing. Tasks were assigned superficially, as they became problems. This has all been rather informal. I'll establish a group to decide who should have responsibility for what so things can return to our previous level of efficiency."

*Adapted from Bernard A. Deitzer and Karl A. Shilliff, *Contemporary Management Incidents* (Columbus, Ohio: Grid, Inc., 1977), 43–46. Copyright © 1997 by John Wiley & Sons, Inc. This material is used by permission of John Wiley & Sons, Inc.

Chapter 2 Workshop: Competing Values and Organizational Effectiveness*

1. Divide into groups of four to six members.
2. Select an organization to "study" for this exercise. It should be an organization for which one of you has worked, or it could be the university.
3. Using the exhibit "Four Approaches to Effectiveness Values" (Exhibit 2.9), your group should list eight potential measures that show a balanced view of performance. These should relate not only to work activities, but also to goal values for the company. Use the table below.
4. How will achieving these goal values help the organization to become more effective? Which values could be given more weight than others? Why?

5. Present your competing values chart to the rest of the class. Each group should explain why it chose those particular values and which are more important. Be prepared to defend your position to the other groups, which are encouraged to question your choices.

*Adapted by Dorothy Marcic from general ideas in Jennifer Howard and Larry Miller, *Team Management*, The Miller Consulting Group, 1994, p. 92.

Goal or Subgoal		Performance Gauge	How to Measure	Source of Data	What Do You Consider Effective?
(Example) Equilibrium		Turnover rates	Compare percentages of workers who left	HRM files	25% reduction in first year
Open system	1.				
	2.				
Human relations	3.				
	4.				
Internal process	5.				
	6.				
Rational goal	7.				
	8.				

Notes

1. Steven Gray, "Starbucks Brews Broader Menu; Coffee Chain's Cup Runneth Over with Breakfast, Lunch, Music," *The Wall Street Journal* (February 9, 2005), B9; Andy Serwer, "Hot Starbucks to Go," *Fortune* (January 26, 2004), 60–74; Jean Patteson, "Warm Hues Hot for Fall; Call It the Starbucks Influence, as Designers Serve Colors from Latte to Espresso Spiked with Vibrant Blues," *Orlando Sentinel* (February 10, 2005), E1; "Starbucks Continues Successful Expansion of Music Experience," *Business Wire* (February 9, 2005), 1; and Monica Soto Ouchi, "No Roast, Just Thanks to Can-Do Coffee Man," *Seattle Times* (February 10, 2005), A1.

2. Amitai Etzioni, *Modern Organizations* (Englewood Cliffs, N.J.: Prentice-Hall, 1964), 6.
3. John P. Kotter, "What Effective General Managers Really Do," *Harvard Business Review* (November December 1982), 156–167; Henry Mintzberg, *The Nature of Managerial Work* (New York: Harper & Row, 1973).
4. Charles C. Snow and Lawrence G. Hrebiniak, "Strategy, Distinctive Competence, and Organizational Performance," *Administrative Science Quarterly* 25 (1980), 317–335.
5. Amy Barrett, "Staying On Top," *Business Week* (May 5, 2003), 60–68.

86   Part 2: Organizational Purpose and Structural Design

6. Forest R. David and Fred R. David, "It's Time to Redraft Your Mission Statement," *Journal of Business Strategy* (January–February 2003), 11–14; John Pearce and Fred David, "Corporate Mission Statements: The Bottom Line," *Academy of Management Executive* 1, no. 2 (May 1987), 109–116; and Christopher Bart and Mark Baetz, "The Relationship Between Mission Statements and Firm Performance: An Exploratory Study," *Journal of Management Studies* 35 (1998).

7. Barbara Bartkus, Myron Glassman, and R. Bruce McAfee, "Mission Statements: Are They Smoke and Mirrors?" *Business Horizons* (November–December 2000), 23–28.

8. Mark C. Suchman, "Managing Legitimacy: Strategic and Institutional Approaches," *Academy of Management Review* 20, no. 3 (1995), 571–610.

9. Kurt Eichenwald, "Miscues, Missteps, and the Fall of Andersen," *The New York Times* (May 8, 2002), C1, C4; Ian Wilson, "The Agenda for Redefining Corporate Purpose: Five Key Executive Actions," *Strategy & Leadership* 32, no. 1 (2004), 21–26.

10. Bill George, "The Company's Mission is the Message," *Strategy & Business*, Issue 33 (Winter 2003), 13–14; Jim Collins and Jerry Porras, *Built to Last: Successful Habits of Visionary Companies* (New York: HarperBusiness, 1994).

11. Charles Perrow, "The Analysis of Goals in Complex Organizations," *American Sociological Review* 26 (1961), 854–866.

12. Johannes U. Stoelwinder and Martin P. Charns, "The Task Field Model of Organization Analysis and Design," *Human Relations* 34 (1981), 743–762; Anthony Raia, *Managing by Objectives* (Glenview, Ill.: Scott, Foresman, 1974).

13. Lee Hawkins Jr. "GM Seeks Chevrolet Revival," *The Wall Street Journal* (December 19, 2003), B4.

14. Alex Taylor III, "Honda Goes Its Own Way," *Fortune* (July 22, 2002), 148–152; Joseph Pereira and Christopher J. Chipello, "Battle of the Block Makers," *The Wall Street Journal* (February 4, 2004), B1.

15. Kevin E. Joyce, "Lessons for Employers from *Fortune*'s '100 Best,'" *Business Horizons* (March–April 2003), 77–84; Ann Harrington, "The 100 Best Companies to Work For Hall of Fame," *Fortune* (January 24, 2005), 94.

16. Michael Arndt, "3M: A Lab for Growth?" *BusinessWeek* (January 21, 2002), 50–51.

17. Kim Cross, "Does Your Team Measure Up?" *Business2.com* (June 12, 2001), 22–28; J. Lynn Lunsford, "Lean Times: With Airbus on Its Tail, Boeing is Rethinking How It Builds Planes," *The Wall Street Journal* (September 5, 2001), A11.

18. Christopher Cooper and Greg Jaffe, "Under Fire: At Abu Ghraib, Soldiers Faced Intense Pressure to Produce Data," *The Wall Street Journal* (June 1, 2004), A1, A6.

19. James D. Thompson, *Organizations in Action* (New York: McGraw-Hill, 1967), 83–98.

20. Michael E. Porter, "What Is Strategy?" *Harvard Business Review* (November–December 1996), 61–78.

21. Michael E. Porter, *Competitive Strategy: Techniques for Analyzing Industries and Competitors* (New York: Free Press, 1980).

22. Alan Ruddock, "Keeping Up with O'Leary," *Management Today* (September 2003), 48–55; Jane Engle, "Flying High for Pocket Change; Regional Carriers Offer Inexpensive Travel Alternative," *South Florida Sun Sentinel* (February 13, 2005), 5; "Ryanair is Top on Net," *The Daily Mirror* (February 3, 2005), 10; and "Ryanair Tops 2m Passengers," *Daily Post* (February 4, 2005), 21.

23. Richard Teitelbaum, "The Wal-Mart of Wall Street," *Fortune* (October 13, 1997), 128–130.

24. Kevin J. O'Brien, "Focusing on Armchair Athletes, Puma Becomes a Leader," *The New York Times* (March 12, 2004), W1.

25. Michael E. Porter, "Strategy and the Internet," *Harvard Business Review* (March 2001), 63–78; and John Magretta, "Why Business Models Matter," *Harvard Business Review* (May 2002), 86.

26. Raymond E. Miles and Charles C. Snow, *Organizational Strategy, Structure, and Process* (New York: McGraw-Hill, 1978).

27. Geraldine Fabrikant, "The Paramount Team Puts Profit Over Splash," *The New York Times* (June 30, 2002), Section 3, 1, 15.

28. "Miles and Snow: Enduring Insights for Managers: Academic Commentary by Sumantra Ghoshal," *Academy of Management Executive* 17, no. 4 (2003), 109–114.

29. Pallavi Gogoi and Michael Arndt, "Hamburger Hell," *BusinessWeek* (March 3, 2003), 104–108; and Michael Arndt, "McDonald's: Fries with That Salad?" *BusinessWeek* (July 5, 2004), 82–84.

30. "On the Staying Power of Defenders, Analyzers, and Prospectors: Academic Commentary by Donald C. Hambrick," *Academy of Management Executive* 17, no. 4 (2003), 115–118.

31. Etzioni, *Modern Organizations*, 8.

32. Etzioni, *Modern Organizations*, 8; and Gary D. Sandefur, "Efficiency in Social Service Organizations," *Administration and Society* 14 (1983), 449–468.

33. Richard M. Steers, *Organizational Effectiveness: A Behavioral View* (Santa Monica, Calif.: Goodyear, 1977), 51.

34. Karl E. Weick and Richard L. Daft, "The Effectiveness of Interpretation Systems," in Kim S. Cameron and David A. Whetten, eds., *Organizational Effectiveness: A Comparison of Multiple Models* (New York: Academic Press, 1982).

35. David L. Blenkhorn and Brian Gaber, "The Use of 'Warm Fuzzies' to Assess Organizational Effectiveness," *Journal of General Management*, 21, no. 2 (Winter 1995), 40–51.

36. Steven Strasser, J. D. Eveland, Gaylord Cummins, O. Lynn Deniston, and John H. Romani, "Conceptualizing the Goal and Systems Models of Organizational Effectiveness—Implications for Comparative Evaluation Research," *Journal of Management Studies* 18 (1981), 321–340.

37. James L. Price, "The Study of Organizational Effectiveness," *Sociological Quarterly* 13 (1972), 3–15.

38. Lucy McCauley, ed., "Unit of One: Measure What Matters," *Fast Company* (May 1999), 97.

39. Richard H. Hall and John P. Clark, "An Ineffective Effectiveness Study and Some Suggestions for Future Research," *Sociological Quarterly* 21 (1980), 119–134; Price, "The Study of Organizational Effectiveness"; and Perrow, "Analysis of Goals."

40. Y. K. Shetty, "New Look at Corporate Goals," *California Management Review* 22, no. 2 (1979), 71–79.

41. Lee Hawkins, Jr., "GM Seeks Chevrolet Revival"; Lee Hawkins, Jr., "Chevy's Small-Car Gambit; Two New Models Aim to Match Rivals in Cost, Ride, Features, and Boost GM Unit's Market," *The Wall Street Journal* (July 15, 2004), B1; and John K. Teahen, Jr., "We've Got a Race! Chevy Closes In on Ford," *Automotive News* (October 11, 2004), 1.

42. The discussion of the resource-based approach is based in part on Michael V. Russo and Paul A. Fouts, "A Resource-Based Perspective on Corporate Environmental Performance and Profitability," *Academy of Management Journal* 40, no. 3 (June 1997), 534–559; and Jay B. Barney, J. L. "Larry" Stempert, Loren T. Gustafson, and Yolanda Sarason, "Organizational Identity within the Strategic Management Conversation: Contributions and Assumptions," in *Identity in Organizations: Building Theory through Conversations*, David A. Whetten and Paul C. Godfrey, eds. (Thousand Oaks, Calif.: Sage Publications, 1998), 83–98.

43. Lucy McCauley, "Measure What Matters."

44. Richard I. Priem, "Is the Resource-Based 'View' a Useful Perspective for Strategic Management Research?" *Academy of Management Review* 26, no. 1 (2001), 22–40.

45. Chris Argyris, *Integrating the Individual and the Organization* (New York: Wiley, 1964); Warren G. Bennis, *Changing Organizations* (New York: McGraw-Hill, 1966); Rensis Likert, *The Human Organization* (New York: McGraw-Hill, 1967); and Richard Beckhard, *Organization Development Strategies and Models* (Reading, Mass.: Addison-Wesley, 1969).

46. Cheri Ostroff and Neal Schmitt, "Configurations of Organizational Effectiveness and Efficiency," *Academy of Man-*

agement Journal 36 (1993), 1345–1361; Peter J. Frost, Larry F. Moore, Meryl Reise Louis, Craig C. Lundburg, and Joanne Martin, *Organizational Culture* (Beverly Hills, Calif.: Sage, 1985).

47. J. Barton Cunningham, "Approaches to the Evaluation of Organizational Effectiveness," *Academy of Management Review* 2 (1977), 463–474; Beckhard, *Organization Development*.

48. Stanley Holmes, "A New Black Eye for Boeing?" *BusinessWeek* (April 26, 2004), 90–92; Robert Levering and Milton Moskowitz, "The 100 Best Companies to Work For," *Fortune* (January 24, 2005), 72–90.

49. Eric J. Walton and Sarah Dawson, "Managers' Perceptions of Criteria of Organizational Effectiveness," *Journal of Management Studies* 38, no. 2 (2001), 173–199.

50. Beth Dickey, "NASA's Next Step," *Government Executive* (April 15, 2004), 34+.

51. Robert E. Quinn and John Rohrbaugh, "A Spatial Model of Effectiveness Criteria: Toward a Competing Values Approach to Organizational Analysis," *Management Science* 29 (1983), 363–377.

52. Regina M. O'Neill and Robert E. Quinn, "Editor's Note: Applications of the Competing Values Framework," *Human Resource Management* 32 (Spring 1993), 1–7.

53. Robert E. Quinn and Kim Cameron, "Organizational Life Cycles and Shifting Criteria of Effectiveness: Some Preliminary Evidence," *Management Science* 29 (1983), 33–51.

54. Larry Bossidy and Ram Charan, *Confronting Reality: Doing What Matters to Get Things Right* (New York: Crown Business, 2004), Chapter 9, 153–168.

3

Fundamentals of Organization Structure

Organization Structure

Information-Processing Perspective on Structure
Vertical Information Linkages • Horizontal Information Linkages

Organization Design Alternatives
Required Work Activities • Reporting Relationships • Departmental Grouping Options

Functional, Divisional, and Geographical Designs
Functional Structure • Functional Structure with Horizontal Linkages • Divisional Structure • Geographical Structure

Matrix Structure
Conditions for the Matrix • Strengths and Weaknesses

Horizontal Structure
Characteristics • Strengths and Weaknesses

Virtual Network Structure
How the Structure Works • Strengths and Weaknesses

Hybrid Structure

Applications of Structural Design
Structural Alignment • Symptoms of Structural Deficiency

Summary and Interpretation

A Look Inside

Ford Motor Company

The demand for hybrid vehicles is growing at a fast clip, but many people want more than the pocket-sized cars from Toyota and Honda that were first on the market. Ford Motor Company vowed to be the first auto manufacturer to come out with a hybrid SUV. CEO Bill Ford raved for years about plans for a new model that would handle like a muscular V6 but sip tiny amounts of gas and produce minuscule emissions. The Escape Hybrid SUV would be the most technologically advanced vehicle Ford had ever made, and perhaps its most important since the Model T.

The problem was, the Escape Hybrid was a dramatically different product for Ford and involved nine major new technologies, which Ford wanted to develop in-house rather than licensing patents from Toyota's hybrid system. Introducing even one major technological breakthrough was a challenge for Ford's traditional design and engineering process. Typically, researchers and product engineers haven't worked closely together at Ford—in fact, they were located in different buildings a half-mile apart. To meet the demanding schedule for getting the Escape Hybrid on the market, Ford created a sort of hybrid team, made up of scientists and product engineers from far-flung departments, now working side-by-side, creating and building software and hardware together, then working with production personnel to bring their creation to life. The team's leader, Prabhaker Patil, was himself a hybrid, a Ph.D. scientist who had started out working in Ford's lab and then crossed over to hands-on product development. Patil was careful to select team members he knew would be open to collaboration. Whereas in the past problems were "tossed over the wall," they would now be ironed out collaboratively. The approach was revolutionary for Ford, and it led to amazing breakthroughs.

The Escape Hybrid team was given nearly complete autonomy, another rarity for Ford. Because the team was allowed to be entrepreneurial, their productivity zoomed. Decisions that once would have taken days were made on the spot. As a result, the team met the demanding schedule, and the Ford Escape Hybrid was introduced right on time—and to amazing success. It was named the best truck of the year at the 2005 North American International Auto Show, and Ford will use the technologies the team developed to introduce four more hybrid vehicles over the next 3 years.[1]

Just as Ford Motor Company first made the automobile accessible to the everyday consumer, it has taken a bold step by introducing a team-based structure to bring the hybrid to a mass market. Booz Allen Hamilton Inc. estimates that hybrids could make up 20 percent of the U.S. market by 2010. Most automakers outside of Japan have been shortsighted by failing to invest in hybrid technology.[2] Ford has an early lead, thanks largely to the communication and collaboration made possible by the team approach. Many of today's organizations are using teams as a way to increase horizontal collaboration, spur innovation, and speed new products and services to market.

Organizations use various structural alternatives to help them achieve their purpose and goals. Nearly every firm needs to undergo structural reorganization at some point to help meet new challenges. Structural changes are needed to reflect new strategies or respond to changes in other contingency factors introduced in

Chapter 2: environment, technology, size and life cycle, and culture. For example, the Catholic Church is reorganizing to meet the challenges of a dwindling and aging corps of priests, financial pressures, shifting demographics, and ethical scandals. The traditional top-down, authoritarian management style is being evaluated in an effort to improve decision making and put resources in places where they're needed most.[3]

■ Purpose of This Chapter

This chapter introduces basic concepts of organization structure and shows how to design structure as it appears on the organization chart. First we define structure and provide an overview of structural design. Then, an information-processing perspective explains how to design vertical and horizontal linkages to provide needed information flow. The chapter next presents basic design options, followed by strategies for grouping organizational activities into functional, divisional, matrix, horizontal, virtual network, or hybrid structures. The final section examines how the application of basic structures depends on the organization's situation and outlines the symptoms of structural misalignment.

Organization Structure

There are three key components in the definition of **organization structure**:
1. Organization structure designates formal reporting relationships, including the number of levels in the hierarchy and the span of control of managers and supervisors.
2. Organization structure identifies the grouping together of individuals into departments and of departments into the total organization.
3. Organization structure includes the design of systems to ensure effective communication, coordination, and integration of efforts across departments.[4]

These three elements of structure pertain to both vertical and horizontal aspects of organizing. For example, the first two elements are the structural *framework*, which is the vertical hierarchy.[5] The third element pertains to the pattern of *interactions* among organizational employees. An ideal structure encourages employees to provide horizontal information and coordination where and when it is needed.

Organization structure is reflected in the organization chart. It isn't possible to see the internal structure of an organization the way we might see its manufacturing tools, offices, or products. Although we might see employees going about their duties, performing different tasks, and working in different locations, the only way to actually see the structure underlying all this activity is through the organization chart. The organization chart is the visual representation of a whole set of underlying activities and processes in an organization. Exhibit 3.1 shows a sample organization chart. The organization chart can be quite useful in understanding how a company works. It shows the various parts of an organization, how they are interrelated, and how each position and department fits into the whole.

The concept of an organization chart, showing what positions exist, how they are grouped, and who reports to whom, has been around for centuries.[6] For example, diagrams outlining church hierarchy can be found in medieval churches in Spain. However, the use of the organization chart for business stems largely from the Industrial Revolution. As we discussed in Chapter 1, as work grew more

Briefcase

As an organization manager, keep these guidelines in mind:

Develop organization charts that describe task responsibilities, reporting relationships, and the grouping of individuals into departments. Provide sufficient documentation so that all people within the organization know to whom they report and how they fit into the total organization picture.

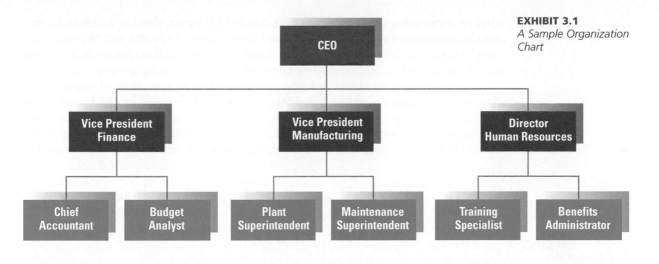

EXHIBIT 3.1
A Sample Organization Chart

complex and was performed by greater and greater numbers of workers, there was a pressing need to develop ways of managing and controlling organizations. The growth of the railroads provides an example. After the collision of two passenger trains in Massachusetts in 1841, the public demanded better control of the operation. As a result, the Board of Directors of the Western Railroad took steps to outline "definite responsibilities for each phase of the company's business, drawing solid lines of authority and command for the railroad's administration, maintenance, and operation."[7]

The type of organization structure that grew out of these efforts in the late nineteenth and early twentieth centuries was one in which the CEO was placed at the top and everyone else was arranged in layers down below, as illustrated in Exhibit 3.1. The thinking and decision making are done by those at the top, and the physical work is performed by employees who are organized into distinct, functional departments. This structure was quite effective and became entrenched in business, nonprofit, and military organizations for most of the twentieth century. However, this type of vertical structure is not always effective, particularly in rapidly changing environments. Over the years, organizations have developed other structural designs, many of them aimed at increasing horizontal coordination and communication and encouraging adaptation to external changes. This chapter's Book Mark argues that business is on the verge of a tremendous historic transformation, in which centralized hierarchical forms of organizing will give way to decentralized structures based on horizontal processes. In this chapter, we will examine five basic structural designs and show how they are reflected in the organization chart.

Information-Processing Perspective on Structure

The organization should be designed to provide both vertical and horizontal information flow as necessary to accomplish the organization's overall goals. If the structure doesn't fit the information requirements of the organization, people either will have too little information or will spend time processing information that is not vital to their tasks, thus reducing effectiveness.[8] However, there is an inherent tension between vertical and horizontal mechanisms in an organization. Whereas vertical linkages are designed primarily for control, horizontal linkages are designed for coordination and collaboration, which usually means reducing control.

Organizations can choose whether to orient toward a traditional organization designed for efficiency, which emphasizes vertical communication and control, or toward a contemporary learning organization, which emphasizes horizontal communication and coordination. Exhibit 3.2 compares organizations designed for efficiency with those designed for learning. An emphasis on efficiency and control is

Book Mark 3.0 (HAVE YOU READ THIS BOOK?)

The Future of Work: How the New Order of Business Will Shape Your Organization, Your Management Style, and Your Life
By Thomas W. Malone

Organizations are experiencing tremendous change, and Thomas W. Malone suggests in his book *The Future of Work* that they are on the verge of a fundamental shift that could be "as important to business as the shift to democracy has been for government." Rigid, highly centralized vertical hierarchies, he says, will essentially be a thing of the past as organizations move to flexible decentralized forms of organizing based on horizontal work processes. Command-and-control management and top-down decision making will give way to empowered teams of employees focused on specific workflows and processes, working across organizational boundaries and making their own decisions based on up-to-the-minute information.

THE BRAVE NEW WORLD OF WORK
Malone describes several decentralized management structures and provides numerous examples of organizations that are experimenting with new forms of organizing and innovative management techniques. Here are some of Malone's key points about the future of work:

- *Information technology is the key driver of the transformation*. The falling cost of communication is making the distribution of power away from the corporate suite both inevitable and desirable. Outsourcing information work to India, for example, is possible because digital communication with India is so cheap. In the same way, accessible information makes it possible for any lower-level employee to plan his or her work more effectively, network and get advice from people anywhere, and make good decisions based on accurate information.
- *Managers will move from command-and-control to coordinate-and-cultivate*. To coordinate is to organize work so that good things happen, whether managers are "in control" or not. To cultivate means to bring out

the best in employees with the right combination of control and freedom. W. L. Gore, the maker of Gore-Tex fabric, lets people decide what they want to do. Leaders emerge based on who has a good idea and can recruit people to work on it. AES, one of the world's largest electric power producers, coordinates and cultivates so well that it lets low-level workers make critical multimillion-dollar decisions about such things as acquiring new subsidiaries.
- *Every organization needs standards*. Many people think clear standards are incompatible with flexibility and decentralization. Malone points out, though, that when employees have guidelines and standards within which to make decisions and take action, they can do their jobs with greater freedom and authority. Consider eBay, which has more than 430,000 people who make their primary living as sellers on the site. EBay managers have no direct control over those 430,000 people, yet they've established clear standards and guidelines for trading that maintain order and accountability.

THE TRANSITION YEARS
Malone, a professor at MIT's Sloan School of Management, acknowledges that hierarchy and centralization continue to provide tremendous advantages for some companies in today's economy. In addition, for most organizations, centralized and decentralized structures and management systems will coexist well into the future. Yet, he is convinced that, ultimately, rigid hierarchical centralized structures will be consigned to the dustbin of history.

The Future of Work: How the New Order of Business Will Shape Your Organization, Your Management Style, and Your Life, by Thomas W. Malone, is published by Harvard Business School Press.

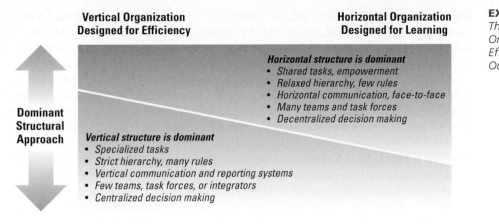

EXHIBIT 3.2
*The Relationship of
Organization Design to
Efficiency versus Learning
Outcomes*

associated with specialized tasks, a hierarchy of authority, rules and regulations, formal reporting systems, few teams or task forces, and **centralized** decision making, which means problems and decisions are funneled to top levels of the hierarchy for resolution. Emphasis on learning is associated with shared tasks, a relaxed hierarchy, few rules, face-to-face communication, many teams and task forces, and informal, **decentralized** decision making. Decentralized decision making means decision-making authority is pushed down to lower organizational levels. Organizations may have to experiment to find the correct degree of centralization or decentralization to meet their needs. For example, a recent study found that three large school districts that shifted to a more flexible, decentralized structure performed better and more efficiently than large districts that were highly centralized.[9] On the other hand, decentralized companies such as Dow Chemical and Procter & Gamble have found a need in recent years to build in more centralized communication and control systems to keep these huge, global corporations functioning efficiently. Thus, managers are always searching for the best combination of vertical control and horizontal collaboration, centralization and decentralization, for their own situations.[10]

■ Vertical Information Linkages

Organization design should facilitate the communication among employees and departments that is necessary to accomplish the organization's overall task. *Linkage* is defined as the extent of communication and coordination among organizational elements. **Vertical linkages** are used to coordinate activities between the top and bottom of an organization and are designed primarily for control of the organization. Employees at lower levels should carry out activities consistent with top-level goals, and top executives must be informed of activities and accomplishments at the lower levels. Organizations may use any of a variety of structural devices to achieve vertical linkage, including hierarchical referral, rules, plans, and formal management information systems.[11]

Hierarchical Referral. The first vertical device is the hierarchy, or chain of command, which is illustrated by the vertical lines in Exhibit 3.1. If a problem arises that employees don't know how to solve, it can be referred up to the next level in the hierarchy. When the problem is solved, the answer is passed back down to lower levels. The lines of the organization chart act as communication channels.

Rules and Plans. The next linkage device is the use of rules and plans. To the extent that problems and decisions are repetitious, a rule or procedure can be established so employees know how to respond without communicating directly with their manager. Rules provide a standard information source enabling employees to be coordinated without actually communicating about every task. A plan also provides standing information for employees. The most widely used plan is the budget. With carefully designed budget plans, employees at lower levels can be left on their own to perform activities within their resource allotment.

Vertical Information Systems. A **vertical information system** is another strategy for increasing vertical information capacity. Vertical information systems include the periodic reports, written information, and computer-based communications distributed to managers. Information systems make communication up and down the hierarchy more efficient. Vertical information systems are an important component of vertical control at software-maker Oracle.

In Practice

Oracle Corporation

In an era of decentralization and empowerment, Larry Ellison, CEO of Oracle, doesn't hesitate to proclaim his belief in stronger vertical control. Oracle got in trouble some years ago because sales managers around the globe were cutting backroom deals or hammering out private, individualized compensation agreements with salespeople in different countries. Today, all the terms, including sales contracts and commissions, are dictated from the top and spelled out in a global database. In addition, Ellison requires that all deals be entered into the database so they can easily be tracked by top managers.

The Internet plays a key part in Ellison's vertical information and control systems, by offering the power to centralize complex operations while also rapidly disseminating information all over the world. Oracle uses its own suite of Internet software applications that work together on a global basis. All employees do their work via the Internet, enabling Ellison to carefully track, analyze, and control the behavior of each unit, manager, and employee. Although many managers weren't happy with the stronger top-down control, Ellison believed it was necessary to effectively manage a sprawling global corporation that was beginning to behave more like a bunch of separate companies. In addition, the system helps to circulate and ensure implementation of standard rules and procedures across divisions. According to Chief Marketing Officer Mark Jarvis, this ultimately provides for greater freedom for lower levels and prevents the hierarchy from becoming overloaded. "Once we have a standard set of global business practices," Jarvis notes, "the [managers] can be allowed more scope for decision making within the broad framework."

Oracle's recent acquisition of PeopleSoft has increased the complexity of the organization, but Ellison and other top managers are focused on smooth integration through the use of vertical information systems. The company is working on developing a super-suite of software applications that combines the best features of products from Oracle, PeopleSoft, and J.D. Edwards and will allow for standardization and centralization across the enterprise. The new super-suite, dubbed Project Fusion, will allow Oracle as well as its customers to automate an entire global infrastructure so that everything is linked and compatible and managers can get the information they need to effectively control the organization.[12]

In today's world of corporate financial scandals and ethical concerns, many top managers, like Larry Ellison, are considering strengthening their organization's linkages for vertical information and control. The other major issue in organizing is to provide adequate horizontal linkages for coordination and collaboration.

Horizontal Information Linkages

Horizontal communication overcomes barriers between departments and provides opportunities for coordination among employees to achieve unity of effort and organizational objectives. **Horizontal linkage** refers to the amount of communication and coordination horizontally across organizational departments. Its importance is articulated by comments made by Lee Iacocca when he took over Chrysler Corporation in the 1980s.

What I found at Chrysler were thirty-five vice presidents, each with his own turf . . . I couldn't believe, for example, that the guy running engineering departments wasn't in constant touch with his counterpart in manufacturing. But that's how it was. Everybody worked independently. I took one look at that system and I almost threw up. That's when I knew I was in really deep trouble . . . Nobody at Chrysler seemed to understand that interaction among the different functions in a company is absolutely critical. People in engineering and manufacturing almost have to be sleeping together. These guys weren't even flirting![13]

During his tenure at Chrysler (now DaimlerChrysler), Iacocca pushed horizontal coordination to a high level. Everyone working on a specific vehicle project—designers, engineers, and manufacturers, as well as representatives from marketing, finance, purchasing, and even outside suppliers—worked together on a single floor so they could constantly communicate.

Horizontal linkage mechanisms often are not drawn on the organization chart, but nevertheless are part of organization structure. The following devices are structural alternatives that can improve horizontal coordination and information flow.[14] Each device enables people to exchange information.

Information Systems. A significant method of providing horizontal linkage in today's organizations is the use of cross-functional information systems. Computerized information systems can enable managers or frontline workers throughout the organization to routinely exchange information about problems, opportunities, activities, or decisions. For example, Siemens uses an organization-wide information system that enables 450,000 employees around the world to share knowledge and collaborate on projects to provide better solutions to customers. The information and communications division recently collaborated with the medical division to develop new products for the healthcare market.[15]

Some organizations also encourage employees to use the company's information systems to build relationships all across the organization, aiming to support and enhance ongoing horizontal coordination across projects and geographical boundaries. CARE International, one of the world's largest private international relief organizations, enhanced its personnel database to make it easy for people to find others with congruent interests, concerns, or needs. Each person in the database has listed past and current responsibilities, experience, language abilities, knowledge of foreign countries, emergency experiences, skills and competencies, and outside interests. The database makes it easy for employees working across borders to seek each other out, share ideas and information, and build enduring horizontal connections.[16]

Briefcase

As an organization manager, keep these guidelines in mind:

Provide vertical and horizontal information linkages to integrate diverse departments into a coherent whole. Achieve vertical linkage through hierarchy referral, rules and plans, and vertical information systems. Achieve horizontal linkage through cross-functional information systems, direct contact, task forces, full-time integrators, and teams.

Direct Contact. A higher level of horizontal linkage is direct contact between managers or employees affected by a problem. One way to promote direct contact is to create a special **liaison role**. A liaison person is located in one department but has the responsibility for communicating and achieving coordination with another department. Liaison roles often exist between engineering and manufacturing departments because engineering has to develop and test products to fit the limitations of manufacturing facilities. At Johnson & Johnson, CEO William C. Weldon has set up a committee made up of managers from research and development (R&D) and sales and marketing. The direct contact between managers in these two departments enables the company to set priorities for which new drugs to pursue and market. Weldon also created a new position to oversee R&D, with an express charge to increase coordination with sales and marketing executives.[17] Another approach is to locate people close together so they will have direct contact on a regular basis.

Task Forces. Liaison roles usually link only two departments. When linkage involves several departments, a more complex device such as a task force is required. A **task force** is a temporary committee composed of representatives from each organizational unit affected by a problem.[18] Each member represents the interest of a department or division and can carry information from the meeting back to that department.

Task forces are an effective horizontal linkage device for temporary issues. They solve problems by direct horizontal coordination and reduce the information load on the vertical hierarchy. Typically, they are disbanded after their tasks are accomplished.

Organizations have used task forces for everything from organizing the annual company picnic to solving expensive and complex manufacturing problems. One example is the Executive Automotive Committee formed by DaimlerChrysler CEO Jürgen Schrempp. This task force was set up specifically to identify ideas for increasing cooperation and component sharing among Chrysler, Mercedes, and Mitsubishi (in which DaimlerChrysler owns a 37 percent stake). The task force started with a product road map, showing all Mercedes, Chrysler, Dodge, Jeep, and Mitsubishi vehicles to be launched over a 10-year period, along with an analysis of the components they would use, so task force members could identify overlap and find ways to share parts and cut time and costs.[19]

Full-time Integrator. A stronger horizontal linkage device is to create a full-time position or department solely for the purpose of coordination. A full-time **integrator** frequently has a title, such as product manager, project manager, program manager, or brand manager. Unlike the liaison person described earlier, the integrator does not report to one of the functional departments being coordinated. He or she is located outside the departments and has the responsibility for coordinating several departments.

The brand manager for Planters Peanuts, for example, coordinates the sales, distribution, and advertising for that product. General Motors set up brand managers who are responsible for marketing and sales strategies for each of GM's new models.[20]

The integrator can also be responsible for an innovation or change project, such as coordinating the design, financing, and marketing of a new product. An organization chart that illustrates the location of project managers for new product development is shown in Exhibit 3.3. The project managers are drawn to the side to

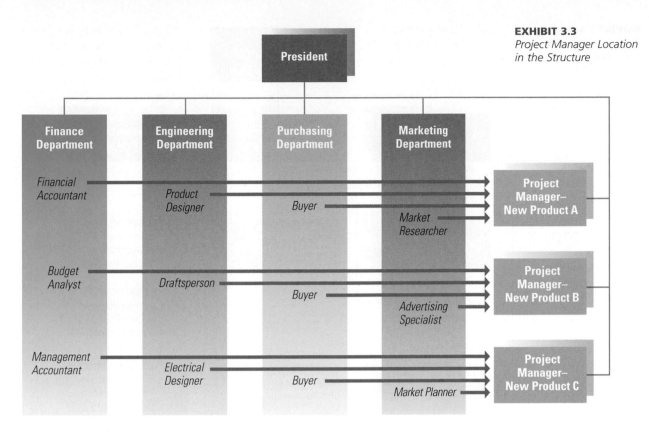

EXHIBIT 3.3
*Project Manager Location
in the Structure*

indicate their separation from other departments. The arrows indicate project members assigned to the new product development. New Product A, for example, has a financial accountant assigned to keep track of costs and budgets. The engineering member provides design advice, and purchasing and manufacturing members represent their areas. The project manager is responsible for the entire project. He or she sees that the new product is completed on time, is introduced to the market, and achieves other project goals. The horizontal lines in Exhibit 3.3 indicate that project managers do not have formal authority over team members with respect to giving pay raises, hiring, or firing. Formal authority rests with the managers of the functional departments, who have formal authority over subordinates.

Integrators need excellent people skills. Integrators in most companies have a lot of responsibility but little authority. The integrator has to use expertise and persuasion to achieve coordination. He or she spans the boundary between departments and must be able to get people together, maintain their trust, confront problems, and resolve conflicts and disputes in the interest of the organization.[21]

Teams. Project teams tend to be the strongest horizontal linkage mechanism. **Teams** are permanent task forces and are often used in conjunction with a full-time integrator. When activities among departments require strong coordination over a long period of time, a cross-functional team is often the solution. Special project teams may be used when organizations have a large-scale project, a major innovation, or a new product line.

EXHIBIT 3.4
*Teams Used for Horizontal
Coordination at Wizard
Software Company*

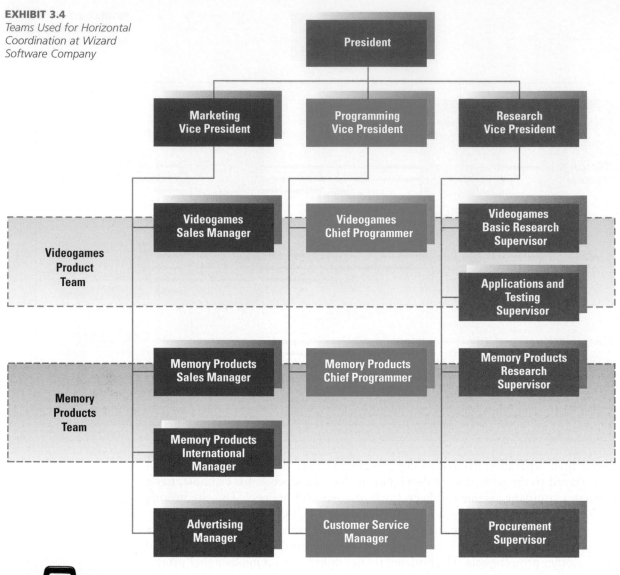

Imagination Ltd., Britain's largest design firm, is based entirely on teamwork. At the beginning of each project, Imagination puts together a team of designers, writers, artists, marketing experts, information specialists, and representatives of other functional areas to carry out the entire project from beginning to end. Hewlett-Packard's Medical Products Group uses *virtual cross-functional teams*, made up of members from various countries, to develop and market medical products and services such as electrocardiograph systems, ultrasound imaging technologies, and patient monitoring systems.[22] A **virtual team** is one that is made up of organizationally or geographically dispersed members who are linked primarily through advanced information and communications technologies. Members frequently use the Internet and collaborative software to work together, rather than meeting face to face.[23]

An illustration of how teams provide strong horizontal coordination is shown in Exhibit 3.4. Wizard Software Company develops and markets software for various

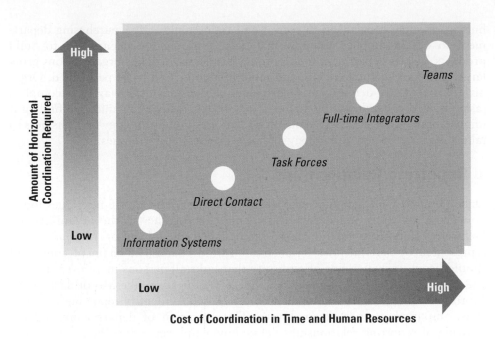

EXHIBIT 3.5
Ladder of Mechanisms for Horizontal Linkage and Coordination

applications, from videogames to financial services. Wizard uses teams to coordinate each product line across the research, programming, and marketing departments, as illustrated by the dashed lines and shaded areas in the exhibit. Members from each team meet at the beginning of each day as needed to resolve problems concerning customer needs, backlogs, programming changes, scheduling conflicts, and any other problem with the product line. The opening example of Ford Motor Company provides another good illustration of the use of teams for horizontal coordination.

Exhibit 3.5 summarizes the mechanisms for achieving horizontal linkages. These devices represent alternatives that managers can select to increase horizontal coordination in any organization. The higher-level devices provide more horizontal information capacity, although the cost to the organization in terms of time and human resources is greater. If horizontal communication is insufficient, departments will find themselves out of synchronization and will not contribute to the overall goals of the organization. When the amount of horizontal coordination required is high, managers should select higher-level mechanisms.

Organization Design Alternatives

The overall design of organization structure indicates three things—required work activities, reporting relationships, and departmental groupings.

Required Work Activities

Departments are created to perform tasks considered strategically important to the company. For example, in a typical manufacturing company, work activities fall into a range of functions that help the organization accomplish its goals, such as a human resource department to recruit and train employees, a purchasing department to obtain supplies and raw materials, a production department to build products, a sales department to sell products, and so forth. As organizations grow larger and more complex, more and more functions need to be performed. Organizations typically define new departments or divisions as a way to accomplish tasks deemed valuable by the organization. Today, many companies are finding it important to establish departments such as information technology or e-business to take advantage of new technology and new business opportunities.

■ Reporting Relationships

Once required work activities and departments are defined, the next question is how these activities and departments should fit together in the organizational hierarchy. Reporting relationships, often called the *chain of command*, are represented by vertical lines on an organization chart. The chain of command should be an unbroken line of authority that links all persons in an organization and shows who reports to whom. In a large organization like Motorola or Ford Motor Company, 100 or more charts are required to identify reporting relationships among thousands of employees. The definition of departments and the drawing of reporting relationships define how employees are to be grouped into departments.

■ Departmental Grouping Options

Options for departmental grouping, including functional grouping, divisional grouping, multifocused grouping, horizontal grouping, and virtual network grouping, are illustrated in Exhibit 3.6. **Departmental grouping** affects employees because they share a common supervisor and common resources, are jointly responsible for performance, and tend to identify and collaborate with one another.[24] For example, at Albany Ladder Company, the credit manager was shifted from the finance department to the marketing department. As a member of the marketing department, the credit manager started working with salespeople to increase sales, thus becoming more liberal with credit than when he was located in the finance department.

Functional grouping places together employees who perform similar functions or work processes or who bring similar knowledge and skills to bear. For example, all marketing people work together under the same supervisor, as do manufacturing and engineering people. All people associated with the assembly process for generators are grouped together in one department. All chemists may be grouped in a department different from biologists because they represent different disciplines.

Divisional grouping means people are organized according to what the organization produces. All people required to produce toothpaste—including personnel in marketing, manufacturing, and sales—are grouped together under one executive. In huge corporations such as EDS, some product or service lines may represent independent businesses, such as A. T. Kearney (management consulting) and Wendover Financial Services.

Multifocused grouping means an organization embraces two structural grouping alternatives simultaneously. These structural forms are often called *matrix* or *hybrid*. They will be discussed in more detail later in this chapter. An organization may need to group by function and product division simultaneously or perhaps by product division and geography.

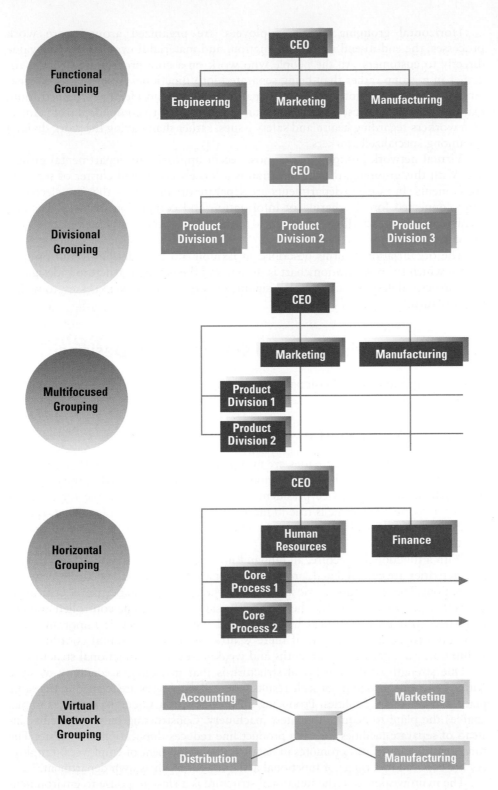

EXHIBIT 3.6
Structural Design Options for Grouping Employees into Departments
Source: Adapted from David Nadler and Michael Tushman, *Strategic Organization Design* (Glenview, Ill.: Scott Foresman, 1988), 68.

Horizontal grouping means employees are organized around core work processes, the end-to-end work, information, and material flows that provide value directly to customers. All the people who work on a core process are brought together in a group rather than being separated into functional departments. For example, at field offices of the U.S. Occupational Safety and Health Administration, teams of workers representing various functions respond to complaints from American workers regarding health and safety issues, rather than having the work divided up among specialized workers.[25]

Virtual network grouping is the most recent approach to departmental grouping. With this grouping, the organization is a loosely connected cluster of separate components. In essence, departments are separate organizations that are electronically connected for the sharing of information and completion of tasks. Departments can be spread all over the world rather than located together in one geographical location.

The organizational forms described in Exhibit 3.6 provide the overall options within which the organization chart is drawn and the detailed structure is designed. Each structural design alternative has significant strengths and weaknesses, to which we now turn.

Functional, Divisional, and Geographical Designs

Functional grouping and divisional grouping are the two most common approaches to structural design.

Functional Structure

In a **functional structure**, activities are grouped together by common function from the bottom to the top of the organization. All engineers are located in the engineering department, and the vice president of engineering is responsible for all engineering activities. The same is true in marketing, R&D, and manufacturing. An example of the functional organization structure was shown in Exhibit 3.1 earlier in this chapter.

With a functional structure, all human knowledge and skills with respect to specific activities are consolidated, providing a valuable depth of knowledge for the organization. This structure is most effective when in-depth expertise is critical to meeting organizational goals, when the organization needs to be controlled and coordinated through the vertical hierarchy, and when efficiency is important. The structure can be quite effective if there is little need for horizontal coordination. Exhibit 3.7 summarizes the strengths and weaknesses of the functional structure.

One strength of the functional structure is that it promotes economy of scale within functions. Economy of scale results when all employees are located in the same place and can share facilities. Producing all products in a single plant, for example, enables the plant to acquire the latest machinery. Constructing only one facility instead of separate facilities for each product line reduces duplication and waste. The functional structure also promotes in-depth skill development of employees. Employees are exposed to a range of functional activities within their own department.[26]

The main weakness of the functional structure is a slow response to environmental changes that require coordination across departments. The vertical hierarchy becomes overloaded. Decisions pile up, and top managers do not respond fast enough.

Strengths	Weaknesses
1. Allows economies of scale within functional departments	1. Slow response time to environmental changes
2. Enables in-depth knowledge and skill development	2. May cause decisions to pile on top, hierarchy overload
3. Enables organization to accomplish functional goals	3. Leads to poor horizontal coordination among departments
4. Is best with only one or a few products	4. Results in less innovation
	5. Involves restricted view of organizational goals

EXHIBIT 3.7
Strengths and Weaknesses of Functional Organization Structure

Source: Adapted from Robert Duncan, "What Is the Right Organization Structure? Decision Tree Analysis Provides the Answer," *Organizational Dynamics* (Winter 1979), 429.

Other disadvantages of the functional structure are that innovation is slow because of poor coordination, and each employee has a restricted view of overall goals.

Some organizations perform very effectively with a functional structure. Consider the case of Blue Bell Creameries.

In Practice

Blue Bell Creameries, Inc.

It's the third best-selling brand of ice cream in the United States and is regularly served to foreign dignitaries visiting President George W. Bush. A standing order is delivered to Camp David every 2 weeks. Yet many Americans have never heard of it. That's because Blue Bell Creameries, with headquarters in Brenham, Texas, sells its ice cream in only fourteen, mostly southern, states. "That allows us to focus on making and selling ice cream," says CEO Paul Kruse, the fourth generation of Kruses to run Blue Bell.

The "little creamery in Brenham," as the company markets itself, doesn't let anyone outside the company touch its product from the plant to the freezer case. Everything from R&D to distribution is handled in-house. The company cannot meet the demand for its ice cream, and it doesn't even try. Blue Bell commands 60 percent of the ice cream market in Texas and Louisiana and 47 percent in Alabama, where it opened a plant in 1997. People outside the region often pay $85 to have four half-gallons packed in dry ice and shipped to them. Despite the demand, management refuses to compromise quality by expanding into regions that cannot be satisfactorily serviced or by growing so fast that it can't adequately train employees in the art of making ice cream.

Blue Bell's major departments are sales, quality control, production, maintenance, and distribution. There is also an accounting department and a small R&D group. Most employees have been with the company for years and have a wealth of experience in making quality ice cream. The environment is stable. The customer base is well established. The only change has been the increase in demand for Blue Bell Ice Cream.

Blue Bell's quality-control department tests all incoming ingredients and ensures that only the best products go into its ice cream. Quality control also tests outgoing ice cream products. After years of experience, quality inspectors can taste the slightest deviation from expected quality. Blue Bell owns its own trucks to make sure the product is handled correctly once it leaves the plant. "If you don't clearly watch the temperature," Chairman Howard Kruse explains, "the taste can suffer." It's no wonder Blue Bell has successfully maintained the image of a small-town creamery making homemade ice cream.[27]

The functional structure is just right for Blue Bell Creameries. The organization has chosen to stay medium-sized and focus on making a single product—quality ice cream. However, as Blue Bell expands, it may have problems coordinating across departments, requiring stronger horizontal linkage mechanisms.

■ Functional Structure with Horizontal Linkages

Today, there is a shift toward flatter, more horizontal structures because of the challenges introduced in Chapter 1. Very few of today's successful companies can maintain a strictly functional structure. Organizations compensate for the vertical functional hierarchy by installing horizontal linkages, as described earlier in this chapter. Managers improve horizontal coordination by using information systems, direct contact between departments, full-time integrators or project managers (illustrated in Exhibit 3.3), task forces, or teams (illustrated in Exhibit 3.4). One interesting use of horizontal linkages occurred at Karolinska Hospital in Stockholm, Sweden, which had forty-seven functional departments. Even after top executives cut that down to eleven, coordination was still woefully inadequate. The team set about reorganizing workflow at the hospital around patient care. Instead of bouncing a patient from department to department, Karolinska now envisions the illness to recovery period as a process with "pit stops" in admissions, X-ray, surgery, and so forth. The most interesting aspect of the approach is the new position of nurse coordinator. Nurse coordinators serve as full-time integrators, troubleshooting transitions within or between departments. The improved horizontal coordination dramatically improved productivity and patient care at Karolinska.[28] Karolinska is effectively using horizontal linkages to overcome some of the disadvantages of the functional structure.

■ Divisional Structure

Briefcase

As an organization manager, keep these guidelines in mind:

When designing overall organization structure, choose a functional structure when efficiency is important, when in-depth knowledge and expertise are critical to meeting organizational goals, and when the organization needs to be controlled and coordinated through the vertical hierarchy. Use a divisional structure in a large organization with multiple product lines and when you wish to give priority to product goals and coordination across functions.

The term **divisional structure** is used here as the generic term for what is sometimes called a *product structure* or *strategic business units*. With this structure, divisions can be organized according to individual products, services, product groups, major projects or programs, divisions, businesses, or profit centers. The distinctive feature of a divisional structure is that grouping is based on organizational outputs.

The difference between a divisional structure and a functional structure is illustrated in Exhibit 3.8. The functional structure can be redesigned into separate product groups, and each group contains the functional departments of R&D, manufacturing, accounting, and marketing. Coordination across functional departments within each product group is maximized. The divisional structure promotes flexibility and change because each unit is smaller and can adapt to the needs of its environment. Moreover, the divisional structure *decentralizes* decision making, because the lines of authority converge at a lower level in the hierarchy. The functional structure, by contrast, is *centralized*, because it forces decisions all the way to the top before a problem affecting several functions can be resolved.

Strengths and weaknesses of the divisional structure are summarized in Exhibit 3.9. The divisional organization structure is excellent for achieving coordination across functional departments. It works well when organizations can no longer be adequately controlled through the traditional vertical hierarchy, and when goals are oriented toward adaptation and change. Giant, complex organizations such as General Electric, Nestlé, and Johnson & Johnson are subdivided

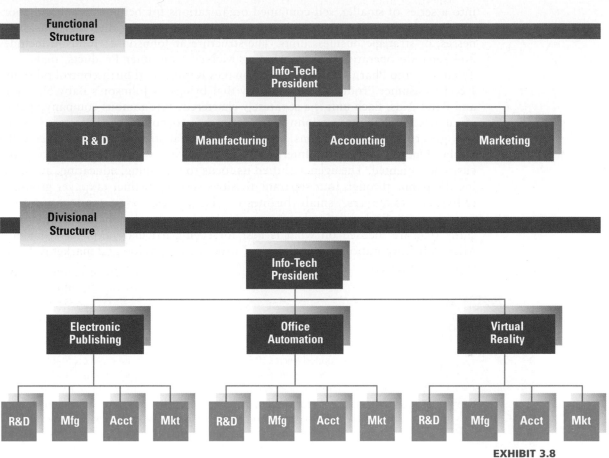

EXHIBIT 3.8
Reorganization from Functional Structure to Divisional Structure at Info-Tech

EXHIBIT 3.9
Strengths and Weaknesses of Divisional Organization Structure

Strengths	Weaknesses
1. Suited to fast change in unstable environment 2. Leads to customer satisfaction because product responsibility and contact points are clear 3. Involves high coordination across functions 4. Allows units to adapt to differences in products, regions, customers 5. Best in large organizations with several products 6. Decentralizes decision making	1. Eliminates economies of scale in functional departments 2. Leads to poor coordination across product lines 3. Eliminates in-depth competence and technical specialization 4. Makes integration and standardization across product lines difficult

Source: Adapted from Robert Duncan, "What Is the Right Organization Structure? Decision Tree Analysis Provides the Answer," *Organization Dynamics* (Winter 1979), 431.

into a series of smaller, self-contained organizations for better control and coordination. In these large companies, the units are sometimes called divisions, businesses, or strategic business units. The structure at Johnson & Johnson includes 204 separate operating units, including McNeil Consumer Products, makers of Tylenol; Ortho Pharmaceuticals, which makes Retin-A and birth-control pills; and J & J Consumer Products, the company that brings us Johnson's Baby Shampoo and Band-Aids. Each unit is a separately chartered, autonomous company operating under the guidance of Johnson & Johnson's corporate headquarters.[29] Some U.S. government organizations also use a divisional structure to better serve the public. One example is the Internal Revenue Service, which wanted to be more customer oriented. The agency shifted its focus to informing, educating, and serving the public through four separate divisions serving distinct taxpayer groups—individual taxpayers, small businesses, large businesses, and tax-exempt organizations. Each division has its own budget, personnel, policies, and planning staffs that are focused on what is best for each particular taxpayer segment.[30] Microsoft Corporation uses a divisional structure to develop and market different software products.

In Practice

Microsoft

Bill Gates co-founded Microsoft in 1975 and built it into the most profitable technology company in the world. But as the company grew larger, the functional structure became ineffective. Employees began complaining about the growing bureaucracy and the snail's pace for decision making. A functional structure was just too slow and inflexible for a large organization operating in the fast-moving technology industry.

To speed things up and better respond to environmental changes, top executives created seven business units based on Microsoft's major products: Windows Group; Server Software Group; Mobile Software Group; Office Software Group; Video Games and XBox Group; Business Software Group; and MSN-Internet Group. Each division is run by a general manager and contains most of the functions of a stand-alone company, including product development, sales, marketing, and finance.

What really makes the new structure revolutionary for Microsoft is that the heads of the seven divisions are given the freedom and authority to run the businesses and spend their budgets as they see fit to meet goals. The general managers and chief financial officers for each division set their own budgets and manage their own profit and loss statements. Previously, the two top executives, Bill Gates and Steven Ballmer, were involved in practically every decision, large and small. Managers of the divisions are charged up by the new authority and responsibility. One manager said he feels "like I am running my own little company."[31]

The divisional structure has several strengths that are of benefit to Microsoft.[32] This structure is suited to fast change in an unstable environment and provides high product or service visibility. Since each product line has its own separate division, customers are able to contact the correct division and achieve satisfaction. Coordination across functions is excellent. Each product can adapt to requirements of individual customers or regions. The divisional structure typically works best in organizations that have multiple products or services and enough personnel to staff separate functional units. At corporations like Johnson & Johnson, PepsiCo, and Microsoft, decision making is pushed down to the lowest levels. Each division is small enough to be quick on its feet, responding rapidly to changes in the market.

One disadvantage of using divisional structuring is that the organization loses economies of scale. Instead of fifty research engineers sharing a common facility in a functional structure, ten engineers may be assigned to each of five product divisions. The critical mass required for in-depth research is lost, and physical facilities have to be duplicated for each product line. Another problem is that product lines become separate from each other, and coordination across product lines can be difficult. As one Johnson & Johnson executive said, "We have to keep reminding ourselves that we work for the same corporation."[33] There is some concern at Microsoft that the newly independent divisions might start offering products and services that conflict with one another.

Companies such as Xerox, Hewlett-Packard, and Sony have a large number of divisions and have had real problems with horizontal coordination. Sony is way behind in the business of digital media products partly because of poor coordination. Apple's iPod quickly captured 60 percent of the U.S. market versus 10 percent for Sony. The digital music business depends on seamless coordination. Currently, Sony's Walkman doesn't even recognize some of the music sets that can be made with the company's SonicStage software, and thus doesn't mesh well with the division selling music downloads. Sony has set up a new company, called Connect Co., specifically to coordinate among the different units for the development of digital media businesses.[34] Unless effective horizontal mechanisms are in place, a divisional structure can cause real problems. One division may produce products or programs that are incompatible with products sold by another division. Customers are frustrated when a sales representative from one division is unaware of developments in other divisions. Task forces and other linkage devices are needed to coordinate across divisions. A lack of technical specialization is also a problem in a divisional structure. Employees identify with the product line rather than with a functional specialty. R&D personnel, for example, tend to do applied research to benefit the product line rather than basic research to benefit the entire organization.

Geographical Structure

Another basis for structural grouping is the organization's users or customers. The most common structure in this category is geography. Each region of the country may have distinct tastes and needs. Each geographic unit includes all functions required to produce and market products or services in that region. Large nonprofit organizations such as the Girl Scouts of the USA, Habitat for Humanity, Make-a-Wish Foundation, and the United Way of America frequently use a type of geographical structure, with a central headquarters and semi-autonomous local units. The national organization provides brand recognition, coordinates fund-raising services, and handles some shared administrative functions, while day-to-day control and decision making is decentralized to local or regional units.[35]

For multinational corporations, self-contained units are created for different countries and parts of the world. Some years ago, Apple Computer reorganized from a functional to a geographical structure to facilitate manufacture and delivery of Apple computers to customers around the world. Exhibit 3.10 contains a partial organization structure illustrating the geographical thrust. Apple used this structure to focus managers and employees on specific geographical customers and sales targets. McDonald's divided its U.S. operations into five geographical divisions, each with its own president and staff functions such as human resources and legal.[36] The regional structure allows Apple and McDonald's to focus on the needs of customers in a geographical area.

EXHIBIT 3.10
Geographical Structure for Apple Computer
Source: Apple Computer, Inc. regions of the world, *http://www.apple.com/find/areas.htm*, April 18, 2000.

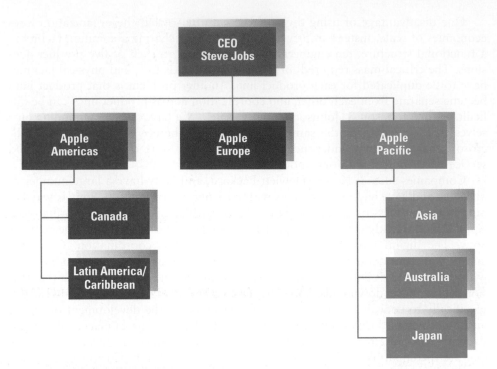

The strengths and weaknesses of a geographic divisional structure are similar to the divisional organization characteristics listed in Exhibit 3.9. The organization can adapt to specific needs of its own region, and employees identify with regional goals rather than with national goals. Horizontal coordination within a region is emphasized rather than linkages across regions or to the national office.

Matrix Structure

Sometimes, an organization's structure needs to be multifocused in that both product and function or product and geography are emphasized at the same time. One way to achieve this is through the **matrix structure**. The matrix can be used when both technical expertise and product innovation and change are important for meeting organizational goals. The matrix structure often is the answer when organizations find that the functional, divisional, and geographical structures combined with horizontal linkage mechanisms will not work.

The matrix is a strong form of horizontal linkage. The unique characteristic of the matrix organization is that both product division and functional structures (horizontal and vertical) are implemented simultaneously, as shown in Exhibit 3.11. The product managers and functional managers have equal authority within the organization, and employees report to both of them. The matrix structure is similar to the use of full-time integrators or product managers described earlier in this chapter (Exhibit 3.3), except that in the matrix structure the product managers (horizontal) are given formal authority equal to that of the functional managers (vertical).

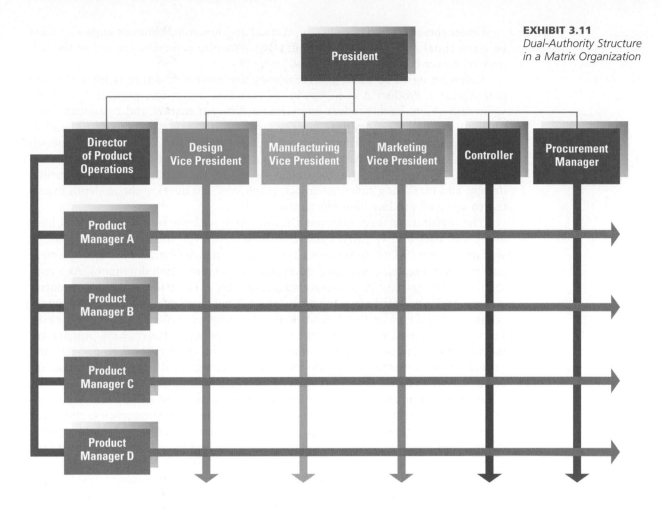

EXHIBIT 3.11
Dual-Authority Structure in a Matrix Organization

◼ Conditions for the Matrix

A dual hierarchy may seem an unusual way to design an organization, but the matrix is the correct structure when the following conditions are met:[37]

- *Condition 1.* Pressure exists to share scarce resources across product lines. The organization is typically medium sized and has a moderate number of product lines. It feels pressure for the shared and flexible use of people and equipment across those products. For example, the organization is not large enough to assign engineers full-time to each product line, so engineers are assigned part-time to several products or projects.
- *Condition 2.* Environmental pressure exists for two or more critical outputs, such as for in-depth technical knowledge (functional structure) and frequent new products (divisional structure). This dual pressure means a balance of power is needed between the functional and product sides of the organization, and a dual-authority structure is needed to maintain that balance.
- *Condition 3.* The environmental domain of the organization is both complex and uncertain. Frequent external changes and high interdependence between departments require a large amount of coordination and information processing in both vertical and horizontal directions.

Under these three conditions, the vertical and horizontal lines of authority must be given equal recognition. A dual-authority structure is thereby created so the balance of power between them is equal.

Referring again to Exhibit 3.11, assume the matrix structure is for a clothing manufacturer. Product A is footwear, product B is outerwear, product C is sleepwear, and so on. Each product line serves a different market and customers. As a medium-size organization, the company must effectively use people from manufacturing, design, and marketing to work on each product line. There are not enough designers to warrant a separate design department for each product line, so the designers are shared across product lines. Moreover, by keeping the manufacturing, design, and marketing functions intact, employees can develop the in-depth expertise to serve all product lines efficiently.

The matrix formalizes horizontal teams along with the traditional vertical hierarchy and tries to give equal balance to both. However, the matrix may shift one way or the other. Many companies have found a balanced matrix hard to implement and maintain because one side of the authority structure often dominates. As a consequence, two variations of matrix structure have evolved—the **functional matrix** and the **product matrix**. In a functional matrix, the functional bosses have primary authority and the project or product managers simply coordinate product activities. In a product matrix, by contrast, the project or product managers have primary authority and functional managers simply assign technical personnel to projects and provide advisory expertise as needed. For many organizations, one of these approaches works better than the balanced matrix with dual lines of authority.[38]

All kinds of organizations have experimented with the matrix, including hospitals, consulting firms, banks, insurance companies, government agencies, and many types of industrial firms.[39] This structure has been used successfully by large, global organizations such as Procter & Gamble, Unilever, and Dow Chemical, which fine-tuned the matrix to suit their own particular goals and culture. General Motors began shifting toward a matrix structure in the company's Information Systems and Services unit. Managers believed the matrix could lead to better, more creative decision making because it requires integrating differing viewpoints.[40]

■ Strengths and Weaknesses

The matrix structure is best when environmental change is high and when goals reflect a dual requirement, such as for both product and functional goals. The dual-authority structure facilitates communication and coordination to cope with rapid environmental change and enables an equal balance between product and functional bosses. The matrix facilitates discussion and adaptation to unexpected problems. It tends to work best in organizations of moderate size with a few product lines. The matrix is not needed for only a single product line, and too many product lines make it difficult to coordinate both directions at once. Exhibit 3.12 summarizes the strengths and weaknesses of the matrix structure based on what we know of organizations that use it.[41]

The strength of the matrix is that it enables an organization to meet dual demands from customers in the environment. Resources (people, equipment) can be flexibly allocated across different products, and the organization can adapt to changing external requirements.[42] This structure also provides an opportunity for employees to acquire either functional or general management skills, depending on their interests.

Briefcase

As an organization manager, keep these guidelines in mind:

Consider a matrix structure when the organization needs to give equal priority to both products and functions because of dual pressures from customers in the environment. Use either a functional matrix or a product matrix if the balanced matrix with dual lines of authority is not appropriate for your organization.

Strengths	Weaknesses
1. Achieves coordination necessary to meet dual demands from customers 2. Flexible sharing of human resources across products 3. Suited to complex decisions and frequent changes in unstable environment 4. Provides opportunity for both functional and product skill development 5. Best in medium-sized organizations with multiple products	1. Causes participants to experience dual authority, which can be frustrating and confusing 2. Means participants need good interpersonal skills and extensive training 3. Is time consuming; involves frequent meetings and conflict resolution sessions 4. Will not work unless participants understand it and adopt collegial rather than vertical type relationships 5. Requires great effort to maintain power balance

EXHIBIT 3.12
Strengths and Weaknesses of Matrix Organization Structure

Source: Adapted from Robert Duncan, "What Is the Right Organization Structure? Decision Tree Analysis Provides the Answer," *Organizational Dynamics* (Winter 1979), 429.

One disadvantage of the matrix is that some employees experience dual authority, reporting to two bosses and sometimes juggling conflicting demands. This can be frustrating and confusing, especially if roles and responsibilities are not clearly defined by top managers.[43] Employees working in a matrix need excellent interpersonal and conflict-resolution skills, which may require special training in human relations. The matrix also forces managers to spend a great deal of time in meetings.[44] If managers do not adapt to the information and power sharing required by the matrix, the system will not work. Managers must collaborate with one another rather than rely on vertical authority in decision making. The successful implementation of one matrix structure occurred at a steel company in Great Britain.

As far back as anyone could remember, the steel industry in England was stable and certain. Then in the 1980s and 1990s, excess European steel capacity, an economic downturn, the emergence of the mini mill electric arc furnace, and competition from steelmakers in Germany and Japan forever changed the English steel industry. By the turn of the century, traditional steel mills in the United States, such as Bethlehem Steel Corp. and LTV Corp., were facing bankruptcy. Mittal Steel in Asia and Europe's leading steelmaker, Arcelor, started acquiring steel companies to become world steel titans. The survival hope of small traditional steel manufacturers was to sell specialized products. A small company could market specialty products aggressively and quickly adapt to customer needs. Complex process settings and operating conditions had to be rapidly changed for each customer's order—a difficult feat for the titans.

Englander Steel employed 2,900 people, made 400,000 tons of steel a year (about 1 percent of Arcelor's output), and was 180 years old. For 160 of those years, a functional structure worked fine. As the environment became more turbulent and competitive, however, Englander Steel managers realized they were not keeping up. Fifty percent of Englander's orders were behind schedule. Profits were eroded by labor, material, and energy cost increases. Market share declined.

In Practice

Englander Steel

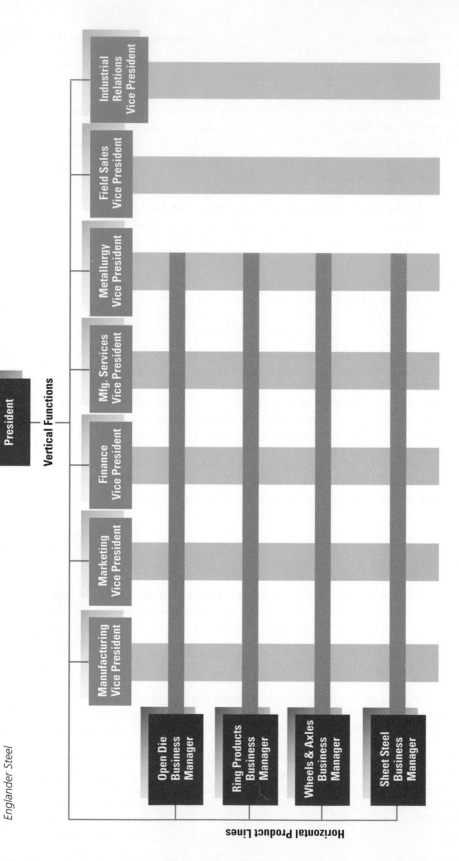

EXHIBIT 3.13
Matrix Structure for Englander Steel

In consultation with outside experts, the president of Englander Steel saw that the company had to walk a tightrope. It had to specialize in a few high-value-added products tailored for separate markets, while maintaining economies of scale and sophisticated technology within functional departments. The dual pressure led to an unusual solution for a steel company: a matrix structure.

Englander Steel had four product lines: open-die forgings, ring-mill products, wheels and axles, and sheet steel. A business manager was given responsibility for and authority over each line, which included preparing a business plan and developing targets for production costs, product inventory, shipping dates, and gross profit. The managers were given authority to meet those targets and to make their lines profitable. Functional vice presidents were responsible for technical decisions. Functional managers were expected to stay abreast of the latest techniques in their areas and to keep personnel trained in new technologies that could apply to product lines. With 20,000 recipes for specialty steels and several hundred new recipes ordered each month, functional personnel had to stay current. Two functional departments—field sales and industrial relations—were not included in the matrix because they worked independently. The final design was a hybrid matrix structure with both matrix and functional relationships, as illustrated in Exhibit 3.13.

Implementation of the matrix was slow. Middle managers were confused. Meetings to coordinate orders across functional departments seemed to be held every day. After about a year of training by external consultants, Englander Steel was on track. Ninety percent of the orders were now delivered on time and market share recovered. Both productivity and profitability increased steadily. The managers thrived on matrix involvement. Meetings to coordinate product and functional decisions provided a growth experience. Middle managers began including younger managers in the matrix discussions as training for future management responsibility.[45]

This example illustrates the correct use of a matrix structure. The dual pressure to maintain economies of scale and to market four product lines gave equal emphasis to the functional and product hierarchies. Through continuous meetings for coordination, Englander Steel achieved both economies of scale and flexibility.

Horizontal Structure

A recent approach to organizing is the **horizontal structure**, which organizes employees around core processes. Organizations typically shift toward a horizontal structure during a procedure called reengineering. **Reengineering**, or *business process reengineering*, basically means the redesign of a vertical organization along its horizontal workflows and processes. A **process** refers to an organized group of related tasks and activities that work together to transform inputs into outputs that create value for customers.[46] Reengineering changes the way managers think about how work is done. Rather than focusing on narrow jobs structured into distinct functional departments, they emphasize core processes that cut horizontally across the organization and involve teams of employees working together to serve customers. Examples of processes include order fulfillment, new product development, and customer service.

A good illustration of process is provided by claims handling at Progressive Casualty Insurance Company. In the past, a customer would report an accident to an agent, who would pass the information to a customer service representative, who, in turn, would pass it to a claims manager. The claims manager would batch the claim with others from the same territory and assign it to an adjuster, who would schedule a time to inspect the vehicle damage. Today, adjusters are organized into teams that handle the entire claims process from beginning to end. One member handles claimant calls to the office while others are stationed in the field. When an adjuster takes a call, he or she does whatever is possible over the phone. If an inspection is needed, the adjuster contacts a team member in the field and schedules an appointment immediately. Progressive now measures the time from call to inspection in hours rather than the 7 to 10 days it once took.[47]

When a company is reengineered to a horizontal structure, all the people throughout the organization who work on a particular process (such as claims handling or order fulfillment) have easy access to one another so they can communicate and coordinate their efforts. The horizontal structure virtually eliminates both the vertical hierarchy and old departmental boundaries. This structural approach is largely a response to the profound changes that have occurred in the workplace and the business environment over the past 15 to 20 years. Technological progress emphasizes computer- and Internet-based integration and coordination. Customers expect faster and better service, and employees want opportunities to use their minds, learn new skills, and assume greater responsibility. Organizations mired in a vertical mindset have a hard time meeting these challenges. Thus, numerous organizations have experimented with horizontal mechanisms such as cross-functional teams to achieve coordination across departments or task forces to accomplish temporary projects. Increasingly, organizations are shifting away from hierarchical, function-based structures to structures based on horizontal processes.

■ Characteristics

An illustration of a company reengineered into a horizontal structure appears in Exhibit 3.14. Such an organization has the following characteristics:[48]

- Structure is created around cross-functional core processes rather than tasks, functions, or geography. Thus, boundaries between departments are obliterated. Ford Motor Company's Customer Service Division, for example, has core process groups for business development, parts supply and logistics, vehicle service and programs, and technical support.
- Self-directed teams, not individuals, are the basis of organizational design and performance.
- Process owners have responsibility for each core process in its entirety. For Ford's parts supply and logistics process, for example, a number of teams may work on jobs such as parts analysis, purchasing, material flow, and distribution, but a process owner is responsible for coordinating the entire process.
- People on the team are given the skills, tools, motivation, and authority to make decisions central to the team's performance. Team members are cross-trained to perform one another's jobs, and the combined skills are sufficient to complete a major organizational task.
- Teams have the freedom to think creatively and respond flexibly to new challenges that arise.
- Customers drive the horizontal corporation. Effectiveness is measured by end-of-process performance objectives (based on the goal of bringing value to the customer), as well as customer satisfaction, employee satisfaction, and financial contribution.
- The culture is one of openness, trust, and collaboration, focused on continuous improvement. The culture values employee empowerment, responsibility, and well-being.

General Electric's Salisbury, North Carolina, plant shifted to a horizontal structure to improve flexibility and customer service.

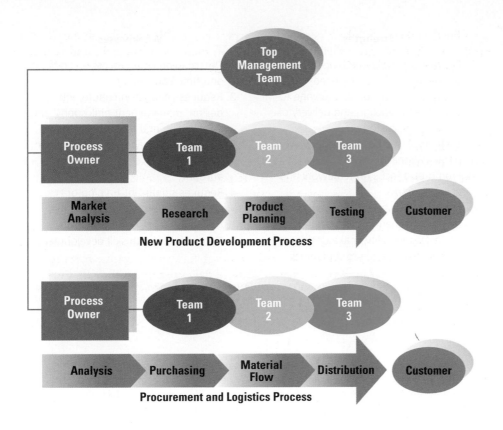

EXHIBIT 3.14
A Horizontal Structure
Source: Based on Frank Ostroff,
The Horizontal Organization
(New York: Oxford University
Press, 1999); John A. Byrne,
"The Horizontal Corporation,"
BusinessWeek (December 20,
1993), 76–81; and Thomas A.
Stewart, "The Search for the
Organization of Tomorrow,"
Fortune (May 18, 1992),
92–98.

In Practice
GE Salisbury

General Electric's plant in Salisbury, North Carolina, which manufactures electrical lighting panel boards for industrial and commercial purposes, used to be organized functionally and vertically. Because no two GE customers have identical needs, each panel board has to be configured and built to order, which frequently created bottlenecks in the standard production process. In the mid-1980s, faced with high product-line costs, inconsistent customer service, and a declining market share, managers began exploring new ways of organizing that would emphasize teamwork, responsibility, continuous improvement, empowerment, and commitment to the customer.

By the early 1990s, GE Salisbury had made the transition to a horizontal structure that links sets of multiskilled teams who are responsible for the entire build-to-order process. The new structure is based on the goal of producing lighting panel boards "of the highest possible quality, in the shortest possible cycle time, at a competitive price, with the best possible service." The process consists of four linked teams, each made up of ten to fifteen members representing a range of skills and functions. A production-control team serves as process owner (as illustrated earlier in Exhibit 3.14) and is responsible for order receipt, planning, coordination of production, purchasing, working with suppliers and customers, tracking inventory, and keeping all the teams focused on meeting objectives. The fabrication team cuts, builds, welds, and paints the various parts that make up the steel box that will house the electrical components panel, which is assembled and tested by the electrical components team. The electrical components team also handles shipping. A maintenance team takes care of heavy equipment maintenance that cannot be performed as part of the regular production process. Managers have become *associate advisors* who serve as guides and coaches and bring their expertise to the teams as needed.

EXHIBIT 3.15
*Strengths and
Weaknesses of Horizontal
Structure*

Strengths	Weaknesses
1. Promotes flexibility and rapid response to changes in customer needs	1. Determining core processes is difficult and time consuming
2. Directs the attention of everyone toward the production and delivery of value to the customer	2. Requires changes in culture, job design, management philosophy, and information and reward systems
3. Each employee has a broader view of organizational goals	3. Traditional managers may balk when they have to give up power and authority
4. Promotes a focus on teamwork and collaboration	4. Requires significant training of employees to work effectively in a horizontal team environment
5. Improves quality of life for employees by offering them the opportunity to share responsibility, make decisions, and be accountable for outcomes	5. Can limit in-depth skill development

Sources: Based on Frank Ostroff, *The Horizontal Organization: What the Organization of the Future Looks Like and How It Delivers Value to Customers* (New York: Oxford University Press, 1999); and Richard L. Daft, *Organization Theory and Design*, 6th ed. (Cincinnati, Ohio: South-Western, 1998), 253.

The key to success of the horizontal structure is that all the operating teams work in concert with each other and have access to the information they need to meet team and process goals. Teams are given information about sales, backlogs, inventory, staffing needs, productivity, costs, quality, and other data, and each team regularly shares information about its part of the build-to-order process with the other teams. Joint production meetings, job rotation, and cross-training of employees are some of the mechanisms that help ensure smooth integration. The linked teams assume responsibility for setting their own production targets, determining production schedules, assigning duties, and identifying and solving problems.

Productivity and performance have dramatically improved with the horizontal structure. Bottlenecks in the workflow, which once wreaked havoc with production schedules, have been virtually eliminated. A 6-week lead time has been cut 2½ days. More subtle but just as important are the increases in employee and customer satisfaction that GE Salisbury has realized since implementing its new structure.[49]

■ Strengths and Weaknesses

As with all structures, the horizontal structure has weaknesses as well as strengths. The strengths and weaknesses of the horizontal structure are listed in Exhibit 3.15.

The most significant strength of the horizontal structure is that it can dramatically increase the company's flexibility and response to changes in customer needs because of the enhanced coordination. The structure directs everyone's attention toward the customer, which leads to greater customer satisfaction as well as improvements in productivity, speed, and efficiency. In addition, because there are no boundaries between functional departments, employees take a broader view of organizational goals rather than being focused on the goals of a single department. The horizontal structure promotes an emphasis on teamwork and cooperation, so that team members share a commitment to meeting common objectives. Finally, the horizontal structure can improve the quality of life for employees by giving them opportunities to share responsibility, make decisions, and contribute significantly to the organization.

A weakness of the horizontal structure is that it can harm rather than help organizational performance unless managers carefully determine which core processes are critical for bringing value to customers. Simply defining the processes around which to organize can be difficult. In addition, shifting to a horizontal structure is complicated and time consuming because it requires significant changes in culture, job design, management philosophy, and information and reward systems. Traditional managers may balk when they have to give up power and authority to serve instead as coaches and facilitators of teams. Employees have to be trained to work effectively in a team environment. Finally, because of the cross-functional nature of work, a horizontal structure can limit in-depth knowledge and skill development unless measures are taken to give employees opportunities to maintain and build technical expertise.

Virtual Network Structure

The virtual network structure extends the concept of horizontal coordination and collaboration beyond the boundaries of the traditional organization. Many of today's organizations farm out some of their activities to other companies that can do it more efficiently. **Outsourcing** means to contract out certain corporate functions, such as manufacturing, information technology, or credit processing, to other companies. This is a significant trend in all industries that is affecting organization structure.[50] Accenture, for example, handles all aspects of information technology for the British food retailer J. Sainsbury's. Companies in India, Malaysia, and Scotland manage call center and technical support for U.S. computer and cell phone companies. Entire chunks of General Motors automobiles and Bombardier airplanes are engineered and built by outside contractors. Fiat Auto is involved in multiple complex outsourcing relationships with other companies handling logistics, maintenance, and the manufacturing of some parts.[51]

These interorganizational relationships reflect a significant shift in organization design. A few organizations carry outsourcing to the extreme and create a virtual network structure. With a **virtual network structure**, sometimes called a *modular structure*, the firm subcontracts many or most of its major processes to separate companies and coordinates their activities from a small headquarters organization.[52]

How the Structure Works

The virtual network organization may be viewed as a central hub surrounded by a network of outside specialists. Rather than being housed under one roof or located within one organization, services such as accounting, design, manufacturing, marketing, and distribution are outsourced to separate companies that are connected electronically to a central office. Organizational partners located in different parts of the world may use networked computers or the Internet to exchange data and information so rapidly and smoothly that a loosely connected network of suppliers, manufacturers, and distributors can look and act like one seamless company. The virtual network form incorporates a free-market style to replace the traditional vertical hierarchy. Subcontractors may flow into and out of the system as needed to meet changing needs.

With a network structure, the hub maintains control over processes in which it has world-class or difficult-to-imitate capabilities and then transfers other

Briefcase

As an organization manager, keep this guideline in mind:

Use a virtual network structure for extreme flexibility and rapid response to changing market conditions. Focus on key activities that give the organization its competitive advantage and outsource other activities to carefully selected partners.

activities—along with the decision making and control over them—to other organizations. These partner organizations organize and accomplish their work using their own ideas, assets, and tools.[53] The idea is that a firm can concentrate on what it does best and contract out everything else to companies with distinctive competence in those specific areas, enabling the organization to do more with less.[54] The network structure is often advantageous for start-up companies, such as TiVo Inc., the company that introduced the personal video recorder.

In Practice

TiVo Inc.

"I love my TiVo more than my wife," says Craig Volpe, a 36-year-old sales manager in Chicago. He says it with a laugh, but many people are feeling a similar passion. The market for personal video recording systems is hot, and major electronics, cable, and satellite companies are getting in on the action. The company that started it all was TiVo Inc., a small organization based in the San Francisco Bay area.

TiVo's founders developed a technology to allow users to record up to 80 hours of television and replay it at their convenience, without commercial interruption and minus the hassles of digital storage media or videotapes. The system can even track down and record favorite shows despite schedule changes.

Company leaders knew speed was of the essence if they were to take this new market by storm. The only way to do it was by outsourcing practically everything. TiVo first developed major manufacturing and marketing partnerships with large companies such as Sony, Hughes Electronics, and Royal Philips Electronics. In addition, the company outsourced distribution, public relations, advertising, and customer support. TiVo managers considered the customer support function particularly critical. Because TiVo was a new concept, ordinary call-center approaches wouldn't work. Company leaders worked closely with ClientLogic to develop processes and training materials that would help customer-service agents "think like a TiVo customer."

Using the virtual network structure enabled a small but growing company like TiVo to get the advanced capabilities it needed without having to spend time and limited financial resources building an organization from scratch. TiVo leaders concentrated on technological innovation and developing and managing the multiple partnerships necessary for TiVo to succeed. Today, TiVo functionality is incorporated into DVR systems from Sony, Toshiba, and Direct TV, as well as Comcast, the nation's no. 1 cable operator. The recent deal with Comcast is critical. Without a cable partner, TiVo would find it difficult to remain a major player in the growing market for digital video recorders.[55]

TiVo faces stiff competition, but using the network structure has enabled it to get a big head start. Exhibit 3.16 illustrates a simplified network structure for TiVo, showing some of the functions that are outsourced to other companies.

■ Strengths and Weaknesses

Exhibit 3.17 summarizes the strengths and weaknesses of the virtual network structure. One of the major strengths is that the organization, no matter how small, can be truly global, drawing on resources worldwide to achieve the best quality and price and then selling products or services worldwide just as easily through subcontractors. The network structure also enables a new or small company, such as TiVo, to develop products or services and get them to market rapidly without huge

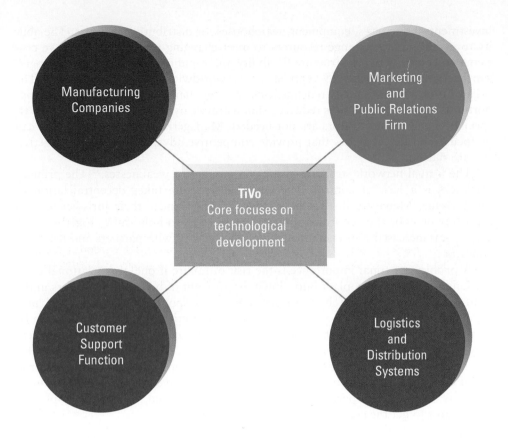

EXHIBIT 3.16
Partial Virtual Network Structure at TiVo

EXHIBIT 3.17
Strengths and Weaknesses of Virtual Network Structure

Strengths	Weaknesses
1. Enables even small organizations to obtain talent and resources worldwide	1. Managers do not have hands-on control over many activities and employees
2. Gives a company immediate scale and reach without huge investments in factories, equipment, or distribution facilities	2. Requires a great deal of time to manage relationships and potential conflicts with contract partners
3. Enables the organization to be highly flexible and responsive to changing needs	3. There is a risk of organizational failure if a partner fails to deliver or goes out of business
4. Reduces administrative overhead costs	4. Employee loyalty and corporate culture might be weak because employees feel they can be replaced by contract services

Sources: Based on Linda S. Ackerman, "Transition Management: An In-Depth Look at Managing Complex Change," *Organizational Dynamics* (Summer 1982), 46–66; and Frank Ostroff, *The Horizontal Organization* (New York: Oxford University Press, 1999), Fig 2.1, 34.

investments in factories, equipment, warehouses, or distribution facilities. The ability to arrange and rearrange resources to meet changing needs and best serve customers gives the network structure flexibility and rapid response. New technologies can be developed quickly by tapping into a worldwide network of experts. The organization can continually redefine itself to meet changing product or market opportunities. A final strength is reduced administrative overhead. Large teams of staff specialists and administrators are not needed. Managerial and technical talent can be focused on key activities that provide competitive advantage while other activities are outsourced.[56]

The virtual network structure also has a number of weaknesses.[57] The primary weakness is a lack of control. The network structure takes decentralization to the extreme. Managers do not have all operations under their jurisdiction and must rely on contracts, coordination, and negotiation to hold things together. This also means increased time spent managing relationships with partners and resolving conflicts.

A problem of equal importance is the risk of failure if one organizational partner fails to deliver, has a plant burn down, or goes out of business. Managers in the headquarters organization have to act quickly to spot problems and find new arrangements. Finally, from a human resource perspective, employee loyalty can be weak in a network organization because of concerns over job security. Employees may feel that they can be replaced by contract services. In addition, it is more difficult to develop a cohesive corporate culture. Turnover may be higher because emotional commitment between the organization and employees is low. With changing products, markets, and partners, the organization may need to reshuffle employees at any time to get the correct mix of skills and capabilities.

Hybrid Structure

As a practical matter, many structures in the real world do not exist in the pure forms we have outlined in this chapter. Organizations often use a **hybrid structure** that combines characteristics of various approaches tailored to specific strategic needs. Most companies combine characteristics of functional, divisional, geographical, horizontal, or network structures to take advantage of the strengths of various structures and to avoid some of the weaknesses. Hybrid structures tend to be used in rapidly changing environments because they offer the organization greater flexibility.

As an organization manager, keep these guidelines in mind:

Implement hybrid structures, when needed, to combine characteristics of functional, divisional, and horizontal structures. Use a hybrid structure in complex environments to take advantage of the strengths of various structural characteristics and avoid some of the weaknesses.

One type of hybrid that is often used is to combine characteristics of the functional and divisional structures. When a corporation grows large and has several products or markets, it typically is organized into self-contained divisions of some type. Functions that are important to each product or market are decentralized to the self-contained units. However, some functions that are relatively stable and require economies of scale and in-depth specialization are also centralized at headquarters. Sun Petroleum Products Corporation (SPPC) reorganized to a hybrid structure to be more responsive to changing markets. The hybrid organization structure adopted by SPPC is illustrated in part 1 of Exhibit 3.18. Three major product divisions—fuels, lubricants, and chemicals—were created, each serving a different market and requiring a different strategy and management style. Each product-line vice president is now in charge of all functions for that product, such as marketing, planning, supply and distribution, and manufacturing. However, activities such as human resources, legal, technology, and finance were centralized as functional

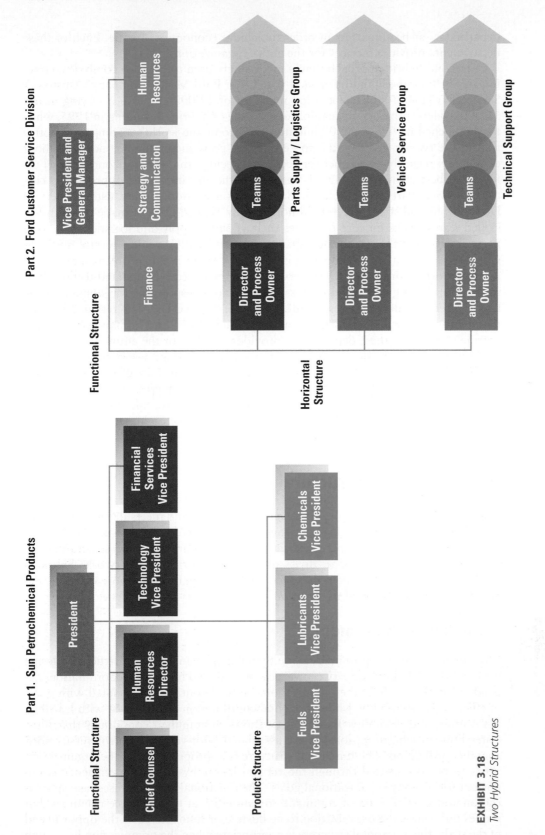

EXHIBIT 3.18
Two Hybrid Structures

departments at headquarters in order to achieve economies of scale. Each of these departments provides services for the entire organization.[58]

A second hybrid approach that is increasingly used today is to combine characteristics of functional and horizontal structures. Ford Motor Company's Customer Service Division, a global operation made up of 12,000 employees serving nearly 15,000 dealers, provides an example of this type of hybrid. Beginning in 1995, when Ford launched its "Ford 2000" initiative to become the world's leading automotive firm in the twenty-first century, top executives grew increasingly concerned about complaints regarding customer service. They decided that the horizontal model offered the best chance to gain a faster, more efficient, integrated approach to customer service. Part 2 of Exhibit 3.18 illustrates a portion of the Customer Service Division's hybrid structure. Several horizontally aligned groups, made up of multi-skilled teams, focus on core processes such as parts supply and logistics (acquiring parts and getting them to dealers quickly and efficiently), vehicle service and programs (collecting and disseminating information about repair problems), and technical support (ensuring that every service department receives updated technical information). Each group has a process owner who is responsible for seeing that the teams meet overall objectives. Ford's Customer Service Division retained a functional structure for finance, strategy and communication, and human resources departments. Each of these departments provides services for the entire division.[59]

In a huge organization such as Ford, managers may use a variety of structural characteristics to meet the needs of the total organization. Like many large organizations, for example, Ford outsources some non-core activities. A hybrid structure is often preferred over the pure functional, divisional, horizontal, or virtual network structure because it can provide some of the advantages of each and overcome some of the disadvantages.

Applications of Structural Design

Each type of structure is applied in different situations and meets different needs. In describing the various structures, we touched briefly on conditions such as environmental stability or change and organizational size that are related to structure. Each form of structure—functional, divisional, matrix, horizontal, network, hybrid—represents a tool that can help managers make an organization more effective, depending on the demands of its situation.

■ Structural Alignment

Briefcase

As an organization manager, keep these guidelines in mind:

Find the correct balance between vertical control and horizontal coordination to meet the needs of the organization. Consider a structural reorganization when symptoms of structural deficiency are observed.

Ultimately, the most important decision that managers make about structural design is to find the right balance between vertical control and horizontal coordination, depending on the needs of the organization. Vertical control is associated with goals of efficiency and stability, while horizontal coordination is associated with learning, innovation, and flexibility. Exhibit 3.19 shows a simplified continuum that illustrates how structural approaches are associated with vertical control versus horizontal coordination. The functional structure is appropriate when the organization needs to be coordinated through the vertical hierarchy and when efficiency is important for meeting organizational goals. The functional structure uses task specialization and a strict chain of command to gain efficient use of scarce resources, but it does not enable the organization to be flexible or innovative. At the opposite end of the scale, the horizontal structure is appropriate when the organization has a high

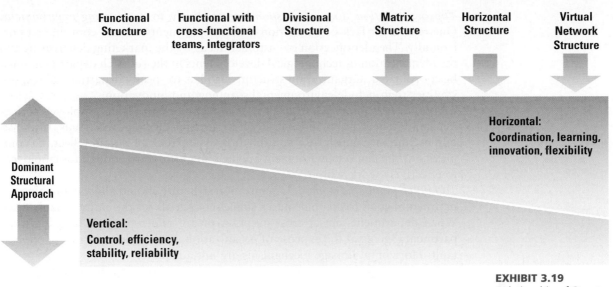

EXHIBIT 3.19
Relationship of Structure to Organization's Need for Efficiency versus Learning

need for coordination among functions to achieve innovation and promote learning. The horizontal structure enables organizations to differentiate themselves and re-spond quickly to changes, but at the expense of efficient resource use. The virtual network structure offers even greater flexibility and potential for rapid response by allowing the organization to add or subtract pieces as needed to adapt and meet changing needs from the environment and marketplace. Exhibit 3.19 also shows how other types of structure defined in this chapter—functional with horizontal linkages, divisional, and matrix—represent intermediate steps on the organization's path to efficiency or innovation and learning. The exhibit does not include all pos-sible structures, but it illustrates how organizations attempt to balance the needs for efficiency and vertical control with innovation and horizontal coordination. In ad-dition, as described in the chapter, many organizations use a hybrid structure to combine characteristics of these structural types.

Symptoms of Structural Deficiency

Top executives periodically evaluate organization structure to determine whether it is appropriate to changing organization needs. Many organizations try one organi-zation structure and then reorganize to another structure in an effort to find the right fit between internal reporting relationships and the needs of the external environment.

As a general rule, when organization structure is out of alignment with orga-nization needs, one or more of the following **symptoms of structural deficiency** appear.[60]

- *Decision making is delayed or lacking in quality.* Decision makers may be over-loaded because the hierarchy funnels too many problems and decisions to them. Delegation to lower levels may be insufficient. Another cause of poor-quality de-cisions is that information may not reach the correct people. Information link-ages in either the vertical or horizontal direction may be inadequate to ensure decision quality.

- *The organization does not respond innovatively to a changing environment.* One reason for lack of innovation is that departments are not coordinated horizontally. The identification of customer needs by the marketing department and the identification of technological developments in the research department must be coordinated. Organization structure also has to specify departmental responsibilities that include environmental scanning and innovation.
- *Employee performance declines and goals are not being met.* Employee performance may decline because the structure doesn't provide clear goals, responsibilities, and mechanisms for coordination. The structure should reflect the complexity of the market environment and be straightforward enough for employees to effectively work within.
- *Too much conflict is evident.* Organization structure should allow conflicting departmental goals to combine into a single set of goals for the entire organization. When departments act at cross-purposes or are under pressure to achieve departmental goals at the expense of organizational goals, the structure is often at fault. Horizontal linkage mechanisms are not adequate.

Summary and Interpretation

Organization structure must accomplish two things for the organization. It must provide a framework of responsibilities, reporting relationships, and groupings, and it must provide mechanisms for linking and coordinating organizational elements into a coherent whole. The structure is reflected on the organization chart. Linking the organization into a coherent whole requires the use of information systems and linkage devices in addition to the organization chart.

It is important to understand the information-processing perspective on structure. Organization structure can be designed to provide vertical and horizontal information linkages based on the information processing required to meet the organization's overall goal. Managers can choose whether to orient toward a traditional organization designed for efficiency, which emphasizes vertical linkages such as hierarchy, rules and plans, and formal information systems, or toward a contemporary learning organization, which emphasizes horizontal communication and coordination. Vertical linkages are not sufficient for most organizations today. Organizations provide horizontal linkages through cross-functional information systems, direct contact between managers across department lines, temporary task forces, full-time integrators, and teams.

Alternatives for grouping employees and departments into overall structural design include functional grouping, divisional grouping, multifocused grouping, horizontal grouping, and network grouping. The choice among functional, divisional, and horizontal structures determines where coordination and integration will be greatest. With functional and divisional structures, managers also use horizontal linkage mechanisms to complement the vertical dimension and achieve integration of departments and levels into an organizational whole. With a horizontal structure, activities are organized horizontally around core work processes. A virtual network structure extends the concept of horizontal coordination and collaboration beyond the boundaries of the organization. Core activities are performed by a central hub while other functions and activities are outsourced to contract partners. The matrix structure attempts to achieve an equal balance between the vertical and horizontal dimensions of structure. Most organizations do not exist in these pure forms, using instead a hybrid structure that incorporates characteristics of two or more types of structure. Ultimately, managers attempt to find the correct balance between vertical control and horizontal coordination.

Finally, an organization chart is only so many lines and boxes on a piece of paper. The purpose of the organization chart is to encourage and direct employees into activities and communications that enable the organization to achieve its goals. The organization chart provides the structure, but employees provide the behavior. The chart is a guideline to encourage people to work together, but management must implement the structure and carry it out.

Key Concepts

centralized
decentralized
departmental grouping
divisional grouping
divisional structure
functional grouping
functional matrix
functional structure
horizontal grouping
horizontal linkage
horizontal structure
hybrid structure
integrator
liaison role
matrix structure

multifocused grouping
organization structure
outsourcing
process
product matrix
reengineering
symptoms of structural deficiency
task force
teams
vertical information system
vertical linkages
virtual network grouping
virtual network structure
virtual team

Discussion Questions

1. What is the definition of *organization structure*? Does organization structure appear on the organization chart? Explain.
2. How do rules and plans help an organization achieve vertical integration?
3. When is a functional structure preferable to a divisional structure?
4. Large corporations tend to use hybrid structures. Why?
5. What are the primary differences between a traditional organization designed for efficiency and a more contemporary organization designed for learning?
6. What is the difference between a task force and a team? Between liaison role and integrating role? Which of these provides the greatest amount of horizontal coordination?
7. What conditions usually have to be present before an organization should adopt a matrix structure?
8. The manager of a consumer products firm said, "We use the brand manager position to train future executives." Do you think the brand manager position is a good training ground? Discuss.
9. Why do companies using a horizontal structure have cultures that emphasize openness, employee empowerment, and responsibility? What do you think a manager's job would be like in a horizontally organized company?
10. How is structure related to the organization's need for efficiency versus its need for learning and innovation? How can managers tell if structure is out of alignment with the organization's needs?
11. Describe the virtual network structure. Why do you think this is becoming a good structural alternative for some of today's organizations?

Chapter 3 Workbook: You and Organization Structure*

To better understand the importance of organization structure in your life, do the following assignment.

Select one of the following situations to organize:

- A copy and printing shop
- A travel agency
- A sports rental (such as jet skis or snowmobiles) in a resort area
- A bakery

Background

Organization is a way of gaining some power against an unreliable environment. The environment provides the organization with inputs, which include raw materials, human resources, and financial resources. There is a service or product to produce that involves technology. The output goes to clients, a group that must be nurtured. The complexities of the environment and the technology determine the complexity of the organization.

Planning Your Organization

1. Write down the mission or purpose of the organization in a few sentences.
2. What are the specific tasks to be completed to accomplish the mission?
3. Based on the specifics in number 2, develop an organization chart. Each position in the chart will perform a specific task or is responsible for a certain outcome.

4. You are into your third year of operation, and your business has been very successful. You want to add a second location a few miles away. What issues will you face running the business at two locations? Draw an organization chart that includes the two business locations.
5. Five more years go by and the business has grown to five locations in two cities. How do you keep in touch with it all? What issues of control and coordination have arisen? Draw an up-to-date organization chart and explain your rationale for it.
6. Twenty years later you have seventy-five business locations in five states. What are the issues and problems that have to be dealt with through organizational structure? Draw an organization chart for this organization, indicating such factors as who is responsible for customer satisfaction, how you will know if customer needs are met, and how information will flow within the organization.

*Adapted by Dorothy Marcic from "Organizing," in Donald D. White and H. William Vroman, *Action in Organizations*, 2nd ed. (Boston: Allyn and Bacon, 1982), 154, and Cheryl Harvey and Kim Morouney, "Organization Structure and Design: The Club Ed Exercise," *Journal of Management Education* (June 1985), 425–429.

Case for Analysis: C & C Grocery Stores, Inc.*

The first C & C grocery store was started in 1947 by Doug Cummins and his brother Bob. Both were veterans who wanted to run their own business, so they used their savings to start the small grocery store in Charlotte, North Carolina. The store was immediately successful. The location was good, and Doug Cummins had a winning personality. Store employees adopted Doug's informal style and "serve the customer" attitude. C & C's increasing circle of customers enjoyed an abundance of good meats and produce.

By 1997, C & C had over 200 stores. A standard physical layout was used for new stores. Company headquarters moved from Charlotte to Atlanta in 1985. The organization chart for C & C is shown in Exhibit 3.20. The central offices in Atlanta handled personnel, merchandising, financial, purchasing, real estate, and legal affairs for the entire chain. For management of individual stores, the organization was divided by regions. The southern, southeastern, and northeastern regions each had about seventy stores. Each region was divided into five districts of ten to

fifteen stores each. A district director was responsible for supervision and coordination of activities for the ten to fifteen district stores.

Each district was divided into four lines of authority based on functional specialty. Three of these lines reached into the stores. The produce department manager within each store reported directly to the produce specialist for the division, and the same was true for the meat department manager, who reported directly to the district meat specialist. The meat and produce managers were responsible for all activities associated with the acquisition and sale of perishable products. The store manager's responsibility included the grocery line, front-end departments, and store operations. The store manager was responsible for appearance of personnel, cleanliness, adequate checkout service, and price accuracy. A grocery manager reported to the

*Prepared by Richard L. Daft, from Richard L. Daft and Richard Steers, *Organizations: A Micro/Macro Approach* (Glenview, Ill.: Scott Foresman, 1986). Reprinted with permission.

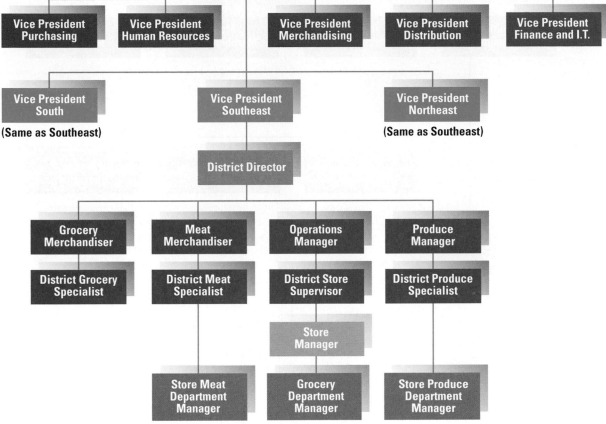

EXHIBIT 3.20
Organization Structure for C & C Grocery Stores, Inc.

store manager, maintained inventories, and restocked shelves for grocery items. The district merchandising office was responsible for promotional campaigns, advertising circulars, district advertising, and attracting customers into the stores. The grocery merchandisers were expected to coordinate their activities with each store in the district.

Business for the C & C chain has dropped off in all regions in recent years—partly because of a declining economy, but mostly because of increased competition from large discount retailers such as Wal-Mart, Target, and Costco Wholesale. When these large discounters entered the grocery business, they brought a level of competition unlike any C & C had seen before. C & C had managed to hold its own against larger supermarket chains, but now even the big chains were threatened by Wal-Mart, which became no. 1 in grocery sales in 2001. C & C managers knew they couldn't compete on price, but they were con-

sidering ways they could use advanced information technology to improve service and customer satisfaction and distinguish the store from the large discounters.

However, the most pressing problem was how to improve business with the resources and stores they now had. A consulting team from a major university was hired to investigate store structure and operations.

The consultants visited several stores in each region, talking to about fifty managers and employees. The consultants wrote a report that pinpointed four problem areas to be addressed by store executives.

1. *The chain was slow to adapt to change.* Store layout and structure were the same as had been designed 15 years ago. Each store did things the same way, even though some stores were in low-income areas and other stores in suburban areas. A new computerized supply chain management system for ordering and stocking

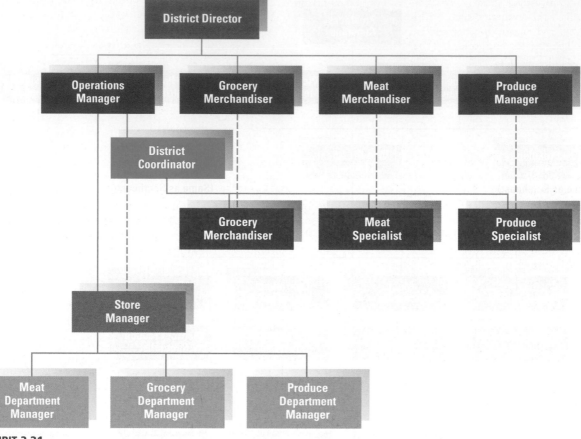

EXHIBIT 3.21
Proposed Reorganization of C & C Grocery Stores, Inc.

had been developed, but after 2 years it was only partially implemented in the stores. Other proposed information technology (IT) initiatives were still "on the back burner," not yet even in the development stage.

2. *Roles of the district store supervisor and the store manager were causing dissatisfaction.* The store managers wanted to learn general management skills for potential promotion into district or regional management positions. However, their jobs restricted them to operational activities and they learned little about merchandising, meat, and produce. Moreover, district store supervisors used store visits to inspect for cleanliness and adherence to operating standards rather than to train the store manager and help coordinate operations with perishable departments. Close supervision on the operational details had become the focus of operations management rather than development, training, and coordination.

3. *Cooperation within stores was low and morale was poor. The informal, friendly atmosphere originally cre-*

ated *by Doug Cummins was gone.* One example of this problem occurred when the grocery merchandiser and store manager in a Louisiana store decided to promote Coke and Diet Coke as a loss leader. Thousands of cartons of Coke were brought in for the sale, but the stockroom was not prepared and did not have room. The store manager wanted to use floor area in the meat and produce sections to display Coke cartons, but those managers refused. The produce department manager said that Diet Coke did not help his sales and it was okay with him if there was no promotion at all.

4. *Long-term growth and development of the store chain would probably require reevaluation of long-term strategy.* The percent of market share going to traditional grocery stores was declining nationwide due to competition from large superstores and discount retailers. In the near future, C & C might need to introduce nonfood items into the stores for one-stop shopping, add specialty or gourmet sections within stores,

and investigate how new technology could help distinguish the company, such as through targeted marketing and promotion, providing superior service and convenience, and offering their customers the best product assortment and availability.

To solve the first three problems, the consultants recommended reorganizing the district and the store structure as illustrated in Exhibit 3.21. Under this reorganization, the meat, grocery, and produce department managers would all report to the store manager. The store manager would have complete store control and would be responsible for coordination of all store activities. The district supervisor's role would be changed from supervision to training and development. The district supervisor would head a team that included himself and several meat, produce, and merchandise specialists who would visit area stores as a team to provide advice and help for the store managers and other employees. The team would act in a liaison capacity between district specialists and the stores.

The consultants were enthusiastic about the proposed structure. With the removal of one level of district operational supervision, store managers would have more freedom and responsibility. The district liaison team would establish a cooperative team approach to management that could be adopted within stores. Focusing store responsibility on a single manager would encourage coordination within stores and adaptation to local conditions. It would also provide a focus of responsibility for storewide administrative changes.

The consultants also believed that the proposed structure could be expanded to accommodate non-grocery lines and gourmet units if these were included in C & C's future plans. Within each store, a new department manager could be added for pharmacy, gourmet/specialty items, or other major departments. The district team could be expanded to include specialists in these lines, as well as an information technology coordinator to act as liaison for stores in the district.

Case for Analysis: Aquarius Advertising Agency*

The Aquarius Advertising Agency is a middle-sized firm that offered two basic services to its clients: (1) customized plans for the content of an advertising campaign (for example, slogans and layouts) and (2) complete plans for media (such as radio, TV, newspapers, billboards, and Internet). Additional services included aid in marketing and distribution of products and marketing research to test advertising effectiveness.

Its activities were organized in a traditional manner. The organization chart is shown in Exhibit 3.22. Each department included similar functions.

Each client account was coordinated by an account executive who acted as a liaison between the client and the various specialists on the professional staff of the operations and marketing divisions. The number of direct communications and contacts between clients and Aquarius specialists, clients and account executives, and Aquarius specialists and account executives is indicated in Exhibit 3.23. These sociometric data were gathered by a consultant who conducted a study of the patterns of formal and informal communication. Each intersecting cell of Aquarius personnel and the clients contains an index of the direct contacts between them.

Although an account executive was designated to be the liaison between the client and specialists within the agency, communications frequently occurred directly between clients and specialists and bypassed the account executive. These direct contacts involved a wide range of interactions, such as meetings, telephone calls, e-mail messages, and so on. A large number of direct communications occurred between agency specialists and their counterparts in the client

organization. For example, an art specialist working as one member of a team on a particular client account would often be contacted directly by the client's in-house art specialist, and agency research personnel had direct communication with research people of the client firm. Also, some of the unstructured contacts often led to more formal meetings with clients in which agency personnel made presentations, interpreted and defended agency policy, and committed the agency to certain courses of action.

Both hierarchical and professional systems operated within the departments of the operations and marketing divisions. Each department was organized hierarchically with a director, an assistant director, and several levels of authority. Professional communications were widespread and mainly concerned with sharing knowledge and techniques, technical evaluation of work, and development of professional interests. Control in each department was exercised mainly through control of promotions and supervision of work done by subordinates. Many account executives, however, felt the need for more influence, and one commented:

Creativity and art. That's all I hear around here. It is hard as hell to effectively manage six or seven hotshots who claim they have to do their own thing. Each of them tries to sell his or her idea to the client, and most of the time I don't know what has happened until a week later. If I were

*Adapted from John F. Veiga and John N. Yanouzas, "Aquarius Advertising Agency," *The Dynamics of Organization Theory* (St. Paul, Minn.: West, 1984), 212–217, with permission.

EXHIBIT 3.22
Aquarius Advertising
Agency Organization Chart

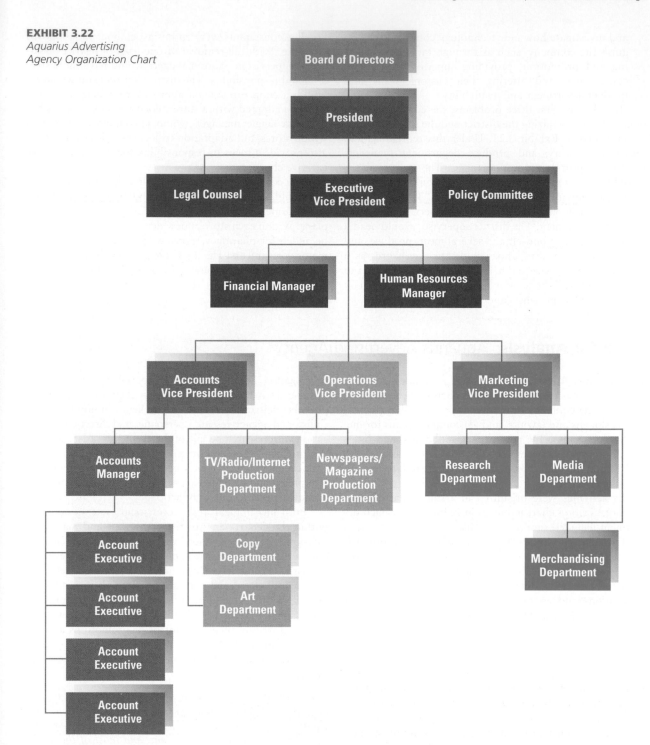

	Clients	Account Manager	Account Executives	TV/Radio Specialists	Newspaper/Magazine Specialists	Copy Specialists	Art Specialists	Merchandising Specialists	Media Specialists	Research Specialists
Clients	X	F	F	N	N	O	O	O	O	O
Account Manager		X	F	N	N	N	N	N	N	N
Account Executives			X	F	F	F	F	F	F	F
TV/Radio Specialists				X	N	O	O	N	N	O
Newspaper/Magazine Specialists					X	O	O	N	O	O
Copy Specialists						X	N	O	O	O
Art Specialists							X	O	O	O
Merchandising Specialists								X	F	F
Media Specialists									X	F
Research Specialists										X

EXHIBIT 3.23
Sociometric Index of Aquarius Personnel and Clients
F = Frequent—daily
O = Occasional—once or twice per project
N = None

a despot, I would make all of them check with me first to get approval. Things would sure change around here.

The need for reorganization was made more acute by changes in the environment. Within a short period of time, there was a rapid turnover in the major accounts handled by the agency. It was typical for advertising agencies to gain or lose clients quickly, often with no advance warning as consumer behavior and lifestyle changes emerged and product innovations occurred.

An agency reorganization was one solution proposed by top management to increase flexibility in this unpredictable environment. The reorganization would be aimed at reducing the agency's response time to environmental changes and at increasing cooperation and communication among specialists from different departments. The top managers are not sure what type of reorganization is appropriate. They would like your help analyzing their context and current structure and welcome your advice on proposing a new structure.

Notes

1. Chuck Salter, "Ford's Escape Route," *Fast Company* (October 2004), 106–110; "Ford Escape Hybrid Named Best Truck in Detroit," *The Jakarta Post* (January 27, 2005), 18; and Bernard Simon, "Ford Aims to Build on Escape Hybrid's Success," *National Post* (January 26, 2005), FP–10.

2. "The Stalling of Motor City," *BusinessWeek* (November 1, 2004), 128.

3. Daniel J. Wakin, "With Shifting Needs and Ebbing Resources, Church is Reorganizing," *The New York Times* (January 4, 2004).

4. John Child, *Organization* (New York: Harper & Row, 1984).

5. Stuart Ranson, Bob Hinings, and Royston Greenwood, "The Structuring of Organizational Structures," *Administrative Science Quarterly* 25 (1980), 1–17; and Hugh Willmott, "The Structuring of Organizational Structure: A Note," *Administrative Science Quarterly* 26 (1981), 470–474.

6. This section is based on Frank Ostroff, *The Horizontal Organization: What the Organization of the Future Looks Like and How It Delivers Value to Customers* (New York: Oxford University Press, 1999).

7. Stephen Salsbury, *The State, the Investor, and the Railroad: The Boston & Albany, 1825–1867* (Cambridge: Harvard University Press, 1967), 186–187.

8. David Nadler and Michael Tushman, *Strategic Organization Design* (Glenview, Ill.: Scott Foresman, 1988).

9. William C. Ouchi, "The Implementation of a Decentralized Organization Design in Three Large Public School Districts: Edmonton, Seattle, and Houston" (unpublished manuscript, Anderson School of Management, University of California–Los Angeles, 2004).

10. "Country Managers: From Baron to Hotelier," *The Economist* (May 11, 2002), 55–56.

11. Based on Jay R. Galbraith, *Designing Complex Organizations* (Reading, Mass.: Addison-Wesley, 1973), and *Organization Design* (Reading, Mass.: Addison-Wesley, 1977), 81–127.

12. G. Christian Hill, "Dog Eats Dog Food. And Damn If It Ain't Tasty," *Ecompany Now* (November 2000), 169–178; "Country Managers: From Baron to Hotelier"; Rochelle Garner and Barbara Darrow, "Oracle Plots Course," *CRN* (January 24, 2005), 3; and Anthony Hilton, "Dangers behind Oracle's Dream," *Evening Standard* (February 11, 2005), 45.

13. Lee Iacocca with William Novak, *Iacocca: An Autobiography* (New York: Phantom Books, 1984), 152–153.

14. Based on Galbraith, *Designing Complex Organizations*.

15. "Mandate 2003: Be Agile and Efficient," *Microsoft Executive Circle* (Spring 2003), 46–48.

16. Jay Galbraith, Diane Downey, and Amy Kates, "How Networks Undergird the Lateral Capability of an Organization— Where the Work Gets Done," *Journal of Organizational Excellence* (Spring 2002), 67–78.

17. Amy Barrett, "Staying on Top," *BusinessWeek* (May 5, 2003), 60–68

18. Walter Kiechel III, "The Art of the Corporate Task Force," *Fortune* (January 28, 1991), 104–105; and William J. Altier,

"Task Forces: An Effective Management Tool," *Management Review* (February 1987), 52–57.

19. Neal E. Boudette, "Marriage Counseling; At Daimler-Chrysler, A New Push to Make Its Units Work Together," *The Wall Street Journal* (March 12, 2003), A1, A15.

20. Keith Naughton and Kathleen Kerwin, "At GM, Two Heads May Be Worse Than One," *Business Week* (August 14, 1995), 46.

21. Paul R. Lawrence and Jay W. Lorsch, "New Managerial Job: The Integrator," *Harvard Business Review* (November–December 1967), 142–151.

22. Charles Fishman, "Total Teamwork: Imagination Ltd.," *Fast Company* (April 2000), 156–168; Thomas L. Legare, "How Hewlett-Packard Used Virtual Cross-Functional Teams to Deliver Healthcare Industry Solutions," *Journal of Organizational Excellence* (Autumn 2001), 29–37.

23. Anthony M. Townsend, Samuel M. DeMarie, and Anthony R. Hendrickson, "Virtual Teams: Technology and the Workplace of the Future," *Academy of Management Executive* 12, no. 3 (August 1998), 17–29.

24. Henry Mintzberg, *The Structuring of Organizations* (Englewood Cliffs, N.J.: Prentice-Hall, 1979).

25. Frank Ostroff, "Stovepipe Stomper," *Government Executive* (April 1999), 70.

26. Based on Robert Duncan, "What Is the Right Organization Structure?" *Organizational Dynamics* (Winter 1979), 59–80; and W. Alan Randolph and Gregory G. Dess, "The Congruence Perspective of Organization Design: A Conceptual Model and Multivariate Research Approach," *Academy of Management Review* 9 (1984), 114–127.

27. Lynn Cook, "How Sweet It Is," *Forbes* (March 1, 2004), 90ff; David Kaplan, "Cool Commander; Brenham's Little Creamery Gets New Leader in Low-Key Switch," *Houston Chronicle* (May 1, 2004), 1; Kristin Hays, "First Family Favorite," *Cincinnati Post* (June 26, 2004), B.8.0; Toni Mack, "The Ice Cream Man Cometh," *Forbes* (January 22, 1990), 52–56; David Abdalla, J. Doehring, and Ann Windhager, "Blue Bell Creameries, Inc.: Case and Analysis" (unpublished manuscript, Texas A&M University, 1981); Jorjanna Price, "Creamery Churns Its Ice Cream into Cool Millions," *Parade* (February 21, 1982), 18–22; and Art Chapman, "Lone Star Scoop—Blue Bell Ice Cream Is a Part of State's Culture," *http://www.bluebell.com/press/FtWorthStar-july2002.htm*.

28. Rahul Jacob, "The Struggle to Create an Organization for the 21st Century," *Fortune* (April 3, 1995), 90–99.

29. Amy Barrett, "Staying On Top"; Joseph Weber, "A Big Company That Works," *BusinessWeek* (May 4, 1992), 124–132; and Elyse Tanouye, "Johnson & Johnson Stays Fit by Shuffling Its Mix of Businesses," *The Wall Street Journal* (December 22, 1992), A1, A4.

30. Eliza Newlin Carney, "Calm in the Storm," *Government Executive* (October 2003), 57–63; and Brian Friel, "Hierarchies and Networks," *Government Executive* (April 2002), 31–39.

31. Robert A. Guth, "Midlife Correction; Inside Microsoft, Financial Managers Winning New Clout," *The Wall Street Journal* (July 23, 2003), A1, A6; and Michael Moeller, with

Steve Hamm and Timothy J. Mullaney, "Remaking Microsoft," *BusinessWeek* (May 17, 1999), 106–114.

32. Based on Duncan, "What Is the Right Organization Structure?"

33. Weber, "A Big Company That Works."

34. Phred Dvorak and Merissa Marr, "Stung by iPod, Sony Addresses a Digital Lag," *The Wall Street Journal* (December 30, 2004), B1.

35. Maisie O'Flanagan and Lynn K. Taliento, "Nonprofits: Ensuring That Bigger Is Better," *McKinsey Quarterly*, Issue 2 (2004), 112ff.

36. John Markoff, "John Sculley's Biggest Test," *The New York Times* (February 26, 1989), sec. 3, 1, 26; and Shelly Branch, "What's Eating McDonald's?" *Fortune* (October 13, 1997), 122–125.

37. Stanley M. Davis and Paul R. Lawrence, *Matrix* (Reading, Mass.: Addison-Wesley, 1977), 11–24.

38. Erik W. Larson and David H. Gobeli, "Matrix Management: Contradictions and Insight," *California Management Review* 29 (Summer 1987), 126–138.

39. Davis and Lawrence, *Matrix*, 155–180.

40. Edward Prewitt, "GM's Matrix Reloads," *CIO* (September 1, 2003), 90–96.

41. Robert C. Ford and W. Alan Randolph, "Cross-Functional Structures: A Review and Integration of Matrix Organizations and Project Management," *Journal of Management* 18 (June 1992), 267–294; and Duncan, "What Is the Right Organization Structure?"

42. Lawton R. Burns, "Matrix Management in Hospitals: Testing Theories of Matrix Structure and Development," *Administrative Science Quarterly* 34 (1989), 349–368.

43. Carol Hymowitz, "Managers Suddenly Have to Answer to a Crowd of Bosses" (In the Lead column), *The Wall Street Journal* (August 12, 2003), B1; and Michael Goold and Andrew Campbell, "Making Matrix Structures Work: Creating Clarity on Unit Roles and Responsibilities," *European Management Journal* 21, no. 3 (June 2003), 351–363.

44. Christopher A. Bartlett and Sumantra Ghoshal, "Matrix Management: Not a Structure, a Frame of Mind," *Harvard Business Review* (July–August 1990), 138–145.

45. This case was inspired by John E. Fogerty, "Integrative Management at Standard Steel" (unpublished manuscript, Latrobe, Pennsylvania, 1980); Stanley Reed with Adam Aston, "Steel: The Mergers Aren't Over Yet," *BusinessWeek* (February 21, 2005), 6; Michael Amdt, "Melting Away Steel's Costs," *BusinessWeek* (November 8, 2004), 48; and "Steeling for a Fight," *The Economist* (June 4, 1994), 63.

46. Michael Hammer, "Process Management and the Future of Six Sigma," *Sloan Management Review* (Winter 2002), 26–32; and Michael Hammer and Steve Stanton, "How Process Enterprises *Really* Work," *Harvard Business Review* 77 (November–December 1999), 108–118.

47. Hammer, "Process Management and the Future of Six Sigma."

48. Based on Ostroff, *The Horizontal Organization*, and Richard L. Daft, *Organization Theory and Design*, 6th ed. (Cincinnati, Ohio: South-Western, 1998), 250–253.

49. Frank Ostroff, *The Horizontal Organization*, 102–114.

50. Melissa A. Schilling and H. Kevin Steensma, "The Use of Modular Organizational Forms: An Industry-Level Analysis," *Academy of Management Journal* 44, no. 6 (2001), 1149–1168; Jane C. Linder, "Transformational Outsourcing," *MIT Sloan Management Review* (Winter 2004), 52–58; and Denis Chamberland, "Is It Core or Strategic? Outsourcing as a Strategic Management Tool," *Ivey Business Journal* (July–August 2003), 1–5.

51. Denis Chamberland, "Is It Core or Strategic?"; Philip Siekman, "The Snap-Together Business Jet," *Fortune* (January 21, 2002), 104[A]–104[H]; Keith H. Hammonds, "Smart, Determined, Ambitious, Cheap: The New Face of Global Competition," *Fast Company* (February 2003), 91–97; Kathleen Kerwin, "GM: Modular Plants Won't Be a Snap," *BusinessWeek* (November 9, 1998), 168–172; and Giuseppe Bonazzi and Cristiano Antonelli, "To Make or To Sell? The Case of In-House Outsourcing at Fiat Auto," *Organization Studies* 24, no. 4 (2003), 575–594.

52. Schilling and Steensma, "The Use of Modular Organizational Forms"; Raymond E. Miles and Charles C. Snow, "The New Network Firm: A Spherical Structure Built on a Human Investment Philosophy," *Organizational Dynamics* (Spring 1995), 5–18; and R. E. Miles, C. C. Snow, J. A. Matthews, G. Miles, and H. J. Coleman Jr., "Organizing in the Knowledge Age: Anticipating the Cellular Form," *Academy of Management Executive* 11, no. 4 (1997), 7–24.

53. Paul Engle, "You *Can* Outsource Strategic Processes," *Industrial Management* (January–February 2002), 13–18.

54. Don Tapscott, "Rethinking Strategy in a Networked World," *Strategy & Business* 24 (Third Quarter, 2001), 34–41.

55. The story of TiVo is described in Jane C. Linder, "Transformational Outsourcing," *MIT Sloan Management Review* (Winter 2004), 52–58; Alison Neumer, "I Want My TiVo; Subscriptions Hike as Nation Gets Hooked," *Chicago Tribune* (February 22, 2005), 8; and David Lieberman, "Deal Will Put TiVo System on Comcast DVRs," *USA Today* (March 14, 2005), *http://www.usatoday.com/money/industries/technology/2005-03-14-tivo-usat_x.htm?POE'click-refer.*

56. Miles and Snow, "The New Network Firm"; Gregory G. Dess, Abdul M. A. Rasheed, Kevin J. McLaughlin, and Richard L. Priem, "The New Corporate Architecture," *Academy of Management Executive* 9, no. 2 (1995), 7–20; and Engle, "You *Can* Outsource Strategic Processes."

57. The discussion of weaknesses is based on Engle, "You *Can* Outsource Strategic Processes"; Henry W. Chesbrough and David J. Teece, "Organizing for Innovation: When Is Virtual Virtuous?" *Harvard Business Review* (August 2002), 127–134; Dess et al., "The New Corporate Architecture"; and N. Anand, "Modular, Virtual, and Hollow Forms of Organization Design," working paper, London Business School, 2000.

58. Linda S. Ackerman, "Transition Management: An In-depth Look at Managing Complex Change," *Organizational Dynamics* (Summer 1982), 46–66.

59. Based on Ostroff, *The Horizontal Organization*, 29–44.

60. Based on Child, *Organization*, Ch. 1; and Jonathan D. Day, Emily Lawson, and Keith Leslie, "When Reorganization Works," *The McKinsey Quarterly*, 2003 Special Edition: The Value in Organization, 21–29.

PART 3
Open System Design Elements

4. The External Environment

5. Interorganizational Relationships

6. Designing Organizations for the International Environment

4 The External Environment

The Environmental Domain
   Task Environment • General Environment • International Context

Environmental Uncertainty
   Simple–Complex Dimension • Stable–Unstable Dimension • Framework

Adapting to Environmental Uncertainty
   Positions and Departments • Buffering and Boundary Spanning • Differentiation and
   Integration • Organic versus Mechanistic Management Processes • Planning, Forecasting,
   and Responsiveness

Framework for Organizational Responses to Uncertainty

Resource Dependence

Controlling Environmental Resources
   Establishing Interorganizational Linkages • Controlling the Environmental
   Domain • Organization–Environment Integrative Framework

Summary and Interpretation

A Look Inside

Nokia

Nokia became the world's leading maker of cell phone handsets in 1998, and the giant Finnish company looked poised to run rivals out of the handset business for good. But by 2004, products that didn't match consumer needs and strained relationships with major customers had cost Nokia nearly a fifth of its 35 percent global market share. Revenue growth shifted into reverse and the stock took a nosedive.

What went wrong? For one thing, Nokia missed the hottest growth sector in cell phones, the market for midrange models with cameras and high-resolution color screens. Nokia's leaders chose instead to pump hundreds of millions of dollars into the development of "smart phones" that allow consumers to get on the Internet, play video games, listen to music, and watch movies or television shows. The problem was, the new phones proved too bulky and expensive for many consumers, who began turning instead to cheaper, stylish models from Motorola, Samsung, and Siemens. The clamshell design, in particular, which allowed users to fold the phone in half when it wasn't in use, fueled a new cell phone boom in Europe and the United States. Nokia had stuck to the "candy bar" handset and was caught without a competitor in the battle. Nokia also neglected some of its biggest customers. Mobile operators such as Orange SA, France Telecom SA's wireless unit, pushed for customized phones with special features that their customers wanted, but Nokia was slow to respond. "Their attitude was that, given their size, they didn't need to listen to us," an executive at one European mobile operator said.

These missteps allowed rivals to gobble up market share. To get Nokia back on track, leaders have cranked up the introduction of new midrange phones, slashed costs on low-end models for developing countries, and promised mobile operators to tailor phones to their specifications. Nokia also continues to invest heavily in gadgets that feature advanced software and run programs just like a computer. The key question is: Are the gadgets Nokia is developing products that customers will want?[1]

Many companies, like Nokia, face tremendous uncertainty in dealing with the external environment. The only way a high-tech company like Nokia can continue to grow is through innovation, yet unless the company makes products that people want to buy, the huge investments in research and development will not pay off. At the time this text is being written, Nokia is getting its strongest sales in China due to a growing demand for less expensive phones in rural areas. It remains to be seen if the company's new, technologically advanced products will catch on in the marketplace. Nokia still holds the largest share of the mobile phone market, but its sales and profits are stagnant while those of rival Samsung Electronics of Korea are zooming.[2]

Some companies get surprised by shifts in the environment and are unable to quickly adapt to new competition, changing consumer interests, or innovative technologies. Tower Records and Wherehouse both filed for bankruptcy, and some smaller retail music chains have simply disappeared, in the wake of Apple's iPod and other new channels that allow music lovers to download just what they want. Traditional music retailers are surviving only by diversifying into new areas or forming partnerships to create their own downloading services. In the airline industry, major carriers that use a traditional hub-and-spoke system, such as United Air Lines, Swissair, and US Airways, have been pummeled by smaller, nimbler competitors like JetBlue, Ryanair, and Southwest, which can prosper in today's difficult environment by keeping operations costs ultra-low.[3]

Numerous factors in the external environment cause turbulence and uncertainty for organizations. The external environment, including international competition and events, is the source of major threats confronting today's organizations. The environment often imposes significant constraints on the choices that managers make for an organization.

■ Purpose of This Chapter

The purpose of this chapter is to develop a framework for assessing environments and how organizations can respond to them. First, we will identify the organizational domain and the sectors that influence the organization. Then, we will explore two major environmental forces on the organization—the need for information and the need for resources. Organizations respond to these forces through structural design, planning systems, and attempts to change and control elements in the environment.

The Environmental Domain

In a broad sense the environment is infinite and includes everything outside the organization. However, the analysis presented here considers only those aspects of the environment to which the organization is sensitive and must respond to survive. Thus, **organizational environment** is defined as all elements that exist outside the boundary of the organization and have the potential to affect all or part of the organization.

The environment of an organization can be understood by analyzing its domain within external sectors. An organization's **domain** is the chosen environmental field of action. It is the territory an organization stakes out for itself with respect to products, services, and markets served. Domain defines the organization's niche and defines those external sectors with which the organization will interact to accomplish its goals.

The environment comprises several **sectors** or subdivisions of the external environment that contain similar elements. Ten sectors can be analyzed for each organization: industry, raw materials, human resources, financial resources, market, technology, economic conditions, government, sociocultural, and international. The sectors and a hypothetical organizational domain are illustrated in Exhibit 4.1. For most companies, the sectors in Exhibit 4.1 can be further subdivided into the task environment and general environment.

■ Task Environment

The **task environment** includes sectors with which the organization interacts directly and that have a direct impact on the organization's ability to achieve its goals. The task environment typically includes the industry, raw materials, and market sectors, and perhaps the human resources and international sectors.

The following examples illustrate how each of these sectors can affect organizations:

*   In the industry sector, Wal-Mart has become the nation's largest food retailer, and nontraditional outlets such as club stores and discounters now account for

EXHIBIT 4.1
*An Organization's
Environment*

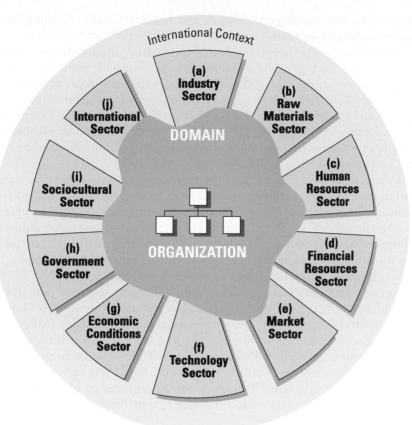

(a) Competitors, industry size and
    competitiveness, related industries

(b) Suppliers, manufacturers, real estate,
    services

(c) Labor market, employment agencies,
    universities, training schools, employees
    in other companies, unionization

(d) Stock markets, banks, savings and loans,
    private investors

(e) Customers, clients, potential users of
    products and services

(f) Techniques of production, science,
    computers, information technology,
    e-commerce

(g) Recession, unemployment rate, inflation
    rate, rate of investment, economics,
    growth

(h) City, state, federal laws and regulations,
    taxes, services, court system, political
    processes

(i) Age, values, beliefs, education, religion,
    work ethic, consumer and green
    movements

(j) Competition from and acquisition by
    foreign firms, entry into overseas
    markets, foreign customs, regulations,
    exchange rate

more than 30 percent of the grocery market. This shift is forcing traditional
supermarkets to find new ways to compete. Recall the discussion of Wegmans in
the Chapter 2 Leading by Design box. Wegmans has stayed competitive by
building larger stores, stocking gourmet foods and ready-made meals, and
adding services such as dry cleaning, child play centers, and wine shops.[4]

• An interesting example in the *raw materials sector* concerns the beverage can
industry. Steelmakers owned the beverage can market until the mid-1960s,
when Reynolds Aluminum Company launched a huge aluminum recycling

program to gain a cheaper source of raw materials and make aluminum cans price-competitive with steel.[5]

- In the *market sector*, keeping up with consumers' rapidly changing tastes is a real headache for big food companies such as Kraft and Nestlé SA. A few years ago, Kraft was at the top of the food chain, with a portfolio of brands including Oscar Mayer, Jell-O, Oreo, and Ritz. But growing consumer concerns over obesity and food-related health issues have taken a huge toll on Kraft's earnings. The company is now looking for growth primarily by expanding its organic and gourmet product offerings rather than pushing macaroni and cheese or cookies and crackers.[6]

- The *human resources sector* is of significant concern to every business. Research groups say U.S. businesses will soon face a shortage of skilled workers. Princeton, New Jersey–based Educational Testing Service, for example, found that the literacy of American adults ranks tenth out of seventeen industrialized countries. Moreover, younger adults underperform Americans over forty, leading researchers to warn that without improved adult training and education, U.S. companies will fall further behind in the global economy.[7]

- For most companies today, the *international sector* is also a part of the task environment because of globalization and intense competition. Outsourcing has become a hot-button issue, with companies in industries from toy manufacturing to information technology sending work to lower-wage countries to become more competitive. Biotechnology and life sciences firms once seemed immune to the trend, but that too is changing. Big U.S. drug manufacturers are facing pressures as smaller firms gain cost advantages by outsourcing to companies such as WuXi Pharmatech in Shanghai or Biocon in India.[8]

■ General Environment

The **general environment** includes those sectors that might not have a direct impact on the daily operations of a firm but will indirectly influence it. The general environment often includes the government, sociocultural, economic conditions, technology, and financial resources sectors. These sectors affect all organizations eventually. Consider the following examples:

- In the *government sector*, new European Union (EU) environmental and consumer protection legislation could cause headaches for many U.S. firms. For example, one new rule requires chemical makers who do business in EU countries to run safety and environmental impact tests on more than 30,000 chemicals, a process that could cost these companies more than $7 billion. Other new regulations require companies to pick up the tab for recycling the products they sell in the EU.[9]

- Shifting demographics is a significant element in the *sociocultural sector*. In the United States, Hispanics have passed African Americans as the nation's largest minority group, and their numbers are growing so fast that Hispanics (or Latinos, as many prefer to be called) are becoming a driving force in U.S. politics, economics, and culture. Kroger has already converted one of its Houston stores to an all-Hispanic *supermercado* to compete with Hispanic merchants, and the growing Hispanic population is forcing gradual changes in organizations from the U.S. Labor Department to the local auto parts store.[10]

- General *economic conditions* often affect the way a company does business. Germany's two most celebrated daily newspapers, the *Frankfurter Allgemeine*

Zeitung and the *Süddeutsche Zeitung*, expanded pell-mell during the economic boom of the late 1990s. When the economy crashed, both papers found themselves in dire financial circumstances and have had to cut jobs, close regional offices, scrap special sections, and cut out customized inserts.[11]

- The *technology sector* is an area in which massive changes have occurred in recent years, from digital music and video recorders to advances in cloning technology and stem-cell research. One technology having a tremendous impact on organizations is online software that allows people to easily create and maintain Web logs, or *blogs*. One estimate is that, in early 2005, 23,000 new Web logs were being created each day, with everyday people widely publishing information on everything from bad customer service to poor product performance.[12]

- All businesses have to be concerned with *financial resources*, but this sector is often first and foremost in the minds of entrepreneurs starting a new business. Ken Vaughan started a gas-mask business to take advantage of a boom in the asbestos-removal business. When the boom ended, it looked like Neoterik Health Technologies Inc. would end too. But after the terrorist attacks of September 11, 2001, Vaughan attracted the attention of venture capitalists, who were eager to invest financial resources in a company that could profit from concerns over homeland security.[13]

■ International Context

The international sector can directly affect many organizations, and it has become extremely important in the last few years. In addition, all domestic sectors can be affected by international events. Despite the significance of international events for today's organizations, many students fail to appreciate the importance of international events and still think domestically. Think again. Even if you stay in your hometown, your company may be purchased tomorrow by the English, Canadians, Japanese, or Germans. For example, General Shale Brick, with headquarters in a small town in East Tennessee, was bought by Wienerberger Baustoffindustrie AG, a Vienna, Austria, company that is the world's largest brickmaker. The Japanese alone own thousands of U.S. companies, including steel mills, rubber and tire factories, automobile assembly plants, and auto parts suppliers.[14]

The distinctions between foreign and domestic operations have become increasingly irrelevant. For example, in the auto industry, Ford owns Sweden's Volvo, while Chrysler, still considered one of America's Big Three automakers, is owned by Germany's DaimlerChrysler and builds its PT Cruiser in Mexico. Toyota, which recently overtook Ford as the world's second largest automaker, is a Japanese company, but it has built more than 10 million vehicles in North American factories. In addition, U.S.-based companies are involved in thousands of partnerships and alliances with firms all around the world. These increasing global interconnections have both positive and negative implications for organizations. Because of the significance of the international sector and its tremendous impact on organization design, this topic will be covered in detail in Chapter 6.

The growing importance of the international sector means that the environment for all organizations is becoming extremely complex and extremely competitive. However, every organization faces uncertainty domestically as well as globally. Consider how changing elements in the various environmental sectors have created uncertainty for advertising agencies such as Ogilvy & Mather.

In Practice

Ogilvy & Mather

It was a sad day in the advertising industry when Ogilvy & Mather, one of the most respected advertising agencies on Madison Avenue, was reduced to competing for business in a live online auction. The agency won the account, but that eased the pain only slightly.

The world has changed dramatically since Ogilvy & Mather's founders made deals with corporate CEOs over golf games and could reach 90 percent of the American public with a prime-time commercial on network television. Today, agency executives frequently have to dicker with people from their client's procurement department, who are used to beating down suppliers on the price of cardboard boxes or paper bags. They want to get the best deal, and they want to see a whole lot more than a couple of television spots.

The economic decline that followed the crash of the dot-coms and the 2001 terrorist attacks in the United States led to the worst advertising recession in more than half a century. Marketing budgets were often the first to be cut, and worldwide ad spending declined 7 percent in 2001. The agencies laid off 40,000 employees, nearly 20 percent of their workforce. The weak economic climate also led to a major change in how corporations pay for advertising. Up until that time, most clients paid their agencies a 15 percent commission on media purchases rather than paying them directly for their work. Today, though, many companies have cut out commissions altogether. Corporate procurement departments are demanding that the agencies clearly spell out their labor costs and how they are billing the client. The agencies are having a hard time making the shift.

And that's not even the biggest problem the ad agencies are having. Traditionally, agencies have relied on television and print media, but that's just not working anymore. The number of prime-time television viewers in the United States, particularly for the networks, continues to decline. And those who are watching often do so via new devices like TiVo that let them skip commercials entirely. New forms of media such as the Internet, video on demand, cellular phones, and video games are taking up a larger and larger percentage of people's time. Corporations are clamoring for more innovative low-key approaches, such as product placements in video games or products integrated into television shows and music events, as well as lower-cost options such as direct mail and Internet advertising. Yet the agencies have been slow to adapt, still clinging to the notion that making good half-a-million dollar 30-second television commercials will pay off.

The combination of weak economic conditions, media fragmentation, new technologies, and changing habits has the advertising industry reeling. Although many of these developments have been predicted for some time, the big agencies got caught flat-footed when they actually came to pass. As Ogilvy & Mather's CEO, Shelly Lazurus, says of the recent past, "These have not been the best years."[15]

Advertising agencies aren't the only organizations that have had a hard time adapting to massive shifts in the environment. In the following sections, we will discuss in greater detail how companies can cope with and respond to environmental uncertainty and instability.

Environmental Uncertainty

How does the environment influence an organization? The patterns and events occurring in the environment can be described along several dimensions, such as whether the environment is stable or unstable, homogeneous or heterogeneous, simple or complex; the *munificence*, or amount of resources available to support the organization's growth; whether those resources are concentrated or dispersed; and the degree of consensus in the environment regarding the organization's intended domain.[16] These dimensions boil down to two essential ways the environment influences organizations: (1) the need for information about the environment and (2) the need for resources from the environment. The environmental conditions of complexity and change create a greater need to gather information and to respond based on that information. The organization also is concerned with scarce material and financial resources and with the need to ensure availability of resources.

Environmental uncertainty pertains primarily to those sectors that an organization deals with on a regular, day-to-day basis. Recall the earlier discussion of the general environment and the task environment. Although sectors of the general environment—such as economic conditions, social trends, or technological changes—can create uncertainty for organizations, determining an organization's environmental uncertainty generally means focusing on sectors of the *task environment*, such as how many elements the organization deals with regularly, how rapidly these elements change, and so forth. To assess uncertainty, each sector of the organization's task environment can be analyzed along dimensions such as stability or instability and degree of complexity.[17] The total amount of uncertainty felt by an organization is the uncertainty accumulated across environmental sectors.

Organizations must cope with and manage uncertainty to be effective. **Uncertainty** means that decision makers do not have sufficient information about environmental factors, and they have a difficult time predicting external changes. Uncertainty increases the risk of failure for organizational responses and makes it difficult to compute costs and probabilities associated with decision alternatives.[18] The remainder of this section will focus on the information perspective, which is concerned with uncertainty created by the extent to which the environment is simple or complex and the extent to which events are stable or unstable. Later in the chapter, we discuss how organizations control the environment to acquire needed resources.

■ Simple–Complex Dimension

The **simple–complex dimension** concerns environmental complexity, which refers to heterogeneity, or the number and dissimilarity of external elements relevant to an organization's operations. The more external factors that regularly influence the organization and the greater number of other companies in an organization's domain, the greater the complexity. A complex environment is one in which the organization interacts with and is influenced by numerous diverse external elements. In a simple environment, the organization interacts with and is influenced by only a few similar external elements.

Aerospace firms such as Boeing Co. and Europe's Airbus operate in a complex environment, as do universities. Universities span a large number of technologies and are continually buffeted by social, cultural, and value changes. Universities also must cope with numerous ever-changing government regulations, competition for quality students and highly educated employees, and scarce financial resources for many programs. They deal with granting agencies, professional and scientific associations, alumni, parents, foundations, legislators, community residents, international agencies, donors, corporations, and athletic teams. This large number of external elements make up the organization's domain, creating a complex environment. On the other hand, a family-owned hardware store in a suburban community is in a simple environment. The store does not have to deal with complex technologies or extensive government regulations, and cultural and social changes have little impact. Human resources is not a problem because the store is run by family members and part-time help. The only external elements of real importance are a few competitors, suppliers, and customers.

■ Stable–Unstable Dimension

The **stable–unstable dimension** refers to whether elements in the environment are dynamic. An environmental domain is stable if it remains the same over a period of months or years. Under unstable conditions, environmental elements shift abruptly. Environmental domains seem to be increasingly unstable for most organizations. This chapter's Book Mark examines the volatile nature of today's business world and gives some tips for managing in a fast-shifting environment.

Book Mark 4.0 (HAVE YOU READ THIS BOOK?)

Confronting Reality: Doing What Matters to Get Things Right
By Lawrence A. Bossidy and Ram Charan

The business world has changed in recent years and will continue to change at an increasingly rapid pace. That's the reality that spurred Larry Bossidy, retired chairman and CEO of Honeywell International, and Ram Charan, a noted author, speaker, and business consultant, to write *Confronting Reality: Doing What Matters to Get Things Right.* Too many managers, they believe, are tempted to hide their heads in the sand of financial issues rather than face the confusion and complexity of the organization's environment.

LESSONS FOR FACING REALITY

For many companies, today's environment is characterized by global hyper-competition, declining prices, and the growing power of consumers. Bossidy and Charan offer some lessons to leaders for navigating a fast-changing world.

- *Understand the environment as it is now and is likely to be in the future, rather than as it was in the past.* Relying on the past and conventional wisdom can lead to disaster. Kmart, for example, stuck to its old formula as Wal-Mart gobbled its customers and carved out a new business model. Few could have predicted in 1990, for example, that Wal-Mart would now be America's biggest seller of groceries.
- *Seek out and welcome diverse and unorthodox ideas.* Managers need to be proactive and open-minded toward conversing with employees, suppliers, customers, colleagues, and anyone else they come in contact with. What are people thinking about? What changes and opportunities do they see? What worries them about the future?
- *Avoid the common causes of manager failure to confront reality: filtered information, selective hearing, wishful thinking, fear, emotional overinvestment in a failing* course of action, and unrealistic expectations. For example, when sales and profits fell off a cliff at data-storage giant EMC in early 2001, managers displayed a bias toward hearing good news and believed the company was only experiencing a blip in the growth curve. When Joe Tucci was named CEO, however, he was determined to find out if the slump was temporary. By talking directly with top leaders at his customers' organization, Tucci was able to face the reality that EMC's existing business model based on high-cost technology was dead. Tucci implemented a new business model to fit that reality.

- *Ruthlessly assess your organization.* Understanding the internal environment is just as important. Managers need to evaluate whether their company has the talent, commitment, and attitude needed to drive the important changes. At EMC, Tucci realized his sales force needed an attitude shift to sell software, services, and business solutions rather than just expensive hardware. The arrogant, hard-driving sales tactics of the past had to be replaced with a softer, more customer-oriented approach.

STAYING ALIVE

Staying alive in today's business environment requires that managers stay alert. Managers should always be looking at their competitors, broad industry trends, technological changes, shifting government policies, changing market forces, and economic developments. At the same time, they work hard to stay in touch with what their customers really think and really want. By doing so, leaders can confront reality and be poised for change.

Confronting Reality: Doing What Matters to Get Things Right, by Lawrence A. Bossidy and Ram Charan, is published by Crown Business Publishing.

Instability may occur when competitors react with aggressive moves and countermoves regarding advertising and new products, as happened with Nokia, described in the chapter opening. Sometimes specific, unpredictable events—such as Janet Jackson's "wardrobe malfunction" at the 2004 Super Bowl halftime show, accounts of anthrax-laced letters being sent through the U.S. Postal Service, or the discovery of heart problems related to pain drugs such as Vioxx and Celebrex—create unstable conditions. Today, "hate sites" on the World Wide Web, such as *Ihatemcdonalds.com* and *Walmartsucks.com*, are an important source of instability for scores of companies. In addition, freewheeling bloggers can destroy a company's reputation virtually overnight. Kryptonite's reputation in bicycle locks plummeted after a Web log was posted that the locks could be opened with a Bic pen. After 10 days of blogging, Kryptonite announced a free product exchange that would cost it about $10 million.[19]

Although environments are more unstable for most organizations today, an example of a traditionally stable environment is a public utility.[20] In the rural Midwest, demand and supply factors for a public utility are stable. A gradual increase in demand may occur, which is easily predicted over time. Toy companies, by contrast, have an unstable environment. Hot new toys are difficult to predict, a problem compounded by the fact that children are losing interest in toys at a younger age, their interest captured by video games, cable TV, and the Internet. Adding to the instability for toymakers such as Mattel and Hasbro is the shrinking retail market, with big toy retailers going out of business trying to compete with discounters such as Wal-Mart. Toy manufacturers often find their biggest products languishing on shelves as shoppers turn to less-expensive knock-offs produced for Wal-Mart by low-cost manufacturers in China.[21]

Framework

The simple–complex and stable–unstable dimensions are combined into a framework for assessing environmental uncertainty in Exhibit 4.2. In the *simple, stable* environment, uncertainty is low. There are only a few external elements to contend with, and they tend to remain stable. The *complex, stable* environment represents somewhat greater uncertainty. A large number of elements have to be scanned, analyzed, and acted upon for the organization to perform well. External elements do not change rapidly or unexpectedly in this environment.

Even greater uncertainty is felt in the *simple, unstable* environment.[22] Rapid change creates uncertainty for managers. Even though the organization has few external elements, those elements are hard to predict, and they react unexpectedly to organizational initiatives. The greatest uncertainty for an organization occurs in the *complex, unstable* environment. A large number of elements impinge upon the organization, and they shift frequently or react strongly to organizational initiatives. When several sectors change simultaneously, the environment becomes turbulent.[23]

A beer distributor functions in a simple, stable environment. Demand for beer changes only gradually. The distributor has an established delivery route, and supplies of beer arrive on schedule. State universities, appliance manufacturers, and insurance companies are in somewhat stable, complex environments. A large number of external elements are present, but although they change, changes are gradual and predictable.

Toy manufacturers are in simple, unstable environments. Organizations that design, make, and sell toys, as well as those that are involved in the clothing or music

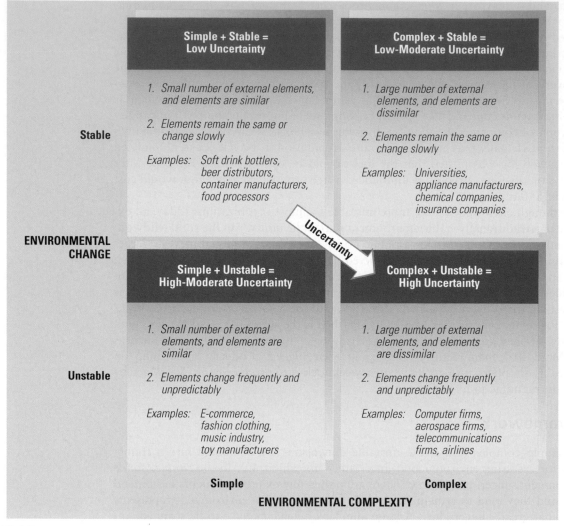

EXHIBIT 4.2

Framework for Assessing Environmental Uncertainty

Source: Adapted and reprinted from "Characteristics of Perceived Environments and Perceived Environmental Uncertainty," by Robert B. Duncan, published in *Administrative Science Quarterly* 17 (1972), 313–327, by permission of *The Administrative Science Quarterly*. Copyright © 1972 by Cornell University.

industry, face shifting supply and demand. Most e-commerce companies focus on a specific competitive niche and, hence, operate in simple but unstable environments as well. Although there may be few elements to contend with—e.g., technology, competitors—they are difficult to predict and change abruptly and unexpectedly.

The telecommunications industry and the airline industry face complex, unstable environments. Many external sectors are changing simultaneously. In the case of airlines, in just a few years they were confronted with an air-traffic controller shortage, price cuts from low-cost carriers such as Southwest Airlines, soaring fuel prices, the entry of new competitors such as JetBlue and AirTran, a series of major air-traffic disasters, and a drastic decline in customer demand following the 2001 terrorist attacks.

Adapting to Environmental Uncertainty

Once you see how environments differ with respect to change and complexity, the next question is, "How do organizations adapt to each level of environmental uncertainty?" Environmental uncertainty represents an important contingency for organization structure and internal behaviors. Recall from Chapter 3 that organizations facing uncertainty generally have a more horizontal structure that encourages cross-functional communication and collaboration to help the company adapt to changes in the environment. In this section we discuss in more detail how the environment affects organizations. An organization in a certain environment will be managed and controlled differently from an organization in an uncertain environment with respect to positions and departments, organizational differentiation and integration, control processes, and future planning and forecasting. Organizations need to have the right fit between internal structure and the external environment.

Positions and Departments

As the complexity and uncertainty in the external environment increases, so does the number of positions and departments within the organization, which in turn increases internal complexity. This relationship is part of being an open system. Each sector in the external environment requires an employee or department to deal with it. The human resource department deals with unemployed people who want to work for the company. The marketing department finds customers. Procurement employees obtain raw materials from hundreds of suppliers. The finance group deals with bankers. The legal department works with the courts and government agencies. Many companies have added e-business departments to handle electronic commerce and information technology departments to deal with the increasing complexity of computerized information and knowledge management systems.

The U.S. government has also responded to environmental uncertainty by creating new positions and departments. Soon after the 2001 terrorist attacks in the United States, Congress created a Department of Homeland Security to merge all or parts of various agencies and create a coordinated national strategy for domestic protection, preparedness, and response.[24]

Buffering and Boundary Spanning

The traditional approach to coping with environmental uncertainty was to establish buffer departments. The purpose of **buffering roles** is to absorb uncertainty from the environment.[25] The technical core performs the primary production activity of an organization. Buffer departments surround the technical core and exchange materials, resources, and money between the environment and the organization. They help the technical core function efficiently. The purchasing department buffers the technical core by stockpiling supplies and raw materials. The human resource department buffers the technical core by handling the uncertainty associated with finding, hiring, and training production employees.

A newer approach some organizations are trying is to drop the buffers and expose the technical core to the uncertain environment. These organizations no longer create buffers because they believe being well connected to customers and suppliers is more important than internal efficiency. For example, John Deere has assembly-line workers visiting local farms to determine and respond to customer concerns. Whirlpool pays hundreds of customers to test computer-simulated products and features.[26] Opening up the organization to the environment makes it more fluid and adaptable.

Boundary-spanning roles link and coordinate an organization with key elements in the external environment. Boundary spanning is primarily concerned with the exchange of information to (1) detect and bring into the organization information about changes in the environment and (2) send information into the environment that presents the organization in a favorable light.[27]

Organizations have to keep in touch with what is going on in the environment so that managers can respond to market changes and other developments. A study of high-tech firms found that 97 percent of competitive failures resulted from lack of attention to market changes or the failure to act on vital information.[28] To detect and bring important information into the organization, boundary personnel scan the environment. For example, a market-research department scans and monitors trends in consumer tastes. Boundary spanners in engineering and research and development (R&D) departments scan new technological developments, innovations, and raw materials. Boundary spanners prevent the organization from stagnating by keeping top managers informed about environmental changes. Often, the greater the uncertainty in the environment, the greater the importance of boundary spanners.[29]

One new approach to boundary spanning is **business intelligence**, which refers to the high-tech analysis of large amounts of internal and external data to spot patterns and relationships that might be significant. For example, Verizon uses business-intelligence to actively monitor customer interactions so that it can catch problems and fix them almost immediately.[30] Tools to automate the process have been the hottest area of software in recent years, with companies spending over $4 billion on business-intelligence software in one recent year and the amount expected to double by 2006.[31]

Business intelligence is related to another important area of boundary spanning, known as *competitive intelligence* (CI). Membership in the Society of Competitive Intelligence Professionals has more than doubled since 1997, and colleges are setting up master's degree programs in CI to respond to the growing demand for these professionals in organizations.[32] Competitive intelligence gives top executives a systematic way to collect and analyze public information about rivals and use it to make better decisions.[33] Using techniques that range from Internet surfing to digging through trash cans, intelligence professionals dig up information on competitors' new products, manufacturing costs, or training methods and share it with top leaders.

In today's turbulent environment, many successful companies involve everyone in boundary-spanning activities. People at the grass-roots level are often able to see and interpret changes or problems sooner than managers, who are typically more removed from the day-to-day work.[34] At Cognos, which sells planning and budgeting programs to large corporations, any of the company's 3,000 employees can submit scoops about competitors through an internal Web site called Street Fighter. Each day, R&D and sales managers pore over the dozens of entries. Good tips are rewarded with prizes.[35]

The boundary task of sending information into the environment to represent the organization is used to influence other people's perception of the organization. In the marketing department, advertising and sales people represent the organization to customers. Purchasers may call on suppliers and describe purchasing needs. The legal department informs lobbyists and elected officials about the organization's needs or views on political matters. Many companies set up their own Web pages to present the organization in a favorable light. For example, to counteract hate sites that criticize their labor practices in Third World countries, Nike and Unocal both created Web sites specifically to tell their side of the story.[36]

All organizations have to keep in touch with the environment. Here's how Genesco, a growing Nashville-based retailer that markets shoes and apparel to trend-savvy teenagers, spans the boundary in the shifting environment of the fashion industry.

James Estepa, the head of Genesco Retail group, lives by the motto, "You're never moving fast enough to satisfy the fickle teen consumer." With teenagers' fashion preferences changing on a weekly basis, how do companies like Genesco stay on top of things? Estepa says his company does it by stepping inside the teenage mind.

For years, Genesco was best known for its Johnston & Murphy brand, the staid brown shoes worn by middle-aged businessmen and U.S. presidents. But recently, the company has transformed itself into a fashion powerhouse with its Journeys teen-focused shoe stores and Underground Station, the nation's second-largest chain of urban-inspired apparel stores. One way Genesco stays on top of trends is by hiring people who are close to the age of its target customers. Sales associates in Journeys and Underground Station stores wear the same kinds of clothes, listen to the same kinds of music, and watch the same movies as their customers. The company's buyers and merchandisers are young too. They spend hours watching music videos, surfing the Internet, and playing the hottest new video games. Staying on top of moment-to-moment shifts in popular culture is the top priority for Genesco's buyers. It is they, rather than managers, who make initial shoe and clothing orders, and they have minimal buying constraints. "If an item shows up on the music videos, the kids are in the stores the next day trying to buy it," Estepa explains. Flexible internal procedures and strong partnerships with vendors enable Genesco to get products into stores fast.

Another key to staying on top of what's hot is continually analyzing sales data. Managers and buyers monitor store and individual shoe sales daily. In many cases, this enables managers to tell how strong a product is going to be from the first day it hits the stores, helping Genesco follow, rather than try to lead, its customers.

"There's a huge amount of fashion risk in this business," says Chris Svezia, an analyst who follows the performance of Genesco. "The important thing is just to stay on top of it. Right now they're on the upswing of getting it right."[37]

In Practice

Genesco

■ Differentiation and Integration

Another response to environmental uncertainty is the amount of differentiation and integration among departments. Organizational **differentiation** is "the differences in cognitive and emotional orientations among managers in different functional departments, and the difference in formal structure among these departments."[38] When the external environment is complex and rapidly changing, organizational departments become highly specialized to handle the uncertainty in their external sector. Success in each sector requires special expertise and behavior. Employees in an R&D department thus have unique attitudes, values, goals, and education that distinguish them from employees in manufacturing or sales departments.

EXHIBIT 4.3
*Organizational
Departments Differentiate
to Meet Needs of
Subenvironments*

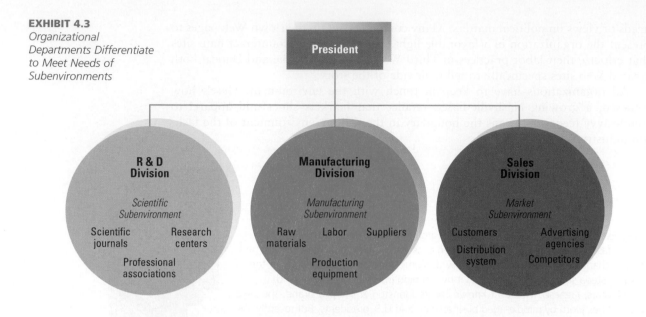

A study by Paul Lawrence and Jay Lorsch examined three organizational departments—manufacturing, research, and sales—in ten corporations.[39] This study found that each department evolved toward a different orientation and structure to deal with specialized parts of the external environment. The market, scientific, and manufacturing subenvironments identified by Lawrence and Lorsch are illustrated in Exhibit 4.3. Each department interacted with different external groups. The differences that evolved among departments within the organizations are shown in Exhibit 4.4. To work effectively with the scientific subenvironment, R&D had a goal of quality work, a long time horizon (up to 5 years), an informal structure, and task-oriented employees. Sales was at the opposite extreme. It had a goal of customer satisfaction, was oriented toward the short term (2 weeks or so), had a very formal structure, and was socially oriented.

One outcome of high differentiation is that coordination among departments becomes difficult. More time and resources must be devoted to achieving coordination when attitudes, goals, and work orientation differ so widely. **Integration** is the quality of collaboration among departments.[40] Formal integrators are often required to coordinate departments. When the environment is highly uncertain, frequent

EXHIBIT 4.4
Differences in Goals and Orientations among Organizational Departments

Characteristic	R&D Department	Manufacturing Department	Sales Department
Goals	New developments, quality	Efficient production	Customer satisfaction
Time horizon	Long	Short	Short
Interpersonal orientation	Mostly task	Task	Social
Formality of structure	Low	High	High

Source: Based on Paul R. Lawrence and Jay W. Lorsch, *Organization and Environment* (Homewood, Ill.: Irwin, 1969), 23–29.

EXHIBIT 4.5
Environmental Uncertainty and Organizational Integrators

Industry	Plastics	Foods	Container
Environmental uncertainty	High	Moderate	Low
Departmental differentiation	High	Moderate	Low
Percent management in integrating roles	22%	17%	0%

Source: Based on Jay W. Lorsch and Paul R. Lawrence, "Environmental Factors and Organizational Integration," *Organizational Planning: Cases and Concepts* (Homewood, Ill.: Irwin and Dorsey, 1972), 45.

changes require more information processing to achieve horizontal coordination, so integrators become a necessary addition to the organization structure. Sometimes integrators are called liaison personnel, project managers, brand managers, or coordinators. As illustrated in Exhibit 4.5, organizations with highly uncertain environments and a highly differentiated structure assign about 22 percent of management personnel to integration activities, such as serving on committees, on task forces, or in liaison roles.[41] In organizations characterized by very simple, stable environments, almost no managers are assigned to integration roles. Exhibit 4.5 shows that, as environmental uncertainty increases, so does differentiation among departments; hence, the organization must assign a larger percentage of managers to coordinating roles.

Lawrence and Lorsch's research concluded that organizations perform better when the levels of differentiation and integration match the level of uncertainty in the environment. Organizations that performed well in uncertain environments had high levels of both differentiation and integration, while those performing well in less uncertain environments had lower levels of differentiation and integration.

▪ Organic versus Mechanistic Management Processes

Another response to environmental uncertainty is the amount of formal structure and control imposed on employees. Tom Burns and G. M. Stalker observed twenty industrial firms in England and discovered that external environment was related to internal management structure.[42] When the external environment was stable, the internal organization was characterized by rules, procedures, and a clear hierarchy of authority. Organizations were formalized. They were also centralized, with most decisions made at the top. Burns and Stalker called this a **mechanistic** organization system.

In rapidly changing environments, the internal organization was much looser, free-flowing, and adaptive. Rules and regulations often were not written down or, if written down, were ignored. People had to find their own way through the system to figure out what to do. The hierarchy of authority was not clear. Decision-making authority was decentralized. Burns and Stalker used the term **organic** to characterize this type of management structure.

Exhibit 4.6 summarizes the differences in organic and mechanistic systems. As environmental uncertainty increases, organizations tend to become more organic, which means decentralizing authority and responsibility to lower levels, encouraging employees to take care of problems by working directly with one another, encouraging teamwork, and taking an informal approach to assigning tasks and responsibility. Thus, the organization is more fluid and is able to adapt continually to changes in the external environment.[43]

Briefcase

As an organization manager, keep these guidelines in mind:

Match internal organization structure to the external environment. If the external environment is complex, make the organization structure complex. Associate a stable environment with a mechanistic structure and an unstable environment with an organic structure. If the external environment is both complex and changing, make the organization highly differentiated and organic, and use mechanisms to achieve coordination across departments.

EXHIBIT 4.6
Mechanistic and Organic Forms

Mechanistic	Organic
1. Tasks are broken down into specialized, separate parts.	1. Employees contribute to the common tasks of the department.
2. Tasks are rigidly defined.	2. Tasks are adjusted and redefined through employee teamwork.
3. There is a strict hierarchy of authority and control, and there are many rules.	3. There is less hierarchy of authority and control, and there are few rules.
4. Knowledge and control of tasks are centralized at the top of the organization.	4. Knowledge and control of tasks are located anywhere in the organization.
5. Communication is vertical.	5. Communication is horizontal.

Source: Adapted from Gerald Zaltman, Robert Duncan, and Jonny Holbek, *Innovations and Organizations* (New York: Wiley, 1973), 131.

The learning organization, described in Chapter 1, and the horizontal and virtual network structures, described in Chapter 3, are organic organizational forms that are used by companies to compete in rapidly changing environments. Guiltless Gourmet, which sells low-fat tortilla chips and other high-quality snack foods, shifted to a flexible network structure to remain competitive when large companies like Frito Lay entered the low-fat snack-food market. The company redesigned itself to become basically a full-time marketing organization, while production and other activities were outsourced. An 18,000-square-foot plant in Austin was closed and the workforce cut from 125 to about 10 core people who handle marketing and sales promotions. The flexible structure allows Guiltless Gourmet to adapt quickly to changing market conditions.[44] Another excellent example of a company that shifted to a more organic system to cope with change and uncertainty is Rowe Furniture Company, described in the Leading by Design box.

■ Planning, Forecasting, and Responsiveness

The whole point of increasing internal integration and shifting to more organic processes is to enhance the organization's ability to quickly respond to sudden changes in an uncertain environment. It might seem that in an environment where everything is changing all the time, planning is useless. However, in uncertain environments, planning and environmental forecasting actually become *more* important as a way to keep the organization geared for a coordinated, speedy response. Japanese electronic giants such as Toshiba and Fujitsu, for example, were caught off guard by a combination of nimble new competitors, rapid technological change, deregulation, the declining stability of Japan's banking system, and the sudden end of the 1990s technology boom. Lulled into complacency by years of success, Japan's industrial electronics companies were unprepared to respond to these dramatic changes and lost billions.[45]

When the environment is stable, the organization can concentrate on current operational problems and day-to-day efficiency. Long-range planning and forecasting are not needed because environmental demands in the future will be the same as they are today.

Leading by Design

Rowe Furniture Company

Nestled in the foothills of the Appalachian Mountains, the Rowe Furniture Company has been cranking out sofas, loveseats, and easy chairs for nearly 60 years. For most of that time, Rowe's workers punched their time cards, turned off their brains, and did exactly what the boss told them to do. Rowe's factory used to be a traditional assembly line, with people performing the same boring tasks over and over—one person cutting, another sewing, another gluing, and so forth. Rowe had been successful with this approach so far, but the marketplace was changing and top executives knew Rowe needed to change to keep pace.

Inexpensive imports had snagged about 16 percent of the upholstered furniture market by early 2005, and Rowe is determined to keep that number from growing much larger. The only way to do that is to offer more styles and fabrics, better quality, and a fast turnaround on custom-made pieces. Furniture shoppers used to be content to buy what was on the showroom floor or else wait several months for a custom-made product. Today's customer wants customized pieces "now." Bruce Birnback, president and chief operating officer of Rowe, believes the custom-order market is the Achilles' heel of low-cost Chinese competitors. He's aiming for an audacious goal of getting custom sofas to retailers in only 10 days.

To meet that difficult challenge, Birnback knew Rowe needed a hyper-efficient assembly process. Managers researched lean manufacturing and realized the operational and cultural factors that made Toyota so successful in automobile manufacturing could be applied in a furniture factory as well. The assembly line was scrapped in favor of a cellular design that has small teams of workers making a piece of furniture from start to finish. A sophisticated computer system was installed so that furniture retailers could send orders to the factory electronically the minute they were placed. The system can immediately start the production process by ordering fabric and assigning the order to a specific team.

The key to success, though, was employee involvement and team commitment. Managers set the basic outline, but employee teams worked closely with engineers to design the new production system. Most supervisory positions were eliminated, and people were cross-trained to perform the different tasks required to build a piece of furniture. Team members signed a pledge of unity agreeing to pitch in and help colleagues, making team goals a priority. Each group selected its own members from the various functional areas and then created the processes, schedules, and routines for a particular product line. Although there was some resistance among employees in the beginning, when the pieces fell into place productivity and quality shot through the roof. Rowe is closing in on its goal of the 10-day sofa. Just as important, employees are enjoying the new sense of involvement and the challenge and responsibility that comes from continuously improving the process. "[The managers] make you feel you're important to this company," said Rhonda Melton, a lead sewer and dispatcher. "They want your opinions."

Open information is an important part of the new culture at Rowe. Everything gets posted, and every team member has instant access to current information about order flows, output, productivity, and quality. Data that were once closely guarded by management are now the common property of the shop floor. The sense of personal control and responsibility has led to some dramatic changes in workers, who often hold impromptu meetings to discuss problems, check each other's progress, or talk about new ideas and better ways of doing things. One group, for example, came together as a "down-pillow task force" to invent a better stuffing process.

The shift to an organic system at Rowe did not happen overnight, but managers believe the results were worth the effort, creating an environment in which workers are constantly learning, solving problems, and creating new and better operational procedures.

Sources: Chuck Salter, "When Couches Fly," *Fast Company* (July 2004), 80–81; Thomas Petzinger, Jr., *The New Pioneers: The Men and Women Who Are Transforming the Workplace and Marketplace* (New York: Simon & Schuster, 1999), 27–32; and Cheryl Lu-Lien Tan, "U.S. Response: Speedier Delivery," *The Wall Street Journal* (November 18, 2004), D1.

With increasing environmental uncertainty, planning and forecasting become necessary.[46] Planning can soften the adverse impact of external shifts. Organizations that have unstable environments often establish a separate planning department. In an unpredictable environment, planners scan environmental elements and analyze potential moves and countermoves by other organizations. Planning can be extensive and may forecast various *scenarios* for environmental contingencies. With scenario building, managers mentally rehearse different scenarios based on anticipating various changes that could affect the organization. Scenarios are like stories that offer alternative, vivid pictures of what the future will look like and how managers will respond. Royal Dutch/Shell Oil has long used scenario building and has been a leader in speedy response to massive changes that other organizations failed to perceive until it was too late.[47]

Planning, however, cannot substitute for other actions, such as effective boundary spanning and adequate internal integration and coordination. The organizations that are most successful in uncertain environments are those that keep everyone in close touch with the environment so they can spot threats and opportunities, enabling the organization to respond immediately.

Framework for Organizational Responses to Uncertainty

The ways environmental uncertainty influences organizational characteristics are summarized in Exhibit 4.7. The change and complexity dimensions are combined and illustrate four levels of uncertainty. The low uncertainty environment is simple and stable. Organizations in this environment have few departments and a mechanistic structure. In a low-moderate uncertainty environment, more departments are needed, along with more integrating roles to coordinate the departments. Some planning may occur. Environments that are high-moderate uncertainty are unstable but simple. Organization structure is organic and decentralized. Planning is emphasized and managers are quick to make internal changes as needed. The high uncertainty environment is both complex and unstable and is the most difficult environment from a management perspective. Organizations are large and have many departments, but they are also organic. A large number of management personnel are assigned to coordination and integration, and the organization uses boundary spanning, planning, and forecasting to enable a high-speed response to environmental changes.

Resource Dependence

Thus far, this chapter has described several ways in which organizations adapt to the lack of information and to the uncertainty caused by environmental change and complexity. We turn now to the third characteristic of the organization-environment relationship that affects organizations, which is the need for material and financial resources. The environment is the source of scarce and valued resources essential to organizational survival. Research in this area is called the *resource-dependence perspective*. **Resource dependence** means that organizations depend on the environment but strive to acquire control over resources to minimize their dependence.[48] Organizations are vulnerable if vital resources are controlled by other organizations, so they try to be as independent as possible. Organizations do not want to become too vulnerable to other organizations because of negative effects on performance.

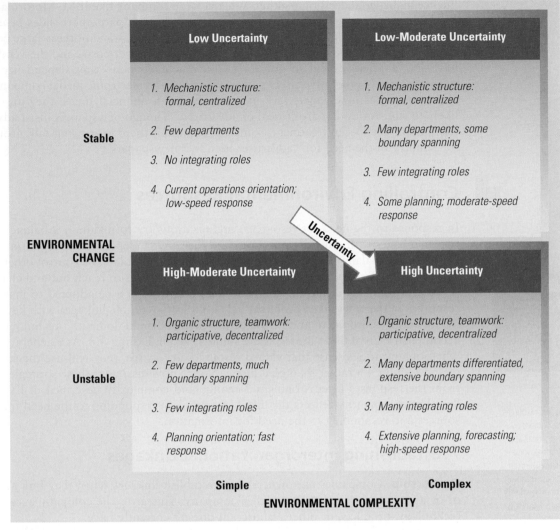

EXHIBIT 4.7
Contingency Framework for Environmental Uncertainty and Organizational Responses

Although companies like to minimize their dependence, when costs and risks are high they also team up to share scarce resources and be more competitive on a global basis. Formal relationships with other organizations present a dilemma to managers. Organizations seek to reduce vulnerability with respect to resources by developing links with other organizations, but they also like to maximize their own autonomy and independence. Organizational linkages require coordination,[49] and they reduce the freedom of each organization to make decisions without concern for the needs and goals of other organizations. Interorganizational relationships thus represent a tradeoff between resources and autonomy. To maintain autonomy, organizations that already have abundant resources will tend not to establish new linkages. Organizations that need resources will give up independence to acquire those resources.

Dependence on shared resources gives power to other organizations. Once an organization relies on others for valued resources, those other organizations can influence managerial decision making. When a large company like IBM, Motorola, or Ford Motor Co. forges a partnership with a supplier for parts, both sides benefit, but each loses a small amount of autonomy. For example, some of these large companies are now putting strong pressure on vendors to lower costs, and the vendors have few alternatives but to go along.[50] In much the same way, dependence on shared resources gives advertisers power over print and electronic media companies. For example, as newspapers face increasingly tough financial times, they are less likely to run stories that are critical of advertisers. Though newspapers insist advertisers don't get special treatment, some editors admit there is growing talk around the country of the need for "advertiser-friendly" newspapers.[51]

Controlling Environmental Resources

In response to the need for resources, organizations try to maintain a balance between linkages with other organizations and their own independence. Organizations maintain this balance through attempts to modify, manipulate, or control other organizations.[52] To survive, the focal organization often tries to reach out and change or control elements in the environment. Two strategies can be adopted to manage resources in the external environment: (1) establish favorable linkages with key elements in the environment and (2) shape the environmental domain.[53] Techniques to accomplish each of these strategies are summarized in Exhibit 4.8. As a general rule, when organizations sense that valued resources are scarce, they will use the strategies in Exhibit 4.8 rather than go it alone. Notice how dissimilar these strategies are from the responses to environmental change and complexity described in Exhibit 4.7. The dissimilarity reflects the difference between responding to the need for resources and responding to the need for information.

Establishing Interorganizational Linkages

Ownership. Companies use ownership to establish linkages when they buy a part of or a controlling interest in another company. This gives the company access to technology, products, or other resources it doesn't currently have.

A greater degree of ownership and control is obtained through acquisition or merger. An *acquisition* involves the purchase of one organization by another so that the buyer assumes control. A *merger* is the unification of two or more organizations into a single unit.[54] In the banking industry, Wells Fargo merged with Norwest and Chase merged with Banc One. Acquisition occurred when IBM bought software developer Lotus Development Corp. and when Wal-Mart purchased Britain's ASDA Group. These forms of ownership reduce uncertainty in an area important to the

Briefcase

As an organization manager, keep these guidelines in mind:

Reach out and control external sectors that threaten needed resources. Influence the domain by engaging in political activity, joining trade associations, and establishing favorable linkages. Establish linkages through ownership, strategic alliances, cooptation, interlocking directorates, and executive recruitment. Reduce the amount of change or threat from the external environment so the organization will not have to change internally.

EXHIBIT 4.8
Organizing Strategies for Controlling the External Environment

Establishing Interorganizational Linkages	Controlling the Environmental Domain
1. Ownership	1. Change of domain
2. Contracts, joint ventures	2. Political activity, regulation
3. Cooptation, interlocking directorates	3. Trade associations
4. Executive recruitment	4. Illegitimate activities
5. Advertising, public relations	

acquiring company. In the past few years, there has been a huge wave of acquisition and merger activity in the telecommunications industry, reflecting the tremendous uncertainty these organizations face.

Cingular and AT&T Wireless. Sprint and Nextel. SBC Communications and AT&T. Verizon and MCI. Western Wireless and Alltel. Between February 2004 and February 2005, it seemed that every month brought news of another acquisition or merger in the telecommunications industry. After $100 billion in deals over the year, two giants are poised to rule the industry if they get regulatory approval of the recent mergers. Verizon and SBC Communications Inc. were both created out of the breakup of AT&T in the mid-1980s. They've spent the past couple of decades acquiring the size and resources they need to remain competitive in the complex and rapidly changing telecommunications industry.

The mergers have given the two "Papa Bells," as they're being called by one Federal Communications Commission official, nationwide reach and a hand in every aspect of modern communications—local, long distance, wireless, Internet, and now even television. With more and more people giving up land lines in favor of wireless, and new competition such as Internet phone service from cable operators, telephone companies have had a tough time. For example, MCI was a long-distance powerhouse in the late 1980s, but long-distance is a losing battle these days. However, the nationwide clout MCI had built, especially with corporate customers, was just what Verizon needed to give it a springboard to compete in the changing arena. Verizon's major competitor, SBC, had similar reasons for buying AT&T Corp. The erosion of SBC's core business (it lost 4 million land lines since 2002) means the company had to gain the size and resources to expand into new areas. Both SBC and Verizon are moving fast to provide a bundle of services that include phone, wireless, Internet, cable television, and on-demand TV.

The cable companies aren't going to just lie down, and the fight is just beginning. However, the recent mergers have put Verizon and SBC in a better position to ride out the waves of change and uncertainty.[55]

In Practice
Verizon and SBC Communications Inc.

Formal Strategic Alliances. When there is a high level of complementarity between the business lines, geographical positions, or skills of two companies, the firms often go the route of a strategic alliance rather than ownership through merger or acquisition.[56] Such alliances are formed through contracts and joint ventures.

Contracts and joint ventures reduce uncertainty through a legal and binding relationship with another firm. Contracts come in the form of *license agreements* that involve the purchase of the right to use an asset (such as a new technology) for a specific time and *supplier arrangements* that contract for the sale of one firm's output to another. Contracts can provide long-term security by tying customers and suppliers to specific amounts and prices. For example, the Italian fashion house Versace has forged a deal to license its primary asset—its name—for a line of designer eyeglasses. McDonald's contracts for an entire crop of russet potatoes to be certain of its supply of french fries. McDonald's also gains influence over suppliers through these contracts and has changed the way farmers grow potatoes and the profit margins they earn, which is consistent with the resource dependence perspective.[57] Large retailers such as Wal-Mart, Target, and Home Depot are gaining so much clout that they can almost dictate contracts, telling manufacturers what to make, how to make it, and how much to charge for it. Many music companies edit songs and visual covers of their CDs to cut out "offensive material" in order to get their products on the shelves of Wal-Mart, which sells more than 50 million CDs annually.[58]

Joint ventures result in the creation of a new organization that is formally independent of the parents, although the parents will have some control.[59] In a joint venture, organizations share the risk and cost associated with large projects or innovations. AOL created a joint venture with Venezuela's Cisneros Group to smooth its entry into the Latin American online market. IBM formed a joint venture with USA Technologies Inc. to test Web-enabled washers and dryers at colleges and universities. Traditional coin-operated technology will be replaced with an IBM micropayment system that allows students to pay by swiping an ID card or pushing a code on a cell phone. They can log onto a Web site to see if a machine is available and have an e-mail sent when a load is done.[60]

Cooptation, Interlocking Directorates. Cooptation occurs when leaders from important sectors in the environment are made part of an organization. It takes place, for example, when influential customers or suppliers are appointed to the board of directors, such as when the senior executive of a bank sits on the board of a manufacturing company. As a board member, the banker may become psychologically coopted into the interests of the manufacturing firm. Community leaders also can be appointed to a company's board of directors or to other organizational committees or task forces. These influential people are thus introduced to the needs of the company and are more likely to include the company's interests in their decision making.

An **interlocking directorate** is a formal linkage that occurs when a member of the board of directors of one company sits on the board of directors of another company. The individual is a communications link between companies and can influence policies and decisions. When one individual is the link between two companies, this is typically referred to as a **direct interlock**. An **indirect interlock** occurs when a director of company A and a director of company B are both directors of company C. They have access to one another but do not have direct influence over their respective companies.[61] Recent research shows that, as a firm's financial fortunes decline, direct interlocks with financial institutions increase. Financial uncertainty facing an industry also has been associated with greater indirect interlocks between competing companies.[62]

Executive Recruitment. Transferring or exchanging executives also offers a method of establishing favorable linkages with external organizations. For example, each year the aerospace industry hires retired generals and executives from the Department of Defense. These generals have personal friends in the department, so the aerospace companies obtain better information about technical specifications, prices, and dates for new weapons systems. They can learn the needs of the defense department and are able to present their case for defense contracts in a more effective way. Companies without personal contacts find it nearly impossible to get a defense contract. Having channels of influence and communication between organizations serves to reduce financial uncertainty and dependence for an organization.

Advertising and Public Relations. A traditional way of establishing favorable relationships is through advertising. Organizations spend large amounts of money to influence the taste of consumers. Advertising is especially important in highly competitive consumer industries and in industries that experience variable demand. Advertising is a major part of Chevrolet's strategy to regain a leading position in the car and truck market. In connection with the introduction of several new models, the company launched a new advertising campaign taglined "An American Revolution," which uses edgy imagery and rock music to provoke a feeling of freedom and "swagger" that Chevy brands were once known for.[63]

Public relations is similar to advertising, except that stories often are free and aimed at public opinion. Public relations people cast an organization in a favorable light in speeches, in press reports, and on television. Public relations attempts to shape the company's image in the minds of customers, suppliers, and government officials. For example, in an effort to survive in this antismoking era, tobacco companies have launched an aggressive public relations campaign touting smokers' rights and freedom of choice.

Controlling the Environmental Domain

In addition to establishing favorable linkages to obtain resources, organizations often try to change the environment. There are four techniques for influencing or changing a firm's environmental domain.

Change of Domain. The ten sectors described earlier in this chapter are not fixed. The organization decides which business it is in, the market to enter, and the suppliers, banks, employees, and location to use, and this domain can be changed.[64] An organization can seek new environmental relationships and drop old ones. An organization may try to find a domain where there is little competition, no government regulation, abundant suppliers, affluent customers, and barriers to keep competitors out.

Acquisition and divestment are two techniques for altering the domain. Canada's Bombardier, maker of Ski-Doo snowmobiles, began a series of acquisitions to alter its domain when the snowmobile industry declined. CEO Laurent Beaudoin gradually moved the company into the aerospace industry by negotiating deals to purchase Canadair, Boeing's deHaviland unit, business-jet pioneer Learjet, and Short Brothers of Northern Ireland.[65] An example of divestment is when JC Penney sold off its chain of Eckerd drug stores to focus on the department store.

Political Activity, Regulation. Political activity includes techniques to influence government legislation and regulation. Political strategy can be used to erect regulatory barriers against new competitors or to squash unfavorable legislation. Corporations also try to influence the appointment to agencies of people who are sympathetic to their needs.

Microsoft has become one of the biggest and most sophisticated lobbying organizations in the country, spending $11.1 million on federal-level lobbyists in 2003 alone. One key issue Microsoft has lobbied against is any legislation that might create an environment favorable to open-source software. Microsoft's widespread lobbying efforts and strong political power make it difficult for the federal government to pass any type of technology-related legislation that the company opposes. Large pharmaceutical companies such as Schering-Plough and Wyeth frequently engage in political activity to influence FDA decisions regarding generic drugs or other changes that might weaken their organization's power and control.[66] Wal-Mart long steered clear of politics but has recently been adding lobbyists to the payroll and becoming heavily involved in political activity.

In Practice
Wal-Mart

In the late 1990s, Wal-Mart discovered a problem that could hamper its ambitious international expansion plans—U.S. negotiators for China's entry into the World Trade Organization had agreed to a thirty-store limit on foreign retailers doing business there. Worse still, executives for the giant retailer realized they didn't know the right people in Washington to talk to about the situation.

Until 1998, Wal-Mart didn't even have a lobbyist on the payroll and spent virtually nothing on political activity. The issue of China's entry into the WTO was a wake-up call, and Wal-Mart began transforming itself from a company that shunned politics to one that works hard to bend public policy to suit its business needs. Hiring in-house lobbyists and working with lobbying organizations favorable to its goals has enabled Wal-Mart to gain significant wins on global trade issues.

In addition to concerns over global trade, Wal-Mart has found other reasons it needs government support. In recent years, the company has been fighting off legal challenges from labor unions, employees' lawyers, and federal investigators. For example, the United Food and Commercial Workers International Union helped Wal-Mart employees file a series of complaints about the company's overtime, health care, and other policies with the National Labor Relations Board, leading to dozens of class-action lawsuits. Wal-Mart in turn poured millions of dollars into a campaign that presses for limits on awards in class-action suits and began lobbying for legislation that bars unions from soliciting outside of retail stores. Although that legislation failed, top executives are pleased with their lobbyists' progress. Yet they admit they still have a lot to learn about the best way to influence government legislation and regulation in Wal-Mart's favor.[67]

In addition to hiring lobbyists and working with other organzations, many CEOs believe they should do their own lobbying. CEOs have easier access than lobbyists and can be especially effective when they do the politicking. Political activity is so important that "informal lobbyist" is an unwritten part of almost any CEO's job description.[68]

Trade Associations. Much of the work to influence the external environment is accomplished jointly with other organizations that have similar interests. For example, most large pharmaceutical companies belong to Pharmaceutical Research and Manufacturers of America. Manufacturing companies are part of the National Association of Manufacturers, and retailers are part of the Retail Industry Leaders Association. Microsoft and other software companies join the Initiative for Software Choice (ISC). By pooling resources, these organizations can pay people to carry out activities such as lobbying legislators, influencing new regulations, developing public relations campaigns, and making campaign contributions. The National Tooling and Machining Association (NTMA) devotes a quarter of a million dollars each year to lobbying, mainly on issues that affect small business, such as taxes, health insurance, or government mandates. NTMA also gives its members statistics and information that help them become more competitive in the global marketplace.[69]

Illegitimate Activities. Illegitimate activities represent the final technique companies sometimes use to control their environmental domain. Certain conditions, such as low profits, pressure from senior managers, or scarce environmental resources, may lead managers to adopt behaviors not considered legitimate.[70] Many well-known companies have been found guilty of unlawful or unethical activities. Examples include payoffs to foreign governments, illegal political contributions, promotional gifts, and wiretapping. At formerly high-flying companies such as Enron and WorldCom, pressure for financial performance encouraged managers to disguise financial problems through complex partnerships or questionable accounting practices. In the defense industry, the intense competition for government contracts for major weapons systems has led some companies to do almost anything to get an edge, including schemes to peddle inside information and to pay off officials. Two former Boeing officials were recently charged with stealing thousands of pages of Lockheed Martin documents to win a rocket-launching contract. In another incident, while Boeing was negotiating a $17 billion deal to replace aerial tankers with 767s, e-mails between Boeing CFO Michael Sears and Air Force procurement officer Darleen Druyan came to light indicating that the Boeing executive had offered Druyan a job.[71]

One study found that companies in industries with low demand, shortages, and strikes were more likely to be convicted for illegal activities, implying that illegal acts are an attempt to cope with resource scarcity. Some nonprofit organizations have been found to use illegitimate or illegal actions to bolster their visibility and reputation as they compete with other organizations for scarce grants and donations.[72]

■ Organization–Environment Integrative Framework

The relationships illustrated in Exhibit 4.9 summarize the two major themes about organization–environment relationships discussed in this chapter. One theme is that the amount of complexity and change in an organization's domain influences the need for information and hence the uncertainty felt within an organization. Greater information uncertainty is resolved through greater structural flexibility and the assignment of additional departments and boundary roles. When uncertainty is low, management structures can be more mechanistic, and the number of departments and boundary roles can be fewer. The second theme pertains to the scarcity of material and financial resources. The more dependent an organization is on other organizations for those resources, the more important it is to either establish favorable linkages with those organizations or control entry into the domain. If dependence on external resources is low, the organization can maintain autonomy and does not need to establish linkages or control the external domain.

■ Summary and Interpretation

The external environment has an overwhelming impact on management uncertainty and organization functioning. Organizations are open social systems. Most are involved with hundreds of external elements. The change and complexity in environmental domains have major implications for organization design and action. Most organizational decisions, activities, and outcomes can be traced to stimuli in the external environment.

Organizational environments differ in terms of uncertainty and resource dependence. Organizational uncertainty is the result of the stable–unstable and

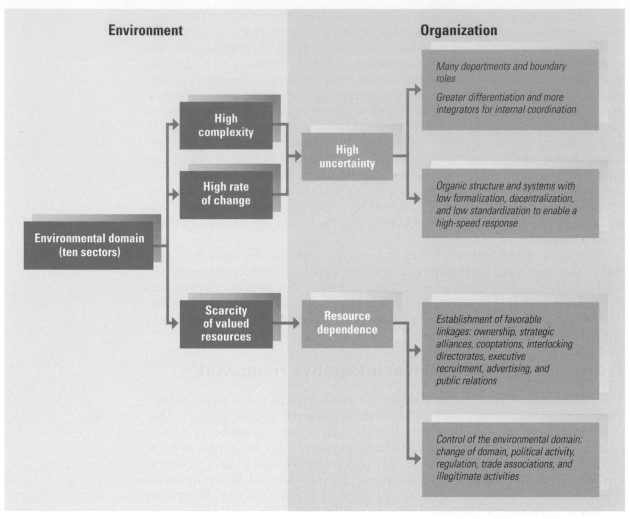

EXHIBIT 4.9
Relationship between Environmental Characteristics and Organizational Actions

simple–complex dimensions of the environment. Resource dependence is the result of scarcity of the material and financial resources needed by the organization.

Organization design takes on a logical perspective when the environment is considered. Organizations try to survive and achieve efficiencies in a world characterized by uncertainty and scarcity. Specific departments and functions are created to deal with uncertainties. The organization can be conceptualized as a technical core and departments that buffer environmental uncertainty. Boundary-spanning roles provide information about the environment.

The concepts in this chapter provide specific frameworks for understanding how the environment influences the structure and functioning of an organization. Environmental complexity and change, for example, have specific impact on internal complexity and adaptability. Under great uncertainty, more resources are allocated to departments that will plan, deal with specific environmental elements, and integrate diverse internal activities. Moreover, when risk is great or resources are scarce, the organization can establish linkages through the acquisition of ownership and through strategic alliances, interlocking directorates, executive recruitment, or advertising and public relations that will minimize risk and maintain a supply of scarce resources. Other techniques for controlling the environment include a change of the domain in which the organization operates, political activity, participation in trade associations, and perhaps illegitimate activities.

Two important themes in this chapter are that organizations can learn and adapt to the environment and that organizations can change and control the environment. These strategies are especially true for large organizations that command many resources. Such organizations can adapt when necessary but can also neutralize or change problematic areas in the environment.

Key Concepts

boundary-spanning roles	interlocking directorate
buffering roles	mechanistic
business intelligence	organic
cooptation	organizational environment
differentiation	resource dependence
direct interlock	sectors
domain	simple–complex dimension
general environment	stable–unstable dimension
indirect interlock	task environment
integration	uncertainty

Discussion Questions

1. Define *organizational environment*. Would the task environment of a new Internet-based company be the same as that of a government welfare agency? Discuss.
2. What are some forces that influence environmental uncertainty? Which typically has the greatest impact on uncertainty—environmental complexity or environmental change? Why?
3. Why does environmental complexity lead to organizational complexity? Explain.
4. Discuss the importance of the international sector for today's organizations, compared to domestic sectors. What are some ways in which the international sector affects organizations in your city or community?
5. Describe differentiation and integration. In what type of environmental uncertainty will differentiation and integration be greatest? Least?
6. Under what environmental conditions is organizational planning emphasized? Is planning an appropriate response to a turbulent environment?
7. What is an organic organization? A mechanistic organization? How does the environment influence organic and mechanistic structures?
8. Why do organizations become involved in interorganizational relationships? Do these relationships affect an organization's dependency? Performance?
9. Assume you have been asked to calculate the ratio of staff employees to production employees in two organizations—one in a simple, stable environment and one in a complex, shifting environment. How would you expect these ratios to differ? Why?
10. Is changing the organization's domain a feasible strategy for coping with a threatening environment? Explain.

Chapter 4 Workbook: Organizations You Rely On*

Below, list eight organizations you somehow rely on in your daily life. Examples might be a restaurant, a clothing or CD store, a university, your family, the post office, the telephone company, an airline, a pizzeria that delivers, your place of work, and so on. In the first column, list those eight organizations. Then, in column 2, choose another organization you could use in case the ones in column 1 were not available. In column 3, evaluate your level of dependence on the organizations listed in column 1 as Strong, Medium, or Weak. Finally, in column 4, rate the certainty of that organization being able to meet your needs as High (certainty), Medium, or Low.

Organization	Backup Organization	Level of dependence	Level of certainty
1.			
2.			
3.			
4.			
5.			
6.			
7.			
8.			

*Adapted by Dorothy Marcic from "Organizational Dependencies," in Ricky W. Griffin and Thomas C. Head, *Practicing Management*, 2nd ed. (Dallas: Houghton Mifflin), 2–3.

Questions

1. Do you have adequate backup organizations for those of high dependence? How might you create even more backups?
2. What would you do if an organization you rated high for dependence and high for certainty suddenly be-

came high-dependence and low-certainty? How would your behavior relate to the concept of resource dependence?
3. Have you ever used any behaviors similar to those in Exhibit 4.8 to manage your relationships with the organizations listed in column 1?

Case for Analysis: The Paradoxical Twins: Acme and Omega Electronics*

Part I

In 1986, Technological Products of Erie, Pennsylvania, was bought out by a Cleveland manufacturer. The Cleveland firm had no interest in the electronics division of Technological Products and subsequently sold to different investors two plants that manufactured computer chips and printed circuit boards. Integrated circuits, or chips, were the first step into microminiaturization in the electronics industry, and both plants had developed some expertise in the technology, along with their superior capabilities in manufacturing printed circuit boards. One of the plants, located in nearby Waterford, was renamed Acme Electronics; the other plant, within the city limits of Erie, was renamed Omega Electronics, Inc.

Acme retained its original management and upgraded its general manager to president. Omega hired a new president who had been a director of a large electronic research laboratory and upgraded several of the existing personnel within the plant. Acme and Omega often competed for the same contracts. As subcontractors, both firms benefited from the electronics boom and both looked forward to future growth and expansion. The world was going digital, and both companies began producing digital microprocessors along with the production of circuit boards. Acme had annual sales of $100 million and employed 550 people. Omega had annual sales of $80 million and employed 480 people. Acme regularly achieved greater net profits, much to the chagrin of Omega's management.

Inside Acme

The president of Acme, John Tyler, was confident that, had the demand not been so great, Acme's competitor would not have survived. "In fact," he said, "we have been able to beat Omega regularly for the most profitable contracts, thereby increasing our profit." Tyler credited his firm's greater effectiveness to his managers' abilities to run a "tight ship." He explained that he had retained the basic structure developed by Technological Products because it was most efficient for high-volume manufacturing. Acme had detailed organization charts and job descriptions. Tyler believed everyone should have clear responsibilities and

narrowly defined jobs, which would lead to efficient performance and high company profits. People were generally satisfied with their work at Acme; however, some of the managers voiced the desire to have a little more latitude in their jobs.

Inside Omega

Omega's president, Jim Rawls, did not believe in organization charts. He felt his organization had departments similar to Acme's, but he thought Omega's plant was small enough that things such as organization charts just put artificial barriers between specialists who should be working together. Written memos were not allowed since, as Rawls expressed it, "the plant is small enough that if people want to communicate, they can just drop by and talk things over."

The head of the mechanical engineering department said, "Jim spends too much of his time and mine making sure everyone understands what we're doing and listening to suggestions." Rawls was concerned with employee satisfaction and wanted everyone to feel part of the organization. The top management team reflected Rawls's attitudes. They also believed that employees should be familiar with activities throughout the organization so that cooperation between departments would be increased. A newer member of the industrial engineering department said, "When I first got here, I wasn't sure what I was supposed to do. One day I worked with some mechanical engineers and the next day I helped the shipping department design some packing cartons. The first months on the job were hectic, but at least I got a real feel for what makes Omega tick."

Part II

In the 1990s, mixed analog and digital devices began threatening the demand for the complex circuit boards manufactured by Acme and Omega. This "system-on-a-chip" technology combined analog functions, such as sound, graphics,

*Adapted from John F. Veiga, "The Paradoxical Twins: Acme and Omega Electronics," in John F. Veiga and John N. Yanouzas, *The Dynamics of Organizational Theory* (St. Paul: West, 1984), 132–138.

and power management, together with digital circuitry, such as logic and memory, making it highly useful for new products such as cellular phones and wireless computers. Both Acme and Omega realized the threat to their futures and began aggressively to seek new customers.

In July 1992, a major photocopier manufacturer was looking for a subcontractor to assemble the digital memory units of its new experimental copier. The projected contract for the job was estimated to be $7 million to $9 million in annual sales.

Both Acme and Omega were geographically close to this manufacturer, and both submitted highly competitive bids for the production of 100 prototypes. Acme's bid was slightly lower than Omega's; however, both firms were asked to produce 100 units. The photocopier manufacturer told both firms that speed was critical because its president had boasted to other manufacturers that the firm would have a finished copier available by Christmas. This boast, much to the designer's dismay, required pressure on all subcontractors to begin prototype production before the final design of the copier was complete. This meant Acme and Omega would have at most 2 weeks to produce the prototypes or would delay the final copier production.

Part III

Inside Acme

As soon as John Tyler was given the blueprints (Monday, July 13, 1992), he sent a memo to the purchasing department asking to move forward on the purchase of all necessary materials. At the same time, he sent the blueprints to the drafting department and asked that it prepare manufacturing prints. The industrial engineering department was told to begin methods design work for use by the production department supervisors. Tyler also sent a memo to all department heads and executives indicating the critical time constraints of this job and how he expected that all employees would perform as efficiently as they had in the past.

The departments had little contact with one another for several days, and each seemed to work at its own speed. Each department also encountered problems. Purchasing could not acquire all the parts on time. Industrial engineering had difficulty arranging an efficient assembly sequence. Mechanical engineering did not take the deadline seriously and parceled its work to vendors so the engineers could work on other jobs scheduled previously. Tyler made it a point to stay in touch with the photocopier manufacturer to let it know things were progressing and to learn of any new developments. He traditionally worked to keep important clients happy. Tyler telephoned someone at the photocopier company at least twice a week and got to know the head designer quite well.

On July 17, Tyler learned that mechanical engineering was far behind in its development work, and he "hit the

roof." To make matters worse, purchasing had not obtained all the parts, so the industrial engineers decided to assemble the product without one part, which would be inserted at the last minute. On Thursday, July 23, the final units were being assembled, although the process was delayed several times. On Friday, July 24, the last units were finished while Tyler paced around the plant. Late that afternoon, Tyler received a phone call from the head designer of the photocopier manufacturer, who told Tyler that he had received a call on Wednesday from Jim Rawls of Omega. He explained that Rawls's workers had found an error in the design of the connector cable and taken corrective action on their prototypes. He told Tyler that he had checked out the design error and that Omega was right. Tyler, a bit overwhelmed by this information, told the designer that he had all the memory units ready for shipment and that, as soon as they received the missing component on Monday or Tuesday, they would be able to deliver the final units. The designer explained that the design error would be rectified in a new blueprint he was sending over by messenger and that he would hold Acme to the Tuesday delivery date.

When the blueprint arrived, Tyler called in the production supervisor to assess the damage. The alterations in the design would call for total disassembly and the unsoldering of several connections. Tyler told the supervisor to put extra people on the alterations first thing Monday morning and to try to finish the job by Tuesday. Late Tuesday afternoon, the alterations were finished and the missing components were delivered. Wednesday morning, the production supervisor discovered that the units would have to be torn apart again to install the missing component. When John Tyler was told this, he again "hit the roof." He called industrial engineering and asked if it could help out. The production supervisor and the methods engineer couldn't agree on how to install the component. John Tyler settled the argument by ordering that all units be taken apart again and the missing component installed. He told shipping to prepare cartons for delivery on Friday afternoon.

On Friday, July 31, fifty prototypes were shipped from Acme without final inspection. John Tyler was concerned about his firm's reputation, so he waived the final inspection after he personally tested one unit and found it operational. On Tuesday, August 4, Acme shipped the last fifty units.

Inside Omega

On Friday, July 10, Jim Rawls called a meeting that included department heads to tell them about the potential contract they were to receive. He told them that as soon as he received the blueprints, work could begin. On Monday, July 13, the prints arrived and again the department heads met to discuss the project. At the end of the meeting, drafting had agreed to prepare manufacturing prints, while industrial engineering and production would begin methods design.

Two problems arose within Omega that were similar to those at Acme. Certain ordered parts could not be delivered on time, and the assembly sequence was difficult to engineer. The departments proposed ideas to help one another, however, and department heads and key employees had daily meetings to discuss progress. The head of electrical engineering knew of a Japanese source for the components that could not be purchased from normal suppliers. Most problems were solved by Saturday, July 18.

On Monday, July 20, a methods engineer and the production supervisor formulated the assembly plans, and production was set to begin on Tuesday morning. On Monday afternoon, people from mechanical engineering, electrical engineering, production, and industrial engineering got together to produce a prototype just to ensure that there would be no snags in production. While they were building the unit, they discovered an error in the connector cable design. All the engineers agreed, after checking and rechecking the blueprints, that the cable was erroneously designed. People from mechanical engineering and electri-cal engineering spent Monday night redesigning the cable, and on Tuesday morning, the drafting department finalized the changes in the manufacturing prints. On Tuesday morning, Rawls was a bit apprehensive about the design changes and decided to get formal approval. Rawls received word on Wednesday from the head designer at the photocopier firm that they could proceed with the design changes as discussed on the phone. On Friday, July 24, the final units were inspected by quality control and were then shipped.

Part IV

Ten of Acme's final memory units were defective, whereas all of Omega's units passed the photocopier firm's tests. The photocopier firm was disappointed with Acme's delivery delay and incurred further delays in repairing the defective Acme units. However, rather than give the entire contract to one firm, the final contract was split between Acme and Omega with two directives added: (1) maintain zero defects and (2) reduce final cost. In 1993, through extensive cost-cutting efforts, Acme reduced its unit cost by 20 percent and was ultimately awarded the total contract.

Notes

1. David Pringle, "Wrong Number; How Nokia Chased Top End of Market, Got Hit in Middle," *The Wall Street Journal* (June 1, 2004), A1; and Andy Reinhardt with Moon Ihlwan, "Will Rewiring Nokia Spark Growth?" *BusinessWeek* (February 14, 2005), 46ff.

2. Andrew Yeh, "China Set To Be Nokia's Top Market," *Financial Times* (February 24, 2005), 24; and Reinhardt and Ihlwan, "Will Rewiring Nokia Spark Growth?"

3. Paul Keegan, "Is the Music Store Over?" *Business 2.0* (March 2004), 115–118; Tom Hansson, Jürgen Ringbeck, and Markus Franke, "Fight for Survival: A New Business Model for the Airline Industry," *Strategy + Business*, Issue 31 (Summer 2003), 78–85.

4. Matthew Boyle, "The Wegmans Way," *Fortune* (January 24, 2005), 62–68.

5. Dana Milbank, "Aluminum Producers, Aggressive and Agile, Outfight Steelmakers," *The Wall Street Journal* (July 1, 1992), A1.

6 Sarah Ellison, "Eating Up; As Shoppers Grow Finicky, Big Food Has Big Problems," *The Wall Street Journal* (May 21, 2004), A1.

7. Aaron Bernstein, "The Time Bomb in the Workforce: Illiteracy," *BusinessWeek* (February 25, 2002), 122.

8. Andrew Pollack, "Yet Another Sector Embraces Outsourcing to Asia: Life Sciences," *International Herald Tribune* (February 25, 2005), 17.

9. Samuel Loewenberg, "Europe Gets Tougher on U.S. Companies," *The New York Times* (April 20, 2003), Section 3, 6.

10. Brian Grow, "Hispanic Nation," *BusinessWeek* (March 15, 2004), 58–70.

11. Mark Landler, "Woes at Two Pillars of German Journalism," *The New York Times* (January 19, 2004), C8.

12. David Kirkpatrick and Daniel Roth, "Why There's No Escaping the Blog," *Fortune* (January 10, 2005), 44–50.

13. Robert Frank, "Silver Lining; How Terror Fears Brought Tiny Firm to Brink of Success," *The Wall Street Journal* (May 8, 2003), A1, A14.

14. Andrew Kupfer, "How American Industry Stacks Up," *Fortune* (March 9, 1992), 36–46.

15. Devin Leonard, "Nightmare on Madison Avenue," *Fortune* (June 28, 2004), 93–108; and Brian Steinberg, "Agency Cost-Accounting Is under Trial," *The Wall Street Journal* (January 28, 2005), B2.

16. Randall D. Harris, "Organizational Task Environments: An Evaluation of Convergent and Discriminant Validity," *Journal of Management Studies* 41, no. 5 (July 2004), 857–882; Allen C. Bluedorn, "Pilgrim's Progress: Trends and Convergence in Research on Organizational Size and Environment," *Journal of Management* 19 (1993), 163–191; Howard E. Aldrich, *Organizations and Environments* (Englewood Cliffs, N.J.: Prentice-Hall, 1979); and Fred E. Emery and Eric L. Trist, "The Casual Texture of Organizational Environments," *Human Relations* 18 (1965), 21–32.

17. Gregory G. Dess and Donald W. Beard, "Dimensions of Organizational Task Environments," *Administrative Science Quarterly* 29 (1984), 52–73; Ray Jurkovich, "A Core Typology of Organizational Environments," *Administrative Science Quarterly* 19 (1974), 380–394; Robert B. Duncan, "Characteristics of Organizational Environment and

Perceived Environmental Uncertainty," *Administrative Science Quarterly* 17 (1972), 313–327.

18. Christine S. Koberg and Gerardo R. Ungson, "The Effects of Environmental Uncertainty and Dependence on Organizational Structure and Performance: A Comparative Study," *Journal of Management* 13 (1987), 725–737; and Frances J. Milliken, "Three Types of Perceived Uncertainty about the Environment: State, Effect, and Response Uncertainty," *Academy of Management Review* 12 (1987), 133–143.

19. Mike France with Joann Muller, "A Site for Soreheads," *BusinessWeek* (April 12, 1999), 86–90; Kirkpatrick and Roth, "Why There's No Escaping the Blog."

20. J. A. Litterer, *The Analysis of Organizations,* 2d ed. (New York: Wiley, 1973), 335.

21. Constance L. Hays, "More Gloom on the Island of Lost Toy Makers," *The New York Times* (February 23, 2005), *http://www.nytimes.com.*

22. Rosalie L. Tung, "Dimensions of Organizational Environments: An Exploratory Study of Their Impact on Organizational Structure," *Academy of Management Journal* 22 (1979), 672–693.

23. Joseph E. McCann and John Selsky, "Hyper-turbulence and the Emergence of Type 5 Environments," *Academy of Management Review* 9 (1984), 460–470.

24. Seth M. M. Stodder, "Fixing Homeland Security; New Leadership and Consolidation Key," *The Washington Times* (February 28, 2005), A21.

25. James D. Thompson, *Organizations in Action* (New York: McGraw-Hill, 1967), 20–21.

26. Sally Solo, "Whirlpool: How to Listen to Consumers," *Fortune* (January 11, 1993), 77–79.

27. David B. Jemison, "The Importance of Boundary Spanning Roles in Strategic Decision-Making," *Journal of Management Studies* 21 (1984), 131–152; and Mohamed Ibrahim Ahmad At-Twaijri and John R. Montanari, "The Impact of Context and Choice on the Boundary-Spanning Process: An Empirical Extension," *Human Relations* 40 (1987), 783–798.

28. Michelle Cook, "The Intelligentsia," *Business 2.0* (July 1999), 135–136.

29. Robert C. Schwab, Gerardo R. Ungson, and Warren B. Brown, "Redefining the Boundary-Spanning Environment Relationship," *Journal of Management* 11 (1985), 75–86.

30. Tom Duffy, "Spying the Holy Grail," *Microsoft Executive Circle* (Winter 2004), 38–39.

31. Julie Schlosser, "Looking for Intelligence in Ice Cream," *Fortune* (March 17, 2003), 114–120.

32. Pia Nordlinger, "Know Your Enemy," *Working Woman* (May 2001), 16.

33. Ken Western, "Ethical Spying," *Business Ethics* (September/October 1995), 22–23; Stan Crock, Geoffrey Smith, Joseph Weber, Richard A. Melcher, and Linda Himelstein, "They Snoop to Conquer," *BusinessWeek* (October 28, 1996), 172–176; and Kenneth A. Sawka, "Demystifying Business Intelligence," *Management Review* (October 1996), 47–51.

34. Edwin M. Epstein, "How to Learn from the Environment about the Environment—A Prerequisite for Organizational Well-Being," *Journal of General Management* 29, no. 1 (Autumn 2003), 68–80.

35. "Snooping on a Shoestring," *Business 2.0* (May 2003), 64–66.

36. Mike France with Joann Muller, "A Site for Soreheads," *BusinessWeek* (April 12, 1999), 86–90.

37. Naomi Snyder, "Close on the Heels of the Followers," *The Tennessean* (February 6, 2005), 1E, 4E; "Stepping into the Teenage Mind" (an Interview with Genesco's Jim Estepa), *Footwear News* (July 28, 2003), 22; Katie Abel, "Smart Journeys," *Footwear News* (November 3, 2003), 14; and "The WWD List: Street Smarts; The Top 10 Streetwear Chains," *WWD* (November 18, 2004), 14.

38. Jay W. Lorsch, "Introduction to the Structural Design of Organizations," in Gene W. Dalton, Paul R. Lawrence, and Jay W. Lorsch, eds., *Organizational Structure and Design* (Homewood, Ill.: Irwin and Dorsey, 1970), 5.

39. Paul R. Lawrence and Jay W. Lorsch, *Organization and Environment* (Homewood, Ill.: Irwin, 1969).

40. Lorsch, "Introduction to the Structural Design of Organizations," 7.

41. Jay W. Lorsch and Paul R. Lawrence, "Environmental Factors and Organizational Integration," in J. W. Lorsch and Paul R. Lawrence, eds., *Organizational Planning: Cases and Concepts* (Homewood, Ill.: Irwin and Dorsey, 1972), 45.

42. Tom Burns and G. M. Stalker, *The Management of Innovation* (London: Tavistock, 1961).

43. John A. Courtright, Gail T. Fairhurst, and L. Edna Rogers, "Interaction Patterns in Organic and Mechanistic Systems," *Academy of Management Journal* 32 (1989), 773–802.

44. Dennis K. Berman, "Crunch Time," *BusinessWeek Frontier* (April 24, 2000), F28–F38.

45. Robert A. Guth, "Eroding Empires: Electronics Giants of Japan Undergo Wrenching Change," *The Wall Street Journal* (June 20, 2002), A1, A9.

46. Thomas C. Powell, "Organizational Alignment as Competitive Advantage," *Strategic Management Journal* 13 (1992), 119–134; Mansour Javidan, "The Impact of Environmental Uncertainty on Long-Range Planning Practices of the U.S. Savings and Loan Industry," *Strategic Management Journal* 5 (1984), 381–392; Tung, "Dimensions of Organizational Environments," 672–693; and Thompson, *Organizations in Action.*

47. Ian Wylie, "There Is No Alternative To . . .," *Fast Company* (July 2002), 106–110.

48. David Ulrich and Jay B. Barney, "Perspectives in Organizations: Resource Dependence, Efficiency, and Population," *Academy of Management Review* 9 (1984), 471–481; and Jeffrey Pfeffer and Gerald Salancik, *The External Control of Organizations: A Resource Dependent Perspective* (New York: Harper & Row, 1978).

49. Andrew H. Van de Ven and Gordon Walker, "The Dynamics of Interorganizational Coordination," *Administrative Science Quarterly* (1984), 598–621; and Huseyin Leblebici and Gerald R. Salancik, "Stability in Interorganizational Exchanges: Rulemaking Processes of the Chicago Board of Trade," *Administrative Science Quarterly* 27 (1982), 227–242.

50. Kevin Kelly and Zachary Schiller with James B. Treece, "Cut Costs or Else: Companies Lay Down the Law to Suppliers," *BusinessWeek* (March 22, 1993), 28–29.

51. G. Pascal Zachary, "Many Journalists See a Growing Reluctance to Criticize Advertisers," *The Wall Street Journal* (February 6, 1992), A1, A9.

52. Judith A. Babcock, *Organizational Responses to Resource Scarcity and Munificence: Adaptation and Modification in Colleges within a University* (Ph.D. diss., Pennsylvania State University, 1981).

53. Peter Smith Ring and Andrew H. Van de Ven, "Developmental Processes of Corporative Interorganizational Relationships," *Academy of Management Review* 19 (1994), 90–118; Jeffrey Pfeffer, "Beyond Management and the Worker: The Institutional Function of Management," *Academy of Management Review* 1 (April 1976), 36–46; and John P. Kotter, "Managing External Dependence," *Academy of Management Review* 4 (1979), 87–92.

54. Bryan Borys and David B. Jemison, "Hybrid Arrangements as Strategic Alliances: Theoretical Issues in Organizational Combinations," *Academy of Management Review* 14 (1989), 234–249.

55. Almar Latour, "Closing Bell; After a Year of Frenzied Deals,Two Telecom Giants Emerge," *The Wall Street Journal* (February 15, 2005), A1, A11; Almar Latour, "New Kid on the Box; To Meet the Threat from Cable, SBC Rushes to Offer TV Service," *The Wall Street Journal* (February 16, 2005), A1, A10; and Murray Sabrin, "No Reason to Fear Telecom Mergers," *The Record* (August 17, 2005), L-09.

56. Julie Cohen Mason, "Strategic Alliances: Partnering for Success," *Management Review* (May 1993), 10–15.

57. Teri Agins and Alessandra Galloni, "After Gianni; Facing a Squeeze, Versace Struggles to Trim the Fat," *The Wall Street Journal* (September 30, 2003), A1, A10; John F. Love, *McDonald's: Behind the Arches* (New York: Bantam Books, 1986).

58. Zachary Schiller and Wendy Zellner with Ron Stodghill II and Mark Maremont, "Clout! More and More, Retail Giants Rule the Marketplace," *Business Week* (December 21, 1992), 66–73.

59. Borys and Jemison, "Hybrid Arrangements as Strategic Alliances."

60. Ian Katz and Elisabeth Malkin, "Battle for the Latin American Net," *Business Week* (November 1, 1999), 194–200; "IBM Joint Venture to Put Laundry on Web," *The Wall Street Journal* (August 30, 2002), B4.

61. Donald Palmer, "Broken Ties: Interlocking Directorates and Intercorporate Coordination," *Administrative Science Quarterly* 28 (1983), 40–55; F. David Shoorman, Max H. Bazerman, and Robert S. Atkin, "Interlocking Directorates: A Strategy for Reducing Environmental Uncertainty," *Academy of Management Review* 6 (1981), 243–251; and

62. James R. Lang and Daniel E. Lockhart, "Increased Environmental Uncertainty and Changes in Board Linkage Patterns," *Academy of Management Journal* 33 (1990), 106–128; and Mark S. Mizruchi and Linda Brewster Stearns, "A Longitudinal Study of the Formation of Interlocking Directorates," *Administrative Science Quarterly* 33 (1988), 194–210.

63. Lee Hawkins Jr. "GM Seeks Chevrolet Revival," *The Wall Street Journal* (December 19, 2003), B4.

64. Kotter, "Managing External Dependence."

65. William C. Symonds, with Farah Nayeri, Geri Smith, and Ted Plafker, "Bombardier's Blitz," *Business Week* (February 6, 1995), 62–66; and Joseph Weber, with Wendy Zellner and Geri Smith, "Loud Noises at Bombardier," *Business Week* (January 26, 1998), 94–95.

66. Ben Worthen, "Mr. Gates Goes to Washington," *CIO* (September 2004), 63–72; Gardiner Harris and Chris Adams, "Delayed Reaction: Drug Manufacturers Step Up Legal Attacks That Slow Generics," *The Wall Street Journal* (July 12, 2001), A1, A10; Leila Abboud, "Raging Hormones: How Drug Giant Keeps a Monopoly on 60–Year-Old Pill," *The Wall Street Journal* (September 9, 2004), A1.

67. Jeanne Cummings, "Joining the PAC; Wal-Mart Opens for Business in a Tough Market: Washington," *The Wall Street Journal* (March 24, 2004), A1.

68. David B. Yoffie, "How an Industry Builds Political Advantage," *Harvard Business Review* (May–June 1988), 82–89; and Jeffrey H. Birnbaum, "Chief Executives Head to Washington to Ply the Lobbyist's Trade," *The Wall Street Journal* (March 19, 1990), A1, A16.

69. David Whitford, "Built by Association," *Inc.* (July 1994), 71–75.

70. Anthony J. Daboub, Abdul M. A. Rasheed, Richard L. Priem, and David A. Gray, "Top Management Team Characteristics and Corporate Illegal Activity," *Academy of Management Review* 20, no. 1 (1995), 138–170.

71. Stewart Toy, "The Defense Scandal," *Business Week* (July 4, 1988), 28–30; and Julie Creswell, "Boeing Plays Defense," *Fortune* (April 19, 2004), 90–98.

72. Barry M. Staw and Eugene Szwajkowski, "The Scarcity-Munificence Component of Organizational Environments and the Commission of Illegal Acts," *Administrative Science Quarterly* 20 (1975), 345–354; and Kimberly D. Elsbach and Robert I. Sutton, "Acquiring Organizational Legitimacy through Illegitimate Actions: A Marriage of Institutional and Impression Management Theories," *Academy of Management Journal* 35 (1992), 699–738.

Ronald S. Burt, *Toward a Structural Theory of Action* (New York: Academic Press, 1982).

5 Interorganizational Relationships

Organizational Ecosystems
Is Competition Dead? • The Changing Role of Management • Interorganizational Framework

Resource Dependence
Resource Strategies • Power Strategies

Collaborative Networks
Why Collaboration? • From Adversaries to Partners

Population Ecology
Organizational Form and Niche • Process of Ecological Change • Strategies for Survival

Institutionalism
The Institutional View and Organization Design • Institutional Similarity

Summary and Interpretation

A Look Inside

International Truck and Engine Corporation

The factory floor of International Truck and Engine Corporation is a beehive of activity. As the nation's largest combined commercial truck, school bus, and mid-range diesel engine producer, the place has to keep humming. But some of the people scurrying around the plant floor don't even work for International; they're on the payroll of Rockwell Automation, one of the company's key suppliers.

Over the past few years, International has negotiated long-term contracts with suppliers to handle more and more of the company's non-core activities. Equipment parts and service management is handled by Rockwell, which can manage inventory, repair parts, upgrade components, and track warranties at a lower cost than International could do in-house. Inventory costs for International have gone way down because the supplier is the one responsible for keeping the most current spare parts available and avoiding obsolete inventory. In addition, on-site parts experts enable the manufacturer to improve machine efficiency. Rockwell benefits from the collaborative arrangement too. By having people on site, Rockwell gets closer to the customer and has greater opportunity for upgrades or sales of other products. Just as important, on-site experience with how parts are used enables the supplier to improve its products and innovate on parts before customers even ask.

International's interest in collaboration isn't limited to parts management. The company has a joint venture with Ford Motor Company to build mid-sized commercial trucks and sell truck and diesel engine parts. A new strategic alliance with MAN Nutzfahrzeuge AG of Munich, Germany, takes collaboration even further. International and MAN will collaborate on the design, development, sourcing, and manufacturing of new components and systems for commercial trucks and engines. Both companies expect to benefit from each other's technologies and achieve greater economies of scale, enabling them to be more competitive on a global basis.[1]

Organizations of all sizes in all industries are rethinking how they do business in response to today's chaotic environment. One of the most widespread trends is to reduce boundaries and increase collaboration between companies, sometimes even between competitors. Today's aerospace companies, for example, depend on strategic partnerships with other organizations. Europe's Airbus Industrie and Boeing, the largest U.S. aerospace company, are both involved in multiple relationships with suppliers, competitors, and other organizations. Global semiconductor makers have been collaborating while competing for years because of the high costs and risks associated with creating and marketing a new generation of semiconductors.

Global competition and rapid advances in technology, communications, and transportation have created amazing new opportunities for organizations, but they have also raised the cost of doing business and made it increasingly difficult for any company to take advantage of those opportunities on its own. In this new economy, webs of organizations are emerging. A large company like General Electric develops a special relationship with a supplier that eliminates middlemen by sharing complete information and reducing the costs of salespersons and distributors. Several small companies may join together to produce and market noncompeting products. You can see the results of interorganizational collaboration when movies such as *War of the Worlds, The Dukes of Hazzard,* or *Star Wars: Episode III—Revenge of the Sith* are launched. Before seeing the movie, you might read a cover story in *People* or *Entertainment Weekly,* see a preview clip or chat live with the stars at an online site such as E online, find action toys being given away at a fast-food franchise, and notice retail stores loaded with movie-related merchandise. For some blockbuster movies, coordinated action among companies can yield millions in addition to box-office and DVD profits. In the new economy, organizations think of themselves as teams that create value jointly rather than as autonomous companies that are in competition with all others.

■ Purpose of This Chapter

This chapter explores the most recent trend in organizing, which is the increasingly dense web of relationships among organizations. Companies have always been dependent on other organizations for supplies, materials, and information. The question is how these relationships are managed. At one time it was a matter of a large, powerful company like General Electric or Johnson & Johnson tightening the screws on small suppliers. Today a company can choose to develop positive, trusting relationships. Or a large company like General Motors might find it difficult to adapt to the environment and hence create a new organizational form, such as Saturn, to operate with a different structure and culture. The notion of horizontal relationships described in Chapter 3 and the understanding of environmental uncertainty in Chapter 4 are leading to the next stage of organizational evolution, which is horizontal relationships *across* organizations. Organizations can choose to build relationships in many ways, such as appointing preferred suppliers, establishing agreements, business partnering, joint ventures, or even mergers and acquisitions.

Interorganizational research has yielded perspectives such as resource-dependence, collaborative networks, population ecology, and institutionalism. The sum total of these ideas can be daunting, because it means managers no longer can rest in the safety of managing a single organization. They have to figure out how to manage a whole set of interorganizational relationships, which is a great deal more challenging and complex.

Organizational Ecosystems

Interorganizational relationships are the relatively enduring resource transactions, flows, and linkages that occur among two or more organizations.[2] Traditionally, these transactions and relationships have been seen as a necessary evil to obtain what an organization needs. The presumption has been that the world is composed of distinct businesses that thrive on autonomy and compete for supremacy. A company may be forced into interorganizational relationships depending on its needs and the instability and complexity of the environment.

A new view described by James Moore argues that organizations are now evolving into business ecosystems. An **organizational ecosystem** is a system formed by the interaction of a community of organizations and their environment. An ecosystem cuts across traditional industry lines. A company can create its own ecosystem. Microsoft travels in four major industries: consumer electronics, information, communications, and personal computers. Its ecosystem also includes hundreds of suppliers, including Hewlett-Packard and Intel, and millions of customers across many markets. Cable companies like Comcast are offering new forms of phone service, and telephone companies like SBC Communications are getting into the television business. Apple Computer is arguably having greater success as an entertainment company with its iPod and iTunes Music Store than it ever had as a computer manufacturer. Apple's success grows out of close partnerships with other organizations, including music companies, consumer electronics firms, cell phone makers, other computer companies, and even car manufacturers.[3] Apple and Microsoft, like other business ecosystems, develop relationships with hundreds of organizations cutting across traditional business boundaries.

■ Is Competition Dead?

No company can go it alone under a constant onslaught of international competitors, changing technology, and new regulations. Organizations around the world are embedded in complex networks of confusing relationships—collaborating in some markets, competing fiercely in others. Indeed, research indicates that a large percentage of new alliances in recent years have been between competitors. These alliances influence organizations' competitive behavior in varied ways.[4]

Traditional competition, which assumes a distinct company competing for survival and supremacy with other stand-alone businesses, no longer exists because each organization both supports and depends on the others for success, and perhaps for survival. However, most managers recognize that the competitive stakes are higher than ever in a world where market share can crumble overnight and no industry is immune from almost instant obsolescence.[5] In today's world, a new form of competition is in fact intensifying.[6]

For one thing, companies now need to coevolve with others in the ecosystem so that everyone gets stronger. Consider the wolf and the caribou. Wolves cull weaker caribou, which strengthens the herd. A strong herd means that wolves must become stronger themselves. With coevolution, the whole system becomes stronger. In the same way, companies coevolve through discussion with each other, shared visions, alliances, and managing complex relationships. Amazon.com Inc. and its retail partners illustrate this approach.

Amazon.com was one of the earliest players in the world of online retailing, opening its virtual bookstore in 1995, before many people had ever heard of the Internet. Since then, Amazon has continued to evolve, from an online bookseller to an online retailer with its own vast warehouses of books, DVDs, kitchen appliances and electronics, and now to a technology provider for other merchants. Today, Amazon sells everything from baby furniture to golf clubs, but its partners own and store most of the inventory. Amazon's Web site serves as a kind of online shopping mall where retailers set up shop to sell their wares to a vast global market. Amazon has partnerships with hundreds of small and large retailers, including Target, Lands End, and Goldsmith International.

Amazon processes the orders and gets a cut of the sale, but retailers fill the orders from their own warehouses. The arrangement gives Amazon a way to expand into new businesses without making huge investments in inventory and developing the expertise to forecast hot products in multiple categories. As for the retailers, they get access to Amazon's global customer traffic,

In Practice
Amazon.com Inc.

$1 billion investment in technology, and Internet savvy, enabling them to focus on their bricks-and-mortar businesses.

The partnership approach is not without its challenges. Toys "R" Us, one of Amazon's earliest partners, recently filed suit against the online firm, charging that Amazon violated its contract when it began allowing other retailers to sell products that compete with Toys "R" Us. Some big companies, including Nike and Callaway Golf, are fighting the sale of their goods on Amazon, fearing it might tarnish their premium brands. Amazon, however, insists that in the long run, the web of partnerships will benefit everyone. One manufacturer that eventually agreed is Sony. Sony executives originally refused to authorize Amazon to sell Sony products, but realized they were fighting a losing battle to try and maintain control and exclusivity in the new world of Internet retailing. Today, Sony products are big sellers on the site.[7]

Amazon and its partners represent an ecosystem, in which each company depends to some extent on the others and each has the opportunity to grow stronger. For example, Amazon is finding that every new retail partner has its own demands for how its products should be presented and sold. Amazon managers welcome the feedback because it enables them to keep improving the site. The retail partners grow stronger too, because Amazon keeps a close watch on factors such as how well the retailers are managing delivery, communication, and customer service.

Exhibit 5.1 illustrates the complexity of an ecosystem by showing the myriad overlapping relationships in which high-tech companies were involved in 1999. Since then, many of these companies have merged, been acquired, or gone out of business during the dot-com crash of 2000 and 2001. Ecosystems constantly change and evolve, with some relationships growing stronger while others weaken or are terminated. The changing pattern of relationships and interactions in an ecosystem contributes to the health and vitality of the system as an integrated whole.[8]

In an organizational ecosystem, conflict and cooperation frequently exist at the same time. Procter & Gamble (P&G) and Clorox are fierce rivals in cleaning products and water purification, but both companies profited when they collaborated on a new plastic wrap. P&G invented a wrap that seals tightly only where it is pressed and won't stick elsewhere. Managers recognized the value of such a product, but P&G didn't have a plastic-wrap category. They thought a joint venture with Clorox to market the new plastic wrap under the well-established Glad brand name would be more profitable than investing the time and money to establish P&G in a new product category. P&G shared the technology with archrival Clorox for a 10 percent stake in the Glad business. Glad's share of the wrap market shot up 23 percent virtually overnight with the introduction of Glad Press 'n Seal. Since then, the two companies have continued the collaboration with the introduction of Glad Force Flex trash bags, which make use of a stretchable plastic invented in P&G labs.[9] Mutual dependencies and partnerships have become a fact of life in business ecosystems. Is competition dead? Companies today may use their strength to win conflicts and negotiations, but ultimately cooperation carries the day.

■ The Changing Role of Management

Within business ecosystems managers learn to move beyond traditional responsibilities of corporate strategy and designing hierarchical structures and control systems. If a top manager looks down to enforce order and uniformity, the company is missing opportunities for new and evolving external relationships.[10] In this new world, managers think about horizontal processes rather than vertical structures.

The largest companies (those with more than 10,000 employees) are, not surprisingly, the hubs of the digital universe: they tend to have the most strategic partnerships (black lines) and investments (red lines).*

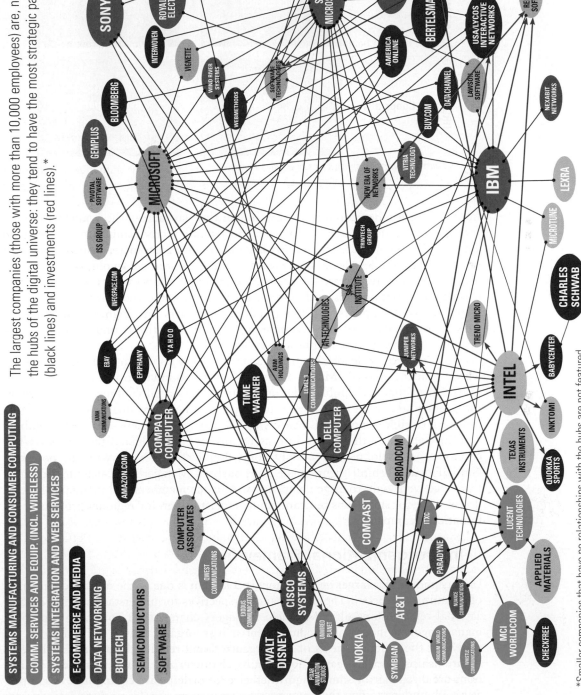

*Smaller companies that have no relationships with the hubs are not featured.

EXHIBIT 5.1

An Organizational Ecosystem (based on 1999 data)

EXHIBIT 5.2
*A Framework of
Interorganizational
Relationships**

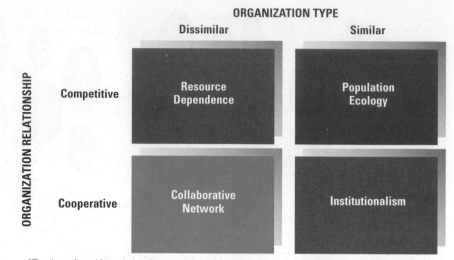

*Thanks to Anand Narasimhan for suggesting this framework.

Important initiatives are not just top down; they cut across the boundaries separating organizational units. Moreover, horizontal relationships, as described in Chapter 3, now include linkages with suppliers and customers, who become part of the team. Business leaders can learn to lead economic coevolution. Managers learn to see and appreciate the rich environment of opportunities that grow from cooperative relationships with other contributors to the ecosystem. Rather than trying to force suppliers into low prices or customers into high prices, managers strive to strengthen the larger system evolving around them, finding ways to understand this big picture and how to contribute.

This is a broader leadership role than ever before. For example, Donovan Neale-May, president of Neale-May & Partners, formed an international alliance of forty independent high-tech public relations agencies, called GlobalFluency, to share information and market their services to acquire business that small, owner-run agencies have trouble winning on their own. "We have companies—our own neighbors here in Colorado—that won't hire us because we don't have offices in sixty-five countries," says John Metzger, CEO of a Boulder firm. Now, with the power of GlobalFluency behind them, small firms such as Metzger's are winning accounts that once went only to large competitors. Alliance members still maintain their independence for small jobs but can join together to pitch for regional projects or international campaigns.[11]

Interorganizational Framework

Understanding this larger organizational ecosystem is one of the most exciting areas of organization theory. The models and perspectives for understanding interorganizational relationships ultimately help managers change their role from top-down management to horizontal management across organizations. A framework for analyzing the different views of interorganizational relationships is in Exhibit 5.2. Relationships among organizations can be characterized by whether the organizations are dissimilar or similar and whether relationships are competitive or cooperative. By understanding these perspectives, managers can assess their environment and adopt strategies to suit their needs. The first perspective is called resource-dependence theory, which was briefly described in Chapter 4. It describes rational ways organizations deal with each other to reduce dependence on the environment. The second perspective is about collaborative networks, wherein organizations allow themselves to become dependent on other organizations to increase value and productivity for both. The third perspective is population ecology, which examines how new organizations fill niches left open by established organizations, and how a rich variety of new organizational forms benefits society. The final approach is called institutionalism and explains why and how organizations legitimate themselves in the larger environment and design structures by borrowing ideas from each other. These four approaches to the study of interorganizational relationships are described in the remainder of this chapter.

Resource Dependence

Resource dependence represents the traditional view of relationships among organizations. As described in Chapter 4, **resource-dependence** theory argues that organizations try to minimize their dependence on other organizations for the supply of important resources and try to influence the environment to make resources available.[12] Organizations succeed by striving for independence and autonomy. When threatened by greater dependence, organizations will assert control over external resources to minimize that dependence. Resource-dependence theory argues that organizations do not want to become vulnerable to other organizations because of negative effects on performance.

The amount of dependence on a resource is based on two factors. First is the importance of the resource to the firm, and second is how much discretion or monopoly power those who control a resource have over its allocation and use.[13] For example, a Wisconsin manufacturer made scientific instruments with internal electronics. It acquired parts from a supplier that provided adequate quality at the lowest price. The supplier was not involved in the manufacturer's product design but was able to provide industry-standard capacitors at 50 cents each. As industry standards changed, other suppliers of the capacitor switched to other products, and in 1 year the cost of the capacitors increased to $2 each. The Wisconsin firm had no choice but to pay the higher price. Within 18 months, the price of the capacitors increased to $10 each, and then the supplier discontinued production altogether. Without capacitors, production came to a halt for 6 months. The scientific instruments manufacturer allowed itself to become dependent on a single supplier and made no plans for redesign to use substitute capacitors or to develop new suppliers. A single supplier had sufficient power to increase prices beyond reason and to almost put the Wisconsin firm out of business.[14]

Organizations aware of resource-dependence tend to develop strategies to reduce their dependence on the environment and learn how to use their power differences.

Resource Strategies

When organizations feel resource or supply constraints, the resource-dependence perspective says they maneuver to maintain their autonomy through a variety of strategies, several of which were described in Chapter 4. One strategy is to adapt to or alter the interdependent relationships. This could mean purchasing ownership in suppliers, developing long-term contracts or joint ventures to lock in necessary

Briefcase

As an organization manager, keep these guidelines in mind:

Reach out and control external sectors that threaten needed resources. Adopt strategies to control resources, especially when your organization is dependent and has little power. Assert your company's influence when you have power and control over resources.

resources, or building relationships in other ways. Another technique is to use interlocking directorships, which means boards of directors include members of the boards of supplier companies. Organizations may also join trade associations to coordinate their needs, sign trade agreements, or merge with another firm to guarantee resources and material supplies. Some organizations may take political action, such as lobbying for new regulations or deregulation, favorable taxation, tariffs, or subsidies, or push for new standards that make resource acquisition easier. Organizations operating under the resource-dependence philosophy will do whatever is needed to avoid excessive dependence on the environment to maintain control of resources and hence reduce uncertainty.

■ Power Strategies

In resource-dependence theory, large, independent companies have power over small suppliers.[15] For example, power in consumer products has shifted from vendors such as Rubbermaid and Procter & Gamble to the big discount retail chains, which can demand—and receive—special pricing deals. Wal-Mart has grown so large and powerful that it can dictate the terms with virtually any supplier. Consider Levi Strauss, which for much of its 150-year history was a powerful supplier with a jeans brand that millions of people wanted and retailers were eager to stock. "When I first started in this business, retailers were a waystation to the consumer," says Levi's CEO Philip Marineau. "Manufacturers had a tendency to tell retailers how to do business." But the balance of power has shifted dramatically. In order to sell to Wal-Mart, Levi Strauss had to overhaul its entire operation, from design and production to pricing and distribution. For example, Levi jeans used to go from factories to a company-owned distribution center where they were labeled, packed, and sent on to retailers. Now, to meet Wal-Mart's need to get products fast, jeans are shipped already tagged from contract factories direct to Wal-Mart distribution centers, where Wal-Mart trucks pick them up and deliver them to individual stores.[16] When one company has power over another, it can ask suppliers to absorb more costs, ship more efficiently, and provide more services than ever before, often without a price increase. Often the suppliers have no choice but to go along, and those who fail to do so may go out of business.

Power is also shifting in other industries. For decades, technology vendors have been putting out incompatible products and expecting their corporate customers to assume the burden and expense of making everything work together. Those days may be coming to an end. When the economy began declining, big corporations cut back their spending on technology, which led to stiffer competition among vendors and gave their corporate customers greater power to make demands. Microsoft and Sun Microsystems, which have been waging war for 15 years, recently buried the hatchet and negotiated a collaboration agreement that will smooth the way for providing compatible software products.[17]

Collaborative Networks

Traditionally, the relationship between organizations and their suppliers has been an adversarial one. Indeed, North American companies typically have worked alone, competing with each other and believing in the tradition of individualism and self-reliance. Today, however, thanks to an uncertain global environment, a realignment in corporate relationships is taking place. The **collaborative-network** perspective is an emerging alternative to resource-dependence theory. Companies join together to become more competitive and to share scarce resources. Technology companies join together to produce next-generation products. Large aerospace firms partner with one another and with smaller companies and suppliers to design next-generation jets. Large pharmaceutical companies join with small biotechnology firms to share resources and knowledge and spur innovation. Consulting firms, investment companies, and accounting firms may join in an alliance to meet customer demands for expanded services.[18] As companies move into their own uncharted territory, they are also racing into alliances.

Why Collaboration?

Why all this interest in interorganizational collaboration? Major reasons are sharing risks when entering new markets, mounting expensive new programs and reducing costs, and enhancing organizational profile in selected industries or technologies. Cooperation is a prerequisite for greater innovation, problem solving, and performance.[19] In addition, partnerships are a major avenue for entering global markets, with both large and small firms developing partnerships overseas and in North America.

North Americans have learned from their international experience just how effective interorganizational relationships can be. Both Japan and Korea have long traditions of corporate clans or industrial groups that collaborate and assist each other. North Americans typically have considered interdependence a bad thing, believing it would reduce competition. However, the experience of collaboration in other countries has shown that competition among companies can be fierce in some areas even as they collaborate in others. It is as if the brothers and sisters of a single family went into separate businesses and want to outdo one another, but they still love one another and will help each other when needed.

Interorganizational linkages provide a kind of safety net that encourages long-term investment and risk taking. Companies can achieve higher levels of innovation and performance as they learn to shift from an adversarial to a partnership mindset.[20] In many cases companies are learning to work closely together. Consider the following examples:

- Chrysler's new Crossfire sports car was designed in collaboration with partners Mercedes and Mitsubishi and assembled almost entirely by outside suppliers using their own factories and employees. The automaker is building a new plant in Canada where suppliers' employees will outnumber Chrysler workers. Suppliers will do everything from bending steel to painting finished bodies, with Chrysler employees handling only the final assembly.[21]
- The pharmaceuticals giant Pfizer collaborates with more than 400 companies on research and development projects and co-marketing campaigns. For example, Pfizer has earned billions from co-promotion of Warner-Lambert's Lipitor, a drug for treating elevated cholesterol.[22]
- The Chicago Mercantile Exchange and the Chicago Board of Trade are crosstown rivals, but they collaborated to build a joint Web-enabled clearing system that enables financial institutions conducting trades to put up money only once to guarantee trades on both exchanges.[23]
- Small companies are banding together to compete against much larger firms. Forty local microbreweries formed the Oregon Brewers Guild to gain the resources needed to compete against craft brews from Miller and Anheuser-Busch.[24]

EXHIBIT 5.3
Changing Characteristics of Interorganizational Relationships

Traditional Orientation: Adversarial	New Orientation: Partnership
Low dependence	High dependence
Suspicion, competition, arm's length	Trust, addition of value to both sides, high commitment
Detailed performance measures, closely monitored	Loose performance measures, problems discussed
Price, efficacy, own profits	Equity, fair dealing, both profit
Limited information and feedback	Electronic linkages to share key information, problem feedback, and discussion
Legal resolution of conflict	Mechanisms for close coordination, people on site
Minimal involvement and up-front investment, separate resources	Involvement in partner's product design and production, shared resources
Short-term contracts	Long-term contracts
Contract limiting the relationship	Business assistance beyond the contract

Source: Based on Mick Marchington and Steven Vincent, "Analysing the Influence of Institutional, Organizational, and Interpersonal Forces in Shaping Inter-Organizational Relations," *Journal of Management Studies* 41, no. 6 (September 2004), 1029–1056; Jeffrey H. Dyer, "How Chrysler Created an American *Keiretsu*," *Harvard Business Review* (July–August 1996), 42–56; Myron Magnet, "The New Golden Rule of Business," *Fortune* (February 21, 1994), 60–64; and Peter Grittner, "Four Elements of Successful Sourcing Strategies," *Management Review* (October 1995), 41–45.

Briefcase

As an organization manager, keep these guidelines in mind:

Seek collaborative partnerships that enable mutual dependence and enhance value and gain for both sides. Get deeply involved in your partner's business, and vice versa, to benefit both.

From Adversaries to Partners

Fresh flowers are blooming on the battle-scarred landscape where once-bitter rivalries among suppliers, customers, and competitors took place. In North America, collaboration among organizations initially occurred in not-for-profit social service and mental health organizations where public interest was involved. Community organizations collaborated to achieve greater effectiveness and better use scarce resources.[25] With the push from international competitors and international examples, hard-nosed American business managers began shifting to a new partnership paradigm on which to base their relationships.

A summary of this change in mindset is in Exhibit 5.3. More companies are changing from a traditional adversarial mindset to a partnership orientation. Evidence from studies of such companies as General Electric, Toyota, Whirlpool, Harley-Davidson, and Microsoft indicate that partnering allows reduced cost and increased value for both parties in a predatory world economy.[26] Rather than organizations maintaining independence, the new model is based on interdependence and trust. Performance measures for the partnership are loosely defined, and problems are resolved through discussion and dialogue. Managing strategic relationships with other firms has become a critical management skill, as discussed in this chapter's Book Mark. In the new orientation, people try to add value to both sides and believe in high commitment rather than suspicion and competition. Companies work toward equitable profits for both sides rather than just for their own benefit. The new model is characterized by lots of shared information, including electronic linkages for automatic ordering and face-to-face discussions to provide corrective feedback and solve problems. Sometimes people from other companies are on site to enable very close coordination, as we saw in the chapter-opening example. Partners are involved in each other's product design and production, and they invest for the long term, with an assumption of continuing relations. Partners develop equitable solutions to conflicts rather than relying on legal contractual relationships. Contracts may be loosely specified, and it is not unusual for business partners to help each other outside whatever is specified in the contract.[27]

For example, AMP, a manufacturer of electronics and electrical connectors, was contacted by a customer about a broken connector that posed serious problems. It wasn't even AMP's connector, but the vice president and his sales manager went to a warehouse on a weekend and found replacement parts to get the customer back on line. They provided the service with no charge as a way to enhance the relationship. Indeed, this kind of teamwork treats partner companies almost like departments of one's own organization.[28]

This new partnership mindset can be seen in a number of industries. Microsoft hired contract manufacturer Flextronics to not only build but also help design Xbox, its electronic game console.[29] Many supermarkets and other retailers rely on key suppliers to help them determine what goes on the store shelves. A large vendor

Book Mark 5.0 (HAVE YOU READ THIS BOOK?)

Managing Strategic Relationships: The Key to Business Success
By Leonard Greenhalgh

What determines organizational success in the twenty-first century? According to Leonard Greenhalgh, author of *Managing Strategic Relationships: The Key to Business Success*, it's how successfully managers support, foster, and protect collaborative relationships both inside and outside the firm. In separate chapters, the book offers strategies for managing relationships between people and groups within the company and with other organizations. Effectively managing relationships generates a sense of commonwealth and consensus, which ultimately results in competitive advantage.

MANAGING RELATIONSHIPS IN A NEW ERA
Greenhalgh says managers need a new way of thinking to fit the realities of the new era. Here are a few guidelines:

- *Recognize that detailed legal contracts can undermine trust and goodwill.* Greenhalgh stresses the need to build relationships that are based on honesty, trust, understanding, and common goals instead of on narrowly defined legal contracts that concentrate on what one business can give to the other.
- *Treat partners like members of your own organization.* Members of partner organizations need to be active participants in the learning experience by becoming involved in training, team meetings, and other activities. Giving a partner organization's employees a chance to make genuine contributions promotes deeper bonds and a sense of unity.
- *Top managers must be champions for the alliance.* Managers from both organizations have to act in ways that signal to everyone inside and outside the organization a new emphasis on partnership and collaboration. Using ceremony and symbols can help instill a commitment to partnership in the company culture.

CONCLUSION
To succeed in today's environment, old-paradigm management practices based on power, hierarchy, and adversarial relationships must be traded for new-era commonwealth practices that emphasize collaboration and communal forms of organization. The companies that will thrive, Greenhalgh believes, "are those that really have their act together—those that can successfully integrate strategy, processes, business arrangements, resources, systems, and empowered workforces." That can be accomplished, he argues, only by effectively creating, shaping, and sustaining strategic relationships.

Managing Strategic Relationships: The Key to Business Success, by Leonard Greenhalgh, is published by The Free Press.

such as Procter & Gamble, for example, analyzes national data and makes recommendations for what products the store should offer, including not just P&G's brands, but products from its competitors as well.[30] A large company in England that supplies pigments to the automobile, plastics, and printing industries has a long-standing interdependent relationship with a key chemicals supplier, with the two organizations sharing information about their long-term business needs so that any changes in products or processes can benefit both sides.[31]

In this new view of partnerships, dependence on another company is seen to reduce rather than increase risks. Greater value can be achieved by both parties. By being embedded in a system of interorganizational relationships, everyone does better by helping each other. This is a far cry from the belief that organizations do best by being autonomous and independent. Sales representatives may have a desk on the customer's factory floor, and they have access to information systems and the research lab.[32] Coordination is so intimate that it's sometimes hard to tell one organization from another. Consider how Canada's Bombardier and its suppliers are linked together almost like one organization in building the Continental, a "super-midsize" business jet that can comfortably fly eight passengers nonstop from coast to coast.

In Practice

Bombardier

In an assembly plant on the edge of Mid-Continent Airport in Wichita, a new plane is taking shape as great chunks of it are rolled in and joined together. Not counting rivets, it takes just a dozen big parts—all manufactured elsewhere—to put Bombardier's new Continental together. Those big subassemblies come from all over the world—the engines from Phoenix in the United States, the nose and cockpit from Montreal, Canada, the mid-fuselage from Belfast, Northern Ireland, the tail from Taichung, Taiwan, the wings from Nagoya, Japan, and other parts from Australia, France, Germany, and Austria. When production is up to full speed, it will take just four days to put a plane together and get it in the air.

In the past, most executive-jet companies have made major parts in-house. Canada's Bombardier, instead, relies heavily on suppliers for design support and the sharing of development costs and market risks. The company is intertwined with about thirty suppliers, a dozen or so of which have been involved since the design stage. At one point, about 250 team members from Bombardier and 250 from outsider suppliers worked together in Montreal to make sure the design was going to be good for everyone involved. Bombardier has so far invested about $250 million in the Continental, but suppliers have equaled that amount in development costs. In addition to sharing costs, the supplier companies also share the risks. "They haven't got a contract that says, 'You're going to sell us twenty-five wings a year for the next 10 years.' If the market's there, it's there, and if it's not, it's not," says John Holding, who is in charge of Bombardier's engineering and product development.

Integrating partners so that everyone benefits from and depends on the others—and managing this multinational, multicompany endeavor—is no easy task, but with development costs for a new plane reaching more than $1 billion, the partnership approach just makes sense.[33]

By breaking down boundaries and becoming involved in partnerships with an attitude of fair dealing and adding value to both sides, today's companies are changing the concept of what makes an organization. The type of collaborative network illustrated by Bombardier is also being used by a growing number of automotive companies, including Volkswagen and General Motors. These companies are push-ing the idea of partnership further than ever before, moving somewhat toward a network approach to organization design, as described in Chapter 3.

Population Ecology

This section introduces a different perspective on relationships among organiza-tions. The **population-ecology perspective** differs from the other perspectives be-cause it focuses on organizational diversity and adaptation within a population of organizations.[34] A **population** is a set of organizations engaged in similar activities with similar patterns of resource utilization and outcomes. Organizations within a population compete for similar resources or similar customers, such as financial in-stitutions in the Seattle area.

Within a population, the question asked by ecology researchers is about the large number and variation of organizations in society. Why are new organizational forms that create such diversity constantly appearing? The answer is that individual organizational adaptation is severely limited compared to the changes demanded by the environment. Innovation and change in a population of organizations take place through the birth of new forms and kinds of organizations more so than by the re-form and change of existing organizations. Indeed, organizational forms are con-sidered relatively stable, and the good of a whole society is served by the develop-ment of new forms of organization through entrepreneurial initiatives. New organizations meet the new needs of society more than established organizations that are slow to change.[35]

What does this theory mean in practical terms? It means that large, established organizations often become dinosaurs. As discussed in the previous chapter, large airlines that rely on a hub-and-spoke system have had tremendous difficulty adapt-ing to a rapidly changing environment. Hence, new organizational forms such as JetBlue are emerging that fit the current environment, fill a new niche, and, over time, take away business from established companies.

Why do established organizations have such a hard time adapting to a rapidly changing environment? Michael Hannan and John Freeman, originators of the population ecology model of organization, argue that there are many limitations on the ability of organizations to change. The limitations come from heavy investment in plants, equipment, and specialized personnel, limited information, established viewpoints of decision makers, the organization's own successful history that justi-fies current procedures, and the difficulty of changing corporate culture. True trans-formation is a rare and unlikely event in the face of all these barriers.[36]

At this very moment, new organizational forms are emerging. Consider Asset Re-covery Center, which buys leftover routers, servers, and other networking equipment from dead or bankrupt corporations for pennies on the dollar and then resells them at a profit. There are thousands of such operations in business today because of the tremendous opportunities—organizations are cutting capital spending, while at the same time widespread corporate troubles have created a glut of nearly new equip-ment for sale. Large equipment makers such as Cisco, Nortel Networks, and Sun Microsystems are feeling the pinch as they lose million-dollar deals to used-equipment brokers.[37] Another recent change is the development of corporate univer-sities within large companies like Motorola and FedEx. There are more than 2,000 corporate universities, compared to just 200 a few years ago. One reason they've developed so fast is that companies can't get desired services from established universities, which are too stuck in traditional ways of thinking and teaching.[38]

According to the population-ecology view, when looking at an organizational population as a whole, the changing environment determines which organizations survive or fail. The assumption is that individual organizations suffer from structural inertia and find it difficult to adapt to environmental changes. Thus, when rapid change occurs, old organizations are likely to decline or fail, and new organizations emerge that are better suited to the needs of the environment.

The population-ecology model is developed from theories of natural selection in biology, and the terms *evolution* and *selection* are used to refer to the underlying behavioral processes. Theories of biological evolution try to explain why certain life forms appear and survive whereas others perish. Some theories suggest the forms that survive are typically best fitted to the immediate environment.

Some years ago, *Forbes* magazine reported a study of American businesses over 70 years, from 1917 to 1987. Have you heard of Baldwin Locomotive, Studebaker, or Lehigh Coal & Navigation? These companies were among 78 percent of the top 100 in 1917 that did not see 1987. Of the 22 that remained in the top 100, only 11 did so under their original names. The environment of the 1940s and 1950s was suitable to Woolworth, but new organizational forms like Wal-Mart became dominant in the 1980s. In 1917, most of the top 100 companies were huge steel and mining industrial organizations, which were replaced by high-technology companies such as IBM and Merck.[39] Two companies that seemed to prosper over a long period were Ford and General Motors, but they are now being threatened by world changes in the automobile industry. No company is immune to the processes of social change. From just 1979 to 1989, 187 of the companies on the *Fortune* 500 list ceased to exist as independent companies. Some were acquired, some merged, and some were liquidated.[40] Meanwhile, technology continues to change the environment. AT&T, once the dominant long-distance carrier and the biggest, healthiest, and wealthiest company in the United States, has steadily declined in importance, while cellular technology has made Verizon almost a household name. The expansion of the Internet into the everyday consumer's household has brought a proliferation of new companies such as Amazon.com, Google, and eBay.

■ Organizational Form and Niche

The population-ecology model is concerned with organizational forms. **Organizational form** is an organization's specific technology, structure, products, goals, and personnel, which can be selected or rejected by the environment. Each new organization tries to find a **niche** (a domain of unique environmental resources and needs) sufficient to support it. The niche is usually small in the early stages of an organization but may increase in size over time if the organization is successful. If a niche is not available, the organization will decline and may perish.

From the viewpoint of a single firm, luck, chance, and randomness play important parts in survival. New products and ideas are continually being proposed by both entrepreneurs and large organizations. Whether these ideas and organizational forms survive or fail is often a matter of chance—whether external circumstances happen to support them. A woman who started a small electrical contracting business in a rapidly growing Florida community would have an excellent chance of success. If the same woman were to start the same business in a declining commu-

EXHIBIT 5.4
*Elements in the
Population-Ecology Model
of Organizations*

nity elsewhere in the United States, the chance of success would be far less. Success or failure of a single firm thus is predicted by the characteristics of the environment as much as by the skills or strategies used by the organization.

Process of Ecological Change

The population-ecology model assumes that new organizations are always appearing in the population. Thus, organization populations are continually undergoing change. The process of change in the population is defined by three principles that occur in stages: variation, selection, and retention. These stages are summarized in Exhibit 5.4.

- *Variation.* **Variation** means the appearance of new, diverse forms in a population of organizations. These new organizational forms are initiated by entrepreneurs, established with venture capital by large corporations, or set up by a government seeking to provide new services. Some forms may be conceived to cope with a perceived need in the external environment. In recent years, a large number of new firms have been initiated to develop computer software, to provide consulting and other services to large corporations, and to develop products and technologies for Internet commerce. Other new organizations produce a traditional product such as steel, but do it using minimal technology and new management techniques that make the new companies, such as the steel company Nucor, far more able to survive. Organizational variations are analogous to mutations in biology, and they add to the scope and complexity of organizational forms in the environment. This chapter's Leading by Design box describes a new organizational form conceived by a British entrepreneur to capitalize on advances in information technology and wireless text messaging.

- *Selection.* **Selection** refers to whether a new organizational form is suited to the environment and can survive. Only a few variations are "selected in" by the environment and survive over the long term. Some variations will suit the external environment better than others. Some prove beneficial and thus are able to find a niche and acquire the resources from the environment necessary to survive. Other variations fail to meet the needs of the environment and perish. When there is insufficient demand for a firm's product and when insufficient resources are available to the organization, that organization will be "selected out." For example, Shazam, described in the Leading by Design box, was launched in mid-2002. If demand for the new service does not continue to grow, or if the company cannot obtain needed resources, the company will be selected out and cease to exist.

Leading by Design

Shazam—It's Magic!

Many people have had the experience of hearing a song they like on the radio or in a dance club and waiting in vain for the DJ to identify it. Shazam, a mobile-phone music service launched in the United Kingdom in August 2002, has come to the rescue. The next time a cell phone user hears that mystery tune, all he or she has to do is dial a four-digit number on the cell phone, let the music play into the handset, and moments later receive a text message with the artist and song title. The user can forward a 30-second clip of the track to friends, or even download the song directly to his or her phone. The song can then be legally copied from the mobile phone to a PC and shared between multiple devices.

Shazam's magic happens through the use of a pattern-recognition software algorithm developed by the company's chief scientist. The algorithm picks out the salient characteristics of a tune and matches them against a massive music database. The company, founded by Californian entrepreneur Chris Barton, calls the process "tagging," and users in the United Kingdom alone have already tagged more than 5.5 million music tracks. Users can go online and see a list of all the songs they've tagged.

Shazam's success depends on collaborative partnerships with mobile phone companies, major record labels, software companies, and others. A recent partnership with Swiss-based SDC (Secure Digital Container) AG provides the technology that enables a complete "tag to download" in three simple steps, allowing users to purchase music on the move. A strategic alliance with MTV Japan helped Shazam expand to about 40 million mobile phone subscribers in Japan. Deals with international mobile operators and media companies throughout the United States, Europe, and Asia make Shazam's service available to more than 1 billion mobile phone users worldwide.

The mobile phone companies offer tagging as a premium service to their customers and pay Shazam a cut of the profits. Since tagging promises to drive up call times, most mobile phone companies are interested. And the record labels' interests are served by getting new music in front of consumers. Word-of-mouth recommendations are a powerful means of driving music sales, so the idea of people all over the world forwarding 30-second clips of their new songs has music companies paying attention. The service has proven to be a good predictor of future hits in Britain, so the music industry closely watches Shazam's weekly chart of tagged pre-release tracks.

Shazam is the world's first in music recognition and one of the brightest new ideas in the world of technology. With multiple deals and a presence in twelve countries, it is clear that Shazam is suited to the environment and has found a solid niche. However, managing the complex network of global relationships will be a challenge for managers of the small company, and it remains to be seen if they can take a good idea and build a lasting organization.

Sources: "SDC Partners with Shazam to Create Simple, Secure Music Download," *M2Presswire* (February 14, 2005), 1; Steve McClure, "Shazam Works Its Magic," *Billboard* (August 21, 2004), 60; Adam Jolly, "Going for a Song and Growth," *Sunday Times* (June 13, 2004), 17; Michael Parsons, "I Got Music, I Got Algorithm," *Red Herring* (May 2002), 54–57; and "MTV and Shazam Lead Japanese Market Extending Music Recognition Offering to KDDI Subscribers and Expanding Local Music Database," *M2Presswire* (February 16, 2005), 1.

- *Retention.* **Retention** is the preservation and institutionalization of selected organizational forms. Certain technologies, products, and services are highly valued by the environment. The retained organizational form may become a dominant part of the environment. Many forms of organization have been institutionalized, such as government, schools, churches, and automobile manufacturers. McDonald's, which owns 43 percent of the fast-food market and provides the first job for many teenagers, has become institutionalized in American life.

Institutionalized organizations like McDonald's seem to be relatively permanent features in the population of organizations, but they are not permanent in the long run. The environment is always changing, and, if the dominant organizational forms do not adapt to external change, they will gradually diminish and be replaced by other organizations. McDonald's is struggling because customers think rivals Burger King and Wendy's provide fresher, higher-quality food at better prices. In addition, chains such as Subway and Quizno's are offering today's health-conscious customer an alternative to fast-food burgers and fries. In an annual consumer satisfaction survey, McDonald's has scored dead last among fast-food restaurants every year since 1992.[41] Unless it adapts, McDonald's might no longer be competitive in the fast-food market.

From the population-ecology perspective, the environment is the important determinant of organizational success or failure. The organization must meet an environmental need, or it will be selected out. The process of variation, selection, and retention leads to the establishment of new organizational forms in a population of organizations.

■ Strategies for Survival

Another principle that underlies the population ecology model is the **struggle for existence**, or competition. Organizations and populations of organizations are engaged in a competitive struggle over resources, and each organizational form is fighting to survive. The struggle is most intense among new organizations, and both the birth and survival frequencies of new organizations are related to factors in the larger environment. Factors such as size of urban area, percentage of immigrants, political turbulence, industry growth rate, and environmental variability have influenced the launching and survival of newspapers, telecommunication firms, railroads, government agencies, labor unions, and even voluntary organizations.[42]

In the population ecology perspective, **generalist** and **specialist** strategies distinguish organizational forms in the struggle for survival. Organizations with a wide niche or domain, that is, those that offer a broad range of products or services or that serve a broad market, are generalists. Organizations that provide a narrower range of goods or services or that serve a narrower market are specialists.

In the natural environment, a specialist form of flora and fauna would evolve in protective isolation in a place like Hawaii, where the nearest body of land is 2,000 miles away. The flora and fauna are heavily protected. In contrast, a place like Costa Rica, which experienced wave after wave of external influences, developed a generalist set of flora and fauna that has better resilience and flexibility for adapting to a broad range of circumstances. In the business world, Amazon.com started with a specialist strategy, selling books over the Internet, but evolved to a generalist strategy with the addition of music, DVDs, greeting cards, and other products, plus partnering with other organizations as an online shopping mall to sell a wide range of products. A company such as Olmec Corporation, which sells African-American and Hispanic dolls, would be considered a specialist, whereas Mattel is a generalist, marketing a broad range of toys for boys and girls of all ages.[43]

Specialists are generally more competitive than generalists in the narrow area in which their domains overlap. However, the breadth of the generalist's domain serves to protect it somewhat from environmental changes. Though demand may decrease for some of the generalist's products or services, it usually increases for others at the same time. In addition, because of the diversity of products, services, and customers, generalists are able to reallocate resources internally to adapt to a changing environment, whereas specialists are not. However, because specialists are often smaller companies, they can sometimes move faster and be more flexible in adapting to changes.[44]

Managerial impact on company success often comes from selecting a strategy that steers a company into an open niche. Consider how Genentech has thrived after a new CEO steered it into a new niche in the pharmaceuticals industry.

In Practice

Genentech

Genentech was the world's first biotechnology firm, founded more than 25 years ago, and its creation spurred the development of a whole new subset in the pharmaceuticals industry. A wide variety of small biotech firms have been established, with each struggling to find a niche that will enable the company to survive in the volatile, competitive world of drug development and manufacturing.

Genentech spent its early years trying to bring out blockbuster drugs and grow into a company on the scale of pharmaceutical giants like Schering Plough or Merck. But its first potential blockbusters fizzled, and the company's fortunes dwindled. Things began to turn around when Genentech's research director, Arthur Levinson, was appointed CEO. Levinson turned the company in a new direction. Rather than betting the farm on blockbusters, Levinson chose a strategy of developing "targeted drugs," lucrative new medicines that are aimed at small sets of patients. For example, Herceptin, Genentech's first targeted therapy launched several years ago, is a breast-cancer drug that is prescribed to only the 25 percent of patients whose tumors reveal a specific genetic characteristic. Other targeted treatments include Rituxan, for treating an immune-cell cancer called non-Hodgkin's lymphoma, and Xolair, a drug pending Food and Drug Administration (FDA) approval for a type of allergic asthma.

Large drug companies are struggling in an industry that is being threatened by changes in managed care, the expiration of numerous drug patents, and the high cost of new drug development. Many have tried to compete with massive marketing campaigns to make up for the decline in blockbuster drugs. Meanwhile, Genentech is achieving remarkable success with its targeted approach. The company recently jumped ahead of giant pharmaceutical companies to become the top seller of branded anti-tumor drugs in the United States. Genentech has an impressive ten drugs on the market and twenty more either in clinical trials or awaiting FDA approval.[45]

Genentech isn't immune from the volatility and uncertainty inherent in the industry, but managers found a niche that put the company on a solid foundation for survival over the long term. CEO Levinson chose a specialist strategy, focusing on specific therapies for relatively small subsets of patients rather than looking for one-size-fits-all blockbuster drugs.

Institutionalism

The institutional perspective provides yet another view of interorganizational relationships.[46] Organizations are highly interconnected. Just as companies need efficient production to survive, the institutional view argues that organizations need legitimacy from their stakeholders. Companies perform well when they are perceived by the larger environment to have a legitimate right to exist. Thus, the **institutional perspective** describes how organizations survive and succeed through congruence between an organization and the expectations from its environment. The **institutional environment** is composed of norms and values from stakeholders (customers, investors, associations, boards, government, collaborating organizations). Thus the institutional view believes that organizations adopt structures and processes to please outsiders, and these activities come to take on rule-like status in organizations. The institutional environment reflects what the greater society views as correct ways of organizing and behaving.[47]

Legitimacy is defined as the general perspective that an organization's actions are desirable, proper, and appropriate within the environment's system of norms, values, and beliefs.[48] Institutional theory thus is concerned with the set of intangible norms and values that shape behavior, as opposed to the tangible elements of technology and structure. Organizations must fit within the cognitive and emotional expectations of their audience. For example, people will not deposit money in a bank unless it sends signals of compliance with norms of wise financial management. Consider also your local government and whether it could raise property taxes for increased school funding if community residents did not approve of the school district's policies and activities.

Most organizations are concerned with legitimacy, as reflected in the annual *Fortune* magazine survey that ranks corporations based on their reputations, and the annual Reputation Quotient study, a survey of public opinion conducted by Harris Interactive and the Reputation Institute.[49] Many corporations actively shape and manage their reputations to increase their competitive advantage, and managers are searching for new ways to bolster legitimacy in the wake of ethical and financial scandals at such well-known companies as Boeing, Enron, and WorldCom. One company that has built a reputation as a highly ethical and socially responsible company is Johnson & Johnson, where managers stress the company's commitment to customers, employees, and the broader community. Johnson & Johnson has ranked in first place for 6 years in a row on the Reputation Quotient, which surveys more than 20,000 people in telephone and online interviews. In contrast, Wal-Mart has seen its reputation decline slightly over the past 2 years.[50]

In Practice
Wal-Mart

"I'm offended by Wal-Mart's ads," says Anthony Leo, a physician in Arvada, Colorado. "The image of a waving American flag with the faces of contented employees and grateful townsfolk welcoming the liberating Wal-Mart—well, for me, it is too much to swallow." For the first time in its history, Wal-Mart is facing a serious legitimacy problem. A combination of factors has led to a decline in the company's reputation and a growing criticism of its practices.

For one thing, people naturally begin to distrust corporations that grow so large and dominant as Wal-Mart. In addition, the company's size has brought a host of new management challenges. Publicity about cleaning contractors using illegal aliens in Wal-Mart stores tarnished the company's All-American image. Wal-Mart's early-1990s claim to "Buy American" has quietly been shelved as the company has more than doubled its imports from China since then. And some critics charge that U.S. manufacturers of everything from bras to bicycles have had to close plants, lay off workers, and outsource to low-wage countries in order to survive in the face of Wal-Mart's cost-cutting demands. Employee complaints about low pay and a damaging gender-discrimination suit have compounded the company's image problems.

Consumers are still captivated by Wal-Mart's low prices, but there is growing concern and criticism about the high social and economic costs of the company's "low-cost" approach. "Shoppers could start feeling guilty about shopping with us," says Wal-Mart spokeswoman Mona Williams. "Communities could make it harder to build our stores." Thus, Wal-Mart's executives have begun to take criticism seriously, vowing to do a better job of telling the right story to the public.[51]

Wal-Mart has not been seriously damaged by these criticisms, but managers know that how the company is perceived by customers and the public plays a big role in long-term success. Wal-Mart is extremely powerful today, but its power could decline if the company's actions are not considered legitimate and appropriate.

The fact that there is a payoff for having a good reputation is verified by a study of organizations in the airline industry. Having a good reputation was significantly related to higher levels of performance measures such as return on assets and net profit margin.[52]

The notion of legitimacy answers an important question for institutional theorists. Why is there so much homogeneity in the forms and practices of established organizations? For example, visit banks, high schools, hospitals, government departments, or business firms in a similar industry, in any part of the country, and they will look strikingly similar. When an organizational field is just getting started, such as in e-commerce, diversity is the norm. New organizations fill emerging niches. However, once an industry becomes established, there is an invisible push toward similarity. *Isomorphism* is the term used to describe this move toward similarity.

The Institutional View and Organization Design

The institutional view also sees organizations as having two essential dimensions—technical and institutional. The technical dimension is the day-to-day work, technology, and operating requirements. The institutional structure is that part of the organization most visible to the outside public. Moreover, the technical dimension is governed by norms of rationality and efficiency, but the institutional dimension is governed by expectations from the external environment. As a result of pressure to do things in a proper and correct way, the formal structures of many organizations reflect the expectations and values of the environment rather than the demand of work activities. This means that an organization may incorporate positions or activities (equal employment officer, e-commerce division, chief ethics officer) perceived as important by the larger society to increase its legitimacy and survival prospects, even though these elements may decrease efficiency. For example, many small companies set up Web sites, even though the benefits gained from the site are sometimes outweighed by the costs of maintaining it. Having a Web site is perceived as essential by the larger society today. The formal structure and design of an organization may not be rational with respect to workflow and products or services, but it will ensure survival in the larger environment.

Organizations adapt to the environment by signaling their congruence with the demands and expectations stemming from cultural norms, standards set by professional bodies, funding agencies, and customers. Structure is something of a facade disconnected from technical work through which the organization obtains approval, legitimacy, and continuing support. The adoption of structures thus might not be linked to actual production needs, and might occur regardless of whether specific internal problems are solved. Formal structure is separated from technical action in this view.[53]

Institutional Similarity

Organizations have a strong need to appear legitimate. In so doing, many aspects of structure and behavior may be targeted toward environmental acceptance rather than toward internal technical efficiency. Interorganizational relationships thus are

EXHIBIT 5.5
Three Mechanisms for Institutional Adaptation

	Mimetic	Coercive	Normative
Reason to become similar:	Uncertainty	Dependence	Duty, obligation
Events:	Innovation visibility	Political law, rules, sanctions	Professionalism—certification, accreditation
Social basis:	Culturally supported	Legal	Moral
Example:	Reengineering, benchmarking	Pollution controls, school regulations	Accounting standards, consultant training

Source: Adapted from W. Richard Scott, *Institutions and Organizations* (Thousand Oaks, Calif.: Sage, 1995).

characterized by forces that cause organizations in a similar population to look like one another. **Institutional similarity**, called *institutional isomorphism* in the academic literature, is the emergence of a common structure and approach among organizations in the same field. Isomorphism is the process that causes one unit in a population to resemble other units that face the same set of environmental conditions.[54]

Exactly how does increasing similarity occur? How are these forces realized? A summary of three mechanisms for institutional adaptation appears in Exhibit 5.5. These three core mechanisms are *mimetic forces*, which result from responses to uncertainty; *coercive forces*, which stem from political influence; and *normative forces*, which result from common training and professionalism.[55]

Mimetic Forces. Most organizations, especially business organizations, face great uncertainty. It is not clear to senior executives exactly what products, services, or technologies will achieve desired goals, and sometimes the goals themselves are not clear. In the face of this uncertainty, **mimetic forces**, the pressure to copy or model other organizations, occur.

Executives observe an innovation in a firm generally regarded as successful, so the management practice is quickly copied. An example is the proliferation of Wi-Fi hotspots in cafes, hotels, and airports. Starbucks was one of the first companies to adopt Wi-Fi, enabling customers to use laptops and handheld computers at Starbucks stores. The practice has rapidly been copied by both large and small companies, from Holiday Inns to the local deli. Many times, this modeling is done without any clear proof that performance will be improved. Mimetic processes explain why fads and fashions occur in the business world. Once a new idea starts, many organizations grab onto it, only to learn that the application is difficult and may cause more problems than it solves. This was the case with the recent merger wave that swept many industries. The past two decades have seen the largest merger and acquisition wave in history, but evidence shows that many of these mergers did not produce the expected financial gains and other benefits. The sheer momentum of the trend was so powerful that many companies chose to merge not because of potential increases in efficiency or profitability but simply because it seemed like the right thing to do.[56] Downsizing of the workforce is another trend that can be attributed partly to mimetic forces. Despite some evidence that massive downsizing actually hurts organizations, managers perceive it as a legitimate and effective means of improving performance.[57]

Briefcase

As an organization manager, keep these guidelines in mind:

Pursue legitimacy with your organization's major stakeholders in the external environment. Adopt strategies, structures, and new management techniques that meet the expectations of significant parties, thereby ensuring their cooperation and access to resources.

Techniques such as outsourcing, reengineering, Six Sigma quality programs, and the balanced scorecard have all been adopted without clear evidence that they will improve efficiency or effectiveness. The one certain benefit is that management's feelings of uncertainty will be reduced, and the company's image will be enhanced because the firm is seen as using the latest management techniques. A recent study of 100 organizations confirmed that those companies associated with using popular management techniques were more admired and rated higher in quality of management, even though these organizations often did not reflect higher economic performance.[58] Perhaps the clearest example of official copying is the technique of benchmarking that occurs as part of the total quality movement. *Benchmarking* means identifying who's best at something in an industry and then duplicating the technique for creating excellence, perhaps even improving it in the process.

The mimetic process works because organizations face continuous high uncertainty, they are aware of innovations occurring in the environment, and the innovations are culturally supported, thereby giving legitimacy to adopters. This is a strong mechanism by which a group of banks, or high schools, or manufacturing firms begin to look and act like one another.

Coercive Forces. All organizations are subject to pressure, both formal and informal, from government, regulatory agencies, and other important organizations in the environment, especially those on which a company is dependent. **Coercive forces** are the external pressures exerted on an organization to adopt structures, techniques, or behaviors similar to other organizations. As with other changes, those brought about because of coercive forces may not make the organization more effective, but it will look more effective and will be accepted as legitimate in the environment. Some pressures may have the force of law, such as government mandates to adopt new pollution control equipment. Health and safety regulations may demand that a safety officer be appointed. New regulations and government oversight boards have been set up for the accounting industry following widespread accounting scandals.[59]

Coercive pressures may also occur between organizations where there is a power difference, as described in the resource-dependence section earlier in this chapter. Large retailers and manufacturers often insist that certain policies, procedures, and techniques be used by their suppliers. When Honda picked Donnelly Corporation to make all the mirrors for its U.S.-manufactured cars, Honda insisted that Donnelly implement an employee empowerment program. Honda managers believed the partnership could work only if Donnelly learned how to foster collaborative internal relationships.

Organizational changes that result from coercive forces occur when an organization is dependent on another, when there are political factors such as rules, laws, and sanctions involved, or when some other contractual or legal basis defines the relationship. Organizations operating under those constraints will adopt changes and relate to one another in a way that increases homogeneity and limits diversity.

Normative Forces. The third reason organizations change according to the institutional view is normative forces. **Normative forces** are pressures to change to achieve standards of professionalism, and to adopt techniques that are considered by the professional community to be up to date and effective. Changes may be in any area, such as information technology, accounting requirements, marketing techniques, or collaborative relationships with other organizations.

Professionals share a body of formal education based on university degrees and professional networks through which ideas are exchanged by consultants and professional leaders. Universities, consulting firms, trade associations, and professional training institutions develop norms among professional managers. People are exposed to similar training and standards and adopt shared values, which are implemented in organizations with which they work. Business schools teach finance, marketing, and human resource majors that certain techniques are better than others, so using those techniques becomes a standard in the field. In one study, for example, a radio station changed from a functional to a multidivisional structure because a consultant recommended it as a "higher standard" of doing business. There was no proof that this structure was better, but the radio station wanted legitimacy and to be perceived as fully professional and up to date in its management techniques.

Companies accept normative pressures to become like one another through a sense of obligation or duty to high standards of performance based on professional norms shared by managers and specialists in their respective organizations. These norms are conveyed through professional education and certification and have almost a moral or ethical requirement based on the highest standards accepted by the profession at that time. In some cases, though, normative forces that maintain legitimacy break down, as they recently did in the accounting industry, and coercive forces are needed to shift organizations back toward acceptable standards.

An organization may use any or all of the mechanisms of mimetic, coercive, or normative forces to change itself for greater legitimacy in the institutional environment. Firms tend to use these mechanisms when they are acting under conditions of dependence, uncertainty, ambiguous goals, and reliance on professional credentials. The outcome of these processes is that organizations become far more homogeneous than would be expected from the natural diversity among managers and environments.

Briefcase

As an organization manager, keep this guideline in mind:

Enhance legitimacy by borrowing good ideas from other firms, complying with laws and regulations, and following procedures considered best for your company.

Summary and Interpretation

This chapter has been about the important evolution in interorganizational relationships. At one time organizations considered themselves autonomous and separate, trying to outdo other companies. Today more organizations see themselves as part of an ecosystem. The organization may span several industries and will be anchored in a dense web of relationships with other companies. In this ecosystem, collaboration is as important as competition. Indeed, organizations may compete and collaborate at the same time depending on the location and issue. In this business ecosystem, the role of management is changing to include the development of horizontal relationships with other organizations.

Four perspectives have been developed to explain relationships among organizations. The resource-dependence perspective is the most traditional, arguing that organizations try to avoid excessive dependence on other organizations. In this view, organizations devote considerable effort to controlling the environment to ensure ample resources while maintaining independence. Moreover, powerful organizations will exploit the dependence of small companies. The collaborative-network perspective is an emerging alternative. Organizations welcome collaboration and interdependence with other organizations to enhance value for both. Many executives are changing mindsets away from autonomy toward collaboration, often with former corporate enemies. The new mindset emphasizes trust, fair dealing, and achieving profits for all parties in a relationship.

The population-ecology perspective explains why organizational diversity continuously increases with the appearance of new organizations filling niches left open by established companies. This perspective says that large companies usually cannot adapt to meet a changing environment; hence, new companies emerge with the appropriate form and skills to serve new needs. Through the process of variation, selection, and retention, some organizations will survive and grow while others perish. Companies may adopt a generalist or specialist strategy to survive in the population of organizations.

The institutional perspective argues that interorganizational relationships are shaped as much by a company's need for legitimacy as by the need for providing products and services. The need for legitimacy means that the organization will adopt structures and activities that are perceived as valid, proper, and up to date by external stakeholders. In this way, established organizations copy techniques from one another and begin to look very similar. The emergence of common structures and approaches in the same field is called institutional similarity or institutional isomorphism. There are three core mechanisms that explain increasing organizational homogeneity: mimetic forces, which result from responses to uncertainty; coercive forces, which stem from power differences and political influences; and normative forces, which result from common training and professionalism.

Each of the four perspectives is valid. They represent different lenses through which the world of interorganizational relationships can be viewed: organizations experience a competitive struggle for autonomy; they can thrive through collaborative relationships with others; the slowness to adapt provides openings for new organizations to flourish; and organizations seek legitimacy as well as profits from the external environment. The important thing is for managers to be aware of interorganizational relationships and to consciously manage them.

Key Concepts

coercive forces	organizational ecosystem
collaborative network	organizational form
generalist	population
institutional environment	population-ecology perspective
institutional perspective	resource dependence
institutional similarity	retention
interorganizational relationships	selection
legitimacy	specialist
mimetic forces	struggle for existence
niche	variation
normative forces	

Discussion Questions

1. The concept of business ecosystems implies that organizations are more interdependent than ever before. From personal experience, do you agree? Explain.
2. How do you feel about the prospect of becoming a manager and having to manage a set of relationships with other companies rather than just managing your own company? Discuss.
3. Assume you are the manager of a small firm that is dependent on a large computer manufacturing customer that uses the resource-dependence perspective. Put yourself in

the position of the small firm, and describe what actions you would take to survive and succeed. What actions would you take from the perspective of the large firm?

4. Many managers today were trained under assumptions of adversarial relationships with other companies. Do you think operating as adversaries is easier or more difficult than operating as partners with other companies? Discuss.

5. Discuss how the adversarial versus partnership orientations work among students in class. Is there a sense of competition for grades? Is it possible to develop true partnerships in which your work depends on others?

6. The population-ecology perspective argues that it is healthy for society to have new organizations emerging and old organizations dying as the environment changes. Do you agree? Why would European countries pass laws to sustain traditional organizations and inhibit the emergence of new ones?

7. Explain how the process of variation, selection, and retention might explain innovations that take place within an organization.

8. Do you believe that legitimacy really motivates a large, powerful organization such as Wal-Mart? Is acceptance by other people a motivation for individuals as well? Explain.

9. How does the desire for legitimacy result in organizations becoming more similar over time?

10. How do mimetic forces differ from normative forces? Give an example of each.

Chapter 5 Workbook: Management Fads*

Look up one or two articles on current trends or fads in management. Then, find one or two articles on a management fad from several years ago. Finally, surf the Internet for information on both the current and previous fads.

Questions

1. How were these fads used in organizations? Use real examples from your readings.

2. Why do you think the fads were adopted? To what extent were the fads adopted to truly improve productivity and morale versus the company's desire to appear current in its management techniques compared to the competition?

3. Give an example in which a fad did not work as expected. Explain the reason it did not work.

*Copyright 1996 by Dorothy Marcic. All rights reserved.

Case for Analysis: Oxford Plastics Company*

Oxford Plastics manufactures high-quality plastics and resins for use in a variety of products, from lawn ornaments and patio furniture to automobiles. The Oxford plant located near Beatty, a town of about 45,000 in a southeastern state, employs about 3,000 workers. It plays an important role in the local economy and, indeed, that of the entire state, which offers few well-paying factory jobs.

In early 1995, Sam Henderson, plant manager of the Beatty facility, notified Governor Tom Winchell that Oxford was ready to announce plans for a major addition to the factory—a state-of-the-art color lab and paint shop that would enable better and faster matching of colors to customer requirements. The new shop would keep Oxford competitive in the fast-paced global market for plastics, as well as bring the Beatty plant into full compliance with U.S. Environmental Protection Agency (EPA) regulations due to take effect within 2 years.

Plans for the new facility were largely complete. The biggest remaining task was identifying the specific location. The new color lab and paint shop would cover approximately 25 acres, requiring Oxford to purchase some additional land adjacent to its 75-acre factory campus. Henderson was somewhat concerned with top management's preferred site because it fell outside the current industrial zoning boundary, and, moreover, would necessitate destruction of several 400- to 500-year-old beech trees.

*Source: Based on "Mammoth Motors' New Paint Shop," a role-play originally prepared by Arnold Howitt, Executive Director of the A. Alfred Taubman Center for State and Local Government at the Kennedy School of Government, Harvard University, and subsequently edited by Gerald Cormick, a principal in the CSE Group and Senior Lecturer for the Graduate School of Public Affairs at the University of Washington.

The owner of the property, a nonprofit agency, was ready to sell, whereas property located on the other side of the campus might be more difficult to obtain in a timely manner. Oxford was on a tight schedule to get the project completed. If the new facility wasn't up and running by the time the new EPA regulations went into effect, there was a chance the EPA could force Oxford to stop using its old process—in effect, shutting down the factory.

The governor was thrilled with Oxford's decision to build the new shop in Beatty and he urged Henderson to immediately begin working closely with local and state officials to circumvent any potential problems. It was essential, he stressed, that the project not be bogged down or thwarted by conflict among different interest groups, as it was too important to the economic development of the region. Governor Winchell assigned Beth Friedlander, director of the Governor's Office of Economic Development, to work closely with Henderson on the project. However, Winchell was not willing to offer his commitment to help push through the rezoning, as he had been an enthusiastic public supporter of environmental causes.

Following his conversation with Governor Winchell, Henderson sat down to identify the various people and organizations that would have an interest in the new color lab project and that would need to collaborate in order for it to proceed in a smooth and timely manner. They are:

Oxford Plastics
- Mark Thomas, Vice President of North American Operations. Thomas would be flying in from Oxford's Michigan headquarters to oversee land purchase and negotiations regarding the expansion.
- Sam Henderson, Beatty Plant Manager, who has spent his entire career at the Beatty facility, beginning on the factory floor fresh out of high school.
- Wayne Talbert, local union president. The union is strongly in favor of the new shop being located in Beatty because of the potential for more and higher-wage jobs.

State Government
- Governor Tom Winchell, who can exert pressure on local officials to support the project.
- Beth Friedlander, Director of the Governor's Office of Economic Development.

- Manu Gottlieb, Director of the State Department of Environmental Quality.

City Government
- Mayor Barbara Ott, a political newcomer, who has been in office for less than a year and who campaigned on environmental issues.
- Major J. Washington, the Chamber of Commerce chair of local economic development.

Public
- May Pinelas, Chairman of Historic Beatty, who argues vociferously that the future of the region lies in historic and natural preservation and tourism.
- Tommy Tompkins, President of the Save Our Future Foundation, a coalition of private individuals and representatives from the local university who have long been involved in public environmental issues and have successfully thwarted at least one previous expansion project.

Henderson is feeling torn about how to proceed. He thinks to himself, "To move forward, how will I build a coalition among these diverse organizations and groups?" He understands the need for Oxford to move quickly, but he wants Oxford to have a good relationship with the people and organizations that will surely oppose destruction of more of Beatty's natural beauty. Henderson has always liked finding a win-win compromise, but there are so many groups with an interest in this project that he's not sure where to start. Maybe he should begin by working closely with Beth Friedlander from the governor's office—there's no doubt this is an extremely important project for the state's economic development. On the other hand, it's the local people who are going to be most affected and most involved in the final decisions. Oxford's vice president has suggested a press conference to announce the new shop at the end of the week, but Henderson is worried about putting the news out cold. Perhaps he should call a meeting of interested parties now and let everyone get their feelings out into the open? He knows it could get emotional, but he wonders if things won't get much uglier later on if he doesn't.

Case for Analysis: Hugh Russel, Inc.*

The following story is a personal recollection by David Hurst of the experience of a group of managers in a mature organization undergoing profound change. . . .The precipitating event in this change was a serious business crisis. . . .

*Source: Reprinted by permission of Harvard Business School Press. From *Crisis and Renewal: Meeting the Challenge of Organizational Change*, by David K. Hurst (Boston: Harvard Business School Press, 1995), pp. 53–73. Copyright © 1995 by the Harvard Business School Publishing Corporation; all rights reserved.

When I joined Hugh Russel Inc. in 1979, it was a medium-sized Canadian distributor of steel and industrial products. With sales of CDN$535 million and 3,000 employees, the business was controlled by the chairman, Archie Russel, who owned 16 percent of the common shares. The business consisted of four groups—the core steel distribution activities (called "Russelsteel"), industrial bearings and valves distribution, a chain of wholesalers of hardware and sporting goods, and a small manufacturing business. . . .

The company was structured for performance. . . . The management was professional, with each of the divisional hierarchies headed by a group president reporting to Peter Foster in his capacity as president of the corporation. Jobs were described in job descriptions, and their mode of execution was specified in detailed standard operating procedures. Three volumes of the corporate manual spelled out policy on everything from accounting to vacation pay. Extensive accounting and data processing systems allowed managers to track the progress of individual operations against budgets and plans. Compensation was performance-based, with return on net assets (RONA) as the primary measure and large bonuses (up to 100 percent of base) for managers who made their targets.

At the senior management level, the culture was polite but formal. The board of directors consisted of Archie's friends and associates together with management insiders. Archie and Peter ran the organization as if they were majority owners. Their interaction with management outside of the head office was restricted to the occasional field trip. . . .

Crisis

Nine months after I joined the company as a financial planner, we were put "in play" by a raider and, after a fierce bidding war, were acquired in a hostile takeover. Our acquirer was a private company controlled by the eldest son of an entrepreneur of legendary wealth and ability, so we had no inkling at the time of the roller-coaster ride that lay ahead of us. We were unaware that not only did the son not have the support of his father in this venture but also he had neglected to consult his two brothers, who were joint owners of the acquiring company! As he had taken on $300 million of debt to do the deal, this left each of the brothers on the hook for a personal guarantee of $100 million. They were not amused, and it showed!

Within days of the deal, we were inundated by waves of consultants, lawyers, and accountants: each shareholder seemed to have his or her own panel of advisers. After 6 weeks of intensive analysis, it was clear that far too much had been paid for us and that the transaction was vastly overleveraged. At the start of the deal, the acquirer had approached our bankers and asked them if they wanted a piece of the "action." Concerned at the possible loss of our

banking business and eager to be associated with such a prominent family, our bankers had agreed to provide the initial financing on a handshake. Now, as they saw the detailed numbers for the first time and became aware of the dissent among the shareholders, they withdrew their support and demanded their money back. We needed to refinance $300 million of debt—fast. . . .

Change

The takeover and the subsequent merger of our new owner's moribund steel-fabricating operations into Hugh Russel changed our agenda completely. We had new shareholders (who fought with each other constantly), new bankers, and new businesses in an environment of soaring interest rates and plummeting demand for our products and services. Almost overnight, the corporation went from a growth-oriented, acquisitive, earnings-driven operation to a broken, cash-starved company, desperate to survive. Closures, layoffs, downsizing, delayering, asset sales, and "rationalization" became our new priorities. . . . At the head office, the clarity of jobs vanished. For example, I had been hired to do financial forecasting and raise capital in the equity markets, but with the company a financial mess, this clearly could not be done. For all of us, the future looked dangerous and frightening as bankruptcy, both personal and corporate, loomed ahead.

And so it was in an atmosphere of crisis that Wayne Mang, the new president (Archie Russel and Peter Foster left the organization soon after the deal), gathered the first group of managers together to discuss the situation. Wayne Mang had been in the steel business for many years and was trusted and respected by the Hugh Russel people. An accountant by training, he used to call himself the "personnel manager" to underscore his belief in both the ability of people to make the difference in the organization and the responsibility of line management to make this happen. The hastily called first meeting consisted of people whom Wayne respected and trusted from all over the organization. They had been selected without regard for their position in the old hierarchy.

The content and style of that first meeting were a revelation to many! Few of them had ever been summoned to the head office for anything but a haranguing over their budgets. Now they were being told the complete gory details of the company's situation and, for the first time, being treated as if they had something to contribute. Wayne asked for their help.

During that first meeting, we counted nineteen major issues confronting the corporation. None of them fell under a single functional area. We arranged ourselves into task forces to deal with them. I say "arranged ourselves" because that was the way it seemed to happen. Individuals volunteered without coercion to work on issues in which they were interested or for which their skills were relevant.

They also volunteered others who were not at the meeting but, it was thought, could help. There was some guidance—each task force had one person from the head office whose function it was to report what was happening back to the "center"—and some members found themselves on too many task forces, which required that substitutes be found. But that was the extent of the conscious management of the process.

The meeting broke up at 2:00 A.M., when we all went home to tell our incredulous spouses what had happened. . . .

The cross-functional project team rapidly became our preferred method of organizing new initiatives, and at the head office, the old formal structure virtually disappeared. The teams could be formed at a moment's notice to handle a fast-breaking issue and dissolved just as quickly. We found, for example, that even when we weren't having formal meetings, we seemed to spend most of our time talking to each other informally. Two people would start a conversation in someone's office, and almost before you knew it, others had wandered in and a small group session was going. Later on, we called these events "bubbles;" they became our equivalent of campfire meetings. . . .

Later, when I became executive vice president, Wayne and I deliberately shared an office so we could each hear what the other was doing in real time and create an environment in which "bubbles" might form spontaneously. As people wandered past our open door, we would wave them in to talk; others would wander in after them. The content of these sessions always had to do with our predicament, both corporate and personal. It was serious stuff, but the atmosphere was light and open. Our fate was potentially a bad one, but at least it would be shared. All of us who were involved then cannot remember ever having laughed so much. We laughed at ourselves and at the desperate situation. We laughed at the foolishness of the bankers in having financed such a mess, and we laughed at the antics of the feuding shareholders, whose outrageous manners and language we learned to mimic to perfection.

I think it was the atmosphere from these informal sessions that gradually permeated all our interactions—with employees, bankers, suppliers, everyone with whom we came into contact. Certainly, we often had tough meetings, filled with tension and threat, but we were always able to "bootstrap" ourselves back up emotionally at the informal debriefings afterward. . . .

Perhaps the best example of both the change in structure and the blurring of the boundaries of the organization was our changing relationships with our bankers. In the beginning, at least for the brief time that the loan was in good standing, the association was polite and at arm's length. Communication was formal. As the bank realized the full horror of what it had financed (a process that took about 18 months), the relationship steadily grew more hostile. Senior executives of the bank became threatening, spelling out what actions they might take if

we did not solve our problem. This hostility culminated in an investigation by the bank for possible fraud (a standard procedure in many banks when faced with a significant loss).

Throughout this period, we had seen a succession of different bankers, each of whom had been assigned to our account for a few months. As a result of our efforts to brief every new face that appeared, we had built a significant network of contacts within the bank with whom we had openly shared a good deal of information and opinion. When no fraud was found, the bank polled its own people on what to do. Our views presented so coherently by our people (because everyone knew what was going on), and shared so widely with so many bankers, had an enormous influence on the outcome of this process. The result was the formation of a joint company-bank team to address a shared problem that together we could solve. The boundary between the corporation and the bank was now blurred: to an outside observer, it would have been unclear where the corporation ended and the bank began. . . .

Our corporation had extensive formal reporting systems to allow the monitoring of operations on a regular basis. After the takeover, these systems required substantial modifications. For example . . . we had to report our results to the public every quarter at a time when we were losing nearly 2 million dollars a week! We knew that unless we got to our suppliers ahead of time, they could easily panic and refuse us credit. Hasty moves on their part could have had fatal consequences for the business.

In addition, our closure plans for plants all over Canada and the United States brought us into contact with unions and governments in an entirely different way. We realized that we had no option but to deal with these audiences in advance of events.

I have already described how our relationship with the bankers changed as a result of our open communication. We found exactly the same effect with these new audiences. Initially, our major suppliers could not understand why we had told them we were in trouble before we had to. We succeeded, however, in framing the situation in a way that enlisted their cooperation in our survival, and by the time the "war story" was news, we had their full support. Similarly, most government and union organizations were so pleased to be involved in the process before announcements were made that they bent over backward to be of assistance. Just as had been the case with the bank, we set up joint task forces with these "outside" agencies to resolve what had become shared problems. A significant contributor to our ability to pull this off was the high quality of our internal communication. Everyone on the teams knew the complete, up-to-date picture of what was happening. An outside agency could talk to anyone on a team and get the same story. In this way, we constructed a formidable network of contacts, many of whom had special skills and experience in areas that would turn out to be of great help to us in the future.

The addition of multiple networks to our information systems enhanced our ability both to gather and to disseminate information. The informality and openness of the networks, together with the high volume of face-to-face dialogues, gave us an early-warning system with which to detect hurt feelings and possible hostile moves on the part of shareholders, suppliers, nervous bankers, and even customers. This information helped us head off trouble before it happened. The networks also acted as a broadcast system through which we could test plans and actions before announcing them formally. In this way, not only did we get excellent suggestions for improvement, but everyone felt that he or she had been consulted before action was taken. . . .

We had a similar experience with a group of people outside the company during the hectic last 6 months of 1983, when we were trying to finalize a deal for the shareholders and bankers to sell the steel distribution business to new owners. The group of people in question comprised the secretaries of the numerous lawyers and accountants involved in the deal. . . .

We made these secretaries part of the network, briefing them in advance on the situation, explaining why things were needed, and keeping them updated on the progress of the deal. We were astounded at the cooperation we received: our calls were put through, our messages received prompt responses, and drafts and opinions were produced on time. In the final event, a complex deal that should have taken 9 months to complete was done in 3. All of this was accomplished by ordinary people going far beyond what might have been expected of them. . . .

We had been thrust into crisis without warning, and our initial activities were almost entirely reactions to issues that imposed themselves upon us. But as we muddled along in the task forces, we began to find that we had unexpected sources of influence over what was happening.

The changing relationship with the bank illustrates this neatly. Although we had no formal power in that situation, we found that by framing a confusing predicament in a coherent way, we could, via our network, influence the outcomes of the bank's decisions. The same applied to suppliers: by briefing them ahead of time and presenting a reasonable scenario for the recovery of their advances, we could influence the decisions they would make.

Slowly we began to realize that, although we were powerless in a formal sense, our networks, together with our own internal coherence, gave us an ability to get things done invisibly. As we discussed the situation with all the parties involved, a strategy began to emerge. A complicated financial/tax structure would allow the bank to "manage" its loss and give it an incentive not to call on the shareholders' personal guarantees. The core steel distribution business could be refinanced in the process and sold to new owners. The wrangle between the shareholders could be resolved, and each could go his or her own way. All that had to be done was to bring all the parties together, including a buyer for the steel business, and have them agree that this was the best course to follow. Using our newfound skills, we managed to pull it off.

It was not without excitement: at the last minute, the shareholders raised further objections to the deal. Only the bank could make them sell, and they were reluctant to do so, fearful that they might attract a lawsuit. Discreet calls to the major suppliers, several of whose executives were on the board of the bank, did the trick. "This business needs to be sold and recapitalized," the suppliers were told. "If the deal does not go through, you should probably reduce your credit exposure." The deal went through. By the end of 1983, we had new owners, just in time to benefit from the general business recovery. The ordeal was over.

Chapter 5 Workshop: Ugli Orange Case*

1. Form groups of three members. One person will be Dr. Roland, one person will be Dr. Jones, and the third person will be an observer.
2. Roland and Jones will read only their own roles, but the observer will read both.
3. Role-play: Instructor announces, "I am Mr./Ms. Cardoza, the owner of the remaining Ugli oranges. My fruit export firm is based in South America. My country does not have diplomatic relations with your country, although we do have strong trade relations."

   The groups will spend about 10 minutes meeting with the other firm's representative and will decide on a course of action. Be prepared to answer the following questions:
   a. What do you plan to do?

   b. If you want to buy the oranges, what price will you offer?
   c. To whom and how will the oranges be delivered?
4. The observers will report the solutions reached. The groups will describe the decision-making process used.
5. The instructor will lead a discussion on the exercise addressing the following questions:
   a. Which groups had the most trust? How did that influence behavior?
   b. Which groups shared more information? Why?
   c. How are trust and disclosure important in negotiations?

*By Dr. Robert House, University of Toronto. Used with permission.

Role of "Dr. Jones"

You are Dr. John W. Jones, a biological research scientist employed by a pharmaceutical firm. You have recently developed a synthetic chemical useful for curing and preventing Rudosen. Rudosen is a disease contracted by pregnant women. If not caught in the first four weeks of pregnancy, the disease causes serious brain, eye, and ear damage to the unborn child. Recently there has been an outbreak of Rudosen in your state, and several thousand women have contracted the disease. You have found, with volunteer patients, that your recently developed synthetic serum cures Rudosen in its early stages. Unfortunately, the serum is made from the juice of the Ugli orange, which is a very rare fruit. Only a small quantity (approximately 4,000) of these oranges were produced last season. No additional Ugli oranges will be available until next season, which will be too late to cure the present Rudosen victims.

You've demonstrated that your synthetic serum is in no way harmful to pregnant women. Consequently, there are no side effects. The Food and Drug Administration has approved production and distribution of the serum as a cure for Rudosen. Unfortunately, the current outbreak was unexpected, and your firm had not planned on having the compound serum available for 6 months. Your firm holds the patent on the synthetic serum, and it is expected to be a highly profitable product when it is generally available to the public.

You have recently been informed on good evidence that Mr. R. H. Cardoza, a South American fruit exporter, is in possession of 3,000 Ugli oranges in good condition. If you could obtain the juice of all 3,000 you would be able to both cure present victims and provide sufficient inoculation for the remaining pregnant women in the state. No other state currently has a Rudosen threat.

You have recently been informed that Dr. P. W. Roland is also urgently seeking Ugli oranges and is also aware of Mr. Cardoza's possession of the 3,000 available. Dr. Roland is employed by a competing pharmaceutical firm. He has been working on biological warfare research for the past several years. There is a great deal of industrial espionage in the pharmaceutical industry. Over the past several years, Dr. Roland's firm and yours have sued each other for infringement of patent rights and espionage law violations several times.

You've been authorized by your firm to approach Mr. Cardoza to purchase the 3,000 Ugli oranges. You have been told he will sell them to the highest bidder. Your firm has authorized you to bid as high as $250,000 to obtain the juice of the 3,000 available oranges.

Role of "Dr. Roland"

You are Dr. P. W. Roland. You work as a research biologist for a pharmaceutical firm. The firm is under contract with the government to do research on methods to combat enemy uses of biological warfare.

Recently several World War II experimental nerve gas bombs were moved from the United States to a small island just off the U.S. coast in the Pacific. In the process of transporting them, two of the bombs developed a leak. The leak is currently controlled by government scientists, who believe that the gas will permeate the bomb chambers within 2 weeks. They know of no method of preventing the gas from getting into the atmosphere and spreading to other islands and very likely to the West Coast as well. If this occurs, it is likely that several thousand people will incur serious brain damage or die.

You've developed a synthetic vapor that will neutralize the nerve gas if it is injected into the bomb chamber before the gas leaks out. The vapor is made with a chemical taken from the rind of the Ugli orange, a very rare fruit. Unfortunately, only 4,000 of these oranges were produced this season.

You've been informed on good evidence that a Mr. R. H. Cardoza, a fruit exporter in South America, is in possession of 3,000 Ugli oranges. The chemicals from the rinds of all 3,000 oranges would be sufficient to neutralize the gas if the vapor is developed and injected efficiently. You have been informed that the rinds of these oranges are in good condition.

You have learned that Dr. J. W. Jones is also urgently seeking to purchase Ugli oranges and that he is aware of Mr. Cardoza's possession of the 3,000 available. Dr. Jones works for a firm with which your firm is highly competitive. There is a great deal of industrial espionage in the pharmaceutical industry. Over the years, your firm and Dr. Jones's have sued each other for violations of industrial espionage laws and infringement of patent rights several times. Litigation on two suits is still in process.

The federal government has asked your firm for assistance. You've been authorized by your firm to approach Mr. Cardoza to purchase 3,000 Ugli oranges. You have been told he will sell them to the highest bidder. Your firm has authorized you to bid as high as $250,000 to obtain the rinds of the oranges.

Before approaching Mr. Cardoza, you have decided to talk to Dr. Jones to influence him so that he will not prevent you from purchasing the oranges.

Notes

1. Tonya Vinas, "IT Starts with Parts," *Industry Week* (September 2003), 40–43; and "Navistar's Operating Company Signs Collaboration Pact with German Truck and Engine Manufacturer," *Business Wire* (December 6, 2004), 1.

2. Christine Oliver, "Determinants of Interorganizational Relationships: Integration and Future Directions," *Academy of Management Review* 15 (1990), 241–265.

3. James Moore, *The Death of Competition: Leadership and Strategy in the Age of Business Ecosystems* (New York: HarperCollins, 1996); Brent Schlender, "How Big Can Apple Get?" *Fortune* (February 21, 2005), 66–76.

4. Howard Muson, "Friend? Foe? Both? The Confusing World of Corporate Alliances," *Across the Board* (March–April 2002), 19–25; and Devi R. Gnyawali and Ravindranath Madhavan, "Cooperative Networks and Competitive Dynamics: A Structural Embeddedness Perspective," *Academy of Management Review* 26, no. 3 (2001), 431–445.

5. Thomas Petzinger, Jr., *The New Pioneers: The Men and Women Who Are Transforming the Workplace and Marketplace* (New York: Simon & Schuster, 1999), 53–54.

6. James Moore, "The Death of Competition," *Fortune* (April 15, 1996), 142–144.

7. Nick Wingfield, "New Chapter: A Web Giant Tries to Boost Profits by Taking On Tenants," *The Wall Street Journal* (September 24, 2003), A1, A10; and Nick Wingfield, "Amazon's eBay Challenge," *The Wall Street Journal* (June 3, 2004), B1, B2.

8. Brian Goodwin, *How the Leopard Changed Its Spots: The Evolution of Complexity* (New York: Touchstone, 1994), 181, quoted in Petzinger, *The New Pioneers*, 53.

9. Alice Dragoon, "A Travel Guide to Collaboration," *CIO* (November 15, 2004), 68–75.

10. Sumantra Ghoshal and Christopher A. Bartlett, "Changing the Role of Top Management: Beyond Structure and Process," *Harvard Business Review* (January–February 1995), 86–96.

11. Susan Greco and Kate O'Sullivan, "Independents' Day," *Inc.* (August 2002), 76–83.

12. J. Pfeffer and G. R. Salancik, *The External Control of Organizations: A Resource Dependence Perspective* (New York: Harper & Row, 1978).

13. Derek S. Pugh and David J. Hickson, *Writers on Organizations*, 5th ed. (Thousand Oaks, Calif.: Sage, 1996).

14. Peter Grittner, "Four Elements of Successful Sourcing Strategies," *Management Review* (October 1996), 41–45.

15. This discussion is based on Matthew Schifrin, "The Big Squeeze," *Forbes* (March 11, 1996), 45–46; Wendy Zellner with Marti Benedetti, "CLOUT!" *BusinessWeek* (December 21, 1992), 62–73; Kevin Kelly and Zachary Schiller with James B. Treece, "Cut Costs or Else," *BusinessWeek* (March 22, 1993), 28–29; and Lee Berton, "Push from Above," *The Wall Street Journal* (May 23, 1996), R24.

16. "Fitting In; In Bow to Retailers' New Clout, Levi Strauss Makes Alterations," *The Wall Street Journal* (June 17, 2004), A1.

17. Robert A. Guth and Don Clark, "Peace Program; Behind Secret Settlement Talks: New Power of Tech Customers," *The Wall Street Journal* (April 5, 2004), A1.

18. Mitchell P. Koza and Arie Y. Lewin, "The Co-Evolution of Network Alliances: A Longitudinal Analysis of an International Professional Service Network," Center for Research on New Organizational Forms, Working Paper 98–09–02; and Kathy Rebello with Richard Brandt, Peter Coy, and Mark Lewyn, "Your Digital Future," *BusinessWeek* (September 7, 1992), 56–64.

19. Christine Oliver, "Determinants of Inter-organizational Relationships: Integration and Future Directions," *Academy of Management Review*, 15 (1990), 241–265; Ken G. Smith, Stephen J. Carroll, and Susan Ashford, "Intra- and Interorganizational Cooperation: Toward a Research Agenda," *Academy of Management Journal*, 38 (1995), 7–23; and Ken G. Smith, Stephen J. Carroll, and Susan Ashford, "Intra- and Interorganizational Cooperation: Toward a Research Agenda," *Academy of Management Journal* 38 (1995), 7–23.

20. Timothy M. Stearns, Alan N. Hoffman, and Jan B. Heide, "Performance of Commercial Television Stations as an Outcome of Interorganizational Linkages and Environmental Conditions," *Academy of Management Journal* 30 (1987), 71–90; and David A. Whetten and Thomas K. Kueng, "The Instrumental Value of Interorganizational Relations: Antecedents and Consequences of Linkage Formation," *Academy of Management Journal* 22 (1979), 325–344.

21. Alex Taylor III, "Just Another Sexy Sports Car?" *Fortune* (March 17, 2003), 76–80.

22. Muson, "Friend? Foe? Both?"

23. Dragoon, "A Travel Guide to Collaboration."

24. Donna Fenn, "Sleeping with the Enemy," *Inc.* (November 1997), 78–88.

25. Keith G. Provan and H. Brinton Milward, "A Preliminary Theory of Interorganizational Network Effectiveness: A Comparative of Four Community Mental Health Systems," *Administrative Science Quarterly* 40 (1995), 1–33.

26. Myron Magnet, "The New Golden Rule of Business," *Fortune* (February 21, 1994), 60–64; Grittner, "Four Elements of Successful Sourcing Strategies"; and Jeffrey H. Dyer and Nile W. Hatch, "Using Supplier Networks to Learn Faster," *MIT Sloan Management Review* (Spring 2004), 57–63.

27. Peter Smith Ring and Andrew H. Van de Ven, "Developmental Processes of Corporate Interorganizational Relationships," *Academy of Management Review* 19 (1994), 90–118; Jeffrey H. Dyer, "How Chrysler Created an American *Keiretsu*," *Harvard Business Review* (July–August 1996), 42–56; Grittner, "Four Elements of Successful Sourcing Strategies"; Magnet, "The New Golden Rule of Business"; and Mick Marchington and Steven Vincent, "Analysing the Influence of Institutional, Organizational and Interpersonal Forces in Shaping Inter-Organizational Relationships," *Journal of Management Studies* 41, no. 6 (September 2004), 1029–1056.

28. Magnet, "The New Golden Rule of Business"; and Grittner, "Four Elements of Successful Sourcing Strategies."

29. Pete Engardio, "The Barons of Outsourcing," *BusinessWeek* (August 28, 2000), 177–178.

30. Andrew Raskin, "Who's Minding the Store?" *Business 2.0* (February 2003), 70–74.

31. Marchington and Vincent, "Analysing the Influence of Institutional, Organizational and Interpersonal Forces in Shaping Inter-Organizational Relationships."

32. Fred R. Blekley, "Some Companies Let Suppliers Work on Site and Even Place Orders," *The Wall Street Journal* (January 13, 1995), A1, A6.

33. Philip Siekman, "The Snap-Together Business Jet," *Fortune* (January 21, 2002), 104[A]–104[H].

34. This section draws from Joel A. C. Baum, "Organizational Ecology," in Stewart R. Clegg, Cynthia Hardy, and Walter R. Nord, eds., *Handbook of Organization Studies* (Thousand Oaks, Calif.: Sage, 1996); Jitendra V. Singh, *Organizational Evolution: New Directions* (Newbury Park, Calif.:

Sage, 1990); Howard Aldrich, Bill McKelvey, and Dave Ulrich, "Design Strategy from the Population Perspective," *Journal of Management* 10 (1984), 67–86; Howard E. Aldrich, *Organizations and Environments* (Englewood Cliffs, N.J.: Prentice Hall, 1979); Michael Hannan and John Freeman, "The Population Ecology of Organizations," *American Journal of Sociology* 82 (1977), 929–964; Dave Ulrich, "The Population Perspective: Review, Critique, and Relevance," *Human Relations* 40 (1987), 137–152; Jitendra V. Singh and Charles J. Lumsden, "Theory and Research in Organizational Ecology," *Annual Review of Sociology* 16 (1990), 161–195; Howard E. Aldrich, "Understanding, Not Integration: Vital Signs from Three Perspectives on Organizations," in Michael Reed and Michael D. Hughes, eds., *Rethinking Organizations: New Directions in Organizational Theory and Analysis* (London: Sage, 1992); Jitendra V. Singh, David J. Tucker, and Robert J. House, "Organizational Legitimacy and the Liability of Newness," *Administrative Science Quarterly* 31 (1986), 171–193; and Douglas R. Wholey and Jack W. Brittain, "Organizational Ecology: Findings and Implications," *Academy of Management Review* 11 (1986), 513–533.

35. Pugh and Hickson, *Writers on Organizations*; and Lex Donaldson, *American Anti-Management Theories of Organization* (New York: Cambridge University Press, 1995).

36. Michael T. Hannan and John Freeman, "The Population Ecology of Organizations."

37. Julie Creswell, "Cisco's Worst Nightmare (And Sun's and IBM's and Nortel's and. . . .)," *Fortune* (February 4, 2002), 114–116.

38. Thomas Moore, "The Corporate University: Transforming Management Education" (presentation in August 1996; Thomas Moore is the Dean of the Arthur D. Little University).

39. Peter Newcomb, "No One is Safe," *Forbes* (July 13, 1987), 121; "It's Tough Up There," *Forbes* (July 13, 1987), 145–160.

40. Stewart Feldman, "Here One Decade, Gone the Next," *Management Review* (November 1990), 5–6.

41. David Stires, "Fallen Arches," *Fortune* (April 29, 2002), 74–76.

42. David J. Tucker, Jitendra V. Singh, and Agnes G. Meinhard, "Organizational Form, Population Dynamics, and Institutional Change: The Founding Patterns of Voluntary Organizations," *Academy of Management Journal* 33 (1990), 151–178; Glenn R. Carroll and Michael T. Hannan, "Density Delay in the Evolution of Organizational Populations: A Model and Five Empirical Tests," *Administrative Science Quarterly* 34 (1989), 411–430; Jacques Delacroix and Glenn R. Carroll, "Organizational Foundings: An Ecological Study of the Newspaper Industries of Argentina and Ireland," *Administrative Science Quarterly* 28 (1983), 274–291; Johannes M. Pennings, "Organizational Birth Frequencies: An Empirical Investigation," *Administrative Science Quarterly* 27 (1982), 120–144; David Marple, "Technological Innovation and Organizational Survival: A Population Ecology Study of Nineteenth-Century American Railroads," *Sociological Quarterly* 23 (1982), 107–116; and Thomas G. Rundall and John O. McClain, "Environmental Selection and Physician Supply," *American Journal of Sociology* 87 (1982), 1090–1112.

43. Robert D. Hof and Linda Himelstein, "eBay vs. Amazon.com," *BusinessWeek* (May 31, 1999), 128–132; and Maria Mallory with Stephanie Anderson Forest, "Waking Up to a Major Market," *BusinessWeek* (March 23, 1992), 70–73.

44. Arthur G. Bedeian and Raymond F. Zammuto, *Organizations: Theory and Design* (Orlando, Fla.: Dryden Press, 1991); and Richard L. Hall, *Organizations: Structure, Process and Outcomes* (Englewood Cliffs, N.J.: Prentice-Hall, 1991).

45. David Stipp, "How Genentech Got It," *Fortune* (June 9, 2003), 81–88.

46. M. Tina Dacin, Jerry Goodstein, and W. Richard Scott, "Institutional Theory and Institutional Change: Introduction to the Special Research Forum," *Academy of Management Journal* 45, no. 1 (2002), 45–47. Thanks to Tina Dacin for her material and suggestions for this section of the chapter.

47. J. Meyer and B. Rowan, "Institutionalized Organizations: Formal Structure as Myth and Ceremony," *American Journal of Sociology* 83 (1990), 340–363.

48. Mark C. Suchman, "Managing Legitimacy: Strategic and Institutional Approaches," *Academy of Management Review* 20 (1995), 571–610.

49. Jerry Useem, "America's Most Admired Companies," *Fortune* (March 7, 2005), 66–70; and Survey Results from Harris Interactive and the Reputation Institute, reported in Ronald Alsop, "In Business Ranking, Some Icons Lose Luster," *The Wall Street Journal* (November 15, 2004), B1.

50. Grahame R. Dowling, "Corporate Reputations: Should You Compete on Yours?" *California Management Review* 46, no. 3 (Spring 2004), 19–36; Ronald Alsop, "In Business Ranking, Some Icons Lose Luster."

51. Jerry Useem, "Should We Admire Wal-Mart?" *Fortune* (March 8, 2004), 118–120; Charles Fishman, "The Wal-Mart You Don't Know: Why Low Prices Have a High Cost," *Fast Company* (December 2003), 68–80; Ronald Alsop, "In Business Ranking, Some Icons Lose Luster," *The Wall Street Journal* (November 15, 2004), B1; and Ronald Alsop, "Corporate Scandals Hit Home," *The Wall Street Journal* (February 19, 2004), B1.

52. Richard J. Martinez and Patricia M. Norman, "Whither Reputation? The Effects of Different Stakeholders," *Business Horizons* 47, no. 5 (September–October 2004), 25–32.

53. Pamela S. Tolbert and Lynne G. Zucker, "The Institutionalization of Institutional Theory," in Stewart R. Clegg, Cynthia Hardy, and Walter R. Nord, eds., *Handbook of Organization Studies* (Thousand Oaks, Calif.: Sage, 1996).

54. Pugh and Hickson, *Writers on Organizations*; and Paul J. DiMaggio and Walter W. Powell, "The Iron Cage Revisited: Institutional Isomorphism and Collective Rationality in Organizational Fields," *American Sociological Review* 48 (1983), 147–160.

55. This section is based largely on DiMaggio and Powell, "The Iron Cage Revisited"; Pugh and Hickson, *Writers on Organizations*; and W. Richard Scott, *Institutions and Organizations* (Thousand Oaks, Calif.: Sage, 1995).

56. Ellen R. Auster and Mark L. Sirower, "The Dynamics of Merger and Acquisition Waves," *The Journal of Applied Behavioral Science* 38, no. 2 (June 2002), 216–244.

57. William McKinley, Jun Zhao, and Kathleen Garrett Rust, "A Sociocognitive Interpretation of Organizational Downsizing," *Academy of Management Review* 25, no. 1 (2000), 227–243.

58. Barry M. Staw and Lisa D. Epstein, "What Bandwagons Bring: Effects of Popular Management Techniques on Corporate Performance, Reputation, and CEO Pay," *Administrative Science Quarterly* 45, no. 3 (September 2000), 523–560.

59. Jeremy Kahn, "Deloitte Restates Its Case," *Fortune* (April 29, 2002), 64–72.

6

Designing Organizations for the International Environment

Entering the Global Arena
Motivations for Global Expansion • Stages of International Development • Global Expansion through International Strategic Alliances

Designing Structure to Fit Global Strategy
Model for Global versus Local Opportunities • International Division • Global Product Division Structure • Global Geographical Division Structure • Global Matrix Structure

Building Global Capabilities
The Global Organizational Challenge • Global Coordination Mechanisms

Cultural Differences in Coordination and Control
National Value Systems • Three National Approaches to Coordination and Control

The Transnational Model of Organization

Summary and Interpretation

A Look Inside

Gruner + Jahr

The plan was to become a top-flight player in the U.S. magazine publishing industry. But after nearly 30 years of trying, Bertelsmann AG's Gruner + Jahr division has begun selling off its U.S. assets, including mainstays such as *Family Circle, Parents,* and *Fitness.* The company's business titles, *Inc.* and *Fast Company*, will soon be sold or disappear.

A clash of cultures is one reason Gruner + Jahr, the largest magazine publisher in Europe, had so much trouble breaking into the U.S. market. Although top executives in Germany wisely hired many American managers at Gruner + Jahr USA Publishing, they still called all the shots about how things should be done. The chief of international magazines, for example, a German former journalist, got involved in every detail of magazine production, even trying to dictate how the borders between articles should look. The CEO of the U.S. division bristled at such micromanaging and insisted that his editors be given more autonomy. At the same time, some say the U.S. chief tended to exploit cultural misunderstandings to win points against his boss with German higher-ups in the company.

There were other conflicts as well. Executives in Germany decided that all Gruner + Jahr units should use Brown Printing, a U.S. printing company that Gruner + Jahr also owned. Managers in New York rebelled, arguing that Brown wasn't as effective as some competitors in handling large-circulation magazines like *Family Circle.* The Germans relented, but they enraged U.S. managers again by directing that they share information with Brown regarding the bids solicited from Brown's competitors. The U.S. managers were concerned about the ethical implications of such a practice, while the German executives couldn't understand what all the fuss was about.

Cultural clashes between German and American managers, differences in business practices between the two countries, a decline in magazine advertising and readership, and the sheer scope and complexity of managing on an international scale took a heavy toll on Gruner + Jahr's business. As the division began dumping its U.S. assets, a business reporter referred to the sell-off as Gruner + Jahr's "exit from a billion-dollar experiment gone horribly wrong."[1]

When an organization decides to do business in another country, managers face a whole new set of challenges. Gruner + Jahr first entered the U.S. magazine market in 1978, but managers soon learned that it wasn't a simple matter to transfer their European success to the United States. Despite the challenges of doing business internationally, most companies today think the potential rewards outweigh the risks. Companies based in the United States have long been involved in international business, but interest in global trade is greater now than ever before. Thousands of U.S.-based companies have set up foreign operations to produce goods and services needed by consumers in other countries, as well as to obtain lower costs for producing products to sell at home. In return, companies from Japan, Germany, and the United Kingdom compete with American companies on their own turf as well as abroad. Domestic markets for many companies are becoming saturated, and the only potential for growth lies overseas. For e-commerce companies, expanding internationally is becoming a priority. The United States' share of total worldwide e-commerce is falling as foreign companies set up their own e-commerce ventures that better respond to local needs.[2] Succeeding on a global scale isn't easy. Organizations have to make decisions about strategic approach, how best to get involved in international markets, and how to design the organization to reap the benefits of international expansion.

■ Purpose of This Chapter

This chapter will explore how managers design the organization for the international environment. We begin by looking at some of the primary motivations for organizations to expand internationally, the typical stages of international development, and the use of strategic alliances as a means for international expansion. Then, the chapter examines global strategic approaches and the application of various structural designs for global advantage. Next, we discuss some of the specific challenges global organizations face, mechanisms for addressing them, and cultural differences that influence the organization's approach to designing and managing a global firm. Finally, the chapter takes a look at an emerging type of global organization, the *transnational model*, that achieves high levels of the varied capabilities needed to succeed in a complex and volatile international environment.

Entering the Global Arena

As recently as 25 years ago, many companies could afford to ignore the international environment. Today's companies must think globally or get left behind. The world is becoming a unified global field. Extraordinary advancements in communications, technology, and transportation have created a new, highly competitive landscape. Products can be made and sold anywhere in the world, communications are instant, and product-development and life cycles are growing shorter. No company is isolated from global influence. Some large so-called American companies such as Coca-Cola and Procter & Gamble rely on international sales for a substantial portion of their sales and profits. On the other hand, organizations in other countries search for customers in the United States. Siemens now gets 24 percent of its annual sales from the United States, compared to 22 percent from its native Germany.[3] And even the smallest companies can be actively involved in international business through exports and online business. Gayle Warwick Fine Linen, for example, has only two employees—Gayle and her assistant. Thanks to electronic connections, the two can effectively manage a company that makes high-end bed and table linens that are woven in Europe, embroidered in Vietnam, and exported to Britain and the United States.[4]

■ Motivations for Global Expansion

Economic, technological, and competitive forces have combined to push many companies from a domestic to a global focus. In some industries, being successful now means succeeding on a global scale. The importance of the global environment for today's organizations is reflected in the shifting global economy. As one indication, *Fortune* magazine's list of the Global 500, the world's 500 largest companies, indicates that economic clout is being diffused across a broad global scale. In Exhibit 6.1, each circle represents the total revenues of all Global 500 companies in each

Note: Each circle represents the total revenues of all Global 500 companies in that country in 2003.
The number in parentheses indicates the number of companies that country had on the Global 500 list in that year.

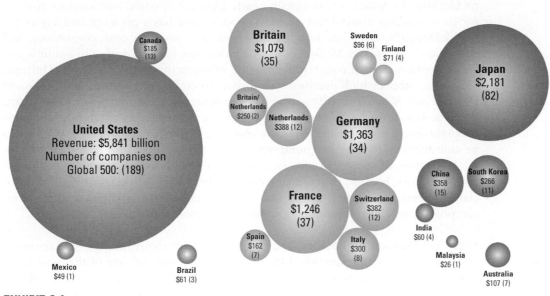

EXHIBIT 6.1
The Global Economy as Reflected in the Fortune *Global 500.*
Source: "The Fortune Global 500," *Fortune* (July 26, 2004) 159–180, figure on page 161.

country. Although the United States accounts for the majority of the Global 500 revenues, a number of smaller and less-developed countries are growing stronger. China, for example, had 15 companies on the Global 500 in 2003, compared to only 3 companies on the list 10 years earlier. Japan, on the other hand, has declined in importance, dropping from 149 companies to 82.[5] In general, three primary factors motivate companies to expand internationally: economies of scale, economies of scope, and low-cost production factors.[6]

Economies of Scale. Building a global presence expands an organization's scale of operations, enabling it to realize **economies of scale**. The trend toward large organizations was initially sparked by the Industrial Revolution, which created pressure in many industries for larger factories that could seize the benefits of economies of scale offered by new technologies and production methods. Through large-volume production, these industrial giants were able to achieve the lowest possible cost per unit of production. However, for many companies, domestic markets no longer provide the high level of sales needed to maintain enough volume to achieve scale economies. In an industry such as automobile manufacturing, for example, a company would need a tremendous share of the domestic market to achieve scale economies. Thus, an organization such as Ford Motor Company is forced to become international in order to survive. Economies of scale also enable companies to obtain volume discounts from suppliers, lowering the organization's cost of production.

Economies of Scope. A second factor is the enhanced potential for exploiting **economies of scope**. *Scope* refers to the number and variety of products and services a company offers, as well as the number and variety of regions, countries, and markets it serves. Having a presence in multiple countries provides marketing power and synergy compared to the same size firm that has presence in fewer countries. For example, an advertising agency with a presence in several global markets gains a competitive edge serving large companies that span the globe. Or consider the case of McDonald's, which has to obtain nearly identical mustard and ketchup packets for its restaurants around the world. A supplier that has a presence in every country McDonald's serves has an advantage because it provides cost, consistency, and convenience benefits to McDonald's, which does not have to deal with a number of local suppliers in each country. Transmatic Manufacturing Co., based in Holland, Michigan, supplies high-precision metal parts to companies such as Motorola and Delphi Corp. When Transmatic began losing contracts to suppliers in China, where the large U.S. firms had manufacturing facilities, owner P. J. Thompson decided to make the international leap. "My customers are multinational and they want me to be multinational too," says Thompson.[7]

Economies of scope can also increase a company's market power as compared to competitors, because the company develops broad knowledge of the cultural, social, economic, and other factors that affect its customers in varied locations and can provide specialized products and services to meet those needs.

Low-Cost Production Factors. The third major force motivating global expansion relates to **factors of production**. One of the earliest, and still one of the most powerful, motivations for U.S. companies to invest abroad is the opportunity to obtain raw materials and other resources at the lowest possible cost. Organizations have long turned overseas to secure raw materials that were scarce or unavailable in their home country. In the early twentieth century, tire companies went abroad to develop rubber plantations to supply tires for America's growing automobile industry. Today, U.S. paper manufacturers such as Weyerhaeuser and U.S. Paper Co., forced by environmental concerns to look overseas for new timberlands, are managing millions of acres of tree farms in New Zealand.[8]

Many companies also turn to other countries as a source of cheap labor. Textile manufacturing in the United States is now practically nonexistent as companies have shifted most production to Asia, Mexico, Latin America, and the Caribbean, where the costs of labor and supplies are much lower. Between 1997 and 2002, the percentage of clothing sold in the United States but manufactured elsewhere rose to around 75 percent, an increase of nearly 20 percent in 5 years. A check of the "Made in" tags at one Gap store found clothing made in twenty-four countries, in addition to the United States.[9] Manufacturing of non-upholstered furniture is rapidly following the same pattern. Companies are closing plants in the United States and importing high-quality wooden furniture from China, where as many as thirty workers can be hired for the cost of one cabinetmaker in the United States.[10] But the trend isn't limited to manufacturing. India's Wipro Ltd., for example, writes software, performs consulting work, integrates back-office solutions, and handles technical support for some of the biggest corporations in the United States—and does the work for 40 percent less than comparable U.S. firms.[11] Other organizations have gone international in search of lower costs of capital, sources of cheap energy, reduced government restrictions, or other factors that lower the company's total production costs. Companies can locate facilities wherever it makes the most economic sense in terms of needed employee education and skill levels, labor and raw materials costs, and other production factors. Automobile manufacturers such as Toyota, BMW, General Motors, and Ford have built plants in South Africa, Brazil, and Thailand, where they can pay workers less than one-tenth of what workers earn

EXHIBIT 6.2
Four Stages of International Evolution

	I. Domestic	II. International	III. Multinational	IV. Global
Strategic Orientation	Domestically oriented	Export-oriented multidomestic	Multinational	Global
Stage of Development	Initial foreign involvement	Competitive positioning	Explosion	Global
Structure	Domestic structure, plus export department	Domestic structure, plus international division	Worldwide geographical, product	Matrix, trans-national
Market Potential	Moderate, mostly domestic	Large, multi-domestic	Very large, multi-national	Whole world

Source: Based on Nancy J. Adler, *International Dimensions of Organizational Behavior,* 4th ed. (Cincinnati, Ohio: South-Western, 2002), 8–9; and Theodore T. Herbert, "Strategy and Multinational Organization Structure: An Interorganizational Relationships Perspective," *Academy of Management Review* 9 (1984), 259–271.

in higher-wage, developed countries. In addition, these countries typically offer dramatically lower costs for factors such as land, water, and electricity.[12] Foreign companies also come to the United States to obtain favorable circumstances. Japan's Honda and Toyota, South Korea's Samsung Electronics, and the Swiss drug company Novartis have all built plants or research centers in the United States to take advantage of tax breaks, find skilled workers, and be closer to major customers and suppliers.[13]

■ Stages of International Development

No company can become a global giant overnight. Managers have to consciously adopt a strategy for global development and growth. Organizations enter foreign markets in a variety of ways and follow diverse paths. However, the shift from domestic to global typically occurs through stages of development, as illustrated in Exhibit 6.2.[14] In stage one, the **domestic stage**, the company is domestically oriented, but managers are aware of the global environment and may want to consider initial foreign involvement to expand production volume and realize economies of scale. Market potential is limited and is primarily in the home country. The structure of the company is domestic, typically functional or divisional, and initial foreign sales are handled through an export department. The details of freight forwarding, customs problems, and foreign exchange are handled by outsiders.

In stage two, the **international stage,** the company takes exports seriously and begins to think multidomestically. **Multidomestic** means competitive issues in each country are independent of other countries; the company deals with each country individually. The concern is with international competitive positioning compared with other firms in the industry. At this point, an international division has replaced the export department, and specialists are hired to handle sales, service, and warehousing abroad. Multiple countries are identified as a potential market. Purafil, a small company with headquarters in Doraville, Georgia, for example, sells air filters that remove pollution and cleanse the air in fifty different countries. Although

Purafil is small, it maintains contracts with independent sales firms in the various countries who know the local markets and cultures.[15] The company first began exporting in the early 1990s and now gets 60 percent of its revenues from overseas.

In stage three, the **multinational stage**, the company has extensive experience in a number of international markets and has established marketing, manufacturing, or research and development (R&D) facilities in several foreign countries. The organization obtains a large percentage of revenues from sales outside the home country. Explosion occurs as international operations take off, and the company has business units scattered around the world along with suppliers, manufacturers, and distributors. Examples of companies in the multinational stage include Siemens of Germany, Sony of Japan, and Coca-Cola of the United States. Wal-Mart, although it is the world's biggest company, is just moving into the multinational stage, with only 18.5 percent of sales and 15.8 percent of profits from international business in 2003.

The fourth and ultimate stage is the **global stage**, which means the company transcends any single country. The business is not merely a collection of domestic industries; rather, subsidiaries are interlinked to the point where competitive position in one country significantly influences activities in other countries.[16] Truly **global companies** no longer think of themselves as having a single home country, and, indeed, have been called *stateless corporations*.[17] This represents a new and dramatic evolution from the multinational company of the 1960s and 1970s.

Global companies operate in truly global fashion, and the entire world is their marketplace. Organization structure at this stage can be extremely complex and often evolves into an international matrix or transnational model, which will be discussed later in this chapter.

Global companies such as Nestlé, Royal Dutch/Shell, Unilever, and Matsushita Electric may operate in more than a hundred countries. The structural problem of holding together this huge complex of subsidiaries scattered thousands of miles apart is immense.

■ Global Expansion through International Strategic Alliances

One of the most popular ways companies get involved in international operations is through international strategic alliances. The average large U.S. corporation, which had no alliances in the early 1990s, now has more than thirty, many of those with international firms. Companies in rapidly changing industries such as media and entertainment, pharmaceuticals, biotechnology, and software might have hundreds of these relationships.[18]

Typical alliances include licensing, joint ventures, and consortia.[19] For example, pharmaceutical companies such as Merck, Eli Lilly, Pfizer, and Warner-Lambert cross-license their newest drugs to one another to support industry-wide innovation and marketing and offset the high fixed costs of research and distribution.[20] A **joint venture** is a separate entity created with two or more active firms as sponsors. This is a popular approach to sharing development and production costs and penetrating new markets. Joint ventures may be with either customers or competitors.[21] Competing firms Sprint, Deutsche Telecom, and Telecom France cooperate with each other and with several smaller firms in a joint venture that serves the telecommunication needs of global corporations in sixty-five countries.[22] The Swiss food company Nestlé and the French cosmetics giant L'Oreal engaged in a joint venture

Briefcase

As an organization manager, keep this guideline in mind:

Develop international strategic alliances, such as licensing, joint ventures, partnerships, and consortia, as fast and inexpensive ways to become involved in international sales and operations.

to develop Inneov, a nutritional supplement intended to improve the health of skin.[23] MTV Networks has joint ventures with companies in Brazil, Australia, and other countries to expand its global media presence.[24]

Companies often seek joint ventures to take advantage of a partner's knowledge of local markets, to achieve production cost savings through economies of scale, to share complementary technological strengths, or to distribute new products and services through another country's distribution channels. An agreement between Robex Resources Inc., a Canadian gold exploration and development company, and Geo Services International, an international company operating in Mali, enables the two firms to combine their technological power and increase the success of gold exploration and drilling projects in certain areas. ICiCI Bank, the largest private sector bank in India, and Prudential plc of the United Kingdom established an Indian asset management joint venture that provides stronger service for ICiCI's corporate customers in India and enables Prudential to expand its presence in Asia.[25] Another growing approach is for companies to become involved in **consortia**, groups of independent companies—including suppliers, customers, and even competitors—that join together to share skills, resources, costs, and access to one another's markets. Airbus Industrie, for example, is a consortium made up of French, British, and German aerospace companies that is successfully battering the U.S. giant Boeing.[26] Consortia are often used in other parts of the world, such as the *keiretsu* family of corporations in Japan. In Korea, these interlocking company arrangements are called *chaebol*.

A type of consortium, the global *virtual organization*, is increasingly being used in the United States and offers a promising approach to meeting worldwide competition. The virtual organization refers to a continually evolving set of company relationships that exist temporarily to exploit unique opportunities or attain specific strategic advantages. A company may be involved in multiple alliances at any one time. Oracle, a software company, is involved in as many as 15,000 short-term organizational partnerships at any time.[27] Some executives believe shifting to a virtual approach is the best way for companies to be competitive in the global marketplace.[28]

Designing Structure to Fit Global Strategy

As we discussed in Chapter 3, an organization's structure must fit its situation by providing sufficient information processing for coordination and control while focusing employees on specific functions, products, or geographical regions. Organization design for international firms follows a similar logic, with special interest in global versus local strategic opportunities.

Model for Global versus Local Opportunities

When organizations venture into the international domain, managers strive to formulate a coherent global strategy that will provide synergy among worldwide operations for the purpose of achieving common organizational goals. One dilemma they face is choosing whether to emphasize global **standardization** versus national responsiveness. Managers must decide whether they want each global affiliate to act autonomously or whether activities should be standardized across countries. These decisions are reflected in the choice between a *globalization* versus a *multidomestic* global strategy.

The **globalization strategy** means that product design, manufacturing, and marketing strategy are standardized throughout the world.[29] For example, the Japanese took business away from Canadian and American companies by developing similar high-quality, low-cost products for all countries. The Canadian and American companies incurred higher costs by tailoring products to specific countries. Black & Decker became much more competitive internationally when it standardized its line of power hand tools. Other products, such as Coca-Cola, are naturals for globalization, because only advertising and marketing need to be tailored for different regions. In general, services are less suitable for globalization because different customs and habits often require a different approach to providing service. Wal-Mart has had trouble transplanting its successful U.S. formula without adjustment. In Indonesia, for example, Wal-Mart closed its stores after only a year. Customers didn't like the brightly lit, highly organized stores, and, because no haggling was permitted, they thought the goods were overpriced.[30]

Other companies in recent years have also begun shifting away from a strict globalization strategy. Economic and social changes, including a backlash against huge global corporations, have prompted consumers to be less interested in global brands and more in favor of products that have a local feel.[31] However, a globalization strategy can help a manufacturing organization reap economy-of-scale efficiencies by standardizing product design and manufacturing, using common suppliers, introducing products around the world faster, coordinating prices, and eliminating overlapping facilities. By sharing technology, design, suppliers, and manufacturing standards worldwide in a coordinated global automotive operation, Ford saved $5 billion during the first 3 years.[32] Similarly, Gillette Company, which makes grooming products such as the Mach3 shaving system for men and the Venus razor for women, has large production facilities that use common suppliers and processes to manufacture products whose technical specifications are standardized around the world.[33]

A **multidomestic strategy** means that competition in each country is handled independently of competition in other countries. Thus, a multidomestic strategy would encourage product design, assembly, and marketing tailored to the specific needs of each country. Some companies have found that their products do not thrive in a single global market. For example, people in different countries have very different expectations for personal-care products such as deodorant or toothpaste. The French do not drink orange juice for breakfast, and laundry detergent is used to wash dishes, not clothes, in parts of Mexico. Domino's Pizza knows that the basics of crust, sauce, and cheese work for a pizza everywhere, but beyond that, there are no hard and fast rules. The company has more than 2,500 international restaurants and offers 100 different pizza pies, including *paneer* pizza in India and *mayo-jaga* in Japan. Domino's franchisees in the various countries often propose variations to suit local tastes. As another example of a multidomestic strategy, Procter & Gamble tried to standardize diaper design, but discovered that cultural values in different parts of the world required style adjustments to make the product acceptable to many mothers. In Italy, for example, designing diapers to cover the baby's navel was critical to successful sales.[34]

Different global organization designs, as well, are better suited to the need for either global standardization or national responsiveness. Recent research on more than 100 international firms based in Spain has provided further support for the connection between international structure and strategic focus.[35] The model in Exhibit 6.3 illustrates how organization design and international strategy fit the needs of the environment.[36]

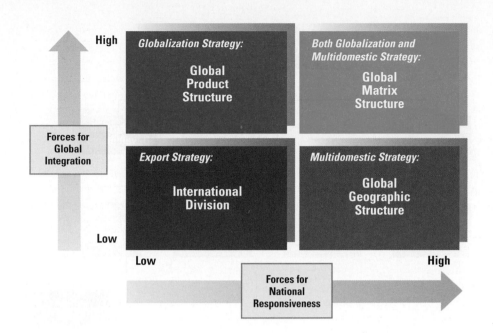

EXHIBIT 6.3
Model to Fit Organization Structure to International Advantages
Source: Roderick E. White and Thomas A. Poynter, "Organizing for Worldwide Advantage," *Business Quarterly* (Summer 1989), 84–89. Adapted by permission of *Business Quarterly*, published by the Western Business School, the University of Western Ontario, London, Ontario, Canada.

Companies can be characterized by whether their product and service lines have potential for globalization, which means advantages through worldwide standardization. Companies that sell diverse products or services across many countries have a globalization strategy. On the other hand, some companies have products and services appropriate for a multidomestic strategy, which means local-country advantages through differentiation and customization to meet local needs.

As indicated in Exhibit 6.3, when forces for both global standardization and national responsiveness in many countries are low, simply using an international division with the domestic structure is an appropriate way to handle international business. For some industries, however, technological, social, or economic forces may create a situation in which selling standardized products worldwide provides a basis for competitive advantage. In these cases, a global product structure is appropriate. This structure provides product managers with authority to handle their product lines on a global basis and enables the company to take advantage of a unified global marketplace. In other cases, companies can gain competitive advantages through national responsiveness—by responding to unique needs in the various countries in which they do business. For these companies, a worldwide geographical structure is appropriate. Each country or region will have subsidiaries modifying products and services to fit that locale. A good illustration is the advertising firm of Ogilvy & Mather, which divides its operations into four primary geographical regions because advertising approaches need to be modified to fit the tastes, preferences, cultural values, and government regulations in different parts of the world.[37] Children are frequently used to advertise products in the United States, but this approach in France is against the law. The competitive claims of rival products regularly seen on U.S. television would violate government regulations in Germany.[38]

In many instances, companies will need to respond to both global and local opportunities simultaneously, in which case the global matrix structure can be used. Part of the product line may need to be standardized globally, and other parts

EXHIBIT 6.4
*Domestic Hybrid Structure
with International Division*

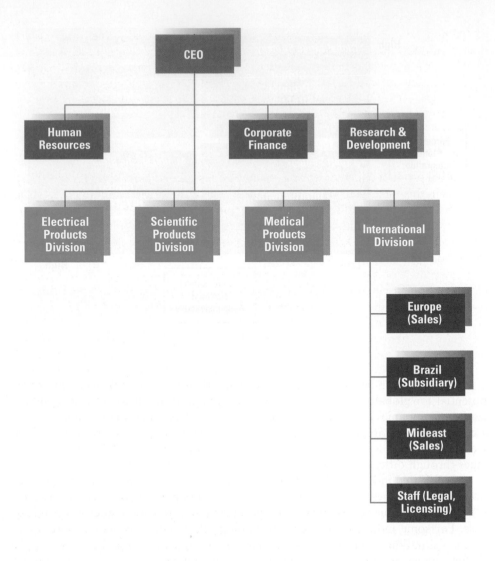

tailored to the needs of local countries. Let's discuss each of the structures in Exhibit 6.2 in more detail.

■ International Division

As companies begin to explore international opportunities, they typically start with an export department that grows into an **international division**. The international division has a status equal to the other major departments or divisions within the company and is illustrated in Exhibit 6.4. Whereas the domestic divisions are typically organized along functional or product lines, the international division is organized according to geographical interests, as illustrated in the exhibit. The international division has its own hierarchy to handle business (licensing, joint ventures) in various countries, selling the products and services created by the domestic divisions, opening subsidiary plants, and in general moving the organization into more sophisticated international operations.

Although functional structures are often used domestically, they are less frequently used to manage a worldwide business.[39] Lines of functional hierarchy running around the world would extend too long, so some form of product or geographical structure is used to subdivide the organization into smaller units. Firms typically start with an international department and, depending on their strategy, later use product or geographical division structures.

Global Product Division Structure

In a **global product structure**, the product divisions take responsibility for global operations in their specific product area. This is one of the most commonly used structures through which managers attempt to achieve global goals because it provides a fairly straightforward way to effectively manage a variety of businesses and products around the world. Managers in each product division can focus on organizing for international operations as they see fit and directing employees' energy toward their own division's unique set of global problems or opportunities.[40] In addition, the structure provides top managers at headquarters with a broad perspective on competition, enabling the entire corporation to respond more rapidly to a changing global environment.[41]

With a global product structure, each division's manager is responsible for planning, organizing, and controlling all functions for the production and distribution of its products for any market around the world. The product-based structure works best when a division handles products that are technologically similar and can be standardized for marketing worldwide. As we saw in Exhibit 6.3, the global product structure works best when the company has opportunities for worldwide production and sale of standard products for all markets, thus providing economies of scale and standardization of production, marketing, and advertising.

Eaton Corporation has used a form of worldwide product structure, as illustrated in Exhibit 6.5. In this structure, the automotive components group, industrial group, and so on are responsible for manufacture and sale of products worldwide. The vice president of international is responsible for coordinators in each region, including a coordinator for Japan, Australia, South America, and northern Europe. The coordinators find ways to share facilities and improve production and delivery across all product lines sold in their regions. These coordinators provide the same function as integrators described in Chapter 3.

The product structure is great for standardizing production and sales around the globe, but it also has problems. Often the product divisions do not work well together, competing instead of cooperating in some countries; and some countries may be ignored by product managers. The solution adopted by Eaton Corporation of using country coordinators who have a clearly defined role is a superb way to overcome these problems.

Global Geographical Division Structure

A regionally based organization is well suited to companies that want to emphasize adaptation to regional or local market needs through a multidomestic strategy, as illustrated in Exhibit 6.3. The **global geographical structure** divides the world into geographical regions, with each geographical division reporting to the CEO. Each

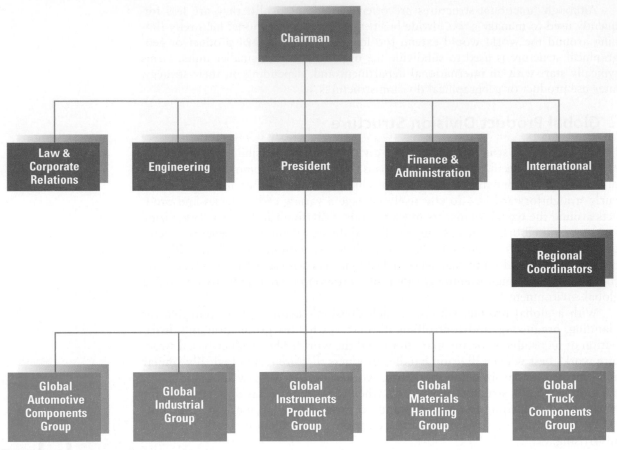

EXHIBIT 6.5
Partial Global Product Structure Used by Eaton Corporation
Source: Based on *New Directions in Multinational Corporate Organization* (New York: Business International Corp., 1981).

division has full control of functional activities within its geographical area. For example, Nestlé, with headquarters in Switzerland, puts great emphasis on the autonomy of regional managers who know the local culture. The largest branded food company in the world, Nestlé rejects the idea of a single global market and uses a geographical structure to focus on the local needs and competition in each country. Local managers have the authority to tinker with a product's flavoring, packaging, portion size, or other elements as they see fit. Many of the company's 8,000 brands are registered in only one country.[42]

Companies that use this type of structure have typically been those with mature product lines and stable technologies. They can find low-cost manufacturing within countries, as well as meeting different needs across countries for marketing and sales. However, several business and organizational trends have led to a broadening of the kinds of companies that use the global geographical structure.[43] The growth of service organizations has outpaced manufacturing for several years, and services by their nature must occur on a local level. In addition, to meet new competitive threats, many manufacturing firms are emphasizing the ability to customize their products to meet specific needs, which requires a greater emphasis on local and regional responsiveness. All organizations are compelled by current environmental and competitive challenges to develop closer relationships with customers, which may lead companies to shift from product-based to geographical-based structures.

The problems encountered by senior management using a global geographical structure result from the autonomy of each regional division. For example, it is difficult to do planning on a global scale—such as new-product R&D—because each division acts to meet only the needs of its region. New domestic technologies and products can be difficult to transfer to international markets because each division thinks it will develop what it needs. Likewise, it is difficult to rapidly introduce products developed offshore into domestic markets, and there is often duplication of line and staff managers across regions.

Nestlé is currently struggling to adapt its global geographical structure in an effort to cut costs and boost efficiency. Because regional divisions act to meet specific needs in their own areas, tracking and maintaining control of costs has been a real problem. One analyst referred to Nestlé as "a holding company, with hundreds of companies reporting in." CEO Peter Brabeck-Letmathe is searching for ways to increase efficiency and coordination without losing the benefits of the global geographical structure. The following example illustrates how executives at Colgate-Palmolive overcame some of the problems associated with this type of structure.

In Practice

Colgate-Palmolive Company

For several years, Colgate-Palmolive Company, which manufactures and markets personal-care, household, and specialty products, used a global geographical structure of the form illustrated in Exhibit 6.6. Colgate has a long, rich history of international involvement and has relied on regional divisions in North America, Europe, Latin America, the Far East, and the South Pacific to stay on the competitive edge. Well over half of the company's total sales are generated outside of the United States.

The regional approach supports Colgate's cultural values, which emphasize individual autonomy, an entrepreneurial spirit, and the ability to act locally. Each regional president reports directly to the chief operating officer, and each division has its own staff functions such as human resources (HR), finance, manufacturing, and marketing. Colgate handled the problem of coordination across geographical divisions by creating an *international business development group* that has responsibility for long-term company planning and worldwide product coordination and communication. It used several product team leaders, many of whom had been former country managers with extensive experience and knowledge. The product leaders are essentially coordinators and advisors to the geographical divisions; they have no power to direct, but they have the ability and the organizational support needed to exert substantial influence. The addition of this business development group quickly reaped positive results in terms of more rapid introduction of new products across all countries and better, lower-cost marketing.

The success of the international business development group prompted Colgate's top management to add two additional coordinating positions—a *vice president of corporate development* to focus on acquisitions, and a *worldwide sales and marketing group* that coordinates sales and marketing initiatives across all geographical locations. With these worldwide positions added to the structure, Colgate maintains its focus on each region and achieves global coordination for overall planning, faster product introductions, and enhanced sales and marketing efficiency.[44]

EXHIBIT 6.6
*Global Geographic
Structure of Colgate-
Palmolive Company*
Source: Based on Robert J.
Kramer, *Organizing for
Global Competitiveness:
The Geographic Design*
(New York: The Conference
Board, 1993), 30.

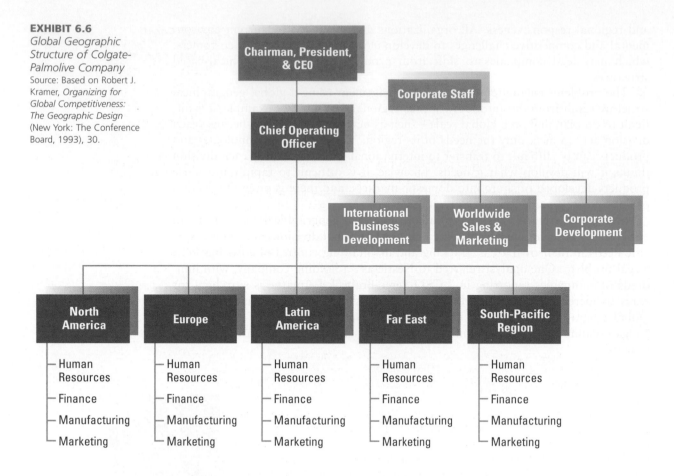

Global Matrix Structure

We've discussed how Eaton used a global product division structure and found ways to coordinate across worldwide divisions. Colgate-Palmolive used a global geographical division structure and found ways to coordinate across geographical regions. Each of these companies emphasized a single dimension. Recall from Chapter 3 that a matrix structure provides a way to achieve vertical and horizontal coordination simultaneously along two dimensions. A **global matrix structure** is similar to the matrix described in Chapter 3, except that for multinational corporations the geographical distances for communication are greater and coordination is more complex.

The matrix works best when pressure for decision making balances the interests of both product standardization and geographical localization and when coordination to share resources is important. For many years, Asea Brown Boveri (ABB), an electrical equipment corporation headquartered in Zurich, used a global matrix structure that worked extremely well to coordinate a 200,000-employee company operating in more than 140 countries.

ABB has given new meaning to the notion of "being local worldwide." ABB owns 1,300 subsidiary companies, divided into 5,000 profit centers located in 140 countries. ABB's average plant has fewer than 200 workers and most of the company's 5,000 profit centers contain only 40 to 50 people, meaning almost everyone stays close to the customer. For many years, ABB used a complex global matrix structure similar to Exhibit 6.7 to achieve worldwide economies of scale combined with local flexibility and responsiveness.

In Practice

Asea Brown Boveri Ltd. (ABB)

At the top are the chief executive officer and an international committee of eight top managers, who hold frequent meetings around the world. Along one side of the matrix are sixty-five or so business areas located worldwide, into which ABB's products and services are grouped. Each business area leader is responsible for handling business on a global scale, allocating export markets, establishing cost and quality standards, and creating mixed-nationality teams to solve problems. For example, the leader for power transformers is responsible for twenty-five factories in sixteen countries.

Along the other side of the matrix is a country structure; ABB has more than 100 country managers, most of them citizens of the country in which they work. They run national companies and are responsible for local balance sheets, income statements, and career ladders. The German president, for example, is responsible for 36,000 people across several business areas that generate annual revenues in Germany of more than $4 billion.

The matrix structure converges at the level of the 1,300 local companies. The presidents of local companies report to two bosses—the business area leader, who is usually located outside the country, and the country president, who runs the company of which the local organization is a subsidiary.

ABB's philosophy is to decentralize things to the lowest levels. Global managers are generous, patient, and multilingual. They must work with teams made up of different nationalities and be culturally sensitive. They craft strategy and evaluate performance for people and subsidiaries around the world. Country managers, by contrast, are regional line managers responsible for several country subsidiaries. They must cooperate with business area managers to achieve worldwide efficiencies and the introduction of new products. Finally, the presidents of local companies have both a global boss—the business area manager—and a country boss, and they learn to coordinate the needs of both.[45]

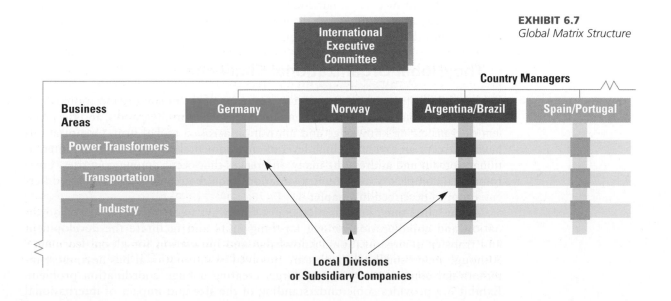

EXHIBIT 6.7
Global Matrix Structure

ABB is a large, successful company that achieved the benefits of both product and geographical organizations through this matrix structure. However, over the past several years, as ABB has faced increasingly complex competitive issues, leaders have transformed the company toward a complex structure called the *transnational model*, which will be discussed later in this chapter.

In the real world, as with the domestic hybrid structure described in Chapter 3, many international firms apply a *global hybrid* or *mixed structure*, in which two or more different structures or elements of different structures are used. Hybrid structures are typical in highly volatile environments. Siemens AG of Germany, for example, combines elements of functional, geographical, and product divisions to respond to dynamic market conditions in the multiple countries where it operates.[46]

Organizations like Siemens, Colgate-Palmolive, and Nestlé that operate on a global scale frequently have to make adjustments to their structures to overcome the challenges of doing business in a global environment. In the following sections, we will look at some of the specific challenges organizations face in the global arena and mechanisms for successfully confronting them.

Building Global Capabilities

There are many instances of well-known companies that have trouble transferring successful ideas, products, and services from their home country to the international domain. We talked earlier about the struggles Wal-Mart is facing internationally, but Wal-Mart isn't alone. In the early 1990s, PepsiCo., Inc., set a 5-year goal to triple its international soft-drink revenues and boldly expanded its presence in international markets. Yet by 1997, the company had withdrawn from some of those markets and had to take a nearly $1 billion loss from international beverage operations.[47] Hundreds of American companies that saw Vietnam as a tremendous international opportunity in the mid-1990s are now calling it quits amid heavy losses. Political and cultural differences sidetracked most of the ventures. Only a few companies, such as Citigroup's Citibank unit and Caterpillar's heavy-equipment business, have found success in that country.[48] Managers taking their companies international face a tremendous challenge in how to capitalize on the incredible opportunities that global expansion presents.

The Global Organizational Challenge

Exhibit 6.8 illustrates the three primary segments of the global organizational challenge: greater complexity and differentiation, the need for integration, and the problem of transferring knowledge and innovation across a global firm. Organizations have to accept an extremely high level of environmental complexity in the international domain and address the many differences that occur among countries. Environmental complexity and country variations require greater organizational differentiation, as described in Chapter 4.

At the same time, organizations must find ways to effectively achieve coordination and collaboration among far-flung units and facilitate the development and transfer of organizational knowledge and innovation for global learning.[49] Although many small companies are involved in international business, most international companies grow very large, creating a huge coordination problem. Exhibit 6.9 provides some understanding of the size and impact of international

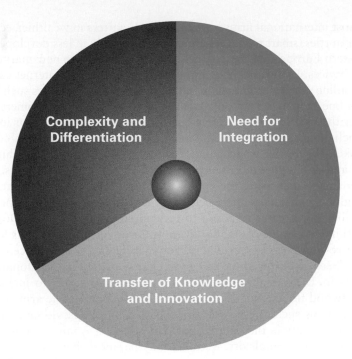

EXHIBIT 6.8
The Global Organizational Challenge

firms by comparing the value added of several large multinational companies with the gross domestic product (GDP) of selected countries.

Increased Complexity and Differentiation. When organizations enter the international arena, they encounter a greater level of internal and external complexity than anything experienced on the domestic front. Companies have to create a structure to operate in numerous countries that differ in economic development, language, political systems and government regulations, cultural norms and values, and infrastructure such as transportation and communication facilities. For example,

Company	Value Added*	Country	Annual GDP†
Wal-Mart	$67.7 billion	Peru	$53.5 billion
Exxon Mobil	$52.6 billion	Czech Republic	$50.8 billion
General Motors	$46.2 billion	Hungary	$45.6 billion
Mitsubishi	$44.3 billion	Nigeria	$41.1 billion
DaimlerChrysler	$37.5 billion	Romania	$36.7 billion
Royal Dutch/Shell	$37.3 billion	Morocco	$33.5 billion
General Electric	$32.5 billion	Vietnam	$31.3 billion
Toyota Motor Co.	$30.4 billion	Kuwait	$29.7 billion

EXHIBIT 6.9
Comparison of Leading Multinational Companies and Selected Countries, 2000 (in U.S. dollars)

*Value added refers to the sum of total wages, pretax profits, and depreciation and amortization for companies.
†Gross domestic product.
Sources: World Bank and *Fortune* magazine, as reported in Paul De Grauwe, University of Leuven and Belgian Senate, and Filip Camerman, Belgian Senate, "How Big are the Big Multinational Companies?" Working paper, 2002.

although most international firms have their headquarters in wealthier, economically advanced countries, smart managers are investing heavily in less developed countries in Asia, Eastern Europe, and Latin America, which offer huge new markets for their goods and services. In the area of e-commerce, the number of Internet users and the amount of online sales are zooming in Latin America, so companies such as Dell and America Online quickly set up online stores and services for customers in that region.[50] Over the past few years, China has become a major center for international business, including burgeoning local companies as well as big foreign corporations such as Nokia, IBM, Volkswagen, and BMW. Yet doing business in China, with its poor roads and developing infrastructure, is not easy, even for big firms.[51]

Another factor increasing the complexity for organizations is that a growing number of global consumers are rejecting the notion of homogenized products and services, calling for greater response to local preferences. Even McDonald's, perhaps the ultimate example of standardization for a world market, has felt the need to be more responsive to local and national differences. In France, where consumers have been resentful of the fast-food chain's incursion, McDonald's boosted sales even as its U.S. restaurants stalled by remodeling stores to include features such as hardwood floors, wood-beam ceilings, and comfortable armchairs, and by adding menu items such as espresso, brioche, and more upscale sandwiches.[52]

All this complexity in the international environment is mirrored in a greater internal organizational complexity. Recall from Chapter 4 that, as environments become more complex and uncertain, organizations grow more highly differentiated, with many specialized positions and departments to cope with specific sectors in the environment. Top management might need to set up specialized departments to deal with the diverse government, legal, and accounting regulations in various countries, for example. More boundary-spanning departments are needed to sense and respond to the external environment. In addition, organizations might implement a variety of strategies, a broader array of activities, and a much larger number of products and services on an international level in order to meet the needs of a diverse market.

Need for Integration. As organizations become more differentiated, with multiple products, divisions, departments, and positions scattered across numerous countries, managers face a tremendous integration challenge. As described in Chapter 4, *integration* refers to the quality of collaboration across organizational units. The question is how to achieve the coordination and collaboration that is necessary for a global organization to reap the benefits of economies of scale, economies of scope, and labor and production cost efficiencies that international expansion offers. Even in a domestic firm, high differentiation among departments requires that more time and resources be devoted to achieving coordination because employees' attitudes, goals, and work orientations differ widely. Imagine what it must be like for an international organization, whose operating units are divided not only by goals and work attitudes but by geographical distance, time differences, cultural values, and perhaps even language as well. Recall how Colgate-Palmolive created several specific units to achieve coordination and integration among regional divisions. Other companies, too, must find ways to share information, ideas, new products, and technologies across the organization. Consider how Sony got blasted by Apple's iPod largely because of integration problems.

In Practice

Sony

Sony once owned the market for mobile music players. With 50 years in the business of providing music on the go—beginning with the transistor radio in the 1950s and continuing with the Walkman, which has sold more than 340 million machines—the consumer electronics giant seemed well-positioned to be the front-runner in the world of digital music. But Sony got blindsided by, of all things, a computer company. With the introduction of Apple's iPod, which Steve Jobs referred to as "the twenty-first-century Walkman," and the iTunes music store, Sony no longer even seemed in the game.

A huge problem for Sony was that its digital music businesses were scattered in many different parts of the vast Sony empire, and cooperation among the parts was woefully inadequate. In addition, Sony's insistence on using only its own technology meant that, until recently, customers couldn't use the Walkman to play MP3s. Sony's Connect music store used its own clunky compression technology that turned users off. In early 2005, Connect ranked number 23 in music sites visited by Internet users, with Yahoo's Launch, AOL Music, and Apple's iTunes the top three sites. Estimates are that Connect lags some 300 million song sales behind iTunes.

In the world of digital music, everything depends on seamless integration, and Apple has gotten it just right. Flawless coordination among hardware, software, and content make buying and playing music ridiculously easy compared to Sony's system. Recently, Sony top executives set up a new division, also called Sony Connect, that is aimed specifically at getting the Tokyo-centered electronics businesses and the U.S. media businesses to work together. In addition, a new CEO, Sir Howard Stringer, the first non-Japanese native to head Sony, is emphasizing cross-company collaboration over technological prowess to get things back on track.

Linking all the scattered pieces together is not an easy job with a company the size of Sony. "The service side and the electronics side have different opinions and priorities," says Koichiro Tsujino, who serves as co-president (with American Phil Wiser) of Sony Connect. "And when you think of Japan and America, the languages are different, the work styles and time zones are different, and they're physically far away from each other." The new CEO's toughest, yet most important, job might be developing effective mechanisms for getting managers around the world from games, music, movies, and hardware to collaborate, share ideas, and set joint priorities.[53]

This example illustrates the tremendous complexity of large global organizations and the difficulties of getting all the pieces working together. Apple had an advantage in creating the iPod and iTunes because the company is smaller and less scattered, meaning coordination is easier. Sony might never be able to catch up with Apple's iPod, which owns 65 percent of the U.S. digital music player market. But new structural mechanisms and a new emphasis on integration should enable the disparate parts of the organization to better coordinate their efforts and help Sony regain some of its lost stature.

Transfer of Knowledge and Innovation. The third piece of the international challenge is for organizations to learn from their international experiences by sharing knowledge and innovations across the enterprise. The diversity of the international environment offers extraordinary opportunities for learning and the development of diverse capabilities.

Organizational units in each location acquire the skills and knowledge to meet environmental challenges that arise in that particular locale. Much of that knowledge, which may be related to product improvements, operational efficiencies, technological advancements, or myriad other competencies, is relevant across multiple countries, so organizations need systems that promote the transfer of knowledge and innovation across the global enterprise. One good example comes from Procter & Gamble. Liquid Tide was one of P&G's most successful U.S. product launches in the 1980s, but the product came about from the sharing of innovations developed in diverse parts of the firm. Liquid Tide incorporated a technology for helping to suspend dirt in wash water from P&G headquarters in the United States, the formula for its cleaning agents from P&G technicians in Japan, and special ingredients for fighting mineral salts present in hard water from company scientists in Brussels.[54]

Most organizations tap only a fraction of the potential that is available from the cross-border transfer of knowledge and innovation.[55] There are several reasons for this:

- Knowledge often remains hidden in various units because language, cultural, and geographical distances prevent top managers from recognizing it exists.
- Divisions sometimes view knowledge and innovation as power and want to hold onto it as a way to gain an influential position within the global firm.
- The "not-invented-here" syndrome makes some managers reluctant to tap into the know-how and expertise of other units.
- Much of an organization's knowledge is in the minds of employees and cannot easily be written down and shared with other units.

Organizations have to find ways to encourage both the development and sharing of knowledge, implement systems for tapping into knowledge wherever it exists, and find ways to share innovations to meet global challenges.

■ Global Coordination Mechanisms

Managers meet the global challenge of coordination and transferring knowledge and innovation across highly differentiated units in a variety of ways. Some of the most common are the use of global teams, stronger headquarters planning and control, and specific coordination roles.

Global Teams. The popularity and success of teams on the domestic front allowed managers to see firsthand how this mechanism can achieve strong horizontal coordination, as described in Chapter 3, and thus recognize the promise teams held for coordination across a global firm as well. **Global teams**, also called *transnational teams*, are cross-border work groups made up of multiskilled, multinational members whose activities span multiple countries.[56] Typically, teams are of two types: intercultural teams, whose members come from different countries and meet face to face, and virtual global teams, whose members remain in separate locations around the world and conduct their work electronically.[57] Heineken formed the European Production Task Force, a thirteen-member team made up of multinational members, to meet regularly and come up with ideas for optimizing the company's production facilities across Europe.[58] The research unit of BT Labs has 660 researchers spread across the United Kingdom and several other countries who work in global virtual teams to investigate virtual reality, artificial intelligence, and other advanced information technologies.[59] The team approach enables technologies, ideas, and learning in one country to rapidly spread across the firm via the constant sharing of information among team members.

The most advanced and competitive use of global teams involves simultaneous contributions in three strategic areas.[60] First, global teams help companies address the differentiation challenge, enabling them to be more locally responsive by providing knowledge to meet the needs of different regional markets, consumer preferences, and political and legal systems. At the same time, teams provide integration benefits, helping organizations achieve global efficiencies by developing regional or worldwide cost advantages and standardizing designs and operations across countries. Finally, these teams contribute to continuous organizational learning, knowledge transfer, and adaptation on a global level.

Headquarters Planning. A second approach to achieving stronger global coordination is for headquarters to take an active role in planning, scheduling, and control to keep the widely distributed pieces of the global organization working together and moving in the same direction. In one survey, 70 percent of global companies reported that the most important function of corporate headquarters was to "provide enterprise leadership."[61] Without strong leadership, highly autonomous divisions can begin to act like independent companies rather than coordinated parts of a global whole. To counteract this, top management may delegate responsibility and decision-making authority in some areas, such as adapting products or services to meet local needs, while maintaining strong control through centralized management and information systems that enable headquarters to keep track of what's going on and that serve to coordinate activities across divisions and countries. Plans, schedules, and formal rules and procedures can help ensure greater communication among divisions and with headquarters and foster cooperation and synergy among far-flung units to achieve the organization's goals in a cost-efficient way. Top managers can provide clear strategic direction, guide far-flung operations, and resolve competing demands from various units. This is one of the primary goals of Sir Howard Stringer at Sony, discussed in the previous section. In his first news conference, Sir Howard emphasized his resolve to promote collaboration and creativity to produce "new products, new ideas, new strategies, new alliances, and a shared vision."[62]

Expanded Coordination Roles. Organizations may also implement structural solutions to achieve stronger coordination and collaboration.[63] Creating specific organizational roles or positions for coordination is a way to integrate all the pieces of the enterprise to achieve a strong competitive position. In successful international firms, the role of top *functional managers*, for example, is expanded to include responsibility for coordinating across countries, identifying and linking the organization's expertise and resources worldwide. In an international organization, the manufacturing manager has to be aware of and coordinate with manufacturing operations of the company in various other parts of the world so that the company achieves manufacturing efficiency and shares technology and ideas across units. A new manufacturing technology developed to improve efficiency in Ford's Brazilian operations may be valuable for European and North American plants as well. Manufacturing managers are responsible for being aware of new developments wherever they occur and for using their knowledge to improve the organization. Similarly, marketing managers, HR managers, and other functional managers at an interna-

Briefcase

As an organization manager, keep these guidelines in mind:

Use mechanisms such as global teams, headquarters planning, and specific coordination roles to provide needed coordination and integration among far-flung international units. Emphasize information and knowledge sharing to help the organization learn and improve on a global scale.

tional company are involved not only in activities for their particular location but in coordinating with their sister units in other countries as well.

Whereas functional managers coordinate across countries, *country managers* coordinate across functions. A country manager for an international firm has to coordinate all the various functional activities to meet the problems, opportunities, needs, and trends in the local market, enabling the organization to achieve multinational flexibility and rapid response. The country manager in Venezuela for a global consumer products firm such as Colgate-Palmolive would coordinate everything that goes on in that country, from manufacturing to HR to marketing, to ensure that activities meet the language, cultural, government, and legal requirements of Venezuela. The country manager in Ireland or Canada would do the same for those countries. Country managers also help with the transfer of ideas, trends, products, and technologies that arise in one country and might have significance on a broader scale.

Some organizations create formal *network coordinator* positions to coordinate information and activities related to key customer accounts. These coordinators would enable a manufacturing organization, for example, to provide knowledge and integrated solutions across multiple businesses, divisions, and countries for a large customer such as Wal-Mart.[64] Top managers in successful global firms also encourage and support informal networks and relationships to keep information flowing in all directions. Much of an organization's information exchange occurs not through formal systems or structures but through informal channels and relationships. By supporting these informal networks, giving people across boundaries opportunities to get together and develop relationships and then ways to keep in close touch, executives enhance organizational coordination.

International companies today have a hard time staying competitive without strong interunit coordination and collaboration. Those firms that stimulate and support collaboration are typically better able to leverage dispersed resources and capabilities to reap operational and economic benefits.[65] Benefits that result from interunit collaboration include the following:

- *Cost savings*. Collaboration can produce real, measurable results in the way of cost savings from the sharing of best practices across global divisions. For example, at BP, a business unit head in the United States improved inventory turns and cut the working capital needed to run U.S. service stations by learning the best practices from BP operations in the United Kingdom and the Netherlands.
- *Better decision making*. By sharing information and advice across divisions, managers can make better business decisions that support their own unit as well as the organization as a whole.
- *Greater revenues*. By sharing expertise and products among various divisions, organizations can reap increased revenues. BP again provides an example. More than seventy-five people from various units around the world flew to China to assist the team developing an acetic acid plant there. As a result, BP finished the project and began realizing revenues sooner than project planners had expected.
- *Increased innovation*. The sharing of ideas and technological innovations across units stimulates creativity and the development of new products and services. Recall the example of Procter & Gamble mentioned earlier, in which P&G developed Liquid Tide based on ideas and innovations that arose in a number of different divisions around the world.

Cultural Differences in Coordination and Control

Just as social and cultural values differ from country to country, the management values and organizational norms of international companies tend to vary depending on the organization's home country. Organizational norms and values are influenced by the values in the larger national culture, and these in turn influence the organization's structural approach and the ways managers coordinate and control an international firm.

National Value Systems

Studies have attempted to determine how national value systems influence management and organizations. One of the most influential was conducted by Geert Hofstede, who identified several dimensions of national value systems that vary widely across countries.[66] For example, two dimensions that seem to have a strong impact within organizations are *power distance* and *uncertainty avoidance*. High **power distance** means that people accept inequality in power among institutions, organizations, and people. Low power distance means that people expect equality in power. High **uncertainty avoidance** means that members of a society feel uncomfortable with uncertainty and ambiguity and thus support beliefs that promise certainty and conformity. Low uncertainty avoidance means that people have a high tolerance for the unstructured, the unclear, and the unpredictable. More recent research by Project GLOBE (Global Leadership and Organizational Behavior Effectiveness) has supported and extended Hofstede's assessment. Project GLOBE used data collected from 18,000 managers in 62 countries to identify 9 dimensions that explain cultural differences, including those identified by Hofstede.[67]

As an organization manager, keep these guidelines in mind:

Appreciate cultural value differences and strive to use coordination mechanisms that are in tune with local values. When broader coordination mechanisms are needed, focus on education and corporate culture as ways to gain understanding and acceptance.

The value dimensions of *power distance* and *uncertainty avoidance* are reflected within organizations in beliefs regarding the need for hierarchy, centralized decision making and control, formal rules and procedures, and specialized jobs.[68] In countries that value high power distance, for example, organizations tend to be more hierarchical and centralized, with greater control and coordination from the top levels of the organization. On the other hand, organizations in countries that value low power distance are more likely to be decentralized. A low tolerance for uncertainty tends to be reflected in a preference for coordination through rules and procedures. Organizations in countries where people have a high tolerance for uncertainty typically have fewer rules and formal systems, relying more on informal networks and personal communication for coordination. This chapter's Book Mark further examines how cultural value patterns influence international organizations.

Although organizations do not always reflect the dominant cultural values, studies have found rather clear patterns of different management structures when comparing countries in Europe, the United States, and Asia.

Three National Approaches to Coordination and Control

Let's look at three primary approaches to coordination and control as represented by Japanese, American, and European companies.[69] It should be noted that companies in each country use tools and techniques from each of the three coordination methods. However, there are broad, general patterns that illustrate cultural differences.

Centralized Coordination in Japanese Companies. When expanding internationally, Japanese companies have typically developed coordination mechanisms that rely on centralization. Top managers at headquarters actively direct and control overseas operations, whose primary focus is to implement strategies handed down from headquarters. A recent study of R&D activities in high-tech firms in Japan and Germany supports the idea that Japanese organizations tend to be more centralized. Whereas the German firms leaned toward dispersing R&D groups out

Book Mark 6.0 (HAVE YOU READ THIS BOOK?)

Cross-Cultural Business Behavior: Marketing, Negotiating and Managing Across Cultures
By Richard R. Gesteland

Richard Gesteland maintains that heeding the "two iron rules of international business" is crucial to success in today's global business environment: "In International Business, the Seller Is Expected to Adapt to the Buyer," and "In International Business, the Visitor Is Expected to Observe Local Customs." In his book *Cross-Cultural Business Behavior*, Gesteland explains and categorizes various cultural patterns of behavior that can help managers follow these rules.

LOGICAL CULTURAL PATTERNS
Gesteland outlines four major cultural value patterns, which he calls *logical patterns*, that characterize countries around the world:

- *Deal-Focused versus Relationship-Focused.* Deal-focused cultures, such as those in North America, Australia, and Northern Europe, are task-oriented, while relationship-focused cultures, including those in Arabia, Africa, Latin America, and Asia, are typically people-oriented. Deal-focused individuals approach business in an objective and impersonal way. Relationship-focused individuals believe in building close personal relationships as the appropriate way to conduct business.
- *Informal versus Formal.* Informal cultures place a low value on status and power differences, whereas formal cultures are typically hierarchical and status-conscious. The unconstrained values of informal cultures, such as those in the United States and Australia, may insult people from formal, hierarchical societies, just as the class-consciousness of formal groups, such as cultures in most of Europe and Latin America, may offend the egalitarian ideals of people in informal cultures.

- *Rigid-Time versus Fluid-Time.* One part of the world's societies is flexible about time and scheduling, while the other group is more rigid and dedicated to clock-time. Conflicts may occur because rigid-time types often consider fluid-time people undisciplined and irresponsible, while fluid-time people regard rigid-time folks as arrogant, demanding, and enslaved by meaningless deadlines.
- *Expressive versus Reserved.* Expressive cultures include those in Latin America and the Mediterranean. Reserved cultures are those in East and Southeast Asia as well as Germanic Europe. This distinction can create a major communication gap. People from expressive cultures tend to talk louder and use more hand gestures and facial expressions. Reserved cultures may interpret raised voices and gesturing as signals of anger or instability.

A PRACTICAL GUIDE
Geographical-cultural differences, and the potential problems that cross-cultural communication can create, "impact our business success throughout the global marketplace," Gesteland asserts. *Cross-Cultural Business Behavior* "is intended as a practical guide for the men and women in the front lines of world trade, those who face every day the frustrating differences in global business customs and practices." By understanding Gesteland's logical patterns of behavior, managers can adapt to varied cultural values and improve their chances for international success.

Cross-Cultural Business Behavior: Marketing, Negotiating and Managing Across Cultures, by Richard R. Gesteland, is published by Copenhagen Business School Press.

into different regions, Japanese companies tended to keep these activities centralized in the home country.[70] This centralized approach enables Japanese companies to leverage the knowledge and resources located at the corporate center, attain global efficiencies, and coordinate across units to obtain synergies and avoid turf battles. Top managers use strong structural linkages to ensure that managers at headquarters remain up-to-date and fully involved in all strategic decisions. However, centralization has its limits. As the organization expands and divisions grow larger, headquarters can become overloaded and decision making slows. The quality of decisions may also suffer as greater diversity and complexity make it difficult for headquarters to understand and respond to local needs in each region.

China is a rapidly growing part of the international business environment, and limited research has been done into management structures of Chinese firms. Many Chinese-based firms are still relatively small and run in a traditional family-like manner. However, similar to Japan, organizations typically reflect a distinct hierarchy of authority and relatively strong centralization. Obligation plays an important role in Chinese culture and management, so employees feel obligated to follow orders directed from above.[71] Interestingly, though, one study found that Chinese employees are loyal not just to the boss, but also to company policies.[72] As Chinese organizations grow larger, more insight will be gained into how these firms handle the balance of coordination and control.

European Firms' Decentralized Approach. A different approach has typically been taken by European companies. Rather than relying on strong, centrally directed coordination and control as in the Japanese firms, international units tend to have a high level of independence and decision-making autonomy. Companies rely on a strong mission, shared values, and informal personal relationships for coordination. Thus, great emphasis is placed on careful selection, training, and development of key managers throughout the international organization. Formal management and control systems are used primarily for financial rather than technical or operational control. With this approach, each international unit focuses on its local markets, enabling the company to excel in meeting diverse needs. One disadvantage is the cost of ensuring, through training and development programs, that managers throughout a huge, global firm share goals, values, and priorities. Decision making can also be slow and complex, and disagreements and conflicts among divisions are more difficult to resolve.

The United States: Coordination and Control through Formalization. U.S.-based companies that have expanded into the international arena have taken still a third direction. Typically, these organizations have delegated responsibility to international divisions, yet retained overall control of the enterprise through the use of sophisticated management control systems and the development of specialist headquarters staff. Formal systems, policies, standards of performance, and a regular flow of information from divisions to headquarters are the primary means of coordination and control. Decision making is based on objective data, policies, and procedures, which provides for many operating efficiencies and reduces conflict among divisions and between divisions and headquarters. However, the cost of setting up complex systems, policies, and rules for an international organization may be quite high. This approach also requires a larger headquarters staff for reviewing, interpreting, and sharing information, thus increasing overhead costs. Finally, standard routines and procedures don't always fit the needs of new problems and situations.

Flexibility is limited if managers pay so much attention to systems that they fail to recognize opportunities and threats in the environment.

Clearly, each of these approaches has advantages. But as international organizations grow larger and more complex, the disadvantages of each tend to become more pronounced. Because traditional approaches have been inadequate to meet the demands of a rapidly changing, complex international environment, many large international companies are moving toward a new kind of organization form, the *transnational model*, which is highly differentiated to address environmental complexity, yet offers very high levels of coordination, learning, and transfer of organizational knowledge and innovations.

The Transnational Model of Organization

The **transnational model** represents the most advanced kind of international organization. It reflects the ultimate in both organizational complexity, with many diverse units, and organizational coordination, with mechanisms for integrating the varied parts. The transnational model is useful for large, multinational companies with subsidiaries in many countries that try to exploit both global and local advantages as well as technological advancements, rapid innovation, and global learning and knowledge sharing. Rather than building capabilities primarily in one area, such as global efficiency, national responsiveness, or global learning, the transnational model seeks to achieve all three simultaneously. Dealing with multiple, interrelated, complex issues requires a complex form of organization and structure.

The transnational model represents the most current thinking about the kind of structure needed by complex global organizations such as Philips NV, illustrated in Exhibit 6.10. Headquartered in the Netherlands, Philips has hundreds of operating units all over the world and is typical of global companies such as Unilever, Matsushita, or Procter & Gamble.[73]

The units in Exhibit 6.10 are far-flung. Achieving coordination, a sense of participation and involvement by subsidiaries, and a sharing of information, knowledge, new technology, and customers is a tremendous challenge. For example, a global corporation like Philips is so large that size alone is a huge problem in coordinating global operations. In addition, some subsidiaries become so large that they no longer fit a narrow strategic role defined by headquarters. While being part of a larger organization, individual units need some autonomy for themselves and the ability to have an impact on other parts of the organization.

The transnational model addresses these challenges by creating an integrated network of individual operations that are linked together to achieve the multidimensional goals of the overall organization.[74] The management philosophy is based on *interdependence* rather than either full divisional independence or total dependence of these units on headquarters for decision making and control. The transnational model is more than just an organization chart. It is a managerial state of mind, a set of values, a shared desire to make a worldwide learning system work, and an idealized structure for effectively managing such a system. Several characteristics distinguish the transnational organization from other global organization forms such as the matrix, described earlier.

1. *Assets and resources are dispersed worldwide into highly specialized operations that are linked together through interdependent relationships.* Resources and

Briefcase

As an organization manager, keep this guideline in mind:

Strive toward a transnational model of organization when the company has to respond to multiple global forces simultaneously and needs to promote worldwide integration, learning, and knowledge sharing.

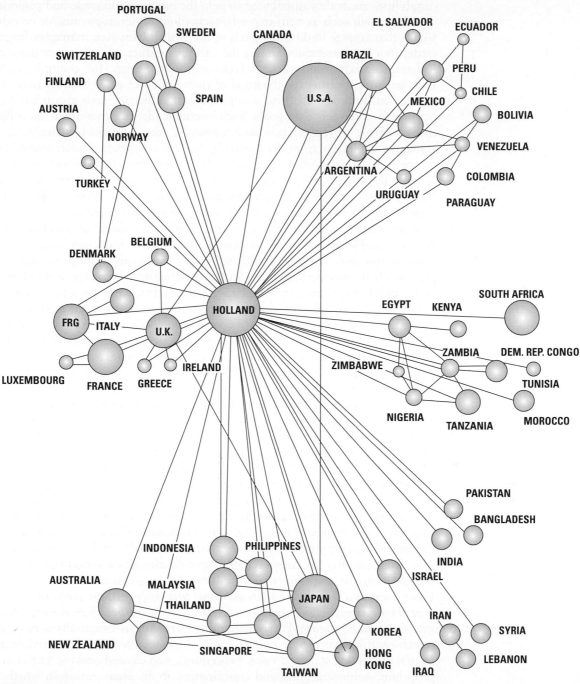

EXHIBIT 6.10
International Organizational Units and Interlinkages within Philips NV
Source: Sumantra Ghoshal and Christopher A. Bartlett, "The Multinational Corporation as an Interorganizational Network," *Academy of Management Review* 15 (1990), 605. Used by permission.

capabilities are widely distributed to help the organization sense and respond to diverse stimuli such as market needs, technological developments, or consumer trends that emerge in different parts of the world. However, managers forge interdependent relationships among the various product, functional, or geographical units. Mechanisms such as cross-subsidiary teams, for example, compel units to work together for the good of their own unit as well as the overall organization. Rather than being completely self-sufficient, each group has to cooperate to achieve its own goals. Such interdependencies encourage the collaborative sharing of information and resources, cross-unit problem solving, and collective implementation demanded by today's competitive international environment. Materials, people, products, ideas, resources, and information are continually flowing among the dispersed parts of the integrated network. In addition, managers actively shape, manage, and reinforce informal information networks that cross functions, products, divisions, and countries.

2. *Structures are flexible and ever-changing.* The transnational operates on a principle of *flexible centralization.* It may centralize some functions in one country, some in another, yet decentralize still other functions among its many geographically dispersed operations. An R&D center may be centralized in Holland and a purchasing center may be located in Sweden, while financial accounting responsibilities are decentralized to operations in many countries. A unit in Hong Kong may be responsible for coordinating activities across Asia, while activities for all other countries are coordinated by a large division headquarters in London. The transnational model requires that managers be flexible in determining structural needs based on the benefits to be gained. Some functions, products, and geographical regions by their nature may need more central control and coordination than others. In addition, coordination and control mechanisms will change over time to meet new needs or competitive threats.

3. *Subsidiary managers initiate strategy and innovations that become strategy for the corporation as a whole.* In traditional structures, managers have a strategic role only for their division. In a transnational structure, various centers and subsidiaries can shape the company from the bottom up by developing creative responses and initiating programs in response to local needs and dispersing those innovations worldwide. Transnational companies recognize each of the worldwide units as a source of capabilities and knowledge that can be used to benefit the entire organization. In addition, environmental demands and opportunities vary from country to country, and exposing the whole organization to this broader range of environmental stimuli triggers greater learning and innovation.

4. *Unification and coordination are achieved primarily through corporate culture, shared vision and values, and management style, rather than through formal structures and systems.* The transnational structure is essentially a horizontal structure. It is diverse and extended, and it exists in a fluctuating environment so that hierarchy, standard rules, procedures, and close supervision are not appropriate. Achieving unity and coordination in an organization in which employees come from a variety of different national backgrounds, are separated by time and geographical distance, and have different cultural norms is more easily accomplished through shared understanding than through formal systems. Top leaders build a context of shared vision, values, and perspectives among managers who in turn cascade these elements through all parts of the organization. Selection and training of managers emphasizes flexibility and open-mindedness. In addition, people are often rotated through different jobs,

divisions, and countries to gain broad experience and become socialized into the corporate culture. Achieving coordination in a transnational organization is a much more complex process than simple centralization or decentralization of decision making and requires shaping and adapting beliefs, culture, and values so that everyone participates in information sharing and learning.

Taken together, these characteristics facilitate strong coordination, organizational learning, and knowledge sharing on a broad global scale. The transnational model is truly a complex and messy way to conceptualize organization structure, but it is becoming increasingly relevant for large, global firms that treat the whole world as their playing field and do not have a single country base. The autonomy of organizational parts gives strength to smaller units and allows the firm to be flexible in responding to rapid change and competitive opportunities on a local level, while the emphasis on interdependency enables global efficiencies and organizational learning. Each part of the transnational company is aware of and closely integrated with the organization as a whole so local actions complement and enhance other company parts.

Summary and Interpretation

This chapter has examined how managers design organizations for a complex international environment. Almost every company today is affected by significant global forces, and many are developing overseas operations to take advantage of global markets. Three primary motivations for global expansion are to realize economies of scale, exploit economies of scope, and achieve scarce or low-cost factors of production such as labor, raw materials, or land. One popular way to become involved in international operations is through strategic alliances with international firms. Alliances include licensing, joint ventures, and consortia.

Organizations typically evolve through four stages, beginning with a domestic orientation, shifting to an international orientation, then changing to a multinational orientation, and finally moving to a global orientation that sees the whole world as a potential market. Organizations typically use an export department, then use an international department, and eventually develop into a worldwide geographical or product structure. Geographical structures are most effective for organizations that can benefit from a multidomestic strategy, meaning that products and services will do best if tailored to local needs and cultures. A product structure supports a globalization strategy, which means that products and services can be standardized and sold worldwide. Huge global firms might use a matrix structure to respond to both local and global forces simultaneously. Many firms use hybrid structures by combining elements of two or more different structures to meet the dynamic conditions of the global environment.

Succeeding on a global scale is not easy. Three aspects of the global organizational challenge are addressing environmental complexity through greater organizational complexity and differentiation, achieving integration and coordination among the highly differentiated units, and implementing mechanisms for the transfer of knowledge and innovations. Common ways to address the problem of integration and knowledge transfer are through global teams, stronger headquarters planning and control, and specific coordination roles. Managers also recognize that diverse national and cultural values influence the organization's approach to coordination and control. Three varied national approaches are the centralized co-ordination and control typically found in many Japanese-based firms, a decentralized approach common among European firms, and the formalization approach often used by U.S.-based international firms. Most companies, however, no matter their home country, use a combination of elements from each of these approaches.

Many are also finding a need to broaden their coordination methods and are moving toward the transnational model of organization. The transnational model is based on a philosophy of interdependence. It is highly differentiated yet offers very high levels of coordination, learning, and transfer of knowledge across far-flung divisions. The transnational model represents the ultimate global design in terms of both organizational complexity and organizational integration. Each part of the transnational organization is aware of and closely integrated with the organization as a whole so that local actions complement and enhance other company parts.

Key Concepts

consortia	globalization strategy
domestic stage	international division
economies of scale	international stage
economies of scope	joint venture
factors of production	multidomestic
global companies	multidomestic strategy
global geographical structure	multinational stage
global matrix structure	power distance
global product structure standardization	standardization
global stage	transnational model
global teams	uncertainty avoidance

Discussion Questions

1. Under what conditions should a company consider adopting a global geographical structure as opposed to a global product structure?
2. Name some companies that you think could succeed today with a globalization strategy and explain why you selected those companies. How does the globalization strategy differ from a multidomestic strategy?
3. Why would a company want to join a strategic alliance rather than go it alone in international operations? What do you see as the potential advantages and disadvantages of international alliances?
4. Why is knowledge sharing so important to a global organization?
5. What are some of the primary reasons a company decides to expand internationally? Identify a company in the news that has recently built a new overseas facility. Which of the three motivations for global expansion described in the chapter do you think best explains the company's decision? Discuss.
6. When would an organization consider using a matrix structure? How does the global matrix differ from the domestic matrix structure described in Chapter 3?
7. Name some of the elements that contribute to greater complexity for international organizations. How do organizations address this complexity? Do you think these elements apply to an online company such as eBay that wants to grow internationally? Discuss.

8. Traditional values in Mexico support high power distance and a low tolerance for uncertainty. What would you predict about a company that opens a division in Mexico and tries to implement global teams characterized by shared power and authority and the lack of formal guidelines, rules, and structure?

9. Do you believe it is possible for a global company to simultaneously achieve the goals of global efficiency and integration, national responsiveness and flexibility, and the worldwide transfer of knowledge and innovation? Discuss.

10. Compare the description of the transnational model in this chapter to the elements of the learning organization described in Chapter 1. Do you think the transnational model seems workable for a huge global firm? Discuss.

11. What does it mean to say that the transnational model is based on a philosophy of interdependence?

Chapter 6 Workbook: Made in the U.S.A.?

Find three different consumer products, such as a shirt, a toy, and a shoe. Try to find out the following information for each product, as shown in the table. To find this information, use Web sites, articles on the company from various business newspapers and magazines, and the labels on the items. You could also try calling the company and talking with someone there.

Product	What country do materials come from?	Where is it manufactured or assembled?	Which country does the marketing and advertising?	In what different countries is the product sold?
1.				
2.				
3.				

What can you conclude about international products and organizations based on your analysis?

Case for Analysis: TopDog Software*

At the age of 39, after working for nearly 15 years at a leading software company on the West Coast, Ari Weiner and his soon-to-be-wife, Mary Carpenter, had cashed in their stock options, withdrew all their savings, maxed out their credit cards, and started their own business, naming it TopDog Software after their beloved Alaskan malamute. The two had developed a new software package for customer relationship management (CRM) applications that they were certain was far superior to anything on the market at that time. TopDog's software was particularly effective for use in call centers because it provided a highly efficient way to integrate massive amounts of customer data and make it almost immediately accessible to call center representatives as they worked the phones. The software, which could be used as a stand-alone product or easily integrated with other major CRM software packages, dramatically expedited customer identification and verification, rapidly selected pertinent bits of data, and provided them in an easily interpreted format so that call center or customer service reps could provide fast, friendly, and customized service.

The timing proved to be right on target. CRM was just getting hot, and TopDog was poised to take advantage of the trend as a niche player in a growing market. Weiner

*Source: Based on Walter Kuemmerle, "Go Global—Or No?" *Harvard Business Review* (June 2001), 37–49.

and Carpenter brought in two former colleagues as partners and were soon able to catch the attention of a venture capitalist firm to gain additional funding. Within a couple of years, TopDog had twenty-eight employees and sales had reached nearly $4 million.

Now, though, the partners are facing the company's first major problem. TopDog's head of sales, Samantha Jenkins, has learned of a new company based in London that is beta-testing a new CRM package that promises to outpace TopDog's—and the London-based company, Fast-Data, has been talking up its global aspirations in the press. "If we stay focused on the United States and they start out as a global player, they'll kill us within months!" Sam moaned. "We've got to come up with an international strategy to deal with this kind of competition."

In a series of group meetings, off-site retreats, and one-on-one conversations, Weiner and Carpenter have gathered opinions and ideas from their partners, employees, advisors, and friends. Now they have to make a decision—should TopDog go global? And if so, what approach would be most effective? There's a growing market for CRM software overseas, and new companies such as FastData will soon be cutting into TopDog's U.S. market share as well. Samantha Jenkins isn't alone in her belief that TopDog has no choice but to enter new international markets or get eaten alive. Others, however, are concerned that TopDog isn't ready for that step. The company's resources are already stretched to the limit, and some advisors have warned that rapid global expansion could spell disaster. TopDog isn't even well established in the United States, they argue, and expanding internationally could strain the company's capabilities and resources. Others have pointed out that none of the managers has any international experience and the company would have to hire someone with significant global exposure to even think about entering new markets.

Although Mary tends to agree that TopDog for the time being should stay focused on building its business in the United States, Ari has come to believe that global expansion of some type is a necessity. But if TopDog does eventually decide on global expansion, he wonders how on earth they should proceed in such a huge, complex environment. Sam, the sales manager, is arguing that the company should set up its own small foreign offices from scratch and staff them primarily with local people. Building a U.K. office and an Asian office, she asserts, would give TopDog an ideal base for penetrating markets around the world. However, it would be quite expensive, not to mention the complexities of dealing with language and cultural differences, legal and government regulations, and other matters. Another option would be to establish alliances or joint ventures with small European and Asian companies that could benefit from adding CRM applications to their suite of products. The companies could share expenses in setting up foreign production facilities and a global sales and distribution network. This would be a much less costly operation and would give TopDog the benefit of the expertise of the foreign partners. However, it might also require lengthy negotiations and would certainly mean giving up some control to the partner companies.

One of TopDog's partners is urging still a third, even lower-cost approach, that of licensing TopDog's software to foreign distributors as a route to international expansion. By giving foreign software companies rights to produce, market, and distribute its CRM software, TopDog could build brand identity and customer awareness while keeping a tight rein on expenses. Ari likes the low-cost approach, but he wonders if licensing would give TopDog enough participation and control to successfully develop its international presence. As another day winds down, Weiner and Carpenter are no closer to a decision about global expansion than they were when the sun came up.

Case for Analysis: Rhodes Industries

David Javier was reviewing the consulting firm's proposed changes in organization structure for Rhodes Industries (RI). As Javier read the report, he wondered whether the changes recommended by the consultants would do more harm than good for RI. Javier had been president of RI for 18 months, and he was keenly aware of the organizational and coordination problems that needed to be corrected in order for RI to improve profits and growth in its international businesses.

Company Background
Rhodes Industries was started in the 1950s in Southern Ontario, Canada, by Robert Rhodes, an engineer who was an entrepreneur at heart. He started the business by first making pipe and then glass for industrial uses, but as soon

as the initial business was established, he quickly branched into new areas such as industrial sealants, coatings, and cleaners, and even into manufacturing mufflers and parts for the trucking industry. Much of this expansion occurred by acquiring small firms in Canada and the United States during the 1960s. RI had a conglomerate-type structure with rather diverse subsidiaries scattered around North America, all reporting directly to the Ontario headquarters. Each subsidiary was a complete local business and was allowed to operate independently so long as it contributed profits to RI.

During the 1970s and 1980s, the president at the time, Clifford Michaels, brought a strong international focus to RI. His strategy was to acquire small companies worldwide with the belief they could be formed into a cohesive unit

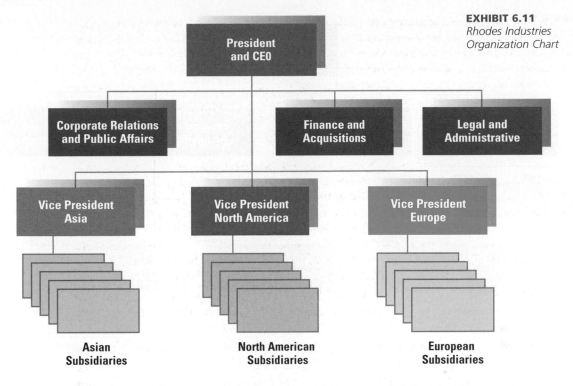

EXHIBIT 6.11
*Rhodes Industries
Organization Chart*

that would bring RI synergies and profits through low cost of manufacturing and by serving businesses in international markets. Some of RI's businesses were acquired simply because they were available at a good price, and RI found itself in new lines of business such as consumer products (paper and envelopes) and electrical equipment (switchboards, lightbulbs, and security systems), in addition to its previous lines of business. Most of these products had local brand names or were manufactured for major international companies such as General Electric or Corning Glass.

During the 1990s, a new president of RI, Sean Rhodes, the grandson of the founder, took over the business and adopted the strategy of focusing RI on three lines of business—Industrial Products, Consumer Products, and Electronics. He led the acquisition of more international businesses that fit these three categories, and divested a few businesses that didn't fit. Each of the three divisions had manufacturing plants as well as marketing and distribution systems in North America, Asia, and Europe. The Industrial Products division included pipe, glass, industrial sealants and coatings, cleaning equipment, and truck parts. The Electronics division included specialty lightbulbs, switchboards, computer chips, and resistors and capacitors for original equipment manufacturers. Consumer Products included dishes and glassware, paper and envelopes, and pencils and pens.

Structure

In 2004 David Javier replaced Sean Rhodes as president. He was very concerned about whether a new organization structure was needed for RI. The current structure was based on three major geographical areas—North America, Asia, and Europe—as illustrated in Exhibit 6.11. The various autonomous units within those regions reported to the office of the regional vice president. When several units existed in a single country, one of the subsidiary presidents was also responsible for coordinating the various businesses in that country, but most coordination was done through the regional vice president. Businesses were largely independent, which provided flexibility and motivation for the subsidiary managers.

The headquarters functional departments in Ontario were rather small. The three central departments—Corporate Relations and Public Affairs, Finance and Acquisitions, and Legal and Administrative—served the corporate business worldwide. Other functions such as HR management, new product development, marketing, and manufacturing all existed within individual subsidiaries and there was little coordination of these functions across geographical regions. Each business devised its own way to develop, manufacture, and market its products in its own country and region.

Organizational Problems

The problems Javier faced at RI, which were confirmed in the report on his desk, fell into three areas. First, each subsidiary acted as an independent business, using its own reporting systems and acting to maximize its own profits. This autonomy made it increasingly difficult to consolidate financial reports worldwide and to gain the efficiencies of uniform information and reporting systems.

EXHIBIT 6.12
Proposed Product Director Structure

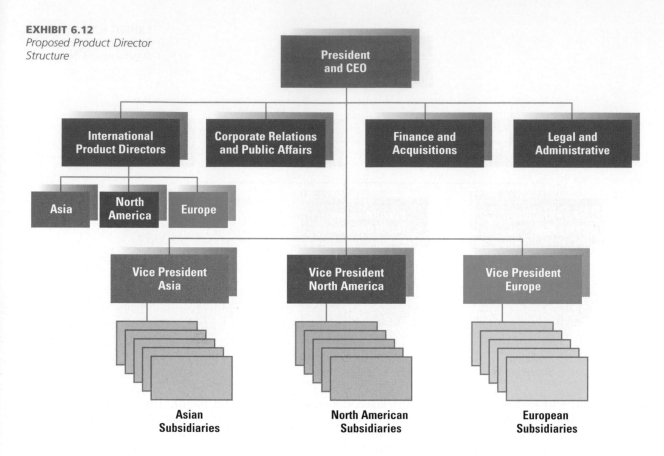

Second, major strategic decisions were made to benefit individual businesses or for a country's or region's local interests. Local projects and profits received more time and resources than did projects that benefited RI worldwide. For example, an electronics manufacturer in Singapore refused to increase production of chips and capacitors for sale in the United Kingdom because it would hurt the bottom line of the Singapore operation. However, the economies of scale in Singapore would more than offset shipping costs to the United Kingdom and would enable RI to close expensive manufacturing facilities in Europe, increasing RI's efficiency and profits.

Third, there had been no transfer of technology, new product ideas, or other innovations within RI. For example, a cost-saving technology for manufacturing lightbulbs in Canada had been ignored in Asia and Europe. A technical innovation that provided homeowners with cell phone access to home security systems developed in Europe has been ignored in North America. The report on Javier's desk stressed that RI was failing to disperse important innovations throughout the organization. These ignored innovations could provide significant improvements in both manufacturing and marketing worldwide. The report said, "No one at RI understands all the prod-

ucts and locations in a way that allows RI to capitalize on manufacturing improvements and new product opportunities." The report also said that better worldwide coordination would reduce RI's costs by 7 percent each year and increase market potential by 10 percent. These numbers were too big to ignore.

Recommended Structure

The report from the consultant recommended that RI try one of two options for improving its structure. The first alternative was to create a new international department at headquarters with the responsibility to coordinate technology transfer and product manufacturing and marketing worldwide (Exhibit 6.12). This department would have a Product Director for each major product line—Industrial, Consumer, and Electronics—who would have authority to coordinate activities and innovations worldwide. Each Product Director would have a team that would travel to each region and carry information on innovations and improvements to subsidiaries in other parts of the world.

The second recommendation was to reorganize into a worldwide product structure, as shown in Exhibit 6.13. All subsidiaries worldwide associated with a product line

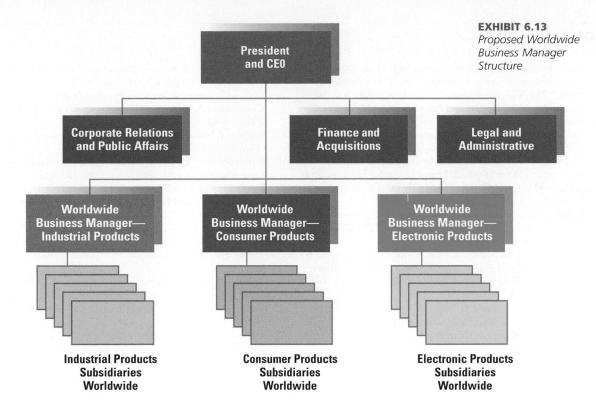

EXHIBIT 6.13
Proposed Worldwide Business Manager Structure

would report to the product line Business Manager. The Business Manager and staff would be responsible for developing business strategies and for coordinating all manufacturing efficiencies and product developments worldwide for its product line.

This worldwide product structure would be a huge change for RI. Many questions came to Javier's mind. Would the subsidiaries still be competitive and adaptive in local markets if forced to coordinate with other sub-sidiaries around the world? Would Business Managers be able to change the habits of subsidiary managers toward more global behavior? Would it be a better idea to appoint Product Director coordinators as a first step, or jump to the Business Manager product structure right away? Javier had a hunch that the move to worldwide product coordination made sense, but he wanted to think through all the potential problems and how RI would implement the changes.

Chapter 6 Workshop: Comparing Cultures*

As a group, rent a video of a foreign movie (or, alternately, go to the cinema when a foreign movie is shown). Take notes as you watch the movie, looking for any differences in cultural norms compared to your own. For example, identify any differences in the following compared to your own cultural norms:

    a. The way people interact with one another
    b. The formality or informality of relationships
    c. The attitudes toward work
    d. The amount of time people spend on work versus family

    e. The connection to family
    f. How people have fun

Questions
1. What were the key differences you observed in the movie's culture versus your own?
2. What are the advantages and disadvantages of using movies to understand another culture?

Notes

1. James Bandler and Matthew Karnitschnig, "Lost in Translation; European Giant in Magazines Finds U.S. a Tough Read," *The Wall Street Journal* (August 19, 2004), A1, A6; David Carr, "The Decline and Fall of Business Magazines," *International Herald Tribune* (May 31, 2005), 11; and James Bandler, "Gruner Cites Latest Miscue Tied to Magazine Circulation," *The Wall Street Journal* (January 13, 2005), B3.

2. Jim Rose and Salim Teja, "The Americans Are Coming!" *Business 2.0* (May 2000), 215; and Mohanbir Sawhney and Sumant Mandal, "What Kind of Global Organization Should You Build?" *Business 2.0* (May 2000), 213.

3. Matthew Karnitschnig, "Identity Question; For Siemens, Move into U.S. Causes Waves Back Home," *The Wall Street Journal* (September 8, 2003), A1, A8.

4. Jane L. Levere, "A Small Company, A Global Approach," *The New York Times* (January 1, 2004), *http://www.nytimes.com*

5. Paola Hject, "The Fortune Global 500," *Fortune* (July 26, 2004), 159–180.

6. This discussion is based heavily on Christopher A. Bartlett and Sumantra Ghoshal, *Transnational Management: Text, Cases, and Readings in Cross-Border Management*, 3rd ed. (Boston: Irwin McGraw-Hill, 2000), 94–96; and Anil K. Gupta and Vijay Govindarajan, "Converting Global Presence into Global Competitive Advantage," *Academy of Management Executive* 15, no. 2 (2001), 45–56.

7. Neil King Jr., "A Whole New World: Competition from China and India Is Changing the Way Businesses Operate Everywhere," *The Wall Street Journal* (September 27, 2004), R1.

8. Jim Carlton, "Branching Out; New Zealanders Now Shear Trees Instead of Sheep," *The Wall Street Journal* (May 29, 2003), A1, A10.

9. "Little Trouble in Big China," *FSB* (March 2004), 56–61; "Trade Gap," sidebar in *Fast Company* (June 2004), 42.

10. Dan Morse, "Cabinet Decisions; In North Carolina, Furniture Makers Try to Stay Alive," *The Wall Street Journal* (February 20, 2004), A1.

11. Keith H. Hammonds, "Smart, Determined, Ambitious, Cheap: The New Face of Global Competition," *Fast Company* (February 2003), 91–97.

12. Todd Zaun, Gregory L. White, Norihiko Shirouzu, and Scott Miller, "More Mileage: Auto Makers Look for Another Edge Farther from Home," *The Wall Street Journal* (July 31, 2002), A1, A8.

13. Ken Belson, "Outsourcing, Turned Inside Out," *The New York Times* (April 11, 2004), Section 3, 1.

14. Based on Nancy J. Adler, *International Dimensions of Organizational Behavior*, 4th ed. (Cincinnati, Ohio: South-Western, 2002); Theodore T. Herbert, "Strategy and Multinational Organizational Structure: An Interorganizational Relationships Perspective," *Academy of Management Review* 9 (1984), 259–271; and Laura K. Rickey, "International Expansion—U.S. Corporations: Strategy, Stages of Development, and Structure" (unpublished manuscript, Vanderbilt University, 1991).

15. Julia Boorstin, "Exporting Cleaner Air," segment of "Small and Global," *FSB* (June 2004), 36–48.

16. Michael E. Porter, "Changing Patterns of International Competition," *California Management Review* 28 (Winter 1986), 9–40.

17. William J. Holstein, "The Stateless Corporation," *BusinessWeek* (May 14, 1990), 98–115.

18. Debra Sparks, "Partners," *BusinessWeek*, Special Report: Corporate Finance (October 25, 1999), 106–112.

19. David Lei and John W. Slocum, Jr., "Global Strategic Alliances: Payoffs and Pitfalls," *Organizational Dynamics* (Winter 1991), 17–29.

20. Joseph Weber with Amy Barrett, "Volatile Combos," *BusinessWeek*, Special Report: Corporate Finance (October 25, 1999), 122; and Lei and Slocum, "Global Strategic Alliances."

21. Stratford Sherman, "Are Strategic Alliances Working?" *Fortune* (September 21, 1992), 77–78; and David Lei, "Strategies for Global Competition," *Long-Range Planning* 22 (1989), 102–109.

22. Cyrus F. Freidheim, Jr., *The Trillion-Dollar Enterprise: How the Alliance Revolution Will Transform Global Business* (New York: Perseus Books, 1998).

23. Carol Matlack, "Nestlé Is Starting to Slim Down at Last; But Can the World's No. 1 Food Colossus Fatten Up Its Profits As It Slashes Costs?" *BusinessWeek* (October 27, 2003), 56ff.

24. Ron Grover and Richard Siklos, "When Old Foes Need Each Other," *BusinessWeek*, Special Report: Corporate Finance (October 25, 1999), 114, 118.

25. "Joint Venture Agreement and Resource Acquisition by Robex," *PR Newswire* (March 8, 2005), 1; "ICiCI Bank and Prudential Strengthen Relationship in India," *Business Wire* (March 11, 2005), 1.

26. Sparks, "Partners."

27. Sparks, "Partners."

28. Kevin Kelly and Otis Port, with James Treece, Gail DeGeorge, and Zachary Schiller, "Learning from Japan," *BusinessWeek* (January 27, 1992), 52–60; and Gregory G. Dess, Abdul M. A. Rasheed, Kevin J. McLaughlin, and Richard L. Priem, "The New Corporate Architecture," *Academy of Management Executive* 9, no. 3 (1995), 7–20.

29. Kenichi Ohmae, "Managing in a Borderless World," *Harvard Business Review* (May–June 1989), 152–161.

30. Constance L. Hays, "From Bentonville to Beijing and Beyond," *The New York Times* (December 6, 2004), *http://www.nytimes.com*.

31. Conrad de Aenlle, "Famous Brands Can Bring Benefit, or a Backlash," *The New York Times* (October 19, 2003), Section 3, 7.

32. Cesare R. Mainardi, Martin Salva, and Muir Sanderson, "Label of Origin: Made on Earth," *Strategy & Business* 15 (Second Quarter 1999), 42–53; and Joann S. Lublin, "Place vs. Product: It's Tough to Choose a Management Model," *The Wall Street Journal* (June 27, 2001), A1, A4.

33. Mainardi, Salva, and Sanderson, "Label of Origin."

34. Gupta and Govindarajan, "Converting Global Presence into Global Competitive Advantage."

35. José Pla-Barber, "From Stopford and Wells's Model to Bartlett and Ghoshal's Typology: New Empirical Evidence," *Management International Review* 42, no. 2 (2002), 141–156.

36. Sumantra Ghoshal and Nitin Nohria, "Horses for Courses: Organizational Forms for Multinational Corporations," *Sloan Management Review* (Winter 1993), 23–35; and Roderick E. White and Thomas A. Poynter, "Organizing for Worldwide Advantage," *Business Quarterly* (Summer 1989), 84–89.

37. Robert J. Kramer, *Organizing for Global Competitiveness: The Country Subsidiary Design* (New York: The Conference Board, 1997), 12.

38. Laura B. Pincus and James A. Belohlav, "Legal Issues in Multinational Business: To Play the Game, You Have to Know the Rules," *Academy of Management Executive* 10, no. 3 (1996), 52–61.

39. John D. Daniels, Robert A. Pitts, and Marietta J. Tretter, "Strategy and Structure of U.S. Multinationals: An Exploratory Study," *Academy of Management Journal* 27 (1984), 292–307.

40. Robert J. Kramer, *Organizing for Global Competitiveness: The Product Design* (New York: The Conference Board, 1994).

41. Robert J. Kramer, *Organizing for Global Competitiveness: The Business Unit Design* (New York: The Conference Board, 1995), 18–19.

42. Carol Matlack, "Nestlé is Starting to Slim Down."

43. Based on Robert J. Kramer, *Organizing for Global Competitiveness: The Geographic Design* (New York: The Conference Board, 1993).

44. Kramer, *Organizing for Global Competitiveness: The Geographic Design*, 29–31.

45. William Taylor, "The Logic of Global Business: An Interview with ABB's Percy Barnevik," *Harvard Business Review* (March–April 1991), 91–105; Carla Rappaport, "A Tough Swede Invades the U.S.," *Fortune* (January 29, 1992), 76–79; Raymond E. Miles and Charles C. Snow, "The New Network Firm: A Spherical Structure Built on a Human Investment Philosophy," *Organizational Dynamics* (Spring 1995), 5–18; and Manfred F. R. Kets de Vries, "Making a Giant Dance," *Across the Board* (October 1994), 27–32.

46. Matthew Karnitschnig, "Identity Question; For Siemens, Move into U.S. Causes Waves Back Home."

47. Gupta and Govindarajan, "Converting Global Presence into Global Competitive Advantage."

48. Robert Frank, "Withdrawal Pains: In Paddies of Vietnam, Americans Once Again Land in a Quagmire," *The Wall Street Journal* (April 21, 2000), A1, A6.

49. The discussion of these challenges is based on Bartlett and Ghoshal, *Transnational Management*.

50. Ian Katz and Elisabeth Malkin, "Battle for the Latin American Net," *BusinessWeek* (November 1, 1999), 194–200; and Pamela Drukerman and Nick Wingfield, "Lost in Translation: AOL's Big Assault in Latin America Hits Snags in Brazil," *The Wall Street Journal* (July 11, 2000), A1.

51. Neil King Jr., "Competition from China and India Is Changing the Way Businesses Operate" and "Little Trouble in Big China."

52. Shirley Leung, "McHaute Cuisine: Armchairs, TVs, and Espresso—Is It McDonald's?" *The Wall Street Journal* (August 30, 2002), A1, A6.

53. Adam Lashinsky, "Saving Face at Sony," *Fortune* (February 21, 2005), 79–86; Phred Dvorak and Merissa Marr, "Stung by iPod, Sony Addresses a Digital Lag," *The Wall Street Journal* (December 30, 2004), A1; Ken Belson, "An Executive Who Could Not Bring the Company into Focus with His Vision," *The New York Times* (March 8, 2005), http://www.nytimes.com; Randall Stross, "How the iPod Ran Circles around the Walkman," *The New York Times* (March 13, 2005), Business Section, 5; Brian Bremner with Cliff Edwards, Ronald Grover, Tom Lowry, and Emily Thornton, "Sony's Sudden Samurai," *BusinessWeek* (March 21, 2005), 28ff; and Lorne Manly and Andrew Ross Sorkin, "At Sony, Diplomacy Trumps Technology," *The New York Times* (March 8, 2005), http://www.nytimes.com.

54. P. Ingrassia, "Industry Is Shopping Abroad for Good Ideas to Apply to Products," *The Wall Street Journal* (April 29, 1985), A1.

55. Based on Gupta and Govindarajan, "Converting Global Presence into Global Competitive Advantage."

56. Vijay Govindarajan and Anil K. Gupta, "Building an Effective Global Business Team," *MIT Sloan Management Review* 42, no. 4 (Summer 2001), 63–71.

57. Charlene Marmer Solomon, "Building Teams across Borders," *Global Workforce* (November 1998), 12–17.

58. Charles C. Snow, Scott A. Snell, Sue Canney Davison, and Donald C. Hambrick, "Use Transnational Teams to Globalize Your Company," *Organizational Dynamics* 24, no. 4 (Spring 1996), 50–67.

59. Jane Pickard, "Control Freaks Need Not Apply," *People Management* (February 5, 1998), 49.

60. Snow et al., "Use Transnational Teams to Globalize Your Company."

61. Robert J. Kramer, *Organizing for Global Competitiveness: The Corporate Headquarters Design* (New York: The Conference Board, 1999).

62. Manly and Sorkin, "At Sony, Diplomacy Trumps Technology."

63. These roles are based on Christopher A. Bartlett and Sumantra Ghoshal, *Managing across Borders: The Transnational Solution*, 2nd ed. (Boston: Harvard Business School Press, 1998), Chapter 11, 231–249.

64. See Jay Galbraith, "Building Organizations around the Global Customer," *Ivey Business Journal* (September–October 2001), 17–24, for a discussion of both formal and informal lateral networks used in multinational companies.

65. This section is based on Morten T. Hansen and Nitin Nohria, "How to Build Collaborative Advantage," *MIT Sloan Management Review* (Fall 2004), 22ff.

66. Geert Hofstede, "The Interaction between National and Organizational Value Systems," *Journal of Management Studies* 22 (1985), 347–357; and Geert Hofstede, *Cultures and Organizations: Software of the Mind* (London: McGraw-Hill, 1991).

67. See Mansour Javidan and Robert J. House, "Cultural Acumen for the Global Manager: Lessons from Project GLOBE," *Organizational Dynamics* 29, no. 4 (2001), 289–305; and R. J. House, M. Javidan, Paul Hanges, and Peter Dorfman, "Understanding Cultures and Implicit Leadership Theories across the Globe: An Introduction to Project GLOBE," *Journal of World Business* 37 (2002), 3–10.

68. This discussion is based on "Culture and Organization," Reading 2–2 in Christopher A. Bartlett and Sumantra Ghoshal, *Transnational Management*, 3rd ed. (Boston: Irwin McGraw-Hill, 2000), 191–216, excerpted from Susan Schneider and Jean-Louis Barsoux, *Managing across Cultures* (London: Prentice-Hall, 1997).

69. Based on Bartlett and Ghoshal, *Managing across Borders*, 181–201.

70. Martin Hemmert, "International Organization of R&D and Technology Acquisition Performance of High-Tech Business Units," *Management International Review* 43, no. 4 (2003), 361–382.

71. Jean Lee, "Culture and Management—A Study of a Small Chinese Family Business in Singapore," *Journal of Small Business Management* 34, no. 3 (July 1996), 63ff; "Olivier Blanchard and Andrei Shleifer, "Federalism with and without Political Centralization: China versus Russia," *IMF Staff Papers* 48 (2001), 171ff.

72. Nailin Bu, Timothy J. Craig, and T. K. Peng, "Reactions to Authority," *Thunderbird International Business Review* 43, no. 6 (November–December 2001), 773–795.

73. Sumantra Ghoshal and Christopher Bartlett, "The Multinational Corporation as an Inter-organizational Network," *Academy of Management Review* 15 (1990), 603–625.

74. The description of the transnational organization is based on Bartlett and Ghoshal, *Transnational Management* and *Managing across Borders*.

PART 4
Internal Design Elements

7. Manufacturing and Service Technologies

8. Information Technology and Control

9. Organization Size, Life Cycle, and Decline

7

Manufacturing and Service Technologies

Core Organization Manufacturing Technology
Manufacturing Firms • Strategy, Technology, and Performance

Contemporary Applications
Flexible Manufacturing Systems • Lean Manufacturing • Performance and Structural Implications

Core Organization Service Technology
Service Firms • Designing the Service Organization

Non-Core Departmental Technology
Variety • Analyzability • Framework

Department Design

Workflow Interdependence among Departments
Types • Structural Priority • Structural Implications

Impact of Technology on Job Design
Job Design • Sociotechnical Systems

Summary and Interpretation

A Look Inside

American Axle & Manufacturing (AAM)

Richard Dauch always wanted to run his own manufacturing company. After more than 28 years in the auto industry, working first as an assembly-line worker and then moving into management at companies such as General Motors, Volkswagen of America, and the Chrysler Corporation, he finally got his chance. General Motors was restructuring and offered five of its axle and drivetrain plants in Detroit, Three Rivers, Michigan, and Buffalo, New York, up for sale. Dauch, with two passive investors, raised more than $300 million and established American Axle & Manufacturing (AAM). Two pressing challenges AAM faced immediately were that the plants were old, neglected, and distressed and the workforce was dispirited and fearful for their future. Dauch's first priority was to work with his people and build a team culture with a commitment to standards of excellence in all that they did. Other top priorities included establishing bulletproof quality and product performance, impeccable delivery, economic discipline, and solid financial performance. To meet these goals, Dauch knew he needed to upgrade product, process, and systems technology in balance.

Friends and family members were questioning Dauch's judgment. However, he was determined to transform the plants into fast, flexible factories that could produce high-quality auto parts and compete with low-cost manufacturers in China and elsewhere. Teams of engineers set out on global missions to locate the best processing equipment and world-class production machinery. In Germany, for example, the team observed and procured high-performance gear-cutting machinery that was exponentially faster than that currently in use, and reduced scrap. Overall, AAM spent $3 billion modernizing and rebuilding factories' capacity and capabilities.

A key component of the redesign is the use of computerized production equipment and information systems in an integrated and simultaneous processing approach. Engineers can now test and validate products by computer before they're manufactured. Images of the parts, along with exact data and specifications, are transmitted directly to production machines. An information system tells managers at a glance how production is proceeding on different assembly lines at each plant. The thoughtful use of new equipment eliminated 5 miles of conveyors, freed up thousands of square feet of floor space, improved quality, and doubled productivity for AAM. Employee training and skills have also been upgraded to run the more complex machinery. AAM provides nearly every associate with 40 hours of training a year, including the availability of college-level courses. Employees now have more opportunities to use their intellect and ingenuity on the job.

In the first 10 years of its existence, AAM more than doubled its top-line revenue and realized a 99.9 percent quality improvement while producing more than 45 million axles and 1.2 billion forgings with no recalls and no product litigation. Combining new technology with new ways of thinking catapulted Richard Dauch's company into the top 10 automotive suppliers in North America and the top 35 in the world. AAM now has 17,000 employees in 18 plants around the world. In 2005, the number of customers had grown from 2 to 100, including U.S., Korean, and European automakers.[1]

Manufacturing plants in the United States are being threatened as never before. Many companies have found it more advantageous to outsource manufacturing to contractors in other countries that can do the work less expensively, as we discussed in a previous chapter. Overall, manufacturing has been on the decline in the United States and other developed countries for years,

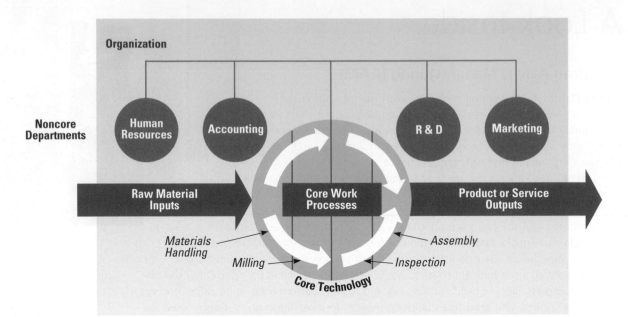

EXHIBIT 7.1

*Core Transformation
Process for a
Manufacturing
Company*

with services becoming an increasingly greater part of the economy. However, some manufacturing companies, like AAM, are applying new technology to gain a new competitive edge. Although AAM also has plants in low-wage countries, Dauch emphasizes that his motivation is to be close to major customers who have their own factories there. In fact, thanks to increased efficiency and productivity in the U.S. plants, AAM has brought some work back to Detroit from Mexico. In addition, AAM recently won a contract to make driveline components in Detroit that a competitor had previously been making in China.[2]

This chapter explores both service and manufacturing technologies and how technology is related to organizational structure. **Technology** refers to the work processes, techniques, machines, and actions used to transform organizational inputs (materials, information, ideas) into outputs (products and services).[3] Technology is an organization's production process and includes work procedures as well as machinery.

An organization's **core technology** is the work process that is directly related to the organization's mission, such as teaching in a high school, medical services in a health clinic, or manufacturing at AAM. For example, at AAM, the core technology begins with raw materials (e.g., steel, aluminum, and composite metals). Employees take action on the raw material to make a change in it (they cut and forge metals and assemble parts), thus transforming the raw material into the output of the organization (axles, drive shafts, crankshafts, transmission parts, etc.). For a service organization like UPS, the core technology includes the production equipment (e.g., sorting machines, package handling equipment, trucks, airplanes) and procedures for delivering packages and overnight mail. In addition, as at companies like UPS and AAM, computers and new information technology have revolutionized work processes in both manufacturing and service organizations. The specific impact of new information technology on organizations will be described in Chapter 8.

Exhibit 7.1 features an example of core technology for a manufacturing plant. Note how the core technology consists of raw material inputs, a transformation work process (milling, inspection, assembly) that changes and adds value to the raw material and produces the ultimate product or service output that is sold to con-

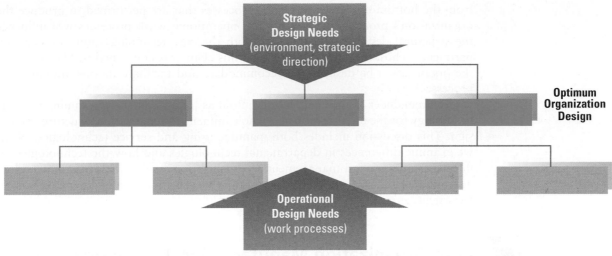

EXHIBIT 7.2
*Pressures Affecting
Organization Design*
Source: Based on David A.
Nadler and Michael L.
Tushman, with Mark B. Nadler,
*Competing by Design: The
Power of Organizational
Architecture* (New York: Oxford
University Press, 1997), 54.

sumers in the environment. In today's large, complex organizations, core work processes vary widely and sometimes can be hard to pinpoint. A core technology can be partly understood by examining the raw materials flowing into the organization,[4] the variability of work activities,[5] the degree to which the production process is mechanized,[6] the extent to which one task depends on another in the workflow,[7] or the number of new product or service outputs.[8]

An important theme in this chapter is how core technology influences organizational structure. Thus, understanding core technology provides insight into how an organization can be structured for efficient performance.[9]

Organizations are made up of many departments, each of which may use a different work process (technology) to provide a good or service within an organization. A **non-core technology** is a department work process that is important to the organization but is not directly related to its primary mission. In Exhibit 7.1, non-core work processes are illustrated by the departments of human resources (HR), accounting, research and development (R&C), and marketing. Thus, R&D transforms ideas into new products, and marketing transforms inventory into sales, each using a somewhat different work process. The output of the HR department is people to work in the organization, and accounting produces accurate statements about the organization's financial condition.

■ Purpose of This Chapter

In this chapter, we will discuss both core and non-core work processes and their relationship to designing organization structure. The nature of the organization's work processes must be considered in designing the organization for maximum efficiency and effectiveness. The optimum organization design is based on a variety of elements. Exhibit 7.2 illustrates that forces affecting organization design come from both outside and inside the organization. External strategic needs, such as environmental conditions, strategic direction, and organizational goals, create top-down pressure for designing the organization in such a way as to fit the environment and accomplish goals. These pressures on design have been discussed in previous chapters. However, decisions about design should also take into consideration pressures from the bottom up—from the work processes that are performed to produce the organization's products or services. The operational work processes will influence the structural design associated with both the core technology and non-core departments. Thus, the subject with which this chapter is concerned is, "How should the organization be designed to accommodate and facilitate its operational work processes?"

The remainder of the chapter will unfold as follows. First, we examine how the technology for the organization as a whole influences organization structure and design. This discussion includes both manufacturing and service technologies. Next, we examine differences in departmental technologies and how the technologies influence the design and management of organizational subunits. Third, we explore how interdependence—flow of materials and information—among departments affects structure.

Core Organization Manufacturing Technology

Manufacturing technologies include traditional manufacturing processes and contemporary applications, such as flexible manufacturing and lean manufacturing.

■ Manufacturing Firms

The first and most influential study of manufacturing technology was conducted by Joan Woodward, a British industrial sociologist. Her research began as a field study of management principles in south Essex. The prevailing management wisdom at the time (1950s) was contained in what were known as universal principles of management. These principles were "one best way" prescriptions that effective organizations were expected to adopt. Woodward surveyed 100 manufacturing firms first-hand to learn how they were organized.[10] She and her research team visited each firm, interviewed managers, examined company records, and observed the manufacturing operations. Her data included a wide range of structural characteristics (span of control, levels of management) and dimensions of management style (written versus verbal communications, use of rewards) and the type of manufacturing process. Data were also obtained that reflected commercial success of the firms.

Woodward developed a scale and organized the firms according to technical complexity of the manufacturing process. **Technical complexity** represents the extent of mechanization of the manufacturing process. High technical complexity means most of the work is performed by machines. Low technical complexity means workers play a larger role in the production process. Woodward's scale of technical complexity originally had ten categories, as summarized in Exhibit 7.3. These categories were further consolidated into three basic technology groups:

*   *Group I: Small-batch and unit production.* These firms tend to be job shop operations that manufacture and assemble small orders to meet specific needs of customers. Custom work is the norm. **Small-batch production** relies heavily on the human operator; it is thus not highly mechanized. Rockwell Collins, which makes electronic equipment for airplanes and other products, provides an example of small-batch manufacturing. Although sophisticated computerized machinery is used for part of the production process, final assembly requires highly skilled human operators to ensure absolute reliability of products used

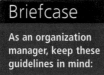

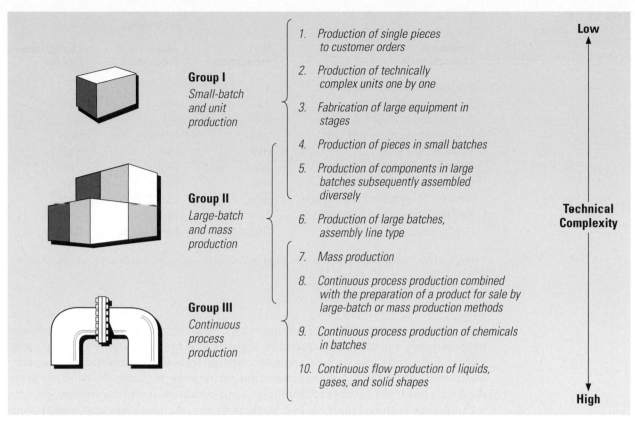

Group I *Small-batch and unit production*	1. Production of single pieces to customer orders	**Low** ↑
	2. Production of technically complex units one by one	
	3. Fabrication of large equipment in stages	
Group II *Large-batch and mass production*	4. Production of pieces in small batches	
	5. Production of components in large batches subsequently assembled diversely	**Technical Complexity**
	6. Production of large batches, assembly line type	
Group III *Continuous process production*	7. Mass production	
	8. Continuous process production combined with the preparation of a product for sale by large-batch or mass production methods	
	9. Continuous process production of chemicals in batches	
	10. Continuous flow production of liquids, gases, and solid shapes	↓ **High**

EXHIBIT 7.3
Woodward's Classification of 100 British Firms According to Their Systems of Production
Source: Adapted from Joan Woodward, *Management and Technology* (London: Her Majesty's Stationery Office, 1958). Used with permission of Her Britannic Majesty's Stationery Office.

by aerospace companies, defense contractors, and the U.S. military. The company's workforce is divided into manufacturing cells, some of which produce only ten units a day. In one plant, 140 workers build Joint Tactical Information Distribution Systems, for managing battlefield communications from a circling plane, at a rate of ten a month.[11]

- *Group II: Large-batch and mass production.* **Large-batch production** is a manufacturing process characterized by long production runs of standardized parts. Output often goes into inventory from which orders are filled, because customers do not have special needs. Examples include most assembly lines, such as for automobiles or trailer homes.

- *Group III: Continuous-process production.* In **continuous-process production**, the entire process is mechanized. There is no starting and stopping. This represents mechanization and standardization one step beyond those in an assembly line. Automated machines control the continuous process, and outcomes are highly predictable. Examples would include chemical plants, oil refineries, liquor producers, pharmaceuticals, and nuclear power plants.

Using this classification of technology, Woodward's data made sense. A few of her key findings are given in Exhibit 7.4. The number of management levels and the manager-to-total personnel ratio, for example, show definite increases as technical complexity increases from unit production to continuous process. This indicates that greater management intensity is needed to manage complex technology.

EXHIBIT 7.4
Relationship between Technical Complexity and Structural Characteristics

Structural Characteristic	Technology		
	Unit Production	Mass Production	Continuous Process
Number of management levels	3	4	6
Supervisor span of control	23	48	15
Direct/indirect labor ratio	9:1	4:1	1:1
Manager/total personnel ratio	Low	Medium	High
Workers' skill level	High	Low	High
Formalized procedures	Low	High	Low
Centralization	Low	High	Low
Amount of verbal communication	High	Low	High
Amount of written communication	Low	High	Low
Overall structure	Organic	Mechanistic	Organic

Source: Joan Woodward, *Industrial Organization: Theory and Practice* (London: Oxford University Press, 1965). Used with permission.

The direct-to-indirect labor ratio decreases with technical complexity because more indirect workers are required to support and maintain complex machinery. Other characteristics, such as span of control, formalized procedures, and centralization, are high for mass-production technology because the work is standardized, but low for other technologies. Unit-production and continuous-process technologies require highly skilled workers to run the machines and verbal communication to adapt to changing conditions. Mass production is standardized and routinized, so few exceptions occur, little verbal communication is needed, and employees are less skilled.

Overall, the management systems in both unit-production and continuous-process technology are characterized as organic, as defined in Chapter 4. They are more free-flowing and adaptive, with fewer procedures and less standardization. Mass production, however, is mechanistic, with standardized jobs and formalized procedures. Woodward's discovery about technology thus provided substantial new insight into the causes of organization structure. In Joan Woodward's own words, "Different technologies impose different kinds of demands on individuals and organizations, and those demands had to be met through an appropriate structure."[12]

Strategy, Technology, and Performance

Another portion of Woodward's study examined the success of the firms along dimensions such as profitability, market share, stock price, and reputation. As indicated in Chapter 2, the measurement of effectiveness is not simple or precise, but Woodward was able to rank firms on a scale of commercial success according to whether they displayed above-average, average, or below-average performance on strategic objectives.

Woodward compared the structure-technology relationship against commercial success and discovered that successful firms tended to be those that had complementary structures and technologies. Many of the organizational characteristics of

Briefcase

As an organization manager, keep this guideline in mind:

When adopting a new technology, realign strategy, structure, and management processes to achieve top performance.

the successful firms were near the average of their technology category, as shown in Exhibit 7.4. Below-average firms tended to depart from the structural characteristics for their technology type. Another conclusion was that structural characteristics could be interpreted as clustering into organic and mechanistic management systems. Successful small-batch and continuous process organizations had organic structures, and successful mass-production organizations had mechanistic structures. Subsequent research has replicated her findings.[13]

What this illustrates for today's companies is that strategy, structure, and technology need to be aligned, especially when competitive conditions change.[14] For example, computer makers had to realign strategy, structure, and technology to compete with Dell in the personal computer market. Manufacturers such as IBM that once tried to differentiate their products and charge a premium price switched to a low-cost strategy, adopted new technology to enable them to customize PCs, revamped supply chains, and began outsourcing manufacturing to other companies that could do the job more efficiently.

Today, many U.S. manufacturers farm production out to other companies. Printronix, a publicly owned company in Irvine, California, however, has gone in the opposite direction and achieved success by carefully aligning technology, structure, and management processes to achieve strategic objectives.

In Practice

Printronix

Printronix makes 60 percent of the electromechanical line printers used in the world's factories and warehouses. To maintain the reliability that makes Printronix products worth $2,600 to $26,000 each, the company does almost everything in-house—from design, to making hundreds of parts, to final assembly, to research on new materials. In the 1970s, Printronix began by making a high-speed line printer that could run with the minicomputers then being used on factory floors. Though it was not the first line printer, it was rugged enough to use in industrial settings and incorporated pioneering software that could print graphics such as charts, graphs, and bar-code labels.

Printronix started as a traditional mass-production operation, but the company faced a tremendous challenge in the late 1980s when factories began switching from minicomputers to personal computers and servers. Within 2 years, sales and profits plunged, and founder and CEO Robert A. Kleist realized Printronix needed new ideas, new technology, and new methods to adapt to a world where printers were no longer stand-alone products but parts of emerging enterprise networks. One change Kleist made was to switch from mass-producing printers that were kept in inventory to a small-batch or unit production system that built printers to order. Products were redesigned and assembly work reorganized so that small groups of workers could configure each printer to a customer's specific needs. Many employees had to be trained in new skills and to take more responsibility than they had on the traditional assembly line. Highly skilled workers were needed to make some of the precision parts needed in the new machines as well. Besides internal restructuring, Kleist decided to pick up on the outsourcing trend and go after the computer industry's factory printer business, winning orders to produce under the labels of IBM, Hewlett-Packard, and Siemens. Kleist doubled the research and development (R&D) budget to be sure the company kept pace with new technological developments. In 2000, Printronix began building thermal printers as well as specialized laser printers that can print adhesive bar-code labels at lightning speed.

By making changes in technology, design, and management methods, Printronix has continued to meet its strategic objective of differentiating its products from the competition. "The restructuring made us a stronger company in both manufacturing and engineering," says Kleist.[15]

Failing to adopt appropriate new technologies to support strategy, or adopting a new technology and failing to realign strategy to match it, can lead to poor performance. Today's increased global competition means more volatile markets, shorter product life cycles, and more sophisticated and knowledgeable consumers; and flexibility to meet these new demands has become a strategic imperative for many companies.[16] Manufacturing companies can adopt new technologies to support the strategy of flexibility. However, organization structures and management processes must also be realigned, as a highly mechanistic structure hampers flexibility and

Book Mark 7.0 (HAVE YOU READ THIS BOOK?)

Inviting Disaster: Lessons from the Edge of Technology
By James R. Chiles

Dateline: Paris, France, July 25, 2000. Less than 2 minutes after Air France Concorde Flight 4590 departs Charles DeGaulle Airport, something goes horribly wrong. Trailing fire and billowing black smoke, the huge plane rolls left and crashes into a hotel, killing all 109 people aboard and 4 more on the ground. It's just one of the technological disasters James R. Chiles describes in his book, *Inviting Disaster: Lessons from the Edge of Technology*. One of Chiles's main points is that advancing technology makes possible the creation of machines that strain the human ability to understand and safely operate them. Moreover, he asserts, the margins of safety are drawing thinner as the energies we harness become more powerful and the time between invention and use grows shorter. Chiles believes that today, "for every twenty books on the pursuit of success, we need a book on how things fly into tiny pieces despite enormous effort and the very highest ideals." All complex systems, he reminds us, are destined to fail at some point.

HOW THINGS FLY INTO PIECES: EXAMPLES OF SYSTEM FRACTURES

Chiles uses historical calamities such as the sinking of the *Titanic* and modern disasters such as the explosion of the space shuttle *Challenger* (the book was published before the 2003 crash of the *Columbia* shuttle) to illustrate the dangers of *system fracture*, a chain of events that involves human error in response to malfunctions in complex machinery. Disaster begins when one weak point links up with others.

- *Sultana* (American steamboat on the Mississippi River near Memphis, Tennessee), April 25, 1865. The boat, designed to carry a maximum of 460 people, was carrying more than 2,000 Union ex-prisoners north—as well as 200 additional crew and passengers—when three of the four boilers exploded, killing 1,800 people. One of the

boilers had been temporarily patched to cover a crack, but the patch was too thin. Operators failed to compensate by resetting the safety valve.
- *Piper Alpha* (offshore drilling rig in the North Sea), July 6, 1988. The offshore platform processed large volumes of natural gas from other rigs via pipe. A daytime work crew, which didn't complete repair of a gas-condensate pump, relayed a verbal message to the next shift, but workers turned the pump on anyway. When the temporary seal on the pump failed, a fire trapped crewmen with no escape route, killing 167 crew and rescue workers.
- *Union Carbide (India) Ltd.* (release of highly toxic chemicals into a community), Bhopal, Mahdya Pradesh, India, December 3, 1984. There are three competing theories for how water got into a storage tank, creating a violent reaction that sent highly toxic methyl isocyanate for herbicides into the environment, causing an estimated 7,000 deaths: (1) poor safety maintenance, (2) sabotage, or (3) worker error.

WHAT CAUSES SYSTEM FRACTURES?

There is a veritable catalog of causes that lead to such disasters, from design errors, insufficient operator training, and poor planning to greed and mismanagement. Chiles wrote this book as a reminder that technology takes us into risky locales, whether it be outer space, up a 2,000-foot tower, or into a chemical processing plant. Chiles also cites examples of potential disasters that were averted by quick thinking and appropriate response. To help prevent system fractures, managers can create organizations in which people throughout the company are expert at picking out the subtle signals of real problems—and where they are empowered to report them and take prompt action.

Inviting Disaster: Lessons from the Edge of Technology, by James R. Chiles, is published by HarperBusiness.

prevents the company from reaping the benefits of the new technology.[17] Managers should always remember that the technological and human systems of an organization are intertwined. This chapter's Book Mark provides a different perspective on technology by looking at the dangers of failing to understand the human role in managing technological advances.

Contemporary Applications

In the years since Woodward's research, new developments have occurred in manufacturing technology. Despite the decline in U.S. manufacturing, it still represents 14 percent of the gross domestic product (GDP) and 11 percent of all employment in the United States.[18] However, the factory of today is far different from the industrial firms Woodward studied in the 1950s. In particular, computers have revolutionized all types of manufacturing—small batch, large batch, and continuous process. At the Marion, North Carolina, plant of Rockwell Automation's Power Systems Division, highly trained employees can quickly handle a build-on-demand unit of one thanks to computers, wireless technology, and radio-frequency systems. In one instance, the Marion plant built, packaged, and delivered a replacement bearing for installation in an industrial air conditioning unit in Texas only 15 hours after the customer called for help.[19] An example in continuous process manufacturing comes from BP's Texas City, Texas, petrochemical plant. Technicians who once manually monitored hundreds of complex processes now focus their energy on surveying long-term production trends. Controlling the continuous production of petrochemicals today is handled faster, smarter, more precisely, and more economically by computer. Productivity at the Texas City plant has increased 55 percent. The plant uses 3 percent less electricity and 10 percent less natural gas, which amounts to millions of dollars in savings and fewer CO_2 emissions.[20]

Mass production manufacturing has seen similar transformations. Two significant contemporary applications of manufacturing technology are flexible manufacturing systems and lean manufacturing.

Flexible Manufacturing Systems

Most of today's factories use a variety of new manufacturing technologies, including robots, numerically controlled machine tools, radio-frequency identification (RFID), wireless technology, and computerized software for product design, engineering analysis, and remote control of machinery. The ultimate automated factories are referred to as **flexible manufacturing systems** (FMS).[21] Also called *computer-integrated manufacturing, smart factories, advanced manufacturing technology, agile manufacturing,* or *the factory of the future,* FMS links together manufacturing components that previously stood alone. Thus, robots, machines, product design, and engineering analysis are coordinated by a single computer.

The result has already revolutionized the shop floor, enabling large factories to deliver a wide range of custom-made products at low mass-production costs.[22] Flexible manufacturing also enables small companies to go toe-to-toe with large factories and low-cost foreign competitors. Techknits, Inc., a small manufacturer located in New York City, competes successfully against low-cost sweater-makers in Asia by using computerized looms and other machinery. The work of designing sweaters, which once took 2 days, can now be accomplished in 2 hours. Looms operate round-the-clock and crank out 60,000 sweaters a week, enabling Techknits to fill customer orders faster than foreign competitors.[23]

Flexible manufacturing is typically the result of three subcomponents:

- *Computer-aided design (CAD)*. Computers are used to assist in the drafting, design, and engineering of new parts. Designers guide their computers to draw specified configurations on the screen, including dimensions and component details. Hundreds of design alternatives can be explored, as can scaled-up or scaled-down versions of the original.[24]
- *Computer-aided manufacturing (CAM)*. Computer-controlled machines in materials handling, fabrication, production, and assembly greatly increase the speed at which items can be manufactured. CAM also permits a production line to shift rapidly from producing one product to any variety of other products by changing the instruction tapes or software codes in the computer. CAM enables the production line to quickly honor customer requests for changes in product design and product mix.[25]
- *Integrated information network*. A computerized system links all aspects of the firm—including accounting, purchasing, marketing, inventory control, design, production, and so forth. This system, based on a common data and information base, enables managers to make decisions and direct the manufacturing process in a truly integrated fashion.

The combination of CAD, CAM, and integrated information systems means that a new product can be designed on the computer and a prototype can be produced untouched by human hands. The ideal factory can switch quickly from one product to another, working fast and with precision, without paperwork or record-keeping to bog down the system.[26]

Van's Aircraft of Aurora, Oregon, used CAD/CAM to become the world's leading producer of airplanes in kit form. Van's business has doubled in the 7 years since founder and CEO Dick VanGrunsven introduced the technology, and profits are up more than 25 percent. The CAD/CAM system enables design data to flow to automated machines that cut, bend, stamp, or drill the appropriate pieces for a single-engine plane that the amateur can put together, almost like a puzzle, in about 2,000 hours.[27]

Some advanced factories have moved to a system called *product life-cycle management* (PLM). PLM software can manage a product from idea through development, manufacturing, testing, and even maintenance in the field. The PLM software provides three primary advantages for product innovation. PLM (1) stores data on ideas and products from all parts of the company; (2) links product design to all departments (and even outside suppliers) involved in new product development; and (3) provides three-dimensional images of new products for testing and maintenance. PLM has been used to coordinate people, tools, and facilities around the world for the design, development, and manufacture of products as diverse as roller skates produced by GID of Yorba Linda, California, product packaging for Procter & Gamble consumer products, and Boeing's new 7E7 Dreamliner passenger jet.[28]

Lean Manufacturing

Flexible manufacturing reaches its ultimate level to improve quality, customer service, and cost cutting when all parts are used interdependently and combined with flexible management processes in a system referred to as lean manufacturing. **Lean manufacturing** uses highly trained employees at every stage of the production process, who take a painstaking approach to details and problem solving to cut waste and improve quality. It incorportes technological elements, such as CAD/CAM and PLM, but the heart of lean manufacturing is not machines or software, but people. Lean manufacturing requires changes in organizational systems, such as decision-making processes and management processes, as well as an organizational culture that supports active employee participation. Employees are trained to "think lean," which means attacking waste and striving for continuous improvement in all areas.[29]

Japan's Toyota Motor Corporation, which pioneered lean manufacturing, is often considered the premier manufacturing organization in the world. The famed Toyota Production System combines techniques such as just-in-time inventory, product life-cycle management, continuous-flow production, quick changeover of assembly lines, continuous improvement, and preventive maintenance with a management system that encourages employee involvement and problem solving. Any employee can stop the production line at any time to solve a problem. In addition, designing equipment to stop automatically so that a defect can be fixed is a key element of the system.[30]

Many North American organizations have studied the Toyota Production System and seen dramatic improvements in productivity, inventory reduction, and quality. Autoliv, a leader in automobile airbag manufacturing, has applied the system so well that it recently won the Utah State University Shingo Prize for Excellence in Manufacturing.

In Practice

Autoliv

Production supervisor Bill Webb thought he was being humble when he suggested to Toyota Motor Corp.'s Takashi Harada that Autoliv ranked around 3 on a scale of 1 to 10. He was stunned when Harada replied, "Maybe a minus-three." It was the opening lecture for Autoliv's education in the Toyota Production System.

Autoliv, which began in 1956 as Morton Automotive Safety and was acquired by Sweden's Autoliv AB in 1996, is a leader in the business of automobile airbag modules, with a commanding share of the market. Toyota was a major customer, though, and, with manufacturing defects rising, Autoliv was more than willing to accept Toyota's offer of help.

One of the first changes Harada made was to set up a system for soliciting and implementing employee suggestions, so that improvements in efficiency and safety began at the bottom. The company also made massive changes in inventory management and production processes.

At the time of Harada's comment, Autoliv was assembling airbag modules on a traditional linear, automated assembly line. The plant held about $23 million in parts—7 to 10 days worth of inventory—in a giant warehouse. Each day, Webb pushed mountains of inventory onto the assembly floor, but since he was never sure of what was needed, he often pushed a lot of it back at the end of the day. After the introduction of lean manufacturing, software was created to track parts automatically as they were being used. The data were communicated to the warehouse and parts were replenished just as they were needed. At the same time, the information was automatically conveyed to Autoliv's suppliers, so they could ship new stock. Inventory was cut by around 50 percent. The assembly process was redesigned into eighty-eight U-shaped production cells, each staffed by a handful of employees. Every 24 minutes, loud rock music signals the arrival of more parts and the rotation of each person to a different task. In addition to being trained to perform different tasks, employees were trained to continuosly look for improvements in every area.

The shift to lean manufacturing has paid off. Defects per million in module parts has been cut dramatically, from more than 1,100 in 1998 to just 16 in 2003. In that same year, Autoliv reported profits of $1 billion on revenues of $5.3 billion. "Their plants are as good as any in the world," said Ross Robson, administrator of the Shingo Prize for Excellence in Manufacturing.[31]

Leading by Design

Dell Computer

It's a tough time in the computer industry, but Dell Computer, like the Energizer bunny, just keeps going and going and going. Even competitors agree that there is just no better way to make, sell, and deliver personal computers (PCs) than the way Dell does it. Dell PCs are made to order and are delivered directly to the consumer. Each customer gets exactly the machine he or she wants—and gets it faster and cheaper than Dell's competitors could provide it.

Dell's speedy, flexible, cost-efficient system is illustrated by the company's newest factory, the Topfer Manufacturing facility near Dell headquarters in Round Rock, Texas, where Dell created a new way of making PCs that helped spur the company from number three to number one in PC sales. The process combines just-in-time delivery of parts from suppliers with a complicated, integrated computer manufacturing system that practically hands a worker the right part—whether it be any of a dozen different microprocessors or a specific combination of software—at just the right moment. The goal is not only to slash costs but also to save time by reducing the number of worker-touches per machine. Dell used to build computers in progressive assembly-line fashion, with up to twenty-five different people building one machine. Now, teams of three to seven workers build a complete computer from start to finish by following precise guidelines and using the components that arrive in carefully indicated racks in front

of them. The combination of baskets, racks, and traffic signals that keeps the whole operation moving is called the Pick-to-Light system. Pick-to-Light is based on an up-to-the minute database and software tying it to a stockroom system. That means the system can make sure teams have everything they need to complete an order, whether it be for 1 PC or 200. The system keeps track of which materials need replenishing and makes sure the racks and baskets are supplied with the proper components. Precise coordination, aided by sophisticated supply chain software, means that Dell can keep just 2 hours' worth of parts inventory and replenish only what it needs throughout the day. The flexible system works so well that 85 percent of orders are built, customized, and shipped within 8 hours.

Dell's new system has dramatically improved productivity, increasing manufacturing speed and throughput of custom-made computers by 150 percent. Employees are happier too because they now use more skills and build a complete machine within the team rather than performing the same boring, repetitive task on an assembly line. The system that began at one cutting-edge factory has been adopted at all of the company's manufacturing plants. With this kind of flexibility, no wonder Dell is number one.

Source: Kathryn Jones, "The Dell Way," *Business 2.0* (February 2003), 61-66; Stewart Deck, "Fine Line," *CIO* (February 1, 2000), 88–92; Andy Serwer, "Dell Does Domination," *Fortune* (January 21, 2002), 71–75; and Betsy Morris, "Can Michael Dell Escape the Box?" *Fortune* (October 16, 2000), 93–110.

Despite the success Autoliv has achieved, managers are continuing to make changes under what they now refer to as the Autoliv Production System. One lesson of lean manufacturing is that there is always room for improvement.

Lean manufacturing and flexible manufacturing systems have paved the way for **mass customization**, which refers to using mass-production technology to quickly and cost-effectively assemble goods that are uniquely designed to fit the demands of individual customers.[32] Mass customization first took hold when Dell Computer Corporation began building computers to order, and has since expanded to products as diverse as farm machinery, water heaters, clothing, and industrial detergents. Today, you can buy jeans customized for your body, glasses molded to precisely fit and flatter your face, windows in the exact shape and size you want for your new home, and pills with the specific combination of vitamins and minerals you need.[33]

Dell, described in the Leading by Design box, still provides an excellent example of the flexible manufacturing needed to make mass customization work.

Oshkosh Truck Company has thrived during an industry-wide slump in sales by offering customized fire, cement, garbage, and military trucks. Firefighters often travel to the plant to watch their new vehicle take shape, sometimes bringing paint chips to customize the color of their fleet.[34] Auto manufacturers, too, are moving toward mass customization. Sixty percent of the cars BMW sells in Europe are built to order.[35] U.S. manufacturers are building and remodeling plants to catch up with Japanese manufacturers such as Nissan and Honda in the ability to offer customers personalized products. For example, Ford's Kansas City, Missouri, plant, one of the largest manufacturing facilities in the world, produces around 490,000 F-150s, Ford Escapes, and Mazda Tributes a year. With just a little tweaking, the assembly lines in Kansas City can be programmed to manufacture any kind of car or truck Ford makes. The new F-150 has so many options that there are more than 1 million possible configurations of that model alone. Robots in wire cages do most of the work, while people act as assistants, taking measurements, refilling parts, and altering the system if something goes wrong. Assembly is synchronized by computers, right down to the last rearview mirror. Ford's flexible manufacturing system is projected to save the company $2 billion over the next 10 years.[36] Plant efficiency experts believe the trend toward mass customization will grow as flexible manufacturing systems become even more sophisticated and adaptive.

■ Performance and Structural Implications

The awesome advantage of flexible manufacturing is that products of different sizes, types, and customer requirements freely intermingle on the assembly line. Bar codes imprinted on a part enable machines to make instantaneous changes—such as putting a larger screw in a different location—without slowing the production line. A manufacturer can turn out an infinite variety of products in unlimited batch sizes, as illustrated in Exhibit 7.5. In traditional manufacturing systems studied by Woodward, choices were limited to the diagonal. Small batch allowed for high product flexibility and custom orders, but because of the "craftsmanship" involved in custom-making products, batch size was necessarily small. Mass production could have large batch size, but offered limited product flexibility. Continuous process could produce a single standard product in unlimited quantities. Flexible manufacturing systems allows plants to break free of this diagonal and to increase both batch size and product flexibility at the same time. When taken to its ultimate level, FMS allows for mass customization, with each specific product tailored to customer specification. This high-level use of FMS has been referred to as *computer-aided craftsmanship*.[37]

Studies suggest that with FMS, machine utilization is more efficient, labor productivity increases, scrap rates decrease, and product variety and customer satisfaction increase.[38] Many U.S. manufacturing companies are reinventing the factory using FMS and lean manufacturing systems to increase productivity.

Research into the relationship between FMS and organizational characteristics is beginning to emerge, and the patterns are summarized in Exhibit 7.6. Compared with traditional mass-production technologies, FMS has a narrow span of control, few hierarchical levels, adaptive tasks, low specialization, and decentralization, and the overall environment is characterized as organic and self-regulative. Employees need the skills to participate in teams; training is broad (so workers are not overly

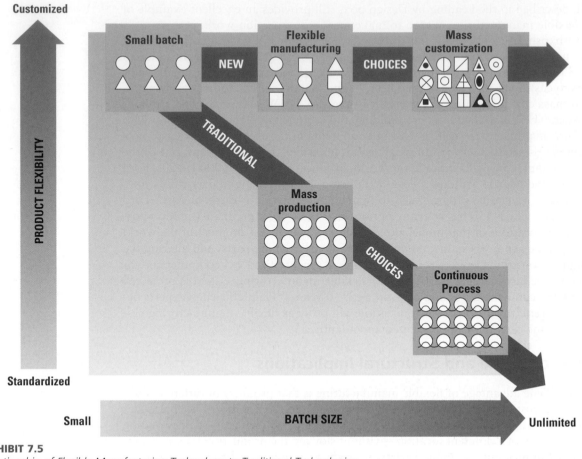

EXHIBIT 7.5

Relationship of Flexible Manufacturing Technology to Traditional Technologies

Source: Based on Jack Meredith, "The Strategic Advantages of New Manufacturing Technologies for Small Firms," *Strategic Management Journal* 8 (1987), 249–258; Paul Adler, "Managing Flexible Automation," *California Management Review* (Spring 1988), 34–56; and Otis Port, "Custom-made Direct from the Plant," *BusinessWeek*/21st Century Capitalism (November 18, 1994), 158–159.

specialized) and frequent (so workers are up-to-date). Expertise tends to be cognitive so workers can process abstract ideas and solve problems. Interorganizational relationships in FMS firms are characterized by changing demand from customers—which is easily handled with the new technology—and close relationships with a few suppliers that provide top-quality raw materials.[39]

Technology alone cannot give organizations the benefits of flexibility, quality, increased production, and greater customer satisfaction. Research suggests that FMS can become a competitive burden rather than a competitive advantage unless organizational structures and management processes are redesigned to take advantage of the new technology.[40] However, when top managers make a commitment to implement new structures and processes that empower workers and support a learning and knowledge-creating environment, FMS can help companies be more competitive.[41]

Characteristic	Mass Production	FMS
Structure		
Span of control	Wide	Narrow
Hierarchical levels	Many	Few
Tasks	Routine, repetitive	Adaptive, craftlike
Specialization	High	Low
Decision making	Centralized	Decentralized
Overall	Bureaucratic, mechanistic	Self-regulating, organic
Human Resources		
Interactions	Standalone	Teamwork
Training	Narrow, one time	Broad, frequent
Expertise	Manual, technical	Cognitive, social
		Solve problems
Interorganizational		
Customer demand	Stable	Changing
Suppliers	Many, arm's length	Few, close relationships

EXHIBIT 7.6

Comparison of Organizational Characteristics Associated with Mass Production and Flexible Manufacturing Systems

Source: Based on Patricia L. Nemetz and Louis W. Fry, "Flexible Manufacturing Organizations: Implications for Strategy Formulation and Organization Design," *Academy of Management Review* 13 (1988), 627–638; Paul S. Adler, "Managing Flexible Automation," *California Management Review* (Spring 1988), 34–56; and Jeremy Main, "Manufacturing the Right Way," *Fortune* (May 21, 1990) 54–64.

Core Organization Service Technology

Another big change occurring in the technology of organizations is the growing service sector. The percentage of the workforce employed in manufacturing continues to decline, not only in the United States, but in Canada, France, Germany, the United Kingdom, and Sweden as well.[42] The service sector has increased three times as fast as the manufacturing sector in the North American economy. More than two-thirds of the U.S. workforce is employed in services, such as hospitals, hotels, package delivery, online services, or telecommunications. Service technologies are different from manufacturing technologies and, in turn, require a specific organization structure.

Service Firms

Definition. Whereas manufacturing organizations achieve their primary purpose through the production of products, service organizations accomplish their primary purpose through the production and provision of services, such as education, health care, transportation, banking, and hospitality. Studies of service organizations have focused on the unique dimensions of service technologies. The characteristics of **service technology** are compared to those of manufacturing technology in Exhibit 7.7.

The most obvious difference is that service technology produces an *intangible output*, rather than a tangible product, such as a refrigerator produced by a manufacturing firm. A service is abstract and often consists of knowledge and ideas rather than a physical product. Thus, whereas manufacturers' products can be inventoried for later sale, services are characterized by *simultaneous production and*

Briefcase

As an organization manager, keep these guidelines in mind:

Use the concept of service technology to evaluate the production process in nonmanufacturing firms. Service technologies are intangible and must be located close to the customer. Hence, service organizations may have an organization structure with fewer boundary roles, greater geographical dispersion, decentralization, highly skilled employees in the technical core, and generally less control than in manufacturing organizations.

Service Technology

1. *Intangible output*
2. *Production and consumption take place simultaneously*
3. *Labor- and knowledge-intensive*
4. *Customer interaction generally high*
5. *Human element very important*
6. *Quality is perceived and difficult to measure*
7. *Rapid response time is usually necessary*
8. *Site of facility is extremely important*

Manufacturing Technology

1. *Tangible product*
2. *Products can be inventoried for later consumption*
3. *Capital asset-intensive*
4. *Little direct customer interaction*
5. *Human element may be less important*
6. *Quality is directly measured*
7. *Longer response time is acceptable*
8. *Site of facility is moderately important*

Service	Product and Service	Product
Airlines	*Fast-food outlets*	*Soft drink companies*
Hotels	*Cosmetics*	*Steel companies*
Consultants	*Real estate*	*Automobile manufacturers*
Health care	*Stockbrokers*	*Mining corporations*
Law firms	*Retail stores*	*Food processing plants*

EXHIBIT 7.7
Differences between Manufacturing and Service Technologies
Source: Based on F. F. Reichheld and W. E. Sasser, Jr., "Zero Defections: Quality Comes to Services," *Harvard Business Review* 68 (September–October 1990), 105–111; and David E. Bowen, Caren Siehl, and Benjamin Schneider, "A Framework for Analyzing Customer Service Orientations in Manufacturing," *Academy of Management Review* 14 (1989), 75–95.

consumption. A client meets with a doctor or attorney, for example, and students and teachers come together in the classroom or over the Internet. A service is an intangible product that does not exist until it is requested by the customer. It cannot be stored, inventoried, or viewed as a finished good. If a service is not consumed immediately upon production, it disappears.[43] This typically means that service firms are *labor- and knowledge-intensive,* with many employees needed to meet the needs of customers, whereas manufacturing firms tend to be *capital-intensive,* relying on mass production, continuous process, and flexible manufacturing technologies.[44]

Direct interaction between customer and employee is generally very high with services, while there is little direct interaction between customers and employees in the technical core of a manufacturing firm. This direct interaction means that the *human element* (employees) becomes extremely important in service firms. Whereas most people never meet the workers who manufactured their cars, they interact directly with the salesperson who sold them their Honda Element or Ford F-150. The treatment received from the salesperson—or from a doctor, lawyer, or hairstylist—affects the perception of the service received and the customer's level of satisfaction. The *quality of a service is perceived* and cannot be directly measured and compared in the same way that the quality of a tangible product can. Another characteristic that affects customer satisfaction and perception of quality service is *rapid response time.* A service must be provided when the customer wants and needs it. When you take a friend to dinner, you want to be seated and served in a timely manner; you would not be very satisfied if the host or manager told you to come back tomorrow when there would be more tables or servers available to accommodate you.

The final defining characteristic of service technology is that *site selection is often much more important* than with manufacturing. Because services are intangible, they have to be located where the customer wants to be served. Services are dispersed and located geographically close to customers. For example, fast-food franchises usually disperse their facilities into local stores. Most towns of even moderate size today have two or more McDonald's restaurants rather than one large one in order to provide service where customers want it.

In reality, it is difficult to find organizations that reflect 100 percent service or 100 percent manufacturing characteristics. Some service firms take on characteristics of manufacturers, and vice versa. Many manufacturing firms are placing a greater emphasis on customer service to differentiate themselves and be more competitive. At General Electric (GE), Chairman and CEO Jeffrey Immelt has implemented a program called "At the Customer, For the Customer," or ACFC. GE is putting customer service at the center of its business, offering to help with problems that often have nothing to do with GE products. A consultant from GE Aircraft Engines, for example, recently went onsite at Southwest Airlines to solve a nagging problem with a component made by another company.[45] In addition, manufacturing organizations have departments such as purchasing, HR, and marketing that are based on service technology. On the other hand, organizations such as gas stations, stockbrokers, retail stores, and restaurants belong to the service sector, but the provision of a product is a significant part of the transaction. The vast majority of organizations involve some combination of products and services. The important point is that all organizations can be classified along a continuum that includes both manufacturing and service characteristics, as illustrated in Exhibit 7.7.

New Directions in Services. Service firms have always tended toward providing *customized output*—that is, providing exactly the service each customer wants and needs. When you visit a hairstylist, you don't automatically get the same cut the stylist gave the three previous clients. The stylist cuts your hair the way you request it. However, the trend toward mass customization that is revolutionizing manufacturing has had a significant impact on the service sector as well. Customer expectations of what constitutes good service are rising.[46] Service companies such as the Ritz-Carlton Hotels, Vanguard, and Progressive Insurance use new technology to keep customers coming back. All Ritz-Carlton hotels are linked to a database filled with the preferences of half a million guests, allowing any desk clerk or bellhop to find out what your favorite wine is, whether you're allergic to feather pillows, and how many extra towels you want in your room.[47] At Vanguard, customer service reps teach customers how to effectively use the company's Web site. That means customers needing simple information now get it quickly and easily over the Web, and reps have more time to help clients with complicated questions. The new approach has had a positive impact on Vanguard's customer retention rates.[48]

The expectation for better service is also pushing service firms in industries from package delivery to banking to take a lesson from manufacturing. Japan Post, under pressure to cut a $191 million loss on operations, hired Toyota's Toshihiro Takahashi to help apply the Toyota Production System to the collection, sorting, and delivery of mail. In all, Takahashi's team came up with 370 improvements and reduced the post office's person-hours by 20 percent. The waste reduction is expected to cut costs by around $350 million a year.[49]

Structural Characteristic	Service	Product
1. Separate boundary roles	Few	Many
2. Geographical dispersion	Much	Little
3. Decision making	Decentralized	Centralized
4. Formalization	Lower	Higher
Human Resources		
1. Employee skill level	Higher	Lower
2. Skill emphasis	Interpersonal	Technical

■ Designing the Service Organization

The feature of service technologies with a distinct influence on organizational structure and control systems is the need for technical core employees to be close to the customer.[50] The differences between service and product organizations necessitated by customer contact are summarized in Exhibit 7.8.

The impact of customer contact on organization structure is reflected in the use of boundary roles and structural disaggregation.[51] Boundary roles are used extensively in manufacturing firms to handle customers and to reduce disruptions for the technical core. They are used less in service firms because a service is intangible and cannot be passed along by boundary spanners, so service customers must interact directly with technical employees, such as doctors or brokers.

A service firm deals in information and intangible outputs and does not need to be large. Its greatest economies are achieved through disaggregation into small units that can be located close to customers. Stockbrokers, doctors' clinics, consulting firms, and banks disperse their facilities into regional and local offices. Some fast-food chains, such as Taco Bell, are taking this a step further, selling chicken tacos and bean burritos anywhere people gather—airports, supermarkets, college campuses, or street corners.

Manufacturing firms, on the other hand, tend to aggregate operations in a single area that has raw materials and an available workforce. A large manufacturing firm can take advantage of economies derived from expensive machinery and long production runs.

Service technology also influences internal organization characteristics used to direct and control the organization. For one thing, the skills of technical core employees typically need to be higher. These employees need enough knowledge and awareness to handle customer problems rather than just enough to perform mechanical tasks. Employees need social and interpersonal skills as well as technical skills.[52] Because of higher skills and structural dispersion, decision making often tends to be decentralized in service firms, and formalization tends to be low. In general, employees in service organizations have more freedom and discretion on the job. However, some service organizations, such as many fast-food chains, have set rules and procedures for customer service. The London-based chain Pret A Manger hopes to differentiate itself in the fast-food market by taking a different approach.

"Would you like fries with that?" The standard line is rattled off by fast-food workers who have been taught to follow a script in serving customers. But at Pret A Manger, a fast-growing chain based in London, you won't hear any standard lines. Employees aren't given scripts for serving customers or pigeonholed into performing the same repetitious tasks all day long. Managers want people to let their own personalities come through in offering each customer the best service possible. "Our customers say, 'I like to be served by human beings,'" explains Ewan Stickley, head of employee training. London's *Sunday Times* recently ranked Pret A Manger as one of the top fifty companies to work for in Britain—the only restaurant to make the cut.

Pret A Manger (faux French for "ready to eat") operates 118 outlets in the United Kingdom and is expanding into the United States. "Nobody has ever gone to America, the home of fast food, with a concept that turned out to be a successful national chain. We think we can do that," says chairman and CEO Andrew Rolfe. Pret's concept is based on organizing a mass-market service business around innovation rather than standardization. The menu is based on salads, fresh-made sandwiches, hot soups, sushi, and a variety of yogurt parfaits and blended juices. Menu items are constantly changing, based on what sells and what customers want. Pret A Manger has built in a number of mechanisms for getting fast feedback. The CEO reviews customer and employee comments every Friday. Employees who send in the best ideas for changes to products or procedures can win up to $1,500. Managers spend one day each quarter working in a store to keep in touch with customers and see how their policies affect employees.

In its native England, Pret A Manger has been a huge hit. Translating that success to the United States has been more of a struggle. To help make the transition, Pret has allied itself with a powerful partner—McDonald's. Some worry that McDonald's might corrupt the company's values and emphasis on fresh, healthy food and individualized service, but Rolfe believes he and his employees are up to the challenge.[53]

In Practice
Pret A Manger

Understanding the nature of its service technology helps managers at Pret A Manger align strategy, structure, and management processes that are quite different from those for a product-based or traditional manufacturing technology. For example, the concept of separating complex tasks into a series of small jobs and exploiting economies of scale is a cornerstone of traditional manufacturing, but researchers have found that applying it to service organizations often does not work so well.[54] Some service firms have redesigned jobs to separate low– and high–customer-contact activities, with more rules and standardization in the low-contact jobs. High-touch service jobs, like those at Pret A Manger, need more freedom and less control to satisfy customers.

Understanding service technology is important for manufacturing firms, too, especially as they put greater emphasis on customer service. Managers can use these concepts and ideas to strengthen their company's service orientation.

Now let's turn to another perspective on technology, that of production activities within specific organizational departments. Departments often have characteristics similar to those of service technology, providing services to other departments within the organization.

Non-Core Departmental Technology

This section shifts to the department level of analysis for departments not necessarily within the technical core. Each department in an organization has a production process that consists of a distinct technology. General Motors has departments for engineering, R&D, HR, advertising, quality control, finance, and dozens of other functions. This section analyzes the nature of departmental technology and its relationship with departmental structure.

The framework that has had the greatest impact on the understanding of departmental technologies was developed by Charles Perrow.[55] Perrow's model has been useful for a broad range of technologies, which made it ideal for research into departmental activities.

Variety

Perrow specified two dimensions of departmental activities that were relevant to organization structure and process. The first is the number of exceptions in the work. This refers to task **variety**, which is the frequency of unexpected and novel events that occur in the conversion process. Task variety concerns whether work processes are performed the same way every time or differ from time to time as employees transform the organization's inputs into outputs.[56] When individuals encounter a large number of unexpected situations, with frequent problems, variety is considered high. When there are few problems, and when day-to-day job requirements are repetitive, technology contains little variety. Variety in departments can range from repeating a single act, such as on a traditional assembly line, to working on a series of unrelated problems or projects.

Analyzability

The second dimension of technology concerns the **analyzability** of work activities. When the conversion process is analyzable, the work can be reduced to mechanical steps and participants can follow an objective, computational procedure to solve problems. Problem solution may involve the use of standard procedures, such as instructions and manuals, or technical knowledge, such as that in a textbook or handbook. On the other hand, some work is not analyzable. When problems arise, it is difficult to identify the correct solution. There is no store of techniques or procedures to tell a person exactly what to do. The cause of or solution to a problem is not clear, so employees rely on accumulated experience, intuition, and judgment. The final solution to a problem is often the result of wisdom and experience and not the result of standard procedures. Philippos Poulos, a tone regulator at Steinway & Sons, has an unanalyzable technology. Tone regulators carefully check each piano's hammers to ensure they produce the proper Steinway sound.[57] These quality-control tasks require years of experience and practice. Standard procedures will not tell a person how to do such tasks.

Framework

The two dimensions of technology and examples of departmental activities on Perrow's framework are shown in Exhibit 7.9. The dimensions of variety and analyzability form the basis for four major categories of technology: routine, craft, engineering, and nonroutine.

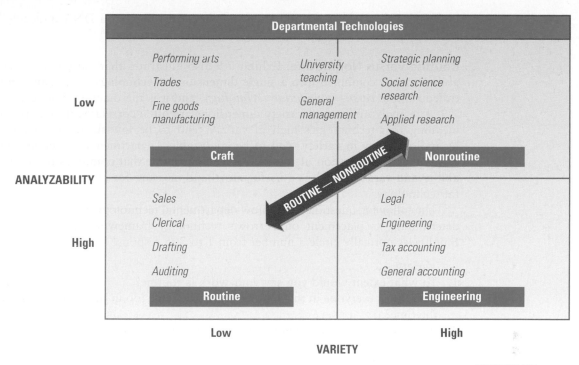

EXHIBIT 7.9
Framework for Department Technologies
Source: Adapted with permission from Richard Daft and Norman Macintosh, "A New Approach to Design and Use of Management Information," *California Management Review* 21 (1978), 82–92. Copyright © 1978 by the Regents of the University of California. Reprinted by permission of the Regents.

Routine technologies are characterized by little task variety and the use of objective, computational procedures. The tasks are formalized and standardized. Examples include an automobile assembly line and a bank teller department.

Craft technologies are characterized by a fairly stable stream of activities, but the conversion process is not analyzable or well understood. Tasks require extensive training and experience because employees respond to intangible factors on the basis of wisdom, intuition, and experience. Although advances in machine technologies seem to have reduced the number of craft technologies in organizations, craft technologies are still important. For example, steel furnace engineers continue to mix steel based on intuition and experience, pattern makers at apparel firms convert rough designers' sketches into salable garments, and teams of writers for television series such as *Everwood* or *OC* convert ideas into story lines.

Engineering technologies tend to be complex because there is substantial variety in the tasks performed. However, the various activities are usually handled on the basis of established formulas, procedures, and techniques. Employees normally refer to a well-developed body of knowledge to handle problems. Engineering and accounting tasks usually fall in this category.

Nonroutine technologies have high task variety, and the conversion process is not analyzable or well understood. In nonroutine technology, a great deal of effort is devoted to analyzing problems and activities. Several equally acceptable options typically can be found. Experience and technical knowledge are used to solve problems and perform the work. Basic research, strategic planning, and other work that involves new projects and unexpected problems are nonroutine. The blossoming biotechnology industry also represents a nonroutine technology. Breakthroughs in understanding metabolism and physiology at a cellular level depend on highly trained employees who use their experience and intuition as well as scientific knowledge. A scientist manipulating the chemical rungs on a DNA molecule has been compared to a musician playing variations on a theme.[58]

Routine versus Nonroutine. Exhibit 7.9 also illustrates that variety and analyzability can be combined into a single dimension of technology. This dimension is called *routine versus nonroutine technology*, and it is the diagonal line in Exhibit 7.9. The analyzability and variety dimensions are often correlated in departments, meaning that technologies high in variety tend to be low in analyzability, and technologies low in variety tend to be analyzable. Departments can be evaluated along a single dimension of routine versus nonroutine that combines both analyzability and variety, which is a useful shorthand measure for analyzing departmental technology.

The following questions show how departmental technology can be analyzed for determining its placement on Perrow's technology framework in Exhibit 7.9.[59] Employees normally circle a number from 1 to 7 in response to each question.

Variety:
1. To what extent would you say your work is routine?
2. Does most everyone in this unit do about the same job in the same way most of the time?
3. Are unit members performing repetitive activities in doing their jobs?

Analyzability:
1. To what extent is there a clearly known way to do the major types of work you normally encounter?
2. To what extent is there an understandable sequence of steps that can be followed in doing your work?
3. To do your work, to what extent can you actually rely on established procedures and practices?

If answers to the above questions indicate high scores for analyzability and low scores for variety, the department would have a routine technology. If the opposite occurs, the technology would be nonroutine. Low variety and low analyzability indicate a craft technology, and high variety and high analyzability indicate an engineering technology. As a practical matter, most departments fit somewhere along the diagonal and can be most easily characterized as routine or nonroutine.

Department Design

Once the nature of a department's technology has been identified, the appropriate structure can be determined. Department technology tends to be associated with a cluster of departmental characteristics, such as the skill level of employees, formalization, and pattern of communication. Definite patterns exist in the relationship between work unit technology and structural characteristics, which are associated with departmental performance.[60] Key relationships between technology and other dimensions of departments are described in this section and are summarized in Exhibit 7.10.

The overall structure of departments may be characterized as either organic or mechanistic. Routine technologies are associated with a mechanistic structure and processes, with formal rules and rigid management processes. Nonroutine

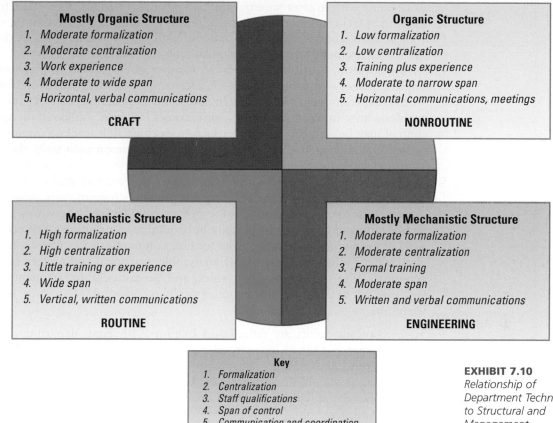

EXHIBIT 7.10
Relationship of Department Technology to Structural and Management Characteristics

---

technologies are associated with an organic structure, and department management is more flexible and free-flowing. The specific design characteristics of formalization, centralization, worker skill level, span of control, and communication and coordination vary, depending on work unit technology.

1. *Formalization.* Routine technology is characterized by standardization and division of labor into small tasks that are governed by formal rules and procedures. For nonroutine tasks, the structure is less formal and less standardized. When variety is high, as in a research department, fewer activities are covered by formal procedures.[61]
2. *Decentralization.* In routine technologies, most decision making about task activities is centralized to management.[62] In engineering technologies, employees with technical training tend to acquire moderate decision authority because technical knowledge is important to task accomplishment. Production employees who have long experience obtain decision authority in craft technologies because they know how to respond to problems. Decentralization to employees is greatest in nonroutine settings, where many decisions are made by employees.
3. *Worker skill level.* Work staff in routine technologies typically require little education or experience, which is congruent with repetitive work activities. In

Briefcase

As an organization manager, keep these guidelines in mind:

Use the two dimensions of variety and analyzability to discover whether the work in a department is routine or nonroutine. If the work in a department is routine, use a mechanistic structure and process. If the work in a department is nonroutine, use an organic management process.

work units with greater variety, staff are more skilled and often have formal training in technical schools or universities. Training for craft activities, which are less analyzable, is more likely to be through job experience. Nonroutine activities require both formal education and job experience.[63]

4. *Span of control.* Span of control is the number of employees who report to a single manager or supervisor. This characteristic is normally influenced by departmental technology. The more complex and nonroutine the task, the more problems arise in which the supervisor becomes involved. Although the span of control may be influenced by other factors, such as skill level of employees, it typically should be smaller for complex tasks because on such tasks the supervisor and subordinate must interact frequently.[64]

5. *Communication and coordination.* Communication activity and frequency increase as task variety increases.[65] Frequent problems require more information sharing to solve problems and ensure proper completion of activities. The direction of communication is typically horizontal in nonroutine work units and vertical in routine work units.[66] The form of communication varies by task analyzability.[67] When tasks are highly analyzable, statistical and written forms of communication (memos, reports, rules, and procedures) are frequent. When tasks are less analyzable, information typically is conveyed face-to-face, over the telephone, or in group meetings.

Two important points are reflected in Exhibit 7.10. First, departments differ from one another and can be categorized according to their workflow technology.[68] Second, structural and management processes differ based on departmental technology. Managers should design their departments so that requirements based on technology can be met. Design problems are most visible when the design is clearly inconsistent with technology. Studies have found that when structure and communication characteristics did not reflect technology, departments tended to be less effective.[69] Employees could not communicate with the frequency needed to solve problems. Consider how the design characteristics of Parkland Memorial Hospital's labor and delivery unit contribute to a smoothly functioning department.

In Practice

Parkland Memorial Hospital

Parkland Memorial Hospital in Dallas, Texas, delivered 16,597 babies in 2001—more than any other hospital in the United States, 40 or 50 babies a day. The hospital's stillbirth and neonatal death rates are lower than the national average, despite the fact that 95 percent of the women who come into the labor and delivery (L&D) unit are indigent and many have drug or alcohol problems. As the county hospital, Parkland takes everyone—from private patients to illegal immigrants—and manages to deliver high-quality care on a shoestring. "We don't have fancy birthing rooms, hardwood floors, and pretty wallpaper," says RN Reina Duerinckx. "But we have the important stuff." Part of the important stuff that helps Parkland achieve such phenomenal results with limited staff and money is L&D's design. Although L&D operates within a set of carefully codified protocols regarding medical care, the rules are applied in a relaxed, informal, and flexible way. The structure gives people a sense of order among the chaos, but flexibility and teamwork by L&D's highly trained professionals translate the rules into appropriate action. Decision making is decentralized so that employees can respond on their own initiative based on problems that arise. "The protocols are not recipes," says Miriam Sibley, senior VP of Parkland's Women and Children's Services. "They give us a way to organize a tremendous amount of work."

Another mechanism for maintaining a sense of order is an elaborate hierarchy that precisely defines duties and authority at every level. This ensures that each patient is served by the best-qualified person for each step of service. However, the L&D unit has an egalitarian, all-hands-on-deck feel. It's not unusual to see a doctor mopping out a delivery room to get ready for the next mother. When shifts change at 7:00 A.M., clerks, nurses, and doctors are all briefing the incoming staff. People call each other by their first (or last) names and everyone wears the same blue scrubs and shares the same locker rooms. Although Parkland managers believe it's important to have defined roles, they make clear that there should be no boundaries. Communication is frequent, face-to-face, and flowing in all directions. It has to be when as many as fourteen babies are delivered in a single hour and the next crisis might be right around the corner.[70]

Workflow Interdependence among Departments

So far, this chapter has explored how organization and department technologies influence structural design. The final characteristic of technology that influences structure is called interdependence. **Interdependence** means the extent to which departments depend on each other for resources or materials to accomplish their tasks. Low interdependence means that departments can do their work independently of each other and have little need for interaction, consultation, or exchange of materials. High interdependence means departments must constantly exchange resources.

Types

James Thompson defined three types of interdependence that influence organization structure.[71] These interdependencies are illustrated in Exhibit 7.11 and are discussed in the following sections.

Pooled. **Pooled interdependence** is the lowest form of interdependence among departments. In this form, work does not flow between units. Each department is part of the organization and contributes to the common good of the organization, but works independently. Subway restaurants or branch banks are examples of pooled interdependence. An outlet in Chicago need not interact with an outlet in Urbana. Pooled interdependence may be associated with the relationships within a *divisional structure*, defined in Chapter 3. Divisions or branches share financial resources from a common pool, and the success of each division contributes to the success of the overall organization.

Thompson proposed that pooled interdependence would exist in firms with what he called a mediating technology. A **mediating technology** provides products or services that mediate or link clients from the external environment and, in so doing, allows each department to work independently. Banks, brokerage firms, and real estate offices all mediate between buyers and sellers, but the offices work independently within the organization.

The management implications associated with pooled interdependence are quite simple. Thompson argued that managers should use rules and procedures to standardize activities across departments. Each department should use the same procedures and financial statements so the outcomes of all departments can be measured and pooled. Very little day-to-day coordination is required among units.

Form of Interdependence	Demands on Horizontal Communication, Decision Making	Type of Coordination Required	Priority for Locating Units Close Together
Pooled (bank) **Clients**	Low communication	Standardization, rules, procedures Divisional structure	Low
Sequential (assembly line) Client	Medium communication	Plans, schedules, feedback Task forces	Medium
Reciprocal (hospital) Client	High communication	Mutual adjustment, cross-departmental meetings, teamwork Horizontal structure	High

Briefcase

As an organization manager, keep these guidelines in mind:

Evaluate the interdependencies among organizational departments. Use the general rule that, as interdependencies increase, mechanisms for coordination must also increase. Consider a divisional structure for pooled interdependence. For sequential interdependence, use task forces and integrators for greater horizontal coordination. At the highest level of interdependence (reciprocal interdependence), a horizontal structure may be appropriate.

Sequential. When interdependence is of serial form, with parts produced in one department becoming inputs to another department, it is called **sequential interdependence.** The first department must perform correctly for the second department to perform correctly. This is a higher level of interdependence than pooled interdependence, because departments exchange resources and depend on others to perform well. Sequential interdependence creates a greater need for horizontal mechanisms such as integrators or task forces.

Sequential interdependence occurs in what Thompson called **long-linked technology,** which "refers to the combination in one organization of successive stages of production; each stage of production uses as its inputs the production of the preceding stage and produces inputs for the following stage."[72] An example of sequential interdependence comes from the shipbuilding industry. Until recently, ship designers made patterns and molds out of paper and plywood, which were passed on to assembly. Mistakes in measurements or pattern mixups, though, often caused errors in the cutting and assembly process, leading to delays and increased costs. Naval architect Filippo Cali created a complex software program that serves as a bridge between design and assembly. The software eliminates the need for paper and plywood molds by putting that crucial part of the design process inside a computer program.[73] Another example of sequential interdependence would be an automobile assembly line, which must have all the parts it needs, such as engines, steering mechanisms, and tires, to keep production rolling.

The management requirements for sequential interdependence are more demanding than those for pooled interdependence. Coordination among the linked plants or departments is required. Since the interdependence implies a one-way flow of materials, extensive planning and scheduling are generally needed. Department B needs to know what to expect from Department A so both can perform effectively. Some day-to-day communication among plants or departments is also needed to handle unexpected problems and exceptions that arise.

Reciprocal. The highest level of interdependence is **reciprocal interdependence**. This exists when the output of operation A is the input to operation B, and the output of operation B is the input back again to operation A. The outputs of departments influence those departments in reciprocal fashion.

Reciprocal interdependence tends to occur in organizations with what Thompson called **intensive technologies**, which provide a variety of products or services in combination to a client. Hospitals are an excellent example because they provide coordinated services to patients. A patient may move back and forth between x-ray, surgery, and physical therapy as needed to be cured. A firm developing new products is another example. Intense coordination is needed between design, engineering, manufacturing, and marketing to combine all their resources to suit the customer's product need.

Management requirements are greatest in the case of reciprocal interdependence. Because reciprocal interdependence requires that departments work together intimately and be closely coordinated, a horizontal structure may be appropriate. The structure must allow for frequent horizontal communication and adjustment as at Parkland Memorial Hospital. Extensive planning is required, but plans will not anticipate or solve all problems. Daily interaction and mutual adjustment among departments are required. Managers from several departments are jointly involved in face-to-face coordination, teamwork, and decision making. Reciprocal interdependence is the most complex interdependence for organizations to handle.

■ Structural Priority

As indicated in Exhibit 7.11, because decision making, communication, and coordination problems are greatest for reciprocal interdependence, reciprocal interdependence should receive first priority in organization structure. New product development is one area of reciprocal interdependence that is of growing concern to managers as companies face increasing pressure to get new products to market fast. Many firms are revamping the design-manufacturing relationship by closely integrating CAD and CAM technologies discussed earlier in this chapter.[74] Activities that are reciprocally interdependent should be grouped close together in the organization so managers have easy access to one another for mutual adjustment. These units should report to the same person on the organization chart and should be physically close so the time and effort for coordination can be minimized. A horizontal structure, with linked sets of teams working on core processes, can provide the close coordination needed to support reciprocal interdependence. Poor coordination will result in poor performance for the organization. If reciprocally interdependent units are not located close together, the organization should design mechanisms for coordination, such as daily meetings between departments or an intranet to facilitate communication. The next priority is given to sequential interdependencies, and finally to pooled interdependencies.

EXHIBIT 7.12
Primary Means to Achieve Coordination for Different Levels of Task Interdependence in a Manufacturing Firm
Source: Adapted from Andrew H. Van de Ven, Andre Delbecq, and Richard Koenig, "Determinants of Communication Modes within Organizations," *American Sociological Review* 41 (1976), 330.

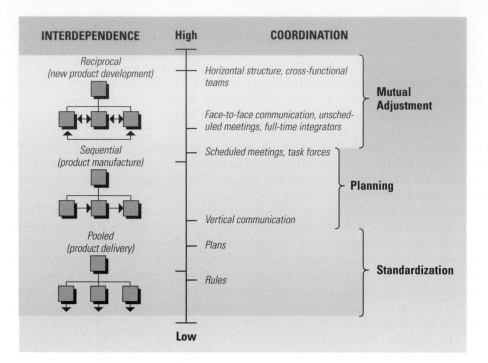

This strategy of organizing keeps the communication channels short where coordination is most critical to organizational success. For example, Boise Cascade Corporation experienced poor service to customers because customer-service reps located in New York City were not coordinating with production planners in Oregon plants. Customers couldn't get delivery as needed. Boise was reorganized, and the two groups were consolidated under one roof, reporting to the same supervisor at division headquarters. Now customer needs are met because customer-service reps work with production planning to schedule customer orders.

■ Structural Implications

Most organizations experience various levels of interdependence, and structure can be designed to fit these needs, as illustrated in Exhibit 7.12.[75] In a manufacturing firm, new product development entails reciprocal interdependence among the design, engineering, purchasing, manufacturing, and sales departments. Perhaps a horizontal structure or cross-functional teams could be used to handle the back-and-forth flow of information and resources. Once a product is designed, its actual manufacture would be sequential interdependence, with a flow of goods from one department to another, such as among purchasing, inventory, production control, manufacturing, and assembly. The actual ordering and delivery of products is pooled interdependence, with warehouses working independently. Customers could place an order with the nearest facility, which would not require coordination among warehouses, except in unusual cases such as a stock outage.

The three levels of interdependence are illustrated by a study of athletic teams that examined interdependency among players and how it influences other aspects of baseball, football, and basketball teams.

A major difference among baseball, football, and basketball is the interdependence among players. Baseball is low in interdependence, football is medium, and basketball represents the highest player interdependence. The relationships among interdependence and other characteristics of team play are illustrated in Exhibit 7.13.

Pete Rose said, "Baseball is a team game, but nine men who reach their individual goals make a nice team." In baseball, interdependence among team players is low and can be defined as pooled. Each member acts independently, taking a turn at bat and playing his or her own position. When interaction does occur, it is between only two or three players, as in a double play. Players are physically dispersed, and the rules of the game are the primary means of coordinating players. Players practice and develop their skills individually, such as by taking batting practice and undergoing physical conditioning. Management's job is to select good players. If each player is successful as an individual, the team should win.

In Practice
Athletic Teams

EXHIBIT 7.13

Relationships among Interdependence and Other Characteristics of Team Play

	Baseball	Football	Basketball
Interdependence	Pooled	Sequential	Reciprocal
Physical dispersion of players	High	Medium	Low
Coordination	Rules that govern the sport	Game plan and position roles	Mutual adjustment and shared responsibility
Key management job	Select players and develop their skills	Prepare and execute game	Influence flow of game

Source: Based on William Pasmore, Carol E. Francis, and Jeffrey Haldeman, "Sociotechnical Systems: A North American Reflection on the Empirical Studies of the 70s," *Human Relations* 35 (1982), 1179–1204.

In football, interdependence among players is higher and tends to be sequential. The line first blocks the opponents to enable the backs to run or pass. Plays are performed sequentially from first down to fourth down. Physical dispersion is medium, which allows players to operate as a coordinated unit. The primary mechanism for coordinating players is developing a game plan along with rules that govern the behavior of team members. Each player has an assignment that fits with other assignments, and management designs the game plan to achieve victory.

In basketball, interdependence tends to be reciprocal. The game is free-flowing, and the division of labor is less precise than in other sports. Each player is involved in both offense and defense, handles the ball, and attempts to score. The ball flows back and forth among players. Team members interact in a dynamic flow to achieve victory. Management skills involve the ability to influence this dynamic process, either by substituting players or by working the ball into certain areas. Players must learn to adapt to the flow of the game and to one another as events unfold.

Interdependence among players is a primary factor explaining the difference among the three sports. Baseball is organized around an autonomous individual, football around groups that are sequentially interdependent, and basketball around the free flow of reciprocal players.[76]

Impact of Technology on Job Design

So far, this chapter has described models for analyzing how manufacturing, service, and department technologies influence structure and management processes. The relationship between a new technology and organization seems to follow a pattern, beginning with immediate effects on the content of jobs followed (after a longer period) by impact on design of the organization. The ultimate impact of technology on employees can be partially understood through the concepts of job design and sociotechnical systems.

Job Design

Job design includes the assignment of goals and tasks to be accomplished by employees. Managers may consciously change job design to improve productivity or worker motivation. For example, when workers are involved in performing boring, repetitive tasks, managers may introduce **job rotation**, which means moving employees from job to job to give them a greater variety of tasks. However, managers may also unconsciously influence job design through the introduction of new technologies, which can change how jobs are done and the very nature of jobs.[77] Managers should understand how the introduction of a new technology may affect employees' jobs. The common theme of new technologies in the workplace is that they in some way substitute machinery for human labor in transforming inputs into outputs. Automated teller machines (ATMs) have replaced thousands of human bank tellers, for example. IBM has even built a plant in Austin, Texas, that can produce laptop computers without the help of a single worker.[78]

In addition to actually replacing human workers, technology may have several different effects on the human jobs that remain. Research has indicated that mass-production technologies tend to produce **job simplification**, which means that the variety and difficulty of tasks performed by a single person are reduced. The consequence is boring, repetitive jobs that generally provide little satisfaction. More advanced technology, on the other hand, tends to cause **job enrichment**, meaning that the job provides greater responsibility, recognition, and opportunities for growth and development. These technologies create a greater need for employee training and education because workers need higher-level skills and greater competence to master their tasks. For example, ATMs took most of the routine tasks (deposits and withdrawals) away from bank tellers and left them with the more complex tasks that require higher-level skills. Studies of flexible manufacturing found that it produces three noticeable results for employees: more opportunities for intellectual mastery and enhanced cognitive skills for workers; more worker responsibility for results; and greater interdependence among workers, enabling more social interaction and the development of teamwork and coordination skills.[79] Flexible manufacturing technology may also contribute to **job enlargement**, which is an expansion of the number of different tasks performed by an employee. Fewer workers are needed with the new technology, and each employee has to be able to perform a greater number and variety of tasks.

With advanced technology, workers have to keep learning new skills because technology is changing so rapidly. Advances in *information technology*, to be discussed in detail in the next chapter, are having a significant effect on jobs in the service industry, including doctors' offices and medical clinics, law firms, financial

Briefcase

As an organization manager, keep these guidelines in mind:

Be aware that the introduction of a new technology has significant impact on job design. Consider using the sociotechnical systems approach to balance the needs of workers with the requirements of the new technological system.

The Social System

- *Individual and team behaviors*
- *Organizational/team culture*
- *Management practices*
- *Leadership style*
- *Degree of communication openness*
- *Individual needs and desires*

Design for Joint Optimization

Work roles, tasks, workflow

Goals and values

Skills and abilities

The Technical System

- *Type of production technology (small batch, mass production, FMS, etc.)*
- *Level of interdependence (pooled, sequential, reciprocal)*
- *Physical work setting*
- *Complexity of production process (variety and analyzability)*
- *Nature of raw materials*
- *Time pressure*

EXHIBIT 7.14
Sociotechnical Systems Model
Sources: Based on T. Cummings, "Self-Regulating Work Groups: A Socio-Technical Synthesis," *Academy of Management Review* 3 (1978), 625–634; Don Hellriegel, John W. Slocum, and Richard W. Woodman, *Organizational Behavior*, 8th ed. (Cincinnati, Ohio: South-Western, 1998), 492; and Gregory B. Northcraft and Margaret A. Neale, *Organizational Behavior: A Management Challenge*, 2nd ed. (Fort Worth, Tex.: The Dryden Press, 1994), 551.

planners, and libraries. Workers may find that their jobs change almost daily because of new software programs, increased use of the Internet, and other advances in information technology.

Advanced technology does not always have a positive effect on employees, but research findings in general are encouraging, suggesting that jobs for workers are enriched rather than simplified, engaging their higher mental capacities, offering opportunities for learning and growth, and providing greater job satisfaction.

■ Sociotechnical Systems

The **sociotechnical systems approach** recognizes the interaction of technical and human needs in effective job design, combining the needs of people with the organization's need for technical efficiency. The *socio* portion of the approach refers to the people and groups that work in organizations and how work is organized and coordinated. The *technical* portion refers to the materials, tools, machines, and processes used to transform organizational inputs into outputs.

Exhibit 7.14 illustrates the three primary components of the sociotechnical systems model.[80] The *social system* includes all human elements—such as individual and team behaviors, organizational culture, management practices, and degree of communication openness—that can influence the performance of work. The *technical system* refers to the type of production technology, the level of interdependence, the complexity of tasks, and so forth. The goal of the sociotechnical systems approach is to design the organization for **joint optimization**, which means that an organization functions best only when the social and technical systems are designed to fit the needs of one another. Designing the organization to meet human needs while ignoring the technical systems, or changing technology to improve efficiency while ignoring human needs, may inadvertently cause performance problems. The sociotechnical systems approach attempts to find a balance between what workers want and need and the technical requirements of the organization's production system.[81]

One example comes from a museum that installed a closed-circuit TV system. Rather than having several guards patrolling the museum and grounds, the television could easily be monitored by a single guard. Although the technology saved money because only one guard was needed per shift, it led to unexpected performance problems. Guards had previously enjoyed the social interaction provided by patrolling; monitoring a closed-circuit television led to alienation and boredom. When a federal agency did an 18-month test of the system, only 5 percent of several thousand experimental covert intrusions were detected by the guard.[82] The system was inadequate because human needs were not taken into account.

Sociotechnical principles evolved from the work of the Tavistock Institute, a research organization in England, during the 1950s and 1960s.[83] Examples of organizational change using sociotechnical systems principles have occurred in numerous organizations, including General Motors, Volvo, the Tennessee Valley Authority (TVA), and Procter & Gamble.[84] Although there have been failures, in many of these applications, the joint optimization of changes in technology and structure to meet the needs of people as well as efficiency improved performance, safety, quality, absenteeism, and turnover. In some cases, work design was not the most efficient based on technical and scientific principles, but worker involvement and commitment more than made up for the difference. Thus, once again research shows that new technologies need not have a negative impact on workers, because the technology often requires higher-level mental and social skills and can be organized to encourage the involvement and commitment of employees, thereby benefiting both the employee and the organization.

The sociotechnical systems principle that people should be viewed as resources and provided with appropriate skills, meaningful work, and suitable rewards becomes even more important in today's world of growing technological complexity.[85] One study of paper manufacturers found that organizations that put too much faith in machines and technology and pay little attention to the appropriate management of people do not achieve advances in productivity and flexibility. Today's most successful companies strive to find the right mix of machines, computer systems, and people and the most effective way to coordinate them.[86]

Although many principles of sociotechnical systems theory are still valid, current scholars and researchers are also arguing for an expansion of the approach to capture the dynamic nature of today's organizations, the chaotic environment, and the shift from routine to nonroutine jobs brought about by advances in technology.[87]

Summary and Interpretation

This chapter reviewed several frameworks and key research findings on the topic of organizational technology. The potential importance of technology as a factor in organizational structure was discovered during the 1960s. Since then, a flurry of research activity has been undertaken to understand more precisely the relationship of technology to other characteristics of organizations.

Five ideas in the technology literature stand out. The first is Woodward's research into manufacturing technology. Woodward went into organizations and collected practical data on technology characteristics, organization structure, and management systems. She found clear relationships between technology and structure in high-performing organizations. Her findings are so clear that managers can analyze their own organizations on the same dimensions of technology and structure. In addition, technology and structure can be co-aligned with organizational strategy to meet changing needs and provide new competitive advantages.

The second important idea is that service technologies differ in a systematic way from manufacturing technologies. Service technologies are characterized by intangible outcomes and direct client involvement in the production process. Service firms do not have the fixed, machine-based technologies that appear in manufacturing organizations; hence, organization design often differs as well.

The third significant idea is Perrow's framework applied to department technologies. Understanding the variety and analyzability of a technology tells one about the management style, structure, and process that should characterize that department. Routine technologies are characterized by mechanistic structure and nonroutine technologies by organic structure. Applying the wrong management system to a department will result in dissatisfaction and reduced efficiency.

The fourth important idea is interdependence among departments. The extent to which departments depend on each other for materials, information, or other resources determines the amount of coordination required between them. As interdependence increases, demands on the organization for coordination increase. Organization design must allow for the correct amount of communication and coordination to handle interdependence across departments.

The fifth important idea is that new flexible manufacturing systems are being adopted by organizations and having impact on organization design. For the most part, the impact is positive, with shifts toward more organic structures both on the shop floor and in the management hierarchy. These technologies replace routine jobs, give employees more autonomy, produce more challenging jobs, encourage teamwork, and let the organization be more flexible and responsive. The new technologies are enriching jobs to the point where organizations are happier places to work.

Several principles of sociotechnical systems theory, which attempts to design the technical and human aspects of an organization to fit one another, are increasingly important as advances in technology alter the nature of jobs and social interaction in today's companies.

Key Concepts

analyzability	long-linked technology
continuous process production	mass customization
core technology	mediating technology
craft technologies	non-core technology
engineering technologies	nonroutine technologies
flexible manufacturing systems	pooled interdependence
intensive technologies	reciprocal interdependence
interdependence	routine technologies
job design	sequential interdependence
job enlargement	service technology
job enrichment	small-batch production
job rotation	sociotechnical systems approach
job simplification	technical complexity
joint optimization	technology
large-batch production	variety
lean manufacturing	

Discussion Questions

1. Where would your university or college department be located on Perrow's technology framework? Look for the underlying variety and analyzability characteristics when making your assessment. Would a department devoted exclusively to teaching be put in a different quadrant from a department devoted exclusively to research?

2. Explain Thompson's levels of interdependence. Identify an example of each level of interdependence in the university or college setting. What kinds of coordination mechanisms should an administration develop to handle each level of interdependence?

3. Describe Woodward's classification of organizational technologies. Explain why each of the three technology groups is related differently to organization structure and management processes.

4. What relationships did Woodward discover between supervisor span of control and technological complexity?

5. How do flexible manufacturing and lean manufacturing differ from other manufacturing technologies? Why are these new approaches needed in today's environment?

6. What is a service technology? Are different types of service technologies likely to be associated with different structures? Explain.

7. Mass customization of products has become a common approach in manufacturing organizations. Discuss ways in which mass customization can be applied to service firms as well.

8. In what primary ways does the design of service firms typically differ from that of product firms? Why?

9. A top executive claimed that top-level management is a craft technology because the work contains intangibles, such as handling personnel, interpreting the environment, and coping with unusual situations that have to be learned through experience. If this is true, is it appropriate to teach management in a business school? Does teaching management from a textbook assume that the manager's job is analyzable, and hence that formal training rather than experience is most important?

10. In which quadrant of Perrow's framework would a mass-production technology be placed? Where would small-batch and continuous process technologies be placed? Why? Would Perrow's framework lead to the same recommendation about organic versus mechanistic structures that Woodward made?

11. To what extent does the development of new technologies simplify and routinize the jobs of employees? How can new technology lead to job enlargement? Discuss.

12. Describe the sociotechnical systems model. Why might some managers oppose a sociotechnical systems approach?

Chapter 7 Workbook: Bistro Technology*

You will be analyzing the technology used in three different restaurants—McDonald's, Subway, and a typical family restaurant. Your instructor will tell you whether to do this assignment as individuals or in a group.

You must visit all three restaurants and infer how the work is done, according to the following criteria. You are not allowed to interview any employees, but instead you will be an observer. Take lots of notes when you are there.

*Adapted loosely by Dorothy Marcic from "Hamburger Technology," in Douglas T. Hall et al., *Experiences in Management and Organizational Behavior*, 2nd ed. (New York: Wiley, 1982), 244–247, as well as "Behavior, Technology, and Work Design" in A. B. Shani and James B. Lau, *Behavior in Organizations* (Chicago: Irwin, 1996), M16–23 to M16–26.

	McDonald's	Subway	Family Restaurant
Organization goals: Speed, service, atmosphere, etc.			
Authority structure			
Type of technology using Woodward's model			
Organization structure: Mechanistic or organic?			
Team versus individual: Do people work together or alone?			
Interdependence: How do employees depend on each other?			
Tasks: Routine versus nonroutine			
Specialization of tasks by employees			
Standardization: How varied are tasks and products?			
Expertise required: Technical versus social			
Decision making: Centralized versus decentralized			

Questions

1. Is the technology used the best one for each restaurant, considering its goals and environment?
2. From the preceding data, determine if the structure and other characteristics fit the technology.
3. If you were part of a consulting team assigned to improve the operations of each organization, what recommendations would you make?

Case for Analysis: Acetate Department*

The acetate department's product consisted of about twenty different kinds of viscous liquid acetate used by another department to manufacture transparent film to be left clear or coated with photographic emulsion or iron oxide.

Before the change: The department was located in an old four-story building as in Exhibit 7.15. The workflow was as follows:

1. Twenty kinds of powder arrived daily in 50-pound paper bags. In addition, storage tanks of liquid would be filled weekly from tank trucks.
2. Two or three acetate helpers would jointly unload pallets of bags into the storage area using a lift truck.
3. Several times during a shift, the helpers would bring the bagged material up in the elevator to the third floor, where it would be temporarily stored along the walls.
4. Mixing batches was under the direction of the group leader and was rather like baking a cake. Following a prescribed formula, the group leader, mixers, and helpers operated valves to feed in the proper solvent and manually dump in the proper weight and mixture of solid material. The glob would be mixed by giant eggbeaters and heated according to the recipe.
5. When the batch was completed, it was pumped to a finished-product storage tank.

6. After completing each batch, the crew would thoroughly clean the work area of dust and empty bags, because cleanliness was extremely important to the finished product.

To accomplish this work, the department was structured as in Exhibit 7.16.

The helpers were usually young men 18 to 25 years of age; the mixers, 25 to 40; and the group leaders and foremen, 40 to 60. Foremen were on salary; group leaders, mixers, and helpers were on hourly pay.

To produce 20 million pounds of product per year, the department operated 24 hours a day, 7 days a week. Four crews rotated shifts: for example, shift foreman A and his two group leaders and crews would work two weeks on the day shift (8:00 A.M. to 4:00 P.M.), then 2 weeks on the evening shift (4:00 P.M. to midnight), then two weeks on the night shift (midnight to 8:00 A.M.). There were 2 days off between shift changes.

*From "Redesigning the Acetate Department," by David L. Hampton, Charles E. Summer, and Ross A. Webber, *Organizational Behavior and the Practice of Management* (Glenview, Ill.: Scott Foresman and Co., 1982), 751–755. Used with permission.

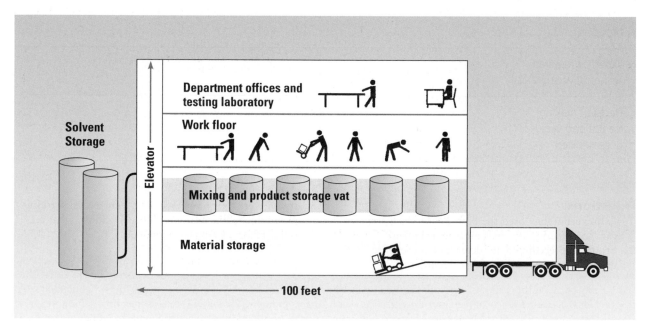

EXHIBIT 7.15
Elevation View of Acetate Department before Change

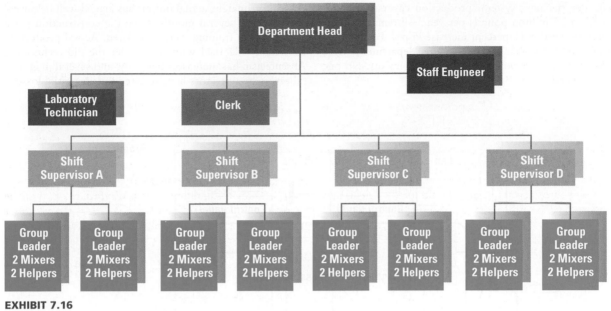

EXHIBIT 7.16
Organizational Chart of Acetate Department before Change

During a typical shift, a group leader and his crew would complete two or three batches. A batch would frequently be started on one shift and completed by the next shift crew. There was slightly less work on the evening and night shifts because no deliveries were made, but these crews engaged in a little more cleaning. The shift foreman would give instructions to the two group leaders at the beginning of each shift as to the status of batches in process, batches to be mixed, what deliveries were expected, and what cleaning was to be done. Periodically throughout the shift, the foreman would collect samples in small bottles, which he would leave at the laboratory technicians' desk for testing.

The management and office staff (department head, staff engineer, lab technician, and department clerk) only worked on the day shift, although if an emergency arose on the other shifts, the foreman might call.

All in all, the department was a pleasant place in which to work. The work floor was a little warm, but well lit, quiet, and clean. Substantial banter and horseplay occurred when the crew wasn't actually loading batches, particularly on the evening and night shifts. The men had a dartboard in the work area and competition was fierce and loud. Frequently a crew would go bowling right after work, even at 1:00 A.M., because the community's alleys were open 24 hours a day. Department turnover and absenteeism were low. Most employees spent their entire career with the company, many in one department. The corporation was large, paternalistic, and well paying and offered attractive

fringe benefits including large, virtually automatic bonuses for all. Then came the change.

The new system: To improve productivity, the acetate department was completely redesigned; the technology changed from batches to continuous processing. The basic building was retained but substantially modified as in Exhibit 7.17. The modified workflow is as follows:

1. Most solid raw materials are delivered via trucks in large aluminum bins holding 500 pounds.
2. One handler (formerly helper) is on duty at all times on the first floor to receive raw materials and to dump the bins into the semiautomatic screw feeder.
3. The head operator (former group leader) directs the mixing operations from his control panel on the fourth floor located along one wall across from the department offices. The mixing is virtually an automatic operation once the solid material has been sent up the screw feed; a tape program opens and closes the necessary valves to add solvent, heat, mix, and so on. Sitting at a table before his panel, the head operator monitors the process to see that everything is operating within specified temperatures and pressures.

This technical change allowed the department to greatly reduce its workforce. The new structure is illustrated in Exhibit 7.18. One new position was created, that of a pump operator who is located in a small, separate shack about 300 feet from the main building. He operates the pumps and valves that move the finished product among various storage tanks.

Under the new system, production capacity was increased to 25 million pounds per year. All remaining employees received a 15 percent increase in pay. Former personnel not retained in the acetate department were transferred to other departments in the company. No one was dismissed.

Unfortunately, actual output has lagged well below capacity in the several months since the construction work and technical training were completed. Actual production is virtually identical with that under the old technology. Absenteeism has increased markedly, and several judgmental errors by operators have resulted in substantial losses.

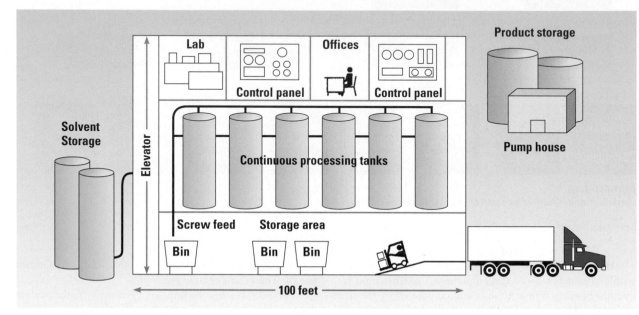

EXHIBIT 7.17
Elevation View of Acetate Department after Change

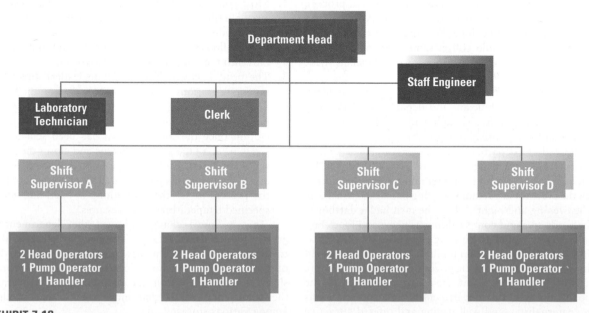

EXHIBIT 7.18
Organizational Chart of Acetate Department after Change

Notes

1. Gene Bylinsky, "Heroes of Manufacturing," *Fortune* (March 8, 2004), 190[B]–190[H].
2. Ibid.
3. Charles Perrow, "A Framework for the Comparative Analysis of Organizations," *American Sociological Review* 32 (1967), 194–208; and R. J. Schonberger, *World Class Manufacturing: The Next Decade* (New York: The Free Press, 1996).
4. Linda Argote, "Input Uncertainty and Organizational Coordination in Hospital Emergency Units," *Administrative Science Quarterly* 27 (1982), 420–434; Charles Perrow, *Organizational Analysis: A Sociological Approach* (Belmont, Calif.: Wadsworth, 1970); and William Rushing, "Hardness of Material as Related to the Division of Labor in Manufacturing Industries," *Administrative Science Quarterly* 13 (1968), 229–245.
5. Lawrence B. Mohr, "Organizational Technology and Organization Structure," *Administrative Science Quarterly* 16 (1971), 444–459; and David Hickson, Derek Pugh, and Diana Pheysey, "Operations Technology and Organization Structure: An Empirical Reappraisal," *Administrative Science Quarterly* 14 (1969), 378–397.
6. Joan Woodward, *Industrial Organization: Theory and Practice* (London: Oxford University Press, 1965); and Joan Woodward, *Management and Technology* (London: Her Majesty's Stationery Office, 1958).
7. Hickson, Pugh, and Pheysey, "Operations Technology and Organization Structure"; and James D. Thompson, *Organizations in Action* (New York: McGraw-Hill, 1967).
8. Edward Harvey, "Technology and the Structure of Organizations," *American Sociological Review* 33 (1968), 241–259.
9. Wanda J. Orlikowski, "The Duality of Technology: Rethinking the Concept of Technology in Organizations," *Organization Science* 3 (1992), 398–427.
10. Based on Woodward, *Industrial Organization* and *Management and Technology*.
11. Philip Siekman, "A Big Maker of Tiny Batches," *Fortune* (May 27, 2002), 152[A]–152[H].
12. Woodward, *Industrial Organization*, vi.
13. William L. Zwerman, *New Perspectives on Organizational Theory* (Westport, Conn.: Greenwood, 1970); and Harvey, "Technology and the Structure of Organizations."
14. Dean M. Schroeder, Steven W. Congden, and C. Gopinath, "Linking Competitive Strategy and Manufacturing Process Technology," *Journal of Management Studies* 32, no. 2 (March 1995), 163–189.
15. Gene Bylinsky, "Heroes of U.S. Manufacturing," *Fortune* (March 18, 2002), 130[A]–130[L].
16. Fernando F. Suarez, Michael A. Cusumano, and Charles H. Fine, "An Empirical Study of Flexibility in Manufacturing," *Sloan Management Review* (Fall 1995), 25–32.
17. Raymond F. Zammuto and Edward J. O'Connor, "Gaining Advanced Manufacturing Technologies' Benefits: The Roles of Organization Design and Culture," *Academy of Management Review* 17, no. 4 (1992), 701–728; and Schroeder, Congden, and Gopinath, "Linking Competitive Strategy and Manufacturing Process Technology."
18. Reported in Grainger David, "One Truck a Minute," *Fortune* (April 5, 2004), 252–258.
19. John S. McClenahen, "Bearing Necessitites," *Industry Week* (October 2004), 63ff.
20. Gene Bylinsky, "Elite Factories," *Fortune*, special section, "Industrial Management and Technology" (September 1, 2003), 154[B]–154[J].
21. Jack R. Meredith, "The Strategic Advantages of the Factory of the Future," *California Management Review* 29 (Spring 1987), 27–41; Jack Meredith, "The Strategic Advantages of the New Manufacturing Technologies for Small Firms," *Strategic Management Journal* 8 (1987), 249–258; and Althea Jones and Terry Webb, "Introducing Computer Integrated Manufacturing," *Journal of General Management* 12 (Summer 1987), 60–74.
22. Raymond F. Zammuto and Edward J. O'Connor, "Gaining Advanced Manufacturing Technologies' Benefits: The Roles of Organization Design and Culture," *Academy of Management Review* 17 (1992), 701–728.
23. John S. DeMott, "Small Factories' Big Lessons," *Nation's Business* (April 1995), 29–30.
24. Paul S. Adler, "Managing Flexible Automation," *California Management Review* (Spring 1988), 34–56.
25. Bela Gold, "Computerization in Domestic and International Manufacturing," *California Management Review* (Winter 1989), 129–143.
26. Graham Dudley and John Hassard, "Design Issues in the Development of Computer Integrated Manufacturing (CIM)," *Journal of General Management* 16 (1990), 43–53.
27. Jeff Wise, "Plane Dealer," *FSB* (July–August 2004), 83–84.
28. Ibid; and Tom Massung, "Manufacturing Efficiency," *Microsoft Executive Circle* (Winter 2004), 28–29.
29. Brian Heymans, "Leading the Lean Enterprise," *Industrial Management* (September–October 2002), 28–33; and Fara Warner, "Think Lean," *Fast Company* (February 2002), 40, 42.
30. Peter Strozniak, "Toyota Alters Face of Production," *Industry Week* (August 13, 2001), 46–48.
31. Abrahm Lustgarten, "Elite Factories," *Fortune*, special section, "Industrial Management and Technology" (September 6, 2004), 240[B]–240[L].
32. B. Joseph Pine II, *Mass Customization: The New Frontier in Business Competition* (Boston: Harvard Business School Press, 1999).
33. Barry Berman, "Should Your Firm Adopt a Mass Customization Strategy?" *Business Horizons* (July–August 2002), 51–60.
34. Mark Tatge, "Red Bodies, Black Ink," *Forbes* (September 18, 2000), 114–115.
35. Erick Schonfeld, "The Customized, Digitized, Have-It-Your-Way Economy," *Fortune* (September 28, 1998), 115–124.
36. Grainger David, "One Truck a Minute," and Scott McMurray, "Ford F-150: Have It Your Way," *Business 2.0* (March 2004), 53–55.
37. Joel D. Goldhar and David Lei, "Variety Is Free: Manufacturing in the Twenty-First Century," *Academy of Management Executive* no. 4 (1995), 73–86.

38. Meredith, "The Strategic Advantages of the Factory of the Future."

39. Patricia L. Nemetz and Louis W. Fry, "Flexible Manufacturing Organizations: Implementations for Strategy Formulation and Organization Design," *Academy of Management Review* 13 (1988), 627–638; Paul S. Adler, "Managing Flexible Automation," *California Management Review* (Spring 1988), 34–56; Jeremy Main, "Manufacturing the Right Way," *Fortune* (May 21, 1990), 54–64; and Frank M. Hull and Paul D. Collins, "High-Technology Batch Production Systems: Woodward's Missing Type," *Academy of Management Journal* 30 (1987), 786–797.

40. Goldhar and Lei, "Variety Is Free: Manufacturing in the Twenty-First Century"; P. Robert Duimering, Frank Safayeni, and Lyn Purdy, "Integrated Manufacturing: Redesign the Organization before Implementing Flexible Technology," *Sloan Management Review* (Summer 1993), 47–56; Zammuto and O'Connor, "Gaining Advanced Manufacturing Technologies' Benefits."

41. Goldhar and Lei, "Variety Is Free: Manufacturing in the Twenty-First Century."

42. "Manufacturing's Decline," *Johnson City Press* (July 17, 1999), 9; Ronald Henkoff, "Service Is Everybody's Business," *Fortune* (June 27, 1994), 48–60; Ronald Henkoff, "Finding, Training, and Keeping the Best Service Workers," *Fortune* (October 3, 1994), 110–122.

43. Byron J. Finch and Richard L. Luebbe, *Operations Management: Competing in a Changing Environment* (Fort Worth, Tex.: The Dryden Press, 1995), 51.

44. David E. Bowen, Caren Siehl, and Benjamin Schneider, "A Framework for Analyzing Customer Service Orientations in Manufacturing," *Academy of Management Review* 14 (1989), 79–95; Peter K. Mills and Newton Margulies, "Toward a Core Typology of Service Organizations," *Academy of Management Review* 5 (1980), 255–265; Peter K. Mills and Dennis J. Moberg, "Perspectives on the Technology of Service Operations," *Academy of Management Review* 7 (1982), 467–478; and G. Lynn Shostack, "Breaking Free from Product Marketing," *Journal of Marketing* (April 1977), 73–80.

45. Diane Brady, "Will Jeff Immelt's New Push Pay Off for GE?" *BusinessWeek* (October 13, 2003), 94–98.

46. Ron Zemke, "The Service Revolution: Who Won?" *Management Review* (March 1997), 10–15; and Wayne Wilhelm and Bill Rossello, "The Care and Feeding of Customers," *Management Review* (March 1997), 19–23.

47. Schonfeld, "The Customized, Digitized, Have-It-Your-Way Economy."

48. Duff McDonald, "Customer, Support Thyself," *Business 2.0* (April 2004), 56.

49. Paul Migliorato, "Toyota Retools Japan," *Business 2.0* (August 2004), 39–41.

50. Richard B. Chase and David A. Tansik, "The Customer Contact Model for Organization Design," *Management Science* 29 (1983), 1037–1050.

51. Ibid.

52. David E. Bowen and Edward E. Lawler III, "The Empowerment of Service Workers: What, Why, How, and When," *Sloan Management Review* (Spring 1992), 31–39: Gregory B. Northcraft and Richard B. Chase, "Managing Service Demand at the Point of Delivery," *Academy of Manage-*

ment Review 10 (1985), 66–75; and Roger W. Schmenner, "How Can Service Businesses Survive and Prosper?" *Sloan Management Review* 27 (Spring 1986), 21–32.

53. Scott Kirsner, "Recipe for Reinvention," *Fast Company* (April 2002), 38–42.

54. Richard Metters and Vincente Vargas, "Organizing Work in Service Firms," *Business Horizons* (July–August 2000), 23–32.

55. Perrow, "A Framework for Comparative Analysis" and *Organizational Analysis.*

56. Brian T. Pentland, "Sequential Variety in Work Processes," *Organization Science* 14, no. 5 (September–October 2003), 528–540.

57. Jim Morrison, "Grand Tour. Making Music: The Craft of the Steinway Piano," *Spirit* (February 1997), 42–49, 100.

58. Stuart F. Brown, "Biotech Gets Productive," *Fortune*, special section, "Industrial Management and Technology" (January 20, 2003), 170[A]–170[H].

59. Michael Withey, Richard L. Daft, and William C. Cooper, "Measures of Perrow's Work Unit Technology: An Empirical Assessment and a New Scale," *Academy of Management Journal* 25 (1983), 45–63.

60. Christopher Gresov, "Exploring Fit and Misfit with Multiple Contingencies," *Administrative Science Quarterly* 34 (1989), 431–453; and Dale L. Goodhue and Ronald L. Thompson, "Task-Technology Fit and Individual Performance," *MIS Quarterly* (June 1995), 213–236.

61. Gresov, "Exploring Fit and Misfit with Multiple Contingencies"; Charles A. Glisson, "Dependence of Technological Routinization on Structural Variables in Human Service Organizations," *Administrative Science Quarterly* 23 (1978), 383–395; and Jerald Hage and Michael Aiken, "Routine Technology, Social Structure and Organizational Goals," *Administrative Science Quarterly* 14 (1969), 368–379.

62. Gresov, "Exploring Fit and Misfit with Multiple Contingencies"; A. J. Grimes and S. M. Kline, "The Technological Imperative: The Relative Impact of Task Unit, Modal Technology, and Hierarchy on Structure," *Academy of Management Journal* 16 (1973), 583–597; Lawrence G. Hrebiniak, "Job Technologies, Supervision and Work Group Structure," *Administrative Science Quarterly* 19 (1974), 395–410; and Jeffrey Pfeffer, *Organizational Design* (Arlington Heights, Ill.: AHM, 1978), Chapter 1.

63. Patrick E. Connor, *Organizations: Theory and Design* (Chicago: Science Research Associates, 1980); Richard L. Daft and Norman B. Macintosh, "A Tentative Exploration into Amount and Equivocality of Information Processing in Organizational Work Units," *Administrative Science Quarterly* 26 (1981), 207–224.

64. Paul D. Collins and Frank Hull, "Technology and Span of Control: Woodward Revisited," *Journal of Management Studies* 23 (1986), 143–164; Gerald D. Bell, "The Influence of Technological Components of Work upon Management Control," *Academy of Management Journal* 8 (1965), 127–132; and Peter M. Blau and Richard A. Schoenherr, *The Structure of Organizations* (New York: Basic Books, 1971).

65. W. Alan Randolph, "Matching Technology and the Design of Organization Units," *California Management Review* 22–23 (1980–81), 39–48; Daft and Macintosh, "Tentative Exploration into Amount and Equivocality of Information Processing"; and Michael L. Tushman, "Work Characteris-

66. Andrew H. Van de Ven and Diane L. Ferry, *Measuring and Assessing Organizations* (New York: Wiley, 1980); and Randolph, "Matching Technology and the Design of Organization Units."

67. Richard L. Daft and Robert H. Lengel, "Information Richness: A New Approach to Managerial Behavior and Organization Design," in Barry Staw and Larry L. Cummings, eds., *Research in Organizational Behavior*, vol. 6 (Greenwich, Conn.: JAI Press, 1984), 191–233; Richard L. Daft and Norman B. Macintosh, "A New Approach into Design and Use of Management Information," *California Management Review* 21 (1978), 82–92; Daft and Macintosh, "A Tentative Exploration into Amount and Equivocality of Information Processing"; W. Alan Randolph, "Organizational Technology and the Media and Purpose Dimensions of Organizational Communication," *Journal of Business Research* 6 (1978), 237–259; Linda Argote, "Input Uncertainty and Organizational Coordination in Hospital Emergency Units," *Administrative Science Quarterly* 27 (1982), 420–434; and Andrew H. Van de Ven and Andre Delbecq, "A Task Contingent Model of Work Unit Structure," *Administrative Science Quarterly* 19 (1974), 183–197.

68. Peggy Leatt and Rodney Schneck, "Criteria for Grouping Nursing Subunits in Hospitals," *Academy of Management Journal* 27 (1984), 150–165; and Robert T. Keller, "Technology-Information Processing," *Academy of Management Journal* 37, no. 1 (1994), 167–179.

69. Gresov, "Exploring Fit and Misfit with Multiple Contingencies"; Michael L. Tushman, "Technological Communication in R&D Laboratories: The Impact of Project Work Characteristics," *Academy of Management Journal* 21 (1978), 624–645; and Robert T. Keller, "Technology-Information Processing Fit and the Performance of R&D Project Groups: A Test of Contingency Theory," *Academy of Management Journal* 37, no. 1 (1994), 167–179.

70. Charles Fishman, "Miracle of Birth," *Fast Company* (October 2002), 106–116.

71. James Thompson, *Organizations in Action* (New York: McGraw-Hill, 1967).

72. Ibid., 40.

73. Gene Bylinsky, "Shipmaking Gets Modern," *Fortune*, special section, "Industrial Management and Technology" (January 20, 2003), 170[K]–170[L].

74. Paul S. Adler, "Interdepartmental Interdependence and Coordination: The Case of the Design/Manufacturing Interface," *Organization Science* 6, no. 2 (March–April 1995), 147–167.

75. Christopher Gresov, "Effects of Dependence and Tasks on Unit Design and Efficiency," *Organization Studies* 11 (1990), 503–529; Andrew H. Van de Ven, Andre Delbecq, and Richard Koenig, "Determinants of Coordination Modes within Organizations," *American Sociological Review* 41 (1976), 322–338; Linda Argote, "Input Uncertainty and Organizational Coordination in Hospital Emergency Units"; Jack K. Ito and Richard B. Peterson, "Effects of Task Difficulty and Interdependence on Information Processing Systems," *Academy of Management Journal* 29 (1986), 139–149; and Joseph L. C. Cheng, "Interdependence and Coordination in Organizations: A Role-System Analysis," *Academy of Management Journal* 26 (1983), 156–162.

76. Robert W. Keidel, "Team Sports Models as a Generic Organizational Framework," *Human Relations* 40 (1987), 591–612; Robert W. Keidel, "Baseball, Football, and Basketball: Models for Business," *Organizational Dynamics* (Winter 1984), 5–18; and Nancy Katz, "Sports Teams as a Model for Workplace Teams: Lessons and Liabilities," *Academy of Management Executive* 15, no. 3 (2001), 56–67.

77. Michele Liu, Héléné Denis, Harvey Kolodny, and Benjt Stymne, "Organization Design for Technological Change," *Human Relations* 43 (January 1990), 7–22.

78. Stephen P. Robbins, *Organizational Behavior* (Upper Saddle River, N.J.: Prentice-Hall, 1998), 521.

79. Gerald I. Susman and Richard B. Chase, "A Sociotechnical Analysis of the Integrated Factory," *Journal of Applied Behavioral Science* 22 (1986), 257–270; and Paul Adler, "New Technologies, New Skills," *California Management Review* 29 (Fall 1986), 9–28.

80. Based on Don Hellriegel, John W. Slocum, Jr., and Richard W. Woodman, *Organizational Behavior*, 8th ed. (Cincinnati, Ohio: South-Western, 1998), 491–495; and Gregory B. Northcraft and Margaret A. Neale, *Organizational Behavior: A Management Challenge*, 2nd ed. (Fort Worth, Tex.: The Dryden Press, 1994), 550–553.

81. F. Emery, "Characteristics of Sociotechnical Systems," Tavistock Institute of Human Relations, document 527, 1959; William Pasmore, Carol Francis, and Jeffrey Haldeman, "Sociotechnical Systems: A North American Reflection on Empirical Studies of the 70s," *Human Relations* 35 (1982), 1179–1204; and William M. Fox, "Sociotechnical System Principles and Guidelines: Past and Present," *Journal of Applied Behavioral Science* 31, no. 1 (March 1995), 91–105.

82. W. S. Cascio, *Managing Human Resources* (New York: McGraw-Hill, 1986), 19.

83. Eric Trist and Hugh Murray, eds., *The Social Engagement of Social Science: A Tavistock Anthology*, vol. II (Philadelphia: University of Pennsylvania Press, 1993); and William A. Pasmore, "Social Science Transformed: The Socio-Technical Perspective," *Human Relations* 48, no. 1 (1995), 1–21.

84. R. E. Walton, "From Control to Commitment in the Workplace," *Harvard Business Review* 63, no. 2 (1985), 76–84; E. W. Lawler, III, *High Involvement Management* (London: Jossey-Bass, 1986), 84; and Hellriegel, Slocum, and Woodman, *Organizational Behavior*, 491.

85. William A. Pasmore, "Social Science Transformed: The Socio-Technical Perspective," *Human Relations* 48, no. 1 (1995), 1–21.

86. David M. Upton, "What Really Makes Factories Flexible?" *Harvard Business Review* (July–August 1995), 74–84.

87. Pasmore, "Social Science Transformed: The Socio-Technical Perspective"; H. Scarbrough, "Review Article: *The Social Engagement of Social Science: A Tavistock Anthology*, Vol. II," *Human Relations* 48, no. 1 (1995), 23–33.

PROGRESSIVE™
DIRECT

1-877-776-4266   E-mai

GET STARTED   VEHICLES   DRIVERS   VIOLATIONS   YOUR RATE

Welcome! In just minutes you can quote and buy a policy online. It's easy!

Help Center

Speak Now with a licen insurance representative

Talk To Me

First name		Middle initial	
Last name		Suffix	
Mailing address ❓		Apt./Room #	
City	, Ohio	Zip code	

Common Questions

→ Why do I have to provid so much information?

→ Will my quote change?

→ Will I be able to compar rates for other companie

Information Disclosure – To offer you an accurate quote in one of Progressive's underwriting companies, we will collect information from consumer reporting agencies, such as driving record, claims, and credit history reports. Future reports may be used to update or renew your insurance. Please review our Privacy Policy.

I have read the Information Disclosure and Privacy Policy and would like to continue   ⦿ Yes ○ No

Information Technology Evolution

Information for Decision Making and Control
Organizational Decision-Making Systems • Feedback Control Model • Management Control Systems • The Balanced Scorecard

Adding Strategic Value: Strengthening Internal Coordination
Intranets • Enterprise Resource Planning • Knowledge Management

Adding Strategic Value: Strengthening External Relationships
The Integrated Enterprise • Customer Relationship Management • E-Business Organization Design

IT Impact on Organization Design

Summary and Interpretation

A Look Inside

The Progressive Group of Insurance Companies

The Progressive Group makes up the third largest auto insurance group in the United States, and it just keeps growing. Not bad for a group of companies that got its start as a niche insurer for high-risk drivers and that, as recently as 1990, was the 15th largest in the United States. How did a relatively small, specialized firm compete with giant insurance companies such as State Farm and Allstate in the larger market for standard and preferred auto insurance? In part, by using information technology to gain a strategic advantage.

Progressive got its start in 1937 and proved itself an innovator from the beginning, when it established the industry's first drive-in claims service. It has been innovating ever since, using technology to provide a more accurate rate, a better customer experience, and auto insurance shopping information not available anywhere else.

Auto insurance rates are developed, in part, using information about past claims history. An insurance company's ability to understand its claims experience and to use that information to even more finely segment its customers and its pricing can help to determine its level of success. Progressive has been using technology to better understand its customers at the most granular level for a very long time, and, in the early 1990s, began to use that understanding to more accurately price the so-called "standard and preferred" markets segment. If they were successful in accurately pricing the high-risk, or "non-standard" segment of the market, they reasoned, why couldn't they apply that talent to the rest of the market?

The 1990s brought other uses of technology that help to explain Progressive's growth from $1.2 billion in net premiums written in 1990 to more than $13 billion in 2004. First was the introduction of Immediate Response claims service, which provided the industry's first 24 hours a day, 7 days a week, in-person response to an auto crash. Using mobile technology, claims representatives would arrive wherever customers wished, write an estimate and be able to "cut them a check on the spot." Progressive has since further refined its approach. In a growing number of markets, it offers a "concierge level" of claims service, which means that the customer need only drop off the car at a specially designated facility and pick up a rental car. The claims representative handles all aspects of the estimate, oversees the repair, and inspects the repair before the customer picks up the car. The customer drives away knowing that the work is guaranteed by the shop that repaired the vehicle and by Progressive.

In the early 1990s, Progressive introduced another first—auto insurance comparison rates. Using publicly filed rates and technology, Progressive became the first—and remains the only—auto insurance company providing consumers with comparison rates. Comparison rates were first offered by phone, but, when Progressive launched the world's first auto insurance Web site in 1995, the rates were available using that technology. Today, visitors to the Web site can buy a policy in as few as 7 minutes. Customers can also use the Web site to manage their policies, make payments, make changes, and print out additional insurance documentation.

Progressive continues to use technology to innovate, most recently announcing the availability of "e-signatures" to some of its customers. Electronic signatures eliminate most of the follow-up paperwork, allowing customers to sign applications online, authorize electronic funds transfer for payment, or sign forms to decline unwanted coverages.

nsurance isn't the only industry that has been transformed by information technology (IT) and the Internet. Effectively using IT in knowledge-based firms such as consulting firm KPMG Peat Marwick, Amerex Worldwide, a brokerage firm specializing in energy resources, and Business Wire, which provides business and corporate information, has long been fundamental to the business. Today, IT has become a crucial factor helping companies in all industries maintain a competitive edge in the face of growing global competition and rising customer demands for speed, convenience, quality, and value. Wood Flooring International (WFI), based in Delran, New Jersey, uses a sophisticated Internet-based system to manage every link of the supply chain, from vendors all the way through to its customers' customers. The small company buys exotic wood overseas, mostly from small, family-owned mills in Latin America, turns it into floorboards, and sells to distributors. WFI used to have three overseas employees just to manage supplier relationships. Now, whenever WFI takes an order, the vendor can see an update instantly on the Web site and adjust its production accordingly. The mills can also check real-time reports of their sales histories, check whether their shipments have arrived, and ensure that WFI's accounting squares with their own.[2] Olive Garden, a restaurant chain, uses computerized systems to measure and control everything from bathroom cleanliness to food preparation time. And Memorial Health Services in Long Beach, California, uses medical identification cards (available over the Internet) that can be swiped into a computer to speed registration and give emergency room personnel immediate access to vital patient information.[3] Even fast-food franchisees are finding highly creative uses for IT. If you've ever ordered a Big Mac at the McDonald's off Interstate 55 near Cape Girardeau, Missouri, you probably had no idea that the order taker was located in a call center more than 900 miles away. Franchisee Shannon Davis has linked four of his restaurants to a call center in Colorado Springs, which is connected to the customer and the restaurant workers by high-speed data lines. A customer's order traverses two states and bounces back to Cape Girardeau before the customer even pulls up to the pickup window. In a business where time is money, shaving even 5 seconds off order processing time makes a difference. The call center approach cuts order time in most restaurants that use it by 30 seconds to 1 minute. Accuracy of orders has also improved.[4]

Yet, the rapidly growing use of IT and the Internet presents not only new opportunities, but also new challenges for managers. For one thing, the balance of power has shifted to the customer. With unlimited access to information on the Internet, customers are much better informed and much more demanding, making customer loyalty harder to build.[5] In addition, the concept of electronically linking suppliers, partners, and customers is forcing companies to rethink their strategies, organization design, and business processes. The pace of business is moving at "warp speed."[6] Planning horizons have become shorter, expectations of customers change rapidly, and new competitors spring up almost overnight. All this means managers, as well as employees throughout the organization, need quality information at their fingertips.

Highly successful organizations today are typically those that most effectively collect, store, distribute, and use information. More than facilities, equipment, or even products, it is the information a company has and how it uses it that defines organization success—some would say even organization survival.[7] Top managers look for ways to manage, leverage, and protect what is rapidly becoming the most valuable asset of any organization: information and knowledge.

■ Purpose of This Chapter

IT is an essential component of successful organizations. Managers spend at least 80 percent of their time actively exchanging information. They need this information to hold the organization together. For example, the vertical and horizontal information linkages described in Chapter 3 are designed to provide managers with relevant information for decision making, evaluation, and control. This chapter examines the evolution of IT. The chapter begins by looking at IT systems applied to organizational operations and then examines how IT is used for decision making and control of the organization. The next sections consider how IT can add strategic value through the use of internal coordination applications such as intranets, enterprise resource planning, and knowledge management systems, as well as applications for external collaboration, such as extranets, customer-relationship management systems, e-business, and the integrated enterprise. The final section of the chapter presents an overview of how IT affects organization design and interorganizational relationships.

■ Information Technology Evolution

The evolution of IT is illustrated in Exhibit 8.1. First-line management is typically concerned with well-defined problems about operational issues and past events. Top management, by contrast, deals mostly with uncertain, ambiguous issues, such as strategy and planning. As the complexity of computer-based IT systems has increased, applications have grown to support effective top management control and decision making about complex and uncertain problems.

Initially, IT systems in organizations were applied to operations. These initial applications were based on the notion of machine-room efficiency—that is, current operations could be performed more efficiently with the use of computer technology. The goal was to reduce labor costs by having computers take over some tasks. These systems became known as **transaction processing systems** (TPS), which automate the organization's routine, day-to-day business transactions. A TPS collects data from transactions such as sales, purchases from suppliers, and inventory changes and stores them in a database. For example, at Enterprise Rent-a-Car, a computerized system keeps track of the 1.4 million transactions the company logs every hour. The system can provide front-line employees with up-to-the-minute information on car availability and other data, enabling them to provide exceptional customer service.[8]

In recent years, the use of data warehousing and business intelligence software has expanded the usefulness of these accumulated data. **Data warehousing** is the use of huge databases that combine all of a company's data and allow users to access the data directly, create reports, and obtain responses to what-if questions. Building a database at a large corporation is a huge undertaking that includes defining hundreds of gigabytes of data from many existing systems, providing a means of continually updating the data, making it all compatible, and linking it to other software that makes it possible for users to search and analyze the data and produce helpful reports. Software for business intelligence helps users make sense of all these data. **Business intelligence** refers to the high-tech analysis of a company's data in order to

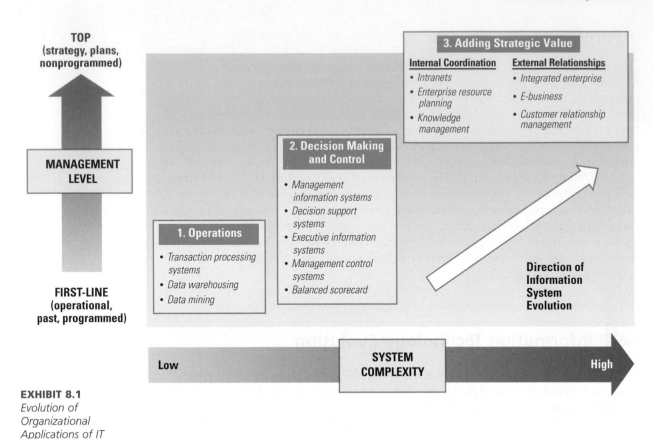

TOP
(strategy, plans,
nonprogrammed)

MANAGEMENT
LEVEL

FIRST-LINE
(operational,
past, programmed)

3. Adding Strategic Value

Internal Coordination
- Intranets
- Enterprise resource planning
- Knowledge management

External Relationships
- Integrated enterprise
- E-business
- Customer relationship management

2. Decision Making and Control
- Management information systems
- Decision support systems
- Executive information systems
- Management control systems
- Balanced scorecard

1. Operations
- Transaction processing systems
- Data warehousing
- Data mining

Direction of Information System Evolution

Low   SYSTEM COMPLEXITY   High

EXHIBIT 8.1
Evolution of
Organizational
Applications of IT

make better strategic decisions.[9] Sometimes referred to as *data mining*, business intelligence means searching out and analyzing data from multiple sources across the enterprise, and sometimes from outside sources as well, to identify patterns and relationships that might be significant.

Organizations spent $4 billion on business intelligence software in 2003, and the amount was expected to double by 2006.[10] Consider how Anheuser-Busch makes profitable use of data warehousing and business intelligence.

In Practice
Anheuser-Busch

Only a few years ago, Anheuser-Busch beer distributors and sales reps were turning their information in on stacks of paper invoices and sales orders. Keeping track of what products were selling and what marketing campaigns were effective was an arduous and time-consuming process. Managers sometimes didn't know for months if a product wasn't selling well in a particular market.

All that changed when Anheuser-Busch introduced BudNet, a corporate data warehouse where distributors and sales reps report in excruciating detail on everything from new orders and level of sales to competitors' shelf stock and current marketing efforts. Sales reps use handheld personal digital assistants and laptops to enter data that are compiled and transmitted nightly to the data warehouse at corporate headquarters. There, business intelligence software goes to work, helping managers find out what beer drinkers are buying, as well as when, where, and even why. They use the intelligence to formulate or alter marketing strategies, design promotions to target certain segments of the population, and get an early warning when rivals might be gaining an edge. For example, business intelligence helps marketing managers tailor campaigns with local precision. They know that Tequiza goes over well in San Antonio but not Peoria; that the Fourth of July is a big beer sales holiday in Atlanta but that St. Patrick's Day isn't; and that beer drinkers in blue-collar neighborhoods prefer cans over bottles.

Every morning, distributors log on to BudNet to access the latest intelligence and get their new marching orders for what products to promote, what displays to use, and what discounts to offer in what neighborhoods. "They're drilling down to the level of the individual store," says Joe Thompson, president of Independent Beverage Group.[11]

Store level data has become the lifeblood of Anheuser-Busch's business. By collecting the right data and using business intelligence to analyze it and spot trends and patterns, Anheuser-Busch managers have been able to make smarter decisions and increase market share compared to competitors. Thus, IT has evolved to more complex systems for managerial decision making and control of the organization, the second stage illustrated in Exhibit 8.1. Further advancements have led to the use of IT to add strategic value, the highest level of application. The remainder of this chapter will focus on these two stages in the evolution of IT.

Information for Decision Making and Control

Through the application of more sophisticated computer-based systems, managers have tools to improve the performance of departments and the organization as a whole. These applications use information stored in corporate databases to help managers control the organization and make important decisions. Exhibit 8.2 illustrates the various elements of information systems used for decision making and control. Management information systems—including information reporting systems, decision support systems, and executive information systems—facilitate rapid and effective decision making. Elements for control include various management control systems and a procedure known as the balanced scorecard. In an organization, these systems are interconnected, as illustrated by the dashed lines in Exhibit 8.2. The systems for decision making and control often share the same basic data, but the data and reports are designed and used for a primary purpose of decision making versus control.

Organizational Decision-Making Systems

A **management information system** (MIS) is a computer-based system that provides information and support for managerial decision making. The MIS is supported by the organization's transaction processing systems and by organizational and external databases. The **information reporting system**, the most common form of MIS, provides mid-level managers with reports that summarize data and support day-to-day decision making. For example, when managers need to make decisions about production scheduling, they can review the data on the

EXHIBIT 8.2
Information Systems for
Managerial Control and
Decision Making

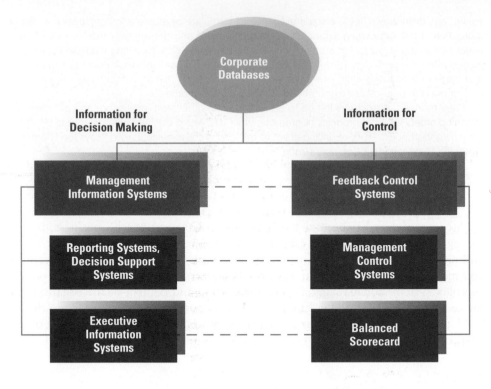

anticipated number of orders within the next month, inventory levels, and availability of human resources.

At Harrah's casinos, an information reporting system keeps track of detailed information on each player and uses quantitative models to predict each customer's potential long-term value. The information helps managers create customized marketing plans, as well as provide customers just the right combination of services and rewards to keep them coming back rather than moving on to another casino. "Almost everything we do in marketing and decision making is influenced by technology," says Harrah's CEO Gary Loveman. Effective use of information helped Harrah's achieve sixteen straight quarters of same-store sales growth, as well as the highest profit growth in the industry.[12]

An **executive information system** (EIS) is a higher-level application that facilitates decision making at the highest levels of management. These systems are typically based on software that can convert large amounts of complex data into pertinent information and provide that information to top managers in a timely fashion. For example, Motorola's Semiconductor Products Sector, based in Austin, Texas, had massive amounts of stored data, but users couldn't easily find what they needed. The company implemented an EIS using online analytical processing software so that more than a thousand senior executives, as well as managers and project analysts in finance, marketing, sales, and accounting departments around the world, could quickly and easily get information about customer buying trends, manufacturing, and so forth, right from their desktop computers, without having to learn complex and arcane search commands.[13]

A **decision support system** (DSS) provides specific benefits to managers at all levels of the organization. These interactive, computer-based systems rely on decision models and integrated databases. Using decision support software, users can pose a series of what-if questions to test possible alternatives. Based on assumptions used in the software or specified by the user, managers can explore various alternatives and receive information to help them choose the alternative that will likely have the best outcome.

Wal-Mart uses an EIS and a DSS that rely on a massive database to make decisions about what to stock, how to price and promote it, and when to reorder. Information about what products are selling and what items are often purchased together is obtained at checkout scanners. Wireless handheld units operated by clerks and department managers help keep close tabs on inventory levels. All these data are sent to Wal-Mart's data warehouse in Bentonville, Arkansas, which has an amazing 460 terabytes of data, according to company representatives. Wal-Mart uses its mountain of data to push for greater efficiency at all levels, as well as to forecast trends and do more business. By analyzing data with a decision support system using predictive technology, for example, Wal-Mart managers learned that six-packs of beer sell out quickly and sales of strawberry Pop-Tarts zoom seven times their normal sales rate in the days ahead of a hurricane.[14]

■ Feedback Control Model

Another primary use of information in organizations is for control. Effective control systems involve the use of feedback to determine whether organizational performance meets established standards to help the organization attain its goals. Managers set up systems for organizational control that consist of the four key steps in the **feedback control model** illustrated in Exhibit 8.3.

The cycle of control includes setting strategic goals for departments or the organization as a whole, establishing metrics and standards of performance, comparing metrics of actual performance to standards, and correcting or changing activities as needed. Feedback control helps managers make needed adjustments in work activities, standards of performance, or goals to help the organization be successful. For example, by evaluating sales performance, customer ratings, and other feedback, managers at McDonald's saw a need to adjust the fast-food chain's menu to include healthier options such as salads, a choice of apple slices and milk instead of fries and soft drinks in Happy Meals, and all-white-meat Chicken McNuggets.[15] In the following sections, we will discuss two commonly used methods that operate as feedback control systems: management control systems and the balanced scorecard.

■ Management Control Systems

Management control systems are broadly defined as the formal routines, reports, and procedures that use information to maintain or alter patterns in organization activities.[16] These control systems include the formalized information-based activities for planning, budgeting, performance evaluation, resource allocation, and employee rewards. Targets are set in advance, outcomes compared to targets, and variance reported to managers for corrective action. Advances in IT have dramatically

Briefcase

As an organization manager, keep this guideline in mind:

Devise control systems that consist of the four essential steps of the feedback control model: set goals, establish standards of performance, measure actual performance and compare to standards, and correct or change activities as needed.

EXHIBIT 8.3
A Simplified Feedback Control Model

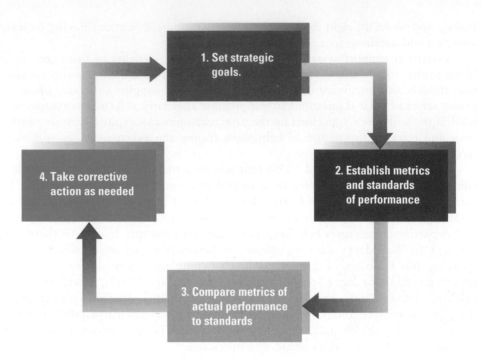

improved the efficiency and effectiveness of these systems. For example, many organizations use *executive dashboards*, which enable managers to see at a glance key control indicators such as sales in relation to targets, number of products on back-order, or percentage of customer service calls resolved within a specified time period.[17] Dashboard systems coordinate, organize, and display the metrics that managers consider most important to monitor on a regular basis, with software automatically updating the figures. At Verizon Communications, a dashboard system keeps track of more than 300 different measures of business performance in three broad categories: market pulse (including daily sales numbers and market share); customer service (for example, call center wait times and problems resolved on the first call); and cost drivers (such as number of repair trucks in the field). Business unit leaders pick a limited set of metrics that matter most for their division's executives and line managers, so that the system provides the right data rather than information overload.[18]

Exhibit 8.4 lists four control system elements that are often considered the core of management control systems: the budget and financial reports; periodic nonfinancial statistical reports; reward systems; and quality-control systems.[19]

The *budget* is typically used to set targets for the organization's expenditures for the year and then report actual costs on a monthly or quarterly basis. As a means of control, budgets report actual as well as planned expenditures for cash, assets, raw materials, salaries, and other resources so that managers can take action to correct variances. Sometimes, the variance between budgeted and actual amounts for each line item is listed as a part of the budget. Managers also rely on a variety of other financial reports. The *balance sheet* shows a firm's financial position with respect to assets and liabilities at a specific point in time. An *income statement*, sometimes called a *profit and loss statement (P&L)*, summarizes the company's financial

Subsystem	Content and Frequency
Budget, financial reports	Financial, resource expenditures, profit and loss; monthly
Statistical reports	Nonfinancial outputs; weekly or monthly, often computer-based
Reward systems	Evaluation of managers based on department goals and performance, set rewards; yearly
Quality control systems	Participation, benchmarking guidelines, Six Sigma goals; continuous

EXHIBIT 8.4
Management Control Systems

Source: Based on Richard L. Daft and Norman B. Macintosh, "The Nature and Use of Formal Control Systems for Management Control and Strategy Implementation," *Journal of Management* 10 (1984), 43–66.

performance for a given time interval, such as for the week, month, or year. This statement shows revenues coming into the organization from all sources and subtracts all expenses, such as cost of goods sold, interest, taxes, and depreciation. The *bottom line* indicates the net income—profit or loss—for the given time period.

Managers use periodic statistical reports to evaluate and monitor nonfinancial performance, such as customer satisfaction, employee performance, or rate of staff turnover. For e-commerce organizations, important measurements of nonfinancial performance include metrics such as *stickiness* (how much attention a site gets over time), the *conversion rate*, the ratio of buyers to site visitors, and *site performance data*, such as how long it takes to load a page or how long it takes to place an order.[20] E-commerce managers regularly review reports on conversion rates, customer dropoff, and other metrics to identify problems and improve their business. For all organizations, nonfinancial reports typically are computer based and may be available daily, weekly, or monthly. The online auction company eBay provides a good illustration of using both financial and nonfinancial statistical reports for feedback control.

Meg Whitman, CEO of eBay, has a guiding mantra: "If you can't measure it, you can't control it." Whitman runs a company that is obsessed with performance measurement. She personally monitors performance metrics such as number of site visitors, percentage of new users, and time spent on the site, as well as profit and loss statements and the ratio of eBay's revenues to the value of goods traded. Managers throughout the company also monitor performance regularly. Category managers, for example, have clear standards of performance for their auction categories (such as sports memorabilia, jewelry and watches, health and beauty, etc.). They continuously measure, tweak, and promote their categories to meet or outperform their targets.

Whitman believes getting a firm grip on performance measurement is essential for a company to know where to spend money, where to assign more personnel, and which projects to promote or abandon. The more statistics that are available, the more early warnings managers have about problems and opportunities. But performance isn't just about numbers at eBay. Measuring customer (user) satisfaction requires a mix of methods, such as surveys, monitoring eBay discussion boards, and personal contact with customers at regular live conferences.

By defining standards and effectively using financial and statistical reports, eBay managers can identify trouble spots and move quickly to take corrective action when and where it is needed.[21]

In Practice

eBay

In addition to performance measurement, eBay also effectively uses the other control system elements listed in Exhibit 8.4—reward systems and quality control systems. Reward systems offer incentives for managers and employees to improve performance and meet departmental goals. Managers and employees evaluate how well previous goals were met, set new goals, and establish rewards for meeting the new targets. Rewards are often tied to the annual performance appraisal process, during which managers assess employee performance and provide feedback to help the employee improve performance and obtain rewards.

The final control element listed in Exhibit 8.4 is quality-control systems, which managers use to train employees in quality-control methods, set targets for employee participation, establish benchmarking guidelines, and assign and measure *Six Sigma* goals. For example, at eBay, Whitman used benchmarking to measure how the company's Web site performs compared to its peers. She found eBay's site weak in the area of adding new features, so managers have taken action to improve the site's performance in that area. **Benchmarking** means the process of continually measuring products, services, and practices against tough competitors or other organizations recognized as industry leaders.[22] **Six Sigma**, originally conceived by Motorola Corp., is a highly ambitious quality standard that specifies a goal of no more than 3.4 defects per million parts.[23]

However, Six Sigma has deviated from its precise definition to become a generic term for a whole set of control procedures that emphasize a relentless pursuit of higher quality and lower costs. The discipline is based on a methodology referred to as DMAIC (Define, Measure, Analyze, Improve, and Control, pronounced de-MAY-ick, for short), which provides a structured way for organizations to approach and solve problems.[24] Companies such as General Electric, ITT Industries, Dow Chemical, ABB Ltd., and 3M have saved millions of dollars by rooting out inefficiencies and waste through Six Sigma processes.[25]

One finding from research into management control systems is that each of the four control systems focuses on a different aspect of the production process. These four systems thus form an overall management control system that provides middle managers with control information about resource inputs, process efficiency, and outputs.[26] Moreover, the use of and reliance on control systems depends on the strategic targets set by top management.

The budget is used primarily to allocate resource inputs. Managers use the budget for planning the future and reducing uncertainty about the availability of human and material resources needed to perform department tasks. Computer-based statistical reports are used to control outputs. These reports contain data about output volume and quality and other indicators that provide feedback to middle management about departmental results. The reward system and quality control systems are directed at the production process. Quality control systems specify standards for employee participation, teamwork, and problem solving. Reward systems provide incentives to meet goals and can help guide and correct employee behavior. Managers also use direct supervision to keep departmental work activities within desired limits.

■ The Balanced Scorecard

In the past, most organizations relied largely on financial accounting measures as the primary basis for measuring organizational performance, but today's companies realize that a balanced view of both financial and operational measures is needed for successful organizational control.

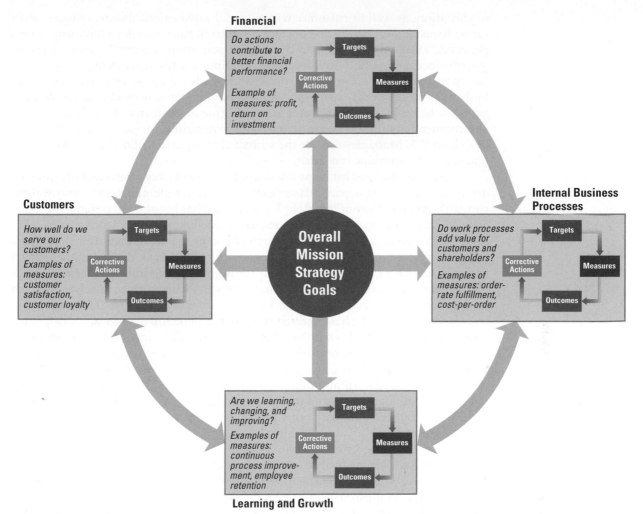

EXHIBIT 8.5

Major Perspectives of the Balanced Scorecard

Source: Based on Robert S. Kaplan and David P. Norton, "Using the Balanced Scorecard as a Strategic Management System," *Harvard Business Review* (January–February 1996), 75–85; Chee W. Chow, Kamal M. Haddad, and James E. Williamson, "Applying the Balanced Scorecard to Small Companies," *Management Accounting* 79, no. 2 (August 1997), 21–27; and Cathy Lazere, "All Together Now," *CFO* (February 1998), 28–36.

The four control elements listed in Exhibit 8.4 help provide managers with a balanced view. In addition, a recent innovation is to integrate internal financial measurements and statistical reports with a concern for markets and customers as well as employees. The **balanced scorecard** is a comprehensive management control system that balances traditional financial measures with operational measures relating to a company's critical success factors.[27] A balanced scorecard contains four major perspectives, as illustrated in Exhibit 8.5: financial performance, customer service, internal business processes, and the organization's capacity for learning and growth.[28] Within these four areas, managers identify key performance indicators the organization will track. The *financial perspective* reflects a concern that the organization's activities contribute to improving short- and long-term financial performance. It includes traditional measures such as net income and return on investment. *Customer service indicators* measure such things as how customers view the organization, as well as customer retention and satisfaction. *Business process indicators* focus on production and operating statistics, such as order fulfillment or cost per order. The final component looks at the organization's *potential for learning and growth*, focusing on how well resources and human capital are being managed for the company's future. Measurements include such things as employee retention, business process improvements, and the introduction of new products. The components of the scorecard are designed in an integrative manner so that they reinforce one another and link short-term actions with long-term strategic goals, as illustrated in Exhibit 8.5. Managers can use the scorecard to set goals, allocate resources, plan budgets, and determine rewards.[29]

The balanced scorecard helps managers focus on the key strategic measures that define the success of a particular organization over time and communicate them clearly throughout the organization. The scorecard has become the core management control system for many organizations today, including Hilton Hotels Corp., Allstate, Bell Emergis (a division of Bell Canada), and Cigna Insurance. British Airways clearly ties its use of the balanced scorecard to the feedback control model shown earlier in Exhibit 8.3. Scorecards serve as the agenda for monthly management meetings, where managers evaluate performance, discuss what corrective actions need to be taken, and set new targets for the various elements.[30] Executive information systems facilitate use of the balanced scorecard by enabling top managers to easily track measurements in multiple areas, rapidly analyze the data, and convert huge amounts of data into clear information reports. The scorecard is not necessarily the best for all situations, and small organizations seem to have been less effective in implementing a balanced-scorecard approach. One study, for example, found that, although many small manufacturing firms measure a wide variety of nonfinancial factors, most did not integrate the data with other peformance measures, a key feature of the balanced scorecard.[31]

Following the use of information systems for managerial decision making and control, IT has evolved further as a strategic tool for organizations such as Wal-Mart, Harrah's Entertainment, and Progressive Insurance. This is the highest level of application, as illustrated in Exhibit 8.1 at the beginning of the chapter. IT can add strategic value by providing better data and information within the organization (internal coordination) as well as redefining and supporting relationships with customers, suppliers, and other organizations (external relationships).

Adding Strategic Value: Strengthening Internal Coordination

Three primary IT tools for internal coordination are intranets, enterprise resource planning (ERP), and knowledge-management systems.

■ Intranets

Networking, which links people and departments within a particular building or across corporate offices, enabling them to share information and cooperate on projects, has become an important strategic tool for many companies. For example, an online database called CareWeb that medical professionals access via a network at Beth Israel Deaconess Medical Center in Boston contains records of more than 9 million patients. Emergency room doctors can instantly review a patient's past medical history, saving seconds that could make a difference between life and death. By managing information and making it available to anyone who needs it across the organization, CareWeb enables Beth Israel to provide better care as well as maintain better cost control.[32]

Networks may take many forms, but the fastest-growing form of corporate networking is the **intranet**, a private, company-wide information system that uses the communications protocols and standards of the Internet and the World Wide Web but is accessible only to people within the company. To view files and information, users simply navigate the site with a standard Web browser, clicking on links.[33] Because intranets are Web based, they can be accessed from any type of computer or workstation.

Today, most companies with intranets have moved their management information systems, executive information systems, and so forth over to the intranet so they are accessible to anyone who needs them. In addition, having these systems as part of the intranet means new features and applications can easily be added and accessed through a standard browser.

Intranets can improve internal communications and unlock hidden information. They enable employees to keep in touch with what's going on around the organization, quickly and easily find information they need, share ideas, and work on projects collaboratively. The most advanced intranets, such as those at SPS, Ford Motor Company, Nike, and Weyerhaeuser, are linked into the proprietary systems that govern a company's business functions. Ford's global intranet connects more than 100,000 workstations to thousands of sites offering proprietary information such as market research, analyses of competitor's components, and product development.[34] Frito-Lay's intranet enables salespeople to rapidly access sales-related customer and corporate information, brainstorm with their colleagues about the best approach for a sales pitch, or locate an expert within the company to assist with promotion planning, costing, or new product announcements.[35]

Enterprise Resource Planning

Another recent approach to information management helps pull together various types of information to see how decisions and actions in one part of the organization affect other parts of the firm. A growing number of companies are setting up broad-scale information systems that take a comprehensive view of the organization's activities. These **enterprise resource planning** (ERP) systems collect, process, and provide information about a company's entire enterprise, including order processing, product design, purchasing, inventory, manufacturing, distribution, human resources (HR), receipt of payments, and forecasting of future demand.[36] An ERP system can serve as the backbone for an entire organization by integrating and optimizing all the various business processes across the entire firm.[37]

Such a system links all of these areas of activity into a network, as illustrated in Exhibit 8.6. When a salesperson takes an order, the ERP system checks to see how the order affects inventory levels, scheduling, HR, purchasing, and distribution. The system replicates organizational processes in software, guides employees through the processes step-by-step, and automates as many of them as possible. For example, ERP software can automatically cut an accounts payable check as soon as a clerk confirms that goods have been received in inventory, send an online purchase order immediately after a manager has authorized a purchase, or schedule production at the most appropriate plant after an order is received.[38]

Briefcase

As an organization manager, keep these guidelines in mind:

Improve internal coordination, integration, and information sharing with intranets, enterprise resource planning (ERP) systems, and knowledge management systems. Use ERP to integrate and optimize business processes across the entire firm.

EXHIBIT 8.6
Example of an ERP Network

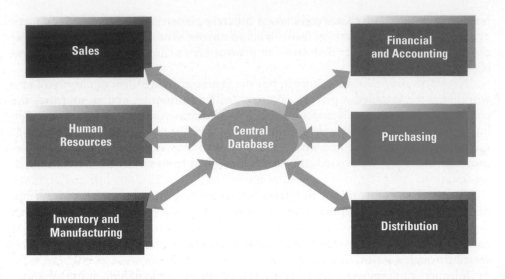

By implementing ERP, Lockport, Louisiana–based Bollinger Shipyards shaved an average of 15 percent off the time it takes to build a boat, translating into huge savings for the company. Each of nine Bollinger shipyards used to require two employees to handle administration, purchasing, and payroll; now they get by with one part-time person at each yard because the ERP system automates these processes. Freed from mundane chores, employees have been reassigned to more knowledge-intensive jobs.[39]

In addition, because the system integrates data about all aspects of operations, managers and employees at all levels can see how decisions and actions in one part of the organization affect other parts, using this information to make better decisions. ERP can provide the kind of information furnished by transaction processing systems, as well as that provided by information reporting systems, decision support systems, or executive information systems. The key is that ERP weaves all of these systems together so people can see the big picture and act quickly, helping the organization be smarter and more effective. Medecins du Monde, an international aid organization, uses an ERP system to keep precise track of expenses, supplies, and needs and enable doctors and volunteers in the field to see what resources are available and where they're most urgently needed.[40]

■ Knowledge Management

A primary goal for IT systems today is to support efforts to manage and leverage organizational knowledge. Increasingly, intellectual capital is the primary way in which businesses measure their value.[41] Therefore, managers see knowledge as an important resource to manage, just as they manage cash flow, raw materials, or other resources. A survey of CEOs attending the World Economic Forum's annual meeting found that 97 percent of senior executives see knowledge management as a critical issue for their organizations.[42] To learn and change, organizations must effectively acquire, create, and transfer knowledge across the company and modify their activities to reflect new knowledge and insight.[43]

Knowledge management is a new way to think about organizing and sharing an organization's intellectual and creative resources. It refers to the efforts to systematically find, organize, and make available a company's intellectual capital and to foster a culture of continuous learning and knowledge sharing so that organizational activities build on what is already known.[44] The company's **intellectual capital** is the sum of its knowledge, experience, understanding, relationships, processes, innovations, and discoveries. Although most of a company's knowledge is within the formal boundaries of the organization, tapping into the knowledge of outside experts is also important because it brings new knowledge into the organization that can be combined with existing knowledge to highlight problems or opportunities and make the organization more competitive.[45] A variety of new software tools support collaboration and knowledge sharing through services such as Web conferencing, knowledge portals, content management, and the use of *wikis*, an emerging collaboration tool. Wikis are an extension of the concept of blogs (Web logs); rather than simply allowing an individual to broadcast his or her views to an online audience, as blogs do, wikis let people edit and add content to the running log.[46]

What Is Knowledge? Knowledge is not the same thing as data or information, although it uses both. **Data** are simple, absolute facts and figures that, in and of themselves, may be of little use. A company might have data that show 30 percent of a particular product is sold to customers in Florida. To be useful to the organization, the data are processed into finished *information* by connecting them with other data—for example, nine out of ten of the products sold in Florida are bought by people over the age of sixty. **Information** is data that have been linked with other data and converted into a useful context for specific use. **Knowledge** goes a step further; it is a conclusion drawn from the information after it is linked to other information and compared to what is already known. Knowledge, as opposed to information and data, always has a human factor. Books can contain information, but the information becomes knowledge only when a person absorbs it and puts it to use.[48]

Organizations deal with both explicit knowledge and implicit, or tacit, knowledge.[49] **Explicit knowledge** is formal, systematic knowledge that can be codified, written down, and passed on to others in documents or general instructions. Tacit knowledge, on the other hand, is often difficult to put into words. **Tacit knowledge** is based on personal experience, rules of thumb, intuition, and judgment. It includes professional know-how and expertise, individual insight and experience, and creative solutions that are difficult to communicate and pass on to others. Explicit knowledge may be equated with *knowing about*; tacit knowledge is equated with *knowing how*.[50]

Finding ways to transfer both explicit and tacit knowledge—the knowing about and the knowing how—across the organization is critical.[51] Although explicit knowledge can easily be captured and shared in documents and through IT systems, as much as 80 percent of an organization's valuable knowledge may be tacit knowledge that is not easily captured and transferred.[52]

Approaches to Knowledge Management. Two distinct approaches to knowledge management are outlined in Exhibit 8.7. The first approach outlined in Exhibit 8.7 deals primarily with the collection and sharing of explicit knowledge, largely through the use of sophisticated IT systems.[53] Explicit knowledge may include intellectual properties such as patents and licenses; work processes such as policies and procedures; specific information on customers, markets, suppliers, or competitors; competitive intelligence reports; benchmark data; and so forth. When an organization uses this approach, the focus is on collecting and codifying knowledge and storing it in databases where it can easily be accessed and reused by anyone in the organization. With this "people-to-documents" approach, knowledge is gath-

Briefcase

As an organization manager, keep this guideline in mind:

Establish systems to facilitate both explicit and tacit knowledge sharing to help the organization learn and improve.

ered from the individuals who possess it and is organized into documents that others can access and reuse. When Barclays Global Investors faces request for proposals, for example, employees have to answer hundreds of complex questions for clients. A knowledge management system enables them to access and reuse answers to similar questions from previous proposals.[54]

Although IT plays an important role in knowledge management by enabling the storage and dissemination of data and information across the organization, IT is only one piece of a larger puzzle.[47] A complete knowledge management system includes not only processes for capturing and storing knowledge and organizing it for easy access, but also ways to generate new knowledge through learning and to share knowledge throughout the organization. As discussed in this chapter's Book Mark, old-fashioned paper might play just as important a role in knowledge work as computer technology.

Book Mark 8.0 (HAVE YOU READ THIS BOOK?)

The Myth of the Paperless Office
By Abigail J. Sellen and Richard H. R. Harper

At first glance, it seems like a great idea. Get rid of all the paper that clutters desktops and put everything on computers. Especially with the proliferation of handheld gadgets, paper seems redundant. Yet paper sales increase every year because paper is woven into the fabric of our lives and organizations—and for very good reasons, argue Abigail Sellen and Richard Harper, authors of *The Myth of the Paperless Office*. Paper actually enables a certain kind of information processing, as well as supporting collaborative knowledge work. People simply can't *think* the same way when looking at a document on a computer screen.

WHY PAPER PERSISTS
Sellen and Harper offer a number of reasons why paper persists. Paper has many advantages, they say, for performing certain kinds of cognitive tasks and supporting certain kinds of collaboration.

- *Paper is flexible and easily manipulated for reading.* Most people still prefer to read newspapers or documents on paper rather than on a computer screen. The authors cite four primary reasons for this: paper allows people to flexibly navigate through documents, it facilitates the cross-referencing of more than one document at a time, it allows for easy annotation, and it enables the interweaving of reading and writing. Paper allows one to pick up a document or newspaper, flip through it, read bits here and there, and quickly get a sense of the overall piece.
- *Paper is a tool for managing and coordinating action among co-workers.* The authors cite a fascinating example of air traffic controllers who, despite the availability

and use of highly sophisticated technology, continue to use paper flight strips to support a seamless teamwork, enable easy manipulation to indicate flight variations, give everyone on the team information at a glance, and facilitate the rapid pace of work required in this high-pressure environment.

- *Paper supports collaboration and sharing of knowledge.* Paper has interactional properties that are not easy to duplicate with digital media and collaborative tools. People working on collaborative documents that require the professional judgment and contributions of many people typically print drafts to read, mark up, and discuss with others while flipping though the pages. Sellen and Harper argue that, without paper drafts, collaborative, iterative knowledge work is much more difficult and time consuming. Paper, they say, "is a versatile medium that can be co-opted, shaped, and adapted to meet the needs of the work."

THE BEST OF BOTH WORLDS
The authors emphasize that digital technologies have their own advantages. Their point in *The Myth of the Paperless Office* is that managers should understand what paper can do and what computers can do and should know how to get the most out of each medium. "The real issue for organizations . . . is not to get rid of paper for its own sake, but to have sufficient motivation to understand their own work process and the ways paper plays a role."

The Myth of the Paperless Office, by Abigail Sellen and Richard Harper, is published by MIT Press.

Explicit Provide high-quality, reliable, and fast information systems for access of codified, reusable knowledge		**Tacit** Channel individual expertise to provide creative advice on strategic problems
People-to-documents approach *Develop an electronic document system that codifies, stores, disseminates, and allows reuse of knowledge*	**Knowledge Management Strategy**	**Person-to-person approach** *Develop networks for linking people so that tacit knowledge can be shared*
Invest heavily in information technology, with a goal of connecting people with reusable, codified knowledge	**Information Technology Approach**	*Invest moderately in information technology, with a goal of facilitating conversations and the personal exchange of tacit knowledge*

EXHIBIT 8.7
Two Approaches to Knowledge Management
Source: Based on Morten T. Hansen, Nitin Nohria, and Thomas Tierney, "What's Your Strategy for Managing Knowledge?" *Harvard Business Review* (March–April 1999), 106–116.

The second approach focuses on leveraging individual expertise and know-how—tacit knowledge—by connecting people face-to-face or through interactive media. Tacit knowledge includes professional know-how, individual insights and creativity, and personal experience and intuition. With this approach, managers concentrate on developing personal networks that link people together for the sharing of tacit knowledge. The organization uses IT systems primarily for facilitating conversation and person-to-person sharing of experience, insight, and ideas. For example, intranets are important for helping employees, especially those who are geographically dispersed, share ideas and tap into expert knowledge throughout the organization.

Organizations typically combine several methods and technologies to facilitate the sharing and transfer of both explicit and tacit knowledge. Consider the example of Montgomery-Watson Harza (MWH), one of the world's leading experts on power, water, and wastewater issues.

In Practice
Montgomery-Watson Harza

Montgomery-Watson Harza designs, builds, finances, and manages some of the largest and most technologically advanced water distribution, drainage, flood control, wastewater treatment, water remediation, and power plant projects in the world. Recent projects, for example, include a $92 million contract for a Lake Houston water plant in Texas and a complex project with the New Zealand Department of Conservation to solve sewerage problems in Abel Tasman National Park.

Innovation is an MWH hallmark, and it isn't limited to serving clients. The firm has implemented sophisticated collaborative systems that enable project teams to share knowledge and manage client work more effectively, giving MWH a competitive edge. Consider the work of design teams, which once had to meet face-to-face on site for development, design, and project management work. On average, teams spent 3 weeks researching a project proposal by searching out documents in various MWH libraries. Getting feedback and comments took more time, and design changes often occurred at the last minute. Project designs typically took months to complete.

Today, teams can access a database that enables them to find out how other projects have handled specific issues and done things better, more efficiently, faster, or more safely (explicit knowledge). In addition, team members can share information and tacit knowledge online and tap into the expertise of anyone who might be able to facilitate or strengthen the project.

The use of knowledge management systems has shortened the design-to-delivery cycle, improved the quality of designs, and increased efficiency for MWH projects.[55]

Adding Strategic Value: Strengthening External Relationships

External applications of IT for strengthening relationships with customers, suppliers, and partners include systems for supply chain management and the integrated enterprise, customer relationship management systems, and e-business organization design. The extension of corporate intranets to include customers and partners has expanded the potential for external collaboration. An **extranet** is an external communications system that uses the Internet and is shared by two or more organizations. Each organization moves certain data outside of its private intranet, but makes the data available only to the other companies sharing the extranet. For example, Pitney Bowes' extranet might enable a small supplier of wood pallets to use an extranet to see how many of its products Pitney Bowes has on hand and how many it will need in the next few days.

Leading by Design

Corrugated Supplies

Rick Van Horne had a vision. What would happen if all his plant's equipment continually fed data to the Internet, where the rest of the company, as well as suppliers and customers, could keep track of what was happening on the factory floor in real time? By using a password, customers could peek into the company's internal workings at any time, calling up Corrugated's production schedules to see exactly where their orders were in the process and when they would arrive. Suppliers could tap into the system to manage their own inventory—inventory they were selling to Corrugated as well as materials stored at Corrugated's plant to sell to someone else.

It cost him millions of dollars, but Van Horne's vision became a reality, making Corrugated one of the world's first completely Web-based production plants. The idea behind the new system is to connect all the plant's manufacturing equipment and then link it to the Web; the integrated system is available to everyone, from machinists on the plant floor to customers and suppliers off-site. The diagram shown here illustrates how the system works for a customer placing an order: The customer logs onto the Web site and types in an order for corrugated paper precisely cut and folded for 20,000 boxes. Computers at Corrugated's factory go to work immediately to determine the best way to blend that order with numerous other orders ranging from a few dozen boxes to 50,000. The computer comes up with the optimum schedule—that is, the one that gets the most orders out of a single roll with little leftover paper. A human operator checks the schedule on one of the numerous linked computer screens scattered around the plant and hits the Send button. Computer software directs the massive corrugators, trimmers, slitters, and other equipment, which begin spewing out paper orders at 800 feet per minute.Computer-controlled conveyor belts carry the order to the loading dock, where forklifts equipped with wireless PCs take the load to the designated trailer. Truck drivers log onto the Web site and are told which trailer to haul to maximize their trip's efficiency. The order is usually delivered to the customer the very next day.

Today, about 70 percent of Corrugated's orders are submitted via the Internet and routed electronically to the plant floor. The system saves time and money for Corrugated by automatically scheduling special-order details and cutting out paper waste. For customers, it means faster service and fewer mix-ups. One customer, Gene Mazurek, co-owner of Suburban Corrugated Box Co., says the first thing he does each morning is log onto Corrugated's Web site to see what's running, what's broken, where his order is, and when it should arrive. The new system has cut Mazurek's delivery time to his own customers from a week down to 2 days, something larger competitiors can't match. It's "the best thing that's ever happened so far," says Mazurek. "It's like Rick put his corrugating machine right inside my plant."

The Integrated Enterprise

Extranets play a critical role in today's integrated enterprise. The **integrated enterprise** is an organization that uses advanced IT to enable close coordination within the company as well as with suppliers, customers, and partners. One good example of the integrated enterprise is Corrugated Supplies, which has linked its entire factory to the Internet, as described in the Leading by Design box. An important aspect of the integrated enterprise is *supply chain management*, which means managing the sequence of suppliers and purchasers covering all stages of processing from obtaining raw materials to distributing finished goods to consumers.[56] For organizations to operate efficiently and provide high-quality items that meet customer needs, the company must have reliable deliveries of high-quality, reasonably priced supplies and materials. It also requires an efficient and reliable system for distributing finished products, making them readily accessible to customers.

Briefcase

As an organization manager, keep this guideline in mind:

Use IT applications such as extranets, systems for supply chain management and enterprise integration, and e-business systems to strengthen relationships with customers, suppliers, and business partners.

Corrugated System in Action

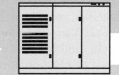

A customer order comes in via the Web and the system suggests the optimum schedule. An employee reviews the schedule and downloads it into the database.

At the scheduled time, software downloads the order to production machinery.

Employees load rolls of paper into the machines, which transform the rolls into corrugated sheets to meet the customer's exact specifications.

Wow, here already?

The truck driver arrives at the loading dock, logs onto the network to see which trailer to take, and delivers the customer's order the next morning.

A wireless PC directs the forklift driver to take the order to the appropriate trailer.

The package is taken by conveyor belt to shipping, which scans the bar code and adds the correct shipping label.

Employees wrap the finished sheets and affix a bar code printed automatically by the system.

Source: Adapted from Bill Richards, "Superplant," *eCompany* (November 2000), 182–196.

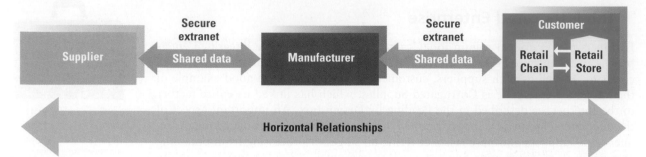

EXHIBIT 8.8
The Integrated Enterprise
Source: Based on Jim Turcotte,
Bob Silveri, and Tom Jobson,
"Are You Ready for the
E-Supply Chain?" *APICS—
The Performance Advantage*
(August 1998), 56–59.

Information Linkages. The most recent advances involve the use of computer networks or extranets to achieve the right balance of low inventory levels and customer responsiveness. Exhibit 8.8 illustrates horizontal information linkages in the integrated enterprise. By establishing electronic linkages between the organization and key partners for the sharing and exchange of data, the integrated enterprise creates a seamless, integrated line stretching from end consumers to raw materials suppliers.[57] For example, in the exhibit, as consumers purchase products in retail stores, the data are automatically fed into the retail chain's information system. In turn, the chain gives access to this constantly updated data to the manufacturing company through a secure extranet. With knowledge of this demand data, the manufacturer can produce and ship products when needed. As products are made by the manufacturer, data about raw materials used in the production process, updated inventory information, and updated forecasted demand are electronically provided to the manufacturer's suppliers, and the suppliers automatically replenish the manufacturer's raw materials inventory as needed.

Horizontal Relationships. The purpose of integrating the supply chain is for everyone to work closely together, moving in lockstep to meet customers' product and time demands. Honeywell Garrett Engine Boosting Systems, which makes turbochargers for cars, trucks, and light aircraft, has used an extranet to give suppliers access to its inventory and production data so they can respond rapidly to the manufacturer's need for parts. Now, Honeywell is working with big customers such as Ford and Volkswagen to integrate their systems so the company will have better information about turbocharger demands from customers as well. "Our goal," says Honeywell's Paul Hopkins, "is seamless value-chain connectivity from customer demand to suppliers."[58]

As with the newer organization designs described in Chapter 3, horizontal relationships get more emphasis than vertical relationships for the integrated enterprise to work. Enterprise integration can create a level of cooperation not previously imaginable if managers approach the practice with an attitude of trust and partnership, as in the interorganizational relationships described in Chapter 5. For example, Wal-Mart and Procter & Gamble (P&G) started simply by sharing sales data so P&G goods could be automatically replaced as they were sold off Wal-Mart's shelves. However, this computer-to-computer exchange evolved into a horizontal relationship that has the two firms sharing customer information, shopper loyalty information, and other data that provides strategic advantages for both sides of the trading partnership.[59]

Customer Relationship Management

Another approach to strengthening external relationships is through the use of **customer relationship (CRM) management** systems. These systems help companies track customers' interactions with the firm and allow employees to call up a customer's past sales and service records, outstanding orders, or unresolved problems.[60] CRM stashes in a database all the customer information that a small-town store owner would keep in his or her head—the names of customers, what they bought, what problems they've had with purchases, and so forth. The system helps coordinate sales, marketing, and customer service departments so that all are smoothly working together.

E-Business Organization Design

CRM and the integrated enterprise are both components of e-business, a new approach to how organizations conduct their business activities. **E-business** can be defined as any business that takes place by digital processes over a computer network rather than in physical space. Most commonly, it refers to electronic linkages over the Internet with customers, partners, suppliers, employees, or other key constituents. Despite the dot-com crash of the early 2000s, the Internet continues to transform traditional ways of doing business, helping companies in industries from banking to manufacturing to music retailing cut costs, speed innovation, and enhance relationships with customers.[61] Many traditional organizations have set up Internet operations to strengthen and improve these external relationships, but managers have to make a decision about how best to integrate *bricks and clicks*—that is, how to blend their traditional operations with an Internet initiative. In the early days of e-business, many organizations set up dot-com initiatives with little understanding of how those activities could and should be integrated with their overall business. As the reality of e-business has evolved, companies have gained valuable lessons in how to merge online and offline activities.[62]

The range of basic strategies for setting up an Internet operation is illustrated in Exhibit 8.9. At one end of the spectrum, companies can set up an in-house division that is closely integrated with the traditional business. The opposite approach is to create a spin-off company that is totally separate from the traditional organization. Many companies take a middle road by forging strategic partnerships with other organizations for their Internet initiative. Each of these options presents distinct advantages and disadvantages.[63]

In-House Division. An in-house division offers tight integration between the Internet operation and the organization's traditional operation. The organization creates a separate unit within the company that functions within the structure and guidance of the traditional organization. This approach gives the new division several advantages by piggybacking on the established company. These include brand recognition, purchasing leverage with suppliers, shared customer information and marketing opportunities, and distribution efficiencies. Tesco achieved success in online grocery delivery by keeping Tesco.com closely integrated with the existing grocery chain.

EXHIBIT 8.9
The Range of Strategies for Integrating Bricks and Clicks

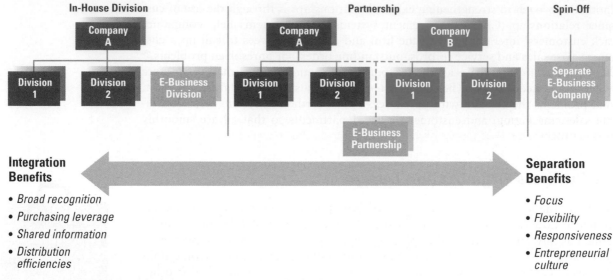

Source: Based on Ranjay Gulati and Jason Garino, "Get the Right Mix of Bricks and Clicks," *Harvard Business Review* (May–June 2000), 107–114.

In Practice

Tesco.com

When Britain's number one supermarket chain, Tesco, decided to launch a dot-com division, creating an electronic version of a 1950s delivery boy, managers evaluated options and decided to set up an in-house division to avoid the huge start-up costs that would be required for a spin-off company. The idea was to start slowly and keep close control over the new operation to maintain profitability. Tesco managers saw their online service as just another way to provide benefits to customers.

By being part of the greater Tesco enterprise, Tesco.com was able to ride on the back of the parent company, leveraging its brand, suppliers, advertising, and customer database. Tesco started by offering delivery from just one store, gradually rolling out service to other areas. By integrating the new operation with the traditional stores, Tesco didn't have to build new warehouses; the Internet division simply used the established warehouses and distribution systems of the chain and picked goods off supermarket shelves to fill customer orders. Using the store-based picking approach kept start-up costs low. Tesco spent only $58 million on its Internet operation during the first 4 years, and the operation was profitable from the beginning. By mid-2004, Tesco.com had grown to cover 95 percent of the United Kingdom and was receiving 70,000 orders per week.[64]

Tesco's success illustrates many of the advantages of the in-house approach. A potential problem with an in-house division, however, is that the new operation doesn't have the flexibility and autonomy needed to move quickly in the Internet world.

Spin-Off. To give the Internet operation greater organizational autonomy, flexibility, and focus, some organizations choose to create a separate spin-off company. For example, Barnes & Noble created a separate division, barnesandnoble.com, which it ultimately spun off as a stand-alone company to compete with Amazon.

Whirlpool created a spin-off called Brandwise.com, a site designed to help consumers find the best products and value—even if that means from other manufacturers. Peter Monticup, owner of retail store Magic Tricks, created an Internet spin-off that became so successful that he eventually closed his bricks-and-mortar establishment.[65] Advantages of a spin-off include faster decision making, increased flexibility and responsiveness to changing market conditions, an entrepreneurial culture, and management that is totally focused on the success of the online operation. Potential disadvantages are the loss of brand recognition and marketing opportunities, higher start-up costs, and loss of leverage with suppliers.

Strategic Partnership. Partnerships, whether through joint ventures or alliances, offer a middle ground, enabling organizations to attain some of the advantages and overcome some of the disadvantages of the purely in-house or spin-off options. For example, when J&R Electronics, a Manhattan store with limited national reach, decided to go online, managers quickly realized that J&R didn't have the resources needed to build a solid online business. The company partnered with Amazon.com to capitalize on the advantages of both integration and separation. Amazon invests around $200 million a year in technology and site content, a rate that a small retailer like J&R simply couldn't do. The partnership approach gave J&R access to Amazon's millions of customers and allowed the firm to build its online identity and reputation. Managers at J&R agree with the advice of Drew Sharma, managing director of Internet marketing agency Mindfire Interactive, for smaller companies going online: "If you can stand on the shoulders of giants, then why not?"[66] A primary disadvantage of partnerships is time spent managing relationships, potential conflicts between partners, and a possibility that one company will fail to deliver as promised or go out of business. For example, if Amazon.com should fail, it would take J&R's online business with it and damage the company's reputation with Internet customers.

IT Impact on Organization Design

Not every organization will become involved in e-business like Tesco, Corrugated Supplies, or J&R Electronics. However, advances in IT are having a tremendous impact on all organizations in every industry. Some specific implications of these advances for organization design are smaller organizations, decentralized structures, improved internal and external coordination, and new network organization structures.

Briefcase

As an organization manager, keep this guideline in mind:

With greater use of IT, consider smaller organizational units, decentralized structures, improved internal coordination, and greater interorganizational collaboration, including the possibility of outsourcing or a network structure.

1. *Smaller organizations.* Some Internet-based businesses exist almost entirely in cyberspace; there is no formal organization in terms of a building with offices, desks, and so forth. One or a few people may maintain the site from their homes or a rented work space. Even for traditional businesses, new IT enables the organization to do more work with fewer people. At Progressive Insurance, described in the chapter opening, customers can buy insurance without ever speaking to an agent or sales rep. In addition, ERP and other IT systems automatically handle many administrative duties, reducing the need for clerical staff. The Michigan Department of Transportation (MDOT) used to need an army of workers to verify contractors' work. Large projects often required as many as twenty inspectors on-site every day to keep track of thousands of work items. Today, MDOT rarely sends more than one field technician to a site. The em-

ployee enters data into a laptop computer using road construction management software tied to computers at headquarters. The system can automatically generate payment estimates and handle other administrative processes that used to take hours of labor.[67] Companies can also outsource many functions and thus use fewer in-house resources.

2. *Decentralized organizational structures.* IT enables organizations to reduce layers of management and decentralize decision making. Information that may have previously been available only to top managers at headquarters can be quickly and easily shared throughout the organization, even across great geographical distances. Managers in varied business divisions or offices have the information they need to make important decisions quickly rather than waiting for decisions from headquarters. Technologies that enable people to meet and coordinate online can facilitate communication and decision making among distributed, autonomous groups of workers. In addition, technology allows for telecommuting, whereby individual workers can perform work that was once done in the office from their computers at home or other remote locations. People and groups no longer have to be located under one roof to collaborate and share information. An organization might be made up of numerous small teams or even individuals who work autonomously but coordinate electronically. Although management philosophy and corporate culture have a substantial impact on whether IT is used to decentralize information and authority or to reinforce a centralized authority structure,[68] most organizations today use technology to further decentralization.

3. *Improved horizontal coordination.* Perhaps one of the greatest outcomes of IT is its potential to improve coordination and communication within the firm. Intranets and other networks can connect people even when their offices, factories, or stores are scattered around the world. For example, General Motors' intranet, dubbed Socrates on the basis that the Greek philosopher's name would be recognizable worldwide, connects some 100,000 staff members around the globe. Managers use the intranet to communicate with one another and to stay aware of organizational activities and outcomes.[69] They can also provide key information to employees throughout the organization with just a few keystrokes.

4. *Improved interorganizational relationships.* IT can also improve horizontal coordination and collaboration with external parties such as suppliers, customers, and partners. Extranets are increasingly important for linking companies with contract manufacturers and outsourcers, as well as for supporting the integrated enterprise, as described earlier. Exhibit 8.10 shows differences between traditional interorganizational relationship characteristics and emerging relationship characteristics. Traditionally, organizations had an arm's-length relationship with suppliers. However, as we discussed in Chapter 5, suppliers are becoming closer partners, tied electronically to the organization for orders, invoices, and payments. In addition, new IT has increased the power of consumers by giving them electronic access to a wealth of information from thousands of companies just by clicking a mouse. Consumers also have direct access to manufacturers, altering their perceptions and expectations regarding convenience, speed, and service.

Studies have shown that interorganizational information networks tend to heighten integration, blur organizational boundaries, and create shared strategic contingencies among firms.[70] One good example of interorganizational collaboration is the PulseNet alliance, sponsored by the Centers for Disease Control and Prevention (CDC). The PulseNet information network uses collaborative tech-

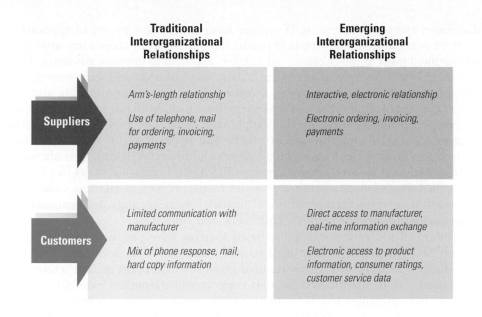

Traditional Interorganizational Relationships	Emerging Interorganizational Relationships
Suppliers Arm's-length relationship Use of telephone, mail for ordering, invoicing, payments	Interactive, electronic relationship Electronic ordering, invoicing, payments
Customers Limited communication with manufacturer Mix of phone response, mail, hard copy information	Direct access to manufacturer, real-time information exchange Electronic access to product information, consumer ratings, customer service data

EXHIBIT 8.10

Key Characteristics of Traditional versus Emerging Interorganizational Relationships
Source: Based on Charles V. Callahan and Bruce A. Pasternack, "Corporate Strategy in the Digital Age," *Strategy & Business*, Issue 15 (Second Quarter 1999), 10–14.

nology to help U.S. state and federal agencies anticipate, identify, and prevent food-borne disease outbreaks. Through more frequent communication and real-time information sharing, rich relationships among the various agencies have evolved. State health labs and the CDC once had infrequent contact but are now involved in joint strategic planning regarding the PulseNet project.[71]

5. *Enhanced network structures.* The high level of interorganizational collaboration needed in a network organization structure, described in Chapter 3, would not be possible without the use of advanced IT. In the business world, these are also sometimes called *modular structures* or *virtual organizations*. Outsourcing has become a major trend, thanks to computer technology that can tie companies together into a seamless information flow. For example, Hong Kong's Li & Fung is one of the biggest providers of clothing for retailers such as Abercrombie & Fitch, Guess, Ann Taylor, the Limited, and Disney, but the company doesn't own any factories, machines, or fabrics. Li & Fung specializes in managing information, relying on an electronically connected web of 7,500 partners in thirty-seven countries to provide raw materials and assemble the clothes. Using an extranet allows Li & Fung to stay in touch with worldwide partners and move items quickly from factories to retailers. It also lets retailers track orders as they move through production and make last-minute changes and additions.[72] With a network structure, most activities are outsourced, so that different companies perform the various functions needed by the organization. The speed and ease of electronic communication makes the network structure a viable option for companies that want to keep costs low but expand activities or market presence.

Summary and Interpretation

This chapter covered a number of important topics related to IT. The information revolution has had a tremendous impact on organizations in all industries. Highly successful organizations today are generally those that most effectively collect, store, distribute, and use information. IT systems have evolved to a variety of applications to meet organizations' information needs. Operations applications are applied to well-defined tasks at lower organization levels and help to improve efficiency. These include transaction processing systems, data warehousing, and data mining. Advanced computer-based systems are also used for better decision making and control of the organization. Decision-making systems include management information systems, reporting systems, decision support systems, and executive information systems, which are typically used at middle and upper levels of the organization. Management control systems include budgets and financial reports, periodic nonfinancial statistical reports, reward systems, and quality control systems. An innovation called the *balanced scorecard* provides managers with a balanced view of the organization by integrating traditional financial measurements and statistical reports with a concern for markets, customers, and employees.

Today, all the various computer-based systems have begun to merge into an overall IT system that can be used to add strategic value. Intranets, ERP, and knowledge management systems are used primarily to support greater internal coordination and flexibility. Systems that support and strengthen external relationships include extranets and the integrated enterprise, customer relationship management, and e-business. The integrated enterprise uses advanced IT to enable close coordination among a company and its suppliers, partners, and customers. Customer relationship management systems help companies keep track of their customers' interactions with the organization and provide better service. To establish an e-business, companies can choose among an in-house division, a spin-off, or a strategic partnership. Each has strengths and weaknesses.

Advanced IT is having a significant impact on organization design. Technology has enabled creation of the network organization structure, in which a company subcontracts most of its major functions to separate companies that are connected electronically to the headquarters organization. Even organizations that do not use a network structure are rapidly evolving toward greater interorganizational collaboration. Other specific implications of advances in technology for organization design include smaller organizations, decentralized organization structures, and improved internal and external coordination.

Key Concepts

balanced scorecard
benchmarking
business intelligence
customer relationship management
data
data mining
data warehousing
decision support system
e-business
enterprise resource planning
executive information system
explicit knowledge
extranet
feedback control model

information
information reporting system
integrated enterprise
intellectual capital
intranet
knowledge
knowledge management
management control systems
management information system
networking
Six Sigma
tacit knowledge
transaction processing systems

Discussion Questions

1. Do you think technology will eventually enable top managers to do their jobs with little face-to-face communication? Discuss.
2. Why might a company consider using an intranet rather than traditional management and executive information systems?
3. How might an enterprise resource planning system be used to improve strategic management of a manufacturing organization?
4. Discuss some ways a large insurance company such as Progressive, described in the chapter opening, might use MIS to improve decision making.
5. Describe how the four management control system elements discussed in the chapter might be used for feedback control within organizations. Compare and contrast this four-part system with use of the balanced scorecard.
6. Describe your use of explicit knowledge when you research and write a term paper. Do you also use tacit knowledge regarding this activity? Discuss.
7. Why is knowledge management particularly important to a company that wants to become a learning organization?
8. What is meant by the *integrated enterprise*? Describe how organizations can use extranets to extend and enhance horizontal relationships required for enterprise integration.
9. What are some competitive issues that might lead a company to take a partnership approach to e-business rather than setting up an in-house Internet division? What are the advantages and disadvantages of each approach?
10. How might the adoption of IT affect how an organization is designed?

Chapter 8 Workbook: Are You Fast Enough to Succeed in Internet Time?*

Does your business have what it takes to move at Internet speed?

What is an Internet year? It's the time in which an e-company needs to accomplish the kind of business goals that once took a year. Conventional wisdom puts an Internet year at anywhere from 60 to 90 days. Regardless, few will argue that companies need to move faster now than ever imagined.

Can you afford the luxury of in-depth analysis, full due diligence, building consensus, test marketing—all the cornerstones of responsible corporate management? Does their value change when you weigh it against the cost to your company's scarcest commodity—time? Kelsey Biggers, executive vice president of Micro Modeling Associates (MMA), offers the following scenarios to help determine whether you are capable of operating at Internet speed. Choose the best course of action from the choices given (answers below):

1. You have met a company that can be a potential strategic partner for marketing your service to a new industry online. The vibes are good, and you want to map out the potential relationship, but to do so you need to share client and billing information. A nondisclosure agreement is necessary, and the company hands you its standard agreement. What do you do?

a. Get a copy of your company's standard nondisclosure agreement and submit it to your potential partner as an alternative to its NDA.
b. Fax the agreement to your lawyer and ask him or her to get back to you ASAP with any amendments so you can continue the conversation.
c. Look over the agreement and sign it right away.

2. You're looking for a creative director for your Web site, and you know the position will be critical to your whole look and feel online. You hope to have three or four excellent candidates to choose from and have considered doing a retained search for the position. Out of nowhere your old college roommate, whom you respect enormously, refers you to an associate for the position. You meet the candidate for breakfast and you are blown away by the person's credentials and personality. You have three choices:

a. Offer the candidate the job before the check arrives.
b. Give the candidate a strong "warm and fuzzy" about the job while you initiate a quick search for a couple of alternative candidates.

*"Are You Fast Enough to Succeed in Internet Time? Does Your Business Have What It Takes to Move at Internet Speed?" Reprinted with permission from *Entrepreneur Magazine*, September 1999, *http://www.entrepreneur.com*.

c. Schedule a round of interviews with your senior colleagues back in the office to confirm your positive instincts, while also identifying one or two alternative candidates for comparison.

3. Your online strategy calls for targeting two vertical markets for your service in the next 9 months. Your service can be tailored to meet the buying needs of companies in several industries, so it's a matter of picking the right industries to target. High-growth, dynamic industries are obviously preferred. Which approach would you select?

   a. Hire an MBA with expertise in finance and marketing to create high-level screening criteria for target industries and identify the five best fits for your services.

   b. Hire your neighbor, who happens to be a doctor, knows the healthcare industry, and can make several introductions to HMOs and pharmaceutical companies.

   c. Ask an intern to research publicly available information from Gartner Group, Forrester Research, and other industry analyst organizations for online spending habits in different industries and make recommendations.

4. Your company has been looking to merge with a strategic partner for some time. You have identified three companies that would be good fits, but each has its advantages and disadvantages. Which would you choose?

   a. Company A offers a service that is perfectly complementary to your own, and the price is right. However, the company has indicated that it doesn't think it has enough scale to do a merger now and would rather wait 9 months until after the holiday selling season to complete the transaction.

   b. Company B is smaller and dynamic, but has grown too fast and has a bad balance sheet. It could be picked up immediately, but your company would have to assume some unwanted debt along with the merger.

   c. Company C has a great offline presence in its space, but has not yet executed its e-commerce plan. The two companies might be a great fit once Company C has established its online presence by midsummer.

5. Your e-commerce strategy requires a real-time fulfillment system that can process orders straight through and provide data on client buying patterns. You have looked outside your firm for technology support to help bring this capability online and have been presented with three alternatives:

   a. A senior programmer from your prior firm is now a freelance consultant. He can get started immediately and hire a dozen coders who promise to get a capability up and running in 60 days and grow out the functionality.

   b. Your internal technology group can staff a team of a dozen people to build out the system in a year and will then have the ability to support and grow the service when it goes live.

   c. An e-solutions consultancy can project manage and build the entire system, but would want to take 60 days to design the technical architecture before starting development. The consultancy insists this time is necessary to ensure a scalable service.

Answers (Each correct answer is worth one point.)

Question 1
c. The objective is to make a decision quickly and to move the process forward without a great deal of red tape and delay. The legal process can oftentimes slow decision making—whether by 3 weeks or 3 months—and time is of the essence in the online world. Moreover, when was the last time an NDA about client information materially affected your business? Better to spend your time building trust than protecting against an unlikely downside.

Question 2
a. Offer the candidate the job while waiting for the check. If this person has been vouched for by someone you trust and you love the person's work, grab the candidate while he or she is available and put that person to work. If you think the candidate is a great hire, chances are, so will your competitors.

Question 3
b. Hire your neighbor. Any list of dynamic industries you put together is bound to include healthcare, and your biggest challenge is to find a credible person with industry know-how and contacts who can take you into the industry. Your neighbor can do that. Now start looking for the other industries you want to focus on.

Question 4
b. Buy Company B. Company B has proven itself fast-moving and dynamic, and its balance sheet issues makes it open to a favorable price. Companies A and C are both tying their success to future events—a strong holiday selling season or a successful online launch—either of which might not happen and both of which are in the distant Internet future.

Question 5
c. The one area a company cannot afford to get wrong is its technical architecture. It must scale and be reliable, or your whole business will be at risk. Programmers without a blueprint cannot ensure a successful online environment, and staffing internally is time-consuming and uncertain. Better to outsource the project immediately while building an internal team to take it over after its launch.

Case for Analysis: Century Medical*

Sam Nolan clicked the mouse for one more round of solitaire on the computer in his den. He'd been at it for more than an hour, and his wife had long ago given up trying to persuade him to join her for a movie or a rare Saturday night on the town. The mind-numbing game seemed to be all that calmed Sam enough to stop thinking about work and how his job seemed to get worse every day.

Nolan was chief information officer at Century Medical, a large medical products company based in Connecticut. He had joined the company 4 years ago, and since that time Century had made great progress integrating technology into its systems and processes. Nolan had already led projects to design and build two highly successful systems for Century. One was a benefits-administration system for the company's HR department. The other was a complex Web-based purchasing system that streamlined the process of purchasing supplies and capital goods. Although the system had been up and running for only a few months, modest projections were that it would save Century nearly $2 million annually.

Previously, Century's purchasing managers were bogged down with shuffling paper. The purchasing process would begin when an employee filled out a materials request form. Then the form would travel through various offices for approval and signatures before eventually being converted into a purchase order. The new Web-based system allowed employees to fill out electronic request forms that were automatically e-mailed to everyone whose approval was needed. The time for processing request forms was cut from weeks to days or even hours. When authorization was complete, the system would automatically launch a purchase order to the appropriate supplier. In addition, because the new system had dramatically cut the time purchasing managers spent shuffling paper, they now had more time to work collaboratively with key stakeholders to identify and select the best suppliers and negotiate better deals.

Nolan thought wearily of all the hours he had put in developing trust with people throughout the company and showing them how technology could not only save time and money but also support team-based work and give people more control over their own jobs. He smiled briefly as he recalled one long-term HR employee, 61-year-old Ethel Moore. She had been terrified when Nolan first began showing her the company's intranet, but she was now one of his biggest supporters. In fact, it had been Ethel who had first approached him with an idea about a Web-based job posting system. The two had pulled together a team and developed an idea for linking Century managers, internal recruiters, and job applicants using artificial intelligence software on top of an integrated Web-based system. When Nolan had presented the idea to his boss, executive vice president Sandra Ivey, she had enthusiastically endorsed it,

and within a few weeks the team had authorization to proceed with the project.

But everything began to change when Ivey resigned her position 6 months later to take a plum job in New York. Ivey's successor, Tom Carr, seemed to have little interest in the project. During their first meeting, Carr had openly referred to the project as a waste of time and money. He immediately disapproved several new features suggested by the company's internal recruiters, even though the project team argued that the features could double internal hiring and save millions in training costs. "Just stick to the original plan and get it done. All this stuff needs to be handled on a personal basis anyway," Carr countered. "You can't learn more from a computer than you can talking to real people—and as for internal recruiting, it shouldn't be so hard to talk to people if they're already working right here in the company." Carr seemed to have no understanding of how and why technology was being used. He became irritated when Ethel Moore referred to the system as "Web-based." He boasted that he had never visited Century's intranet site and suggested that "this Internet fad" would eventually blow over anyway. Even Ethel's enthusiasm couldn't get through to him. She tried to show him some of the HR resources available on the intranet and explain how it had benefited the department and the company, but he waved her away. "Technology is for those people in the IT department. My job is people, and yours should be too." Ethel was crushed, and Nolan realized it would be like beating his head against a brick wall to try to persuade Carr to the team's point of view. Near the end of the meeting, Carr even jokingly suggested that the project team should just buy a couple of filing cabinets and save everyone some time and money.

Just when the team thought things couldn't get any worse, Carr dropped the other bomb. They would no longer be allowed to gather input from users of the new system. Nolan feared that without the input of potential users, the system wouldn't meet their needs, or even that users would boycott the system because they hadn't been allowed to participate. No doubt that would put a great big "I told you so" smile right on Carr's face.

Nolan sighed and leaned back in his chair. The project had begun to feel like a joke. The vibrant and innovative HR department his team had imagined now seemed like nothing more than a pipe dream. But despite his frustration, a new thought entered Nolan's mind: "Is Carr just stubborn and narrow-minded or does he have a point that HR is a people business that doesn't need a high-tech job-posting system?"

*Based on Carol Hildebrand, "New Boss Blues," *CIO Enterprise*, Section 2 (November 15, 1998), 53–58; and Megan Santosus, "Advanced Micro Devices' Web-Based Purchasing System," *CIO*, Section 1 (May 15, 1998), 84.

Case for Analysis: Product X*

Several years ago the top management of a multibillion-dollar corporation decided that Product X was a failure and should be disbanded. The losses involved exceeded $100 million. At least five people knew that Product X was a failure 6 years before the decision was made to stop producing it. Three of those people were plant managers who lived daily with the production problems. The other two were marketing officials who realized that the manufacturing problems were not solvable without expenditures that would raise the price of the product to the point where it would no longer be competitive in the market.

There are several reasons why this information did not get to the top sooner. At first, the subordinates believed that with exceptionally hard work they might turn the errors into successes. But the more they struggled, the more they realized the massiveness of the original error. The next task was to communicate the bad news upward so that it would be heard. They knew that in their company bad news would not be well received at the upper levels if it was not accompanied with suggestions for positive action. They also knew that the top management was enthusiastically describing Product X as a new leader in its field. Therefore, they spent much time composing memos that would communicate the realities without shocking top management.

Middle management read the memos and found them too open and forthright. Since they had done the production and marketing studies that resulted in the decision to produce X, the memos from lower-level management questioned the validity of their analysis. They wanted time to really check these gloomy predictions and, if they were accurate, to design alternative corrective strategies. If the pessimistic information was to be sent upward, middle management wanted it accompanied with optimistic action alternatives. Hence further delay.

Once middle management was convinced that the gloomy predictions were valid, they began to release some of the bad news to the top—but in carefully measured doses. They managed the releases carefully to make certain they were covered if top management became upset. The tactic they used was to cut the memos drastically and summarize the findings. They argued that the cuts were necessary because top management was always complaining about receiving long memos; indeed, some top executives had let it be known that good memos were memos of one page or less. The result was that top management received fragmented information underplaying the intensity of the problem (not the problem itself) and overplaying the degree to which middle management and the technicians were in control of the problem.

Top management therefore continued to speak glowingly about the product, partially to ensure that it would get the financial backing it needed from within the company. Lower-level management became confused and eventually depressed because they could not understand this continued top management support, nor why studies were ordered to evaluate the production and marketing difficulties that they had already identified. Their reaction was to reduce the frequency of their memos and the intensity of their alarm, while simultaneously turning over the responsibility for dealing with the problem to middle-management people. When local plant managers, in turn, were asked by their foremen and employees what was happening, the only response they gave was that the company was studying the situation and continuing its support. This information bewildered the foremen and led them to reduce their own concern.

*Excerpted from C. Argyris and D. Schon, *Organizational Learning: A Theory of Action Perspective.* Argyris/Schon, *Organizational Learning,* © 1978, Addison–Wesley Publishing Co., Inc., Reading, Massachusetts. Pages 1–2. Reprinted with permission. Case appeared in Gareth Morgan, *Creative Organization Theory* (1989), Sage Publications.

Notes

1. Patrick Barwise and Sean Meehan, "The Benefits of Getting the Basics Right," *Financial Times* (October 8, 2004), 4ff; Lisa A. Lewins and Tim R. V. Davis, "Progressive Insurance Competes with the Strategic Application of Information Technology," *Journal of Organizational Excellence* (Spring 2002), 31–38; and "Auto Insurance Gets Even Easier for Progressive Direct Customers Buying Online; New Electronic Signature Capability Cuts Down on Paperwork," *Business Wire* (February 17, 2005), 1.

2. Leigh Buchanan, "Working Wonders on the Web," *Inc. Magazine* (November 2003), 76–84, 104.

3. James Cox, "Changes at Olive Garden Have Chain Living 'La Dolce Vita,'" *USA Today,* (December 18, 2000), B1; Bernard Wysocki Jr., "Hospitals Cut ER Waits," *The Wall Street Journal* (July 3, 2002), D1, D3.

4. Michael Fitzgerald, "A Drive-Through Lane to the Next Time Zone," *The New York Times* (July 18, 2004), Section 3, 3.

5. Charles V. Callahan and Bruce A. Pasternack, "Corporate Strategy in the Digital Age," *Strategy & Business,* Issue 15 (Second Quarter 1999), 10–14.

6. Ibid.

7. Bill Richards, "A Total Overhaul," *The Wall Street Journal* (December 7, 1998), R30.

8. Erik Berkman, "How to Stay Ahead of the Curve," *CIO* (February 1, 2002), 72–80; and Heather Harreld, "Pick-Up Artists," *CIO* (November 1, 2000), 148–154.

9. "Business Intelligence," special advertising section, *Business 2.0* (February 2003), S1–S4; and Alice Dragoon, "Business Intelligence Gets Smart," *CIO* (September 15, 2003), 84–91.

10. Julie Schlosser, "Looking for Intelligence in Ice Cream," *Fortune* (March 17, 2003), 114–120.

11. Kevin Kelleher, "66,207,896 Bottles of Beer on the Wall," *Business 2.0* (January–February 2004), 47–49.

12. Gary Loveman, "Diamonds in the Data Mine," *Harvard Business Review* (May 2003), 109–113; Joe Ashbrook Nickell, "Welcome to Harrah's," *Business 2.0* (April 2002), 48–54; and Meridith Levinson, "Harrah's Knows What You Did Last Night," *Darwin Magazine* (May 2001), 61–68.

13. Megan Santosus, "Motorola's Semiconductor Products Sector's EIS," Working Smart column, *CIO*, Section 1 (November 15, 1998), 84.

14. Constance L. Hays, "What They Know About You; Wal-Mart—An Obsessive Monitor of Customer Behavior," *The New York Times* (November 14, 2004), Section 3, 1.

15. Michael Arndt, "McDonald's: Fries With That Salad?" *BusinessWeek* (July 5, 2004), 82–84.

16. Robert Simons, "Strategic Organizations and Top Management Attention to Control Systems," *Strategic Management Journal* 12 (1991), 49–62.

17. Kevin Ferguson, "Mission Control," *Inc. Magazine* (November 2003), 27–28; and Russ Banham, "Seeing the Big Picture: New Data Tools Are Enabling CEOs to Get a Better Handle on Peformance Across Their Organizations," *Chief Executive* (November 2003), 46ff.

18. Christopher Koch, "How Verizon Flies by Wire," *CIO* (November 1, 2004), 94–96.

19. Richard L. Daft and Norman B. Macintosh, "The Nature and Use of Formal Control Systems for Management Control and Strategy Implementation," *Journal of Management* 10 (1984), 43–66.

20. Susannah Patton, "Web Metrics That Matter," *CIO* (November 14, 2002), 84–88; and Ramin Jaleshgari, "The End of the Hit Parade," *CIO* (May 14, 2000), 183–190.

21. Adam Lashinsky, "Meg and the Machine," *Fortune* (September 1, 2003), 68–78.

22. Howard Rothman, "You Need Not Be Big to Benchmark," *Nation's Business* (December 1992), 64–65.

23. Tom Rancour and Mike McCracken, "Applying 6 Sigma Methods for Breakthrough Safety Performance," *Professional Safety* 45, no. 10 (October 2000), 29–32; Lee Clifford, "Why You Can Safely Ignore Six Sigma," *Fortune* (January 22, 2001), 140.

24. Michael Hammer and Jeff Goding, "Putting Six Sigma in Perspective," *Quality* (October 2001), 58–62; Michael Hammer, "Process Management and the Future of Six Sigma," *Sloan Management Review* (Winter 2002), 26–32.

25. Michael Arndt, "Quality Isn't Just for Widgets," *BusinessWeek* (July 22, 2002), 72–73.

26. Daft and Macintosh, "The Nature and Use of Formal Control Systems for Management Control and Strategy Imple-mentation"; Scott S. Cowen and J. Kendall Middaugh II, "Matching an Organization's Planning and Control System to Its Environment," *Journal of General Management* 16 (1990), 69–84.

27. "On Balance," a CFO Interview with Robert Kaplan and David Norton, *CFO* (February 2001), 73–78; Chee W. Chow, Kamal M. Haddad, and James E. Williamson, "Applying the Balanced Scorecard to Small Companies," *Management Accounting* 79, No. 2 (August 1997), 21–27; and Robert Kaplan and David Norton, "The Balanced Scorecard: Measures That Drive Performance," *Harvard Business Review* (January–February 1992), 71–79.

28. Based on Kaplan and Norton, "The Balanced Scorecard"; Chow, Haddad, and Williamson, "Applying the Balanced Scorecard"; Cathy Lazere, "All Together Now," *CFO* (February 1998), 28–36.

29. Debby Young, "Score It a Hit," *CIO Enterprise*, Section 2 (November 15, 1998), 27ff.

30. Nils–Göran Olve, Carl-Johan Petri, Jan Roy, and Sofie Roy, "Twelve Years Later: Understanding and Realizing the Value of Balanced Scorecards," *Ivey Business Journal* (May–June 2004), 1–7.

31. William Davig, Norb Elbert, and Steve Brown, "Implementing a Strategic Planning Model for Small Manufacturing Firms: An Adaptation of the Balanced Scorecard," *SAM Advanced Management Journal* (Winter 2004), 18–24.

32. Melanie Warner, "Under the Knife," *Business 2.0* (January–February 2004), 84–89.

33. Wayne Kawamoto, "Click Here for Efficiency," *BusinessWeek Enterprise* (December 7, 1998), Ent. 12–Ent. 14.

34. Mary J. Cronin, "Ford's Intranet Success," *Fortune* (March 30, 1998), 158; Eryn Brown, "9 Ways to Win on the Web," *Fortune* (May 24, 1999), 112–125.

35. Esther Shein, "The Knowledge Crunch," *CIO* (May 1, 2001), 128–132.

36. Derek Slater, "What is ERP?" *CIO Enterprise*, Section 2 (May 15, 1999), 86; and Jeffrey Zygmont, "The Ties That Bind," *Inc. Tech* no. 3 (1998), 70–84.

37. Vincent A. Mabert, Ashok Soni, and M. A. Venkataramanan, "Enterprise Resource Planning: Common Myths versus Evolving Reality," *Business Horizons* (May–June 2001), 69–76.

38. Slater, "What Is ERP?"

39. Owen Thomas, "E-Business Software: Bollinger Shipyards," *eCompany* (May 2001), 119–120.

40. Susannah Patton, "Doctors' Group Profits from ERP," *CIO* (September 1, 2003), 32.

41. Research reported in Eric Seubert, Y. Balaji, and Mahesh Makhija, "The Knowledge Imperative," *CIO Advertising Supplement* (March 15, 2000), S1–S4.

42. Andrew Mayo, "Memory Bankers," *People Management* (January 22, 1998), 34–38; Gary Abramson, "On the KM Midway," *CIO Enterprise*, Section 2 (May 15, 1999), 63–70.

43. David A. Garvin, "Building a Learning Organization," in *Harvard Business Review on Knowledge Management* (Boston, Mass.: President and Fellows of Harvard College, 1998), 47–80.

44. Based on Mayo, "Memory Bankers"; William Miller, "Building the Ultimate Resource," *Management Review* (January

1999), 42–45; and Todd Datz, "How to Speak Geek," *CIO Enterprise*, Section 2 (April 15, 1999), 46–52.

45. Vikas Anand, William H. Glick, and Charles C. Manz, "Thriving on the Knowledge of Outsiders: Tapping Organizational Social Capital," *Academy of Management Executive* 16, no. 1 (2002), 87–101.

46. Tony Kontzer, "Kitchen Sink: Many Collaborative Options," *Information Week* (May 5, 2003), 35; sidebar in Tony Kontzer, "Learning to Share," *Information Week* (May 5, 2003), 29–37.

47. Louisa Wah, "Behind the Buzz," *Management Review* (April 1999), 17–26.

48. Richard McDermott, "Why Information Technology Inspired but Cannot Deliver Knowledge Management," *California Management Review* 41, no. 4 (Summer 1999), 103–117.

49. Based on Ikujiro Nonaka and Hirotaka Takeuchi, *The Knowledge-Creating Company: How Japanese Companies Create the Dynamics of Innovation* (New York: Oxford University Press, 1995), 8–9; and Robert M. Grant, "Toward a Knowledge-Based Theory of the Firm," *Strategic Management Journal* 17 (Winter 1996), 109–122.

50. Grant, "Toward a Knowledge-Based Theory of the Firm."

51. Martin Schulz, "The Uncertain Relevance of Newness: Organizational Learning and Knowledge Flows," *Academy of Management Journal* 44, no. 4 (2001), 661–681.

52. C. Jackson Grayson, Jr., and Carla S. O'Dell, "Mining Your Hidden Resources," *Across the Board* (April 1998), 23–28.

53. Based on Morten T. Hansen, Nitin Nohria, and Thomas Tierney, "What's Your Strategy for Managing Knowledge?" *Harvard Business Review* (March–April 1999), 106–116.

54. Kontzer, "Learning to Share."

55. Michael A. Fontaine, Salvatore Parise, and David Miller, "Collaborative Environments: An Effective Tool for Transforming Business Processes," *Ivey Business Journal* (May–June 2004); Mary Flood, "Hawk Vote for California Firm Unanimous," *Houston Chronicle* (May 15, 2001), 15; and "Firm Finalist for Innovation," *The Nelson Mail* (May 23, 2003), 4.

56. Steven A. Melnyk and David R. Denzler, *Operations Management: A Value-Driven Approach* (Burr Ridge, Ill.: Richard D. Irwin, 1996), 613.

57. Jim Turcotte, Bob Silveri, and Tom Jobson, "Are You Ready for the E-Supply Chain?" *APICS—The Performance Advantage* (August 1998), 56–59.

58. Sandra Swanson, "Get Together," *Information Week* (July 1, 2002), 47–48.

59. Christopher Koch, "It All Began with Drayer," *CIO* (August 1, 2002), 56–60.

60. Brian Caulfield, "Facing Up to CRM," *Business 2.0* (August–September 2001), 149–150; and "Customer Relationship Management: The Good, The Bad, The Future," special advertising section, *BusinessWeek* (April 28, 2003), 53–64.

61. Timothy J. Mullaney, "E-Biz Strikes Again," *BusinessWeek* (May 10, 2004), 80–90.

62. Christopher Barnatt, "Embracing E-Business," *Journal of General Management* 30, no. 1 (Autumn 2004), 79–96.

63. This discussion is based on Ranjay Gulati and Jason Garino, "Get the Right Mix of Bricks and Clicks," *Harvard Business Review* (May–June 2000), 107–114.

64. Andy Reinhardt, "Tesco Bets Small—and Wins Big," *BusinessWeek E.Biz* (October 1, 2001), EB26–EB32; and Patrick Barwise and Sean Meehan, "The Benefits of Getting the Basics Right," *Financial Times* (October 8, 2004), 4.

65. Buchanan, "Working Wonders on the Web."

66. Andrew Blackman, "A Strong Net Game," *The Wall Street Journal* (October 25, 2004), R1, R11.

67. Stephanie Overby, "Paving over Paperwork," *CIO* (February 1, 2002), 82–86.

68. Siobhan O'Mahony and Stephen R. Barley, "Do Digital Telecommunications Affect Work and Organization? The State of Our Knowledge," *Research in Organizational Behavior* 21 (1999), 125–161.

69. Sari Kalin, "Overdrive," *CIO Web Business*, Section 2 (July 2, 1999), 36–40.

70. O'Mahony and Barley, "Do Digital Telecommunications Affect Work and Organization?"

71. Michael A. Fontaine, Salvatore Parise, and David Miller, "Collaborative Environments: An Effective Tool for Transforming Business Processes," *Ivey Business Journal* (May–June 2004).

72. Joanne Lee-Young and Megan Barnett, "Furiously Fast Fashions," *The Industry Standard* (June 11, 2001), 72–79.

9 Organization Size, Life Cycle, and Decline

Organization Size: Is Bigger Better?
Pressures for Growth • Dilemmas of Large Size

Organizational Life Cycle
Stages of Life Cycle Development • Organizational Characteristics during the Life Cycle

Organizational Bureaucracy and Control
What Is Bureaucracy? • Size and Structural Control

Bureaucracy in a Changing World
Organizing Temporary Systems for Flexibility and Innovation • Other Approaches to
Reducing Bureaucracy

Organizational Control Strategies
Bureaucratic Control • Market Control • Clan Control

Organizational Decline and Downsizing
Definition and Causes • A Model of Decline Stages • Downsizing Implementation

Summary and Interpretation

A Look Inside

Interpol

Ron Noble, secretary general of Interpol, is managing one of the most complex organizations in the world. Interpol has to work with countries from every corner of the globe, fostering cooperation among people with different cultural values, languages, and legal and political systems. Moreover, it must do it all with a budget about one-tenth the size of the New York City Police Department's.

When Interpol works, it works very well, leading to the quick capture of international terrorists, murderers, and other fugitives. But when Noble took over the international police organization, it wasn't working very well. Rather than a fast-moving, crime-fighting organization, Noble found at Interpol a clumsy, slow-moving, bureaucratic agency that was ill-equipped to respond to the massive challenges of a world increasingly reliant on worldwide coordinated law enforcement to prevent tragedies such as the World Trade Center attacks of September 2001. If a request for assistance and information on Mohammed Atta, one of the terrorist leaders, for example, came into Interpol on a weekend, too bad—the agency was closed until Monday morning. Interpol "Red Notices" (urgent, global wanted-persons alerts) took up to 6 months to process and were sent out by third class mail to save postage costs.

Noble knew that kind of slow response had to change. Since taking over as head of Interpol, he has moved the organization forward by leaps and bounds, reducing bureaucracy and transforming Interpol into a modern, fast-moving organization. Keeping Interpol open 24 hours a day, 7 days a week, was one of his first changes. A policy of issuing red alerts for terrorists within 24 hours and notices for less threatening criminals within 72 hours went into effect immediately after the U.S. attacks on September 11, 2001. Noble has reorganized Interpol to increase speed and flexibility and to focus on the "customer" (law enforcement groups in 179 member countries). Today, the most critical notices are translated immediately, posted online, and sent via express delivery service.

The reorganization also includes mechanisms for better coordination and information gathering. Noble's goal is for Interpol to become the number 1 global police agency, one that coordinates and leads a multidimensional crime-fighting approach. Combatting terrorism and organized crime, Noble knows, requires that everyone have the information they need when they need it and that local police, judicial, intelligence, diplomatic, and military services all work together. A major step toward a more coordinated worldwide effort came when Interpol recently appointed its first-ever representative to the United Nations.[1]

As organizations grow large and complex, they need more complex systems and procedures for guiding and controlling the organization. Unfortunately, these characteristics can also cause problems of inefficiency, rigidity, and slow response time. Every organization—from international agencies like Interpol to locally owned restaurants and auto body shops—wrestles with questions about organizational size, bureaucracy, and control. Most entrepreneurs who start a business want their company to grow. Yet, as organizations become larger, they often find it difficult to respond quickly to changes in the environment. Today's organizations, just like Interpol, are looking for ways to be more flexible and responsive to a rapidly changing marketplace.

During the twentieth century, large organizations became widespread, and bureaucracy has become a major topic of study in organization theory.[2] Most large organizations have bureaucratic characteristics, which can be very effective. These organizations provide us with abundant goods and services and accomplish astonishing feats—explorations of Mars, overnight delivery of packages to any location in the world, the scheduling and coordination of 20,000 airline flights a day in the United States—that are testimony to their effectiveness. On the other hand, bureaucracy is also accused of many sins, including inefficiency, rigidity, and demeaning routinized work that alienates both employees and the customers an organization tries to serve.

Purpose of This Chapter

In this chapter, we explore the question of large versus small organizations and how size relates to structure and control. Organization size is a contextual variable that influences organizational design and functioning just as do the contextual variables—technology, environment, goals—discussed in previous chapters. In the first section, we look at the advantages of large versus small size. Then, we explore what is called an organization's life cycle and the structural characteristics at each stage. Next, we examine the historical need for bureaucracy as a means to control large organizations and compare bureaucratic control to various other control strategies. Finally, the chapter looks at the causes of organizational decline and discusses some methods for dealing with downsizing. By the end of this chapter, you should be able to recognize when bureaucratic control can make an organization effective and when other types of control are more appropriate.

Organization Size: Is Bigger Better?

The question of big versus small begins with the notion of growth and the reasons so many organizations feel the need to grow large.

Pressures for Growth

The dream of practically every businessperson is to have his or her company become a member of the *Fortune* 500 list—to grow fast and to grow large.[3] Sometimes this goal is more urgent than to make the best products or show the greatest profits. A decade ago, analysts and management scholars were heralding a shift away from "bigness" toward small, nimble companies that could quickly respond in a fast-changing environment. Yet, despite the proliferation of new, small organizations, the giants such as Procter & Gamble, General Motors, Toyota, and Wal-Mart continued to grow. Wal-Mart, for example, employs more people than the U.S military and in 2003 sold 36 percent of all dog food, 32 percent of all disposable diapers, and 26 percent of all toothpaste purchased in the United States.[4]

Today, the business world has entered an era of the mega-corporation. Merger mania has given rise to behemoths such as DaimlerChrysler AG and Citigroup.[5] The advertising industry is controlled by four giant agencies—the Omnicom Group and the Interpublic Group of Companies, both with headquarters in New York, London's WPP Group, and Publicis Groupe, based in Paris.[6] These huge conglomerates own scores of companies that soak up more than half the ad industry's revenues and reach into the advertising, direct-mail marketing, and public relations of every region on the planet. Moreover, these agencies grew primarily to better serve their clients, who were themselves growing larger and more global. Companies in all industries, from aerospace to consumer products to media, strive for growth to acquire the size and resources needed to compete on a global scale, to invest in new technology, and to control distribution channels and guarantee access to markets.[7]

There are other pressures for organizations to grow. Many executives have found that firms must grow to stay economically healthy. To stop growing is to stagnate. To be stable means that customers may not have their demands fully met or that competitors will increase market share at the expense of your company. Wal-Mart, for example, keeps growing because executives have, as one phrased it, Sam Walton's "inferiority complex." They are ingrained with the idea that to stop growing is to stagnate and die.[8] Cardinal Health, one of the top pharmaceutical distributors in the United States, searched for new ways to grow in an industry that is squeezed between cost-conscious customers and the demands of powerful drug manufacturers. Cardinal found new opportunities by providing services that could help their suppliers and customers improve their own businesses. For example, rather than just shipping drugs, Cardinal offers pharmacy management services to hospitals. Thanks to new lines of business, Cardinal registered compound annual growth of 40 percent from 1991 to 2001, at a time when many other drug distributors saw declining profits.[9]

Scale is crucial to economic health in marketing-intensive companies such as Coca-Cola, Procter & Gamble, and Anheuser-Busch. Greater size gives these companies power in the marketplace and thus increases revenues.[10] In addition, growing organizations are vibrant, exciting places to work, which enables these companies to attract and keep quality employees. When the number of employees is expanding, the company can offer many challenges and opportunities for advancement.

■ Dilemmas of Large Size

Organizations feel compelled to grow, but how much and how large? What size organization is better poised to compete in a global environment? The arguments are summarized in Exhibit 9.1.

Large. Huge resources and economies of scale are needed for many organizations to compete globally. Only large organizations can build a massive pipeline in Alaska. Only a large corporation like Airbus Industrie can afford to build the A380, the world's first double-deck passenger airline, and only a large Virgin Atlantic Airways can buy it. Only a large Johnson & Johnson can invest hundreds of millions in new products such as bifocal contact lenses and a patch that delivers contraceptives through the skin. In addition, large organizations have the resources to be a supportive economic and social force in difficult times. In 2005, after Hurricane Katrina wiped out New Orleans and much of the Gulf Coast, Wal-Mart gave thousands of employees $1000 for emergency assistance, offered residents of the affected areas a free 7-day emergency supply of prescription drugs, shipped more than 100 truckloads of supplies to evacuation centers, and donated millions to relief organizations.[11] Similarly, following the 2001 terrorist attacks in the United States, American Express had the resources to help stranded customers get home and waive delinquent fees on late payments.[12] Large organizations also are able to get back to

Briefcase

As an organization manager, keep these guidelines in mind:

Decide whether your organization should act like a large or small company. To the extent that economies of scale, global reach, and complexity are important, introduce greater bureaucratization as the organization increases in size. As it becomes necessary, add rules and regulations, written documentation, job specialization, technical competence in hiring and promotion, and decentralization.

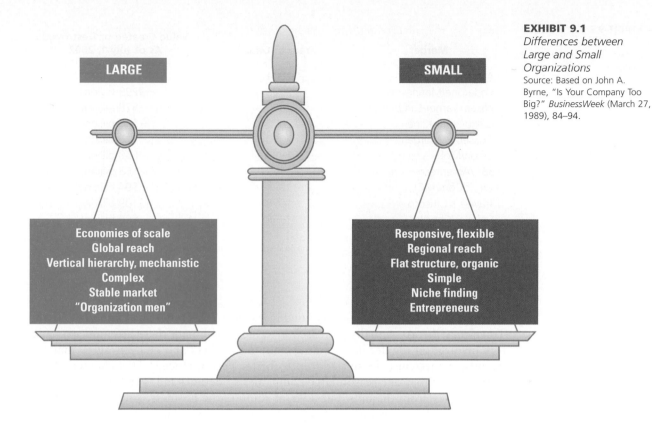

EXHIBIT 9.1
Differences between Large and Small Organizations
Source: Based on John A. Byrne, "Is Your Company Too Big?" *BusinessWeek* (March 27, 1989), 84–94.

business more quickly following a disaster, giving employees a sense of security and belonging during an uncertain time.

Large companies are standardized, often mechanistically run, and complex. The complexity offers hundreds of functional specialties within the organization to perform multifaceted tasks and to produce varied and complicated products. Moreover, large organizations, once established, can be a presence that stabilizes a market for years. Managers can join the company and expect a career reminiscent of the "organization men" of the 1950s and 1960s. The organization can provide longevity, raises, and promotions.

Small. The competing argument says small is beautiful because the crucial requirements for success in a global economy are responsiveness and flexibility in fast-changing markets. Small scale can provide significant advantages in terms of quick reaction to changing customer needs or shifting environmental and market conditions.[13] Although the U.S. economy contains many large and successful organizations, research shows that as global trade has accelerated, smaller organizations have become the norm. Since the mid-1960s, most of the then-existing large businesses have lost market share worldwide.[14] Many large companies have grown even larger through merger or acquisition in recent years, yet research indicates that few of these mergers live up to their expected performance levels.[15] A study of ten of the largest mergers of all time, including AOL/Time Warner, Glaxo/SmithKline, and Daimler/Chrysler, showed a significant decline in shareholder value for eight of the

EXHIBIT 9.2
Effect of Ten Mega-Mergers on Shareholder Wealth

Merger	Year of Deal	Value Created or Destroyed As of July 1, 2002
AOL/Time Warner	2001	−$148 billion
Vodafone/Mannesmann	2000	−$299 billion
Pfizer/Warner-Lambert	2000	−$78 billion
Glaxo/SmithKline	2000	−$40 billion
Chase/J.P. Morgan	2000	−$26 billion
Exxon/Mobil	1999	+$8 billion
SBC/Ameritech	1999	−$68 billion
WorldCom/MCI	1998	−$94 billion
Travelers/Citicorp	1998	+$109 billion
Daimler/Chrysler	1998	−$36 billion

Source: Reported in Keith Hammonds, "Size Is Not a Strategy," *Fast Company* (September 2002), 78–86.

ten combined companies, as illustrated in Exhibit 9.2. Only two, Exxon/Mobil and Travelers/Citicorp, actually increased in value.[16] Although there are numerous factors involved in the decline in value, many researchers and analysts agree that frequently, bigness just doesn't add up to better performance.[17] This chapter's Book Mark argues that one reason large companies sometimes fail is that top leaders get too far away from the nuts and bolts of running the business. Any major strategic initiative, such as a merger, falters without proper execution.

Despite the increasing size of many companies, the economic vitality of the United States, as well as most of the rest of the developed world, is tied to small and mid-sized businesses. There are an estimated 15 to 17 million small businesses in the United States, which account for a tremendous portion of goods and services provided. In addition, a large percentage of exporters are small businesses.[18] The growth of the Internet and other information technologies is making it easier for small companies to act big, as described in Chapter 8. The growing service sector also contributes to a decrease in average organization size, as many service companies remain small to better serve customers.

Small organizations have a flat structure and an organic, free-flowing management style that encourages entrepreneurship and innovation. Today's leading biotechnological drugs, for example, were all discovered by small firms, such as Gilead Sciences, which developed anti-retroviral drugs to treat HIV, rather than by huge pharmaceutical companies such as Merck.[19] Moreover, the personal involvement of employees in small firms encourages motivation and commitment, because employees personally identify with the company's mission.

Big-Company/Small-Company Hybrid. The paradox is that the advantages of small companies sometimes enable them to succeed and, hence, grow large. Most of the 100 firms on *Fortune* magazine's list of the fastest-growing companies in America are small firms characterized by an emphasis on being fast and flexible in responding to the environment.[20] Small companies, however, can become victims of their own success as they grow large, shifting to a mechanistic structure emphasizing vertical hierarchies and spawning "organization men" rather than entrepreneurs. Giant companies are "built for optimization, not innovation."[21] Big companies become committed to their existing products and technologies and have a hard time supporting innovation for the future.

The solution is what Jack Welch, retired chairman of General Electric (GE), called the "big-company/small-company hybrid" that combines a large corporation's resources and reach with a small company's simplicity and flexibility. Full-service global firms need a strong resource base and sufficient complexity and hierarchy to serve clients around the world. Size is not necessarily at odds with speed and flexibility, as evidenced by large companies such as GE, Wal-Mart, and eBay, which continue to try new things and move quickly to change the rules of business. The divisional structure, described in Chapter 3, is one way some large organizations attain a big-company/small-company hybrid. By reorganizing into groups of small companies, huge corporations such as Johnson & Johnson capture the

Briefcase

As an organization manager, keep this guideline in mind:

If responsiveness, flexibility, simplicity, and niche finding are important, subdivide the organization into simple, autonomous divisions that have freedom and a small-company approach.

Book Mark 9.0 (HAVE YOU READ THIS BOOK?)

Execution: The Discipline of Getting Things Done
By Larry Bossidy and Ram Charan, with Charles Burke

Why do so many grand strategies fail and so many large companies go wrong? This is the central question addressed by Larry Bossidy, chairman and former CEO of Allied Signal, and management consultant Ram Charan in their book, *Execution: The Discipline of Getting Things Done*. Success for any organization, large or small, is found in the details. *Execution* offers a practical guide for translating great ideas into successful action. Companies that deliver on their promises year after year are those whose CEOs are skilled in the discipline of execution.

BASIC BUILDING BLOCKS
The discipline of execution is based on the following three basic building blocks:

- *Essential leadership behaviors.* The authors emphasize that execution is the primary job of a leader. This doesn't mean leaders should micromanage, but they must be actively and passionately involved, putting in place a culture, structure, and the right people to make things happen. Seven essential leader behaviors form the first basic building block of execution: (1) know your people and your business, (2) insist on realism and confronting problems head-on, (3) set clear goals and priorities, (4) follow through, (5) reward the "doers," (6) expand people's capabilities, and (7) know yourself.
- *A corporate culture that reinforces a discipline of execution.* Leaders focus on changing people's beliefs and behaviors so that they produce *results*, not just ideas, plans, and strategies. To shift toward a results-oriented culture, leaders make clear the results they want, coach people on

how to achieve them, and reward them for doing so. When people consistently fail to achieve results, leaders need the courage to give them other jobs or let them go. Consistently acting in this manner produces a culture of getting things done.
- *The right people in the right place.* One job no leader should delegate, the authors insist, is recruiting, hiring, promoting, and developing the right people. Even though most leaders claim that "people are our most important asset," they pay very little attention to this aspect of their business, choosing instead to pass it off to the human resources department. Having the right people in the right place, particularly those in the leadership pool, is a key element of successful companies, and one leaders can directly control. As CEO of Allied Signal, Larry Bossidy devoted as much as 40 percent of his day to hiring and developing leaders throughout the company.

THE IMPORTANCE OF EXECUTION
Execution is not simply getting things done; it means understanding the elements that have to be in place in order to get things done. As the authors put it, "Execution is a systematic process of rigorously discussing hows and whats, questioning, tenaciously following through, and ensuring accountability." By having the right people—individually and collectively—focusing on the right details at the right time, organizations can effectively execute and accomplish amazing results.

Execution: The Discipline of Getting Things Done, by Larry Bossidy and Ram Charan, is published by Crown Business.

mindset and advantages of smallness. Johnson & Johnson is actually a group of 204 separate companies. When a new product is created in one of Johnson & Johnson's fifty-six labs, a new company is created along with it.[22]

The development of new organizational forms, with an emphasis on decentralizing authority and cutting out layers of the hierarchy, combined with the increasing use of information technology described in Chapter 8, is making it easier than ever for companies to be simultaneously large and small, thus capturing the advantages of each. The shift can even be seen in the U.S. military. Unlike World War II, for example, which was fought with large masses of soldiers guided by decisions made at top levels, today's "war on terrorism" depends on decentralized decision making and smaller forces of highly skilled soldiers with access to up-to-the minute information.[23] Big companies also find a variety of ways to act both large and small. Retail giants Home Depot and Wal-Mart, for example, use the advantage of size in areas such as advertising, purchasing, and raising capital; however, they also give each individual store the autonomy needed to serve customers as if it were a small, hometown shop.[24] To encourage innovation, the giant corporation Royal Dutch/Shell created a strategy in its exploration-and-production division to set aside 10 percent of the division's research budget for "crazy" ideas. Anyone can apply for the funds, and decisions are made not by managers but by a small group of nonconformist employees.[25] Small companies that are growing can also use these ideas to help their organizations retain the flexibility and customer focus that fueled their growth.

Organizational Life Cycle

A useful way to think about organizational growth and change is the concept of an organizational **life cycle**,[26] which suggests that organizations are born, grow older, and eventually die. Organization structure, leadership style, and administrative systems follow a fairly predictable pattern through stages in the life cycle. Stages are sequential and follow a natural progression.

■ Stages of Life Cycle Development

Research on organizational life cycle suggests that four major stages characterize organizational development.[27] These stages are illustrated in Exhibit 9.3, along with the problems associated with transition to each stage. Growth is not easy. Each time an organization enters a new stage in the life cycle, it enters a whole new ball game with a new set of rules for how the organization functions internally and how it relates to the external environment.[28] For technology companies today, life cycles are getting shorter; to stay competitive, companies like eBay and Google have to successfully progress through stages of the cycle faster.

1. *Entrepreneurial stage.* When an organization is born, the emphasis is on creating a product or service and surviving in the marketplace. The founders are entrepreneurs, and they devote their full energies to the technical activities of production and marketing. The organization is informal and nonbureaucratic. The hours of work are long. Control is based on the owners' personal supervision. Growth is from a creative new product or service. For example, Ross Perot started Electronic Data Systems (EDS) in 1962 after failing to convince his

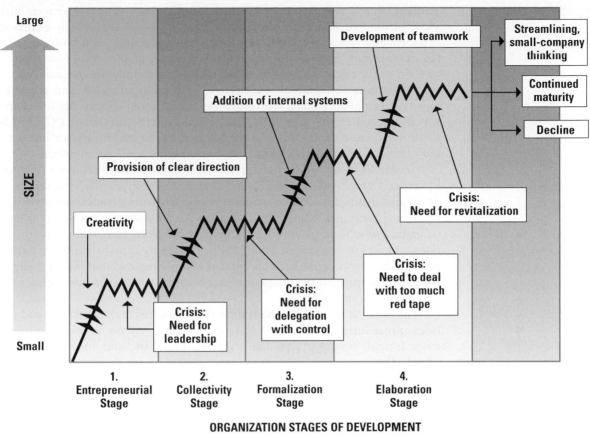

ORGANIZATION STAGES OF DEVELOPMENT

EXHIBIT 9.3
Organizational Life Cycle
Source: Adapted from Robert E. Quinn and Kim Cameron, "Organizational Life Cycles and Shifting Criteria of Effectiveness: Some Preliminary Evidence," *Management Science* 29 (1983), 33–51; and Larry E. Greiner, "Evolution and Revolution as Organizations Grow," *Harvard Business Review* 50 (July–August 1972), 37–46.

superiors at IBM that companies would someday want to take advantage of computer technology without having to understand or manage it themselves. After a few rocky years, demand for the new service EDS offered zoomed, and the company grew rapidly.[29] Apple Computer was in the **entrepreneurial stage** when it was created by Steve Jobs and Stephen Wozniak in Wozniak's parents' garage.

Crisis: Need for leadership. As the organization starts to grow, the larger number of employees causes problems. The creative and technically oriented owners are confronted with management issues, but they may prefer to focus their energies on making and selling the product or inventing new products and services. At this time of crisis, entrepreneurs must either adjust the structure of the organization to accommodate continued growth or else bring in strong managers who can do so. When Apple began a period of rapid growth, A. C. Markkula was brought in as a leader because neither Jobs nor Wozniak was qualified or cared to manage the expanding company.

2. *Collectivity stage.* If the leadership crisis is resolved, strong leadership is obtained and the organization begins to develop clear goals and direction. Departments are established along with a hierarchy of authority, job assignments, and a beginning division of labor. Web search engine Google has quickly moved from the entrepreneurial to the collectivity stage. Founders Larry Page and Sergey Brin devoted their full energy to making sure Google is the most powerful, fastest, and

simplest search engine available, then brought in a skilled manager, former Novell CEO Eric Schmidt, to run the company. Google is currently hiring other experienced executives to manage various functional areas and business units as the organization grows.[30] In the collectivity stage, employees identify with the mission of the organization and spend long hours helping the organization succeed. Members feel part of a collective, and communication and control are mostly informal although a few formal systems begin to appear. Apple Computer was in the **collectivity stage** during the rapid growth years from 1978 to 1981. Employees threw themselves into the business as the major product line was established and more than 2,000 dealers signed on.

Crisis: Need for delegation. If the new management has been successful, lower-level employees gradually find themselves restricted by the strong top-down leadership. Lower-level managers begin to acquire confidence in their own functional areas and want more discretion. An autonomy crisis occurs when top managers, who were successful because of their strong leadership and vision, do not want to give up responsibility. Top managers want to make sure that all parts of the organization are coordinated and pulling together. The organization needs to find mechanisms to control and coordinate departments without direct supervision from the top.

3. *Formalization stage.* The **formalization stage** involves the installation and use of rules, procedures, and control systems. Communication is less frequent and more formal. Engineers, human resource specialists, and other staff may be added. Top management becomes concerned with issues such as strategy and planning and leaves the operations of the firm to middle management. Product groups or other decentralized units may be formed to improve coordination. Incentive systems based on profits may be implemented to ensure that managers work toward what is best for the overall company. When effective, the new coordination and control systems enable the organization to continue growing by establishing linkage mechanisms between top management and field units. Apple Computer was in the formalization stage in the mid- to late 1980s.

Crisis: Too much red tape. At this point in the organization's development, the proliferation of systems and programs may begin to strangle middle-level executives. The organization seems bureaucratized. Middle management may resent the intrusion of staff. Innovation may be restricted. The organization seems too large and complex to be managed through formal programs. It was at this stage of Apple's growth that Jobs resigned from the company and a new CEO took control to face his own management challenges.

4. *Elaboration stage.* The solution to the red tape crisis is a new sense of collaboration and teamwork. Throughout the organization, managers develop skills for confronting problems and working together. Bureaucracy may have reached its limit. Social control and self-discipline reduce the need for additional formal controls. Managers learn to work within the bureaucracy without adding to it. Formal systems may be simplified and replaced by manager teams and task forces. To achieve collaboration, teams are often formed across functions or divisions of the company. The organization may also be split into multiple divisions to maintain a small-company philosophy. Apple Computer is currently in the **elaboration stage** of the life cycle, as are such large companies as EDS, Caterpillar, and Motorola.

Crisis: Need for revitalization. After the organization reaches maturity, it may enter periods of temporary decline.[31] A need for renewal may occur every

10 to 20 years. The organization shifts out of alignment with the environment or perhaps becomes slow moving and overbureaucratized and must go through a stage of streamlining and innovation. Top managers are often replaced during this period. At Apple, the top spot has changed hands a number of times as the company struggled to revitalize. CEOs John Sculley, Michael Spindler, and Gilbert Amelio were each ousted by the board as Apple's problems deepened. Steve Jobs returned in mid-1997 to run the company he had founded nearly 25 years earlier. During those 25 years, Jobs had gained management skills and experience he needed to help Apple through its problems. An older and smarter Jobs quickly reorganized the company, weeded out inefficiencies, and refocused Apple on innovative products for the consumer market, introducing a sleek new iMac in one of the hottest new product launches ever. Even more important, Jobs brought the entrepreneurial spirit back to Apple by moving the company into a whole new direction with the iPod music system. The iPod jump-started growth at Apple as the personal computer market continued to decline. Sales and profits are zooming at Apple thanks to the iPod and an expanding line of innovative consumer electronics products.[32] All mature organizations have to go through periods of revitalization or they will decline, as shown in the last stage of Exhibit 9.3.

Summary. Eighty-four percent of businesses that make it past the first year still fail within 5 years because they can't make the transition from the entrepreneurial stage.[33] The transitions become even more difficult as organizations progress through future stages of the life cycle. Organizations that do not successfully resolve the problems associated with these transitions are restricted in their growth and may even fail. From within an organization, the life cycle crises are very real. For example, Nike suffered in recent years because it seemed to get stuck in a prolonged adolescence and had difficulty resolving the need for discipline and formal control systems.

In Practice

Nike

Nike has always been sort of the "bad boy" of sports marketing. Phil Knight and his college track coach, Bill Bowerman, started the company with $500 each and got the inspiration for their first training shoe from a waffle iron (the shoe was named the Waffle Trainer because of its unique treads). Nike reveres creativity above all; leaders have supported a free-wheeling culture and seemed to almost scoff at the business side of things. Until recently, the company had been run largely on instinct and bravado.

But Nike began to suffer from its antiestablishment attitude, and Phil Knight recently made some major changes to move the company out of its lingering adolescence into a new stage of the life cycle. After hitting the $9.6 billion mark in 1998, sales stagnated. The company's previous approach of guessing how many shoes to manufacture and then flooding the market with them backfired when Nikes were left gathering dust on store shelves. A series of poorly conceived acquisitions and accusations that workers were being exploited in Nike's Asian factories didn't help matters. Nike didn't have the discipline and the formal systems it needed to cope with these kinds of problems. Consider that for a couple of years in the 1990s, the huge company didn't even have a chief financial officer. When Nike's French division went millions over budget in a promotional effort, Wall Street started asking if anyone was in charge at the company.

Although the Nike culture was powerful in terms of design and marketing, Knight realized the company could no longer operate like it was a young, small, entrepreneurial firm. Getting the basic pieces of the business side right—operating principles, financial management, supply chain and inventory management, and so forth—became a priority. He started by putting together a new team of experienced managers, including some Nike veterans but also some outsiders, such as CFO Donald Blair, who was lured from Pepsi. These managers, in turn, have brought the discipline Nike needs, such as establishing clear lines of authority, setting up top-flight systems for inventory and supply chain management, and creating a department to deal with labor issues.

Nike seems to have successfully moved into the formalization stage, and the newfound discipline is paying off. After 4 years under the new management team, Nike's sales climbed 15 percent and the company earned almost $1 billion.[34]

Phil Knight's management overhaul didn't stop until it reached the top. In early 2005, Knight retired as CEO of the company and picked Bill Perez, former CEO of S. C. Johnson Company, as his successor. Some observers worry that without Knight, Nike will again flounder. However, Knight believes Perez is the right leader for the organization's current stage of the life cycle. He continues to provide vision and guidance in his role as chairman, but the day-to-day running of the company is now in the hands of others.[35]

◼ Organizational Characteristics during the Life Cycle

As organizations evolve through the four stages of the life cycle, changes take place in structure, control systems, innovation, and goals. The organizational characteristics associated with each stage are summarized in Exhibit 9.4.

Entrepreneurial. Initially, the organization is small, nonbureaucratic, and a one-person show. The top manager provides the structure and control system. Organizational energy is devoted to survival and the production of a single product or service. The U.K.-based organization, Shazam, which allows mobile phone users to access a database to identify songs by title and artist, is in the entrepreneurial stage. Shazam was described in detail in Chapter 5's Leading by Design box.

Collectivity. This is the organization's youth. Growth is rapid, and employees are excited and committed to the organization's mission. The structure is still mostly informal, although some procedures are emerging. Strong charismatic leaders like Steve Jobs of Apple Computer or Phil Knight at Nike provide direction and goals for the organization. Continued growth is a major goal.

Formalization. At this point, the organization is entering midlife. Bureaucratic characteristics emerge. The organization adds staff support groups, formalizes procedures, and establishes a clear hierarchy and division of labor. At the formalization stage, organizations may also develop complementary products to offer a complete product line. Innovation may be achieved by establishing a separate research and development (R&D) department. Major goals are internal stability and market expansion. Top management to delegates, but it also implements formal control systems.

At this stage, for example, Microsoft founder Bill Gates turned the daily management of the company over to Steven Ballmer, who developed and implemented formal planning, management, and financial systems throughout the company. Gates wanted someone who could manage daily business operations so that he could focus his energies on technological innovation.[36]

Elaboration. The mature organization is large and bureaucratic, with extensive control systems, rules, and procedures. Organization managers attempt to develop a team orientation within the bureaucracy to prevent further bureaucratization. Top

EXHIBIT 9.4
Organization Characteristics during Four Stages of Life Cycle

Characteristic	1. Entrepreneurial Nonbureaucratic	2. Collectivity Prebureaucratic	3. Formalization Bureaucratic	4. Elaboration Very Bureaucratic
Structure	Informal, one-person show	Mostly informal, some procedures	Formal procedures, division of labor, new specialties added	Teamwork within bureaucracy, small-company thinking
Products or services	Single product or service	Major product or service, with variations	Line of products or services	Multiple product or service lines
Reward and control systems	Personal, paternalistic	Personal, contribution to success	Impersonal, formal-ized systems	Extensive, tailored to product and department
Innovation	By owner-manager	By employees and managers	By separate innovation group	By institutionalized R&D department
Goal	Survival	Growth	Internal stability, market expansion	Reputation, complete organization
Top management style	Individualistic, entrepreneurial	Charismatic, direction-giving	Delegation with control	Team approach, attack bureaucracy

Source: Adapted from Larry E. Greiner, "Evolution and Revolution as Organizations Grow," *Harvard Business Review* 50 (July–August 1972), 37–46; G. L. Lippitt and W. H. Schmidt, "Crises in a Developing Organization," *Harvard Business Review* 45 (November–December 1967), 102–112; B. R. Scott, "The Industrial State: Old Myths and New Realities," *Harvard Business Review* 51 (March–April 1973), 133–148; Robert E. Quinn and Kim Cameron, "Organizational Life Cycles and Shifting Criteria of Effectiveness," *Management Science* 29 (1983), 33–51.

managers are concerned with establishing a complete organization. Organizational stature and reputation are important. Innovation is institutionalized through an R&D department. Management may attack the bureaucracy and streamline it.

Summary. Growing organizations move through stages of a life cycle, and each stage is associated with specific characteristics of structure, control systems, goals, and innovation. The life cycle phenomenon is a powerful concept used for understanding problems facing organizations and how managers can respond in a positive way to move an organization to the next stage.

Organizational Bureaucracy and Control

As organizations progress through the life cycle, they usually take on bureaucratic characteristics as they grow larger and more complex. The systematic study of bureaucracy was launched by Max Weber, a sociologist who studied government organizations in Europe and developed a framework of administrative characteristics that would make large organizations rational and efficient.[37] Weber wanted to understand how organizations could be designed to play a positive role in the larger society.

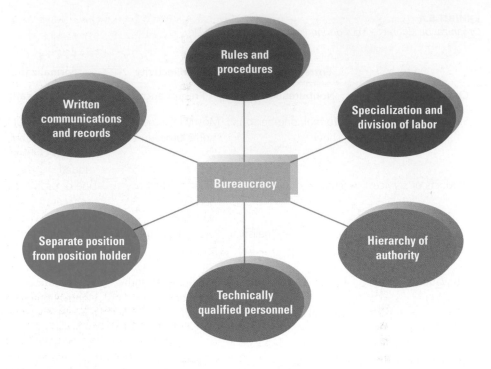

What Is Bureaucracy?

Although Weber perceived **bureaucracy** as a threat to basic personal liberties, he also recognized it as the most efficient possible system of organizing. He predicted the triumph of bureaucracy because of its ability to ensure more efficient functioning of organizations in both business and government settings. Weber identified a set of organizational characteristics, listed in Exhibit 9.5, that could be found in successful bureaucratic organizations.

Rules and standard procedures enabled organizational activities to be performed in a predictable, routine manner. Specialized duties meant that each employee had a clear task to perform. Hierarchy of authority provided a sensible mechanism for supervision and control. Technical competence was the basis by which people were hired rather than friendship, family ties, and favoritism, which dramatically reduced work performance. The separation of the position from the position holder meant that individuals did not own or have an inherent right to the job, which promoted efficiency. Written records provided an organizational memory and continuity over time.

Although bureaucratic characteristics carried to an extreme are widely criticized today, the rational control introduced by Weber was a significant idea and a new form of organization. Bureaucracy provided many advantages over organization forms based on favoritism, social status, family connections, or graft. For example, when he was appointed as commissioner of internal revenue in the Philippines some 30 years ago, Efren Plana found massive corruption, including officials hiring their relatives for high-ranking jobs and tax assessors winning promotions by bribing their superiors.[38] In Mexico, an American lawyer had to pay a $500 bribe to get a telephone. The tradition of giving government posts to relatives is widespread in places such as China. China's emerging class of educated people doesn't like seeing the best jobs going to children and other relatives of officials.[39] By comparison, the logical and rational form of organization described by Weber allows work to be conducted efficiently and according to established rules.

The bureaucratic characteristics listed in Exhibit 9.5 can have a positive impact on many large firms. Consider United Parcel Service (UPS), one of the most efficient large organizations in the United States and Canada.

In Practice

United Parcel Service

UPS, sometimes called *Big Brown* for the color of delivery trucks and employee uniforms, is the largest package-distribution company in the world, delivering more than 13 million packages every business day. UPS is also gaining market share in air service, logistics, and information services. Television commercials ask, "What can Brown do for you today?" signifying the company's expanding global information services.

How did UPS become so successful? Many efficiencies were realized through adoption of the bureaucratic model of organization. UPS is bound up in rules and regulations. It teaches drivers an astounding 340 precise steps to correctly deliver a package. For example, it tells them how to load their trucks, how to fasten their seat belts, how to walk, and how to carry their keys. Strict dress codes are enforced—clean uniforms (called *browns*) every day, black or brown polished shoes with nonslip soles, no shirt unbuttoned below the first button, no hair below the shirt collar, no beards, no smoking in front of customers, and so on. The company conducts 3-minute physical inspections of its drivers each day, a practice begun by the founder in the early 1900s. There are safety rules for drivers, loaders, clerks, and managers. Employees are asked to clean off their desks at the end of each day so they can start fresh the next morning. Managers are given copies of policy books with the expectation that they will use them regularly, and memos on various policies and rules circulate by the hundreds every day.

Despite the strict rules, employees are satisfied and UPS has a retention rate of more than 90 percent. Employees are treated well and paid well, and the company has maintained a sense of equality and fairness. Everyone is on a first-name basis. The policy book states, "A leader does not have to remind others of his authority by use of a title. Knowledge, performance, and capacity should be adequate evidence of position and leadership." Technical qualification, not favoritism, is the criterion for hiring and promotion. Top executives started at the bottom—the current chief executive, James Kelly, for example, began as a temporary holiday-rush driver. The emphasis on equality, fairness, and a promote-from-within mentality inspires loyalty and commitment throughout the ranks.

UPS has also been a leader in using new technology to enhance reliability and efficiency. Drivers use a computerized clipboard, called DIAD (Delivery Information Acquisition Device), to record everything from driver's miles per gallon to data on parcel delivery. Technology is enabling UPS to expand its services and become a global mover of knowledge and information as well as packages. Top managers know the new technology means some of UPS's rigid procedures may have to bend. However, it's likely they won't bend too far. When you're moving more than 13 million items a day, predictability and stability are the watchwords, whether you're using the company's first Model T Ford or its latest technological wizardry.[40]

UPS illustrates how bureaucratic characteristics increase with large size. UPS is so productive and dependable that it dominates the small package delivery market. As it expands and transitions into a global, knowledge-based logistics business, UPS managers may need to find effective ways to reduce the bureaucracy. The new technology and new services place more demands on workers, who may need more flexibility and autonomy to perform well. Now, let's look at some specific ways size affects organizational structure and control.

■ Size and Structural Control

In the field of organization theory, organization size has been described as an important variable that influences structural design and methods of control. Should an organization become more bureaucratic as it grows larger? In what size organizations are bureaucratic characteristics most appropriate? More than 100 studies have attempted to answer these questions.[41] Most of these studies indicate that large organizations are different from small organizations along several dimensions of bureaucratic structure, including formalization, centralization, and personnel ratios.

Formalization and Centralization. **Formalization**, as described in Chapter 1, refers to rules, procedures, and written documentation, such as policy manuals and job descriptions, that prescribe the rights and duties of employees.[42] The evidence supports the conclusion that large organizations are more formalized, as at UPS. The reason is that large organizations rely on rules, procedures, and paperwork to achieve standardization and control across their large numbers of employees and departments, whereas top managers can use personal observation to control a small organization.[43]

Centralization refers to the level of hierarchy with authority to make decisions. In centralized organizations, decisions tend to be made at the top. In decentralized organizations, similar decisions would be made at a lower level.

Decentralization represents a paradox because, in the perfect bureaucracy, all decisions would be made by the top administrator, who would have perfect control. However, as an organization grows larger and has more people and departments, decisions cannot be passed to the top because senior managers would be overloaded. Thus, the research on organization size indicates that larger organizations permit greater decentralization.[44] Consider Microsoft, where CEO Steven Ballmer and Chairman Bill Gates used to make every important decision. In a company with 50,000 employees and multiple product lines, however, the traditional structure was too top heavy. Decision making had slowed to a snail's pace. Ballmer reorganized the 50,000-employee firm into 7 divisions and gave division heads greater decision-making authority.[45] In small start-up organizations, on the other hand, the founder or top executive can effectively be involved in every decision, large and small.

Personnel Ratios. Another characteristic of bureaucracy relates to **personnel ratios** for administrative, clerical, and professional support staff. The most frequently studied ratio is the administrative ratio.[46] Two patterns have emerged. The first is that the ratio of top administration to total employees is actually smaller in large organizations,[47] indicating that organizations experience administrative economies as they grow larger. The second pattern concerns clerical and professional support staff ratios.[48] These groups tend to *increase* in proportion to organization size. The clerical ratio increases because of the greater communication and reporting requirements needed as organizations grow larger. The professional staff ratio increases because of the greater need for specialized skills in larger, complex organizations.

Exhibit 9.6 illustrates administrative and support ratios for small and large organizations. As organizations increase in size, the administrative ratio declines and the ratios for other support groups increase.[49] The net effect for direct workers is that they decline as a percentage of total employees. In summary, whereas top administrators do not make up a disproportionate number of employees in large organizations, the

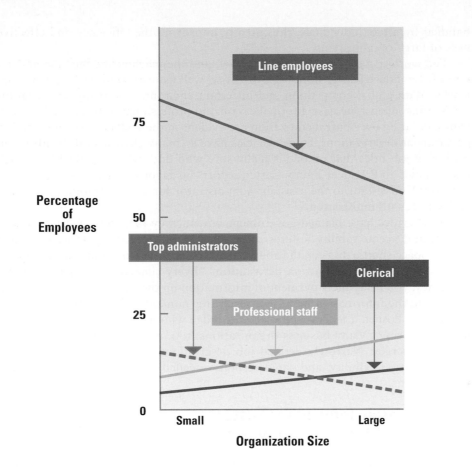

idea that proportionately greater overhead is required in large organizations is supported. Although large organizations reduced overhead during the difficult economic years of the 1980s, overhead costs for many American corporations began creeping back up again as revenues soared during the late 1990s.[50] With the declining U.S. economy following the crash of the technology sector, threats of war and terrorism, and general feelings of uncertainty, many companies have again been struggling to cut overhead costs. Keeping costs for administrative, clerical, and professional support staff low represents an ongoing challenge for large organizations.[51]

Bureaucracy in a Changing World

Weber's prediction of the triumph of bureaucracy proved accurate. Bureaucratic characteristics have many advantages and have worked extremely well for many of the needs of the industrial age.[52] By establishing a hierarchy of authority and specific rules and procedures, bureaucracy provided an effective way to bring order to large groups of people and prevent abuses of power. Impersonal relationships based on roles rather than people reduced the favoritism and nepotism characteristic of many preindustrial organizations. Bureaucracy also provided for systematic and rational ways to organize and manage tasks too complex to be understood and handled by a few individuals, thus greatly improving the efficiency and effectiveness of large organizations.

The world is rapidly changing, however, and the machinelike bureaucratic system of the industrial age no longer works so well as organizations face new challenges. With global competition and uncertain environments, many organizations are fighting against increasing formalization and professional staff ratios. The problems caused by over bureaucratization are evident in the inefficiencies of some U.S. government organizations. Some agencies have so many clerical staff members and confusing job titles that no one is really sure who does what. Richard Cavanagh, once an aide to President Jimmy Carter, reports his favorite federal title as the "administrative assistant to the assistant administrator for administration of the General Services Administration."[53]

Some critics have blamed government bureaucracy for intelligence, communication, and accountability failures related to the 2001 terrorist attacks, the Columbia space shuttle disaster, the abuses at Abu Ghraib prison, and a slow response to the 2005 Hurricane Katrina devastation. "Every time you add a layer of bureaucracy, you delay the movement of information up the chain of command...And you dilute the information because at each step some details are taken out," said Richard A. Posner, a federal appeals court judge who has written a book on intelligence reform.[54] Many business organizations, too, need to reduce formalization and bureaucracy. Narrowly defined job descriptions, for example, tend to limit the creativity, flexibility, and rapid response needed in today's knowledge-based organizations.

■ Organizing Temporary Systems for Flexibility and Innovation

How can organizations overcome the problems of bureaucracy in rapidly changing environments? Some are implementing innovative structural solutions. One structural concept, called the *incident command system* (ICS), is commonly used by organizations that have to respond rapidly to emergency or crisis situations, such as police and fire departments or other emergency management agencies. The **incident command system** was developed to maintain the efficiency and control benefits of bureaucracy yet prevent the problem of slow response to crises.[55] The approach is being adapted by other types of organizations to help them respond quickly to new opportunities, unforeseen competitive threats, or organizational crises.

The basic idea behind the ICS is that the organization can glide smoothly between a highly formalized, hierarchical structure that is effective during times of stability and a more flexible, loosely structured one needed to respond well to unexpected and demanding environmental conditions. The hierarchical side with its rules, procedures, and chain of command helps maintain control and ensure adherence to rules that have been developed and tested over many years to cope with well-understood problems and situations. However, during times of high uncertainty, the most effective structure is one that loosens the lines of command and enables people to work across departmental and hierarchical lines to anticipate, avoid, and solve unanticipated problems within the context of a clearly understood mission and guidelines.

The approach can be seen on the deck of a nuclear aircraft carrier, where there is a rigid chain of command and people are expected to follow orders promptly and without question.[56] Formalization is high, with manuals detailing proper procedures for every known situation. However, at times of high uncertainty, such as the launching and recovery of planes during real or simulated warfare, an important shift occurs. The rigid hierarchy seems to dissolve, and a loosely organized, collaborative structure in which sailors and officers work together as colleagues takes its place. People discuss the best procedures to use, and everyone typically follows the lead of whoever has the most experience and knowledge in a particular area. During this time, no one is thinking about job titles, authority, or chain of command; they are just thinking about the best way to accomplish the mission safely.

A variety of mechanisms ensure smooth functioning of the ICS.[57] For example, despite the free-flowing and flexible nature of crisis response, someone is always in charge. The *incident commander* is ultimately responsible for all activities that occur, and everyone knows clearly who is in charge of what aspect of the situation. This helps maintain order in a chaotic environment. The key is that, whereas formal authority relationships are fixed, decision-making authority is dispersed to individuals who best understand the particular situation. The system is based on trust that lower-level workers have a clear understanding of the mission and make decisions and take actions within guidelines that support the organization's goals. Developing an ICS requires a significant commitment of time and resources, but it offers great potential for organizations that require extremely high reliability, flexibility, and innovation. One organization that effectively uses the incident command model is the Salvation Army, as described in this chapter's Leading by Design box.

■ Other Approaches to Reducing Bureaucracy

Organizations are taking a number of other, less dramatic steps to reduce bureaucracy. Many are cutting layers of the hierarchy, keeping headquarters staff small, and giving lower-level workers greater freedom to make decisions rather than burdening them with excessive rules and regulations. Centex Corporation, which has annual revenues of about $3.8 billion, is run from a modest headquarters in Dallas by a staff of less than 100. Centex decentralizes authority and responsibility to the operating divisions.[58] The point is to not overload headquarters with lawyers, accountants, and financial analysts who inhibit the flexibility and autonomy of divisions.

Of course, many companies must be large to have sufficient resources and complexity to produce products for a global environment but companies such as Wal-Mart, 3M, Coca-Cola, Emerson Electric, and Heinz are striving toward greater decentralization and leanness. They are giving frontline workers more authority and responsibility to define and direct their own jobs, often by creating self-directed teams that find ways to coordinate work, improve productivity, and better serve customers.

Another attack on bureaucracy is from the increasing professionalism of employees. *Professionalism* is defined as the length of formal training and experience of employees. More employees need college degrees, MBAs, and other professional degrees to work as attorneys, researchers, or doctors at General Motors, Kmart, and Bristol-Myers Squibb Company. In addition, Internet-based companies may be staffed entirely by well-educated knowledge workers. Studies of professionals show that formalization is not needed because professional training regularizes a high

Briefcase

As an organization manager, keep these guidelines in mind:

Consider using the incident command system to maintain the efficiency and control benefits of bureaucracy but prevent the problem of slow response to rapid environmental change. Enable the organization to glide smoothly from a formalized system during times of stability to a more flexible, loosely structured one when facing threats, crises, or unexpected environmental changes.

Leading by Design

The Salvation Army

The Salvation Army has been called "the most effective organization in the world" by a leading management scholar. One reason the organization is so effective and powerful is its approach to organizing, which makes use of the incident command system to provide the right amount of structure, control, and flexibility to meet the requirements of each situation. The Salvation Army refers to its approach as "organizing to improvise."

The Salvation Army provides day-to-day assistance to the homeless and economically disadvantaged. In addition, the organization rushes in whenever there is a major disaster—whether it be a tornado, flood, hurricane, airplane crash, or terrorist attack—to network with other agencies to provide disaster relief. Long after the most desperate moments of the initial crisis have passed, the Salvation Army continues helping people rebuild their lives and communities—offering financial assistance; meeting physical needs for food, clothing, and housing; and providing emotional and spiritual support to inspire hope and help people build a foundation for the future. The Army's management realizes that emergencies demand high flexibility. At the same time, the organization must have a high level of control and accountability to ensure its continued existence and meet its day-to-day responsibilities. As a former national commander puts it, "We have to have it both ways. We can't choose to be flexible and reckless or to be accountable and responsive…We have to be several different kinds of organizations at the same time."

In the early emergency moments of a crisis, the Salvation Army deploys a temporary organization that has its own command structure. People need to have a clear sense of who's in charge to prevent the rapid response demands from degenerating into chaos. For example, if the Army responds to a flood in Tennessee or a tornado in Oklahoma, manuals clearly specify in advance who is responsible for talking to the media, who is in charge of supply inventories, who liaises duties with other agencies, and so forth. This model for the temporary organization keeps the Salvation Army responsive and consistent. In the later recovery and rebuilding phases of a crisis, supervisors frequently give people general guidelines and allow them to improvise the best solutions. There isn't time for supervisors to review and sign off on every decision that needs to be made to get families and communities reestablished.

Thus, the Salvation Army actually has people simultaneously working in all different types of organization structures, from traditional vertical command structures, to horizontal teams, to a sort of network form that relies on collaboration with other agencies. Operating in such a fluid way enables the organization to accomplish amazing results. In one year, the Army assisted more than 2.3 million people caught in disasters in the United States, in addition to many more served by regular day-to-day programs. It has been recognized as a leader in putting money to maximal use, meaning donors are willing to give because they trust the organization to be responsible and accountable at the same time it is flexible and innovative in meeting human needs.

Source: Robert A. Watson and Ben Brown, *The Most Effective Organization in the U.S.: Leadership Secrets of the Salvation Army* (New York: Crown Business, 2001), 159–181.

standard of behavior for employees that acts as a substitute for bureaucracy.[59] Companies also enhance this trend when they provide ongoing training for *all* employees, from the front office to the shop floor, in a push for continuous individual and organizational learning. Increased training substitutes for bureaucratic rules and procedures that can constrain the creativity of employees in solving problems and increases organizational capability.

A form of organization called *professional partnership* has emerged that is made up completely of professionals.[60] These organizations include medical practices, law firms, and consulting firms, such as McKinsey & Company and PricewaterhouseCoopers. The general finding concerning professional partnerships is that branches have substantial autonomy and decentralized authority to make necessary decisions.

They work with a consensus orientation rather than the top-down direction typical of traditional business and government organizations. Thus, the trend of increasing professionalism combined with rapidly changing environments is leading to less bureaucracy in corporate North America.

Organizational Control Strategies

Even though many organizations are trying to decrease bureaucracy and reduce rules and procedures that constrain employees, every organization needs systems for guiding and controlling the organization. Employees may have more freedom in today's companies, but control is still a major responsibility of management.

Managers at the top and middle levels of an organization can choose among three overall control strategies. These strategies come from a framework for organizational control proposed by William Ouchi of the University of California at Los Angeles. Ouchi suggested three control strategies that organizations could adopt—bureaucratic, market, and clan.[61] Each form of control uses different types of information. However, all three types may appear simultaneously in an organization. The requirements for each control strategy are given in Exhibit 9.7.

Bureaucratic Control

Bureaucratic control is the use of rules, policies, hierarchy of authority, written documentation, standardization, and other bureaucratic mechanisms to standardize behavior and assess performance. Bureaucratic control uses the bureaucratic characteristics defined by Weber and illustrated in the UPS case. The primary purpose of bureaucratic rules and procedures is to standardize and control employee behavior.

Recall that as organizations progress through the life cycle and grow larger, they become more formalized and standardized. Within a large organization, thousands of work behaviors and information exchanges take place both vertically and horizontally. Rules and policies evolve through a process of trial and error to regulate these behaviors. Some degree of bureaucratic control is used in virtually every organization. Rules, regulations, and directives contain information about a range of behaviors.

To make bureaucratic control work, managers must have the authority to maintain control over the organization. Weber argued that legitimate, rational authority granted to managers was preferred over other types of control (e.g., favoritism or payoffs) as the basis for organizational decisions and activities. Within the larger society, however, Weber identified three types of authority that could explain the creation and control of a large organization.[62]

Type	Requirements
Bureaucracy	Rules, standards, hierarchy, legitimate authority
Market	Prices, competition, exchange relationship
Clan	Tradition, shared values and beliefs, trust

EXHIBIT 9.7
Three Organizational Control Strategies

Source: Based on William G. Ouchi, "A Conceptual Framework for the Design of Organizational Control Mechanisms," *Management Science* 25 (1979), 833–848.

Rational-legal authority is based on employees' belief in the legality of rules and the right of those elevated to positions of authority to issue commands. Rational-legal authority is the basis for both creation and control of most government organizations and is the most common base of control in organizations worldwide. **Traditional authority** is the belief in traditions and in the legitimacy of the status of people exercising authority through those traditions. Traditional authority is the basis for control for monarchies, churches, and some organizations in Latin America and the Persian Gulf. **Charismatic authority** is based on devotion to the exemplary character or to the heroism of an individual person and the order defined by him or her. Revolutionary military organizations are often based on the leader's charisma, as are North American organizations led by charismatic individuals such as Steve Jobs. The organization reflects the personality and values of the leader.

More than one type of authority—such as long tradition and the leader's special charisma—may exist in organizations, but rational-legal authority is the most widely used form to govern internal work activities and decision making, particularly in large organizations.

Market Control

Market control occurs when price competition is used to evaluate the output and productivity of an organization. The idea of market control originated in economics.[63] A dollar price is an efficient form of control, because managers can compare prices and profits to evaluate the efficiency of their corporation. Top managers nearly always use the price mechanism to evaluate performance in corporations. Corporate sales and costs are summarized in a profit-and-loss statement that can be compared against performance in previous years or with that of other corporations.

The use of market control requires that outputs be sufficiently explicit for a price to be assigned and that competition exist. Without competition, the price does not accurately reflect internal efficiency. Even some government and traditionally not-for-profit organizations are turning to market control. For example, the U.S. Federal Aviation Administration took bids to operate its payroll computers. The Department of Agriculture beat out IBM and two other private companies to win the bid. Seventy-three percent of local governments now use private janitorial services, and 54 percent use private garbage collectors.[64] The city of Indianapolis requires all its departments to bid against private companies. When the transportation department was underbid by a private company on a contract to fill potholes, the city's union workers made a counterproposal that involved eliminating most of the department's middle managers and reengineering union jobs to save money. Eighteen supervisors were laid off, costs were cut by 25 percent, and the department won the bid.[65]

Market control was once used primarily at the level of the entire organization, but it is increasingly used in product divisions. Profit centers are self-contained product divisions, such as those described in Chapter 3. Each division contains resource inputs needed to produce a product. Each division can be evaluated on the basis of profit or loss compared with other divisions. Asea Brown Boveri (ABB), a multinational electrical contractor and manufacturer of electrical equipment, includes three different types of profit centers, all operating according to their own bottom line and all interacting through buying and selling with one another and with outside customers.[66] The network organization, also described in Chapter 3, illustrates market control as well. Different companies compete on price to provide the functions and services required by the hub organization. The organization typically contracts with the company that offers the best price and value.

Some firms require that individual departments interact with one another at market prices—buying and selling products or services among themselves at prices equivalent to those quoted outside the firm. To make the market control system work, internal units also have the option to buy and sell with outside companies. Imperial Oil Limited of Canada (formerly Esso) transformed its R&D department into a semiautonomous profit center several years ago.

In the early 1990s, Imperial Oil's R&D was a monopoly service provider allocated an annual budget of about $45 million. Imperial Oil felt that this method of operating gave the 200 scientists and staff little incentive to control costs or advance quality.

Today, R&D receives a much smaller budget and essentially supports itself through applied research and lab-services contracts negotiated with internal and external customers. Contracts spell out the costs of each program, analysis, or other service, and cost-conscious Imperial-Oil managers can shop for lower prices among external labs.

R&D has even introduced competition within its own small unit. For example, research teams are free to buy some lab services outside the company if they feel their own laboratories are overpriced or inefficient. However, quality and efficiency have dramatically improved at Imperial Oil's R&D, and the unit's high-quality, low-cost services are attracting a great deal of business from outside the company. Canadian companies routinely send samples of used motor oil to the R&D labs for analysis. Manufacturers use R&D to autopsy equipment failures. Vehicle makers like General Motors and Ford test new engines at Imperial Oil's R&D's chassis dynamometer lab. According to John Charlton, Imperial Oil's corporate strategic planning manager, applying market control to R&D has led to an increase in the amount of work the unit does, as well as a 12 percent reduction in internal costs.[67]

In Practice

Imperial Oil Limited

Market control can only be used when the output of a company, division, or department can be assigned a dollar price and when there is competition. Companies are finding that they can apply the market control concept to internal departments such as accounting, data processing, legal, and information services.

■ Clan Control

Clan control is the use of social characteristics, such as corporate culture, shared values, commitment, traditions, and beliefs, to control behavior. Organizations that use clan control require shared values and trust among employees.[68] Clan control is important when ambiguity and uncertainty are high. High uncertainty means the organization cannot put a price on its services, and things change so fast that rules and regulations are not able to specify every correct behavior. Under clan control, people may be hired because they are committed to the organization's purpose, such as in a religious organization. New employees may be subjected to a long period of socialization to gain acceptance by colleagues. Clan control is most often used in small, informal organizations or in organizations with a strong culture, because of personal involvement in and commitment to the organization's purpose. For example, St. Luke's Communications Ltd., a London advertising firm committed to equal employee ownership, is especially careful to bring in only new employees who believe in the agency's philosophy and mission. The company even turned down a $90 million contract because it meant rapidly recruiting new employees who might not fit with St. Luke's distinctive culture. Clan control works for St. Luke's; the agency is highly respected and its revenues continue to grow.[69]

Traditional control mechanisms based on strict rules and close supervision are ineffective for controlling behavior in conditions of high uncertainty and rapid change.[70] In addition, the growing use of computer networks and the Internet, which often leads to a democratic spread of information throughout the organization, may force many companies to depend less on bureaucratic control and more on shared values that guide individual actions for the corporate good.[71] Southwest Airlines represents one of the best examples of clan control in today's corporate world.

In Practice

Southwest Airlines

When oil prices soar, the airlines suffer. But at Southwest Airlines, employees have sometimes voluntarily given up vacation pay to help the airline pay for rising fuel costs. Loyalty, commitment, and peer pressure are strong components of control at Southwest Airlines, where a "we're all family" culture spurs employees to give their best and make sure others do too.

New hires are selected carefully to fit in with the culture, and each employee goes through a long period of socialization and training. The peer pressure to work hard and help the company cut costs and boost productivity is powerful. Workers routinely challenge each other on matters such as questionable sick-day calls or overuse of office supplies. Employees frequently go above and beyond the call of duty. Flight attendants who are traveling off-duty pitch in to help clean planes. Pilots help ramp agents load bags to keep flights on time. When founder and former CEO Herb Kelleher asked employees several years ago to find a way to help the company save $5 a day, one employee began taking the stairs instead of the elevator to save electricity.

The strong culture and clan control has helped Southwest Airlines remain profitable for more than 30 consecutive years and turned it into the fourth largest airline in terms of U.S. domestic service. However, as the company grows larger, the culture is beginning to show signs of strain. Unlike the old days, when top leaders could send handwritten notes of compliments or condolence to most of the employees, they now reach only a fraction of the 35,000 workers spread all over the country. In addition, with growth and success, Southwest Airlines has lost its underdog status and the motivation it provided for employees to work hard and conquer new territory. Labor negotiations with unions have been significantly less amicable than in the past as well.

Despite these tensions, clan control still works. Leaders are currently in the process of reinforcing the family-like culture to ensure that heavy bureaucratic controls are not needed.[72]

Southwest Airlines has successfully used clan control throughout its history, but this story illustrates that large size increases the demands on managers to maintain strong cultural values that support this type of control. Today's companies that are trying to become learning organizations often use clan control or *self-control* rather than relying on rules and regulations. Self-control is similar to clan control, but whereas clan control is a function of being socialized into a group, self-control stems from individual values, goals, and standards. The organization attempts to induce a change such that individual employees' own internal values and work preferences are brought in line with the organization's values and goals.[73] With self-control, employees generally set their own goals and monitor their own performance, yet companies relying on self-control need strong leaders who can clarify boundaries within which employees exercise their own knowledge and discretion.

Clan control or self-control may also be used in some departments, such as strategic planning, where uncertainty is high and performance is difficult to measure. Managers of departments that rely on these informal control mechanisms must not assume that the absence of written, bureaucratic control means no control is present. Clan control is invisible yet very powerful. One study found that the actions of employees were controlled even more powerfully and completely with clan control than with a bureaucratic hierarchy.[74] When clan control works, bureaucratic control is not needed.

Organizational Decline and Downsizing

Earlier in the chapter, we discussed the organizational life cycle, which suggests that organizations are born, grow older, and eventually die. Every organization goes through periods of temporary decline. In addition, a reality in today's environment is that for some companies, continual growth and expansion may not be possible.

All around, we see evidence that some organizations have stopped growing, and many are declining. Huge organizations such as Enron, WorldCom, and Arthur Andersen have collapsed partly as a result of rapid growth and ineffective control. The Catholic church continues to lose membership following reports of child molestation by priests and the failure in higher levels of the organization to remove molesters and prevent further abuse. Local governments have been forced to close schools and lay off teachers as tax revenues have declined. Many big companies, including DaimlerChrysler, Nortel Networks, Charles Schwab, and General Electric, have had significant job cuts in recent years, and hundreds of Internet companies that once looked poised for rapid growth have gone out of business.

In this section, we examine the causes and stages of organizational decline and then discuss how leaders can effectively manage the downsizing that is a reality in today's companies.

Definition and Causes

The term **organizational decline** is used to define a condition in which a substantial, absolute decrease in an organization's resource base occurs over a period.[75] Organizational decline is often associated with environmental decline in the sense that an organizational domain experiences either a reduction in size (such as shrinkage in customer demand or erosion of a city's tax base) or a reduction in shape (such as a shift in customer demand). In general, three factors are considered to cause organizational decline.

1. *Organizational atrophy.* Atrophy occurs when organizations grow older and become inefficient and overly bureaucratized. The organization's ability to adapt to its environment deteriorates. Often, atrophy follows a long period of success, because an organization takes success for granted, becomes attached to practices and structures that worked in the past, and fails to adapt to changes in the environment.[76] For example, Blockbuster Inc., which was king of the video-store

industry in the 1980s and 1990s, has had trouble adapting to the new world of video-on-demand (VOD) and digital downloading. Blockbuster is way behind upstarts like Netflix in pay VOD delivery because managers had trouble giving up the traditional successful approach of renting out videos in stores and online. Experts warn that companies risk becoming obsolete by sticking to patterns that were successful in the past but might no longer be effective.[77] Some warning signals for organizational atrophy include excess administrative and support staff, cumbersome administrative procedures, lack of effective communication and co-ordination, and outdated organizational structure.[78]

2. *Vulnerability.* Vulnerability reflects an organization's strategic inability to prosper in its environment. This often happens to small organizations that are not yet fully established. They are vulnerable to shifts in consumer tastes or in the economic health of the larger community. Small e-commerce companies that had not yet become established were the first to go out of business when the technology sector began to decline. Some organizations are vulnerable because they are unable to define the correct strategy to fit the environment. Vulnerable organizations typically need to redefine their environmental domain to enter new industries or markets.

3. *Environmental decline or competition.* Environmental decline refers to reduced energy and resources available to support an organization. When the environment has less capacity to support organizations, the organization has to either scale down operations or shift to another domain.[79] New competition increases the problem, especially for small organizations. Consider what's happening to U.S. toolmakers, the companies that make the dies, molds, jigs, fixtures, and gauges used on factory floors to manufacture everything from car doors to laser-guided bombs. Hundreds of these companies—including one of only two firms in the United States capable of making tools used to build components of stealth aircraft—have gone out of business in recent years, unable to compete with the super-low prices their counterparts in China are offering. One Chinese company, for example, is making tools to stamp metal car-jack parts for a U.S. manufacturer at less than half the cost a U.S. company could make them. The National Tooling and Machining Association estimates that 30 percent of the toolmakers in the United States have shut down since 2000.[80]

A Model of Decline Stages

Based on an extensive review of organizational decline research, a model of decline stages has been proposed and is summarized in Exhibit 9.8. This model suggests that decline, if not managed properly, can move through five stages resulting in organizational dissolution.[81]

1. *Blinded stage.* The first stage of decline is the internal and external change that threatens long-term survival and may require the organization to tighten up. The organization may have excess personnel, cumbersome procedures, or lack of harmony with customers. Leaders often miss the signals of decline at this point, and the solution is to develop effective scanning and control systems that indicate when something is wrong. With timely information, alert executives can bring the organization back to top performance.

2. *Inaction stage.* The second stage of decline is called *inaction* in which denial occurs despite signs of deteriorating performance. Leaders may try to persuade employees that all is well. "Creative accounting" may make things look fine during

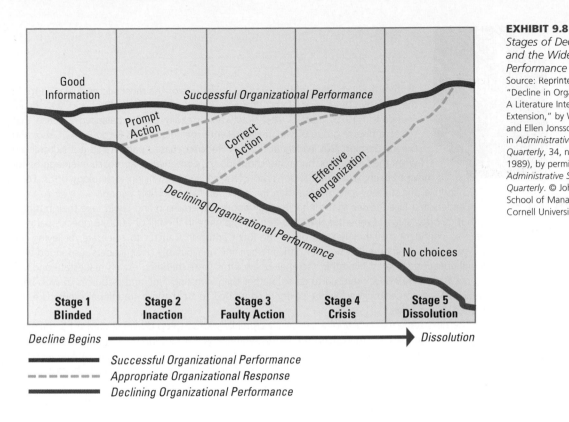

EXHIBIT 9.8
Stages of Decline and the Widening Performance Gap
Source: Reprinted from "Decline in Organizations: A Literature Integration and Extension," by William Weitzel and Ellen Jonsson, published in *Administrative Science Quarterly*, 34, no. 1 (March 1989), by permission of *Administrative Science Quarterly*. © Johnson Graduate School of Management, Cornell University.

this period. The solution is for leaders to acknowledge decline and take prompt action to realign the organization with the environment. Leadership actions may include new problem-solving approaches, increasing decision-making participation, and encouraging expression of dissatisfaction to learn what is wrong.

3. *Faulty action stage.* In the third stage, the organization is facing serious problems, and indicators of poor performance cannot be ignored. Failure to adjust to the declining spiral at this point can lead to organizational failure. Leaders are forced by severe circumstances to consider major changes. Actions may involve retrenchment, including downsizing personnel. Leaders should reduce employee uncertainty by clarifying values and providing information. A major mistake at this stage decreases the oganization's chance for a turnaround.

4. *Crisis stage.* In the fourth stage, the organization still has not been able to deal with decline effectively and is facing a panic. The organization may experience chaos, efforts to go back to basics, sharp changes, and anger. It is best for managers to prevent a stage-4 crisis, and the only solution is major reorganization. The social fabric of the organization is eroding, and dramatic actions, such as replacing top administrators and revolutionary changes in structure, strategy, and culture, are necessary. Workforce downsizing may be severe.

5. *Dissolution stage.* This stage of decline is irreversible. The organization is suffering loss of markets and reputation, the loss of its best personnel, and capital depletion. The only available strategy is to close down the organization in an orderly fashion and reduce the separation trauma of employees.

The following example of a once-respected law firm shows how failure to respond appropriately to signs of decline can lead to disaster.

In Practice

**Brobeck, Phleger
& Harrison LLP**

At the turn of the twenty-first century, it was one of the most successful law firms in the country. Three years later, Brobeck, Phleger & Harrison (Brobeck) was dead. Founded in 1926, Brobeck had slowly and steadily built a balanced practice that served a diverse group of well-heeled clients, including Wells Fargo Bank, Cisco, and Owens Corning. But leaders at the San Francisco–based partnership got sidetracked when the technology boom hit, shunning the conservative approach in an aggressive move to become a national powerhouse by serving high-flying technology firms. For a while, the strategy paid off, but then things began to go horribly wrong.

Leaders first failed to see that the technology boom was crashing and could take their business with it *(blinded stage)*. Even after NASDAQ began its plunge in the fall of 2000, Brobeck's partners were so confident that they headed off to the Ritz-Carlton in Cancun to celebrate, believing the downturn was temporary. As signs of difficulty became unavoidably clear, leaders responded with denial *(inaction stage)*. While other tech-heavy law firms were shedding excess real estate and laying off attorneys, Brobeck refused to do so. Rather than investing time and resources to woo back the loyalty of nontechnology clients, partners continued to treat these traditional clients like unwanted stepchildren.

The next stage *(faulty action)* is where things really started to go downhill. Brobeck's chairman convinced other partners to increase the firm's credit line with Citigroup so that the firm could hire even more lawyers and increase its presence in high-tech areas such as San Diego, Austin, and Silicon Valley. The idea was that the firm needed to take advantage of the downturn to beef up its resources and be ready when things picked back up.

In the *crisis stage*, profits were rapidly sinking, and debt had climbed to $82 million. Partners met to consider their options and decided to seek a merger partner, spend some $26 million of their own money to pay down the debt, and renegotiate leases under more favorable terms. But things had already gone too far.

When Brobeck staffers at offices around the country attended a videoconference at the end of January 2003, they expected to celebrate a merger with Morgan, Lewis & Bockius LLP, a combination that would have created one of the five largest law firms in the United States. Instead, they learned that Brobeck was folding and they were all out of a job. The loss of some key partners and Brobeck's declining reputation had spooked Morgan, Lewis & Bockius and the deal was called off. With still-dropping profits and no other potential merger partner on the horizon, Brobeck's partners realized *dissolution* was inevitable.[82]

As this example shows, properly managing organizational decline is necessary if an organization is to avoid dissolution. Leaders have a responsibility to detect the signs of decline, acknowledge them, implement necessary action, and reverse course. Some of the most difficult decisions pertain to downsizing, which refers to intentionally reducing the size of a company's workforce.

■ Downsizing Implementation

The economic downturn that began in 2000 has made **downsizing** a common practice in America's corporations. In addition, downsizing is a part of many change initiatives in today's organizations.[83] Reengineering projects, mergers and acquisitions, global competition, and the trend toward outsourcing have all led to job reductions.[84]

Some researchers have found that massive downsizing has often not achieved the intended benefits and in some cases has significantly harmed the organization.[85] Nevertheless, there are times when downsizing is a necessary part of managing organizational decline. A number of techniques can help smooth the downsizing process and ease tensions for employees who leave and for those who remain.[86]

1. *Communicate more, not less.* Some organizations seem to think the less that's said about a pending layoff, the better. Not so. Organizational managers should provide advance notice with as much information as possible. At 3Com Corporation, managers drew up a three-stage plan as they prepared for layoffs. First, they warned employees several months ahead that layoffs were inevitable. Soon thereafter, they held on-site presentations at all locations to explain to employees why the layoffs were needed and to provide as much information as they could about what employees should expect. Employees being cut were given a full 60 days' notice (required by a new federal regulation called the Worker Adjustment and Retraining Notification Act).[87] Managers should remember that it is impossible to "overcommunicate" during turbulent times. Remaining employees need to know what is expected of them, whether future layoffs are a possibility, and what the organization is doing to help co-workers who have lost their jobs.

2. *Provide assistance to displaced workers.* The organization has a responsibility to help displaced workers cope with the loss of their jobs and get reestablished in the job market. The organization can provide training, severance packages, extended benefits, and outplacement assistance. At Kaiser-Hill, a company running the cleanup and dismantling of the Rocky Flats nuclear site in Colorado, managers set up a Workforce Transition Program, sponsor an online job bank, and fund grants for entrepreneurs. Because Kaiser-Hill has to motivate employees to work themselves out of a job in a couple of years, it knows people need the security of feeling that they can provide for their families when the job is over.[88] In addition, counseling services for both employees and their families can ease the trauma associated with a job loss. Another key step is to allow employees to leave with dignity, giving them an opportunity to say goodbye to colleagues and meet with leaders to express their hurt and anger.

3. *Help the survivors thrive.* Leaders should remember the emotional needs of survivors as well. Many people experience guilt, anger, confusion, and sadness after the loss of colleagues, and these feelings should be acknowledged. They might also be concerned about their own jobs and have difficulty adapting to the changes in job duties, responsibilities, and so forth. The state of Oregon hired consultant Al Siebert to help employees adapt following the elimination of more than a thousand jobs. Most people "just aren't emotionally prepared to handle major disruptions," Siebert says. Through a series of workshops, Siebert helped people acknowledge their anger and unhappiness and then helped them become "change-resilient" by developing coping skills such as flexibility, curiosity, and optimism.[89]

Even the best-managed organizations may sometimes need to lay off employees in a turbulent environment or to revitalize the organization and reverse decline. Leaders can attain positive results if they handle downsizing in a way that lets departing employees leave with dignity and enables remaining organization members to be motivated, productive, and committed to a better future. Charles Schwab & Company turned to downsizing as a last resort and used techniques to make the process less painful.

In Practice

Charles Schwab & Company

Chuck Schwab founded Charles Schwab & Company (Schwab) in 1974 to "help real people reach their financial dreams." His mission was for a company that wasn't in business just to make money but to make a difference. Since those days, Schwab has maintained a reputation based on integrity and fair play, a principle that extends to clients and employees alike.

The company has always shunned layoffs, which it refers to as "the L word." Until recently, the only people laid off in the company's history were 150 people let go after the stock market decline of 1987. But when the bear market took over in the early 2000s, Schwab got mauled. Annual revenue plunged 29 percent, daily average revenue trades declined more than 50 percent, and the company's stock dropped nearly 75 percent from its all-time high. Something had to give, but managers had a toolbox filled with all sorts of belt-tightening measures to take before resorting to layoffs.

Managers first put projects on hold and cut back on expenses such as catered staff lunches, travel, and entertainment. When it became clear that more savings were needed, top executives took hefty pay cuts, with the top two slashing their pay by 50 percent and refusing bonuses. The company also began encouraging people to take unpaid vacation days, shift to part-time work or job sharing, and take Fridays off.

Unfortunately, the moves just weren't enough. Managers realized layoffs were inevitable and announced it to the entire workforce. They were also careful to keep people informed throughout the process, releasing information as it was available. The company eventually shed around 6,500 workers, a full 25 percent of the workforce. The cuts have been painful for everyone, but Schwab has tried to smooth the process as much as possible. For example, severance packages included as much as 18 months' pay, everyone let go was promised a $7,000 signing bonus if they were hired back, and Chuck Schwab and his wife put $10 million of their own money into a fund for anyone who wanted to earn an advanced degree until the market picked back up.

Although morale and satisfaction is down at Schwab, for most remaining employees it makes a difference that the company handled the layoffs in a way that showed genuine concern for employees rather than regarding them simply as costs to be cut.[90]

Summary and Interpretation

The material covered in this chapter contains several important ideas about organizations. Organizations evolve through distinct life cycle stages as they grow and mature. Organization structure, internal systems, and management issues are different for each stage of development. Growth creates crises and revolutions along the way toward large size. A major task of managers is to guide the organization through the entrepreneurial, collectivity, formalization, and elaboration stages of development. As organizations progress through the life cycle and grow larger and more complex, they generally take on bureaucratic characteristics, such as rules, division of labor, written records, hierarchy of authority, and impersonal procedures. Bureaucracy is a logical form of organizing that lets firms use resources efficiently. However, in many large corporate and government organizations, bureaucracy has come under attack with attempts to decentralize authority, flatten organization structure, reduce rules and written records, and create a small-company mindset. These companies are willing to trade economies of scale for responsive, adaptive organizations. Many companies are subdividing to gain small-company advantages. Another approach to overcoming the problems of bureaucracy is to use a structural concept called the *incident command system*, which enables the organization to glide smoothly between a highly formalized, hierarchical style that is effective during times of stability and a more flexible, loosely structured one needed to respond to unexpected or volatile environmental conditions.

In large organizations, greater support is required from clerical and professional staff specialists. This is a logical outcome of employee specialization and the division of labor. By dividing an organization's tasks and having specialists perform each part, the organization can become more efficient.

All organizations, large and small, need systems for control. Managers can choose among three overall control strategies: market, bureaucratic, and clan. Bureaucratic control relies on standard rules and the rational-legal authority of managers. Market control is used where product or service outputs can be priced and competition exists. Clan control, and more recently self-control, are associated with uncertain and rapidly changing organization processes. They rely on commitment, tradition, and shared values for control. Managers may use a combination of control approaches to meet the organization's needs.

Many organizations have stopped growing, and some are declining. Organizations go through stages of decline, and it is the responsibility of managers to detect the signs of decline, implement necessary action, and reverse course. One of the most difficult decisions pertains to downsizing the workforce. To smooth the downsizing process, managers can communicate with employees and provide as much information as possible, provide assistance to displaced workers, and remember to address the emotional needs of those who remain with the organization.

Key Concepts

bureaucracy	formalization
bureaucratic control	formalization stage
centralization	incident command system
charismatic authority	life cycle
clan control	market control
collectivity stage	organizational decline
downsizing	personnel ratios
elaboration stage	rational-legal authority
entrepreneurial stage	traditional authority

Discussion Questions

1. Discuss the key differences between large and small organizations. Which kinds of organizations would be better off acting as large organizations, and which are best trying to act as big-company/small-company hybrids?
2. Why do large organizations tend to be more formalized?
3. If you were managing a department of college professors, how might you structure the department differently than if you were managing a department of bookkeepers? Why?
4. Apply the concept of life cycle to an organization with which you are familiar, such as a university or a local business. What stage is the organization in now? How did the organization handle or pass through its life cycle crises?
5. Describe the three bases of authority identified by Weber. Is it possible for each of these types of authority to function at the same time within an organization?
6. In writing about types of control, William Ouchi said, "The Market is like the trout and the Clan like the salmon, each a beautiful highly specialized species which re-

quires uncommon conditions for its survival. In comparison, the bureaucratic method of control is the catfish—clumsy, ugly, but able to live in the widest range of environments and ultimately, the dominant species." Discuss what Ouchi meant with that analogy.

7. Government organizations often seem more bureaucratic than for-profit organizations. Could this partly be the result of the type of control used in government organizations? Explain.

8. The incident command system has been used primarily by organizations that regularly deal with crisis situations. Discuss whether this approach seems workable for a large media company that wants to reduce bureaucracy. How about for a manufacturer of cell phones?

9. Refer to the Xerox case at the beginning of Chapter 1 and discuss how Xerox illustrates the major causes of organizational decline. In what stage of decline does Xerox seem to be?

10. Do you think a "no growth" philosophy of management should be taught in business schools? Discuss.

Chapter 9 Workbook: Control Mechanisms*

Think of two situations in your life: your work and your school experiences. How is control exerted? Fill out the tables.

On the Job

Your job responsibilities	How your boss controls	Positives of this control	Negatives of this control	How you would improve control
1.				
2.				
3.				
4.				

At the University

Items	How professor A (small class) controls	How professor B (large class) controls	How these controls influence you	What you think is a better control
1. Exams				
2. Assignments/ papers				
3. Class participation				
4. Attendance				
5. Other				

Questions

1. What are the advantages and disadvantages of the various controls?
2. What happens when there is too much control? Too little?
3. Does the type of control depend on the situation and the number of people involved?
4. *Optional:* How do the control mechanisms in your tables compare to those of other students?

Case for Analysis: Sunflower Incorporated*

Sunflower Incorporated is a large distribution company with more than 5,000 employees and gross sales of more than $550 million (2003). The company purchases salty snack foods and liquor and distributes them to independent retail stores throughout the United States and Canada. Salty snack foods include corn chips, potato chips, cheese curls, tortilla chips, pretzels, and peanuts. The United States and Canada are divided into twenty-two regions, each with its own central warehouse, salespeople, finance department, and purchasing department. The company distributes national and local brands and packages some items under private labels. Competition in this industry is intense. The demand for liquor has been declining, and competitors like Procter & Gamble and Frito-Lay have developed new snack foods and low-carb options to gain market share from smaller companies like Sunflower. The head office encourages each region to be autonomous because of local tastes and practices. In the northeastern United States, for example, people consume a greater percentage of Canadian whiskey and American bourbon, whereas in the West, they consume more light liquors, such as vodka, gin, and rum. Snack foods in the Southwest are often seasoned to reflect Mexican tastes, and customers in the Northeast buy a greater percent of pretzels.

Early in 1998, Sunflower began using a financial reporting system that compared sales, costs, and profits across company regions. Each region was a profit center, and top management was surprised to learn that profits varied widely. By 2001, the differences were so great that management decided some standardization was necessary. Managers believed highly profitable regions were sometimes using lower-quality items, even seconds, to boost profit margins. This practice could hurt Sunflower's image. Most regions were facing cutthroat price competition to hold market share. Triggered by price cuts by Anheuser-Busch Company's Eagle Snacks division, national distributors, such as Frito-Lay, Borden, Nabisco, Procter & Gamble (Pringles), and Standard Brands (Planters Peanuts), were pushing to hold or increase market share by cutting prices and launching new products. Independent snack food distributors had a tougher and tougher time competing, and many were going out of business.

As these problems accumulated, Joe Steelman, president of Sunflower, decided to create a new position to monitor pricing and purchasing practices. Loretta Williams was hired from the finance department of a competing organization. Her new title was director of pricing and purchasing, and she reported to the vice president of finance, Peter Langly. Langly gave Williams great latitude in organizing her job and encouraged her to establish whatever rules and procedures were necessary. She was also encouraged to gather information from each region. Each region was notified of her appointment by an official memo sent to the twenty-two regional directors. A copy of the memo was posted on each warehouse bulletin board. The announcement was also made in the company newspaper.

After 3 weeks on the job, Williams decided two problems needed her attention. Over the long term, Sunflower should make better use of information technology. Williams believed information technology could provide more information to headquarters for decision making. Top managers in the divisions were connected to headquarters by an intranet, but lower-level employees and salespeople were not connected. Only a few senior managers in about half the divisions used the system regularly.

In the short term, Williams decided fragmented pricing and purchasing decisions were a problem and these decisions should be standardized across regions. This should be undertaken immediately. As a first step, she wanted the financial executive in each region to notify her of any change in local prices of more than 3 percent. She also decided that all new contracts for local purchases of more than $5,000 should be cleared through her office. (Approximately 60 percent of items distributed in the regions were purchased in large quantities and supplied from the home office. The other 40 percent were purchased and distributed within the region.) Williams believed the only way to standardize op-

*This case was inspired by "Frito-Lay May Find Itself in a Competition Crunch," *BusinessWeek* (July 19, 1982), 186; Jim Bohman, "Mike-Sells Works to Remain on Snack Map," *Dayton Daily News* (February 27, 2005) D; "Dashman Company" in Paul R. Lawrence and John A. Seiler, *Organizational Behavior and Administration: Cases, Concepts, and Research Findings* (Homewood, Ill: Irwin and Dorsey, 1965), 16–17; and Laurie M. Grossman, "Price Wars Bring Flavor to Once Quiet Snack Market," *The Wall Street Journal* (May 23, 1991), B1, B3.

erations was for each region to notify the home office in advance of any change in prices or purchases. She discussed the proposed policy with Langly. He agreed, so they submitted a formal proposal to the president and board of directors, who approved the plan. The changes represented a complicated shift in policy procedures, and Sunflower was moving into peak holiday season, so Williams wanted to implement the new procedures right away. She decided to send an e-mail message followed by a fax to the financial and purchasing executives in each region notifying them of the new procedures. The change would be inserted in all policy and procedure manuals throughout Sunflower within 4 months.

Williams showed a draft of the message to Langly and invited his comments. Langly said the message was a good idea but wondered if it was sufficient. The regions handled hundreds of items and were accustomed to decentralized decision making. Langly suggested that Williams ought to visit the regions and discuss purchasing and pricing policies with the executives. Williams refused, saying that such trips would be expensive and time-consuming. She had so many things to do at headquarters that trips were impossible. Langly also suggested waiting to implement the proce-

dures until after the annual company meeting in 3 months, when Williams could meet the regional directors personally. Williams said this would take too long, because the procedures would then not take effect until after the peak sales season. She believed the procedures were needed now. The messages went out the next day.

During the next few days, e-mail replies came in from seven regions. The managers said they were in agreement and were happy to cooperate.

Eight weeks later, Williams had not received notices from any regions about local price or purchase changes. Other executives who had visited regional warehouses indicated to her that the regions were busy as usual. Regional executives seemed to be following usual procedures for that time of year. She telephoned one of the regional managers and discovered that he did not know who she was and had never heard of her position. Besides, he said, "we have enough to worry about reaching profit goals without additional procedures from headquarters." Williams was chagrined that her position and her suggested changes in procedure had no impact. She wondered whether field managers were disobedient or whether she should have used another communication strategy.

Chapter 9 Workshop: Windsock, Inc.*

1. *Introduction*. Class is divided into four groups: Central Office, Product Design, Marketing/Sales, and Production. Central Office is a slightly smaller group. If groups are large enough, assign observers to each one. Central Office is given 500 straws and 750 pins. Each person reads *only* the role description relevant to that group. *Materials needed*: plastic milk straws (500) and a box of straight pins (750).
2. *Perform task*. Depending on length of class, step 2 may take 30 to 60 minutes. Groups perform functions and prepare for a 2-minute report for stockholders.
3. *Group reports*. Each group gives a 2-minute presentation to stockholders.
4. *Observers' reports (optional)*. Observers share insights with subgroups.
5. *Class discussion*.
   a. What helped or blocked intergroup cooperation and coordination?
   b. To what extent was there open versus closed communication? What impact did that have?
   c. What styles of leadership were exhibited?
   d. What types of team interdependencies emerged?

Roles
Central Office
Your team is the central management and administration of Windsock, Inc. You are the heart and pulse of the organization, because without your coordination and resource

allocation, the organization would go under. Your task is to manage the operations of the organization, which is not an easy responsibility because you have to coordinate the activities of three distinct groups of personnel: the Marketing/Sales group, the Production group, and the Product Design group. In addition, you have to manage resources including materials (pins and straws), time deadlines, communications, and product requirements.

In this exercise, you are to do whatever is necessary to accomplish the mission and to keep the organization operating harmoniously and efficiently.

Windsock, Inc., has a total of 30 minutes (more if instructor assigns) to design an advertising campaign and ad copy, to design the windmill, and to produce the first windmill prototypes for delivery. Good luck to you all.

Product Design
Your team is the research and product design group of Windsock, Inc. You are the brain and creative aspect of the operation, because without an innovative and successfully designed product, the organization would go under. Your

---

*Adapted by Dorothy Marcic from Christopher Taylor and Saundra Taylor in "Teaching Organizational Team-Building through Simulations," *Organizational Behavior Teaching Review* XI(3), 86–87.

duties are to design products that compete favorably in the marketplace, keeping in mind function, aesthetics, cost, ease of production, and available materials.

In this exercise, you are to come up with a workable plan for a product that will be built by your production team. Your windmill must be light, portable, easy to assemble, and aesthetically pleasing. Central Office controls the budget and allocates material for your division.

Windsock, Inc., as an organization has a total of 30 minutes (more if instructor assigns) to design an advertising campaign, to design the windmill (your group's task), and to produce the first windmill prototypes for delivery. Good luck to you all.

Marketing/Sales

Your team is the marketing/sales group of Windsock, Inc. You are the backbone of the operation, because without customers and sales the organization would go under. Your task is to determine the market, develop an advertising campaign to promote your company's unique product, produce ad copy, and develop a sales force and sales procedures for both potential customers and the public at large.

For the purpose of this exercise, you may assume that a market analysis has been completed. Your team is now in a position to produce an advertising campaign and ad copy for the product. To be effective, you have to become very familiar with the characteristics of the product and how it is different from those products already on the market. The Central Office controls your budget and allocates materials for use by your division.

Windsock, Inc., has a total of 30 minutes (more if instructor assigns) to design an advertising campaign and ad (your group's task), to design the windmill, and to produce the first windmill prototypes for delivery. Good luck to you all.

Production

Your team is the production group of Windsock, Inc. You are the heart of the operation, because without a group to produce the product, the organization would go under. You have the responsibility to coordinate and produce the product for delivery. The product involves an innovative design for a windmill that is cheaper, lighter, more portable, more flexible, and more aesthetically pleasing than other designs currently available in the marketplace. Your task is to build windmills within cost guidelines, according to specifications, and within a prescribed period, using predetermined materials.

For the purpose of this exercise, you are to organize your team, set production schedules, and build the windmills. Central Office controls your budget, materials, and specifications.

Windsock, Inc., has a total of 30 minutes (more if instructor assigns) to design an advertising campaign, to design the windmill, and to produce the first windmill prototypes (your group's task) for delivery. Good luck to you all.

Notes

1. Chuck Salter, "Terrorists Strike Fast...Interpol Has to Move Faster...Ron Noble Is on the Case," *Fast Company* (October 2002), 96–104; and "Interpol Pushing to Be UN Globocop," *The New American* (November 1, 2004), 8.

2. James Q. Wilson, *Bureaucracy* (New York: Basic Books, 1989); and Charles Perrow, *Complex Organizations: A Critical Essay* (Glenview, Ill.: Scott, Foresman, 1979), 4.

3. Tom Peters, "Rethinking Scale," *California Management Review* (Fall 1992), 7–29.

4. Jerry Useem, "One Nation Under Wal-Mart," *Fortune* (March 3, 2003), 65–78.

5. Matt Murray, "Critical Mass: As Huge Companies Keep Growing, CEOs Struggle to Keep Pace," *The Wall Street Journal* (February 8, 2001), A1, A6.

6. Stuart Elliott, "Advertising's Big Four: It's Their World Now," *The New York Times* (March 31, 2002), Section 3, 1, 10.

7. Donald V. Potter, "Scale Matters," *Across the Board* (July–August 2000), 36–39.

8. Jim Collins, "Bigger, Better, Faster," *Fast Company* (June 2003), 74–78.

9. Adrian Slywotzky and Richard Wise, "Double-Digit Growth in No-Growth Times," *Fast Company* (April 2003), 66.

10. James B. Treece, "Sometimes, You've Still Gotta Have Size," *BusinessWeek/Enterprise* (1993), 200–201 (April, 2003), 66ff.

11. Alan Murray, "The Profit Motive Has a Limit: Tragedy," *The Wall Street Journal* (September 7, 2005), A2.

12. John A. Byrne and Heather Timmons, "Tough Times for a New CEO," *BusinessWeek* (October 29, 2001), 64–70; and Patrick McGeehan, "Sailing Into a Sea of Trouble," *The New York Times* (October 5, 2001), C1, C4.

13. Frits K. Pil and Matthias Holweg, "Exploring Scale: The Advantages of Thinking Small," *MIT Sloan Management Review* (Winter 2003), 33–39.

14. David Friedman, "Is Big Back? Or Is Small Still Beautiful?" *Inc.* (April 1998), 23–28.

15. David Henry, "Mergers: Why Most Big Deals Don't Pay Off," *BusinessWeek* (October 14, 2002), 60–70.

16. Keith H. Hammonds, "Size Is Not a Strategy," *Fast Company* (September 2002), 78–86.

17. See Hammonds, "Size Is Not a Strategy," Henry, "Mergers: Why Most Big Deals Don't Pay Off," and Tom Brown, "How Big Is Too Big?" *Across the Board* (July–August 1999), 15–20, for a discussion.

18. Reported in John Case, "Counting Companies," *Inc.*, State of Small Business 2001 (May 29, 2001), 21–23; and Peter Drucker, "Toward the New Organization," *Executive Excellence* (February 1997), 7.

19. "The Hot 100," *Fortune* (September 5, 2005), 75–80.

20. Ibid.

21. Gary Hamel, quoted in Hammonds, "Size Is Not a Strategy."

22. Richard A. Melcher, "How Goliaths Can Act Like Davids," *BusinessWeek/Enterprise* (1993), 192–201.

23. Michael Barone, "Not a Victory for Big Government," *The Wall Street Journal* (January 15, 2002), A16.

24. Ibid.

25. Hammonds, "Size Is Not a Strategy."

26. John R. Kimberly, Robert H. Miles, and associates, *The Organizational Life Cycle* (San Francisco: Jossey-Bass, 1980); Ichak Adices, "Organizational Passages—Diagnosing and Treating Lifecycle Problems of Organizations," *Organizational Dynamics* (Summer 1979), 3–25; Danny Miller and Peter H. Friesen, "A Longitudinal Study of the Corporate Life Cycle," *Management Science* 30 (October 1984), 1161–1183; and Neil C. Churchill and Virginia L. Lewis, "The Five Stages of Small Business Growth," *Harvard Business Review* 61 (May–June 1983), 30–50.

27. Larry E. Greiner, "Evolution and Revolution as Organizations Grow," *Harvard Business Review* 50 (July–August 1972), 37–46; and Robert E. Quinn and Kim Cameron, "Organizational Life Cycles and Shifting Criteria of Effectiveness: Some Preliminary Evidence," *Management Science* 29 (1983), 33–51.

28. George Land and Beth Jarman, "Moving beyond Breakpoint," in Michael Ray and Alan Rinzler, eds., *The New Paradigm* (New York: Jeremy P. Tarcher/Perigee Books, 1993), 250–266; and Michael L. Tushman, William H. Newman, and Elaine Romanelli, "Convergence and Upheaval: Managing the Unsteady Pace of Organizational Evolution," *California Management Review* 29 (1987), 1–16.

29. David A. Mack and James Campbell Quick, "EDS: An Inside View of a Corporate Life Cycle Transition," *Organizational Dynamics* 30, no. 3 (2002), 282–293.

30. Adam Lashinsky, "Google Hires a Grown-up," *Business 2.0* (February 2002), 22.

31. David A. Whetten, "Sources, Responses, and Effects of Organizational Decline," in John R. Kimberly, Robert H. Miles, and associates, *The Organizational Life Cycle*, 342–374.

32. Brent Schlender, "How Big Can Apple Get?" *Fortune* (February 21, 2005), 67–76; and Josh Quittner with Rebecca Winters, "Apple's New Core—Exclusive: How Steve Jobs Made a Sleek Machine That Could Be the Home-Digital Hub of the Future," *Time* (January 14, 2002), 46.

33. Land and Jarman, "Moving beyond Breakpoint."

34. Stanley Holmes, "The New Nike," *BusinessWeek* (September 20, 2004), 78–86.

35. Daniel Roth, "Can Nike Still Do It without Phil Knight?" *Fortune* (April 4, 2005), 58–68.

36. Jay Greene, "Microsoft's Midlife Crisis," *BusinessWeek* (April 19, 2004), 88–98.

37. Max Weber, *The Theory of Social and Economic Organizations*, translated by A. M. Henderson and T. Parsons (New York: Free Press, 1947).

38. Tina Rosenberg, "The Taint of the Greased Palm," *The New York Times Magazine* (August 10, 2003), 28.

39. John Crewdson, "Corruption Viewed as a Way of Life," *Bryan-College Station Eagle* (November 28, 1982), 13A; Barry Kramer, "Chinese Officials Still Give Preference to Kin, Despite Peking Policies," *The Wall Street Journal* (October 29, 1985), 1, 21.

40. Kelly Barron, "Logistics in Brown," *Forbes* (January 10, 2000), 78–83; Scott Kirsner, "Venture Vérité: United Parcel Service," *Wired* (September 1999), 83–96; and Kathy Goode, Betty Hahn, and Cindy Seibert, *United Parcel Service: The Brown Giant* (unpublished manuscript, Texas A&M University, 1981).

41. Allen C. Bluedorn, "Pilgrim's Progress: Trends and Convergence in Research on Organizational Size and Environment," *Journal of Management Studies* 19 (Summer 1993), 163–191; John R. Kimberly, "Organizational Size and the Structuralist Perspective: A Review, Critique, and Proposal," *Administrative Science Quarterly* (1976), 571–597; Richard L. Daft and Selwyn W. Becker, "Managerial, Institutional, and Technical Influences on Administration: A Longitudinal Analysis," *Social Forces* 59 (1980), 392–413.

42. James P. Walsh and Robert D. Dewar, "Formalization and the Organizational Life Cycle," *Journal of Management Studies* 24 (May 1987), 215–231.

43. Nancy M. Carter and Thomas L. Keon, "Specialization as a Multidimensional Construct," *Journal of Management Studies* 26 (1989), 11–28; Cheng-Kuang Hsu, Robert M. March, and Hiroshi Mannari, "An Examination of the Determinants of Organizational Structure," *American Journal of Sociology* 88 (1983), 975–996; Guy Geeraerts, "The Effect of Ownership on the Organization Structure in Small Firms," *Administrative Science Quarterly* 29 (1984), 232–237; Bernard Reimann, "On the Dimensions of Bureaucratic Structure: An Empirical Reappraisal," *Administrative Science Quarterly* 18 (1973), 462–476; Richard H. Hall, "The Concept of Bureaucracy: An Empirical Assessment," *American Journal of Sociology* 69 (1963), 32–40; and William A. Rushing, "Organizational Rules and Surveillance: A Proposition in Comparative Organizational Analysis," *Administrative Science Quarterly* 10 (1966), 423–443.

44. Jerald Hage and Michael Aiken, "Relationship of Centralization to Other Structural Properties," *Administrative Science Quarterly* 12 (1967), 72–91.

45. Steve Lohr and John Markoff, "You Call This a Midlife Crisis?" *The New York Times* (August 31, 2003), Section 3, 1.

46. Peter Brimelow, "How Do You Cure Injelitance?" *Forbes* (August 7, 1989), 42–44; Jeffrey D. Ford and John W. Slocum, Jr., "Size, Technology, Environment and the Structure of Organizations," *Academy of Management Review* 2 (1977), 561–575; and John D. Kasarda, "The Structural Implications of Social System Size: A Three-Level Analysis," *American Sociological Review* 39 (1974), 19–28.

47. Graham Astley, "Organizational Size and Bureaucratic Structure," *Organization Studies* 6 (1985), 201–228; Spyros K. Lioukas and Demitris A. Xerokostas, "Size and Administrative Intensity in Organizational Divisions," *Management Science* 28 (1982), 854–868; Peter M. Blau, "Interdependence and Hierarchy in Organizations," *Social Science Research* 1 (1972), 1–24; Peter M. Blau and R. A. Schoenherr, *The Structure of Organizations* (New York: Basic Books, 1971); A. Hawley, W. Boland, and M. Boland, "Population Size and Administration in Institutions of Higher Education," *American Sociological Review* 30 (1965), 252–255; Richard L. Daft, "System Influence on Organization Decision-Making: The Case of Resource Allocation," *Academy of Management Journal* 21 (1978), 6–22; and B. P. Indik,

"The Relationship between Organization Size and the Supervisory Ratio," *Administrative Science Quarterly* 9 (1964), 301–312.

48. T. F. James, "The Administrative Component in Complex Organizations," *Sociological Quarterly* 13 (1972), 533–539; Daft, "System Influence on Organization Decision-Making"; E. A. Holdaway and E. A. Blowers, "Administrative Ratios and Organization Size: A Longitudinal Examination," *American Sociological Review* 36 (1971), 278–286; and John Child, "Parkinson's Progress: Accounting for the Number of Specialists in Organizations," *Administrative Science Quarterly* 18 (1973), 328–348.

49. Richard L. Daft and Selwyn Becker, "School District Size and the Development of Personnel Resources," *Alberta Journal of Educational Research* 24 (1978), 173–187.

50. Thomas A. Stewart, "Yikes! Deadwood is Creeping Back," *Fortune* (August 18, 1997), 221–222.

51. Cathy Lazere, "Resisting Temptation: The Fourth Annual SG&A Survey," *CFO* (December 1997), 64–70.

52. Based on Gifford and Elizabeth Pinchot, *The End of Bureaucracy and the Rise of the Intelligent Organization* (San Francisco: Berrett-Koehler Publishers, 1993), 21–29.

53. Jack Rosenthal, "Entitled: A Chief for Every Occasion, and Even a Chief Chief," *New York Times Magazine* (August 26, 2001), 16.

54. Scott Shane, "The Beast That Feeds on Boxes: Bureaucracy," *The New York Times* (April 10, 2005), http://www.nytimes.com.

55. Gregory A. Bigley and Karlene H. Roberts, "The Incident Command System: High-Reliability Organizing for Complex and Volatile Task Environments," *Academy of Management Journal* 44, no. 6 (2001), 1281–1299.

56. Robert Pool, "In the Zero Luck Zone," *Forbes ASAP* (November 27, 2000), 85.

57. Based on Bigley and Roberts, "The Incident Command System."

58. Lazere, "Resisting Temptation."

59. Philip M. Padsakoff, Larry J. Williams, and William D. Todor, "Effects of Organizational Formalization on Alienation among Professionals and Nonprofessionals," *Academy of Management Journal* 29 (1986), 820–831.

60. Royston Greenwood, C. R. Hinings, and John Brown, "'P2-Form' Strategic Management: Corporate Practices in Professional Partnerships," *Academy of Management Journal* 33 (1990), 725–755; Royston Greenwood and C. R. Hinings, "Understanding Strategic Change: The Contribution of Archetypes," *Academy of Management Journal* 36 (1993), 1052–1081.

61. William G. Ouchi, "Markets, Bureaucracies, and Clans," *Administrative Science Quarterly* 25 (1980), 129–141; idem, "A Conceptual Framework for the Design of Organizational Control Mechanisms," *Management Science* 25 (1979), 833–848.

62. Weber, *The Theory of Social and Economic Organizations*, 328–340.

63. Oliver A. Williamson, *Markets and Hierarchies: Analyses and Antitrust Implications* (New York: Free Press, 1975).

64. David Wessel and John Harwood, "Capitalism is Giddy with Triumph: Is It Possible to Overdo It?" *The Wall Street Journal* (May 14, 1998), A1, A10.

65. Anita Micossi, "Creating Internal Markets," *Enterprise* (April 1994), 43–44.

66. Raymond E. Miles, Henry J. Coleman, Jr., and W. E. Douglas Creed, "Keys to Success in Corporate Redesign," *California Management Review* 37, no. 3 (Spring 1995), 128–145.

67. Micossi, "Creating Internal Markets."

68. Ouchi, "Markets, Bureaucracies, and Clans."

69. Anna Muoio, ed., "Growing Smart," *Fast Company* (August 1998), 73–83.

70. Richard Leifer and Peter K. Mills, "An Information Processing Approach for Deciding upon Control Strategies and Reducing Control Loss in Emerging Organizations," *Journal of Management* 22, no. 1 (1996), 113–137.

71. Stratford Sherman, "The New Computer Revolution," *Fortune* (June 14, 1993), 56–80.

72. Melanie Trottman, "New Atmosphere: Inside Southwest Airlines, Storied Culture Feels Strain," *The Wall Street Journal* (July 11, 2003), A1, A6.

73. Leifer and Mills, "An Information Processing Approach for Deciding upon Control Strategies"; and Laurie J. Kirsch, "The Management of Complex Tasks in Organizations: Controlling the Systems Development Process," *Organization Science* 7, no. 1 (January–February 1996), 1–21.

74. James R. Barker, "Tightening the Iron Cage: Concertive Control in Self-Managing Teams," *Administrative Science Quarterly* 38 (1993), 408–437.

75. Kim S. Cameron, Myung Kim, and David A. Whetten, "Organizational Effects of Decline and Turbulence," *Administrative Science Quarterly* 32 (1987), 222–240.

76. Danny Miller, "What Happens after Success: The Perils of Excellence," *Journal of Management Studies* 31, no. 3 (May 1994), 325–358.

77. Kris Frieswick, "The Turning Point: What Options Do Companies Have When Their Industries Are Dying?" *CFO Magazine* (April 1, 2005), http://www.cfo.com.

78. Leonard Greenhalgh, "Organizational Decline," in Samuel B. Bacharach, ed., *Research in the Sociology of Organizations* 2 (Greenwich, Conn.: JAI Press, 1983), 231–276; and Peter Lorange and Robert T. Nelson, "How to Recognize—and Avoid—Organizational Decline," *Sloan Management Review* (Spring 1987), 41–48.

79. Kim S. Cameron and Raymond Zammuto, "Matching Managerial Strategies to Conditions of Decline," *Human Resources Management* 22 (1983), 359–375; and Leonard Greenhalgh, Anne T. Lawrence, and Robert I. Sutton, "Determinants of Workforce Reduction Strategies in Organizations," *Academy of Management Review* 13 (1988), 241–254.

80. Timothy Aeppel, "Die Is Cast; Toolmakers Know Precisely What's the Problem: Price," *The Wall Street Journal* (November 21, 2003), A1, A6.

81. William Weitzel and Ellen Jonsson, "Reversing the Downward Spiral: Lessons from W. T. Grant and Sears Roebuck," *Academy of Management Executive* 5 (1991), 7–21; William Weitzel and Ellen Jonsson, "Decline in Organizations: A Literature Integration and Extension," *Administrative Science Quarterly* 34 (1989), 91–109.

82. Linda Himelstein with Heather Timmons, "Meltdown of a Highflier," *BusinessWeek* (February 24, 2003), 130–131.

83. William McKinley, Carol M. Sanchez, and Allen G. Schick, "Organizational Downsizing: Constraining, Cloning, Learning," *Academy of Management Executive* 9, no. 3 (1995), 32–42.

84. Gregory B. Northcraft and Margaret A. Neale, *Organizational Behavior: A Management Challenge*, 2nd ed. (Fort Worth, Tex: The Dryden Press, 1994), 626; and A. Catherine Higgs, "Executive Commentary" on McKinley, Sanchez, and Schick, "Organizational Downsizing: Constraining, Cloning, Learning," 43–44.

85. Wayne Cascio, "Strategies for Responsible Restructuring," *Academy of Management Executive* 16, no. 3 (2002), 80–91; James R. Morris, Wayne F. Cascio, and Clifford E. Young, "Downsizing after All These Years: Questions and Answers about Who Did It, How Many Did It, and Who Benefited from It," *Organizational Dynamics* (Winter 1999), 78–86; Stephen Doerflein and James Atsaides, "Corporate Psychology: Making Downsizing Work," *Electrical World* (September–October 1999), 41–43; and Brett C. Luthans and Steven M. Sommer, "The Impact of Downsizing on Workplace Attitudes," *Group and Organization Management* 2, no. 1 (1999), 46–70.

86. These techniques are based on Bob Nelson, "The Care of the Un-Downsized," *Training and Development* (April 1997), 40–43; Shari Caudron, "Teach Downsizing Sur-

vivors How to Thrive," *Personnel Journal* (January 1996), 38; Joel Brockner, "Managing the Effects of Layoffs on Survivors," *California Management Review* (Winter 1992), 9–28; Ronald Henkoff, "Getting beyond Downsizing," *Fortune* (January 10, 1994), 58–64; Kim S. Cameron, "Strategies for Successful Organizational Downsizing," *Human Resource Management* 33, no. 2 (Summer 1994), 189–211; and Doerflein and Atsaides, "Corporate Psychology: Making Downsizing Work."

87. Matt Murray, "Stress Mounts as More Firms Announce Large Layoffs, But Don't Say Who or When" (Your Career Matters column), *The Wall Street Journal* (March 13, 2001), B1, B12.

88. Jena McGregor, "Rocky Mountain High," and sidebar, "Downsizing Decently," *Fast Company* (July 2004), 58ff.

89. Caudron, "Teach Downsizing Survivors How to Thrive."

90. Betsy Morris, "When Bad Things Happen to Good Companies," *Fortune* (December 8, 2003), 78–88; and Wayne F. Cascio, "Strategies for Responsible Restructuring," *Academy of Management Executive* 16, no. 3 (2002), 80–91.

PART 5
Managing
Dynamic
Processes

10. Organizational Culture and
    Ethical Values

11. Innovation and Change

12. Decision-Making Processes

13. Conflict, Power, and Politics

10 Organizational Culture and Ethical Values

Organizational Culture
What Is Culture? • Emergence and Purpose of Culture • Interpreting Culture

Organization Design and Culture
The Adaptability Culture • The Mission Culture • The Clan Culture • The Bureaucratic Culture • Culture Strength and Organizational Subcultures

Organizational Culture, Learning, and Performance

Ethical Values and Social Responsibility
Sources of Individual Ethical Principles • Managerial Ethics and Social Responsibility • Does It Pay to Be Good?

Sources of Ethical Values in Organizations
Personal Ethics • Organizational Culture • Organizational Systems • External Stakeholders

How Leaders Shape Culture and Ethics
Values-based Leadership • Formal Structure and Systems

Corporate Culture and Ethics in a Global Environment

Summary and Interpretation

A Look Inside

Boots Company PLC

Boots. For many years, people in the United Kingdom didn't think of sturdy footwear but rather of the local pharmacy and tempting shelves stocked with all manner of health items, cosmetics, and toiletries. Boots is a much-loved and trusted retail brand in the United Kingdom, but when Richard Baker took over as chief executive in 2003, the company was looking—well, a bit broken down at the heels. Baker found himself facing one of the most difficult jobs in retailing, helping the troubled company find a way to compete with the growing power of supermarkets like Tesco and Asda (Baker's former employer).

Baker immediately recognized many of the problems, such as antiquated distribution and information technology (IT) systems, high costs and inefficient processes, cluttered stores, and excessive headquarters personnel. But he soon realized there would be no quick fixes, because the roots of Boots's troubles went very deep, right to the heart of the organization. Indeed, the cultural values at Boots Co. PLC, he found, were woefully out of sync with today's fast-moving, competitive environment.

Baker came to Boots from Asda, which is owned by U.S. discount giant Wal-Mart. At Asda, he'd gotten accustomed to a culture of openness and innovation. Ideas that could promote useful change were encouraged and acted on quickly. At Boots, though, change was almost viewed as the enemy. Boots had its greatest years of success in an era when the world moved more slowly and gently. A "civil service" culture developed at the firm, with people signing on for lifetime careers and expecting to have a comfortable ride straight to the top. The highly insular culture meant that outsiders and outside ideas were not welcome. With home-grown managers and a long tradition of doing things a certain way, Boots had grown culturally incapable of change. For example, one previous chairman says his efforts to encourage Boots to concentrate on aspects of the business with the most potential for growth were ignored by a team of long-serving executives who tended to focus on current profits at the expense of the future.

Over the past few years, all of the top management at Boots has changed, and Baker has taken a number of steps to improve efficiency, spruce up the stores, and be more price-competitive. However, the 1,400-store chain is still struggling. After a promising Christmas 2004 season, sales and profits went flat. Baker's biggest challenge is to reverse years of underspending and status-quo thinking. Cultural values do not change overnight, and it remains to be seen if the new leader can find the right prescription to instill new values and put the shine back on Boots.[1]

E very organization, like Boots Co. PLC and Asda, has a set of values that characterize how people behave and how the organization carries out everyday business. Sometimes, these values get out of alignment with the environment and cause problems for the organization. One of the most important jobs organizational leaders do is instill and support the kind of values needed for the company to thrive.

Strong cultures can have a profound impact on a company, which can be either positive or negative for the organization. For example, at J. M. Smucker & Co., which in 2004 became the first manufacturer to earn the top spot on *Fortune* magazine's list of "The 100 Best Companies to Work For," strong values of cooperation, caring for employees and customers, and an "all for one, one for all" attitude enable the company to consistently meet productivity, quality, and customer-service goals in the challenging environment of the food industry.[2] Negative cultural norms, however, can damage a company just as powerfully as positive ones can strengthen it. Consider the case of Enron Corp., where the corporate culture supported pushing everything to the limits: business practices, rules, personal behavior, and laws. Executives drove expensive cars, challenged employees to participate in risky competitive behavior, and often celebrated big deals by heading off to a bar or dance club.[3]

A related concept concerning the influence of norms and values on how people work together and how they treat one another and customers is called *social capital*. **Social capital** refers to the quality of interactions among people and whether they share a common perspective. In organizations with a high degree of social capital, for example, relationships are based on trust, mutual understandings, and shared norms and values that enable people to cooperate and coordinate their activities to achieve organizational goals.[4] An organization can have either a high or a low level of social capital. One way to think of social capital is as *goodwill*. When relationships both within the organization and with customers, suppliers, and partners are based on honesty, trust, and respect, a spirit of goodwill exists and people willingly cooperate to achieve mutual benefits. A high level of social capital enables frictionless social interactions and exchanges that help to facilitate smooth organizational functioning.

Think of eBay, which relies largely on social capital to bring millions of buyers and sellers together on its Web site, leading to 2004 profits of $778 million.[5] The company builds goodwill through such mechanisms as a feedback system that enables buyers and sellers to rate one another, discussion boards that build a sense of community among site users, and regular all-day focus groups with representative buyers and sellers. Another example of a company with high social capital is Microsoft UK. Of employees surveyed by the *Sunday Times*, 89 percent reported that they "love working there" and 93 percent feel that the company "makes a positive difference to the world we live in." Although employees work long, hard hours, Microsoft UK has a *Department of People and Culture* to focus on the characteristics that create and strengthen social capital. For example, in 1998, Microsoft UK developed a long-term vision for a culture that fostered "honesty, openness, an entrepreneurial spirit, and respect for the customer."[6] Other organizations also build social capital by being open and honest and cultivating positive social relationships among employees and with outsiders. Relationships based on cutthroat competition, self-interest, and subterfuge, such as those at Enron, can be devastating to a company. Social capital relates to both corporate culture and ethics, which is the subject matter of this chapter.

■ Purpose of This Chapter

This chapter explores ideas about corporate culture and associated ethical values and how these are influenced by organizations. The first section describes the nature of corporate culture, its origins and purpose, and how to identify and interpret culture through ceremonies, stories, and symbols. We then examine how culture reinforces the strategy and structural design the organization needs to be effective in its environment and discuss the important role of culture in organizational learning and high performance. Next, the chapter turns to ethical values and social responsibility. We consider how managers implement the structures and systems that influence ethical and socially responsible behavior. The chapter also discusses how leaders shape culture and ethical values in a direction suitable for strategy and performance outcomes. The chapter closes with a brief overview of the complex cultural and ethical issues that managers face in an international environment.

Organizational Culture

The popularity of the organizational culture topic raises a number of questions. Can we identify cultures? Can culture be aligned with strategy? How can cultures be managed or changed? The best place to start is by defining culture and explaining how it can be identified in organizations.

What Is Culture?

Culture is the set of values, norms, guiding beliefs, and understandings that is shared by members of an organization and is taught to new members.[7] It represents the unwritten, feeling part of the organization. Everyone participates in culture, but culture generally goes unnoticed. It is only when organizations try to implement new strategies or programs that go against basic cultural norms and values that they come face to face with the power of culture.

Organizational culture exists at two levels, as illustrated in Exhibit 10.1. On the surface are visible artifacts and observable behaviors—the ways people dress and act and the symbols, stories, and ceremonies organization members share. The visible elements of culture, however, reflect deeper values in the minds of organization members. These underlying values, assumptions, beliefs, and thought processes are the true culture.[8] For example, Steelcase Corp. built a new pyramid-shaped corporate development center with scattered, open "thought stations" with white boards and idea-inspiring features. The six-floor building also has an open atrium from ground floor to top, with a giant ticking pendulum. The new building is a visible symbol; the underlying values are an emphasis on openness, collaboration, teamwork, innovation, and constant change.[9] The attributes of culture display themselves in many ways but typically evolve into a patterned set of activities carried out through social interactions.[10] Those patterns can be used to interpret culture.

Emergence and Purpose of Culture

Culture provides members with a sense of organizational identity and generates in them a commitment to beliefs and values that are larger than themselves. Though ideas that become part of culture can come from anywhere within the organization, an organization's culture generally begins with a founder or early leader who articulates and implements particular ideas and values as a vision, philosophy, or business strategy.

When these ideas and values lead to success, they become institutionalized, and an organizational culture emerges that reflects the vision and strategy of the founder or leader.[11] For example, the culture at Les Schwab Tire Centers is based on the down-home values and beliefs of 87-year-old founder Les Schwab, who several years ago was still tooling to work several days a week in his 1962 Jeep. Schwab

EXHIBIT 10.1
*Levels of Corporate
Culture*

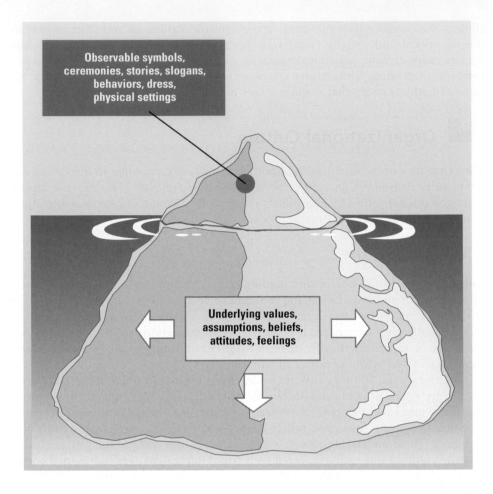

grew up in a logging camp and was orphaned at 15. He believes people are here on Earth to help each other; employees at Schwab Tire Centers fix flats for free and have been known to install new tires hours before opening time for an emergency trip. At stores in Oregon, March is "free beef month," when every customer who buys four new tires gets a package of steaks.[12]

Cultures serve two critical functions in organizations: (1) to integrate members so that they know how to relate to one another, and (2) to help the organization adapt to the external environment. **Internal integration** means that members develop a collective identity and know how to work together effectively. It is culture that guides day-to-day working relationships and determines how people communicate within the organization, what behavior is acceptable or not acceptable, and how power and status are allocated. **External adaptation** refers to how the organization meets goals and deals with outsiders. Culture helps guide the daily activities of workers to meet certain goals. It can help the organization respond rapidly to customer needs or the moves of a competitor. As discussed in this chapter's Book Mark, culture plays a key role in transforming an organization's performance from average to truly great.

The organization's culture also guides employee decision making in the absence of written rules or policies.[13] Thus, both functions of culture are related to building

Type of Rite	Example	Social Consequences
Passage	Induction and basic training, U.S. Army	Facilitate transition of persons into social roles and statuses that are new for them
Enhancement	Annual awards night	Enhance social identities and increase status of employees
Renewal	Organization development activities	Refurbish social structures and improve organization functioning
Integration	Office holiday party	Encourage and revive common feelings that bind members together and commit them to the organization

EXHIBIT 10.2
A Typology of Organization Rites and Their Social Consequences

Source: Adapted from Harrison M. Trice and Janice M. Beyer, "Studying Organizational Cultures through Rites and Ceremonials," *Academy of Management Review* 9 (1984), 653–659. Used with permission.

the organization's social capital, by forging either positive or negative relationships both within the organization and with outsiders.

Interpreting Culture

To identify and interpret culture requires that people make inferences based on observable artifacts. Artifacts can be studied but are hard to decipher accurately. An award ceremony in one company may have a different meaning than in another company. To decipher what is really going on in an organization requires detective work and probably some experience as an insider. Some of the typical and important observable aspects of culture are rites and ceremonies, stories, symbols, and language.[14]

Rites and Ceremonies. Important artifacts for culture are **rites and ceremonies,** the elaborate, planned activities that make up a special event and are often conducted for the benefit of an audience. Managers can hold rites and ceremonies to provide dramatic examples of what a company values. These are special occasions that reinforce specific values, create a bond among people for sharing an important understanding, and anoint and celebrate heroes and heroines who symbolize important beliefs and activities.[15]

Four types of rites that appear in organizations are summarized in Exhibit 10.2. *Rites of passage* facilitate the transition of employees into new social roles. *Rites of enhancement* create stronger social identities and increase the status of employees. *Rites of renewal* reflect training and development activities that improve organization functioning. *Rites of integration* create common bonds and good feelings among employees and increase commitment to the organization. The following examples illustrate how these rites and ceremonies are used by top managers to reinforce important cultural values.

- In a major bank, election as an officer was seen as the key event in a successful career. A series of activities accompanied every promotion to bank officer, including a special method of notification, taking the new officer to the officers'

Briefcase

As an organization manager, keep these guidelines in mind:

Pay attention to corporate culture. Understand the underlying values, assumptions, and beliefs on which culture is based as well as its observable manifestations. Evaluate corporate culture based on rites and ceremonies, stories and heroes, symbols, and language.

dining room for the first time, and the new officer buying drinks on the Friday after his or her notification.[16] This is a rite of passage.

- Mary Kay Cosmetics Company holds elaborate awards ceremonies, presenting gold and diamond pins, furs, and luxury cars to high-achieving sales consultants. The most successful consultants are introduced by film clips, such as the kind used to introduce award nominees in the entertainment industry. This is a rite of enhancement.
- An important event at Walt Disney Company is the "Gong Show." Three times a year, executives hold events around the country at which any employee, down

Book Mark 10.0 (HAVE YOU READ THIS BOOK?)

Good to Great: Why Some Companies Make the Leap…And Others Don't
By Jim Collins

How and why do some companies move from merely good to truly great long-term performance, while others can't make the leap—or if they do, can't sustain it? This is the question Jim Collins set out to answer in a 6-year study that culminated in the book *Good to Great: Why Some Companies Make the Leap… And Others Don't*. Collins identifies eleven great companies—those that averaged returns 6.9 times the general stock market over a 15-year period—and compares them to a group of companies that had similar resources but failed either to make the leap or to sustain it.

A CULTURE OF DISCIPLINE

Collins identifies a number of characteristics that define truly great companies. One aspect is a culture of discipline, in which everyone in the organization is focused on doing whatever is needed to keep the company successful. How is a culture of discipline built? Here are some of the key factors:

- *Level 5 leadership.* All good-to-great companies begin with a top leader who exemplifies what Collins calls level 5 leadership. Level 5 leaders are characterized by an almost complete lack of personal ego, coupled with a strong will and ambition for the success of the organization. They develop a strong corps of leaders throughout the organization so that when they leave, the company can grow even more successful. Values of selfishness, greed, and arrogance have no place in a great company.
- *The right values.* Leaders build a culture based on values of individual freedom and responsibility, but within a framework of organizational purpose, goals, and systems. People have the autonomy to do whatever it takes—within well-defined boundaries and clear, consistent guidelines—to move the organization toward achieving its goals and vision.
- *The right people in the right jobs.* Leaders of good-to-great organizations look for self-disciplined people who embody values that fit the culture. These people are described using terms such as *determined*, *diligent*, *precise*, *systematic*, *consistent*, *focused*, *accountable*, and *responsible*. They are willing to go the extra mile to become the best they can be and help the organization continuously improve.
- *Knowing where to go.* Good-to-great companies base their success on a deep understanding throughout the organization of three essential ideas, conceptualized as three intersecting circles: what they can be the best in the world at, what they are deeply passionate about, and what makes economic sense for the organization. This understanding is translated into a vision and strategy that guides all actions.

THE FLYWHEEL CONCEPT

No company makes the leap from good to great in one fell swoop. The process is one of buildup followed by breakthrough, similar to pushing a giant flywheel in one direction, turn after turn, building momentum until a breakthrough is reached. Once leaders get the right people in the right jobs, support the right values, and focus on activities that fit within the three intersecting circles, people begin to see positive results, which pushes the flywheel to full momentum. As success builds on success, the organization makes the move from good to great.

Good to Great: Why Some Companies Make the Leap…And Others Don't, by Jim Collins, is published by HarperBusiness.

to the level of secretaries, janitors, and mailroom personnel, can pitch movie ideas to top executives. The fun event is a way to symbolize and support the company's commitment to employee involvement and innovation.[17] This is a rite of renewal.

- Whenever a Wal-Mart executive visits one of the stores, he or she leads employees in the Wal-Mart cheer: "Give me a W! Give me an A! Give me an L! Give me a squiggly! (All do a version of the twist.) Give me an M! Give me an A! Give me an R! Give me a T! What's that spell? Wal-Mart! What's that spell? Wal-Mart! Who's No. 1? THE CUSTOMER!" The cheer strengthens bonds among employees and reinforces their commitment to common goals.[18] This is a rite of integration.

Stories. Stories are narratives based on true events that are frequently shared among organizational employees and told to new employees to inform them about an organization. Many stories are about company **heroes** who serve as models or ideals for serving cultural norms and values. Some stories are considered **legends** because the events are historic and may have been embellished with fictional details. Other stories are **myths**, which are consistent with the values and beliefs of the organization but are not supported by facts.[19] Stories keep alive the primary values of the organization and provide a shared understanding among all employees. Examples of how stories shape culture are as follows:

- At 3M Corp., the story is told of a vice president who was fired early in his career for persisting with a new product even after his boss had told him to stop because the boss thought it was a stupid idea. After the worker was fired, he stayed in an unused office, working without a salary on the new product idea. Eventually he was rehired, the product was a success, and he was promoted to vice president. The story symbolizes the 3M value of persisting in what you believe in.[20]
- Employees at IBM often hear a story about the female security guard who challenged IBM's chairman. Although she knew who he was, the guard insisted that the chairman could not enter a particular area because he wasn't carrying the appropriate security clearance. Rather than getting reprimanded or fired, the guard was praised for her diligence and commitment to maintaining the security of IBM's buildings.[21] By telling this story, employees emphasize both the importance of following the rules and the value of every employee from the bottom to the top of the organization.

Symbols. Another tool for interpreting culture is the **symbol**. A symbol is something that represents another thing. In one sense, ceremonies, stories, slogans, and rites are all symbols. They symbolize deeper values of an organization. Another symbol is a physical artifact of the organization. Physical symbols are powerful because they focus attention on a specific item. Examples of physical symbols are as follows:

- Nordstrom's department store symbolizes the importance of supporting lower-level employees with the organization chart in Exhibit 10.3. Nordstrom's is known for its extraordinary customer service, and the organization chart symbolizes that managers are to support the employees who give the service rather than control them.[22]
- Symbols can also represent negative elements of corporate culture. At Enron, premium parking spots were symbols of power, wealth, and winning at any cost.

EXHIBIT 10.3
*Organization Chart for
Nordstrom, Inc.*
Source: Used with permission
of Nordstrom, Inc.

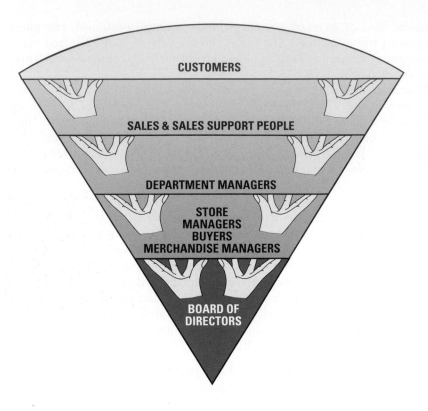

At the company's London office, executives submitted blind e-mail bids for the limited spaces. One top manager paid more than $6,000 to use a well-placed company spot for a year.[23]

Language. The final technique for influencing culture is **language.** Many companies use a specific saying, slogan, metaphor, or other form of language to convey special meaning to employees. Slogans can be readily picked up and repeated by employees as well as customers of the company. Averitt Express's motto, "Our driving force is people," applies to both employees and customers. The trucking company's culture emphasizes treating employees as well as they are expected to treat customers. Drivers and customers, not top executives, are seen as the power that fuels the company's success. Other significant uses of language to shape culture are as follows:

- Before it was acquired by Oracle in a hostile takeover, PeopleSoft Inc. prided itself on a close-knit, family-like culture. Employees called themselves PeoplePeople, shopped at the company PeopleStore, and munched on company-funded PeopleSnacks. The use of this special lingo reinforced the distinctive cultural values. The loss of the culture has been painful for employees, many of whom were laid off after the takeover. PeopleSoft's founder Dave Duffield has set up a fund to help laid-off workers.[24]

- Milacron Inc., the Cincinnati-based global leader in plastics processing and metalworking technologies, used the term "Wolfpack" for the teams that would redesign the company's machine tool product lines to better compete in an in-

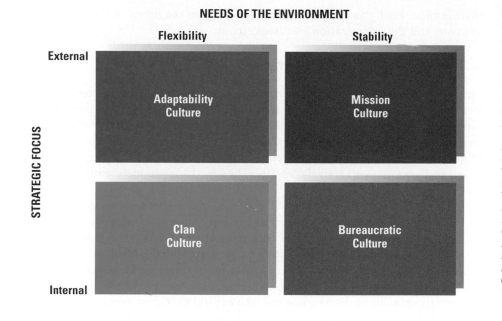

NEEDS OF THE ENVIRONMENT

Flexibility | Stability

External

Adaptability Culture

Mission Culture

STRATEGIC FOCUS

Clan Culture

Bureaucratic Culture

Internal

EXHIBIT 10.4
Relationship of Environment and Strategy to Corporate Culture
Source: Based on Daniel R. Denison and Aneil K. Mishra, "Toward a Theory of Organizational Culture and Effectiveness," *Organization Science* 6, no. 2 (March–April 1995), 204–223; R. Hooijberg and F. Petrock, "On Cultural Change: Using the Competing Values Framework to Help Leaders Execute a Transformational Strategy," *Human Resource Management* 32 (1993), 29–50; and R. E. Quinn, *Beyond Rational Management: Mastering the Paradoxes and Competing Demands of High Performance* (San Francisco: Jossey-Bass, 1988).

creasingly aggressive and hostile industry environment. The word proved to be highly motivating as a metaphor for promoting change and innovation.[25]

Recall that culture exists at two levels—the underlying values and assumptions and the visible artifacts and observable behaviors. The slogans, symbols, and ceremonies just described are artifacts that reflect underlying company values. These visible artifacts and behaviors can be used by managers to shape company values and to strengthen organizational culture.

Organization Design and Culture

Corporate culture should reinforce the strategy and structural design that the organization needs to be effective within its environment. For example, if the external environment requires flexibility and responsiveness, such as the environment for Internet-based companies like eBay, the culture should encourage adaptability. The correct relationship among cultural values, organizational strategy and structure, and the environment can enhance organizational performance.[26]

Culture can be assessed along many dimensions, such as the extent of collaboration versus isolation among people and departments, the importance of control and where control is concentrated, or whether the organization's time orientation is short range or long range.[27] Here, we will focus on two specific dimensions: (1) the extent to which the competitive environment requires flexibility or stability; and (2) the extent to which the organization's strategic focus and strength are internal or external. Four categories of culture associated with these differences, as illustrated in Exhibit 10.4, are adaptability, mission, clan, and bureaucratic.[28] These four categories relate to the fit among cultural values, strategy, structure, and the environment. Each can be successful, depending on the needs of the external environment and the organization's strategic focus.

■ The Adaptability Culture

The **adaptability culture** is characterized by strategic focus on the external environment through flexibility and change to meet customer needs. The culture encourages entrepreneurial values, norms, and beliefs that support the capacity of the organization to detect, interpret, and translate signals from the environment into new behavior responses. This type of company, however, doesn't just react quickly to environmental changes—it actively creates change. Innovation, creativity, and risk taking are valued and rewarded.

An example of the adaptability culture is 3M, a company whose values promote individual initiative and entrepreneurship. All new employees attend a class on risk-taking, where they are told to pursue their ideas even if it means defying their supervisors. IBM has been shifting to an adaptability culture to support a new strategy that requires flexibility, speed, and innovation. CEO Sam Palmisano has implemented practices and procedures that support teamwork, egalitarianism, and creativity, such as dismantling the 92-year-old executive committee that previously ruled the company and replacing it with three cross-functional and cross-hierarchical teams for strategy, operations, and technology. He symbolized his commitment to the new values by asking the board to slash his 2003 bonus and set the money aside to be shared with the top executive team. Listening to both employees and customers has also become a priority at IBM. Palmisano believes an external focus emphasizing the importance of employee empowerment, flexibility, and initiative is critical to IBM's success in coming decades.[29] Most e-commerce companies, such as eBay, Amazon, and Google, as well as companies in the marketing, electronics, and cosmetics industries, use this type of culture because they must move quickly to satisfy customers.

■ The Mission Culture

An organization concerned with serving specific customers in the external environment, but without the need for rapid change, is suited to the mission culture. The **mission culture** is characterized by emphasis on a clear vision of the organization's purpose and on the achievement of goals, such as sales growth, profitability, or market share, to help achieve the purpose. Individual employees may be responsible for a specified level of performance, and the organization promises specified rewards in return. Managers shape behavior by envisioning and communicating a desired future state for the organization. Because the environment is stable, they can translate the vision into measurable goals and evaluate employee performance for meeting them. In some cases, mission cultures reflect a high level of competitiveness and a profit-making orientation.

One example of a mission culture is Siebel Systems, which thrives on an intense, ambitious culture. Professionalism and aggressiveness are key values. Siebel keeps employees focused on achieving high sales and profit levels, and those who meet the demanding goals are handsomely rewarded.[30] Another example is J.C. Penney, where a new CEO has been instilling values of a mission culture to put the department store back on the fashion map.

Briefcase

As an organization manager, keep these guidelines in mind:

Make sure corporate culture is consistent with strategy and the environment. Culture can be shaped to fit the needs of both. Four types of culture are adaptability culture, mission culture, clan culture, and bureaucratic culture.

Perhaps you can't imagine Britney Spears shopping at J.C. Penney, but Allen Questrom is out to change your mind. The new CEO has signed an exclusive deal with designer Michele Bohbot and her marketing husband, Marc, to become the nation's only distributor of the trendy Bisou Bisou line, a collection of sexy clothes worn by stars like Spears and Sharon Stone.

Questrom is the first outsider head in J.C. Penney's 103-year history, and he's shaking things up at the previously stodgy retailer. Questrom's vision is to turn J.C. Penney into a shopping destination of choice for 25- to 35-year-old women, a group that spends almost $15 billion a year on clothes. To support the new vision, Questrom is instilling values of assertiveness and competitiveness at the company. For one thing, he has centralized the chain's buying operation rather than allowing each store manager to buy merchandise for his or her individual store. The CEO has recruited new top executives and established clear goals and strict accountability. Many of the new managers are young and aggressive, reflecting the cultural shift going on at all levels of the company. Managers can no longer just follow the status quo; they are required to take the steps needed to move the chain toward the new vision.

Although Questrom admits J.C. Penney has a long way to go, results of the changes so far are impressive. By emphasizing a clear vision and keeping managers at all levels focused on meeting ambitious targets, Questrom has begun a transformation that has sales and profits rising.[31]

In Practice

J.C. Penney

■ The Clan Culture

The **clan culture** has a primary focus on the involvement and participation of the organization's members and on rapidly changing expectations from the external environment. This culture is similar to the clan form of control described in Chapter 9. More than any other, this culture focuses on the needs of employees as the route to high performance. Involvement and participation create a sense of responsibility and ownership and, hence, greater commitment to the organization.

In a clan culture, an important value is taking care of employees and making sure they have whatever they need to help them be satisfied as well as productive. Companies in the fashion and retail industries often adopt this culture because it releases the creativity of employees to respond to rapidly changing tastes. Wegmans, a Rochester, New York–based chain of supermarkets, has succeeded with a clan culture. Employee commitment and satisfaction is considered key to success. Wegmans pays good wages, sends employees on learning trips, and offers college scholarships for both full- and part-time employees. Employees are empowered to use their own initiative and creativity in serving customers.[32] Wegmans was described in detail in Chapter 2's Leading by Design box.

■ The Bureaucratic Culture

The **bureaucratic culture** has an internal focus and a consistency orientation for a stable environment. This organization has a culture that supports a methodical approach to doing business. Symbols, heroes, and ceremonies support cooperation, tradition, and following established policies and practices as ways to achieve goals.

Personal involvement is somewhat lower here, but that is outweighed by a high level of consistency, conformity, and collaboration among members. This organization succeeds by being highly integrated and efficient.

Today, most managers are shifting away from bureaucratic cultures because of a need for greater flexibility. However, one thriving new company, Pacific Edge Software, has successfully implemented some elements of a bureaucratic culture, ensuring that all its projects are on time and on budget. The husband-and-wife team of Lisa Hjorten and Scott Fuller implanted a culture of order, discipline, and control from the moment they founded the company. The emphasis on order and focus means employees can generally go home by 6:00 P.M. rather than working all night to finish an important project. Hjorten insists that the company's culture isn't rigid or uptight, just *careful*. Although sometimes being careful means being slow, so far Pacific Edge has managed to keep pace with the demands of the external environment.[33]

■ Culture Strength and Organizational Subcultures

A strong organizational culture can have a powerful impact on company performance. **Culture strength** refers to the degree of agreement among members of an organization about the importance of specific values. If widespread consensus exists about the importance of those values, the culture is cohesive and strong; if little agreement exists, the culture is weak.[34]

A strong culture is typically associated with the frequent use of ceremonies, symbols, stories, heroes, and slogans. These elements increase employee commitment to the values and strategy of a company. In addition, managers who want to create and maintain strong corporate cultures often give emphasis to the selection and socialization of employees.[35] TechTarget, a Needham, Massachusetts, interactive media company, uses a painstaking hiring process to find the kind of employees who will mesh with the company's unique values. TechTarget has an "open-leave" policy, meaning that employees are free to come and go as they please. The culture emphasizes individual autonomy and personal responsibility; founder and CEO Greg Strakosch tries to hire people who are independent, achievement oriented, conscientious, and capable of managing their own time.[36]

However, culture is not always uniform throughout the organization, particularly in large companies. Even in organizations that have strong cultures, there may be several sets of subcultures. **Subcultures** develop to reflect the common problems, goals, and experiences that members of a team, department, or other unit share. An office, branch, or unit of a company that is physically separated from the company's main operations may also take on a distinctive subculture.

For example, although the dominant culture of an organization may be a mission culture, various departments may also reflect characteristics of adaptability, clan, or bureaucratic cultures. The manufacturing department of a large organization may thrive in an environment that emphasizes order, efficiency, and obedience to rules, whereas the research and development (R&D) department may be characterized by employee empowerment, flexibility, and customer focus. This is similar to the concept of differentiation described in Chapter 4, where employees in manufacturing, sales, and research departments studied by Paul Lawrence and Jay Lorsch[37] developed different values with respect to time horizon, interpersonal relationships, and formality in order to perform the job of each particular department most effectively. The credit division of Pitney Bowes, a huge corporation that manufactures postage meters, copiers, and other office equipment, developed a distinctive subculture to encourage innovation and risk taking.

In Practice

**Pitney Bowes
Credit
Corporation**

Pitney Bowes, a maker of postage meters and other office equipment, has long thrived in an environment of order and predictability. Its headquarters reflects a typical corporate environment and an orderly culture with its blank walls and bland carpeting. But step onto the third floor of the Pitney Bowes building in Shelton, Connecticut, and you might think you're at a different company. The domain of Pitney Bowes Credit Corporation (PBCC) looks more like an indoor theme park, featuring cobblestone-patterned carpets, faux gas lamps, and an ornate town square-style clock. It also has a French-style café, a 1950s-style diner, and the "Cranial Kitchen," where employees sit in cozy booths to surf the Internet or watch training videos. The friendly hallways encourage impromptu conversations, where people can exchange information and share ideas they wouldn't otherwise share.

PBCC traditionally helped customers finance their business with the parent company. However, Matthew Kisner, PBCC's president and CEO, has worked with other managers to redefine the division as a *creator* of services rather than just a provider of services. Rather than just financing sales and leasing of existing products, PBCC now creates new services for customers to buy. For example, Purchase Power is a revolving line of credit that helps companies finance their postage costs. It was profitable within 9 months and now has more than 400,000 customers. When PBCC redefined its job, it began redefining its subculture to match, by emphasizing values of teamwork, risk taking, and creativity. "We wanted a fun space that would embody our culture," Kisner says. "No straight lines, no linear thinking. Because we're a financial services company, our biggest advantage is the quality of our ideas." So far, PBCC's new approach is working. In one recent year, the division, whose 600 employees make up less than 2 percent of Pitney Bowes' total workforce, generated 36 percent of the company's net profits.[38]

Subcultures typically include the basic values of the dominant organizational culture plus additional values unique to members of the subculture. However, subcultural differences can sometimes lead to conflicts between departments, especially in organizations that do not have strong overall corporate cultures. When subcultural values become too strong and outweigh the corporate cultural values, conflicts may emerge and hurt organizational performance. Conflict will be discussed in detail in Chapter 13.

Organizational Culture, Learning, and Performance

Culture can play an important role in creating an organizational climate that enables learning and innovative response to challenges, competitive threats, or new opportunities. A strong culture that encourages adaptation and change enhances organizational performance by energizing and motivating employees, unifying people around shared goals and a higher mission, and shaping and guiding employee behavior so that everyone's actions are aligned with strategic priorities. Thus,

Leading by Design

JetBlue Airways

The airline industry isn't a very happy place to be these days. Unless, that is, you're at JetBlue Airways, the fastest growing domestic carrier in the United States and the only U.S. airline except Southwest that is making money. JetBlue, based at New York's JFK airport, grew revenues more than threefold in its first 4 years. The company now operates nearly 300 daily flights to 29 destinations, including Puerto Rico, the Dominican Republic, and the Bahamas. JetBlue topped the Airline Quality Ratings for 2 years in a row (2004–2005) and placed number 1 in J. D. Powers' 2005 rankings of consumer satisfaction.

A large part of JetBlue's success can be attributed to its culture. From its beginning, JetBlue has incorporated strong customer-focused values that encourage continual adaptation. Founder David Neeleman based JetBlue's culture on the values he developed while working as a missionary in the slums of Brazil. The corporate philosophy is that the greatest satisfaction a person can achieve comes from serving others. Today, every new employee is asked to make a commitment to the basic corporate commandments: safety, caring, integrity, fun, and passion. JetBlue's People Department actively scrutinizes all applicants to see how well they'll mesh with the values, then provides them with comprehensive training that gives them the tools they need to make good decisions and do the right thing in serving customers.

JetBlue's response to the September 11, 2001, terrorist attacks in New York illustrates the values in action. When employees realized the airports would be shutting down and passengers would be stranded, they immediately started re-serving buses and shuttling people (even some customers of other airlines) to hotels, where they were put up at JetBlue's expense. Soon after the attacks, JetBlue became the first airline to install bulletproof, dead-bolted cockpit doors on all its aircraft, even before the Federal Aviation Administration issued a mandate. Instead of encouraging Americans to shake off their fear of flying, JetBlue ran ads telling people it was okay to take time to heal. Yet, rather than laying off workers and cutting routes during the slowdown in air travel, JetBlue expanded its service and picked up some new markets where larger carriers had scaled back.

JetBlue doesn't believe in waiting around for others to determine what needs to be done; instead, leaders take a proactive approach and move quickly to implement changes that can provide customers with better service, greater safety, and a happier flying experience. The company initially differentiated itself by offering only one class, providing assigned seats with more leg room, and installing free satellite television on the backs of all seats. But leaders continue to push the envelope in trying to give customers what they want, exploring, for example, options such as airplane Internet service and phone-to-plane communications.

When JetBlue first started flying in February of 2000, skeptics said it was doomed to fail. Five years later, JetBlue's adaptive, customer-focused culture has made it one of the few bright spots in the turbulent airline industry.

Sources: Paul C. Judge, "How Will Your Company Adapt?" *Fast Company* (December 2001), 128ff; "Lessons from the Slums of Brazil: David Neeleman on the Origins of JetBlue's Culture," *Harvard Business Review* (March 2005), Reprint F0503K, http://www.hbr.org; Eve Tahmincioglu, "True Blue," *Workforce Management* (February 2005), 47–50; and Ben Mutzabaugh, "JetBlue Tries to Make Flying Less of a Pain," *USA Today* (April 6, 2005), B3.

Briefcase

As an organization manager, keep this guideline in mind:

Consciously manage culture to shift values toward high performance and goal accomplishment.

creating and influencing an adaptive culture is one of the most important jobs for organizational leaders. The right culture can drive high performance.[39] JetBlue Airways, described in this chapter's Leading by Design box, has achieved phenomenal success partly because of its strong adaptive culture.

A number of studies have found a positive relationship between culture and performance.[40] In *Corporate Culture and Performance*, Kotter and Heskett provided evidence that companies that intentionally managed cultural values outperformed similar companies that did not. Some companies have developed systematic ways to measure and manage the impact of culture on organizational performance. At Caterpillar Inc., leaders used a tool called the Cultural Assessment Process (CAP), which gave top executives hard data documenting millions of dollars in savings they could attribute directly to cultural factors.[41] Even the U.S. federal government is recognizing the link between culture and effectiveness. The U.S. Office of Personnel Management created its Organizational Assessment Survey as a way for federal agencies to measure culture factors and shift values toward high performance.[42]

Strong cultures that don't encourage adaptation, however, can hurt the organization. A danger for many successful organizations is that the culture becomes set and the company fails to adapt as the environment changes, as we saw in the chapter-opening example of Boots Co. PLC. When organizations are successful, the values, ideas, and practices that helped attain success become institutionalized. As the environment changes, these values may become detrimental to future performance. Many organizations become victims of their own success, clinging to outmoded and even destructive values and behaviors. Thus, the impact of a strong culture is not always positive. Typically, healthy cultures not only provide for smooth internal integration but also encourage adaptation to the external environment. Nonadaptive cultures encourage rigidity and stability. Strong adaptive cultures often incorporate the following values:

1. *The whole is more important than the parts and boundaries between parts are minimized.* People are aware of the whole system, how everything fits together, and the relationships among various organizational parts. All members consider how their actions affect other parts and the total organization. This emphasis on the whole reduces boundaries both within the organization and with other companies. Although subcultures may form, everyone's primary attitudes and behaviors reflect the organization's dominant culture. The free flow of people, ideas, and information allows coordinated action and continuous learning.

2. *Equality and trust are primary values.* The culture creates a sense of community and caring for one another. The organization is a place for creating a web of relationships that allows people to take risks and develop to their full potential. The emphasis on treating everyone with care and respect creates a climate of safety and trust that allows experimentation, frequent mistakes, and learning. Managers emphasize honest and open communications as a way to build trust.

3. *The culture encourages risk taking, change, and improvement.* A basic value is to question the status quo. Constant questioning of assumptions opens the gates to creativity and improvement. The culture rewards and celebrates the creators of new ideas, products, and work processes. To symbolize the importance of taking risks, an adaptive culture may also reward those who fail in order to learn and grow.

As illustrated in Exhibit 10.5, adaptive corporate cultures have different values and behavior patterns than nonadaptive cultures.[43] In adaptive cultures, managers are concerned with customers and employees as well as with the internal processes and procedures that bring about useful change. Behavior is flexible and managers initiate change when needed, even if it involves risk. In unadaptive cultures, managers are more concerned about themselves or their own special projects, and their values discourage risk taking and change. Thus, strong, healthy cultures, such as those in learning companies, help organizations adapt to the external environment, whereas strong, unhealthy cultures can encourage an organization to march resolutely in the wrong direction.

Briefcase

As an organization manager, keep these guidelines in mind:

To support a learning orientation, emphasize cultural values of openness and collaboration, equality and trust, continuous improvement, and risk taking. Build a strong internal culture that encourages adaptation to changing environmental conditions.

EXHIBIT 10.5
*Adaptive versus
Nonadaptive Corporate
Cultures*

	Adaptive Corporate Cultures	Nonadaptive Corporate Cultures
Core Values	Managers care deeply about customers, stockholders, and employees. They also strongly value people and processes that can create useful change (for example, leadership initiatives up and down the management hierarchy).	Managers care mainly about themselves, their immediate work group, or some product (or technology) associated with that work group. They value the orderly and risk-reducing management process much more highly than leadership initiatives.
Common Behavior	Managers pay close attention to all their constituencies, especially customers, and initiate change when needed to serve their legitimate interests, even if it entails taking some risks.	Managers tend to be somewhat isolated, political, and bureaucratic. As a result, they do not change their strategies quickly to adjust to or take advantage of changes in their business environments.

Source: Adapted and reprinted with the permission of The Free Press, a division of Simon & Schuster Adult Publishing Group, from *Corporate Culture and Performance* by John P. Kotter and James L. Heskett. Copyright © 1992 by Kotter Associates, Inc. and James L. Heskett.

Ethical Values and Social Responsibility

Of the values that make up an organization's culture, ethical values are now considered among the most important. Widespread corporate accounting scandals, allegations that top managers of some organizations made personal use of company funds, and charges of insider trading have blanketed the newspapers and airwaves in recent years. Top corporate managers are under scrutiny from the public as never before, and even small companies are finding a need to put more emphasis on ethics to restore trust among their customers and the community.

Sources of Individual Ethical Principles

Ethics is the code of moral principles and values that governs the behaviors of a person or group with respect to what is right or wrong. Ethical values set standards as to what is good or bad in conduct and decision making.[44] Ethics are personal and unique to each individual, although in any given group, organization, or society there are many areas of concensus about what constitutes ethical behavior.[45] Exhibit 10.6 illustrates the varied sources of individual ethical principles. Each person is a creation of his or her time and place in history. National culture, religious heritage, historical background, and so forth lead to the development of societal morality, or society's view of what is right and wrong. Societal morality is often reflected in norms of behavior and values about what makes sense for an orderly society. Some principles are codified into laws and regulations, such as laws against drunk driving, robbery, or murder.

These laws, as well as unwritten societal norms and values, shape the local environment within which each individual acts, such as a person's community, family, and place of work. Individuals absorb the beliefs and values of their family, community, culture, society, religious community, and geographic environment, typically

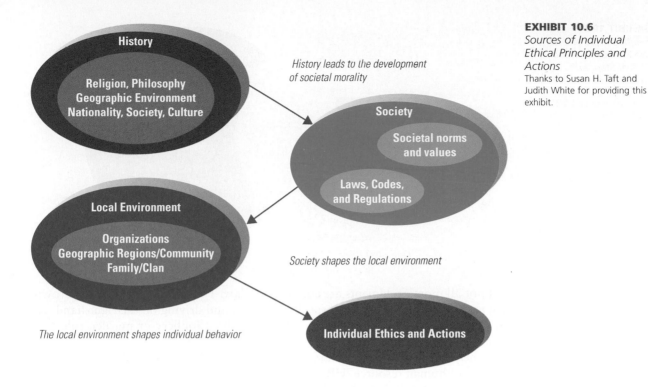

EXHIBIT 10.6
Sources of Individual Ethical Principles and Actions
Thanks to Susan H. Taft and Judith White for providing this exhibit.

discarding some and incorporating others into their own personal ethical standards. Each person's ethical stance is thus a blending of his or her historical, cultural, societal, and family backgrounds and influences.

It is important to look at individual ethics because ethics always involve an individual action, whether it be a decision to act or the failure to take action against wrongdoing by others. In organizations, an individual's ethical stance may be affected by peers, subordinates, and supervisors, as well as by the organizational culture. Organizational culture often has a profound influence on individual choices and can support and encourage ethical actions or promote unethical and socially irresponsibe behavior.

■ Managerial Ethics and Social Responsibility

Recent events have demonstrated the powerful influence of organizational standards on ethical behavior. Strict ethical standards are becoming part of the formal policies and informal cultures of many organizations, and courses in ethics are taught in many business schools. Many of the recent scandals in the news have dealt with people and corporations that broke the law. But it is important to remember that ethics goes far beyond behaviors governed by law.[46] The **rule of law** arises from a set of codified principles and regulations that describe how people are required to act, that are generally accepted in society, and that are enforceable in the courts.[47]

The relationship between ethical standards and legal requirements is illustrated in Exhibit 10.7. Ethical standards for the most part apply to behavior not covered by the law, and the rule of law applies to behaviors not necessarily covered by ethical standards. Current laws often reflect combined moral judgments,

Briefcase

As an organization manager, keep these guidelines in mind:

Take control of ethical values in the organization. Ethics is not the same as following the law. Ethical decisions are influenced by management's personal background, by organizational culture, and by organizational systems.

EXHIBIT 10.7

Relationship between the Rule of Law and Ethical Standards

Source: LaRue Tone Hosmer, *The Ethics of Management,* 2d ed. (Homewood, Ill.: Irwin, 1991).

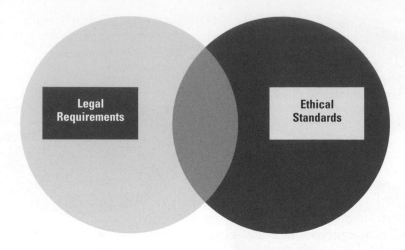

but not all moral judgments are codified into law. The morality of aiding a drowning person, for example, is not specified by law, and driving on the right-hand side of the road has no moral basis; but in acts such as robbery or murder, rules and moral standards overlap.

Unethical conduct in organizations is surprisingly widespread. More than 54 percent of human resource (HR) professionals polled by the Society for Human Resource Management and the Ethics Resource Center reported observing employees lying to supervisors or coworkers, falsifying reports or records, or abusing drugs or alcohol while on the job.[48] Many people believe that if you are not breaking the law, then you are behaving in an ethical manner, but this is not always true. Many behaviors have not been codified, and managers must be sensitive to emerging norms and values about those issues.

Managerial ethics are principles that guide the decisions and behaviors of managers with regard to whether they are right or wrong. The notion of **social responsibility** is an extension of this idea and refers to management's obligation to make choices and take action so that the organization contributes to the welfare and interest of all organizational stakeholders, such as employees, customers, shareholders, the community, and the broader society.[49]

Examples of the need for managerial ethics are as follows:[50]

- Top executives are considering promoting a rising sales manager who consistently brings in $70 million a year and has cracked open new markets in places like Brazil and Turkey that are important to the organization's international growth. However, female employees have been complaining for years that the manager is verbally abusive to them, tells offensive jokes, and throws temper tantrums if female employees don't do exactly as he says.

- The manager of a beauty supply store is told that she and her salespeople can receive large bonuses for selling a specified number of boxes of a new product, a permanent-wave solution that costs nearly twice as much as what most of her salon customers typically use. She orders the salespeople to store the old product in the back and tell customers there's been a delay in delivery.

- The project manager for a construction planning project wondered whether some facts should be left out of a report because the community where the facility would be built might object if they discovered certain environmental aspects of the project.

- A North American manufacturer operating abroad was asked to make cash payments (a bribe) to government officials and was told it was consistent with local customs, despite being illegal in North America.

As these examples illustrate, ethics and social responsibility is about making decisions. Managers make choices every day about whether to be honest or deceitful with suppliers, treat employees with respect or disdain, and be a good or a harmful corporate citizen. Some issues are exceedingly difficult to resolve and often represent ethical dilemmas. An **ethical dilemma** arises in a situation concerning right and wrong in which values are in conflict.[51] Right or wrong cannot be clearly identified in such situations. For example, for a salesperson at the beauty supply store, the value conflict is between being honest with customers and adhering to the boss's expectations. The manufacturing manager may feel torn between respecting and following local customs in a foreign country or adhering to U.S. laws concerning bribes. Sometimes, each alternative choice or behavior seems undesirable.

Ethical dilemmas are not easy to resolve, but top executives can aid the process by establishing organizational values that provide people with guidelines for making the best decision from a moral standpoint.

■ Does It Pay to Be Good?

The relationship of an organization's ethics and social responsibility to its performance concerns both organizational managers and organization scholars. Studies have provided varying results but generally have found that there is a small positive relationship between ethical and socially responsible behavior and financial results.[52] For example, a recent study of the financial performance of large U.S. corporations considered "best corporate citizens" found that they have both superior reputations and superior financial performance.[53] Similarly, Governance Metrics International, an independent corporate governance ratings agency, found that the stocks of companies run on more selfless principles perform better than those run in a self-serving manner. Top-ranked companies such as Pfizer, Johnson Controls, and Sunoco also outperformed lower-ranking firms on measures like return on assets, return on investment, and return on capital.[54]

As discussed earlier in the chapter, long-term organizational success relies largely on social capital, which means companies need to build a reputation for honesty, fairness, and doing the right thing. Researchers have found that people prefer to work for companies that demonstrate a high level of ethics and social responsibility, so these companies can attract and retain high-quality employees.[55] Timberland, for example, which gives employees 40 hours of unpaid leave annually to do community volunteer work and supports a number of charitable causes, is consistently ranked on *Fortune* magazine's list of the 100 best companies to work for. One vice president says she has turned down lucrative offers from other companies because she prefers to work at a company that puts ethics and social responsibility ahead of just making a profit.[56]

Customers pay attention, too. A study by Walker Research indicates that, price and quality being equal, two-thirds of people say they would switch brands to do business with a company that makes a high commitment to ethics.[57]

Companies that put ethics on the back burner in favor of fast growth and short-term profits ultimately suffer. To gain and keep the trust of employees, customers, investors, and the general public, organizations must put ethics first. "Just saying you're ethical isn't very useful," says Charles O. Holliday, Jr., chairman and CEO of DuPont Co. "You have to earn trust by what you do every day."[58]

Sources of Ethical Values in Organizations

Ethics in organizations is both an individual and an organizational matter. The standards for ethical or socially responsible conduct are embodied within each employee as well as within the organization itself. In addition, external stakeholders can influence standards of what is ethical and socially responsible. The immediate forces that impinge on ethical decisions in organizations are summarized in Exhibit 10.8. Individual beliefs and values, a person's ethical decision framework, and moral development influence personal ethics. Organizational culture, as we have already discussed, shapes the overall framework of values within the organization. Moreover, formal organization systems influence values and behaviors according to the organization's policy framework and reward systems. Companies also respond to numerous stakeholders in determining what is right. They consider how their actions may be viewed by customers, government agencies, shareholders, and the general community, as well as the impact each alternative course of action may have on various stakeholders. All of these factors can be explored to understand ethical and socially responsible decisions in organizations.[59]

Personal Ethics

Every individual brings a set of personal beliefs and values into the workplace. Personal values and the moral reasoning that translates these values into behavior are an important aspect of ethical decision making in organizations.[60]

As we discussed earlier, the historical, cultural, family, religious, and community backgrounds of managers shape their personal values and provide principles by which they carry out business. In addition, people go through stages of moral development that affect their ability to translate values into behavior. For example, children have a low level of moral development, making decisions and behaving to obtain rewards and avoid physical punishment. At an intermediate level of development, people learn to conform to expectations of good behavior as defined by colleagues and society. Most managers are at this level, willingly upholding the law and responding to societal expectations. At the highest level of moral development are people who develop an internal set of standards. These are self-chosen ethical principles that are more important to decisions than external expectations. Only a few people reach this high level, which can mean breaking laws if necessary to sustain higher moral principles.[61]

The other personal factor is whether managers have developed an *ethical framework* that guides their decisions. *Utilitarian theory*, for example, argues that ethical decisions should be made to generate the greatest benefits for the largest number of people. This framework is often consistent with business decisions because costs and benefits can be calculated in dollars. The *personal liberty* framework argues that decisions should be made to ensure the greatest possible freedom of choice and liberty for individuals. Liberties include the freedom to act on one's conscience, freedom of speech, due process of law, and the right to privacy. The *distributive justice* framework holds that moral decisions are those that promote equity, fairness, and impartiality with respect to the distribution of rewards and the administration of rules, which are essential for social cooperation.[62]

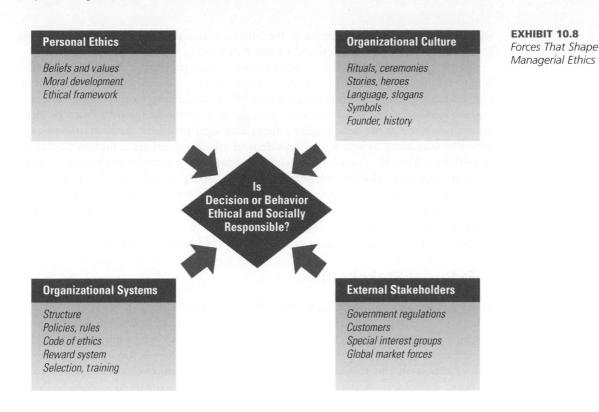

EXHIBIT 10.8
Forces That Shape Managerial Ethics

Organizational Culture

Rarely can ethical or unethical business practices be attributed entirely to the personal ethics of a single individual. Business practices also reflect the values, attitudes, and behavior patterns of an organization's culture. To promote ethical behavior in the workplace, companies should make ethics an integral part of the organization's culture. Kevin Kelly, who runs Emerald Packaging, a family-owned business started by Kelly's father in 1963, strives to continue the tradition of ethical business that earned his dad the nickname "Honest Jim." Kelly knows that some of his competitors try to secure customers' loyalty by giving them expensive gifts, but the culture at Emerald emphasizes that the best way to attract and keep customers is by being honest and treating them fairly.[63]

Organizational culture has a powerful impact on individual ethics because it helps to guide employees in making daily decisions. When the culture supports wrongdoing, it is easier for individual employees to go along. One young Enron employee explained how he slid into unethical decisions and practices in his job: "It was easy to get into, 'Well, everybody else is doing it, so maybe it isn't so bad.'"[64]

Organizational Systems

The third category of influences that shape managerial ethics is formal organizational systems. This includes the basic architecture of the organization, such as whether ethical values are incorporated in policies and rules; whether an explicit code of ethics is available and issued to members; whether organizational rewards, including praise, attention, and promotions, are linked to ethical behavior; and whether ethics is a consideration in the selection and training of employees. These formal efforts can reinforce ethical values that exist in the informal culture.

Many companies have established formal ethics programs. For example, after being maligned by the national press and pursued by federal officials for questionable billing practices and fraud, Columbia/HCA Healthcare Corp., a large hospital chain based in Nashville, Tennessee, brought in a new management team to clean up the mess and make sure similar ethical and legal problems never happen again. When he was hired as senior vice president of ethics, compliance, and corporate responsibility, Alan R. Yuspeh found only a rudimentary compliance program and a set of perfunctory ethical guidelines that no one could understand. Yuspeh drafted a clear and concise code of conduct that emphasized the values of compassion, honesty, fairness, loyalty, respect, and kindness. In addition, Yuspeh's office developed a massive ethics program that includes comprehensive training for all employees and an ethics hotline that answers about 1,200 employee calls annually.[65]

■ External Stakeholders

Managerial ethics and social responsibility are also influenced by a variety of external stakeholders, groups outside the organization that have a stake in the organization's performance. Ethical and socially responsible decision making recognizes that the organization is part of a larger community and considers the impact of a decision or action on all stakeholders.[66] Important external stakeholders are government agencies, customers, and special-interest groups such as those concerned with the natural environment.

Companies must operate within the limits of certain government regulations, such as safety laws, environmental protection requirements, and many other laws and regulations. Numerous companies, including Global Crossing, WorldCom, Merrill Lynch, and Xerox, have come under investigation by the Securities and Exchange Commission for alleged violations of laws related to financial controls and accounting practices. Companies in the health care industry have to respond to numerous laws and regulations, as do organizations such as schools and day care centers. Customers are another important stakeholder group. Customers are primarily concerned about the quality, safety, and availability of goods and services. For example, McDonald's has reduced trans–fatty acids in its fried foods in response to growing customer concerns about possible health risks associated with a fast-food diet.[67]

Special-interest groups continue to be one of the largest stakeholder concerns that companies face. Today, those concerned with corporate responsibility to the natural environment are particularly vocal. Thus, environmentalism is becoming an integral part of organizational planning and decision making for leading companies. The concept of *sustainable development*, a dual concern for economic growth and environmental sustainability, has been gaining ground among many business leaders. The public is no longer comfortable with organizations focusing solely on profit at the expense of the natural environment. Environmental sustainability—meaning that what is taken out of the environmental system for food, shelter, clothing, energy, and other human uses is restored to the system in waste that can be reused—is a part of strategy for companies like Monsanto, Interface, IKEA, Electrolux, Scandic Hotels, and MacMillan-Bloedel. Interface, the $1 billion leader in the floor-covering industry, is instituting changes that will allow the company to manufacture without pollution, waste, or fossil fuels. From the factory floor to the R&D lab, sustainability is as important a consideration at Interface as profitability. The emphasis on environmentalism hasn't hurt Interface. Over a 1-year period, sales increased from $800 million to $1 billion. During that time, the amount of raw materials used by the company dropped almost 20 percent per dollar of sales.[68]

How Leaders Shape Culture and Ethics

In a study of ethics policy and practice in successful, ethical companies such as Johnson & Johnson and General Mills, no point emerged more clearly than the role of top management in providing commitment, leadership, and examples for ethical behavior.[69] The CEO and other top managers must be committed to specific values and provide constant leadership in tending and renewing the values. Values can be communicated in a number of ways—speeches, company publications, policy statements, and, especially, personal actions. Top leaders are responsible for creating and sustaining a culture that emphasizes the importance of ethical behavior for all employees every day. When the CEO engages in unethical practices or fails to take firm and decisive action in response to the unethical practices of others, this attitude filters down through the organization. Formal ethics codes and training programs are worthless if leaders do not set and live up to high standards of ethical conduct.[70]

The following sections examine how managers signal and implement values through leadership as well as through the formal systems of the organization.

Values-based Leadership

The underlying value system of an organization cannot be managed in the traditional way. Issuing an authoritative directive, for example, has little or no impact on an organization's value system. Organizational values are developed and strengthened primarily through **values-based leadership**, a relationship between a leader and followers that is based on shared, strongly internalized values that are advocated and acted upon by the leader.[71]

Leaders influence cultural and ethical values by clearly articulating a vision for organizational values that employees can believe in, communicating the vision throughout the organization, and institutionalizing the vision through everyday behavior, rituals, ceremonies, and symbols, as well as through organizational systems and policies. When Vic Sarni was CEO of PPG Industries, he often called himself the chief ethics officer. Sarni didn't believe in using special staff departments to investigate ethical complaints; instead, he personally headed the firm's ethics committee. This sent a powerful symbolic message that ethics was important in the organization.[72]

Managers should remember that every statement and action has an impact on culture and values. For example, a survey of readers of the magazine *The Secretary* found that employees are acutely aware of their bosses' ethical lapses. Something as simple as having a secretary notarize a document without witnessing the signature may seem insignificant, but it communicates that the manager doesn't value honesty.[73] Employees learn about values, beliefs, and goals from watching managers, just as students learn which topics are important for an exam, what professors like, and how to get a good grade from watching professors. To be effective values-based leaders, executives often use symbols, ceremonies, speeches, and slogans that match the values. Citigroup's new CEO, Charles Prince, is devoting a tremendous amount of time to talking about values with both employees and customers. Prince knows that for a company the size of Citigroup, just strengthening rules and systems isn't enough. To get the company to "internalize" a strong code of ethics around the

Briefcase

As an organization manager, keep these guidelines in mind:

Act as a leader for the internal culture and ethical values that are important to the organization. Influence the value system through values-based leadership, including the use of ceremonies, slogans, symbols, and stories. Communicate important values to employees to enhance organizational effectiveness, and remember that actions speak louder than words.

globe, Prince is making a visible commitment to values through speeches, video addresses, and regular communication.[74] Prince also says he will be "ruthless" with managers and employees who don't follow the rules. Actions speak louder than words, so values-based leaders "walk their talk."[75]

Values-based leaders engender a high level of trust and respect from employees, based not only on their stated values but also on the courage, determination, and self-sacrifice they demonstrate in upholding them. Leaders can use this respect and trust to motivate employees toward high-level performance and a sense of purpose in achieving the organizational vision. When leaders are willing to make personal sacrifices for the sake of values, employees also become more willing to do so. This element of self-sacrifice puts a somewhat spiritual connotation on the process of leadership. Indeed, one writer in organization theory, Karl Weick, has said that "managerial work can be viewed as managing myth, symbols, and labels…; because managers traffic so often in images, the appropriate role for the manager may be evangelist rather than accountant."[76]

John Tu and David Sun, cofounders of Kingston Technology Co., provide an example of values-based leadership.

In Practice

Kingston Technology Co.

"Business is not about money," says David Sun, vice president and chief operating officer of Kingston Technology Co., which manufactures memory products for personal computers, laser printers, digital cameras, and other products. "It's about relationships." Sun and his cofounder, president John Tu, strive to develop deep, caring, trusting relationships with employees. "They are part of the team," says one employee of the partnership that workers feel with leaders at Kingston. "They are not owners; they are employees. And that…value system is passed on."

Sun and Tu believe everyone in the company is a leader, so they share the wealth with employees. When the two sold 80 percent of Kingston to Softbank Corp. of Japan for $1.5 billion, they set aside $100 million of the proceeds for employee bonuses. The initial distribution of $38 million went to about 550 employees who were with the company at the time of its sale. Another $40 million has since been divvied up among the company's current 1,500 workers. Sun and Tu seem genuinely puzzled by people's astonishment that they would give $100 million to employees. It seems only right to them.

Despite this amazing generosity, when people talk about why they like working for Kingston, they rarely mention money and benefits. Instead, they talk about personal acts of gentleness or kindness performed by the two top leaders. There are many stories of these leaders quietly offering money, time, other resources—or just genuine concern—to employees who were dealing with family or personal troubles. This approach to leadership creates an emotional bond with employees that builds mutual trust and respect. Employees feel that they are part of a caring family. And because employees are treated with kindness, care, and respect, they pass that attitude on in their relationships with each other and with customers, suppliers, and other outsiders. Employees are highly motivated to meet organizational goals and keep the company's reputation for doing the right thing. Says one, "We try to keep the family name a good name."[77]

■ Formal Structure and Systems

Another set of tools leaders can use to shape cultural and ethical values is the formal structure and systems of the organization. These systems have been especially effective in recent years for influencing managerial ethics.

Structure. Managers can assign responsibility for ethical values to a specific position. This not only allocates organization time and energy to the problem but symbolizes to everyone the importance of ethics. One example is an **ethics committee**, which is a cross-functional group of executives who oversee company ethics. The committee provides rulings on questionable ethical issues and assumes responsibility for disciplining wrongdoers. By appointing top-level executives to serve on the committee, the organization signals the importance of ethics.

Today, many organizations are setting up ethics departments that manage and coordinate all corporate ethics activities. These departments are headed by a **chief ethics officer**, a high-level company executive who oversees all aspects of ethics, including establishing and broadly communicating ethical standards, setting up ethics training programs, supervising the investigation of ethical problems, and advising managers on the ethical aspects of corporate decisions.[78] The title of chief ethics officer was almost unheard of a decade ago, but recent ethical and legal problems have created a growing demand for these specialists. Between 1992 and early 2005, membership in the Ethics Officer Association, a trade group, soared from only twelve companies to more than a thousand.[79]

Ethics offices sometimes also work as counseling centers to help employees resolve difficult ethical dilemmas. The focus is as much on helping employees make the right decisions as on disciplining wrongdoers. Most ethics offices have confidential **ethics hotlines** that employees can use to seek guidance as well as report questionable behavior. One organization calls its hotline a "Guide Line" to emphasize its use as a tool for making ethical decisions as well as reporting lapses.[80] According to Gary Edwards, president of the Ethics Resource Center, between 65 and 85 percent of calls to hotlines in the organizations he advises are calls for counsel on ethical issues. Northrup Grumman's "Openline" fields about 1,400 calls a year, of which only one fourth are reports of misdeeds.[81]

Disclosure Mechanisms. A confidential hotline is also an important mechanism for employees to voice concerns about ethical practices. Holding organizations accountable depends to some degree on individuals who are willing to speak up if they suspect illegal, dangerous, or unethical activities. Organizations can establish policies and procedures to support and protect *whistle-blowers*. **Whistle-blowing** is employee disclosure of illegal, immoral, or illegitimate practices on the part of the organization.[82] One value of corporate policy is to protect whistle-blowers so they will not be transferred to lower-level positions or fired because of their ethical concerns. A policy can also encourage whistle-blowers to stay within the organization—for instance, to quietly blow the whistle to responsible managers.[83] Whistle-blowers have the option to stop organizational activities by going to newspaper or television reporters, but as a last resort. As ethical problems in the corporate world increase, many companies are looking for ways to protect whistle-blowers. In addition, calls are increasing for stronger legal protection for those who report illegal or unethical business activities.[84] When there are no protective measures, whistle-blowers suffer, and the company may continue its unethical or illegal practices.

Many whistle-blowers suffer financial and personal loss to maintain their personal ethical standards. When Colleen Rowley of the Federal Bureau of Investigation (FBI) wrote a 13-page memo to FBI director Robert Mueller about agency failures and lapses that may have contributed to the September 11, 2001, terrorist attacks, she was well aware of the risks. "Due to the frankness with which I have expressed myself," Rowley wrote, "I hope my continued employment with the FBI is not somehow placed in jeopardy." Fearing recriminations and concerned that the

Briefcase

As an organization manager, keep these guidelines in mind:

Use the formal systems of the organization to implement desired cultural and ethical values. These systems include an ethics committee, a chief ethics officer, disclosure mechanisms, a code of ethics, a mission statement, and training in ethical decision-making frameworks.

agency would suppress her allegations, Rowley also sent a copy of the memo to the Senate Intelligence Committee.[85]

Enlightened companies strive to create a climate and a culture in which employees feel free to point out problems and managers take swift action to address concerns about unethical or illegal activities. Organizations can view whistle-blowing as a benefit to the company, helping to prevent the kind of disasters that have hit companies such as Enron, Arthur Andersen, and WorldCom, and make dedicated efforts to encourage and protect whistle-blowers.

Code of Ethics. A survey of *Fortune* 1,000 companies found that 98 percent address issues of ethics and business conduct in formal corporate policies, and 78 percent have separate codes of ethics that are widely distributed to employees.[86] A **code of ethics** is a formal statement of the company's values concerning ethics and social responsibility; it clarifies to employees what the company stands for and its expectations for employee conduct. The code of ethics at Lockheed Martin, for example, states that the organization "aims to set the standard for ethical conduct" through adhering to the values of honesty, integrity, respect, trust, responsibility, and citizenship. The code specifies the types of behaviors expected to honor these values and encourages employees to use available company resources to help make ethical choices and decisions.[87] Codes of ethics may cover a broad range of issues, including statements of the company's guiding values; guidelines related to issues such as workplace safety, the security of proprietary information, or employee privacy; and commitments to environmental responsibility, product safety, and other matters of concern to stakeholders.

Some companies use broader values statements within which ethics is a part. These statements define ethical values as well as corporate culture and contain language about company responsibility, quality of product, and treatment of employees. A formal statement of values can serve as a fundamental organizational document that defines what the organization stands for and legitimizes value choices for employees.[88] For example, Citigroup is implementing a new statement of cultural and ethical values after being stung by a series of scandals in the United States, Japan, and Europe. CEO Charles Prince explains: "Our goal is to make explicit what is implicit. Every employee, starting with me, has the ability to refocus our reputation and our integrity."[89]

Written codes of ethics are important because they clarify and formally state the company's values and expected ethical behaviors. However, it is essential that top managers support and reinforce the codes through their actions, including rewards for compliance and discipline for violations. Otherwise, a code of ethics is nothing more than a piece of paper. Indeed, one study found that companies with a written code of ethics are just as likely as those without a code to be found guilty of illegal activities.[90] Many of the companies currently in hot water with the U.S. Securities and Exchange Commission (SEC)—for example, Halliburton and Arthur Andersen—had well-developed codes of ethics, but managers failed to support and enforce the ethical values.

Training Programs. To ensure that ethical issues are considered in daily decision making, companies can supplement a written code of ethics with employee training programs.[91] At Citigroup, a new online ethics training program is mandatory for all 300,000 employees worldwide.[92] All Texas Instruments (TI) employees go through an 8-hour ethics training course that includes case examples giving people a chance to wrestle with ethical dilemmas. In addition, TI incorporates an ethics component into every training course it offers.[93]

In an important step, ethics programs also include frameworks for ethical decision making, such as the utilitarian approach described earlier in this chapter. Learning these frameworks helps managers act autonomously and still think their way through a difficult decision. In a few companies, managers are also taught about the stages of moral development, which helps to bring them to a high level of ethical decision making. This training has been an important catalyst for establishing ethical behavior and integrity as critical components of strategic competitiveness.[94]

These formal systems and structures can be highly effective. However, they alone are not sufficient to build and sustain an ethical company. Leaders should integrate ethics into the organizational culture and support and renew ethical values through their words and actions. Jeffrey Immelt, chairman and chief executive officer of General Electric, is striving to integrate ethical and socially responsible values into the very core of the giant industrial and financial services company.

In Practice
General Electric

Two hundred corporate officers of General Electric (GE), the world's most valuable and most admired company, listened as chairman and CEO Jeffrey Immelt outlined the four elements it would take to keep GE on top. They had heard most of it before: execution, growth, and great people. But Immelt stunned some listeners when he put a new point at the top of the list: *virtue*. Moreover, Immelt insisted that virtue is not just the nice thing to do but a business imperative. To be a great company today, he believes, means you have to be a good company.

Immelt is emphasizing values as the center of corporate decision making. The shift is reflected in how the company runs itself and treats employees, the kinds of companies it does business with, and the new technologies it invests in. For example, Immelt appointed GE's first vice president for corporate citizenship in 2002. Part of the manager's job is to help Immelt spread the gospel of virtue to GE's far-flung business units. The company is now auditing suppliers in the developing world to make sure they comply with labor, environmental, health, and safety standards. HR policies have been revised to include domestic partner benefits and move more women and African Americans into the upper ranks. GE is also investing in new environmentally friendly technologies, such as solar-energy equipment and wind-energy businesses. And it's spending $20 million on a health care project in rural Ghana.

General Electric has long had a strong ethics program, including a values statement, an ethics policy, an integrity policy that every employee signs, training programs, compliance policies, and so forth. The big difference Immelt is bringing to the company is moving values to the center of the business and focusing everyone more carefully on how GE relates to the world around it. Immelt believes the approach is good for the company, for society, and for employees. "The reason people come to work for GE is that they want to be about something that is bigger than themselves," he says. "People want . . . to work for a company that's doing great things in the world."[95]

By integrating ethics and corporate social responsibility into the core of the organization, Immelt is making organizational integrity a part of day-to-day business. Only when employees are convinced that ethical values play a key role in all management decisions and actions can they become committed to making them a part of their everyday behavior. In a company the size and scale of GE, it's a huge challenge to keep ethical values entrenched in the culture. Other organizations that operate on a global scale also face challenges related to culture and ethics.

Corporate Culture and Ethics in a Global Environment

A Hudson Institute report, *Workforce 2020*, states, "The rest of the world matters to a degree that it never did in the past."[96] Managers are finding this to be true not only in terms of economics or HR issues, but also in terms of cultural and ethical values. Organizations operating in many different areas of the world have a tough time because of the various cultural and market factors they must deal with. The greater complexity of the environment and organizational domain create a greater potential for ethical problems or misunderstandings.[97] Consider that in Europe, privacy has been defined as a basic human right and there are laws limiting the amount and kind of information companies can collect and governing how they use it. In U.S. organizations, on the other hand, collecting data, trading it with partners, using it for marketing, and even selling it are all common practice.[98] How do managers translate the ideas for developing strong corporate cultures to a complex global environment? How do they develop ethics codes or other ethical structures and systems that address the complex issues associated with doing business on a global scale?

Corporate culture and national culture are often intertwined, and the global diversity of many of today's companies presents a challenge to managers trying to build a strong organizational culture. Employees who come from different countries often have varied attitudes and beliefs that make it difficult to establish a sense of community and cohesiveness based on the corporate culture. In fact, research has indicated that national culture has a greater impact on employees than does corporate culture.[99] For example, a study of effectiveness and cultural values in Russia found that flexibility and collectivism (working together in groups), which are key values in the national culture, are considerably more important to organizational effectiveness than they are for most U.S.-based companies.[100] When these values are not incorporated into the organizational culture, employees do not perform as well. Another recent study found that differences in national cultural values and preferences also create significant variance in ethical attitudes among people from different countries.[101]

Some companies have been successful in developing a broad global perspective that permeates the entire organizational culture. For example, Omron, a global company with headquarters in Kyoto, Japan, has offices on six continents. However, until a few years ago, Omron had always assigned Japanese managers to head them. Today, it relies on local expertise in each geographical area and blends the insights and perspectives of local managers into a global whole. Global planning meetings are held in offices around the world. In addition, Omron established a global database and standardized its software to ensure a smooth exchange of information among its offices worldwide. It takes time to develop a broad cultural mind-set and spread it throughout the company, but firms such as Omron try to bring a multicultural approach to every business issue.[102]

Vijay Govindarajan, a professor of international business and director of the "Global Leadership 2020" management program at Dartmouth College, offers some guidance for managers trying to build a global culture. His research indicates that, even though organizational cultures may vary widely, there are specific components that characterize a global culture. These include an emphasis on multicultural rather than national values, basing status on merit rather than nationality, being open to new ideas from other cultures, showing excitement rather than trepidation when entering new cultural environments, and being sensitive to cultural differences without being limited by them.[103]

Global ethics is also challenging today's organizations to think more broadly. Many are using a wide variety of mechanisms to support and reinforce their ethics initiatives on a global scale. One of the most useful mechanisms for building global ethics is the **social audit,** which measures and reports the ethical, social, and environmental impact of a company's operations.[104] Concerns about the labor practices and working conditions of many major U.S. corporations' overseas suppliers originally spurred the Council on Economic Priorities Accreditation Agency to propose a set of global social standards to deal with issues such as child labor, low wages, and unsafe working conditions. Today, the Social Accountability 8000, or SA 8000, is the only auditable social standard in the world. The system is designed to work like the ISO 9000 quality-auditing system of the International Standards Organization.

Many companies, such as Avon, Eileen Fisher, and Toys "R" Us, are taking steps to ensure that their factories and suppliers meet SA 8000 standards. Eileen Fisher, a clothing company, has trained all its suppliers and even picked up the bill for their SA 8000 audits.[105] Companies can also ask an outside company to perform an independent social audit to measure how well the company is living up to its ethical and social values and how it is perceived by different stakeholder groups.

In the coming years, organizations will continue to evolve in their ability to work with varied cultures, combine them into a cohesive whole, live up to high social and ethical standards worldwide, and cope with the conflicts that may arise when working in a multicultural environment.

Summary and Interpretation

This chapter covered a range of material on corporate culture, the importance of cultural and ethical values, and techniques managers can use to influence these values. Cultural and ethical values help determine the organization's social capital, and the right values can contribute to organizational success.

Culture is the set of key values, beliefs, and norms shared by members of an organization. Organizational cultures serve two critically important functions—to integrate members so that they know how to relate to one another and to help the organization adapt to the external environment. Culture can be observed and interpreted through rites and ceremonies, stories and heroes, symbols, and language.

Organizational culture should reinforce the strategy and structure that the organization needs to be successful in its environment. Four types of culture that may exist in organizations are adaptability culture, mission culture, clan culture, and bureaucratic culture. When widespread consensus exists about the importance of specific values, the organizational culture is strong and cohesive. However, even in organizations with strong cultures, several sets of subcultures may emerge, particularly in large organizations. Strong cultures can be either adaptive or nonadaptive. Adaptive cultures have different values and different behavior patterns than nonadaptive cultures. Strong but unhealthy cultures can be detrimental to a company's chances for success. On the other hand, strong adaptive cultures can play an important role in creating high performance and innovative response to challenges, competitive threats, or new opportunities.

An important aspect of organizational values is managerial ethics, which is the set of values governing behavior with respect to what is right or wrong. Ethical decision making in organizations is shaped by many factors: personal characteristics, which include personal beliefs, moral development, and the adoption of ethical frameworks for decision making; organizational culture, which is the extent to which values, heroes, traditions, and symbols reinforce ethical decision making; organizational systems, which pertain to the formal structure, policies, codes of ethics, and reward systems that reinforce ethical or unethical choices; and the interests and concerns of external stakeholders, which include government agencies, customers, and special interest groups.

The chapter also discussed how leaders can shape culture and ethics. One important idea is values-based leadership, which means leaders define a vision of proper values, communicate it throughout the organization, and institutionalize it through everyday behavior, rituals, ceremonies, and symbols. We also discussed formal systems that are important for shaping ethical values. Formal systems include an ethics committee, an ethics department, disclosure mechanisms for whistle-blowing, ethics training programs, and a code of ethics or values statement that specifies ethical values. As business increasingly crosses geographical and cultural boundaries, leaders face difficult challenges in establishing strong cultural and ethical values with which all employees can identify and agree. Companies that develop global cultures emphasize multicultural values, base status on merit rather than nationality, are excited about new cultural environments, remain open to ideas from other cultures, and are sensitive to different cultural values without being limited by them. Social audits are important tools for companies trying to maintain high ethical standards on a global basis.

Key Concepts

adaptability culture	legends
bureaucratic culture	managerial ethics
chief ethics officer	mission culture
clan culture	myths
code of ethics	rites and ceremonies
culture	rule of law
culture strength	social audit
ethical dilemma	social capital
ethics	social responsibility
ethics committee	stories
ethics hotlines	subcultures
external adaptation	symbol
heroes	values-based leadership
internal integration	whistle-blowing
language	

Discussion Questions

1. Describe observable symbols, ceremonies, dress, or other aspects of culture and the underlying values they represent for an organization where you have worked.
2. What might be some of the advantages of having several subcultures within an organization? The disadvantages?
3. Explain the concept of social capital. Name an organization currently in the business news that seems to have a high degree of social capital and one that seems to have a low degree.
4. Do you think a bureaucratic culture would be less employee oriented than a clan culture? Discuss.

5. Why is values-based leadership so important to the influence of culture? Does a symbolic act communicate more about company values than an explicit statement? Discuss.

6. Are you aware of a situation in which either you or someone you know was confronted by an ethical dilemma, such as being encouraged to inflate an expense account? Do you think the person's decision was affected by individual moral development or by the accepted values within the company? Explain.

7. Why is equality an important value to support learning and innovation? Discuss.

8. What importance would you attribute to leadership statements and actions for influencing ethical values and decision making in an organization?

9. How do external stakeholders influence ethical decision making in an organization? Discuss why globalization has contributed to more complex ethical issues related to external stakeholders.

10. Codes of ethics have been criticized for transferring responsibility for ethical behavior from the organization to the individual employee. Do you agree? Do you think a code of ethics is valuable for an organization?

11. Top executives at numerous technology companies, including AOL/Time Warner, Gateway, Sun Microsystems, and Cisco, made millions of dollars from the sale of stock during the "bubble years" of 1999–2001. When the bubble burst, ordinary investors lost 70 to 90 percent of their holdings. Do you see anything wrong with this from an ethical standpoint? How do you think this affects the social capital of these organizations?

Chapter 10 Workbook: Shop 'til You Drop: Corporate Culture in the Retail World*

To understand more about corporate culture, visit two retail stores and compare them according to various factors. Go to one discount or low-end store, such as Kmart or Wal-Mart, and to one high-end store, such as Saks Fifth Avenue, Dayton/Hudson's, Goldwater's, or Dillard's. Do not interview any employees, but instead be an observer or a shopper. After your visits, fill out the following table for each store. Spend at least 2 hours in each store on a busy day and be very observant.

Culture Item	Discount Store	High-End Department Store
1. Mission of store: What is it, and is it clear to employees?		
2. Individual initiative: Is it encouraged?		
3. Reward system: What are employees rewarded for?		
4. Teamwork: Do people within one department or across departments work together or talk with each other?		
5. Company loyalty: Is there evidence of loyalty or of enthusiasm to be working there?		

Continued

Culture Item	Discount Store	High-End Department Store
6. Dress: Are there uniforms? Is there a dress code? How strong is it? How do you rate employees' personal appearance in general?		
7. Diversity or commonality of employees: Is there diversity or commonality in age, education, race, personality, and so on?		
8. Service orientation: Is the customer valued or tolerated?		
9. Human resource development: Is there opportunity for growth and advancement?		

Questions

1. How does the culture seem to influence employee behavior in each store?
2. What effect does employees' behavior have on customers?
3. Which store was more pleasant to be in? How does that relate to the mission of the store?

Case for Analysis: Implementing Change at National Industrial Products*

Curtis Simpson sat staring out the window of his office. What would he say to Tom Lawrence when they met this afternoon? Tom had clearly met the challenge Simpson set for him when he hired him as president of National Industrial Products (National) a little more than a year ago, but the company seemed to be coming apart at the seams. As chairman and CEO of Simpson Industries, which had bought National several years ago, Simpson was faced with the task of understanding the problem and clearly communicating his ideas and beliefs to Lawrence.

National Industrial Products is a medium-sized producer of mechanical seals, pumps, and other flow-control products. When Simpson Industries acquired the company, it was under the leadership of Jim Carpenter, who had been CEO for almost three decades and was very well liked by employees. Carpenter had always treated his employees like family. He knew most of them by name, often visited them in their homes if they were ill, and spent part of each day just chatting with workers on the factory floor. National sponsored an annual holiday party for its workers, as well as company picnics and other social events several times a year, and Carpenter was always in attendance. He considered these activities to be just as important as his visits with customers or negotiations with suppliers. Carpen-

*Based on Gary Yukl, "Consolidated Products," in *Leadership in Organizations*, 4th ed. (Englewood Cliffs, N.J.: Prentice-Hall, 1998), 66–67; John M. Champion and John H. James, "Implementing Strategic Change," in *Critical Incidents in Management: Decision and Policy Issues*, 6th ed. (Homewood, Ill.: Irwin, 1989), 138–140; and William C. Symonds, "Where Paternalism Equals Good Business," *BusinessWeek* (July 20, 1998), 16E4, 16E6.

ter believed it was important to treat people right so they would have a sense of loyalty to the company. If business was slow, he would find something else for workers to do, even if it was just sweeping the parking lot, rather than lay people off. He figured the company couldn't afford to lose skilled workers who were so difficult to replace. "If you treat people right," he said, "they'll do a good job for you without your having to push them."

Carpenter had never set performance objectives and standards for the various departments, and he trusted his managers to run their departments as they saw fit. He offered training programs in communications and HR for managers and team leaders several times each year. Carpenter's approach had seemed to work quite well for much of National's history. Employees were very loyal to Carpenter and the company, and there were many instances in which workers had gone above and beyond the call of duty. For example, when two National pumps that supplied water to a U.S. Navy ship failed on a Saturday night just before the ship's scheduled departure, two employees worked throughout the night to make new seals and deliver them for installation before the ship left port. Most managers and employees had been with the company for many years, and National boasted the lowest turnover rate in the industry.

However, as the industry began to change in recent years, National's competitiveness began to decline. Four of National's major rivals had recently merged into two large companies that were better able to meet customer needs, which was one factor that led to National being acquired by Simpson Industries. Following the acquisition, National's sales and profits had continued to decline, while costs kept going up. In addition, Simpson Industries's top executives were concerned about low productivity at National. Although they had been happy to have Carpenter stay on through the transition, within a year they had gently pressured him into early retirement. Some of the top managers believed Carpenter tolerated poor performance and low productivity in order to maintain a friendly atmosphere. "In today's world, you just can't do that," one had said. "We've got to bring in someone who can implement change and turn this company around in a hurry, or National's going to go bankrupt." That's when Tom Lawrence was brought on board, with a mandate to cut costs and improve productivity and profits.

Lawrence had a growing reputation as a young, dynamic manager who could get things done fast. He quickly began making changes at National. First, he cut costs by discontinuing the company-sponsored social activities, and he even refused to allow the impromptu birthday celebrations that had once been a regular part of life at National. He cut the training programs in communications and HR, arguing that they were a waste of time and money. "We're not here to make people feel good," he told his managers. "If people don't want to work, get rid of them and find someone else who does." He often referred to workers who complained about the changes at National as "crybabies."

Lawrence established strict performance standards for his vice presidents and department managers and ordered them to do the same for their employees. He held weekly meetings with each manager to review department performance and discuss problems. All employees were now subject to regular performance reviews. Any worker who had substandard performance was to be given one warning and then fired if performance did not improve within 2 weeks. And, whereas managers and sales representatives had once been paid on a straight salary basis, with seniority being the sole criterion for advancement, Lawrence implemented a revised system that rewarded them for meeting productivity, sales, and profit goals. For those who met the standards, rewards were generous, including large bonuses and perks such as company cars and first-class air travel to industry meetings. Those who fell behind were often chided in front of their colleagues to set an example, and if they didn't shape up soon, Lawrence didn't hesitate to fire them.

By the end of Lawrence's first year as president of National, production costs had been reduced by nearly 20 percent, while output was up 10 percent and sales increased by nearly 10 percent as well. However, three experienced and well-respected National managers had left the company for jobs with competitors, and turnover among production workers had increased alarmingly. In the tight labor market, replacements were not easily found. Most disturbing to Simpson were the results of a survey he had commissioned by an outside consultant. The survey indicated that morale at National was in the pits. Workers viewed their supervisors with antagonism and a touch of fear. They expressed the belief that managers were obsessed with profits and quotas and cared nothing about workers' needs and feelings. They also noted that the collegial, friendly atmosphere that had made National a great place to work had been replaced by an environment of aggressive internal competition and distrust.

Simpson was pleased that Lawrence has brought National's profits and productivity up to the standards Simpson Industries expects. However, he was concerned that the low morale and high turnover would seriously damage the company in the long run. Was Lawrence correct that many of the employees at National are just being "crybabies?" Were they so accustomed to being coddled by Carpenter that they weren't willing to make the changes necessary to keep the company competitive? Finally, Simpson wondered if a spirit of competition can exist in an atmosphere of collegiality and cooperativeness such as that fostered by Carpenter.

Case for Analysis: Does This Milkshake Taste Funny?*

George Stein, a college student working for Eastern Dairy during the summer, was suddenly faced with an ethical dilemma. George had very little time to think about his choices, less than a minute. On the one hand, he could do what Paul told him to do, and his shift could go home on time. However, he found it tough to shake the gross mental image of all those innocent kids drinking milkshakes contaminated with pulverized maggots. If he chose instead to go against Paul, what would the guys say? He could almost hear their derisive comments already: "wimp... college kid..."

Background

George Stein had lived his entire life in various suburbs of a major city on the East Coast. His father's salary as a manager provided the family with a solid middle-class lifestyle. His mother was a homemaker. George's major interests in life were the local teenage gathering place—a drive-in restaurant—hot rod cars, and his girlfriend, Cathy. He had not really wanted to attend college, but relentless pressure by his parents convinced him to try it for a year. He chose mechanical engineering as his major, hoping there might be some similarity between being a mechanical engineer and being a mechanic. After 1 year of engineering school, however, he has not seen any similarity yet. Once again this summer, his parents had to prod and cajole him to agree to return to school in the fall. They only succeeded by promising to give their blessing to his marriage to Cathy following his sophomore year.

George had worked at menial jobs each of the last four summers to satisfy his immediate need for dating and car money. He did manage to put away a bit to be used for spending money during the school year. He had saved very little for the day that he and Cathy would start their life together, but they planned for Cathy to support them with her earnings as a customer service representative until George either finished or quit school.

The day after George returned home this summer, he heard that Eastern Dairy might hire summer help. He applied at the local plant the next day. Eastern Dairy was unionized, and the wages paid were more than twice the minimum wage George had been paid on previous jobs, so he was quite interested in a position.

Eastern Dairy manufactured milkshake and ice cream mix for a number of customers in the metropolitan area. It sold the ice cream mix in 5- and 10-gallon containers to other firms, which then added the flavoring ingredients (e.g., strawberries or blueberries), packaged and froze the mix, and sold the ice cream under their own brand names. Eastern Dairy sold the milkshake mix in 5-gallon cardboard cartons, which contained a plastic liner. These packages were delivered to many restaurants in the area. The packaging was designed to fit into automatic milkshake machines used in many types of restaurants, including most fast-food restaurants and drive-ins.

George was elated when he received the call asking him to come to the plant on June 8. After a brief visit with the HR director, at which time George filled out the necessary employment forms, he was instructed to report for work at 11:00 P.M. that night. He was assigned to the night shift, working from 11:00 P.M. until 7:00 A.M. six nights per week—Sunday through Friday. With the regular wages paid at Eastern Dairy, supplemented by time and one-half pay for 8 hours of guaranteed overtime each week, George thought he could save a tidy sum before he had to return to school at the end of the first week in September.

When George reported to work, he discovered that there were no managers assigned to the night shift. The entire plant was run by a six-person crew of operators. One member of this crew, a young man named Paul Burnham, received each night's production orders from the day shift superintendent as the superintendent left for the day. Although Paul's status was no different from that of his five colleagues, the other crew members looked to him for direction. Paul passed the production orders to the mixer (who was the first stage of the production process) and kept the production records for the shift.

The production process was really quite simple. Mixes moved between various pieces of equipment (including mixing vats, pasteurizers, coolers, homogenizers, and filling machines) through stainless steel pipes suspended from the ceiling. All of the pipes had to be disassembled, thoroughly cleaned, and reinstalled by the conclusion of the night shift. This process took approximately 1 hour, so all the mix had to be run by 6:00 A.M. in order to complete the cleanup by the 7:00 A.M. quitting time. Paul and one other worker, Fred (the mixer), cleaned the giant mixing vats while the other four on the shift, including George, cleaned and reinstalled the pipes and filters.

George soon learned that Paul felt a sense of responsibility for completing all of the assigned work before the end of the shift. However, as long as that objective was

*This case was prepared by Roland B. Cousins, LaGrange College, and Linda E. Benitz, InterCel, Inc., as a basis for class discussion and not to illustrate either effective or ineffective handling of an administrative situation. The names of the firm and individuals and the location involved have been disguised to preserve anonymity. The situation reported is factual. The authors thank Anne T. Lawrence for her assistance in the development of this case.

achieved, he did not seem to care about what else went on during the shift. A great deal of story-telling and horseplay was the norm, but the work was always completed by quitting time. George was soon enjoying the easy camaraderie of the work group, the outrageous pranks they pulled on one another, and even the work itself.

George's position required that he station himself beside the conveyor in a large freezer room. He removed containers of mix as they came down the line and stacked them in the appropriate places. Periodically, Paul would decide that they had all worked hard enough and would shut down the line for a while so that they could engage in some nonwork activity like joke telling, hiding each other's lunch boxes, or "balloon" fights. The balloons were actually the 5-gallon, flexible liners for the cardboard boxes in which the mix was sold.

While George did not relish being hit by an exploding bag containing 5 gallons of heavy mix, he found it great fun to lob one at one of his co-workers. The loss of 10 to 40 gallons of mix on a shift did not seem to concern anyone, and these fights were never curtailed. George quickly learned that management had only two expectations of the night shift. First, the shift was expected to complete the production orders each night. Second, management expected the equipment, including the pipes, to be spotlessly clean at the conclusion of the shift. Paul told George that inspectors from the county health department would occasionally drop by unannounced at the end of the shift to inspect the vats and pipes after they had been disassembled and scrubbed. Paul also told George that management would be very upset if the inspectors registered any complaints about cleanliness.

George did join the union but saw very little evidence of its involvement in the day-to-day operations of the plant. Labor relations seemed quite amicable, and George thought of the union only when he looked at a pay stub and noticed that union dues had been deducted from his gross pay. The difference George noticed in working for Eastern Dairy compared to his previous employers was not the presence of the union but the absence of management.

The Current Situation

Things seemed to be going quite well for George on the job—until a few minutes ago. The problem first surfaced when the milkshake mix that was being run started spewing out of one of the joints in the overhead pipe network. The pumps were shut down while George disassembled the joint to see what the problem was. George removed the filter screen from the pipe at the leaking joint and saw that it was completely packed with solid matter. Closer inspection revealed that maggots were the culprits. George hurriedly took the filter to Paul to show him the blockage. Paul did not seem too concerned and told George to clean the filter and reassemble the joint. When George asked how this could have happened, Paul said maggots occasionally got into the bags of certain ingredients that were stored in

a warehouse at the back of the lot. "But you don't have to worry," said Paul. "The filters will catch any solid matter."

Feeling somewhat reassured, George cleaned the filter and reassembled the pipe. But still, the image of maggots floating in a milkshake was hard to shake. And, unfortunately for George, that was not the end of it.

Shortly after the pumps were restarted, the mix began to flow out of another joint. Once again, a filter plugged with maggots was found to be the cause.

For the second time, George cleaned the filter and reassembled the connection. This time Paul had seemed a bit more concerned as he noted that they barely had enough time to run the last 500 gallons remaining in the vats before they needed to clean up in preparation for the end of the shift.

Moments after the equipment was again restarted, another joint started to spew. When maggots were found to be clogging this filter, too, Paul called George over and told him to remove all five filters from the line so the last 500 gallons could be run without any filters. Paul laughed when he saw the shocked look on George's face.

"George," he said, "don't forget that all of this stuff goes through the homogenizer, so any solid matter will be completely pulverized. And when it's heated in the pasteurization process, any bacteria will be killed. No one will ever know about this, the company can save a lot of mix—that's money—and, most important, we can run this through and go home on time."

George knew that they would never get this lot packaged if they had to shut down every minute to clean filters, and there was no reason to believe it would not be this way for the rest of the run. The product had been thoroughly mixed in the mixing vats at the beginning of the process, which meant that contaminants would be distributed uniformly throughout the 500 gallons. George also knew that the 500 gallons of milkshake was very expensive. He did not think management would just want it dumped down the drain.

Finally, Paul was definitely right about one thing—removing all of the filters, a 10-minute job at most, would ensure that they could get everything cleaned up and be out on time.

As George walked to the first filter joint, he felt a knot forming in his stomach as he thought of kids drinking all of the milkshakes they were about to produce. He had already decided he would not have another milkshake for at least a month, in order to be absolutely sure that this batch was no longer being served at restaurants. After all, he did not know exactly which restaurants would receive this mix. As he picked up his wrench and approached the first pipe joint that contained a filter, he still could not help wondering if he should do or say something more.

NOTE: This case appeared in Paul F. Buller and Randall S. Schuler, *Managing Organizations and People*, South-Western © 2000.

Chapter 10 Workshop: The Power of Ethics*

This exercise will help you to better understand the concept of ethics and what it means to you.

1. Spend about 5 minutes individually answering the questions below.
2. Divide into groups of four to six members.
3. Have each group try to achieve consensus with answers to each of the four questions. For question 3, choose one scenario to highlight. You will have 20 to 40 minutes for this exercise, depending on the instructor.
4. Have groups share their answers with the whole class, after which the instructor will lead a discussion on ethics and its power in business.

Questions

1. In your own words, define the concept of ethics in one or two sentences.

2. If you were a manager, how would you motivate your employees to follow ethical behavior? Use no more than two sentences.
3. Describe a situation in which you were faced with an ethical dilemma. What was your decision and behavior? How did you decide to do that? Can you relate your decision to any concept in the chapter?
4. What do you think is a powerful ethical message for others? Where did you get it from? How will it influence your behavior in the future?

*Adapted by Dorothy Marcic from Allayne Barrilleaux Pizzolatto's "Ethical Management: An Exercise in Understanding Its Power," *Journal of Management Education* 17, no. 1 (February 1993), 107–109.

Notes

1. Susanna Voyle "Encouraging an Ageing Colossus," *Financial Times* (September 13, 2003), 3; Susanna Voyle, "Baker's Challenge on Joining Boots," *Financial Times* (September 13, 2003) 3; Mickey Clark, "The Bad News is Behind but Boots Still Faces Stiff Climb," *Evening Standard* (April 4, 2005), 62; and Patience Wheatcroft, "Back to Basics May Just Save Boots," *The Times* (March 2, 2005), 49.
2. Julia Boorstin, "Secret Recipe: J. M. Smucker," *Fortune* (January 12, 2004), 58–59.
3. Anita Raghavan, Kathryn Kranhold, and Alexei Barrionuevo, "Full Speed Ahead: How Enron Bosses Created a Culture of Pushing Limits," *The Wall Street Journal* (August 26, 2002), A1, A7.
4. Mark C. Bolino, William H. Turnley, and James M. Bloodgood, "Citizenship Behavior and the Creation of Social Capital in Organizations," *Academy of Management Review* 27, no. 4 (2002), 505–522; and Don Cohen and Laurence Prusak, *In Good Company: How Social Capital Makes Organizations Work* (Boston, Mass.: Harvard Business School Press, 2001), 3–4.
5. "*Fortune* 1,000 Ranked within Industries," *Fortune* (April 18, 2005), F–46–F–69; Erick Shonfeld, "eBay's Secret Ingredient," *Business 2.0* (March 2002), 52–58.
6. Joy Persaud, "Keep the Faithful," *People Management* (June 2003), 37–38.
7. W. Jack Duncan, "Organizational Culture: 'Getting a Fix' on an Elusive Concept," *Academy of Management Executive* 3 (1989), 229–236; Linda Smircich, "Concepts of Culture and Organizational Analysis," *Administrative Science Quarterly* 28 (1983), 339–358; and Andrew D. Brown and Ken Starkey, "The Effect of Organizational Culture on Communication and Information," *Journal of Management Studies* 31, no. 6 (November 1994), 807–828.
8. Edgar H. Schein, "Organizational Culture," *American Psychologist* 45 (February 1990), 109–119.
9. James H. Higgins and Craig McAllaster, "Want Innovation? Then Use Cultural Artifacts That Support It," *Organizational Dynamics* 31, no. 1 (2002), 74–84.
10. Harrison M. Trice and Janice M. Beyer, "Studying Organizational Cultures through Rites and Ceremonials," *Academy of Management Review* 9 (1984), 653–669; Janice M. Beyer and Harrison M. Trice, "How an Organization's Rites Reveal Its Culture," *Organizational Dynamics* 15 (Spring 1987), 5–24; Steven P. Feldman, "Management in Context: An Essay on the Relevance of Culture to the Understanding of Organizational Change," *Journal of Management Studies* 23 (1986), 589–607; and Mary Jo Hatch, "The Dynamics of Organizational Culture," *Academy of Management Review* 18 (1993), 657–693.
11. This discussion is based on Edgar H. Schein, *Organizational Culture and Leadership*, 2d ed. (Homewood, Ill.: Richard D. Irwin, 1992); and John P. Kotter and James L. Heskett, *Corporate Culture and Performance* (New York: Free Press, 1992).
12. Cheryl Dahle, "Four Tires, Free Beef," *Fast Company* (September 2003), 36.
13. Larry Mallak, "Understanding and Changing Your Organization's Culture," *Industrial Management* (March–April 2001), 18–24.
14. For a list of various elements that can be used to assess or interpret corporate culture, see "10 Key Cultural Elements," sidebar in Micah R. Kee, "Corporate Culture Makes a Fiscal

Difference," *Industrial Management* (November–December 2003), 16–20.

15. Charlotte B. Sutton, "Richness Hierarchy of the Cultural Network: The Communication of Corporate Values" (unpublished manuscript, Texas A&M University, 1985); and Terrence E. Deal and Allan A. Kennedy, "Culture: A New Look through Old Lenses," *Journal of Applied Behavioral Science* 19 (1983), 498–505.

16. Thomas C. Dandridge, "Symbols at Work" (working paper, School of Business, State University of New York at Albany, 1978), 1.

17. Jennifer A. Chatman and Sandra Eunyoung Cha, "Leading by Leveraging Culture," *California Management Review* 45, no. 4 (Summer 2003), 20–34.

18. Don Hellriegel and John W. Slocum, Jr., *Management*, 7th ed. (Cincinnati, Ohio: South-Western, 1996), 537.

19. Trice and Beyer, "Studying Organizational Cultures through Rites and Ceremonials."

20. Sutton, "Richness Hierarchy of the Cultural Network"; and Terrence E. Deal and Allan A. Kennedy, *Corporate Cultures: The Rites and Rituals of Corporate Life* (Reading, Mass.: Addison-Wesley, 1982).

21. Joanne Martin, *Organizational Culture: Mapping the Terrain* (Thousand Oaks, Calif.: Sage Publications, 2002), 71–72.

22. "FYI," *Inc.* (April 1991), 14.

23. Raghavan, Kranhold, and Barrionuevo, "Full Speed Ahead."

24. David Bank, "Fund Helps PeopleSoft Ex-Workers," *The Wall Street Journal* (April 4, 2005), B4.

25. Higgins and McAllaster, "Want Innovation?"

26. Jennifer A. Chatman and Sandra Eunyoung Cha, "Leading by Leveraging Culture," *California Management Review* 45, no. 4 (Summer 2003), 20–34; and Abby Ghobadian and Nicholas O'Regan, "The Link between Culture, Strategy, and Performance in Manufacturing SMEs," *Journal of General Management* 28, no. 1 (Autumn 2002), 16–34.

27. James R. Detert, Roger G. Schroeder, and John J. Mauriel, "A Framework for Linking Culture and Improvement Initiatives in Organizations," *Academy of Management Review* 25, no. 4 (2000), 850–863.

28. Based on Daniel R. Denison, *Corporate Culture and Organizational Effectiveness* (New York: Wiley, 1990), 11–15; Daniel R. Denison and Aneil K. Mishra, "Toward a Theory of Organizational Culture and Effectiveness," *Organization Science* 6, no. 2 (March–April 1995), 204–223; R. Hooijberg and F. Petrock, "On Cultural Change: Using the Competing Values Framework to Help Leaders Execute a Transformational Strategy," *Human Resource Management* 32 (1993), 29–50; and R. E. Quinn, *Beyond Rational Management: Mastering the Paradoxes and Competing Demands of High Performance* (San Francisco: Jossey-Bass, 1988).

29. Steve Lohr, "Big Blue's Big Bet: Less Tech, More Touch," *The New York Times* (January 25, 2004), Sec. 3, 1.

30. Melanie Warner, "Confessions of a Control Freak," *Fortune* (September 4, 2000), 130–140.

31. Cora Daniels, "J.C. Penney Dresses Up," *Fortune* (June 9, 2003), 127–130.

32. Matthew Boyle, "The Wegmans Way, " *Fortune* (January 24, 2005), 62–68.

33. Rekha Balu, "Pacific Edge Projects Itself," *Fast Company* (October 2000), 371–381.

34. Bernard Arogyaswamy and Charles M. Byles, "Organizational Culture: Internal and External Fits," *Journal of Management* 13 (1987), 647–659.

35. Chatman and Cha, "Leading by Leveraging Culture."

36. Patrick J. Sauer, "Open-Door Management," *Inc.* (June 2003), 44.

37. Paul R. Lawrence and Jay W. Lorsch, *Organization and Environment* (Homewood, Ill.: Irwin, 1969).

38. Scott Kirsner, "Designed for Innovation," *Fast Company* (November 1998), 54, 56.

39. Chatman and Cha, "Leading by Leveraging Culture"; Jeff Rosenthal and Mary Ann Masarech, "High-Performance Cultures: How Values Can Drive Business Results," *Journal of Organizational Excellence* (Spring 2003), 3–18.

40. Ghobadian and O'Regan, "The Link between Culture, Strategy and Performance"; G. G. Gordon and N. DiTomaso, "Predicting Corporate Performance from Organisational Culture," *Journal of Management Studies* 29, no. 6 (1992), 783–798; and G. A. Marcoulides and R. H. Heck, "Organizational Culture and Performance: Proposing and Testing a Model," *Organization Science* 4 (1993), 209–225.

41. Micah Kee, "Corporate Culture Makes a Fiscal Difference."

42. Tressie Wright Muldrow, Timothy Buckley, and Brigitte W. Schay, "Creating High-Performance Organizations in the Public Sector," *Human Resource Management* 41, no. 3 (Fall 2002), 341–354.

43. John P. Kotter and James L. Heskett, *Corporate Culture and Performance* (New York: The Free Press, 1992).

44. Gordon F. Shea, *Practical Ethics* (New York: American Management Association, 1988); Linda K. Treviño, "Ethical Decision Making in Organizations: A Person–Situation Interactionist Model," *Academy of Management Review* 11 (1986), 601–617; and Linda Klebe Treviño and Katherine A. Nelson, *Managing Business Ethics: Straight Talk about How to Do It Right*, 2nd ed. (New York: John Wiley & Sons, Inc., 1999).

45. Thanks to Susan H. Taft, Kent State University, and Judith White, University of Redlands, for this overview of the sources of individual ethics.

46. Dawn-Marie Driscoll, "Don't Confuse Legal and Ethical Standards," *Business Ethics* (July–August 1996), 44.

47. LaRue Tone Hosmer, *The Ethics of Management*, 2d ed. (Homewood, Ill.: Irwin, 1991).

48. Geanne Rosenberg, "Truth and Consequences," *Working Woman* (July–August 1998), 79–80.

49. N. Craig Smith, "Corporate Social Responsibility: Whether or How?" *California Management Review* 45, no. 4 (Summer 2003), 52–76; and Eugene W. Szwajkowski, "The Myths and Realities of Research on Organizational Misconduct," in James E. Post, ed., *Research in Corporate Social Performance and Policy*, vol. 9 (Greenwich, Conn.: JAI Press, 1986), 103–122.

50. Some of these incidents are from Hosmer, *The Ethics of Management*.

51. Linda K. Treviño and Katherine A. Nelson, *Managing Business Ethics: Straight Talk about How to Do It Right* (New York: John Wiley & Sons, Inc., 1995), 4.

52. Curtis C. Verschoor and Elizabeth A. Murphy, "The Financial Performance of Large U.S. Firms and Those with Global Prominence: How Do the Best Corporate Citizens Rate?" *Business and Society Review* 107, no. 2 (Fall 2002), 371–381; Homer H. Johnson, "Does It Pay to Be Good? Social Responsibility and Financial Performance," *Business Horizons* (November–December 2003), 34–40; Quentin R. Skrabec, "Playing By the Rules: Why Ethics Are Profitable," *Business Horizons* (September–October 2003), 15–18; Marc Gunther, "Tree Huggers, Soy Lovers, and Profits," *Fortune* (June 23, 2003), 98–104; Dale Kurschner, "5 Ways Ethical Business Creates Fatter Profits," *Business Ethics* (March–April 1996), 20–23. Also see various studies reported in Lori Ioannou, "Corporate America's Social Conscience," *Fortune*, special advertising section (May 26, 2003), S1–S10.

53. Verschoor and Murphy, "The Financial Performance of Large U.S. Firms."

54. Gretchen Morgenson, "Shares of Corporate Nice Guys Can Finish First," *The New York Times* (April 27, 2003), Section 3, 1.

55. Daniel W. Greening and Daniel B. Turban, "Corporate Social Performance as a Competitive Advantage in Attracting a Quality Workforce," *Business and Society* 39, no. 3 (September 2000), 254.

56. Christopher Marquis, "Doing Well and Doing Good," *The New York Times* (July 13, 2003), Section 3, 2; and Joseph Pereira, "Career Journal: Doing Good and Doing Well at Timberland," *The Wall Street Journal* (September 9, 2003), B1.

57. "The Socially Correct Corporate Business," segment in Leslie Holstrom and Simon Brady, "The Changing Face of Global Business," *Fortune*, special advertising section (July 24, 2000), S1–S38.

58. Carol Hymowitz, "CEOs Must Work Hard to Maintain Faith in the Corner Office" (In the Lead column), *The Wall Street Journal* (July 9, 2002), B1.

59. Linda Klebe Treviño, "A Cultural Perspective on Changing and Developing Organizational Ethics," in Richard Woodman and William Pasmore, eds., *Research and Organizational Change and Development*, vol. 4 (Greenwich, Conn.: JAI Press, 1990); and Lynn Sharp Paine, "Managing for Organizational Integrity," *Harvard Business Review* (March/April 1994), 106–117.

60. James Weber, "Exploring the Relationship between Personal Values and Moral Reasoning," *Human Relations* 46 (1993), 435–463.

61. L. Kohlberg, "Moral Stages and Moralization: The Cognitive-Developmental Approach," in T. Likona, ed., *Moral Development and Behavior: Theory, Research, and Social Issues* (New York: Holt, Rinehart & Winston, 1976).

62. Hosmer, *The Ethics of Management*.

63. Kevin Kelly, "My Slithery Rivals," *FSB* (February 2005), 27–28.

64. John A. Byrne with Mike France and Wendy Zellner, "The Environment Was Ripe for Abuse," *BusinessWeek* (February 25, 2002), 118–120.

65. Jennifer Bresnahan, "For Goodness Sake," *CIO Enterprise*, Section 2 (June 15, 1999), 54–62.

66. David M. Messick and Max H. Bazerman, "Ethical Leadership and the Psychology of Decision Making," *Sloan Management Review* (Winter 1996), 9–22; Dawn-Marie Driscoll, "Don't Confuse Legal and Ethical Standards," *Business Ethics* (July–August 1996), 44; and Max B. E. Clarkson, "A Stakeholder Framework for Analyzing and Evaluating Corporate Social Performance," *Academy of Management Review* 20, no. 1 (1995), 92–117.

67. Roger Parloff, "Is Fat the Next Tobacco?" *Fortune* (February 3, 2003), 51–54.

68. Gwen Kinkead, "In the Future, People Like Me Will Go to Jail," *Fortune* (May 24, 1999), 190–200.

69. *Corporate Ethics: A Prime Business Asset* (New York: The Business Round Table, February 1988).

70. Andrew W. Singer, "The Ultimate Ethics Test," *Across the Board* (March 1992), 19–22; Ronald B. Morgan, "Self and Co-Worker Perceptions of Ethics and Their Relationships to Leadership and Salary," *Academy of Management Journal* 36, no. 1 (February 1993), 200–214; and Joseph L. Badaracco, Jr., and Allen P. Webb, "Business Ethics: A View from the Trenches," *California Management Review* 37, no. 2 (Winter 1995), 8–28.

71. This discussion is based on Robert J. House, Andre Delbecq, and Toon W. Taris, "Value Based Leadership: An Integrated Theory and an Empirical Test" (working paper).

72. Treviño and Nelson, *Managing Business Ethics*, 201.

73. Michael Barrier, "Doing the Right Thing," *Nation's Business* (March 1998), 33–38.

74. Mitchell Pacelle, "Citigroup CEO Makes 'Value' a Key Focus," *The Wall Street Journal* (October 1, 2004), C1.

75. Thomas J. Peters and Robert H. Waterman, Jr., *In Search of Excellence* (New York: Harper & Row, 1982).

76. Karl E. Weick, "Cognitive Processes in Organizations," in B. M. Staw, ed., *Research in Organizations*, vol. 1 (Greenwich, Conn.: JAI Press, 1979), 42.

77. Richard Osborne, "Kingston's Family Values," *Industry Week* (August 13, 2001), 51–54.

78. Alan Yuspeh, "Do the Right Thing," *CIO* (August 1, 2000), 56–58.

79. Information in Amy Zipkin, "Getting Religion on Corporate Ethics," *The New York Times* (October 18, 2000), C1, C10; and *http://www.eoa.org*, accessed April 20, 2005.

80. Treviño and Nelson, *Managing Business Ethics*, 212.

81. Beverly Geber, "The Right and Wrong of Ethics Offices," *Training* (October 1995), 102–118.

82. Janet P. Near and Marcia P. Miceli, "Effective Whistle-Blowing," *Academy of Management Review* 20, no. 3 (1995), 679–708.

83. Richard P. Nielsen, "Changing Unethical Organizational Behavior," *Academy of Management Executive* 3 (1989), 123–130.

84. Jene G. James, "Whistle-Blowing: Its Moral Justification," in Peter Madsen and Jay M. Shafritz, eds., *Essentials of Business Ethics* (New York: Meridian Books, 1990), 160–190; and Janet P. Near, Terry Morehead Dworkin, and Marcia P. Miceli, "Explaining the Whistle-Blowing Process: Suggestions from Power Theory and Justice Theory," *Organization Science* 4 (1993), 393–411.

85. Steven L. Schooner, "Badge of Courage," *Government Executive* (August 2002), 65.

86. Linda Klebe Treviño, Gary R. Weaver, David G. Gibson, and Barbara Ley Toffler, "Managing Ethics and Legal Compli-

ance: What Works and What Hurts?" *California Management Review* 41, no. 2 (Winter 1999), 131–151.

87. "Setting the Standard," Lockheed Martin's Web site, *http://www.lockheedmartin.com/exeth/html/code/code.html*, accessed August 7, 2001.

88. Carl Anderson, "Values-Based Management," *Academy of Management Executive* 11, no. 4 (1997), 25–46.

89. "Citigroup Begins Implementing 5-Point Ethics Program," *Dow Jones Newswires*, March 1, 2005, *http://online.wsj.com*.

90. Ronald E. Berenbeim, *Corporate Ethics Practices* (New York: The Conference Board, 1992).

91. James Weber, "Institutionalizing Ethics into Business Organizations: A Model and Research Agenda," *Business Ethics Quarterly* 3 (1993), 419–436.

92. Landon Thomas Jr. "On Wall Street, a Rise in Dismissals over Ethics," *The New York Times* (March 25, 2005), *http://www.nytimes.com*.

93. Mark Henricks, "Ethics in Action," *Management Review* (January 1995), 53–55; Dorothy Marcic, *Management and the Wisdom of Love* (San Francisco: Jossey-Bass, 1997); and Beverly Geber, "The Right and Wrong of Ethics Offices," *Training* (October 1995), 102–118.

94. Susan J. Harrington, "What Corporate America Is Teaching about Ethics," *Academy of Management Executive* 5 (1991), 21–30.

95. Marc Gunther, "Money and Morals at GE," *Fortune* (November 15, 2004), 176–182.

96. Richard W. Judy and Carol D'Amico, *Workforce 2020: Work and Workers in the 21st Century* (Indianapolis, Ind.: Hudson Institute, 1997).

97. Jerry G. Kreuze, Zahida Luqmani, and Mushtaq Luqmani, "Shades of Gray," *Internal Auditor* (April 2001), 48.

98. David Scheer, "For Your Eyes Only; Europe's New High-Tech Role: Playing Privacy Cop to the World," *The Wall Street Journal* (October 10, 2003), A1, A16.

99. S. C. Schneider, "National vs. Corporate Culture: Implications for Human Resource Management," *Human Resource Management* (Summer 1988), 239.

100. Carl F. Fey and Daniel R. Denison, "Organizational Culture and Effectiveness: Can American Theory Be Applied in Russia?" *Organization Science* 14, no. 6 (November–December 2003), 686–706.

101. Terence Jackson, "Cultural Values and Management Ethics: A 10-Nation Study," *Human Relations* 54, no. 10 (2001), 1267–1302.

102. Gail Dutton, "Building a Global Brain," *Management Review* (May 1999), 34–38.

103. Ibid.

104. Homer H. Johnson, "Corporate Social Audits—This Time Around," *Business Horizons* (May–June 2001), 29–36.

105. Cassandra Kegler , "Holding Herself Accountable," *Working Woman* (May 2001), 13; Louisa Wah, "Treading the Sacred Ground," *Management Review* (July–August 1998), 18–22.

11

Innovation and Change

Innovate or Perish: The Strategic Role of Change
Incremental versus Radical Change • Strategic Types of Change

Elements for Successful Change

Technology Change
The Ambidextrous Approach • Techniques for Encouraging Technology Change

New Products and Services
New Product Success Rate • Reasons for New Product Success • Horizontal Coordination
Model • Achieving Competitive Advantage: The Need for Speed

Strategy and Structure Change
The Dual-Core Approach • Organization Design for Implementing Administrative Change

Culture Change
Forces for Culture Change • Organization Development Culture Change Interventions

Strategies for Implementing Change
Leadership for Change • Barriers to Change • Techniques for Implementation

Summary and Interpretation

A Look Inside

Toyota Motor Corporation

In auto manufacturing, Japanese companies rule, and one manufacturer outshines them all. Toyota increasingly dominates the global auto market, pushing ever closer to its goal of overtaking General Motors (GM) as the world's number 1 automaker. The basis of Toyota's supremacy lies primarily in its steady stream of technological and product innovation. Toyota executives created the doctrine of *kaizen*, or continuous improvement, and the company applies it relentlessly. Toyota hands the responsibility for continuous improvement to every employee. People on the shop floor can get cash rewards for searching out production glitches and finding ways to solve them.

Although thinking big can be important, Toyota knows that sweating the details is just as critical for driving innovation. Consider this: Several years ago, Toyota made a small change to its production lines by using a single master brace to hold automobile frames in place as they were welded, instead of the dozens of braces used in a standard auto factory. It seemed almost insignificant in the context of the company's complex manufacturing system, yet it was a radical manufacturing innovation. That one change, referred to now as the Global Body Line system, slashed 75 percent off the cost of retrofitting a production line and made it possible for Toyota to produce different car and truck models on a single line. The result has been billions of dollars in annual cost savings.

For developing new models, Toyota applies the concept of *obeya*, which literally means "big room." To make sure all the critical factors are considered from the beginning, product development teams made up of manufacturing and product engineers, designers, marketers, and suppliers hold regular face-to-face brainstorming sessions. New software programs, including the product life cycle management software discussed in Chapter 8, also make it possible for these cross-functional teams to collaborate digitally, viewing product design changes and associated costs. That way, if a designer makes a change that conflicts with manufacturing's needs or a supplier's capability, it can be noted and adjusted immediately. This collaborative process created Toyota's sturdy small truck, the Hilux, which is sold mostly in developing countries and is favored by oil companies and other organizations working in areas where a pickup breakdown can mean life or death. A new version of the Hilux is key to Toyota's strategy of overtaking GM by capturing 15 percent of the world auto market by 2010.[1]

Today, every company must change and innovate to survive. New discoveries and inventions quickly replace standard ways of doing things. Organizations like Toyota, Microsoft, Nokia, and Procter & Gamble are searching for any innovation edge they can find. Some companies, like 3M, the maker of Post-it Notes, Thinsulate insulation, Scotch-Brite scouring pads, and thousands of other products, are known for innovation. 3M's culture supports a risk-taking and entrepreneurial spirit that keeps it bubbling over with new ideas and new products. However, many large, established companies have a hard time being entrepreneurial and continually look for ways to encourage change and innovation to keep pace with changes in the external environment.

The pace of change is revealed in the fact that the parents of today's college-age students grew up without debit cards, video on demand, iPods, laser checkout systems, cellular phones, TiVo, instant messaging, and the Internet. The idea of communicating instantly with people around the world was unimaginable to many people as recently as a decade ago.

■ Purpose of This Chapter

This chapter will explore how organizations change and how managers direct the innovation and change process. The next section describes the difference between incremental and radical change, the four types of change—technology, product, structure, people—occurring in organizations, and how to manage change successfully. The organization structure and management approach for facilitating each type of change is then discussed. Management techniques for influencing both the creation and implementation of change are also covered.

Innovate or Perish: The Strategic Role of Change

If there is one theme or lesson that emerges from previous chapters, it is that organizations must run fast to keep up with changes taking place all around them. Large organizations must find ways to act like small, flexible organizations. Manufacturing firms need to reach out for new, flexible manufacturing technology and service firms for new information technology (IT). Today's organizations must poise themselves to innovate and change, not only to prosper but merely to survive in a world of increased competition.[2] As illustrated in Exhibit 11.1, a number of environmental forces drive this need for major organizational change. Powerful forces associated with advancing technology, international economic integration, the maturing of domestic markets, and the shift to capitalism in formerly communist regions have brought about a globalized economy that affects every business, from the largest to the smallest, creating more threats as well as more opportunities. To recognize and manage the threats and take advantage of the opportunities, today's companies are undergoing dramatic changes in all areas of their operations.

As we have seen in previous chapters, many organizations are responding to global forces by adopting self-directed teams and horizontal structures that enhance communication and collaboration, streamlining supply and distribution channels, and overcoming barriers of time and place through IT and e-business. Others become involved in joint ventures or consortia to exploit opportunities and extend operations or markets internationally. Some adopt structural innovations such as the virtual network approach to focus on their core competencies while outside specialists handle other activities. In addition, today's organizations face a need for dramatic strategic and cultural change and for rapid and continuous innovations in technology, services, products, and processes.

Change, rather than stability, is the norm today. Whereas change once occurred incrementally and infrequently, today it is dramatic and constant. A key element of the success of companies such as 3M Corporation, Starbucks Coffee, and eBay has been their passion for creating change.

■ Incremental versus Radical Change

The changes used to adapt to the environment can be evaluated according to scope—that is, the extent to which changes are incremental or radical for the organization.[3] As summarized in Exhibit 11.2, **incremental change** represents a series of

EXHIBIT 11.1
Forces Driving the Need for Major Organizational Change
Source: Based on John P. Kotter, *The New Rules: How to Succeed in Today's Post-Corporate World* (New York: The Free Press, 1995).

continual progressions that maintain the organization's general equilibrium and often affect only one organizational part. **Radical change**, by contrast, breaks the frame of reference for the organization, often transforming the entire organization. For example, an incremental change is the implementation of sales teams in the marketing department, whereas a radical change is shifting the entire organization from a vertical to a horizontal structure, with all employees who work on specific core processes brought together in teams rather than being separated into functional departments such as marketing, finance, production, and so forth. Although bold, transforming change gets a lot of attention and can be powerful for an organization, recent research indicates that incremental change—the constant implementation of small ideas, such as at Toyota—more often results in a sustainable competitive advantage. At the Danish subsidiary of textile manufacturer Milliken & Co., for example, a machine supplier discovered that his company's looms were running four times faster and producing more varied products than the engineers believed was possible. The advances came via the implementation of hundreds of small changes suggested by the textile maker's front-line employees.[4] The search engine company Google, based in Mountain View, California, also thrives on a culture that encourages continuous incremental change, as described in the Leading by Design box.

EXHIBIT 11.2
Incremental versus Radical Change
Source: Based on Alan D. Meyer, James B. Goes, and Geoffrey R. Brooks, "Organizations in Disequilibrium: Environmental Jolts and Industry Revolutions," in George Huber and William H. Glick, eds., *Organizational Change and Redesign* (New York: Oxford University Press, 1992), 66–111; and Harry S. Dent, Jr., "Growth through New Product Development," *Small Business Reports* (November 1990), 30–40.

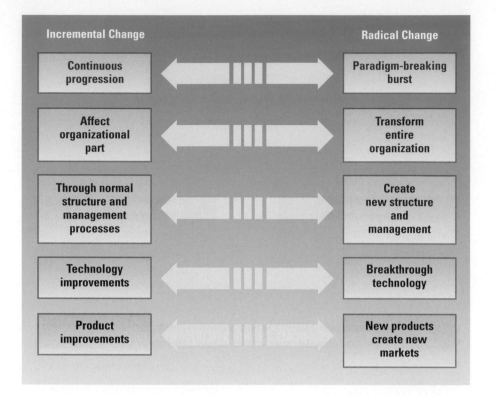

For the most part, incremental change occurs through the established structure and management processes, and it may include technology improvements—such as the introduction of flexible manufacturing systems—or product improvements—such as Procter & Gamble's addition to Tide detergent of cleaning agents that protect colors and fabrics. Radical change involves the creation of a new structure and new management processes. The technology is likely to be breakthrough, and new products thereby created will establish new markets.

As we have just discussed, there is a growing emphasis on the need for radical change because of today's turbulent, unpredictable environment.[5] One example of radical change is Apple Computer, which has transformed itself from a personal computer (PC) manufacturer to a dominant force in the digital entertainment business. By creating the iPod and iTunes online store, giving people easy, legal access to lots of songs, Apple has changed the rules of the game in consumer electronics, entertainment, and software.[6] Corporate transformations and turnarounds, such as Larry Bossidy's turnaround of Allied Signal or Lou Gerstner's transformation of IBM, are also considered radical change. Major turnarounds involve changes in all areas of the organization, including structure, management systems, culture, technology, and products or services.

■ Strategic Types of Change

Managers can focus on four types of change within organizations to achieve strategic advantage. These four types of change are summarized in Exhibit 11.3 as products and services, strategy and structure, culture, and technology. We touched on

Leading by Design

Google

Google quickly became the most popular search engine on the Internet with its smarter, faster approach to providing users with what they are looking for. But to maintain that success, managers knew the company needed to continuously innovate.

Product manager Marissa Mayer suggested that the company come up with new ideas the same way its search engine scours the Web. To provide users with the best Web search experience possible, Google searches far and wide, combing through billions of documents. Then it ranks the search results by relevance and zaps them to the user quickly. The idea search process works much the same way by casting a wide net across the organization. The process begins with an easy-to-use intranet. Even employees with limited technology expertise can quickly set up a page of ideas. "We never say, 'This group should innovate and the rest should just do their jobs,'" says Jonathan Rosenberg, vice president of product management. "Everyone spends a fraction of [the] day on R&D." The intranet has also tapped into more ideas from technologically savvy Google employees who may not be very vocal or assertive in meetings. Mayer says some engineers had lots of good ideas but were shy about putting them forth in open meetings. Now, employees can post their ideas on the intranet and see what kind of response they get.

Mayer searches the site each day to see which ideas are generating the most excitement and comments. Once a week, she sits down with a team to hash over the ideas and flesh out at least six or seven that can be fast-tracked into development. In addition to the internal search process, users continue to play a key role in innovation. Ten full-time employees read and respond to user e-mails and pass along ideas to project teams, who are constantly tweaking Google's service. Engineers work in teams of three and have the authority to make any changes that improve the quality of the user experience and get rid of anything that gets in the way. Moreover, Google allows any software developer to integrate its search engine into their own applications. The download is easy and the license is free. It sounds crazy to some businesses, but Google says it "turns the world into Google's development team."

Google's organic approach to innovation has been highly successful. Indeed, the company is no longer just a hugely successful search engine. Google has evolved into a software company that is emerging as a major threat to Microsoft's dominance. While Microsoft has been struggling to catch up in the game of search, Google has quietly been launching products such as desktop search; Gmail; software to manage, edit, and send digital photos; and programs for creating, editing, and posting documents. The idea that Google could one day marginalize Microsoft's operating system and bypass Windows applications is being taken seriously by Microsoft managers. Microsoft is ten times the size of Google and has plenty of cash with which to compete. But Microsoft leaders know that, for now, Google's innovation process gives it an edge. "Here Microsoft was spending $600 million a year in R&D for MSN, $1 billion a year for Office, and $1 billion a year for Windows, and Google [got] desktop search out before us," said a Microsoft executive. "It was a real wake-up call."

Source: Fara Warner, "How Google Searches Itself," *Fast Company* (July 2002), 50–52; Fred Vogelstein, "Search and Destroy," *Fortune* (May 2, 2005), 72–82; and Keith H. Hammonds, "How Google Grows…and Grows…and Grows," *Fast Company* (April 2003), 74.

overall leadership and organizational strategy in Chapter 2 and in the previous chapter on corporate culture. These factors provide an overall context within which the four types of change serve as a competitive wedge to achieve an advantage in the international environment. Each company has a unique configuration of products and services, strategy and structure, culture, and technologies that can be focused for maximum impact upon the company's chosen markets.[7]

Technology changes are changes in an organization's production process, including its knowledge and skill base, that enable distinctive competence. These changes are designed to make production more efficient or to produce greater volume. Changes in technology involve the techniques for making products or services.

Briefcase

As an organization manager, keep this guideline in mind:

Recognize that the four types of change are interdependent and that changes in one area often require changes in others.

EXHIBIT 11.3
The Four Types of Change Provide a Strategic Competitive Wedge
Source: Joseph E. McCann, "Design Principles for an Innovating Company," *Academy of Management Executive* 5 (May 1991), 76–93. Used by permission.

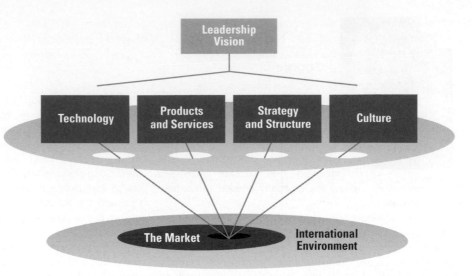

They include work methods, equipment, and workflow. For example, a technology change at UPS was the implementation of the DIAD (Delivery Information Acquisition Device). When a customer signs for a package on a computerized clipboard, the device automatically zaps the information to the Web site, where the sender can verify that the package has been delivered before the driver even gets back to the truck.[8]

Product and service changes pertain to the product or service outputs of an organization. New products include small adaptations of existing products or entirely new product lines. New products and services are normally designed to increase the market share or to develop new markets, customers, or clients. Toyota's Hilux truck is a new product designed to increase market share, whereas Apple's iPod is a new product that created a new market for the company. An example of a new service designed to reach new markets and customers is Starbucks' development of Hear Music Coffeehouses, where people can pick from hundreds of thousands of songs and make custom CDs at a dollar a tune.[9]

Strategy and structure changes pertain to the administrative domain in an organization. The administrative domain involves the supervision and management of the organization. These changes include changes in organization structure, strategic management, policies, reward systems, labor relations, coordination devices, management information and control systems, and accounting and budgeting systems. Structure and system changes are usually top-down, that is, mandated by top management, whereas product and technology changes may often come from the bottom up. A system change instituted by management in a university might be a new merit pay plan. Corporate downsizing and the shift to horizontal teams are other examples of top-down structure change.

Culture changes refer to changes in the values, attitudes, expectations, beliefs, abilities, and behavior of employees. Culture changes pertain to changes in how employees think; these are changes in mind-set rather than technology, structure, or products.

The four types of change in Exhibit 11.3 are interdependent—a change in one often means a change in another. A new product may require changes in the production technology, or a change in structure may require new employee skills. For example, when Shenandoah Life Insurance Company acquired new computer technology to process claims, the technology was not fully utilized until clerks were restructured into teams of five to seven members that were compatible with the technology. The structural change was an outgrowth of the technology change. Organizations are interdependent systems, and changing one part often has implications for other organization elements.

Elements for Successful Change

Regardless of the type or scope of change, there are identifiable stages of innovation, which generally occur as a sequence of events, though innovation stages may overlap.[10] In the research literature on innovation, **organizational change** is considered the adoption of a new idea or behavior by an organization.[11] **Organizational innovation**, in contrast, is the adoption of an idea or behavior that is new to the organization's industry, market, or general environment.[12] The first organization to introduce a new product is considered the innovator, and organizations that copy are considered to adopt changes. For purposes of managing change, however, the terms *innovation* and *change* will be used interchangeably because the **change process** within organizations tends to be identical whether a change is early or late with respect to other organizations in the environment. Innovations typically are assimilated into an organization through a series of steps or elements. Organization members first become aware of a possible innovation, evaluate its appropriateness, and then evaluate and choose the idea.[13] The required elements of successful change are summarized in Exhibit 11.4. For a change to be successfully implemented, managers must make sure each element occurs in the organization. If one of the elements is missing, the change process will fail.

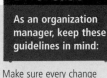

Briefcase

As an organization manager, keep these guidelines in mind:

Make sure every change undertaken has a definite need, idea, adoption decision, implementation strategy, and resources. Avoid failure by not proceeding until each element is accounted for.

1. *Ideas.* No company can remain competitive without new ideas; change is the outward expression of those ideas.[14] An idea is a new way of doing things. It may be a new product or service, a new management concept, or a new procedure for working together in the organization. Ideas can come from within or from outside the organization. Internal creativity is a dramatic element of organizational change. **Creativity** is the generation of novel ideas that may meet perceived needs or respond to opportunities. An employee at Boardroom Inc., a publisher of books and newsletters, came up with the idea of cutting the dimensions of the company's books by a quarter inch. Managers learned that the smaller size would reduce postal rates, and implementation of the idea led to annual savings of more than $500,000.[15] Some techniques for spurring internal creativity are to increase the diversity within the organization, make sure employees have plenty of opportunities to interact with people different from themselves, give employees time and freedom for experimentation, and support risk taking and making mistakes.[16] Eli Lilly & Co., the Indianapolis-based pharmaceutical company, holds "failure parties," to commemorate brilliant, efficient scientific work that nevertheless resulted in failure. The company's scientists are encouraged to take risks and look for alternative uses for failed drugs. Lilly's osteoporosis drug Evista was a failed contraceptive. Strattera, which treats attention deficit/hyperactivity disorder, had been unsuccessful as an antidepressant. The blockbuster impotence drug Viagra was originally developed to treat severe heart pain.[17]

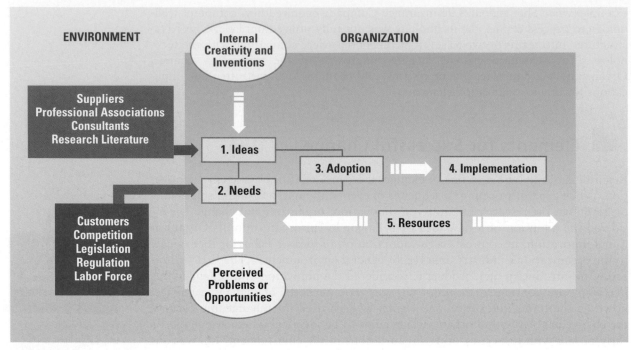

ENVIRONMENT   Internal Creativity and Inventions   **ORGANIZATION**

Suppliers
Professional Associations
Consultants
Research Literature

1. Ideas   3. Adoption   4. Implementation

2. Needs   5. Resources

Customers
Competition
Legislation
Regulation
Labor Force

Perceived Problems or Opportunities

EXHIBIT 11.4
*Sequence of Elements for
Successful Change*

2. *Need*. Ideas are generally not seriously considered unless there is a perceived need for change. A perceived need for change occurs when managers see a gap between actual performance and desired performance in the organization. Managers try to establish a sense of urgency so that others will understand the need for change. Sometimes a crisis provides an undoubted sense of urgency. In many cases, however, there is no crisis, so managers have to recognize a need and communicate it to others.[18] A study of innovativeness in industrial firms, for example, suggests that organizations that encourage close attention to customers and market conditions and support for entrepreneurial activity produce more ideas and are more innovative.[19] Jeffrey Immelt, the new CEO of General Electric (GE), is trying to create just those conditions at the sprawling industrial giant, which has grown in recent years largely through acquisition. By combining an emphasis on marketing, a renewed basic research effort, and a company-wide focus on learning and sharing ideas, Immelt is recharging GE into a house of technological innovation, calling for constant reinvention to generate more growth from internal operations.[20]

3. *Adoption*. Adoption occurs when decision makers choose to go ahead with a proposed idea. Key managers and employees need to be in agreement to support the change. For a major organizational change, the decision might require the signing of a legal document by the board of directors. For a small change, adoption might occur with informal approval by a middle manager.

4. *Implementation*. Implementation occurs when organization members actually use a new idea, technique, or behavior. Materials and equipment may have to be acquired, and workers may have to be trained to use the new idea. Implementation is a very important step because without it, previous steps are to no avail. Implementation of change is often the most difficult part of the change process. Until people use the new idea, no change has actually taken place.

5. *Resources*. Human energy and activity are required to bring about change. Change does not happen on its own; it requires time and resources, for both creating and implementing a new idea. Employees have to provide energy to see both the need and the idea to meet that need. Someone must develop a proposal and provide the time and effort to implement it. 3M has an unwritten but widely understood rule that its 8,300 researchers can spend up to 15 percent of their time working on any idea of their choosing, without management approval. Most innovations go beyond ordinary budget allocations and require special funding. At 3M, exceptionally promising ideas become "pacing programs" and receive high levels of funding for further development.[21] Some companies use task forces, as described in Chapter 3, to focus resources on a change. Others set up seed funds or venture funds that employees with promising ideas can tap into. At Eli Lilly, a "blue sky fund" pays researchers for working on projects that don't appear to make immediate commercial sense.[22]

One point about Exhibit 11.4 is especially important. Needs and ideas are listed simultaneously at the beginning of the change sequence. Either may occur first. Many organizations adopted the computer, for example, because it seemed a promising way to improve efficiency. The search for a vaccine against the AIDS virus, on the other hand, was stimulated by a severe need. Whether the need or the idea occurs first, for the change to be accomplished, each of the steps in Exhibit 11.4 must be completed.

Technology Change

In today's business world, any company that isn't continually developing, acquiring, or adapting new technology will likely be out of business in a few years. However, organizations face a contradiction when it comes to technology change, because the conditions that promote new ideas are not generally the best for implementing those ideas for routine production. An innovative organization is characterized by flexibility and empowered employees and the absence of rigid work rules.[23] As discussed earlier in this book, an organic, free-flowing organization is typically associated with change and is considered the best organization form for adapting to a chaotic environment.

The flexibility of an organic organization is attributed to people's freedom to be creative and introduce new ideas. Organic organizations encourage a bottom-up innovation process. Ideas bubble up from middle- and lower-level employees because they have the freedom to propose ideas and to experiment. A mechanistic structure, in contrast, stifles innovation with its emphasis on rules and regulations, but it is often the best structure for efficiently producing routine products. The challenge for managers is to create both organic and mechanistic conditions within the organization to achieve both innovation and efficiency. To attain both aspects of technological change, many organizations use the ambidextrous approach.

The Ambidextrous Approach

Recent thinking has refined the idea of organic versus mechanistic structures with respect to innovation creation versus innovation utilization. For example, sometimes an organic structure generates innovative ideas but is not the best structure for using those ideas.[24] In other words, the initiation and the utilization of change are

Briefcase

As an organization manager, keep these guidelines in mind:

Facilitate frequent changes in internal technology by adopting an organic organizational structure. Give technical personnel freedom to analyze problems and develop solutions or create a separate, organically structured department or venture group to conceive and propose new ideas.

EXHIBIT 11.5
*Division of Labor
in the Ambidextrous
Organization*

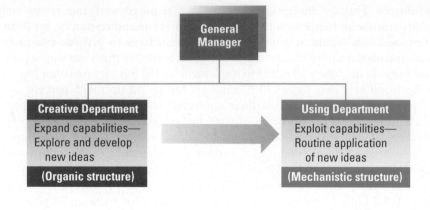

two distinct processes. Organic characteristics such as decentralization and employee freedom are excellent for initiating ideas; but these same conditions often make it hard to implement a change because employees are less likely to comply. Employees can ignore the innovation because of decentralization and a generally loose structure.

How does an organization solve this dilemma? One remedy is for the organization to use an **ambidextrous approach**—to incorporate structures and management processes that are appropriate to both the creation and the implementation of innovation.[25] Another way to think of the ambidextrous approach is to look at the organization design elements that are important for *exploring* new ideas versus the design elements that are most suitable for *exploiting* current capabilities. Exploration means encouraging creativity and developing new ideas, whereas exploitation means implementing those ideas to produce routine products. The organization can be designed to behave in an organic way for exploring new ideas and in a mechanistic way to exploit and use the ideas. Exhibit 11.5 illustrates how one department is structured organically to explore and develop new ideas and another department is structured mechanistically for routine implementation of innovations. Research has shown that organizations that use an ambidextrous approach by designing for both exploration and exploitation are significantly more successful in launching innovative new products or services.[26]

For example, a study of long-established Japanese companies such as Honda and Canon that have succeeded in breakthrough innovations found that these companies use an ambidextrous approach.[27] To develop ideas related to a new technology, the companies assign teams of young staff members who are not entrenched in the "old way of doing things" to work on the project. The teams are headed by an esteemed elder and are charged with doing whatever is needed to develop new ideas and products, even if it means breaking rules that are important in the larger organization for implementing the new ideas.

■ Techniques for Encouraging Technology Change

Some of the techniques used by companies to maintain an ambidextrous approach are switching structures, separate creative departments, venture teams, and corporate entrepreneurship.

Switching Structures. **Switching structures** means an organization creates an organic structure when such a structure is needed for the initiation of new ideas.[28] Some of the ways organizations have switched structures to achieve the ambidextrous approach are as follows:

- Philips Corporation, a building materials producer based in Ohio, each year creates up to 150 transient teams—made up of members from various departments—to develop ideas for improving Philips products and work methods. After five days of organic brainstorming and problem solving, the company reverts to a more mechanistic basis to implement the changes.[29]
- Gardetto's, a family-run snack-food business, sends small teams of workers to Eureka Ranch, where they may engage in a Nerf gun battle to set the tone for fun and freedom and then participate in brainstorming exercises with the idea of generating as many new ideas as possible by the end of the day. After 2½ days, the group returns to the regular organizational structure to put the best of the ideas into action.[30]
- The NUMMI plant, a Toyota subsidiary located in Fremont, California, creates a separate, organically organized, cross-functional subunit, called the Pilot Team, to design production processes for new car and truck models. When the model they are preparing moves into production, workers return to their regular jobs on the shop floor.[31]

Each of these organizations found creative ways to be ambidextrous, establishing organic conditions for developing new ideas in the midst of more mechanistic conditions for implementing and using those ideas.

Creative Departments. In many large organizations the initiation of innovation is assigned to separate **creative departments**.[32] Staff departments, such as research and development (R&D), engineering, design, and systems analysis, create changes for adoption in other departments. Departments that initiate change are organically structured to facilitate the generation of new ideas and techniques. Departments that use those innovations tend to have a mechanistic structure more suitable for efficient production.

One example of a creative department is the research lab at Oksuka Pharmaceutical Company. Although most big U.S. drug firms have switched to using robots and other high-tech tools to perform large-scale drug experiments, Japanese companies such as Oksuka are achieving success by continuing to emphasize human creativity. To get the kind of creative spirit that is willing to try new things and look for the unexpected, Oksuka's president Tatsuo Higuchi says its research labs "put a high value on weird people."[33] However, in the department that manufactures drugs, where routine and precision is important, a pharmaceutical company would prefer to have less unusual people who are comfortable following rules and standard procedures.

Another type of creative department is the **idea incubator**, an increasingly popular way to facilitate the development of new ideas within the organization. An idea incubator provides a safe harbor where ideas from employees throughout the organization can be developed without interference from company bureaucracy or politics.[34] The incubator gives people throughout the organization a place to go rather than having to shop a new idea all over the company and hope someone will pay attention. Companies as diverse as Boeing, Adobe Systems, Ziff-Davis, and United Parcel Service (UPS) are using incubators to support the development of creative ideas.

Venture Teams. Venture teams are a technique used to give free rein to creativity within organizations. Venture teams are often given a separate location and facilities so they are not constrained by organizational procedures. A venture team is like a small company within a large company. Numerous organizations have used the venture team concept to free creative people from the bureaucracy of a large corporation. At 3M, a program called *3M Acceleration* allows an employee with a promising idea for a new technology or product to recruit people from around the company to serve on a new venture team. 3M provides the space, funding, and freedom the team needs to fast-track the idea into a marketable product.[35] Most established companies that have successful Internet-based operations have set them up as venture teams so they have the freedom and authority to explore and develop the new technology. To establish its online news services, for example, *USA Today* gave the new unit a separate location and the freedom to establish its own distinctive management processes, hiring strategies, structure, and culture. At the same time, senior leaders at the online unit are tightly integrated with the print business to attain synergy and cross-unit collaboration.[36]

One type of venture team is called a *skunkworks*.[37] A **skunkworks** is a separate, small, informal, highly autonomous, and often secretive group that focuses on breakthrough ideas for the business. The original skunkworks was created by Lockheed Martin more than 50 years ago and is still in operation. The essence of a skunkworks is that highly talented people are given the time and freedom to let creativity reign.

A variation of the venture team concept is the **new-venture fund**, which provides financial resources for employees to develop new ideas, products, or businesses. In order to tap into its employees' entrepreneurial urges, Lockheed Martin allows workers to take up to 2 years' unpaid leave to explore a new idea, using company labs and equipment and paying company rates for health insurance. If the idea is successful, the corporation's venture fund invests about $250,000 in the start-up company. One successful start-up is Genase, which created an enzyme that "stonewashes" denim.[38]

Corporate Entrepreneurship. Corporate entrepreneurship attempts to develop an internal entrepreneurial spirit, philosophy, and structure that will produce a higher-than-average number of innovations. Corporate entrepreneurship may involve the use of creative departments and new venture teams, but it also attempts to release the creative energy of all employees in the organization. Managers can create systems and structures that encourage entrepreneurship. For example, at the giant oil company BP, top executives establish contracts with the heads of all BP's business units. Then, the unit managers are given free rein to deliver on the contract in whatever way they see fit, within clearly identified constraints.[39]

An important outcome of corporate entrepreneurship is to facilitate **idea champions**. These go by a variety of names, including *advocate*, *intrapreneur*, or *change agent*. Idea champions provide the time and energy to make things happen. They fight to overcome natural resistance to change and to convince others of the merit of a new idea.[40] Idea champions need not be within the organization. Some companies have found that fostering idea champions among regular customers can be a highly successful approach.[41] An example is Anglian Water, where every innovation project has a sponsor or champion who is a customer seeking a solution to a specific problem.[42] The importance of the idea champion is illustrated by a fascinating fact discovered by Texas Instruments (TI): When TI reviewed fifty successful and unsuccessful technical projects, it discovered that every failure was characterized by the absence of a volunteer champion. There was no one who passionately believed in the idea, who pushed the idea through every obstacle to make it work. TI took this finding so seriously that now its number-one criterion for approving new technical projects is the presence of a zealous champion.[43]

Idea champions usually come in two types. The **technical champion**, or *product champion*, is the person who generates or adopts and develops an idea for a technological innovation and is devoted to it, even to the extent of risking position or prestige. The **management champion** acts as a supporter and sponsor to shield and promote an idea within the organization.[44] The management champion sees the potential application and has the prestige and authority to get the idea a fair hearing and to allocate resources to it. Technical and management champions often work together because a technical idea will have a greater chance of success if a manager can be found to sponsor it. Numerous studies have identified the importance of idea champions as a factor in the success of new products.[45]

Companies encourage idea champions by providing freedom and slack time to creative people. Companies such as IBM, General Electric, and 3M allow employees to develop new technologies without company approval. Known as *bootlegging*, the unauthorized research often pays big dividends. As one IBM executive said, "We wink at it. It pays off. It's just amazing what a handful of dedicated people can do when they are really turned on."[46] W. L. Gore also relies on idea champions for successful innovation.

In Practice
W. L. Gore

W. L. Gore, a privately held company best known as the maker of Gore-Tex fabric, is so good at innovating that it has become a major player in areas as diverse as guitar strings, dental floss, fuel cells, and medical devices. Everyone at Gore is expected to become an idea champion at some time in their career with the company. Gore provides the environment for that to happen by letting employees figure out what they want to do.

Gore's employees, known as associates, don't have job titles or bosses. Rather than being assigned to tasks, people make commitments to work on projects where they think they can make the biggest contribution. That means employees tend to be "very passionate about what they're doing," says researcher Jeff Kolde. Kolde himself is an excellent example of an idea champion. Gore researchers had developed an improved kind of ionic membrane that separates positive and negative ions, but the company wasn't sure what to do with it. Kolde got excited about the potential use in the fuel cell industry and began sending out prototypes. The fuel cell industry got really excited too. W. L. Gore became the first commercial supplier of membrane-electron assemblies (MEAs), a critical technology for fuel cells. But Kolde first had to convince others that the project was worth their time and effort, no easy task in a new area like fuel cells. His passion for the project enabled him to recruit people from around the company, including two Ph.Ds.

Gore research associates get to spend 10 percent of their time as "dabble time," developing their own ideas. A senior colleague serves as a mentor and guide; if the idea is promising and the associate is passionate about it, the mentor becomes a management champion to make sure the project gets the attention and resources needed to pursue it. Gore has found that having associates recruit volunteers to work on projects turns out to be a pretty good indication of whether an innovation is likely to succeed.[47]

New Products and Services

Although the ideas just discussed are important to product and service as well as technology changes, other factors also need to be considered. In many ways, new products and services are a special case of innovation because they are used by customers outside the organization. Since new products are designed for sale in the environment, uncertainty about the suitability and success of an innovation is very high.

New Product Success Rate

Research has explored the enormous uncertainty associated with the development and sale of new products.[48] To understand what this uncertainty can mean to organizations, just consider such flops as RCA's VideoDisc player, which lost an estimated $500 million, or Time Incorporated's *TV-Cable Week*, which lost $47 million. Pfizer Inc. invested more than $70 million in the development and testing of an anti-aging drug before it flopped in the final testing stages.[49] Developing and producing products that fail is a part of business in all industries. Packaged food companies spend billions on R&D for new products such as Kraft's Rip-Ums, a pull-apart cheese snack; P.B. Slices, Kennedy Foods' answer to making peanut butter easy; or ConAgra's Squeez 'n Go portable pudding, but hundreds of new food products fail each year. Organizations take the risk because product innovation is one of the most important ways companies adapt to changes in markets, technologies, and competition.[50]

Experts estimate that about 80 percent of new products fail upon introduction and another 10 percent disappear within 5 years. Considering that it can cost $50 million or more to successfully launch a new product, new product development is a risky, high-stakes game for organizations. Nevertheless, more than 25,000 new products appeared in one year alone, including more than 5,000 new toys.[51]

A survey some years ago examined 200 projects in nineteen chemical, drug, electronics, and petroleum laboratories to learn about success rates.[52] To be successful, the new product had to pass three stages of development: technical completion, commercialization, and market success. The findings about success rates are given in Exhibit 11.6. On the average, only 57 percent of all projects undertaken in the R&D laboratories achieved technical objectives, which means all technical problems were solved and the projects moved on to production. Of all projects that were started, less than one third (31 percent) were fully marketed and commercialized. Several projects failed at this stage because production estimates or test market results were unfavorable.

Finally, only 12 percent of all projects originally undertaken achieved economic success. Most of the commercialized products did not earn sufficient returns to cover the cost of development and production. This means that only about one project in eight returned a profit to the company.

Reasons for New Product Success

The next question to be answered by research was, Why are some products more successful than others? Why did products such as Frappuccino and Mountain Dew Code Red succeed in the marketplace while Miller Clear Beer and Frito-Lay's

	Probability
Technical completion (technical objectives achieved)	.57
Commercialization (full-scale marketing)	.31
Market success (earns economic return)	.12

Source: Based on Edwin Mansfield, J. Rapaport, J. Schnee, S. Wagner, and M. Hamburger, *Research and Innovation in Modern Corporations* (New York: Norton, 1971), 57.

EXHIBIT 11.6
Probability of New Product Success

lemonade failed? Further studies indicated that innovation success is related to collaboration between technical and marketing departments. Successful new products and services seem to be technologically sound and also carefully tailored to customer needs.[53] A study called Project SAPPHO examined seventeen pairs of new product innovations, with one success and one failure in each pair, and concluded the following:

1. Successful innovating companies had a much better understanding of customer needs and paid much more attention to marketing.
2. Successful innovating companies made more effective use of outside technology and outside advice, even though they did more work in-house.
3. Top management support in the successful innovating companies was from people who were more senior and had greater authority.

Thus there is a distinct pattern of tailoring innovations to customer needs, making effective use of technology, and having influential top managers support the project. These ideas taken together indicate that the effective design for new product innovation is associated with horizontal coordination across departments.

■ Horizontal Coordination Model

The organization design for achieving new product innovation involves three components—departmental specialization, boundary spanning, and horizontal coordination. These components are similar to the horizontal coordination mechanisms discussed in Chapter 3, such as teams, task forces, and project managers, and the differentiation and integration ideas discussed in Chapter 4. Exhibit 11.7 illustrates these components in the **horizontal coordination model**.

Specialization. The key departments in new product development are R&D, marketing, and production. The specialization component means that the personnel in all three of these departments are highly competent at their own tasks. The three departments are differentiated from each other and have skills, goals, and attitudes appropriate for their specialized functions.

Boundary Spanning. This component means each department involved with new products has excellent linkage with relevant sectors in the external environment. R&D personnel are linked to professional associations and to colleagues in other R&D departments. They are aware of recent scientific developments. Marketing personnel are closely linked to customer needs. They listen to what customers have to say, and they analyze competitor products and suggestions by distributors. For

Briefcase

As an organization manager, keep this guideline in mind:

Encourage marketing, research, and production departments to develop linkages to each other and to their environments when new products or services are needed.

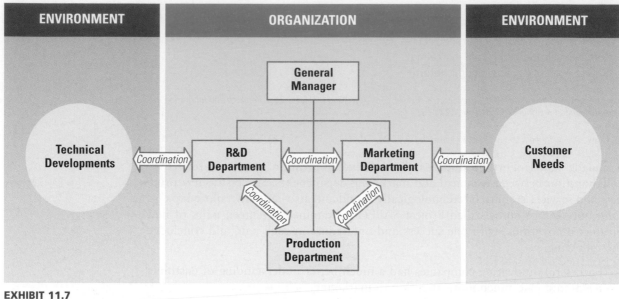

EXHIBIT 11.7
Horizontal Coordination Model for New Product Innovations

example, Kimberly-Clark had amazing success with Huggies Pull-Ups because marketing researchers worked closely with customers in their own homes and recognized the emotional appeal of pull-on diapers for toddlers. By the time competitors caught on, Kimberly-Clark was selling $400 million worth of Huggies annually.[54]

Horizontal Coordination. This component means that technical, marketing, and production people share ideas and information. Research people inform marketing of new technical developments to learn whether the developments are applicable to customers. Marketing people provide customer complaints and information to R&D to use in the design of new products. People from both R&D and marketing coordinate with production because new products have to fit within production capabilities so costs are not exorbitant. The decision to launch a new product is ultimately a joint decision among all three departments. Horizontal coordination, using mechanisms such as cross-functional teams, increases both the amount and the variety of information for new product development, enabling the design of products that meet customer needs and circumventing manufacturing and marketing problems.[55]

Recall the chapter-opening example of Toyota, which uses a product development technique called *obeya*. The idea behind *obeya* is to change the way people think about product innovation and development by changing how they share information. "There are no taboos in *obeya*," explains Takeshi Yoshida, chief engineer for the 2003 Corolla. "Everyone in that room is an expert. They all have a part to play in building the car."[56] Consumer products firm Procter & Gamble is also taking a bold new approach to innovation.

A few years ago, Procter & Gamble (P&G) was a stodgy consumer products company selling successful but tired brands such as Tide, Crest, and Pampers. Today, the 169-year-old company has reemerged as a master brand-builder and a hot growth company, thanks largely to a new approach to innovation initiated by CEO A. G. Lafley. Between 2002 and 2004, P&G raised its new product hit rate from 70 percent to 90 percent. Products such as Olay Regenerist, Swiffer dusters, and Mr. Clean AutoDry have made Procter & Gamble look like a nimble start-up company.

There are several key elements to Lafley's innovation machine. One is a stronger connection with consumers. Rather than relying on focus groups, P&G marketers now spend time with people in their homes, watching how they wash their dishes or clean their floors and asking questions about their habits and frustrations with household chores or child rearing. Another key is getting people from different functions and divisions to exchange ideas and collaborate. Lafley conducts half-day "innovation reviews" in each unit once a year and evaluates how well marketers and researchers are sharing ideas. Besides opportunities for face-to-face meetings and internal trade shows, an internal Web site called InnovationNet connects employees from all divisions and departments worldwide. R&D people located in twenty technical facilities in nine countries can post a question such as "How can you clean without rinsing?" and get suggestions from employees across the company and around the world. The technologies that enable Mr. Clean AutoDry, a power gun that sprays your car clean and dry, came from P&G's Cascade division, which knew how to reduce water spots on dishes, and the PuR water filter unit, which had a technology for reducing minerals in water.

The most revolutionary part of Lafley's approach is encouraging collaboration with outside people and other firms, even competitors. For example, Glad Press 'n Seal was developed collaboratively with Clorox, which competes fiercely with P&G in floor mops and water purification products. Lafley is pushing for half of P&G's innovations to be derived from outside sources. "Inventors are evenly distributed in the population," he says, "and we're as likely to find invention in a garage as in our labs."[57]

Research findings show that collaboration with other firms and with customers can be a significant source of product innovation, and can even stimulate stronger internal coordination. Cooperating with external parties requires the involvement of people from different areas of the company, which in turn necessitates that organizations set up stronger internal coordination mechanisms.[58]

Companies such as Procter & Gamble, W. L. Gore, and Boeing routinely turn to customers and other organizations for advice. Gore worked with physicians to develop its thoracic graft, and with hunters to create Supprescent, a fabric intended to block human odors.[59] During development of new planes such as the Boeing 787, Boeing's engineers work closely with flight attendants, pilots, engineers from major airlines, suppliers, and even banks that finance aircraft purchases, to make sure the plane is designed for maximum functionality and compatibility with suppliers' capabilities and the airlines' needs.[60]

These companies use the concept of horizontal coordination to achieve competitive advantage. Famous innovation failures—such as McDonald's Arch Deluxe or the baby-food company Gerber's Singles for Adults—usually violate the horizontal linkage model. Employees fail to connect with customer needs and market forces or internal departments fail to adequately share needs and coordinate with one another.

Recent research has confirmed a connection between effective boundary spanning that keeps the organization in touch with market forces, smooth coordination among departments, and successful product development.[61]

■ Achieving Competitive Advantage: The Need for Speed

The rapid development of new products is becoming a major strategic weapon in the shifting international marketplace.[62] To remain competitive, companies are learning to develop ideas into new products and services incredibly fast. Whether the approach is called the *horizontal linkage model, concurrent engineering, companies without walls, the parallel approach,* or *simultaneous coupling of departments*, the point is the same—get people working together simultaneously on a project rather than in sequence. Many companies are learning to sprint to market with new products.

Time-based competition means delivering products and services faster than competitors, giving companies a competitive edge. For example, Russell Stover got a line of low-carb candies, called Net Carb, on store shelves within 3 months after perfecting the recipe, rather than the 12 months it usually takes the company to get a new product to market. This gave Russell Stover an early lead over other national candy companies and allowed it to establish a strong foothold in the new market for low-carb snacks. Some companies use what are called *fast cycle teams* as a way to support highly important projects and deliver products and services faster than competitors. A fast cycle team is a multifunctional, and sometimes multinational, team that works under stringent timelines and is provided with high levels of company resources and empowerment to accomplish an accelerated product development project.[63] By using the Internet to collaborate on new designs among various functional departments and with suppliers, teams at Moen take a new kitchen or bath faucet from drawing board to store shelf in only 16 months. The time savings means Moen's teams can work on three times as many projects as previously and introduce up to fifteen new designs a year for today's fashion-conscious consumers.[64] Similarly, using virtual reality, collaborative software, and a horizontal, integrated design process, GM has cut its time from concept to production on a new vehicle model down to a mere 18 months. Not so long ago, it took GM an astounding 4 years to complete that process. The new approach to product development has given GM a speed advantage over competitors in the design and production of hot new car models that capitalize on fashion trends and capture the market for younger car buyers.[65]

Another critical issue is designing products that can compete on a global scale and successfully marketing those products internationally. Companies such as Quaker Oats, Häagen Dazs, and Levi's are trying to improve horizontal communication and collaboration across geographical regions, recognizing that they can pick up winning product ideas from customers in other countries. A new Häagen Dazs flavor, *dulce de leche*, developed primarily for sale in Argentina, has quickly become a favorite in the United States.[66]

Many new product development teams today are global teams because organizations have to develop products that will meet diverse needs of consumers all over the world.[67] GM's collaborative, computer-based product development system enables engineers and suppliers from all over the world to work together on a project. Ford Motor Company also uses an intranet and global teleconferencing to link car design teams around the world into a single unified group.[68] When companies enter the arena of intense international competition, horizontal coordination across countries is essential to new product development.

Strategy and Structure Change

The preceding discussion focused on new production processes and products, which are based in the technology of an organization. The expertise for such innovation lies within the technical core and professional staff groups, such as research and engineering. This section turns to an examination of strategy and structure changes.

All organizations need to make changes in their strategies, structures, and administrative procedures from time to time. In the past, when the environment was relatively stable, most organizations focused on small, incremental changes to solve immediate problems or take advantage of new opportunities. However, over the past decade, companies throughout the world have faced the need to make radical changes in strategy, structure, and management processes to adapt to new competitive demands.[69] Many organizations are cutting out layers of management and decentralizing decision making. There is a strong shift toward more horizontal structures, with teams of front-line workers empowered to make decisions and solve problems on their own. Some companies are breaking totally away from traditional organization forms and shifting toward virtual network strategies and structures. Numerous companies are reorganizing and shifting their strategies as the expansion of e-business changes the rules. Global competition and rapid technological change will likely lead to even greater strategy-structure realignments over the next decade.

These types of changes are the responsibility of the organization's top managers, and the overall process of change is typically different from the process for innovation in technology or new products.

The Dual-Core Approach

The **dual-core approach** to organizational change compares administrative and technical changes. Administrative changes pertain to the design and structure of the organization itself, including restructuring, downsizing, teams, control systems, information systems, and departmental grouping. Research into administrative change suggests two things. First, administrative changes occur less frequently than do technical changes. Second, administrative changes occur in response to different environmental sectors and follow a different internal process than do technology-based changes.[70] The dual-core approach to organizational change identifies the unique processes associated with administrative change.[71]

Organizations—schools, hospitals, city governments, welfare agencies, government bureaucracies, and many business firms—can be conceptualized as having two cores: a *technical core* and an *administrative core*. Each core has its own employees, tasks, and environmental domain. Innovation can originate in either core.

The administrative core is above the technical core in the hierarchy. The responsibility of the administrative core includes the structure, control, and coordination of the organization itself and concerns the environmental sectors of government, financial resources, economic conditions, human resources, and competitors. The technical core is concerned with the transformation of raw materials into

Briefcase

As an organization manager, keep this guideline in mind:

Facilitate changes in strategy and structure by adopting a top-down approach. Use a mechanistic structure when the organization needs to adopt frequent administrative changes in a top-down fashion.

EXHIBIT 11.8
Dual-Core Approach to Organization Change

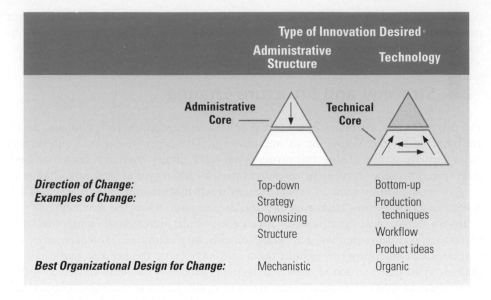

organizational products and services and involves the environmental sectors of customers and technology.[72]

The point of the dual-core approach is that many organizations—especially not-for-profit and government organizations—must adopt frequent administrative changes and need to be structured differently from organizations that rely on frequent technical and product changes for competitive advantage.

■ Organization Design for Implementing Administrative Change

The findings from research comparing administrative and technical change suggest that a mechanistic organization structure is appropriate for frequent administrative changes, including changes in goals, strategy, structure, control systems, and personnel.[73] Administrative changes in policy, regulations, or control systems are more critical than technical changes in many government organizations that are bureaucratically structured. Organizations that successfully adopt many administrative changes often have a larger administrative ratio, are larger in size, and are centralized and formalized compared with organizations that adopt many technical changes.[74] The reason is the top-down implementation of changes in response to changes in the government, financial, or legal sectors of the environment. If an organization has an organic structure, lower-level employees have more freedom and autonomy and, hence, may resist top-down initiatives.

The innovation approaches associated with administrative versus technical change are summarized in Exhibit 11.8. Technical change, such as changes in production techniques and innovation technology for new products, is facilitated by an organic structure, which allows ideas to bubble upward from lower- and middle-level employees. Organizations that must adopt frequent administrative changes, in contrast, tend to use a top-down process and a mechanistic structure. For example, policy changes, such as the adoption of no-smoking policies, sexual harassment policies, or new safety procedures, are facilitated by a top-down approach. Downsizing and restructuring are nearly always managed top down, such as when the president of Oracle Corp. split the sales force into two teams (one focused on selling database software and the other on selling applications), cut out two levels of management, and placed himself directly in charge of U.S. sales.[75]

For organizations that must adopt frequent administrative changes, a mechanistic structure may be appropriate. Research into civil service reform found that the implementation of administrative innovation was extremely difficult in organizations that had an organic technical core. The professional employees in a decentralized agency could resist civil service changes. By contrast, organizations that were considered more bureaucratic in the sense of high formalization and centralization adopted administrative changes readily.[76]

What about business organizations that are normally technologically innovative in bottom-up fashion but suddenly face a crisis and need to reorganize? Or a technically innovative, high-tech firm that must reorganize frequently to accommodate changes in production technology or the environment? Technically innovative firms may suddenly have to restructure, reduce the number of employees, alter pay systems, disband teams, or form a new division.[77] The answer is to use a top-down change process. The authority for strategy and structure change lies with top management, who should initiate and implement the new strategy and structure to meet environmental circumstances. Employee input may be sought, but top managers have the responsibility to direct the change. When Ed Breen took over as Chairman and CEO of Tyco, he knew that strong, swift top-down change was needed to help the organization weather a crisis and get back on track.

The name Tyco ranks right up there with Enron, WorldCom, and HealthSouth as a model of corporate greed and corrupt leadership. But rather than seeing disaster, Ed Breen saw opportunity. He knew that Tyco had "all the attributes of what could be a great company." That's why he left his cozy job as president and heir apparent of Motorola to take on the challenge of transforming the scandal-ridden Tyco.

Breen set about to remake Tyco's management and governance from the ground up. He set up an internal audit staff and a confidential hotline where employees could report anything they perceive as wrongdoing. In the first year, Tyco conducted over 1,000 investigations, a quarter of which resulted in disciplinary action or changes in policies and procedures.

Breen's next major change was to clean up top and middle management, firing 290 of Tyco's highest-ranking managers within the first few months. Because it was next to impossible to determine who knew what about the former wrongdoing at Tyco, Breen wanted to start with a clean slate. He also changed the bonus policy, making it clear that no bonuses would be paid until the numbers on which they were based were clearly explained and justified. Other top-down changes included centralizing purchasing for Tyco's five divisions, revising IT procedures, and reducing the number of suppliers the company deals with.

The strong top-down change at Tyco has had positive results. Employees and investors are feeling better about the company, as evidenced in rising morale and a surging share price. Now the challenge for Breen is to develop the stuctures and systems that can enable Tyco to innovate in technologies and products and get growing again.[78]

In Practice

Tyco International

Throughout his management career, Breen has shown that he is a master at getting companies out of tough spots through carefully planned and firmly implemented top-down changes. Some top-down changes, particularly those related to restructuring and downsizing, can be painful for employees, so top managers should move quickly and authoritatively to make them as humane as possible.[79] A study of successful corporate transformations, which frequently involve painful changes, found that managers followed a fast, focused approach. When top managers spread difficult changes such as downsizing over a long time period, employee morale suffers and the change is much less likely to lead to positive outcomes.[80]

Top managers should also remember that top-down change means initiation of the idea occurs at upper levels and is implemented downward. It does not mean that lower-level employees are not educated about the change or allowed to participate in it.

Culture Change

Organizations are made up of people and their relationships with one another. Changes in strategy, structure, technologies, and products do not happen on their own, and changes in any of these areas involve changes in people as well. Employees must learn how to use new technologies, or market new products, or work effectively in a team-based structure. Sometimes achieving a new way of thinking requires a focused change in the underlying corporate cultural values and norms. Changing corporate culture fundamentally shifts how work is done in an organization and generally leads to renewed commitment and empowerment of employees and a stronger bond between the company and its customers.[81]

Forces for Culture Change

A number of recent trends have contributed to a need for cultural makeovers at companies such as Electronic Data Systems (EDS), Alberto-Culver, Marriott, and IBM. Some of the primary changes requiring a shift in culture and employee mindset are reengineering and the move toward horizontal forms of organizing, greater employee and customer diversity, and the shift to the learning organization.

Reengineering and Horizontal Organizing. As described in Chapter 3, reengineering involves redesigning a vertical organization along its horizontal workflows. This changes the way managers and employees need to think about how work is done and requires greater focus on employee empowerment, collaboration, information sharing, and meeting customer needs. In his book *The Reengineering Revolution*, Michael Hammer refers to people change as "the most perplexing, annoying, distressing, and confusing part" of reengineering.[82] Managers may confront powerful emotions as employees react to rapid, massive change with fear or anger.

In the horizontal organization, managers and front-line workers need to understand and embrace the concepts of teamwork, empowerment, and cooperation. Managers shift their thinking to view workers as colleagues rather than cogs in a wheel; and workers learn to accept not only greater freedom and power, but also the higher level of responsibility that comes with them. Mutual trust, risk taking, and tolerance for mistakes become key cultural values in the horizontal organization.

Diversity. Diversity is a fact of life for today's organizations, and many are implementing new recruiting, mentoring, and promotion methods, diversity training programs, tough policies regarding sexual harassment and racial discrimination, and new benefits programs that respond to a more diverse workforce. However, if the underlying culture of an organization does not change, all other efforts to support diversity will fail. Managers at Mitsubishi are still struggling with this reality. Even though the company settled a sexual harassment lawsuit filed by women at its Normal, Illinois, plant, established a zero tolerance policy, and fired workers who were guilty of blatant sexual or racial harassment, employees said the work environment at the plant remained deeply hostile to women and minorities. Incidents of blatant harassment declined, but women and minority workers still felt threatened and powerless because the culture that allowed the harassment to occur had not changed.[83]

The Learning Organization. The learning organization involves breaking down boundaries both within and between organizations to create companies that are focused on knowledge sharing and continuous learning. Recall from Chapter 1 that shifting to a learning organization involves changes in a number of areas. For example, structures become horizontal and involve empowered teams working directly with customers. There are few rules and procedures for performing tasks, and knowledge and control of tasks are located with employees rather than supervisors. Information is broadly shared rather than being concentrated with top managers. In addition, employees, customers, suppliers, and partners all play a role in determining the organization's strategic direction. Clearly, all of these changes require new values, new attitudes, and new ways of thinking and working together. A learning organization cannot exist without a culture that supports openness, equality, adaptability, and employee participation.

One organization that has undergone culture change to support greater participation, collaboration, and adaptability is X-Rite, a color technology company with headquarters in Grandville, Michigan.

In Practice
X-Rite Inc.

X-Rite provides products that measure and track color data, helping their customers ensure color accuracy in products as diverse as consumer packages, paint, outdoor furniture, or dental restorations. Founded in 1958, X-Rite enjoyed years of success by leveraging superior engineering ability and innovation. But by the 1990s, the company had become unfocused, out of touch with customers, and change resistant. New product development had slowed to a near standstill; sales had fallen sharply; and employee morale was in the pits. When Michael Ferrara joined X-Rite as president in 2001, he knew he needed to do something to get X-Rite moving forward again.

He started by assessing the organization according to a culture survey questionnaire, which evaluated the organization's adaptability, focus on a clear mission, consistency in meeting customer needs, and employee involvement. The results were even worse than Ferrara expected. "It was like someone telling you your baby's ugly," he said. The disappointment and hurt soon turned to action. Ferrara started by refocusing everyone on a clear direction. Over the years, X-Rite had gotten involved in so many businesses that no one knew what they were supposed to be doing. Ferrara issued a company-wide message that said simply, "We are in the color business," signalling that X-Rite would focus its energies on providing hardware and software to support color accuracy. He also established a theme for the new culture: *Play to Win*. Those two steps, though simple, had a powerful impact on employees.

A harder step was breaking down the boundaries in the company. X-Rite was so territorial that departmental managers weren't just not working together; they were actually working against one another. Constant blaming and criticism was the rule. Ferrara demanded that the finger-pointing stop. He gathered managers in a brainstorming session to set new "rules of engagement" for how people would interact with one another. Managers also hammered out a new product-development process that required cooperation among engineering, manufacturing, procurement, marketing, and other departments. The physical layout was changed so that all members of the management team were located in the same area, encouraging communication and collaboration. Managers who weren't committed to the new culture were let go, and some managers and employees were reassigned to new positions. To get everyone more focused on the customer, managers scheduled brown bag lunches called "Meet Your Customers." People spent time working directly with internal and external customers and had a chance to get involved in developing proposals to win new business.

When Ferrara and his top management team did a second culture survey, they found significant improvements, particularly in the areas of coordination and integration, customer focus, and clear strategic direction. In 2003, X-Rite introduced twenty-two new products, an increase of 250 percent from 2001, when the culture change initiative was begun. Moreover, the Play to Win culture has significantly improved morale. "I love my job. I love my customers," said one employee. "I actually look forward to being here."[84]

■ Organization Development Culture Change Interventions

Briefcase

As an organization manager, keep this guideline in mind:

Work with organization development consultants for large-scale changes in the attitudes, values, or skills of employees, and when shifting to a learning organization culture.

Managers use a variety of approaches and techniques for changing corporate culture, some of which we discussed in Chapter 10. One method of quickly bringing about culture change is known as **organization development** (OD), which focuses on the human and social aspects of the organization as a way to improve the organization's ability to adapt and solve problems. OD emphasizes the values of human development, fairness, openness, freedom from coercion, and individual autonomy that allows workers to perform the job as they see fit, within reasonable organizational constraints.[85] In the 1970s, OD evolved as a separate field that applied the behavioral sciences in a process of planned organization-wide change, with the goal of increasing organizational effectiveness. Today, the concept has been enlarged to examine how people and groups can change to a learning organization culture in a complex and turbulent environment. Organization development is not a step-by-step procedure to solve a specific problem but a process of fundamental change in the human and social systems of the organization, including organizational culture.[86]

OD uses knowledge and techniques from the behavioral sciences to create a learning environment through increased trust, open confrontation of problems, employee empowerment and participation, knowledge and information sharing, the design of meaningful work, cooperation and collaboration between groups, and the full use of human potential.

OD interventions involve training of specific groups or of everyone in the organization. For OD interventions to be successful, senior management in the organization must see the need for OD and provide enthusiastic support for the change.

Techniques used by many organizations for improving people skills through OD include the following.

Large Group Intervention. Most early OD activities involved small groups and focused on incremental change. However, in recent years, there has been growing interest in the application of OD techniques to large group settings, which are more attuned to bringing about radical or transformational change in organizations operating in complex environments.[87] The **large group intervention** approach[88] brings together participants from all parts of the organization—often including key stakeholders from outside the organization as well—in an off-site setting to discuss problems or opportunities and plan for change. A large group intervention might involve 50 to 500 people and last for several days. The off-site setting limits interference and distractions, enabling participants to focus on new ways of doing things. General Electric's "Work Out" program, an ongoing process of solving problems, learning, and improving, begins with large-scale off-site meetings that get people talking across functional, hierarchical, and organizational boundaries. Hourly and salaried workers come together from many different parts of the organization and join with customers and suppliers to discuss and solve specific problems.[89] The process forces a rapid analysis of ideas, the creation of solutions, and the development of a plan for implementation. Over time, Work Out creates a culture where ideas are rapidly translated into action and positive business results.[90]

Team Building. **Team building** promotes the idea that people who work together can work as a team. A work team can be brought together to discuss conflicts, goals, the decision-making process, communication, creativity, and leadership. The team can then plan to overcome problems and improve results. Team-building activities are also used in many companies to train task forces, committees, and new product development groups. These activities enhance communication and collaboration and strengthen the cohesiveness of organizational groups and teams.

Interdepartmental Activities. Representatives from different departments are brought together in a mutual location to expose problems or conflicts, diagnose the causes, and plan improvements in communication and coordination. This type of intervention has been applied to union–management conflict, headquarters–field office conflict, interdepartmental conflict, and mergers.[91] A box-storage business, which stores archived records for other companies, found interdepartmental meetings to be a key means of building a culture based on team spirit and customer focus. People from different departments met for hour-long sessions every 2 weeks and shared their problems, told stories about their successes, and talked about things they'd observed in the company. The meetings helped people understand the problems faced in other departments and see how everyone depended on each other to do their jobs successfully.[92]

One current area in which OD can provide significant value is in spurring culture change toward valuing diversity.[93] In addition, today's organizations are continuously adapting to environmental uncertainty and increasing global competition, and OD interventions can respond to these new realities as companies strive to create greater capability for learning and growth.[94]

Strategies for Implementing Change

Managers and employees can think of inventive ways to improve the organization's technology, creative ideas for new products and services, fresh approaches to strategies and structures, or ideas for fostering adaptive cultural values, but until the ideas are put into action, they are worthless to the organization. Implementation is the most crucial part of the change process, but it is also the most difficult. Change is frequently disruptive and uncomfortable for managers as well as employees. The Book Mark

Book Mark 11.0 (HAVE YOU READ THIS BOOK?)

The Change Monster: The Human Forces That Fuel or Foil Corporate Transformation and Change
By Jeanie Daniel Duck

The change monster is lurking in every organization, just waiting to gobble up unsuspecting managers who are striving to implement new strategies, accomplish re-organizations, or complete mergers. Jeanie Daniel Duck uses the term *change monster* in her book by the same name to refer to all the complex human emotions and social dynamics that emerge during major change efforts. Many managers, she says, simplify or ignore the people issues of change, a sure prescription for failure.

MASTERING THE CHANGE CURVE
Duck says that major organizational change typically follows a change curve—a roller-coaster ride that brings out myriad unexpected and conflicting emotions.

- *Stagnation*. This is the period during which the organization has lost direction or is moving in the wrong direction. The change monster is generally quiet—people feel comfortable and safe. However, it is the job of managers to recognize stagnation and create a sense of urgency for change.
- *Preparation*. In this stage, Duck says, "the change monster is rudely awakened from its hibernating slumber and stretches itself, causing all kinds of emotional tremors." This is the period during which change leaders define and refine their vision for change and begin to involve others in the change process. Emotions range from excitement and hopefulness to anxiety and betrayal. Everyone is jittery and distracted.
- *Implementation*. This phase is the actual tactical start of the change journey, and as such is the longest and typically the most painful. There is an explosion of emotions, both positive and negative, in the organization. During this phase, employees often feel in limbo. Everything has

changed, and yet the changes haven't been solidified. Many people feel uncertain about their ability to function in the new environment.

- *Determination*. During this period, Duck says, the change monster is roaming the hallways, ready to do its worst damage. Many managers think the change has been accomplished and turn their attention elsewhere right at the time when reinforcement is most needed. People often exhibit *retroactive resistance*, a sort of change fatigue and a desire to revert to the old familiar patterns.
- *Fruition*. Ahhhh…the time when all the hard work pays off at last. In this phase, the changes have become a part of the accepted way of doing things. The whole organization may feel new and different. Employees have gained confidence and are optimistic and energized. The change monster has been corralled.

COMING FULL CIRCLE
It is the goal of every change initiative to reach fruition. But Duck cautions that a new period of stagnation is just around the corner. When an organization accomplishes a major change, people need to take time to bask in the success. But managers must be on guard that basking doesn't turn to napping. Managers can teach their organizations how to perpetually adapt and help them muster the will to do so. "When an organization sees itself as a hearty band of monster slayers, change becomes a challenge they're ready to meet rather than a threat that signals retreat."

The Change Monster: The Human Forces That Fuel or Foil Corporate Transformation and Change, by Jeanie Daniel Duck, is published by Crown Business.

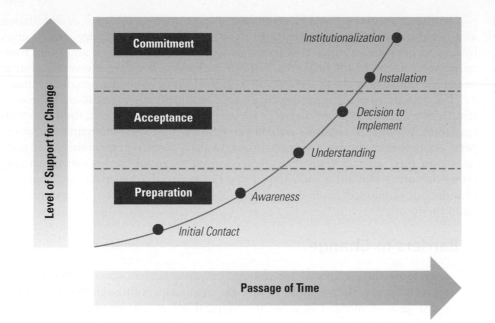

EXHIBIT 11.9
*Stages of Commitment
to Change*
Source: Adapted from Daryl R.
Conner, *Managing at the
Speed of Change* (New York:
Villard Books, 1992), 148.
Used with permission.

explores how managers can improve change implementation by understanding the emotional aspects of the change process. Change is complex, dynamic, and messy, and implementation requires strong and persistent leadership. In this final section, we briefly discuss the role of leadership for change, some reasons for resistance to change, and techniques that managers can use to overcome resistance and successfully implement change.

Leadership for Change

The need for change within organizations and the need for leaders who can successfully manage change continues to grow. The leadership style of the top executive sets the tone for how effective the organization is at continuous adaptation and innovation. One style of leadership, referred to as *transformational leadership*, is particularly suited for bringing about change. Top leaders who use a transformational leadership style enhance organizational innovation both directly, by creating a compelling vision, and indirectly, by creating an environment that supports exploration, experimentation, risk taking, and sharing of ideas.[95]

Successful change can happen only when employees are willing to devote the time and energy needed to reach new goals, as well as endure possible stress and hardship. Having a clearly communicated vision that embodies flexibility and openness to new ideas, methods, and styles sets the stage for a change-oriented organization and helps employees cope with the chaos and tension associated with change.[96] Leaders also build organization-wide commitment by taking employees through three stages of the change commitment process, illustrated in Exhibit 11.9.[97] In the first stage, *preparation*, employees hear about the change through memos, meetings, speeches, or personal contact and become aware that the change will directly affect their work. In the second stage, *acceptance*, leaders should help employees develop an understanding of the full impact of the change and the positive outcomes of making the change. When employees perceive the change as positive, the decision to implement is made. In the third stage, the true *commitment* process begins. The commitment stage involves the steps of installation and institutionalization. Installation is a trial process for the change, which gives leaders an opportunity to discuss problems and employee concerns and build commitment to action. In the final step, *institutionalization*, employees view the change not as something new but as a normal and integral part of organizational operations.

The pressures on organizations to change will probably increase over the next few decades. Leaders must develop the personal qualities, skills, and methods needed to help their companies remain competitive. Indeed, some management experts argue that to survive the upheaval of the early twenty-first century, managers must turn their organizations into *change leaders* by using the present to actually create the future—breaking industry rules, creating new market space, and routinely abandoning outmoded products, services, and processes to free up resources to build the future.[98]

■ Barriers to Change

Visionary leadership is crucial for change; however, leaders should expect to encounter resistance as they attempt to take the organization through the three stages of the change commitment process. It is natural for people to resist change, and many barriers to change exist at the individual and organizational levels.[99]

1. *Excessive focus on costs*. Management may possess the mind-set that costs are all-important and may fail to appreciate the importance of a change that is not focused on costs—for example, a change to increase employee motivation or customer satisfaction.
2. *Failure to perceive benefits*. Any significant change will produce both positive and negative reactions. Education may be needed to help managers and employees perceive more positive than negative aspects of the change. In addition, if the organization's reward system discourages risk taking, a change process might falter because employees think that the risk of making the change is too high.
3. *Lack of coordination and cooperation*. Organizational fragmentation and conflict often result from the lack of coordination for change implementation. Moreover, in the case of new technology, the old and new systems must be compatible.
4. *Uncertainty avoidance*. At the individual level, many employees fear the uncertainty associated with change. Constant communication is needed so that employees know what is going on and understand how it affects their jobs.
5. *Fear of loss*. Managers and employees may fear the loss of power and status—or even their jobs. In these cases, implementation should be careful and incremental, and all employees should be involved as closely as possible in the change process.

Implementation can typically be designed to overcome many of the organizational and individual barriers to change.

■ Techniques for Implementation

Top leaders articulate the vision and set the tone, but managers and employees throughout the organization are involved in the process of change. A number of techniques can be used to successfully implement change.[100]

1. *Establish a sense of urgency for change.* Once managers identify a true need for change, they need to thaw resistance by creating a sense of urgency that change is really needed. Organizational crises can help unfreeze employees and make them willing to invest the time and energy needed to adopt new techniques or procedures. For example, American Airlines has lost billions since 2001, and top managers have undertaken a massive change effort to try to save the company. Although the changes will be painful, the crisis has made employees more receptive to them because otherwise the organization is not likely to survive.[101] However, in many cases there is no public crisis and managers have to make others aware of the need for change.

2. *Establish a coalition to guide the change.* Change managers have to build a coalition of people throughout the organization who have enough power and influence to steer the change process. For implementation to be successful, there must be a shared commitment to the need and possibilities for change. Top management support is crucial for any major change project, and lack of top management support is one of the most frequent causes of implementation failure.[102] In addition, the coalition should involve lower-level supervisors and middle managers from across the organization. For smaller changes, the support of influential managers in the affected departments is important.

3. *Create a vision and strategy for change.* Leaders who have taken their companies through major successful transformations often have one thing in common: They focus on formulating and articulating a compelling vision and strategy that will guide the change process. Even for a small change, a vision of how the future can be better and strategies to get there are important motivations for change.

4. *Find an idea that fits the need.* Finding the right idea often involves search procedures—talking with other managers, assigning a task force to investigate the problem, sending out a request to suppliers, or asking creative people within the organization to develop a solution. The creation of a new idea requires organic conditions. This is a good opportunity to encourage employee participation, because employees need the freedom to think about and explore new options.[103] ALLTEL set up a program called Team Focus to gather input from all employees. In twenty group meetings over a period of 2 weeks, managers gathered 2,800 suggestions, which they then narrowed down to 170 critical action items that specifically addressed problems that were affecting employee morale and performance.[104]

5. *Develop plans to overcome resistance to change.* Many good ideas are never used because managers failed to anticipate or prepare for resistance to change by consumers, employees, or other managers. No matter how impressive the performance characteristics of an innovation, its implementation will conflict with some interests and jeopardize some alliances in the organization. To increase the chance of successful implementation, management must acknowledge the conflict, threats, and potential losses perceived by employees. Several strategies can be used by managers to overcome the resistance problem:

   - *Alignment with needs and goals of users.* The best strategy for overcoming resistance is to make sure change meets a real need. Employees in R&D often come up with great ideas that solve nonexistent problems. This happens because initiators fail to consult with the intended users. Resistance can be frustrating for managers, but moderate resistance to change is good for an organization. Resistance provides a barrier to frivolous changes and to

Briefcase

As an organization manager, keep these guidelines in mind:

Lead employees through the three stages of commitment to change—preparation, acceptance, and commitment—and use techniques to achieve successful implementation. These include obtaining top management support, implementing the change in a series of steps, assigning change teams or idea champions, and overcoming resistance by actively communicating with workers and encouraging their participation in the change process.

change for the sake of change. The process of overcoming resistance to change normally requires that the change be good for its users.

- *Communication and training.* Communication means informing users about the need for change and the consequences of a proposed change, preventing rumors, misunderstanding, and resentment. In one study of change efforts, the most commonly cited reason for failure was that employees learned of the change from outsiders. Top managers concentrated on communicating with the public and shareholders but failed to communicate with the people who would be most intimately involved with and most affected by the change—their own employees.[105] Open communication often gives management an opportunity to explain what steps will be taken to ensure that the change will have no adverse consequences for employees. Training is also needed to help employees understand and cope with their role in the change process.

- *An environment that affords psychological safety.* Psychological safety means that people feel a sense of confidence that they will not be embarrassed or rejected by others in the organization. People need to feel secure and capable of making the changes that are asked of them.[106] Change requires that people be willing to take risks and do things differently, but many people are fearful of trying something new if they think they might be embarrassed by mistakes or failure. Managers support psychological safety by creating a climate of trust and mutual respect in the organization. "Not being afraid someone is laughing at you helps you take genuine risks," says Andy Law, one of the founders of St. Luke's, an advertising agency based in London.[107]

- *Participation and involvement.* Early and extensive participation in a change should be part of implementation. Participation gives those involved a sense of control over the change activity. They understand it better, and they become committed to successful implementation. One study of the implementation and adoption of technology systems at two companies showed a much smoother implementation process at the company that introduced the new technology using a participatory approach.[108] The team-building and large group intervention activities described earlier can be effective ways to involve employees in a change process.

- *Forcing and coercion.* As a last resort, managers may overcome resistance by threatening employees with the loss of jobs or promotions or by firing or transferring them. In other words, management power is used to overwhelm resistance. In most cases, this approach is not advisable because it leaves people angry at change managers, and the change may be sabotaged. However, this technique may be needed when speed is essential, such as when the organization faces a crisis. It may also be required for needed administrative changes that flow from the top down, such as downsizing the workforce.[109]

6. *Create change teams.* Throughout this chapter the need for resources and energy to make change happen has been discussed. Separate creative departments, new-venture groups, and ad hoc teams or task forces are ways to focus energy on both creation and implementation. A separate department has the freedom to create a new technology that fits a genuine need. A task force can be created to see that implementation is completed. The task force can be responsible for communication, involvement of users, training, and other activities needed for change.

7. *Foster idea champions.* One of the most effective weapons in the battle for change is the idea champion. The most effective champion is a volunteer champion who is deeply committed to a new idea. The idea champion sees that all technical activities are correct and complete. An additional champion, such as a manager sponsor, may also be needed to persuade people about implementation, even using coercion if necessary.

Summary and Interpretation

Organizations face a dilemma. Managers prefer to organize day-to-day activities in a predictable, routine manner. However, change—not stability—is the natural order of things in today's global environment. Thus, organizations need to build in change as well as stability, to facilitate innovation as well as efficiency.

Most change in organizations is incremental, but there is a growing emphasis on the need for radical change. Four types of change—technology, products and services, strategy and structure, and culture—may give an organization a competitive edge, and managers can make certain each of the necessary ingredients for change is present.

For technical innovation, which is of concern to most organizations, an organic structure that encourages employee autonomy works best because it encourages a bottom-up flow of ideas. Other approaches are to establish a separate department charged with creating new technical ideas, establish venture teams or idea incubators, and encourage idea champions. New products and services generally require cooperation among several departments, so horizontal linkage is an essential part of the innovation process.

For changes in strategy and structure, a top-down approach is typically best. These innovations are in the domain of top administrators who take responsibility for restructuring, for downsizing, and for changes in policies, goals, and control systems.

Culture changes are also generally the responsibility of top management. Some recent trends that may create a need for broad-scale culture change in the organization are reengineering, the shift to horizontal forms of organizing, greater organizational diversity, and the learning organization. All of these changes require significant shifts in employee and manager attitudes and ways of working together. One method for bringing about this level of culture change is organization development (OD). OD focuses on the human and social aspects of the organization and uses behavioral science knowledge to bring about changes in attitudes and relationships.

Finally, the implementation of change can be difficult. Strong leadership is needed to guide employees through the turbulence and uncertainty and build organization-wide commitment to change. A number of barriers to change exist, including excessive focus on cost, failure to perceive benefits, lack of organizational coordination, and individual uncertainty avoidance and fear of loss. Managers can thoughtfully plan how to deal with resistance to increase the likelihood of success. Techniques that will facilitate implementation are to establish a sense or urgency that change is needed; create a powerful coalition to guide the change; formulate a vision and strategy to achieve the change; and overcome resistance by aligning with the needs and goals of users, including users in the change process, providing psychological safety, and, in rare cases, forcing the innovation if necessary. Change teams and idea champions are also effective.

Key Concepts

ambidextrous approach
change process
creative departments
creativity
culture changes
dual-core approach
horizontal coordination model
idea champion
idea incubator
incremental change
large group intervention
management champion
new-venture fund

organization development
organizational change
organizational innovation
product and service changes
radical change
skunkworks
strategy and structure changes
switching structures
team building
technical champion
technology changes
time-based competition
venture teams

Discussion Questions

1. How is the management of radical change likely to differ from the management of incremental change?
2. How are organic characteristics related to changes in technology? To administrative changes?
3. Describe the dual-core approach. How does administrative change normally differ from technology change? Discuss.
4. How might organizations manage the dilemma of needing both stability and change? Discuss.
5. Why do organizations experience resistance to change? What steps can managers take to overcome this resistance?
6. "Bureaucracies are not innovative." Discuss.
7. A noted organization theorist said, "Pressure for change originates in the environment; pressure for stability originates within the organization." Do you agree? Discuss.
8. Of the five elements required for successful change, which element do you think managers are most likely to overlook? Discuss.
9. How do the underlying values of organization development compare to the values underlying other types of change? Why do the values underlying OD make it particularly useful in shifting to a learning organization?
10. The manager of R&D for a drug company said that only 5 percent of the company's new products ever achieve market success. He also said the industry average is 10 percent and wondered how his organization might increase its success rate. If you were acting as a consultant, what advice would you give him concerning organization structure?
11. Review the stages of commitment to change illustrated in Exhibit 11.9 and the seven techniques for implementing change discussed at the end of the chapter. At which stage of change commitment would each of the seven techniques most likely be used?

Chapter 11 Workbook: Innovation Climate*

In order to examine differences in the level of innovation encouragement in organizations, you will be asked to rate two organizations. The first should be an organization in which you have worked, or the university. The second

*Adapted by Dorothy Marcic from Susanne G. Scott and Reginald A. Bruce, "Determinants of Innovative Behavior: A Path Model of Individual Innovation in the Workplace," *Academy of Management Journal* 37, no. 3 (1994), 580–607.

should be someone else's workplace, that of a family member, a friend, or an acquaintance. You will have to interview that person to answer the questions below. You should put your own answers in column A, your interviewee's answers in column B, and what you think would be the ideal in column C.

Innovation Measures

Item of Measure	A Your Organization	B Other Organization	C Your Ideal
Score items 1–5 on this scale: 1 = *don't agree at all* to 5 = *agree completely*			
1. Creativity is encouraged here.†			
2. People are allowed to solve the same problems in different ways.†			
3. I get to pursue creative ideas.‡			
4. The organization publicly recognizes and also rewards those who are innovative.‡			
5. Our organization is flexible and always open to change.†			
Score items 6–10 on the *opposite* scale: 1 = *agree completely* to 5 = *don't agree at all*			
6. The primary job of people here is to follow orders that come from the top.†			
7. The best way to get along here is to think and act like the others.†			
8. This place seems to be more concerned with the status quo than with change.†			
9. People are rewarded more if they don't rock the boat.‡			
10. New ideas are great, but we don't have enough people or money to carry them out.‡			

†These items indicate the organization's innovation climate.
‡These items show resource support.

Questions

1. What comparisons in terms of innovation climates can you make between these two organizations?

2. How might productivity differ between a climate that supports innovation and a climate that does not?

3. Where would you rather work? Why?

Case for Analysis: Shoe Corporation of Illinois*

Shoe Corporation of Illinois (SCI) produces a line of women's shoes that sell in the lower-price market for $27.99 to $29.99 per pair. Profits averaged 30 cents to 50 cents per pair 10 years ago, but according to the president and the controller, labor and materials costs have risen so much in the intervening period that profits today average only 25 cents to 30 cents per pair.

Production at both the company's plants totals 12,500 pairs per day. The two factories are located within a radius of 60 miles of Chicago: one at Centerville, which produces 4,500 pairs per day, and the other at Meadowvale, which produces 8,000 pairs per day. Company headquarters is located in a building adjacent to the Centerville plant.

It is difficult to give an accurate picture of the number of items in the company's product line. Shoes change in style perhaps more rapidly than any other style product, including garments. This is chiefly because it is possible to change production processes quickly and because, historically, each company, in attempting to get ahead of competitors, gradually made style changes more frequently. At present, including both major and minor style changes, SCI offers 100 to 120 different products to customers each year.

A partial organizational chart, showing the departments involved in this case, appears in Exhibit 11.10.

Competitive Structure of the Industry

Very large general shoe houses, such as International and Brown, carry a line of women's shoes and are able to undercut prices charged by SCI, principally because of the policy in the big companies of producing large numbers of "stable" shoes, such as the plain pump and the loafer. They do not attempt to change styles as rapidly as their smaller competitors. Thus, without constant changes in production processes and sales presentations, they are able to keep costs substantially lower.

Charles F. Allison, the president of SCI, feels that the only way for a small independent company to be competitive is to change styles frequently, taking advantage of the flexibility of a small organization to create designs that appeal to customers. Thus, demand can be created and a price set high enough to make a profit. Allison, incidentally, appears to have an artistic talent in styling and a record of successful judgments in approving high-volume styles over the years.

Regarding how SCI differs from its large competitors, Allison has said:

You see, Brown and International Shoe Company both produce hundreds of thousands of the same pair of shoes. They store them in inventory at their factories. Their customers, the large wholesalers and retailers, simply know

their line and send in orders. They do not have to change styles nearly as often as we do. Sometimes I wish we could do that, too. It makes for a much more stable and orderly system. There is also less friction between people inside the company. The salespeople always know what they're selling; the production people know what is expected of them. The plant personnel are not shook up so often by someone coming in one morning and tampering with their machine lines or their schedules. The styling people are not shook up so often by the plant saying, "We can't do your new style the way you want it."

To help SCI be more competitive against larger firms, Allison recently created an e-commerce department. Although his main interest was in marketing over the Internet, he also hoped new technology would help reduce some of the internal friction by giving people an easier way to communicate. He invested in a sophisticated new computer system and hired consultants to set up a company intranet and provide a few days' training to upper and middle managers. Katherine Olsen came on board as director of e-commerce, charged primarily with coordinating Internet marketing and sales. When she took the job, she had visions of one day offering consumers the option of customized shoe designs. However, Olsen was somewhat surprised to learn that most employees still refused to use the intranet even for internal communication and coordination. The process for deciding on new styles, for example, had not changed since the 1970s.

Major Style Changes

The decision about whether to put a certain style into production requires information from a number of different people. Here is what typically happens in the company. It may be helpful to follow the organization chart (see Exhibit 11.10) tracing the procedure.

M. T. Lawson, the styling manager, and his designer, John Flynn, originate most of the ideas about shape, size of heel, use of flat sole or heels, and findings (the term used for ornaments attached to, but not part of, the shoes—bows, straps, and so forth). They get their ideas principally from reading style and trade magazines or by copying top-flight designers. Lawson corresponds with publications and friends in large stores in New York, Rome, and Paris to obtain pictures and samples of up-to-the-minute style innovations. Although he uses e-mail occasionally, Lawson prefers telephone contact and receiving drawings or samples by overnight mail. Then, he and Flynn discuss various ideas and come up with design options.

*Written by Charles E. Summer. Copyright 1978. Revised with permission.

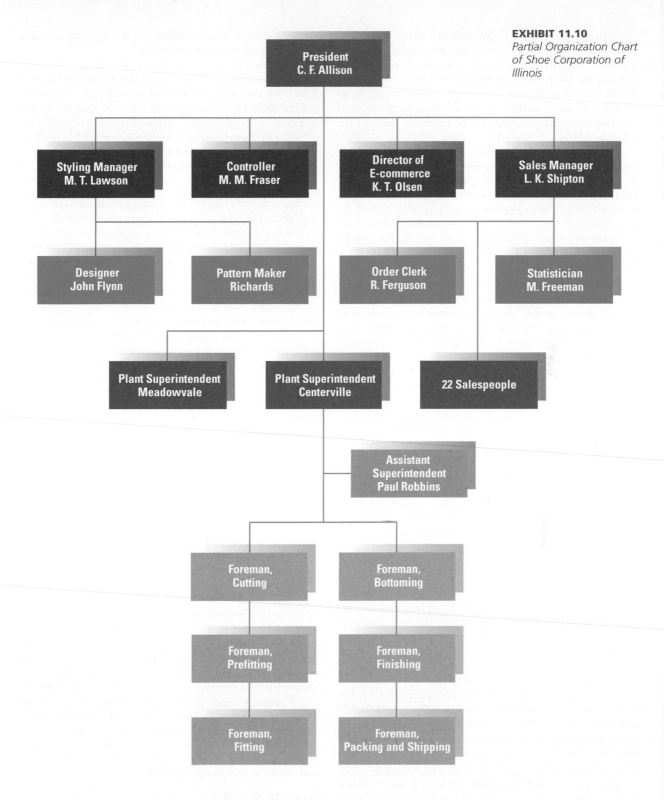

EXHIBIT 11.10
Partial Organization Chart of Shoe Corporation of Illinois

President
C. F. Allison

Styling Manager
M. T. Lawson

Controller
M. M. Fraser

Director of
E-commerce
K. T. Olsen

Sales Manager
L. K. Shipton

Designer
John Flynn

Pattern Maker
Richards

Order Clerk
R. Ferguson

Statistician
M. Freeman

Plant Superintendent
Meadowvale

Plant Superintendent
Centerville

22 Salespeople

Assistant
Superintendent
Paul Robbins

Foreman,
Cutting

Foreman,
Bottoming

Foreman,
Prefitting

Foreman,
Finishing

Foreman,
Fitting

Foreman,
Packing and Shipping

When Lawson decides on a design, he takes a sketch to Allison, who either approves or disapproves it. If Allison approves, he (Allison) then passes the sketch on to L. K. Shipton, the sales manager, to find out what lasts (widths) should be chosen. Shipton, in turn, forwards the design to Martin Freeman, a statistician in the sales department, who maintains summary information on customer demand for colors and lasts.

To compile this information, Freeman visits salespeople twice a year to get their opinions on the colors and lasts that are selling best, and he keeps records of shipments by color and by last. For these needs, he simply totals data that are sent to him by the shipping foreman in each of the two plants.

When Freeman has decided on the lasts and colors, he sends Allison a form that lists the colors and lasts in which the shoe should be produced. Allison, if he approves this list, forwards the information to Lawson, who passes it on to Jenna Richards, an expert pattern maker. Richards makes a paper pattern and then constructs a prototype in leather and paper. She sends this to Lawson, who in turn approves or disapproves it. He forwards any approved prototype to Allison. Allison, if he, too, approves, notifies Lawson, who takes the prototype to Paul Robbins, assistant to the superintendent of the Centerville plant. Only this plant produces small quantities of new or experimental shoe styles. This is referred to as a "pilot run" by executives at the plant.

Robbins then literally carries the prototype through the six production departments of the plant—from cutting to finishing—discussing it with each foreman, who in turn works with employees on the machines in having a sample lot of several thousand pairs made. When the finished lot is delivered by the finishing foreman to the shipping foreman (because of the importance of styling, Allison has directed that each foreman personally deliver styling goods in process to the foreman of the next department), the latter holds the inventory in storage and sends one pair each to Allison and Lawson. If they approve of the finished product, Allison instructs the shipping foreman to mail samples to each of the company's twenty-two salespeople throughout the country. Olsen also receives samples, photos, and drawings to post on the Web page and gauge customer interest.

Salespeople have instructions to take the samples immediately (within 1 week) to at least ten customers. Orders for already-established shoes are normally sent to Ralph Ferguson, a clerk in Shipton's office, who records them and forwards them to the plant superintendents for production. However, salespeople have found by experience that Martin Freeman has a greater interest in the success of new "trials," so they rush these orders to him by overnight mail, and he in turn places the first orders for a new style in the interoffice mail to the plant superintendents. He then sends off a duplicate of the order, mailed in by the sales-people, to Ferguson for entering in his statistical record of all orders received by the company.

Three weeks after the salespeople receive samples, Allison requires Ralph Ferguson to give him a tabulation of orders. At that time, he decides whether the salespeople and the Web page should push the item and the superintendents should produce large quantities, or whether he will tell them that although existing orders will be produced, the item will be discontinued in a short time.

The procedures outlined here have, according to Allison,

worked reasonably well. The average time from when Lawson decides on a design until we notify the Centerville plant to produce the pilot run is two weeks to a month. Of course, if we could speed that up, it would make the company just that much more secure in staying in the game against the big companies, and in taking sales away from our competitors. There seems to be endless bickering among people around here involved in the styling phase of the business. That's to be expected when you have to move fast—there isn't much time to stop and observe all of the social amenities. I have never thought that a formal organization chart would be good in this company—we've worked out a customary system here that functions well.

M. T. Lawson, manager of styling, said that within his department all work seems to get out in minimum time; he also stated that both Flynn and Richards are good employees and skilled in their work. He mentioned that Flynn had been in to see him twice in the last year

to inquire about his [Flynn's] future in the company. He is 33 years old and has three children. I know that he is eager to make money, and I assured him that over the years we can raise him right along from the $60,000 we are now paying. Actually, he has learned a lot about shoe styles since we hired him from the design department of a fabric company 6 years ago.

John Flynn revealed:

I was actually becoming dissatisfied with this job. All shoe companies copy styles—it's generally accepted practice within the industry. But I've picked up a real feel for designs, and several times I've suggested that the company make all its own original styles. We could make SCI a style leader and also increase our volume. When I ask Lawson about this, he says it takes too much time for the designer to create originals—that we have all we can handle to do research in trade magazines and maintain contracts feeding us the results of experts. Beside, he says our styles are standing the test of the marketplace.

Projects X and Y

Flynn also said that he and Martin Freeman had frequently talked about the styling problem. They felt that

Allison is really a great president, and the company surely would be lost without him. However, we've seen times when he lost a lot of money on bad judgments in styles. Not many times—perhaps six or seven times in the last 18 months. Also, he is, of course, extremely busy as president of the corporation. He must look after everything from financing from the banks to bargaining with the union. The result is that he is sometimes unavailable to do his styling approvals for several days, or even 2 weeks. In a business like this, that kind of delay can cost money. It also makes him slightly edgy. It tends, at times when he has many other things to do, to make him look quickly at the styles we submit, or the prototypes Richards makes, or even the finished shoes that are sent for approval by the shipping foreman. Sometimes I worry that he makes two kinds of errors. He simply rubber-stamps what we've done, which makes sending these things to him simply a waste of time. At other times he makes snap judgments of his own, overruling those of us who have spent so much time and expertise on the shoe. We do think he has good judgment, but he himself has said at times that he wishes he had more time to concentrate on styling and approval of prototypes and final products.

Flynn further explained (and this was corroborated by Freeman) that the two had worked out two plans, which they referred to as "project X" and "project Y." In the first, Flynn created an original design that was not copied from existing styles. Freeman then gave special attention to color and last research for the shoe and recommended a color line that didn't exactly fit past records on consumer purchases—but one he and Flynn thought would have "great consumer appeal." This design and color recommendation were accepted by Lawson and Allison; the shoe went into production and was one of the three top sellers during the calendar year. The latter two men did not know that the shoe was styled in a different way from the usual procedure.

The result of a second, similar project (Y) was put into production the next year, but this time sales were discontinued after 3 weeks.

Problem between Lawson and Robbins

Frequently, perhaps ten to twelve times a year, disagreement arises between Mel Lawson, manager of styling, and Paul Robbins, assistant to the superintendent of the Centerville plant. Robbins said,

The styling people don't understand what it means to produce a shoe in the quantities that we do, and to make the changes in production that we have to. They dream up a style quickly, out of thin air. They do not realize that we have a lot of machines that have to be adjusted and that some things they dream up take much longer on certain machines than others, thus creating a bottleneck in the production line. If they put a bow or strap in one position

rather than another, it may mean we have to keep people idle on later machines while there is a pileup on the sewing machines on which this complicated little operation is performed. This costs the plant money. Furthermore, there are times when they get the prototype here late, and either the foremen and I work overtime or the trial run won't get through in time to have new production runs on new styles, to take the plant capacity liberated by our stopping production on old styles. Lawson doesn't know much about production and sales and the whole company. I think all he does is to bring shoes down here to the plant, sort of like a messenger boy. Why should he be so hard to get along with? He isn't getting paid any more than I am, and my position in the plant is just as important as his.

Lawson, in turn, said that he has a difficult time getting along with Robbins:

There are many times when Robbins is just unreasonable. I take prototypes to him five or six times a month, and other minor style changes to him six or eight times. I tell him every time that we have problems in getting these ready, but he knows only about the plant, and telling him doesn't seem to do any good. When we first joined the company, we got along all right, but he has gotten harder and harder to get along with.

Other Problems

Ralph Ferguson, the clerk in the sales department who receives orders from salespeople and forwards totals for production schedules to the two plant superintendents, has complained that the salespeople and Freeman are bypassing him in their practice of sending experimental shoe orders to Freeman. He insisted that his job description (one of only two written descriptions in the company) gives him responsibility for receiving all orders throughout the company and for maintaining historical statistics on shipments.

Both the salespeople and Freeman, on the other hand, said that before they started the new practice (that is, when Ferguson still received the experimental shoe orders), there were at least eight or ten instances a year when these were delayed from 1 to 3 days on Ferguson's desk. They reported that Ferguson just wasn't interested in new styles, so the salespeople "just started sending them to Freeman." Ferguson acknowledged that there were times of short delay, but said that there were good reasons for them:

They [the salespeople and Freeman] are so interested in new designs, colors, and lasts that they can't understand the importance of a systematic handling of the whole order procedure, including both old and new shoe styles. There must be accuracy. Sure, I give some priority to experimental orders, but sometimes when rush orders for existing company products are piling up, and when there's a lot of planning I have to do to allocate production between Centerville and Meadowvale, I decide which comes first—

processing of these, or processing the experimental shoe orders. Shipton is my boss, not the salespeople or Freeman. I'm going to insist that these orders come to me.

The Push for New Technology

Katherine Olsen believes many of these problems could be solved through better use of technology. She has approached Charles Allison several times about the need to make greater use of the expensive and sophisticated computer information systems he had installed. Although Allison always agrees with her, he has so far done nothing to help solve the problem. Olsen thinks the new technology could dramatically improve coordination at SCI.

Everyone needs to be working from the same data at the same time. As soon as Lawson and Flynn come up with a new design, it should be posted on the intranet so all of us can be informed. And everyone needs access to sales and order information, production schedules, and shipping deadlines. If everyone—from Allison down to the people in the production plants—was kept up to date throughout the entire process, we wouldn't have all this confusion and bickering. But no one around here wants to give up any control—they all have their own little operations and don't want to share information with anyone else. For example, I sometimes don't even know there's a new style in the works until I get finished samples and photos. No one seems to recognize that one of the biggest advantages of the Internet is to help stay ahead of changing styles. I know that Flynn has a good feel for design, and we're not taking advantage of his abilities. But I also have information and ideas that could help this company keep pace with changes and really stand out from the crowd. I don't know how long we expect to remain competitive using this cumbersome, slow-moving process and putting out shoes that are already behind the times.

Case for Analysis: Southern Discomfort*

Jim Malesckowski remembered the call of 2 weeks ago as if he had just put down the telephone receiver: "I just read your analysis and I want you to get down to Mexico right away," Jack Ripon, his boss and chief executive officer, had blurted in his ear. "You know we can't make the plant in Oconomo work anymore—the costs are just too high. So go down there, check out what our operational costs would be if we move, and report back to me in a week."

As president of the Wisconsin Specialty Products Division of Lamprey, Inc., Jim knew quite well the challenge of dealing with high-cost labor in a third-generation, unionized, U.S. manufacturing plant. And although he had done the analysis that led to his boss's knee-jerk response, the call still stunned him. There were 520 people who made a living at Lamprey's Oconomo facility, and if it closed, most of them wouldn't have a chance of finding another job in the town of 9,900 people.

Instead of the $16-per-hour average wage paid at the Oconomo plant, the wages paid to the Mexican workers—who lived in a town without sanitation and with an unbelievably toxic effluent from industrial pollution—would amount to about $1.60 an hour on average. That would be a savings of nearly $15 million a year for Lamprey, to be offset in part by increased costs for training, transportation, and other matters.

After 2 days of talking with Mexican government representatives and managers of other companies in the town, Jim had enough information to develop a set of comparative figures of production and shipping costs. On the way home, he started to outline the report, knowing full well that unless some miracle occurred, he would be ushering in a blizzard of pink slips for people he had come to appreciate.

The plant in Oconomo had been in operation since 1921, making special apparel for people suffering from injuries and other medical conditions. Jim had often talked with employees who would recount stories about their fathers or grandfathers working in the same Lamprey company plant—the last of the original manufacturing operations in town.

But friendship aside, competitors had already edged past Lamprey in terms of price and were dangerously close to overtaking it in product quality. Although both Jim and the plant manager had tried to convince the union to accept lower wages, union leaders resisted. In fact, on one occasion when Jim and the plant manager tried to discuss a cell manufacturing approach, which would cross-train employees to perform up to three different jobs, local union leaders could barely restrain their anger. Jim thought he sensed an underlying fear, meaning the union reps were aware of at least some of the problems, but he had been unable to get them to acknowledge this and move on to open discussion.

A week passed and Jim had just submitted his report to his boss. Although he didn't specifically bring up the point, it was apparent that Lamprey could put its investment dollars in a bank and receive a better return than what its Oconomo operation was currently producing.

The next day, he would discuss the report with the CEO. Jim didn't want to be responsible for the plant's dis-

*Doug Wallace, "What Would You Do?" *Business Ethics* (March/April 1996), 52–53. Reprinted with permission from *Business Ethics*, PO Box 8439, Minneapolis, MN 55408; phone: 612-879-0695.

mantling, an act he personally believed would be wrong as long as there was a chance its costs can be lowered. "But Ripon's right," he said to himself. "The costs are too high, the union's unwilling to cooperate, and the company needs to make a better return on its investment if it's to continue at all. It sounds right but feels wrong. What should I do?"

Notes

1. Robert D. Hof, "Building an Idea Factory," *BusinessWeek* (October 11, 2004), 194–200; Brian Bremner and Chester Dawson, "Can Anything Stop Toyota?" *BusinessWeek* (November 17, 2003), 114–122; and Norihiko Shirouzu and Jathon Sapsford, "Heavy Load; For Toyota, a New Small Truck Carries Hopes for Topping GM," *The Wall Street Journal* (May 12, 2005), A1, A6.

2. Based on John P. Kotter, *Leading Change* (Boston, Mass.: Harvard Business School Press, 1996), 18–20.

3. David A. Nadler and Michael L. Tushman, "Organizational Frame Bending: Principles for Managing Reorientation," *Academy of Management Executive* 3 (1989), 194–204; and Michael L. Tushman and Charles A. O'Reilly III, "Ambidextrous Organizations: Managing Evolutionary and Revolutionary Change," *California Management Review* 38, no. 4 (Summer 1996), 8–30.

4. Alan G. Robinson and Dean M. Schroeder, *Ideas Are Free: How the Idea Revolution Is Liberating People and Transforming Organizations* (San Francisco: Berrett-Koehler, 2004), as reported in John Grossman, "Strategies: Thinking Small," *Inc. Magazine* (August 2004), 34–35.

5. William A. Davidow and Michael S. Malone, *The Virtual Corporation* (New York: HarperBusiness, 1992); and Gregory G. Dess, Abdul M. A. Rasheed, Kevin J. McLaughlin, and Richard L. Priem, "The New Corporate Architecture," *Academy of Management Executive* 9, no. 3 (1995), 7–20.

6. Brent Schlender, "How Big Can Apple Get?" *Fortune* (February 21, 2005), 66–76.

7. Joseph E. McCann, "Design Principles for an Innovating Company," *Academy of Management Executive* 5 (May 1991), 76–93.

8. Kelly Barron, "Logistics in Brown," *Forbes* (January 10, 2000), 78–83; and Scott Kirsner, "Venture Vérité: United Parcel Service," *Wired* (September 1999), 83–96.

9. Robert D. Hof, "Building an Idea Factory."

10. Richard A. Wolfe, "Organizational Innovation: Review, Critique and Suggested Research Directions," *Journal of Management Studies* 31, no. 3 (May 1994), 405–431.

11. John L. Pierce and Andre L. Delbecq, "Organization Structure, Individual Attitudes and Innovation," *Academy of Management Review* 2 (1977), 27–37; and Michael Aiken and Jerald Hage, "The Organic Organization and Innovation," *Sociology* 5 (1971), 63–82.

12. Richard L. Daft, "Bureaucratic versus Non-bureaucratic Structure in the Process of Innovation and Change," in Samuel B. Bacharach, ed., *Perspectives in Organizational Sociology: Theory and Research* (Greenwich, Conn.: JAI Press, 1982), 129–166.

13. Alan D. Meyer and James B. Goes, "Organizational Assimilation of Innovations: A Multilevel Contextual Analysis," *Academy of Management Journal* 31 (1988), 897–923.

14. Richard W. Woodman, John E. Sawyer, and Ricky W. Griffin, "Toward a Theory of Organizational Creativity," *Academy of Management Review* 18 (1993), 293–321; and Alan Farnham, "How to Nurture Creative Sparks," *Fortune* (January 10, 1994), 94–100.

15. J. Grossman, "Strategies: Thinking Small."

16. Robert I. Sutton, "Weird Ideas That Spark Innovation," *MIT Sloan Management Review* (Winter 2002), 83–87; Robert Barker, "The Art of Brainstorming," *BusinessWeek* (August 26, 2002), 168–169; Gary A. Steiner, ed., *The Creative Organization* (Chicago, Ill.: University of Chicago Press, 1965), 16–18; and James Brian Quinn, "Managing Innovation: Controlled Chaos," *Harvard Business Review* (May–June 1985), 73–84.

17. Thomas M. Burton, "Flop Factor: By Learning from Failures, Lilly Keeps Drug Pipeline Full," *The Wall Street Journal* (April 21, 2004), A1, A12.

18. Kotter, *Leading Change*, 20–25; and John P. Kotter, "Leading Change," *Harvard Business Review* (March–April 1995), 59–67.

19. G. Tomas M. Hult, Robert F. Hurley, and Gary A. Knight, "Innovativeness: Its Antecedents and Impact on Business Performance," *Industrial Marketing Management* 33 (2004), 429–438.

20. Erick Schonfeld, "GE Sees the Light," *Business 2.0* (July 2004), 80–86.

21. L. D. DiSimone, comments about 3M in "How Can Big Companies Keep the Entrepreneurial Spirit Alive?" *Harvard Business Review* (November– December 1995), 184–185; and Thomas A. Stewart, "3M Fights Back," *Fortune* (February 1996), 94–99.

22. T. M. Burton, "Flop Factor."

23. D. Bruce Merrifield, "Intrapreneurial Corporate Renewal," *Journal of Business Venturing* 8 (September 1993), 383–389; Linsu Kim, "Organizational Innovation and Structure," *Journal of Business Research* 8 (1980), 225–245; and Tom Burns and G. M. Stalker, *The Management of Innovation* (London: Tavistock Publications, 1961).

24. James Q. Wilson, "Innovation in Organization: Notes toward a Theory," in James D. Thompson, ed., *Approaches to Organizational Design* (Pittsburgh, Penn.: University of Pittsburgh Press, 1966), 193–218.

25. Charles A. O'Reilly III and Michael L. Tushman, "The Ambidextrous Organization," *Harvard Business Review* (April 2004), 74–81; M. L. Tushman and C. A. O'Reilly III, "Building an Ambidextrous Organization: Forming Your Own 'Skunk Works,'" *Health Forum Journal* 42, no. 2 (March– April 1999), 20–23; J. C. Spender and Eric H. Kessler, "Managing the Uncertainties of Innovation: Extending Thompson (1967)," *Human Relations* 48, no. 1 (1995), 35–56; and Robert B. Duncan, "The Ambidextrous Organization:

Designing Dual Structures for Innovation," in Ralph H. Killman, Louis R. Pondy, and Dennis Slevin, eds., *The Management of Organization*, vol. 1 (New York: North-Holland,
1976), 167–188.

26. C. A. O'Reilly III and M. L. Tushman, "The Ambidextrous
    Organization."

27. Tushman and O'Reilly, "Building an Ambidextrous Organi-
    zation."

28. Edward F. McDonough III and Richard Leifer, "Using Simul-
    taneous Structures to Cope with Uncertainty," *Academy of
    Management Journal* 26 (1983), 727–735.

29. John McCormick and Bill Powell, "Management for the
    1990s," *Newsweek* (April 25, 1988), 47–48.

30. Todd Datz, "Romper Ranch," *CIO Enterprise* Section 2
    (May 15, 1999), 39–52.

31. Paul S. Adler, Barbara Goldoftas, and David I. Levine, "Er-
    gonomics, Employee Involvement, and the Toyota Produc-
    tion System: A Case Study of NUMMI's 1993 Model Intro-
    duction," *Industrial and Labor Relations Review* 50, no. 3
    (April 1997), 416–437.

32. Judith R. Blau and William McKinley, "Ideas, Complexity,
    and Innovation," *Administrative Science Quarterly* 24
    (1979), 200–219.

33. Peter Landers, "Back to Basics; With Dry Pipelines, Big Drug
    Makers Stock Up in Japan," *The Wall Street Journal* (No-
    vember 24, 2003), A1, A7.

34. Sherri Eng, "Hatching Schemes," *The Industry Standard*
    (November 27–December 4, 2000), 174–175.

35. Christine Canabou, "Fast Ideas for Slow Times," *Fast Com-
    pany* (May 2003), 52.

36. O'Reilly and Tushman, "The Ambidextrous Organization."

37. Christopher Hoenig, "Skunk Works Secrets," *CIO* (July 1,
    2000), 74–76.

38. Phaedra Hise, "New Recruitment Strategy: Ask Your Best
    Employees to Leave," *Inc.* (July 1997), 2.

39. Daniel F. Jennings and James R. Lumpkin, "Functioning
    Modeling Corporate Entrepreneurship: An Empirical Integra-
    tive Analysis," *Journal of Management* 15 (1989), 485–502;
    and Julian Birkinshaw, "The Paradox of Corporate Entrepre-
    neurship," *Strategy & Business*, issue 30 (Spring 2003),
    46–57.

40. Jane M. Howell and Christopher A. Higgins, "Champions of
    Technology Innovation," *Administrative Science Quarterly*
    35 (1990), 317–341; and Jane M. Howell and Christopher
    A. Higgins, "Champions of Change: Identifying, Understand-
    ing, and Supporting Champions of Technology Innovations,"
    Organizational Dynamics (Summer 1990), 40–55.

41. Peter F. Drucker, "Change Leaders," *Inc.* (June 1999),
    65–72; and Peter F. Drucker, *Management Challenges for the
    21st Century* (New York: HarperBusiness, 1999).

42. Stuart Crainer and Des Dearlove, "Water Works," *Manage-
    ment Review* (May 1999), 39–43.

43. Thomas J. Peters and Robert H. Waterman, Jr., *In Search of
    Excellence* (New York: Harper & Row, 1982).

44. Peter J. Frost and Carolyn P. Egri, "The Political Process of
    Innovation," in L. L. Cummings and Barry M. Staw, eds.,
    Research in Organizational Behavior, vol. 13 (New York:
    JAI Press, 1991), 229–295; Jay R. Galbraith, "Designing the
    Innovating Organization," *Organizational Dynamics* (Winter

1982), 5–25; and Marsha Sinatar, "Entrepreneurs, Chaos,
and Creativity—Can Creative People Really Survive Large
Company Structure?" *Sloan Management Review* (Winter
1985), 57–62.

45. See Lionel Roure, "Product Champion Characteristics in
    France and Germany," *Human Relations* 54, no. 5 (2001),
    663–682 for a recent review of the literature related to prod-
    uct champions.

46. Ibid., p. 205.

47. Ann Harrington, "Who's Afraid of a New Product?" *Fortune*
    (November 10, 2003), 189–192.

48. Christopher Power with Kathleen Kerwin, Ronald Grover,
    Keith Alexander, and Robert D. Hof, "Flops," *BusinessWeek*
    (August 16, 1993), 76–82; Modesto A. Maidique and Billie
    Jo Zirger, "A Study of Success and Failure in Product Inno-
    vation: The Case of the U.S. Electronics Industry," *IEEE
    Transactions in Engineering Management* 31 (November
    1984), 192–203.

49. Scott Hensley, "Bleeding Cash: Pfizer 'Youth Pill' Ate Up $71
    Million Before It Flopped," *The Wall Street Journal* (May 2,
    2002), A1, A8.

50. Deborah Dougherty and Cynthia Hardy, "Sustained Product
    Innovation in Large, Mature Organizations: Overcoming
    Innovation-to-Organization Problems," *Academy of Manage-
    ment Journal* 39, no. 5 (1996), 1120–1153.

51. Cliff Edwards, "Many Products Have Gone Way of the Ed-
    sel," *Johnson City Press* (May 23, 1999), 28, 30; Paul Lukas,
    "The Ghastliest Product Launches," *Fortune* (March 16,
    1998), 44; Robert McMath, *What Were They Thinking?
    Marketing Lessons I've Learned from Over 80,000 New-
    Product Innovations and Idiocies* (New York: Times Busi-
    ness, 1998).

52. Edwin Mansfield, J. Rapaport, J. Schnee, S. Wagner, and
    M. Hamburger, *Research and Innovation in Modern Corpo-
    rations* (New York: Norton, 1971); and Antonio J. Bailetti
    and Paul F. Litva, "Integrating Customer Requirements into
    Product Designs," *Journal of Product Innovation Manage-
    ment* 12 (1995), 3–15.

53. Shona L. Brown and Kathleen M. Eisenhardt, "Product
    Development: Past Research, Present Findings, and Future
    Directions," *Academy of Management Review* 20, no. 2
    (1995), 343–378; F. Axel Johne and Patricia A. Snelson,
    "Success Factors in Product Innovation: A Selective Review
    of the Literature," *Journal of Product Innovation Manage-
    ment* 5 (1988), 114–128; and Science Policy Research Unit,
    University of Sussex, *Success and Failure in Industrial Inno-
    vation* (London: Centre for the Study of Industrial Innova-
    tion, 1972).

54. Dorothy Leonard and Jeffrey F. Rayport, "Spark Innovation
    through Empathic Design," *Harvard Business Review*
    (November–December 1997), 102–113.

55. Brown and Eisenhardt, "Product Development"; Dan
    Dimancescu and Kemp Dwenger, "Smoothing the Product
    Development Path," *Management Review* (January 1996),
    36–41.

56. Fara Warner, "In a Word, Toyota Drives for Innovation,"
    Fast Company (August 2002), 36–38.

57. Patricia Sellers, "P&G: Teaching an Old Dog New Tricks,"
    Fortune (May 31, 2004), 167–180; Robert D. Hof, "Building

an Idea Factory"; and Bettina von Stamm, "Collaboration with Other Firms and Customers: Innovation's Secret Weapon," *Stategy & Leadership* 32, no. 3 (2004), 16–20.

58. Bettina von Stamm, "Collaboration with Other Firms and Customers"; Bas Hillebrand and Wim G. Biemans, "Links between Internal and External Cooperation in Product Development: An Exploratory Study," *The Journal of Product Innovation Management* 21 (2004), 110–122.

59. Ann Harrington, "Who's Afraid of a New Product?" *Fortune* (November 10, 2003), 189–192.

60. Melissa A. Schilling and Charles W. L. Hill, "Managing the New Product Development Process," *Academy of Management Executive* 12, no. 3 (1998), 67–81; and J. Lynn Lunsford and Daniel Michaels, "New Orders; After Four Years in the Rear, Boeing Is Set to Jet Past Airbus," *The Wall Street Journal* (June 10, 2005), A1, A5.

61. Kenneth B. Kahn, "Market Orientation, Interdepartmental Integration, and Product Development Performance," *The Journal of Product Innovation Management* 18 (2001), 314–323; and Ali E. Akgün, Gary S. Lynn, and John C. Byrne, "Taking the Guesswork Out of New Product Development: How Succcessful High-Tech Companies Get That Way," *Journal of Business Strategy* 25, no. 4 (2004), 41–46.

62. John A. Pearce II, "Speed Merchants," *Organizational Dynamics* 30, no. 3 (2002), 191–205; Kathleen M. Eisenhardt and Behnam N. Tabrizi, "Accelerating Adaptive Processes: Product Innovation in the Global Computer Industry," *Administrative Science Quarterly* 40 (1995), 84–110; Dougherty and Hardy, "Sustained Product Innovation in Large, Mature Organizations"; and Karne Bronikowski, "Speeding New Products to Market," *Journal of Business Strategy* (September–October 1990), 34–37.

63. V. K. Narayanan, Frank L. Douglas, Brock Guernsey, and John Charnes, "How Top Management Steers Fast Cycle Teams to Success," *Strategy & Leadership* 30, no. 3 (2002), 19–27.

64. Faith Keenan, "Opening the Spigot," *Business-Week e.biz* (June 4, 2001), EB17–EB20.

65. Steve Konicki, "Time Trials," *Information Week* (June 3, 2002), 36–44.

66. David Leonhardt, "It Was a Hit in Buenos Aires—So Why Not Boise?" *BusinessWeek* (September 7, 1998), 56, 58.

67. Edward F. McDonough III, Kenneth B. Kahn, and Gloria Barczak, "An Investigation of the Use of Global, Virtual, and Colocated New Product Development Teams," *The Journal of Product Innovation Management* 18 (2001), 110–120.

68. Dimancescu and Dwenger, "Smoothing the Product Development Path."

69. Raymond E. Miles, Henry J. Coleman, Jr., and W. E. Douglas Creed, "Keys to Success in Corporate Redesign," *California Management Review* 37, no. 3 (Spring 1995), 128–145.

70. Fariborz Damanpour and William M. Evan, "Organizational Innovation and Performance: The Problem of 'Organizational Lag,'" *Administrative Science Quarterly* 29 (1984), 392–409; David J. Teece, "The Diffusion of an Administrative Innovation," *Management Science* 26 (1980), 464–470; John R. Kimberly and Michael J. Evaniski, "Organizational Innovation: The Influence of Individual, Organizational and Contextual Factors on Hospital Adoption of Technological and Administrative Innovation," *Academy of Management Journal* 24 (1981), 689–713; Michael K. Moch and Edward V. Morse, "Size, Centralization, and Organizational Adoption of Innovations," *American Sociological Review* 42 (1977), 716–725; and Mary L. Fennell, "Synergy, Influence, and Information in the Adoption of Administrative Innovation," *Academy of Management Journal* 27 (1984), 113–129.

71. Richard L. Daft, "A Dual-Core Model of Organizational Innovation," *Academy of Management Journal* 21 (1978), 193–210.

72. Daft, "Bureaucratic versus Nonbureaucratic Structure"; Robert W. Zmud, "Diffusion of Modern Software Practices: Influence of Centralization and Formalization," *Management Science* 28 (1982), 1421–1431.

73. Daft, "A Dual-Core Model of Organizational Innovation"; Zmud, "Diffusion of Modern Software Practices."

74. Fariborz Damanpour, "The Adoption of Technological, Administrative, and Ancillary Innovations: Impact of Organizational Factors," *Journal of Management* 13 (1987), 675–688.

75. Steve Hamm, "Is Oracle Finally Seeing Clearly?" *BusinessWeek* (August 3, 1998), 86–88.

76. Gregory H. Gaertner, Karen N. Gaertner, and David M. Akinnusi, "Environment, Strategy, and the Implementation of Administrative Change: The Case of Civil Service Reform," *Academy of Management Journal* 27 (1984), 525–543.

77. Claudia Bird Schoonhoven and Mariann Jelinek, "Dynamic Tension in Innovative, High Technology Firms: Managing Rapid Technology Change through Organization Structure," in Mary Ann Von Glinow and Susan Albers Mohrman, eds., *Managing Complexity in High Technology Organizations* (New York: Oxford University Press, 1990), 90–118.

78. Shawn Tully, "Mr. CleanUp," *Fortune* (November 15, 2004), 151–163.

79. David Ulm and James K. Hickel, "What Happens after Restructuring?" *Journal of Business Strategy* (July–August 1990), 37–41; and John L. Sprague, "Restructuring and Corporate Renewal: A Manager's Guide," *Management Review* (March 1989), 34–36.

80. Stan Pace, "Rip the Band-Aid Off Quickly," *Strategy & Leadership* 30, no. 1 (2002), 4–9.

81. Benson L. Porter and Warrington S. Parker, Jr., "Culture Change," *Human Resource Management* 31 (Spring–Summer 1992), 45–67.

82. Quoted in Anne B. Fisher, "Making Change Stick," *Fortune* (April 17, 1995), 122.

83. Reed Abelson, "Can Respect Be Mandated? Maybe Not Here," *The New York Times* (September 10, 2000), Section 3, 1.

84. Patricia Carr, "Riding the Tiger of Culture Change," *TD* (August 2004), 33–41.

85. W. Warner Burke, "The New Agenda for Organization Development," in Wendell L. French, Cecil H. Bell, Jr., and Robert A. Zawacki, *Organization Development and Transformation: Managing Effective Change* (Burr Ridge, Ill.: Irwin McGraw-Hill, 2000), 523–535.

86. W. Warner Burke, *Organization Development: A Process of Learning and Changing*, 2nd ed. (Reading, Mass.: Addison-Wesley, 1994); and Wendell L. French and Cecil H. Bell, Jr., "A History of Organization Development," in French, Bell, and Zawacki, *Organization Development and Transformation*, 20–42.

87. French and Bell, "A History of Organization Development."

88. The information on large group intervention is based on Kathleen D. Dannemiller and Robert W. Jacobs, "Changing the Way Organizations Change: A Revolution of Common Sense," *The Journal of Applied Behavioral Science* 28, no. 4 (December 1992), 480–498; Barbara B. Bunker and Billie T. Alban, "Conclusion: What Makes Large Group Interventions Effective?" *The Journal of Applied Behavioral Science* 28, no. 4 (December 1992), 570–591; and Marvin R. Weisbord, "Inventing the Future: Search Strategies for Whole System Improvements," in French, Bell, and Zawacki, *Organization Development and Transformation*, 242–250.

89. J. Quinn, "What a Workout!" *Performance* (November 1994), 58–63; and Bunker and Alban, "Conclusion: What Makes Large Group Interventions Effective?"

90. Dave Ulrich, Steve Kerr, and Ron Ashkenas, with Debbie Burke and Patrice Murphy, *The GE Work Out: How to Implement GE's Revolutionary Method for Busting Bureaucracy and Attacking Organizational Problems—Fast!* (New York: McGraw-Hill, 2002).

91. Paul F. Buller, "For Successful Strategic Change: Blend OD Practices with Strategic Management," *Organizational Dynamics* (Winter 1988), 42–55.

92. Norm Brodsky, "Everybody Sells," (Street Smarts column), *Inc. Magazine* (June 2004), 53–54.

93. Richard S. Allen and Kendyl A. Montgomery, "Applying an Organizational Development Approach to Creating Diversity," *Organizational Dynamics* 30, no. 2 (2001), 149–161.

94. Jyotsna Sanzgiri and Jonathan Z. Gottlieb, "Philosophic and Pragmatic Influences on the Practice of Organization Development, 1950–2000," *Organizational Dynamics* (Autumn 1992), 57–69.

95. Bernard M. Bass, "Theory of Transformational Leadership Redux," *Leadership Quarterly* 6, no. 4 (1995), 463–478; and Dong I. Jung, Chee Chow, and Anne Wu, "The Role of Transformational Leadership in Enhancing Organizational Innovation: Hypotheses and Some Preliminary Findings," *The Leadership Quarterly* 14 (2003), 525–544.

96. Ronald Recardo, Kathleen Molloy, and James Pellegrino, "How the Learning Organization Manages Change," *National Productivity Review* (Winter 1995/96), 7–13.

97. Based on Daryl R. Conner, *Managing at the Speed of Change* (New York: Villard Books, 1992), 146–160.

98. Drucker, *Management Challenges for the 21st Century*; Tushman and O'Reilly, "Ambidextrous Organizations"; Gary Hamel and C. K. Prahalad, "Seeing the Future First," *Fortune* (September 4, 1994), 64–70; and Linda Yates and Peter Skarzynski, "How Do Companies Get to the Future First?" *Management Review* (January 1999), 16–22.

99. Based on Carol A. Beatty and John R. M. Gordon, "Barriers to the Implementation of CAD/CAM Systems," *Sloan Management Review* (Summer 1988), 25–33.

100. These techniques are based partly on John P. Kotter's eight-stage model of planned organizational change, Kotter, *Leading Change*, 20–25.

101. Scott McCartney, "Clipped Wings: American Airlines to Retrench in Bid to Beat Discount Carriers," *The Wall Street Journal* (August 13, 2002), A1, A8; and Christine Y. Chen, "American Airlines: Blastoff or Bust?" *Fortune* (October 28, 2002), 37.

102. Everett M. Rogers and Floyd Shoemaker, *Communication of Innovations: A Cross Cultural Approach*, 2d ed. (New York: Free Press, 1971); Stratford P. Sherman, "Eight Big Masters of Innovation," *Fortune* (October 15, 1984), 66–84.

103. Richard L. Daft and Selwyn W. Becker, *Innovation in Organizations* (New York: Elsevier, 1978); and John P. Kotter and Leonard A. Schlesinger, "Choosing Strategies for Change," *Harvard Business Review* 57 (1979), 106–114.

104. Jim Cross, "Back to the Future," *Management Review* (February 1999), 50–54.

105. Peter Richardson and D. Keith Denton, "Communicating Change," *Human Resource Management* 35, no. 2 (Summer 1996), 203–216.

106. Edgar H. Schein and Warren Bennis, *Personal and Organizational Change via Group Methods* (New York: Wiley, 1965); and Amy Edmondson, "Psychological Safety and Learning Behavior in Work Teams," *Administrative Science Quarterly* 44 (1999), 350–383.

107. Diane L. Coutu, "Creating the Most Frightening Company on Earth; An Interview with Andy Law of St. Luke's," *Harvard Business Review* (September–October 2000), 143–150.

108. Philip H. Mirvis, Amy L. Sales, and Edward J. Hackett, "The Implementation and Adoption of New Technology in Organizations: The Impact on Work, People, and Culture," *Human Resource Management* 30 (Spring 1991), 113–139; Arthur E. Wallach, "System Changes Begin in the Training Department," *Personnel Journal* 58 (1979), 846–848, 872; and Paul R. Lawrence, "How to Deal with Resistance to Change," *Harvard Business Review* 47 (January–February 1969), 4–12, 166–176.

109. Dexter C. Dunphy and Doug A. Stace, "Transformational and Coercive Strategies for Planned Organizational Change: Beyond the O.D. Model," *Organizational Studies* 9 (1988), 317–334; and Kotter and Schlesinger, "Choosing Strategies for Change."

Definitions

Individual Decision Making
Rational Approach • Bounded Rationality Perspective

Organizational Decision Making
Management Science Approach • Carnegie Model • Incremental Decision Process Model

The Learning Organization
Combining the Incremental Process and Carnegie Models • Garbage Can Model

Contingency Decision-Making Framework
Problem Consensus • Technical Knowledge about Solutions • Contingency Framework

Special Decision Circumstances
High-Velocity Environments • Decision Mistakes and Learning • Escalating Commitment

Summary and Interpretation

A Look Inside

Maytag

The repairman isn't the only one feeling lonely at Maytag these days. Once an American icon of high-quality appliance manufacturing, Maytag has fallen on some seriously hard times. By the late 1990s, costs at the appliance maker had spiraled out of control, rivals such as Whirlpool, General Electric (GE), and Electrolux were snatching market share, and the stock was on a downhill slide. Even worse, Maytag's reputation for quality and dependability had taken a beating due to leaking problems with the new Neptune washer. When Ralph Hake took over as CEO in 2001, he knew he had to do something drastic to return Maytag to its glory days. Hake quickly took charge, diving headfirst into the mess at Maytag and making several major decisions designed to boost sales and return the company to profitability. For example, the acquisition of stove and refrigerator maker Amana helped push sales up. To cut costs, he closed warehouses, centralized information technology (IT) operations, trimmed the number of Maytag vendors, and slashed the research and development (R&D) budget. Unfortunately, some of Hake's decisions just exacerbated the deeper problems at Maytag. The severe cost cutting jeopardized quality control efforts, leading to a continued decline in customer satisfaction. Whereas Maytag used to be the leader in customer satisfaction, surveys show it's now near the bottom of the heap. Moreover, by cutting the R&D budget, Hake hamstrung new product development. "Maytag realized it too late," says one appliance industry veteran, "but innovation is the name of the game today." Maytag also lost touch with consumers, and the few new products it has brought out haven't caught on. The much-heralded Neptune Drying Center, for example, is so large that few people can fit it in their existing laundry rooms.

On a positive note, Hake has begun investing more in new product initiatives, including a laundry R&D center in Newton, Iowa. However, it could be too little too late. Unless Maytag can fix its quality problems, repair its reputation, and regain market share, the turnaround Hake envisioned will turn into a dead end.[1]

Every organization grows, prospers, or fails as a result of decisions by its managers, and decisions can be risky and uncertain, without any guarantee of success. Sometimes, decision making is a trial-and-error process, in which top managers continue to search for appropriate ways to solve complex problems. At Maytag, Ralph Hake and his top management team continue to evaluate the company's troubles and search for the correct alternatives to mend them. Decision making is done amid constantly changing factors, unclear information, and conflicting points of view. The 2002 decision to merge Hewlett-Packard (H-P) and Compaq, for example, was highly controversial. Former H-P CEO Carly Fiorina and her supporters believed it was essential for H-P's future success, but other managers and board members argued that it was insane to risk H-P's printer business and move the company more deeply into the highly competitive computer world. Fiorina's side ultimately won out, but results of the merger have been disappointing. Hewlett-Packard's board ousted Fiorina in early 2005, partly due to issues related to the Compaq merger. Now, new CEO Mark Hurd faces his own challenges, with managers, consultants, and observers offering different, often conflicting views of what is needed to get H-P back on track.[2]

Many organizational decisions are complete failures. A classic example is the 1985 introduction of New Coke, which Coca-Cola executives were sure was the company's answer to winning back market share from Pepsi. Within 3 months, the company had gotten more than 400,000 angry letters and phone calls, and New Coke quietly faded from store shelves.[3] A similar example comes from Interstate Bakeries, which makes Wonder Bread and Twinkies. When the company tinkered with its recipe to give bread a longer shelf life, sales began falling. Consumers rejected the stale, gummy new products, contributing to a net loss of $25.7 million in 2004. Interstate is now in bankruptcy.[4]

Even the most successful companies sometimes make big blunders. Dream-Works, the studio that made *Shrek 2*, the biggest box-office hit of 2004, poured tens of millions into marketing for the DVD release of the monster hit. Sales during the initial release period boomed, so DreamWorks flooded the market. But managers got a shock when retailers began returning millions of unsold copies. Based on patterns in the past, DreamWorks wrongly assumed the strong early sales would continue and perhaps even grow.[5]

Yet managers also make many successful decisions every day. Meg Whitman made eBay today's model of what an Internet company should be by steering clear of get-rich-quick schemes and keeping the company focused on nurturing its community of buyers and sellers. Cadillac managers' decision to ditch stuffy golf and yachting sponsorships in favor of tying in with popular Hollywood movies has boosted sales and revived Cadillac's image. And Carlos Ghosn implemented structural, management, and product changes that transformed Nissan from a directionless, debt-ridden company into one of the most dynamic and profitable automakers in the world.[6]

◼ Purpose of This Chapter

At any time, an organization may be identifying problems and implementing alternatives for hundreds of decisions. Managers and organizations somehow muddle through these processes.[7] The purpose here is to analyze these processes to learn what decision making is actually like in organizational settings. Decision-making processes can be thought of as the brain and nervous system of an organization. Decision making is the end use of the information and control systems described in Chapter 8. Decisions are made about organization strategy, structure, innovation, and acquisitions. This chapter explores how organizations can and should make decisions about these issues.

The first section defines decision making. The next section examines how individual managers make decisions. Then several models of organizational decision making are explored. Each model is used in a different organizational situation. The final section in this chapter combines the models into a single framework that describes when and how they should be used and discusses special issues, such as decision mistakes.

◼ Definitions

Organizational decision making is formally defined as the process of identifying and solving problems. The process has two major stages. In the **problem identification** stage, information about environmental and organizational conditions is monitored

to determine if performance is satisfactory and to diagnose the cause of shortcomings. The **problem solution** stage is when alternative courses of action are considered and one alternative is selected and implemented.

Organizational decisions vary in complexity and can be categorized as programmed or nonprogrammed.[8] **Programmed decisions** are repetitive and well defined, and procedures exist for resolving the problem. They are well structured because criteria of performance are normally clear, good information is available about current performance, alternatives are easily specified, and there is relative certainty that the chosen alternative will be successful. Examples of programmed decisions include decision rules, such as when to replace an office copy machine, when to reimburse managers for travel expenses, or whether an applicant has sufficient qualifications for an assembly-line job. Many companies adopt rules based on experience with programmed decisions. For example, a rule for large hotels staffing banquets is to allow one server per thirty guests for a sit-down function and one server per forty guests for a buffet.[9]

Nonprogrammed decisions are novel and poorly defined, and no procedure exists for solving the problem. They are used when an organization has not seen a problem before and may not know how to respond. Clear-cut decision criteria do not exist. Alternatives are fuzzy. There is uncertainty about whether a proposed solution will solve the problem. Typically, few alternatives can be developed for a nonprogrammed decision, so a single solution is custom-tailored to the problem.

Many nonprogrammed decisions involve strategic planning, because uncertainty is great and decisions are complex. One recent example of a nonprogrammed decision comes from Tupperware, the maker of unique food storage products and kitchen gadgets traditionally sold at home Tupperware parties. Managers hit a home run with the decision to set up booths in shopping malls and push sales over the Internet. Thus, a further push into retail sales by placing Tupperware in Target stores, with volunteer salespeople to demonstrate the products, seemed destined for success. But moving into Target turned out to be one of the biggest disasters in Tupperware's history. Some Target stores and shoppers didn't know how to deal with the influx of Tupperware salespeople, who ended up feeling slighted and stopped volunteering for store duty. Sales were slow. At the same time, the availability of Tupperware in Target stores decreased the interest in home parties, further hurting sales and alienating independent sales reps. Although overseas sales remained strong, sales of Tupperware in North America fell to a 3-year low and profits plummeted nearly 50 percent. Managers are currently considering new decisions about how to turn things around.[10]

Particularly complex nonprogrammed decisions have been referred to as "wicked" decisions, because simply defining the problem can turn into a major task. Wicked problems are associated with manager conflicts over objectives and alternatives, rapidly changing circumstances, and unclear linkages among decision elements. Managers dealing with a wicked decision may hit on a solution that merely proves they failed to correctly define the problem to begin with.[11]

Today's managers and organizations are dealing with a higher percentage of nonprogrammed decisions because of the rapidly changing business environment. As outlined in Exhibit 12.1, today's environment has increased both the number and complexity of decisions that have to be made and has created a need for new decision-making processes. Managers in rapidly changing e-business departments, for example, often have to make quick decisions based on very limited information. Another example is globalization. The trend toward moving production to low-

Today's Business Environment

- *Demands more large-scale change via new strategies, reengineering, restructuring, mergers, acquisitions, downsizing, new product or market development, and so on*

⬇

Decisions Made Inside the Organization

- *Are based on bigger, more complex, more emotionally charged issues*
- *Are made more quickly*
- *Are made in a less certain environment, with less clarity about means and outcomes*
- *Require more cooperation from more people involved in making and implementing decisions*

⬇

A New Decision-Making Process

- *Is required because no one individual has the information needed to make all major decisions*
- *Is required because no one individual has the time and credibility needed to convince lots of people to implement the decision*
- *Relies less on hard data as a basis for good decisions*
- *Is guided by a powerful coalition that can act as a team*
- *Permits decisions to evolve through trial and error and incremental steps as needed*

EXHIBIT 12.1
Decision Making in Today's Environment
Source: Reprinted by permission of Harvard Business School Press. From *Leading Change* by John P. Kotter. Boston, MA, 1996, p. 56. Copyright © 1996 by the Harvard Business School Publishing Corporation, all rights reserved.

wage countries has managers all over corporate America struggling with ethical decisions concerning working conditions in the Third World and the loss of manufacturing jobs in small American communities. In one Tennessee community where the unemployment rate is 18 percent, 600 workers lost their jobs because the company decided to send garment manufacturing overseas.[12]

Individual Decision Making

Individual decision making by managers can be described in two ways. First is the **rational approach,** which suggests how managers should try to make decisions. Second is the **bounded rationality perspective,** which describes how decisions actually have to be made under severe time and resource constraints. The rational approach is an ideal managers may work toward but never reach.

Rational Approach

The rational approach to individual decision making stresses the need for systematic analysis of a problem followed by choice and implementation in a logical, step-by-step sequence. The rational approach was developed to guide individual decision making because many managers were observed to be unsystematic and arbitrary in their approach to organizational decisions.

EXHIBIT 12.2
*Steps in the Rational
Approach to Decision
Making*

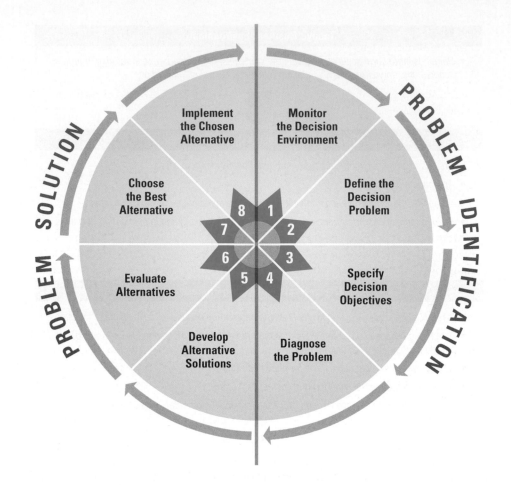

Although the rational model is an ideal not fully achievable in the real world of uncertainty, complexity, and rapid change highlighted in Exhibit 12.1, the model does help managers think about decisions more clearly and rationally. Managers should use systematic procedures to make decisions whenever possible. When managers have a deep understanding of the rational decision-making process, it can help them make better decisions even when there is a lack of clear information. The authors of a recent book on decision making use the example of the U.S. Marines, who have a reputation for handling complex problems quickly and decisively. The Marines are trained to quickly go through a series of mental routines that help them analyze the situation and take action.[13]

According to the rational approach, decision making can be broken down into eight steps, as illustrated in Exhibit 12.2 and demonstrated by the department store Marshall Field's.[14]

1. *Monitor the decision environment.* In the first step, a manager monitors internal and external information that will indicate deviations from planned or acceptable behavior. He or she talks to colleagues and reviews financial statements,

performance evaluations, industry indices, competitors' activities, and so forth. For example, during the pressure-packed 5-week Christmas season, Linda Koslow, general manager of Marshall Field's Oakbrook, Illinois, store, checks out competitors around the mall, eyeing whether they are marking down merchandise. She also scans printouts of her store's previous day's sales to learn what is or is not moving.[15]

2. *Define the decision problem.* The manager responds to deviations by identifying essential details of the problem: where, when, who was involved, who was affected, and how current activities are influenced. For Koslow, this means defining whether store profits are low because overall sales are less than expected or because certain lines of merchandise are not moving as expected.

3. *Specify decision objectives.* The manager determines what performance outcomes should be achieved by a decision.

4. *Diagnose the problem.* In this step, the manager digs below the surface to analyze the cause of the problem. Additional data might be gathered to facilitate this diagnosis. Understanding the cause enables appropriate treatment. For Koslow at Marshall Field's, the cause of slow sales might be competitors' marking down of merchandise or Marshall Field's failure to display hot-selling items in a visible location.

5. *Develop alternative solutions.* Before a manager can move ahead with a decisive action plan, he or she must have a clear understanding of the various options available to achieve desired objectives. The manager may seek ideas and suggestions from other people. Koslow's alternatives for increasing profits could include buying fresh merchandise, running a sale, or reducing the number of employees.

6. *Evaluate alternatives.* This step may involve the use of statistical techniques or personal experience to gauge the probability of success. The merits of each alternative are assessed, as well as the probability that it will reach the desired objectives.

7. *Choose the best alternative.* This step is the core of the decision process. The manager uses his or her analysis of the problem, objectives, and alternatives to select a single alternative that has the best chance for success. At Marshall Field's, Koslow may choose to reduce the number of staff as a way to meet the profit goals rather than increase advertising or markdowns.

8. *Implement the chosen alternative.* Finally, the manager uses managerial, administrative, and persuasive abilities and gives directions to ensure that the decision is carried out. The monitoring activity (step 1) begins again as soon as the solution is implemented. For Linda Koslow, the decision cycle is a continuous process, with new decisions made daily based on monitoring her environment for problems and opportunities.

The first four steps in this sequence are the problem identification stage, and the next four steps are the problem solution stage of decision making, as indicated in Exhibit 12.2. A manager normally goes through all eight steps in making a decision, although each step may not be a distinct element. Managers may know from experience exactly what to do in a situation, so one or more steps will be minimized. The following In Practice illustrates how the rational approach is used to make a decision about a personnel problem.

In Practice

Alberta Consulting

1. *Monitor the decision environment.* It is Monday morning, and Joe DeFoe, Alberta's accounts receivable supervisor, is absent again.
2. *Define the decision problem.* This is the fourth consecutive Monday DeFoe has been absent. Company policy forbids unexcused absenteeism, and DeFoe has been warned about his excessive absenteeism on the last two occasions. A final warning is in order but can be delayed, if warranted.
3. *Specify decision objectives.* DeFoe should attend work regularly and establish the invoice collection levels of which he is capable. The time period for solving the problem is 2 weeks.
4. *Diagnose the problem.* Discreet discussions with DeFoe's co-workers and information gleaned from DeFoe indicate that DeFoe has a drinking problem. He apparently uses Mondays to dry out from weekend benders. Discussion with other company sources confirms that DeFoe is a problem drinker.
5. *Develop alternative solutions.* (1) Fire DeFoe. (2) Issue a final warning without comment. (3) Issue a warning and accuse DeFoe of being an alcoholic to let him know you are aware of his problem. (4) Talk with DeFoe to see if he will discuss his drinking. If he admits he has a drinking problem, delay the final warning and suggest that he enroll in Alberta's new employee assistance program for help with personal problems, including alcoholism. (5) Talk with DeFoe to see if he will discuss his drinking. If he does not admit he has a drinking problem, let him know that the next absence will cost him his job.
6. *Evaluate alternatives.* The cost of training a replacement is the same for each alternative. Alternative 1 ignores cost and other criteria. Alternatives 2 and 3 do not adhere to company policy, which advocates counseling where appropriate. Alternative 4 is designed for the benefit of both DeFoe and the company. It might save a good employee if DeFoe is willing to seek assistance. Alternative 5 is primarily for the benefit of the company. A final warning might provide some incentive for DeFoe to admit he has a drinking problem. If so, dismissal might be avoided, but further absences will no longer be tolerated.
7. *Choose the best alternative.* DeFoe does not admit that he has a drinking problem. Choose alternative 5.
8. *Implement the chosen alternative.* Write up the case and issue the final warning.[16]

In the preceding example, issuing the final warning to Joe DeFoe was a programmed decision. The standard of expected behavior was clearly defined, information on the frequency and cause of DeFoe's absence was readily available, and acceptable alternatives and procedures were described. The rational procedure works best in such cases, when the decision maker has sufficient time for an orderly, thoughtful process. Moreover, Alberta Consulting had mechanisms in place to implement the decision, once made.

When decisions are nonprogrammed, ill-defined, and piling on top of one another, the individual manager should still try to use the steps in the rational approach, but he or she often will have to take shortcuts by relying on intuition and experience. Deviations from the rational approach are explained by the bounded rationality perspective.

◼ Bounded Rationality Perspective

The point of the rational approach is that managers should try to use systematic procedures to arrive at good decisions. When organizations are facing little competition and are dealing with well-understood issues, managers generally use rational

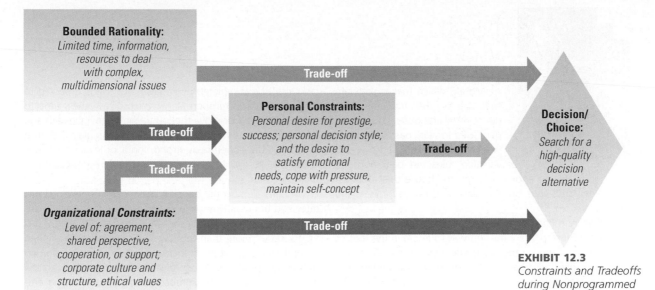

EXHIBIT 12.3
Constraints and Tradeoffs during Nonprogrammed Decision Making
Source: Adapted from Irving L. Janis, *Crucial Decisions* (New York: Free Press, 1989); and A. L. George, *Presidential Decision Making in Foreign Policy: The Effective Use of Information and Advice* (Boulder, Colo.: Westview Press, 1980).

procedures to make decisions.[17] Yet research into managerial decision making shows that managers often are unable to follow an ideal procedure. Many decisions must be made very quickly. Time pressure, a large number of internal and external factors affecting a decision, and the ill-defined nature of many problems make systematic analysis virtually impossible. Managers have only so much time and mental capacity and, hence, cannot evaluate every goal, problem, and alternative. The attempt to be rational is bounded (limited) by the enormous complexity of many problems. There is a limit to how rational managers can be. For example, an executive in a hurry may have a choice of fifty ties on a rack but will take the first or second one that matches his suit. The executive doesn't carefully weigh all fifty alternatives because the short amount of time and the large number of plausible alternatives would be overwhelming. The manager simply selects the first tie that solves the problem and moves on to the next task.

Constraints and Tradeoffs. Not only are large organizational decisions too complex to fully comprehend, but several other constraints impinge on the decision maker, as illustrated in Exhibit 12.3. For many decisions, the circumstances are ambiguous, requiring social support, a shared perspective on what happens, and acceptance and agreement. For example, consider the early U.S. decision to disband the Iraqi army and disagreements over which of three new security forces to build up. These events left the United States without any sizeable Iraqi force to subdue the growing violence, compelling American troops to be more visible and active and making them targets of attack and criticism. In addition, U.S. leaders' lack of agreement to use military force to stop the looting that occurred when troops first enterred Iraq alienated many Iraqi citizens, allowed insurgents to gain strength, and made it more difficult to implement later police and military decisions.[18]

Corporate culture and ethical values also influence decision making, as discussed in Chapter 10. This chapter's Leading by Design box describes how the founder of

Briefcase

As an organization manager, keep these guidelines in mind:

Use rational decision processes when possible, but recognize that many constraints may impinge on decision makers and prevent a perfectly rational decision. Apply the bounded rationality perspective and use intuition when confronting ill-defined, nonprogrammed decisions.

Leading by Design

Motek

At Motek, which makes software that tracks the movement of goods in warehouses, no one is permitted to work past 5:00 P.M. or on weekends. Everyone gets 5 weeks of vacation, plus ten paid holidays, and people get to choose their own assignments and vote on the size of their pay raises and bonuses.

When Ann Price founded Motek, she wanted to create a company whose primary mission was to improve the lives of its employees and customers rather than to reward shareholders or investors. She decided early on to take a long-term approach to business. "We know we're revolutionizing the warehouse automation industry," Price says. "We know we'll get there. But instead of doing it in five years, we'll do it in ten and have a life along the way." Her emphasis on treating people well has guided every major company decision as Motek grows and changes.

Decision making at Motek is a democratic process. Every Monday morning, the company's technical staff gathers to discuss what needs to be done that week, poring over a to-do list of hundreds of tasks. Rather than having a manager determine which people should perform which jobs, individuals volunteer for various chores and decide among themselves the best way to accomplish all the work. "We decide what happens," explains employee Ran Ever-Hadani. "Things are rarely decreed from above." If someone sees that all the tasks can't be completed by Friday, he or she is expected to give a Thursday-afternoon alert, which gives others time to pitch in and help or move the job to the following week and inform the customer. Customers rarely complain because Motek has developed such strong bonds of loyalty that they know the job will be done right and within an acceptable time frame.

Motek's democratic decision making also applies to pay rates and bonuses. Everyone except the CIO and sales manager makes one of three salaries at Motek, and the highest is only $30,000 more than the lowest. Employees recently had an opportunity to vote on increasing their compensation by distributing profits, but they decided instead to look to the long run and pay down company debt. Each founding employee has been promised 1 percent of Motek's value when it is sold to a large company, which Price believes could happen within the next few years.

Price has emphasized hiring the right people, socializing them into the corporate culture, providing them with complete information, and then trusting them to make their own decisions. It's a decision formula that seems to be working. As Motek continues to grow, Price's challenge will be maintaining an environment that encourages the kind of decisions that create both happy employees and a successful organization.

Source: Ellyn Spragins, "Is This the Best Company to Work for Anywhere?" *FSB* (November 2002), 66–70.

software company Motek created a culture where decisions are made based on a primary goal of improving the lives of employees and customers. Managers also often make decisions within a context of trying to please upper managers, people who are perceived to have power within the organization, or others they respect and want to emulate.[19] Personal constraints—such as decision style, work pressure, desire for prestige, or simple feelings of insecurity—may constrain either the search for alternatives or the acceptability of an alternative. All of these factors constrain a perfectly rational approach that should lead to an obviously ideal choice.[20] Even seemingly simple decisions, such as selecting a job on graduation from college, can quickly become so complex that a bounded rationality approach is used. Graduating students have been known to search for a job until they have two or three acceptable job offers, at which point their search activity rapidly diminishes. Hundreds of firms may be available for interviews, and two or three job offers are far short of the maximum number that would be possible if students made the decision based on perfect rationality.

The Role of Intuition. The bounded rationality perspective is often associated with intuitive decision processes. In **intuitive decision making**, experience and judgment rather than sequential logic or explicit reasoning are used to make decisions.[21] Intuition is not arbitrary or irrational because it is based on years of practice and hands-on experience, often stored in the subconscious. When managers use their intuition based on long experience with organizational issues, they more rapidly perceive and understand problems, and they develop a gut feeling or hunch about which alternative will solve a problem, speeding the decision-making process.[22] The value of intuition for effective decision making is supported by a growing body of research from psychology, organizational science, and other disciplines.[23] Indeed, many universities are offering courses in creativity and intuition so business students can learn to understand and use these processes.

In a situation of great complexity or ambiguity, previous experience and judgment are needed to incorporate intangible elements at both the problem identification and problem solution stages.[24] A study of manager problem finding showed that thirty of thirty-three problems were ambiguous and ill-defined.[25] Bits and scraps of unrelated information from informal sources resulted in a pattern in the manager's mind. The manager could not prove a problem existed but knew intuitively that a certain area needed attention. A too-simple view of a complex problem is often associated with decision failure.[26] Intuition plays an increasingly important role in problem identification in today's fast-paced and uncertain business environment.

Intuitive processes are also used in the problem solution stage. Executives frequently make decisions without explicit reference to the impact on profits or to other measurable outcomes.[27] As we saw in Exhibit 12.3, many intangible factors—such as a person's concern about the support of other executives, fear of failure, and social attitudes—influence selection of the best alternative. These factors cannot be quantified in a systematic way, so intuition guides the choice of a solution. Managers may make a decision based on what they sense to be right rather than on what they can document with hard data. A survey of managers conducted in May 2002 by executive search firm Christian & Timbers found that 45 percent of corporate executives say they rely more on instinct than on facts and figures to make business decisions.[28]

Howard Schultz turned Starbucks into a household name by pursuing his intuition that the leisurely caffeine-and-conversation *caffe* model he observed in Italy would work in the United States, despite market research that indicated Americans would never pay $3 for a cup of coffee. Jerry Jones based his decision to buy the losing Dallas Cowboys on intuition, then made a series of further intuitive decisions that turned the team back into a winner. Similarly, the vice president for talent development and casting at MTV relied on intuition to create the show *The Osbournes*. "We never tested the show," he says. "We just knew it would make great TV."[29]

However, there are also many examples of intuitive decisions that turned out to be complete failures.[30] This chapter's Book Mark discusses how managers can give their intuition a better chance of leading to successful decisions.

Managers may walk a fine line between two extremes: on the one hand, making arbitrary decisions without careful study, and on the other, relying obsessively on numbers and rational analysis.[31] Remember that the bounded rationality perspective and the use of intuition apply mostly to nonprogrammed decisions. The novel, unclear, complex aspects of nonprogrammed decisions mean hard data and logical procedures are not available. One study of executive decision making found that managers simply could not use the rational approach for nonprogrammed decisions, such as when to buy a computed tomography (CT) scanner for an osteopathic hospital or whether a city had a need for and could reasonably adopt an enterprise resource planning system.[32] In those cases, managers had limited time and resources, and some factors simply couldn't be measured and analyzed. Trying to quantify such information could cause mistakes because it may oversimplify decision criteria. Intuition can also balance and supplement rational analysis to help organization leaders make better decisions. At Paramount Pictures, a top management team combined intuition and analysis to keep the studio consistently profitable.

Book Mark 12.0 (HAVE YOU READ THIS BOOK?)

Blink: The Power of Thinking without Thinking
By Malcolm Gladwell

Snap decisions can be just as good as—and sometimes better than—decisions that are made cautiously and deliberately. Yet they can also be seriously flawed or even dangerously wrong. That's the premise of Malcolm Gladwell's *Blink: The Power of Thinking without Thinking*. Gladwell explores how our "adaptive unconscious" arrives at complex, important decisions in an instant—and how we can train it to make those decisions good ones.

SHARPENING YOUR INTUITION
Even when we think our decision making is the result of careful analysis and rational consideration, Gladwell says, most of it actually happens subconsciously in a split second. This process, which he refers to as "rapid cognition," provides room for both amazing insight and grave error. Here are some tips for improving rapid cognition:

- *Remember that more is not better.* Gladwell argues that giving people too much data and information hampers their ability to make good decisions. He cites a study showing that emergency room doctors who are best at diagnosing heart attacks gather less information from their patients than other doctors do. Rather than overloading on information, search out the most meaningful parts.
- *Practice thin-slicing.* The process Gladwell refers to as *thin-slicing* is what harnesses the power of the adaptive unconscious and enables us to make smart decisions with minimal time and information. Thin-slicing means focusing on a thin slice of pertinent data or information and allowing your intuition to do the work for you. Gladwell

cites the example of a Pentagon war game, in which an enemy team of commodities traders defeated a U.S. Army that had "an unpredented amount of information and intelligence" and "did a thoroughly rational and rigorous analysis that covered every conceivable contingency." The commodities traders were used to making thousands of instant decisions an hour based on limited information. Managers can practice spontaneous decision making until it becomes second nature.

- *Know Your Limits.* Not every decision should be based on intuition. When you have a depth of knowledge and experience in an area, you can put more trust in your gut feelings. Gladwell also cautions to beware of biases that interfere with good decision making. *Blink* suggests that we can teach ourselves to sort through first impressions and figure out which are important and which are based on subconscious biases such as stereotypes or emotional baggage.

CONCLUSION
Blink is filled with lively and interesting anecdotes, such as how firefighters can "slow down a moment" and create an environment where spontaneous decision making can take place. Gladwell asserts that a better understanding of the process of split-second decision making can help people make better decisions in all areas of their lives, as well as help them anticipate and avoid miscalculations.

Blink: The Power of Thinking without Thinking, by Malcolm Gladwell, is published by Little, Brown.

When she was head of Paramount Pictures, Shery Lansing and her boss, Jonathan Dolgen, head of Viacom Entertainment Group, made a powerful team. Unlike many studios, which lose money despite successful box-office films, Paramount has consistently turned a profit every year since Lansing and Dolgen were put in charge.

As a former independent producer, Lansing relied on her experience and intuition to pick good scripts and the right actors to make them work. Consider 1994's *Forrest Gump*. "It was a film about a guy on a bench," said Lansing. "It was one of the riskiest films ever made." But Lansing's intuition told her that Tom Hanks sitting on a bench talking about life being "like a box of chocolates" would work, and the film reaped $329 million at the box office. More recent successes under the leadership of Lansing and Dolgen include *Along Came a Spider*, *Vanilla Sky*, and *Lara Croft: Tomb Raider*. Dolgen, a former lawyer, provided the analytical side of the partnership. Dolgen's intelligence and careful attention to detail helped Paramount generate consistently good returns. Sometimes, his analysis would suggest that a risk was just not worth taking, even though it meant the studio turned down a potential blockbuster.

Lansing and Dolgen were considered one of the most effective management teams in Hollywood. They combined their natural strengths—one intuitive, the other analytical—to make good decisions that kept Paramount consistently profitable in a difficult, high-risk, unpredictable business. However, although Paramount has turned out a string of well-planned, reliable movies, top executives at Viacom are pushing the studio to take bigger risks and come up with some box office blockbusters. Lansing recently left Paramount and a new leader will try his hand at the business of picking successful movies. Like Lansing, though, he will likely rely largely on intuition. There's no formula for accurately predicting which stories will resonate with today's fickle movie-going audience.[33]

In Practice
Paramount Pictures

Organizational Decision Making

Organizations are composed of managers who make decisions using both rational and intuitive processes; but organization-level decisions are not usually made by a single manager. Many organizational decisions involve several managers. Problem identification and problem solution involve many departments, multiple viewpoints, and even other organizations, which are beyond the scope of an individual manager.

The processes by which decisions are made in organizations are influenced by a number of factors, particularly the organization's own internal structures and the degree of stability or instability of the external environment.[34] Research into organization-level decision making has identified four primary types of organizational decision-making processes: the management science approach, the Carnegie model, the incremental decision process model, and the garbage can model.

■ Management Science Approach

The **management science approach** to organizational decision making is the analog to the rational approach by individual managers. Management science came into being during World War II.[35] At that time, mathematical and statistical techniques were applied to urgent, large-scale military problems that were beyond the ability of individual decision makers.

Mathematicians, physicists, and operations researchers used systems analysis to develop artillery trajectories, antisubmarine strategies, and bombing strategies such as salvoing (discharging multiple shells simultaneously). Consider the problem of a

Briefcase

As an organization manager, keep this guideline in mind:

Use a rational decision approach—computation, management science—when a problem situation is well understood.

battleship trying to sink an enemy ship several miles away. The calculation for aiming the battleship's guns should consider distance, wind speed, shell size, speed and direction of both ships, pitch and roll of the firing ship, and curvature of the earth. Methods for performing such calculations using trial and error and intuition are not accurate, take far too long, and may never achieve success.

This is where management science came in. Analysts were able to identify the relevant variables involved in aiming a ship's guns and could model them with the use of mathematical equations. Distance, speed, pitch, roll, shell size, and so on could be calculated and entered into the equations. The answer was immediate, and the guns could begin firing. Factors such as pitch and roll were soon measured mechanically and fed directly into the targeting mechanism. Today, the human element is completely removed from the targeting process. Radar picks up the target, and the entire sequence is computed automatically.

Management science yielded astonishing success for many military problems. This approach to decision making diffused into corporations and business schools, where techniques were studied and elaborated. Today, many corporations have assigned departments to use these techniques. The computer department develops quantitative data for analysis. Operations research departments use mathematical models to quantify relevant variables and develop a quantitative representation of alternative solutions and the probability of each one solving the problem. These departments also use such devices as linear programming, Bayesian statistics, PERT charts, and computer simulations.

Management science is an excellent device for organizational decision making when problems are analyzable and when the variables can be identified and measured. Mathematical models can contain a thousand or more variables, each one relevant in some way to the ultimate outcome. Management science techniques have been used to correctly solve problems as diverse as finding the right spot for a church camp, test-marketing the first of a new family of products, drilling for oil, and radically altering the distribution of telecommunications services.[36] Other problems amenable to management science techniques are the scheduling of ambulance technicians, telephone operators, and turnpike toll collectors.[37] The following example describes how Continental Airlines uses management science techniques to optimize crew recovery solutions.

In Practice

Continental Airlines

Airlines spend a tremendous amount of time and energy planning and scheduling their operations, yet schedule disruptions due to bad weather, unexpected events, mechanical problems, or ill crew members are unavoidable. That means flight delays and cancellations, and lost revenue for the airline. Continental Airlines wanted a way to deal with crew disruptions in real time, so that pilots and flight attendants could be reassigned quickly and cost-effectively. By reassigning crews quickly, airlines can avoid additional delays and cancellations, improve on-time performance, preserve passenger goodwill, and save money.

Crew assignments and reassignments are limited by several employee qualification factors, including the type of aircraft a pilot is qualified to fly, qualifications for landing at specific airports, foreign language ability for flight attendants on international flights, employees' quality-of-life preferences, and so forth. In addition, numerous governmental regulations and contractual labor laws and rules, such as the number of hours or days in a row an employee can work, must be taken into account. Without a computerized decision support system, Continental had to produce recovery solutions manually, which could take days even for a moderate disruption because of the number and complexity of factors that have to be considered.

Continental managers and crew coordinators worked closely with CALEB Technologies to develop CrewSolver, a computerized system that takes all the legal and governmental requirements, crew qualifications, and quality-of-life issues into account. Mathematical formulations generate up to three possible solutions. Continental estimates that it saved approximately $40 million in 2001 as a direct result of using CrewSolver to recover from four major disruptions, including the terrorist attacks in September. After the attacks, the problem of recovery involved more cancellations and a larger time window than Continental or CALEB had ever imagined. Yet the system returned optimal solutions in less than 17 minutes. This gave Continental an advantage over other major airlines. When airspace was reopened, Continental offered passengers more consistent and reliable service because it suffered fewer delays caused by crew unavailability. Continental executives believe that without CrewSolver, the airline could not have recovered from the disruptions and schedule changes caused by the September 11 attacks.[38]

Since then, Continental has continued to use management science to improve operations efficiency, reliability, and service. Other airlines, including Southwest Airlines and Northwest Airlines, have since implemented their own customized versions of CrewSolver to quickly and effectively solve scheduling problems that affect millions of people every day.

Management science can accurately and quickly solve problems that have too many explicit variables for human processing. This system is at its best when applied to problems that are analyzable, are measurable, and can be structured in a logical way. Increasingly sophisticated computer technology and software programs are allowing the expansion of management science to cover a broader range of problems than ever before. For example, some retailers, including Home Depot, Bloomingdale's, and Gap, now use software to analyze current and historical sales data and determine when, where, and how much to mark down prices. Managers at Harrah's Entertainment Inc. have turned the company into one of the hottest operators of casinos by amassing tons of data about customers and using sophisticated computer systems to make decisions about everything from casino layout to hotel room pricing. Prices quoted for rooms, for instance, are based on a complex mathematical formula that takes into account how long the customers typically stay, what games they play and how often, and other details.[39]

Management science has also produced many failures.[40] In recent years, many banks have begun using computerized scoring systems to rate those applying for credit, but some argue that human judgment is needed to account for extenuating circumstances. In one case, a member of the Federal Reserve Board, the agency that sets interest rates and regulates banks, was denied a Toys "R" Us credit card based on his computerized score.[41]

One problem with the management science approach is that quantitative data are not rich and do not convey tacit knowledge, as described in Chapter 8. Informal cues that indicate the existence of problems have to be sensed on a more personal basis by managers.[42] The most sophisticated mathematical analyses are of no value if the important factors cannot be quantified and included in the model. Such things as competitor reactions, consumer tastes, and product warmth are qualitative dimensions. In these situations, the role of management science is to supplement manager decision making. Quantitative results can be given to managers for discussion and interpretation along with their informal opinions, judgment, and intuition. The final decision can include both qualitative factors and quantitative calculations.

Carnegie Model

The **Carnegie model** of organizational decision making is based on the work of Richard Cyert, James March, and Herbert Simon, who were all associated with Carnegie-Mellon University.[43] Their research helped formulate the bounded rationality approach to individual decision making, as well as provide new insights about organizational decisions.

Until their work, research in economics assumed that business firms made decisions as a single entity, as if all relevant information were funneled to the top decision maker for a choice. Research by the Carnegie group indicated that organization-level decisions involved many managers and that a final choice was based on a coalition among those managers. A **coalition** is an alliance among several managers who agree about organizational goals and problem priorities.[44] It could include managers from line departments, staff specialists, and even external groups, such as powerful customers, bankers, or union representatives.

Management coalitions are needed during decision making for two reasons. First, organizational goals are often ambiguous, and operative goals of departments are often inconsistent. When goals are ambiguous and inconsistent, managers disagree about problem priorities. They must bargain about problems and build a coalition around the question of which problems to solve.

The second reason for coalitions is that individual managers intend to be rational but function with human cognitive limitations and other constraints, as described earlier. Managers do not have the time, resources, or mental capacity to identify all dimensions and to process all information relevant to a decision. These limitations lead to coalition-building behavior. Managers talk to each other and exchange points of view to gather information and reduce ambiguity. People who have relevant information or a stake in a decision outcome are consulted. Building a coalition will lead to a decision that is supported by interested parties.

The process of coalition formation has several implications for organizational decision behavior. First, decisions are made to *satisfice* rather than to optimize problem solutions. **Satisficing** means organizations accept a satisfactory rather than a maximum level of performance, enabling them to achieve several goals simultaneously. In decision making, the coalition will accept a solution that is perceived as satisfactory to all coalition members. Second, managers are concerned with immediate problems and short-run solutions. They engage in what Cyert and March called *problemistic search*.[45]

Problemistic search means managers look around in the immediate environment for a solution to quickly resolve a problem. Managers don't expect a perfect solution when the situation is ill-defined and conflict-laden. This contrasts with the management science approach, which assumes that analysis can uncover every reasonable alternative. The Carnegie model says that search behavior is just sufficient to produce a satisfactory solution and that managers typically adopt the first satisfactory solution that emerges. Third, discussion and bargaining are especially important in the problem identification stage of decision making. Unless coalition members perceive a problem, action will not be taken.

The decision process described in the Carnegie model is summarized in Exhibit 12.4. The Carnegie model points out that building agreement through a managerial coalition is a major part of organizational decision making. This is especially true at upper management levels. Discussion and bargaining are time consuming, so search procedures are usually simple and the selected alternative satisfices rather than optimizes problem solution. When problems are programmed—are clear and have

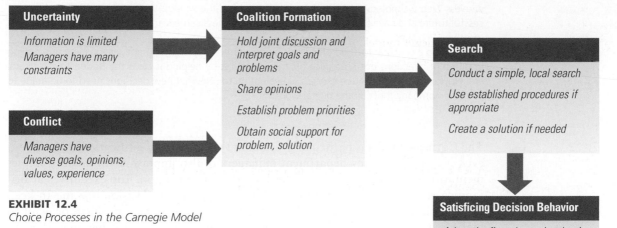

EXHIBIT 12.4
Choice Processes in the Carnegie Model

been seen before—the organization will rely on previous procedures and routines. Rules and procedures prevent the need for renewed coalition formation and political bargaining. Nonprogrammed decisions, however, require bargaining and conflict resolution.

Organizations suffer when managers are unable to build a coalition around goals and problem priorities, as illustrated by the case of Encyclopaedia Britannica.

For most of its 231-year history, the *Encyclopaedia Britannica* had been viewed as an illustrious repository of cultural and historical knowledge—almost a national treasure. Generations of students and librarians relied on the *Britannica*—but that was before CD-ROMs and the Internet became the study tools of choice. Suddenly, the thirty-two-volume collection of encyclopedias, stretching 4 feet on a bookshelf and costing as much as a personal computer (PC), seemed destined to fade into history.

When Swiss-based financier Joseph Safra bought Britannica, he discovered one of the reasons. For nearly a decade, managers had bickered over goals and priorities. Some top executives believed the company needed to invest more in electronic media, but others supported Britannica's traditional direct-to-home sales force. Eventually, the company's Compton unit, a CD-ROM pioneer now being used by millions of consumers, was sold, leaving Britannica without any presence in the new market. In the 1980s, Microsoft had approached Britannica to develop a CD-ROM encyclopedia; when it didn't work out, Microsoft went with Funk & Wagnalls and developed Encarta. Microsoft arranged to have Encarta preinstalled on PCs, so the CD-ROM was essentially free to new PC buyers. When Britannica finally came out with its CD-ROM version, however, it was priced at a staggering $1,200. The squabbling among managers, owners, and editors about product development, pricing, distribution, and other important decisions contributed to the company's decline.

The first step in Safra's turnaround strategy was to install a new top management team, led by one of his longtime advisors. The team immediately coalesced around the important problem of establishing a presence in the world of electronic media. With this goal, the company rushed out a revamped, lower-cost CD-ROM package and launched the Britannica.com Web site, which allows users to call up encyclopedia entries online as well as get a list of links to related Web sites. The team also created a separate digital media division to focus on new product development, such as for

In Practice

Encyclopaedia Britannica

wireless Web technology. Managers are looking toward the wireless Web as the best route to a successful future and have teamed up with numerous wireless carriers and licensed Britannica's content to other Web sites.

Building a coalition focused on common goals rather than having managers pushing and pulling in different directions got Britannica off the critical list by helping it cross the bridge to the digital era. Now, managers are in the process of evaluation to see what new decisions need to be made to help the company thrive in the digital world.[46]

The Carnegie model is particularly useful at the problem identification stage. However, a coalition of key department managers is also important for smooth implementation of a decision, particularly a major reorganization. Top executives at Britannica realize the importance of building coalitions for decision making to keep the company moving forward. When top managers perceive a problem or want to make a major decision, they need to reach agreement with other managers to support the decision.[47]

■ Incremental Decision Process Model

Henry Mintzberg and his associates at McGill University in Montreal approached organizational decision making from a different perspective. They identified twenty-five decisions made in organizations and traced the events associated with these decisions from beginning to end.[48] Their research identified each step in the decision sequence. This approach to decision making, called the **incremental decision process model**, places less emphasis on the political and social factors described in the Carnegie model, but tells more about the structured sequence of activities undertaken from the discovery of a problem to its solution.[49]

Sample decisions in Mintzberg's research included choosing which jet aircraft to acquire for a regional airline, developing a new supper club, developing a new container terminal in a harbor, identifying a new market for a deodorant, installing a controversial new medical treatment in a hospital, and firing a star radio announcer.[50] The scope and importance of these decisions are revealed in the length of time taken to complete them. Most of these decisions took more than a year, and one third of them took more than 2 years. Most of these decisions were nonprogrammed and required custom-designed solutions.

One discovery from this research is that major organization choices are usually a series of small choices that combine to produce the major decision. Thus, many organizational decisions are a series of nibbles rather than a big bite. Organizations move through several decision points and may hit barriers along the way. Mintzberg called these barriers *decision interrupts*. An interrupt may mean an organization has to cycle back through a previous decision and try something new. Decision loops or cycles are one way the organization learns which alternatives will work. The ultimate solution may be very different from what was initially anticipated.

The pattern of decision stages discovered by Mintzberg and his associates is shown in Exhibit 12.5. Each box indicates a possible step in the decision sequence. The steps take place in three major decision phases: identification, development, and selection.

Identification Phase. The identification phase begins with *recognition*. Recognition means one or more managers become aware of a problem and the need to make a decision. Recognition is usually stimulated by a problem or an opportunity.

Briefcase

As an organization manager, keep these guidelines in mind:

Take risks and move the company ahead by increments when a problem is defined but solutions are uncertain. Try solutions step by step to learn whether they work.

A problem exists when elements in the external environment change or when internal performance is perceived to be below standard. In the case of firing a radio announcer, comments about the announcer came from listeners, other announcers, and advertisers. Managers interpreted these cues until a pattern emerged that indicated a problem had to be dealt with.

The second step is *diagnosis*, in which more information is gathered if needed to define the problem situation. Diagnosis may be systematic or informal, depending upon the severity of the problem. Severe problems do not allow time for extensive diagnosis; the response must be immediate. Mild problems are usually diagnosed in a more systematic manner.

Development Phase. In the development phase, a solution is shaped to solve the problem defined in the identification phase. The development of a solution takes one of two directions. First, *search* procedures may be used to seek out alternatives within the organization's repertoire of solutions. For example, in the case of firing a star announcer, managers asked what the radio station had done the last time an announcer had to be let go. To conduct the search, organization participants may look into their own memories, talk to other managers, or examine the formal procedures of the organization.

The second direction of development is to *design* a custom solution. This happens when the problem is novel so that previous experience has no value. Mintzberg found that in these cases, key decision makers have only a vague idea of the ideal solution. Gradually, through a trial-and-error process, a custom-designed alternative will emerge. Development of the solution is a groping, incremental procedure, building a solution brick by brick.

Selection Phase. The selection phase is when the solution is chosen. This phase is not always a matter of making a clear choice among alternatives. In the case of custom-made solutions, selection is more an evaluation of the single alternative that seems feasible.

Evaluation and choice may be accomplished in three ways. The *judgment* form of selection is used when a final choice falls upon a single decision maker, and the choice involves judgment based upon experience. In analysis, alternatives are evaluated on a more systematic basis, such as with management science techniques. Mintzberg found that most decisions did not involve systematic analysis and evaluation of alternatives. *Bargaining* occurs when selection involves a group of decision makers. Each decision maker may have a different stake in the outcome, so conflict emerges. Discussion and bargaining occur until a coalition is formed, as in the Carnegie model described earlier.

When a decision is formally accepted by the organization, *authorization* takes place. The decision may be passed up the hierarchy to the responsible hierarchical level. Authorization is often routine because the expertise and knowledge rest with the lower-level decision makers who identified the problem and developed the solution. A few decisions are rejected because of implications not anticipated by lower-level managers.

Dynamic Factors. The lower part of the chart in Exhibit 12.5 shows lines running back toward the beginning of the decision process. These lines represent loops or cycles that take place in the decision process. Organizational decisions do not follow an orderly progression from recognition through authorization. Minor problems arise that force a loop back to an earlier stage. These are decision interrupts. If a

EXHIBIT 12.5
The Incremental Decision Process Model

Source: Adapted and reprinted from "The Structure of Unstructured Decision Processes" by Henry Mintzberg, Duru Raisinghani, and André Théorêt, published in *Administrative Science Quarterly* 21, no. 2 (1976), 266, by permission of *The Administrative Science Quarterly*. Copyright © 1976 Cornell University.

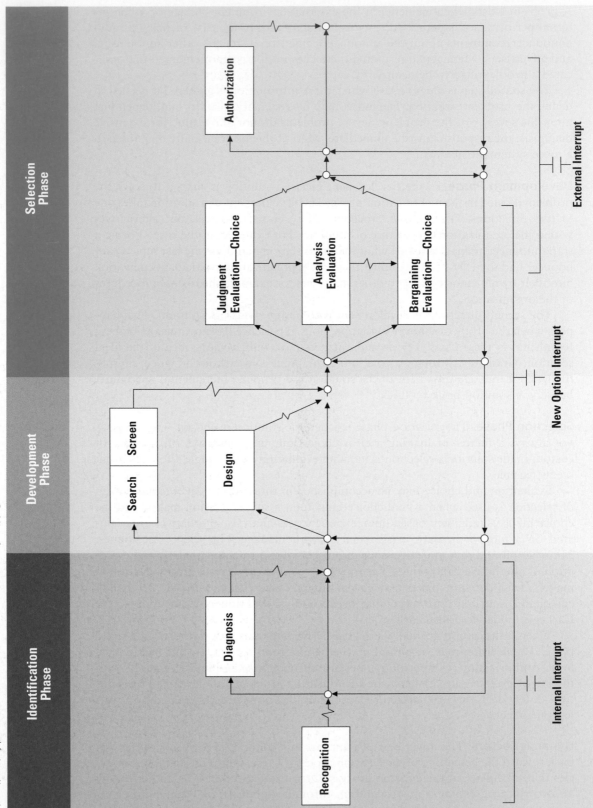

custom-designed solution is perceived as unsatisfactory, the organization may have to go back to the very beginning and reconsider whether the problem is truly worth solving. Feedback loops can be caused by problems of timing, politics, disagreement among managers, inability to identify a feasible solution, turnover of managers, or the sudden appearance of a new alternative. For example, when a small Canadian airline made the decision to acquire jet aircraft, the board authorized the decision, but shortly after, a new chief executive was brought in who canceled the contract, recycling the decision back to the identification phase. He accepted the diagnosis of the problem but insisted upon a new search for alternatives. Then a foreign airline went out of business and two used aircraft became available at a bargain price. This presented an unexpected option, and the chief executive used his own judgment to authorize the purchase of the aircraft.[51]

Because most decisions take place over an extended period of time, circumstances change. Decision making is a dynamic process that may require a number of cycles before a problem is solved. An example of the incremental process and cycling that can take place is illustrated in Gillette's decision to create a new razor.

In Practice

Gillette Company

The Gillette Company uses incremental decision making to perfect the design of razors such as the Sensor, the Mach3, or the vibrating M3Power. Consider the development of the Mach3. While searching for a new idea to increase sales in Gillette's mature shaving market, researchers at the company's British research lab came up with a bright idea to create a razor with three blades to produce a closer, smoother, more comfortable shave (recognition and diagnosis). Ten years later, the Mach3 reached the market, after thousands of shaving tests, numerous design modifications, and a development and tooling cost of $750 million, roughly the amount a pharmaceutical firm invests in developing a blockbuster drug.

The technical demands of building a razor with three blades that would follow a man's face and also be easy to clean had several blind alleys. Engineers first tried to find established techniques (search, screen), but none fit the bill. Eventually a prototype called Manx was built (design), and in shaving tests it "beat the pants off" Gillette's Sensor Excel, the company's best-selling razor at the time. However, Gillette's CEO insisted that the razor had to have a radically new blade edge so the razor could use thinner blades (internal interrupt), so engineers began looking for new technology that could produce a stronger blade (search, screen). Eventually, the new edge, known as DLC for diamond-like carbon coating, would be applied atom by atom with chip-making technology (design).

The next problem was manufacturing (diagnosis), which required an entirely new process to handle the complexity of the triple-bladed razor (design). Although the board gave the go-ahead to develop manufacturing equipment (judgment, authorization), some members became concerned because the new blades, which are three times stronger than stainless steel, would last longer and cause Gillette to sell fewer cartridges (internal interrupt). The board eventually made the decision to continue with the new blades, which have a blue indicator strip that fades to white and signals when it's time for a new cartridge.

The board gave final approval for production of the Mach3 to begin in the fall of 1997. The new razor was introduced in the summer of 1998 and began smoothly sliding off shelves. Gillette recovered its huge investment in record time. Gillette then started the process of searching for the next shaving breakthrough all over again, using new technology that can examine a razor blade at the atomic level and high-speed video that can capture the act of cutting a single whisker. The company has moved ahead in increments and is expected to roll out its next major shaving product sometime before the end of 2006.[52]

At Gillette, the identification phase occurred because executives were aware of the need for a new razor and became alert to the idea of using three blades to produce a closer shave. The development phase was characterized by the trial-and-error custom design leading to the Mach3. During the selection phase, certain approaches were found to be unacceptable, causing Gillette to cycle back and redesign the razor, including using thinner, stronger blades. Advancing once again to the selection phase, the Mach3 passed the judgment of top executives and board members, and manufacturing and marketing budgets were quickly authorized. This decision took more than a decade, finally reaching completion in the summer of 1998.

The Learning Organization

At the beginning of this chapter, we discussed how the rapidly changing business environment is creating greater uncertainty for decision makers. Some organizations that are particularly affected by this trend are shifting to the learning organization concept. These organizations are marked by a tremendous amount of uncertainty at both the problem identification and problem solution stages. Two approaches to decision making have evolved to help managers cope with this uncertainty and complexity. One approach is to combine the Carnegie and incremental process models just described. The second is a unique approach called the garbage can model.

◾ Combining the Incremental Process and Carnegie Models

The Carnegie description of coalition building is especially relevant for the problem identification stage. When issues are ambiguous, or if managers disagree about problem severity, discussion, negotiation, and coalition building are needed. Once agreement is reached about the problem to be tackled, the organization can move toward a solution.

The incremental process model tends to emphasize the steps used to reach a solution. After managers agree on a problem, the step-by-step process is a way of trying various solutions to see what will work. When problem solution is unclear, a trial-and-error solution may be designed. For example, in 1999, executives from three of the world's largest music companies formed a coalition to provide online consumers with a legal alternative to the digital piracy of Internet song-swapping services. However, making the joint venture MusicNet an appealing choice was a challenge. As originally conceived, the service didn't provide music lovers with the features they wanted, so managers took an incremental approach to try to make MusicNet more user-friendly. Today, as the leading online music service provider, MusicNet creates customized downloads and subscription services distributed through providers such as Yahoo!, AOL, and Virgin Digital. Managers have continued to use an incremental approach as the industry evolves with the introduction of Apple's iTunes and other new distribution channels. As one executive put it, "This is a business of trial and error."[53]

The two models do not disagree with one another. They describe how organizations make decisions when either problem identification or solution is uncertain. The application of these two models to the stages in the decision process is illustrated in Exhibit 12.6. When both parts of the decision process are simultaneously

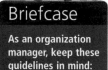

Briefcase

As an organization manager, keep these guidelines in mind:

Apply both the Carnegie model and the incremental process model in a situation with high uncertainty about both problems and solutions. Decision making may also employ garbage can procedures. Move the organization toward better performance by proposing new ideas, spending time working in important areas, and persisting with potential solutions.

Problem Identification	Problem Solution
When problem identification is uncertain, Carnegie model *applies*	*When problem solution is uncertain,* incremental process model *applies*
Political and social process is needed	*Incremental, trial-and-error process is needed*
Build coalition, seek agreement, and resolve conflict about goals and problem priorities	*Solve big problems in little steps*
	Recycle and try again when blocked

EXHIBIT 12.6
Decision Process When Problem Identification and Problem Solution Are Uncertain

highly uncertain, which is often the case in learning organizations, the organization is in an extremely difficult position. Decision processes in that situation may be a combination of Carnegie and incremental process models, and this combination may evolve into a situation described in the garbage can model.

▪ Garbage Can Model

The **garbage can model** is one of the most recent and interesting descriptions of organizational decision processes. It is not directly comparable to the earlier models, because the garbage can model deals with the pattern or flow of multiple decisions within organizations, whereas the incremental and Carnegie models focus on how a single decision is made. The garbage can model helps you think of the whole organization and the frequent decisions being made by managers throughout.

Organized Anarchy. The garbage can model was developed to explain the pattern of decision making in organizations that experience extremely high uncertainty, such as the growth and change required in a learning organization. Michael Cohen, James March, and Johan Olsen, the originators of the model, called the highly uncertain conditions an **organized anarchy**, which is an extremely organic organization.[54] Organized anarchies do not rely on the normal vertical hierarchy of authority and bureaucratic decision rules. They result from three characteristics:

1. *Problematic preferences.* Goals, problems, alternatives, and solutions are ill-defined. Ambiguity characterizes each step of a decision process.
2. *Unclear, poorly understood technology.* Cause-and-effect relationships within the organization are difficult to identify. An explicit database that applies to decisions is not available.
3. *Turnover.* Organizational positions experience turnover of participants. In addition, employees are busy and have only limited time to allocate to any one problem or decision. Participation in any given decision will be fluid and limited.

An organized anarchy is characterized by rapid change and a collegial, nonbureaucratic environment. No organization fits this extremely organic circumstance all the time, although learning organizations and today's Internet-based companies may experience it much of the time. Many organizations will occasionally find themselves in positions of making decisions under unclear, problematic circumstances. The garbage can model is useful for understanding the pattern of these decisions.

Streams of Events. The unique characteristic of the garbage can model is that the decision process is not seen as a sequence of steps that begins with a problem and ends with a solution. Indeed, problem identification and problem solution may not be connected to each other. An idea may be proposed as a solution when no problem is specified. A problem may exist and never generate a solution. Decisions are the outcome of independent streams of events within the organization. The four streams relevant to organizational decision making are as follows:

1. *Problems.* Problems are points of dissatisfaction with current activities and performance. They represent a gap between desired performance and current activities. Problems are perceived to require attention. However, they are distinct from solutions and choices. A problem may lead to a proposed solution or it may not. Problems may not be solved when solutions are adopted.
2. *Potential solutions.* A solution is an idea somebody proposes for adoption. Such ideas form a flow of alternative solutions through the organization. Ideas may be brought into the organization by new personnel or may be invented by existing personnel. Participants may simply be attracted to certain ideas and push them as logical choices regardless of problems. Attraction to an idea may cause an employee to look for a problem to which the idea can be attached and, hence, justified. The point is that solutions exist independent of problems.
3. *Participants.* Organization participants are employees who come and go throughout the organization. People are hired, reassigned, and fired. Participants vary widely in their ideas, perception of problems, experience, values, and training. The problems and solutions recognized by one manager will differ from those recognized by another manager.
4. *Choice opportunities.* Choice opportunities are occasions when an organization usually makes a decision. They occur when contracts are signed, people are hired, or a new product is authorized. They also occur when the right mix of participants, solutions, and problems exists. Thus, a manager who happened to learn of a good idea may suddenly become aware of a problem to which it applies and, hence, can provide the organization with a choice opportunity. Match-ups of problems and solutions often result in decisions.

With the concept of four streams, the overall pattern of organizational decision making takes on a random quality. Problems, solutions, participants, and choices all flow through the organization. In one sense, the organization is a large garbage can in which these streams are being stirred, as illustrated in Exhibit 12.7. When a problem, solution, and participant happen to connect at one point, a decision may be made and the problem may be solved; but if the solution does not fit the problem, the problem may not be solved.

Thus, when viewing the organization as a whole and considering its high level of uncertainty, one sees problems arise that are not solved and solutions tried that do not work. Organization decisions are disorderly and not the result of a logical, step-by-step sequence. Events may be so ill-defined and complex that decisions, problems, and solutions act as independent events. When they connect, some problems are solved, but many are not.[55]

Consequences. There are four specific consequences of the garbage can decision process for organizational decision making:

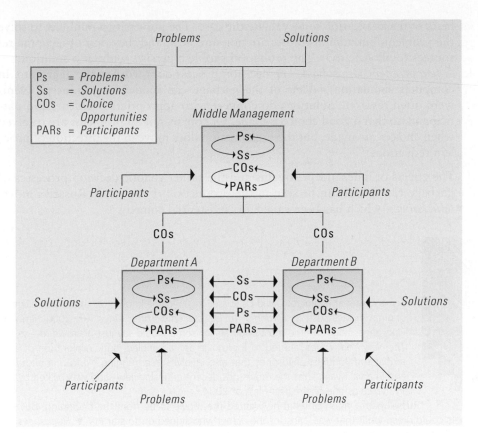

EXHIBIT 12.7
*Illustration of
Independent Streams
of Events in the Garbage
Can Model of Decision
Making*

1. *Solutions may be proposed even when problems do not exist.* An employee might be sold on an idea and might try to sell it to the rest of the organization. An example was the adoption of computers by many organizations during the 1970s. The computer was an exciting solution and was pushed by both computer manufacturers and systems analysts within organizations. The computer did not solve any problems in those initial applications. Indeed, some computers caused more problems than they solved.

2. *Choices are made without solving problems.* A choice such as creating a new department may be made with the intention of solving a problem; but, under conditions of high uncertainty, the choice may be incorrect. Moreover, many choices just seem to happen. People decide to quit, the organization's budget is cut, or a new policy bulletin is issued. These choices may be oriented toward problems but do not necessarily solve them.

3. *Problems may persist without being solved.* Organization participants get used to certain problems and give up trying to solve them; or participants may not know how to solve certain problems because the technology is unclear. A university in Canada was placed on probation by the American Association of University Professors because a professor had been denied tenure without due process. The probation was a nagging annoyance that the administrators wanted to remove. Fifteen years later, the nontenured professor died. The probation continues because the university did not acquiesce to the demands of the

heirs of the association to reevaluate the case. The university would like to solve the problem, but administrators are not sure how, and they do not have the resources to allocate to it. The probation problem persists without a solution.

4. *A few problems are solved.* The decision process does work in the aggregate. In computer simulation models of the garbage can model, important problems were often resolved. Solutions do connect with appropriate problems and participants so that a good choice is made. Of course, not all problems are resolved when choices are made, but the organization does move in the direction of problem reduction.

The effects of independent streams and the rather chaotic decision processes of the garbage can model can be seen in the production of David O. Russell's movie *I ♥ Huckabees*, which has been called an "existential comedy."

In Practice

I ♥ Huckabees

Screenwriter and director David O. Russell has become known for creating intelligent, original movies such as *Flirting with Disaster* and *Three Kings*. His 2004 film *I ♥ Huckabees* might be the most original—or some would say just plain weird—so far. *The New York Times* referred to the movie as "a jumbled, antic exploration of existential and Buddhist philosophy that also involves tree-hugging, African immigrants, and Shania Twain." Yet the movie got decent critical reviews and was picked by the *Village Voice* as one of the best films of 2004.

Russell had a vision of what he wanted the movie to be from the beginning, but few others could grasp what that was. Most of the actors who signed on to star in *I ♥ Huckabees* admit that they didn't really understand the script, but trusted Russell's vision and imagination. Two of the biggest actors in Hollywood, Jude Law and Gwyneth Paltrow, signed on to play employees at a department store chain called Huckabees. But Paltrow backed out before filming ever started. Nicole Kidman was interested but had a conflict. Jennifer Aniston became—and as quickly unbecame—a possibility. Finally, Naomi Watts, who had been Russell's original choice for the role, was able to free herself from scheduling conflicts to take the part. The casting wasn't quite set though. Jude Law dropped out for unknown reasons—but just as quickly dropped back in.

Filming was chaotic. As the actors were on camera saying the lines they'd memorized, Russell was a few feet away continually calling out new lines to them. In one scene, Law became so exhausted and frustrated that he started pounding his fists in the grass and shouting expletives. Russell loved the improvisation and kept the cameras rolling. Actors were unsure of how to develop their characterizations, so they just did whatever seemed right at the time, often based on Russell's efforts to keep them off balance. Scenes were often filmed blindly with no idea of how they were supposed to fit in the overall story.

After Russell's hours in the editing room, the final film turned out to be quite different from what the actors thought they'd shot. Some major scenes, including one that was supposed to articulate the film's theme that everything is connected, were cut entirely.

Amazingly, considering the chaos on the set, the film was completed on schedule and on budget. Although *I ♥ Huckabees* is emotionally and intellectually dense, and not the kind of movie that reaps big bucks, the haphazard process worked to create the movie David O. Russell wanted to make.[56]

The production of *I ♥ Huckabees* was not a rational process that started with a clear problem and ended with a logical solution. Many events occurred by chance and were intertwined, which characterizes the garbage can model. Everyone from the director to the actors continuously added to the stream of new ideas for the story. Some solutions were connected to emerging problems: Naomi Watts cleared her schedule just in time to take the role after Gwyneth Paltrow dropped out, for example. The actors (participants) daily made personal choices regarding characterization that proved to be right for the story line. The garbage can model, however, doesn't always work—in the movies or in organizations. A similar haphazard process during the filming of *Waterworld* led to the most expensive film in Hollywood history and a decided box-office flop for Universal Pictures.[57]

Contingency Decision-Making Framework

This chapter has covered several approaches to organizational decision making, including management science, the Carnegie model, the incremental decision process model, and the garbage can model. It has also discussed rational and intuitive decision processes used by individual managers. Each decision approach is a relatively accurate description of the actual decision process, yet all differ from each other. Management science, for example, reflects a different set of decision assumptions and procedures than does the garbage can model.

One reason for having different approaches is that they appear in different organizational situations. The use of an approach is contingent on the organization setting. Two characteristics of organizations that determine the use of decision approaches are (1) problem consensus and (2) technical knowledge about the means to solve those problems.[58] Analyzing organizations along these two dimensions suggests which approach will be used to make decisions.

Problem Consensus

Problem consensus refers to the agreement among managers about the nature of a problem or opportunity and about which goals and outcomes to pursue. This variable ranges from complete agreement to complete disagreement. When managers agree, there is little uncertainty—the problems and goals of the organization are clear, and so are standards of performance. When managers disagree, organization direction and performance expectations are in dispute, creating a situation of high uncertainty. One example of problem uncertainty occurred at Wal-Mart stores regarding the use of parking lot patrols. Some managers presented evidence that golf-cart patrols significantly reduced auto theft, assault, and other crimes in the stores' lots and increased business because they encouraged more nighttime shopping. These managers argued that the patrols should be used, but others believed the patrols were not needed and were too expensive, emphasizing that parking lot crime was a society problem rather than a store problem.[59]

Problem consensus tends to be low when organizations are differentiated, as described in Chapter 4. Recall that uncertain environments cause organizational departments to differentiate from one another in goals and attitudes to specialize in specific environmental sectors. This differentiation leads to disagreement and conflict, so managers must make a special effort to build coalitions during decision making. For example, NASA has been criticized for failing to identify problems with the *Columbia* space shuttle that might have prevented the February 2003 disaster. Part of the reason was high differentiation and conflicting opinions between safety managers and scheduling managers, in which pressure to launch on time overrode safety concerns. In addition, after the launch, engineers three times requested—and were denied—better photos to assess the damage from a piece of foam debris that struck the shuttle's left wing just seconds after launch. Investigations now indicate that the damage caused by the debris may have been the primary physical cause of the explosion. Mechanisms for hearing dissenting opinions and building coalitions can improve decision making at NASA and other organizations dealing with complex problems.[60]

Problem consensus is especially important for the problem identification stage of decision making. When problems are clear and agreed on, they provide clear standards and expectations for performance. When problems are not agreed on, problem identification is uncertain and management attention must be focused on gaining agreement about goals and priorities.

◼ Technical Knowledge about Solutions

Technical knowledge refers to understanding and agreement about how to solve problems and reach organizational goals. This variable can range from complete agreement and certainty to complete disagreement and uncertainty about cause–effect relationships leading to problem solution. One example of low technical knowledge occurred at PepsiCo's 7-Up division. Managers agreed on the problem to be solved—they wanted to increase market share from 6 percent to 7 percent. However, the means for achieving this increase in market share were not known or agreed on. A few managers wanted to use discount pricing in supermarkets. Other managers believed they should increase the number of soda fountain outlets in restaurants and fast-food chains. A few other managers insisted that the best approach was to increase advertising through radio and television. Managers did not know what would cause an increase in market share. Eventually, the advertising judgment prevailed at 7-Up, but it did not work very well. The failure of its decision reflected 7-Up's low technical knowledge about how to solve the problem.

When means are well understood, the appropriate alternatives can be identified and calculated with some degree of certainty. When means are poorly understood, potential solutions are ill-defined and uncertain. Intuition, judgment, and trial and error become the basis for decisions.

◼ Contingency Framework

Exhibit 12.8 describes the **contingency decision-making framework**, which brings together the two dimensions of problem consensus and technical knowledge about solutions. Each cell represents an organizational situation that is appropriate for the decision-making approaches described in this chapter.

Cell 1. In cell 1 of Exhibit 12.8, rational decision procedures are used because problems are agreed on and cause–effect relationships are well understood, so there is little uncertainty. Decisions can be made in a computational manner. Alternatives can be identified and the best solution adopted through analysis and calculations. The rational models described earlier in this chapter, both for individuals and for the organization, are appropriate when problems and the means for solving them are well defined.

Cell 2. In cell 2, there is high uncertainty about problems and priorities, so bargaining and compromise are used to reach consensus. Tackling one problem might mean the organization must postpone action on other issues. The priorities given

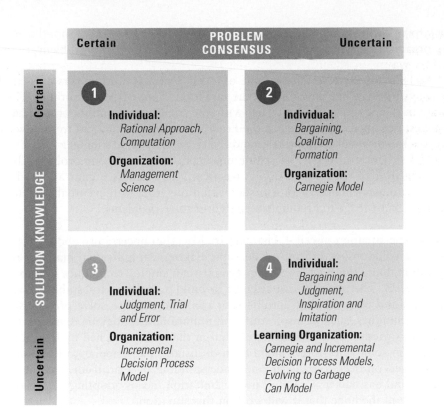

EXHIBIT 12.8
*Contingency Framework
for Using Decision Models*

to respective problems are decided through discussion, debate, and coalition building.

Managers in this situation should use broad participation to achieve consensus in the decision process. Opinions should be surfaced and discussed until compromise is reached. The organization will not otherwise move forward as an integrated unit. In the case of Wal-Mart, managers will discuss conflicting opinions about the benefits and costs of parking lot patrols.

The Carnegie model applies when there is dissension about organizational problems. When groups within the organization disagree, or when the organization is in conflict with constituencies (government regulators, suppliers, unions), bargaining and negotiation are required. The bargaining strategy is especially relevant to the problem identification stage of the decision process. Once bargaining and negotiation are completed, the organization will have support for one direction.

Cell 3. In a cell 3 situation, problems and standards of performance are certain, but alternative technical solutions are vague and uncertain. Techniques to solve a problem are ill defined and poorly understood. When an individual manager faces this situation, intuition will be the decision guideline. The manager will rely on past experience and judgment to make a decision. Rational, analytical approaches are not effective because the alternatives cannot be identified and calculated. Hard facts and accurate information are not available.

The incremental decision process model reflects trial and error on the part of the organization. Once a problem is identified, a sequence of small steps enables the organization to learn a solution. As new problems arise, the organization may recycle back to an earlier point and start over. Eventually, over a period of months or years, the organization will acquire sufficient experience to solve the problem in a satisfactory way.

McDonald's provides an example of a cell 3 situation. Managers are searching for ways to revive flagging sales at the fast-food chain's U.S. restaurants. They are using trial and error to come up with the right combination of management changes, new menu items such as the Fruit and Walnut Salad, and fresh advertising approaches that will rekindle sales and recharge McDonald's image.

The situation in cell 3, of senior managers agreeing about problems but not knowing how to solve them, occurs frequently in business organizations. If managers use incremental decisions in such situations, they will eventually acquire the technical knowledge to accomplish goals and solve problems.

Cell 4. The situation in cell 4, characterized by high uncertainty about both problems and solutions, is difficult for decision making. An individual manager making a decision under this high level of uncertainty can employ techniques from both cell 2 and cell 3. The manager can attempt to build a coalition to establish goals and priorities and use judgment, intuition, or trial and error to solve problems. Additional techniques, such as inspiration and imitation, also may be required. **Inspiration** refers to an innovative, creative solution that is not reached by logical means. Inspiration sometimes comes like a flash of insight, but—similar to intuition—it is often based on deep knowledge and understanding of a problem that the unconscious mind has had time to mull over.[61] **Imitation** means adopting a decision tried elsewhere in the hope that it will work in this situation.

For example, in one university, accounting department faculty were unhappy with their current circumstances but could not decide on the direction the department should take. Some faculty members wanted a greater research orientation, whereas others wanted greater orientation toward business firms and accounting applications. The disagreement about goals was compounded because neither group was sure about the best technique for achieving its goals. The ultimate solution was inspirational on the part of the dean. An accounting research center was established with funding from major accounting firms. The funding was used to finance research activities for faculty interested in basic research and to provide contact with business firms for other faculty. The solution provided a common goal and unified people within the department to work toward that goal.

When an entire organization is characterized by high uncertainty regarding both problems and solutions, as in learning organizations, elements of the garbage can model will appear. Managers may first try techniques from both cells 2 and 3, but logical decision sequences starting with problem identification and ending with problem solution will not occur. Potential solutions will precede problems as often as problems precede solutions. In this situation, managers should encourage widespread discussion of problems and idea proposals to facilitate the opportunity to make choices. Eventually, through trial and error, the organization will solve some problems.

Research has found that decisions made following the prescriptions of the contingency decision-making framework tend to be more successful. However, the study noted that nearly six of ten strategic management decisions failed to follow the framework, leading to a situation in which misleading or missing information decreased the chance of an effective decision choice.[62] Managers can use the contingency framework in Exhibit 12.8 to improve the likelihood of successful organizational decisions.

Special Decision Circumstances

In a highly competitive world beset by global competition and rapid change, decision making seldom fits the traditional rational, analytical model. Today's managers have to make high-stakes decisions more often and more quickly than ever before in an environment that is increasingly less predictable. For example, interviews with CEOs in high-tech industries found that they strive to use some type of rational process, but the uncertainty and change in the industry often make that approach unsuccessful. The way these managers actually reach decisions is through a complex interaction with other managers, subordinates, environmental factors, and organizational events.[63]

Three issues of particular concern for today's decision makers are coping with high-velocity environments, learning from decision mistakes, and avoiding escalating commitment.

High-Velocity Environments

In some industries today, the rate of competitive and technological change is so extreme that market data are either unavailable or obsolete, strategic windows open and shut quickly, perhaps within a few months, and the cost of poor decisions is company failure. Research has examined how successful companies make decisions in these **high-velocity environments**, especially to understand whether organizations abandon rational approaches or have time for incremental implementation.[64]

A comparison of successful with unsuccessful decisions in high-velocity environments found the following patterns:

- Successful decision makers tracked information in real time to develop a deep and intuitive grasp of the business. Two to three intense meetings per week with all key players were usual. Decision makers tracked operating statistics about cash, scrap, backlog, work in process, and shipments to constantly feel the pulse of what was happening. Unsuccessful firms were more concerned with future planning and forward-looking information, with only a loose grip on immediate happenings.
- During a major decision, successful companies began immediately to build multiple alternatives. Implementation of alternatives sometimes ran in parallel before they finally settled on a final choice. Companies that made decisions slowly developed just one alternative, moving to another only after the first one failed.
- Fast, successful decision makers sought advice from everyone and depended heavily on one or two savvy, trusted colleagues as counselors. Slow companies were unable to build trust and agreement among the best people.
- Fast companies involved everyone in the decision and tried for consensus; but if consensus did not emerge, the top manager made the choice and moved ahead. Waiting for everyone to be on board created more delays than was warranted. Slow companies delayed decisions to achieve a uniform consensus.
- Fast, successful choices were well integrated with other decisions and the overall strategic direction of the company. Less successful choices considered the decision in isolation from other decisions; the decision was made in the abstract.[65]

When speed matters, a slow decision is as ineffective as the wrong decision. As we discussed in Chapter 11, speed is a crucial competitive weapon in a growing number of industries, and companies can learn to make decisions quickly. To improve the chances of a good decision under high-velocity conditions, some organizations stimulate constructive conflict through a technique called **point–counterpoint**, which divides decision makers into two groups and assigns them different, often competing responsibilities.[66] The groups develop and exchange proposals and debate options until they arrive at a common set of understandings and recommendations. Groups can often make better decisions because multiple and diverse opinions are considered. In the face of complexity and uncertainty, the more people who have a say in the decision making, the better. At Intel Corp., the decision-making process typically involves people from several different areas and levels of hierarchy, "jousting with one another about the pros and cons of this or that," says CEO Craig Barrett.[67]

In group decision making, a consensus may not always be reached, but the exercise gives everyone a chance to consider options and state their opinions, and it gives top managers a broader understanding. Typically, those involved support the final choice. However, if a very speedy decision is required, top managers are willing to make the decision and move forward. Once a decision has been made at Intel, for example, it is everyone's responsibility to be involved and commit, even if they disagree. As Barrett says, "No backbiting, no second-guessing. We make a decision, we charge ahead."[68]

Decision Mistakes and Learning

Organizational decisions result in many errors, especially when made in conditions of great uncertainty. Managers simply cannot determine or predict which alternative will solve a problem. In these cases, the organization must make the decision—and take the risk—often in the spirit of trial and error. If an alternative fails, the organization can learn from it and try another alternative that better fits the situation. Each failure provides new information and insight. The point for managers is to move ahead with the decision process despite the potential for mistakes. "Chaotic action is preferable to orderly inaction."[69]

In some organizations, managers are encouraged to instill a climate of experimentation to facilitate creative decision making. If one idea fails, another idea should be tried. Failure often lays the groundwork for success, such as when technicians at 3M developed Post-it Notes based on a failed product—a not-very-sticky glue. Companies such as PepsiCo believe that if all their new products succeed, they're doing something wrong, not taking the necessary risks to develop new markets.[70]

Only by making mistakes can managers and organizations go through the process of **decision learning** and acquire sufficient experience and knowledge to perform more effectively in the future. Robert Townsend, who was president at Avis Corporation, gives the following advice:

Admit your mistakes openly, maybe even joyfully. Encourage your associates to do likewise by commiserating with them. Never castigate. Babies learn to walk by falling down. If you beat a baby every time he falls down, he'll never care much for walking.

My batting average on decisions at Avis was no better than a .333. Two out of every three decisions I made were wrong. But my mistakes were discussed openly and most of them corrected with a little help from my friends.[71]

■ Escalating Commitment

A much more dangerous mistake is to persist in a course of action when it is failing, a tendency referred to as **escalating commitment**. Research suggests that organizations often continue to invest time and money in a solution despite strong evidence that it is not working. Two explanations are given for why managers escalate commitment to a failing decision. The first is that managers block or distort negative information when they are personally responsible for a negative decision. They simply don't know when to pull the plug. In some cases, they continue to throw good money after bad even when a strategy seems incorrect and goals are not being met.[72]

A second explanation for escalating commitment to a failing decision is that consistency and persistence are valued in contemporary society. Consistent managers are considered better leaders than those who switch around from one course of action to another. Even though organizations learn through trial and error, organizational norms value consistency. These norms may result in a course of action being maintained, resources being squandered, and learning being inhibited. Emphasis on consistent leadership was partly responsible for the Long Island Lighting Company's (LILCO's) refusal to change course in the construction of the Shoreham Nuclear Power Plant, which was eventually abandoned—after an investment of more than $5 billion—without ever having begun operation. Shoreham's cost was estimated at $75 million when the project was announced in 1966, but by the time a construction permit was granted, LILCO had already spent $77 million. Opposition to nuclear power was growing. Critics continued to decry the huge sums of money being pumped into Shoreham. Customers complained that LILCO was cutting back on customer service and maintenance of current operations. Shoreham officials, however, seemed convinced that they would triumph in the end; their response to criticism was, "If people will just wait until the end, they are going to realize that this is a hell of an investment."

The end came in 1989, when a negotiated agreement with the state of New York led LILCO to abandon the $5.5 billion plant in return for rate increases and a $2.5 billion tax write-off. By the time Governor Mario Cuomo signed an agreement with the company, LILCO had remained firmly committed to a losing course of action for more than 23 years.[73]

Failure to admit a mistake and adopt a new course of action is far worse than an attitude that tolerates mistakes to encourage learning. Based on what has been said about decision making in this chapter, one can expect companies to be ultimately successful in their decision making by adopting a learning approach toward solutions. They will make mistakes along the way, but they will resolve uncertainty through the trial-and-error process.

Briefcase

As an organization manager, keep these guidelines in mind:

Do not persist in a course of action that is failing. Some actions will not work if uncertainty is high, so encourage organizational learning by readily trying new alternatives. Seek information and evidence that indicates when a course of action is failing, and allocate resources to new choices rather than to unsuccessful ventures.

■ Summary and Interpretation

The most important idea in this chapter is that most organizational decisions are not made in a logical, rational manner. Most decisions do not begin with the careful analysis of a problem, followed by systematic analysis of alternatives, and finally implementation of a solution. On the contrary, decision processes are characterized by conflict, coalition building, trial and error, speed, and mistakes. Managers operate under many constraints that limit rationality; hence, intuition and hunch often are the criteria for choice.

Another important idea is that individuals make decisions, but organizational decisions are not made by a single individual. Organizational decision making is a social process. Only in rare circumstances do managers analyze problems and find solutions by themselves. Many problems are not clear, so widespread discussion and coalition building take place. Once goals and priorities are set, alternatives to achieve those goals can be tried. When a manager does make an individual decision, it is often a small part of a larger decision process. Organizations solve big problems through a series of small steps. A single manager may initiate one step but should be aware of the larger decision process to which it belongs.

The greatest amount of conflict and coalition building occurs when problems are not agreed on. Priorities must be established to indicate which goals are important and what problems should be solved first. If a manager attacks a problem other people do not agree with, the manager will lose support for the solution to be implemented. Thus, time and activity should be spent building a coalition in the problem identification stage of decision making. Then the organization can move toward solutions. Under conditions of low technical knowledge, the solution unfolds as a series of incremental trials that will gradually lead to an overall solution.

The most novel description of decision making is the garbage can model. This model describes how decision processes can seem almost random in highly organic organizations such as learning organizations. Decisions, problems, ideas, and people flow through organizations and mix together in various combinations. Through this process, the organization gradually learns. Some problems may never be solved, but many are, and the organization will move toward maintaining and improving its level of performance.

Finally, many organizations must make decisions with speed, which means staying in immediate touch with operations and the environment. Moreover, in an uncertain world, organizations will make mistakes, and mistakes made through trial and error should be encouraged. Encouraging trial-and-error increments facilitates organizational learning. On the other hand, an unwillingness to change from a failing course of action can have serious negative consequences for an organization. Norms for consistency and the desire to prove one's decision correct can lead to continued investment in a useless course of action.

Key Concepts

bounded rationality perspective

Carnegie model

coalition

contingency decision-making framework

decision learning

escalating commitment

garbage can model

high-velocity environments

imitation

incremental decision process model

inspiration

intuitive decision making

management science approach

nonprogrammed decisions

organizational decision making

organized anarchy

point–counterpoint

problem consensus

problem identification

problem solution

problemistic search

programmed decisions

rational approach

satisficing

technical knowledge

Discussion Questions

1. When you are faced with choosing between several valid options, how do you typically make your decision? How do you think managers typically choose between several options? What are the similarities between your decision process and what you think managers do?
2. A professional economist once told his class, "An individual decision maker should process all relevant information and select the economically rational alternative." Do you agree? Why or why not?
3. Do you think intuition is a valid way to make important business decisions? Why or why not? Can you think of a time when you used intuition to make a decision?
4. The Carnegie model emphasizes the need for a political coalition in the decision-making process. When and why are coalitions necessary?
5. What are the three major phases in Mintzberg's incremental decision process model? Why might an organization recycle through one or more phases of the model?
6. An organization theorist once told her class, "Organizations never make big decisions. They make small decisions that eventually add up to a big decision." Explain the logic behind this statement.
7. How would you make a decision to select a building site for a new waste-treatment plant in the Philippines? Where would you start with this complex decision, and what steps would you take? Explain which decision model in the chapter best describes your approach.
8. Why would managers in high-velocity environments worry more about the present than the future? Discuss.
9. Describe the four streams of events in the garbage can model of decision making. Do you think those streams are independent of each other? Why?
10. Why are decision mistakes usually accepted in organizations but penalized in college courses and exams that are designed to train managers?

Chapter 12 Workbook: Decision Styles*

Think of some recent decisions that have influenced your life. Choose two significant decisions that you made and two decisions that other people made. Fill out the following table, using Exhibit 12.8 to determine decision styles.

*Adapted by Dorothy Marcic from "Action Assignment" in Jennifer M. Howard and Lawrence M. Miller, *Team Management* (Miller Consulting Group, 1994), 205.

Your decisions	Approach used	Advantages and disadvantages	Your recommended decision style
1.			
2.			
Decisions by others			
1.			
2.			

Questions

1. How can a decision approach influence the outcome of the decision? What happens when the approach fits the decision? When it doesn't fit?

2. How can you know which approach is best?

Case for Analysis: Cracking the Whip*

Harmon Davidson stared dejectedly at the departing figure of his management survey team leader. Their meeting had not gone well. Davidson had relayed to Al Pitcher complaints about his handling of the survey. Pitcher had responded with adamant denial and unveiled scorn.

Davidson, director of headquarters management, was prepared to discount some of the criticism as resentment of outsiders meddling with "the way we've always done business," exacerbated by the turbulence of continual reorganization. But Davidson could hardly ignore the sheer volume of complaints or his high regard for some of their sources. "Was I missing danger signals about Pitcher from the start?" Davidson asked himself. "Or was I just giving a guy I didn't know a fair chance with an inherently controversial assignment?"

With his division decimated in the latest round of downsizing at the Department of Technical Services (DTS) earlier that year, Davidson had been asked to return to the headquarters management office after a 5-year hiatus. The director, Walton Drummond, had abruptly taken early retirement.

One of the first things Davidson had learned about his new job was that he would be responsible for a comprehensive 6-month survey of the headquarters management structure and processes. The DTS secretary had promised the survey to the White House as a prelude to the agency's next phase of management reform. Drummond had already picked the five-person survey team consisting of two experienced management analysts, a promising younger staff member, an intern, and Pitcher, the team leader. Pitcher was fresh from the Treasury Department, where he had participated in a similar survey. But having gone off after retirement for an extended mountain-climbing expedition in Asia, Drummond was unavailable to explain his survey plans or any understandings he had reached with Pitcher.

Davidson had been impressed with Pitcher's energy and motivation. He worked long hours, wrote voluminously if awkwardly, and was brimming with the latest organizational theory. Pitcher had other characteristics, however, that were disquieting. He seemed uninterested in DTS's history and culture and was paternalistic toward top managers, assuming they were unsophisticated and unconcerned about modern management.

A series of presurvey informational briefings for headquarters office heads conducted by Davidson and Pitcher seemed to go swimmingly. Pitcher deferred to his chief on matters of philosophy and confined his remarks to schedule and procedures. He closed his segment on a friendly note, saying, "If we do find opportunities for improvement, we'll try to have recommendations for you."

But the survey was barely a week old when the director of management received his first call from an outraged customer. It was the assistant secretary for public affairs, Erin Dove, and she was not speaking in her usual upbeat tones. "Your folks have managed to upset my whole supervisory staff with their comments about how we'll have to change our organization and methods," she said. "I thought you were going through a fact-finding study. This guy Pitcher sounds like he wants to remake DTS headquarters overnight. Who does he think he is?"

When Davidson asked him about the encounter with public affairs, Pitcher expressed puzzlement that a few summary observations shared with supervisors in the interest of "prompt informal feedback" had been interpreted as such disturbing conclusions. "I told them we'll tell them how to fix it," he reassured his supervisor.

"Listen, Al," Davidson remonstrated gently. "These are very accomplished managers who aren't used to being told they have to fix anything. This agency's been on a roll for years, and the need for reinvention isn't resonating all that well yet. We've got to collect and analyze the information and assemble a convincing case for change, or we'll be spinning our wheels. Let's hold off on the feedback until you and I have reviewed it together."

But 2 weeks later, Technology Development Director Phil Canseco, an old and treasured colleague, was on Davidson's doorstep looking as unhappy as Erin Dove had sounded on the phone. "Harmon, buddy, I think you have to rein in this survey team a bit," he said. "Several managers who were scheduled for survey interviews were working on a 24-hour turnaround to give a revised project budget to the Appropriations subcommittee that day. My deputy says Pitcher was put out about postponing interviews and grumbled about whether we understood the new priorities. Is he living in the real world?"

Canseco's comments prompted Davidson to call a few of his respected peers who had dealt with the survey team. With varying degrees of reluctance, they all criticized the team leader and, in some cases, team members, as abrasive and uninterested in the rationales offered for existing structure and processes.

*This case was prepared by David Hornestay and appeared in *Government Executive*, August 1998, 45–46, as part of a series of case studies examining workplace dilemmas confronting federal managers. Reprinted by permission of *Government Executive*.

And so Davidson marshaled all of his tact for a review with the survey team leader. But Pitcher was in no mood for either introspection or reconsideration. He took the view that he had been brought in to spearhead a White House–inspired management improvement initiative in a glamour agency that had never had to think much about efficiency. He reminded Davidson that even he had conceded that managers were due some hard lessons on this score. Pitcher didn't see any way to meet his deadline except by adhering to a rigorous schedule, since he was working with managers disinclined to cooperate with an outsider pushing an unpopular exercise.

He felt Davidson's role was to hold the line against unwarranted criticisms from prima donnas trying to discredit the survey.

Many questions arose in Davidson's mind about the survey plan and his division's capacity to carry it out. Had they taken on too much with too little? Had the right people been picked for the survey team? Had managers and executives, and even the team, been properly prepared for the survey?

But the most immediate question was whether Al Pitcher could help him with these problems.

Case for Analysis: The Dilemma of Aliesha State College: Competence versus Need*

Until the 1980s, Aliesha was a well-reputed, somewhat sleepy state teachers college located on the outer fringes of a major metropolitan area. Then with the rapid expansion of college enrollments, the state converted Aliesha to a 4-year state college (and the plans called for it to become a state university with graduate work and perhaps even with a medical school in the late 1990s). Within 10 years, Aliesha grew from 1,500 to 9,000 students. Its budget expanded even faster than the enrollment, increasing twentyfold during that period.

The only part of Aliesha that did not grow was the original part, the teachers' college; there enrollment actually went down. Everything else seemed to flourish. In addition to building new 4-year schools of liberal arts, business, veterinary medicine, and dentistry, Aliesha developed many community service programs. Among them were a rapidly growing evening program, a mental health clinic, and a speech-therapy center for children with speech defects—the only one in the area. Even within education one area grew—the demonstration high school attached to the old teachers' college. Even though the high school enrolled only 300 students, its teachers were the leading experts in teacher education, and it was considered the best high school in the area.

Then, in 1992, the budget was suddenly cut quite sharply by the state legislature. At the same time the faculty demanded and got a fairly hefty raise in salary. It was clear that something had to give—the budget deficit was much too great to be covered by ordinary cost reductions. When the faculty committee sat down with the president and the board of trustees, two candidates for abandonment emerged after long and heated wrangling: the speech-therapy program and the demonstration high school. Both

cost about the same—and both were extremely expensive. The speech-therapy clinic, everyone agreed, addressed itself to a real need and one of high priority. But—and everyone had to agree because the evidence was overwhelming—it did not do the job. Indeed, it did such a poor, sloppy, disorganized job that pediatricians, psychiatrists, and psychologists hesitated to refer their patients to the clinic. The reason was that the clinic was a college program run to teach psychology students rather than to help children with serious speech impediments.

The opposite criticism applied to the high school. No one questioned its excellence and the impact it made on the education students who listened in on its classes and on many young teachers in the area who came in as auditors. But what need did it fill? There were plenty of perfectly adequate high schools in the area.

"How can we justify," asked one of the psychologists connected with the speech clinic, "running an unnecessary high school in which each child costs as much as a graduate student at Harvard?"

"But how can we justify," asked the dean of the school of education, himself one of the outstanding teachers in the demonstration high school, "a speech clinic that has no results even though each of its patients costs the state as much as one of our demonstration high school students, or more?"

*"The Dilemma of Aliesha State College: Competence versus Need" (pp. 23–24), from *Management Cases* by Peter F. Drucker. Copyright © 1977 by Peter F. Drucker. Reprinted by permission of the author.

Notes

1. Michael V. Copeland, "Stuck in the Spin Cycle," *Business 2.0* (May 2005), 74–75.

2. Carol J. Loomis, "Why Carly's Big Bet Is Failing," *Fortune* (February 7, 2005), 50–64; David Bank and Joann S. Lublin, "For H-P, No Shortage of Ideas; Turnaround Experts Offer Wide Range of Conflicting Strategies," *Asian Wall Street Journal* (February 14, 2005), M5; and James B. Stewart, "Common Sense: Finding a New CEO Won't Help Unless H-P Finds New Products," *The Wall Street Journal* (February 23, 2005), D3.

3. Alex Markels, "10 Biggest Business Blunders," *U.S. News & World Report* (November 8, 2004), EE2–EE8.

4. Adam Horowitz, Mark Athitakis, Mark Lasswell, and Owen Thomas, "101 Dumbest Moments in Business," *Business 2.0* (January–February 2005), 103–112.

5. Merissa Marr, "Return of the Ogre; How DreamWorks Misjudged DVD Sales of Its Monster Hit," *The Wall Street Journal* (May 31, 2005), A1, A9.

6. Saul Hansell, "Meg Whitman and eBay, Net Survivors," *The New York Times* (May 5, 2002), 17; Michael V. Copeland and Owen Thomas, "Hits (& Misses)," *Business 2.0* (January–February 2004), 126; Carlos Ghosn, "Saving the Business without Losing the Company," *Harvard Business Review* (January 2002), 37–45.

7. Charles Lindblom, "The Science of 'Muddling Through,'" *Public Administration Review* 29 (1954), 79–88.

8. Herbert A. Simon, *The New Science of Management Decision* (Englewood Cliffs, N.J.: Prentice-Hall, 1960), 1–8.

9. Paul J. H. Schoemaker and J. Edward Russo, "A Pyramid of Decision Approaches," *California Management Review* (Fall 1993), 9–31.

10. Rick Brooks, "Sealing Their Fate; A Deal with Target Put Lid on Revival at Tupperware," *The Wall Street Journal* (February 18, 2004), A1, A9.

11. Michael Pacanowsky, "Team Tools for Wicked Problems," *Organizational Dynamics* 23, no. 3 (Winter 1995), 36–51.

12. Doug Wallace, "What Would You Do? Southern Discomfort," *Business Ethics* (March/April 1996), 52–53; Renee Elder, "Apparel Plant Closings Rip Fabric of Community's Employment," *The Tennessean* (November 3, 1996), 1E.

13. Karen Dillon, "The Perfect Decision" (an interview with John S. Hammond and Ralph L. Keeney), *Inc.* (October 1998), 74–78; John S. Hammond and Ralph L. Keeney, *Smart Choices: A Practical Guide to Making Better Decisions* (Boston, Mass.: Harvard Business School Press, 1998).

14. Earnest R. Archer, "How to Make a Business Decision: An Analysis of Theory and Practice," *Management Review* 69 (February 1980), 54–61; and Boris Blai, "Eight Steps to Successful Problem Solving," *Supervisory Management* (January 1986), 7–9.

15. Francine Schwadel, "Christmas Sales' Lack of Momentum Test Store Managers' Mettle," *The Wall Street Journal* (December 16, 1987), 1.

16. Adapted from Archer, "How to Make a Business Decision," 59–61.

17. James W. Dean, Jr., and Mark P. Sharfman, "Procedural Rationality in the Strategic Decision-Making Process," *Journal of Management Studies* 30 (1993), 587–610.

18. Farnaz Fassihi, Greg Jaffe, Yaroslav Trofimov, Carla Anne Robbins, and Yochi J. Dreazen, "Winning the Peace; Early U. S. Decisions on Iraq Now Haunt American Efforts," *The Wall Street Journal* (April 19, 2004), A1, A14.

19. Art Kleiner, "Core Group Therapy," *Strategy & Business*, issue 27 (Second Quarter, 2002), 26–31.

20. Irving L. Janis, *Crucial Decisions: Leadership in Policymaking and Crisis Management* and (New York: The Free Press, 1989); and Paul C. Nutt, "Flexible Decision Styles and the Choices of Top Executives," *Journal of Management Studies* 30 (1993), 695–721.

21. Herbert A. Simon, "Making Management Decisions: The Role of Intuition and Emotion," *Academy of Management Executive* 1 (February 1987), 57–64; and Daniel J. Eisenberg, "How Senior Managers Think," *Harvard Business Review* 62 (November–December 1984), 80–90.

22. Sefan Wally and J. Robert Baum, "Personal and Structural Determinants of the Pace of Strategic Decision Making," *Academy of Management Journal* 37, no. 4 (1994), 932–956; and Orlando Behling and Norman L. Eckel, "Making Sense Out of Intuition," *Academy of Management Executive* 5, no. 1 (1991), 46–54.

23. Gary Klein, *Intuition at Work: Why Developing Your Gut Instincts Will Make You Better at What You Do* (New York: Doubleday, 2002); Milorad M. Novicevic, Thomas J. Hench, and Daniel A. Wren, "'Playing By Ear . . . In an Incessant Din of Reasons': Chester Barnard and the History of Intuition in Management Thought," *Management Decision* 40, no. 10 (2002), 992–1002; Alden M. Hayashi, "When to Trust Your Gut," *Harvard Business Review* (February 2001), 59–65; Brian R. Reinwald, "Tactical Intuition," *Military Review* 80, no. 5 (September–October 2000), 78–88; Thomas A. Stewart, "How to Think with Your Gut," *Business 2.0* (November 2002), accessed at *http://www.business2.com/articles* on November 7, 2002; Bill Breen, "What's Your Intuition?" *Fast Company* (September 2000), 290–300; and Henry Mintzberg and Frances Westley, "Decision Making: It's Not What You Think," *MIT Sloan Management Review* (Spring 2001), 89–93.

24. Thomas F. Issack, "Intuition: An Ignored Dimension of Management," *Academy of Management Review* 3 (1978), 917–922.

25. Marjorie A. Lyles, "Defining Strategic Problems: Subjective Criteria of Executives," *Organizational Studies* 8 (1987), 263–280; and Marjorie A. Lyles and Ian I. Mitroff, "Organizational Problem Formulation: An Empirical Study," *Administrative Science Quarterly* 25 (1980), 102–119.

26. Marjorie A. Lyles and Howard Thomas, "Strategic Problem Formulation: Biases and Assumptions Embedded in Alternative Decision-Making Models," *Journal of Management Studies* 25 (1988), 131–145.

27. Ross Stagner, "Corporate Decision-Making: An Empirical Study," *Journal of Applied Psychology* 53 (1969), 1–13.

28. Reported in Eric Bonabeau, "Don't Trust Your Gut," *Harvard Business Review* (May 2003), 116ff.

29. Thomas George, "Head Cowboy Gets Off His High Horse," *The New York Times* (December 21, 2003), Section 8, 1; Stewart, "How to Think with Your Gut."

30. Bonabeau, "Don't Trust Your Gut."

31. Ann Langley, "Between 'Paralysis by Analysis' and 'Extinction by Instinct,'" *Sloan Management Review* (Spring 1995), 63–76.

32. Paul C. Nutt, "Types of Organizational Decision Processes," *Administrative Science Quarterly* 29 (1984), 414–450.

33. Geraldine Fabrikant, "The Paramount Team Puts Profit Over Splash," *The New York Times* (June 30, 2002), 1, 15.

34. Nandini Rajagopalan, Abdul M. A. Rasheed, and Deepak K. Datta, "Strategic Decision Processes: Critical Review and Future Decisions," *Journal of Management* 19 (1993), 349–384; Paul J. H. Schoemaker, "Strategic Decisions in Organizations: Rational and Behavioral Views," *Journal of Management Studies* 30 (1993), 107–129; Charles J. McMillan, "Qualitative Models of Organizational Decision Making," *Journal of Management Studies* 5 (1980), 22–39; and Paul C. Nutt, "Models for Decision Making in Organizations and Some Contextual Variables Which Stimulate Optimal Use," *Academy of Management Review* 1 (1976), 84–98.

35. Hugh J. Miser, "Operations Analysis in the Army Air Forces in World War II: Some Reminiscences," *Interfaces* 23 (September–October 1993), 47–49; Harold J. Leavitt, William R. Dill, and Henry B. Eyring, *The Organizational World* (New York: Harcourt Brace Jovanovich, 1973), chap. 6.

36. Stephen J. Huxley, "Finding the Right Spot for a Church Camp in Spain," *Interfaces* 12 (October 1982), 108–114; James E. Hodder and Henry E. Riggs, "Pitfalls in Evaluating Risky Projects," *Harvard Business Review* (January–February 1985), 128–135.

37. Edward Baker and Michael Fisher, "Computational Results for Very Large Air Crew Scheduling Problems," *Omega* 9 (1981), 613–618; Jean Aubin, "Scheduling Ambulances," *Interfaces* 22 (March–April, 1992), 1–10.

38. Gang Yu, Michael Argüello, Gao Song, Sandra M. McCowan, and Anna White, "A New Era for Crew Recovery at Continental Airlines," *Interfaces* 33, no. 1 (January–February 2003), 5–22.

39. Julie Schlosser, Markdown Lowdown," *Fortune* (January 12, 2004), 40; Christina Binkley, "Numbers Game; Taking Retailers' Cues, Harrah's Taps Into Science of Gambling," *The Wall Street Journal* (November 22, 2004), A1, A8.

40. Harold J. Leavitt, "Beyond the Analytic Manager," *California Management Review* 17 (1975), 5–12; and C. Jackson Grayson, Jr., "Management Science and Business Practice," *Harvard Business Review* 51 (July–August 1973), 41–48.

41. David Wessel, "A Man Who Governs Credit Is Denied a Toys 'R' Us Card," *The Wall Street Journal* (December 14, 1995), B1.

42. Richard L. Daft and John C. Wiginton, "Language and Organization," *Academy of Management Review* (1979), 179–191.

43. Based on Richard M. Cyert and James G. March, *A Behavioral Theory of the Firm* (Englewood Cliffs, N.J.: Prentice-Hall, 1963); and James G. March and Herbert A. Simon, *Organizations* (New York: Wiley, 1958).

44. William B. Stevenson, Joan L. Pearce, and Lyman W. Porter, "The Concept of 'Coalition' in Organization Theory and Research," *Academy of Management Review* 10 (1985), 256–268.

45. Cyert and March, *A Behavioral Theory of the Firm*, 120–222.

46. Pui-Wing Tam, "One for the History Books: The Tale of How Britannica Is Trying to Leap from the Old Economy Into the New One," *The Wall Street Journal* (December 11, 2000), R32; and Richard A. Melcher, "Dusting Off the *Britannica*," *BusinessWeek* (October 20, 1997), 143–146.

47. Lawrence G. Hrebiniak, "Top-Management Agreement and Organizational Performance," *Human Relations* 35 (1982), 1139–1158; and Richard P. Nielsen, "Toward a Method for Building Consensus during Strategic Planning," *Sloan Management Review* (Summer 1981), 29–40.

48. Based on Henry Mintzberg, Duru Raisinghani, and André Théorêt, "The Structure of 'Unstructured' Decision Processes," *Administrative Science Quarterly* 21 (1976), 246–275.

49. Lawrence T. Pinfield, "A Field Evaluation of Perspectives on Organizational Decision Making," *Administrative Science Quarterly* 31 (1986), 365–388.

50. Mintzberg et al., "The Structure of 'Unstructured' Decision Processes."

51. Ibid., 270.

52. William C. Symonds with Carol Matlack, "Gillette's Edge," *BusinessWeek* (January 19, 1998), 70–77; William C. Symonds, "Would You Spend $1.50 for a Razor Blade?" *BusinessWeek* (April 27, 1998), 46; and Peter J. Howe, "Innovative; For the Past Half Century, 'Cutting Edge' Has Meant More at Gillette Co. Than a Sharp Blade," *Boston Globe* (January 30, 2005), D1.

53. Anna Wilde Mathews, Martin Peers, and Nick Wingfield, "Off-Key: The Music Industry Is Finally Online, but Few Listen," *The Wall Street Journal* (May 7, 2002), A1, A20; and *http://www.musicnet.com*.

54. Michael D. Cohen, James G. March, and Johan P. Olsen, "A Garbage Can Model of Organizational Choice," *Administrative Science Quarterly* 17 (March 1972), 1–25; and Michael D. Cohen and James G. March, *Leadership and Ambiguity: The American College President* (New York: McGraw-Hill, 1974).

55. Michael Masuch and Perry LaPotin, "Beyond Garbage Cans: An AI Model of Organizational Choice," *Administrative Science Quarterly* 34 (1989), 38–67.

56. Sharon Waxman, "The Nudist Buddhist Borderline-Abusive Love-In," *The New York Times* (September 19, 2004), Section 2, 1; and V. A. Musetto, "Crix Pick Best Pix," *The New York Post* (May 29, 2005), 93.

57. Thomas R. King, "Why 'Waterworld,' with Costner in Fins, Is Costliest Film Ever," *The Wall Street Journal* (January 31, 1995), A1.

58. Adapted from James D. Thompson, *Organizations in Action* (New York: McGraw-Hill, 1967), chap. 10; and McMillan, "Qualitative Models of Organizational Decision Making," 25.

59. Louise Lee, "Courts Begin to Award Damages to Victims of Parking-Area Crime," *The Wall Street Journal* (April 23, 1997), A1, A8.

60. Beth Dickey, "NASA's Next Step," *Government Executive* (April 15, 2004), 34ff; and Jena McGregor, "Gospels of Failure," *Fast Company* (February 2005), 61–67.

61. Mintzberg and Wheatley, "Decision Making: It's Not What You Think."

62. Paul C. Nutt, "Selecting Decision Rules for Crucial Choices: An Investigation of the Thompson Framework," *The Journal of Applied Behavioral Science* 38, no. 1 (March 2002), 99–131; and Paul C. Nutt, "Making Strategic Choices," *Journal of Management Studies* 39, no. 1 (January 2002), 67–95.

63. George T. Doran and Jack Gunn, "Decision Making in High-Tech Firms: Perspectives of Three Executives," *Business Horizons* (November–December 2002), 7–16.

64. L. J. Bourgeois III and Kathleen M. Eisenhardt, "Strategic Decision Processes in High Velocity Environments: Four Cases in the Microcomputer Industry," *Management Science* 34 (1988), 816–835.

65. Kathleen M. Eisenhardt, "Speed and Strategic Course: How Managers Accelerate Decision Making," *California Management Review* (Spring 1990), 39–54.

66. David A. Garvin and Michael A. Roberto, "What You Don't Know about Making Decisions," *Harvard Business Review* (September 2001), 108–116.

67. Janes Surowiecki, *The Wisdom of Crowds: Why the Many Are Smarter Than the Few and How Collective Wisdom Shapes Business, Economies, Societies, and Nations* (New York: Doubleday, 2004); Doran and Gunn, "Decision Making in High-Tech Firms."

68. Doran and Gunn, "Decision Making in High-Tech Firms."

69. Karl Weick, *The Social Psychology of Organizing*, 2d ed. (Reading, Mass.: Addison-Wesley, 1979), 243.

70. Christopher Power with Kathleen Kerwin, Ronald Grover, Keith Alexander, and Robert D. Hof, "Flops," *BusinessWeek* (August 16, 1993), 76–82.

71. Robert Townsend, *Up the Organization* (New York: Knopf, 1974), 115.

72. Helga Drummond, "Too Little Too Late: A Case Study of Escalation in Decision Making," *Organization Studies* 15, no. 4 (1994), 591–607; Joel Brockner, "The Escalation of Commitment to a Failing Course of Action: Toward Theoretical Progress," *Academy of Management Review* 17 (1992), 39–61; Barry M. Staw and Jerry Ross, "Knowing When to Pull the Plug," *Harvard Business Review* 65 (March–April 1987), 68–74; and Barry M. Staw, "The Escalation of Commitment to a Course of Action," *Academy of Management Review* 6 (1981), 577–587.

73. Jerry Ross and Barry M. Staw, "Organizational Escalation and Exit: Lessons from the Shoreham Nuclear Power Plant," *Academy of Management Journal* 36 (1993), 701–732.

13 Conflict, Power, and Politics

Intergroup Conflict in Organizations
  Sources of Conflict • Rational versus Political Model

Power and Organizations
  Individual versus Organizational Power • Power versus Authority • Vertical Sources of Power • Horizontal Sources of Power

Political Processes in Organizations
  Definition • When Is Political Activity Used?

Using Power, Politics, and Collaboration
  Tactics for Increasing Power • Political Tactics for Using Power • Tactics for Enhancing Collaboration

Summary and Interpretation

A Look Inside

Morgan Stanley

"This is like *People* magazine for Wall Street," said one observer. Another referred to it as *Peyton Place.* They were talking about the spectacle at Morgan Stanley, one of the oldest and most established securities firms on Wall Street. In the summer of 2005, the firm that once prided itself on refinement and discretion was engaged in an all-out war that made front-page headlines. Morgan Stanley's merger with Dean Witter Discover & Co. in 1997 was intended to create a financial services powerhouse. But the two sides clashed from the start.

The bankers at Morgan Stanley, with a list of blue-chip clients stretching back to the ninteenth century, viewed themselves as Wall Street's elite. Dean Witter, on the other hand, was a purveyor of credit cards to bargain hunters and a stockbroker to middle America. "They treated us like we were the Clampetts," said one Dean Witter manager. Conflicting goals between the Morgan Stanley side and the Dean Witter side were evident from the beginning, but the discord burst into public view when a group of eight stockholders, all former Morgan Stanley executives, launched a public campaign calling for the ouster of chairman and CEO Philip J. Purcell. When Purcell, head of Dean Witter, got the top job in 1997, the arrangement was that he would serve for 5 years and then be succeeded by John Mack, from the Morgan Stanley side of the merger. But Purcell made a series of moves that effectively forced Mack from the company and gave Purcell almost total control over management changes and the nomination of new directors. Purcell continued building his power by stacking the board with allies and placing loyal Dean Witter managers in key positions in the firm. As Morgan Stanley executives saw their responsibilities and authority taken away, they began leaving the firm in droves. A management shake-up in early 2005, in which Purcell appointed two Dean Witter loyalists as co-presidents, led to the departure of three more high-level Morgan Stanley executives and prompted the call for Purcell's ouster.

Although Purcell had strong support among the board, the public antagonism combined with weak financial performance and a sagging stock price caused the board and Purcell to reconsider. They made a joint decision that Purcell would resign from the firm. New leadership may resolve the discord and set Morgan Stanley on a smoother course with a united vision.[1]

Although the conflict at Morgan Stanley is an extreme example, all organizations are a complex mix of individuals and groups pursuing various goals and interests. Conflict is a natural and inevitable outcome of the close interaction of people who may have diverse opinions and values, pursue different objectives, and have differential access to information and resources within the organization. Individuals and groups will use power and political activity to handle their differences and manage conflict.[2]

Too much conflict can be harmful to an organization, as with the case at Morgan Stanley. However, conflict can also be a positive force because it challenges the status quo, encourages new ideas and approaches, and leads to change.[3] Some degree of conflict occurs in all human relationships—between friends, romantic partners, and teammates, as well as between parents and children, teachers and students, and bosses and employees. Conflict is not necessarily a negative force; it results from the normal interaction of varying human interests. Within organizations, individuals and groups frequently have different interests and goals they wish to achieve through the organization. In learning organizations, which encourage a democratic push and pull of ideas, the forces of conflict, power, and politics may be particularly evident. Managers in all organizations regularly deal with conflict and struggle with decisions about how to get the most out of employees, enhance job satisfaction and team identification, and realize high organizational performance.

Purpose of This Chapter

In this chapter we discuss the nature of conflict and the use of power and political tactics to manage and reduce conflict among individuals and groups. The notion of conflict has appeared in previous chapters. In Chapter 3, we talked about horizontal linkages such as task forces and teams that encourage collaboration among functional departments. Chapter 4 introduced the concept of differentiation, which means that different departments pursue different goals and may have different attitudes and values. Chapter 10 discussed the emergence of subcultures, and in Chapter 12, coalition building was proposed as one way to resolve disagreements among departments.

The first sections of this chapter explore the nature of intergroup conflict, characteristics of organizations that contribute to conflict, and the use of a political versus a rational model of organization to manage conflicting interests. Subsequent sections examine individual and organizational power, the vertical and horizontal sources of power for managers and other employees, and how power is used to attain organizational goals. The latter part of the chapter looks at politics, which is the application of power and authority to achieve desired outcomes. We also discuss some tactics managers can use to enhance collaboration among people and departments.

Intergroup Conflict in Organizations

Intergroup conflict requires three ingredients: group identification, observable group differences, and frustration. First, employees have to perceive themselves as part of an identifiable group or department.[4] Second, there has to be an observable group difference of some form. Groups may be located on different floors of the building, members may have different social or educational backgrounds, or members may work in different departments. The ability to identify oneself as a part of one group and to observe differences in comparison with other groups is necessary for conflict.[5]

The third ingredient is frustration. Frustration means that if one group achieves its goal, the other will not; it will be blocked. Frustration need not be severe and only needs to be anticipated to set off intergroup conflict. Intergroup conflict will appear when one group tries to advance its position in relation to other groups. **Intergroup conflict** can be defined as the behavior that occurs among organizational groups when participants identify with one group and perceive that other groups may block their group's goal achievement or expectations.[6] In the chapter-opening example, the Morgan Stanley bankers were opposed to moves by Purcell and Dean Witter executives to move the company into a wide range of new consumer markets, believing the firm should focus more strongly on its key businesses of securities underwriting, mergers and acquisitions, and investment banking. Conflict means that groups clash directly, that they are in fundamental opposition. Conflict is similar to competition but more severe. **Competition** is rivalry among groups in the pursuit of a common prize, whereas conflict presumes direct interference with goal achievement.

Intergroup conflict within organizations can occur horizontally across departments or vertically between different levels of the organization.[7] The production department of a manufacturing company may have a dispute with quality control because new quality procedures reduce production efficiency. Teammates may argue about the best way to accomplish tasks and achieve goals. Workers may clash with bosses about new work methods, reward systems, or job assignments. Another typical area of conflict is between groups such as unions and management or franchise owners and headquarters. For example, the United Auto Workers (UAW) is clashing with General Motors (GM) over demands from management that union workers accept decreased benefits to alleviate GM's rising healthcare costs. Franchise owners for McDonald's, Taco Bell, Burger King, and KFC have clashed with headquarters because of the increase of company-owned stores in neighborhoods that compete directly with franchisees.[8]

Conflict can also occur between different divisions or business units within an organization, such as between the auditing and consulting units of big firms such as PricewaterhouseCoopers and Deloitte Touche.[9] In global organizations, conflicts between regional managers and business division managers, among different divisions, or between divisions and headquarters are common because of the complexities of international business, as described in Chapter 6.

Sources of Conflict

Some specific organizational characteristics can generate conflict. These **sources of intergroup conflict** are goal incompatibility, differentiation, task interdependence, and limited resources. These characteristics of organizational relationships are determined by the contextual factors of environment, size, technology, strategy and goals, and organizational structure, which have been discussed in previous chapters. These characteristics, in turn, help shape the extent to which a rational model of behavior versus a political model of behavior is used to accomplish objectives.

Goal Incompatibility. Goal incompatibility is probably the greatest cause of intergroup conflict in organizations.[10] The goals of each department reflect the specific objectives members are trying to achieve. The achievement of one department's goals often interferes with another department's goals. University police, for example, have a goal of providing a safe and secure campus. They can achieve their goal by locking all buildings on evenings and weekends and not distributing keys. Without easy access to buildings, however, progress toward the science department's research goals will proceed slowly. On the other hand, if scientists come and go at all hours and security is ignored, police goals for security will not be met. Goal incompatibility throws the departments into conflict with each other.

The potential for conflict is perhaps greater between marketing and manufacturing than between other departments because the goals of these two departments are frequently at odds. Exhibit 13.1 shows examples of goal conflict between typical marketing and manufacturing departments. Marketing strives to increase the breadth of the product line to meet customer tastes for variety. A broad product line means short production runs, so manufacturing has to bear higher costs.[11] Other

Briefcase

As an organization manager, keep these guidelines in mind:

Recognize that some interdepartmental conflict is natural and can benefit the organization. Associate the organizational design characteristics of goal incompatibility, differentiation, task interdependence, and resource scarcity with greater conflict among groups. Expect to devote more time and energy to resolving conflict in these situations.

EXHIBIT 13.1
Marketing-Manufacturing Areas of Potential Goal Conflict

	MARKETING versus MANUFACTURING	
Goal Conflict	**Operative Goal is Customer Satisfaction**	**Operative Goal is Production Efficiency**
Conflict Area	**Typical Comment**	**Typical Comment**
1. Breadth of product line	"Our customers demand variety."	"The product line is too broad—all we get are short, uneconomical runs."
2. New product introduction	"New products are our lifeblood."	"Unnecessary design changes are prohibitively expensive."
3. Product scheduling	"We need faster response. Our customer lead times are too long."	"We need realistic commitments that don't change like wind direction."
4. Physical distribution	"Why don't we ever have the right merchandise in inventory?"	"We can't afford to keep huge inventories."
5. Quality	"Why can't we have reasonable quality at lower cost?"	"Why must we always offer options that are too expensive and offer little customer utility?"

Source: Based on Benson S. Shapiro, "Can Marketing and Manufacturing Coexist?" *Harvard Business Review* 55 (September–October 1977), 104–114; and Victoria L. Crittenden, Lorraine R. Gardiner, and Antonie Stam, "Reducing Conflict between Marketing and Manufacturing," *Industrial Marketing Management* 22 (1993), 299–309.

areas of goal conflict are quality, cost control, and new products or services. For example, at Rockford Health Systems, the human resources (HR) department wanted to implement a new self-service benefits system that would let employees manage their benefits from their home computers, but the high price of the software licenses conflicted with the finance department's goal of controlling costs.[12] Goal incompatibility exists among departments in most organizations.

Differentiation. *Differentiation* was defined in Chapter 4 as "the differences in cognitive and emotional orientations among managers in different functional departments." Functional specialization requires people with specific education, skills, attitudes, and time horizons. For example, people may join a sales department because they have ability and aptitude consistent with sales work. After becoming members of the sales department, they are influenced by departmental norms and values.

Departments or divisions within an organization often differ in values, attitudes, and standards of behavior, and these subcultural differences lead to conflicts.[13] Consider an encounter between a sales manager and a research and development (R&D) scientist about a new product:

The sales manager may be outgoing and concerned with maintaining a warm, friendly relationship with the scientist. He may be put off because the scientist seems withdrawn and disinclined to talk about anything other than the problems in which he is interested. He may also be annoyed that the scientist seems to have such freedom in choosing what he will work on. Furthermore, the scientist is probably often late for appointments, which, from the salesman's point of view, is no way to run a business. Our scientist, for his part, may feel uncomfortable because the salesman

Leading by Design

Advanced Cardiovascular Systems

Advanced Cardiovascular Systems (ACS; now Guidant Corporation) was the darling of the medical devices industry. The company, owned by pharmaceutical giant Eli Lilly, reached $100 million in sales within 5 years of launching its first product and revolutionized the field of angioplasty by producing one innovation after another. But when Ginger Graham took over as president and CEO of the medical device manufacturer, she realized that something was terribly wrong. Even though top managers were still touting ACS's strong internal and external relationships as key to the company's success, the reality was that these relationships were increasingly marked by conflict and discord rather than harmony and cooperation.

When Graham gave her first address to the company, she decided to tell the truth: "I've always heard about what a wonderful company ACS is," she began, "but frankly, that's not what I see. What I see is deteriorating morale, disillusioned customers, and finger-pointing. I see a place where R&D and manufacturing are practically at war. You folks in sales blame manufacturing. R&D blames marketing. We're all so busy blaming each other that nothing gets done." The response of employees—standing and cheering their approval—confirmed Graham's suspicions. People just wanted to hear that someone at the top knew the truth and was willing to admit it. From that moment, Graham began building a culture at ACS in which everyone feels free to tell the truth without fear of negative consequences.

ACS has established a number of practices that foster open and honest communications. To start, Graham reversed the top-down communication structure in an immediately visible way. Each top manager was assigned a coach from lower ranks of the organization. The coaches were trained to ask questions and gather specific information from everyone throughout the organization about the manager's openness and honest communication skills. Managers met with their coaches once a quarter. Because it had support from the top, the coaching program worked to close the communication gap between managers and employees. Managers also began sharing all information with employees—good and bad—and asking for their help in solving company problems. Employees who went above and beyond the call of duty to meet organizational goals were recognized and rewarded.

Rallying everyone around company goals rather than departmental goals helped alleviate much of the tension and conflict between departments. The war between R&D and manufacturing, however, had become so entrenched that stronger methods were needed.

Even though it cost the company dearly, Graham shut down product development altogether while representatives from R&D, manufacturing, clinical, and marketing worked with a professional facilitator to confront the issues head-on and come up with a new approach to product development. The process meant that no new products went out the door for 18 months, but the results were worth it. The company now repeatedly launches innovative new products every year, can produce enough to supply the entire market in a matter of weeks, completes clinical studies in record-setting time, and has improved quality while cutting costs.

Source: Ginger L. Graham, "If You Want Honesty, Break Some Rules," *Harvard Business Review* (April 2002), 42–47.

seems to be pressing for immediate answers to technical questions that will take a long time to investigate. All the discomforts are concrete manifestations of the relatively wide differences between these two men in respect to their working and thinking styles.[14]

A lack of trust within the organization can magnify these natural differences and increase the potential for conflict among departments and with top managers, as a new CEO discovered at Advanced Cardiovascular Systems. Her solution was to build a new culture of honesty, as discussed in this chapter's Leading by Design.

Task Interdependence. Task interdependence refers to the dependence of one unit on another for materials, resources, or information. As described in Chapter 7, *pooled interdependence* means there is little interaction; *sequential interdepen-*

dence means the output of one department goes to the next department; and *reciprocal interdependence* means that departments mutually exchange materials and information.[15]

Generally, as interdependence increases, the potential for conflict increases.[16] In the case of pooled interdependence, units have little need to interact. Conflict is at a minimum. Sequential and reciprocal interdependence require employees to spend time coordinating and sharing information. Employees must communicate frequently, and differences in goals or attitudes will surface. Conflict is especially likely to occur when agreement is not reached about the coordination of services to each other. Greater interdependence means departments often exert pressure for a fast response because departmental work has to wait on other departments.[17]

Limited Resources. Another major source of conflict involves competition between groups for what members perceive as limited resources.[18] Organizations have limited money, physical facilities, staff resources, and human resources to share among departments. In their desire to achieve goals, groups want to increase their resources. This throws them into conflict. Managers may develop strategies, such as inflating budget requirements or working behind the scenes, to obtain a desired level of resources.

Resources also symbolize power and influence within an organization. The ability to obtain resources enhances prestige. Departments typically believe they have a legitimate claim on additional resources. However, exercising that claim results in conflict. For example, in almost every organization, conflict occurs during the annual budget exercise, often creating political activity.

■ Rational versus Political Model

The sources of intergroup conflict are listed in Exhibit 13.2. The degree of goal incompatibility, differentiation, interdependence, and conflict over limited resources determines whether a rational or political model of behavior is used within the organization to accomplish goals.

When goals are in alignment, there is little differentiation, departments are characterized by pooled interdependence, and resources seem abundant, managers can use a **rational model** of organization, as outlined in Exhibit 13.2. As with the rational approach to decision making described in Chapter 12, the rational model of organization is an ideal that is not fully achievable in the real world, though managers strive to use rational processes whenever possible. In the rational organization, behavior is not random or accidental. Goals are clear and choices are made in a logical way. When a decision is needed, the goal is defined, alternatives are identified, and the choice with the highest probability of success is selected. The rational model is also characterized by centralized power and control, extensive information systems, and an efficiency orientation.[19] The opposite view of organizational processes is the **political model**, also described in Exhibit 13.2. When differences are great, organization groups have separate interests, goals, and values. Disagreement and conflict are normal, so power and influence are needed to reach decisions. Groups will engage in the push and pull of debate to decide goals and reach decisions. Information is ambiguous and incomplete. The political model particularly describes organizations that strive for democracy and participation in decision making by empowering workers. Purely rational procedures do not work in democratic organizations, such as learning organizations.

When Conflict is Low, Rational Model Describes Organization		When Conflict is High, Political Model Describes Organization
Consistent across participants	Goals	Inconsistent, pluralistic within the organization
Centralized	Power and control	Decentralized, shifting coalitions and interest groups
Orderly, logical, rational	Decision process	Disorderly, result of bargaining and interplay among interests
Norm of efficiency	Rules and norms	Free play of market forces; conflict is legitimate and expected
Extensive, systematic, accurate	Information	Ambiguous; information used and withheld strategically

Sources of Potential Intergroup Conflict

- Goal incompatibility
- Differentiation
- Task interdependence
- Limited resources

EXHIBIT 13.2
Sources of Conflict and Use of Rational versus Political Model

Both rational and political processes are normally used in organizations. In most organizations, neither the rational model nor the political model characterizes things fully, but each will be used some of the time. At Amazon.com, founder and CEO Jeff Bezos emphasizes a rational approach to planning and decision making whenever possible. "The great thing about fact-based decisions," he says, "is that they overrule the hierarchy. The most junior person in the company can win an argument with the most senior person with a fact-based decision." For decisions and situations that are complex, ill-defined, and controversial, however, Bezos uses a political model, discussing the issues with people, building agreement among senior executives, and relying on his own judgment.[20]

Managers may strive to adopt rational procedures but will find that politics is needed to accomplish objectives. The political model means managers learn to acquire, develop, and use power to accomplish objectives.

Power and Organizations

Power is an intangible force in organizations. It cannot be seen, but its effect can be felt. *Power* is often defined as the potential ability of one person (or department) to influence other people (or departments) to carry out orders[21] or to do something they would not otherwise have done.[22] Other definitions stress that power is the ability to achieve goals or outcomes that power holders desire.[23] The achievement of desired outcomes is the basis of the definition used here: **Power** is the ability of one person or department in an organization to influence other people to bring about desired outcomes. It is the potential to influence others within the organization with the goal of attaining desired outcomes for power holders.

Power exists only in a relationship between two or more people, and it can be exercised in either vertical or horizontal directions. The source of power often derives from an exchange relationship in which one position or department provides scarce or valued resources to other departments. When one person is dependent on another person, a power relationship emerges in which the person with the resources has greater power.[24]

When power exists in a relationship, the power holders can achieve compliance with their requests. Powerful individuals are often able to get bigger budgets for their departments, more favorable production schedules, and more control over the organization's agenda.[25]

As an illustration, consider how power is shifting in the game of baseball. Seasoned team managers, who typically base their decisions on instinct and experience, are losing power to general managers using business theories and new analytical tools to come up with statistical benchmarks and operational standards that are believed to improve performance. As a result of their increased power, some general managers are now suggesting player lineups, handpicking members of the coaching staff, and generally telling team managers how to run the team.[26]

■ Individual versus Organizational Power

In popular literature, power is often described as a personal characteristic, and a frequent topic is how one person can influence or dominate another person.[27] You probably recall from an earlier management or organizational behavior course that managers have five sources of personal power.[28] *Legitimate power* is the authority granted by the organization to the formal management position a manager holds. *Reward power* stems from the ability to bestow rewards—a promotion, raise, or pat on the back—to other people. The authority to punish or recommend punishment is called *coercive power*. *Expert power* derives from a person's greater skill or knowledge about the tasks being performed. The last, *referent power*, is derived from personal characteristics: people admire the manager and want to be like or identify with the manager out of respect and admiration. Each of these sources may be used by individuals within organizations.

Power in organizations, however, is often the result of structural characteristics.[29] Organizations are large, complex systems that contain hundreds, even thousands, of people. These systems have a formal hierarchy in which some tasks are more important regardless of who performs them. In addition, some positions have access to greater resources, or their contribution to the organization is more critical. Thus, the important power processes in organizations reflect larger organizational relationships, both horizontal and vertical.

■ Power versus Authority

Anyone in an organization can exercise power to achieve desired outcomes. When the Discovery Channel wanted to extend its brand beyond cable television, Tom Hicks began pushing for a focus on the Internet. Even though Discovery's CEO favored exploring interactive television, Hicks organized a grassroots campaign that eventually persuaded the CEO to focus instead on Web publishing, indicating that Hicks had power within the organization. Today, Hicks runs Discovery Channel Online.[30]

The concept of formal authority is related to power but is narrower in scope. **Authority** is also a force for achieving desired outcomes, but only as prescribed by the formal hierarchy and reporting relationships. Three properties identify authority:

1. *Authority is vested in organizational positions.* People have authority because of the positions they hold, not because of personal characteristics or resources.

2. *Authority is accepted by subordinates.* Subordinates comply because they believe position holders have a legitimate right to exercise authority.[31] In most North American organizations, employees accept that supervisors can legitimately tell them what time to arrive at work, the tasks to perform while they're there, and what time they can go home.
3. *Authority flows down the vertical hierarchy.*[32] Authority exists along the formal chain of command, and positions at the top of the hierarchy are vested with more formal authority than are positions at the bottom.

Organizational power can be exercised upward, downward, and horizontally in organizations. Formal authority is exercised downward along the hierarchy and is the same as legitimate power. In the following sections, we will examine vertical and horizontal sources of power for employees throughout the organization.

Vertical Sources of Power

All employees along the vertical hierarchy have access to some sources of power. Although a large amount of power is typically allocated to top managers by the organization structure, employees throughout the organization often obtain power disproportionate to their formal positions and can exert influence in an upward direction, as Tom Hicks did at the Discovery Channel. There are four major sources of vertical power: formal position, resources, control of decision premises and information, and network centrality.[33]

Briefcase

As an organization manager, keep this guideline in mind:

Understand and use the vertical sources of power in organizations, including formal position, resources, control of decision premises and information, and network centrality.

Formal Position. Certain rights, responsibilities, and prerogatives accrue to top positions. People throughout the organization accept the legitimate right of top managers to set goals, make decisions, and direct activities. Thus, the power from formal position is sometimes called *legitimate power*.[34] Senior managers often use symbols and language to perpetuate their legitimate power. For example, the new administrator at a large hospital in the San Francisco area symbolized his formal power by issuing a newsletter with his photo on the cover and airing a 24-hour-a-day video to personally welcome patients.[35]

The amount of power provided to middle managers and lower-level participants can be built into the organization's structural design. The allocation of power to middle managers and staff is important because power enables employees to be productive. When job tasks are nonroutine, and when employees participate in self-directed teams and problem-solving task forces, this encourages employees to be flexible and creative and to use their own discretion. Allowing people to make their own decisions increases their power.

Power is also increased when a position encourages contact with high-level people. Access to powerful people and the development of a relationship with them provide a strong base of influence.[36] For example, in some organizations an administrative assistant to the president might have more power than a department head because the assistant has access to the senior executive on a daily basis.

The logic of designing positions for more power assumes that an organization does not have a limited amount of power to be allocated among high-level and low-level employees. The total amount of power in an organization can be increased by designing tasks and interactions along the hierarchy so everyone can exert more influence. eBay CEO Meg Whitman, for example, tops *Fortune* magazine's list of the most powerful women in American business. Yet Whitman believes that to have power, you have to give it away. She makes sure executives and employees at eBay have the power and authority they need to contribute to the company's astounding success.[37] If the distribution of power is skewed too heavily toward the top, research suggests that the organization will be less effective.[38]

Resources. Organizations allocate huge amounts of resources. Buildings are constructed, salaries are paid, and equipment and supplies are purchased. Each year, new resources are allocated in the form of budgets. These resources are allocated downward from top managers. Top managers often own stock, which gives them property rights over resource allocation. However, in many of today's organizations, employees throughout the organization also share in ownership, which increases their power.

In most cases, top managers control the resources and, hence, can determine their distribution. Resources can be used as rewards and punishments, which are additional sources of power. Resource allocation also creates a dependency relationship. Lower-level participants depend on top managers for the financial and physical resources needed to perform their tasks. Top management can exchange resources in the form of salaries and bonuses, personnel, promotions, and physical facilities for compliance with the outcomes they desire. When he was CEO of American International Group, Inc. (AIG), Hank Greenberg used preferred shares of a private partnership called C.V. Starr & Co. to reward executives for hard work and loyalty. In connection with alleged wrongdoing at AIG, Greenberg and the incentive program are now under investigation, but for years the practice enabled Greenberg to wield tremendous power over AIG executives, for whom admission to the "Starr Club" was both emotionally and financially gratifying.[39]

Control of Decision Premises and Information. Control of **decision premises** means that top managers place constraints on decisions made at lower levels by specifying a decision frame of reference and guidelines. In one sense, top managers make big decisions, whereas lower-level participants make small decisions. Top management decides which goal an organization will try to achieve, such as increased market share. Lower-level participants then decide how the goal is to be reached. In one company, top management appointed a committee to select a new marketing vice president. The CEO provided the committee with detailed qualifications that the new vice president should have. He also selected people to serve on the committee. In this way, the CEO shaped the decision premises within which the marketing vice president would be chosen. Top manager actions and decisions such as these place limits on the decisions of lower-level managers and thereby influence the outcome of their decisions.[40]

The control of information can also be a source of power. Managers in today's organizations recognize that information is a primary business resource and that by controlling what information is collected, how it is interpreted, and how it is shared, they can influence how decisions are made.[41] In many of today's companies, especially in learning organizations, information is openly and broadly shared, which increases the power of people throughout the organization.

However, top managers generally have access to more information than do other employees. This information can be released as needed to shape the decision outcomes of other people. In one organization, Clark, Ltd., the senior information technology (IT) manager controlled information given to the board of directors and thereby influenced the board's decision to purchase a sophisticated computer system.[42] The board of directors had formal authority to decide from which company

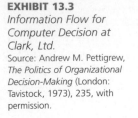

EXHIBIT 13.3
*Information Flow for
Computer Decision at
Clark, Ltd.*
Source: Andrew M. Pettigrew,
*The Politics of Organizational
Decision-Making* (London:
Tavistock, 1973), 235, with
permission.

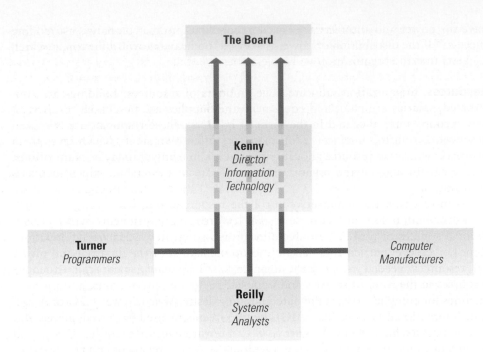

the system would be purchased. The management services group was asked to recommend which of six computer manufacturers should receive the order. Jim Kenny was in charge of the management services group, and Kenny disagreed with other managers about which system to purchase. As shown in Exhibit 13.3, other managers had to go through Kenny to have their viewpoints heard by the board. Kenny shaped the board's thinking toward selecting the system he preferred by controlling information given to them.

Control of information can also be used to shape decisions for self-serving, unethical, and even illegal purposes. For example, at Hollinger International, Inc., which owns newspapers including the *Chicago Sun-Times* and *Jerusalem Post,* the board approved a series of transactions that allowed CEO Lord Conrad Black and his colleagues to improperly draw off millions of dollars from the company for personal gain. Although the board has been criticized for its lax governance, several directors insist that their decisions were based on false, skewed, or misleading information provided by Lord Black.[43]

Middle managers and lower-level employees may also have access to information that can increase their power. A secretary to a senior executive can often control information that other people want and will thus be able to influence those people. Top executives depend on people throughout the organization for information about problems or opportunities. Middle managers or lower-level employees may manipulate the information they provide to top managers in order to influence decision outcomes.

Network Centrality. **Network centrality** means being centrally located in the organization and having access to information and people that are critical to the company's success. Top executives are more successful when they put themselves at the center of a communication network, building connections with people throughout the company. Sir Howard Stringer, the new CEO of Sony, is known as a skilled corporate politician who builds trust and alliances across different divisions and hierarchical levels. Stringer has been praised for his ability to network with almost everyone. He will need those political skills to gain an understanding of the sprawling Sony empire and get the various divisions working together. "He's the only one I know who can manage the Japanese [electronics side] and the show-bizzers [entertainment side]," said a former head of Sony Pictures Entertainment.[44] Middle managers and lower-level employees can also use the ideas of network centrality. For example, several years ago at Xerox, Cindy Casselman, who had little formal power and authority, began selling her idea for an intranet site to managers all over the company. Working behind the scenes, Casselman gradually gained the power she needed to make her vision a reality—and win a promotion.[45]

Employees also have more power when their jobs are related to current areas of concern or opportunity. When a job pertains to pressing organizational problems, power is more easily accumulated. For example, managers at all levels who possess crisis leadership skills have gained power in today's world of terror alerts, major natural disasters, and general uncertainty. A communications manager at Empire Blue Cross and Blue Shield, for instance, gained power following the September 11, 2001, terrorist attacks in New York because he acted on his own and worked around the clock to get phone lines and voice mail restored.[46]

Employees increase their network centrality by becoming knowledgeable and expert about certain activities or by taking on difficult tasks and acquiring specialized knowledge that makes them indispensable to managers above them. People who show initiative, work beyond what is expected, take on undesirable but important projects, and show interest in learning about the company and industry often find themselves with influence. Physical location also helps because some locations are in the center of things. Central location lets a person be visible to key people and become part of important interaction networks.

People. Top leaders often increase their power by surrounding themselves with a group of loyal executives.[47] Loyal managers keep the top leader informed and in touch with events and report possible disobedience or troublemaking in the organization. Top executives can use their central positions to build alliances and exercise substantial power when they have a management team that is fully in support of their decisions and actions.

This works in the opposite direction too. Lower-level people have greater power when they have positive relationships and connections with higher-ups. By being loyal and supportive of their bosses, employees sometimes gain favorable status and exert greater influence.

The chapter-opening example illustrates how Phillip Purcell gained power after the merger of Morgan Stanley and Dean Witter Discover & Co. by surrounding himself with loyal allies and edging out Morgan Stanley executives. Purcell is by no means alone in using this tactic. As a senior banker at a rival firm referred to the Morgan Stanley situation, "What do you really have here? A CEO who isn't terribly popular, who gets rid of any executive who isn't loyal to him. He packs the board with his pals, and the company's stock performance is mediocre. So what? That's like most companies on the S&P 500."[48]

Indeed, many top executives strive to build a cadre of loyal and supportive executives to help them achieve their goals for the organization. For example, former New York Stock Exchange Chairman Dick Grasso placed his friends and allies in

EXHIBIT 13.4
Ratings of Power among Departments in Industrial Firms
Source: Charles Perrow, "Departmental Power and Perspective in Industrial Firms," in Mayer N. Zald, ed., *Power in Organizations* (Nashville, Tenn.: Vanderbilt University Press, 1970), 64.

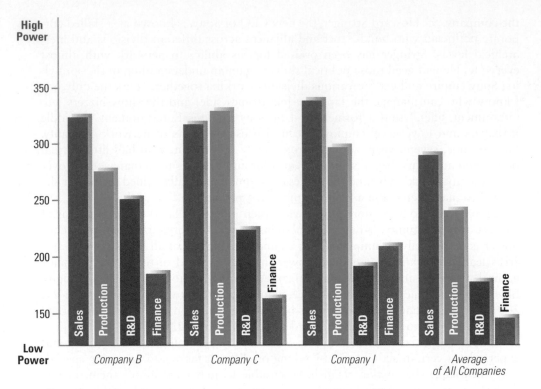

critical positions and pushed favored candidates for board posts. As another example, the U.S. government hand picked the advisers and committee members who would influence decisions made by the interim Iraqi government.[49]

■ Horizontal Sources of Power

Horizontal power pertains to relationships across departments or divisions. All vice presidents are usually at the same level on the organization chart. Does this mean each department has the same amount of power? No. Horizontal power is not defined by the formal hierarchy or the organization chart. Each department makes a unique contribution to organizational success. Some departments will have greater say and will achieve their desired outcomes, whereas others will not. For example, Charles Perrow surveyed managers in several industrial firms.[50] He bluntly asked, "Which department has the most power?" among four major departments: production, sales and marketing, R&D, and finance and accounting. Partial survey results are given in Exhibit 13.4.

In most firms, sales had the greatest power. In a few firms, production was also quite powerful. On average, the sales and production departments were more powerful than R&D and finance, although substantial variation existed. Differences in the amount of horizontal power clearly occurred in those firms. Today, IT departments have growing power in many organizations.

Horizontal power is difficult to measure because power differences are not defined on the organization chart. However, some initial explanations for departmen-

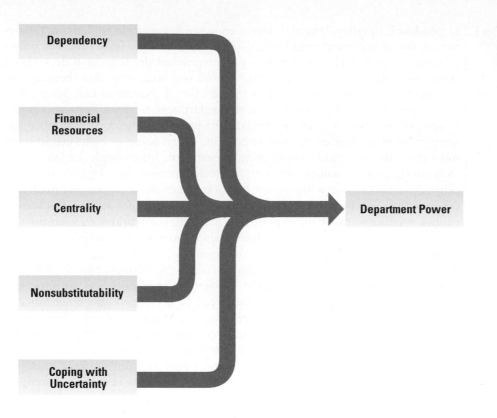

tal power differences, such as those shown in Exhibit 13.4, have been found. The theoretical concept that explains relative power is called strategic contingencies.[51]

Strategic Contingencies. Strategic contingencies are events and activities both inside and outside an organization that are essential for attaining organizational goals. Departments involved with strategic contingencies for the organization tend to have greater power. Departmental activities are important when they provide strategic value by solving problems or crises for the organization. For example, if an organization faces an intense threat from lawsuits and regulations, the legal department will gain power and influence over organizational decisions because it copes with such a threat. If product innovation is the key strategic issue, the power of R&D can be expected to be high.

The strategic contingency approach to power is similar to the resource dependence model described in Chapters 4 and 5. Recall that organizations try to reduce dependency on the external environment. The strategic contingency approach to power suggests that the departments most responsible for dealing with key resource issues and dependencies in the environment will become most powerful.

Power Sources. Jeffrey Pfeffer and Gerald Salancik, among others, have been instrumental in conducting research on the strategic contingency theory.[52] Their findings indicate that a department rated as powerful may possess one or more of the characteristics illustrated in Exhibit 13.5.[53] In some organizations these five **power sources** overlap, but each provides a useful way to evaluate sources of horizontal power.

1. **Dependency.** Interdepartmental dependency is a key element underlying relative power. Power is derived from having something someone else wants. The power of department A over department B is greater when department B depends on department A.[54] Materials, information, and resources may flow between departments in one direction, such as in the case of sequential task interdependence (see Chapter 7). In such cases, the department receiving resources is in a lower power position than the department providing them. The number and strength of dependencies are also important. When seven or eight departments must come for help to the engineering department, for example, engineering is in a strong power position. In contrast, a department that depends on many other departments is in a low power position. Likewise, a department in an otherwise low power position might gain power through dependencies. If a factory cannot produce without the expertise of maintenance workers to keep the machines working, the maintenance department is in a strong power position because it has control over a strategic contingency.

2. **Financial resources.** There's a new golden rule in the business world: "The person with the gold makes the rules."[55] Control over resources is an important source of power in organizations. Money can be converted into other kinds of resources that are needed by other departments. Money generates dependency; departments that provide financial resources have something other departments want. Departments that generate income for an organization have greater power. Exhibit 13.4 showed sales as the most powerful unit in most industrial firms. This is because salespeople find customers and bring in money, thereby removing an important problem for the organization. An ability to provide financial resources also explains why certain departments are powerful in other organizations, such as universities.

In Practice

University of Illinois

You might expect budget allocation in a state university to be a straightforward process. The need for financial resources can be determined by such things as the number of undergraduate students, the number of graduate students, and the number of faculty in each department.

In fact, resource allocation at the University of Illinois is not clear-cut. The University of Illinois has a relatively fixed resource inflow from state government. Beyond that, important resources come from research grants and the quality of students and faculty. University departments that provide the most resources to the university are rated as having the most power. Some departments have more power because of their resource contribution to the university. Departments that generate large research grants are more powerful because research grants contain a sizable overhead payment to university administration. This overhead money pays for a large share of the university's personnel and facilities. The size of a department's graduate student body and the national prestige of the department also add to power. Graduate students and national prestige are nonfinancial resources that add to the reputation and effectiveness of the university.

How do university departments use their power? Generally, they use it to obtain even more resources from the rest of the university. Very powerful departments receive university resources, such as graduate-student fellowships, internal research support, and summer faculty salaries, far in excess of their needs based on the number of students and faculty.[56]

As shown in the example of the University of Illinois, power accrues to departments that bring in or provide resources that are highly valued by an organization. Power enables those departments to obtain more of the scarce resources allocated within the organization. "Power derived from acquiring resources is used to obtain more resources, which in turn can be employed to produce more power—the rich get richer."[57]

3. **Centrality.** Centrality reflects a department's role in the primary activity of an organization.[58] One measure of centrality is the extent to which the work of the department affects the final output of the organization. For example, the production department is more central and usually has more power than staff groups (assuming no other critical contingencies). Centrality is associated with power because it reflects the contribution made to the organization. The corporate finance department of an investment bank generally has more power than the stock research department. By contrast, in the manufacturing firms described in Exhibit 13.4, finance tends to be low in power. When the finance department has the limited task of recording money and expenditures, it is not responsible for obtaining critical resources or for producing the products of the organization. Today, however, finance departments have greater power in many organizations because of the greater need for controlling costs.

4. **Nonsubstitutability.** Power is also determined by *nonsubstitutability*, which means that a department's function cannot be performed by other readily available resources. Similarly, if an employee cannot be easily replaced, his or her power is greater. If an organization has no alternative sources of skill and information, a department's power will be greater. This can be the case when management uses outside consultants. Consultants might be used as substitutes for staff people to reduce the power of staff groups.

   The impact of substitutability on power was studied for programmers in computer departments.[59] When computers were first introduced, programming was a rare and specialized occupation. Programmers controlled the use of organizational computers because they alone possessed the knowledge to program them. Over a period of about 10 years, computer programming became a more common activity. People could be substituted easily, and the power of programming departments dropped.

5. **Coping with Uncertainty.** Elements in the environment can change swiftly and can be unpredictable and complex. In the face of uncertainty, little information is available to managers on appropriate courses of action. Departments that reduce this uncertainty for the organization will increase their power.[60] When market research personnel accurately predict changes in demand for new products, they gain power and prestige because they have reduced a critical uncertainty. But forecasting is only one technique. Sometimes uncertainty can be reduced by taking quick and appropriate action after an unpredictable event occurs.

   Departments can cope with critical uncertainties by (1) obtaining prior information, (2) prevention, and (3) absorption.[61] *Obtaining prior information* means a department can reduce an organization's uncertainty by forecasting an event. Departments increase their power through *prevention* by predicting and forestalling negative events. *Absorption* occurs when a department takes action after an event to reduce its negative consequences. Consider the following case from the health care industry.

Briefcase

As an organization manager, keep these guidelines in mind:

Be aware of the important horizontal power relationships that come from the ability of a department to deal with strategic contingencies that confront the organization. Increase the horizontal power of a department by increasing involvement in strategic contingencies.

In Practice

**HCA and
Aetna Inc.**

Not so long ago, insurers called the shots, forcing hospitals to take lower reimbursements, forego price increases, and discharge patients more quickly. HCA, based in Nashville, Tennessee, says it routinely signed contracts that barely covered its costs. But HCA is now the largest hospital owner in the United States and controls a huge percentage of the hospital market in major metropolitan areas such as Denver, Las Vegas, and Houston. Now, it has enough power to push around large insurance companies such as Aetna Inc.

HCA's legal department has been instrumental in absorbing critical uncertainties for the organization. Beginning in 1996, when a Medicare scandal surfaced, the legal department swung into action to help the organization weather the storm and develop clear guidelines and compliance programs to make sure similar legal problems didn't happen again. The department again played a critical role in negotiating a series of mergers and acquisitions that enabled HCA to grow in size and power and turn the tables on big insurers. In Houston, for example, HCA now operates ten hospitals, a 22 percent share of the market. In that city, HCA officials began warning doctors that it will terminate its contract with Aetna, the country's largest health insurer, unless the company meets its demands for price increases.

At the same time, hospitals are facing another critical uncertainty concerning billing practices that sometimes require uninsured patients to pay excessively high rates. A congressional committee has been investigating billing practices at HCA and other large hospitals, again requiring shrewd attention from the legal department. So long as legal issues represent a critical strategic contingency for HCA, the legal department will remain a powerful force in the organization.[62]

Because hospitals have to deal with so many complex legal and regulatory matters, it is likely that the legal department at systems such as HCA and Tenet Healthcare is usually in a high power position. At HCA, the department coped with a critical uncertainty (questionable Medicare practices) by absorption. It took action to reduce the uncertainty after it appeared. Horizontal power relationships in organizations change as strategic contingencies change. In a hospital dealing with a major health crisis, the public relations department might gain power, for example, by soothing public fears and keeping people informed about the hospital's efforts to control the spread of disease. As another example, large retailers such as Wal-Mart and Home Depot attempting to build new stores often face challenges from community activists fighting urban sprawl. The public relations department can gain power by helping the organization present a positive side to the story and counteract the arguments of protestors. Departments that help organizations cope with new strategic issues will have greater power.

Political Processes in Organizations

Politics, like power, is intangible and difficult to measure. It is hidden from view and is hard to observe in a systematic way. Two surveys uncovered the following reactions of managers toward political behavior.[63]

1. Most managers have a negative view toward politics and believe that politics will more often hurt than help an organization in achieving its goals.

2. Managers believe that political behavior is common in practically all organizations.

3. Most managers think that political behavior occurs more often at upper rather than lower levels in organizations.

4. Political behavior arises in certain decision domains, such as structural change, but is absent from other decisions, such as handling employee grievances.

Based on these surveys, politics seems more likely to occur at the top levels of an organization and around certain issues and decisions. Moreover, managers do not approve of political behavior. The remainder of this chapter explores more fully what political behavior is, when it should be used, the type of issues and decisions most likely to be associated with politics, and some political tactics that may be effective.

◼ Definition

Power has been described as the available force or potential for achieving desired outcomes. *Politics* is the use of power to influence decisions in order to achieve those outcomes. The exercise of power and influence has led to two ways to define politics—as self-serving behavior or as a natural organizational decision process. The first definition emphasizes that politics is self-serving and involves activities that are not sanctioned by the organization.[64]

In this view, politics involves deception and dishonesty for purposes of individual self-interest and leads to conflict and disharmony within the work environment. This dark view of politics is widely held by laypeople, and political activity certainly can be used in this way. Recent studies have shown that workers who perceive this kind of political activity within their companies often have related feelings of anxiety and job dissatisfaction. Studies also support the belief that inappropriate use of politics is related to low employee morale, inferior organizational performance, and poor decision making.[65] This view of politics explains why managers in the aforementioned surveys did not approve of political behavior.

Although politics can be used in a negative, self-serving way, the appropriate use of political behavior can serve organizational goals.[66] The second view sees politics as a natural organizational process for resolving differences among organizational interest groups.[67] Politics is the process of bargaining and negotiation that is used to overcome conflicts and differences of opinion. In this view, politics is similar to the coalition-building decision processes defined in Chapter 12.

The organization theory perspective views politics as described in the second definition—as a normal decision-making process. Politics is simply the activity through which power is exercised in the resolution of conflicts and uncertainty. Politics is neutral and is not necessarily harmful to the organization. The formal definition of organizational politics is as follows: **Organizational politics** involves activities to acquire, develop, and use power and other resources to obtain the preferred outcome when there is uncertainty or disagreement about choices.[68]

Political behavior can be either a positive or a negative force. Politics is the use of power to get things accomplished—good things as well as bad. Uncertainty and conflict are natural and inevitable, and politics is the mechanism for reaching agreement. Politics includes informal discussions that enable participants to arrive at consensus and make decisions that otherwise might be stalemated or unsolvable.

■ When Is Political Activity Used?

Politics is a mechanism for arriving at consensus when uncertainty is high and there is disagreement over goals or problem priorities. Recall the rational versus political models described in Exhibit 13.2. The political model is associated with conflict over goals, shifting coalitions and interest groups, ambiguous information, and uncertainty. Thus, political activity tends to be most visible when managers confront nonprogrammed decisions, as discussed in Chapter 12, and is related to the Carnegie model of decision making. Because managers at the top of an organization generally deal with more nonprogrammed decisions than do managers at lower levels, more political activity will appear at higher levels. Moreover, some issues are associated with inherent disagreement. Resources, for example, are critical for the survival and effectiveness of departments, so resource allocation often becomes a political issue. Rational methods of allocation do not satisfy participants. Three **domains of political activity** (areas in which politics plays a role) in most organizations are structural change, management succession, and resource allocation.

Structural reorganizations strike at the heart of power and authority relationships. Reorganizations such as those discussed in Chapter 3 change responsibilities and tasks, which also affects the underlying power base from strategic contingencies. For these reasons, a major reorganization can lead to an explosion of political activity.[69] Managers may actively bargain and negotiate to maintain the responsibilities and power bases they have. Mergers and acquisitions also frequently create tremendous political activity, as we saw with the chapter-opening example of Morgan Stanley.

Organizational changes such as hiring new executives, promotions, and transfers have great political significance, particularly at top organizational levels where uncertainty is high and networks of trust, cooperation, and communication among executives are important.[70] Hiring decisions can generate uncertainty, discussion, and disagreement. Managers can use hiring and promotion to strengthen network alliances and coalitions by putting their own people in prominent positions.

The third area of political activity is resource allocation. Resource allocation decisions encompass all resources required for organizational performance, including salaries, operating budgets, employees, office facilities, equipment, use of the company airplane, and so forth. Resources are so vital that disagreement about priorities exists, and political processes help resolve the dilemmas.

Using Power, Politics, and Collaboration

One theme in this chapter has been that power in organizations is not primarily a phenomenon of the individual. It is related to the resources departments command, the role departments play in an organization, and the environmental contingencies with which departments cope. Position and responsibility, more than personality and style, determine a manager's influence on outcomes in the organization.

Power is used through individual political behavior, however. Individual managers seek agreement about a strategy to achieve their departments' desired outcomes. Individual managers negotiate decisions and adopt tactics that enable them to acquire and use power. In addition, managers develop ways to increase cooperation and collaboration within the organization to reduce damaging conflicts.

EXHIBIT 13.6
Power and Political Tactics in Organizations

Tactics for Increasing the Power Base	Political Tactics for Using Power	Tactics for Enhancing Collaboration
1. Enter areas of high uncertainty. 2. Create dependencies. 3. Provide scarce resources. 4. Satisfy strategic contingencies. 5. Make a direct appeal.	1. Build coalitions and expand networks. 2. Assign loyal people to key positions. 3. Control decision premises. 4. Enhance legitimacy and expertise. 5. Create superordinate goals.	1. Create integration devices. 2. Use confrontation and negotiation. 3. Schedule intergroup consultation. 4. Practice member rotation.

To fully understand the use of power within organizations, it is important to look at both structural components and individual behavior.[71] Although the power comes from larger organizational forms and processes, the political use of power involves individual-level activities. For instance, all managers use tactics to exert influence, but research indicates that managers in HR departments may use softer, more subtle approaches than do managers in more powerful finance departments. In one study, HR executives, who were not seen as having centrality to the firm's mission, took a low-key approach to try to influence others, whereas finance executives, who had a more central and powerful position, used harder, more direct influence tactics.[72] The following sections briefly summarize various tactics that managers can use to increase the power base of their departments, political tactics they can use to achieve desired outcomes, and tactics for increasing collaboration. These tactics are summarized in Exhibit 13.6.

Tactics for Increasing Power

Four **tactics for increasing power** for the organization are as follows:

1. *Enter areas of high uncertainty.* One source of departmental power is to cope with critical uncertainties.[73] If department managers can identify key uncertainties and take steps to remove those uncertainties, the department's power base will be enhanced. Uncertainties could arise from stoppages on an assembly line, from the quality demanded of a new product, or from the inability to predict a demand for new services. Once an uncertainty is identified, the department can take action to cope with it. By their very nature, uncertain tasks will not be solved immediately. Trial and error will be needed, which is to the advantage of the department. The trial-and-error process provides experience and expertise that cannot easily be duplicated by other departments.

2. *Create dependencies.* Dependencies are another source of power.[74] When the organization depends on a department for information, materials, knowledge, or skills, that department will hold power over others. This power can be increased by incurring obligations. Doing additional work that helps out other departments will obligate the other departments to respond at a future date. The power accumulated by creating a dependency can be used to resolve future disagree-

ments in the department's favor. An equally effective and related strategy is to reduce dependency on other departments by acquiring necessary information or skills. IT departments have created dependencies in many organizations because of the rapid changes in this area. Employees in other departments depend on the IT unit to master complex software programs, changing use of the Internet, and other advances so that they will have the information they need to perform effectively.

3. *Provide scarce resources.* Resources are always important to organizational survival. Departments that accumulate resources and provide them to an organization in the form of money, information, or facilities will be powerful. An earlier In Practice described how university departments with the greatest power are those that obtain external research funds for contributions to university overhead. Likewise, sales departments are powerful in industrial firms because they bring in financial resources.

4. *Satisfy strategic contingencies.* The theory of strategic contingencies says that some elements in the external environment and within the organization are especially important for organizational success. A contingency could be a critical event, a task for which there are no substitutes, or a central task that is interdependent with many others in the organization. An analysis of the organization and its changing environment will reveal strategic contingencies. To the extent that contingencies are new or are not being satisfied, there is room for a department to move into those critical areas and increase its importance and power.

In summary, the allocation of power in an organization is not random. Power is the result of organizational processes that can be understood and predicted. The abilities to reduce uncertainty, increase dependency on one's own department, obtain resources, and cope with strategic contingencies all enhance a department's power. Once power is available, the next challenge is to use it to attain helpful outcomes.

■ Political Tactics for Using Power

The use of power in organizations requires both skill and willingness. Many decisions are made through political processes because rational decision processes do not fit. Uncertainty or disagreement is too high. **Political tactics for using power** to influence decision outcomes include the following:

1. *Build coalitions and expand networks.* Coalition building means taking the time to talk with other managers to persuade them to your point of view.[75] Most important decisions are made outside of formal meetings. Managers discuss issues with each other and reach agreement. Effective managers are those who huddle, meeting in groups of twos and threes to resolve key issues.[76] Effective managers also build networks of relationships across hierarchical and functional boundaries. Networks can be expanded by (1) reaching out to establish contact with additional managers and (2) coopting dissenters. A recent research project found that the ability to build networks has a positive impact on both employees' perception of a manager's effectiveness and the ability of the manager to influence performance.[77] Establishing contact with additional managers means building good interpersonal relationships based on liking, trust, and respect. Reliability and the motivation to work with rather than exploit others are part of both

networking and coalition building.[78] The second approach to expanding networks, cooptation, is the act of bringing a dissenter into one's network. One example of cooptation involved a university committee whose membership was based on promotion and tenure. Several professors who were critical of the tenure and promotion process were appointed to the committee. Once a part of the administrative process, they could see the administrative point of view. Cooptation effectively brought them into the administrative network.[79]

2. *Assign loyal people to key positions.* Another political tactic is to assign trusted and loyal people to key positions in the organization or department. Top managers as well as department heads often use the hiring, transfer, and promotion processes to place in key positions people who are sympathetic to the outcomes of the department, thus helping to achieve departmental goals.[80] Top leaders frequently use this tactic, as we discussed earlier. For example, since he became CEO at Merrill Lynch & Co., Stan O'Neal has gotten rid of a whole generation of top talent and moved in other managers who support his vision and goals for the organization. He recently brought back a popular retired executive, countering charges that he was stacking the management ranks only with people who wouldn't challenge his power and authority.[81]

3. *Control decision premises.* To control decision premises means to constrain the boundaries of a decision. One technique is to choose or limit information provided to other managers. A common method is simply to put your department's best foot forward, such as selectively presenting favorable criteria. A variety of statistics can be assembled to support the departmental point of view. A university department that is growing rapidly and has a large number of students can make claims for additional resources by emphasizing its growth and large size. Such objective criteria do not always work, but they are a valuable step.

   Decision premises can be further influenced by limiting the decision process. Decisions can be influenced by the items put on an agenda for an important meeting or even by the sequence in which items are discussed.[82] Items discussed last, when time is short and people want to leave, will receive less attention than those discussed earlier. Calling attention to specific problems and suggesting alternatives also will affect outcomes. Stressing a specific problem to get it—rather than problems not relevant to your department—on the agenda is an example of agenda setting.

4. *Enhance legitimacy and expertise.* Managers can exert the greatest influence in areas in which they have recognized legitimacy and expertise. If a request is within the task domain of a department and is consistent with the department's vested interest, other departments will tend to comply. Members can also identify external consultants or other experts within the organization to support their cause.[83] For example, a financial vice president in a large retail firm wanted to fire the director of HR management. She hired a consultant to evaluate the HR projects undertaken to date. A negative report from the consultant provided sufficient legitimacy to fire the director, who was replaced with a director loyal to the financial vice president.

5. *Make a direct appeal.* If managers do not ask, they seldom receive. Political activity is effective only when goals and needs are made explicit so the organization can respond. Managers should bargain aggressively and be persuasive. An assertive proposal may be accepted because other managers have no better alternatives. Moreover, an explicit proposal will often receive favorable treatment because other alternatives are ambiguous and less well defined. Effective politi-

cal behavior requires sufficient forcefulness and risk taking to at least ask for what you need to achieve desired outcomes.

The use of power, however, should not be obvious.[84] If you formally draw on your power base in a meeting by saying, "My department has more power, so the rest of you have to do it my way," your power will be diminished. Power works best when it is used quietly. To call attention to power is to lose it. People know who has power. Explicit claims to power are not necessary and can even harm the department's cause.

Book Mark 13.0 (HAVE YOU READ THIS BOOK?)

Influence: Science and Practice
By Robert B. Cialdini

Managers use a variety of political tactics to influence others and bring about desired outcomes. In his book *Influence: Science and Practice*, Robert Cialdini examines the social and psychological pressures that cause people to respond favorably to these various tactics. Over years of study, Cialdini, Regents' Professor of Psychology at Arizona State University, has identified some basic *influence principles*, "those that work in a variety of situations, for a variety of practitioners, on a variety of topics, for a variety of prospects."

INFLUENCE PRINCIPLES
Having a working knowledge of the basic set of persuasion tools can help managers predict and influence human behavior, which is valuable for interacting with colleagues, employees, customers, partners, and even friends. Some basic psychological principles that govern successful influence tactics are as follows:

- *Reciprocity*. The principle of reciprocity refers to the sense of obligation people feel to give back in kind what they have received. For example, a manager who does favors for others creates in them a sense of obligation to return the favors in the future. Smart managers find ways to be helpful to others, whether it be helping a colleague finish an unpleasant job or offering compassion and concern for a subordinate's personal problems.
- *Liking*. People say yes more often to those they like. Companies such as Tupperware Corp. have long understood that familiar faces and congenial characteristics sell products. In-home Tupperware parties allow customers to buy from a friend instead of an unknown salesperson. Salespeople in all kinds of companies often try to capitalize on this principle by finding interests they share with cus-

tomers as a way to establish rapport. In general, managers who are pleasant, generous with praise, cooperative, and considerate of others' feelings find that they have greater influence.
- *Credible authority*. Legitimate authorities are particularly influential sources. However, research has discovered that the key to successful use of authority is to be knowledgeable, credible, and trustworthy. Managers who become known for their expertise, who are honest and straightforward with others, and who inspire trust can exert greater influence than those who rely on formal position alone.
- *Social validation*. One of the primary ways people decide what to do in any given situation is to consider what others are doing. That is, people examine the actions of others to validate correct choices. For instance, when homeowners were shown a list of neighbors who had donated to a local charity during a fundraiser, the frequency of contributions increased dramatically. By demonstrating, or even implying, that others have already complied with a request, managers gain greater cooperation.

THE PROCESS OF SOCIAL INFLUENCE
Because life as a manager is all about influencing others, learning to be genuinely persuasive is a valuable management skill. Cialdini's book helps managers understand the basic psychological rules of persuasion—how and why people are motivated to change their attitudes and behaviors. When managers use this understanding in an honest and ethical manner, they improve their effectiveness and the success of their organizations.

Influence: Science and Practice (4th edition), by Robert B. Cialdini, is published by Allyn & Bacon.

When using any of the preceding tactics, recall that most people think self-serving behavior hurts rather than helps an organization. If managers are perceived to be throwing their weight around or pursuing goals that are self-serving rather than beneficial to the organization, they will lose respect. On the other hand, managers must recognize the relational and political aspect of their work. It is not sufficient to be rational and technically competent. Politics is a way to reach agreement. This chapter's Book Mark describes some basic psychological principles that underlie successful political influence tactics. Managers can use this understanding to assert influence and get things done within the organization. When managers ignore political tactics, they may find themselves failing without understanding why. This is partly the reason Tim Koogle failed to accomplish a key acquisition at Yahoo!.

In late March of 2000, Yahoo! began negotiating to buy online auction leader eBay Inc. Tim Koogle, Yahoo!'s CEO at the time, was fully in support of the deal, believing it would enable the company to beef up its e-commerce revenues and bring needed new blood to the increasingly insular Yahoo! culture. But the deal never happened, and while Yahoo!'s fortunes flagged, eBay's revenues and net income continued to climb.

What happened? Jeffrey Mallett, Yahoo!'s president, opposed the acquisition of eBay, and he used political tactics to quash it. Koogle had always been a consensus-style manager. He believed the top leaders would debate the pros and cons of the acquisition and arrive at the best decision. In addition, he felt sure the merits of the eBay deal would ultimately win the day. But Mallett, who insiders say was already angling to take over the CEO job, began courting co-founders Jerry Yang and David Filo. Eventually, he convinced them that the eBay culture was a poor fit with Yahoo!. With Koogle outnumbered, the deal fell apart. A former Yahoo! manager called it management by persuasion.

By failing to build a coalition, Koogle allowed Mallett to control this important decision. It's only one example of several that ultimately led to Koogle being pushed out as CEO. Despite Mallett's political moves, he was passed over for the top job in favor of an outsider who board members felt could turn the struggling company around. Koogle took the decision to seek a new CEO calmly and blamed himself for not keeping a closer eye on Mallett.[85]

In Practice

Yahoo!

■ Tactics for Enhancing Collaboration

Power and political tactics are important means for getting things done within organizations. Most organizations today have at least moderate interunit conflict. An additional approach in many organizations is to overcome conflict by stimulating cooperation and collaboration among departments to support the attainment of organizational goals. **Tactics for enhancing collaboration** include the following:

1. *Create integration devices.* As described in Chapter 3, teams, task forces, and project managers who span the boundaries between departments can be used as integration devices. Bringing together representatives from conflicting departments in joint problem-solving teams is an effective way to enhance collaboration because representatives learn to understand each other's point of view.[86] Sometimes a full-time integrator is assigned to achieve cooperation and collaboration by meeting with members of the respective departments and exchanging

Briefcase

As an organization manager, keep these guidelines in mind:

If conflict becomes too strong, use tactics for enhancing collaboration, including integration devices, confrontation, intergroup consultation, member rotation, and superordinate goals. Select the technique that fits the organization and the conflict.

information. The integrator has to understand each group's problems and must be able to move both groups toward a solution that is mutually acceptable.[87]

Teams and task forces reduce conflict and enhance cooperation because they integrate people from different departments. Integration devices can also be used to enhance cooperation between labor and management, as the example of Aluminum Company of America and the International Association of Machinists illustrates.

In Practice

Aluminum Company of America/ International Association of Machinists

When representatives from the International Association of Machinists (IAM) approached David Groetsch, president of a division of Aluminum Company of America (Alcoa), and offered to help create a new work system, Groetsch immediately agreed to give it a try. Alcoa managers joined union leaders for a week-long course at the union's school in Maryland, where they learned how to set up a labor–management partnership to spur productivity. Working together, labor and management studied everything from the history of high-performance systems to new accounting methods for measuring them. After the course, the union sent experts free of charge to help union leaders and managers from manufacturing to marketing create teams and joint decision-making councils.

The IAM is at the forefront of a revolutionary change in the relationship between labor and management. After decades of suspicion about company-sponsored teams, many unions are now actively embracing the concept of partnership. According to Groetsch, relationships on the shop floor at Alcoa have improved because each side better understands the other's concerns. "The days of 1950s-style table-banging aren't gone yet," says Arthur C. Coia, former president of the Laborers' International Union of North America, whose union is also involved in cooperative ventures.[88] However, the use of integration devices is dramatically improving cooperative relationships between labor and management.

Labor–management teams, which are designed to increase worker participation and provide a cooperative model for solving union–management problems, are increasingly being used at companies such as Goodyear, Ford Motor Company, and Xerox. In the steel industry, companies such as USX and Wheeling-Pittsburgh Steel Corp. have signed pacts that give union representatives seats on the board.[89] Although unions continue to battle over traditional issues such as wages, these integration devices are creating a level of cooperation that many managers would not have believed possible just a few years ago.

2. *Use confrontation and negotiation.* **Confrontation** occurs when parties in conflict directly engage one another and try to work out their differences. **Negotiation** is the bargaining process that often occurs during confrontation and that enables the parties to systematically reach a solution. These techniques bring appointed representatives from the departments together to work out a serious dispute. Representatives of the United Auto Workers (UAW) and GM are using confrontation and negotiation to try to resolve the issue of rising healthcare costs. The UAW wants to find a way to solve the problem without changing the current contract, which is set to expire in 2007, while GM management would like to reopen the contract for further negotiations.[90]

Confrontation and negotiation involve some risk. There is no guarantee that discussions will focus on a conflict or that emotions will not get out of hand. However, if members are able to resolve the conflict on the basis of face-to-face

Win–Win Strategy	Win–Lose Strategy
1. Define the conflict as a mutual problem.	1. Define the problem as a win–lose situation.
2. Pursue joint outcomes.	2. Pursue own group's outcomes.
3. Find creative agreements that satisfy both groups.	3. Force the other group into submission.
4. Be open, honest, and accurate in communicating the group's needs, goals, and proposals.	4. Be deceitful, inaccurate, and misleading in communicating the group's needs, goals, and proposals.
5. Avoid threats (to reduce the other's defensiveness).	5. Use threats (to force submission).
6. Communicate flexibility of position.	6. Communicate strong commitment (rigidity) regarding one's position.

EXHIBIT 13.7
Negotiating Strategies

Source: Adapted from David W. Johnson and Frank P. Johnson, *Joining Together: Group Theory and Group Skills* (Englewood Cliffs, N.J.: Prentice-Hall, 1975), 182–183.

discussions, they will find new respect for each other, and future collaboration becomes easier. The beginnings of relatively permanent attitude change are possible through direct negotiation.

Confrontation and negotiation are successful when managers engage in a *win–win strategy*. Win–win means both sides adopt a positive attitude and strive to resolve the conflict in a way that will benefit each other.[91] If the negotiations deteriorate into a strictly win–lose strategy (each group wants to defeat the other), the confrontation will be ineffective. The differences between win–win and win–lose strategies of negotiation are shown in Exhibit 13.7. With a win–win strategy—which includes defining the problem as mutual, communicating openly, and avoiding threats—understanding can be changed while the dispute is resolved.

One type of negotiation, used to resolve a disagreement between workers and management, is referred to as **collective bargaining.** The bargaining process is usually accomplished through a union and results in an agreement that specifies each party's responsibilities for the next 2 to 3 years, as with the contract between GM and the UAW.

3. *Schedule intergroup consultation.* When conflict is intense and enduring, and department members are suspicious and uncooperative, top managers may intervene as third parties to help resolve the conflict or bring in third-party consultants from outside the organization.[92] This process, sometimes called *workplace mediation*, is a strong intervention to reduce conflict because it involves bringing the disputing parties together and allowing each side to present its version of the situation. The technique has been developed by such psychologists as Robert Blake, Jane Mouton, and Richard Walton.[93]

Department members attend a workshop, which may last for several days, away from day-to-day work problems. This approach is similar to the organization development (OD) approach described in Chapter 11. The conflicting groups are separated, and each group is invited to discuss and make a list of its perceptions of itself and the other group. Group representatives publicly share these perceptions, and together the groups discuss the results.

Intergroup consultation can be quite demanding for everyone involved. Although it is fairly easy to have conflicting groups list perceptions and identify discrepancies, exploring their differences face-to-face and agreeing to change is more difficult. If handled correctly, these sessions can help department employees understand each other much better and lead to improved attitudes and better working relationships for years to come.

4. *Practice member rotation.* Rotation means that individuals from one department can be asked to work in another department on a temporary or permanent basis. The advantage is that individuals become submerged in the values, attitudes, problems, and goals of the other department. In addition, individuals can explain the problems and goals of their original departments to their new colleagues. This enables a frank, accurate exchange of views and information. Rotation works slowly to reduce conflict but is very effective for changing the underlying attitudes and perceptions that promote conflict.[94]

5. *Create shared mission and superordinate goals.* Another strategy is for top management to create a shared mission and establish superordinate goals that require cooperation among departments.[95] As discussed in Chapter 10, organizations with strong, adaptive cultures, where employees share a larger vision for their company, are more likely to have a united, cooperative workforce. Studies have shown that when employees from different departments see that their goals are linked together, they will openly share resources and information.[96] To be effective, superordinate goals must be substantial, and employees must be granted the time and incentives to work cooperatively in pursuit of the superordinate goals rather than departmental subgoals.

Summary and Interpretation

The central message of this chapter is that conflict, power, and politics are natural outcomes of organizing. Differences in goals, backgrounds, and tasks are necessary for organizational excellence, but these differences can throw groups into conflict. Managers use power and politics to manage and resolve conflict. Two views of organization were presented. The rational model of organization assumes that organizations have specific goals and that problems can be logically solved. The other view, the political model of organization, is the basis for much of the chapter. This view assumes that the goals of an organization are not specific or agreed upon. Departments have different values and interests, so managers come into conflict. Decisions are made on the basis of power and political influence. Bargaining, negotiation, persuasion, and coalition building decide outcomes.

The chapter also discussed the vertical and horizontal sources of power. Vertical sources of power include formal position, resources, control of decision premises, and network centrality. In general, managers at the top of the organizational hierarchy have more power than people at lower levels. However, positions all along the hierarchy can be designed to increase the power of employees. As organizations face increased competition and environmental uncertainty, top executives are finding that increasing the power of middle managers and lower-level employees can help the organization be more competitive. Research into horizontal power processes has revealed that certain characteristics make some departments more powerful than others. Such factors as dependency, resources, and nonsubstitutability determine the influence of departments.

Managers can use political tactics such as coalition building, expanded networks, and control of decision premises to help departments achieve desired outcomes. Many people distrust political behavior, fearing that it will be used for selfish ends that benefit the individual but not the organization. However, politics is often needed to achieve the legitimate goals of a department or organization. Three areas in which politics often plays a role are structural change, management succession, and resource allocation because these are areas of high uncertainty. Although conflict and political behavior are natural and can be used for beneficial purposes, managers also strive to enhance collaboration so that conflict between groups does not become too strong. Tactics for enhancing collaboration include integration devices, confrontation and negotiation, intergroup consultation, member rotation, and shared mission and superordinate goals.

Key Concepts

authority	network centrality
centrality	nonsubstitutability
collective bargaining	organizational politics
competition	political model
confrontation	political tactics for using power
coping with uncertainty	power
decision premises	power sources
dependency	rational model
domains of political activity	sources of intergroup conflict
financial resources	strategic contingencies
intergroup conflict	tactics for enhancing collaboration
labor–management teams	tactics for increasing power
negotiation	

Discussion Questions

1. Give an example from your personal experience of how differences in tasks, personal background, and training lead to conflict among groups. How might task interdependence have influenced that conflict?
2. A noted expert on organizations said that some conflict is beneficial to organizations. Discuss.
3. In a rapidly changing organization, are decisions more likely to be made using the rational or political model of organization? Discuss.
4. What is the difference between power and authority? Is it possible for a person to have formal authority but no real power? Discuss.
5. Discuss ways in which a department at an insurance company might help the organization cope with the increased power of large hospital systems by obtaining prior information, prevention, or absorption.
6. In Exhibit 13.4, R&D has greater power in company B than in the other firms. Discuss possible strategic contingencies that give R&D greater power in this firm.
7. State University X receives 90 percent of its financial resources from the state and is overcrowded with students. It is trying to pass regulations to limit student enrollment. Private University Y receives 90 percent of its income from student tuition and has barely enough students to make ends meet. It is actively recruiting students for next year. In which university will students have greater power? What implications will this have for professors and administrators? Discuss.
8. A bookkeeper at HealthSouth Corp., which is currently embroiled in a financial scandal, tried for several years to expose fraud in the organization's accounting department, but he couldn't get anyone to pay attention to his claims. How would you

evaluate this employee's power? What might he have done to increase his power and call notice to the ethical and legal problems at the firm?

9. The engineering college at a major university brings in three times as many government research dollars as does the rest of the university combined. Engineering appears wealthy and has many professors on full-time research status. Yet, when internal research funds are allocated, engineering gets a larger share of the money, even though it already has substantial external research funds. Why would this happen?

10. Which do you believe would have a greater long-term impact on changing employee attitudes toward increased collaboration—intergroup consultation or confrontation and negotiation? Discuss.

Chapter 13 Workbook: How Do You Handle Conflict?*

Think of some disagreements you have had with a friend, relative, manager, or co-worker. Then indicate how frequently you engage in each of the following behaviors. There are no right or wrong answers. Respond to all items using the following scale from 1 to 7:

*From "How Do You Handle Conflict?" in Robert E. Quinn et al., *Becoming a Master Manager* (New York: Wiley, 1990), 221–223. Copyright © 1990 by John Wiley & Sons, Inc. This material is used by permission of John Wiley & Sons, Inc.

Scale

Always	Very often	Often	Sometimes	Seldom	Very seldom	Never
1	2	3	4	5	6	7

_____ 1.   I blend my ideas to create new alternatives for resolving a disagreement.

_____ 2.   I shy away from topics that are sources of disputes.

_____ 3.   I make my opinion known in a disagreement.

_____ 4.   I suggest solutions that combine a variety of viewpoints.

_____ 5.   I steer clear of disagreeable situations.

_____ 6.   I give in a little on my ideas when the other person also gives in.

_____ 7.   I avoid the other person when I suspect that he or she wants to discuss a disagreement.

_____ 8.   I integrate arguments into a new solution from the issues raised in a dispute.

_____ 9.   I will go 50–50 to reach a settlement.

_____ 10. I raise my voice when I'm trying to get the other person to accept my position.

_____ 11. I offer creative solutions in discussions of disagreements.

_____ 12. I keep quiet about my views in order to avoid disagreements.

_____ 13. I give in if the other person will meet me halfway.

_____ 14. I downplay the importance of a disagreement.

_____ 15. I reduce disagreements by making them seem insignificant.

_____ 16. I meet the other person at a midpoint in our differences.

_____ 17. I assert my opinion forcefully.

_____ 18. I dominate arguments until the other person understands my position.

_____ 19. I suggest we work together to create solutions to disagreements.

_____ 20. I try to use the other person's ideas to generate solutions to problems.

_____ 21. I offer tradeoffs to reach solutions in disagreements.

_____ 22. I argue insistently for my stance.

_____ 23. I withdraw when the other person confronts me about a controversial issue.

_____ 24. I sidestep disagreements when they arise.

_____ 25. I try to smooth over disagreements by making them appear unimportant.

_____ 26. I insist my position be accepted during a disagreement with the other person.

_____ 27. I make our differences seem less serious.

_____ 28. I hold my tongue rather than argue with the other person.

_____ 29. I ease conflict by claiming our differences are trivial.

_____ 30. I stand firm in expressing my viewpoints during a disagreement.

Scoring and Interpretation: Three categories of conflict-handling strategies are measured in this instrument: solution oriented, nonconfrontational, and control. By comparing your scores on the following three scales, you can see which of the three is your preferred conflict-handling strategy.

To calculate your three scores, add the individual scores for the items and divide by the number of items measuring the strategy. Then subtract each of the three mean scores from seven.

Solution oriented: Items 1, 4, 6, 8, 9, 11, 13, 16, 19, 20, 21 (total = 11)

Nonconfrontational: Items 2, 5, 7, 12, 14, 15, 23, 24, 25, 27, 28, 29 (total = 12)

Control: Items 3, 10, 17, 18, 22, 26, 30 (total = 7)

Solution-oriented strategies tend to focus on the problem rather than on the individuals involved. Solutions reached are often mutually beneficial, with neither party defining himself or herself as the winner and the other party as the loser.

Nonconfrontational strategies tend to focus on avoiding the conflict by either avoiding the other party or by simply allowing the other party to have his or her way. These strategies are used when there is more concern with avoiding a confrontation than with the actual outcome of the problem situation.

Control strategies tend to focus on winning or achieving one's goals without regard for the other party's needs or desires. Individuals using these strategies often rely on rules and regulations in order to win the battle.

Questions

1. Which strategy do you find easiest to use? Most difficult? Which do you use more often?
2. How would your answers have differed if the other person was a friend, family member, or co-worker?
3. What is it about the conflict situation or strategy that tells you which strategy to use in dealing with a conflict situation?

Case for Analysis: The Daily Tribune*

The *Daily Tribune* is the only daily newspaper serving a six-county region of eastern Tennessee. Even though its staff is small and it serves a region of mostly small towns and rural areas, the *Tribune* has won numerous awards for news coverage and photojournalism from the Tennessee Press Association and other organizations.

Rick Arnold became news editor almost 15 years ago. He has spent his entire career with the *Tribune* and feels a great sense of pride that it has been recognized for its journalistic integrity and balanced coverage of issues and events. The paper has been able to attract bright, talented young writers and photographers thanks largely to Rick's commitment and his support of the news staff. In his early years, the newsroom was a dynamic, exciting place to work—reporters thrived on the fast pace and the chance to occasionally scoop the major daily paper in Knoxville.

But times have changed at the *Daily Tribune*. Over the past 5 years or so, the advertising department has continued to grow, in terms of both staff and budget, while the news department has begun to shrink. "Advertising pays the bills," publisher John Freeman reminded everyone at this month's managers' meeting. "Today, advertisers can go to direct mail, cable television, even the Internet, if they don't like what we're doing for them."

Rick has regularly clashed with the advertising department regarding news stories that are critical of major advertisers, but the conflicts have increased dramatically over the past few years. Now, Freeman is encouraging greater

"horizontal collaboration," as he calls it, asking that managers in the news department and the ad department consult with one another regarding issues or stories that involve the paper's major advertisers. The move was prompted in part by a growing number of complaints from advertisers about stories they deemed unfair. "We print the news," Freeman said, "and I understand that sometimes we've got to print things that some people won't like. But we've got to find ways to be more advertiser-friendly. If we work together, we can develop strategies that both present good news coverage and serve to attract more advertisers."

Rick left the meeting fuming, and he didn't fail to make his contempt for the new "advertiser-friendly" approach known to all, including the advertising manager, Fred Thomas, as he headed down the hallway back to the newsroom. Lisa Lawrence, his managing editor, quietly agreed but pointed out that advertisers were readers too, and the newspaper had to listen to all its constituencies. "If we don't handle this carefully, we'll have Freeman and Thomas in here dictating to us what we can write and what we can't."

Lawrence has worked with Rick since he first came to the paper, and even though the two have had their share of

*This case was inspired by G. Pascal Zachary, "Many Journalists See a Growing Reluctance to Criticize Advertisers," *The Wall Street Journal* (February 6, 1992), A1, A9; and G. Bruce Knecht, "Retail Chains Emerge as Advance Arbiters of Magazine Content," *The Wall Street Journal* (October 22, 1997), A1, A13.

conflicts, the relationship is primarily one of mutual respect and trust. "Let's just be careful," she emphasized. "Read the stories about big advertisers a little more carefully, make sure we can defend whatever we print, and it will all work out. I know this blurring of the line between advertising and editorial rubs you the wrong way, but Thomas is a reasonable man. We just need to keep him in the loop."

Late that afternoon, Rick received a story from one of his corresponding reporters that had been in the works for a couple of days. East Tennessee Healthcorp (ETH), which operated a string of health clinics throughout the region, was closing three of its rural clinics because of mounting financial woes. The reporter, Elisabeth Fraley, who lived in one of the communities, had learned about the closings from her neighbor, who worked as an accountant for ETH, before the announcement had been made just this afternoon. Fraley had written a compelling human-interest story about how the closings would leave people in two counties with essentially no access to health care, while clinics in larger towns that didn't really need them were being kept open. She had carefully interviewed both former patients of the clinics and ETH employees, including the director of one of the clinics and two high-level managers at the corporate office, and she had carefully documented her sources. After this morning's meeting, Rick knew he should run the story by Lisa Lawrence, since East Tennessee Healthcorp was one of the *Tribune's* biggest advertisers, but Lawrence had left for the day. And he simply couldn't bring himself to consult with the advertising department—that political nonsense was for Lawrence to handle. If he held the story for Lawrence's approval, it wouldn't make the Sunday edition. His only other option was to write a brief story simply reporting the closings and leaving out the human-interest aspect. Rick was sure the major papers from Knoxville and other nearby cities would have the report in their Sunday papers, but none of them would have the time to develop as comprehensive and interesting an account as Fraley had presented. With a few quick strokes of the pen to make some minor editorial changes, Rick sent the story to production.

When he arrived at work the next day, Rick was called immediately to the publisher's office. He knew it was bad news for Freeman to be in on a Sunday. After some general yelling and screaming, Rick learned that tens of thousands of copies of the Sunday paper had been destroyed and a new edition printed. The advertising manager had called Freeman at home in the wee hours of Sunday morning and informed him of the ETH story, which was appearing the same day the corporation was running a full-page ad touting its service to the small towns and rural communities of East Tennessee.

"The story's accurate, and I assumed you'd want to take advantage of a chance to scoop the big papers," Rick began, but Freeman cut his argument short with his favorite line: "When you assume," he screamed, "you make an ass out of you and me. You could have just reported the basic facts without implying that the company doesn't care about the people of this region. The next time something like this happens, you'll find yourself and your reporters standing in the unemployment line!"

Rick had heard it before, but somehow this time he almost believed it. "What happened to the days when the primary purpose of a newspaper was to present the news?" Rick mumbled. "Now, it seems we have to dance to the tune played by the ad department."

Case for Analysis: Pierre Dux*

Pierre Dux sat quietly in his office considering the news. A third appointment to regional management had been announced and, once again, the promotion he had expected had been given to someone else. The explanations seemed insufficient this time. Clearly, this signaled the end to his career at INCO. Only 1 year ago, the company president had arrived at Dux's facility with national press coverage to publicize the success of his innovations in the management of manufacturing operations. The intervening year had brought improved operating results and further positive publicity for the corporation but a string of personal disappointments for Pierre Dux.

Four years earlier, the INCO manufacturing plant had been one of the least productive of the thirteen facilities operating in Europe. Absenteeism and high employee turnover were symptoms of the low morale among the work group. These factors were reflected in mediocre production levels and the worst quality record in INCO. Pierre Dux had been in his current position 1 year and had derived his only satisfaction from the fact that these poor results might have been worse had he not instituted minor reforms in organizational communication. These allowed workers and supervisors to vent their concerns and frustrations. Although nothing substantial had changed during that first year, operating results had stabilized, ending a period of rapid decline. But this honeymoon was ending. The expectation of significant change was growing, particularly

*This case was prepared by Michael Brimm, Associate Professor of INSEAD. It is intended to be used as a basis for class discussion rather than to illustrate either effective or ineffective handling of an administrative situation. Copyright © 1983 INSEAD Foundation, Fontainebleau, France. Revised 1987.

among workers who had been vocal in expressing their dissatisfaction and suggesting concrete proposals for change.

The change process, which had begun 3 years before, had centered on a redesign of production operations from a single machine-paced assembly line to a number of semi-autonomous assembly teams. Although the change had been referred to as the INCO "Volvo project" or "INCO's effort at Japanese-style management," it had really been neither of these. Rather, it had been the brainchild of a group of managers, led by Dux, who believed that both productivity and working conditions in the plant could be improved through a single effort. Of course, members of the group had visited other so-called innovative production facilities, but the new work groups and job classifications had been designed with the particular products and technology at INCO in mind.

After lengthy discussions among the management group, largely dedicated to reaching agreement on the general direction that the new project would take, the actual design began to emerge. Equally lengthy discussions (often referred to as negotiations) with members of the workforce, supervisors, and representatives of the local unions were part of the design process. The first restructuring into smaller work groups was tried in an experimental project that received tentative approval from top management in INCO headquarters and a "wait and see" response from the union. The strongest initial resistance had come from the plant engineers. They were sold neither on the new structure nor on the process of involving the workforce in the design of operating equipment and production methods. Previously, the engineering group had itself fulfilled these functions, and it felt the present problems were a result of a lack of skill among employees or managerial unwillingness to make the system work.

The experiment was staffed by volunteers supported by a few of the better-trained workers in the plant. The latter were necessary to ensure a start-up of the new equipment, which had been modified from the existing technology on the assembly line.

The initial experiment met with limited success. Although the group was able to meet the productivity levels of the existing line within a few weeks, critics of the new plan attributed the low level of success to the unrepresentative nature of the experimental group or the newness of the equipment on which they were working. However, even this limited success attracted the attention of numerous people at INCO headquarters and in other plants. All were interested in seeing the new experiment. Visits soon became a major distraction, and Dux declared a temporary halt to permit the project to proceed, although this produced some muttering at headquarters about his "secretive" and "uncooperative" behavior.

Because of the experiment's success, Dux and his staff prepared to convert the entire production operation to the new system. The enthusiasm of workers in the plant grew as training for the changeover proceeded. In fact, a group of production workers asked to help with the installation of the new equipment as a means of learning more about its operation.

Dux and his staff were surprised at the difficulties encountered at this phase. Headquarters seemed to drag its feet in approving the necessary funding for the changeover. Even after the funding was approved, there was a stream of challenges to minor parts of the plan. "Can't you lay the workers off during the changeover?" "Why use workers on overtime to do the changeover when you could hire temporary workers more cheaply?" These criticisms reflected a lack of understanding of the basic operating principles of the new system, and Dux rejected them.

The conversion of the entire assembly line to work groups was finally achieved, with the local management group making few concessions from their stated plans. The initial change and the first days of operation were filled with crises. The design process had not anticipated many of the problems that arose with full-scale operations. However, Dux was pleased to see managers, staff, and workers clustered together at the trouble areas, fine-tuning the design when problems arose. Just as the start-up finally appeared to be moving forward, a change in product specifications from a headquarters group dictated additional changes in the design of the assembly process. The new changes were handled quickly and with enthusiasm by the workforce. While the period was exhausting and seemingly endless to those who felt responsible for the change, the new design took only 6 months to reach normal operating levels (1 year had been forecast as the time needed to reach that level—without the added requirement for a change in product specifications).

Within a year, Dux was certain that he had a major success on his hands. Productivity and product quality measures for the plant had greatly improved. In this relatively short period his plant had moved from the worst, according to these indicators, to the third most productive in the INCO system. Absenteeism had dropped only slightly, but turnover had been reduced substantially. Morale was not measured formally but was considered by all members of the management team to be greatly improved. Now, after 3 years of full operations, the plant was considered the most productive in the entire INCO system.

Dux was a bit surprised when no other facility in INCO initiated a similar effort or called upon him for help. Increases of the early years had leveled off, with the peak being achieved in the early part of year 3. Now the facility seemed to have found a new equilibrium. The calm of smoother operations had been a welcome relief to many who had worked so hard to launch the new design. For Dux it provided the time to reflect on his accomplishment and think about his future career.

It was in this context that he considered the news that he had once again been bypassed for promotion to the next level in the INCO hierarchy.

Notes

1. Bethany McLean and Andy Serwer, "Brahmins at the Gate," *Fortune* (May 2, 2005), 59–68; Ann Davis and Anita Raghavan, "Fault Lines; Behind Morgan Stanley Turmoil: Competing Visions of Its Future," *The Wall Street Journal* (April 15, 2005), A1, A7; Ann Davis and Randall Smith, "Battle Ready; In Morgan Stanley Rebellion, Purcell Puts Up Tough Fight," *The Wall Street Journal* (April 4, 2005), A1, A10; Landon Thomas Jr., "High-Stakes Tit for Tat at Morgan Stanley," *The New York Times* (April 13, 2005), Business section, page 1; and Ann Davis, "Closing Bell; How Tide Turned against Purcell in Struggle at Morgan Stanley," *The Wall Street Journal* (June 14, 2005), A1, A11.

2. Lee G. Bolman and Terrence E. Deal, *Reframing Organizations: Artistry, Choice, and Leadership* (San Francisco: Jossey-Bass, 1991).

3. Paul M. Terry, "Conflict Management," *The Journal of Leadership Studies* 3, no. 2 (1996), 3–21; and Kathleen M. Eisenhardt, Jean L. Kahwajy, and L. J. Bourgeois III, "How Management Teams Can Have a Good Fight," *Harvard Business Review* (July–August 1997), 77–85.

4. Clayton T. Alderfer and Ken K. Smith, "Studying Intergroup Relations Imbedded in Organizations," *Administrative Science Quarterly* 27 (1982), 35–65.

5. Muzafer Sherif, "Experiments in Group Conflict," *Scientific American* 195 (1956), 54–58; and Edgar H. Schein, *Organizational Psychology*, 3d ed. (Englewood Cliffs, N.J.: Prentice-Hall, 1980).

6. M. Afzalur Rahim, "A Strategy for Managing Conflict in Complex Organizations," *Human Relations* 38 (1985), 81–89; Kenneth Thomas, "Conflict and Conflict Management," in M.D. Dunnette, ed., *Handbook of Industrial and Organizational Psychology* (Chicago, Ill.: Rand McNally, 1976); and Stuart M. Schmidt and Thomas A. Kochan, "Conflict: Toward Conceptual Clarity," *Administrative Science Quarterly* 13 (1972), 359–370.

7. L. David Brown, "Managing Conflict among Groups," in David A. Kolb, Irwin M. Rubin, and James M. McIntyre, eds., *Organizational Psychology: A Book of Readings* (Englewood Cliffs, N.J.: Prentice-Hall, 1979), 377–389; and Robert W. Ruekert and Orville C. Walker, Jr., "Interactions between Marketing and R&D Departments in Implementing Different Business Strategies," *Strategic Management Journal* 8 (1987), 233–248.

8. Joseph B. White, Lee Hawkins, Jr., and Karen Lundegaard, "UAW Is Facing Biggest Battles in Two Decades," *The Wall Street Journal* (June 10, 2005), B1; Amy Barrett, "Indigestion at Taco Bell," *BusinessWeek* (December 14, 1994), 66–67; Greg Burns, "Fast-Food Fight," *BusinessWeek* (June 2, 1997), 34–36.

9. Nanette Byrnes, with Mike McNamee, Ronald Grover, Joann Muller, and Andrew Park, "Auditing Here, Consulting Over There," *BusinessWeek* (April 8, 2002), 34–36.

10. Thomas A. Kochan, George P. Huber, and L. L. Cummings, "Determinants of Intraorganizational Conflict in Collective Bargaining in the Public Sector," *Administrative Science Quarterly* 20 (1975), 10–23.

11. Victoria L. Crittenden, Lorraine R. Gardiner, and Antonie Stam, "Reducing Conflict between Marketing and Manufac-turing," *Industrial Marketing Management* 22 (1993), 299–309; and Benson S. Shapiro, "Can Marketing and Manufacturing Coexist?" *Harvard Business Review* 55 (September–October 1977), 104–114.

12. Ben Worthen, "Cost-Cutting versus Innovation: Reconcilable Differences," *CIO* (October 1, 2004), 89–94.

13. Eric H. Neilsen, "Understanding and Managing Intergroup Conflict," in Jay W. Lorsch and Paul R. Lawrence, eds., *Managing Group and Intergroup Relations* (Homewood, Ill.: Irwin and Dorsey, 1972), 329–343; and Richard E. Walton and John M. Dutton, "The Management of Interdepartmental Conflict: A Model and Review," *Administrative Science Quarterly* 14 (1969), 73–84.

14. Jay W. Lorsch, "Introduction to the Structural Design of Organizations," in Gene W. Dalton, Paul R. Lawrence, and Jay W. Lorsch, eds., *Organization Structure and Design* (Homewood, Ill.: Irwin and Dorsey, 1970), 5.

15. James D. Thompson, *Organizations in Action* (New York: McGraw-Hill, 1967), 54–56.

16. Walton and Dutton, "The Management of Interdepartmental Conflict."

17. Joseph McCann and Jay R. Galbraith, "Interdepartmental Relations," in Paul C. Nystrom and William H. Starbuck, eds., *Handbook of Organizational Design*, vol. 2 (New York: Oxford University Press, 1981), 60–84.

18. Roderick M. Cramer, "Intergroup Relations and Organizational Dilemmas: The Role of Categorization Processes," in L. L. Cummings and Barry M. Staw, eds., *Research in Organizational Behavior*, vol. 13 (New York: JAI Press, 1991), 191–228; Neilsen, "Understanding and Managing Intergroup Conflict"; and Louis R. Pondy, "Organizational Conflict: Concepts and Models," *Administrative Science Quarterly* 12 (1968), 296–320.

19. Jeffrey Pfeffer, *Power in Organizations* (Marshfield, Mass.: Pitman, 1981).

20. Alan Deutschman, "The Mind of Jeff Bezos," *Fast Company* (August 2004), 53–58.

21. Robert A. Dahl, "The Concept of Power," *Behavioral Science* 2 (1957), 201–215.

22. W. Graham Astley and Paramijit S. Sachdeva, "Structural Sources of Intraorganizational Power: A Theoretical Synthesis," *Academy of Management Review* 9 (1984), 104–113; Abraham Kaplan, "Power in Perspective," in Robert L. Kahn and Elise Boulding, eds., *Power and Conflict in Organizations* (London: Tavistock, 1964), 11–32.

23. Gerald R. Salancik and Jeffrey Pfeffer, "The Bases and Use of Power in Organizational Decision-Making: The Case of the University," *Administrative Science Quarterly* 19 (1974), 453–473.

24. Richard M. Emerson, "Power-Dependence Relations," *American Sociological Review* 27 (1962), 31–41.

25. Rosabeth Moss Kanter, "Power Failure in Management Circuits," *Harvard Business Review* (July–August 1979), 65–75.

26. Sam Walker, "On Sports: Meet the Micro Manager," *The Wall Street Journal* (July 11, 2003), W12.

27. Examples are Robert Greene and Joost Elffers, *The 48 Laws of Power* (New York: Viking, 1999); Jeffrey J. Fox, *How to Become CEO* (New York: Hyperion, 1999).

28. John R. P. French, Jr., and Bertram Raven, "The Bases of Social Power," in *Group Dynamics*, D. Cartwright and A. F. Zander, eds. (Evanston, Ill.: Row Peterson, 1960), 607–623.

29. Ran Lachman, "Power from What? A Reexamination of Its Relationships with Structural Conditions," *Administrative Science Quarterly* 34 (1989), 231–251; and Daniel J. Brass, "Being in the Right Place: A Structural Analysis of Individual Influence in an Organization," *Administrative Science Quarterly* 29 (1984), 518–539.

30. Michael Warshaw, "The Good Guy's Guide to Office Politics," *Fast Company* (April–May 1998), 157–178.

31. A. J. Grimes, "Authority, Power, Influence, and Social Control: A Theoretical Synthesis," *Academy of Management Review* 3 (1978), 724–735.

32. Astley and Sachdeva, "Structural Sources of Intraorganizational Power."

33. Jeffrey Pfeffer, *Managing with Power: Politics and Influence in Organizations* (Boston, Mass.: Harvard Business School Press, 1992).

34. Robert L. Peabody, "Perceptions of Organizational Authority," *Administrative Science Quarterly* 6 (1962), 479.

35. Monica Langley, "Columbia Tells Doctors at Hospital to End Their Outside Practice," *The Wall Street Journal* (May 2, 1997), A1, A6.

36. Richard S. Blackburn, "Lower Participant Power: Toward a Conceptual Integration," *Academy of Management Review* 6 (1981), 127–131.

37. Patricia Sellers, "eBay's Secret," *Fortune* (October 18, 2004), 161–178.

38. Kanter, "Power Failure in Management Circuits," 70.

39. Ianthe Jeanne Dugan and George Anders, "Members Only; At AIG, Exclusive 'Club' Gave Greenberg Powerful Infuence," *The Wall Street Journal* (April 11, 2005), A1, A10.

40. Pfeffer, *Power in Organizations*.

41. Erik W. Larson and Jonathan B. King, "The Systemic Distortion of Information: An Ongoing Challenge to Management," *Organizational Dynamics* 24, no. 3 (Winter 1996), 49–61; and Thomas H. Davenport, Robert G. Eccles, and Laurence Prusak, "Information Politics," *Sloan Management Review* (Fall 1992), 53–65.

42. Andrew M. Pettigrew, *The Politics of Organizational Decision-Making* (London: Tavistock, 1973).

43. Robert Frank and Elena Cherney, "Paper Tigers; Lord Black's Board: A-List Cast Played Acquiescent Role," *The Wall Street Journal* (September 27, 2004), A1.

44. Lorne Manly and Andrew Ross Sorkin, "At Sony, Diplomacy Trumps Technology," *The New York Times* (March 8, 2005), http://www.nytimes.com.

45. Warshaw, "The Good Guy's Guide to Office Politics."

46. Carol Hymowitz, "Companies Experience Major Power Shifts as Crises Continue" (In the Lead column), *The Wall Street Journal* (October 9, 2001), B1.

47. Astley and Sachdeva, "Structural Sources of Intraorganizational Power"; and Noel M. Tichy and Charles Fombrun, "Network Analysis in Organizational Settings," *Human Relations* 32 (1979), 923–965.

48. McLean and Serwer, "Brahmins at the Gate."

49. Greg Ip, Kate Kelly, Susanne Craig, and Ianthe Jeanne Dugan, "A Bull's Market; Dick Grasso's NYSE Legacy: Buffed Image, Shaky Foundation," *The Wall Street Journal* (December 30, 2003), A1, A6; Yochi J. Dreazen and Christopher Cooper, "Lingering Presence; Behind the Scenes, U.S. Tightens Grip on Iraq's Future," *The Wall Street Journal* (May 13, 2004), A1.

50. Charles Perrow, "Departmental Power and Perspective in Industrial Firms," in Mayer N. Zald, ed., *Power in Organizations* (Nashville, Tenn.: Vanderbilt University Press, 1970), 59–89.

51. D. J. Hickson, C. R. Hinings, C. A. Lee, R. E. Schneck, and J. M. Pennings, "A Strategic Contingencies Theory of Intraorganizational Power," *Administrative Science Quarterly* 16 (1971), 216–229; and Gerald R. Salancik and Jeffrey Pfeffer, "Who Gets Power—and How They Hold onto It: A Strategic-Contingency Model of Power," *Organizational Dynamics* (Winter 1977), 3–21.

52. Pfeffer, *Managing with Power*; Salancik and Pfeffer, "Who Gets Power"; C. R. Hinings, D. J. Hickson, J. M. Pennings, and R. E. Schneck, "Structural Conditions of Intraorganizational Power," *Administrative Science Quarterly* 19 (1974), 22–44.

53. Carol Stoak Saunders, "The Strategic Contingencies Theory of Power: Multiple Perspectives," *Journal of Management Studies* 27 (1990), 1–18; Warren Boeker, "The Development and Institutionalization of Sub-Unit Power in Organizations," *Administrative Science Quarterly* 34 (1989), 388–510; and Irit Cohen and Ran Lachman, "The Generality of the Strategic Contingencies Approach to Sub-Unit Power," *Organizational Studies* 9 (1988), 371–391.

54. Emerson, "Power-Dependence Relations."

55. Pfeffer, *Managing with Power*.

56. Jeffrey Pfeffer and Gerald Salancik, "Organizational Decision-Making as a Political Process: The Case of a University Budget," *Administrative Science Quarterly* (1974), 135–151.

57. Salancik and Pfeffer, "Bases and Use of Power in Organizational Decision-Making," 470.

58. Hickson et al., "A Strategic Contingencies Theory."

59. Pettigrew, *The Politics of Organizational Decision-Making*.

60. Hickson et al., "A Strategic Contingencies Theory."

61. Ibid.

62. Barbara Martinez, "Strong Medicine; With New Muscle, Hospitals Squeeze Insurers on Rates," *The Wall Street Journal* (April 12, 2002), A1; James V. DeLong, "Rule of Law: Just What Crime Did Columbia/HCA Commit?" *The Wall Street Journal* (August 20, 1997), A15; and Lucette Lagnado, "House Panel Begins Inquiry into Hospital Billing Practices," *The Wall Street Journal* (July 17, 2003), B1.

63. Jeffrey Gantz and Victor V. Murray, "Experience of Workplace Politics," *Academy of Management Journal* 23 (1980), 237–251; and Dan L. Madison, Robert W. Allen, Lyman W. Porter, Patricia A. Renwick, and Bronston T. Mayes, "Organizational Politics: An Exploration of Managers' Perception," *Human Relations* 33 (1980), 79–100.

64. Gerald R. Ferris and K. Michele Kacmar, "Perceptions of Organizational Politics," *Journal of Management* 18 (1992), 93–116; Parmod Kumar and Rehana Ghadially, "Organizational Politics and Its Effects on Members of Organizations," *Human Relations* 42 (1989), 305–314; Donald J. Vredenburgh and John G. Maurer, "A Process Framework of Organizational Politics," *Human Relations* 37 (1984), 47–66; and Gerald R. Ferris, Dwight D. Frink, Maria Carmen Galang, Jing Zhou, Michele Kacmar, and Jack L. Howard, "Perceptions of Organizational Politics: Prediction, Stress-Related

Implications, and Outcomes," *Human Relations* 49, no. 2 (1996), 233–266.

65. Ferris et al., "Perceptions of Organizational Politics: Prediction, Stress-Related Implications, and Outcomes"; John J. Voyer, "Coercive Organizational Politics and Organizational Outcomes: An Interpretive Study," *Organization Science* 5, no. 1 (February 1994), 72–85; and James W. Dean, Jr., and Mark P. Sharfman, "Does Decision Process Matter? A Study of Strategic Decision-Making Effectiveness," *Academy of Management Journal* 39, no. 2 (1996), 368–396.

66. Jeffrey Pfeffer, *Managing with Power: Politics and Influence in Organizations* (Boston, Mass.: Harvard Business School Press, 1992).

67. Amos Drory and Tsilia Romm, "The Definition of Organizational Politics: A Review," *Human Relations* 43 (1990), 1133–1154; and Vredenburgh and Maurer, "A Process Framework of Organizational Politics"; and Lafe Low, "It's Politics, As Usual," *CIO* (April 1, 2004), 87–90.

68. Pfeffer, *Power in Organizations*, 70.

69. Madison et al., "Organizational Politics"; Jay R. Galbraith, *Organizational Design* (Reading, Mass.: Addison-Wesley, 1977).

70. Gantz and Murray, "Experience of Workplace Politics"; Pfeffer, *Power in Organizations*.

71. Daniel J. Brass and Marlene E. Burkhardt, "Potential Power and Power Use: An Investigation of Structure and Behavior," *Academy of Management Journal* 38 (1993), 441–470.

72. Harvey G. Enns and Dean B. McFarlin, "When Executives Influence Peers, Does Function Matter?" *Human Resource Management* 4, no. 2 (Summer 2003), 125–142.

73. Hickson et al., "A Strategic Contingencies Theory."

74. Pfeffer, *Power in Organizations*.

75. Ibid.

76. V. Dallas Merrell, *Huddling: The Informal Way to Management Success* (New York: AMACON, 1979).

77. Ceasar Douglas and Anthony P. Ammeter, "An Examination of Leader Political Skill and Its Effect on Ratings of Leader Effectiveness," *The Leadership Quarterly* 15 (2004), 537–550.

78. Vredenburgh and Maurer, "A Process Framework of Organizational Politics."

79. Pfeffer, *Power in Organizations*.

80. Ibid.

81. Ann Davis and Randall Smith, "Merrill Switch: Popular Veteran Is In, Not Out," *The Wall Street Journal* (August 13, 2003), C1.

82. Pfeffer, *Power in Organizations*.

83. Ibid.

84. Kanter, "Power Failure in Management Circuits"; Pfeffer, *Power in Organizations*.

85. Ben Elgin, "Inside Yahoo!" *BusinessWeek* (May 21, 2001), 114–122.

86. Robert R. Blake and Jane S. Mouton, "Overcoming Group Warfare," *Harvard Business Review* (November–December 1984), 98–108.

87. Blake and Mouton, "Overcoming Group Warfare"; Paul R. Lawrence and Jay W. Lorsch, "New Management Job: The Integrator," *Harvard Business Review* 45 (November–December 1967), 142–151.

88. Aaron Bernstein, "Look Who's Pushing Productivity," *BusinessWeek* (April 7, 1997), 72–75.

89. Ibid.

90. White, et al., "UAW Is Facing Biggest Battles in Two Decades."

91. Robert R. Blake, Herbert A. Shepard, and Jane S. Mouton, *Managing Intergroup Conflict in Industry* (Houston: Gulf Publishing, 1964); Doug Stewart, "Expand the Pie before You Divvy It Up," *Smithsonian* (November 1997), 78–90.

92. Patrick S. Nugent, "Managing Conflict: Third-Party Interventions for Managers," *Academy of Management Executive* 16, no. 1 (2002), 139–155.

93. Blake and Mouton, "Overcoming Group Warfare"; Schein, *Organizational Psychology*; Blake, Shepard, and Mouton, *Managing Intergroup Conflict in Industry*; and Richard E. Walton, *Interpersonal Peacemaking: Confrontation and Third-Party Consultations* (Reading, Mass.: Addison-Wesley, 1969).

94. Neilsen, "Understanding and Managing Intergroup Conflict"; McCann and Galbraith, "Interdepartmental Relations."

95. Neilsen, "Understanding and Managing Intergroup Conflict"; McCann and Galbraith, "Interdepartmental Relations"; Sherif et al., *Intergroup Conflict and Cooperation*.

96. Dean Tjosvold, Valerie Dann, and Choy Wong, "Managing Conflict between Departments to Serve Customers," *Human Relations* 45 (1992), 1035–1054.

Integrative Cases

Integrative Case 1.0

It Isn't So Simple: Infrastructure Change at Royce Consulting

Background
Infrastructure and Proposed Changes
Work Patterns
Organizational Culture
Current Situation
The Feasibility Study
The Challenge

Integrative Case 2.0

Custom Chip, Inc.

Introduction
Company Background
The Manufacturing Process
Role of the Product Engineer
Weekly Meeting
Coordination with Applications
    Engineers
Coordination with Manufacturing
Later in the Day

Integrative Case 3.0

W. L. Gore & Associates, Inc. Entering 1998

The First Day on the Job
Company Background
Company Products
W. L. Gore & Associates' Approach
    to Organization and Structure
The Lattice Organization
Features of W. L. Gore's Culture
W. L. Gore & Associates' Sponsor
    Program

Compensation Practices
W. L. Gore & Associates' Guiding
    Principles and Core Values
Research and Development
Development of Gore Associates
Marketing Approaches and Strategy
Adapting to Changing Environmental
    Forces
W. L. Gore & Associates' Financial
    Performance
Acknowledgments
Excerpts from Interviews with
    Associates

Integrative Case 4.0

XEL Communications, Inc. (C): Forming a Strategic Partnership

XEL Communications, Inc.
The XEL Vision
Which Path to Choose
Staying the Course
Going Public
Strategic Partnership
The Case Against Strategic
    Partnership
Choosing a Partner
Going Forward

Integrative Case 5.0

Empire Plastics

A Project to Remember
Conflict Ahead
Failing . . . Forward

Integrative Case 6.0

The Audubon Zoo, 1993

The Decision
Purpose of the Zoo
New Directions
Operations
Financial
Management
The Zoo in the Late 1980s
The Future

Integrative Case 7.0

Moss Adams, LLP

Company Background
The Industry and the Market
The Wine Industry Niche
The Aftermath

Integrative Case 8.1

Littleton Manufacturing (A)

The Problems
The Company
The Financial Picture
The Quality Improvement System
How Different Levels Perceived the
    Problems
Top Management
Recommendation Time

Integrative Case 8.2

Littleton Manufacturing (B)

Integrative Case 1.0

It Isn't So Simple: Infrastructure Change at Royce Consulting*

1.0

The lights of the city glittered outside Ken Vincent's twelfth-floor office. After nine years of late nights and missed holidays, Ken was in the executive suite with the words "Associate Partner" on the door. Things should be easier now, but the proposed changes at Royce Consulting had been more challenging than he had expected. "I don't understand," he thought. "At Royce Consulting our clients, our people, and our reputation are what count, so why do I feel so much tension from the managers about the changes that are going to be made in the office? We've analyzed why we have to make the changes. Heck, we even got an outside person to help us. The administrative support staff are pleased. So why aren't the managers enthusiastic? We all know what the decision at tomorrow's meeting will be—Go! Then it will all be over. Or will it?" Ken thought as he turned out the lights.

Background

Royce Consulting is an international consulting firm whose clients are large corporations, usually with long-term contracts. Royce employees spend weeks, months, and even years working under contract at the client's site. Royce consultants are employed by a wide range of industries, from manufacturing facilities to utilities to service businesses. The firm has over 160 consulting offices located in 65 countries. At this location Royce employees included 85 staff members, 22 site managers, 9 partners and associate partners, 6 administrative support staff, 1 human resource professional, and 1 financial support person.

For the most part, Royce Consulting hired entry-level staff straight out of college and promoted from within. New hires worked on staff for five or six years; if they did well, they were promoted to manager. Managers were responsible for maintaining client contracts and assisting partners in creating proposals for future engagements. Those who were not promoted after six or seven years generally left the company for other jobs.

Newly promoted managers were assigned an office, a major perquisite of their new status. During the previous year, some new managers had been forced to share an office because of space limitations. To minimize the friction of sharing an office, one of the managers was usually assigned to a long-term project out of town. Thus, practically speaking, each manager had a private office.

Infrastructure and Proposed Changes

Royce was thinking about instituting a hoteling office system—also referred to as a "nonterritorial" or "free-address" office. A hoteling office system made offices available to managers on a reservation or drop-in basis. Managers are not assigned a permanent office; instead, whatever materials and equipment the manager needs are moved into the temporary office. These are some of the features and advantages of a hoteling office system:

- No permanent office assigned
- Offices are scheduled by reservations
- Long-term scheduling of an office is feasible
- Storage space would be located in a separate file room
- Standard manuals and supplies would be maintained in each office
- Hoteling coordinator is responsible for maintaining offices
- A change in "possession of space"
- Eliminates two or more managers assigned to the same office
- Allows managers to keep the same office if desired
- Managers would have to bring in whatever files they needed for their stay
- Information available would be standardized regardless of office
- Managers do not have to worry about "housekeeping issues"

The other innovation under consideration was an upgrade to state-of-the-art electronic office technology. All managers would receive a new notebook computer with updated communications capability to use Royce's integrated and proprietary software. Also, as part of the electronic office technology, an electronic filing system was considered. The electronic filing system meant information regarding proposals, client records, and promotional materials would be electronically available on the Royce Consulting network.

The administrative support staff had limited experience with many of the application packages used by the managers. While they used word processing extensively, they had little experience with spreadsheets, communications, or graphics packages. The firm had a graphics department and the managers did most of their own work, so the administrative staff did not have to work with those application software packages.

*Presented to and accepted by the Society for Case Research. All rights reserved to the authors and SCR.

This case was prepared by Sally Dresdow of the University of Wisconsin at Green Bay and Joy Benson of the University of Illinois at Springfield and is intended to be used as a basis for class discussion. The views represented here are those of the case authors and do not necessarily reflect the views of the Society for Case Research. The authors' views are based on their own professional judgments. The names of the organization, individuals, and location have been disguised to preserve the organization's request for anonymity.

Work Patterns

Royce Consulting was located in a large city in the Midwest. The office was located in the downtown area, but it was easy to get to. Managers assigned to in-town projects often stopped by for a few hours at various times of the day. Managers who were not currently assigned to client projects were expected to be in the office to assist on current projects or work with a partner to develop proposals for new business.

In a consulting firm, managers spend a significant portion of their time at client sites. As a result, the office occupancy rate at Royce Consulting was about 40 to 60 percent. This meant that the firm paid lease costs for offices that were empty approximately half of the time. With the planned growth over the next ten years, assigning permanent offices to every manager, even in doubled-up arrangements, was judged to be economically unnecessary given the amount of time offices were empty.

The proposed changes would require managers and administrative support staff to adjust their work patterns. Additionally, if a hoteling office system was adopted, managers would need to keep their files in a centralized file room.

Organizational Culture

Royce Consulting had a strong organizational culture, and management personnel were highly effective at communicating it to all employees.

Stability of Culture

The culture at Royce Consulting was stable. The leadership of the corporation had a clear picture of who they were and what type of organization they were. Royce Consulting had positioned itself to be a leader in all areas of large business consulting. Royce Consulting's CEO articulated the firm's commitment to being client-centered. Everything that was done at Royce Consulting was because of the client.

Training

New hires at Royce Consulting received extensive training in the culture of the organization and the methodology employed in consulting projects. They began with a structured program of classroom instruction and computer-aided courses covering technologies used in the various industries in which the firm was involved. Royce Consulting recruited top young people who were aggressive and who were willing to do whatever was necessary to get the job done and build a common bond. Among new hires, camaraderie was encouraged along with a level of competition. This kind of behavior continued to be cultivated throughout the training and promotion process.

Work Relationships

Royce Consulting employees had a remarkably similar outlook on the organization. Accepting the culture and norms of the organization was important for each employee. The

norms of Royce Consulting revolved around high performance expectations and strong job involvement.

By the time people made manager, they were aware of what types of behaviors were acceptable. Managers were formally assigned the role of coach to younger staff people, and they modeled acceptable behavior. Behavioral norms included when they came into the office, how late they stayed at the office, and the type of comments they made about others. Managers spent time checking on staff people and talking with them about how they were doing.

The standard for relationships was that of professionalism. Managers knew they had to do what the partners asked and they were to be available at all times. A norms survey and conversations made it clear that people at Royce Consulting were expected to help each other with on-the-job problems, but personal problems were outside the realm of sanctioned relationships. Personal problems were not to interfere with performance on a job. To illustrate, vacations were put on hold and other kinds of commitments were set aside if something was needed at Royce Consulting.

Organizational Values

Three things were of major importance to the organization: its clients, its people, and its reputation. There was a strong client-centered philosophy communicated and practiced. Organization members sought to meet and exceed customer expectations. Putting clients first was stressed. The management of Royce Consulting listened to its clients and made adjustments to satisfy the client.

The reputation of Royce Consulting was important to those leading the organization. They protected and enhanced it by focusing on quality services delivered by quality people. The emphasis on clients, Royce Consulting personnel, and the firm's reputation was cultivated by developing a highly motivated, cohesive, and committed group of employees.

Management Style and Hierarchical Structure

The company organization was characterized by a directive style of management. The partners had the final word on all issues of importance. It was common to hear statements like "Managers are expected to solve problems, and do whatever it takes to finish the job" and "Whatever the partners want, we do." Partners accepted and asked for managers' feedback on projects, but in the final analysis, the partners made the decisions.

Current Situation

Royce Consulting had an aggressive five-year plan that was predicated on a continued increase in business. Increases in the total number of partners, associate partners, managers, and staff were forecast. Additional office space would be required to accommodate the growth in staff; this would increase rental costs at a time when Royce's fixed and variable costs were going up.

The partners, led by managing partner Donald Gray and associate partner Ken Vincent, believed that something had to be done to improve space utilization and the productivity of the managers and administrative personnel. The partners approved a feasibility study of the innovations and their impact on the company.

1.0

The ultimate decision makers were the partner group who had the power to approve the concepts and commit the required financial investment. A planning committee consisted of Ken Vincent; the human resources person; the financial officer; and an outside consultant, Mary Schrean.

The Feasibility Study

Within two working days of the initial meeting, all the partners and managers received a memo announcing the hoteling office feasibility study. The memo included a brief description of the concept and stated that it would include an interview with the staff. By this time, partners and managers had already heard about the possible changes and knew that Gray was leaning toward hoteling offices.

Interviews with the Partners

All the partners were interviewed. One similarity in the comments was that they thought the move to hoteling offices was necessary but they were glad it would not affect them. Three partners expressed concern about managers' acceptance of the change to a hoteling system. The conclusion of each partner was that if Royce Consulting moved to hoteling offices, with or without electronic office technology, the managers would accept the change. The reason given by the partners for such acceptance was that the managers would do what the partners wanted done.

The partners all agreed that productivity could be improved at all levels of the organization: in their own work as well as among the secretaries and the managers. Partners acknowledged that current levels of information technology at Royce Consulting would not support the move to hoteling offices and that advances in electronic office technology needed to be considered.

Partners viewed all filing issues as secondary to both the office layout change and the proposed technology improvement. What eventually emerged, however, was that ownership and control of files was a major concern, and most partners and managers did not want anything centralized.

Interviews with the Managers

Personal interviews were conducted with all ten managers who were in the office. During the interviews, four of the managers asked Schrean whether the change to hoteling offices was her idea. The managers passed the question off as a joke; however, they expected a response from her. She stated that she was there as an adviser, that she had not generated the idea, and that she would not make the final decision regarding the changes.

The length of time that these managers had been in their current positions ranged from six months to five years. None of them expressed positive feelings about the hoteling system, and all of them referred to how hard they had worked to make manager and gain an office of their own. Eight managers spoke of the status that the office gave them and the convenience of having a permanent place to keep their information and files. Two of the managers said they did not care so much about the status but were concerned about the convenience. One manager said he would come in less frequently if he did not have his own office. The managers believed that a change to hoteling offices would decrease their productivity. Two managers stated that they did not care how much money Royce Consulting would save on lease costs; they wanted to keep their offices.

However, for all the negative comments, all the managers said that they would go along with whatever the partners decided to do. One manager stated that if Royce Consulting stays busy with client projects, having a permanently assigned office was not a big issue.

During the interviews, every manager was enthusiastic and supportive of new productivity tools, particularly the improved electronic office technology. They believed that new computers and integrated software and productivity tools would definitely improve their productivity. Half the managers stated that updated technology would make the change to hoteling offices "a little less terrible," and they wanted their secretaries to have the same software as they did.

The managers' responses to the filing issue varied. The volume of files managers had was in direct proportion to their tenure in that position: The longer a person was a manager, the more files he or she had. In all cases, managers took care of their own files, storing them in their offices and in whatever filing drawers were free.

As part of the process of speaking with managers, their administrative assistants were asked about the proposed changes. Each of the six thought that the electronic office upgrade would benefit the managers, although they were somewhat concerned about what would be expected of them. Regarding the move to hoteling offices, each said that the managers would hate the change, but that they would agree to it if the partners wanted to move in that direction.

Results of the Survey

A survey developed from the interviews was sent to all partners, associate partners, and managers two weeks after the interviews were conducted. The completed survey was returned by 6 of the 9 partners and associate partners and 16 of the 22 managers. This is what the survey showed.

Work Patterns. It was "common knowledge" that managers were out of the office a significant portion of their time, but there were no figures to substantiate this belief, so the respondents were asked to provide data on where they spent their time. The survey results indicated that partners spent 38 percent of their time in the office; 54 percent at client sites; 5 percent at home; and 3 percent in other places, such as airports. Managers reported spending 32 percent of their time in the office, 63 percent at client sites, 4 percent at home, and 1 percent in other places.

For 15 workdays, the planning team also visually checked each of the 15 managers' offices four times each day: at 9 a.m., 11 a.m., 2 p.m., and 4 p.m. These times were selected because initial observations indicated that these were the peak occupancy times. An average of six offices (40 percent of all manager offices) were empty at any given time; in other words, there was a 60 percent occupancy rate.

Alternative Office Layouts. One of the alternatives outlined by the planning committee was a continuation of and expansion of shared offices. Eleven of the managers responding to the survey preferred shared offices to hoteling offices. Occasions when more than one manager was in the shared office at the same time were infrequent. Eight managers reported 0 to 5 office conflicts per month; three managers reported 6 to 10 office conflicts per month. The type of problems encountered with shared offices included not having enough filing space, problems in directing telephone calls, and lack of privacy.

Managers agreed that having a permanently assigned office was an important perquisite. The survey confirmed the information gathered in the interviews about managers' attitudes: All but two managers preferred shared offices over hoteling, and managers believed their productivity would be negatively impacted. The challenges facing Royce Consulting if they move to hoteling offices centered around tradition and managers' expectations, file accessibility and organization, security and privacy issues, unpredictable work schedules, and high-traffic periods.

Control of Personal Files. Because of the comments made during the face-to-face interviews, survey respondents were asked to rank the importance of having personal control of their files. A 5-point scale was used, with 5 being "strongly agree" and 1 being "strongly disagree." Here are the responses.

Electronic Technology. Royce Consulting had a basic network system in the office that could not accommodate the current partners and managers working at a remote site. The administrative support staff had a separate network, and the managers and staff could not communicate electronically. Of managers responding to the survey, 95 percent wanted to use the network but only 50 percent could actually do so.

Option Analysis

A financial analysis showed that there were significant cost differences between the options under consideration:

Option 1: Continue private offices with some office sharing
- Lease an additional floor in existing building; annual cost, $360,000

- Build out the additional floor (i.e., construct, furnish, and equip offices and work areas): one-time cost, $600,000

Option 2: Move to hoteling offices with upgraded office technology
- Upgrade office electronic technology: one-time cost, $190,000

Option 1 was expensive because under the terms of the existing lease, Royce had to commit to an entire floor if it wanted additional space. Hoteling offices showed an overall financial advantage of $360,000 per year and a one-time savings of $410,000 over shared or individual offices.

The Challenge

Vincent met with Mary Schrean to discuss the upcoming meeting of partners and managers, where they would present the results of the study and a proposal for action. Included in the report were proposed layouts for both shared and hoteling offices. Vincent and Gray were planning to recommend a hoteling office system, which would include storage areas, state-of-the-art electronic office technology for managers and administrative support staff, and centralized files. The rationale for their decision emphasized the amount of time that managers were out of the office and the high cost of maintaining the status quo and was built around the following points:

1. Royce's business is different: offices are empty from 40 to 60 percent of the time.
2. Real estate costs continue to escalate.
3. Projections indicate there will be increased need for offices and cost-control strategies as the business develops.
4. Royce Consulting plays a leading role in helping organizations implement innovation.

"It's still a go," thought Vincent as he and the others returned from a break. "The cost figures support it and the growth figures support it. It's simple—or is it? The decision is the easy part. What is it about Royce Consulting that will help or hinder its acceptance? In the long run, I hope we strengthen our internal processes and don't hinder our effectiveness by going ahead with these simple changes."

Respondents	Sample	Rank
Partners	6	4.3
Managers:		
0–1 year	5	4.6
2–3 years	5	3.6
4+ years	6	4.3

Integrative Case 2.0

Custom Chip, Inc.*

2.0

Introduction

It was 7:50 on Monday morning. Frank Questin, product engineering manager at Custom Chip, Inc., was sitting in his office making a TO DO list for the day. From 8:00 to 9:30 a.m., he would have his weekly meeting with his staff of engineers. After the meeting, Frank thought he would begin developing a proposal for solving what he called "Custom Chip's manufacturing documentation problem"— inadequate technical information regarding the steps to manufacture many of the company's products. Before he could finish his TO DO list, he answered a phone call from Custom Chip's human resource manager, who asked him about the status of two overdue performance appraisals and reminded him that this day marked Bill Lazarus's fifth-year anniversary with the company. Following this call, Frank hurried off to the Monday morning meeting with his staff.

Frank had been product engineering manager at Custom Chip for fourteen months. This was his first management position, and he sometimes questioned his effectiveness as a manager. Often he could not complete the tasks he set out for himself due to interruptions and problems brought to his attention by others. Even though he had not been told exactly what results he was supposed to accomplish, he had a nagging feeling that he should have achieved more after these fourteen months. On the other hand, he thought maybe he was functioning pretty well in some of his areas of responsibility given the complexity of the problems his group handled and the unpredictable changes in the semiconductor industry—changes caused not only by rapid advances in technology, but also by increased foreign competition and a recent downturn in demand.

Company Background

Custom Chip, Inc., was a semiconductor manufacturer specializing in custom chips and components used in radars, satellite transmitters, and other radio frequency devices. The company had been founded in 1977 and had grown rapidly with sales exceeding $25 million in 1986. Most of the company's 300 employees were located in the main plant in Silicon Valley, but overseas manufacturing facilities in Europe and the Far East were growing in size and importance. These overseas facilities assembled the less complex, higher-volume products. New products and the more complex ones were assembled in the main plant. Approximately one-third of the assembly employees were in overseas facilities.

While the specialized products and markets of Custom Chip provided a market niche that had thus far shielded the company from the major downturn in the semiconductor industry, growth had come to a standstill. Because of this, cost reduction had become a high priority.

The Manufacturing Process

Manufacturers of standard chips have long production runs of a few products. Their cost per unit is low and cost control is a primary determinant of success. In contrast, manufacturers of custom chips have extensive product lines and produce small production runs of special applications. Custom Chip, Inc., for example, had manufactured over 2,000 different products in the last five years. In any one quarter the company might schedule 300 production runs for different products, as many as one-third of which might be new or modified products that the company had not made before. Because they must be efficient in designing and manufacturing many product lines, all custom chip manufacturers are highly dependent on their engineers. Customers are often first concerned with whether Custom Chip can design and manufacture the needed product *at all*; second, with whether they can deliver it on time; and only third, with cost.

After a product is designed, there are two phases to the manufacturing process. (See Exhibit 1.) The first is wafer fabrication. This is a complex process in which circuits are etched onto the various layers added to a silicon wafer. The number of steps that the wafer goes through plus inherent problems in controlling various chemical processes make it very difficult to meet the exacting specifications required for the final wafer. The wafers, which are typically "just a few" inches in diameter when the fabrication process is complete, contain hundreds, sometimes thousands, of tiny identical die. Once the wafer has been tested and sliced up to produce these die, each die will be used as a circuit component.

If the completed wafer passes the various quality tests, it moves on to the assembly phase. In assembly, the die from the wafers, very small wires, and other components are attached to a circuit in a series of precise operations. This finished circuit is the final product of Custom Chip, Inc.

Each product goes through many independent and delicate operations, and each step is subject to operator or machine error. Due to the number of steps and tests involved, the wafer fabrication takes eight to twelve weeks

Pre-production

- *Application engineers design and produce prototype*
- *Product engineers translate design into manufacturing instructions*

Production

- *Wafer fabrication*

EXHIBIT 1
Manufacturing Process

2.0

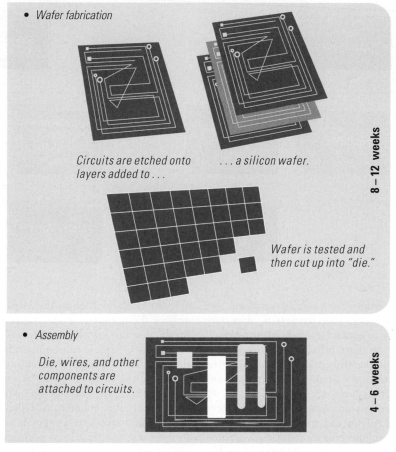

Circuits are etched onto layers added to . . .

. . . a silicon wafer.

Wafer is tested and then cut up into "die."

8 – 12 weeks

- *Assembly*

Die, wires, and other components are attached to circuits.

4 – 6 weeks

and the assembly process takes four to six weeks. Because of the exacting specifications, products are rejected for the slightest flaw. The likelihood that every product starting the run will make it through all of the processes and still meet specifications is often quite low. For some products, average yield[1] is as low as 40 percent, and actual yields can vary considerably from one run to another. At Custom Chip, the average yield for all products is in the 60 to 70 percent range.

Because it takes so long to make a custom chip, it is especially important to have some control of these yields. For example, if a customer orders one thousand units of a product and typical yields for that product average 50 percent, Custom Chip will schedule a starting batch of 2,200 units. With this approach, even if the yield falls as low as 45.4 percent (45.4 percent of 2,200 is 1,000) the company

can still meet the order. If the actual yield falls below 45.4 percent, the order will not be completed in that run, and a very small, costly run of the item will be needed to complete the order. The only way the company can effectively control these yields and stay on schedule is for the engineering groups and operations to cooperate and coordinate their efforts efficiently.

Role of the Product Engineer

The product engineer's job is defined by its relationship to applications engineering and operations. The applications engineers are responsible for designing and developing prototypes when incoming orders are for new or modified products. The product engineer's role is to translate the applications engineering group's design into a set of manufacturing instructions and then to work alongside manufactur-

EXHIBIT 2
Custom Chip, Inc., Partial Organization Chart

2.0

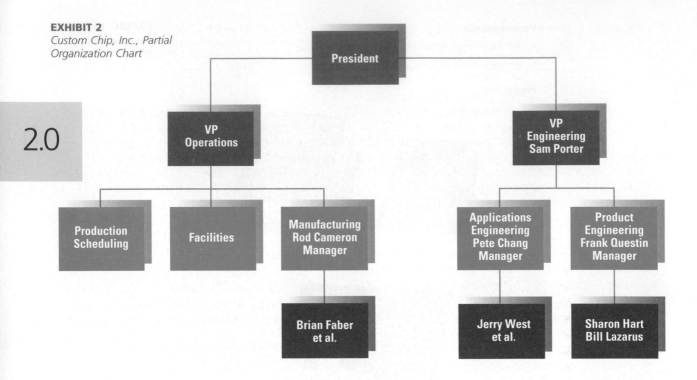

ing to make sure that engineering-related problems get solved. The product engineers' effectiveness is ultimately measured by their ability to control yields on their assigned products. The organization chart in Exhibit 2 shows the engineering and operations departments. Exhibit 3 summarizes the roles and objectives of manufacturing, applications engineering, and product engineering.

The product engineers estimate that 70 to 80 percent of their time is spent in solving day-to-day manufacturing problems. The product engineers have cubicles in a room directly across the hall from the manufacturing facility. If a manufacturing supervisor has a question regarding how to build a product during a run, that supervisor will call the engineer assigned to that product. If the engineer is avail-

able, he or she will go to the manufacturing floor to help answer the question. If the engineer is not available, the production run may be stopped and the product put aside so that other orders can be manufactured. This results in delays and added costs. One reason that product engineers are consulted is that documentation—the instructions for manufacturing the product—is unclear or incomplete.

The product engineer will also be called if a product is tested and fails to meet specifications. If a product fails to meet test specifications, production stops, and the engineer must diagnose the problem and attempt to find a solution. Otherwise, the order for that product may be only partially met. Test failures are a very serious problem, which can result in considerable cost increases and

EXHIBIT 3
Departmental Roles and Objectives

Department	Role	Primary Objective
Applications Engineering	Designs and develops prototypes for new or modified products	Satisfy customer needs through innovative designs
Product Engineering	Translates designs into manufacturing instructions and works alongside manufacturing to solve "engineering-related" problems	Maintain and control yields on assigned products
Manufacturing	Executes designs	Meet productivity standards and time schedules

schedule delays for customers. Products do not test properly for many reasons, including operator errors, poor materials, a design that is very difficult to manufacture, a design that provides too little margin for error, or a combination of these.

On a typical day, the product engineer may respond to half a dozen questions from the manufacturing floor, and two to four calls to the testing stations. When interviewed, the engineers expressed a frustration with this situation. They thought they spent too much time solving short-term problems, and, consequently, they were neglecting other important parts of their jobs. In particular, they felt they had little time in which to:

- *Coordinate with applications engineers during the design phase.* The product engineers stated that their knowledge of manufacturing could provide valuable input to the applications engineer. Together they could improve the manufacturability and thus, the yields of the new or modified product.
- *Engage in yield improvement projects.* This would involve an in-depth study of the existing process for a specific product in conjunction with an analysis of past product failures.
- *Accurately document the manufacturing steps for their assigned products, especially for those that tend to have large or repeat orders.* They said that the current state of the documentation is very poor. Operators often have to build products using only a drawing showing the final circuit, along with a few notes scribbled in the margins. While experienced operators and supervisors may be able to work with this information, they often make incorrect guesses and assumptions. Inexperienced operators may not be able to proceed with certain products because of this poor documentation.

Weekly Meeting

As manager of the product engineering group, Frank Questin had eight engineers reporting to him, each responsible for a different set of Custom Chip products. According to Frank:

When I took over as manager, the product engineers were not spending much time together as a group. They were required to handle operations problems on short notice. This made it difficult for the entire group to meet due to constant requests for assistance from the manufacturing area.

I thought that my engineers could be of more assistance and support to each other if they all spent more time together as a group, so one of my first actions as a manager was to institute a regularly scheduled weekly meeting. I let the manufacturing people know that my staff would not respond to requests for assistance during the meeting.

The meeting on this particular Monday morning followed the usual pattern. Frank talked about upcoming company plans, projects, and other news that might be of interest to the group. He then provided data about current yields for each product and commended those engineers who had maintained or improved yields on most of their products. This initial phase of the meeting lasted until about 8:30 a.m. The remainder of the meeting was a meandering discussion of a variety of topics. Since there was no agenda, engineers felt comfortable in raising issues of concern to them.

The discussion started with one of the engineers describing a technical problem in the assembly of one of his products. He was asked a number of questions and given some advice. Another engineer raised the topic of a need for new testing equipment and described a test unit he had seen at a recent demonstration. He claimed the savings in labor and improved yields from this machine would allow it to pay for itself in less than nine months. Frank immediately replied that budget limitations made such a purchase unfeasible, and the discussion moved into another area. They briefly discussed the increasing inaccessibility of the applications engineers and then talked about a few other topics.

In general, the engineers valued these meetings. One commented that:

The Monday meetings give me a chance to hear what's on everyone's mind and to find out about and discuss company-wide news. It's hard to reach any conclusions because the meeting is a freewheeling discussion. But I really appreciate the friendly atmosphere with my peers.

Coordination with Applications Engineers

Following the meeting that morning, an event occurred that highlighted the issue of the inaccessibility of the applications engineers. An order of 300 units of custom chip 1210A for a major customer was already overdue. Because the projected yield of this product was 70 percent, they had started with a run of 500 units. A sample tested at one of the early assembly points indicated a major performance problem that could drop the yield to below 50 percent. Bill Lazarus, the product engineer assigned to the 1210A, examined the sample and determined that the problem could be solved by redesigning the wiring. Jerry West, the applications engineer assigned to that product category, was responsible for revising the design. Bill tried to contact Jerry, but he was not immediately available, and didn't get back to Bill until later in the day. Jerry explained that he was on a tight schedule trying to finish a design for a customer who was coming into town in two days, and could not get to "Bill's problem" for a while.

Jerry's attitude that the problem belonged to product engineering was typical of the applications engineers. From their point of view there were a number of reasons for making the product engineers' needs for assistance a lower priority. In the first place, applications engineers

2.0

2.0

were rewarded and acknowledged primarily for satisfying customer needs through designing new and modified products. They got little recognition for solving manufacturing problems. Second, applications engineering was perceived to be more glamorous than product engineering because of opportunities to be credited with innovative and groundbreaking designs. Finally, the size of the applications engineering group had declined over the past year, causing the workload on each engineer to increase considerably. Now they had even less time to respond to the product engineers' requests.

When Bill Lazarus told Frank about the situation, Frank acted quickly. He wanted this order to be in process again by tomorrow, and he knew manufacturing was also trying to meet this goal. He walked over to see Pete Chang, head of applications engineering (see the organizational chart in Exhibit 2). Meetings like this with Pete to discuss and resolve interdepartmental issues were common.

Frank found Pete at a workbench talking with one of his engineers. He asked Pete if he could talk to him in private, and they walked to Pete's office.

Frank: We've got a problem in manufacturing in getting out an order of 1210As. Bill Lazarus is getting little or no assistance from Jerry West. I'm hoping you can get Jerry to pitch in and help Bill. It should take no more than a few hours of his time.

Pete: I do have Jerry on a short leash trying to keep him focused on getting out a design for Teletronics. We can't afford to show up empty-handed at our meeting with them in two days.

Frank: Well, we are going to end up losing one customer in trying to please another. Can't we satisfy everyone here?

Pete: Do you have an idea?

Frank: Can't you give Jerry some additional support on the Teletronics design?

Pete: Let's get Jerry in here to see what we can do.

Pete brought Jerry back to the office, and together they discussed the issues and possible solutions. When Pete made it clear to Jerry that he considered the problem with the 1210As a priority, Jerry offered to work on the 1210A problem with Bill. He said, "This will mean I'll have to stay a few hours past 5:00 this evening, but I'll do what's required to get the job done."

Frank was glad he had developed a collaborative relationship with Pete. He had always made it a point to keep Pete informed about activities in the product engineering group that might affect the applications engineers. In addition, he would often chat with Pete informally over coffee or lunch in the company cafeteria. This relationship with Pete made Frank's job easier. He wished he had the same rapport with Rod Cameron, the manufacturing manager.

Coordination with Manufacturing

The product engineers worked closely on a day-to-day basis with the manufacturing supervisors and workers. The problems between these two groups stemmed from an inherent conflict between their objectives (see Exhibit 3). The objective of the product engineers was to maintain and improve yields. They had the authority to stop production of any run that did not test properly. Manufacturing, on the other hand, was trying to meet productivity standards and time schedules. When a product engineer stopped a manufacturing run, he or she was possibly preventing the manufacturing group from reaching its objectives.

Rod Cameron, the current manufacturing manager, had been promoted from his position as a manufacturing supervisor a year ago. His views on the product engineers:

The product engineers are perfectionists. The minute a test result looks a little suspicious they want to shut down the factory. I'm under a lot of pressure to get products out the door. If they pull a few $50,000 orders off the line when they are within a few days of reaching shipping, I'm liable to miss my numbers by $100,000 that month.

Besides that, they are doing a lousy job of documenting the manufacturing steps. I've got a lot of turnover, and my new operators need to be told or shown exactly what to do for each product. The instructions for a lot of our products are a joke.

At first, Frank found Rod very difficult to deal with. Rod found fault with the product engineers for many problems and sometimes seemed rude to Frank when they talked. For example, Rod might tell Frank to "make it quick; I haven't got much time." Frank tried not to take Rod's actions personally, and through persistence was able to develop a more amicable relationship with him. According to Frank:

Sometimes, my people will stop work on a product because it doesn't meet test results at that stage of manufacturing. If we study the situation, we might be able to maintain yields or even save an entire run by adjusting the manufacturing procedures. Rod tries to bully me into changing my engineers' decisions. He yells at me or criticizes the competence of my people, but I don't allow his temper or ravings to influence my best judgment in a situation. My strategy in dealing with Rod is to try not to respond defensively to him. Eventually he cools down, and we can have a reasonable discussion of the situation.

Despite this strategy, Frank could not always resolve his problems with Rod. On these occasions, Frank took the issue to his own boss, Sam Porter, the vice president in charge of engineering. However, Frank was not satisfied with the support he got from Sam. Frank said:

Sam avoids confrontations with the operations VP. He doesn't have the influence or clout with the other VPs or the president to do justice to engineering's needs in the organization.

Early that afternoon, Frank again found himself trying to resolve a conflict between engineering and manufacturing. Sharon Hart, one of his most effective product engineers, was responsible for a series of products used in radars—the 3805A–3808A series. Today she had stopped a large run of 3806As. The manufacturing supervisor, Brian Faber, went to Rod Cameron to complain about the impact of this stoppage on his group's productivity. Brian felt that yields were low on that particular product because the production instructions were confusing to his operators, and that even with clearer instructions, his operators would need additional training to build it satisfactorily. He stressed that the product engineer's responsibility was to adequately document the production instructions and provide training. For these reasons, Brian asserted that product engineering, and not manufacturing, should be accountable for the productivity loss in the case of these 3806As.

Rod called Frank to his office, where he joined the discussion with Sharon, Brian, and Rod. After listening to the issues, Frank conceded that product engineering had responsibility for documenting and training. He also explained, even though everyone was aware of it, that the product engineering group had been operating with reduced staff for over a year now, so training and documentation were lower priorities. Because of this staffing situation, Frank suggested that manufacturing and product engineering work together and pool their limited resources to solve the documentation and training problem. He was especially interested in using a few of the long-term experienced workers to assist in training newer workers. Rod and Brian opposed his suggestion. They did not want to take experienced operators off of the line because it would decrease productivity. The meeting ended when Brian stormed out, saying that Sharon had better get the 3806As up and running again that morning.

Frank was particularly frustrated by this episode with manufacturing. He knew perfectly well that his group had primary responsibility for documenting the manufacturing steps for each product. A year ago he told Sam Porter that the product engineers needed to update and standardize all of the documentation for manufacturing products. At that time, Sam told Frank that he would support his efforts to develop the documentation, but would not increase his staff. In fact, Sam had withheld authorization to fill a recently vacated product engineering slot. Frank was reluctant to push the staffing issue because of Sam's adamance about reducing costs. "Perhaps," Frank thought, "if I develop a proposal clearly showing the ben-

efits of a documentation program in manufacturing and detailing the steps and resources required to implement the program, I might be able to convince Sam to provide us with more resources." But Frank could never find the time to develop that proposal. And so he remained frustrated.

Later in the Day

Frank was reflecting on the complexity of his job when Sharon came to the doorway to see if he had a few moments. Before he could say "Come in," the phone rang. He looked at the clock. It was 4:10 p.m. Pete was on the other end of the line with an idea he wanted to try out on Frank, so Frank said he could call him back shortly. Sharon was upset, and told him that she was thinking of quitting because the job was not satisfying for her.

Sharon said that although she very much enjoyed working on yield improvement projects, she could find no time for them. She was tired of the applications engineers acting like "prima donnas," too busy to help her solve what they seemed to think were mundane day-to-day manufacturing problems. She also thought that many of the day-to-day problems she handled wouldn't exist if there was enough time to document manufacturing procedures to begin with.

Frank didn't want to lose Sharon, so he tried to get into a frame of mind where he could be empathetic to her. He listened to her and told her that he could understand her frustration in this situation. He told her the situation would change as industry conditions improved. He told her that he was pleased that she felt comfortable in venting her frustrations with him, and he hoped she would stay with Custom Chip.

After Sharon left, Frank realized that he had told Pete that he would call back. He glanced at the TO DO list he had never completed, and realized that he hadn't spent time on his top priority—developing a proposal relating to solving the documentation problem in manufacturing. Then, he remembered that he had forgotten to acknowledge Bill Lazarus's fifth-year anniversary with the company. He thought to himself that his job felt like a roller coaster ride, and once again he pondered his effectiveness as a manager.

Note

1. Yield refers to the ratio of finished products that meet specifications relative to the number that initially entered the manufacturing process.

Integrative Case 3.0

W. L. Gore & Associates, Inc. Entering 1998*

3.0

"To make money and have fun." W. L. Gore

The First Day on the Job

Bursting with resolve, Jack Dougherty, a newly minted M.B.A. from the College of William and Mary, reported to his first day at W. L. Gore & Associates on July 26, 1976. He presented himself to Bill Gore, shook hands firmly, looked him in the eye, and said he was ready for anything.

Jack was not ready, however, for what happened next. Gore replied, "That's fine, Jack, fine. Why don't you look around and find something you'd like to do?" Three frustrating weeks later he found that something: trading in his dark blue suit for jeans, he loaded fabric into the mouth of a machine that laminated the company's patented GORE-TEX®[1] membrane to fabric. By 1982, Jack had become responsible for all advertising and marketing in the fabrics group. This story is part of the folklore of W. L. Gore & Associates.

Today the process is more structured. Regardless of the job for which they are hired, new Associates[2] take a journey through the business before settling into their own positions. A new sales Associate in the fabrics division may spend six weeks rotating through different areas before beginning to concentrate on sales and marketing. Among other things the newcomer learns is how GORE-TEX fabric is made, what it can and cannot do, how Gore handles customer complaints, and how it makes its investment decisions.

Anita McBride related her early experience at W. L. Gore & Associates this way: "Before I came to Gore, I had worked for a structured organization. I came here, and for the first month it was fairly structured because I was going through training and this is what we do and this is how Gore is and all of that. I went to Flagstaff for that training. After a month I came down to Phoenix and my sponsor said, 'Well, here's your office; it's a wonderful office,' and 'Here's your desk,' and walked away. And I thought, 'Now what do I do?' You know, I was waiting for a memo or something, or a job description. Finally after another month I was so frustrated, I felt, 'What have I gotten myself into?' And so I went to my sponsor and I said, 'What the heck do you want from me? I need something from you.' And he said, 'If you don't know what you're supposed to do, examine your commitment, and opportunities.'"

Company Background

W. L. Gore & Associates was formed by the late Wilbert L. Gore and his wife in 1958. The idea for the business sprang from his personal, organizational, and technical experiences at E. I. DuPont de Nemours, and, particu-

larly, his discovery of a chemical compound with unique properties. The compound, now widely know as GORE-TEX, has catapulted W. L. Gore & Associates to a high ranking on the *Forbes* 1998 list of the 500 largest private companies in the United States, with estimated revenues of more than $1.1 billion. The company's avant-garde culture and people management practices resulted in W. L. Gore being ranked as the seventh best company to work for in America by *Fortune* in a January 1998 article.

Wilbert Gore was born in Meridian, Idaho, near Boise in 1912. By age six, according to his own account, he was an avid hiker in the Wasatch Mountain Range in Utah. In those mountains, at a church camp, he met Genevieve, his future wife. In 1935, they got married—in their eyes, a partnership. He would make breakfast and Vieve, as everyone called her, would make lunch. The partnership lasted a lifetime.

He received both a bachelor of science in chemical engineering in 1933 and a master of science in physical chemistry in 1935 from the University of Utah. He began his professional career at American Smelting and Refining in 1936. He moved to Remington Arms Company in 1941 and then to E. I. DuPont de Nemours in 1945. He held positions as research supervisor and head of operations research. While at DuPont, he worked on a team to develop applications for polytetrafluoroethylene, referred to as PTFE in the scientific community and known as "Teflon" by DuPont's consumers. (Consumers know it under other names from other companies.) On this team Wilbert Gore, called Bill by everyone, felt a sense of excited commitment, personal fulfillment, and self-direction. He followed the development of computers and transistors and felt that PTFE had the ideal insulating characteristics for use with such equipment.

He tried many ways to make a PTFE-coated ribbon cable without success. A breakthrough came in his home basement laboratory while he was explaining the problem to his nineteen-year-old son, Bob. The young Gore saw some PTFE sealant tape made by 3M and asked his father, "Why don't you try this tape?" Bill then explained that everyone knew that you cannot bond PTFE to itself. Bob went on to bed.

Bill Gore remained in his basement lab and proceeded to try what everyone knew would not work. At about

*Prepared by Frank Shipper, Department of Management and Marketing, Franklin P. Perdue School of Business, Salisbury State University and Charles C. Manz, Nirenberg Professor of Business Leadership, School of Management, University of Massachusetts. Used with permission.

4 a.m. he woke up his son, waving a small piece of cable around and saying excitedly, "It works, it works." The following night father and son returned to the basement lab to make ribbon cable coated with PTFE. Because the breakthrough idea came from Bob, the patent for the cable was issued in Bob's name.

For the next four months Bill Gore tried to persuade DuPont to make a new product—PTFE-coated ribbon cable. By this time in his career Bill Gore knew some of the decision makers at DuPont. After talking to a number of them, he came to realize that DuPont wanted to remain a supplier of raw materials and not a fabricator.

Bill and his wife, Vieve, began discussing the possibility of starting their own insulated wire and cable business. On January 1, 1958, their wedding anniversary, they founded W. L. Gore & Associates. The basement of their home served as their first facility. After finishing dinner that night, Vieve turned to her husband of twenty-three years and said, "Well, let's clear up the dishes, go downstairs, and get to work."

Bill Gore was forty-five years old with five children to support when he left DuPont. He put aside a career of seventeen years, and a good, secure salary. To finance the first two years of the business, he and Vieve mortgaged their house and took $4,000 from savings. All their friends told them not to do it.

The first few years were rough. In lieu of salary, some of their employees accepted room and board in the Gore home. At one point eleven Associates were living and working under one roof. One afternoon, while sifting PTFE powder, Vieve received a call from the City of Denver's water department. The caller indicated that he was interested in the ribbon cable, but wanted to ask some technical questions. Bill was out running some errands. The caller asked for the product manager. Vieve explained that he was out at the moment. Next he asked for the sales manager and finally, the president. Vieve explained that they were also out. The caller became outraged and hollered, "What kind of company is this anyway?" With a little diplomacy the Gores were able eventually to secure an order for $100,000. This order put the company on a profitable footing and it began to take off.

W. L. Gore & Associates continued to grow and develop new products, primarily derived from PTFE. Its best-known product would become GORE-TEX fabric. In 1986, Bill Gore died while backpacking in the Wind River Mountains of Wyoming. He was then Chairman of the Board. His son, Bob, continued to occupy the position of president. Vieve remained as the only other officer, secretary-treasurer.

Company Products

In 1998, W. L. Gore & Associates has a fairly extensive line of high-tech products that are used in a variety of applications, including electronic, waterproofing, industrial filtration, industrial seals, and coatings.

Electronic & Wire Products

Gore electronic products have been found in unconventional places where conventional products will not do—in space shuttles, for example, where Gore wire and cable assemblies withstand the heat of ignition and the cold of space. In addition, they have been found in fast computers, transmitting signals at up to 93 percent of the speed of light. Gore cables have even gone underground, in oil-drilling operations, and underseas, on submarines that require superior microwave signal equipment and no-fail cables that can survive high pressure. The Gore electronic products division has a history of anticipating future customer needs with innovative products. Gore electronic products have been well received in industry for their ability to last under adverse conditions. For example, Gore has become, according to Sally Gore, leader in Human Resources and Communications, "one of the largest manufacturers of ultrasound cable in the world, the reason being that Gore's electronic cables' signal transmission is very, very accurate and it's very thin and extremely flexible and has a very, very long flex life. That makes it ideal for things like ultrasound and many medical electronic applications."

Medical Products

The medical division began on the ski slopes of Colorado. Bill was skiing with a friend, Dr. Ben Eiseman of Denver General Hospital. As Bill Gore told the story: "We were just to start a run when I absentmindedly pulled a small tubular section of GORE-TEX out of my pocket and looked at it. 'What is that stuff?' Ben asked. So I told him about its properties. 'Feels great,' he said. 'What do you use it for?' 'Got no idea,' I said. 'Well give it to me,' he said, 'and I'll try it in a vascular graft on a pig.' Two weeks later, he called me up. Ben was pretty excited. 'Bill,' he said, 'I put it in a pig and it works. What do I do now?' I told him to get together with Pete Cooper in our Flagstaff plant, and let them figure it out." Not long after, hundreds of thousands of people throughout the world began walking around with GORE-TEX vascular grafts.

GORE-TEX's expanded PTFE proved to be an ideal replacement for human tissue in many situations. In patients suffering from cardiovascular disease the diseased portion of arteries has been replaced by tubes of expanded PTFE—strong, biocompatible structures capable of carrying blood at arterial pressures. Gore has a strong position in this product segment. Other Gore medical products have included patches that can literally mend broken hearts by sealing holes, and sutures that allow for tissue attachment and offer the surgeon silk-like handling coupled with extreme strength. In 1985, W. L. Gore & Associates won Britain's Prince Philip Award for Poly-

3.0

mers in the Service of Mankind. The award recognized especially the lifesaving achievements of the Gore medical products team.

Two recently developed products by this division are a new patch material that is intended to incorporate more tissue into the graft more quickly and the GORE™ RideOn®[3] Cable System for bicycles. According to Amy LeGere of the medical division, "All the top pro riders in the world are using it. It was introduced just about a year ago and it has become an industry standard." This product had a positive cash flow very soon after its introduction. Some Associates who were also outdoor sports enthusiasts developed the product and realized that Gore could make a great bicycle cable that would have 70 percent less friction and need no lubrication. The Associates maintain that the profitable development, production, and marketing of such specialized niche products are possible because of the lack of bureaucracy and associated overhead, Associate commitment, and the use of product champions.

Industrial Products

The output of the industrial products division has included sealants, filter bags, cartridges, clothes, and coatings. Industrial filtration products, such as GORE-TEX filter bags, have reduced air pollution and recovered valuable solids from gases and liquids more completely than alternatives—and they have done so economically. In the future they may make coal-burning plants completely smoke-free, contributing to a cleaner environment. The specialized and critical applications of these products, along with Gore's reputation for quality, have had a strong influence on industrial purchasers.

This division has developed a unique joint sealant—a flexible cord of porous PTFE—that can be applied as a gasket to the most complex shapes, sealing them to prevent leakage of corrosive chemicals, even at extreme temperature and pressure. Steam valves packed with GORE-TEX have been sold with a lifetime guarantee, provided the valve is used properly. In addition, this division has introduced Gore's first consumer product—GLIDE®[4]—a dental floss. "That was a product that people knew about for a while and they went the route of trying to persuade industry leaders to promote the product, but they didn't really pursue it very well. So out of basically default almost, Gore decided, Okay, they're not doing it right. Let's go in ourselves. We had a champion, John Spencer, who took that and pushed it forward through the dentists' offices and it just skyrocketed. There were many more people on the team but it was basically getting that one champion who focused on that product and got it out. They told him it 'couldn't be done,' 'It's never going to work,' and I guess that's all he needed. It was done and it

worked," said Ray Wnenchak of the industrial products division. Amy LeGere added, "The champion worked very closely with the medical people to understand the medical market like claims and labeling so that when the product came out on the market it would be consistent with our medical products. And that's where, when we cross divisions, we know whom to work with and with whom we combine forces so that the end result takes the strengths of all of our different teams." As of 1998, GLIDE has captured a major portion of the dental floss market and the mint flavor is the largest-selling variety in the U.S. market based on dollar volume.

Fabric Products

The Gore fabrics division has supplied laminates to manufacturers of foul weather gear, ski wear, running suits, footwear, gloves, and hunting and fishing garments. Firefighters and U.S. Navy pilots have worn GORE-TEX fabric gear, as have some Olympic athletes. The U.S. Army adopted a total garment system built around a GORE-TEX fabric component. Employees in high-tech clean rooms also wear GORE-TEX garments.

GORE-TEX membrane has 9 billion pores randomly dotting each square inch and is feather-light. Each pore is 700 times larger than a water vapor molecule, yet thousands of times smaller than a water droplet. Wind and water cannot penetrate the pores, but perspiration can escape.

As a result, fabrics bonded with GORE-TEX membrane are waterproof, windproof, and breathable. The laminated fabrics bring protection from the elements to a variety of products—from survival gear to high-fashion rainwear. Other manufacturers, including 3M, Burlington Industries, Akzo Nobel Fibers, and DuPont, have brought out products to compete with GORE-TEX fabrics. Earlier, the toughest competition came from firms that violated the patents on GORE-TEX. Gore successfully challenged them in court. In 1993, the basic patent on the process for manufacturing ran out. Nevertheless, as Sally Gore explained, "what happens is you get an initial process patent and then as you begin to create things with this process you get additional patents. For instance we have patents protecting our vascular graft, different patents for protecting GORE-TEX patches, and still other patents protecting GORE-TEX industrial sealants and filtration material. One of our patent attorneys did a talk recently, a year or so ago, when the patent expired and a lot of people were saying, Oh, golly, are we going to be in trouble! We would be in trouble if we didn't have any patents. Our attorney had this picture with a great big umbrella, sort of a parachute, with Gore under it. Next he showed us lots of little umbrellas scattered all over the sky. So you protect certain niche markets and niche areas, but indeed competition increases as your initial patents expire." Gore, however, has continued to have a commanding position in the active-wear market.

To meet a variety of customer needs, Gore introduced a new family of fabrics in the 1990s (Exhibit 1). The introduction posed new challenges. According to Bob Winterling, "we did such a great job with the brand GORE-TEX that we actually have hurt ourselves in many ways. By that I mean it has been very difficult for us to come up with other new brands, because many people didn't even know Gore. We are the GORE-TEX company. One thing we decided to change about Gore four or five years ago was instead of being the GORE-TEX company we wanted to become the Gore company and that underneath the Gore company we had an umbrella of products that fall out of being the great Gore company. So it was a shift in how we positioned GORE-TEX. Today GORE-TEX is stronger than ever as it's turned out, but now we've ventured into such things as WindStopper®[5] fabric that is very big in the golf market. It could be a sweater or a fleece piece or even a knit shirt with the WindStopper behind it or closer to your skin and what it does is it stops the wind. It's not waterproof; it's water resistant. What we've tried to do is position the Gore name and beneath that all of the great products of the company."

W. L. Gore & Associates' Approach to Organization and Structure

W. L. Gore & Associates has never had titles, hierarchy, or any of the conventional structures associated with enterprises of its size. The titles of president and secretary-treasurer continue to be used only because they are required by the laws of incorporation. In addition, Gore has never had a corporate-wide mission or code of ethics statement, nor has Gore ever required or prohibited business units from developing such statements for themselves. Thus, the Associates of some business units who have felt a need for such statements have developed them on their own. When questioned about this issue, one Associate stated, "The company belief is that (1) its four basic operating principles cover ethical practices required of people in business; (2) it will not tolerate illegal practices." Gore's management style has been referred to as unmanagement. The organization has been guided by Bill's experiences on teams at DuPont and has evolved as needed.

For example, in 1965 W. L. Gore & Associates was a thriving company with a facility on Paper Mill Road in Newark, Delaware. One Monday morning in the summer, Bill Gore was taking his usual walk through the plant. All of a sudden he realized that he did not know everyone in the plant. The team had become too big. As a result, he established the practice of limiting plant size to approximately two hundred Associates. Thus was born the expansion policy of "Get big by staying small." The purpose of maintaining small plants was to accentuate a close-knit atmosphere and encourage communication among Associates in a facility.

At the beginning of 1998, W. L. Gore & Associates consisted of over forty-five plants worldwide with approximately seven thousand Associates. In some cases, the plants are grouped together on the same site (as in Flagstaff, Arizona, with ten plants). Overseas, Gore's manufacturing facilities are located in Scotland, Germany, and China, and the company has two joint ventures in Japan (Exhibit 2). In addition, it has sales facilities located in fifteen other countries. Gore manufactures electronic, medical, industrial, and fabric products. In addition, it has numerous sales offices worldwide, including offices in Eastern Europe and Russia.

3.0

EXHIBIT 1

Gore's Family of Fabrics

Brand Name	Activity/Conditions	Breathability	Water Protection	Wind Protection
GORE-TEX®	rain, snow, cold, windy	very breathable	waterproof	windproof
Immersion™ technology	for fishing and paddle sports	very breathable	waterproof	windproof
Ocean technology	for offshore and coastal sailing	very breathable	waterproof	windproof
WindStopper®	cool/cold, windy	very breathable	no water resistance	windproof
Gore Dryloft™	cold, windy, light precipitation	extremely breathable	water-resistant	windproof
Activent™	cool/cold, windy, light precipitation	extremely breathable	water-resistant	windproof

3.0

EXHIBIT 2
International Locations of W. L. Gore & Associates

The Lattice Organization

W. L. Gore & Associates has been described not only as unmanaged, but also as unstructured. Bill Gore referred to the structure as a lattice organization (Exhibit 3). The characteristics of this structure are:

1. Direct lines of communication—person to person—no intermediary
2. No fixed or assigned authority
3. Sponsors, not bosses
4. Natural leadership defined by followership
5. Objectives set by those who must "make them happen"
6. Tasks and functions organized through commitments

The structure within the lattice is complex and evolves from interpersonal interactions, self commitment to group-known responsibilities, natural leadership, and group-imposed discipline. Bill Gore once explained the structure this way: "Every successful organization has an underground lattice. It's where the news spreads like lightning, where people can go around the organization to get things done." An analogy might be drawn to a structure of constant cross-area teams—the equivalent of quality circles going on all the time. When a puzzled interviewer told Bill that he was having trouble understanding how planning and accountability worked, Bill replied with a grin: "So am I. You ask me how it works? Every which way."

The lattice structure has not been without its critics. As Bill Gore stated, "I'm told from time to time that a lattice organization can't meet a crisis well because it takes too long to reach a consensus when there are no bosses. But this isn't true. Actually, a lattice by its very nature works particularly well in a crisis. A lot of useless effort is avoided because there is no rigid management hierarchy to conquer before you can attack a problem."

The lattice has been put to the test on a number of occasions. For example, in 1975, Dr. Charles Campbell of the University of Pittsburgh reported that a GORE-TEX arterial graft had developed an aneurysm. If the bubble-like protrusion continued to expand, it would explode.

Obviously, this life-threatening situation had to be resolved quickly and permanently. Within only a few days of Dr. Campbell's first report, he flew to Newark to present his findings to Bill and Bob Gore and a few other Associates. The meeting lasted two hours. Dan Hubis, a former policeman who had joined Gore to develop new production methods, had an idea before the meeting was over. He returned to his work area to try some different production techniques. After only three hours and twelve tries, he had developed a permanent solution. In other words, in three hours a potentially damaging problem to both patients and the company was resolved. Furthermore, Hubis's redesigned graft went on to win widespread acceptance in the medical community.

Eric Reynolds, founder of Marmot Mountain Works Ltd. of Grand Junction, Colorado, and a major Gore customer, raised another issue: "I think the lattice has its prob-

EXHIBIT 3
The Lattice Structure

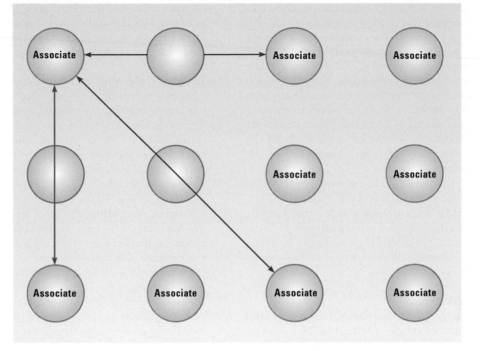

3.0

lems with the day-to-day nitty-gritty of getting things done on time and out the door. I don't think Bill realizes how the lattice system affects customers. I mean, after you've established a relationship with someone about product quality, you can call up one day and suddenly find that someone new to you is handling your problem. It's frustrating to find a lack of continuity." He went on to say: "But I have to admit that I've personally seen at Gore remarkable examples of people coming out of nowhere and excelling."

When Bill Gore was asked if the lattice structure could be used by other companies, he answered: "No. For example, established companies would find it very difficult to use the lattice. Too many hierarchies would be destroyed. When you remove titles and positions and allow people to follow who they want, it may very well be someone other than the person who has been in charge. The lattice works for us, but it's always evolving. You have to expect problems." He maintained that the lattice system worked best when it was put in place in start-up companies by dynamic entrepreneurs.

Not all Gore Associates function well in this unstructured work environment, especially initially. For those accustomed to a more structured work environment, there can be adjustment problems. As Bill Gore said: "All our lives most of us have been told what to do, and some people don't know how to respond when asked to do something—and have the very real option of saying no—on their job. It's the new Associate's responsibility to find out

what he or she can do for the good of the operation." The vast majority of the new Associates, after some initial floundering, have adapted quickly.

Others, especially those who require more structured working conditions, have found that Gore's flexible workplace is not for them. According to Bill, for those few, "It's an unhappy situation, for both the Associate and the sponsor. If there is no contribution, there is no paycheck."

As Anita McBride, an Associate in Phoenix, noted: "It's not for everybody. People ask me do we have turnover, and yes we do have turnover. What you're seeing looks like utopia, but it also looks extreme. If you finally figure the system, it can be real exciting. If you can't handle it, you gotta go. Probably by your own choice, because you're going to be so frustrated." Overall, the Associates appear to have responded positively to the Gore system of unmanagement and unstructure. And the company's lattice organization has proven itself to be good from a bottom-line perspective. Bill estimated the year before he died that "the profit per Associate is double" that of DuPont.

Features of W. L. Gore's Culture
Outsiders have been struck by the degree of informality and humor in the Gore organization. Meetings tend to be only as long as necessary. As Trish Hearn, an Associate in Newark, Delaware, said, "No one feels a need to pontificate." Words such as "responsibilities" and "commitments" are commonly heard, whereas words such as "em-

3.0

ployees," "subordinates," and "managers" are taboo in the Gore culture. This is an organization that has always taken what it does very seriously, without its members taking themselves too seriously.

For a company of its size, Gore has always had a very short organizational pyramid. As of 1995 the pyramid consists of Bob Gore, the late Bill Gore's son, as president and Vieve, Bill Gore's widow, as secretary-treasurer. He has been the chief executive officer for more than twenty years. No second-in-command or successor has been designated. All the other members of the Gore organization were, and continue to be, referred to as Associates.

Some outsiders have had problems with the idea of no titles. Sarah Clifton, an Associate at the Flagstaff facility, was being pressed by some outsiders as to what her title was. She made one up and had it printed on some business cards: SUPREME COMMANDER (see Exhibit 4). When Bill Gore learned what she did, he loved it and recounted the story to others.

Leaders, Not Managers

Within W. L. Gore & Associates, the various people who take lead roles are thought of as being leaders, not managers. Bill Gore described in an internal memo the kinds of leadership and the role of leadership as follows:

1. The Associate who is recognized by a team as having a special knowledge, or experience (for example, this could be a chemist, computer expert, machine operator, salesman, engineer, lawyer). This kind of leader gives the team *guidance in a special area.*

2. The Associate the team looks to for coordination of individual activities in order to achieve the agreed-upon objectives of the team. The role of this leader is to persuade team members to *make the commitments* necessary for success (commitment seeker).

3. The Associate who proposes necessary objectives and activities and seeks agreement and team *consensus on objectives.* This leader is perceived by the team members as having a good grasp of how the objectives of the team fit in with the broad objective of the enterprise. This kind of leader is often also the "commitment-seeking" leader.

4. The leader who evaluates relative contribution of team members (in consultation with other sponsors), and reports these contribution evaluations to a compensation committee. This leader may also participate in the compensation committee on relative contribution and pay and *reports changes in compensation* to individual Associates. This leader is then also a compensation sponsor.

5. *Product specialists* who coordinate the research, manufacturing, and marketing of one product type within a business, interacting with team leaders and individual Associates who have commitments regarding the product type. They are respected for their knowledge and dedication to their products.

6. *Plant leaders* who help coordinate activities of people within a plant.

7. *Business leaders* who help coordinate activities of people in a business.

8. *Functional leaders* who help coordinate activities of people in a "functional" area.

9. *Corporate leaders* who help coordinate activities of people in different businesses and functions and who try to promote communication and cooperation among all Associates.

10. *Entrepreneuring Associates* who organize new teams for new businesses, new products, new processes, new devices, new marketing efforts, new or better methods of all kinds. These leaders invite other Associates to "sign up" for their project.

It is clear that leadership is widespread in our lattice organization and that it is continually changing and evolving. The situation that leaders are frequently also sponsors should not imply that these are different activities and responsibilities.

Leaders are not authoritarians, managers of people, or supervisors who tell us what to do or forbid us to do things; nor are they "parents" to whom we transfer our own self-responsibility. However, they do often advise us of the consequences of actions we have done or propose to do. Our actions result in contributions, or lack of contribution, to the success of our enterprise. Our pay depends on the magnitude of our contributions. This is the basic discipline of our lattice organization.

EXHIBIT 4
The Supreme Commander

GORE

W. L. GORE & ASSOCIATES, Inc.

SARAH CLIFTON

SUPREME COMMANDER

1505 NORTH FOURTH STREET
FLAGSTAFF, ARIZONA 86001
PHONE: 602-774-0611
TWX 910-972-0969

Egalitarian and Innovative

Other aspects of the Gore culture have been aimed at promoting an egalitarian atmosphere, such as parking lots with no reserved parking spaces except for customers and disabled workers or visitors and dining areas—only one in each plant—set up as focal points for Associate interaction. As Dave McCarter of Phoenix explained: "The design is no accident. The lunchroom in Flagstaff has a fireplace in the middle. We want people to like to be here." The location of a plant is also no accident. Sites have been selected on the basis of transportation access, a nearby university, beautiful surroundings, and climate appeal. Land cost has never been a primary consideration. McCarter justified the selection by stating: "Expanding is not costly in the long run. The loss of money is what you make happen by stymieing people into a box."

Bob Gore is a champion of Gore culture. As Sally Gore related, "We have managed surprisingly to maintain our sense of freedom and our entrepreneurial spirit. I think what we've found is that we had to develop new ways to communicate with Associates because you can't communicate with six thousand people the way that you can communicate with five hundred people. It just can't be done. So we have developed a newsletter that we didn't have before. One of the most important communication mediums that we developed, and this was Bob Gore's idea, is a digital voice exchange which we call our Gorecom. Basically everyone has a mailbox and a password. Lots of companies have gone to e-mail and we use e-mail, but Bob feels very strongly that we're very much an oral culture and there's a big difference between cultures that are predominantly oral and predominantly written. Oral cultures encourage direct communication, which is, of course, something that we encourage."

In rare cases an Associate "is trying to be unfair," in Bill's own words. In one case the problem was chronic absenteeism and in another, an individual was caught stealing.

"When that happens, all hell breaks loose," said Bill Gore. "We can get damned authoritarian when we have to."

Over the years, Gore & Associates has faced a number of unionization drives. The company has neither tried to dissuade Associates from attending an organizational meeting nor retaliated when flyers were passed out. As of 1995, none of the plants had been organized. Bill believed that no need existed for third-party representation under the lattice structure. He asked the question, "Why would Associates join a union when they own the company? It seems rather absurd."

Commitment has long been considered a two-way street. W. L. Gore & Associates has tried to avoid layoffs. Instead of cutting pay, which in the Gore culture would be disastrous to morale, the company has used a system of temporary transfers within a plant or cluster of plants and voluntary layoffs. Exhibit 7 at the end of this case example contains excerpts of interviews with two Gore Associates that further indicate the nature of the culture and work environment at W. L. Gore & Associates.

W. L. Gore & Associates' Sponsor Program

Bill Gore knew that products alone did not a company make. He wanted to avoid smothering the company in thick layers of formal "management." He felt that hierarchy stifled individual creativity. As the company grew, he knew that he had to find a way to assist new people and to follow their progress. This was particularly important when it came to compensation. W. L. Gore & Associates developed its "sponsor" program to meet these needs.

When people apply to Gore, they are initially screened by personnel specialists. As many as ten references might be

EXHIBIT 5

Growth of Gore's Sales vs. Gross Domestic Product

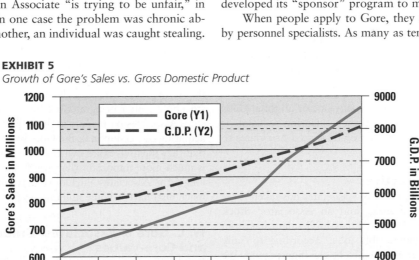

Years	1989	1990	1991	1992	1993	1994	1995	1996	1997
Gore	60	660	700	750	804	828	958	1064	1160
G.D.P.	5438.7	5743.8	5916.7	6244.4	6553	6935.7	7265.4	7636	8079.9

contacted on each applicant. Those who meet the basic criteria are interviewed by current Associates. The interviews have been described as rigorous by those who have gone through them. Before anyone is hired, an Associate must agree to be his or her sponsor. The sponsor is to take a personal interest in the new Associate's contributions, problems, and goals, acting as both a coach and an advocate. The sponsor tracks the new Associate's progress, helping and encouraging, dealing with weaknesses, and concentrating on strengths. Sponsoring is not a short-term commitment. All Associates have sponsors and many have more than one. When individuals are hired initially, they are likely to have a sponsor in their immediate work area. If they move to another area, they may have a sponsor in that work area. As Associates' commitments change or grow, they may acquire additional sponsors. Because the hiring process looks beyond conventional views of what makes a good Associate, some anomalies have occurred. Bill Gore proudly told the story of "a very young man" of 84 who walked in, applied, and spent five very good years with the company. The individual had thirty years of experience in the industry before joining Gore. His other Associates had no problems accepting him, but the personnel computer did. It insisted that his age was 48. The individual success stories at Gore have come from diverse backgrounds.

An internal memo by Bill Gore described three roles of sponsors:

1. *Starting sponsor*—a sponsor who helps a new Associate get started on a first job, or a present Associate get started on a new job.
2. *Advocate sponsor*—a sponsor who sees that an Associate's accomplishments are recognized.
3. *Compensation sponsor*—a sponsor who sees to it that an Associate is fairly paid for contributions to the success of the enterprise.

A single person can perform any one or all three kinds of sponsorship. Quite frequently, a sponsoring Associate is a good friend and it is not unknown for two Associates to sponsor each other.

Compensation Practices

Compensation at W. L. Gore & Associates has taken three forms: salary, profit sharing, and an Associates' Stock Ownership Program (ASOP).[6] Entry-level salary has been in the middle for comparable jobs. According to Sally Gore: "We do not feel we need to be the highest paid. We never try to steal people away from other companies with salary. We want them to come here because of the opportunities for growth and the unique work environment." Associates' salaries have been reviewed at least once a year and more commonly twice a year. The reviews are conducted by a compensation team at each facility, with sponsors for the Associates acting as their advocates during the review process. Prior to meeting with the compensation committee, the sponsor checks with customers or Associates familiar with the person's work to find out what contribution the Associate has made. The compensation team relies heavily on this input. In addition, the compensation team considers the Associate's leadership ability and willingness to help others develop to their fullest.

Profit sharing follows a formula based on economic value added (EVA). Sally Gore had the following to say about the adoption of a formula: "It's become more formalized, and in a way, I think that's unfortunate because it used to be a complete surprise to receive a profit share. The thinking of the people like Bob Gore and other leaders was that maybe we weren't using it in the right way and we could encourage people by helping them know more about it and how we made profit-share decisions. The fun of it before was people didn't know when it was coming and all of a sudden you could do something creative about passing out checks. It was great fun and people would have a wonderful time with it. The disadvantage was that Associates then did not focus much on, 'What am I doing to create another profit share?' By using EVA as a method of evaluation for our profit share, we know at the end of every month how much EVA was created that month. When we've created a certain amount of EVA, we then get another profit share. So everybody knows and everyone says, 'We'll do it in January,' so it is done. Now Associates feel more part of the happening to make it work. What have you done? Go make some more sales calls, please! There are lots of things we can do to improve our EVA and everybody has a responsibility to do that." Every month EVA is calculated and every Associate is informed. John Mosko of electronic products commented, "...(EVA) lets us know where we are on the path to getting one (a profit share). It's very critical—every Associate knows."

Annually, Gore also buys company stock equivalent to a fixed percent of the Associates' annual incomes, placing it in the ASOP retirement fund. Thus, an Associate can become a stockholder after being at Gore for a year. Gore's ASOP ensures Associates participate in the growth of the company by acquiring ownership in it. Bill Gore wanted Associates to feel that they themselves are owners. One Associate stated, "This is much more important than profit sharing." In fact, some long-term Associates (including a twenty-five-year veteran machinist) have become millionaires from the ASOP.

W. L. Gore & Associates' Guiding Principles and Core Values

In addition to the sponsor program, Bill Gore articulated four guiding principles:

1. Try to be fair.
2. Encourage, help, and allow other Associates to grow in knowledge, skill, and scope of activity and responsibility.
3. Make your own commitments, and keep them.
4. Consult with other Associates before taking actions that may be "below the water line."

The four principles have been referred to as Fairness, Freedom, Commitment, and Waterline. The *waterline* terminology is drawn from an analogy to ships. If someone pokes a hole in a boat above the water line, the boat will be in relatively little real danger. If someone, however, pokes a hole below the water line, the boat is in immediate danger of sinking. "Water line" issues must be discussed across teams and plants before decisions are made.

The operating principles were put to a test in 1978. By this time word about the qualities of GORE-TEX fabric was being spread throughout the recreational and outdoor markets. Production and shipment had begun in volume. At first a few complaints were heard. Next some of the clothing started coming back. Finally, much of the clothing was being returned. The trouble was that the GORE-TEX fabric was leaking. Waterproofing was one of the major properties responsible for GORE-TEX fabric's success. The company's reputation and credibility were on the line.

Peter W. Gilson, who led Gore's fabrics division, recalled: "It was an incredible crisis for us at that point. We were really starting to attract attention; we were taking off—and then this." In the next few months, Gilson and a number of his Associates made a number of those below-the-water-line decisions.

First, the researchers determined that oils in human sweat were responsible for clogging the pores in the GORE-TEX fabric and altering the surface tension of the membrane. Thus, water could pass through. They also discovered that a good washing could restore the waterproof property. At first this solution, known as the "Ivory Snow solution," was accepted. A single letter from "Butch," a mountain guide in the Sierras, changed the company's position. Butch described what happened while he was leading a group: "My parka leaked and my life was in danger." As Gilson noted, "That scared the hell out of us. Clearly our solution was no solution at all to someone on a mountaintop." All the products were recalled. Gilson remembered: "We bought back, at our own expense, a fortune in pipeline material—anything that was in the stores, at the manufacturers, or anywhere else in the pipeline."

In the meantime, Bob Gore and other Associates set out to develop a permanent fix. One month later, a second-generation GORE-TEX fabric had been developed. Gilson, furthermore, told dealers that if a customer ever returned a leaky parka, they should replace it and bill the company. The replacement program alone cost Gore roughly $4 million.

The popularity of GORE-TEX outerwear took off. Many manufacturers now make numerous pieces of apparel such as parkas, gloves, boots, jogging outfits, and wind shirts from GORE-TEX laminate. Sometimes when customers are dissatisfied with a garment, they return them directly to Gore. Gore has always stood behind any product made of GORE-TEX fabric. Analysis of the returned garments found that the problem was often not the GORE-TEX fabric. The manufacturer, "...had created a design flaw so that the water could get in here or get in over the zipper and we found that when there was something negative about it, everyone knew it was GORE-TEX. So we had to make good on products that we were not manufacturing. We now license the manufacturers of all our GORE-TEX fabric products. They pay a fee to obtain a license to manufacture GORE-TEX products. In return we oversee the manufacture and we let them manufacture only designs that we are sure are guaranteed to keep you dry, that really will work. Then it works for them and for us—a win-win for them as well as for us," according to Sally Gore.

To further ensure quality, Gore & Associates has its own test facility including a rain room for garments made from GORE-TEX. Besides a rain/storm test, all garments must pass abrasion and washing machine tests. Only the garments that pass these tests will be licensed to display the GORE-TEX label.

Research and Development

Like everything else at Gore, research and development has always been unstructured. Even without a formal R&D department, the company has been issued many patents, although most inventions have been held as proprietary or trade secrets. For example, few Associates are allowed to see GORE-TEX being made. Any Associate can, however, ask for a piece of raw PTFE (known as a silly worm) with which to experiment. Bill Gore believed that all people had it within themselves to be creative.

One of the best examples of Gore inventiveness occurred in 1969. At the time, the wire and cable division was facing increased competition. Bill Gore began to look for a way to straighten out the PTFE molecules. As he said, "I figured out that if we ever unfold those molecules, get them to stretch out straight, we'd have a tremendous new kind of material." He thought that if PTFE could be stretched, air could be introduced into its molecular structure. The result would be greater volume per pound of raw material with no effect on performance. Thus, fabricating costs would be reduced and profit margins would be increased. Going about this search in a scientific manner, Bob Gore heated rods of PTFE to various temperatures and then slowly stretched them. Regardless of the temperature or how carefully he stretched them, the rods broke.

Working alone late one night after countless failures, Bob in frustration stretched one of the rods violently. To his surprise, it did not break. He tried it again and again with the same results. The next morning Bob demonstrated his breakthrough to his father, but not without some drama. As Bill Gore recalled: "Bob wanted to surprise me so he took a rod and stretched it slowly. Naturally, it broke. Then he pretended to get mad. He grabbed another rod and said, 'Oh, the hell with this,' and gave it a pull. It didn't break—he'd done it." The new arrangement of molecules not only changed the wire and cable division, but led to the development of GORE-TEX fabric.

3.0

3.0

Bill and Vieve did the initial field-testing of GORE-TEX fabric the summer of 1970. Vieve made a hand-sewn tent out of patches of GORE-TEX fabric. They took it on their annual camping trip to the Wind River Mountains in Wyoming. The very first night in the wilderness, they encountered a hail storm. The hail tore holes in the top of the tent, and the bottom filled up like a bathtub from the rain. Undaunted, Bill Gore stated: "At least we knew from all the water that the tent was waterproof. We just needed to make it stronger, so it could withstand hail."

Gore Associates have always been encouraged to think, experiment, and follow a potentially profitable idea to its conclusion. At a plant in Newark, Delaware, Fred L. Eldreth, an Associate with a third-grade education, designed a machine that could wrap thousands of feet of wire a day. The design was completed over a weekend. Many other Associates have contributed their ideas through both product and process breakthroughs.

Even without an R&D department, innovation and creativity continue at a rapid pace at Gore & Associates. The year before he died, Bill Gore claimed that "the creativity, the number of patent applications and innovative products is triple" that of DuPont.

Development of Gore Associates

Ron Hill, an Associate in Newark, noted that Gore "will work with Associates who want to advance themselves." Associates have been offered many in-house training opportunities, not only in technical and engineering areas but also in leadership development. In addition, the company has established cooperative education programs with universities and other outside providers, picking up most of the costs for the Gore Associates. The emphasis in Associate development, as in many parts of Gore, has always been that the Associate must take the initiative.

Marketing Approaches and Strategy

Gore's business philosophy incorporates three beliefs and principles: (1) that the company can and should offer the best-valued products in the markets and market segments where it chooses to compete, (2) that buyers in each of its markets should appreciate the caliber and performance of the items it manufactures, and (3) that Gore should become a leader with unique expertise in each of the product categories where it competes. To achieve these outcomes, the company's approach to marketing (it has no formally organized marketing department) is based on the following principles:

1. *Marketing a product requires a leader, or product champion.* According to Dave McCarter: "You marry your technology with the interests of your champions,

since you've got to have champions for all these things no matter what. And that's the key element within our company. Without a product champion you can't do much anyway, so it is individually driven. If you get people interested in a particular market or a particular product for the marketplace, then there is no stopping them." Bob Winterling of the Fabrics Division elaborated further on the role and importance of the product champion.

The product champion is probably the most important resource we have at Gore for the introduction of new products. You look at that bicycle cable. That could have come out of many different divisions of Gore, but it really happened because one or two individuals said, "Look, this can work. I believe in it; I'm passionate about it; and I want it to happen." And the same thing with GLIDE floss. I think John Spencer in this case—although there was a team that supported John, let's never forget that—John sought the experts out throughout the organization. But without John making it happen on his own, GLIDE floss would never have come to fruition. He started with a little chain of drugstores here, Happy Harry's I think, and we put a few cases in and we just tracked the sales and that's how it all started. Who would have ever believed that you could take what we would have considered a commodity product like that, sell it direct for $3–$5 apiece. That is so unGorelike it's incredible. So it comes down to people and it comes down to the product champion to make things happen.

2. *A product champion is responsible for marketing the product through commitments with sales representatives.* Again, according to Dave McCarter: "We have no quota system. Our marketing and our sales people make their own commitments as to what their forecasts have been. There is no person sitting around telling them that is not high enough, you have to increase it by 10 percent, or whatever somebody feels is necessary. You are expected to meet your commitment, which is your forecast, but nobody is going to tell you to change it. . . . There is no order of command, no chain involved. These are groups of independent people who come together to make unified commitments to do something and sometimes when they can't make those agreements...you may pass up a marketplace...but that's OK, because there's much more advantage when the team decides to do something."

3. *Sales Associates are on salary, not commission.* They participate in the profit sharing and ASOP plans in which all other Associates participate. As in other areas of Gore, individual success stories have come from diverse backgrounds. Dave McCarter related another

success of the company relying on a product champion as follows:

I interviewed Sam one day. I didn't even know why I was interviewing him actually. Sam was retired from AT&T. After twenty-five years, he took the golden parachute and went down to Sun Lakes to play golf. He played golf a few months and got tired of that. He was selling life insurance. I sat reading the application; his technical background interested me. . . . He had managed an engineering department with six hundred people. He'd managed manufacturing plants for AT&T and had a great wealth of experience at AT&T. He said, "I'm retired. I like to play golf but I just can't do it every day, so I want to do something else. Do you have something around here I can do?" I was thinking to myself, "This is one of these guys I would sure like to hire but I don't know what I would do with him." The thing that triggered me was the fact that he said he sold insurance and here is a guy with a high degree of technical background selling insurance. He had marketing experience, international marketing experience. So, the bell went off in my head that we were trying to introduce a new product into the marketplace that was a hydrocarbon leak protection cable. You can bury it in the ground and in a matter of seconds it could detect a hydrocarbon-like gasoline. I had a couple of other guys working on the product who hadn't been very successful with marketing it. We were having a hard time finding a customer. Well, I thought, that kind of product would be like selling insurance. If you think about it, why should you protect your tanks? It's an insurance policy that things are not leaking into the environment. That has implications, big-time monetary. So, actually, I said, "Why don't you come back Monday? I have just the thing for you." He did. We hired him; he went to work, a very energetic guy. Certainly a champion of the product, he picked right up on it, ran with it single-handed.

Now it's a growing business. It certainly is a valuable one too for the environment. In the implementation of its marketing strategy, Gore has relied on cooperative and word-of-mouth advertising. Cooperative advertising has been especially used to promote GORE-TEX fabric products. These high-dollar, glossy campaigns include full-color ads and dressing the sales force in GORE-TEX garments. A recent slogan used in the ad campaigns has been, "If it doesn't say GORE-TEX, it's not." Some retailers praise the marketing and advertising efforts as the best. Leigh Gallagher, managing editor of *Sporting Goods Business* magazine, describes Gore & Associates' marketing as "unbeatable."

Gore has stressed cooperative advertising because the Associates believe positive experiences with any one prod-

uct will carry over to purchases of other and more GORE-TEX fabric products. Apparently, this strategy has paid off. When the Grandoe Corporation introduced GORE-TEX gloves, its president, Richard Zuckerwar, noted: "Sports activists have had the benefit of GORE-TEX gloves to protect their hands from the elements.... With this handsome collection of gloves ...you can have warm, dry hands without sacrificing style." Other clothing manufacturers and distributors who sell GORE-TEX garments include Apparel Technologies, Lands' End, Austin Reed, Hudson Trail Outfitters, Timberland, Woolrich, North Face, L.L. Bean, and Michelle Jaffe.

3.0

The power of these marketing techniques extends beyond consumer products. According to Dave McCarter: "In the technical end of the business, company reputation probably is most important. You have to have a good reputation with your company." He went on to say that without a good reputation, a company's products would not be considered seriously by many industrial customers. In other words, the sale is often made before the representative calls. Using its marketing strategies, Gore has been very successful in securing a market leadership position in a number of areas, ranging from waterproof outdoor clothing to vascular grafts. Its market share of waterproof, breathable fabrics is estimated to be 90 percent.

Adapting to Changing Environmental Forces

Each of Gore's divisions has faced from time to time adverse environmental forces. For example, the fabric division was hit hard when the fad for jogging suits collapsed in the mid-1980s. The fabric division took another hit from the recession of 1989. People simply reduced their purchases of high-end athletic apparel. By 1995, the fabric division was the fastest-growing division of Gore again.

The electronic division was hit hard when the mainframe computer business declined in the early 1990s. By 1995, that division was seeing a resurgence for its products partially because that division had developed some electronic products for the medical industry. As can be seen, not all the forces have been negative.

The aging population of America has increased the need for health care. As a result, Gore has invested in the development of additional medical products and the medical division is growing.

W. L. Gore & Associates' Financial Performance

As a closely held private corporation, W. L. Gore has kept its financial information as closely guarded as proprietary information on products and processes. It has been estimated that Associates who work at Gore own 90 percent of the stock. According to Shanti Mehta, an Associate,

Gore's returns on assets and sales have consistently ranked it among the top 10 percent of the *Fortune 500* companies. According to another source, W. L. Gore & Associates has been doing just fine by any financial measure. For thirty-seven straight years (from 1961 to 1997) the company has enjoyed profitability and positive return on equity. The compounded growth rate for revenues at W. L. Gore & Associates from 1969 to 1989 was more than 18 percent, discounted for inflation.[7] In 1969, total sales were about $6 million; by 1989, the figure was $600 million. As should be expected with the increase in size, the percentage increase in sales has slowed over the last seven years (Exhibit 6). The company projects sales to reach $1.4 billion in 1998. Gore financed this growth without long-term debt unless it made sense. For example, "We used to have some industrial revenue bonds where, in essence, to build facilities the government allows banks to lend you money tax-free. Up to a couple of years ago we were borrowing money through industrial revenue bonds. Other than that, we are totally debt-free. Our money is generated out of the operations of the business, and frankly we're looking for new things to invest in. I know that's a challenge for all of us today," said Bob Winterling. *Forbes* magazine estimates Gore's operating profits for 1993, 1994, 1995, 1996, and 1997 to be $120, $140, $192, $213, and $230 million, respectively (see Exhibit 6). Bob Gore predicts that the company will reach $2 billion in sales by 2001.

Recently, the company purchased Optical Concepts Inc., a laser, semiconductor technology company, of Lom-

poc, California. In addition, Gore & Associates is investing in test-marketing a new product, guitar strings, which was developed by its Associates.

When asked about cost control, Sally Gore had the following to say:

You have to pay attention to cost or you're not an effective steward of anyone's money, your own or anyone else's. It's kind of interesting, we started manufacturing medical products in 1974 with the vascular graft and it built from there. The Gore vascular graft is the Cadillac or BMW or the Rolls Royce of the business. There is absolutely no contest, and our medical products division became very successful. People thought this was Mecca. Nothing had ever been manufactured that was so wonderful. Our business expanded enormously, rapidly out there (Flagstaff, Arizona) and we had a lot of young, young leadership. They spent some time thinking they could do no wrong and that everything they touched was going to turn to gold.

They have had some hard knocks along the way and discovered it wasn't as easy as they initially thought it was. And that's probably good learning for everyone somewhere along the way. That's not how business works. There's a lot of truth in that old saying that you learn more from your failures than you do your successes. One failure goes a long way toward making you say, Oh, wow!

Acknowledgments

Many sources were helpful in providing background material for this case. The most important sources of all were the W. L. Gore Associates, who generously shared their time and viewpoints about the company. They provided

EXHIBIT 6
Operating and Net Profits of W. L. Gore & Associates

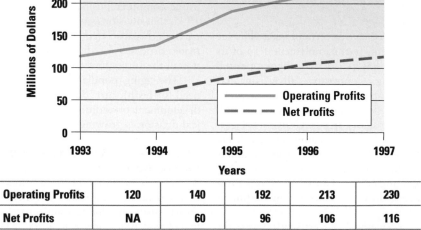

	1993	1994	1995	1996	1997
Operating Profits	120	140	192	213	230
Net Profits	NA	60	96	106	116

Data from *Forbes* Magazine's Annual Report on the 500 Largest Private Companies in the U.S.

many resources, including internal documents, and added much to this case through sharing their personal experiences as well as ensuring that the case accurately reflected the Gore company and culture.

Excerpts from Interviews with Associates

The first excerpt is from an Associate that was formerly with IBM and has been with Gore for two years:

Q. What is the difference between being with IBM and Gore?

A. I spent twenty-four years working for IBM, and there's a big difference. I can go ten times faster here at Gore because of the simplicity of the lattice organization. Let me give you an example. If I wanted to purchase chemicals at IBM (I am an industrial chemist), the first thing I would need to do is get accounting approval, then I would need at least two levels of managers' approval, then a secretary to log in my purchase and the purchase order would go to Purchasing where it would be assigned a buyer. Some time could be saved if you were willing to "walk" the paperwork through the approval process, but even after computerizing the process, it typically would take one month from the time you initiated the purchase requisition till the time the material actually arrived. Here they have one simple form. Usually, I get the chemicals the next day and a copy of the purchase order will arrive a day or two after that. It happens so fast. I wasn't used to that.

Q. Do you find that a lot more pleasant?

A. Yeah, you're unshackled here. There's a lot less bureaucracy that allows you to be a lot more productive. Take Lab Safety, for example. In my lab at IBM, we were cited for not having eyewash taped properly. The first time, we were cited for not having a big enough area taped off. So we taped off a bigger area. The next week the same eyewash was cited again, because the area we taped off was three inches too short in one direction. We retaped it and the following week, it got cited again for having the wrong color tape. Keep in mind that the violation was viewed as serious as a pail of gasoline next to a lit Bunsen burner. Another time I had the dubious honor of being selected the functional safety representative in charge of getting the function's labs ready for a Corporate Safety Audit. (The function was a third level in the pyramidal organization—[1] department, [2] project, and [3] function.) At the same time I was working on developing a new surface mount package. As it turned out, I had no time to work on development, and the function spent a lot of time and money getting ready for the Corporate Auditors who in the end never showed. I'm not belittling the importance of safety, but you really don't need all that bureaucracy to be safe.

The second interview is with an Associate who is a recent engineering graduate:

Q. How did you find the transition coming here?

A. Although I never would have expected it to be, I found my transition coming to Gore to be rather challenging. What attracted me to the company was the opportunity to "be my own boss" and determine my own commitments. I am very goal-oriented, and enjoy taking a project and running with it—all things that you are able to do and encouraged to do within the Gore culture. Thus, I thought, a perfect fit!

However, as a new Associate, I really struggled with where to focus my efforts—I was ready to make my own commitments, but to what?! I felt a strong need to be sure that I was working on something that had value, something that truly needed to be done. While I didn't expect to have the "hottest" project, I did want to make sure that I was helping the company to "make money" in some way.

At the time, though, I was working for a plant that was pretty typical of what Gore was like when it was originally founded—after my first project (which was designed to be a "quick win"—a project with meaning, but one that had a definite end point), I was told, "Go find something to work on." While I could have found something, I wanted to find something with at least a small degree of priority! Thus, the whole process of finding a project was very frustrating for me—I didn't feel that I had the perspective to make such a choice and ended up in many conversations with my sponsor about what would be valuable....

In the end, of course, I did find that project—and it did actually turn out to be a good investment for Gore. The process to get there, though, was definitely trying for someone as inexperienced as I was—so much ground would have been gained by suggesting a few projects to me and then letting me choose from that smaller pool.

What's really neat about the whole thing, though, is that my experience has truly made a difference. Due in part to my frustrations, my plant now provides college grads with more guidance on their first several projects. (This guidance obviously becomes less and less critical as each Associate grows within Gore.) Associates still are choosing their own commitments, but they're doing so with additional perspective, and the knowledge that they are making a contribution to Gore—which is an important thing within our culture. As I said, though, it was definitely rewarding to see that the company was so responsive, and to feel that I had helped to shape someone else's transition!

3.0

Notes

1. GORE-TEX is a registered trademark of W. L. Gore & Associates.
2. In this case the word *Associates* is used and capitalized because in W. L. Gore & Associates' literature the word is always used instead of *employees* and is capitalized. In fact, case writers were told that Gore "never had 'employees'—always 'Associates.'"
   3. GORE RideOn is a registered trademark of W. L. Gore & Associates.
   4. Glide is a registered trademark of W. L. Gore & Associates.
5. WindStopper is a registered trademark of W. L. Gore & Associates.
6. Similar legally to an ESOP (Employee Stock Ownership Plan). Again, Gore simply has never allowed the word *employee* in any of its documentation.
7. In comparison, only 11 of the 200 largest companies in the *Fortune* 500 had positive ROE each year from 1970 to 1988 and only 2 other companies missed a year. The revenue growth rate for these 13 companies was 5.4 percent, compared with 2.5 percent for the entire *Fortune* 500.

References

Aburdene, Patricia, and John Nasbitt. *Re-inventing the Corporation* (New York: Warner Books, 1985).

Angrist, S. W. "Classless Capitalists," *Forbes* (May 9, 1983), 123–124.

Franlesca, L. "Dry and Cool," *Forbes* (August 27, 1984), 126.

Hoerr, J. "A Company Where Everybody Is the Boss," *Business Week* (April 15, 1985), 98.

Levering, Robert. *The 100 Best Companies to Work for in America*. See the chapter on W. L. Gore & Associates, Inc. (New York: Signet, 1985).

McKendrick, Joseph. "The Employees as Entrepreneur," *Management World* (January 1985), 12–13.

Milne, M. J. "The Gorey Details," *Management Review* (March 1985), 16–17.

Posner, B. G. "The First Day on the Job," *Inc.* (June 1986), 73–75.

Price, Debbie M. "GORE-TEX style," *Baltimore Sun* (April 20, 1997), 1D & 4D.

Price, Kathy. "Firm Thrives Without Boss," *AZ Republic* (February 2, 1986).

Rhodes, Lucien. "The Un-manager," *Inc.* (August 1982), 34.

Simmons, J. "People Managing Themselves: Un-management at W. L. Gore Inc.," *The Journal for Quality and Participation* (December 1987), 14–19.

"The Future Workplace," *Management Review* (July 1986), 22–23.

Trachtenberg, J. A. "Give Them Stormy Weather," *Forbes* (March 24, 1986), 172–174.

Ward, Alex. "An All-Weather Idea," *The New York Times Magazine* (November 10, 1985), Sec. 6.

Weber, Joseph. "No Bosses. And Even 'Leaders' Can't Give Orders," *Business Week* (December 10, 1990), 196–197.

"Wilbert L. Gore," *Industry Week* (October 17, 1983), 48–49.

Integrative Case 4.0

XEL Communications, Inc. (C): Forming a Strategic Partnership*

In the fall of 1995, Bill Sanko, president of XEL Communications, Inc., strolled around in the new 115,000-square-foot facility with its spacious conference rooms and computer-based skills training center, into which the company had just moved. Their former facility had been a 53,000-square-foot building that just could not accommodate XEL's growth. During the upcoming round of strategic planning sessions, Bill wondered how XEL and its management team would decide to grapple with the two-edged sword of rapid growth. Would it be possible for XEL to maintain its entrepreneurial culture while it experienced rapid growth? Would it find the resources necessary to sustain growth without harming its culture? From where?

XEL Communications, Inc.

XEL Communications, Inc.[1]—located in the outskirts of Denver, Colorado—designed and manufactured various telecommunications products for a number of companies—primarily large U.S. telephone operating companies. Originally a division within GTE headed by Bill Sanko, it was in the process of being closed when Bill and a few key managers persuaded GTE to sell the division to them. In July 1984, Sanko and fellow managers signed a letter of intent to buy the division from GTE. Two months later, the bill of sale was signed, and XEL Communications, Inc., became an independent company. Ironically, GTE remained as one of XEL's major customer accounts.

In terms of overall financial performance, XEL was profitable. Its revenues increased from $16.8 million in 1992 to $23.6 million in 1993 and $52.3 million in 1994—over a threefold increase in three years. In 1996, XEL employed approximately 300 people.

XEL designed and manufactured more than 300 individual products that enabled network operators to upgrade existing infrastructures and cost-effectively enhance the speed and functionality of their networks while reducing operating expenses and overhead costs. The firm's products provided access to telecommunications services and automated monitoring and maintenance of network performance, and extended the distance over which network operators were able to offer their services.[2] For example, XEL produced equipment that "conditioned" existing lines to make them acceptable for business use and sold products that facilitated the transmission of data and information over phone lines. Driving the need for XEL's products was the keen interest in electronic data transference: "Businesses are more and more dependent on the transfer of information," Bill Sanko noted. In addition, more businesses, including XEL, were operating by taking and filling orders through electronic data exchanges. Instead of dialing in to inside salespeople, businesses often accessed databases directly.

One of XEL's strengths was its ability to adapt one manufacturer's equipment to another's. XEL provided the bits and pieces of telecommunications equipment to the "network," allowing the smooth integration of disparate transmission pieces. XEL also sold central office transmission equipment and a full range of mechanical housings, specialty devices, power supplies, and shelves.

In 1995, XEL began developing a hybrid fiber/cable broadband modem for use by cable television firms seeking to provide enhanced data communication services over their network facilities. Cable modems were one of the hottest new products in telecommunications. The devices would enable computers to send and receive information about one hundred times faster than standard modems used with phone lines. Given that 34 million homes had personal computers, cable modems were seen as a surefire way to exploit the personal computer (PC) boom and the continuing convergence of computers and television. Media analysts estimated that cable modem users would rise to 11.8 million by the end of 2005 from a handful in 1996.[3]

"Business customers and their changing telecommunications needs drive the demand for XEL's products. That, in turn, presents a challenge to the company," said Sanko. Sanko cited the constant stream of new products developed by XEL—approximately two per month—as the driving force behind the growth. Throughout the industry, product life-cycle times were getting even shorter. Before the breakup of the Bell System in 1984, transmission switches and other telecommunications devices enjoyed a thirty- to forty-year life. In 1995, with technology moving so fast, XEL's products had about a three-year to five-year life.

XEL sold products to all of the Regional Bell Operating Companies (RBOCs), as well as such companies as GTE and Centel. Railroads, with their own telephone networks, were also customers. In addition to its domestic

*This case was prepared by Professors Robert P. McGowan and Cynthia V. Fukami, Daniels College of Business, as a basis for classroom discussion rather than to illustrate either effective or ineffective handling of an administrative situation. Copyright © 1995 by the authors: © 1997 by the Case Center, Daniels College of Business, University of Denver. Published by South-Western College Publishing.

For information regarding this and other CaseNet* cases, please visit CaseNet* on the World Wide Web at *http://casenet.thomson.com*.

business, products were sold in Canada, Mexico, and Central and South America.[4] XEL's field salespeople worked with engineers to satisfy client requests for specific services. Over a period of time, the salespeople developed a rapport with these engineers, providing XEL with new product leads.

4.0

With all the consolidations and ventures in telecommunications, those who watched the industry often concluded that the overall market would become more difficult. Sanko believed, however, that "out of change comes opportunity. The worst-case scenario would be a static situation. Thus, a small company, fast to respond to customer needs and able to capitalize on small market niches, will be successful. Often, a large company like AT&T will forsake a smaller market and XEL will move in. Also, XEL's size allows it to design a project in a very short time."

Sanko watched federal legislation keenly. The Telecommunications Act of 1996, which removed numerous barriers to competition, had clearly changed the rules of the game. Consequently, said Sanko, "we need to expand our market and be prepared to sell to others as the regulatory environment changes." The joint venture between Time Warner and US West also signaled that telephone and cable companies would be pooling their resources to provide a broader array of information services. As for the future, Sanko saw "a lot of opportunities we can't even now imagine."

The XEL Vision

A feature that set XEL apart from other companies was its strong, healthy corporate culture. Developing a culture of innovation and team decision making was instrumental in providing the results XEL prided itself on.[5] An early attempt to define culture in a top-down fashion was less successful than the management team had hoped,[6] so the team had embarked on a second journey to determine what their core values were and what they would like the company to look like in five years. The team had then gone off-site for several days and finalized the XEL Vision statement (Exhibit 1). By the summer of 1987, the statement had been signed by members of the senior team and been hung up by the bulletin board. Employees were not required to sign the statement, but were free to do so when each was ready.

Julie Rich, vice president of human resources, described the management team's approach to getting the rest of the organization to understand as well as become comfortable with the XEL Vision: "Frequently, organizations tend to take a combination top-down/bottom-up approach in instituting cultural change. That is, the top level will develop a statement about values and overall vision. They will then communicate it down to the bottom level and hope that results will percolate upward through the middle levels. Yet it is often the middle level of management which is most skeptical, and they will block it or resist change. We decided to take a 'cascade' approach in which the process begins at the top and gradually cascades from one level to the next so that the critical players are slowly acclimated to the process. We also did a number of other things—including sending a copy of the vision statement to the homes of the employees and dedicating a section of the company newspaper to communicate what key sections of the vision mean from the viewpoint of managers and employees."

The vision statement became a living symbol of the XEL culture and the degree to which XEL embraced and empowered its employees. When teams or managers made decisions, they routinely brought out the XEL Vision document so workers might consult various parts of the statement to help guide and direct decisions. According to Julie, the statement was used to help evaluate new products, emphasize quality (a specific XEL strategic objective was to be the top quality vendor for each product), support teams, and drive the performance-appraisal process.

The XEL Vision was successfully implemented as a key first step; but it was far from being a static document. Key XEL managers continually revisited the statement to ensure that it became a reflection of where they wanted to go, not where they had been. Julie believed this regular appraisal was a large factor in the success of the vision. "Our values are the key," Julie explained. "They are strong, they are truly core values, and they are deeply held." Along with the buy-in process, the workers also saw that the managers experimented with the statement, which reflected the strong entrepreneurial nature of XEL's founders—a common bond that they all shared. They were not afraid of risk, or of failure, and this spirit was reinforced in all employees through the vision itself, as well as through the yearly process of revisiting the statement. Once a year, Bill Sanko sat with all employees and directly challenged (and listened to direct challenges to) the XEL Vision. From 1987 to 1995, only two relatively minor additions had altered the original statement.

Which Path to Choose

When the 1995 annual strategic planning process got under way, XEL was in good shape on any one of a number of indicators. Profits were growing, new products were being developed, the culture and vision of the company were strong, employee morale was high, and the self-directed work teams were achieving exceptional quality.[7] Rapid growth, however, was also presenting a challenge. Would it be possible for XEL to maintain its entrepreneurial culture in the face of rapid growth? Could they sustain their growth without harming their culture? Would they find the resources necessary to sustain the growth? From where?

As the strategic planning retreat progressed, three options seemed apparent to the team. First, they could stay the course and remain privately held. Second, they could initiate a public offering of stock. Third, they could seek a strategic partnership. Which would be the right choice for XEL?

EXHIBIT 1
The XEL Vision

XEL will become the leader in our selected telecommunications markets through innovation in products and services. Every XEL product and service will be rated Number One by our customers.

XEL will set the standards by which our competitors are judged. We will be the best, most innovative, responsive designer, manufacturer and provider of quality products and services as seen by customers, employees, competitors, and suppliers.*

We will insist upon the highest quality from everyone in every task.

We will be an organization where each of us is a self-manager who will:
- initiate action, commit to, and act responsibly in achieving objectives
- be responsible for XEL's performance
- be responsible for the quality of individual and team output
- invite team members to contribute based on experience, knowledge and ability

We will:
- be ethical and honest in all relationships
- build an environment where creativity and risk taking is promoted
- provide challenging and satisfying work
- ensure a climate of dignity and respect for all
- rely on interdepartmental teamwork, communications and cooperative problem solving to attain common goals**
- offer opportunities for professional and personal growth
- recognize and reward individual contribution and achievement
- provide tools and services to enhance productivity
- maintain a safe and healthy work environment

XEL will be profitable and will grow in order to provide both a return to our investors and rewards to our team members.

XEL will be an exciting and enjoyable place to work while we achieve success.

*Responsiveness to customers' new product needs as well as responding to customers' emergency delivery requirements have been identified as key strategic strengths. Therefore, the vision statement has been updated to recognize this important element.
**The importance of cooperation and communication was emphasized with this update of the Vision Statement.

4.0

Staying the Course

The most obvious option was to do nothing. Bill Sanko indicated that the management team did not favor staying the course and remaining privately held. "We had a venture capitalist involved who, after being with us for ten years, wanted out. In addition, the founders—ourselves—also wanted out from a financial standpoint. You also have to understand that one of the original founders, Don Donnelly, had passed away; and his estate was looking to make his investment more liquid. So, there were a lot of things that converged at the same time."

Once they determined they would not remain privately held, Bill mentioned that the decision boiled down to two main avenues: XEL would do an initial public offering and go public, or it would find a strategic partner. "To guide us in this process, we decided to retain the services of an outside party; we talked to about a dozen investment houses.

In October 1994, we decided to hire Alex Brown, a long time investment house out of Baltimore. What we liked about this firm was that they had experience with doing both options—going public or finding a partner."

Going Public

One avenue open to XEL was initiating a public offering of stock. Alex Brown advised them of the pluses and minuses of this option. Sanko reviewed their recommendations:

The plus side for XEL doing an initial public offering was that technology was really hot about this time [October 1994]. In addition, we felt that XEL would be valued pretty highly in the market. The downside of going public was that XEL was really not a big firm, and institutional investors usually like doing offerings of firms that generate revenues of over $100 million. Another downside was that *you had to deal with analysts, and their projections become your plan, which really turned me off. Also, shareholders want a steady and predictable rate of return. Technology stocks are not steady—there are frequent ups and downs in this marketplace—caused by a number of factors, such as a major telecommunications company deciding not to upgrade at the last minute or Congress considering sweeping regulatory changes. Finally, Alex Brown felt that the stock would have traded thinly. This, coupled with SEC restrictions on trading, made the option of going public less desirable.*

Strategic Partnership

After taking these factors into account, Sanko said,

. . . we decided to take the third path and look for a potential partner. But you have to also note that there was always the first option available as a safety valve. We could not do anything and stay the way we were. That's the nice thing about all of this. We were not under any pressure to go public or seek a partner. We could also wait and do one of these things later on. So, we had the luxury of taking our time.

In terms of finding a potential partner, there were certain key items that we wanted Alex Brown to consider in helping us in this process. The first was that we, management, wanted to remain with XEL. We had really grown XEL as a business and were not interested in going off and doing something else. The second key item was that we were not interested in being acquired by someone who was interested in consolidating our operations with theirs, closing this facility and moving functions from here to there. To us, this would destroy the essence of XEL. The third item was that we wanted a partner that would bring something to the table but would not try to micromanage our business.

The Case Against Strategic Partnership

In the 1990s, "merger mania" swept the United States. In the first nine months of 1995, the value of all announced mergers and acquisitions reached $248.5 billion, surpassing the record full-year volume of $246.9 billion reached in 1988. This volume occurred in the face of strong evidence that over the past thirty-five years, mergers and acquisitions had hurt organizations more than they had helped.[8] Among the reasons for failure in mergers and acquisitions were the following:

- Inadequate due diligence
- Lack of strategic rationale
- Unrealistic expectations of possible synergies
- Paying too much
- Conflicting corporate cultures
- Failure to move quickly to meld the two companies

Nevertheless, there had been successful mergers and acquisitions. Most notably, small and midsized deals had been found to have a better chance for success. Michael Porter argued that the best acquisitions were "gap-filling," that is, a deal in which one company bought another to strengthen its product line or expand its territory, including globally. Anslinger and Copeland argued that successful acquisitions were more likely when preacquisition managers were kept in their positions, big incentives were offered to top-level executives so that their net worths were on the line, and the holding company was kept flat (that is, the business was kept separate from other operating units and retained a high degree of autonomy).[9]

More often than not, however, the deal was won or lost after it was done. Bad post-merger planning and integration could doom the acquisition. "While there is clearly a role for thoughtful and well-conceived mergers in American business, all too many don't meet that description."[10]

Choosing a Partner

"With these issues in mind, Alex Brown was able to screen out possible candidates," said Sanko. "In January, 1995, this plan was presented to our board of directors for approval, and by February, we had developed the 'book' about XEL that was to be presented to these candidates. We then had a series of meetings with the candidates in the conference room at our new facility. The interesting aside on these meetings was that, often, senior management from some of these firms didn't know what pieces of their business that they still had or had gotten rid of. We did not see this as a good sign."

One of the firms with which XEL met was Gilbert Associates, based in Reading, Pennsylvania. Gilbert Associates was founded in the 1940s as an engineering and construction firm, primarily in the area of power plants. They embarked on a strategy of reinventing themselves by divesting their energy-related companies and becoming a holding company whose subsidiaries operated in the high-growth markets of telecommunications and technical services. Gilbert also owned a real estate management-and-development subsidiary. After due diligence and due deliberation, Gilbert was chosen by the management team as XEL's strategic partner. The letter of intent was signed on October 5, 1995, and the deal was closed on October 27, 1995. Gilbert paid $30 million in cash.[11]

Why was Gilbert chosen as the partner from among six or seven suitors? Not because they made the highest bid. XEL was attracted to Gilbert by three factors: (1) Gilbert's long-term strategy to enter the telecommunications industry; (2) its intention of keeping XEL as a separate, autonomous company; and (3) its willingness to pay cash (as opposed to stock or debt). "It was a clean deal," said Sanko.

The deal was also attractive because it was structured with upside potential. XEL was given realistic performance targets for the next three years. If these targets were achieved, and Sanko had every expectation that they would be, approximately $6-$8 million would be earned. Gilbert did not place a cap on the upside.

In spite of the attractive financial package, more was necessary to seal the deal. "At the end of the day," said Sanko, "culture, comfort, and trust—those were more important than money." It was important to XEL's board that Gilbert presented a good fit. Sanko was encouraged because he felt comfortable with Gilbert's chief executive officer. Vice president of Human Resources Julie Rich also noted, "The management team was to remain intact. Gilbert recognized that the XEL Vision was part of our success and our strength. They wanted to keep it going."

As one way of gaining confidence in Gilbert, Bill Sanko personally spoke with the CEOs of other companies Gilbert had recently acquired. In these conversations, Sanko was assured that Gilbert would keep its promises.

Timothy S. Cobb, chair, president, and CEO of Gilbert Associates, commented at the time of the acquisition: "This transaction represented the first clear step toward the attainment of our long-term strategy of focusing on the higher margin areas of telecommunications and technical services. XEL's superior reputation for quality throughout the industry, its innovative design and manufacturing capabilities, and its focus on products aimed at the emerging information highway markets, will serve us well as we seek to further penetrate this important segment of the vast communications market."[12]

Cobb continued, "We see long-term growth opportunities worldwide for XEL's current proprietary and Original Equipment Manufacturer [OEM] products as well as for the powerful new products being developed. These products fall into two families: (1) fiber optic network interfaces designed specifically to meet the needs of telephone companies, interexchange carriers (e.g., AT&T, Sprint, MCI), and specialized network carriers installing fiber-optic facilities; and (2) a hybrid fiber/cable broadband modem for use by cable television firms seeking to provide enhanced data communications services over their network facilities. Going forward, we expect to leverage Gilbert's knowledge and relationships with the RBOCs to significantly increase sales to those important customers, while also utilizing our GAI-Tronics subsidiary's established international sales organization to further penetrate the vast global opportunities which exist. As a result, revenues from Gilbert Associates' growing telecommunications segment could represent over half of our total revenues by the end of 1996."

Timothy Cobb had come to Gilbert from Ameritech, an RBOC which covered the Midwestern United States. He had been president of GAI-Tronics Corporation, an international supplier of industrial communication equipment, a subsidiary of Gilbert, prior to his appointment as Gilbert's CEO.

Bill Sanko offered, "When all the dust had settled, the one firm that we really felt good about was Gilbert.... Gilbert is an interesting story in itself. Ironically, they had contacted us in August, 1994, based on the advice of their consultant who had read about us in an *Inc.* magazine article. Unfortunately, at the time, they did not have the cash to acquire us since they were in the process of selling off one of their divisions. In the intervening period, Gilbert Associates divested itself of one of its companies, Gilbert/Commonwealth. This sale provided needed funds for the acquisition of XEL."

4.0

Once Sanko was confident that the deal would go, but before the letter of intent was signed, the pending acquisition was announced to the management team, and a general meeting was held with all employees. SEC regulations prohibited sharing particular information (and common sense seconded this directive), but Sanko and his associates felt it was important to keep employees informed before the letter was signed.

During the meeting, Sanko told the employees that the board was "seriously considering" an offer. Sanko assured the employees that the suitor was not a competitor, and that he felt that the suitor was a good fit in culture and values. Sanko reiterated that this partnership would give XEL the resources it needed to grow. Questions were not allowed because of SEC regulations. Employees left the meeting concerned and somewhat nervous, but members of the management team and Julie Rich were positioned in the audience and made themselves available to talk.

During the closing of the deal, Sanko held another general meeting, attended by Timothy Cobb, where more detailed information was shared with employees. Managers had been informed in a premeeting so that they would be prepared to meet with their teams directly following the general meeting.

Employees wanted to know about Gilbert. They wanted to know simple information, such as where Gilbert was located and what businesses it was in. They also wanted to know strategic plans, such as whether Gilbert had plans to consolidate manufacturing operations. Finally, they wanted to know about the near future of XEL—they wanted to know if their benefits would change, if they would still have profit sharing, and if the management team would stay in place. "We have a track record of being open," says Sanko. "Good news or bad is always shared. This history stemmed much of the rumor mill."

In the next few weeks, Tim Cobb returned to hold a series of meetings with the management team and with a focus group of thirty employees representing a cross-section of the organization. Cobb also met with managers and their spouses at an informal reception. Sanko wanted to ease the management team into the realization that they were now part of a larger whole in Gilbert. He asked Cobb to make the same presentation to XEL that he was currently making to stockholders throughout the country—a presentation that emphasized the role XEL would play in the long-term strategy of Gilbert.

4.0

Going Forward

The human resource systems remained in place with no changes. The management bonus system would change slightly because it included stock options, which were no longer available. XEL's internal advisory board, the "management team," remained intact, but XEL's external advisory board was disbanded. Bill Sanko reported to Gilbert's chairman.

XEL's strategic plan was to follow the process it already had in place, and which was not unlike Gilbert's. The cycle did not change: Gilbert expected XEL's next strategic plan in early November 1996.

XEL's strategic objectives also remained the same. Nothing was put on hold. Plans were still in place to penetrate Brazil, Mexico, and South America.[13] Sanko hoped to capitalize on the synergies of Gilbert's existing international distribution network. XEL met with Gilbert's international representatives to see if this was an avenue for XEL to gain a more rapid presence in South America. Finally, XEL was planning to move into Radio Frequency (RF) engineering and manufacturing, potentially opening the door for wireless support.

Whether XEL would grow depended on the success of these new ventures. In 1996, slight growth was forecasted. But if these new markets really took off, Julie Rich was concerned about hiring enough people in Colorado when the labor market was approaching full employment. Julie considered more creative ways of attracting new hires: for example, by offering more flexible scheduling, or by hiring unskilled workers and training them internally. A new U.S. Department of Education grant to test computer-based training systems was being implemented. Nevertheless, employment was strong in the Denver metro area in 1996, and migration to Colorado had slowed. It would be a challenge to staff XEL if high growth became the business strategy.

Approximately six weeks after the acquisition, Sanko noted that few changes had taken place. Now that they were a publicly held company, there was a great deal more interest in meeting quarterly numbers. "If there has been a change," said Sanko, "it is that there is more attention to numbers." Julie Rich noted that there had been no turnover in the six-week period following the acquisition. She took this calm in the workforce as a sign that things were going well so far.

One reason things went well was that the management team had all worked for GTE prior to the spin-off of XEL. Having all worked for a large public company, they did not experience a terrible culture shock when the Gilbert acquisition took place. Time would tell if the remaining XEL employees would feel the same way.

As Sanko awaited Cobb's upcoming visit, he wondered how to prepare for the event and for the year ahead. He wondered whether XEL would attempt new ventures into RF technology, or how the planned fiber/cable broadband modem would progress. He wondered whether Gilbert's experience in selling in South America would prove valuable for XEL's international strategy. In addition, he wondered how he could encourage XEL and its employees to become members of Gilbert's "team." Would XEL's vision survive the new partnership?

Finally, according to one study of CEO turnover after acquisition, 80 percent of acquired CEOs left their companies by the sixth year after the acquisition, but 87 percent of those who did leave, did so within two years. The key factor in their turnover was post-acquisition autonomy.[14] After nearly twelve years as the captain of his own ship, Sanko wondered what his own future, and the future of the XEL management team, would hold.

Notes

1. For additional information on XEL Communications, Inc., and the key strategic issues facing XEL, see Robert P. McGowan and Cynthia V. Fukami, "XEL Communications, Inc. (A)," Daniels College of Business, University of Denver © 1995, published by South-Western Publishing.
2. *PR Newsletter* (October 5, 1995).
3. Bill Menezes "Modern Times," *Rocky Mountain News* (April 28, 1996).
4. *PR Newswire* (October 5, 1995).
5. John Sheridan, "America's Best Plants: XEL Communications," *IndustryWeek* (October 16, 1995).
6. See McGowan and Fukami, "XEL Communications, Inc. (A)," for a larger discussion of corporate culture at XEL.
7. Sheridan, "America's Best Plants."
8. Philip Zweig "The Case Against Mergers," *BusinessWeek* (October 30, 1995).
9. Patricia Anslinger and Thomas Copeland, "Growth Through Acquisitions: A Fresh Look," *Harvard Business Review* (January–February 1996).
10. Zweig, "The Case Against Mergers."
11. Dina Bunn "XEL to be Sold in $30 Million Deal," *Rocky Mountain News* (October 27, 1995).
12. *PR Newswire* (October 5, 1995).
13. For more information on XEL's global penetration, see McGowan and Allen, "XEL Communications, Inc. (B): Going Global."
14. Kim A. Stewart, "After the Acquisition: A Study of Turnover of Chief Executives of Target Companies," doctoral dissertation, University of Houston, 1992.

Integrative Case 5.0

Empire Plastics*

A Project to Remember

In June 1991, **Ian Jones** a production manager with **Empire Plastics Northern (EPN)** was pondering the latest project to increase the production rate of oleic acid. This was the third project in 6 years targeting the oleic acid plant for improvement and arose from the policy followed by the group's directors. This was to identify profitable plants and invest in improving their productivity and profitability, thus avoiding the need for investment in new facilities.

The installation of the "wet end" went well and no problems were experienced. However, the "dry end" was a different story. It wasn't working a year after practical completion, except in short bursts. They were still making changes to it. Jones had known all along that the technology on the dry end was relatively new and might prove troublesome, but the procurement department at **Empire Consultants** in their wisdom recommended its use. Granted, they did send a couple of guys over to Italy to see some similar plants first.

Jones constructed an organizational chart and set about examining the key issues raised by this project (Exhibit 1).

Jones had been appointed as commissioning manager at the commencement of the project. He remembered some of the nightmares experienced by colleagues during two earlier oleic acid projects and firmly resolved to make this one different; it was going to be "his" to manage on completion, and he was going to make his presence felt from the outset.

The execution of the project had been overseen by the group's engineering arm, **Empire Consultants (EC),** headed up by **Henry Holdsworth** as site project manager and **John Marshall** as construction engineer. It was a good team. The project was ambitious, but there were several signs of progress in the beginning. What did perplex him, though, was Marshall's apparent lack of enthusiasm.

Holdsworth described the project as a double management contract, and in this respect it was an unusual project. Empire Consultants traditionally assumed the role of management contactor and directly organized the trade contractors and discipline consultants. Times were changing, though, and both Holdsworth and Marshall had commented on the increasing frequency with which projects were now being tendered as complete packages to outside management contractors. This was their first project that involved two management contractors simultaneously, and neither Marshall nor Holdsworth was happy. Their own involvement had not been clearly defined. **Western Construction** had a £3.1 million contract for the "wet end" and **Teknibuild** a £6.0 million contract for the "dry end." These two contractors provided all the design and management ef-

fort during the project. EC's role was effectively reduced to acting as construction policemen; checking that design and construction were being carried out in accordance with the original process diagram and that EPN's demanding process control and safety requirements were being maintained.

Selecting the management contractors turned out to be extremely protracted and Holdsworth, encouraged by Jones, went ahead and ordered reactors for the wet end and a fluidized bed dryer for the dry end. Over 50% of the total material requirements were in order before either contractor had been formally appointed. Jones was confident that by doing this they could cut the project duration by several months. Nobody had asked Marshall for his opinion.

Conflict Ahead

The first line breaks were in October 1988. Site operations were supervised by Marshall and the two contractor site managers: **Bob Weald** from Western and **Vic Mason** from Teknibuild.

As a construction engineer, Marshall was familiar with the antics of clients and client representatives, especially regarding their tendency to try to make changes. He commented:

Clients always try and change things! When they see the job in the flesh as it were they go "Oh, we need some extra paving round here, or extra railings there!" But if they didn't ask for that at the start, they won't get it. If they want an extra 100 metres of paving they have to pay for it. In this project we had about £500k set aside for contingency purposes, that is unforeseen eventualities over and above the price fixed with the management contractors. If that is not used up by the end of the contract, as in this case, then we can give the clients some extras.

Jones recalled that by June 1989 relationships were not going at all well at the dry end. EC had procured a fluidized bed dryer, a cooler, and more than 300 associated parts, and, as the purchasers of this equipment, they were

*This case was prepared by Dr. Paul D. Gardiner, Department of Business Organisation, Heriot-Watt University, Edinburgh. It is intended to be used as the basis for class discussion rather than to illustrate either effective or ineffective handling of a management situation.

The case was made possible by the cooperation of an organization which wishes to remain anonymous.

EXHIBIT 1
Organizational and Contractual Relationships

5.0

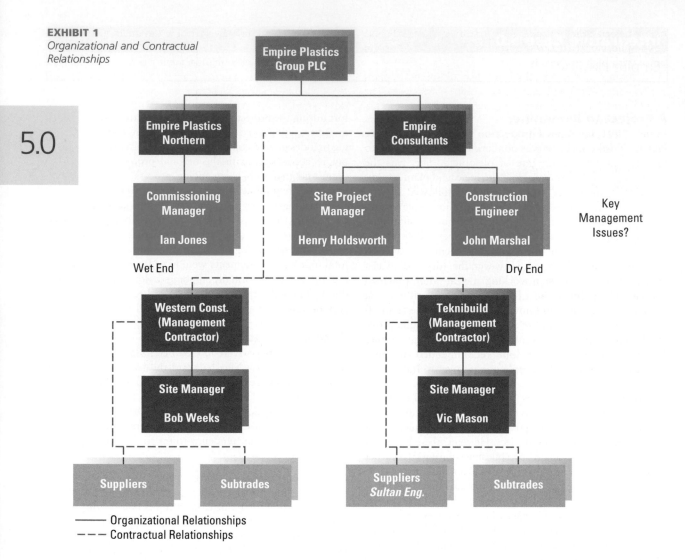

Key Management Issues?

—— Organizational Relationships
- - - Contractual Relationships

the ones responsible for chasing up design drawings from the supplier, **Sultan Engineering.**

Unfortunately, Teknibuild, who, as management contractors, were supposed to design and build the plant, had problems getting the necessary information from Sultan to design the steelwork and foundations. As Marshall had noted earlier:

They [Teknibuild] *were constantly at our doors and throats looking for more information to get on. They didn't seem to have enough data to design properly, which led to conflict very early on. We got off to a bad start and that feeling carried on right to the end of the job. I think in every discipline we had problems with Teknibuild. Our discipline engineer against their discipline engineer.*

The only exception to this was with the electrical and instrumentation (E & I) work. Marshall had put that down

to the E & I subcontractor coming in at the end of the log jam of information, giving them more time to get it right.

While this was going on, Jones got more and more frustrated. In his opinion a lot of time was wasted between Teknibuild and EC for no good reason. He was sure that Teknibuild had more than enough design information to do their job.

When confronted by Jones, Marshall remarked that the truth probably lay somewhere in between, but added that he was *"particularly dismayed at Teknibuild's unwillingness to spend man-hours on the design until they had 100% definition from Sultan Engineering,"* almost to the point where they knew where every nut and bolt was. It was a real mess . . . and Marshall was accepting none of the blame.

On the other hand, things went fine with Western Construction. Their approach was much more relaxed; they had a design office on site with low overheads, whereas Teknibuild worked from the head office in a large design office with high overheads.

On one occasion Marshall asked for Teknibuild's planner to come down and take some site measurements. The reply he received was not very constructive: *"I don't know if I can do that, it's at least a couple of hours to get down there."* Holdsworth agreed that Teknibuild were constantly watching their man-hours:

You felt all the time that they were looking for profit rather than trying to get the job done. Even Teknibuild's construction man, Vic Mason, had internal conflict with his own designers. But with Western it was the other way round, you really felt they were seeking to set a good impression.

Jones thought that perhaps communication with Western had been good because their design and construction people operated side by side, communication was just across the corridor; whereas Teknibuild's site men had difficulty getting answers out of their Head Office. Marshall had always maintained that the best-run jobs are the ones in which you get a good design-construction liaison, particularly by having the designers on site with you.

Failing . . . Forward

Jones considered that in the future it might be a good idea to insist that management contractors set up a local design team on site. Current practice was to leave it up to the contractor, but these days EC had few designers of their own to help.

The trouble with management contractors, he surmised, is that you create an extra link in the communications chain—a large link that can easily break down, and, in his experience, did break down.

Relationships had been better at the wet end, he felt, because Marshall and Weald had worked together before. Marshall knew Weald, knew how he worked and where he was coming from. They could trust each other.

At the Teknibuild end, Vic Mason, their site manager, caused no end of conflict. He was a bit belligerent; thought he knew best, had done it all before, and couldn't be told anything. It never really got out of hand . . . just a bit heated at times. At the end of the day, Marshall maintained that Mason's intentions were ultimately to get the job built. But Jones remained unimpressed, even if Mason's main trouble was his own designers and suppliers.

Driving home, Jones wondered what the effect of the company's new policy on managing projects would be on people like Harry Holdsworth and John Marshall. He couldn't help remembering what Marshall had said about Teknibuild and Western independently setting up their own enquiries and going out for bids separately; there did seem to be a lot of repetition—maybe Marshall was right in viewing the new system as *"a very inefficient way of doing projects."*

5.0

Integrative Case 6.0

The Audubon Zoo, 1993*

6.0

The Audubon Zoo was the focus of national concern in the early 1970s, with well-documented stories of animals kept in conditions that were variously termed an "animal ghetto,"[1] "the New Orleans antiquarium," and even "an animal concentration camp."[2] In 1971, the Bureau of Governmental Research recommended a $5.6 million zoo improvement plan to the Audubon Park Commission and the City Council of New Orleans. The local *Times Picayune* commented on the new zoo: "It's not going to be quite like the Planet of the Apes situation in which the apes caged and studied human beings but something along those broad general lines."[3] The new zoo confined people to bridges and walkways while the animals roamed amidst grass, shrubs, trees, pools, and fake rocks. The gracefully curving pathways, generously lined with luxuriant plantings, gave the visitor a sense of being alone in a wilderness, although crowds of visitors might be only a few yards away.

The Decision

The Audubon Park Commission launched a $5.6 million development program, based on the Bureau of Governmental Research plan for the zoo, in March 1972. A bond issue and a property tax dedicated to the zoo were put before the voters on November 7, 1972. When it passed by an overwhelming majority, serious discussions began about what should be done. The New Orleans City Planning Commission finally approved the master plan for the Audubon Park Zoo in September 1973. But the institution of the master plan was far from smooth.

The Zoo Question Goes Public

Over two dozen special interests were ultimately involved in choosing whether to renovate/expand the existing facilities or move to another site. Expansion became a major community controversy. Some residents opposed the zoo expansion, fearing "loss of green space" would affect the secluded character of the neighborhood. Others opposed the loss of what they saw as an attractive and educational facility.

Most of the opposition came from the zoo's affluent neighbors. Zoo Director John Moore ascribed the criticism to "a select few people who have the money and power to make a lot of noise." He went on to say, "[T]he real basis behind the problem is that the neighbors who live around the edge of the park have a selfish concern because they want the park as their private backyard." Legal battles over the expansion plans continued until early 1976. At that time, the 4th Circuit Court of Appeals ruled that the expansion was legal.[4] An out-of-court agreement with the zoo's neighbors (the Upper Audubon Association) followed shortly.

Physical Facilities

The expansion of the Audubon Park Zoo took it from fourteen to fifty-eight acres. The zoo was laid out in geographic sections: the Asian Domain, World of Primates, World's Grasslands, Savannah, North American Prairie, South American Pampas, and Louisiana Swamp, according to the zoo master plan developed by the Bureau of Governmental Research. Additional exhibits included the Wisner Discovery Zoo, Sea Lion exhibit, and Flight Cage. Exhibit 1 is a map of the new zoo.

Purpose of the Zoo

The main outward purpose of the Audubon Park Zoo was entertainment. Many of the promotional efforts of the zoo were aimed at creating an image of the zoo as an entertaining place to go. Obviously, such a campaign was necessary to attract visitors to the zoo. Behind the scenes, the zoo also preserved and bred many animal species, conducted research, and educated the public. The mission statement of the Audubon Institute is given in Exhibit 2.

New Directions

A chronology of major events in the life of the Audubon Zoo is given in Exhibit 3. One of the first significant changes made was the institution of an admission charge in 1972. Admission to the zoo had been free to anyone prior to the adoption of the renovation plan. Ostensibly, the initial purpose behind instituting the admission charge was to prevent vandalism,[5] but the need for additional income was also apparent. Despite the institution of and increases in admission charges, attendance increased dramatically (Exhibit 4).

Operations
Friends of the Zoo

The Friends of the Zoo was formed in 1974 and incorporated in 1975 with four hundred members. The stated purpose of the group was to increase support and awareness of the Audubon Park Zoo. Initially, the Friends of the Zoo tried to increase interest in and commitment to the zoo, but its activities increased dramatically over the following

*By Claire J. Anderson, Old Dominion University, and Caroline Fisher, Loyola University, New Orleans. © 1993, 1991, 1989, 1987, Claire J. Anderson and Caroline Fisher. This case was designed for classroom discussion only, not to depict effective or ineffective handling of administrative situations.

EXHIBIT 1
The Audubon Park Zoo

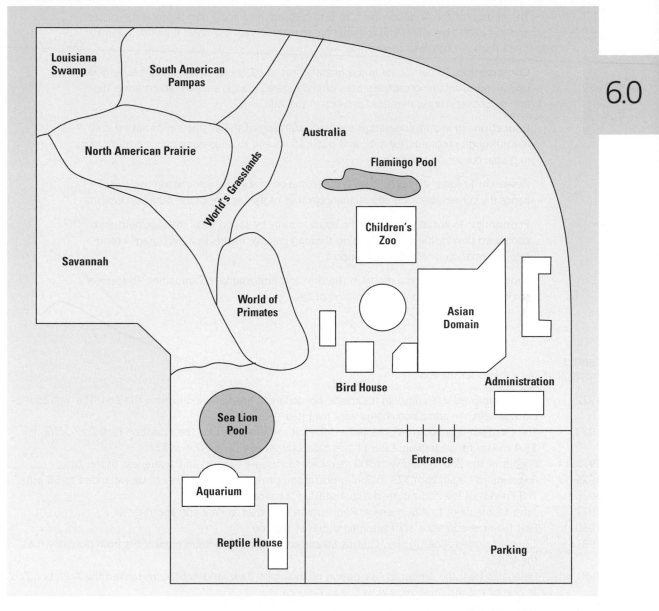

6.0

years to where it was involved in funding, operating, and governing the zoo.

The Friends of the Zoo had a 24-member governing board. Yearly elections were held for six members of the board, who served four-year terms. The board oversaw the policies of the zoo and set guidelines for memberships, concessions, fund-raising, and marketing. Actual policy making and operations were controlled by the Audubon Park Commission, however, which set zoo hours, admission prices, and so forth.

Through its volunteer programs, the Friends of the Zoo staffed many of the zoo's programs. Members of the Friends of the Zoo served as "edZOOcators," education volunteers who were specially trained to conduct interpretive educational programs, and "Zoo Area Patrollers," who provided general information at the zoo and helped with crowd control. Other volunteers assisted in the commissary, the Animal Health Care Center, and the Wild Bird Rehabilitation Center or helped with membership, public relations, graphics, clerical work, research, or horticulture.

EXHIBIT 2
Audubon Institute Mission Statement

6.0

> The mission of the Audubon Institute is to cultivate awareness and appreciation of life and the earth's resources and to help conserve and enrich our natural world. The Institute's primary objectives toward this are:
>
> **Conservation:** To participate in the global effort to conserve natural resources by developing and maintaining captive stocks of endangered plants, animals, and marine life, and by cooperating with related projects in the wild.
>
> **Education:** To impart knowledge and understanding of the interaction of nature and man through programs, exhibits, and publications and to encourage public participation in global conservation efforts.
>
> **Research:** To foster the collection and dissemination of scientific information that will enhance the conservation and educational objectives of the facilities of the Audubon Institute.
>
> **Economics:** To ensure long-range financial security by sound fiscal management and continued development, with funding through creative means that encourage corporate, foundation, and individual support.
>
> **Leadership:** To serve as a model in the civic and professional communities. To foster a spirit of cooperation, participation, and pride.

Source: The Audubon Institute.

EXHIBIT 3
Chronology of Major Events for the Zoo

1972	Voters approved a referendum to provide tax dollars to renovate and expand the Zoo. The first Zoo-To-Do was held. An admission charge was instituted.
1973	The City Planning Commission approved the initial master plan for the Audubon Park Zoo calling for $3.4 million for upgrading. Later phases called for an additional $2.1 million.
1974	Friends of the Zoo formed with 400 members to increase support and awareness of the Zoo.
1975	Renovations began with $25 million in public and private funds; 14 acres to be expanded to 58 acres.
1976	The Friends of the Zoo assumed responsibility for concessions.
1977	John Moore went to Albuquerque; Ron Forman took over as Park and Zoo director.
1980	First full-time education staff assumed duties at the Zoo.
1981	Contract signed allowing New Orleans Steamboat Company to bring passengers from downtown to the Park.
1981	Delegates from the American Association of Zoological Parks and Aquariums ranked the Audubon Zoo as one of the top three zoos of its size in America.
1981	Zoo accredited.
1982	The Audubon Park Commission reorganized under Act 352, which required the Commission to contract with a nonprofit organization for the daily management of the Park.
1985	The Zoo was designated as a Rescue Center for Endangered and Threatened Plants.
1986	Voters approved a $25 million bond issue for the Aquarium.
1988	The Friends of the Zoo became the Audubon Institute.
1990	The Aquarium of the Americas opened in September.

Source: The Audubon Institute.

EXHIBIT 4
Admission Charges

Admission Charges		
Year	**Adult**	**Child**
1972	$0.75	$0.25
1978	1.00	0.50
1979	1.50	0.75
1980	2.00	1.00
1981	2.50	1.25
1982	3.00	1.50
1983	3.50	1.75
1984	4.00	2.00
1985	4.50	2.00
1986	5.00	2.50
1987	5.50	2.50
1988	5.50	2.50
1989	6.00	3.00
1990	6.50	3.00
1991	7.00	3.25

Admission		
Year	**Number of Paid Admissions**	**Number of Member Admissions**
1972	163,000	
1973	310,000	
1974	345,000	
1975	324,000	
1976	381,000	
1977	502,000	
1978	456,000	
1979	561,000	
1980	707,000	
1981	741,000	
1982	740,339	78,950
1983	835,044	118,665
1984	813,025	128,538
1985	856,064	145,020
1986	916,865	187,119
1987	902,744	193,926
1988	899,181	173,313
1989	711,709	239,718
1990	725,469	219,668

Source: The Audubon Institute.

In 1988, the name of the Friends of the Zoo was changed to the Audubon Institute to reflect its growing interest in activities beyond the zoo alone. It planned to promote the development of other facilities and manage these facilities once they were a reality.

6.0

Fund-Raising. The Audubon Park Zoo and the Friends of the Zoo raised funds through five major types of activities: Friends of the Zoo membership, concessions, "Adopt an Animal," "Zoo-To-Do," and capital fund drives. Zoo managers from around the country came to the Audubon Park Zoo for tips on fund-raising.

Membership. Membership in the Friends of the Zoo was open to anyone. The membership fees increased over the years as summarized in Exhibit 5, yet the number of members increased steadily from the original 400 members in 1974 to 38,000 members in 1990, but declined to 28,000 in 1992. Membership allowed free entry to the Audubon Park Zoo and many other zoos around the United States. Participation in Zoobilations (annual members-only evenings at the zoo) and the many volunteer programs described earlier were other benefits of membership.

Expanding membership required a special approach to marketing the zoo. Chip Weigand, director of marketing for the zoo, stated:

. . . [I]n marketing memberships we try to encourage repeat visitations, the feeling that one can visit as often as one wants, the idea that the zoo changes from visit to visit and that there are good reasons to make one large payment or donation for a membership card, rather than paying for

each visit.... [T]he overwhelming factor is a good zoo that people want to visit often, so that a membership makes good economical sense.

Results of research on visitors to the zoo are contained in Exhibits 6 and 7.

In 1985, the zoo announced a new membership designed for business, the Audubon Zoo Curator Club, with four categories of membership: bronze, $250; silver, $500; gold, $1,000; and platinum, $2,500 and more.

Concessions. The Friends of the Zoo took over the Audubon Park Zoo concessions for refreshments and gifts in 1976 through a public bidding process. The concessions were run by volunteer members of the Friends of the Zoo and all profits went directly to the zoo. Before 1976, concession rentals brought in $1,500 in a good year. Profits from operation of the concessions by the Friends of the Zoo brought in $400,000 a year by 1980 and almost $700,000 in profits in 1988. In 1993, FOTZ was considering leasing the concessions to a third-party vendor.

Adopt an Animal. Zoo Parents paid a fee to "adopt" an animal, the fee varying with the animal chosen. Zoo Parents' names were listed on a large sign inside the zoo. They also had their own annual celebration, Zoo Parents Day.

Zoo-To-Do. Zoo-To-Do was an annual black-tie fundraiser held with live music, food and drink, and original, high-class souvenirs, such as posters or ceramic necklaces. Admission tickets, limited to 3,000 annually, were priced starting at $100 per person. A raffle was conducted in conjunction with the Zoo-To-Do, with raffle items varying

EXHIBIT 5
Membership Fees and Membership

Year	Family Membership Fees	Individual Membership Fees	Number of Memberships
1979	$20	$10	1,000
1980	20	10	7,000
1981	20	10	11,000
1982	25	15	18,000
1983	30	15	22,000
1984	35	20	26,000
1985	40	20	27,000
1986	45	25	28,616
1987	45	25	29,318
1988	45	25	33,314
1989	49	29	36,935
1990	49	29	38,154

Source: The Audubon Institute.

EXHIBIT 6
Respondent Characteristics of Zoo Visitors According to Visitation Frequency (in %)

Respondent Characteristic	Number of Zoo Visits Over Past Two Years			
	Four or More	Two or Three	One or None	Never Visited
Age				
Under 27	26	35	31	9
27 to 35	55	27	15	3
36 to 45	48	32	11	9
46 to 55	18	20	37	25
Over 55	27	29	30	14
Marital status				
Married	41	28	20	11
Not married	30	34	24	13
Children at home				
Yes	46	30	15	9
No	34	28	27	12
Interested in visiting New Orleans Aquarium				
Very, with emphasis	47	26	18	9
Very, without emphasis	45	24	23	12
Somewhat	28	37	14	11
Not too	19	32	27	22
Member of Friends of the Zoo				
Yes	67	24	6	4
No, but heard of it	35	30	24	12
Never heard of it	25	28	35	13
Would you be interested in joining FOTZ (non-members only)?				
Very/somewhat	50	28	14	8
No/don't know	33	29	26	12

Source: The Audubon Institute.

6.0

from an opportunity to be zoo curator for a day to the use of a Mercedes-Benz for a year. Despite the rather stiff price, the Zoo-To-Do was a popular sellout every year. Local restaurants and other businesses donated most of the necessary supplies, decreasing the cost of the affair. In 1985, the Zoo-To-Do raised almost $500,000 in one night, more money than any other nonmedical fund-raiser in the county.[6]

Advertising

The Audubon Zoo launched impressive marketing campaigns in the 1980s. The zoo received ADDY awards from the New Orleans Advertising Club year after year.[7] In 1986, the film *Urban Eden*, produced by Alford Advertis-

ing and Buckholtz Productions Inc. in New Orleans, finished first among fifty entries in the "documentary films, public relations" category of the Eighth Annual Houston International Film Festival. The first-place Gold Award recognized the film for vividly portraying Audubon Zoo as a conservation, rather than a confining, environment.

During the same year, local television affiliates of ABC, CBS, and NBC produced independent TV spots using the theme: "One of the World's Greatest Zoos Is in Your Own Backyard...Audubon Zoo!" Along with some innovative views of the Audubon Zoo being in someone's "backyard," local news anchor personalities enjoyed "monkeying around" with the animals, and the zoo enjoyed some welcome free exposure.[8]

EXHIBIT 7
Relative Importance of Seven Reasons Respondent Does Not Visit the Zoo More Often (in %)

Reason (Closed-Ended)	Very Imp. w/ Emphasis	Very Imp. w/o Emphasis	Somewhat Important	Unimportant
The distance of the Zoo from where you live	7	11	21	60
The cost of a Zoo visit	4	8	22	66
Not being all that interested in Zoo animals	2	12	18	67
The parking problems on weekends	7	11	19	62
The idea that you get tired of seeing the same exhibits over and over	5	18	28	49
It's too hot during summer months	25	23	22	30
Just not having the idea occur to you	8	19	26	48

Source: The Audubon Institute.

6.0

In 1993, the marketing budget was over $800,000, including group sales, public relations, advertising, and special events. Not included in this budget was developmental fund-raising or membership. Percentage breakdowns of the marketing budget can be found in Exhibit 8.

The American Association of Zoological Parks and Aquariums reported that most zoos find the majority of their visitors live within a single population center in close proximity to the park.[9] Thus, to sustain attendance over the years, zoos must attract the same visitors repeatedly. A

EXHIBIT 8
1991 Marketing Budget

Marketing		Advertising	
General and Administrative	$ 30,900	Media	$244,000
Sales	96,300	Production	50,000
Public Relations	109,250	Account Service	10,800
Advertising	304,800	TOTAL	$304,800
Special Events	157,900		
TOTAL	$699,150	**Special Events**	
		General and Administrative	$ 27,900
Public Relations		LA Swamp Fest	35,000
Education, Travel, and Subscriptions	$ 5,200	Earthfest	25,000
Printing and Duplicating	64,000	Ninja Turtle Breakfast	20,000
Professional Services	15,000	Jazz Search	15,000
Delivery and Postage	3,000	Fiesta Latina	10,000
Telephone	1,250	Crescent City Cats	10,000
Entertainment	2,000	Other Events	15,000
Supplies	16,600	TOTAL	$157,900
Miscellaneous	2,200		
TOTAL	$109,250		

Source: The Audubon Institute.

EXHIBIT 9

Selected Audubon Park Zoo Promotional Programs

6.0

Month	Activity
March	**Louisiana Black Heritage Festival.** A two-day celebration of Louisiana's black history and its native contributions through food, music, and arts and crafts.
March	**Earth Fest.** The environment and our planet are the focus of this fun-filled and educational event. Recycling, conservation displays, and puppet shows.
April	**Jazz Search.** This entertainment series is aimed at finding the best new talent in the area with the winners featured at the New Orleans Jazz & Heritage Festival.
April	**Zoo-To-Do for kids.** At this "pint-sized" version of the Zoo-To-Do, fun and games abound for kids.
May	**Zoo-To-Do.** Annual black tie fund-raiser featuring over 100 of New Orleans' finest restaurants and three music stages.
May	**Irma Thomas Mother's Day Concert.** The annual celebration of Mother's Day with a buffet.
August	**Lego Invitational.** Architectural firms turn thousands of Lego pieces into original creations.
September	**Fiesta Latina.** Experience the best the Hispanic community has to offer through music, cuisine, and arts and crafts.
October	**Louisiana Swamp Festival.** Cajun food, music, and crafts highlight this four-day salute to Louisiana's bayou country; features hands-on contact with live swamp animals.
October	**Boo at the Zoo.** This annual Halloween extravaganza features games, special entertainment, trick or treat, a haunted house, and the Zoo's Spook Train.

Source: The Audubon Institute

large number of the zoo's promotional programs and special events were aimed at just that.

Progress was slow among non-natives. For example, Simon & Schuster, a reputable publishing firm, in its 218-page [Frommer's] *1983–84 Guide to New Orleans*, managed only a three-word allusion to a "very nice zoo." A 1984 study found that only 36 percent of the visitors were tourists, and even this number was probably influenced to some extent by an overflow from the World's Fair.

Promotional Programs
The Audubon Park Zoo and the Friends of the Zoo conducted a multitude of very successful promotional programs. The effect was to have continual parties and celebrations going on, attracting a variety of people to the zoo (and raising additional revenue). Exhibit 9 lists the major annual promotional programs conducted by the zoo.

In addition to these annual promotions, the zoo scheduled concerts of well-known musicians, such as Irma Thomas, Pete Fountain, The Monkees, and Manhattan

Transfer, and other special events throughout the year. As a result, a variety of events occurred each month.

Many educational activities were conducted all year long. These included (1) a junior zookeeper program for seventh and eighth graders; (2) a student intern program for high school and college students; and (3) a ZOOmobile that took live animals to such locations as special education classes, hospitals, and nursing homes.

Admission Policy
The commission recommended the institution of an admission charge. Arguments generally advanced against such a charge held that it results in an overall decline in attendance and a reduction of nongate revenues. Proponents held that gate charges control vandalism, produce greater revenues, and result in increased public awareness and appreciation of the facility. In the early 1970s, no major international zoo charged admission, and 73 percent of the 125 zoos in the United States charged admission.

The commission argued that there is no such thing as a free zoo; someone must pay. If the zoo is tax-supported, then locals carry a disproportionate share of the cost. At the time, neighboring Jefferson Parish was growing by leaps and bounds and surely would bring a large, nonpaying [constituency] to the new zoo. Further, since most zoos are tourist attractions, tourists should pay since they contribute little to the local tax revenues.

The average yearly attendance for a zoo may be estimated using projected population figures multiplied by a "visitor generating factor." The average visitor generating factor of fourteen zoos similar in size and climate to the Audubon Zoo was 1.34, with a rather wide range from a low of 0.58 in the cities of Phoenix and Miami to a high of 2.80 in Jackson, Mississippi.

Attracting More Tourists and Other Visitors

A riverboat ride on the romantic paddle wheeler *Cotton Blossom* took visitors from downtown New Orleans to the zoo. Originally, the trip began at a dock in the French Quarter, but it was later moved to a dock immediately adjacent to New Orleans' newest attraction, the Riverwalk, a Rouse development, on the site of the 1984 Louisiana World Exposition. Not only was the riverboat ride great fun, it also lured tourists and conventioneers from the downtown attractions of the French Quarter and the new Riverwalk to the zoo, some six miles upstream. A further allure of the riverboat ride was a return trip to downtown on the New Orleans Streetcar, one of the few remaining trolley cars in the United States. The Zoo Cruise not only drew more visitors but also generated additional revenue through landing fees paid by the New Orleans Steamboat Company and [helped keep] traffic out of uptown New Orleans.[10]

Financial

The zoo's ability to generate operating funds has been ascribed to the dedication of the Friends of the Zoo, continuing increases in attendance, and creative special events and programs. A history of adequate operating funds allowed the zoo to guarantee capital donors that their gifts would be used to build and maintain top-notch exhibits. A comparison of the 1989 and 1990 Statements of Operating Income and Expense for the Audubon Institute is in Exhibit 10.

Capital Fund Drives

The Audubon Zoo Development Fund was established in 1973. Corporate/industrial support of the zoo has been very strong—many corporations have underwritten construction of zoo displays and facilities. A partial list of major corporate sponsors is in Exhibit 11. A sponsorship was considered to be for the life of the exhibit. The development department operated on a 12 percent overhead rate,

EXHIBIT 10

The Audubon Institute, Inc. The Audubon Park and Zoological Garden Statement of Operating Income and Expenses

	1989	1990 (Zoo)	1990 (Aquarium)
Operating Income			
Admissions	$2,952,000	$3,587,000	$3,664,000
Food and Gift Operations	2,706,000	3,495,500	711,000
Membership	1,476,000	1,932,000	2,318,000
Recreational Programs	410,000	396,000	0
Visitor Services	246,000	218,000	0
Other	410,000	32,000	650,000
TOTAL INCOME	$8,200,000	$9,660,500	$7,343,000
Operating Expenses			
Maintenance	$1,394,000	$1,444,000	$1,316,000
Educational/Curatorial	2,296,000	2,527,500	2,783,000
Food and Gift Operations	1,804,000	2,375,000	483,000
Membership	574,000	840,000	631,000
Recreational	328,000	358,000	362,000
Marketing	410,000	633,000	593,000
Visitor Services	574,000	373,000	125,000
Administration	820,000	1,110,000	1,050,000
TOTAL EXPENSES	$8,200,000	$9,660,500	$7,343,000

Source: The Audubon Institute.

EXHIBIT 11
Major Corporate Sponsors

Amoco Foundation	Louisiana Coca-Cola Bottling Company, Ltd.
American Express	Louisiana Land and Exploration Company
Anheuser-Busch, Inc.	Martin Marietta Manned Space Systems
Arthur Andersen and Company	McDonald's Operators of New Orleans
J. Aron Charitable Foundation, Inc.	Mobil Foundation, Inc.
Bell South Corporation	National Endowment for the Arts
BP America	National Science Foundation
Chevron USA, Inc.	Ozone Spring Water
Conoco, Inc.	Pan American Life Insurance Company
Consolidated Natural Gas Corporation	Philip Morris Companies Inc.
Entergy Corporation	Shell Companies Foundation, Inc.
Exxon Company, USA	Tenneco, Inc.
Freeport-McMoRan, Inc.	Texaco USA
Host International, Inc.	USF&G Corporation
Kentwood Spring Water	Wendy's of New Orleans, Inc.

Source: The Audubon Institute.

6.0

which meant 88 cents of every dollar raised went toward the projects. By 1989, the master plan for development was 75 percent complete. The fund-raising goal for the zoo in 1989 was $1,500,000.

Management
The Zoo Director
Ron Forman, Audubon Zoo director, was called a "zoomaster extraordinaire" and was described by the press as a "cross between Doctor Doolittle and the Wizard of Oz," as a "practical visionary," and as "serious, but with a sense of humor."[11] A native New Orleanian . . . Forman quit an MBA program to join the city government as an administrative assistant and found himself doing a business analysis project on the Audubon Park. Once the city was committed to a new zoo, Forman was placed on board as an assistant to the zoo director, John Moore. In early 1977, Moore gave up the battle between the "animal people" and the "people people,"[12] and Forman took over as park and zoo director.

Forman was said to bring an MBA-meets-menagerie style to the zoo, which was responsible for transforming it from a public burden into an almost completely self-sustaining operation. The result not only benefited the citizens of the city but also added a major tourist attraction to the economically troubled city of the 1980s.

Staffing
The zoo used two classes of employees, civil service, through the Audubon Park Commission, and noncivil service. The civil service employees included the curators and zookeepers. They fell under the jurisdiction of the city civil service system but were paid out of the budget of the Friends of the Zoo. Employees who worked in public rela-

tions, advertising, concessions, fund-raising, and so on were hired through the Friends of the Zoo and were not part of the civil service system. See Exhibit 12 for further data on staffing patterns.

EXHIBIT 12
Employee Structure

Year	Number of Paid Employees	Number of Volunteers
1972	36	
1973	49	
1974	69	
1975	90	
1976	143	
1977	193	
1978	184	
1979	189	
1980	198	
1981	245	
1982	305	
1983	302	56
1984	419	120
1985	454	126
1986	426	250
1987	431	300
1988	462	310
1989	300	270
1990	450	350

Source: The Audubon Institute.

The Zoo in the Late 1980s

A visitor to the new Audubon Park Zoo could quickly see why New Orleanians were so proud of their zoo. In a city that was termed among the dirtiest in the nation, the zoo was virtually spotless. This was a result of adequate staffing and the clear pride of both those who worked at and those who visited the zoo. One of the first points made by volunteers guiding school groups was that anyone seeing a piece of trash on the ground must pick it up.[13] A 1986 city poll showed that 93 percent of the citizens surveyed gave the zoo a high approval rating—an extremely high rating for any public facility.

Kudos came from groups outside the local area as well. Delegates from the American Association of Zoological Parks and Aquariums ranked the Audubon Park Zoo as one of the three top zoos of its size in America. In 1982, the American Association of Nurserymen gave the zoo a Special Judges Award for its use of plant materials. In 1985, the Audubon Park Zoo received the Phoenix Award from the Society of American Travel Writers for its achievements in conservation, preservation, and beautification.

By 1987, the zoo was virtually self-sufficient. The small amount of money received from government grants amounted to less than 10 percent of the budget. The master plan for the development of the zoo was 75 percent complete, and the reptile exhibit was scheduled for completion in the fall. The organization had expanded with a full complement of professionals and managers. (See Exhibit 13 for the organizational structure of the zoo.)

While the zoo made great progress in fifteen years, all was not quiet on the political front. In a court battle, the city won over the state on the issue of who wielded ultimate authority over Audubon Park and Zoo. Indeed, the zoo benefited from three friendly mayors in a row, starting with Moon Landrieu, who championed the new zoo, to Ernest "Dutch" Morial, to Sidney Barthelemy who threw his support to both the zoo and the aquarium proposal championed by Ron Forman.

The Future
New Directions for the Zoo

Zoo Director Ron Forman demonstrated that zoos have almost unlimited potential. A 1980 New Orleans magazine article cited some of Forman's ideas, ranging from a safari train to a breeding center for rare animals. The latter has an added attraction as a potential money-maker since an Asiatic lion cub, for example, sells for around $10,000. This wealth of ideas was important because expanded facilities and programs are required to maintain attendance at any public attraction. The most ambitious of Forman's ideas was for an aquarium and riverfront park to be located at the foot of Canal Street.

Although the zoo enjoyed political support in 1992, New Orleans was still suffering from a high unemployment rate and a generally depressed economy resulting from the slump in the oil industry. Some economists predicted the beginning of a gradual turnaround in 1988, but any significant improvement in the economy was still forecasted to be years away in 1993. (A few facts about New Orleans are given in Exhibit 14.) In addition, the zoo operated in a city where many attractions competed for the leisure dollar of citizens and visitors. The Audubon Zoological Garden had to vie with the French Quarter, Dixieland jazz, the Superdome, and even the greatest of all attractions in the city—Mardi Gras.

The New Orleans Aquarium

In 1986, Forman and a group of supporters proposed the development of an aquarium and riverfront park to the New Orleans City Council. In November 1986, the electorate voted to fund an aquarium and a riverfront park by a 70 percent margin—one of the largest margins the city has ever given to any tax proposal. Forman[14] hailed this vote of confidence from the citizens as a mandate to build a world-class aquarium that would produce new jobs, stimulate the local economy, and create an educational resource for the children of the city.

The Aquarium of the Americas opened in September 1990. The $40 million aquarium project was located providing a logical pedestrian link for visitors between [major] attractions of the Riverwalk and the Jax Brewery, a shopping center in the French Quarter. Management of the aquarium was placed under the Audubon Institute, the same organization that ran the Audubon Zoo. A feasibility study prepared by Harrison Price Company[15] projected a probable 863,000 visitors by the year 1990, with 75 percent of the visitors coming from outside the metropolitan area. That attendance figure was reached in only four months and six days from the grand opening. Attendance remained strong through 1992, after a slight drop from the initial grand opening figures.

Meanwhile, the zoo had its own future to plan. The new physical facilities and professional care paid off handsomely in increased attendance and new animal births. But the zoo could not expand at its existing location because of lack of land within the city. Forman and the zoo considered several alternatives. One was little "neighborhood" zoos to be located all over the city. A second was a special survival center, a separate breeding area to be located outside the city boundaries where land was available.

Forman presented plans for a project called Riverfront 2000, which included expansion of the aquarium, the Woldenberg Riverfront Park, a species survival center, an arboretum, an insectarium, a natural history museum, and a further expansion of the zoo. With the zoo running smoothly, the staff seemed to need new challenges to tackle, and the zoo needed new facilities or programs to continue to increase attendance.

EXHIBIT 13
Audubon Park Commission

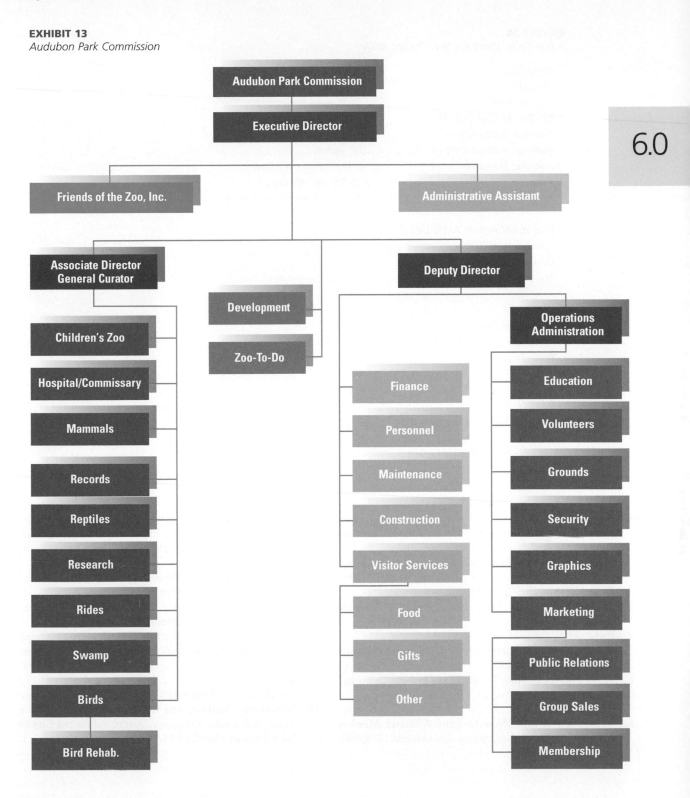

6.0

EXHIBIT 14
A Few Facts About the New Orleans MSA

6.0

Population	1,324,400
Households	489,900
Median Age	30.8 years
Median Household EBI	$29,130
Average Temperature	70 degrees
Average Annual Rainfall	63 inches
Average Elevation	5 feet below sea level
Area	363.5 square miles
	199.4 square miles of land

Major Economic Activities
Tourism (5 million visitors per year)
Oil and Gas Industry
The Port of New Orleans (170 million tons of cargo/year)

Taxes

State Sales Tax	4.0%
Parish (County) Sales Tax	5.0% (Orleans)
State Income Tax	2.1%–2.6% on first $20,000
	3.0%–3.5% on next $30,000
	6.0% on $51,000 and over

Parish property tax of 126.15 mills (Orleans) is based on 10% of appraised value over $75,000 homestead exemption.

Source: Sales and Marketing Management. South Central Bell Yellow Pages, 1991.

Notes

1. Millie Ball, "The New Zoo of '82," *Dixie Magazine, Sunday Times Picayune* (June 24, 1979).
2. Merikaye Presley, "Neighbors Objecting to Audubon Zoo Expansion Project in Midst of Work," *Times Picayune* (March 30, 1975), A3.
3. "Zoo Expansion Is Ruled Illegal," *Times Picayune* (January 20, 1976).
4. Ibid.
5. "Society Seeks Change at Zoo," *Times Picayune* (April 29, 1972), D25.
6. "Zoo Thrives Despite Tough Times in New Orleans," *Jefferson Business* (August 1985), A1.
7. Ibid.
8. Sharon Donovan, "New Orleans Affiliates Monkey Around for Zoo," *Advertising Age* (March 17, 1986).
9. Karen Sausmann, ed., *Zoological Park and Aquarium Fundamentals* (Wheeling, W. Va.: American Association of Zoological Parks and Aquariums, 1982), 111.
10. Diane Luope, "Riverboat Rides to Zoo Are Planned," *Times Picayne* (November 30, 1981), A17.
11. Steve Brooks, "Don't Say 'No Can Do' to Audubon Zoo Chief," *Jefferson Business* (May 5, 1986), 1.
12. Ross Yuchey, "No Longer Is Heard a Discouraging Word at the Audubon Zoo," *New Orleans* (August 1980), 53.
13. Ibid., 49.
14. "At the Zoo" (Winter 1987).
15. "Feasibility Analysis and Conceptual Planning for a Major Aquarium Attraction," prepared for the City of New Orleans (March 1985).

References

Ball, Millie. "The New Zoo of '82," *Dixie Magazine, Sunday Times Picayune* (June 24, 1978).

Beaulieu, Lovell. "It's All Happening at the Zoo," *Sunday Times Picayune* (January 28, 1978).

Brooks, Steve. "Don't Say 'No Can Do' to Audubon Zoo Chief," *Jefferson Business* (May 5, 1986).

Bureau of Governmental Research, City of New Orleans, "Audubon Park Zoo Study, Part I, Zoo Improvement Plan" (New Orleans, La.: Bureau of Governmental Research, August 1971).

Bureau of Governmental Research, City of New Orleans, "Audubon Park Zoo Study, Part II, An Operational Analysis," (New Orleans, La.: Bureau of Governmental Research, August 1971).

Donovan, S. "The Audubon Zoo: A Dream Come True," *New Orleans* (May 1986), 52–66.

"Feasibility Analysis and Conceptual Planning for a Major Aquarium Attraction," prepared for the City of New Orleans (March 1985).

Forman, R., J. Logsdon, and J. Wilds. "Audubon Park: An Urban Eden" (New Orleans, La.: The Friends of the Zoo, 1985).

Poole, Susan. *Frommer's 1983–84 Guide to New Orleans,* (New York: Simon & Schuster, 1983).

Sausmann, Karen, ed., *Zoological Park and Aquarium Fundamentals* (Wheeling, WVa.: American Association of Zoological Parks and Aquariums, 1982).

Yuchey, Ross "No Longer Is Heard a Discouraging Word at the Audubon Zoo," *New Orleans* (August 1980), 49–60.

Zuckerman, S., ed. *Great Zoos of the World* (Boulder, Co.: Westview Press, 1980).

6.0

Integrative Case 7.0

Moss Adams, LLP

7.0

In early January, 2001, Jeff Gutsch, senior manager at Moss Adams LLP, an accounting firm located in Santa Rosa, California, met with his team to discuss the progress of a new initiative for developing the firm's accounting practice to serve clients in the Northern California wine industry. At the meeting, Gutsch and his wine niche team reviewed the strategic plan for the coming year (Exhibit 1).

EXHIBIT 1

Moss Adams's Wine Niche Strategic Plan, 2001

Moss Adams LLP
Santa Rosa Office
Wine Industry Advisors
2001 Strategic Plan

Mission Statement

Our goal is to become the dominant accounting and business consulting firm serving the wine industry by providing superior, value-added services tailored to the needs of Northern California vineyards and wineries, as well as becoming experts in the industry.
• We expect to achieve this goal by December 31, 2004.

Five-Year Vision

We are recognized as the premier wine industry accounting and business consulting firm in Sonoma, Mendocino, and Napa counties. We are leaders in the Moss Adams firm-wide wine industry group, helping to establish Moss Adams as the dominant firm in the Washington and Oregon wine regions. We have trained and developed recognized industry experts in tax, accounting, and business consulting. Our staff is enthusiastic and devoted to the niche.

The Market

• A firmwide objective is to increase the average size of our business client. We expect to manage the wine niche with that objective in mind. However, during the first two to three years, we intend to pursue vineyards and wineries smaller than the firm's more mature niches would. When this niche is more mature we will increase our minimum prospect size. This strategy will help us gain experience, and build confidence in Moss Adams in the industry, as it is an industry that tends to seek firms that are well established in the Wine Industry.
• There are approximately 122 wineries in Sonoma County, 168 in Napa County and 25 in Mendocino County. Of these, approximately 55% have sales over $1 million, and up to one-third have sales in excess of $10 million. In addition to these, there are over 450 vineyards within the same three counties.
• The wine industry appears to be extremely provincial. That combined with the fact that most of our stronger competitors (see "Competition" on the next page) are in Napa County, we consider Sonoma County to be our primary geographic market. However, Mendocino County has a growing wine industry, and we certainly will not pass up opportunities in Napa and other nearby counties in 2001.

Our Strengths

The strengths Moss Adams has in competing in this industry are:
• We are large enough to provide the specific services demanded by this industry.
• Our firm's emphasis is on serving middle-market businesses, while the "Big 5" firms are continually increasing their minimum client size. The majority of the wine industry

EXHIBIT 1
Moss Adams's Wine Niche Strategic Plan, 2001 (continued)

is made up of middle-market companies. This "Big 5" trend increases our market each year.

- We do not try to be all things to all people. We focus our efforts in specialized industries/niches, with the goal of ultimately becoming dominant in those industries.
- We emphasize value-added services, which create more client satisfaction, loyalty, and name recognition.
- We have offices located throughout the West Coast wine regions.
- We have individuals within the firm with significant wine industry experience, including tax, accounting and consulting. We also have experts in closely related industries such as orchards, beverage, and food manufacturing.
- Within California, we have some high profile wine industry clients.
- The majority of our niche members have roots in Sonoma County, which is important to Sonoma County wineries and grape growers.
- Our group is committed to being successful in and ultimately dominating the industry in Sonoma, Napa, and Mendocino counties.

Challenges

- Our experience and credibility in the wine industry are low compared to other firms.
- There has been a perception in the Sonoma County area that we are not local to the area. As we continue to grow and become better known, this should be less of an issue.

If we can minimize our weaknesses by emphasizing our strengths, we will be successful in marketing to the wine industry, allowing us to achieve our ultimate goal of being dominant in the industry.

Competition

There are several CPA firms in Northern California that service vineyards and wineries. The "Big 5" firms are generally considered our biggest competitors in many of the industries we serve, and some have several winery clients. But as noted earlier, their focus seems to be on larger clients, which has decreased their ability to compete in this industry. Of the firms with significant wine industry practices, the following firms appear to be our most significant competitors:

- Motto Kryla & Fisher. This firm is a well-established wine industry leader, with the majority of their client base located in Napa County, although they have many Sonoma County clients. They are moving away from the traditional accounting and tax compliance services, concentrating their efforts on consulting and research projects. We can take advantage of this, along with the perception of many in the industry that they are becoming too much of an insider, and gain additional market share.
- Dal Pagetto & Company. This firm was a split off from Deloitte & Touche several years ago. They are located in Santa Rosa, and have several vineyard and winery clients. At this time, they are probably our biggest Sonoma County competitor. However, they may be too small to compete once our momentum builds.
- Other firms that have significant wine industry practices that we will compete against include G & J Seiberlich & Co., Brotemarkle Davis & Co., Zainer Reinhart & Clarke, Pisenti & Brinker, Deloitte & Touche, and PriceWaterhouseCoopers. The first two are wine industry specialists headquartered in Napa County, and although very competitive there, they each do not appear to have a large Sonoma County client base. The next two are general practice firms with several wine industry clients. However, each of these firms has struggled to hold themselves together in recent years, and they do not appear to have well coordinated wine industry practices. The last two firms listed above are "Big 5" firms that, as noted earlier, focus mostly on the largest wineries.

7.0

(continued)

EXHIBIT 1
Moss Adams's Wine Niche Strategic Plan, 2001 (continued)

7.0

Annual Marketing Plan

Our marketing strategy will build on the foundation we laid during the prior two years. We have established the following as our marketing plan:

- Increase and develop industry knowledge and expertise:
  1. Work with other Moss Adams offices, particularly Stockton, to gain knowledge and experience from their experienced staff. Additionally, work with Stockton to have Santa Rosa Wine Niche staff assigned to two of their winery audits.
  2. Continue to attend industry CPE, including the Vineyard Symposium, the Wine Industry Symposium, the California State Society of CPAs–sponsored wine industry conferences in Napa and San Luis Obispo, and selected Sonoma State University and UC Davis courses. We would like eight hours of wine industry specific CPE for each Senior Level and above committed member of the Wine Niche. Jeff will have final approval on who will attend which classes.
  3. Continue to build our relationship with Sonoma State University (SSU). Our Wine Niche has agreed to be the subject of an SSU case study on the development of a CPA firm wine industry practice. We feel this case study will help us gain additional insight into what it will take to be competitive, as well as give us increased exposure both at SSU and in the industry. We will also seek to become more involved in SSU's wine industry educational program by providing classroom guest speakers twice a year.
  4. Attract and hire staff with wine industry experience. We should strongly consider candidates who have attained a degree through the SSU Wine Business Program. We should also work to recruit staff within the office that have an interest in the industry.
- Continue to form alliances with industry experts both inside and outside the firm. We are building relationships with Ray Blatt of the Moss Adams Los Angeles office who has expertise in wine industry excise and property tax issues. Cheryl Mead of the Santa Rosa office has developed as a Cost Segregation specialist with significant winery experience.
- Develop and use relationships with industry referral sources:
  1. Bankers and attorneys that specialize in the wine industry. From these bankers and attorneys, we would like to see three new leads per year.
  2. Partner with other CPA firms in the industry. Smaller firms may need to enlist the services of a larger firm with a broader range of services, while the "Big 5" firms may want to use a smaller firm to assist with projects that are below their minimum billing size for the project type. We will obtain at least two projects per year using this approach.
  3. Leverage the relationships we have to obtain five referrals and introductions to other wine industry prospects per year.
  4. We will maintain a matrix of Sonoma, Mendocino, and Napa County wineries and vineyards, including addresses, controller or top financial officer, current CPA, and banking relationship. This matrix will be updated as new information becomes available. From this matrix, we will send at least one mailing per quarter.
- Increase our involvement in the following industry trade associations by attending regular meetings and getting to know association members. In one of the following associations, each committed niche member will seek to obtain an office or board position:
  1. Sonoma County Wineries Association
  2. Sonoma County Grape Growers Association

EXHIBIT 1
Moss Adams's Wine Niche Strategic Plan, 2001 (continued)

    3. Sonoma State University Wine Business Program
    4. Zinfandel Advocates and Producers
    5. Women for Winesense
    6. California Association of Winegrape Growers
    7. Wine Institute
- Establish an environment within the niche that promotes and practices the PILLAR concept. Encourage staff in the niche to be creative and strive to be the best. Provide interesting projects and events for the niche to make participation more interesting.
- Use the existing services that Moss Adams offers to market the firm, which include:
    1. BOSS
    2. Business Valuations
    3. Cost Segregation
    4. SCORE!
    5. SALT
    6. Business Assurance Services
    7. Income Tax Compliance Services
- Make use of Firm Resources
    1. Use Moss Adams's Info Edge (document management system) to share and refer to industry related proposals and marketing materials.
        a. All Wine Niche Proposals will be entered into and updated in InfoEdge as completed.
        b. All Wine Niche Marketing letters will be entered into InfoEdge as created.
- Continue to have monthly wine industry niche meetings. We will review the progress on this plan at our March, April, and September niche meetings. Within our niche, we should focus our marketing efforts on Sonoma County, concentrating on smaller prospects that we can grow with, which will enable us to increase our prospect size over time. We would like to be in position to attract the largest wineries in the industry by 2004.
- Establish a Quarterly CFO/Controller roundtable group, with the Moss Adams Wine Industry Group working as facilitator. We will have the Group established and have our first meeting in the summer.
- Quarterly, at our niche meetings, monitor progress on the quantifiable goals in this strategic plan.

Summary

In 2001, one of our goals is to add a minimum of three winery clients to our client base. We feel this is a reasonable goal as long as we continue to implement our plan as written.

We believe we can make the wine industry niche a strong niche in the Santa Rosa office. The firm defines niche dominance as having a minimum of $500,000 in billings, a 20% market share, and having 40% of the services provided be in value-added service codes. We expect to become the dominant industry force in Sonoma, Mendocino, and Napa counties by 2004.

We are also willing to assist other offices within the firm to establish wine industry niches, eventually leading to a mature niche within the firm. We believe with the proper effort we can accomplish each of these goals.

The meeting took place just before the height of the busy tax and audit season. Gutsch, 39, had been concentrating on the firm's clients in its construction industry niche. He had not made as much headway developing new business with wine industry clients as he had hoped and opened the meeting by saying:

7.0

I think the issue we are all struggling with is how to break into a well-established mature niche. Do we discount fees? If so, is that our desired position in servicing the wine industry? Do we advertise? Seems like a big commitment for something that we can't be sure will produce results. Do we just get on every panel we can and shake as many hands as we can? I'm still trying to find the right formula.

Chris Pritchard, an accounting manager who had worked with Gutsch for 2 years to develop the wine niche, said:

Sorry, Jeff, but I've been too busy working in health care. Health care is taking off, so my time is limited on the wine side. There's something missing, sort of a spark in this niche. There's not as much of a hunger to close, to go out and actually close a deal, or at least go out and meet with somebody. I think that's what's lacking for our success right now. I think we have all of the tools we need. But we don't have an aggressive nature to go out and start shaking hands and asking for business. We're doing everything else except asking for the business. We don't follow up.

Neysa Sloan, a senior accountant, nodded in assent:

I personally do not see us making our objectives of gathering 20% of the market share in the regional wine industry over the next 3–5 years. Our marketing tactics are not up to the challenge. We need to seriously look at what we have done in the last year or two, what we are currently doing, and what we are proposing to do in regards to marketing. If we looked at this objectively, we would see that we have not gained much ground in the past using our current tactics—why would it work now? If you allowed more individuals to market and be involved, we might get somewhere.

Cheryl Mead, a senior manager whose specialty was conducting cost segregation (cost segregation is a process of breaking a large asset into its smaller components so that depreciation may be taken on an accelerated basis) studies, commented:

Growing wineries are looking for help. We need to focus on wineries that are expanding their facilities, and then grow with their growing businesses. Value-added services like cost segregation could represent as much as 40% of our wine industry practice. If we want to get in, we've got to do much more networking, marketing, and presentations. The challenge for us here in Santa Rosa is how to manage our resources. Career choices are changing; you

can't be a generalist anymore. We need both people-related and technical skills, but those don't usually go hand-in-hand. We need someone who is famous in the field, a "who's who" in the wine accounting industry.

Claire Calderon, also a senior tax manager, said to the team:

This is a hard niche to break into, Jeff. It takes a long time to develop relationships in specific industries. It could take a couple of years. First you find forums to meet people, get to know people, get people to trust you and then you get an opportunity to work on a project and you do a good job. It takes a while. Our goal is to become a trusted advisor and that doesn't happen overnight.

Gutsch replied:

While consolidation is happening in the wine industry, many of the wineries we are targeting are still privately owned. When you're dealing with privately owned businesses it's much more personal than with public companies.

Calderon added:

That might explain part of it, Jeff, but the reality is that there are two other fledgling niches that are doing well and going like gangbusters. This niche is off to a slow start!

Barbara Korte, a senior accountant, reassured him:

Jeff, you have been very focused, very enthusiastic about this project. You've put a lot of time into it. As a leader, I think you are a real good manager.

At stake was the opportunity to generate significant incremental client fee revenues. More than 600 wine producers and vineyards (grape growers) were in business in the premium Northern California wine-growing region encompassing Napa, Sonoma, and Mendocino counties. According to the Summer 2000 issue of *Marketplace*, there were 168 wine producers and 228 vineyards in Napa; 122 wine producers and 196 vineyards in Sonoma; and 25 wine producers and 61 vineyards in Mendocino. Few of these operations were large, according to *Marketplace*. Napa and Sonoma each had 14 wine producers reporting over $10 million in sales, and Mendocino, only one.

Company Background

Moss Adams was a regional accounting firm. It had four regional hubs within the firm: Southern California, Northern California, Washington, and Oregon. By late 2000, Moss Adams had become one of the 15 largest accounting firms in the United States, with 150 partners, 740 CPAs, and 1,200 employees. Founded in 1913 and headquartered in Seattle, the full-service firm specialized in middle-market companies, those with annual revenues of $10–$200 million.

Each office had a managing partner. Art King was the managing partner of the Santa Rosa office (Exhibit 2). The

EXHIBIT 2
Moss Adams's Organizational Chart

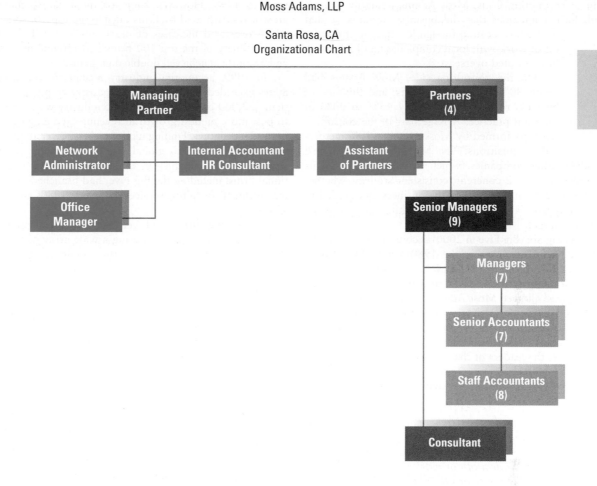

Moss Adams, LLP

Santa Rosa, CA
Organizational Chart

7.0

firm was considered mid-size and its client base tended to mirror that size. King reflected on Moss Adams's advantages of size and location:

. . . it is an advantage to be a regional firm with a strong local presence. For one thing, there just aren't that many regional firms, especially out here on the West Coast. In fact, I think we're the only true West Coast regional firm. That gives us access to a tremendous number of resources that the larger firms have. We have the added advantage of being a big part of Sonoma County. Sonoma County companies want the same kind of services they can get from the Big Five operating out of places like San Francisco, but they also like to deal with local firms that are active in the community. Our staff is active in Rotary, 20–30, the local chambers of commerce, and so on, and that means a lot to the businesspeople in the area. Sonoma County companies will go to San Francisco for professional services, but only if they have to, so we offer the best of both worlds.

Each office within the firm was differentiated. An office like Santa Rosa had the ability to be strong in more niches because it was one of the dominant firms in the area. Moss Adams did not have to directly compete with the Big Five accounting firms because they were not interested in providing services to small to mid-size businesses. Since it was a regional firm, Moss Adams was able to offer a depth of services that most local firms were not able to match. This gave Moss Adams a competitive advantage when selling services to the middle market company segment.

Moss Adams provided services in four main areas of expertise: business assurance (auditing), tax, international, and consulting. Auditing comprised approximately 35% to 40% of Moss Adams's practice, the remainder being divided among tax work in corporate, partnerships, trusts and estates, and individual taxation. In its Santa Rosa office, Moss Adams serviced corporate business and high-wealth individuals.

On the international side, Moss Adams was a member of Moores Rowland International, a worldwide association of accounting firms. Moss Adams primarily worked with local companies that did business overseas or that wanted to set up a foreign location. It also did a lot of work with local companies that had parent firms located overseas.

7.0

On the consulting side, Moss Adams had about 80 full-time consultants, and this line of business represented probably 15% to 20% of the total practice. A large part of the consulting work performed by Moss Adams was in mergers and acquisitions. Its M&A division helped middle-market companies, which formed the bulk of its clientele, develop a coherent, consistent strategy, whether they were planning on selling the business and needed to find an appropriate buyer or were looking for a good acquisition target.

The Big Six (Big Five in 2000) accounting firms had developed niche strategies in the 1980s, and Moss Adams had been one of the first mid-level accounting firms in the nation to identify niches as a strategy. Adopting a niche strategy had allowed Moss Adams to target a basket of services to a particular industry of regional importance. As each practice developed a niche, it also identified the "famous people" in that niche. These people became the "go-to" people, the leaders of that niche.

The high-technology sector represented one of the fastest-growing parts of Moss Adams's business. According to King:

It's big in the Seattle area (where Moss Adams has its headquarters), and with the development of Telecom Valley, it's certainly becoming big in Sonoma County. We're finding that a great deal of our work is coming from companies that are offshoots of other large high-tech companies in the area. Financial institutions represent another client group that's growing rapidly, as is health care. With all of the changes in the health care and medical fields, there's been a good deal of turmoil. We have a lot of expertise in the health care and medical areas, so that's a big market for us. Have I seen a drop-off? No, not really. The interesting thing about the accounting industry is that even when the economy slows down, there's still a lot of work for a CPA firm. There might not be as many large, special projects as when the economy is really rolling, but the work doesn't slow down.

The Industry and the Market

Accounting was a large and relatively stable service industry, according to *The Journal of Accountancy*, the industry's most widely read trade publication. The Big Five accounting firms (Andersen Worldwide, PriceWaterhouseCoopers, Ernst & Young, Deloitte & Touche, and KPMG) dominated the global market in 1998 with combined global revenue ex-

ceeding $58 billion, well over half of the industry's total revenue. All of the Big Five firms reported double-digit growth rates in 1998. However, some of the most spectacular growth was achieved by firms outside the top 10, some of which registered increases of nearly 60% over 1997 revenues. Ninety of the top 100 firms had revenue increases, and 58 of them achieved double-digit gains.

In 1999, accounting industry receipts in the United States exceeded $65 billion. The industry employed more than 632,000 people. However, the industry was expected to post more modest growth in revenues and employment in the 21st century. Finding niche markets, diversifying services, and catering to global markets were key growth strategies for companies in the industry. Large international firms, including the Big Five, had branched out into management consulting services in the late 1980s and early 1990s.

Accounting firms and certified public accountants (CPAs) nationwide began offering a wide array of services in addition to traditional accounting, auditing, and bookkeeping services. This trend was partially a response to clients' demand for "one-stop shopping" for all their professional services needs. Another cause was the relatively flat growth in demand for traditional accounting and auditing services over the past 10 years, as well as the desire of CPAs to develop more value-added services. The addition of management consulting, legal, and other professional services to the practice mix of large national accounting networks was transforming the industry.

Many firms began offering technology consulting because of growing client demand for Internet and e-commerce services. *Accounting Today*'s 1999 survey of CPA clients indicated that keeping up with technology was *the* strategic issue of greatest concern, followed by recruiting and retaining staff, competing with larger companies, planning for executive succession, and maximizing productivity.

However, according to *The CPA Journal*, the attractive consulting fees may have led many firms to ignore potential conflicts of interest in serving as an auditor and as a management consultant to the same client. The profession's standards could be jeopardized by the entrance of non-CPA partners and owners in influential accounting firms. Many companies facing these problems split their accounting and management consulting operations. In January 2001, Arthur Andersen spun off its consulting division and renamed it "Accenture" to avoid accusations of impropriety.

Still, CPA firms could be expected to continue to develop their capabilities and/or strategic alliances to meet clients' demands. Some other areas of expansion among accounting firms included administrative services, financial and investment planning services, general management services, government administration, human resources, international operations, information technology and computer systems consulting, litigation support, manufacturing administration, marketing, and research and development. Many small and medium-size independent firms were merging or forming alliances with large service companies such as American Express, H&R Block, and Century Business Services.

By the late 1990s, a trend toward consolidation got under way in the accounting industry. Several factors were fueling the drive toward consolidation. Large increases in revenue among the top 100 accounting firms between 1997 and 1998 may have been partially attributable to this trend toward consolidation. Consolidators wanted access to the large volume of business currently being done by independent CPAs. The trust that small businesses and individuals had in their CPAs was considered very valuable, and consolidators wanted to leverage the potential of an individual firm's integrity to expand their own businesses. Consolidation caused a decline in the number of independent accounting firms that offered only tax and accounting services. The New York State Society of CPAs estimated that there was a strong possibility that up to 50 of the largest accounting firms in the United States would dissolve or merge with other entities by the end of the year 2000. In the San Franciso Bay area, for example, the Big Five dominated the industry (Exhibit 3).

The Wine Industry Niche

The wine industry practice was a new niche for the Santa Rosa office, as well as for Moss Adams in general. Moss Adams allowed any employee to propose a niche. All accounting firms bill at fairly standard rates, so the more business generated, the greater the profit. Moss Adams felt it was in their long-term best interest to allow employees to focus on areas in which they were interested. The firm would benefit from revenues generated, but, more importantly, employees would likely stay with a firm that allowed a degree of personal freedom and promoted professional growth.

Gutsch and Pritchard had begun this niche in mid-1998 for several reasons. First, both had an interest in the industry. Second, Sonoma and Napa counties had 200 wineries and numerous vineyard operations. Third, Moss Adams had expertise in related or similar business lines such as orchards, as well as significant related experience in providing services to the manufacturing sector. Finally, the wine industry had been historically serviced by either large firms that considered the typical winery a small client, or by smaller firms that were not able to offer the range of services that Moss Adams could provide.

Sara Rogers, a senior accountant and member of the wine niche team, recalled:

It first started with Jeff Gutsch and Chris Pritchard and another senior manager, who was in our office until November 1999. Anyway, I think it was their motivation that really started the group. The three of them were doing everything in building the niche. When the senior manager left, it sort of fell flat on its face for a little while. I think it

got stagnant. Pretty much nobody said anything about it until last summer, when Jeff started the organization of it again and brought in more people, and then he approached people that he wanted to work with.

Gutsch felt that Moss Adams was in position to move forward to make the wine industry niche a strong niche both in the Santa Rosa office and, eventually, the firm as a whole. He was committed to that goal and expected to achieve it within 5 years. Gutsch saw this niche as his door to future partnership. Moss Adams's marketing strategy included the following:

1. Develop industry marketing materials that communicate Moss Adams's strengths and commitment.
2. Develop a distinctive logo for use in the industry.
3. Create an industry brochure similar to that of the firm's construction industry group.
4. Develop industry service information flyers such as the business lifecycle, R&E (Research & Exploration) credit, excise tax compliance, and BOSS (Business Ownership Succession Services).
5. Develop relationships with industry referral sources (e.g., bankers and attorneys that specialized in the wine industry or current clients who served or had contacts in the industry).
6. Join and become active in industry trade associations.
7. Use existing relationships with industry contacts to obtain leads into prospective wineries and vineyards.
8. Use the existing services that Moss Adams offered to market the firm, particularly in Cost Segregation.
9. Focus efforts on Sonoma County, as well as adjacent wine-growing regions, which would enable Moss Adams to increase its prospect size over time.

Pritchard reflected on those early days:

The first thing we did was to develop a database of regional wineries and send out an introduction letter. The other thing we did was to develop marketing materials. Jeff developed a logo. We used a top-down approach pyramid for an introduction letter, starting out general and then with an action step at the end to call us. So, we used that at first. Usually with that we'd get about 2% response, which is good, out of 300 letters or whatever we sent out.

However, according to King, the major issue in growing the wine industry practice was selling:

The thing about selling in public accounting is that you have to have a lot of confidence in what you do and what you can do for the client. You have to have confidence that you know something about the industry. If you go into a marketing meeting, or a proposal meeting and you're saying, "Well, we do a couple of wineries but we really want to do more and get better at it," you're not going to get the work. You gain confidence by knowing how to talk the lan-

7.0

EXHIBIT 3

Top 20 Accounting Firms in the San Francisco Bay Area, Ranked by Number of Bay Area CPAs, June 2000

Rank	1999 Rank	Company	No. Bay Area CPAs	No. Company CPAs	No. Bay Area Employees	1999 Billings Bay Area	No. Partners in Bay Area	No. Company Partners	FYE	US Net Revenue ($mil)	% Chg. vs. Prev. Yr.
1	2	Deloitte & Touche LLP	439	8,380	1,437	NR	172	2,066	May 99	$5,336.00	24.2
2	1	PricewaterhouseCoopers LLP	430	430	2,000	NR	138	9,000	Sep. 99	6,956.00	18.7
3	3	KPMG Peat Marwick LLP	316	NR	1,778	NR	157	6,800	Jun. 99	4,112.00	21.5
4	4	Arthur Andersen**	312	6,161	821	NR	63	3,059	Aug. 99	3,300.00	17.9
5	5	Ernst & Young LLP	300	NR	850	NR	77	2,465	Sep. 99	6,100.00	10.0
6	6	BDO Seldman LLP	72	1,650	122	NR	15	360	Jun. 00	408.00	36.9
7	14	Seiler & Co. LLP	44	44	110	NR	12	12	NR	NR	NR
8	7	Frank, Runerman & Co. LLP	43	51	76	NR	12	13	May 99	17.23	9.2
9	9	Hood & Strong LLP	42	42	89	NR	12	12	NR	NR	NR
10*	10	Harb, Levy & Weiland LLP	38	38	80	NR	13	13	NR	NR	NR
10*	13	Ireland San Filippo LLP	38	38	81	12.7M	13	17	Apr. 00	12.71	15.8
12	15	Burr, Pilger & Mayer	35	35	110	NR	10	10	NR	NR	NR
13	11	Armanino McKenna LLP	34	34	87	NR	13	13	NR	NR	NR
14	14	Novogradac & Co. LLP	31	36	80	NR	6	8	NR	NR	NR
15	12	RINA Accountancy Corp.	26	29	59	7.3M	13	14	NR	NR	NR
16*	16	Grant Thornton LLP	25	1,300	90	NR	10	300	Jul. 00	416.00	10.9
16*	18	Shea Labagh Dobberstein	25	25	35	NR	3	3	NR	NR	NR
18	18	Moss Adams LLP	24	800	39	NR	7	144	Dec. 99	109.00	31.3
19	16	Lindquist, von Husen & Joyce	23	23	47	NR	5	5	NR	NR	NR
20	21	Lautze & Lautze	21	28	39	NR	9	11	NR	NR	NR

Sources: Viva Chan, *San Francisco Business Times*, 14 146, June 16, 2000, p. 28; Strafford Publications, *Public Accounting Reports*, vol. XXIV, June 2000.

NR = Not reported.

*Indicates tie in ranking.

**Excludes consulting.

guage, knowing the buzzwords, knowing some of the players in the industry. You go into a meeting, all of a sudden you're on an equal footing with them. From a confidence standpoint, that's huge. You can't sell public accounting services unless you're confident about you and your firm and the people that are going to do the work. Over the last 2 years, Jeff has gone to the classes, gone to the meetings and his confidence level is much higher than it was a year ago. When he goes into these meetings he's going to be at a level where he doesn't have to make excuses for not having a lot of winery clients, because we have a lot of activity in the wine and the beverage processing industries. So, I think that's going to help a lot. That's where he's going to have more success because we're getting the at bats, we just need to get some hits.

One of the roles of the managing partner was to mentor potential partners and help them attain the role of partner. The training process included marketing and helping them build a practice, according to King:

When we're talking with senior managers, I explain to them what they need to do to get to that next level. I had this conversation with Jeff because his primary focus when he came was, "I need to build a big practice, nothing else matters." He trusts the system now. He's transferred some clients to others and received some clients. You have to work well with people, you have to train people, you have to have some responsibilities, and you have to get along with your peers.

The firm's philosophy was to encourage people to really enjoy what they did. Anyone was allowed to propose a niche, even a senior manager. Pritchard explained:

Well, part of the way our firm works is, there is a "four-bucket" tier to make partner. One of the buckets is to become a famous person and the fastest way of doing that is through the niche base; within a niche you get the experience and the reputation faster than you would as a generalist. Jeff is a senior manager, so now he's trying to figure out a way to become partner. I work on Bonny Doon Winery. I have a grower client in Kenwood, so I do have some experience with that. I also like wine because I make wine. It's an untapped market in Sonoma County for our firm. So we both got together—I had the entrepreneurial spirit to start and Jeff had the need.

King described in detail the "four bucket" evaluation system at Moss Adams:

We have four criteria that get evaluated by the partners and the compensation committee on a scale of one to ten. All of these are weighted equally, 25%, with a possibility of 40 points. The first is financial. We take a look at the potential partner's financial responsibilities, what their billings are, what their fee adjustments are, what their charge hours are. I've transferred many clients to people in the of-

fice. That's one way I help others grow their practices. I'm still responsible for some of those clients, because I'm the one who brought them in and I'm still the primary contact. My billing numbers may be this, but my overall financial responsibility may be bigger. That's an objective measure because we look at the numbers, we look at the trends.

The second is responsibility. Managing partner of a big office gets more points than the managing partner of a smaller office does, who in turn gets more points than a person in charge of a niche, who in turn gets more points than a line partner. Somebody who is a partner and is responsible for the tax department, let's say, might get an extra point or half a point, whereas someone in charge of a niche might get an extra point. If they're in charge of an office they get more points.

The third is personnel. Personnel is a very big initiative within Moss Adams. Upstream and downstream evaluations are conducted by our HR person for each office and measures staff retention and the quality of our mentoring program. Each partner is also evaluated up or down from an overall office rating score. For example, our office may get a "seven," but I may get an "eight" because I'm really good with people. Somebody who's really hard on people would get a lower rating.

The fourth and final "bucket" is peer evaluation. We have three other partners evaluate each partner. They evaluate the partner for training, mentoring, marketing, and involvement in their community. Then, evaluations are used by the compensation committee to review individual partner compensation. They are also used for partner counseling sessions.

King also assured a "soft landing" to the participants of the niche teams. This meant that if a niche didn't work out, he would assure the individuals that another niche in the firm would be found for them. This, it was hoped, fostered entrepreneurial behavior. According to King:

A high level of practice responsibility for a partner would be $1 million in this office. The range is anywhere from $600,000 to $1 million in billings a year. The overall picture is where we try to get people involved in at least two niches in the office, until a niche becomes large enough that you can spend full-time in it. The upside, potentially, of the wine niche would be a practice of from $500,000 to $1,000,000 based on Sonoma and maybe some Napa County wineries. So, the upside is a very mature, profitable niche that fits right into our model of our other niches of middle market companies that have the need, not only for client services, but also our value-added services.

If for some reason the wine niche didn't take off, Jeff would become more involved in the manufacturing niche—well, wine is manufacturing anyway, but it's just a subset of manufacturing. It might slow his rate to partner. It could

7.0

also turn out that—all of a sudden—Jeff gets four great referrals in the manufacturing niche this year, he builds this great big practice in manufacturing, and as a result he has less time for the wine niche. The downside is we've spent some money on marketing, and Jeff has spent some time on marketing when he could have been doing something else. Then, we abandon the project. If that happens, then Jeff's time becomes available and the money becomes available to go after some other initiative or something we're already doing or some new initiative. Nobody is going to lose his or her job over it. We haven't lost a lot of money over it.

The Aftermath

After the January 2001 meeting. Gutsch pondered how he should proceed to overcome some major roadblocks to building his team. King took Gutsch aside for counseling:

. . . target the $10 million to under $20 million winery for which we can provide a full range of services. There's nobody else with our range of services that's really doing a good job in that area. There's an under-served market for those middle-market companies. When you started, I knew it would take 2 to 3 years to really get the ball rolling. This is really going to be your year, Jeff. If it isn't, well, we'll reevaluate at the end of the year. Our overall marketing budget is probably in the area of 1.5% to 2% of total client

billings. In 1999, the first year for the wineries, we probably spent somewhere in the neighborhood of $5,000 to $8,000, which wasn't a lot but you joined some organizations and you did some training. Last year we probably spent $10,000 to $12,000. Now, Jeff, I know that some of our other offices spend a lot more on marketing than we do. We'll have to decide: is this the best use of your time? Is this the best use of our resources to try to go after an industry where we just tried for three years and haven't made any inroads?

The decision to develop a niche had been based upon a gut feeling. Moss Adams did not use any litmus test or hurdle rate of return to screen possible niches. This was because, with the exception of nonprofits, most clients had similar fee realization rates. Moss Adams looked at the potential volume of business and determined whether it could handle that volume. Yet Moss Adams remained unknown in the wine industry. Time was running out.

This case study was prepared by Professors Armand Gilinsky, Jr. and Sherri Anderson at Sonoma State University as a basis for class discussion rather than to illustrate either effective or ineffective handling of an administrative situation. This case was originally presented at the 2001 meeting of the North American Case Research Association in Memphis, Tenn. The authors gratefully acknowledge the support of Moss Adams PLC and the Wine Business Program at Sonoma State University for assistance in preparation of this case.

7.0

Integrative Case 8.1

Littleton Manufacturing (A)*

Rule #1 for business organizations: People, not structure, make a business work or fail. Blindly following organizational concepts that have worked elsewhere is a sure way to waste talent and get poor results. Organizational change alone achieves nothing, while dedicated people can make any structure work. This doesn't mean that organizational changes shouldn't happen. But design any changes to get the most out of people in the company's unique circumstances. Top management should never dictate change as a cure-all to avoid facing fundamental problems.

Quotation from the Harvard Business Review
(title and author uncited) posted on the wall of
Bill Larson, Plant Manager of Littleton Manufacturing

On June 21, 1990, Paul Winslow, the director of human resources at Littleton Manufacturing, was told by his boss, Bill Larson, to put together a team of employees to address a number of issues that Larson thought were hurting Littleton's bottom line. Winslow's assignment had come about as a result of his making a presentation on those problems to Larson. Larson had then met with his executive staff, and he and Winslow had subsequently gone to the plant's Quality Steering Committee to discuss what to do. They decided to form a Human Resources Process Improvement Team (PIT) to prioritize the issues and propose a corrective course of action. Winslow, who had been at the plant for seventeen years, had been asked by Larson to chair the PIT.

The Quality Steering Committee decided that the PIT should include two representatives each from Sales and Marketing, Fabrication, and Components. Two managers from each of these areas were chosen, including Dan Gordon, the fabrication manufacturing manager, and Phil Hanson, the components manufacturing manager. There were no supervisors or hourly employees on the team.

At the first meeting, the PIT discussed the six widely recognized problem areas that Winslow had identified to Larson. Each member's assignment for the next meeting, on June 28, was to prioritize the issues and propose an action plan.

The Problems

A course in management and organizational studies carried out by students at a nearby college had started the chain of events that led to the formation of the Human Resources PIT. In late 1989, Winslow was approached by a faculty member at a local college who was interested in using Littleton as a site for a field-project course. Because of ongoing concerns about communication at the plant by all lev-els, Winslow asked that the students assess organizational communication at Littleton. Larson gave his approval, and in the spring of 1990 the students carried out the project, conducting individual and group interviews with employees at all levels of the plant.

Winslow and his staff combined the results of the students' assessment with the results of an in-house survey done several years earlier. The result was the identification of six problem areas that they thought were critical for the plant to address:

- Lack of organizational unity
- Lack of consistency in enforcing rules and procedures
- Supervisor's role poorly perceived
- Insufficient focus on Littleton's priorities
- Change is poorly managed
- Lack of a systematic approach to training

The Company

Littleton Manufacturing, located in rural Minnesota, was founded in 1925. In 1942, Littleton was bought by Brooks Industries, a major manufacturer of domestic appliances and their components. At that time, Littleton manufactured custom-made and precision-machined components from special metals for a variety of industries.

In 1983, through the purchase of a larger competitor, Frühling, Inc., Brooks was able to increase its domestic market share from 8 percent to about 25 percent. Brooks then decided to have only one facility produce the components that were used in most of the products it made in the United States. The site chosen was Littleton Manufacturing. To do this, Brooks added a whole new business (Components) to Littleton's traditional activity. To accommodate the new line, a building of 80,000 square feet was added to the old Littleton plant, bringing the total to 220,000 square feet of plant space. Because of the addition of this new business, Littleton went from 150 employees in 1984 to 600 in 1986. In mid-1990, there were about 500 employees.

The older part of the plant (the Fabrication side) manufactured its traditional custom-made products and sold them to a variety of industrial customers. It also supplied the newer side of the plant (the Components side) with a variety of parts that were further processed and used to make electrical components. These components were used by all other Brooks plants in the assembly of domestic appliances that were sold worldwide. About 95 percent of the products made on the Components side of the plant originated on the Fabrication side.

The plant was also headquarters for Brooks Industries' sales and marketing department, known as the "commercial group," which had worldwide sales responsibilities for products made by the Fabrication side. These included international and domestic sales of products to several industries, including the semiconductor, consumer electronics, and nuclear furnace industry. This group marketed products made not only by Littleton Manufacturing but also those made by Brooks's other fourteen plants, all located in the United States.

Bill Larson, the plant manager, reported to the executive vice president of manufacturing of Brooks, whose corporate office was in Chicago, Illinois. Larson met once a month with his boss and the other plant managers. Reporting directly to Larson were six functional line managers and the manager of the Quality Improvement System (QIS). This group of seven managers, known as the "staff," met weekly to plan and discuss how things were going. (See Exhibit 1 for an organizational chart.)

In December 1989, there were 343 hourly and 125 salaried employees at the plant. About 80 percent of the workforce was under 45. Seventy-seven percent were male,

and 23 percent were female. Seventy-six percent had been at the plant 10 years or less. All of the hourly workers were represented by the Teamsters union.

The Financial Picture
Brooks Industries

Brooks was the second largest producer of its kind of domestic appliances in the United States. Its three core business units were commercial/industrial, consumer, and original equipment manufacturing. The major U.S. competitors for its domestic appliances were Eagleton, Inc., and Universal Appliances, Inc. In the United States, Eagleton's market share was 47 percent; Brooks had about 23 percent; and Universal Appliances and a number of small companies had the remaining 30 percent. However, U.S. manufacturers were facing increasing competition, primarily based on lower prices, from companies in Asia and eastern Europe.

In 1989, Brooks's sales declined 4 percent, and in 1990, they declined another 5 percent, to $647 million. Their 1989 annual report contained the following statement about the company's financial condition: "There was fierce competition...which led to a decline in our share of a stable market and a fall in prices, resulting in a lower level of sales.... With sales volume showing slower growth, we failed to reduce our costs proportionately and there was underutilization of capacity." In May 1990, after announcing unexpected first-quarter losses, Brooks started a corporation-wide efficiency drive, including planned layoffs of 16 percent of its workforce, a corporate restructuring, and renewed emphasis on managerial accountability for bottom-line results.

Because of its worsening financial condition, for the past few years Brooks had been reducing the resources

EXHIBIT 1
Littleton Manufacturing Organizational Chart

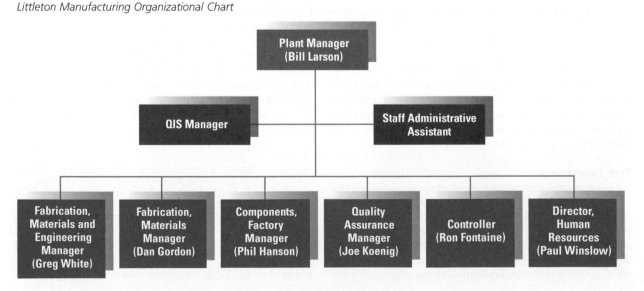

available to Littleton. For example, Larson's budget for salaries had been increased by only 4 percent each year for the past several years. As a result, supervisors and middle managers complained strongly that recent salary increases had been too little and that plant salaries were too low. They also felt that the forced-ranking performance appraisal system used by the plant, which was based on a bell curve, did not reward good performance adequately. One middle manager commented: "All we get now for good performance is a card and a turkey." In April 1990, the company cut Littleton's capital budget by half and stipulated that any new project involving nonessential items had to have a one-year payback.

In addition, in both 1988 and 1989 Brooks had charged the Littleton plant around $300,000 for various services provided, such as technical support, but in 1990 this charge was increased by $1 million. Many of the Littleton plant managers felt that this was done to help offset Brooks's deteriorating financial condition and were frustrated by it. Indicating that he thought Brooks was using Littleton as a cash cow, one staff member said, "The more profitable we get, the more corporate will charge us."

Many managers, especially those on the Fabrication side, felt that even though they had made money for the plant, corporate's increase in charges nullified their success and hard work. A number of managers on the Fabrication side also feared that if their operation did not do well financially, the company might close it down.

In discussing the increasing lack of resources available from corporate and the plant's own decline in profits, Larson said: "There needs to be a change in the way people here think about resources. They have to think more in terms of efficiency." He was proud of the fact that the company had achieved its goal of reducing standard costs by 1 percent for each of the past three years and that in 1990 cost reductions would equal 5 percent of production value. He thought that if the company reduced the number of reworks, costs could be lowered by another 20 to 30 percent.

Littleton Manufacturing

The Fabrication and the Components operations at Littleton Manufacturing were managed as cost centers by Brooks while the commercial group was a profit center. (A *profit center* is a part of an organization that is responsible for accumulating revenues as well as costs. A *cost center* is an organizational division or unit of activity in which accounts are maintained containing direct costs for which the center's head is responsible.) In 1989 and 1990, the Fabrication side of Littleton had done well in terms of budgeted costs, while the Components side had incurred significant losses for both years.

Littleton's net worth increased from $319,000 in 1989 to $3,094,000 in 1990 due to the addition of a new Fabrication-side product that was sold on the external market and had required no additional assets or resources.

In 1990, sales for the plant as a whole were $41,196,000, with an operating profit of 3.7 percent, down from 7.3 percent in 1989. Larson estimated that the current recession, which was hurting the company, would lower sales in 1991 by 10 percent. Exhibit 2 presents an operating statement for Littleton Manufacturing from 1988 to 1990.

The Quality Improvement System

8.1

In 1985, corporate mandated a total quality management effort, the Quality Improvement System (QIS), which replaced the quality circles that the plant had instituted in 1980. Posted throughout the plant was a Quality Declaration, which had been developed by Larson and his staff. It read:

We at Littleton Manufacturing are dedicated to achieving lasting quality. This means that each of us must understand and meet the requirements of our customers and coworkers. We all must continually strive for improvement and error-free work in all we do—in every job . . . on time . . . all the time.

Bill Larson was enthusiastic about QIS. He saw QIS as a total quality approach affecting not just products but all of the plant's processes, one that would require a long-term effort at changing the culture at the plant. He felt that QIS was already reaping benefits in terms of significant improvements in quality, and that the system had also greatly helped communication at the plant.

In the QIS all employees were required to participate in Departmental Quality Teams (DQTs) that met in groups of six to twelve every two weeks for at least an hour to identify ways to improve quality. Most hourly employees were on only one DQT; middle managers were, on average, on three DQTs. Some managers were on as many as six. The results of each team's efforts were exhibited in graphs and charts by their work area and updated monthly. There were about sixty teams in the plant.

The leader from each Departmental Quality Team, a volunteer, served also as a member of a Quality Improvement Team (QIT), whose goals were to support the DQTs and help them link their goals to the company's goals. QITs consisted of six to eight people; each was chaired by a member of the executive staff. These staff members, along with Bill Larson, composed the Quality Steering Committee (QSC) for the plant. The QSC's job was to oversee the direction and implementation of the Quality Improvement System for the plant and to coordinate with corporate's quality improvement programs. The QSC also sometimes formed corrective action teams to work on special projects. Unlike DQTs, which were composed of employees from a single department or work area, corrective action teams had members from different functions or departments. By 1986, there were nine corrective action teams, but by 1989, none were functioning. When asked

8.1

EXHIBIT 2
Littleton Manufacturing Operating Profit Statement

	1988	1989	1990
Fabrication			
Sales	$16,929	$18,321	$19,640
Direct costs	11,551	11,642	11,701
Contribution margin	5,378	6,679	7,939
% of sales	31.8%	36.5%	40.4%
All other operating costs	4,501	4,377	4,443
Operating profit	877	2,301	3,496
% to sales	5.2%	12.6%	17.8%
Components			
Sales	$20,468	$15,590	$21,556
Direct costs	16,049	10,612	18,916
Contribution margin	4,419	4,978	2,640
% of sales	21.6%	31.9%	12.2%
All other operating costs	4,824	4,797	4,628
Operating profit	(405)	180	(1,988)
% to sales	−2.0%	1.2%	−9.2%
Total Littleton Manufacturing			
Sales	$37,397	$33,911	$41,196
Direct costs	27,599	22,254	30,617
Contribution margin	9,798	11,657	10,579
% to sales	26.2%	34.4%	25.7%
All other operating costs	9,326	9,175	9,071
Operating profit	472	2,482	1,508
% to sales	1.3%	7.3%	3.7%

Note: Changes in Operating Profit from year to year are posted to retained earnings (net worth) account on the corporate balance sheet. It must be noted, however, that the balance sheet figures include the impact of headquarters, national organization changes, and extraordinary income from other operations, which are not reflected on the operating profit statement shown above.
Source: Controller, Littleton Manufacturing.

about them, Winslow said, "I'm not sure what happened to them. They just sort of died out."

Larson and most managers believed that the QIS had improved quality. On most of its Fabrication products, the company competed on the basis of quality and customer service, and the vice president of sales and marketing thought that their quality was the best in the industry. In 1988 and 1989, the plant won several Brooks awards for quality and was publicly cited by a number of customers for quality products.

Hourly employees in general also thought that QIS had improved quality, although they were less enthusiastic about the system than management. A number of hourly employees complained that since participation was mandatory, many groups were held back by unmotivated members. They thought participation should be voluntary. Another complaint was that there was inadequate training for

group leaders, with the result that some groups were not productive.

In the spring of 1990, the company decided that the QIS effort was "stagnating" and that DQTs should be changed to include members from different departments. It was thought that this would improve communication and coordination between departments and lead to further improvements in quality, productivity, and on-time delivery. DQTs became known is IDQTs (Interdepartmental Quality Teams). IDQTs were scheduled to begin in November 1990. In addition, the company decided to begin Process Improvement Teams (PITs), which would focus on various ongoing processes at the plant, such as budgeting and inventory management. A PIT, composed of managers from different functions, would not be ongoing but only last as long as it took to achieve its particular goals.

How Different Levels Perceived the Problems

In order to choose the issues to tackle first and to devise a tentative plan for addressing them, Winslow reflected on the background information he had on the six problem areas that he and his staff had identified on the basis of their own analysis and the students' assessment of organizational communication.

A Lack of Organizational Unity

People often talked about "this side of the wall and that side of the wall" in describing the plant. They were referring to the wall separating the newer Components side and the older Fabrication side of the plant. (Some parts of the Fabrication side had been built in the twenties.) The Components side was brighter, cleaner, and more open, and, in summer, it was cooler. In comparing the two sides, one manager said, "At the end of the shift in Fabrication, you come out looking like you've been through the wringer." On the whole, the equipment in the Components side was also newer, with most of it dating from the 1970s and 1980s and some of it state-of-the-art machinery that was developed at the plant. Much of the equipment on the Fabrication side went back to the 1950s and 1960s. These differences in age meant that, in general, the machinery on the Fabrication side required more maintenance.

It was generally agreed that Components jobs were cleaner and easier, and allowed more social interaction. On the Fabrication side many of the machines could run only two to three hours before needing attention, whereas on the Components side the machines might run for days without worker intervention. On the Fabrication side, because of the placement of the machines and the need for frequent maintenance, people tended to work more by themselves and to "be on the go all the time." It was not uncommon for senior hourly employees in Fabrication to request a transfer to Components.

Hourly workers described Components as "a country club" compared to the Fabrication side. Many attributed this to how the different sides were managed. Enforcement of rules was more lax on the Components side. For example, rules requiring safety shoes and goggles were not as strictly enforced, and some operators were allowed to eat on the job.

One Human Resources staff member described Components supervisors as "laid-back about sticking to the rules" and those in Fabrication as "sergeants." He saw the manufacturing manager of Fabrication, Dan Gordon, as having a clear vision of what he wanted for the Fabrication side and a definite plan on how to get there. He also saw Gordon as keeping a tight rein on his supervisors and holding them accountable. The same Human Resources employee described the factory manager of Components, Phil Hanson, as dealing with things as they came up—as more reactive. Hanson allowed his supervisors more freedom

and did not get involved on the floor unless there was a problem. When there was a problem, however, he reacted strongly and swiftly. For example, to combat a recent tendency for employees to take extended breaks, he had begun posting supervisors outside of the bathrooms right before and after scheduled breaks.

Bill Larson attributed the differences in the two sides "to the different performance and accountability needs dictated by their business activities and by the corporate office." Components met the internal production needs of Brooks by supplying all of the other Brooks plants with a product that they, in turn, used to manufacture a household product that sold in the millions each year. Fabrication, however, had to satisfy the needs of a variety of industrial customers while competing on the open market. Larson felt that Fabrication had to have a more entrepreneurial ethic than Components because "Fabrication lives or dies by how they treat their customers—they have to woo them and interact well with them," whereas Components had a ready-made market.

Larson also thought that some of the differences were due to the fact that the plant was "held prisoner by what goes on in corporate." Although the corporate office set financial targets for both sides of the plant, it exercised more control over the financial and productivity goals of the Components side because no other Brooks plant was in the Fabrication business and Brooks understood the Components business much better. In addition, corporate was dependent on the Components side for the standardized parts—primarily wire coils—used in many of its finished products. The Components side produced as many as 2 million of some of these small parts a day.

Larson also indicated that the requirements for the number of workers on the two sides of the plant were different. For example, depending on what business was like for each side, the overtime requirements could vary. Hourly employees on the side of the plant that had more overtime felt the side that was working less was getting "easier" treatment. Larson knew that the overtime disparity was due to need, not preferential treatment of one side over the other, but as he put it: "You can talk your head off, but you're not going to be able to explain it to them to their satisfaction. So that causes a lot of frustration among the ranks down there."

The Manager of QIS traced the differences between the Fabrication side and the Components side to the consolidation at Littleton of all of Brooks's production of wire coils needed for its domestic appliances after Brooks bought Frühling, Inc., in 1984. Most of the upper managers hired to start the Components business were brought in from Frühling, and, as he put it, "They had a different way of doing things. It wasn't a tightly run ship." He said that some of the old managers at the plant wondered about the wisdom of bringing in managers from a company that

8.1

had not been successful. People asked, "Why use them here? They must have been part of what was wrong." One Fabrication manager added that the manager brought in to start the Components business, Bob Halperin, had the view: "We're going to start a new business here and do whatever is necessary to make it run and to hell with Littleton Manufacturing policies." Also, when the new Components business was started, its manager reported directly to the Brooks corporate office and not to the plant manager. In 1986 the structure was changed so that the factory manager of Components reported to the Littleton Manufacturing plant manager.

A union steward at the plant attributed some of the differences between the two sides to the fact that the workforce on the Components side tended to be younger and had more women with young children (67 percent of the hourly women in the plant worked in Components). The demands of raising children, he thought, resulted in the women needing to take more time off from work. One of the Fabrication supervisors thought that since the supervisors on the Components side were younger, they expected more from management and were more outspoken, especially about how much an hour they should be paid. A number of these supervisors had also been brought in from Frühling, and were not originally from Littleton.

Lack of Consistency in Enforcing Rules and Procedures

A major complaint of both hourly and salaried workers was the inconsistent application of policies and procedures. Although most people mentioned the differences from one side of the plant to the other, there were also differences from one department to another. As the chief union steward put it, "This is the number-one problem here—nobody is the same!" Some Components supervisors were letting people take longer breaks and going for breaks earlier than they were supposed to. Some supervisors allowed hourly employees to stand around and talk for a while before getting them to start their machines. In some departments on the Components side, employees were allowed to gather in the bathrooms and "hang out" anywhere from five to twenty minutes before quitting time. The chief steward cited an example where, contrary to previous policy, some workers on the Components side were allowed to have radios. "When people on the Fabrication side found out," he said, "they went wild."

Some other examples of inconsistencies cited by employees were as follows:

1. Fighting in the plant was supposed to result in automatic dismissal, but the Human Resources administrator recalled two incidents of fighting where the people involved were not disciplined.
2. Another incident that had been much discussed throughout the plant involved an employee who was "caught in a cloud of marijuana smoke" by his supervisor. Since the supervisor did not observe the man smoking but just smelled the marijuana, the person was only given a written warning. One manager said, "We need to take a stand on these things. We need to make a statement. That way we would gain some respect." Describing the same incident, another manager said, "It makes us close to thinking we're giving them (hourly employees) the key to the door."
3. Several people also mentioned the case of a mother who claimed she missed work several times because of doctors' appointments for her children and was suspended for three days, which they compared with the case of an operator who also missed work several times, and was suspected of drug or alcohol abuse, but was not disciplined.

In discussing differences in the enforcement of safety regulations throughout the plant, the administrator of plant safety and security said that when he confronted people who were wearing sneakers, often they would just say they forgot to wear their safety shoes. He said, "If I had to punish everyone, I'd be punishing 50 to 100 people a day."

There were also differences in absenteeism for the two sides of the plant. Absenteeism on the Components side was around 2.2 percent, whereas it was slightly less than 1 percent on the Fabrication side. Some attributed this to a looser enforcement of the rules governing absenteeism by supervisors on the Components side.

Winslow had tried to estimate the annual cost of failure to enforce the rules governing starting and stopping work. His estimate was that the plant was losing $2,247.50 per day, for a total of $539,400 a year. Winslow's memo detailing how he arrived at his overall estimate had been part of his presentation to Larson; it is included as Exhibit 3. Although Winslow had not said so in the memo, he later estimated that 70 percent of the total loss occurred on the Components side of the plant.

Supervisors complained that when they tried to discipline subordinates, they often did not feel confident of backing by management. They referred to incidents where they had disciplined hourly employees only to have their decisions changed by management or the Human Resources department. One supervisor told of an incident in which he tried to fire someone in accordance with what he thought was company policy, but the termination was changed to a suspension. He was told he had been too harsh. In a subsequent incident he had another decision overruled and was told he had been too lenient. He said, "We feel our hands are tied; we're not sure what we can do." Supervisors' decisions that were changed were usually communicated directly to the union by the Human Resources department. In these instances, the supervisors felt they wound up with "egg on their faces."

EXHIBIT 3
Memo from Paul Winslow to Bill Larson

MEMORANDUM

From: Paul Winslow, Director of Human Resources
To: Bill Larson
Subject: Estimated Cost of Loss of Manufacturing Time
Date: 6/18/90

Loss of Manufacturing Time*
(Based on 348 Hourly Employees)

Delay at start of shift	10 minutes × 25% (87) =	14.50 hours
Washup before AM break	5 minutes × 75% (261) =	21.75 hours
Delayed return from break	10 minutes × 50% (174) =	29.00 hours
Early washup—lunch avg.	10 minutes × 50% (174) =	29.00 hours
Delayed return from lunch	10 minutes × 25% (87) =	14.50 hours
Early washup before PM break	5 minutes × 75% (261) =	21.75 hours
Delayed return from break	10 minutes × 50% (174) =	29.00 hours
Early washup—end of shift	5 minutes × 75% (261) =	65.25 hours
	Total =	224.75 hours/day

Cost: 224.75 × avg. $10 hr. = $2,247.50/day
        240 days × $2,247.50 = $539,400.00/year
*1. Does not include benefits.
  2. Does not include overtime abuses.
  3. Does not include instances of employees exiting building while punched in.

Winslow attributed some of these problems to a lack of communication regarding the company's policies and procedures. He thought that if the supervisors understood company policy better, their decisions would not need to be changed so frequently. There was no Human Resources policy manual, for example, although the work rules were contained in the union contract.

Dan Gordon disagreed with the view that these problems were a result of the supervisors' lack of understanding of the plant's policies and procedures. He claimed: "Ninety-nine percent of the supervisors know the policies but they lack the skills and willingness to enforce them. Just like a police officer needs to be trained to read a prisoner his rights, the supervisors need to be taught to do their jobs." He thought that in some of the cases where a supervisor's decision was changed, the supervisor had made a mistake in following the proper disciplinary procedure. Then, when the supervisor's decision was overturned, no explanation was provided, so the supervisor would be left with his or her own erroneous view of what happened.

The Human Resources administrator thought that some of the supervisors were reluctant to discipline or confront people because "They're afraid to hurt people's feelings and want to stay on their good side."

Supervisor's Role Is Poorly Perceived

On the first shift in Fabrication there were about 70 hourly workers and 7 supervisors, and in Components there were about 140 hourly workers and 11 supervisors. Supervisors were assisted by group leaders, hourly employees who were appointed by the company and who received up to an extra 10 cents an hour.

All levels of the plant were concerned about the role of supervisors. "Supervisors feel like a nobody," said one senior manager. In the assessment of organizational communication done by the students, hourly employees, middle managers, and supervisors all reported that supervisors had too much to do and that this limited their effectiveness. A typical observation by one hourly employee was: "The supervisors can't be out on the floor because of meetings and paperwork. They have a tremendous amount of things on their mind.... The supervisor has become a paperboy, which prevents him from being able to do his job." In speaking about how busy the supervisors were and how they responded to suggestions by hourly employees, another hourly person said, "The supervisor's favorite word is, 'I forgot.'"

Supervisors also wanted more involvement in decision making. "You will! You will! You will!" is the way one supervisor characterized the dominant decision-making style of managers at the plant. He thought that most managers expected supervisors to just do what they were told to do. "We have a lot of responsibility but little authority," was how another supervisor put it. Many supervisors felt that they were ordered to do things by their managers, but when something went wrong, they were blamed.

Another factor contributing to the low morale of supervisors was a perceived lack of the resources that they felt were necessary to do a good job. Many complained that they were often told there was no money to make changes to improve things. They also complained of too few engineering, housekeeping, and maintenance personnel. Some supervisors thought there were too few supervisors on the second and third shifts. They thought this resulted in inadequate supervision and allowed some hourly workers to goof off, since the employees knew when these few supervisors would and would not be around.

The combination of these factors—job overload, too much paperwork, lack of authority, not enough involvement in decision making, lack of resources to make changes, inadequate training, and few rewards—made it difficult to find hourly people at the plant who would accept an offer to become a supervisor.

In discussing the role of supervisors, Larson said, "We don't do a good job of training our supervisors. We tell them what we want and hold them accountable, but we don't give them the personal tools for them to do what we want them to do. They need to have the confidence and ability to deal with people and to hold them accountable without feeling badly." He continued by praising one supervisor who he thought was doing a good job. In particular, Larson felt, this supervisor's subordinates knew what to expect from him. This person had been a chief petty officer in the Navy for many years, and Larson thought this had helped him feel comfortable enforcing rules. Reflecting on this, he said, "Maybe we should just look for people with military backgrounds to be supervisors."

Insufficient Focus on Littleton's Priorities

The phrase "insufficient focus on Littleton's priorities" reflected two concerns expressed by employees. First, there was a lack of understanding of Littleton's goals. Second, there was a questioning of the plant's commitment to these goals. However, various levels saw these matters differently.

Although the plant had no mission statement, senior managers said that they thought that they understood Littleton's priorities. A typical senior management description of the plant's goals was, "To supply customers with quality products on time at the lowest possible cost in order to make a profit."

Each year, Larson and the executive staff developed a four-year strategic plan for Littleton. Sales and marketing would first project the amounts and types of products that they thought they could sell. Then manufacturing would look at the machine and labor capabilities of the plant. The sales projections and capabilities were then adjusted as necessary. Throughout the process, goals were set for improving quality and lowering costs. Larson then took the plan to Brooks for revision and/or approval. Next, Larson turned the goals in the strategic plan into specific objectives for each department. These departmental objectives were used to set measurable objectives for each executive staff member. These then formed the basis for annual performance appraisals. Because of this process, all of the executive staff felt that they knew what was expected of them and how their jobs contributed to achieving the company's goals.

At the same time, both senior and middle managers thought there was insufficient communication and support from corporate headquarters. They mentioned not knowing enough about corporate's long-term plans for the company. A number of the managers on the Fabrication side wondered about corporate's commitment to the Fabrication business. They thought that if their operation did not do well financially, the company might end it. In discussing the status of the Fabrication side of the plant, Gordon said that Brooks considered it a "noncore business." The Quality Assurance manager felt that corporate was not providing enough support and long-term direction for the QIS. Winslow was concerned about the lack of consistency in corporate's Human Resources policies and felt that he did not have enough say in corporate Human Resources planning efforts.

All levels below the executive staff complained that they did not have a good understanding of Littleton's own long-range goals. Some middle managers thought there was a written, long-range plan for the company but others disagreed. One member of the executive staff reported that as far as he knew, the entire strategic plan was seen only by the executive staff, although some managers would see the portions of it that concerned their departments. He also reported that the strategic plan was never discussed at operations review meetings. Most hourly employees said that they relied on the grapevine for information about "the big picture." In discussing the flow of information at the plant, one union steward said, "Things get lost in the chain of command." He said he got more than 80 percent of his information from gossip on the floor.

The primary mechanism used to communicate Littleton's goals and the plant's status with regard to achieving them was the operations review meeting held once a month by the plant manager, to which all salaried employees were ostensibly invited. At these meetings, usually attended by about eighty people, the plant manager provided figures on how closely the plant had hit selected business indicators. At one recent and typical meeting, for example, the Manager of QIS described various in-place efforts to improve quality. Bill Larson then reviewed the numbers. He presented data on budgeted versus actual production, variances between budgeted and actual manufacturing costs, profits, the top ten products in sales, standard margins on various products, shipments of products, information on backlogs, and the top ten customers.[1] When he asked for questions at the end of his presentation, there were none.

The students' organizational assessment reported that all levels appreciated the intent of the operations review meetings, but there were a number of concerns. Everyone interviewed wanted more two-way communication but thought the size and format of the meetings inhibited discussion. Middle managers thought the meetings focused too much on what had happened and not enough on the future. As one manager said: "It's like seeing Lubbock in the rearview mirror. We want to know where we're going—not where we've been. We want to know what's coming up, how it's going to affect our department, and what we can do to help." Others, including some of the executive staff, complained about the difficulty of understanding the financial jargon. Some hourly employees interviewed did not know there were operations review meetings, and others did not know what was discussed at them.

A number of middle managers in manufacturing thought that having regular departmental meetings would improve communication within their departments. They also said that they would like to see minutes of the executive staff meetings.

When interviewed by the students for their assessment of organizational communication, a number of middle managers, supervisors, and hourly workers thought the company was not practicing what it preached with regard to its stated goals. A primary goal was supposed to be a quality product; however, they reported that there was too much emphasis on "hitting the numbers," or getting the required number of products shipped, even if there were defects. They said this especially occurred toward the end of the month when production reports were submitted. One worker's comment reflected opinions held by many hourly employees: "Some foremen are telling people to push through products that are not of good quality. This passes the problem from one department to another and the end result is a lousy product. They seem too interested in reaching the quota and getting the order out on time rather than quality. It's a big problem because when the hourly workers believe that quality isn't important, they start not to care about their work. They pass it on to the next guy, and the next guy gets mad."

The perception by a number of hourly workers that their suggestions to improve quality were not responded to because of a lack of money also resulted in their questioning the company's commitment to quality.

Change Is Poorly Managed

Most of the employees interviewed by the students thought there were too many changes at the plant and that the numerous changes resulted in confusion.

1. QIS was initiated in 1985.
2. In 1986, 100 hourly employees were laid off.
3. In 1984, there were 154 managers; in 1990, there were 87 managers.
4. In 1989, corporate initiated a restructuring that changed the reporting relationships of several senior managers.
5. In 1989, as part of QIS, the plant began using statistical process control techniques and began efforts to attain ISO certification. (ISO is an internationally recognized certification of excellence.)
6. In 1989, a new production and inventory control system was introduced, with the help of a team of outside consultants who were at the plant for almost a year studying its operations.
7. In 1990, the Components side reorganized its production flow.

A number of complaints were voiced about the effect of all the changes. People felt that some roles and responsibilities were not clear. There was a widespread belief that the reasons for changes were not communicated well enough and that people found out about changes affecting them too late. In addition, many were uncertain how long a new program, once started, would be continued. Larson thought that many hourly employees were resistant to the changes being made because they thought the changes would require more work for them and they were already "running all the time." One union steward observed, "There's never a gradual easing in of things here." A middle manager said: "We're mandated for speed. We pride ourselves on going fast. We rush through today to get to tomorrow."

Larson thought the culture of the plant was gradually changing due to the implementation of QIS, but he noted that a lot of time had to be spent giving the employees reasons for changes.

Dan Gordon thought the plant needed to "communicate change in a single voice." He said that Larson's style was to leave it to the staff to tell others about upcoming changes. He commented, "By the time it gets to the last person, it's lost something." He felt that Larson needed to communicate changes to those on lower levels in person.

The QIS manager thought that Brooks did not provide enough resources and support for changes at the plant. In explaining his view of corporate's approach to change, he said, "Step one is to not give much. Step two is to not give anything. Step three is they take what's left away." Another middle manager commented, "We're always being asked to do more with less, but the requirements by corporate don't get cut back."

8.1

A frequently mentioned example of change that was frustrating to many people was the introduction of the Manufacturing Assisted Production and Inventory Control System (MAPICS) in 1989. MAPICS was a computerized system that was supposed to keep track of materials, productivity, and labor efficiency. Theoretically, it tracked orders from time of entry to payment of the bill, and one could find out where an order was at any point in the system by calling it up on a computer. However, the system was time-consuming (data had to be entered manually by the supervisors), and was not as well suited to the Fabrication side of the plant as it was to the Components side, where production was more standardized. One senior manager commented, "MAPICS was sold as the savior for the supervisors, and the company was supposed to get all of the data it needed. But it's never happened. It's only half-installed, and there are systems problems and input problems." Recently, there had been some question as to whether MAPICS was giving an accurate inventory count.

Hourly workers felt put upon by the way in which changes were made. One person said, "We were all of a sudden told to start monitoring waste and then all of a sudden we were told to stop." Another said, "One day the MAPICS room is over here, and then the next day it's over there. They also put a new system in the stockroom, and we didn't know about it." Many resented the outside consultants that had been brought in by corporate, reporting that they did not know why the consultants were brought in or what they were doing. They feared that the consultants' recommendations might result in layoffs.

Hourly people felt that a lot of their information about upcoming changes came through the grapevine. "Rumors fly like crazy" is the way one hourly person described communication on the floor. Another said, "The managers don't walk through the plant much. We only see them when things are going bad."

In discussing communication about changes, one middle manager said: "It's a standing joke. The hourly know what's going to happen before we do." One steward said, "Lots of times, you'll tell the supervisors something that's going to happen and they will be surprised. It raises hell with morale and creates unstable working conditions. But nine out of ten times it's true."

Hourly workers also felt that they were not involved enough in management decisions about changes to be made. One hourly worker said, "They don't ask our input. We could tell them if something is not going to work. They should keep us informed. We're not idiots."

Lack of a Systematic Approach to Training

The company had carried out a well-regarded training effort when employees were hired to begin the Components side of the plant and when the QIS program was started. In addition, every two years each employee went through refresher training for the QIS. There was no other formal company training or career development at the plant.

Hourly employees and supervisors in particular complained about the lack of training. One hourly employee expressed the predominant view: "When you start work here, it's sink or swim." In discussing the promotion of supervisors, the chief union steward said he did not know how people got to be supervisors and that as far as he knew there was no training that one had to have to become a supervisor.

When they were hired, new hourly and salaried employees attended an orientation session in which they were informed about benefits, attendance policies, their work schedule, parking regulations, and safety issues. After the orientation session, further training for new salaried employees was left up to individual departments. Standard practice was for the department supervisor to assign the hourly person to an experienced hourly operator for one-on-one job training for two weeks. Winslow expressed some of his reservations about this approach by commenting, "You don't know if the department is assigning the best person to train the new employee or if they always use the same person for training."

The Human Resources department had no separate training budget. Individual departments, however, did sometimes use their money for training and counted the money used as a variance from their budgeted goals. The training that did occur with some regularity tended to be technical training for maintenance personnel.

When asked to explain why there was not more training, Winslow replied, "We would like to do more but we haven't been able to because of the cost and staffing issues." For example, in 1986 Winslow's title was manager of training and development, and he had been responsible for the training program for all of the new employees hired to begin the Components unit. After the initial training was completed, he requested that the plant provide ongoing training for Components operators. However, his request was turned down by Larson, who did not want to spend the money. Winslow also recalled the over 160 hours he had spent the previous year developing a video training package for hourly workers in one part of the Components side of the plant. He said that the program had been piloted, but when it came time to send people through the training course, production management was unwilling to let people take time off the floor.

Winslow also cited a lack of support from corporate as a factor in the plant's sporadic training efforts. At one time Brooks had employed a director of training for its plants, but in 1987, the person left and the company never hired anyone to replace him. Now, Brooks had no training department; each plant was expected to provide its own training. The training Brooks did provide, according to Winslow, was for the "promising manager" and was purchased from an outside vendor.

Top Management

As he sat in his office thinking about what to do, Winslow knew that any plan would have to be acceptable to Larson, Gordon, and Hanson—the plant manager and the two factory managers—and he spent some time thinking about their management styles.

Bill Larson was in his late forties, had a B.S. in mechanical engineering, and had started at Littleton in 1970. He had been plant manager since 1983. His direct reports considered him bright, analytical, and down to earth. When asked once how he would describe himself to someone who didn't know him, he said, "I keep my emotions out of things. I can remember when I was in the Army, standing at attention in my dress blues at the Tomb of the Unknown Soldier. People would come up a foot from my face and look me in the eye and try to get me to blink. But I was able to remove myself from that. I wouldn't even see it." He added that he had built most of his own home and repaired his own equipment, including the diesels on a cabin cruiser he used to own. Being raised on a farm in the rural Midwest, he said he learned at an early age how to repair equipment with baling wire to keep it going.

Although Larson was considered accessible by the executive staff, he rarely got out on the floor to talk to people. Many managers saw him as a "numbers" person who readily sprinkled his conversations about the plant with quantitative data about business indicators, variances, budgeted costs, etc. In referring to his discomfort discussing personal things, he somewhat jokingly said about himself, "I can talk on the phone for about thirty-five seconds and then I can't talk any longer."

In describing his own management style, Larson said, "I like to support people and get them involved. I like to let them know what I am thinking and what they need to accomplish. I like to let ideas come from them. I want them to give me recommendations, and if I feel they're OK, I won't change them. They need to be accountable, but I don't want them to feel I'm looking over their shoulders. I don't want to hamper their motivation." He estimated that 40 percent of his job responsibility consisted of managing change.

Dan Gordon, who was 38, had been at Littleton for fifteen years and had been manufacturing manager of Fabrication for seven years. In describing himself, he said, "I'm a stickler for details, and I hate to not perform well. My superiors tell me I'm a Theory X manager and that I have a strong personality—that I can intimidate people."

In speaking about how much he communicated with hourly employees, Gordon said that he didn't do enough of it, adding that "Our platters are all so loaded, we don't spend as much time talking to people as we should." He said he seldom walked through the plant and never talked to hourly workers one-on-one. Once a year, though, he met formally with all the hourly employees on the Fabrication side to have an operations review meeting like the salaried people had in order to discuss what the plant was doing, profits, new products, etc. "The hourly people love it," he reported.

Reflecting on why he didn't communicate more with hourly workers, Gordon said, "Since the accounting department's data depends, in part, on our data collection, a lot of my time is eaten up with this. Maybe I'm too busy with clerical activities to be more visible." He based his management decisions on documented data and regularly studied the financial and productivity reports issued by the accounting department. He said he would like to see the supervisors go around in the morning to just talk to people but acknowledged that they had too many reports to fill out and too many meetings to attend.

When asked to explain what one needed to do to succeed as a manager at Littleton, Gordon answered, "You have to get things done. Bill Larson wants certain things done within a certain time span. If you do this, you'll succeed."

Phil Hanson, in his early fifties, had been at Littleton for seven years. He was hired as materials manager for Components and was promoted to Components factory manager in mid-1989. Phil estimated that he spent 50 percent of his time on the factory floor talking to people. He felt it gave him a better insight as to what was going on at the plant and created trust. He thought that too many of the managers at the plant were "office haunts"—they felt it was beneath them to talk with hourly workers. It appeared to other managers that Hanson often made decisions based on what he learned in informal conversations with hourly employees. He tried to delegate as much as he could to his managers. When asked what a manager had to do to succeed there, he said, "You have to be a self-starter and make things happen."

Winslow remembered how a few years ago, when he was manager of training and development, the executive staff had gone to one of those management development workshops where you find out about your management style. All of the staff had scored high on the authoritarian end of the scale.

This triggered a memory of a recent debate in which he had passed along a suggestion by his staff to the executive staff to "do something nice for the workers on the floor." To celebrate the arrival of summer, his staff wanted the company to pay for buying hamburgers, hot dogs, and soft drinks so the workers could have a cookout during their lunch break. Those on the executive staff who resisted the idea cited the "jellybean theory of management." As one manager explained it, "If you give a hungry bear jellybeans, you can keep it happy and get it to do what you want. But watch out when you run out of jellybeans! You're going to have a helluva angry bear to deal with!" The jelly bean argument carried the day, and the cookout was not held.

8.1

Recommendation Time

8.1

As Winslow turned on the computer to write down his recommendations concerning the six problem areas, he recalled how Larson had reacted when the students made their presentation on organizational communication at Littleton. After praising the students' efforts, Larson had said, in an offhanded way, "This mainly confirms what we already knew. Most of this is not a surprise." Winslow was hopeful that now some of these issues would be addressed.

One potential sticking point, he knew, was the need for the meetings that would be necessary to discuss the problems and plan a strategy. People were already strapped for time and complaining about the number of meetings. Yet unless they took time to step back and look at what they were doing, nothing would change.

On a more hopeful note, he recalled that Larson had been impressed when the Human Resources staff empha-

sized in their presentation to him that these issues were impacting Littleton's bottom line. Winslow felt that the decline in sales and profits at Brooks, the increasing domestic and foreign competition, the current recession, and declining employee morale made it even more important that the issues be dealt with. People at all levels of the plant were starting to worry about the possibility of more layoffs.

Note

1. At Littleton, the manufacturing, engineering, and accounting departments estimated the standard labor costs for making each of the plant's products and a budget was prepared based on those estimates. The budgeted costs were plant goals. A variance is the difference between actual and standard costs. A variance could be positive (less than) or negative (greater than) with respect to the budgeted costs.

Integrative Case 8.2

Littleton Manufacturing (B)*

Winslow met with his staff to develop a list of proposed corrective actions. Exhibit 1 is the memo that Winslow sent, in June 1990, to the Human Resources PIT, outlining suggested corrective actions. (The action steps were not prioritized.)

The PIT did not meet to discuss what to do about the six issues identified by the Human Resources department until the middle of September. The first issue the PIT decided to address was the inconsistent application of disciplinary policies and procedures. They chose this issue first because they thought that if this could be improved, many of the other issues would be resolved as well.

The PIT decided to first find out how well supervisors understood the work rules and the extent to which they had different interpretations of them. To do this they developed a quiz covering Littleton's twenty-eight work rules and gave the quiz to all supervisors. One question, for example, was "If you came in and found an employee who had just dozed off at his/her workstation, what would you do?" The supervisor then had to choose from several alternatives. This question was followed by, "If you came in and found an employee away from the job and asleep on top of some packing materials, what would you do?" Again, there was a choice of several responses. After taking the exam, the answers were discussed and the correct answer explained by Winslow and the Human Resources staff. The results revealed to the PIT that there was much less knowledge of these rules and how to apply them than management had expected.

The PIT then theorized that a number of supervisors were not comfortable with confronting employees about their failure to follow the company's policies and procedures, especially the wearing of safety shoes and goggles. They decided to seek the assistance of an outside consultant to help them develop a training program for the supervisors. However, on September 1, 1991, as a continuation of its "efficiency drive," Brooks had imposed a freeze on salaries and a reduction in travel, and prohibited the use of outside consultants at all of its plants. When Winslow asked Bill Larson for approval to hire the consultant, he was reminded that because of the freeze they would have to do the training in-house.

As a consequence, Winslow began a series of meetings with union stewards and supervisors—called "Sup and Stew" meetings—to discuss what the work rules were, different interpretations of them, and how violations of work rules should be handled. For scheduling reasons, it was planned so that half of the supervisors and the stewards would attend each meeting. These meetings were held biweekly for over a year. Winslow believed that the meetings were helping to clarify and support the role of the supervisors and were beginning to have a positive effect on the enforcement of policies and procedures.

In 1991, because the plants that bought the wire coils made by Components had excess finished goods inventory, Brooks shut them down for a month during the Christmas holidays, leading Littleton to eliminate 125 positions from the Components side for the same month, to reduce production. "If we hadn't," Winslow said, "we would have had a horrendous amount of inventory." The employees filling those positions had, in general, less seniority than their counterparts from Fabrication, and no one from the Fabrication side was laid off. A few of the more senior employees from the Components side were hired to work on the Fabrication side. At the time of the layoffs, business on the Fabrication side was booming. In January, the plant started rehiring the laid-off workers, and by the end of June, all of them had been rehired.

In November 1991, Bill Larson learned that he had cancer, and in June 1992, he died. Because of Larson's illness, the lack of resources, and time pressures, there was no formal attempt to address any of the issues identified by Winslow other than inconsistent enforcement of policies and procedures.

The new plant manager, Bob Halperin, took over in the fall of 1992; Halperin had been managing another Brooks plant in the south for three years. One of the reasons he was chosen was his familiarity with Littleton. He had been at Littleton as an industrial engineer from 1973 to 1980, when he left to manage another facility. In 1984 he was sent back to Littleton to start and manage Components. He held this position for four years before leaving to manage the plant in the southern United States.

Shortly after Halperin arrived, Winslow acquainted him with the problem areas defined the previous year, gave him a copy of the (A) case, and met with him to discuss the issues. At that time, although Winslow felt that progress had been made on having more consistent enforcement of policies and procedures from one side of the plant to the other, he did not feel much had changed with regard to the other issues. With the exception of the Sup and Stew meetings, none of the specific action steps recommended by him and his staff had been implemented.

*By David E. Whiteside, organizational development consultant. This case was written at Lewiston-Auburn College of the University of Southern Maine with the cooperation of management, solely for the purpose of stimulating student discussion. Data are based on field research; all events are real, although the names of organizations, locations, and individuals have been disguised. Faculty members in nonprofit institutions are encouraged to reproduce this case for distribution to their students without charge or written permission. All other rights reserved jointly to the author and the North American Case Research Association (NACRA). Copyright © 1994 by the *Case Research Journal* and David E. Whiteside.

EXHIBIT 1
Memorandum from Paul Winslow to Human Resources

8.2

MEMORANDUM

From: Paul Winslow, Director of Human Resources
To: Human Resources Process Improvement Team
Subject: Proposed Corrective Actions
Date: 6/14/90

Lack of Organizational Unity
1. Use job shadowing or rotation to help people understand each other's jobs, e.g., do this across functions.
2. Reformat the Operations Review meetings, e.g., have a program committee.
3. Have a smaller group forum, e.g., have supervisors from the two sides meet.
4. Provide teamwork training for salaried employees.

Lack of Consistency in Enforcing Rules and Procedures
1. Hold meetings with department managers and supervisors to discuss how to enforce policies and procedures. Have these led by Bill Larson.
2. Develop a policy and procedures review and monitoring system.

Supervisor's Role Poorly Perceived
1. Have department managers meet with supervisors to determine priorities or conflicts between priorities.
2. Have supervisory training for all manufacturing supervisors.
3. Time assessment. (How is their time being spent?)

Insufficient Focus on Littleton's Priorities
1. Use the in-house newsletter to communicate priorities.
2. Develop an internal news sheet.
3. Have a question box for questions to be answered at Operations Review meetings.
4. Have a restatement of Littleton's purpose (do at Operations Review).
5. Have an Operations Review for hourly workers.
6. Use payroll stuffers to communicate information about goals.
7. Hold department meetings; have the manager of the department facilitate the meeting.

Change Is Poorly Managed
1. Provide training in managing change.
2. Communicate changes.

Lack of a Systematic Approach to Training
1. Establish annual departmental training goals.
2. Link training goals to organizational priorities.
3. Have a systematic approach to training the hourly workforce.
4. Have a training plan for each salaried employee.
5. Have an annual training budget.

HR Dept.
6/90

Glossary

A

adaptability culture a culture characterized by strategic focus on the external environment through flexibility and change to meet customer needs.

administrative principles a closed systems management perspective that focuses on the total organization and grows from the insights of practitioners.

ambidextrous approach a characteristic of an organization that can behave in both an organic and a mechanistic way.

analyzability a dimension of technology in which work activities can be reduced to mechanical steps and participants can follow an objective, computational procedure to solve problems.

analyzer a business strategy that seeks to maintain a stable business while innovating on the periphery.

authority a force for achieving desired outcomes that is prescribed by the formal hierarchy and reporting relationships.

B

balanced scorecard a comprehensive management control system that balances traditional financial measures with operational measures relating to an organization's critical success factors.

benchmarking process whereby companies find out how others do something better than they do and then try to imitate or improve on it.

boundary spanning roles activities that link and coordinate an organization with key elements in the external environment.

bounded rationality perspective how decisions are made when time is limited, a large number of internal and external factors affect a decision, and the problem is ill-defined.

buffering roles activities that absorb uncertainty from the environment.

bureaucracy an organizational framework marked by rules and procedures, specialization and division of labor, hierarchy of authority, technically qualified personnel, separate position and incumbent, and written communications and records.

bureaucratic control the use of rules, policies, hierarchy of authority, written documentation, standardization, and other bureaucratic mechanisms to standardize behavior and assess performance.

bureaucratic culture a culture that has an internal focus and a consistency orientation for a stable environment.

bureaucratic organization a perspective that emphasizes management on an impersonal, rational basis through such elements as clearly defined authority and responsibility, formal recordkeeping, and uniform application of standard rules.

business intelligence high-tech analysis of large amounts of internal and external data to identify patterns and relationships.

C

Carnegie model organizational decision making involving many managers and a final choice based on a coalition among those managers.

centrality a trait of a department whose role is in the primary activity of an organization.

centralization refers to the level of hierarchy with authority to make decisions.

centralized decision making is limited to higher authority.

change process the way in which changes occur in an organization.

chaos theory a scientific theory that suggests that relationships in complex, adaptive systems are made up of numerous interconnections that create unintended effects and render the environment unpredictable.

charismatic authority based in devotion to the exemplary character or heroism of an individual and the order defined by him or her.

chief ethics officer high-level company executive who oversees all aspects of ethics, including establishing and broadly communicating ethical standards, setting up ethics training programs, supervising the investigation of ethical problems, and advising managers in the ethical aspects of corporate decisions.

clan control the use of social characteristics, such as corporate culture, shared values, commitments, traditions, and beliefs, to control behavior.

clan culture a culture that focuses primarily on the involvement and participation of the organization's members and on rapidly changing expectations from the external environment.

closed system a system that is autonomous, enclosed, and not dependent on its environment.

coalition an alliance among several managers who agree through bargaining about organizational goals and problem priorities.

code of ethics A formal statement of the company's values concerning ethics and social responsibility.

coercive forces external pressures such as legal requirements exerted on an organization to adopt structures, techniques, or behaviors similar to other organizations.

collaborative network an emerging perspective whereby organizations allow themselves to become dependent on other organizations to increase value and productivity for all.

collective bargaining the negotiation of an agreement between management and workers.

collectivity stage the life cycle phase in which an organization has strong leadership and begins to develop clear goals and direction.

competing values approach a perspective on organizational effectiveness that combines diverse indicators of performance that represent competing management values.

competition rivalry between groups in the pursuit of a common prize.

confrontation a situation in which parties in conflict directly engage one another and try to work out their differences.

consortia groups of firms that venture into new products and technologies.

contextual dimensions traits that characterize the whole organization, including its size, technology, environment, and goals.

contingency a theory meaning one thing depends on other things; the organization's situation dictates the correct management approach.

contingency decision-making framework a perspective that brings together the two organizational dimensions of problem consensus and technical knowledge about solutions.

continuous process production a completely mechanized manufacturing process in which there is no starting or stopping.

cooptation occurs when leaders from important sectors in the environment are made part of an organization.

coping with uncertainty a source of power for a department that reduces uncertainty for other departments by obtaining prior information, prevention, and absorption.

core technology the work process that is directly related to the organization's mission.

craft technology technology characterized by a fairly stable stream of activities but in which the conversion process is not analyzable or well understood.

creative departments organizational departments that initiate change, such as research and development, engineering, design, and systems analysis.

creativity the generation of novel ideas that may meet perceived needs or respond to opportunities.

culture the set of values, guiding beliefs, understandings, and ways of thinking that are shared by members of an organization and are taught to new members as correct.

culture changes changes in the values, attitudes, expectations, beliefs, abilities, and behavior of employees.

culture strength the degree of agreement among members of an organization about the importance of specific values.

customer relationship management systems that help companies track customer interactions with the firm and allow employees to call up a customer's past sales and service records, outstanding orders, or unresolved problems.

D

data the input of a communication channel.

data mining software that uses sophisticated decision-making processes to search raw data for patterns and relationships that may be significant.

data warehousing the use of a huge database that combines all of an organization's data and allows users to access the data directly, create reports, and obtain answers to "what-if" questions.

decentralized decision making and communication are spread out across the company

decision learning a process of recognizing and admitting mistakes that allows managers and organizations to acquire the experience and knowledge to perform more effectively in the future.

decision premises constraining frames of reference and guidelines placed by top managers on decisions made at lower levels.

decision support system a system that enables managers at all levels of the organization to retrieve, manipulate, and display information from integrated databases for making specific decisions.

defender a business strategy that seeks stability or even retrenchment rather than innovation or growth.

departmental grouping a structure in which employees share a common supervisor and resources, are jointly responsible for performance, and tend to identify and collaborate with each other.

dependency one aspect of horizontal power: when one department is dependent on another, the latter is in a position of greater power.

differentiation the cognitive and emotional differences among managers in various functional departments of an organization and formal structure differences among these departments.

direct interlock a situation that occurs when a member of the board of directors of one company sits on the board of another.

divisional grouping a grouping in which people are organized according to what the organization produces.

divisional structure the structuring of the organization according to individual products, services, product groups, major projects, or profit centers; also called *product structure* or *strategic business units*.

domain an organization's chosen environmental field of activity.

domains of political activity areas in which politics plays a role. Three domains in organizations are structural change, management succession, and resource allocation.

domestic stage the first stage of international development in which a company is domestically oriented while managers are aware of the global environment.

downsizing intentionally reducing the size of a company's workforce by laying off employees.

dual-core approach an organizational change perspective that identifies the unique processes associated with administrative change compared to those associated with technical change.

E

e-business any business that takes place by digital processes over a computer network rather than in physical space.

economies of scale achieving lower costs through large volume production; often made possible by global expansion.

economies of scope achieving economies by having a presence in many product lines, technologies, or geographic areas.

effectiveness the degree to which an organization achieves its goals.

efficiency the amount of resources used to produce a unit of output.

elaboration stage the organizational life cycle phase in which the red tape crisis is resolved through the development of a new sense of teamwork and collaboration.

electronic data interchange (EDI) the linking of organizations through computers for the transmission of data without human interference.

empowerment the delegation of power or authority to subordinates; also called *power sharing*.

engineering technology technology in which there is substantial variety in the tasks performed, but activities are usually handled on the basis of established formulas, procedures, and techniques.

enterprise resource planning (ERP) sophisticated computerized systems that collect, process, and provide information about a company's entire enterprise, including order processing, product design, purchasing, inventory, manufacturing, distribution, human resources, receipt of payments, and forecasting of future demand.

entrepreneurial stage the life cycle phase in which an organization is born and its emphasis is on creating a product and surviving in the marketplace.

escalating commitment persisting in a course of action when it is failing; occurs because managers block or distort negative information and because consistency and persistence are valued in contemporary society.

ethical dilemma when each alternative choice or behavior seems undesirable because of a potentially negative ethical consequence.

ethics the code of moral principles and values that governs the behavior of a person or group with respect to what is right or wrong.

ethics committee a group of executives appointed to oversee company ethics.

ethics hotline a telephone number that employees can call to seek guidance and to report questionable behavior

executive information system (EIS) interactive systems that help top managers monitor and control organizational operations by processing and presenting data in usable form.

explicit knowledge formal, systematic knowledge that can be codified, written down, and passed on to others in documents or general instructions.

external adaptation the manner in which an organization meets goals and deals with outsiders.

extranet private information network.

F

factors of production supplies necessary for production, such as land, raw materials, and labor.

feedback control model a control cycle that involves setting goals, establishing standards of performance, measuring actual performance and comparing it to standards, and changing activities as needed based on the feedback.

financial resources control over money is an important source of power within an organization.

flexible manufacturing systems (FMS) using computers to link together manufacturing components such as robots, machines, product design, and engineering analysis to enable fast switching from one product to another.

focus an organization's dominant perspective value, which may be internal or external.

focus strategy a strategy in which an organization concentrates on a specific regional market or buyer group.

formalization the degree to which an organization has rules, procedures, and written documentation.

formalization stage the phase in an organization's life cycle involving the installation and use of rules, procedures, and control systems.

functional grouping the placing together of employees who perform similar functions or work processes or who bring similar knowledge and skills to bear.

functional matrix a structure in which functional bosses have primary authority and product or project managers simply coordinate product activities.

functional structure the grouping of activities by common function.

G

garbage can model model that describes the pattern or flow of multiple decisions within an organization.

general environment includes those sectors that may not directly affect the daily operations of a firm but will indirectly influence it.

generalist an organization that offers a broad range of products or services and serves a broad market.

global company a company that no longer thinks of itself as having a home country.

global geographical structure a form in which an organization divides its operations into world regions, each of which reports to the CEO.

global matrix structure a form of horizontal linkage in an international organization in which both product and geographical structures are implemented simultaneously to achieve a balance between standardization and globalization.

global product structure a form in which product divisions take responsibility for global operations in their specific product areas.

global stage the stage of international development in which the company transcends any one country.

global teams work groups made up of multinational members whose activities span multiple countries; also called *transnational teams*.

globalization strategy the standardization of product design and advertising strategy throughout the world.

goal approach an approach to organizational effectiveness that is concerned with output and whether the organization achieves its output goals.

H

Hawthorne Studies a series of experiments on worker productivity begun in 1924 at the Hawthorne plant of Western Electric Company in Illinois; attributed employees' increased output to managers' better treatment of them during the study.

heroes organizational members who serve as models or ideals for serving cultural norms and values.

high-velocity environments industries in which competitive and technological change is so extreme that market data is either unavailable or obsolete, strategic windows open and shut quickly, and the cost of a decision error is company failure.

horizontal coordination model a model of the three components of organizational design needed to achieve new product innovation: departmental specialization, boundary spanning, and horizontal linkages.

horizontal grouping the organizing of employees around core work processes rather than by function, product, or geography.

horizontal linkage the amount of communication and coordination that occurs horizontally across organizational departments.

horizontal structure a structure that virtually eliminates both the vertical hierarchy and departmental boundaries by organizing teams of employees around core work processes; the end-to-end work, information, and material flows that provide value directly to customers.

human relations model emphasis on an aspect of the competing values model that incorporates the values of an internal focus and a flexible structure.

hybrid structure a structure that combines characteristics of various structural approaches (functional, divisional, geographical, horizontal) tailored to specific strategic needs.

I

idea champions organizational members who provide the time and energy to make things happen; sometimes called *advocates, intrapreneurs,* and *change agents.*

idea incubator safe harbor where ideas from employees throughout the organization can be developed without interference from company bureaucracy or politics.

imitation the adoption of a decision tried elsewhere in the hope that it will work in the present situation.

incident command system developed to maintain the efficiency and control benefits of bureaucracy yet prevent the problems of slow response to crises.

incremental change a series of continual progressions that maintain an organization's general equilibrium and often affect only one organizational part.

incremental decision process model a model that describes the structured sequence of activities undertaken from the discovery of a problem to its solution.

indirect interlock a situation that occurs when a director of one company and a director of another are both directors of a third company.

information that which alters or reinforces understanding.

information reporting systems the most common form of management information system, these computerized systems provide managers with reports that summarize data and support day-to-day decision making.

inspiration an innovative, creative solution that is not reached by logical means.

institutional environment norms and values from stakeholders (customers, investors, boards, government, etc.) that organizations try to follow in order to please stakeholders.

institutional perspective an emerging view that holds that under high uncertainty, organizations imitate others in the same institutional environment.

institutional similarity the emergence of common structures, management approaches, and behaviors among organizations in the same field.

integrated enterprise an organization that uses advanced information technology to enable close coordination within the company as well as with suppliers, customers, and partners.

integration the quality of collaboration between departments of an organization.

integrator a position or department created solely to coordinate several departments.

intellectual capital the sum of an organization's knowledge, experience, understanding, processes, innovations, and discoveries.

intensive technologies a variety of products or services provided in combination to a client.

interdependence the extent to which departments depend on each other for resources or materials to accomplish their tasks.

intergroup conflict behavior that occurs between organizational groups when participants identify with one group and perceive that other groups may block their group's goal achievements or expectations.

interlocking directorate a formal linkage that occurs when a member of the board of directors of one company sits on the board of another company.

internal integration a state in which organization members develop a collective identity and know how to work together effectively.

internal process approach an approach that looks at internal activities and assesses effectiveness by indicators of internal health and efficiency.

internal process emphasis an aspect of the competing values model that reflects the values of internal focus and structural control.

international division a division that is equal in status to other major departments within a company and has its own hierarchy to handle business in various countries.

international stage the second stage of international development, in which the company takes exports seriously and begins to think multidomestically.

interorganizational relationships the relatively enduring resource transactions, flows, and linkages that occur among two or more organizations.

intranet a private, company-wide information network that uses the communications protocols and standards of the Internet but is accessible only to people within the company.

intuitive decision making the use of experience and judgment rather than sequential logic or explicit reasoning to solve a problem.

J

job design the assignment of goals and tasks to be accomplished by employees.

job enlargement the designing of jobs to expand the number of different tasks performed by an employee.

job enrichment the designing of jobs to increase responsibility, recognition, and opportunities for growth and achievement.

job rotation moving employees from job to job to give them a greater variety of tasks and alleviate boredom.

job simplification the reduction of the number and difficulty of tasks performed by a single person.

joint optimization the goal of the sociotechnical systems approach, which states that an organization will function best only if its social and technical systems are designed to fit the needs of one another.

joint venture a separate entity for sharing development and production costs and penetrating new markets that is created with two or more active firms as sponsors.

K

knowledge a conclusion drawn from information that has been linked to other information and compared to what is already known.

knowledge management the efforts to systematically find, organize, and make available a company's intellectual capital and to foster a culture of continuous learning and knowledge sharing so that organizational activities build on existing knowledge.

L

labor–management teams a cooperative approach designed to increase worker participation and provide a cooperative model for union-management problems.

language slogans, sayings, metaphors, or other expressions that convey a special meaning to employees.

large-batch production a manufacturing process characterized by long production runs of standardized parts.

large group intervention an approach that brings together participants from all parts of the organization (and may include outside stakeholders as well) to discuss problems or opportunities and plan for change.

lean manufacturing uses highly trained employees at every stage of the production process who take a painstaking approach to details and continuous problem solving to cut waste and improve quality.

learning organization an organization in which everyone is engaged in identifying and solving problems, enabling the organization to continuously experiment, improve, and increase its capability.

legends stories of events based in history that may have been embellished with fictional details.

legitimacy the general perspective that an organization's actions are desirable, proper, and appropriate within the environment's system of norms, values, and beliefs.

level of analysis in systems theory, the subsystem on which the primary focus is placed; four levels of analysis normally characterize organizations.

liaison role the function of a person located in one department who is responsible for communicating and achieving coordination with another department.

life cycle a perspective on organizational growth and change that suggests that organizations are born, grow older, and eventually die.

long-linked technology the combination within one organization of successive stages of production, with each stage using as its inputs the production of the preceding stage.

low-cost leadership a strategy that tries to increase market share by emphasizing low cost when compared with competitors' products.

M

management champion a manager who acts as a supporter and sponsor of a technical champion to shield and promote an idea within the organization.

management control systems the formalized routines, reports, and procedures that use information to maintain or alter patterns in organizational activity.

management information system a comprehensive, computerized system that provides information and supports day-to-day decision making.

management science approach organizational decision making that is the analog to the rational approach by individual managers.

managerial ethics principles that guide the decisions and behaviors of managers with regard to whether they are morally right or wrong.

market control a situation that occurs when price competition is used to evaluate the output and productivity of an organization.

mass customization the use of computer-integrated systems and flexible work processes to enable companies to mass produce a variety of products or services designed to exact customer specification.

matrix structure a strong form of horizontal linkage in which both product and functional structures (horizontal and vertical) are implemented simultaneously.

mechanistic an organization system marked by rules, procedures, a clear hierarchy of authority, and centralized decision making.

mediating technology the provision of products or services that mediate or link clients from the external environment and allow each department to work independently.

meso theory a new approach to organization studies that integrates both micro and macro levels of analysis.

mimetic forces under conditions of uncertainty, the pressure to copy or model other organizations that appear to be successful in the environment.

mission the organization's reason for its existence.

mission culture a culture that places emphasis on a clear vision of the organization's purpose and on the achievement of specific goals.

multidomestic company a company that deals with competitive issues in each country independent of other countries.

multidomestic strategy one in which competition in each country is handled independently of competition in other countries.

multifocused grouping a structure in which an organization embraces structural grouping alternatives simultaneously.

multinational stage the stage of international development in which a company has marketing and production facilities in many countries and more than one-third of its sales outside its home country.

myths stories that are consistent with the values and beliefs of the organization but are not supported by facts.

N

negotiation the bargaining process that often occurs during confrontation and enables the parties to systematically reach a solution.

network centrality top managers increase their power by locating themselves centrally in an organization and surrounding themselves with loyal subordinates.

networking linking computers within or between organizations.

new-venture fund a fund that provides financial resources to employees to develop new ideas, products, or businesses.

niche a domain of unique environmental resources and needs.

non-core technology a department work process that is important to the organization but is not directly related to its central mission.

nonprogrammed decisions novel and poorly defined, these are used when no procedure exists for solving the problem.

nonroutine technology technology in which there is high task variety and the conversion process is not analyzable or well understood.

nonsubstitutability a trait of a department whose function cannot be performed by other readily available resources.

normative forces pressures to adopt structures, techniques, or management processes because they are considered by the community to be up-to-date and effective.

O

official goals the formally stated definition of business scope and outcomes the organization is trying to achieve; another term for *mission*.

open system a system that must interact with the environment to survive.

open systems emphasis an aspect of the competing values model that reflects a combination of external focus and flexible structure.

operative goals descriptions of the ends sought through the actual operating procedures of the organization; these explain what the organization is trying to accomplish.

organic an organization system marked by free-flowing, adaptive processes, an unclear hierarchy of authority, and decentralized decision making.

organization development a behavioral science field devoted to improving performance through trust, open confrontation of problems, employee empowerment and participation, the design of meaningful work, cooperation between groups, and the full use of human potential.

organization structure designates formal reporting relationships, including the number of levels in the hierarchy and the span of control of managers and supervisors; identifies the grouping together of individuals into departments and of departments into the total organization; and includes the design of systems to ensure effective communication, coordination, and integration of efforts across departments.

organization theory a macro approach to organizations that analyzes the whole organization as a unit.

organizational behavior a micro approach to organizations that focuses on the individuals within organizations as the relevant units for analysis.

organizational change the adoption of a new idea or behavior by an organization.

organizational decision making the organizational process of identifying and solving problems.

organizational decline a condition in which a substantial, absolute decrease in an organization's resource base occurs over a period of time.

organizational ecosystem a system formed by the interaction of a community of organizations and their environment, usually cutting across traditional industry lines.

organizational environment all elements that exist outside the boundary of the organization and have the potential to affect all or part of the organization.

organizational form an organization's specific technology, structure, products, goals, and personnel.

organizational goal a desired state of affairs that the organization attempts to reach.

organizational innovation the adoption of an idea or behavior that is new to an organization's industry, market, or general environment.

organizational politics activities to acquire, develop, and use power and other resources to obtain one's preferred outcome when there is uncertainty or disagreement about choices.

organizations social entities that are goal-directed, deliberately structured activity systems linked to the external environment.

organized anarchy extremely organic organizations characterized by highly uncertain conditions.

outsourcing to contract out certain corporate functions, such as manufacturing, information technology, or credit processing, to other companies.

P

personnel ratios the proportions of administrative, clerical, and professional support staff.

point–counterpoint a decision-making technique that divides decision makers into two groups and assigns them different, often competing responsibilities.

political model a definition of an organization as being made up of groups that have separate interests, goals, and values in which power and influence are needed to reach decisions.

political tactics for using power these include building coalitions, expanding networks, controlling decision premises, enhancing legitimacy and expertise, and making a direct appeal.

pooled interdependence the lowest form of interdependence among departments, in which work does not flow between units.

population a set of organizations engaged in similar activities with similar patterns of resource utilization and outcomes.

population ecology perspective a perspective in which the focus is on organizational diversity and adaptation within a community or population or organizations.

power the ability of one person or department in an organization to influence others to bring about desired outcomes.

power distance the level of inequality people are willing to accept within an organization.

power sources there are five sources of horizontal power in organizations: dependency, financial resources, centrality, nonsubstitutability, and the ability to cope with uncertainty.

problem consensus the agreement among managers about the nature of problems or opportunities and about which goals and outcomes to pursue.

problem identification the decision-making stage in which information about environmental and organizational conditions is monitored to determine if performance is satisfactory and to diagnose the cause of shortcomings.

problem solution the decision-making stage in which alternative courses of action are considered and one alternative is selected and implemented.

problemistic search occurs when managers look around in the immediate environment for a solution to resolve a problem quickly.

process organized group of related tasks and activities that work together to transform inputs into outputs that create value for customers.

product and service changes changes in an organization's product or service outputs.

product matrix a variation of the matrix structure in which project or product managers have primary authority and functional managers simply assign technical personnel to projects and provide advisory expertise.

programmed decisions repetitive and well-defined procedures that exist for resolving problems.

prospector a business strategy characterized by innovation, risk-taking, seeking out new opportunities, and growth.

R

radical change a breaking of the frame of reference for an organization, often creating a new equilibrium because the entire organization is transformed.

rational approach a process of decision making that stresses the need for systematic analysis of a problem followed by choice and implementation in a logical sequence.

rational goal emphasis an aspect of the competing values model that reflects values of structural control and external focus.

rational-legal authority based on employees' belief in the legality of rules and the right of those in authority to issue commands.

rational model a description of an organization characterized by a rational approach to decision making, extensive and reliable information systems, central power, a norm of optimization, uniform values across groups, little conflict, and an efficiency orientation.

reactor a business strategy in which environmental threats and opportunities are responded to in an ad hoc fashion.

reasons organizations grow growth occurs because it is an organizational goal, it is necessary to attract and keep quality managers, or it is necessary to maintain economic health.

reciprocal interdependence the highest level of interdependence, in which the output of one operation is the input of a second, and the output of the second operation is the input of the first (for example, a hospital).

reengineering redesigning a vertical organization along its horizontal workflows and processes.

resource dependence a situation in which organizations depend on the environment but strive to acquire control over resources to minimize their dependence.

resource-based approach an organizational perspective that assesses effectiveness by observing how successfully the organization obtains, integrates, and manages valued resources.

retention the preservation and institutionalization of selected organizational forms.

rites and ceremonies the elaborate, planned activities that make up a special event and often are conducted for the benefit of an audience.

role a part in a dynamic social system that allows an employee to use his or her discretion and ability to achieve outcomes and meet goals.

routine technology technology characterized by little task variety and the use of objective, computational procedures.

rule of law that which arises from a set of codified principles and regulations that describe how people are required to act, are generally accepted in society, and are enforceable in the courts.

S

satisficing the acceptance by organizations of a satisfactory rather than a maximum level of performance.

scientific management a classical approach that claims decisions about organization and job design should be based on precise, scientific procedures.

sectors subdivisions of the external environment that contain similar elements.

selection the process by which organizational variations are determined to fit the external environment; variations that fail to fit the needs of the environment are "selected out" and fail.

sequential interdependence a serial form of interdependence in which the output of one operation becomes the input to another operation.

service technology technology characterized by simultaneous production and consumption, customized output, customer participation, intangible output, and being labor intensive.

simple-complex dimension the number and dissimilarity of external elements relevant to an organization's operation.

Six Sigma quality standard that specifies a goal of no more than 3.4 defects per million parts; expanded to refer to a set of control procedures that emphasize the relentless pursuit of higher quality and lower costs.

skunkworks separate, small, informal, highly autonomous, and often secretive group that focuses on breakthrough ideas for the business.

small-batch production a manufacturing process, often custom work, that is not highly mechanized and relies heavily on the human operator.

social audit measures and reports the ethical, social, and environmental impact of a company's operations.

social capital the quality of interactions among people, affected by whether they share a common perspective.

social responsibility management's obligation to make choices and take action so that the organization contributes to the welfare and interest of society as well as itself.

sociotechnical systems approach an approach that combines the needs of people with the needs of technical efficiency.

sources of intergroup conflict factors that generate conflict, including goal incompatibility, differentiation, task interdependence, and limited resources.

specialist an organization that has a narrow range of goods or services or serves a narrow market.

stable-unstable dimension the state of an organization's environmental elements.

stakeholder any group within or outside an organization that has a stake in the organization's performance.

stakeholder approach also called the *constituency approach,* this perspective assesses the satisfaction of stakeholders as an indicator of the organization's performance.

standardization a policy that ensures all branches of the company at all locations operate in the same way

stories narratives based on true events that are frequently shared among organizational employees and told to new employees to inform them about an organization.

strategic contingencies events and activities inside and outside an organization that are essential for attaining organizational goals.

strategy the current set of plans, decisions, and objectives that have been adopted to achieve the organization's goals.

strategy and structure changes changes in the administrative domain of an organization, including structure, policies, reward systems, labor relations, coordination devices, management information control systems, and accounting and budgeting.

structural dimensions descriptions of the internal characteristics of an organization

structure the formal reporting relationships, groupings, and systems of an organization.

struggle for existence a principle of the population ecology model that holds that organizations are engaged in a competitive struggle for resources and fighting to survive.

subcultures cultures that develop within an organization to reflect the common problems, goals, and experiences that members of a team, department, or other unit share.

subsystems divisions of an organization that perform specific functions for the organization's survival; organizational subsystems perform the essential functions of boundary spanning, production, maintenance, adaptation, and management.

switching structures an organization creates an organic structure when such a structure is needed for the initiation of new ideas.

symbol something that represents another thing.

symptoms of structural deficiency signs of the organization structure being out of alignment, including delayed or poor-quality decision making, failure to respond innovatively to environmental changes, and too much conflict.

system a set of interacting elements that acquires inputs from the environment, transforms them, and discharges outputs to the external environment.

T

tacit knowledge knowledge that is based on personal experience, intuition, rules of thumb, and judgment, and cannot be easily codified and passed on to others in written form.

tactics for enhancing collaboration techniques such as integration devices, confrontation and negotiation, intergroup consultation, member rotation, and shared mission and superordinate goals that enable groups to overcome differences and work together.

tactics for increasing power these include entering areas of high uncertainty, creating dependencies, providing resources, and satisfying strategic contingencies.

task a narrowly defined piece of work assigned to a person.

task environment sectors with which the organization interacts directly and that have a direct effect on the organization's ability to achieve its goals.

task force a temporary committee composed of representatives from each department affected by a problem.

team building activities that promote the idea that people who work together can work together as a team.

teams permanent task forces often used in conjunction with a full-time integrator.

technical champion a person who generates or adopts and develops an idea for a technological innovation and is devoted to it, even to the extent of risking position or prestige; also called *product champion*.

technical complexity the extent of mechanization in the manufacturing process.

technical knowledge understanding and agreement about how to solve problems and reach organizational goals.

technology the tools, techniques, and actions used to transform organizational inputs into outputs.

technology changes changes in an organization's production process, including its knowledge and skills base, that enable distinctive competence.

time-based competition delivering products and services faster than competitors, giving companies a competitive edge.

traditional authority based in the belief in traditions and the legitimacy of the status of people exercising authority through those traditions.

transaction processing systems (TPS) automation of the organization's routine, day-to-day business transactions.

transnational model a form of horizontal organization that has multiple centers, subsidiary managers who initiate strategy and innovations for the company as a whole, and unity and coordination achieved through corporate culture and shared vision and values.

U

uncertainty occurs when decision makers do not have sufficient information about environmental factors and have a difficult time predicting external changes.

uncertainty avoidance the level of tolerance for and comfort with uncertainty and individualism within a culture.

V

values-based leadership a relationship between a leader and followers that is based on strongly shared values that are advocated and acted upon by the leader.

variation appearance of new organizational forms in response to the needs of the external environment; analogous to mutations in biology.

variety in terms of tasks, the frequency of unexpected and novel events that occur in the conversion process.

venture teams a technique to foster creativity within organizations in which a small team is set up as its own company to pursue innovations.

vertical information system the periodic reports, written information, and computer-based communications distributed to managers.

vertical linkages communication and coordination activities connecting the top and bottom of an organization.

virtual network grouping organization that is a loosely connected cluster of separate components.

virtual network structure the firm subcontracts many or most of its major processes to separate companies and coordinates their activities from a small headquarters organization.

virtual team made up of organizationally or geographically dispersed members who are linked through advanced information and communications technologies. Members frequently use the Internet and collaborative software to work together, rather than meeting face-to-face.

W

whistle-blowing employee disclosure of illegal, immoral, or illegitimate practices on the part of the organization.

Name Index

Page numbers followed by the letter n indicate the note in which the entry is located.

A

Abboud, Leila, 169n66
Abdalla, David, 132n27
Abel, Katie, 168n37
Abelson, Reed, 439n83
Abizaid, John, 30
Abramson, Gary, 317n42
Ackerman, Linda S., 119, 133n58
Ackerman, Val, 71
Adams, Chris, 169n66
Adices, Ichak, 354n26
Adler, Nancy J., 209, 240n14
Adler, Paul S., 258–259, 283n24, 284n39, 285n74, 285n79, 438n31
Aenlle, Conrad de, 240n31
Aeppel, Timothy, 355n80
Agins, Teri, 169n57
Aiken, Michael, 284n61, 354n44, 437n11
Akgün, Ali E., 439n61
Akinnusi, David M., 439n76
Alban, Billie T., 440n88, 440n89
Alderfer, Clayton T., 514n4
Aldrich, Howard E., 49n14, 167n16, 202n34
Alexander, Keith, 438n48, 480n70
Allaire, Paul, 4–5
Allen, Richard S., 440n93
Allen, Robert W., 515n63
Allison, Charles F., 432, 434–435
Alsop, Ronald, 202n49, 202n50, 202n51
Altier, William J., 132n18
Amdt, Michael, 133n45
Amelio, Gilbert, 329
Ammeter, Anthony P., 516n77
Anand, N., 133n57
Anand, Vikas, 318n45
Anders, George, 515n39
Andersen, Arthur, 8
Anderson, Carl, 397n88

Aniston, Jennifer, 466
Antonelli, Cristiano, 133n51
Archer, Earnest R., 478n14, 478n16
Argote, Linda, 283n4, 285n67, 285n75
Argüello, Michael, 479n38
Argyris, Chris, 74, 87n45, 316
Arndt, Michael, 86n16, 86n29, 317n15, 317n25
Arnold, Rick, 511–512
Arogyaswamy, Bernard, 395n34
Arthur, Mr., 41
Ashford, Susan, 201n19
Ashkenas, Ron, 440n90
Astley, W. Graham, 354n47, 514n22, 515n32, 515n47
Aston, Adam, 133n45
At-Twaijri, Mohamed Ibrahim Ahmad, 168n27
Athitakis, Mark, 478n4
Atkin, Robert S., 169n61
Atsaides, James, 356n85, 356n86
Aubin, Jean, 479n37
Auster, Ellen R., 202n56
Austin, Nancy, 41
Ayers, Nicholas, 28

B

Babcock, Judith A., 169n52
Bacharach, Samuel B., 437n12
Badaracco, Joseph L. Jr., 396n70
Baetz, Mark, 86n6
Bailetti, Antonio J., 438n52
Baker, Edward, 479n37
Baker, Richard, 358
Balaji, Y., 317n41
Ballmer, Steven, 106, 330, 334
Balu, Rekha, 395n33
Bandler, James, 240n1
Banham, Russ, 317n17
Bank, David, 395n24, 478n2
Bannon, Lisa, 50n17
Barbara, Mayor, 196
Barczak, Gloria, 439n67
Barkema, Harry G., 49n3, 49n4
Barker, James R., 355n74
Barker, Robert, 437n16

Barley, Stephen R., 50n18, 318n68, 318n70
Barnatt, Christopher, 318n62
Barnett, Megan, 318n72
Barney, Jay B., 87n42, 168n48
Barone, Michael, 354n23
Barrett, Amy, 85n5, 132n17, 132n29, 240n20, 241n49, 514n8
Barrett, Craig, 472
Barrier, Michael, 396n73
Barrionuevo, Alexei, 394n3, 395n23
Barron, Kelly, 354n40, 437n8
Barsoux, Jean-Louis, 242n68
Bart, Christopher, 86n6
Bartkus, Barbara, 86n7
Bartlett, Christopher A., 133n44, 201n10, 231, 240n6, 241n63, 242n68, 242n69, 242n73, 242n74
Barton, Chris, 186
Barwise, Patrick, 316n1, 318n64
Bass, Bernard M., 440n95
Baum, J. Robert, 478n22
Baum, Joel A. C., 49n3, 201n34
Bazerman, Max H., 169n61, 396n66
Beard, Donald W., 167n17
Beatty, Carol A., 440n99
Beaudoin, Laurent, 159
Becker, Selwyn W., 354n41, 355n49, 440n103
Beckhard, Richard, 74, 87n45
Bedeian, Arthur G., 202n44
Behling, Orlando, 478n22
Bell, Cecil H. Jr., 439n85, 440n86
Bell, Gerald D., 284n64
Belohlav, James A., 241n38
Belson, Ken, 240n13, 241n53
Benedetti, Marti, 201n15
Benitz, Linda E., 392
Bennett, Amanda, 50n35
Bennis, Warren G., 74, 87n45, 440n106
Berenbeim, Ronald E., 397n90
Bergquist, William, 50n38
Berkman, Erik, 317n8
Berman, Barry, 283n33

Berman, Dennis K., 168n44
Bernstein, Aaron, 49n5, 167n7, 516n88
Berrett-Koehler, 437n4
Beyer, Janice M., 363, 394n10, 395n19
Bezos, Jeff, 488
Bianco, Anthony, 49n1
Biemans, Wim G., 439n58
Biggers, Kelsey, 313
Bigley, Gregory A., 355n55, 355n57
Binkley, Christina, 479n39
Birkinshaw, Julian, 438n39
Birnback, Bruce, 153
Birnbaum, Jeffrey H., 169n68
Black, Lord Conrad, 492
Blackburn, Richard S., 515n36
Blackman, Andrew, 318n66
Blai, Boris, 478n14
Blair, Donald, 330
Blake, Robert R., 507, 516n86, 516n87, 516n91, 516n93
Blanchard, Olivier, 242n71
Blau, Judith R., 438n32
Blau, Peter M., 284n64, 354n47
Blekley, Fred R., 201n32
Blenkhorn, David L., 86n35
Bloodgood, James M., 394n4
Bluedorn, Allen C., 167n16, 354n41
Boeker, Warren, 515n53
Bohbot, Michele, 369
Bohman, Jim, 351
Boland, M., 354n47
Boland, W., 354n47
Bolino, Mark C., 394n4
Bolman, Lee G., 514n2
Bonabeau, Eric, 479n28, 479n30
Bonazzi, Giuseppe, 133n51
Boorstin, Julia, 240n15, 394n2
Borys, Bryan, 169n54, 169n58
Bossidy, Larry, 87n54, 325, 402
Bossidy, Lawrence A., 144
Boudette, Neal E., 132n19
Boulding, Elise, 514n22
Bourgeois, L. J. III, 480n64, 514n3

Bowen, David E., 260, 284n44, 284n52
Bower, Carolyn, 50n28
Bowerman, Bill, 329
Boyle, Matthew, 61, 167n4, 395n32
Brabeck-Letmathe, Peter, 217
Brady, Diane, 284n45
Brady, Simon, 396n57
Branch, Shelly, 133n36
Brandt, Richard, 201n18
Brannigan, Martha, 49n2
Brass, Daniel J., 515n29, 516n71
Breen, Bill, 478n23
Breen, Ed, 419–420
Bremner, Brian, 241n53, 437n1
Bresnahan, Jennifer, 396n65
Brewster, Linda, 169n62
Brimelow, Peter, 354n46
Brimm, Michael, 512
Brin, Sergey, 327
Brittain, Jack W., 202n34
Brockner, Joel, 356n86, 480n72
Brodsky, Norm, 50n44, 440n92
Bronikowski, Karne, 439n62
Brooks, Geoffrey R., 402
Brooks, Rick, 50n28, 478n10
Brown, Andrew D., 394n7
Brown, Ben, 338
Brown, Eryn, 317n34
Brown, John, 355n60
Brown, L. David, 514n7
Brown, Shona L., 438n53, 438n55
Brown, Steve, 317n31
Brown, Stuart F., 284n58
Brown, Tom, 353n17
Brown, Warren B., 168n29
Bruce, Reginald A., 430
Bu, Nailin, 242n72
Buchanan, Leigh, 316n2, 318n65
Buckley, Ron, 24
Buckley, Timothy, 395n42
Buller, Paul F., 393, 440n91
Bunker, Barbara B., 440n88, 440n89
Burke, Charles, 325
Burke, Debbie, 440n90
Burke, W. Warner, 439n85, 440n86
Burkhardt, Marlene E., 516n71
Burns, Greg, 514n8
Burns, Lawton R., 133n42
Burns, Tom, 151, 168n42, 437n23
Burt, Ronald S., 169n61
Burton, Thomas M., 437n17, 437n22
Bush, George W., 103
Byles, Charles M., 395n34
Bylinsky, Gene, 283n1, 283n15, 283n20, 285n73
Byrne, John A., 115, 323, 353n12, 396n64
Byrne, John C., 439n61
Byrnes, Nanette, 514n9

C

Cadieux, Chester II, 31
Cali, Filippo, 270
Callahan, Charles V., 311, 316n5
Camerman, Filip, 221
Cameron, Kim S., 76, 86n34, 87n53, 327, 331, 354n27, 355n75, 355n79, 356n86
Campbell, Andrew, 133n43
Canabou, Christine, 438n35
Canseco, Phil, 476
Cardoza, Mr. R. H., 199–200
Cardoza, Ms., 199
Carlton, Jim, 240n8
Carney, Eliza Newlin, 132n30
Carpenter, Jim, 390–391
Carpenter, Mary, 235–236
Carr, David, 240n1
Carr, Patricia, 439n84
Carr, Tom, 315
Carroll, Glenn R., 202n42
Carroll, Stephen J., 201n19
Carter, Jimmy, 336
Carter, Nancy M., 354n43
Cartwright, D., 515n28
Cascio, W. S., 285n82
Cascio, Wayne F., 356n85, 356n90
Case, John, 353n18
Casselman, Cindy, 493
Caudron, Shari, 356n86, 356n89
Caulfield, Brian, 318n60
Cavanagh, Richard, 336
Cha, Sandra Eunyoung, 395n17, 395n26, 395n35, 395n39
Chamberland, Denis, 133n50, 133n51
Champion, John M., 390
Chapman, Art, 132n27
Charan, Ram, 87n54, 144, 325
Charnes, John, 439n63
Charns, Martin P., 86n12
Chase, Richard B., 284n50, 284n52, 285n79
Chatman, Jennifer A., 395n17, 395n26, 395n35, 395n39
Chen, Christine Y., 440n101
Cheng, Joseph L. C., 285n75
Cherney, Elena, 515n43
Chesbrough, Henry W., 133n57
Child, John, 132n4, 133n60, 355n48
Chiles, James R., 252
Chipello, Christopher J., 86n14
Chow, Chee W., 297, 317n27, 317n28, 440n95
Churchill, Neil C., 354n26
Cialdini, Robert B., 504
Clark, Don, 201n17
Clark, John P., 86n39
Clark, Mickey, 394n1
Clarkson, Max B. E., 396n66
Clegg, Stewart R., 201n34, 202n53
Clifford, Lee, 317n23
Cohen, Don, 394n4
Cohen, Irit, 515n53

Cohen, Michael D., 463, 479n54
Coia, Arthur C., 506
Coleman, Henry J. Jr., 68, 133n52, 355n66, 439n69
Collins, Jim, 86n10, 353n8, 364
Collins, Paul D., 284n39, 284n64
Congden, Steven W., 283n14, 283n17
Conlon, Edward J., 50n29
Conner, Daryl R., 425, 440n97
Connolly, Terry, 50n29
Connor, Patrick E., 284n63
Cook, Lynn, 132n27
Cook, Michelle, 168n28
Cooper, Christopher, 86n18, 515n49
Cooper, William C., 284n59
Copeland, Michael V., 478n1, 478n6
Cormick, Gerald, 195
Courtright, John A., 168n43
Cousins, Roland B., 392
Coutu, Diane L., 440n107
Cowen, Scott S., 317n26
Cox, James, 316n3
Coy, Peter, 201n18
Craig, Susanne, 515n49
Craig, Timothy J., 242n72
Crainer, Stuart, 438n42
Cramer, Roderick M., 514n18
Creed, W. E. Douglas, 355n66, 439n69
Creswell, Julie, 169n72, 202n37
Crewdson, John, 354n39
Crittenden, Victoria L., 485, 514n11
Crock, Stan, 168n33
Cronin, Mary J., 317n34
Cross, Jim, 440n104
Cross, Kim, 86n17
Cummings, Jeanne, 169n67
Cummings, Larry L., 285n67, 438n44, 514n10, 514n18
Cummings, T., 275
Cummins, Doug, 126
Cummins, Gaylord, 86n36
Cunningham, J. Barton, 87n47
Cuomo, Mario, 473
Cusumano, Michael A., 283n16
Cyert, Richard M., 456, 479n43, 479n45

D

Daboub, Anthony J., 169n70
Dacin, M. Tina, 202n46
Daft, Richard L., 33, 86n34, 116, 126, 133n48, 264, 284n59, 284n63, 284n65, 285n67, 295, 317n19, 317n26, 354n41, 354n47, 355n48, 355n49, 437n12, 439n71, 439n72, 439n73, 440n103, 479n42
Dahl, Robert A., 514n21
Dahle, Cheryl, 394n12

Dalton, Gene W., 168n38, 514n14
Damanpour, Fariborz, 439n70, 439n74
D'Amico, Carol, 49n12, 397n96
Dandridge, Thomas C., 395n16
Daniels, Cora, 395n31
Daniels, John D., 241n39
Dann, Valerie, 516n96
Dannemiller, Kathleen D., 440n88
Darrow, Barbara, 132n12
Datta, Deepak K., 479n34
Datz, Todd, 318n44, 438n30
Dauch, Richard, 245
Davenport, Thomas H., 515n41
David, Forest R., 86n6
David, Fred R., 86n6
David, Grainger, 283n18, 283n36
Davidow, William A., 437n5
Davidson, Harmon, 476–477
Davig, William, 317n31
Davis, Ann, 514n1, 516n81
Davis, Eileen, 49n3
Davis, Stanley M., 133n37, 133n39
Davis, Tim R. V., 316n1
Davison, Sue Canney, 241n58
Dawson, Chester, 437n1
Dawson, Sarah, 87n49
Day, Jonathan D., 133n60
Deal, Terrence E., 395n15, 395n20, 514n2
Dean, James W. Jr., 478n17, 516n65
Dearlove, Des, 438n42
Deere, John, 147
DeFoe, Joe, 448
DeGeorge, Gail, 240n28
Deitzer, Bernard A., 84
Delacroix, Jacques, 202n42
Delbecq, Andre L., 272, 285n67, 285n75, 396n71, 437n11
DeLong, James V., 515n62
DeMarie, Samuel M., 132n23
DeMott, John S., 283n23
Denis, Hélène, 285n77
Denison, Daniel R., 367, 395n28, 397n100
Deniston, O. Lynn, 86n36
Dent, Harry S. Jr., 402
Denton, D. Keith, 440n105
Denzler, David R., 318n56
DePeters, Jack, 61
Dess, Gregory G., 132n26, 133n56, 133n57, 167n17, 240n28, 437n5
Detert, James R., 395n27
Deutsch, Claudia H., 49n1
Deutsch, Stuart Jay, 50n29
Deutschman, Alan, 514n20
Dewar, Robert D., 354n42
Dickey, Beth, 87n50, 480n60
Digate, Charles, 73
Dill, William R., 479n35
Dillon, Karen, 478n13
DiMaggio, Paul J., 202n54, 202n55

Dimancescu, Dan, 438n55, 439n68
DiSimone, L. D., 437n21
DiTomaso, N., 395n40
Doehring, J., 132n27
Doerflein, Stephen, 356n85, 356n86
Dolgen, Jonathan, 453
Donald, Jim, 55
Donaldson, T., 50n29
Doran, George T., 480n63, 480n67, 480n68
Dorfman, Peter, 242n67
Dougherty, Deborah, 438n50, 439n62
Dougherty, Jack, 21
Douglas, Ceasar, 516n77
Douglas, Frank L., 439n63
Dove, Erin, 476
Dowling, Grahame R., 202n50
Downey, Diane, 132n16
Dragoon, Alice, 201n9, 201n22, 317n9
Dreazen, Yochi J., 478n18, 515n49
Driscoll, Dawn-Marie, 395n46, 396n66
Drory, Amos, 516n67
Drucker, Peter F., 49n15, 81, 353n18, 438n41, 440n98, 477
Drukerman, Pamela, 241n50
Drummond, Helga, 480n72
Drummond, Walton, 476
Druyan, Darleen, 161
Duck, Jeanie Daniel, 424
Dudley, Graham, 283n26
Duerinckx, Reina, 268
Duffield, Dave, 366
Duffy, Tom, 168n30
Dugan, Ianthe Jeanne, 515n39, 515n49
Duimering, P. Robert, 284n40
Duncan, Robert B., 103, 105, 111, 132n26, 133n32, 133n41, 146, 152, 167n17, 437n25
Duncan, W. Jack, 394n7
Dunnette, M.D., 514n6
Dunphy, Dexter C., 440n109
Dutton, Gail, 397n102
Dutton, John M., 514n13, 514n16
Dux, Pierre, 512–513
Dvorak, Phred, 133n34, 241n53
Dwenger, Kemp, 438n55, 439n68
Dworkin, Terry Morehead, 396n84
Dwyer, Paula, 49n13
Dyer, Jeffrey H., 180, 201n26, 201n27

E

Eccles, Robert G., 515n41
Eckel, Norman L., 478n22
Edmondson, Amy, 440n106
Edwards, Cliff, 241n53, 438n51

Edwards, Gary, 383
Egri, Carolyn P., 438n44
Eichenwald, Kurt, 86n9
Eisenberg, Daniel J., 478n21
Eisenhardt, Kathleen M., 438n53, 438n55, 439n62, 480n64, 480n65, 514n3
Elbert, Norb, 317n31
Elder, Renee, 478n12
Elffers, Joost, 514n27
Elgin, Ben, 516n85
Elliott, Stuart, 353n6
Ellison, Larry, 94
Ellison, Sarah, 167n6
Elsbach, Kimberly D., 169n72
Emerson, Richard M., 514n24, 515n54
Emery, F., 285n81
Emery, Fred E., 167n16
Eng, Sherri, 438n34
Engardio, Pete, 49n5, 201n29
Engle, Jane, 86n22
Engle, Paul, 133n53, 133n56, 133n57
Enns, Harvey G., 516n72
Epstein, Edwin M., 168n34
Epstein, Lisa D., 203n58
Estepa, James, 149
Estepa, Jim, 168n37
Etzioni, Amitai, 85n2, 86n31, 86n32
Evan, William M., 439n70
Evaniski, Michael J., 439n70
Eveland, J. D., 86n36
Eyring, Henry B., 479n35

F

Fabrikant, Geraldine, 86n27, 479n33
Fairhurst, Gail T., 168n43
Farnham, Alan, 50n34, 437n14
Fassihi, Farnaz, 478n18
Fayol, Henri, 26
Feldman, Steven P., 394n10
Feldman, Stewart, 202n40
Fenn, Donna, 201n22
Fennell, Mary L., 439n70
Ferguson, Kevin, 317n17
Ferguson, Ralph, 434–435
Ferrara, Michael, 421
Ferris, Gerald R., 515n64, 516n65
Ferry, Diane L., 33, 285n66
Fey, Carl F., 397n100
Fields, Gary, 50n33
Filo, David, 505
Finch, Byron J., 284n43
Fine, Charles H., 283n16
Finnigan, Annie, 49n13
Fiorina, Carly, 442
Fisher, Anne B., 439n82
Fisher, Michael, 479n37
Fishman, Charles, 50n30, 132n22, 202n51, 285n70
Fitzgerald, Michael, 316n4
Fletcher, Joyce K., 49n13
Flood, Mary, 318n55
Flynn, John, 432, 434–435

Fogerty, John E., 133n45
Fombrun, Charles, 50n29, 50n32, 515n47
Fontaine, Michael A., 318n55, 318n71
Ford, Bill, 89
Ford, Jeffrey D., 354n46
Ford, Robert C., 133n41
Forest, Stephanie Anderson, 202n43
Forsythe, Jason, 49n12
Foster, Peter, 197
Fouts, Paul A., 87n42
Fox, Jeffrey J., 514n27
Fox, William M., 285n81
Fraley, Elisabeth, 512
France, Mike, 168n19, 168n36, 396n64
Francis, Carol E., 273, 285n81
Frank, Robert, 167n13, 241n48, 515n43
Franke, Markus, 167n3
Freedberg, Sydney J., 50n42
Freeman, John, 183, 202n34, 202n36
Freeman, Martin, 434–435
Freidheim, Cyrus F. Jr., 240n22
French, Bell, 440n86, 440n87, 440n88
French, John R. P. Jr., 515n28
French, Wendell L., 439n85, 440n86, 440n87, 440n88
Friedlander, Beth, 196
Friedman, David, 353n14
Friesen, Peter H., 354n26
Frieswick, Kris, 355n77
Frink, Dwight D., 515n64
Frost, Peter J., 87n46, 438n44
Fry, Louis W., 259, 284n39
Fuller, Scott, 370

G

Gaber, Brian, 86n35
Gaertner, Gregory H., 439n76
Gaertner, Karen N., 439n76
Gajilan, Arlyn Tobias, 50n22
Galang, Maria Carmen, 515n64
Galbraith, Jay R., 132n11, 132n14, 132n16, 241n64, 438n44, 514n17, 516n94, 516n95
Galloni, Alessandra, 169n57
Gantz, Jeffrey, 515n63, 516n70
Gardiner, Lorraine R., 485, 514n11
Garino, Jason, 308, 318n63
Garner, Rochelle, 132n12
Garvin, David A., 317n43, 480n66
Gates, Bill, 13, 106, 330, 334
Geber, Beverly, 396n81, 397n93
Geeraerts, Guy, 354n43
George, A. L., 449
George, Bill, 86n10
George, Thomas, 479n29
Gerstner, Louis, 4, 402
Gesteland, Richard R., 228

Ghadially, Rehana, 515n64
Ghobadian, Abby, 395n26, 395n40
Ghoshal, Sumantra, 133n44, 201n10, 231, 240n6, 241n36, 241n49, 241n63, 242n68, 242n69, 242n73, 242n74
Ghosn, Carlos, 443, 478n6
Gibson, David G., 396n86
Gladwell, Malcolm, 452
Glassman, Myron, 86n7
Glick, William H., 318n45, 402
Glinow, Mary Ann Von, 439n77
Glisson, Charles A., 284n61
Gnyawali, Devi R., 201n4
Gobeli, David H., 133n38
Godfrey, Joline, 49n13
Godfrey, Paul C., 87n42
Goding, Jeff, 317n24
Goes, James B., 402, 437n13
Gogoi, Pallavi, 86n29
Gold, Bela, 283n25
Goldhar, Joel D., 283n37, 284n40, 284n41
Goldoftas, Barbara, 438n31
Goode, Kathy, 354n40
Goodhue, Dale L., 284n60
Goodstein, Jerry, 202n46
Goodwin, Brian, 201n8
Goold, Michael, 133n43
Gopinath, C., 283n14, 283n17
Gordon, G. G., 395n40
Gordon, John R. M., 440n99
Gore, Bill, 21
Gore, W. L., 92
Gottlieb, Jonathan Z., 440n94
Gottlieb, Manu, 196
Govindarajan, Vijay, 240n6, 241n34, 241n47, 241n55, 241n56, 386
Graham, Ginger L., 486
Grant, Robert M., 318n49, 318n50
Grasso, Dick, 493
Grauwe, Paul De, 221
Gray, David A., 169n70
Gray, Steven, 85n1
Grayson, C. Jackson Jr., 318n52, 479n40
Greco, Susan, 201n11
Greenberg, Hank, 491
Greene, Jay, 354n36
Greene, Robert, 514n27
Greenhalgh, Leonard, 181, 355n78, 355n79
Greenhouse, Steven, 49n12
Greening, Daniel W., 396n55
Greenwood, Royston, 132n5, 355n60
Greiner, Larry E., 327, 331, 354n27
Gresov, Christopher, 284n60, 284n61, 284n62, 285n69, 285n75
Griffin, Ricky W., 164, 437n14
Grimes, A. J., 284n62, 515n31

Grittner, Peter, 180, 201n14, 201n26, 201n27
Groetsch, David, 506
Grossman, Allen, 50n16
Grossman, John, 437n4, 437n15
Grossman, Laurie M., 351
Grossman, Robert J., 49n1
Grover, Ron, 240n24
Grover, Ronald, 241n53, 438n48, 480n70, 514n9
Grow, Brian, 167n10
Guernsey, Brock, 439n63
Guillén, Mauro F., 50n34
Gulati, Ranjay, 308, 318n63
Gunn, Jack, 480n63, 480n67, 480n68
Gunther, Marc, 396n52, 397n95
Gupta, Anil K., 240n6, 241n34, 241n47, 241n55, 241n56
Gupta, Rajat, 9
Gustafson, Loren T., 87n42
Guth, Robert A., 132n31, 168n45, 201n17

H

Hackett, Edward J., 440n108
Haddad, Kamal M., 297, 317n27, 317n28
Hage, Jerald, 284n61, 354n44, 437n11
Hahn, Betty, 354n40
Hake, Ralph, 442
Haldeman, Jeffrey, 273, 285n81
Hale, Wayne, 75
Hall, Douglas T., 278
Hall, Richard H., 50n26, 86n39, 354n43
Hall, Richard L., 202n44
Hambrick, Donald C., 86n30, 241n58
Hamburger, M., 413, 438n52
Hamel, Gary, 354n21, 440n98
Hamm, Steve, 133n31, 439n75
Hammer, Michael, 133n46, 133n47, 317n24, 420
Hammond, John S., 478n13
Hammonds, Keith H., 49n5, 50n21, 133n51, 240n11, 324, 353n16, 354n25, 403
Hammonds, See, 353n17
Hampton, David L., 280
Hancock, Herbie, 55
Hanges, Paul, 242n67
Hanks, Tom, 453
Hannan, Michael T., 183, 202n34, 202n36, 202n42
Hansell, Saul, 478n6
Hansen, Morten T., 241n65, 303, 318n53
Hansson, Tom, 167n3
Harada, Takashi, 255
Harari, Oren, 51n46
Hardy, Cynthia, 201n34, 202n53, 438n50, 439n62
Harper, Richard H. R., 302
Harreld, Heather, 317n8

Harrington, Ann, 50n27, 50n34, 51n45, 86n15, 438n47, 439n59
Harrington, Richard, 78
Harrington, Susan J., 397n94
Harris, Gardiner, 169n66
Harris, Randall D., 167n16
Harvey, Cheryl, 126
Harvey, Edward, 283n8
Harwood, John, 355n64
Hassard, John, 283n26
Hatch, Mary Jo, 394n10
Hatch, Nile W., 201n26
Hawkins, Lee Jr., 86n13, 87n41, 169n63, 514n8
Hawley, A., 354n47
Hayashi, Alden M., 478n23
Hays, Constance L., 168n21, 240n30, 317n14
Hays, Kristin, 132n27
Head, Thomas C., 164
Heck, R. H., 395n40
Heide, Jan B., 201n20
Hellriegel, Don, 275, 285n80, 395n18
Hellriegel, Slocum, 285n84
Hemmert, Martin, 242n70
Hench, Thomas J., 478n23
Henderson, A. M., 354n37
Henderson, Sam, 195–196
Hendrickson, Anthony R., 132n23
Henkoff, Ronald, 284n42, 356n86
Henricks, Mark, 397n93
Henry, David, 353n15
Hensley, Scott, 438n49
Herbert, Theodore T., 209, 240n14
Heskett, James L., 372, 374, 394n11, 395n43
Heymans, Brian, 283n29
Hickel, James K., 439n79
Hicks, Tom, 489–490
Hickson, David J., 50n26, 201n13, 202n35, 202n54, 202n55, 283n5, 283n7, 515n51, 515n52, 515n58, 515n60, 516n73
Higgins, Christopher A., 438n40
Higgins, James H., 394n9, 395n25
Higgs, A. Catherine, 356n84
Higuchi, Tatsuo, 409
Hildebrand, Carol, 315
Hill, Charles W. L., 439n60
Hill, G. Christian, 132n12
Hillebrand, Bas, 439n58
Hilton, Anthony, 132n12
Himelstein, Linda, 168n33, 202n43, 355n82
Hinings, Bob, 132n5
Hinings, C. R., 50n26, 355n60, 515n51, 515n52
Hise, Phaedra, 438n38
Hitt, Michael, 68
Hject, Paola, 240n5
Hjorten, Lisa, 370
Hodder, James E., 479n36

Hof, Robert D., 202n43, 437n1, 437n9, 438n48, 480n70
Hoffman, Alan N., 201n20
Hofstede, Geert, 225, 241n66
Holbek, Jonny, 152
Holliday, Charles O. Jr., 378
Holmes, Stanley, 87n48
Holstein, William J., 7, 49n5, 240n17
Holstrom, Leslie, 396n57
Holweg, Matthias, 353n13
Hooijberg, R., 367, 395n28
Hopkins, Paul, 306
Hornestay, David, 476
Horowitz, Adam, 478n4
Hoskisson, Robert E., 68
Hosmer, LaRue Tone, 376, 395n47, 395n50, 396n62
House, Robert J., 51n47, 199, 202n34, 242n67, 396n71
Howard, Jack L., 515n64
Howard, Jennifer M., 85, 475
Howe, Peter J., 479n52
Howell, Jane M., 438n40
Howitt, Arnold, 195
Hrebiniak, Lawrence G., 85n4, 284n62, 479n47
Hsu, Cheng-Kuang, 354n43
Huber, George P., 402, 514n10
Huey, John, 50n27
Hughes, Michael D., 202n34
Hull, Frank M., 284n39, 284n64
Hult, G. Tomas M., 437n19
Hurd, Mark, 442
Hurley, Robert F., 437n19
Hurst, David K., 29, 50n43, 196
Huxley, Stephen J., 479n36
Hymowitz, Carol, 133n43, 396n58, 515n46

I

Iacocca, Lee, 95, 132n13
Ihlwan, Moon, 167n1, 167n2
Immelt, Jeffrey, 261, 385, 406
Indik, B. P., 354n47
Ingrassia, P., 241n54
Ioannou, Lori, 396n52
Ip, Greg, 49n8, 515n49
Ireland, R. Duane, 68
Issack, Thomas F., 478n24
Ito, Jack K., 285n75

J

Jackson, Janet, 145
Jackson, Terence, 397n101
Jacob, Rahul, 132n28
Jacobs, Robert W., 440n88
Jaffe, Greg, 50n40, 86n18, 478n18
Jagger, Mick, 7
James, Jene G., 396n84
James, John H., 390
James, T. F., 355n48
Janis, Irving L., 449, 478n20
Jarman, Beth, 354n28, 354n33
Jarvis, Mark, 94

Javidan, Mansour, 168n46, 242n67
Javier, David, 236–239
Jelinek, Mariann, 439n77
Jemison, David B., 168n27, 169n54, 169n58
Jenkins, Samantha, 236
Jennings, Daniel F., 438n39
Jobs, Steve, 223, 327, 329–330, 340
Jobson, Tom, 318n57
Johne, F. Axel, 438n53
Johnson, David W., 507
Johnson, Frank P., 507
Johnson, Homer H., 396n52, 397n104
Johnston, Marsha, 49n13
Jolly, Adam, 186
Jones, Althea, 283n21
Jones, Dr. John W., 199–200
Jones, Jerry, 451
Jones, Kathryn, 256
Jonsson, Ellen, 345, 355n81
Joyce, Kevin E., 86n15
Joyce, William F., 66
Judge, Paul C., 372
Judy, Richard W., 49n12, 397n96
Jung, Dong I., 440n95
Jurkovich, Ray, 167n17

K

Kacmar, K. Michele, 515n64
Kahn, Jeremy, 49n1, 203n59
Kahn, Kenneth B., 439n61, 439n67
Kahn, Robert L., 514n22
Kahwajy, Jean L., 514n3
Kalin, Sari, 318n69
Kanigel, Robert, 50n34
Kanter, Rosabeth Moss, 514n25, 515n38, 516n84
Kaplan, Abraham, 514n22
Kaplan, David, 132n27
Kaplan, Robert S., 297, 317n27, 317n28
Karnitschnig, Matthew, 240n1, 240n3, 241n46
Kasarda, John D., 354n46
Katel, Peter, 51n46
Kates, Amy, 132n16
Katz, Ian, 169n60, 241n50
Katz, Nancy, 285n76
Kawamoto, Wayne, 317n33
Kearns, David, 3–4
Kee, Micah R., 394n14, 395n41
Keegan, Paul, 167n3
Keenan, Faith, 439n64
Keeney, Ralph L., 478n13
Kegler, Cassandra, 397n105
Keidel, Robert W., 285n76
Kelleher, Herb, 342
Kelleher, Kevin, 317n11
Keller, Robert T., 285n68, 285n69
Kelly, Kate, 515n49
Kelly, Kevin, 168n50, 201n15, 240n28, 379, 396n63

Kennedy, Allan A., 395n15, 395n20
Kenny, Jim, 492
Keon, Thomas L., 354n43
Kerr, Steve, 440n90
Kerwin, Kathleen, 132n20, 133n51, 438n48, 480n70
Kessler, Eric H., 437n25
Kets de Vries, Manfred F. R., 241n45
Kharif, Olga, 49n1
Kidman, Nicole, 466
Kiechel, Walter III, 132n18
Killman, Ralph H., 438n25
Kim, Linsu, 437n23
Kim, Myung, 355n75
Kimberly, John R., 354n26, 354n31, 354n41, 439n70
King, Jonathan B., 515n41
King, Neil Jr., 240n7, 241n51
King, Thomas R., 479n57
Kinkead, Gwen, 396n68
Kirkoff, Miss, 81–82
Kirkpatrick, David, 167n12, 168n19
Kirsch, Laurie J., 355n73
Kirsner, Scott, 284n53, 395n38, 437n8
Kisner, Matthew, 371
Klein, Gary, 478n23
Kleiner, Art, 478n19
Kleist, Robert A., 251
Kline, S. M., 284n62
Knecht, G. Bruce, 511
Knight, Gary A., 437n19
Knight, Phil, 329–330
Koberg, Christine S., 168n18
Koch, Christopher, 317n18, 318n59
Kochan, Thomas A., 514n6, 514n10
Koenig, Richard, 272, 285n75
Kohlberg, L., 396n61
Kolb, David A., 514n7
Kolde, Jeff, 411
Kolodny, Harvey, 285n77
Könen, Roland, 65
Konicki, Steve, 439n65
Kontzer, Tony, 318n46, 318n54
Koogle, Tim, 505
Koslow, Linda, 447
Kotter, John P., 85n3, 169n53, 169n64, 372, 374, 394n11, 395n43, 401, 437n2, 437n18, 440n100, 440n103, 440n109, 445
Koza, Mitchell P., 201n18
Kramer, Barry, 354n39
Kramer, Robert J., 217, 241n37, 241n40, 241n41, 241n43, 241n44, 241n61
Kranhold, Kathryn, 394n3, 395n23
Kreuze, Jerry G., 397n97
Kripalani, Manjeet, 49n5
Kruse, Howard, 103
Kruse, Paul, 103
Kuemmerle, Walter, 235
Kueng, Thomas K., 201n20

Kumar, Parmod, 515n64
Kupfer, Andrew, 167n14
Kurschner, Dale, 396n52

L

LaBarre, Polly, 50n41
Lachman, Ran, 515n29, 515n53
Lafley, A. G., 415
Lagnado, Lucette, 515n62
Land, George, 354n28, 354n33
Landers, Peter, 438n33
Landler, Mark, 167n11
Lang, James R., 169n62
Langley, Ann, 479n31
Langley, Monica, 515n35
Langly, Peter, 351–352
Lansing, Shery, 453
LaPotin, Perry, 479n55
Larson, Erik W., 133n38, 515n41
Lashinsky, Adam, 241n53, 317n21, 354n30
Lasswell, Mark, 478n4
Latour, Almar, 169n55
Lau, James B., 278
Law, Andy, 428
Law, Jude, 466
Lawler, Edward E. III, 284n52, 285n84
Lawrence, Anne T., 355n79, 392
Lawrence, Lisa, 512
Lawrence, Paul R., 132n21, 133n37, 133n39, 150–151, 168n38, 168n39, 168n41, 351, 370, 395n37, 440n108, 514n13, 514n14, 516n87
Lawrence, Tom, 390–391
Lawson, Emily, 133n60
Lawson, M. T., 432, 434–435
Lazere, Cathy, 297, 317n28, 355n51, 355n58
Lazurus, Shelly, 142
Leatt, Peggy, 285n68
Leavitt, Harold J., 479n35, 479n40
Leblebici, Huseyin, 168n49
Lee, C. A., 515n51
Lee, Jean, 242n71
Lee, Louise, 480n59
Lee-Young, Joanne, 318n72
Legare, Thomas L., 132n22
Lei, David, 240n19, 240n20, 283n37, 284n40, 284n41
Leifer, Richard, 355n70, 355n73, 438n28
Lengel, Robert H., 285n67
Lennox, Annie, 55
Leo, Anthony, 189
Leonard, Devin, 167n15
Leonard, Dorothy, 438n54
Leonhardt, David, 439n66
Leslie, Keith, 133n60
Letts, Christine W., 50n16
Leung, Shirley, 241n52
Levere, Jane L., 240n4
Levering, Robert, 51n45, 87n48
Levine, David I., 438n31

Levinson, Arthur, 188
Levinson, Meridith, 317n12
Lewin, Arie Y., 57, 201n18
Lewins, Lisa A., 316n1
Lewis, Virginia L., 354n26
Lewyn, Mark, 201n18
Lieberman, David, 133n55
Lindblom, Charles, 478n7
Linder, Jane C., 133n50, 133n55
Lioukas, Spyros K., 354n47
Lippitt, G. L., 331
Litterer, J. A., 168n20
Litva, Paul F., 438n52
Liu, Michele, 285n77
Lockhart, Daniel E., 169n62
Loewenberg, Samuel, 167n9
Lohr, Steve, 354n45, 395n29
Loomis, Carol J., 478n2
Lorange, Peter, 355n78
Lorsch, Jay W., 132n21, 150–151, 168n38, 168n39, 168n40, 168n41, 370, 395n37, 514n13, 514n14, 516n87
Louis, Meryl Reise, 87n46
Love, John F., 169n57
Loveman, Gary, 292, 317n12
Low, Lafe, 516n67
Lowry, Tom, 241n53
Lublin, Joann S., 49n6, 240n32, 478n2
Luebbe, Richard L., 284n43
Lukas, Paul, 438n51
Lumpkin, James R., 438n39
Lumsden, Charles J., 202n34
Lundburg, Craig C., 87n46
Lundegaard, Karen, 514n8
Lunsford, J. Lynn, 86n17, 439n60
Luqmani, Mushtaq, 397n97
Luqmani, Zahida, 397n97
Lustgarten, Abrahm, 283n31
Luthans, Brett C., 356n85
Lyles, Marjorie A., 478n25, 478n26
Lynn, Gary S., 439n61

M

Mabert, Vincent A., 317n37
Macintosh, Norman B., 264, 284n63, 284n65, 285n67, 295, 317n19, 317n26
Mack, David A., 354n29
Mack, John, 482
Mack, Toni, 132n27
Madhavan, Ravindranath, 201n4
Madison, Dan L., 515n63, 516n69
Madsen, Peter, 396n84
Magnet, Myron, 180, 201n26, 201n27, 201n28
Main, Jeremy, 259, 284n39
Mainardi, Cesare R., 240n32, 240n33
Makhija, Mahesh, 317n41

Malesckowski, Jim, 436
Malkin, Elisabeth, 169n60, 241n50
Mallak, Larry, 394n13
Mallett, Jeffrey, 505
Mallory, Maria, 202n43
Malone, Michael S., 437n5
Malone, Thomas W., 92
Mandal, Sumant, 240n2
Mang, Wayne, 197–198
Manly, Lorne, 241n53, 241n62, 515n44
Mannari, Hiroshi, 354n43
Mannix, Elizabeth A., 49n3
Mansfield, Edwin, 413, 438n52
Manz, Charles C., 318n45
March, James G., 456, 463, 479n43, 479n45, 479n54
March, Robert M., 354n43
Marchington, Mick, 180, 201n27, 201n31
Marcic, Dorothy, 38, 80, 85, 126, 164, 195, 239, 278, 351–352, 389, 394, 430, 475
Marcoulides, G. A., 395n40
Maremont, Mark, 169n58
Margulies, Newton, 284n44
Marineau, Philip, 178
Markels, Alex, 478n3
Markkula, A. C., 327
Markoff, John, 133n36, 354n45
Marple, David, 202n42
Marquis, Christopher, 396n56
Marr, Merissa, 133n34, 241n53, 478n5
Martin, Joanne, 87n46, 395n21
Martin, Lockheed, 397n87
Martinez, Barbara, 515n62
Martinez, Richard J., 202n52
Masarech, Mary Ann, 395n39
Mason, Julie Cohen, 169n56
Masuch, Michael, 479n55
Mathews, Anna Wilde, 479n53
Matlack, Carol, 240n23, 241n42, 479n52
Matthews, J. A., 133n52
Maurer, John G., 515n64, 516n67, 516n78
Mauriel, John J., 395n27
Mayer, John, 55
Mayer, Marissa, 403
Mayes, Bronston T., 515n63
Mayo, Andrew, 317n42, 317n44
Mazurek, Gene, 304
McCowan, Sandra M., 479n38
McAfee, R. Bruce, 86n7
McAllaster, Craig, 394n9, 395n25
McCann, Joseph E., 168n23, 404, 437n7, 514n17, 516n94, 516n95
McCartney, Scott, 440n101
McCauley, Lucy, 86n38, 87n43
McClain, John O., 202n42
McClenahen, John S., 283n19
McClure, Steve, 186
McCormick, John, 438n29
McCracken, Mike, 317n23

McDermott, Richard, 318n48
McDonald, Duff, 284n48
McDonough, Edward F. III, 438n28, 439n67
McFarlin, Dean B., 516n72
McGeehan, Patrick, 353n12
McGregor, Jena, 356n88, 480n60
McIntyre, James M., 514n7
McKelvey, Bill, 202n34
McKinley, William, 203n57, 355n83, 356n84, 438n32
McLaughlin, Kevin J., 133n56, 240n28, 437n5
McLean, Bethany, 514n1, 515n48
McMath, Robert, 438n51
McMillan, Charles J., 479n34, 480n58
McNamee, Mike, 514n9
Meehan, Sean, 316n1, 318n64
Meinhard, Agnes G., 202n42
Melcher, Richard A., 168n33, 354n22, 479n46
Melnyk, Steven A., 318n56
Melton, Rhonda, 153
Meredith, Jack R., 258, 283n21, 284n38
Merrell, V. Dallas, 516n76
Merrifield, D. Bruce, 437n23
Merrion, Paul, 50n28
Messick, David M., 396n66
Metters, Richard, 284n54
Metzger, John, 176
Meyer, Alan D., 68, 402, 437n13
Meyer, J., 202n47
Meyerson, Debra E., 49n13
Miceli, Marcia P., 396n82, 396n84
Michaels, Clifford, 236
Michaels, Daniel, 439n60
Michener, James, 39
Micklethwait, John, 12
Micossi, Anita, 355n65, 355n67
Middaugh, J. Kendall II, 317n26
Migliorato, Paul, 284n49
Milbank, Dana, 167n5
Miles, G., 133n52, 133n56
Miles, Raymond E., 65, 68, 79–80, 86n26, 133n52, 241n45, 355n66, 439n69
Miles, Robert H., 354n26, 354n31
Miller, Danny, 354n26, 355n76
Miller, David, 318n55, 318n71
Miller, Karen Lowry, 49n13
Miller, Larry, 85
Miller, Lawrence M., 475
Miller, Scott, 240n12
Miller, William, 317n44
Milliken, Frances J., 168n18
Mills, Peter K., 284n44, 355n70, 355n73
Milward, H. Brinton, 201n25
Mintzberg, Henry, 16, 37, 50n24, 85n3, 132n24, 458–460, 478n23, 479n48, 479n50, 480n61

Mirvis, Philip H., 440n108
Miser, Hugh J., 479n35
Mishra, Aneil K., 367, 395n28
Mitroff, Ian I., 478n25
Mizruchi, Mark S., 169n62
Moberg, Dennis J., 284n44
Moch, Michael K., 439n70
Moeller, Michael, 132n31
Mohr, Lawrence B., 283n5
Mohrman, Susan Albers, 439n77
Molloy, Kathleen, 440n96
Montanari, John R., 168n27
Montgomery, Kendyl A., 440n93
Monticup, Peter, 309
Moore, Ethel, 315
Moore, James, 172, 201n3, 201n6
Moore, Larry F., 87n46
Moore, Pamela L., 49n1
Moore, Thomas, 202n38
Morgan, Gareth, 316
Morgan, Ronald B., 396n70
Morgan, Roy, 84
Morgenson, Gretchen, 396n54
Morouney, Kim, 126
Morris, Betsy, 256, 356n90
Morris, James R., 356n85
Morrison, Jim, 284n57
Morse, Dan, 240n10
Morse, Edward V., 439n70
Moskowitz, Milton, 51n45, 87n48
Mouton, Jane S., 507, 516n86, 516n87, 516n91, 516n93
Mueller, Robert, 383
Mulcahy, Anne, 5, 17, 49n1
Muldrow, Tressie Wright, 395n42
Mullaney, Timothy J., 133n31, 318n61
Muller, Joann, 168n19, 168n36, 514n9
Muoio, Anna, 355n69
Murphy, Elizabeth A., 396n52, 396n53
Murphy, Patrice, 440n90
Murray, Alan, 353n11
Murray, Hugh, 285n83
Murray, Matt, 353n5, 356n87
Murray, Victor V., 515n63, 516n70
Musetto, V. A., 479n56
Muson, Howard, 201n4, 201n22
Mutzabaugh, Ben, 372

N

Nadler, David A., 101, 132n8, 247, 437n3
Nagl, Major John, 28
Narasimhan, Anand, 176
Narayanan, V. K., 439n63
Naughton, Keith, 132n20
Nayeri, Farah, 169n65
Neale, Margaret A., 275, 285n80, 356n84

Neale-May, Donovan, 176
Near, Janet P., 396n82, 396n84
Neeleman, David, 31, 372
Neilsen, Eric H., 514n13, 514n18, 516n94, 516n95
Nelson, Bob, 356n86
Nelson, Katherine A., 395n44, 395n51, 396n72, 396n80
Nelson, Robert T., 355n78
Nemetz, Patricia L., 259, 284n39
Neumer, Alison, 133n55
Newcomb, Peter, 202n39
Newman, William H., 354n28
Nicholas O'Regan, 395n40
Nickell, Joe Ashbrook, 317n12
Nielsen, Richard P., 396n83, 479n47
Noble, Ron, 320
Nohria, Nitin, 66, 241n36, 241n65, 303, 318n53
Nolan, Sam, 315
Nonaka, Ikujiro, 318n49
Nord, Walter R., 201n34, 202n53
Nordlinger, Pia, 168n32
Norman, Patricia M., 202n52
Northcraft, Gregory B., 275, 284n52, 285n80, 356n84
Norton, David P., 297, 317n27, 317n28
Novak, William, 132n13
Novicevic, Milorad M., 478n23
Nugent, Patrick S., 516n92
Nutt, Paul C., 478n20, 479n32, 479n34, 480n62
Nystrom, Paul C., 514n17

O

O'Brien, Kevin J., 86n24
O'Connor, Edward J., 283n17, 283n22, 284n40
O'Dell, Carla S., 318n52
O'Flanagan, Maisie, 133n35
Ohmae, Kenichi, 240n29
O'Leary, Michael, 64
Oliver, Christine, 200n2, 201n19
Olsen, Johan P., 463, 479n54
Olsen, Katherine, 432, 436
Olve, Nils–Göran, 317n30
O'Mahony, Siobhan, 318n68, 318n70
O'Neal, Stan, 503
O'Neill, Regina M., 87n52
O'Regan, Nicholas, 395n26
O'Reilly, Charles A. III, 437n3, 437n25, 438n26, 438n27, 438n36, 440n98
Orlikowski, Wanda J., 283n9
Osborne, Richard, 396n77
Ostroff, Cheri, 87n46
Ostroff, Frank, 115–116, 119, 132n6, 132n25, 133n48, 133n49, 133n59
O'Sullivan, Kate, 201n11
Ouchi, Monica Soto, 85n1
Ouchi, William C., 132n9

Ouchi, William G., 339, 349–350, 355n61, 355n68
Overby, Stephanie, 318n67

P

Pacanowsky, Michael, 478n11
Pace, Stan, 439n80
Pacelle, Mitchell, 396n74
Padsakoff, Philip M., 355n59
Page, Larry, 327
Paine, Lynn Sharp, 396n59
Palmer, Donald, 169n61
Palmisano, Sam, 368
Paltrow, Gwyneth, 466–467
Parise, Salvatore, 318n55, 318n71
Park, Andrew, 514n9
Parker, Warrington S. Jr., 439n81
Parloff, Roger, 396n67
Parsons, Michael, 186
Parsons, T., 354n37
Pascale, Richard T., 50n39
Pasmore, William A., 273, 285n81, 285n83, 285n85, 285n87, 396n59
Pasternack, Bruce A., 311, 316n5
Patil, Prabhaker, 89
Patteson, Jean, 85n1
Patton, Susannah, 317n20, 317n40
Peabody, Robert L., 515n34
Pearce, Joan L., 479n44
Pearce, John, 86n6
Pearce, John A. II, 439n62
Peers, Martin, 479n53
Pellegrino, James, 440n96
Peng, T. K., 242n72
Penney, J.C., 159
Pennings, Johannes M., 50n36, 202n42, 515n51, 515n52
Pentland, Brian T., 284n56
Perdue, Arthur W., 39
Perdue, Franklin Parsons, 39, 41–44, 49
Perdue, James A. (Jim), 39, 41, 47, 49
Pereira, Joseph, 86n14, 396n56
Perez, Bill, 330
Perot, Ross, 326
Perrow, Charles, 86n11, 86n39, 264, 276, 283, 283n4, 284n55, 353n2, 494, 515n50
Persaud, Joy, 394n6
Peters, Thomas J., 396n75, 438n43
Peters, Tom, 41, 353n3
Peterson, Richard B., 285n75
Petri, Carl-Johan, 317n30
Petrock, F., 367, 395n28
Pettigrew, Andrew M., 492, 515n42, 515n59
Petzinger, Thomas Jr., 51n46, 153, 201n5

Pfeffer, Jeffrey, 168n48, 169n53, 201n12, 284n62, 495, 514n19, 514n23, 515n33, 515n40, 515n51, 515n52, 515n55, 515n56, 515n57, 516n66, 516n68, 516n74, 516n79, 516n82
Pheysey, Diana, 283n5, 283n7
Pickard, Jane, 241n59
Pierce, John L., 437n11
Pil, Frits K., 353n13
Pinchot, Elizabeth, 355n52
Pinchot, Gifford, 355n52
Pincus, Laura B., 241n38
Pine, B. Joseph II, 283n32
Pinelas, May, 196
Pinfield, Lawrence T., 479n49
Pitcher, Al, 476–477
Pitts, Robert A., 241n39
Pla-Barber, José, 241n35
Plafker, Ted, 169n65
Plana, Efren, 332
Pollack, Andrew, 167n8
Pondy, Louis R., 438n25, 514n18
Pool, Robert, 355n56
Porras, Jerry, 86n10
Port, Otis, 240n28, 258
Porter, Benson L., 439n81
Porter, Lyman W., 479n44, 515n63
Porter, Michael E., 63, 65, 68, 79–80, 86n20, 86n21, 86n25, 240n16
Posner, Richard A., 336
Post, James E., 395n49
Potter, Donald V., 353n7
Poulos, Philippos, 264
Powell, Bill, 438n29
Powell, Thomas C., 168n46
Powell, Walter W., 202n54, 202n55
Power, Christopher, 438n48, 480n70
Poynter, Thomas A., 213, 241n36
Prahalad, C. K., 440n98
Preston, L. E., 50n29
Prewitt, Edward, 133n40
Price, Ann, 450
Price, James L., 86n37
Price, Jorjanna, 132n27
Priem, Richard L., 87n44, 133n56, 169n70, 240n28, 437n5
Prince, Charles, 381–382, 384
Pringle, David, 167n1
Provan, Keith G., 201n25
Prusak, Laurence, 394n4, 515n41
Pugh, Derek S., 50n26, 201n13, 202n35, 202n54, 202n55, 283n5, 283n7
Purcell, Philip J., 482–483, 493
Purdy, Lyn, 284n40

Q

Questrom, Allen, 369
Quick, James Campbell, 354n29

Quinn, E., 510
Quinn, J., 440n89
Quinn, James Brian, 437n16
Quinn, Robert E., 75–76, 87n51, 87n52, 87n53, 327, 331, 354n27, 367, 395n28
Quittner, Josh, 354n32

R

Raghavan, Anita, 394n3, 395n23, 514n1
Rahim, M. Afzalur, 514n6
Raia, Anthony, 86n12
Raisinghani, Duru, 479n48
Rajagopalan, Nandini, 479n34
Rancour, Tom, 317n23
Randolph, W. Alan, 132n26, 133n41, 284n65, 285n67
Ranson, Stuart, 132n5
Rapaport, J., 413, 438n52
Rappaport, Carla, 241n45
Rasheed, Abdul M. A., 133n56, 169n70, 240n28, 437n5, 479n34
Raskin, Andrew, 201n30
Raven, Bertram, 515n28
Rawls, Jim, 165–166
Ray, Michael, 354n28
Rayport, Jeffrey F., 438n54
Rebello, Kathy, 201n18
Recardo, Ronald, 440n96
Reed, Michael, 202n34
Reed, Stanley, 133n45
Reese, Shelley, 45
Reichheld, F. F., 260
Reimann, Bernard, 354n43
Reinhardt, Andy, 49n9, 167n1, 167n2, 318n64
Reinwald, Brian R., 478n23
Renwick, Patricia A., 515n63
Rhodes, Robert, 236
Rhodes, Sean, 237
Richards, Bill, 305, 317n7
Richards, Jenna, 434
Richards, Keith, 7
Richardson, Peter, 440n105
Rickey, Laura K., 240n14
Rigby, Darrell, 61
Riggs, Henry E., 479n36
Ring, Peter Smith, 169n53, 201n27
Ringbeck, Jürgen, 167n3
Rinzler, Alan, 354n28
Ripon, Jack, 436
Robbins, Carla Anne, 478n18
Robbins, Paul, 434–435
Robbins, Stephen P., 285n78
Roberson, Bruce, 66
Roberto, Michael A., 480n66
Roberts, Karlene H., 355n55, 355n57
Robinson, Alan G., 437n4
Robinson, Jim, 84
Robson, Ross, 255
Rogers, Everett M., 440n102
Rogers, L. Edna, 168n43
Rohrbaugh, John, 75–76, 87n51
Roland, Dr. P. W., 199–200

Rolfe, Andrew, 263
Romanelli, Elaine, 354n28
Romani, John H., 86n36
Romm, Tsilia, 516n67
Rose, Jim, 240n2
Rose, Pete, 273
Rosenberg, Geanne, 395n48
Rosenberg, Jonathan, 403
Rosenberg, Tina, 354n38
Rosenthal, Jack, 355n53
Rosenthal, Jeff, 395n39
Ross, Jerry, 480n72, 480n73
Roth, Daniel, 167n12, 168n19, 354n35
Rothman, Howard, 317n22
Roure, Lionel, 438n45
Rousseau, Denise M., 51n47
Rowan, B., 202n47
Rowley, Colleen, 383
Roy, Jan, 317n30
Roy, Sofie, 317n30
Rubenson, George C., 39
Rubin, Irwin M., 514n7
Ruddock, Alan, 86n22
Ruekert, Robert W., 514n7
Rundall, Thomas G., 202n42
Rushing, William A., 283n4, 354n43
Russel, Archie, 197
Russell, David O., 466
Russo, J. Edward, 478n9
Russo, Michael V., 87n42
Rust, Kathleen Garrett, 203n57
Ryan, William P., 50n16

S

Sabrin, Murray, 169n55
Sachdeva, Paramjit S., 514n22, 515n32, 515n47
Safayeni, Frank, 284n40
Safra, Joseph, 457
Salancik, Gerald R., 168n48, 168n49, 201n12, 495, 514n23, 515n51, 515n52, 515n56, 515n57
Sales, Amy L., 440n108
Salsbury, Stephen, 132n7
Salter, Chuck, 132n1, 153, 353n1
Salva, Martin, 240n32, 240n33
Sanchez, Carol M., 355n83, 356n84
Sanderson, Muir, 240n32, 240n33
Santana, Carlos, 55
Santosus, Megan, 315, 317n13
Sanzgiri, Jyotsna, 440n94
Sapsford, Jathon, 437n1
Sarason, Yolanda, 87n42
Sarni, Vic, 381
Sasser, W. E. Jr., 260
Sauer, Patrick J., 395n36
Saunders, Carol Stoak, 515n53
Sawhney, Mohanbir, 240n2
Sawka, Kenneth A., 168n33
Sawyer, John E., 437n14
Scannell, Kara, 49n6
Scarbrough, H., 285n87

Schay, Brigitte W., 395n42
Scheer, David, 397n98
Schein, Edgar H., 394n8, 394n11, 440n106, 514n5
Schick, Allen G., 355n83, 356n84
Schiller, Zachary, 168n50, 169n58, 201n15, 240n28
Schilling, Melissa A., 133n50, 133n52, 439n60
Schlender, Brent, 50n20, 50n21, 201n3, 354n32, 437n6
Schlesinger, Leonard A., 440n103, 440n109
Schlosser, Julie, 168n31, 317n10, 479n39
Schmenner, Roger W., 284n52
Schmidt, Eric, 328
Schmidt, Stuart M., 514n6
Schmidt, W. H., 331
Schmitt, Neal, 87n46
Schneck, R. E., 515n51, 515n52
Schneck, Rodney, 285n68
Schnee, J., 413, 438n52
Schneider, Benjamin, 260, 284n44
Schneider, S. C., 397n99
Schneider, Susan, 242n68
Schoemaker, Paul J. H., 478n9, 479n34
Schoenherr, Richard A., 284n64, 354n47
Schon, D., 316
Schonberger, R. J., 283n3
Schonfeld, Erick, 283n35, 284n47, 437n20
Schooner, Steven L., 396n85
Schoonhoven, Claudia Bird, 439n77
Schrempp, Jürgen, 96
Schroeder, Dean M., 283n14, 283n17, 437n4
Schroeder, Roger G., 395n27
Schuler, Randall S., 393
Schultz, Howard, 55, 451
Schulz, Martin, 318n51
Schwab, Chuck, 348
Schwab, Les, 361
Schwab, Robert C., 168n29
Schwadel, Francine, 478n15
Scott, B. R., 331
Scott, Susanne G., 430
Scott, W. Richard, 191, 202n46, 202n55
Sculley, John, 329
Sears, Michael, 161
Seibert, Cindy, 354n40
Seiler, John A., 351
Sellen, Abigail J., 302
Sellers, Patricia, 438n57, 515n37
Selsky, John, 168n23
Serwer, Andy, 7, 85n1, 256, 514n1, 515n48
Seubert, Eric, 317n41
Shafritz, Jay M., 396n84
Shane, Scott, 355n54
Shani, A. B., 278
Shanley, Mark, 50n29, 50n33

Shapiro, Benson S., 485, 514n11
Sharfman, Mark P., 478n17, 516n65
Sharma, Drew, 309
Shea, Gordon F., 395n44
Shein, Esther, 317n35
Shepard, Herbert A., 516n91, 516n93
Sherif, Muzafer, 514n5, 516n95
Sherman, Stratford P., 240n21, 355n71, 440n102
Shetty, Y. K., 72, 86n40
Shilliff, Karl A., 84
Shipper, Frank M., 39
Shipton, L. K., 434
Shirouzu, Norihiko, 240n12, 437n1
Shleifer, Andrei, 242n71
Shoemaker, Floyd, 440n102
Shonfeld, Erick, 394n5
Shoorman, F. David, 169n61
Shostack, G. Lynn, 284n44
Sibley, Miriam, 268
Siebert, Al, 347
Siehl, Caren, 260, 284n44
Siekman, Philip, 50n19, 133n51, 201n33, 283n11
Siklos, Richard, 240n24
Silveri, Bob, 318n57
Simon, Bernard, 132n1
Simon, Herbert A., 456, 478n8, 478n21, 479n43
Simons, Robert, 317n16
Simpson, Curtis, 390
Sinatar, Marsha, 438n44
Singer, Andrew W., 396n70
Singh, Jitendra V., 201n34–202n34, 202n42
Sirower, Mark L., 202n56
Skarzynski, Peter, 440n98
Skrabec, Quentin R., 396n52
Slater, Derek, 317n36, 317n38
Slevin, Dennis, 438n25
Slocum, John W. Jr., 240n19, 240n20, 275, 285n80, 354n46, 395n18
Slywotzky, Adrian, 353n9
Smircich, Linda, 394n7
Smith, Geoffrey, 168n33
Smith, Geri, 169n65
Smith, Ken G., 201n19
Smith, Ken K., 514n4
Smith, N. Craig, 395n49
Smith, Orin, 55
Smith, Randall, 514n1, 516n81
Smith, Rebecca, 49n6
Snell, Scott A., 241n58
Snelson, Patricia A., 438n53
Snow, Charles C., 65, 68, 79–80, 85n4, 86n26, 133n52, 133n56, 241n45, 241n58, 241n60
Snyder, Naomi, 168n37
Socrates, 310
Solo, Sally, 168n26
Solomon, Charlene Marmer, 241n57
Sommer, Steven M., 356n85
Song, Gao, 479n38

Soni, Ashok, 317n37
Sorenson, Ralph Z., 41
Sorkin, Andrew Ross, 241n53, 241n62, 515n44
Sparks, Debra, 240n18, 240n26, 240n27
Spears, Britney, 369
Spender, J. C., 437n25
Spindler, Michael, 329
Spragins, Ellyn, 450
Sprague, John L., 439n79
Stace, Doug A., 440n109
Stagner, Ross, 479n27
Stalker, G. M., 151, 168n42, 437n23
Stam, Antonie, 485, 514n11
Stamm, Bettina von, 439n57, 439n58
Stanton, Steve, 133n46
Starbuck, William H., 514n17
Starkey, Ken, 394n7
Staw, Barry M., 169n72, 203n58, 285n67, 438n44, 480n72, 480n73, 514n18
Staw, M., 396n76
Stearns, Timothy M., 201n20
Steensma, H. Kevin, 133n50, 133n52
Steers, Richard M., 33, 86n33, 126
Steinberg, Brian, 167n15
Steiner, Gary A., 437n16
Stempert, J. L., 87n42
Stephens, Carroll U., 57
Sterling, Bill, 39
Stern, Robert N., 50n18
Stevenson, William B., 479n44
Stewart, Doug, 516n91
Stewart, James B., 478n2
Stewart, Martha, 8
Stewart, Thomas A., 115, 355n50, 437n21, 478n23, 479n29
Stickley, Ewan, 263
Sting, 55
Stipp, David, 202n45
Stires, David, 202n41
Stodder, Seth M. M., 168n24
Stodghill, Ron II, 169n58
Stoelwinder, Johannes U., 86n12
Stone, Sharon, 369
Stonecipher, Harry, 75
Strakosch, Greg, 370
Strasser, Steven, 86n36
Stringer, Sir Howard, 223, 225, 493
Stross, Randall, 241n53
Strozniak, Peter, 283n30
Stymne, Benjt, 285n77
Suarez, Fernando F., 283n16
Suchman, Mark C., 86n8, 202n48
Summer, Charles E., 280, 432
Sun, David, 382
Surowiecki, Janes, 480n67
Susman, Gerald I., 285n79
Sutton, Charlotte B., 395n15, 395n20

Sutton, Robert I., 169n72, 355n79, 437n16
Svezia, Chris, 149
Swanson, Sandra, 318n58
Symonds, William C., 169n65, 390, 479n52
Szwajkowski, Eugene W., 169n72, 395n49

T

Tabrizi, Behnam N., 439n62
Taft, Susan H., 375, 395n45
Takahashi, Toshihiro, 261
Takeuchi, Hirotaka, 318n49
Talbert, Wayne, 196
Taliento, Lynn K., 133n35
Tam, Pui-Wing, 479n46
Tan, Cheryl Lu-Lien, 153
Tanouye, Elyse, 132n29
Tansik, David A., 284n50
Tapscott, Don, 133n54
Taris, Toon W., 396n71
Tatge, Mark, 283n34
Taylor, Alex III, 86n14, 201n21
Taylor, Christopher, 352
Taylor, Frederick Winslow, 25
Taylor, Saundra, 352
Taylor, William, 241n45
Teahen, John K., 87n41
Teece, David J., 133n57, 439n70
Teitelbaum, Richard, 86n23
Teja, Salim, 240n2
Terry, Paul M., 514n3
Tetenbaum, Toby J., 50n37, 50n39
Théorêt, André, 479n48
Thoman, Richard, 4–5
Thomas, Fred, 511–512
Thomas, Howard, 478n26
Thomas-Hunt, Melissa, 51n47
Thomas, Kenneth, 514n6
Thomas, Landon Jr., 397n92, 514n1
Thomas, Mark, 196
Thomas, Owen, 317n39, 478n4, 478n6
Thompson, James D., 50n23, 86n19, 168n25, 269–271, 283n7, 285n71, 437n24, 480n58, 514n15
Thompson, Joe, 291
Thompson, P. J., 208
Thompson, Ronald L., 284n60
Thornton, Emily, 241n53
Tichy, Noel M., 515n47
Tierney, Thomas, 303, 318n53
Timmons, Heather, 353n12, 355n82
Tjosvold, Dean, 516n96
Todor, William D., 355n59
Toffler, Barbara Ley, 396n86
Tolbert, Pamela S., 202n53
Tompkins, Tommy, 196
Townsend, Anthony M., 132n23
Townsend, Robert, 472, 480n71
Toy, Stewart, 169n71
Treacy, Michael, 68

Treece, James B., 168n50, 201n15, 240n28, 353n10
Tretter, Marietta J., 241n39
Treviño, Linda Klebe, 395n44, 395n51, 396n59, 396n72, 396n80, 396n86
Trice, Harrison M., 363, 394n10, 395n19
Trist, Eric L., 167n16, 285n83
Trofimov, Yaroslav, 478n18
Trottman, Melanie, 355n72
Tsujino, Koichiro, 223
Tu, John, 382
Tucci, Joe, 144
Tucker, David J., 202n34, 202n42
Tully, Shawn, 439n78
Tung, Rosalie L., 168n22, 168n46
Turban, Daniel B., 396n55
Turcotte, Jim, 318n57
Turner, C., 50n26
Tushman, Michael L., 101, 132n8, 247, 284n65, 285n69, 354n28, 394n4, 437n3, 437n25, 438n26, 438n27, 438n36, 440n98
Tusi, Anne S., 50n29, 50n31
Tyler, John, 165–166

U

Ulm, David, 439n79
Ulrich, David, 168n48, 202n34, 440n90
Ungson, Gerardo R., 168n18, 168n29
Upton, David M., 285n86
Useem, Jerry, 202n49, 202n51, 353n4

V

Van de Ven, Andrew H., 33, 168n49, 169n53, 201n27, 272, 285n66, 285n67, 285n75
Van Horne, Rick, 304
VanGrunsven, Dick, 254
Vargas, Vincente, 284n54
Vaughan, Ken, 141
Veiga, John F., 129, 165
Venkataramanan, M. A., 317n37
Verschoor, Curtis C., 396n52, 396n53
Vinas, Tonya, 200n1
Vincent, Steven, 180, 201n27, 201n31
Vogelstein, Fred, 403
Volpe, Craig, 118
Voyer, John J., 516n65
Voyle, Susanna, 394n1
Vredenburgh, Donald J., 515n64, 516n67, 516n78
Vroman, H. William, 126

W

Wagner, S., 413, 438n52
Wah, Louisa, 318n47
Wakin, Daniel J., 132n3
Walker, Gordon, 168n49
Walker, Orville C. Jr., 514n7
Walker, Sam, 514n26
Wallace, Doug, 436, 478n12
Wallach, Arthur E., 440n108
Wally, Sefan, 478n22
Walsh, James P., 354n42
Walton, Eric J., 87n49
Walton, Richard E., 285n84, 507, 514n13, 514n16
Walton, Sam, 322
Warner, Fara, 283n29, 403, 438n56
Warner, Melanie, 317n32, 395n30
Warshaw, Michael, 515n30, 515n45
Washington, Major J., 196
Waterman, Robert H. Jr., 396n75, 438n43
Watson, Robert A., 338
Watts, Charlie, 7
Watts, Naomi, 466–467
Waxman, Sharon, 479n56
Weaver, Gary R., 396n86
Webb, Allen P., 396n70
Webb, Bill, 255
Webb, Terry, 283n21
Webber, Ross A., 280
Weber, James, 396n60, 397n91
Weber, Joseph, 132n29, 133n33, 168n33, 169n65, 240n20
Weber, Max, 331, 339, 354n37, 355n62

Wegman, Danny, 61
Wegman, Robert, 61
Weick, Karl E., 86n34, 382, 396n76, 480n69
Weil, Jonathan, 49n6
Weiner, Ari, 235–236
Weisbord, Marvin R., 440n88
Weitzel, William, 345, 355n81
Weldon, William C., 57, 96
Weller, Timothy, 60
Wessel, David, 49n7, 355n64, 479n41
Western, Ken, 168n33
Westley, Frances, 478n23
Wheatcroft, Patience, 394n1
Whetten, David A., 86n34, 87n42, 201n20, 354n31, 355n75
White, Anna, 479n38
White, Donald D., 126
White, Gregory L., 240n12
White, Joseph B., 514n8, 516n90
White, Judith, 375, 395n45
White, Roderick E., 213, 241n36
Whitford, David, 169n69
Whitman, Meg, 295–296, 443, 490
Wholey, Douglas R., 202n34
Wiersema, Fred, 68
Wiginton, John C., 479n42
Wilhelm, Wayne, 284n46
Wilke, John R., 50n33
Williams, Larry J., 355n59
Williams, Loretta, 351–352
Williams, Mona, 189
Williamson, James E., 297, 317n27, 317n28

Williamson, Oliver A., 355n63
Willmott, Hugh, 132n5
Wilson, Ian, 86n9
Wilson, James Q., 353n2, 437n24
Wilson, Joseph C., 3
Winchell, Tom, 195–196
Windhager, Ann, 132n27
Wingfield, Nick, 201n7, 241n50, 479n53
Winters, Rebecca, 354n32
Wise, Jeff, 283n27
Wise, Richard, 353n9
Wiser, Phil, 223
Withey, Michael, 284n59
Wolf, Thomas, 49n15
Wolfe, Richard A., 437n10
Wong, Choy, 516n96
Wood, Ronnie, 7
Woodman, Richard W., 275, 285n80, 285n84, 396n59, 437n14
Woodward, Joan, 248–250, 253, 276, 283n6, 283n10, 28312
Wooldridge, Adrian, 12
Worthen, Ben, 169n66, 514n12
Wozniak, Stephen, 327
Wren, Daniel A., 478n23
Wu, Anne, 440n95
Wylie, Ian, 168n47
Wysocki, Bernard Jr., 49n9, 316n3

X

Xerokostas, Demitris A., 354n47

Y

Yang, Jerry, 505
Yanouzas, John N., 129, 165
Yates, Linda, 440n98
Yee, Amy, 49n1
Yeh, Andrew, 167n1
Yoffie, David B., 169n68
Yoshida, Takeshi, 414
Young, Clifford E., 356n85
Young, Debby, 317n29
Yu, Gang, 479n38
Yukl, Gary, 390
Yuspeh, Alan R., 380, 396n78

Z

Zachary, G. Pascal, 49n11, 169n51, 511
Zald, Mayer N., 494, 515n50
Zaltman, Gerald, 152
Zammuto, Raymond F., 202n44, 283n17, 283n22, 284n40, 355n79
Zander, A. F., 515n28
Zaun, Todd, 240n12
Zawacki, Robert A., 439n85, 439n86, 440n88
Zeitz, Jochen, 65
Zellner, Wendy, 169n58, 169n65, 201n15, 396n64
Zemke, Ron, 284n46
Zhao, Jun, 203n57
Zhou, Jing, 515n64
Zipkin, Amy, 396n79
Zirger, Jo, 438n48
Zmud, Robert W., 439n72, 439n73

Corporate Name Index

A

A. T. Kearney, 100
Abercrombie & Fitch, 311
Acetate Department, 280–282
Acme Electronics, 165–167
Adobe Systems, 409
Advanced Cardiovascular
    Systems (ACS), 486
AES Corporation, 14, 92
Aetna Inc., 498
Aflac Insurance, 64
AgriRecycle Inc., 47
Ahold USA, 61
Airbus Industrie, 143, 171, 211,
    322
Airstar, Inc., 84
AirTran Airways, 6, 146
Akamai Technologies, 60
Albany Ladder Company,
    100
Alberta Consulting, 448
Alberto-Culver, 420
Albertson's, 61
Allied Signal, 325, 402
Allstate, 287, 298
ALLTEL, 427
Aluminum Company of America
    (Alcoa), 506
Amana, 442
Amazon.com Inc., 173–174,
    184, 187, 308–309, 368,
    488
Amerex Worldwide, 288
America Online (AOL), 158,
    222–223, 323, 389, 462
American Airlines, 427
American Axle &
    Manufacturing (AAM),
    245–246
American Express, 322
American Humane Association, 6
American International Group,
    Inc. (AIG), 491
AMP, 181
Anglian Water, 410
Anheuser-Busch Company, 7,
    179, 290–291, 322, 351
Ann Taylor, 311

Apple Computer, 107–108, 137,
    173, 222–223, 327–330,
    402, 404, 462
Aquarius Advertising Agency,
    129–131
Arcelor, 111
Arthur Andersen, 58, 343, 384
ASDA Group, 156, 359
Asea Brown Boveri Ltd. (ABB),
    218–220, 296, 340
Asset Recovery Center, 183
AT&T, 157, 184
Athletic Teams, 273
Autoliv AB, 255–256
Avis Corporation, 472
Avon, 387
A.W. Perdue and Son, Inc., 39

B

Bain & Company, 61
Baldwin Locomotive, 184
Banc One, 156
Barclays Global Investors, 302
Barnes & Noble, 308
Bell Canada, 298
Bell Emergis, 298
Bertelsmann AG, 205
Bethlehem Steel Corp., 25, 111
Biocon, 140
Bistro Technology, 278
Black & Decker, 212
Blackwell Library, 39
Blockbuster Inc., 343
Bloomingdale's, 455
Blue Bell Creameries, Inc.,
    103–104
BMW, 208, 222, 257
Boardroom Inc., 405
Boeing Company, 60–61, 74–75,
    143, 159, 161, 171, 189,
    211, 409, 415
Boise Cascade Corporation, 272
Bombardier, 159, 182
Boots Company PLC, 359, 373
Booz Allen Hamilton Inc., 89
Borden, 351

BP, 226, 253
Bristol-Myers Squibb Company,
    337
British Airways, 298
Brobeck, Phleger & Harrison
    LLP, 346
Brown, 432
Brown Printing, 205
BT Labs, 224
Burger King, 187, 484
Business Wire, 288

C

C & C Grocery Stores, Inc.,
    126–129
Cadillac, 443
CALEB Technologies, 455
Callaway Golf, 174
Canadair, 159
Canada's Mega Bloks Inc., 60
Cannondale Associates, 61
Canon, 4–5, 408
Cardinal Health, 322
CARE International, 95
CareWeb, 298–299
Carroll's Foods, 41
Caterpillar Inc., 220, 328, 372
Cementos Mexicanos (Cemex),
    32
Centex Corporation, 337
Century Medical, 315
Chamber of Commerce, 196
Charles Schwab & Company,
    343, 347–348
Chase, 156
Chevrolet, 72–73, 158–159
Chicago Board of Trade, 179
Chicago Electric Company, 26
Chicago Mercantile Exchange,
    179
Chrysler Corporation, 95, 141,
    179, 245, 323
Cigna Insurance, 298
Cingular, 157
Cisco, 183, 346, 389
Cisneros Group, 158
Citibank, 220

Citicorp, 324
Citigroup, 321, 346, 381, 384
Clark, Ltd., 491
ClientLogic, 118
Clorox, 174, 415
CNA Life, 7
Coca-Cola, 14, 69, 206, 210,
    212, 322, 337, 443
Cognos, 148
Colgate-Palmolive Company,
    217–218, 220, 222, 226
Columbia/HCA Healthcare
    Corp., 380
Comcast, 118, 173
Compaq, 442
ConAgra, 412
Connect Co., 107
Contact USA, 60
Continental Airlines, 454–455
Corning Glass, 237
Corrugated Supplies, 304, 309
Costco Wholesale, 127
C.V. Starr & Co., 491

D

DaimlerChrysler, 95–96, 141,
    321, 323, 343
Dayton/Hudson, 389
Dean Witter Discover & Co.,
    482–483, 493
Dell Computer Corporation, 7,
    9, 222, 251, 256–257
Deloitte Touche, 484
Delphi Corp., 208
Deluca, 43
Denmark's Lego, 60
Deutsche Telecom, 210
Dillard's, 389
Direct TV, 118
Discovery Channel, 489–490
Disney, 311
Dodge, 96
Domino's Pizza, 212
Donnelly Corporation, 192
Dow Chemical, 110, 296
DreamWorks, 443
DuPont Co, 378

E

East Tennessee Healthcorp (ETH), 512
Eaton Corporation, 215, 218
eBay Inc., 11, 26, 65, 92, 184, 295–296, 325–326, 368, 400, 443, 490, 505
Eckerd, 159
Edward Jones, 65
Eileen Fisher, 387
Electrolux, 380, 442
Electronic Data Systems (EDS), 100, 327–328, 420
Eli Lilly & Co., 210, 405, 407
EMC, 144
Emerald Packaging, 379
Emerson Electric, 337
Empire Blue Cross and Blue Shield, 493
Encyclopaedia Britannica, 457–458
Englander Steel, 111–113
Enron Corporation, 8, 58, 161, 189, 343, 360, 365, 379, 384, 419
Esso, 341
Ethics Officer Association, 383
Ethics Resource Center, 383
Eureka Ranch, 409
Exxon, 324

F

Fast-Data, 236
Federal Bureau of Investigation (FBI), 383
Federal Reserve Board, 455
FedEx Corporation, 65, 183
Fiat Auto, 117
Financial Services., 100
Flextronics, 181
Ford Motor Company, 6, 72, 89, 100, 114, 121–122, 141, 156, 171, 184, 207–208, 212, 225, 257, 260, 299, 341, 416, 506
Forrester Research, 314
Four Seasons Hotels, 64, 75
France Telecom SA, 137
Frankfurter Allgemeine Zeitung, 140
Frito-Lay, 152, 299, 351, 412
Fujitsu, 152
Funk & Wagnalls, 457

G

Gap, 455
Gardetto, 409
Gartner Group, 314
Gateway, 389
Gayle Warwick Fine Linen, 206
Genase, 410
Genentech, 188

General Electric (GE), 69, 84,
104, 171–172, 180, 237, 261, 296, 325, 343, 385, 406, 411, 442
General Electric (GE) Salisbury, 114–116
General Mills, 381
General Motors, 59, 72–73, 96, 110, 117, 183–184, 208, 245, 264, 276, 310, 321, 337, 341, 399, 416, 484, 506
General Shale Brick, 141
Genesco, 149
Geo Services International, 211
Gerber, 415
GID, 254
Gilead Sciences, 324
Gillette Company, 212, 461–462
Girl Scouts, 6, 107
GlaxoSmithKline, 323
Global Crossing, 380
GlobalFluency, 176
Goldsmith International, 173
Goldwater, 389
Goodyear, 506
Google, 13–14, 26, 65, 184, 326–327, 368, 401, 403
Governance Metrics International, 377
Gruner + Jahr, 205
Guess, 311
Guidant Corporation, 486
Guiltless Gourmet, 152

H

Häagen Dazs, 416
Halliburton, 384
Haloid Company, 3
Harley-Davidson Motorcycles, 64, 180
Harrah's Entertainment Inc., 292, 298, 455
Harris Interactive and the Reputation Institute, 189, 202
Hasbro, 145
HCA, 498
HealthSouth Corp., 419, 509
Heineken Breweries, 14, 224
Heinz, 337
Hewlett-Packard, 5–6, 107, 173, 251, 442
Hewlett-Packard's Medical Products Group, 98
Hilton Hotels Corp., 298
Holiday Inn, 11, 191
Hollinger International, Inc., 492
Home Depot, 7, 66, 157, 326, 455, 498
Honda Motor Company, 60, 192, 209, 257, 260, 408
Honest Jim, 379
Honeywell Garrett Engine Boosting Systems, 306

Honeywell International, 144
Hudson Foods, 48
Hudson Institute, 386
Hugh Russel Inc., 196–197
Hughes Electronics, 118

I

IBM, 4, 6, 14, 156, 158, 184, 222, 251, 327, 340, 365, 368, 402, 411, 420
ICiCI Bank, 211
IKEA, 380
Imagination Ltd., 98
ImClone Systems, 8
Imperial Oil Limited, 341
INCO, 512–513
Indiana Children's Wish Fund, 12
INSEAD, 512
Intel Corp., 173, 472
InterCel, Inc., 392
Interface, 380
Internal Revenue Service, 60, 106
International Association of Machinists (IAM), 506
International Shoe Company, 432
International Standards Organization, 387
International Truck and Engine Corporation, 171
Interpol, 320
Interpublic Group of Companies, 321
Interstate Bakeries, 443
ITT Industries, 296

J

J & J Consumer Products, 106
J. M. Smucker & Co., 359
J. Sainsbury's, 117
J&R Electronics, 309
Jaguar Automobiles, 64
J.C. Penney, 368–369
J.D. Edwards, 94
Jeep, 96
JetBlue Airways, 14, 31, 138, 146, 372
Johnson & Johnson, 57–58, 96, 104, 106–107, 172, 189, 322, 325–326, 381

K

Kaiser-Hill, 347
Karolinska Hospital, 104
Keiretsu, 211
Kennedy Foods, 412
KFC, 484
Kimberly-Clark, 414
Kingston Technology Co., 382
Kmart, 66, 144, 337, 389
Kodak, 67
KPMG Peat Marwick, 288

Kraft, 140, 412
Kroger, 61, 140
Kryptonite, 145

L

Lamprey Inc., 436
Lands End, 173
Learjet, 159
Lehigh Coal & Navigation, 184
Les Schwab Tire Centers, 361–362
Levi Strauss, 178, 416
Li & Fung, 311
Liberty Mutual's, 59
Limited, The, 311
Lockheed Martin, 161, 384, 410
Lockport, 300
Long Island Lighting Company (LILCO), 473
L'Oreal, 210
Lotus Development Corp., 156
LTV Corp., 111
Lufthansa, 64

M

MacMillan-Bloedel, 380
Make-a-Wish Foundation, 107
MAN Nutzfahrzeuge AG, 171
Marriott, 420
Marshall Field's, 446–447
Mary Kay Cosmetics Company, 364
Mathsoft, Inc., 73
Matsushita Electric, 210, 230
Mattel, 145, 187
Maytag, 442
Mazda, 257
McDonald's, 67, 107, 157, 186–187, 208, 222, 261, 263, 278–279, 288, 293, 380, 415, 470, 484
MCI, 157
McKinsey & Company, 9, 338
McNeil Consumer Products, 106
Medtronic, 59
Memorial Health Services, 288
Mercedes, 96, 179
Merck, 184, 188, 210, 324
Merrill Lynch & Co., 380, 503
Micro Modeling Associates (MMA), 313
Microsoft Corporation, 7, 12–13, 66, 106–107, 159–160, 172–173, 178, 180–181, 330, 334, 360, 399, 403, 457
Milacron Inc., 366
Miller, 179
Milliken & Co., 401
Mindfire Interactive, 309
Mitsubishi, 96, 179, 421
Mittal Steel, 111
Mobil, 324
Moen, 416
Monsanto, 380

Montgomery-Watson Harza
(MWH), 303
Morgan, Lewis & Bockius LLP,
346
Morgan Stanley, 482–483, 493
Morton Automotive Safety, 255
Motek, 450
Motorola, 100, 137, 156, 183,
208, 292, 296, 328
MTV Japan, 186
MTV Networks, 211
MusicNet, 462
Musidor, 7

N

Nabisco, 351
National Industrial Products,
390
Neale-May & Partners, 176
Neoterik Health Technologies
Inc., 141
Nestlé, 104, 140, 210, 216–217,
220
Netflix, 344
New Line Cinema, 58
New York Stock Exchange,
493
Newport News Shipbuilding, 13
Nextel, 157
Nike, 149, 174, 299, 329–330
Nissan, 60, 257, 443
Nokia, 137, 145, 222, 399
Nordstrom Inc., 365–366
Nortel Networks, 183, 343
Northrup Grumman Newport
News, 13, 383
Northwest Airlines, 455
Norwest, 156
Novartis, 209
Novell, 328
Nucor, 66
NUMMI, 409

O

Ogilvy & Mather, 141–142,
213
Oksuka Pharmaceutical
Company, 409
Olive Garden, 288
Olmec Corporation, 187
Omega Electronics, Inc.,
165–167
Omnicom Group, 321
Omron, 386
Oracle Corporation, 94, 211,
366, 419
Orange SA, 137
Oregon Brewers Guild, 179
Ortho Pharmaceuticals, 106
Oshkosh Truck Company, 257
Oticon Holding A/S, 30
Owens Corning, 346
Oxford Plastics Company,
195–196

P

Pacific Edge Software, 370
Paramount Pictures, 66–67,
452–453
P.B. Slices, 412
PeopleSoft Inc., 94, 366
PepsiCo. Inc., 106, 220, 330,
443, 468
Perdue AgriRecycle, 48
Perdue Farms Inc., 39, 41–49
Pfizer Inc., 179, 210, 412
Philips Corporation, 409
Philips NV, 230–231
Piper Alpha, 252
Pitney Bowes Credit Corporation
(PBCC), 304, 370–371
Planters Peanuts, 96
PPG Industries, 381
Pratt & Whitney, 84
Pret A Manger, 262–263
Pricewaterhouse-Coopers, 338,
484
Princeton, 140
Printronix, 251
Procter & Gamble (P&G), 110,
174, 178, 182, 206, 212,
224, 226, 230, 254, 276,
306, 321–322, 351, 399,
402, 414–415
Progressive Casualty Insurance
Company, 113–114, 261,
287, 298
Prudential plc, 211
Publicis Groupe, 321
PulseNet, 310
Puma, 65
Purafil, 209–210
Purvis Farms, 41

Q

Quaker Oats, 416
QuikTrip, 31
Quizno's, 187

R

RCA, 412
Reynolds Aluminum Company,
139
Rhodes Industries (RI), 236
Ricoh, 4
Ritz-Carlton Hotels, 261, 346
Robex Resources Inc., 211
Rockford Health Systems, 485
Rockwell Automation, 171, 253
Rockwell Collins, 248
Rolling Stones Inc., 6–7
Rowe Furniture Company,
152–153
Royal Dutch/Shell, 154, 210,
326
Royal Philips Electronics, 118
Rubbermaid, 178
Russell Stover, 416
Ryanair, 64–65, 138

S

S. C. Johnson Company, 330
Safeway, 61
Saks Fifth Avenue, 389
Salisbury State University, 39, 42
Samsung Electronics, 7, 137,
209
Saturn, 172
Salvation Army, The, 11,
337–338
SBC Communications, 157, 173
Scandic Hotels, 380
Schering-Plough, 159, 188
SDC (Secure Digital Container)
AG, 186
Shazam, 185–186, 330
Shell Oil, 154, 210, 326
Shenandoah Farms, 41
Shenandoah Life Insurance
Company, 405
Shenandoah Valley Poultry
Company, 41
Shoe Corporation of Illinois
(SCI), 432
Short Brothers, 159
Siebel Systems, 368
Siemens AG, 95, 137, 210, 220,
251
Simpson Industries, 390–391
Sony Connect, 223
Sony Corp., 7, 67, 69, 107, 118,
174, 210, 222–223, 225,
493
Sony Pictures Entertainment, 493
Southwest Airlines, 138, 146,
342, 455
Sprint, 7, 157, 210
SPS, 299
St. Luke's Communications Ltd,
342, 428
Standard Brands, 351
Starbucks Coffee, 11, 55–56, 64,
400, 404, 451
State Farm, 58, 59, 287
Steelcase Corp., 361
Steinway & Sons, 264
Studebaker, 184
Suburban Corrugated Box Co.,
304
Subway, 187, 278–279
Süddeutsche Zeitung, 141
Sun Microsystems, 178, 183,
389
Sun Petroleum Products Corpora-
tion (SPPC), 120–121
Sunflower Incorporated, 351
Swissair, 138

T

Taco Bell, 262, 484
Target, 66, 127, 157, 173, 444
Techknits, Inc., 253
Technological Products, 165
TechTarget, 370
Telecom France, 210

Tenet Healthcare, 498
Tesco.com, 308–309, 359
Texas Instruments (TI), 384, 410
Thomson Corporation, 78
3Com Corporation, 347
3M Corporation, 60, 296, 337,
365, 368, 399–400, 407,
410–411, 472
Time Incorporated, 412
Time Warner, 323, 389
TiVo Inc., 118–119, 142
Tommy Hilfiger clothing, 64
TopDog Software, 235–236
Toshiba, 118, 152
Tower Records, 137
Toyota Motor Corporation, 60,
141, 180, 208–209, 255,
321, 399, 404, 409, 414
Toys "R" Us, 174, 387, 455
Transmatic Manufacturing Co.,
208
Travelers, 324
Tupperware Corp., 444, 504
Tyco International, 419

U

Ugli Orange, 199
Unilever, 110, 210, 230
United Air Lines, 138
United Parcel Service (UPS), 12,
22, 246, 333–334, 339,
404, 409
Universal Pictures, 467
Unocal, 149
U.S. Airways, 138
USA Technologies Inc., 158
USX, 506

V

Vanguard, 261
Van's Aircraft, 254
Verizon Communications, 148,
157, 184, 294
Versace, 157
Viacom Entertainment Group,
453
Virgin Atlantic Airways, 322
Virgin Digital, 462
Virginia Company, 12
Volkswagen, 183, 222, 245
Volvo, 141, 276

W

W. L. Gore & Associates, Inc.,
21–22, 411, 415
Wal-Mart, 21–23, 47, 61, 64,
66, 127, 138, 144–145,
156–157, 159–160, 178,
184, 189–190, 195, 210,
212, 220, 226, 293, 298,
306, 321–322, 325–326,
337, 359, 365, 389, 467,
469, 498

Walker Research, 377
Walt Disney Company, 364
Warner-Lambert, 179, 210
Weber, 333
Wegmans Food Markets, 60–61, 139, 369
Wells Fargo Bank, 156, 346
Wendover, 100
Wendy's, 187
Western Railroad, 91
Weyerhaeuser, 208, 299

Wheeling-Pittsburgh Steel Corp., 506
Wherehouse, 137
Whirlpool, 148, 180, 442
Wienerberger Baustoffindustrie AG, 141
Windsock, Inc., 352–353
Wipro Ltd., 7, 208
Wizard Software Company, 98–99
Wood Flooring International (WFI), 288
Woolworth, 184

WorldCom, 161, 189, 343, 380, 384, 419
WPP Group, 321
WuXi Pharmatech, 140
Wyeth, 159

X

X-Rite Inc., 421–422
Xerox Corporation, 3–6, 10, 12, 15–17, 24, 31, 67, 107, 350, 380, 493, 506

Y

Yahoo!, 223, 462, 505

Z

Ziff-Davis, 409

Subject Index

A

Absorption, 497
Abu Ghraib prison, abuses at, 336
Acceptance, 425
Achieving competitive advantage, 416–417
Acquisition, 156
Adaptability culture, 368
Adaptive versus nonadaptive corporate cultures, *exhibit*, 374
Administrative principles, 25–26
Adoption, 406
Advanced manufacturing technology, 253
Adversaries to partners, 180–183
Advocate, 410
Agile manufacturing, 253
Ambidextrous approach, 407–408
Authority, 489
Authorization, 459
Automated teller machines (ATMs), 274

B

Balance sheet, 294
Balanced scorecard, 296–298, 312
 major perspectives of the, *exhibit*, 297
Bargaining, 459
Barriers to change, 426
Bayesian statistics, 454
Benchmarking, 192, 296
Better decision making, 226
Blinded stage, 344, 346
Blogs, 141
Boeing 787, 415
Bootlegging, 411
Bottom line, 295
Boundary spanning, 17, 413–414
 roles, 148
Bounded rationality perspective, 448
 constraints and tradeoffs, 449–451
 role of intuition, 451–453

Budget, 294
Buffering roles, 147
Bureaucracy, 26, 332–333
 Weber's dimensions of, *exhibit*, 332
Bureaucracy in changing world, 335
 flexibility, innovation, organizing temporary systems for, 336–337
 other approaches to reducing, 337–339
Bureaucratic control, 339–340, 349
Bureaucratic culture, 369–370
Bureaucratic organizations, 26
Burox, 3–4
Business intelligence, 148, 289
Business process indicators, 298
Business process reengineering, 113

C

CAD. *See* Computer-aided design (CAD)
CAM. *See* Computer-aided manufacturing (CAM)
Capital-intensive, service firms, 260
Carnegie model, 453, 456–459, 463, 467
 choice processes in the, *exhibit*, 457
 of decision making, 500
Centralization, 334
Centralized decision making, 104
Ceremonies, 363–365
Chaebol, 211
Chain of command, 100
Change
 elements for successful, 405–407
 process, 405
 stages of commitment to, *exhibit*, 425
Change agent, 410
Change leaders, 426

Change, strategic role of
 incremental versus radical change, 400–402
 strategic types of change, 402–405
Change, strategies for implementing, 424
 barriers to change, 426
 leadership for change, 425–426
 techniques for implementation, 426–429
Chaos theory, 27
Charismatic authority, 340
Clan control, 341–343, 349
Clan culture, 369
Closed system, 14
Coalition, 456
Code of ethics, 384
Coercive forces, 191–192
Coercive power, 489
Collaborative networks, 178
 adversaries to partners, 180–183
 why collaboration, 179
Collective bargaining, 507
Columbia space shuttle disaster, 336, 467
Commitment, 426
Communication and coordination, 268
Companies without walls, 416
Comparison of organizational characteristics associated with mass production and flexible manufacturing systems, *exhibit*, 259
Competing values model, 75
Competition, 484
Competitive intelligence (CI), 148
Complex, stable environment, 145
Complex, unstable environment, 145
Computer-aided craftsmanship, 257
Computer-aided design (CAD), 254

Computer-aided manufacturing (CAM), 254
Computer simulations, 454
Computer-integrated manufacturing, 253
Concurrent engineering, 416
Configuration and structural characteristics of service organizations versus product organizations, *exhibit*, 262
Confrontation, 506
Consortia, 211
Constraints and tradeoffs, 449–451
Constraints and tradeoffs during nonprogrammed decision making, *exhibit*, 449
Contemporary applications
 flexible manufacturing systems, 253–254
 lean manufacturing, 254–257
 performance and structural implications, 257–258
Contemporary organization design, 27–28
Contextual dimensions of organization design, 17, 21–22
Contingency, 27
Contingency decision-making framework
 contingency framework, 468–470
 problem consensus, 467–468
 technical knowledge about solutions, 468
Contingency effectiveness approaches, 70
 goal approach, 71–73
 internal process approach, 74–75
 measurement of, *exhibit*, 71
 resource-based approach, 73–74
Contingency framework, 468–470
 for using decision models, *exhibit*, 469

Contingency framework for environmental uncertainty and organizational responses, *exhibit*, 155
Continuous improvement, 399
Continuous-process production, 249
Control mechanisms, 350
Conversion rate, 295
Cooptation, 158
Coordination and control, cultural differences in national value systems, 227
three national approaches to coordination and control, 227–230
Coordination and control, three national approaches to, 227
European firms' decentralized approach, 229
Japanese companies centralized coordination, 228–229
United States coordination and control formalization, 229–230
Coordination roles, expanded, 225–226
Core organization manufacturing technology manufacturing firms, 248–250
performance, 250–253
strategy, 250–253
technology, 250–253
Core organization service technology designing the service organization, 262–263
service firms, 259–260
Core technology, 246
Core transformation process for a manufacturing company, *exhibit*, 246
Corporate culture and ethics in a global environment, 386–387
Corporate Culture and Performance, 372
Corporate entrepreneurship, 410–411
Corrugated system in action, 305
Cost savings, 226
Council on Economic Priorities Accreditation Agency, 387
Country managers, 226
Craft technologies, 265
Creative departments, 409
Creativity, 405
Crisis stage, 345
Cultural Assessment Process (CAP), 372
Culture, 361
emergence and purpose of, 361–363
interpreting, 363–367
levels of corporate, *exhibit*, 362

Culture and ethics, how leaders shape
formal structure and systems, 382–385
values-based leadership, 381–382
Culture change
forces for, 420
organization development culture change interventions, 422–423
Culture changes, 404
Culture strength, 370–371
Customer relationship management (CRM), 235, 306
Customer service indicators, 297–298
Customized output, 261

D

Data, 301
Data mining, 290
Data warehousing, 289
Decentralization, 267
Decentralized decision making, 93, 104
Decentralized organizational structures, 310
Decision interrupts, 458
Decision learning, 472
Decision making and control, information for
balanced scorecard, 296–298
feedback control model, 293
management control systems, 293–296
organizational decision-making systems, 291–293
Decision making in today's environment, *exhibit*, 444
Decision mistakes and learning, 472
Decision process when problem identification and problem solution are uncertain, *exhibit*, 463
Decision support system (DSS), 293
Defender strategy, 66–67
Department design, 266
communication and coordination, 268
decentralization, 267
formalization, 267
span of control, 268
worker skill level, 267–268
Departmental grouping options divisional grouping, 100
functional grouping, 100
horizontal grouping, 102
multifocused grouping, 100
virtual network grouping, 102
Design, 459
Designing the service organization, 262–263

Desktop search, 403
DIAD (Delivery Information Acquisition Device), 333, 404
Diagnosis, 459
Differences between large and small organizations, *exhibit*, 323
Differences between manu-facturing and service technologies, *exhibit*, 260
Differences in goals and orientations among organizational departments, *exhibit*, 150
Differentiation, 149–151
strategy, 64
Digital downloading, 344
Digital workplace, 9
Dilemmas of large (organization) size, 322–326
big-company/small-company hybrid, 324–326
large, 322–323
small, 323–324
Direct interlock, 158
Disclosure mechanisms, 383–384
Dissolution stage, 345
Distributive justice, 378
Diversity, 9, 421
Division of labor in the ambidextrous organization, *exhibit*, 408
Divisional organization structure, 104–107
Divisional structure, 269
DMAIC (Define, Measure, Analyze, Improve, and Control), 296
Domestic hybrid structure with international division, *exhibit*, 214
Domestic stage of international development, 209
Dual-authority structure in a matrix organization, *exhibit*, 109
Dual-core approach
administrative core, 417–418
organization change, *exhibit*, 418
technical core, 417–418

E

E-business organization design, 307–309
Economic conditions, 140
Economies of scale, 207
Economies of scope, 207–208
Effect of ten mega-mergers on shareholder wealth, *exhibit*, 324
Effectiveness, 22, 70
Efficiency, 22, 70

Efficient performance versus learning organization
competitive to collaborative strategy, 31
formal control systems to shared information, 30–31
rigid to adaptive culture, 31–32
routine tasks to empowered roles, 30
vertical to horizontal structure, 28–30
Element in the population ecology model of organizations, *exhibit*, 185
Engineering technologies, 265
Enhanced network structures, 311
Enterprise resource planning (ERP), 299–300
Environmental decline (competition), 344
Environmental domain
general environment, 140–141
international context, 141–142
task environment, 138–140
Environmental domain, controlling the
change of domain, 159
illegitimate activities, 160–161
political activity, 159–160
regulation, 159–160
trade associations, 160
Environmental resources, controlling
controlling the environmental domain, 159–161
establishing interorganizational linkages, 156–159
organization-environment integrative framework, 161
Environmental uncertainty, 142
framework, 145–146
and organizational integrators, *exhibit*, 151
Simple–complex dimension, 143–144
Stable–unstable dimension, 144–145
Environmental uncertainty, adapting to
buffering and boundary spanning, 147–149
differentiation, 149–151
forecasting, 152–154
integration, 149–151
organic versus mechanistic management processes, 151–152
planning, 152–154
positions and departments, 147
responsiveness, 152–154
Escalating Commitment, 473

Essential leadership behaviors, 325
Establishing interorganizational linkages
  advertising, 158–159
  cooptation, 158
  executive recruitment, 158
  formal strategic alliances, 157–158
  interlocking directorates, 158
  ownership, 156–157
  public relations, 158–159
Ethical dilemma, 377
Ethical framework, 378
Ethical values and social responsibility
  does it pay to be good, 377–378
  managerial ethics and social responsibility, 375–377
  sources of individual ethical principles, 374–375
Ethical values in organizations, sources of
  external stakeholders, 380–381
  organizational culture, 379
  organizational systems, 379–380
  personal ethics, 378
Ethics, 374
Ethics committee, 383
Ethics hotlines, 383
Ethics officer, 383
European Production Task Force, 224
European Union (EU) environmental and consumer protection legislation, 140
Evolution, 184
Evolution of organizational applications of IT, *exhibit*, 290
Example of an ERP network, *exhibit*, 300
Excessive focus on costs, 426
Execution, 325
Executive dashboards, 294
Executive information system (EIS), 292
Expert power, 489
Explicit knowledge, 301
External adaptation, 362
External stakeholders, 380–381
Extranet, 304

F

Factors of production, 208
Factory of the future, 253
Failure to perceive benefits, 426
Famous innovation failures, 415
Fast cycle teams, 416
Faulty action stage, 345–346
Fear of loss, 426
Federal Aviation Administration, 372

Federal Bureau of Investigation (FBI), 24
Feedback control model, 293
Financial perspective, 297
Financial resources, 141
Five basic parts of an organization, *exhibit*, 16
Flexible manufacturing systems (FMS), 253
FMS. *See* Flexible manufacturing systems (FMS)
Focus strategy, 65
Focused differentiation, 63
Focused low cost, 63
Food and Drug Administration (FDA), 188
Forces driving the need for major organizational change, *exhibit*, 401
Forces for culture change
  diversity, 421
  horizontal organizing, 420
  learning organization, 421–422
  reengineering, 420
Forces that shape managerial ethics, *exhibit*, 379
Forecasting, 152–154
Formal structure and systems, 382
  code of ethics, 384
  disclosure mechanisms, 383–384
  structure, 383
  training programs, 384–385
Formalization, 267, 334, 337
Four stages of international evolution, *exhibit*, 209
Four types of change provide a strategic competitive wedge, *exhibit*, 404
Framework, 145–146
Framework for assessing environmental uncertainty, *exhibit*, 146
Framework for department technologies, *exhibit*, 265
Framework for this book, *exhibit*, 35
Framework of interorganizational relationships, *exhibit*, 176
Functional, divisional, and geographical organization designs
  divisional structure, 104–107
  functional structure, 102–104
  functional structure with horizontal linkages, 104
  geographical structure, 107–108
Functional managers, 225
Functional matrix, 110
Functional organization structure, 102–104

G

Garbage can model, 453, 467
  consequences, 464–467
  organized anarchy, 463
  streams of events, 464

General organization environment, 140–141
Generalist strategy, 187
Geographical organization structure, 107–108
Geographical structure for Apple Computer, *exhibit*, 108
Global arena, entering
  global expansion through international strategic alliances, 210–211
  motivations for global expansion, 206–209
  stages of international development, 209–210
Global Body Line System, 399
Global capabilities, building
  global coordination mechanisms, 224–226
  global organizational challenge, 220–224
Global companies, 210
Global coordination mechanisms
  expanded coordination roles, 225–226
  global teams, 224–225
  headquarters planning, 225
Global economy as reflected in the *Fortune* Global 500, *exhibit*, 207
Global expansion
  motivations for, 206–209
  through international strategic alliances, 210–211
Global geographical division structure, 215–217
Global hybrid, 220
"Global Leadership 2020" management program, 386
Global Leadership and Organizational Behavior Effectiveness (Project GLOBE), 227
Global matrix structure, 218–220
Global organizational challenge, 220
  exhibit, 221
  increased complexity and differentiation, 221–222
  innovation, 223–224
  need for integration, 222–223
  transfer of knowledge, 223–224
Global product division structure, 215
Global stage of international development, 210
Global standardization, 211
Global teams, 224–225
Globalization strategy, 211–212
Goal approach, 70
  indicators, 71
  usefulness, 71–73
Goals, 62
Goodwill, 360
Government sector, 140
Greater revenues, 226
Gross domestic product (GDP), 221, 253

H

Hawthorne studies, 26
Headquarters planning, 225
High-velocity environments, 471–472
Horizontal coordination model, 413, 415–416
  boundary spanning, 413–414
  for new product innovations, *exhibit*, 414
  specialization, 413
Horizontal information linkages
  direct contact, 96
  full-time integrator, 96–97
  information systems, 95
  task forces, 96
  teams, 97–99
Horizontal linkage, 95
  model, 416
Horizontal organization structure, 113
  characteristics, 114–116
  exhibit, 115
  strengths, 116–117
  strengths, *exhibit*, 116
  weaknesses, 116–117
  weaknesses, *exhibit*, 116
Horizontal organizing, 420
Horizontal relationships, 306
Horizontal sources of power
  power sources, 495–498
  strategic contingencies, 495
Human relations emphasis, 77
Human resources sector, 140
Hurricane Katrina, 322
Hybrid, 100
Hybrid organization structure, 120–122

I

I ♥ Huckabees, 466
Idea champions, 410
Idea incubator, 409
Ideas, 405
Illustration of independent streams of events in the garbage can model of decision making, *exhibit*, 465
Imitation, 470
Immigration and Naturalization Service (INS), 48
Implementation, 406
Improved horizontal coordination, 310
Improved interorganizational relationships, 310–311
In-house division, 307
Inaction stage, 344, 346
Incident command system (ICS), 336, 348
Incident commander, 337
Income statement, 294
Increased innovation, 226
Incremental change, 400
Incremental decision process model, 453, 467
  development phase, 459

dynamic factors, 459–462
  exhibit, 460
  identification phase, 458
  selection phase, 459
Incremental process model, 463
Incremental versus radical
  change, 400–402
Indirect interlock, 158
Individual decision making
  bounded rationality
    perspective, 448–453
  rational approach, 445–448
Individual versus organizational
  power, 489
Industry sector, 138
Information, 301
Information linkages, 306
Information-processing
  perspective on structure,
  91–92
  horizontal information
    linkages, 95–99
  vertical information linkages,
  93–95
Information reporting system,
  291
Information systems for
  managerial control and
  decision making, *exhibit*,
  292
Information technology
  evolution, 289–291
Initiative for Software Choice
  (ISC), 160
Inspiration, 470
Institutional environment, 188
Institutional isomorphism, 191
Institutional perspective, 188
Institutional similarity, 190
  coercive forces, 192
  mimetic forces, 191–192
  normative forces, 192–193
Institutional view, 190
Institutionalism, 188–189
  institutional similarity,
    190–193
  institutional view, 190
  organization design, 190
Institutionalization, 426
Intangible output, 259
Integrated effectiveness model,
  75
  effectiveness values for two
    organizations, *exhibit*, 77
  four approaches to
    effectiveness values,
    exhibit, 76
  indicators, 76–78
  usefulness, 78–79
Integrated enterprise, 305–306
  exhibit, 306
Integration, 149–151, 222
Integration of bricks and clicks,
  307
  range of strategies for, *exhibit*,
  308
Intellectual capital, 301
Interaction of contextual and
  structural dimensions of

organization design,
  exhibit, 18
Interdepartmental activities, 423
Interdependence, 230
Intergroup conflict in
  organizations
  rational versus political
    model, 487–488
  sources of conflict, 484–487
Interlocking directorate, 158
Internal integration, 362
Internal process approach, 70
  indicators, 74
  usefulness, 74–75
Internal process emphasis,
  76–77
International business
  development group, 217
International division, 214–215
International sector, 140
International stage of international development, 209
Interorganizational framework,
  176–177
Interorganizational relationships,
  172
  changing characteristics of,
    exhibit, 180
Interpreting culture
  ceremonies, 363–365
  language, 366–367
  rites, 363–365
  stories, 365
  symbols, 365–366
Intranets, 298, 312
Intrapreneur, 410
Intuitive decision making, 451
iPod, 223, 329, 399, 402, 404
ISO 9000 quality-auditing
  system, 387
Isomorphism, 190
iTunes, 223, 402, 462

J

J. D. Powers' 2005 rankings of
  consumer satisfaction, 372
Job design, 274–275
Job enlargement, 274
Job enrichment, 274
Job rotation, 274
Job simplification, 274
Joint optimization, 275
Joint ventures, 158
Judgment, 459

K

Kaizen, 399
Key characteristics of traditional
  versus emerging
  interorganizational
  relationships, *exhibit*, 311
Knowledge, 301
Knowledge management,
  300–303
  systems, 312
  two approaches to, *exhibit*,
  303

L

Labor- and knowledge-intensive,
  service firms, 260
Labor–management teams, 506
Lack of coordination and
  cooperation, 426
Ladder of mechanisms for
  horizontal linkage and
  coordination, *exhibit*, 99
Language, 366
Large-batch production, 249
Large group intervention, 423
Leadership for change, 425–426
Lean manufacturing, 254–257
Learning organization, 28,
  421–422
  combining the incremental
    process and Carnegie
    models, 462–463
  garbage can model,
    463–467
Legitimacy, 189
Legitimate power, 489–490
Levels of analysis in
  organizations, 33–34
  exhibit, 34
Liaison role, 96
License agreements, 157
Life cycle development, stages of
  collectivity stage, 327–328
  elaboration stage, 328–329
  entrepreneurial stage,
    326–327
  formalization stage, 328
Linear programming, 454
Liquid Tide, 224, 226, 402,
  415
Long-linked technology, 270
Low-cost leadership strategy,
  64–65
Low-cost production factors,
  208–209

M

Major stakeholder groups and
  their expectations, *exhibit*,
  23
Management
  changing role of, 174–176
Management champion, 411
Management control systems,
  293–296
  exhibit, 295
Management information system
  (MIS), 291
Management science approach,
  453–455
Managerial ethics, 376
Managerial ethics and social
  responsibility, 375–377
Manufacturing firms, 248–250
Market control, 340–341, 349
Market sector, 140
Marketing-manufacturing areas
  of potential goal conflict,
  exhibit, 485
Mass customization, 256
Matrix, 100

Matrix organization structure,
  108
  conditions for the matrix,
    109–110
  strengths, 110–113
  strengths, *exhibit*, 111
  weaknesses, 110–113
  weaknesses, *exhibit*, 111
Measuring dimensions of
  organizations, 38
Mechanical system design,
  exhibit, 29
Mechanistic and organic forms,
  exhibit, 152
Mediating technology, 269
Membrane-electron assemblies
  (MEAs), 411
Merger, 156
Meso theory, 34
Miles and Snow's Strategy
  Typology, 63
  analyzer, 67
  defender, 66–67
  prospector, 65–66
  reactor, 67
Mimetic forces, 191–192
Mintzberg's research, 458
Mission culture, 368–369
Mission statement, 58
Mixed structure, 220
Model to fit organization
  structure to international
  advantages, *exhibit*, 213
Modular organization structure,
  117
Modular structures, 311
Multidomestic strategy, 211–212
Multinational stage of
  international development,
  210
Munificence, 142

N

NASDAQ, 346
National Association of
  Manufacturers, 160
National responsiveness, 211
National Tooling and Machining
  Association (NTMA), 160
National value systems, 227
Natural system design, *exhibit*,
  29
Need, 406
Negotiating strategies, 507
Negotiation, 506
Network coordinator, 226
Networking, 298
New product success rate, 412
  probability of, *exhibit*, 413
New products and services
  achieving competitive
    advantage, 416–417
  horizontal coordination
    model, 413–416
  reasons for new product
    success, 412–413
  success rate, 412
New-venture fund, 410

Niche, 184–185
Non-core departmental
   technology
   analyzability, 264
   framework, 264–266
   variety, 264
Non-core technology, 247
Nonprogrammed decisions, 444
Nonroutine technologies, 265
Normative forces, 191, 192–193
NTMA. *See* National Tooling
   and Machining Association
   (NTMA)

O

Obeya, 399, 414
Obtaining prior information,
   497
Occupational Safety and Health
   Administration (OSHA), 48
Office Software Group, 106
Official goals, 58
Open systems, 14–15
   emphasis, 76
Operative goals
   employee development, 60
   innovation and change, 60
   market, 60
   overall performance, 59–60
   productivity, 60–61
   resources, 60
Organic versus mechanistic
   management processes,
   151–152
Organization. *See* also
   Organizational and
   Organizations
   defined, 10–11
   importance of, 12–14
   perspectives on, 14–15
   types of, 11–12
Organization chart illustrating
   hierarchy of authority,
   exhibit, 19
Organization chart sample,
   exhibit, 91
Organization design, 190
   contingency factors affecting,
      exhibit, 69
   how strategies affect, 67–68
   IT impact on, 309–311
   other factors affecting, 69
   outcomes of strategy, *exhibit*,
      68
   pressures affecting, *exhibit*,
      247
Organization design alternatives
   departmental grouping
      options, 100–102
   reporting relationships, 100
   required work activities,
      99–100
Organization design and culture,
   367
   adaptability culture, 368
   bureaucratic culture, 369–370
   clan culture, 369

culture strength and
   organizational
   subcultures, 370–371
   mission culture, 368–369
Organization design, dimensions
   of
   contextual dimensions, 17,
      20–22
   performance and effectiveness
      outcomes, 22–24
   structural dimensions, 17–20
Organization design for
   implementing
   administrative change,
   418–420
Organization design, strategic
   direction in, 56–58
   top management role in,
      exhibit, 57
Organization development
   culture change interventions
   interdepartmental activities,
      423
   large group intervention, 423
   team building, 423
Organization development (OD),
   422, 429
   approach, 507
Organization-environment
   integrative framework, 161
Organization size
   dilemmas of large size,
      322–326
   pressures for growth,
      321–322
Organization structure, 76,
   90–91
Organization theory, 34
   current challenges, 6–10
   topics, 6
Organization theory and design,
   evolution of
   contemporary design, 27–28
   efficient performance vs
      learning organization,
      28–32
   historical perspectives,
      25–26
Organizational Assessment
   Survey, 373
Organizational atrophy, 343
Organizational behavior, 34
Organizational bureaucracy and
   control, 331
   bureaucracy, 332–333
   size and structural control,
      334–335
Organizational change, 405
Organizational characteristics
   during the life cycle,
      330–331
   four stages, *exhibit*, 331
Organizational configuration
   administrative support, 16–17
   management, 17
   technical core, 16
   technical support, 16
Organizational control strategies

bureaucratic control, 339–340
   clan control, 341–343
   market control, 340–341
   three, *exhibit*, 339
Organizational culture,
   371–373, 379
   emergence and purpose of
      culture, 361–363
   interpreting culture, 363–367
Organizational decision making,
   443–445
   Carnegie model, 456–458
   incremental decision process
      model, 458–462
   management science
      approach, 453–455
Organizational decision-making
   systems, 291–293
Organizational decline and
   downsizing
   definition and causes,
      343–344
   downsizing implementation,
      346–348
   model of decline stages,
      344–346
Organizational departments
   differentiate to meet needs
   of subenvironments,
   exhibit, 150
Organizational differentiation,
   149
Organizational domain, 138
Organizational ecosystems,
   172
   changing role of management,
      174–176
   exhibit, 175
   interorganizational
      framework, 176–177
   is competition dead, 173–174
Organizational effectiveness,
   assessing, 70
Organizational environment, 138
   exhibit, 139
Organizational form, 184–185
Organizational goal, 55
Organizational innovation, 405
Organizational learning,
   371–373
Organizational life cycle
   characteristics during the life
      cycle, 330–331
   exhibit, 327
   stages of life cycle
      development, 326–330
Organizational performance,
   371–373
Organizational politics, 499
Organizational purpose
   goals, importance of, 62
   mission, 58
   operative goals, 59–61
Organizational responses to
   uncertainty, 154
Organizational systems,
   379–380
Outsourcing, 117

P

Parallel approach, 416
Percentage of personnel
   allocated to administrative
   and support activities,
   exhibit, 335
Performance, 250–253
   and structural implications,
      257–258
Performance and effectiveness
   outcomes, 22–24
Perrow's
   framework, 277
   model, 264
   technology framework, 266
Personal ethics, 378
Personal liberty framework, 378
Personnel ratios, 334
Pharmaceutical Research and
   Manufacturers of America,
   160
Planning, 152–154
PLM. *See* Product life-cycle
   management (PLM)
Point–counterpoint, 472
Political activity, three domains
   of, 500
Political model, 487
Political processes in
   organizations, 498
   definition, 499
   when is political activity used,
      500
Political tactics for using power,
   502–505
Politics, 499
Pooled interdependence, 269,
   486
Population, 183
Population ecology, 183
   niche, 184–185
   organizational form, 184–185
   process of ecological change,
      185–187
   strategies for survival,
      187–188
Population-ecology perspective,
   183
Porter's competitive strategies,
   63
   differentiation, 64
   exhibit, 63
   focus, 65
   low-cost leadership, 64–65
Positions and departments, 147
Power, 488
Power and organizations, 488
   horizontal sources of power,
      494–498
   individual versus
      organizational power,
      489
   power versus authority,
      489–490
   vertical sources of power,
      490–494
Power and political tactics in
   organizations, *exhibit*, 501

Power distance, 227
Power sources, 495
    centrality, 497
    coping with uncertainty,
        497–498
    dependency, 496
    financial resources, 496–497
    nonsubstitutability, 497
Power strategies, 178
Power versus authority, 489–490
Preparation, 425
Pressures for (organization)
    growth, 321–322
Prevention, 497
Primary responsibility of top
    management, 56
Problem consensus, 467–468
Problem identification stage, 443
Problem solution, 443
Problemistic search, 456
Process, 113
Process of ecological change,
    187
    retention, 186
    selection, 185
    variation, 185
Product and service changes,
    404
Product champion, 411
Product life-cycle management
    (PLM), 254
Product matrix, 110
Product structure, 104
Professional partnership, 338
Professionalism, 337
Profit and loss statement (P&L),
    294
Programmed decisions, 444
Project GLOBE (Global
    Leadership and
    Organizational Behavior
    Effectiveness), 227
Project SAPPHO, 413

Q

Quality of service, 260

R

Radical change, 401
    incremental versus, *exhibit*,
        402
Radio-frequency identification
    (RFID), 253
Ratings of power among
    departments in industrial
    firms, *exhibit*, 494
Rational approach, 445–448
Rational goal emphasis, 76
Rational-legal authority, 340
Rational model, 487
Rational versus political model,
    487–488
Raw materials sector, 139
Reactor strategy, 67
Reasons for new product
    success, 412–413

Reciprocal interdependence,
    271, 487
Recognition, 458
Reengineering, 113, 420
Referent power, 489
Relationship between
    environmental
    characteristics and
    organizational actions,
    exhibit, 162
Relationship between technical
    complexity and structural
    characteristics, *exhibit*,
    250
Relationship between the rule of
    law and ethical standards,
    exhibit, 376
Relationship of department
    technology to structural
    and management
    characteristics, *exhibit*, 267
Relationship of environment and
    strategy to corporate
    culture, *exhibit*, 367
Relationship of flexible
    manufacturing technology
    to traditional technologies,
    exhibit, 258
Relationship of organization
    design to efficiency
    versus learning outcomes,
    exhibit, 93
Relationship of structure to
    organization's need for
    efficiency versus learning,
    exhibit, 123
Reputation Quotient study, 189
Resource-based approach, 70
    indicators, 73
    usefulness, 73–74
Resource dependence, 154–156
    power strategies, 178
    resource strategies, 177–178
Resource strategies, 177–178
Resources, 407
Responsiveness, 152–154
Retail Industry Leaders
    Association, 160
Retention, 186
Return on net assets (RONA),
    196
Reward power, 489
Rites, 363–365
Rites of enhancement, 363
Rites of integration, 363
Rites of passage, 363
Rites of renewal, 363
Role of intuition, 451–453
Routine technologies, 265
Routine versus nonroutine
    technology, 266
Rule of law, 375

S

S&P 500, 493
SA 8000 audits, 387
Satisficing, 456

Scientific management, 14,
    25–26
Search, 459
Securities and Exchange
    Commission (SEC), 3, 380
Selection, 184–185
Self-control, 342
Sequence of elements for
    successful change, *exhibit*,
    406
Sequential interdependence, 270,
    486
Service firms
    definition, 259–261
    new directions in services,
        261
Service technology, 259
Shoreham Nuclear Power Plant,
    473
Simple, stable environment,
    145
Simple, unstable environment,
    145
Simple–complex dimension,
    143–144
Simplified feedback control
    model, *exhibit*, 294
Simultaneous coupling
    departments, 416
Simultaneous production and
    consumption, 259–260
Site performance data, 295
Six Sigma
    goals, 296
    quality programs, 192
Size and structural control of
    organizational bureaucracy,
    334–335
Skunkworks, 410
Small-batch production, 248
Smaller organizations, 309–310
Smart factories, 253
Social Accountability 8000 (SA
    8000), 387
Social audit, 387
Social capital, 360
Social responsibility, 376
Social system, 275
Society for Human Resource
    Management, 376
Society of Competitive
    Intelligence Professionals,
    148
Sociocultural sector, 140
Sociotechnical systems,
    275–276
    model, *exhibit*, 275
Sources of conflict
    differentiation, 485–486
    goal incompatibility, 484–485
    limited resources, 487
    task interdependence,
        486–487
Sources of conflict and use of
    rational versus political
    model, *exhibit*, 488
Sources of individual ethical
    principles, 374–375

Sources of individual ethical
    principles and actions,
    exhibit, 375
Span of control, 268
Special decision circumstances
    decision mistakes and
        learning, 472
    escalating commitment, 473
    high-velocity environments,
        471–472
Specialist strategy, 187
Specialization, 413
Spin-off, 308–309
Stable–unstable dimension,
    144–145
Stages of decline and the
    widening performance gap,
    exhibit, 345
Stages of international
    development, 209–210
Stakeholder approach, 23
State Farm's mission statement,
    exhibit, 59
Stateless corporations, 210
Steps in the rational approach to
    decision making, *exhibit*,
    446
Stickiness, 295
Stories, 365
Strategic business units, 104
Strategic contingencies, 495
Strategic contingencies that
    influence horizontal power
    among departments,
    exhibit, 495
Strategic partnership, 309
Strategic types of change,
    402–405
Strategies for survival, 187–188
Strategy, 62, 250–253
Strategy and design, framework
    for selecting, 62
    Miles and Snow's strategy
        typology, 63, 65–67
    organization design,
        contingency factors
        affecting, *exhibit*, 69
    organization design, how
        strategies affect, 67–68
    organization design, other
        factors affecting, 69
    organization design, outcomes
        of strategy, *exhibit*, 68
    Porter competitive strategies,
        63–65
Strategy and structure change,
    404
    dual-core approach, 417–418
    organization design for imple-
        menting administrative
        change, 418–420
Strengthening external
    relationships, 304
    customer relationship
        management (CRM), 307
    e-business organization
        design, 307–309
    integrated enterprise, 305–306

Strengthening internal
    coordination
    enterprise resource planning
        (ERP), 299–300
    intranets, 298–299
    knowledge management,
        300–303
Strengths and weaknesses of
    divisional organization
    structure, *exhibit*, 105
Strengths and weaknesses of
    functional organization
    structure, *exhibit*, 103
Structural design, applications of
    structural alignment, 122–123
    symptoms of structural
        deficiency, 123–124
Structural design, options for
    grouping employees into
    departments, *exhibit*, 101
Structural dimensions of
    organization design
    centralization, 18
    formalization, 17–18
    hierarchy of authority, 18
    personnel ratios, 20
    professionalism, 20
    specialization, 18
Structural framework, 90
Structural implications, 272–273
Structural priority, 271–272
Structure, 383
Structure, designing to fit global
    strategy
    global geographical structure,
        215–217
    global matrix structure,
        218–220
    global product structure, 215
    international division,
        214–215
    model for global vs local
        opportunities, 211–214
Struggle for existence, 187
Subcultures, 370–371
Subsystems, 15
Supplier arrangements, 157
Supply chain management, 305
Sustainable development, 380
Switching structures, 409

Symbols, 365
System, 15

T

Tacit knowledge, 301
Tactics for enhancing
    collaboration, 505–508
Tactics for increasing power,
    501–502
Task, 30
Task environment, 138, 143
Team building, 423
Team focus, 427
Teams, 97
Technical champion, 411
Technical complexity, 248
Technical knowledge, 468
Technical system, 275
Techniques for encouraging
    technology change, 408
    corporate entrepreneurship,
        410–411
    creative departments, 409
    switching structures, 409
    venture teams, 410
Techniques for implementation
    of change, 426–429
Technology, 250–253
Technology change, 403
    ambidextrous approach,
        407–408
    techniques for encouraging,
        408–411
Technology, impact of on job
    design
    job design, 274–275
    sociotechnical systems,
        275–276
Terrorist attacks (2001), 336
Technology sector, 141
The Reengineering Revolution,
    420
Thompson's classification of
    interdependence and
    management implications,
    exhibit, 270
Three mechanisms for
    institutional adaptation,
    exhibit, 191

Time-based competition, 416
Traditional authority, 340
Training programs, 384–385
Transaction processing systems
    (TPS), 289
Transformational leadership,
    425
Transnational model, 220
    of organization, 230–233
Transnational teams, 224
Two hybrid structures, *exhibit*,
    121
Typology of organization rites
    and their social
    consequences, *exhibit*, 363

U

Uncertainty avoidance, 227, 426
Using power, politics, and
    collaboration, 500
    political tactics for using
        power, 502–505
    tactics for enhancing
        collaboration, 505–508
    tactics for increasing power,
        501–502
Utilitarian theory, 378

V

Values-based leadership,
    381–382
Variation, 185
Venture teams, 410
Vertical information linkages
    hierarchical referral, 93
    rules and plans, 94
    vertical information system,
        94–95
Vertical information systems, 94
Vertical linkages, 93
Vertical sources of power
    control of decision premises,
        491–492
    formal position, 490–491
    information, 491–492
    network centrality, 492–493
    people, 493–494
    resources, 491

Virtual cross-functional
    teams, 98
Virtual network organization
    structure
    how the structure works,
        117–118
    strengths, 118–120
    strengths, *exhibit*, 119
    weaknesses, 118–120
    weaknesses, *exhibit*, 119
Virtual organizations, 211,
    311
Virtual team, 98
Vulnerability, 344

W

Web logs, 141, 301
Whistle-blowers, 383
Whistle-blowing, 383–384
Wikis, 301
Windows Group, 106
Win–lose strategy, 507
Win–win strategy, 507
Woodward's classification of
    100 British firms according
    to their systems of
    production, *exhibit*, 249
Woodward's research into
    manufacturing technology,
    276
Worker Adjustment and
    Retraining Notification Act,
    347
Worker skill level, 267–268
Workflow interdependence
    among departments
    structural implications,
        272–273
    structural priority, 271–272
    types, 269–271
Workforce Transition Program,
    347
Workforce 2020, 386
Workplace mediation, 507
World Economic Forum's annual
    meeting, 300
World Trade Center attacks of
    September 2001, 319